J.J.P. Oud

# Poetic Functionalist

# J.J.P. Oud

1890-1963

**The Complete Works**


**Ed Taverne**
**Cor Wagenaar**
**Martien de Vletter**

With contributions of:

Dolf Broekhuizen
Bernard Colenbrander
Maartje Taverne
Sander van Wees


**NAi Publishers**

Contents

# 1 Formative Years

# 2 Pioneer of the 'New Architecture'

# 3 New Architecture in Crisis

# 4 War and Recovery

# Preface

J.J.P. Oud is probably one of the most controversial Dutch architects from the first half of the twentieth century. During his lifetime he aroused both admiration and irritation with the self-willed course he pursued, a course he charted not only for himself, but also for the so-called Modern Movement in architecture. Even after he died, he managed to wrong-foot many a historian with his writings and statements. This qualifies Oud as one of the most enigmatic and unknown architects in the history of modern architecture in the Netherlands.

Oud is typically an exponent of a building culture that was not afraid of experimenting and taking risks. When he worked as an architect in government service just after World War I, Oud, challenged by developments in neighbouring countries, managed to convince politicians and civil servants that realising mass produced, low budget house-construction was not only a technical ands social task, but also a cultural and artistic duty. Oud managed to persuade town councils, housing corporations and other architects to experiment and take risks, an achievement that won him great respect, especially from abroad.

All this fell silent when Oud, in the mid thirties, left the scene of public housing – in his view a completed project – and subsequently managed to persuade the international business world – in this case Shell – to identify themselves with an extraordinary, exceptionally wilful and classic-modern office building in The Hague. To Oud, the architect, this was the logical step on the road to *complete* architecture, that is, an urban way of building representative of feelings and movements in society. However, to many colleagues and critics this actually meant a return to the previously renounced nineteenth-century architecture.

Notwithstanding this criticism Oud pursued his leanings towards all sorts of complex and often controversial building projects during and after the war, such as the Hofplein project in Rotterdam (1942). Town councils, consultants, architects and project developers were played off against one another by Oud in a manner that was as intractable as it was a matter of principle, or he would direct them on the basis of clear, sound architectonic choices.
Whereas, even today, there are those among Dutch architects who start foaming at the mouth when they hear J.J.P. Oud's name mentioned, there were the inspired *angry young men* of the Italian group *Tendenza,* in particular Aldo Rossi and Giorgio Grassi, who in the early sixties, in their designs, in speech and in writing, drew attention to Oud's integrity as a modern architect who was motivated by his traditional professionalism. They managed to convince the international architectural world of Oud's significance, which lay not so much in the realisation of a few world-famous blocks in Rotterdam and Stuttgart, but first and foremost in the fact that in a systematic manner he had exposed the crisis facing modern construction both with his theoretic stand and with his architecture.

The research that forms the basis for this monograph – published on the occasion of an extensive special exhibition in the Netherlands Architecture Institute – could be seen as a historic foundation of the presuppositions and intuitive views of a generation of architects and critics who began to take a fresh interest in Oud's personality and work in the mid sixties. Not for the purpose of projecting it on their own contemporary designs, but to reposition themselves in the light of the many faces of modernism, so abundantly present in Oud's works. At the time, this was a positioning that was as authentic as it was productive and to this very day it has lost none of its validity.

The combination of this book and the exhibition marks the conclusion and the public account of an extensive research project carried out by staff members of the Art and Architectural History Department of the University of Groningen. Over

**the years they enjoyed the support of the Nederlandse Organisatie voor Wetenschappelijk Onderzoek (Netherlands Organization for Scientific Research, NWO) and the Koninklijke Nederlandse Akademie van Wetenschappen (Royal Dutch Academy of Sciences, KNAW).**
**However, this programme could never have been completed without the moral and technical support received from the Netherlands Architecture Institute. This Institute not only manages the major part of Oud's estate, but also runs a study centre offering ample facilities for research. The long-standing co-operation between the Netherlands Architecture Institute and the University of Groningen finally led to the organisation and the execution of a joint initiative: the Oud-manifestation, with an exhibition and this monograph as its highlights. In their different ways both try to do justice to the import and the depth of the personality and the oeuvre of Jacobus Johannes Pieter Oud.**

**Kristin Feireiss**
**Director, Netherlands Architecture Institute**

**Ed Taverne**
**Professor, History of Architecture and Urban Development, University of Groningen**

# Introduction

## The manifestation

J.J.P. Oud (1890-1963) is a name synonymous with modern Dutch architecture in the first half of the twentieth century. Yet his life and work have never been extensively documented like those of other founding fathers of the international Modern Movement, such as Walter Gropius and Le Corbusier. The manifestation *J.J.P. Oud, Poetic Functionalist* is designed to fill this gap. The main elements are a major retrospective exhibition in the summer of 2001 in the Netherlands Architecture Institute in Rotterdam, and this catalogue of his oeuvre. This manifestation is a joint initiative of the Netherlands Architecture Institute and the History of Art and Architecture department at the university of Groningen, who entered into a covenant for this purpose in 1997. Final responsibility was in the hands of the director of the Netherlands Architecture Institute, Kristin Feireiss, and the head of the architecture section of the History of Art and Architecture department, Ed Taverne. Day-to-day management was entrusted to two project managers: Bernard Colenbrander and Cor Wagenaar. When Colenbrander left to take up a position at the Ministry of Education, Culture and Science, his position was filled by Martien de Vletter but he remained closely involved in the realization of this book. In 1998 a project group was formed, made up of Dolf Broekhuizen, Maartje Taverne, Martien de Vletter and Sander van Wees. This project group, with Martien de Vletter as its pivot, prepared a very detailed description of all of Oud's works as well as making an inventory of the most important of his other activities, including his commitment to several associations and magazines, and his travels.

The preparation of this manifestation was able to take advantage of various other projects. Martien de Vletter made a fresh inventory of Oud's archives at the Netherlands Architecture Institute: 20,000 drawings, 15,000 letters, 5,000 photographs, and countless papers; Oud's library, handed down almost intact, had already been inventoried. The new inventory turned out to be essential to the writing of the project descriptions. Dolf Broekhuizen had done doctoral research on Oud's later work and this too proved to be invaluable for the description of Oud's post-war work. Cor Wagenaar charted the development of Oud's theories as reflected in his correspondence. During her practical year, Marieke van Rooij explored the archives of the Rotterdam Woningdienst; Marinke Steenhuis conducted a study of Oud's Hoek van Holland housing estate for Camp & Kamphuis. Furthermore, the group was able to draw on the expertise of Bernard Colenbrander, the Oud expert at the Netherlands Architecture Institute, and of Ed Taverne, who has published extensively on Oud's work. Last but not least, Donald Langmead's 'bio-bibliography' devoted to publications by and about Oud proved exceptionally useful.

Some of the funding required for this ambitious project was provided by the initiators, but the greater part came from other sources. The Dutch Organisation for Scientific Research (NWO) financed Dolf Broekhuizen's doctoral research as well as the work done by Sander van Wees and Maartje Taverne; the latter began her work with a start-up grant from the Sikkens Foundation. The Royal Dutch Academy of Sciences (KNAW) took care of the cost of Cor Wagenaar's postgraduate research. Nonetheless, the production of this catalogue would not have been possible without the generous contributions made by the Prins Bernhard Cultuurfonds and the Oranje Nassau Group. The makers of this catalogue also owe a debt of gratitude to Jean-Paul Baeten (NAI Study Centre), Marie-Agnes Benoit (CCA), Herman van Bergeijk, Eva Dockal, Michelle Elligot (MOMA), Robert Elwall (RIBA), Henk Engel, the Fondation Custodia in Paris, Simon Franke (NAi Publishers), Charles Hind (RIBA), Robyn de Jong-Dalziel, Marjanne

**Kok (NAI), Marianne Lahr, Julie Leclerc (CCA), Letje Lips (NAI), Jonathan Makepeace (RIBA), Philipa Martin (RIBA), Cammie Mcatee (CCA), Wendy van Os, Ton Overtoom, Irene Philips-Lotspeich (Getty Research Institute), Sal and Daniel Poolman, Elizabeth Reinhartz-Tergau, D. Renes, James Viloria (CCA), Astrid Vorstermans (NAi Publishers) Mariet Willinge (NAI), Wim de Wit (Getty Research Institute).**

### The book

**This book was written with the express intention of presenting Oud's life and work in an accessible manner. Although the catalogue contains all the works, only a relatively small part of the archival materials is shown. Not all the available drawings make for a better understanding of a given subject and where this was not the case they have not been included in this book. Instead, the text received special emphasis: indeed, the catalogue was conceived as a reader, in which it deliberately differs from the general run of monographic reference books. The layout, by Peter Kingma (Joseph Plateau bureau), was designed with the same aim in mind.**

**The catalogue contains four types of text: an introduction in the form of an essay, detailed project descriptions, original documents by Oud and his contemporaries, connecting texts sketching the historical background, and several short, thematic essays dealing with standardization, material and colour, the ornament and the library order (Bernard Colenbrander), the design process and office organization (Dolf Broekhuizen) and visual arts (Martien de Vletter). The project descriptions were written by the project group and edited by Ed Taverne and Cor Wagenaar, who also wrote the connecting texts and the introductory essay. The essay, the opening item of the book, analyses Oud's – continually changing – position in relation to his contemporaries. The catalogue itself consists of four sections representing clearly distinguishable periods in Oud's life. Within these sections the projects are arranged in thematic clusters, each introduced by a connecting text.**

The **Sources** from which the project descriptions were gathered fall into three categories: archival material (heading: Sources), contemporary articles (heading: Articles) and (historical) literature. Under Sources the locations are given of Oud's original records relating to the project concerned. These are housed not only at the NAI, but also in the Canadian Centre of Architecture in Montreal, the Getty Research Institute in Los Angeles, the Rijksbureau Kunsthistorische Documentatie (Netherlands Institute for Art History) and in a few Dutch municipal archives. Since the inventory systems differ from institution to institution, the descriptions given vary. The CCA identifies all records page by page with a letter code indicating whether it concerns a drawing (dr), or a photograph (ph), and the year it was acquired; the page number is given after the colon. At the Getty Research Institute the records are bundled and coded per group. The first group of numbers refers to the Oud archive in general (890126), the second code denotes the particular bundle (box 2-folder 17). At the NAI the drawings and photographs have been individually numbered and given a filing code (OUDJ), a project code (e.g. kh = Kiefhoek) and a page number. The written documents have been given a filing code; if they relate to a specific design they also have a project code and a number in the 1000 (for written documents), 2000 (for plans) and 3000 (for articles and publications). The models, which are part of the NAI's model collection, have a different filing code (MAQV).

Texts written and published before Oud's death in 1963 come under the category of **Articles**. The reason for listing them separately in this way is that it is often difficult to find them outside the Oud Archive. In a few instances this category includes a book or a publication in which reference is made to the project (for instance, *Architecturalia* written by Oud, 1963).

The final category, **Literature**, contains references. That is to say, general and more specific books and articles published after Oud's death and publications that provide insight into particular aspects of the project. Two separate bibliographies are included at the back of the book: Oud's own publications (arranged chronologically) and publications about Oud (in alphabetical order).

Both the source acknowledgements and the annotations in the connecting texts have been deliberately kept to a minimum. Where inventory numbers are not needed to trace a document (e.g. a letter) quickly, they have been omitted. Frequently consulted archives are identified by an abbreviation:

CCA: Canadian Center of Architecture, Montreal, Canada (Oud Archives)

Getty: Getty Research Institute, Los Angeles, United States of America (Oud Archives)

GAR: Gemeentearcief Rotterdam (Rotterdam Municipal Archives)

GTA: Institut für Geschichte und Theorie der Architektur, Eidgenossiche Technische Hochschule, Zurich (Giedion bequest and CIAM Archives)

ICN: Instituut Collectie Nederland (Netherlands Institute for Cultural Heritage)

MOMA: Museum of Modern Art, New York, (Johnson Papers, Barr Papers)

NAI: Netherlands Architecture Institute, Rotterdam (Oud Archive)

RKD: Rijksbureau Kunsthistorische Documentatie (Netherlands Institute for Art History)

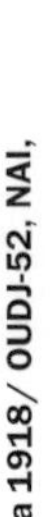
J.J.P. Oud, circa 1918/ OUDJ-52, NAI, Rotterdam

# Lonely Explorations along the Horizon of our Times

## J.J.P. Oud and the Modern Movement

**'The Tragedy of the Transitional Years'**

In the spring of 1916 J.J.P. Oud ('Bob' to his friends) read an article in *De Beweging* which brought an abrupt end to a period of nervous exploration of the direction architecture would take in the future. He was, no doubt, curious to read yet another contribution by H.P. Berlage (1856-1934) and encountered the first instalment of 'De nieuwe beweging in de schilderkunst' (The new movement in painting) by Theo van Doesburg (1883-1931). Oud was 26 years old at the time and had been running his own architectural practice in Leiden since 1913. As yet, his circle of acquaintances had largely been limited to Berlage, whom he regularly visited in Amsterdam, and, most especially, W.M. Dudok (1884-1974), whom he met in Purmerend and with whom he had built an unpretentious, small estate of working-class housing in Leiderdorp. The four housing blocks, like the private houses he had previously built in Purmerend (chiefly for relatives), did not look very urban, thanks primarily to the preponderance of slanting roofs and the picturesque effect of carefully distributed glazing bars in the strip windows. The complex shows the extent of Oud's – and, of course, Dudok's – fascination at the time with developments in garden cities and country-house architecture in England and Germany, and how closely he followed the illustrated publications of Raymond Unwin and Hermann Muthesius.

At that time Oud was not the only architect who, in his pursuit of the fundamentals of a well-considered and almost traditional design approach, derived inspiration from the rich tradition of the vernacular. That interest was part of a national and even international programme for a new type of architecture which initially was tangible in everyday building practice, but on which trade press speculations were highly confusing and incoherent. After all, from the 1890s onwards, growing numbers of buildings were being designed – not only in New York, Berlin and London, but also in smaller cities like Amsterdam and Rotterdam – according to ever-newer technical, constructional, as well as aesthetic principles. Take Amsterdam, for instance: the building of Central Station in 1889 heralded a complete spatial rearrangement of the historical city centre, which did not end with the upgrading of existing streets like the Damrak, but also included the setting out of new traffic axes and shopping streets like the Raadhuisstraat, which, with Hausmannian dynamism, pushed its way through the seventeenth-century concentric canal ring. That urban planning operation also triggered another, architectural orchestration of the Amsterdam cityscape, with new types of buildings, including shopping arcades, hotels, banks, insurance offices, department and clothing stores; buildings, the scale and measurements of which were just as new as the businesses they housed. Although few of these buildings seemed, on the face of it, to have much in common stylistically, nearly all reflected the same mentality: they made extensive use of new technical possibilities as regards construction and interior design, and revealed to the outside the spa-

Erich Mendelsohn/ NAI, Rotterdam (Photo M. Schmiegelski)

**tial make-up and arrangement of the inside. Regardless of whether the influences were Romanesque, Gothic or Renaissance, or local variations on the international Art Nouveau, the vocabulary was little more than a transparent masquerade of a new formal, architectural ideal: to achieve a simple spatial effect, economical use of resources and a strong, businesslike statement. As a child, Oud had followed the metamorphosis of the centre of Amsterdam from the moment he began travelling every day to the city from Purmerend, at the age of thirteen – first to the Quellinus School and later to the Rijksnormaalschool (State School for Art Education), where, incidentally, he encountered the leading figures of the Modern Movement: Berlage, K.P.C. de Bazel (1869-1923), W. Kromhout (1864-1940) and J.L.M. Lauweriks (1864-1932). Although Oud – like Le Corbusier (1887-1965) – carefully stage-managed almost every step in his career and repeatedly reviewed it afterwards, he was never particularly communicative about his professional training. There probably was not much for him to learn in Amsterdam, apart from certain skills relating to technical drawing, design by means of proportional systems and elementary architecture. As an architect, J.J.P. Oud was in fact a self-made man. He taught himself design and construction, thanks to generous clients in Purmerend and surroundings, and especially thanks to his almost boundless curiosity to see, understand and put into words what was taking place elsewhere in the field of architecture. The latter was harder to do than the former. He did not have much money for travel, but that was compensated by his personal acquaintance and friendship with the 'learned' H.P. Berlage. It is doubtful whether Berlage – who was at the peak of his fame, having just completed the Exchange – was able to teach young Oud much about the building trade itself; however, he certainly introduced the young man to the mysteries of contemporary architecture theory and stimulated him in his ambitions in architecture journalism. On 26 September 1910 Mrs Berlage sent a short letter to Oud, who was on the point of going to Delft Technical College: *Dear Oud. I do not know whether you are entirely happy about the decision to go to Delft and if you would prefer to talk things over again with my husband, do come and stay for a couple of days. Lectures at Delft haven't actually started yet and I noticed you were rather nervous; it might well do you good to get away for a while.*[1] It is not known whether the talk was of any help. At all events, Oud did go to Delft, soon became depressed there and left to join the famous architect and urban planner Theodor Fischer (1862-1938) in Munich as a trainee draughtsman, probably at Berlage's intercession. Prior to that, Fischer had helped along Bruno Taut (1880-1938) and Erich Mendelsohn (1887-1953), although, the year before, he had not managed to hold on to the young, unknown Swiss architect Charles-Eduard Jeanneret (Le Corbusier) for long. Oud only stayed a few months in Munich. It is not clear what fascinated him most there: Theodor Fischer's personality and undogmatic pedagogy, the simplicity and clear arrangement of the Classicist cityscape or, most probably, the liveliness of local artistic life which was dominated by the 'Neue Künstlervereinigung' and its offshoot 'Der Blaue Reiter', which in 1911 first exhibited work by Kandinsky, Franz Marc, August Macke and Paul Klee. Fischer, a versatile designer, managed to convince the inexperienced Oud, as he did Le Corbusier, of the significance of proportions and 'design by means of proportional systems' – the use of what Le Corbusier later termed 'les tracés régulateurs' – for architectural composition, firmly paving the way for Oud's essentially classical interpretation of architecture. In addition, Oud was able to see with his own eyes, in various working-class enclaves on the outskirts of Munich, what Fischer intended with the traditional 'farm-house', and how it could be transformed into an organic and modern serial house by means of well-considered site layout, well-planned, differentiated housing types and a meticulous, rugged finish.**

**In Oud's intellectual education, his short stay in Munich was therapeutic rather than practical. It is unlikely that Fischer was able to help him with what concerned him most at that time (as it did Le Corbusier): the quest for a consistent theory of the new direction which contemporary architecture appeared to be taking, nationally and internationally. As a new, generally applicable aesthetic ideal, it resembled a fusion of seemingly contradictory preferences for the vernacular, classical, rationalist, technological and monumentally-ceremonial. In other words, Oud was looking for a 'spiritual ideal', of the kind he admired in the Leiden philosopher Bolland, formulated in one of his earliest 'Thoughts on architecture':**

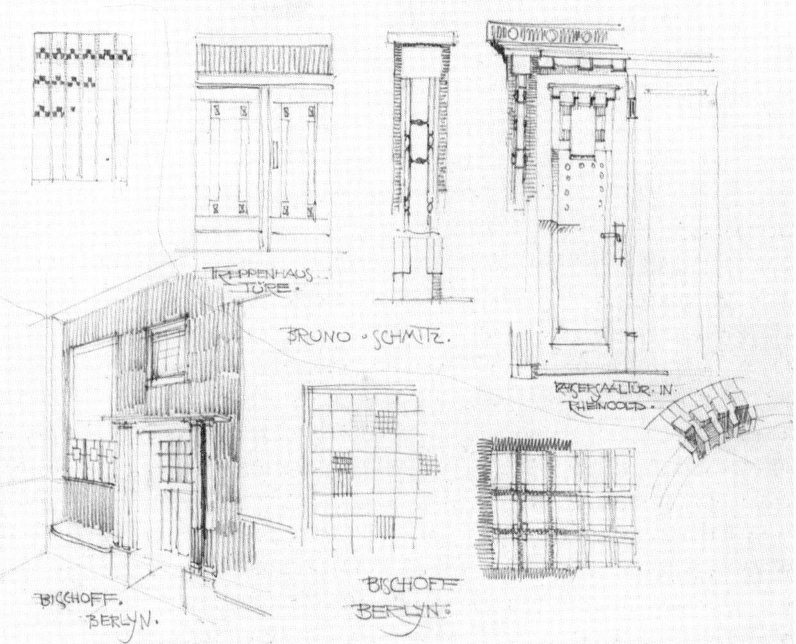


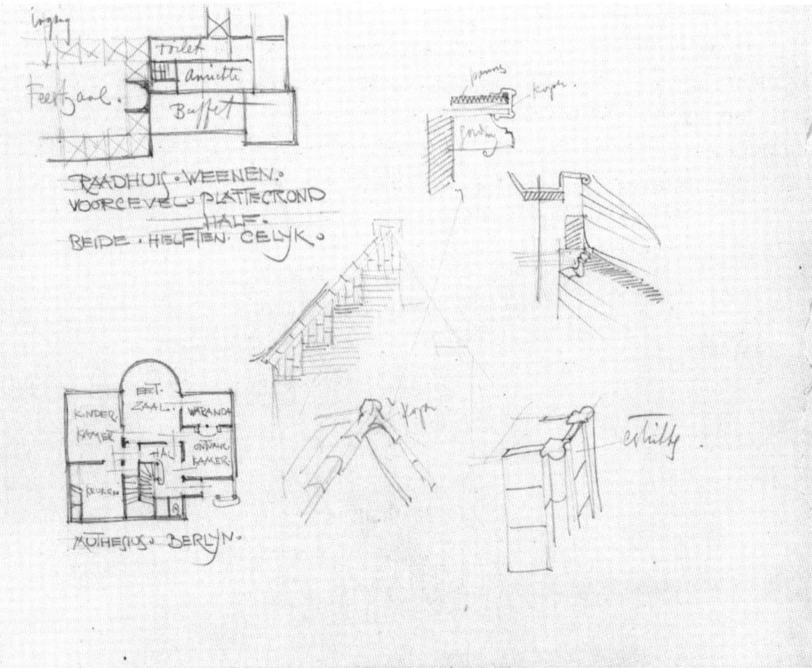




Pages from Oud's sketchbook/ 890126-box 1, F2, Getty, Los Angeles

Harm Kamerlingh Onnes, drawn by Oud/ 890126-box 1, F2, Getty, Los Angeles

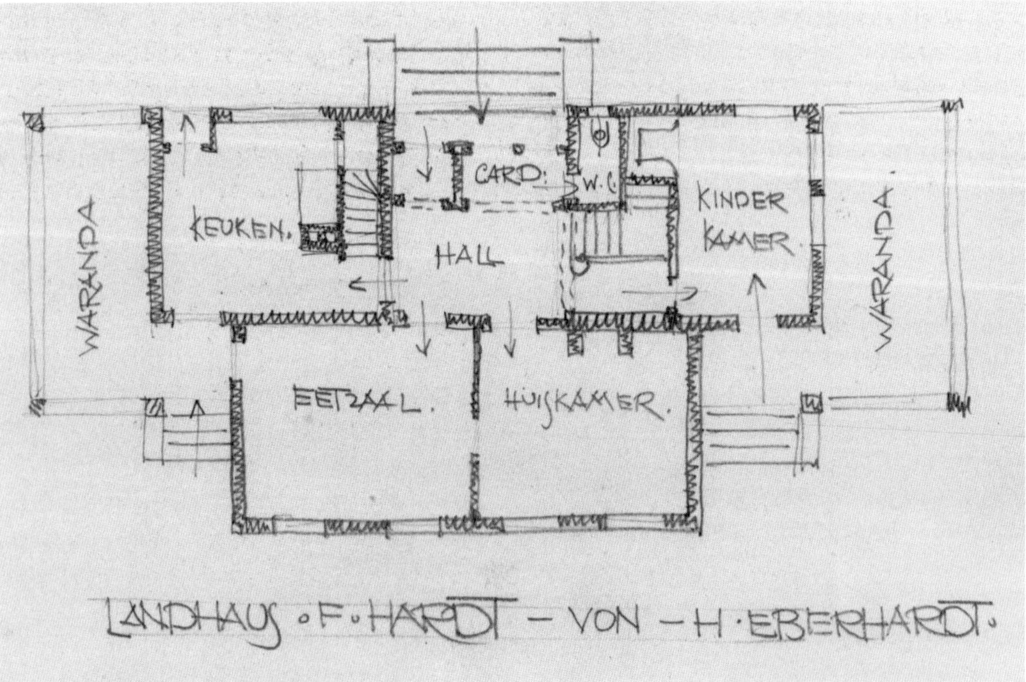


Pages from Oud's sketchbook/ 890126-box 1, F2, Getty, Los Angeles

*because when that has been found, what Scheffler calls the 'tragedy of the transitional years' will have ended and the demoralizing search can make way for a conscious striving and concentration of forces in one direction. That direction is already visible, giving us a very, very great advantage over the architects of a few decades ago, as we have been able to arrange things accordingly, since the beginning of our studies.*

### Art and Crafts

Oud must soon have realized that Purmerend was not the inspiring environment where his brooding on the 'conscious direction of art' would produce sensational results. Admittedly, his move to Leiden (1913) – as it happens, in Dudok's footsteps – did put him back in a small-town environment, but there artistic life was more lively and, especially, more daring. De Lakenhal Municipal Museum had a reputation as regards lectures and exhibitions on modern painting in France and Germany. They were a welcome addition to what was to be seen and heard about Cubism and particularly Futurism in Amsterdam for instance, from 1911 onwards. In Leiden he immediately joined the artists' group 'Kunst om de Kunst'. One of the friends he made there was the wealthy and charming Harm Kamerlingh Onnes (1893-1985), who introduced him into better-off and more artistic circles in Leiden and surroundings (Katwijk and Noordwijk). His contact with the wayward potter W.C. Brouwer (1877-1933) was quite different and more profound. Brouwer had a passion for sturdy, almost primitive design, which was not limited to the applied arts, but at that time was also evident in his socio-political ideas on the role of art and the artist in society. Later correspondence revealed that Oud, in his youthful idealism and pursuit of 'beauty by and for all' in his early Leiden years, was very much under the spell of Brouwer's radical personality and his artistic and social convictions. Brouwer's aesthetic views were largely influenced by the English Arts and Crafts movement and the concomitant idealization of the medieval guild as the social framework for unadorned, traditional craft. Brouwer, with his pragmatic yet idealistic operations, seemed to move between the socio-radical objectives of C.R. Ashbee's Guild and School of Handicraft (1888) and the ensuing workshops, and Walter Crane's *The Claims of Decorative Arts*, published in Dutch in 1894 by Jan Veth. E. Thorn Prikker had written in 1905: *Brouwer makes his pots in the curious hope that beauty will disappear at some time in the future, making way for a beauty which is contained in functionality.*[2] The association with Brouwer was highly formative for Oud for various reasons. Brouwer's monumental building ceramics in terracotta opened perspectives of new unity in the visual, applied and monumental arts which did not violate the autonomous character of architecture. Moreover, Brouwer was the most passionate and radical among Oud's friends and acquaintances in convincing him of the necessity of a new *gemeenschapskunst* or integrated art, and of the artist's social responsibility. Of course, Oud was also impressed by Brouwer's technical knowledge and skill, and the innovative character of his aesthetic theory of form. Brouwer demonstrated the inextricability of artistic innovation and social innovation, for which the causal connection was production according to traditional methods. But it was precisely on that point that Van Doesburg was to open Oud's eyes in 1916.

### 'The Visual Artillery of Cubism'

*There are works of Architecture which we admire for what they are. We admire a cathedral, not because there is an organ playing inside, or because certain religious acts take place inside, but because it is a rhythmic, balanced, mathematical entity, a* building, *which moves us because of its architectural characteristics. A cathedral moves us, because, in its spatial relationships of mathematical forms, it has assumed the air of beauty, in such a way that we accept it,* unreservedly, *as Architecture. If you stand in front of such a building with someone and he asks you what is the* purpose *of this building, you can be sure that he has missed the Purpose of Architecture as such.* With these masterly lines Van Doesburg opened his essay on 'De nieuwe beweging in de schilderkunst' (The new movement in painting) in *De Beweging* in 1916. His abrupt opening had the effect of a manifesto on Oud, who at that point was alive to the significance of medieval buildings for his own times: the essence of architecture lies in the capacity to touch someone, a power to which all else – technology, style, form – is subservient and contributory. So emotion was the key word of a new aesthetics giving meaning to the changing architectural reality which Oud had perceived with his own eyes and for which no consistent theory yet existed. Oud himself contributed over the years to the formulation of such a theory, always reasoning that *the true value of architecture lies in the fact that it conveys the emotion of one person (the architect) to another (the spectator)*, though he never actually referred to Van Doesburg's key text of 1916. And that does not only apply to emotion as the foundation of the artistic value of architecture. Van Doesburg's keen observations on developments in contemporary art were far more significant than any other text, be it by Berlage, Muthesius (1861-1927), Fischer or Wagner (1841-1918), in triggering Oud's consideration of 'future architecture and its architectural possibilities'. And they caused a dramatic rupture with the traditionally-minded W.C. Brouwer.

Van Doesburg wrote: *What is painting? Painting is: being driven by an inner perception – emotion, feeling, idea – to determine the mutual relationships between colours and shapes, and their combined relationship with the plane.*[3] The true subject of painting is the emotional condition upon observation – not the forms present in nature, like a bird, horse, tree or town – but their actual content: the universal. In Van Doesburg's view, that has always been the concern of painting, from Giotto to Picasso, but in modern times our *impression* of the universal has changed fundamentally, due to science and technology. It may have been acceptable in Giotto's day, for the Madonna, and in Rembrandt's day, for the landscape to figure as the visible expression of the universal, but today art is looking for a 'purely expressive construction', which 'translates' the emotion immediately in the paint, without complication from the representation. According to Van Doesburg, the quest for the fundamentals of a new kind of painting as a purely visual expression began with the Impressionists and had achieved its critical point, by way of Gauguin (form/plane), Cézanne (colour) and Cubism, because by then the literary elements had finally been ousted by the visual. Accordingly, Cubism – as a formal concept as well as an aesthetic theory – was the movement which laid the foundations for a 'strong, monumental artistic expression of the future', a new *gemeenschapskunst* which differed from that of the Middle Ages in form only.

Van Doesburg devoted the rest of the five-instalment essay to a detailed analysis of the 'Cubist method', on the basis of which painting rediscovered form as an independent visual expression. Those at times lyrical pages no doubt immediately convinced Oud of the importance of the development of modern art for the technical and theoretical reform of contemporary architecture. The extent of Oud's obsession in those crucial years of 1916 and 1917 with Van Doesburg's ideas is apparent both from a hastily written short article on Cubism (1916) and the surprising design for a seaside promenade (1917). The latter can correctly be seen an architectural exercise in the Cubist working method.

In Van Doesburg's view there are two moments in the Cubist procedure: that of 'visual perception' or observation of the object, and that of composition – the arrangement and and linking of formal impressions into an expressive construction. If the Cubist succeeds in restoring the pure form with plane, colour and line, it is primarily the result of intensified observation. Picasso *does not only look at his model, but also handles it, weighs it, measures it in all its dimensions, and goes to work on it like an anatomist with a corpse.* At the same time, he sees his model move, *as a construction moving in space.* Composition marks the moment when the painter creates order and rhythm from the cacophony of formal impressions. After all, the Cubist does not show us the objects themselves, but their characteristics: *he shows us how the objects influence, cut across, penetrate or entirely destroy*

Design for a logo or bookplate, *circa* 1915/ OUDJ-to 1, NAI, Rotterdam

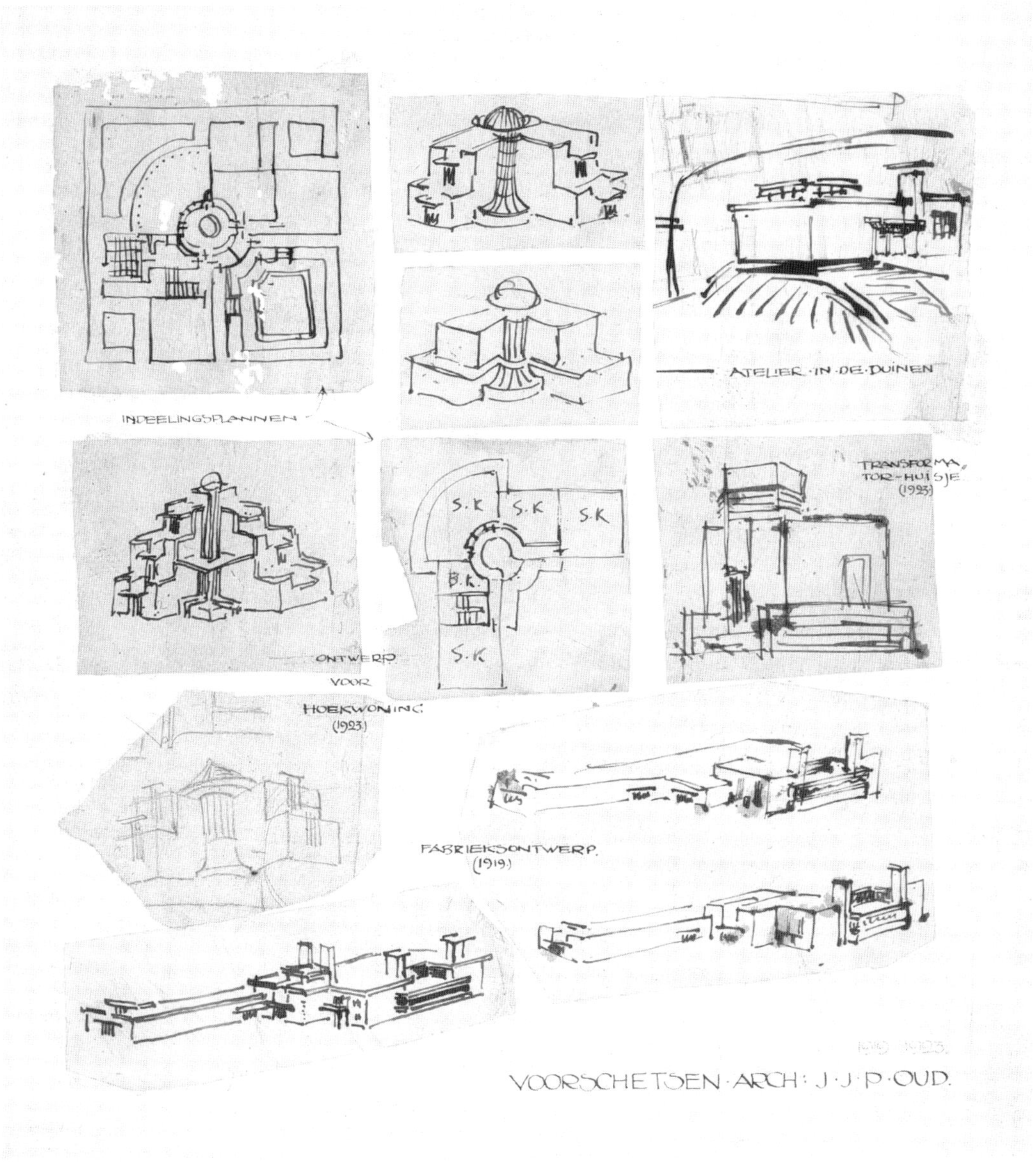

21

**Exhibition panel, sketches for a corner house, a studio for Van Doesburg, a transformer kiosk and the Factory at Purmerend, 1919-1922/ OUDJ-hw 5, NAI, Rotterdam**

*one another.* With the problems of contrasting and harmonizing shapes and colours, the painter is entering the territory of the visual arts, in which the sole concern is to reveal *the relationship between horizontal and vertical; round and angular; heavy and light; fast and slow; hanging and standing and floating; gradual and sudden; jumbled and separate; simultaneous and successive.* The ultimate goal being to shape all these universal characteristics *into a rhythmical, balanced totality, in which each part contributes to expressing the moving, visual perception.*

Oud's reaction to Van Doesburg's article proves that he appreciated the remarkable combination, inherent to Cubism, of abstract and classical concepts of form, but also the connotation of a new *gemeenschapskunst* which Van Doesburg linked with it. However, Oud had his reservations, especially with respect to Van Doesburg's assessment of the significance of plane and space for painting and architecture, respectively. On 30 May 1916 – a few days after publication of the first instalment in *De Beweging* – Oud wrote his first long letter to Van Doesburg which he evidently felt was so good that he adapted it into a short article 'Over cubisme, futurisme, moderne bouwkunst, enz.' (On cubism, futurism, modern architecture, etc.) for *Bouwkundig Weekblad.* This text, three years after Bruno Taut had first put forward the work of Delaunay, Léger, Kandinsky and others as a model for contemporary architecture, contains almost all the ingredients for the many misunderstandings and arguments Oud was to have in the course of his architectural career with artists, starting with Van Doesburg. The plane is for Van Doesburg the painter the same as silence for the composer and space for the architect: the true foundation of painting. Yet it is interrupted by relationships of colour and form, in the same way as the architect 'interrupts space with relationships in stone'. Consequently, the plane has a metaphysical meaning for Van Doesburg: it is the symbol of space. After all, the Cubists had liberated the plane from its subservient role as the backing for the three-dimensional *portrayal* of space, and reinstated it as the expression of universal space. However, Oud adhered to a purely architectural, even physical interpretation of the plane, as advocated since the 1890s by the new school of thought in architecture. It was felt that the basic form of the modern building should be extremely sober in detail and simple in composition, and have a characteristic outline. That ideal of 'profound planarity' undoubtedly meant that Oud could but interpret Van Doesburg's text as a step towards 'applied painting', which was subservient to architecture and would ultimately lead to a new *gemeenschapskunst.* Opinions differed greatly as to its exact form. Van Doesburg envisaged a 'monumentally expressive style', in which the achievements of Cubism, Futurism and Expressionism blended imperceptibly, whereas Oud still thought in terms of monumental art, a dramatic *Gesamtkunstwerk*, to which painting contributed as an art form complying with architecture. His hastily penned article in *Bouwkundig Weekblad* left no room for doubt about his views: *It [i.e. painting] will be able to 'animate' the planes with which we, as spatial artists, express our emotions, turning them into an essential element of space, capable of making it more intimate and moving. In the hallowed space, the gold and blue images will harmonize with the sublime chorales; in the banquet hall the brightly-coloured visions will intensify the revellers' excitement.* With that prospect, he summoned his fellow-architects to follow developments in modern art closely and, one day before the official opening, asked Van Doesburg to admit architects to the new Leiden art society, the Sphinx.



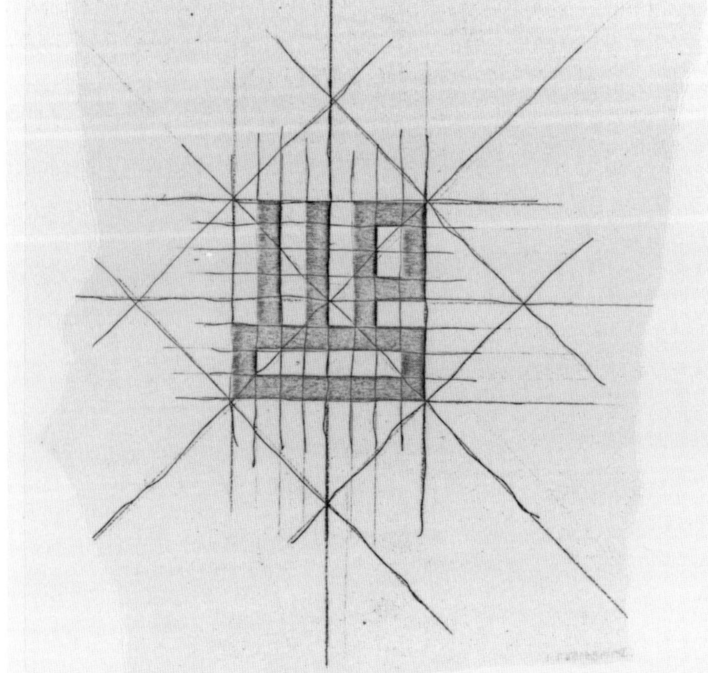
T. van Doesburg, monogram design for J.J.P. Oud, 1919/ dr1984: 0567, CCA, Montreal

**Russia, Europe and America: Großstadt**

The 'visual artillery of Cubism' achieved in painting what the canons achieved on the battle field and the first aerial bombardments in some cities: it destroyed the old culture. It seemed pointless to continue building on traditional concepts. The old European civilization was exhausted, the power stations of new energy were located outside the old continent. For the first time, the United States and Russia emerged as the vehicles of a vital, new culture. Van Doesburg and Oud drew inspiration from the Soviet Union and – even more – the United States. Since the end of the nineteenth century, Europe had been observing the economic and technological superiority of the United States with a mixture of amazement and admiration; it was little consolation that the official American culture was based entirely on the European. However, commercial mass culture was quite a different matter. Thanks to radio, film and gramophone it began to filter through to all levels of European population and was of particular fascination to the 'man in the street'. But the skirmishes in the trenches were hardly conducive to the self-assurance required to stop this offensive. Fuel was added to the fire by the Russian Revolution, heralding the great experiment of Socialism. The unstoppable advance of the United States and the fascination with the first serious attempt to build an entirely new society – these are the base lines in the ideas of the European avant-garde in the 1920s.

The obliteration of traditional values, the rise of the masses, the progressively greater influence of technology and the birth of a commercial culture, supported by neon advertising signs, were contributed by America and Russia. The final synthesis was the new phenomenon of the Großstadt (metropolis), which also occurred in Europe. Großstadt implied chaos, feverishness, bustle, dynamism and, above all, simultaneity. It was impossible to experience everything at once, the sensation of the Großstadt was never more than one of a seemingly accidental collage of fragments. Yet the Großstadt operated as an unfailing machine, and the simultaneity of the infinite number of phenomena and events seemed to coincide amazingly with the simultaneity of innovations in art and culture, making the Großstadt the symbol of that innovation. Paris was the most important European Großstadt, but in the 1920s faced competition from Berlin. The Großstadt sensation stemmed from American metropolitan culture: neon lights, dance halls with jazz, streets full of cars, the experience of the mobile masses as the vehicle for the future culture – and they had even come to power in Russia. Van Doesburg's exaltation about Paris is telling: *Paris is a seemingly very complicated machine, yet when you understand the structure, it is amazing how soon you become part of it.*[4]

America was, in the eyes of the European champions of the new culture, superlative in many respects to Berlin and Paris. It was the source of a new, unofficial, spontaneous and, to quote Van Doesburg and Oud, 'unintentional' popular culture, in which sports and leisure played an essential part (as the Dutch historian J. Huizinga observed).[5] The masses benefited to the full as well – the automobile was, for example, already widely available in the 1920s. Oud's first real introduction to the new continent took place in 1912, at Berlage's home, at an evening of slides in which Berlage had recorded the experiences of his visit to America.[6] On that occasion Oud saw much work by F.L. Wright (1867-1959) and L. Sullivan (1856-1924) for the first time. In the 1920s he was in close touch with numerous kindred spirits who wanted to see America for themselves and invariably began the voyage in Rotterdam – having called on Oud first. The flood of excited reports from the New World was endless. *All night New York lies before my eyes with its gigantic Dada neon signs. And the rhythm of the city fascinates me*, K. Lönberg Holm wrote to Oud, who ensured that *Bouwkundig Weekblad* published the impressions of his trip to America.[7] Admittedly, E. Mendelsohn, whose *Rußland – Europa – Amerika* assessed the value of the various cultures for the new civilization, saw Russia as *a fact in its sacrifice toward the beginning of a new order*, but still expected most from America. The war *brought America's energy to fantastic circulation, and transformed Russia's lethargy into a peak of vitality. The new Russia grabs for America which has become master of the world.*[8] Accordingly, in the 1920s America appeared to be ousting the gridlocked, self-destroying European culture.

**Architecture, Art and Life**

Van Doesburg introduced Oud to the work of P. Mondrian, who continued to fascinate Oud for the rest of his life. Oud exchanged views with Mondrian, the painter-theoretician, on the relationship between painting and architecture in general, as well as its social roots. *I am convinced I could build nothing which wasn't art – in a higher or lesser sense*, Oud let slip in a letter to Mondrian.[9] But Mondrian was by no means certain. If the new architecture wished to be art, it would have to meet the conditions of Neo-Plasticism. If it did, there would be friction with everyday life. *N.P. need not and cannot adapt to people. So-called 'actual practice' can never produce an architecture as N.P. Only an entirely different kind of practice could do that.*[10] The necessary ties between architecture and the practical demands of society set architecture outside the territory of art. For Mondrian that also explained the failure of Van Doesburg's experiment with colour in Spangen: art clashed with everyday practice and municipal red tape.[11] Oud had fundamentally different views on the subject. He admired the new painting and especially Mondrian's work, *provided it did not relate to space.*[12] In his attempt to transmit the dynamism of the Großstadt to Oud's housing estate in the bright yellow of the window frames, Van Doesburg was in fact seeking to replace architecture with spatial painting, as proposed by Mondrian in his three-dimensional experiments. The principles of the 'Nieuwe Beelding' (Neo-Plasticism) were applied without being related to the function, to the lives being lived in these buildings. Mondrian called it 'form fixing'.[13] In his opinion there was no other option – Neo-Plasticism just happened to be far in advance of life.[14] Oud opposed this, which almost caused Mondrian to break off the friendship. The new art also had a spiritual character for Oud, as it did for Mondrian, though for Oud it was rooted in everyday life, in technical and social trends which were starting up everywhere and which were at their most concentrated and unmistakably intense in the modern Großstadt. The new architecture's task was not to force this life into a Neo-Plasticist straitjacket, but actually to create a new style from that life. That was a crucial difference, coinciding with the distinction between painting and architecture. *Your life is painting, mine is building*, Oud impressed on Mondrian,[15] and Mondrian admitted that architecture was 'a different category'.[16]

Oud's quarrel with Van Doesburg about Spangen and his difference of opinion with Mondrian mark a new stage in his personal development. He had not long bidden a final farewell to the vernacular, yet the way in which he adjusted his view of painting was no less fundamental. He had barely recovered from the shock he had received from Van Doesburg's article a few years previously, when he realized at the beginning of the 1920s that the revolution in painting actually entailed risks for architecture. The pioneers of the new art could boast two important achievements: they had dared to jettison old ballast, and they had proved that the new art was a spiritual matter. However, the way in which they transformed

Piet Mondrian/ NAI, Rotterdam

their perception of the objects they painted – and deformed – and their perception of space proved unsuitable as a basis for a new architecture. Van Doesburg demonstrated that in Spangen, Mondrian did so in the way his theory deliberately forgot about 'life', which still had to be the substance of architecture, even new architecture. New architecture could not but be part and parcel of modern life. It was not a drug to introduce the spectator into a world of 'sweet apathy' and 'spiritual intoxication', but the expression of everyday, city life, which should no longer be camouflaged in 'dreamy forms'.[17] Oud used the term 'social' to describe that engagement: architecture, unlike painting, was a social art – but an art, nevertheless. From then on, the new form of painting was not only a source of inspiration for Oud, but also an enormous danger. He decided to stop his Cubist experiments because, even though they might be a springboard to a new architecture, they could never themselves mature into that new architecture.[18]

**Unintentionality**

Oud's resistance to Mondrian's 'form fixing' corresponded to his dislike of what he called 'intentionality' – his attitude to 'unintentionality' analogous to his changing view on painting. This theme prevailed within *De Stijl*. Everything proceeding from life, not conceived outside and then added, was unintentional. Architectural beauty was not, as Oud stressed time and again, the starting-point of a design process, but the end result. However, the artist's and architect's personality stood between life and the design. His task consisted of *subordination to the assignment, to the verge of self-renunciation.*[19] A difficult position, which forced him into an extremely important, yet subordinate role. It was his job to *transform formless life into a disciplined form*, with life as the starting-point, not the designer's chance imaginings.[20] That ambivalence is crucial. On the one hand, Oud championed the fundamental role of the designer, on the other hand the designer was not expected to impose on his assignment all kinds of forms, regardless, for Oud, whether they were entirely haphazard or underpinned by inappropriate theories.

Of course, industry and particularly industrial engineering, provided the main example of unintentional design generated by 'life' (i.e. function). It was also invading everyday life, thanks to the boom in electrical domestic appliances. Oud was overly fascinated by the way Mendelsohn integrated the hustle of the Großstadt – traffic, advertising – into his megaprojects.[21] Mendelsohn showed how modern life could evidently be the direct trigger for a new style. It proved possible for the social ideal of the vernacular to assume new forms, apart from the traditional ideal of the Arts and Crafts, which was, moreover, artificial and forced, so anything but unintentional. Consequently, attempts to arrive at a new style pursuing that course were doomed to fail.[22] Industrial engineering attested to the possibilities of an unintentional, convincing design, founded on social developments. G. Rietveld (1888-1964) and P. Behrens (1868-1940) put things in perspective,

Theo van Doesburg (left) and Cornelis van Eesteren, Paris 1923/ Van Doesburg Archive, AB5396, NAI, Rotterdam

**but their comments were wasted on Oud. *Be particularly wary about seeing too much unintentionality in mechanical things. At present they are inferior to you and me,* Rietveld warned.[23] Behrens also sensed attempts to tone down technology with aesthetics. *It becomes increasingly clear to me that all earlier attempts to exert an aesthetic influence on technology, to include it in the beautiful cityscape, have led to a situation where it is robbed of its character, where the new and the exotic are toned down, where it is made proper i.e. fashionable, adapted to fit the daily routine, instead of to the fairy-like improbability of taking the grotesque capriciousness of its often bizarre forms as its principal motif.* [24] And Oud was also concerned with the latter. He wanted new architecture to be just as self-evident as the design of aeroplanes and ocean liners. And that was the crux of Oud's break with Van Doesburg in 1921. *I really should have told you back in Weimar ... that "De Stijl" is changing for the worse (and not me), and no longer has anything to do with "forming". That, under the influence of the German Expressionism, it is degenerating into Baroque, and that the original motto of "unintentionality" will be replaced by out-and-out "intentionality", while the intellectual level in Leiden drops to that of Magdeburg!*[25]**

**The essence of architecture in Oud's opinion around 1920 was that it conveyed modern life and its excitement, an emotion which was not the same as that of being immersed in the Großstadt, but was related to it. Life was the starting-point, its design a process of careful composition, in which the dynamic force of modern life and that of the search for clear, direct forms of expression, what determined the ultimate emotional connotation of a building or neighbourhood. As universal as the new modern civilization was, so strictly personal was the design process – which with Oud was just as deliberate as it was with Mondrian. The effect was meant to be just as self-evident, just as convincing and emotional as a Mondrian painting, and never betray a sign of intentionality. However unintentional and spontaneous it might have been, the emotion Oud wished to convey was still profound, thus surpassing the admittedly clever, but superficial and coquettish formal world of, say, the Amsterdam School. For Oud, new architecture was not a matter of taste or fashion, but of supporting a new spirituality. He was not gloomy; suffering from architecture, as some German architects were inclined to do, was at odds with Oud's views.[26] His ideal was architecture which was indeed as self-evident as the 'mechanical' design of industrial engineering: direct, spontaneous, unaffected, not forced, and so an expression of modern life, of the new civilization, which was emerging everywhere and had the same character everywhere: hopeful, positive and containing the promise that the 'tragedy of the transitional years' would soon be overcome.**

**'Let them throw caution to the winds'**

**The essence of Oud's theory of architecture is that there is no point in theorizing, it only damages the case of new architecture. Here, again, the credo of unintentionality all round. Admittedly, new architecture was to be discussed and criticized: however, not by people in institutions or on the basis of codified manifestos, but by sound journalistic work, in which architects also had a part to play. Oud's aversion to theorizing stemmed from his ideas on style, and especially the view that style does not result from the effort of individual artists and architects – albeit a necessary requirement – but from a new spiritual unity. That individually experienced and individually wrought spiritual unity was felt to be a communal, collective fact, penetrating the whole of life, including its artistic expression. That explained the simultaneous occurrence of renewal in various art forms, the fact that the innovative movements pursued a parallel course and that they were**

Gerrit Rietveld (seated) in front of his workshop in Utrecht, *circa* 1918.
From: M. Küper, I. van Zijl, *Gerrit Th. Rietveld, het volledige werk,* Utrecht 1992

inspired in a similar way by new social developments like technology, the masses and mass-orientated commercialism (advertising!). Self-evidence was a key word for Oud – it was all about the inevitability of the new art. Words would only confuse things, because, as he wrote to Mendelsohn, the 'weaker brethren' might concentrate too much on the words and miss the meaning behind them, *as in architecture they always see just the form and never the essence from which it was born and that – for its development at least – alone is of significance in the end.*[27] The first friendship – and not the last – to be ruined by this conviction was that with Van Doesburg. Many were to follow. Behne, Giedion, Le Corbusier – all were, in Oud's opinion, guilty of intentionality, which he equated with propaganda and considered to be a symptom of failing trust. He used the same argument to explain his break with *Opbouw* and his decision to cold-shoulder CIAM, and he used it with remarkable consistency. *Let them throw away all that theory, all that advertising, all that calculating and justifying; in other words, let them throw caution to the winds and just get on with it. Let them 'jolly well' get on with it. Just build a house, one they'd like to live in, too. Not thinking about behaving properly as a theoretician should and possibly going against the principles, but the real thing, from the heart,* Oud wrote in 1941 to *De Opbouw* secretarial office.[28] Was that argument genuine? Was Oud really convinced of the 'self-evidence' of the new architecture? Or was it a convenient way of discarding troublesome alliances? He certainly could not stomach anything hinting of 'propaganda', but, equally, the 'propagandists' were certainly persuasive, in their texts as well as in their architecture, but their cogency had done more for a collective International Style than Oud's oeuvre, which was produced in relative isolation. However, the collectivity of the International Style was not, for Oud, one of a new style, but of an ideology propagated by inadmissible means and squandering the artistic principles of the European avant-garde. The ideology of the International Style was one of 'business-like' teamwork, tying in with the methods of international (American) business practice, not with the spiritual essence of Modernism. Even Mondrian's theories, which inspired Oud throughout his life, were ultimately unacceptable for him, and thus even Mondrian's work lost its ultimate lustre: *If someone were to ask me now if I believe that this painting might ever rise to the highest possible peaks of painting, I would say, in no uncertain terms: 'no'. It is too domineeringly abstract-aesthetic, not general enough for that. Despite the proof to the contrary which is advanced so well, theoretically!*[29] Mondrian intrigued him on account of his boundless dedication, his integrity and, above all, his paintings – not the way in which he tried to legitimate them theoretically.

### 'Das Waschen einer Architektur' (The Development of an Architecture)

Oud, like Mondrian, was absolutely convinced of the inevitability of the new art and architecture. *Yes, as you say,* Mondrian wrote to him, *I do indeed have reason to be satisfied that we are making progress. Our art is so beautiful that it is to be expected, if we believe in evolution.*[30] That belief in a gradual evolution of art was not new. It sometimes resulted, in combination with ideas on style, in a far broader view of the evolution of art as part of social developments in general, with 'unity' of art, architecture and society the starting-point. For Marxism-focused architects like Berlage, the moment at which unity actually came about coincided with the realization of Socialism. The work of the art historian H. Wölfflin, whom Oud greatly admired, has less emphasis on the social component of the new *gemeenschapskunst*, and more on the evolution of art and architecture as such. Oud regularly referred to Wölfflin's theory of artistic evolution, for instance in his correspondence with Giedion. *The development of an architecture is like the development of a forest: there are thousands of nourishing currents, producing thousands of trees, plants, flowers (unimportant and small ones like houses, important and very beautiful ones like the building of the League of Nations!)*[31]

Wölfflin envisaged the goal of the artistic evolution as the emergence of a completely lucid, clear style. It could only be lucid and clear if it had contemporary foundations, in a spiritual and a material sense. Style was a historical and dynamic phenomenon, brought about by a temporary harmony between culture, on the one hand, and social and economic circumstances on the other. When they altered, the balance was upset and the next stage in the cultural evolution began, leading to a new style. Wölfflin sought to chart that process and fathom its dynamics. His work can be interpreted in different ways, and appealed to Oud because of the legitimation of replacing one style by another, whilst referring to the connection of art to a deeper social essence.

In keeping with Darwin's description of biological evolution some decades earlier, artistic evolution was felt to be a prolonged affair, in which the individual artist's role was decisive and, at the same time, slight. Can the avant-gardist, the artist, fighting for 'the new', speed up that evolution? This question is open to speculations along the lines of the debate prevailing around 1918 between Leninists and classical Marxists within the socialist movement: the Leninist group tried to get a grip on the historical process, while the Marxists maintained that it could not be steered, but had already been determined by social developments. Oud was not unaware of the analogy; within the spectrum ranging from the revolutionary throwing himself wholeheartedly into propaganda, and the artist working steadily on the new style, Oud had most affinity with the latter.

Evolution means progress, but also leaving the past behind. For Oud, however, it did not mean that the architecture of the past was less perfect. In his view, the closer architecture was to the life from which it originated (so the more style it had), the more perfect it was. In that sense, architectural quality was relative. The task of new architecture was to at least equal the quality of the past. *So, I want to try to explain that, from a spiritual point of view, the new architecture does not measure up to the earlier architecture and that it is part of evolution that we to try to catch up.*[32] Throughout his life, Oud was fascinated by architecture of the past, and, as a member of the Rijkscommissie voor de Monumentenzorg (National Historic Monuments Commission), for decades strove to protect it wherever necessary. It did not impede his striving for a new architecture – on the contrary, it provided direction, urgency and a qualitative touchstone.

Oud's belief in the evolution of a new architecture also had consequences for the way he presented his own work. He attached great importance to publishing his latest work, possibly adding the most successful preceding projects. He refused on principle to show outdated work. For instance, when his little row of houses at Hoek van Holland was completed, he no longer thought his housing at Tusschendijken was important. They were 'alte Dinge' – old things – echoes from a 'conquered' past, 'lästige Vergangenheit' – irksome past – which he did not want to go on dragging behind him.[33] His diffidence about showing old work was partly due to his belief in the need to sever himself from previous stages in the development of architecture, at both the universal and the personal level. Accordingly, he kept a careful watch on developments in international architecture and on the evolution of his own work. However interesting it might have been to look at 'old' art and architecture, it could also damage the evolution towards new things. That was particularly true for stages

Sigfried Giedion/ Archiv GTH, Zurich

which Oud felt had only just been conquered. He was, for example, wary of the effect of an exhibition dedicated to Van Doesburg in 1936. However interesting it might be, he *would regret it if it were to cause the revival of an approach, which had had a great benefit, but should now remain "history"*.[34] What was past had to be conquered or, in the revolutionary rhetoric of the 1920s, 'destroyed'.

**Construction and Destruction**

The construction of 'unintentional', self-evident architecture required that everything hampering such unintentionality be eradicated. Innovative architecture had to be revolutionary, and that feature was exactly what Berlage lacked. Oud considered Berlage too much of a theoretician and too little of an activist. What appealed to him about Henry van de Velde (1863-1957) was that he remained loyal to the revolution. Van de Velde, who began his career as a painter and went on to master architecture, lived in Wassenaar from 1917 to 1926, from 1921 in a prefabricated house he designed himself and christened 'The Tent'. Oud visited him many times. Van de Velde was, for them, the embodiment of the ongoing battle for 'the new'. Around 1900 Van de Velde had already drawn attention to the beauty of the ocean liner and compared a cabin window with a Greek capital.[35] In Weimar he had been the director of the Kunstgewerbeschule, which is seen as the predecessor of the Bauhaus. There, he had emerged as a Classicist with a desire to derive inspiration from the continuity of architectural history, in the same tradition as Wölfflin.[36] Van de Velde reasoned in the same vein as Nietzsche, who had a veritable cult following in Weimar, and emphasized the fundamental role of the individual artist's will in paving the way for a new, collective style. The title of his best-known book, *Der Wille zum Stil*, is a direct reference to one of Nietzsche's famous writings – and was borrowed by Van Doesburg as the title for one of his lectures.[37] Van de Velde basked in his role of 'Nestor' of revolutionary art. *My task is to fight, not to inaugurate officially. Whenever I am given the opportunity to introduce and defend the young people from all countries, I, above all others, will be the right person to do so, because I have been a pioneer, a rebel and an iconoclast, and because my entire work is founded on the debris of something I first knocked down.*[38]

The idea of knocking down and building on the ruins greatly appealed to Oud. He saw the clearing up of something which could not be developed further as a prerequisite for the continued evolution of architecture. Therein lay an essential difference between Oud and the preceding generation, with the exception of Van de Velde. Hegemann, the publisher of authoritative journals like *Städtebau* and *Wasmuths Monatshefte für Baukunst*, did not believe in such a radical break with the past, and stuck to his belief, however hard Oud tried to change his mind. *You admire Goethe, and his balance is something of an ideal to me, like you (to me especially, in architecture!). But in art there is always a concentration (per-*

Henry van de Velde/ Bauhaus Archiv, Berlin

***fection – Goethe) and destruction to prepare for new values (Nietzsche). This destruction is necessary, because perfection can no longer be developed.***[39] **Oud also believed it was occasionally useful to do something 'artistic' in his own work, as he had in Café De Unie, for instance. For him, it was an example of a building which could not contribute to architectural evolution, if only because it was intended soon to be pulled down. However, after such provocations control once more prevailed.**[40]

## Classicism and Romanticism

**Control was Oud's architectural ideal. He was convinced that the new style could only be Classical; accordingly, he was known among like-minded architects as a Classicist. Of which he was not ashamed – on the contrary. Classicism was not, in his opinion, a historical style – such styles had exhausted their scope for development and had to go – but a universal approach to architecture: 'Order as opposed to arbitrariness'.**[41] **The contours of a new Classicism were taking form everywhere, in the same way as a new Classicism had replaced the late Baroque a century before, leading to the conscious pursuit of severity. Behrens had already brought it to Oud's attention**[42]**, and the Swiss art historian E. Stockmeyer noted striking similarities with that evolution, which Giedion had described in his book on Baroque and Classicism. For Stockmeyer, Giedion's book *brings back vivid memories of the double artistic aspirations of your architecture...here severely classical, there form destruction or in this case, even better, mass destruction.***[43] **Unlike Behrens, who could only envisage the emotional content of architecture in its romanticism, seeing everything lacking romanticism as barren and intellectual, Oud believed that the two concepts were directly opposed to each other.**[44] **Oud decided, having visited the project, that Behrens's attempt to unite them in his 'Dombauhütte' – stonemason's lodge – in Munich would lead nowhere.**

**The new Classicism which Oud championed would only recall Classical movements of the past spiritually, not stylistically. Hegemann and Wölfflin also recalled the evolution of architecture in a classical direction, but did not deny its historical roots. *In your case as well as in his,* Oud wrote to Hegemann, *I have asked myself again and again why such clever brains do not progress a little further and, instead of linking their conclusions to traditional material, cannot simply be content with the results in an abstract form...After all, we could agree to the extent that you and I strive for an architecture that is severe, systematic, clear, symmetric (when necessary) etc.; since in this respect you recognize only one possibility (the Greeks, why not – albeit different – the Egyptians, too??), whereas I believe in a realization of this ideal in a form fitting to our time and am in fact making an effort to realize this ideal.***[45]

**Classicism and Romanticism were complete antitheses: the former construction, the latter destruction. Destruction was also needed, but as such could never lead to new archi-**

Philip Johnson (left), Alfred Barr and Margreth Barr, during a tour of Europe (Italy) in 1930. MOMA, New York

tecture. Oud felt that the greatest threat to the new architecture was that it might be affected by Romanticism, which, in the final analysis, could never amount to more than individualstic intentionality and a danger to the construction of a new style, embedded in collective spirituality. In that respect, the Amsterdam School was the worst thing Oud could imagine. In his vocabulary, Romanticism was a term of abuse – the worst he could conceive. And there was ample opportunity to apply it.

## Publicity: Adolf Behne, Werner Hegemann, Sigfried Giedion and Philip Johnson

The relationship with the press was very important in disseminating the new art. Berlage had been the first to familiarize Oud with international exposure and Van Doesburg tried deliberately to force his international breakthrough. The magazine was the best medium and Germany the country where reputations were made and broken. In the early 1920s, the journalist Adolf Behne dominated German architecture criticism. Oud was in close contact with him for many years. Behne was a useful go-between for Oud at the start of the 1920s, in disseminating his ideas in Germany, in magazines such as *Das Feuer*, *Der Städtebau* and *Cicerone*. Of course, Oud kept a close eye on the image that was portrayed of him – he was against publication of the 'dune house', for instance, which had only been a remodelling job, and primarily Kamerlingh Onnes's work at that.[46] Oud ordered books from Behne (including P. Scheerbart's *Glasarchitektur*, which was more poetry than professional literature, according to Behne), and 'modern' sheet music for his wife. In October 1921 Oud received a commission through Behne for a villa in the Berlin Grünewald for a lady who was very interested in music; L. Moholy-Nagy acted as a go-between.[47] Behne introduced people with similar interests, including Otto Bartning (1883-1959), who visited Oud in Rotterdam, and travelled to Rotterdam himself to give a lecture – which was a way for Oud to support his German friends, who were having a very hard time during the years of inflation. On that occasion Behne went with Oud to call on Van de Velde, the 'old' revolutionary, who at the time lived in Wassenaar.[48] Although Behne was an important contact for Oud, their views differed on key issues. Behne, like Oud, had an aversion to dogmatism. In the wide range of innovative movements in art and architecture, he refused to make a few exceptions which were thought to be of special importance in heralding the new style. For Behne, the main thing was individual artistic skill. He considered the artist's soul to be a requirement for *Die Wiederkehr der Kunst* (the return of art) – the title of a book he had written when he was a soldier in the First World War.[49] He did not think it mattered whether a work was Expressionist, Cubist or typical of Neo-Plasticism: if he perceived sufficient desire for creative innovation, a work would pass muster: *I don't happen to know of dogma in art*.[50] Behne was not the only one to hold this opinion. Mendelsohn's views were identical and he even attempted to reconcile Van Doesburg (*De Stijl* and Nieuwe

Adolf Behne/ Behne Collection, Landesarchiv, Berlin

Beelding) and H.T. Wijdeveld (1886-1987; *Wendingen* and Expressionism). The very sight of Wijdeveld ('a provincial-German type wearing a floppy hat') made Van Doesburg nauseous and the entire business was extra proof of the Germans' indecisive attitude.[51] The gap between Expressionism and Nieuwe Beelding was unbridgeable for Oud too. He could not stand Behne's attitude either. After all, Behne was guilty of what Oud considered a cardinal sin: instead of informing the public, he engaged in propaganda, and in a way that harmed the essence of new architecture. Oud believed that it was generated 'automatically' by life; incorrect propaganda could only be damaging.

Oud's belief in the self-evidence of modern architecture stopped him from pursuing an initiative of Behne's, who was organizing a boycott of *Wasmuths Monatshefte* in 1925. The reason was an article by the new editor-in-chief, W. Hegemann, who wrote very disparagingly about Van de Velde and Berlage. The protest against it was an important stimulus for the 'Ring', a group of modern architects including Mendelsohn, W. Gropius (1883-1969), H. Scharoun (1893-1972) and H. Häring (1882-1958). The boycott was to entail refusal to continue to supply Hegemann with material. When Oud heard that it would not only affect Hegemann, but De Fries as well, he decided not to join in. As he wrote to Mendelsohn: *I am not in favour of the press just saying 'yes, great' to everything that is presented as 'modern'. Now and again the modern formalism very much needs proper criticism and on several occasions I have found remarks made by Hegemann I agree with wholeheartedly. On the other hand there were many comments that often irritated me immensely!!! All the same, I believe that the new movement is so full of vigour and so unassailably strong that I can laugh about these things and grant someone the pleasure of his dissenting disposition: our work and not the suppression of an opinion shall be our strength.*[52] He informed Hegemann that he considered a boycott to be pointless...*because even Hegemann's glowing pen will prove to be powerless against the development of the architecture that is so unavoidably necessary that I can only consider any resistance a waste of time for those concerned and believe it to be of little consequence.*[53] He was against 'intellectual dictatorship'.[54] When the Nazis robbed and exiled Hegemann in the early nineteen-thirties, Oud tried to help him in what was now the customary way: he organized lectures and articles in magazines – admittedly without much success. Oud also tried to arrange a press card for him, to enable him to travel to New York at a reduced fare. After he had arrived in the United States, Hegemann sought to convince J. Hudnut, who was then the dean of Columbia University, to offer Oud a professorship. It is not known whether Hudnut followed Hegemann's advice at that stage, but when, two years later, he was looking for someone for the Graduate School of Design which he had established at Harvard University, Oud was his first choice. After the Hegemann business, relations between Oud and Behne cooled off.

Henry-Russell Hitchcock. From: H. Searing (ed.), *In search of modern architecture. A tribute to Henry-Russell Hitchcock Jr*, New York/Cambridge (Mass.) 1982

**Oud had an unusual relationship with Giedion, a student of Wölfflin's. He first met Giedion in the summer of 1926, when L. Moholy-Nagy was visiting Rotterdam and introduced them. Giedion promised to expose the long lines of architectural evolution, entirely in agreement with Wölfflin, and thus the roots of the new architecture. *What I hold dear as a historian – and this could be a subject for debate – is to expose the unknown 19th century and to learn to see things, viewed as modern and new (Neues Bauen) today, in the total continuity of history as silent links in the development.*[55] But, according to Oud, this was exactly what he failed to do. Instead of providing a historically-based opinion, he dished up propaganda full of sensationalism. His *Bauen in Frankreich* was nothing but a Behne-like cinematographic collage, which hopelessly neglected the essence of the new architecture. Giedion's visual manipulation ignored the social commitment of architecture and was, basically, antisocial. *A sentence such as "there is a draught in my house" is hurtful to me, because it is an antisocial sentence. Why is only the biggest window modern, why only the airiest house? To me that is 'formalism'.*[56] Oud pulled the book completely to pieces. Worst of all, Giedion had turned out to be a romantic, and moreover, as a historian, understood nothing of the practicalities of building. *To me they still are a bit of 'cloud cuckoo land', a little romanticism.*[57] The collages with bridges and cranes had nothing to do with architecture: they were *large constructions transposed to the field of small buildings: technical romanticism of the worst kind.*[58] Giedion's eulogies for Le Corbusier and his dwellings on pilotis were merely *aesthetic hobbies, dear Giedion, romantic constructions. Antisocial just like the whole of your book.*[59] And why wasn't there a picture of a working-class house anywhere in the book? Probably because Giedion could not use them in his theory, *a theory that wants to be a 'general' theory, but the most general: that does not tolerate mass-produced houses and terraced houses (or do you reject towns, as a modern person?).*[60] He extolled architecture for the rich. There was absolutely no trace in Giedion's work of a carefully composed theory of evolution. *But I expect a student of Wölfflin's to look deeper into temporary things, to see a deeper truth with regard to a closed and an open (lighter) form, to have a deeper understanding of Thomas Mann and classical flawlessness.*[61] And that put paid to Giedion. The friendship lasted, but they no longer mentioned architecture.**

**As Oud closed the door on Giedion, someone of fresh promise was being ushered in – Philip Johnson (1906). He, like Giedion, was an art and architecture historian, and first visited Oud in 1930. He accompanied Henry-Russell Hitchcock, who was to become the American chronicler of modern architecture. Johnson's opinion of Giedion's book proved, if nothing else, that he was indeed in agreement with Oud. *Giedion is the incarnation of the point of view that Russell and I, and you as well I think, especially disagree with. It is interesting that the great architects all disagree with him in this fundamental point of view. You and Mies and Corbusier, and of***

**W. Kandinsky (left), Walter Gropius (centre) and J.J.P. Oud, *circa* 1923/ OUDJ-52, NAI, Rotterdam**

*course the Swedes all disagree. But the Swiss architects except perhaps Schmidt of Basel all belong to the group, which Giedion and Stam head. They sacrifice their ideas of beauty which they regard as wrong, in order to have windows that God knows only the Swiss would find practical.*[62] Johnson was profoundly impressed with Oud's housing at Hoek van Holland. For him, it was one of the absolute masterpieces of new architecture, together with the Tugendhat House by L. Mies van der Rohe (1886-1969) in Brno. The visit caused Hitchcock to change his mind about Oud (about whom he had published a far from complimentary article not long before), and the result was one of the first foreign monographs on Oud. Johnson, curator for architecture at the prestigious Museum of Modern Art (MOMA) in New York, gave Oud a place of honour in the now famous exhibition entitled *The International Style. Architecture since 1922*, which got off to a slow start, but was ultimately a great success. The exhibition was one of the first attempts to codify the new architecture. *Today a new style has come into existence*, Hitchcock and Johnson wrote. They went on to emphasize that it was the result of the spontaneous creative process of a handful of pioneers. *The aesthetic conceptions on which its disciplines are based derive from the experimentation of the individualists.* The characteristics of the new style could be summarized in a few points. *There is, first , a new conception of architecture as volume rather than as mass. Secondly, regularity rather than axial symmetry serves as the chief means of ordering design. These two principles, with a third proscribing arbitrarily applied decoration, mark the productions of an international style.*[63] Work by Oud on show included the row of houses at Hoek van Holland, his contribution to the Weissenhofsiedlung in Stuttgart and the Kiefhoek estate in Rotterdam. His work was hung with that of Raymond Hood (1881-1934), Frank Lloyd Wright, Richard Neutra (1892-1970), Howe & Lescaze, and Bowman Brothers, all from the United States, and from Europe Mies van der Rohe, Gropius and Le Corbusier. The key exhibit was a collection of newly made models; there were also photographs on display. Oud's model cost more than the other three from Europe combined; it was of a design for a villa for Johnson's mother. Oud's prominent presence at the exhibition also established him in the New World as one of the pioneers of the new architecture.

## The Movement

The 1920s in Europe seemed literally to be producing a revolution in the design of society. Architecture and urban planning, sculpture and painting, music, theatre, literature, dance – innovative trends were taking shape everywhere. The same descriptions were applicable, time and again: destruction of what was traditional, omission of the subject in the traditional sense, focus on newly discovered essentials, abstraction, fascination with collective phenomena like the masses, rationalism, industrial techniques as inspiration and, when possible, as the supplier of new technological design processes. This common focus was experienced as positive, as the symptom of a freshly emerging style based on a new feeling about life deriving from new social relationships. Now, thanks to a long series of breakthroughs in science and technology, what had seemed insurmountable in the past was now possible and inescapable, and could, to some extent, be typified by the same adjectives. What was new was everywhere, universal and spontaneous, because, in Oud's words, it sprang directly and unintentionally from life.

It was hard to reconcile this unintentionality, this spontaneous bubbling up from the wells of modern life with attempts to organize and institutionalize. Oud's attitude towards such efforts was ambivalent. On the one hand, associations and magazines – which often went hand in hand – were useful weapons in achieving something new, on the other hand they entailed a risk of ossification, ideologization and dogmatism. It called for permanent alertness and Oud sized up the situation constantly. Those who were part of the movement and those who were not were assessed for their usefulness on behalf of 'the new'; it was an ever-changing scene. To start with, the hub of the movement was Paris, in the 1920s it switched to Germany, which was to be the centre of the new architecture into the 1930s. Added to which Germany, more than other countries, was the home base of numerous associations and groups, militant or otherwise.

The main reason why Oud became a key figure in the Modern Movement in the 1920s and '30s was not so much his membership of various associations and his participation in several prominent joint initiatives, but his exceptionally wide, international network, which he maintained by way of extensive correspondence. In the mid-1920s the correspondence peaked. He must have spent hours and hours every day, letter-writing, which he did himself, without a secretary or assistant, unlike Frank Lloyd Wright, for instance. He was in touch with all the well-known and with some meanwhile forgotten pioneers of the Modern Movement, largely in German. His vast network was one of the tools with which Oud acquired a wider audience. He received invitations for lectures in Belgium and, above all, Germany. In the 1920s, the fulcrum of the Modern Movement was in Germany, and that is the country he visited most.

The universal character of 'the new' explains why Oud considered magazines dealing not only with architecture but also with literature, sculpture and dance to be more important than journals on architecture. There were, in his opinion, more than enough of the latter. During the 1920s the Bauhaus emerged as the most successful institution, covering almost all aspects of the Modern Movement. It became an absolutely unique institute and one of the centres of modern architecture. But the process was by no means a matter of course. When Van Doesburg visited the Bauhaus in 1921, he was wildly enthusiastic, as well as amazed ... *those Bauhaus modernists race around like mad people, baring as much as possible, bare, bare feet, necks, chests, legs*, Van Doesburg wrote. He himself was inclined to wear tight American suits or ditto American sportswear. *Ravens and grasshoppers build nests in their hair and lobsters lay eggs in their ears.*[64] The Bauhaus reading-room was a ... *meeting-place for long-haired mental gymnasts, poisoned with the nicotine of ruin romanticism.*[65] Much missionary work was needed, and Van Doesburg threw himself into it with dedication. A year later he was out of favour, as tends to happen in revolutionary circles. The Bauhaus, led by W. Gropius, was examining the 'scientific' basis of design, which was sought in social commitment (the masses and mass production), in technology and in theories about visual and spatial perception. That was at the other extreme, and irreconcilable with Van Doesburg's mentality. Moreover, the Bauhaus was thus embarking on the slippery slope of collectivism, which embodied two dangers, from Oud's point of view: it threatened to push art into political territory, and it whittled away at the personal element in the design process, although that was the seat of the emotion which made art of architecture. Nevertheless, Oud made an effort to keep the Bauhaus for the movement. Undoubtedly partly because, at the Bauhaus, innovations were allowed to be mutually reinforcing. The curriculum reflected the whole gamut of disciplines: painting, cabinetmaking, music. It was unique, and it was just what Oud approved of. Moreover, the Bauhaus was vital, as a platform – thanks, amongst other things, to the *Bauhausbücher* series to which Mondrian and Oud both contributed. Even after the Nazis had forced the Bauhaus in Weimar to close and it had moved to Dessau, Oud continued to support it initially. After Gropius left, the politicization Oud head feared began to accelerate and he felt it was lost to the movement. However, in those hard times Oud became personally involved in an initiative for a new, comprehensive magazine.

Around 1920 Oud no longer had *De Stijl* in which to air his views, and there was no other magazine with a similarly broad base for him to use. That changed when in 1926 Arthur Müller Lehning invited him to become an editor of the *Internationale Revue i10*. Piet Mondrian had brought Oud to Lehning's attention.[66] Apart from Dutch contributors like Van Eesteren (1897-1988), Rietveld, Van der Leck, Domela, Huszár, Vordemberge-Gildewart and Vantongerloo, Lehning also looked for interested parties in the Bauhaus. Van Doesburg was not asked, on account of his conflicts with a number of contributors. Gropius, Kandinsky and Moholy-Nagy promised to take part.[67] Willem Pijper was the editor of the music section. Oud, who was after all a civil servant working for the municipal authority, had only one reservation: the fact that the magazine might take a politically revolutionary tone. *It would be extremely unpleasant for me personally to be pushed or inadvertently manoeuvred into a political alliance which does not appeal to me: for that same reason the "Bauhaus" in Weimar went under, and I am not keen on any political party at all, and so do not wish to get saddled with any difficulties or efforts (opposition on behalf of work is enough as it is: so I don't want any groundless pretexts).*[68] Lehning replied by return: *We want a magazine for the fundamentally new, progressive, pioneering movements in all areas, in art and science. Why not just the relationship between Man and society: soci-*

*ology? We want revolutionaries from all directions. Why only exclude those who emphasize revolutionizing society... There are people who believe that social revolution is enough in itself and that innovation will automatically follow; there are others who believe that art has nothing to do with society. Our magazine wants to challenge both and seeks to demonstrate the connection, where it exists, and where it doesn't exist, just arrange the different movements side by side, to prove that what is new takes on many different guises, and is not just found in the fanatical bias of a particular group.*[69] Evidently that set Oud's mind at rest. In 1927 the first number was published, containing a personal 'guideline' by Oud, in which he set forth his views on cooperation between the arts.[70] *i10* was not to last long. Attempts to raise funds for it in Switzerland failed and in 1929 it ceased publication.

Oud was bitterly disappointed when *i10* folded, particularly because no similar ventures materialized. The Congrès Internationaux d'Architecture Moderne (CIAM) proved not to be an option either, and, after his initial enthusiasm, Oud decided not to participate. The impetus for this international association came from experiences with the Weissenhofsiedlung in Stuttgart and was stimulated by negative experiences with the competition for a League of Nations Palace in Geneva. The jury had awarded first prize to Le Corbusier's design, but in the end opted for something less explicitly modern. As a result, Hélène de Mandrot, who had been directly involved in the competition, invited a number of modern architects for a reunion at her château at La Sarraz. Le Corbusier wrote the programme, S. Giedion was in charge of organization and one of his first basic decisions was to exclude the visual arts, to which modern architecture in fact owed so much.[71] And that immediately established the nature of the CIAM: it was for architects, not a platform for all aspects of the new movement. The list of prospective participants was discussed at length. The group of modern architects in Berlin was bothered by what they considered to be the informal nature of the meeting. They did not turn up, but sent Hugo Häring as an observer. Their refusal to travel to La Sarraz meant that at least two branches of modern architecture were left out of the CIAM: taut, cubist Expressionism and organic architecture by designers like H. Scharoun. Oud and Van Eesteren intervened when they discovered that Giedion also intended to invite J. Wils (1891-1972) and W.M. Dudok: their names were scrapped. H.P. Berlage, A. Loos (1870-1933) and K. Moser (1860-1936) were approached, as representatives of the previous generation of modern architects. Only Berlage attended.

Despite the selective set-up and the squabbles over the list of participants, Oud warmly welcomed Giedion's initiative. It was the intention to discuss topical themes in smaller configurations and Oud was asked to chair the working group dealing with urban planning. Illness forced him to call off at the last minute. Van Eesteren and Stam were not able to attend either, so there was no-one from the Netherlands except Berlage. At later congresses the absences were fully

Willem Dudok (second row, third from left)/ H. van Bergeijk collection.

compensated, the more so as Giedion appointed Van Eesteren (who from 1928 on was commissioned to design the General Extension Plan for Amsterdam at the Amsterdam department of City Development) as president. Giedion was very keen to have Oud participate, as was demonstrated by the fact that he got Moser to try and involve him in the congresses.[72] Oud finally pulled out when he discovered that Giedion pursued an almost military approach for the congresses. Giedion set up a Central Council (Comité International pour la Réalisation des Problèmes Architecturaux Contemporains, CIRPAC), operating as the executive committee; he created the post of Secretary General for himself. He succeeded, from that central position, in applying his own historical and theoretical views for the delineation of modern architecture. That produced a clearly identifiable CIAM orthodoxy, which by no means included all the movements considered at that time as belonging to Modernism. Oud had envisaged it quite differently. *You know the admiration with which I welcomed the Sarraz Congress: to be happily together with our colleagues, a little conversation (not too much and not too profound), a few walks in the beautiful surroundings, some dancing, a few final conclusions of a general nature and then: The End.*[73] Moreover, he wanted to rid himself of the stigma of a spoilt prima donna who was inclined to shun all too worldly concerns.[74] When CIAM turned out to be a propaganda machine and threatened to become a vehicle for a dogmatic doctrine, Oud turned his back on it. Added to which, he was not keen on the list of participants. *What do I have to do with an untalented hanger-on like Hoste? What with Häring? What really with the quantity-freak May? With the hothouse plant Corbusier?*[75]

### Le Corbusier

Oud never wrote as much or as intensely about any fellow architect as he did about Le Corbusier. He continued to praise him until 1927 as one of the pioneers of new architecture, but after his contribution to the Weissenhofsiedlung and the consolidation of his development in a programmatical manifesto – a kind of profession of faith, with building on pilotis as one of its propositions – disappointment prevailed. Oud thought of Le Corbusier as a genius, but a misguided genius. For Oud he had turned out to be 'the biggest disappointment'. As Oud put it to Giedion: *I don't like Le Corbusier because with every day he flaunts an increasing virtuosity, because he combines a rare clarity of vision with a nowadays rare unclarity of form.*[76] True, Oud admired Le Corbusier's gift for stimulating ideas and the clarity of his vision, but those talents were cancelled out by aspects which, for Oud, were fundamental sins. Le Corbusier abused his talent, he lost sight of reality and ignored the problems which the new architecture was supposed to solve, in order to concentrate fully on purely programmatical architecture – architecture as an ongoing manifesto. *He has not created a standard for architecture, but a standard-architecture (at the rich man's level) and that is a different thing.*[77] Le Corbusier's contribution to the Weissenhofsiedlung demonstrated the extent to which his architecture had degenerated into show: *Theatre, very beautiful now and again, to be sure, but for evolution useless and dangerous. The worst romanticism. You may not wish to admit this to me, but just watch this abstract 'Wright'.*[78] Le Corbusier's work was *far too coquettish and feminine in its airiness and desire to please.*[79] Romanticism was Le Corbusier's cardinal sin, and was all the more unpardonable because all he did was convert painting into architecture.[80] In other words, Le Corbusier's architecture did not have roots in modern life. Oud's judgement was harsh, but clear, and he never had cause to revise it. On the contrary, the 'floating' houses on pilotis merely proved that Le Corbusier was lost to the new architecture. Architecture which did arise from life, unlike that Le Corbusier's, would never stand on pilotis, because there was absolutely no practical reason for it to do so: the garden beneath did not get any sun and the fact that the rooms above also had to be insulated on the underside meant that such architecture – like that of the Stuttgart houses – was only suitable for the wealthy upper class.[81] The more celebrated Le Corbusier became in the 1930s, particularly with the younger architects, the more irritated Oud became. In 1938 he maintained that Le Corbusier was outmoded; you could learn more from 'an old farmhouse'.[82]

Oud took leave of Le Corbusier in the 1927-1928 period, which marked another crucial stage in Oud's development. Ten years earlier he had renounced the vernacular, and, without relinquishing his admiration or even his affection for Berlage, had put a distance between himself and his important role model. At the beginning of the 1920s he again set out a new course: he now believed that modern painting and architecture could not possibly be united in a concrete architectural design, even though they were imbued with the same spirit. Modern architecture had to follow its own programme. Around 1927 Oud deliberately opposed the prime representatives of that same modern architecture, deliberately refused to join their most sensational movement and finally broke with Berlage, who had already indicated that he was increasingly disenchanted with Oud's work, and, as a member of the jury for the competition for an Exchange in Rotterdam, had rejected Oud's entry. Oud was all the more disappointed because he was convinced that Berlage was departing from the course he had himself charted. How else could he explain why Berlage supported the Expressionists of the Amsterdam School and rejected Oud, who believed he was following in Berlage's footsteps? *I am still deeply disappointed to see you moving among a catagory of architects, as if you felt at home with them, but for whom I have only the greatest aversion. After all, they drag our profession, in which I have learnt to see what is beautiful thanks primarily to you, down to a level which in no way deserves the name of architecture.*[83] A few years later, Oud saw Berlage as 'conquered' i.e. past history. *I have virtually distanced myself from Berlage. In spite of his initial pursuit of a wider recognition of modern life, I see him much more as a renewer on the basis of art-historical development of form than as a designer of modern life.*[84] Oud appears to have finally dissociated himself from the Modern Movement around 1928 and deliberately opted for a position as a solitary pioneer. That did not initially detract from his international fame; quite the reverse.

### Lonely Prophet

Thanks partly to his collaboration in undertakings like *i10* and his participation in the Weissenhofsiedlung, Oud became an international celebrity. His reputation can be measured by the large number of requests from abroad to accept posts at universities or housing agencies. In May 1927

Le Corbusier/ Fondation Le Corbusier, Paris (Photo Studio Limo)

he was asked to succeed Wilhelm Kreis at the 'Staatliche Kunstakademie' in Düsseldorf. Having consulted the Rotterdam municipal authorities, Oud refused. A year later the 'Eidegenössische Technische Hochschule' in Zurich invited him to succeed Karl Moser as professor there.[85] Again Oud let it be known that he was not interested. During that period he had various requests for architectural work. In 1927 there were rumours in the press from abroad of an offer in Munich, where some people were advocating a similar position for him to Ernst May's in Frankfurt, but again Oud turned it down.[86] Evidently he did not consider the offer realistic and he was fed up with public housing. He gave his passion for building as an explanation for his systematic refusal of professorships. Oud feared that the two would be hard to combine.

Five years later, Oud's work figured prominently at the New York exhibition *The International Style. Architecture since 1922* and he established his reputation in America, the country which fascinated him. Oud's contribution to the exhibition did not generate concrete assignments; there was no follow-up to the house he designed for Johnson's mother. In the mid-1930s it looked as if things were about to change. In June 1936 Oud, who had left the Rotterdam housing authority in 1933 and set up as an independent architect, had a visit from A.H. Barr, director of the MOMA in New York. Barr had something special to offer him: J. Hudnut, the dean of Harvard University, educational reformer and founder of the Graduate School of Design, had asked Barr to persuade Oud to organize teaching at his college. So another potential professorship, but there was more: the MOMA was looking for an architect for its new building and Barr would have preferred a European. Oud topped the list; Gropius and Mies van der Rohe were also possible candidates. In other words, Barr had the ideal 'package deal' for Oud: a combination of a professorship and a concrete design assignment, and for America's most prominent institution in the field of modern art and architecture at that. But again Oud refused to take the plunge. Barr wrote to the Board of the MOMA that Oud wanted to stay in the Netherlands, *where his position, as a prophet in his own country, is rapidly improving.*[87] The Board decided to stop looking for a European architect. The MOMA's new premises were designed by P. Goodwin, who came up with a dazzlingly white, 'New Objectivity' temple. In the years that followed, the MOMA was to become one of the most influential centres of propaganda for Modernism, which was promoted in the 1940s to the house-style of American social-capitalism, and was exported to Europe in the 1950s with support from American public authorities. However, Oud's name did not feature on the long list of retrospective exhibitions devoted to the work of the pioneers of the 1920s. His rejection of Barr's unique offer obliged Hudnut to look for another European pioneer for his school. Gropius was appointed, at Oud's suggestion. Gropius transformed the school into a 'Harvard Bauhaus' and also got Giedion over to Cambridge. As a result, the centre of the movement effectively moved to the United States. Harvard played a leading role in defining a Modernism geared to the American situation which was far removed from the pre-war European roots and in many respects was irreconcilable with Oud's personal opinions. Even before he had rejected Barr's proposal, he had been a lonely prophet, now he was permanently out on a limb, in terms of modern architecture. The situation was not only aggravated by his self-imposed isolation, but by the work he produced in the 1930s after his move from the municipal housing authority.

### Social Housing or Monument

Oud's international reputation rested almost exclusively on his social housing work in Rotterdam. Between 1918 and 1933, the year he left the Rotterdam Woningdienst (Rotterdam Housing Authority), he built several thousands of dwellings in such noteworthy complexes as the large blocks at Spangen, Kiefhoek and the small row of houses at Hoek van Holland. He demonstrated that mass housing could be very well designed, architecture as art. Yet his attitude to social housing was ambivalent. The battle with budgets that were always too tight and the constant need to cut costs made it a tough assignment. The euphoria about the 'Wohnung für das Existenzminimum' (housing for the subsistence level) puzzled Oud. *I am not so fond of 'Minimum-Existenz' building in general. They are part of the world and not the whole of it thank God.*[88] The favourable reactions to his contribution to the Weissenhofsiedlung also struck him as strange: *it is nothing more than an attempt to build a proper residence:*

*a problem that hardly belongs to the world of architecture.*[89] In the early 1920s he was already feeling the strict financial constraints of social housing to be so limiting that he would have preferred to leave the Woningdienst. When his housing blocks at Spangen were completed at the start of the 1920s he was longing for different assignments. *I would like to build a bigger railway station for a town, or something for the community of a grand nature: would you know of something for me? Starting in three months?* he wrote to Giedion in 1928; the three months' respite referred to his term of notice for the municipality.[90]

What caused his ambivalence? Was Oud starting at the end of the 1920s to have doubts about the architectural scope of social housing? He was certainly convinced that housing could never be the starting-point of urban planning, and that the element which turned a building into architecture was easier to achieve in public buildings. The latter allowed more freedom, were less tied down to bureaucratic regulations and procedures, and had larger budgets. His designs for a Volksuniversiteit (Adult Education Institute) and, in particular, his famous entry for the Rotterdam Exchange competition (both of which were made in the 1920s, coinciding with his well-known social housing projects) reveal how he envisaged such buildings. It is not Oud's design approach which distinguishes the plans for public buildings from those for housing, but his attempt to create buildings which, on account of their institutional embeddedness, were dominant in urban planning terms. Oud sought to give these public buildings a 'representative' character and make them the crowning features of their surroundings. In other words, public buildings were more architecture than a series of working-class dwellings. It was unthinkable that working-class housing might reach the same architectural standard as public buildings, in Oud's view.[91] His conviction that representational buildings were on a higher plane coincided with his views on society: unlike many of his European colleagues around 1930, he believed that this difference corresponded with a hierarchic make-up of society, which he considered to be meritorious, comparing it with relationships within a family. At a later stage he presented this theme to counter criticism of his Shell Building, although it originated from the 1930s. *Just as little as a child has the same rights as the father in a family (and this will soon be proved right again!) so little does the house have the same rights as the town hall in architecture (this will also be proved right again soon).* Oud felt this view did not demonstrate a lack of democratic conviction. *There is a bad democracy where everyone is equal (and where there is no order: just anarchy!) and a good democracy in which masters and servants live together as fathers and sons. With order of rank, to be sure. The latter I love!*[92] The city ought to reflect the hierarchy of social life in the design and siting of its buildings: working-class houses were at the bottom of the ladder, then churches and offices, and in many respects the town hall was the apex. Even with these basic assumptions, Oud still managed to build modern architecture; his designs for public buildings in the 1920s show that he, unlike many of his colleagues at the time, did not consider modernism and 'representation' to be irreconcilable. However, in the 1930s he began to wonder whether representational architecture could indeed be produced in the same way as social housing. The latter was the result of abstraction, reduction and spatial differentiation of the building block, which had been broken down into rows. The designs for the Volksuniversiteit and the Exchange came about in the same way, but with far more differentiation. Did the modern representational building not in fact require an extra layer, which was more than strictly functional. Was representation not identical to embellishment?

**Beyond Modernism?**

In the 1930s Oud began to differentiate systematically between building and architecture. Building was nothing more than competently solving a building task in a technical and functional sense. It was the work of engineers, without artistic pretensions, and should not be called architecture. He disliked the term 'nieuwe bouwen' (new building): *an insipid and nasty word for 'new architecture', if you don't mind me saying.*[93] He was particularly annoyed by the fact that new trends in society were identified with socialism – something of which leftist colleagues, including J.B. van Loghem (1881-1940), were especially guilty, in his view. And that caused increasing tension within the Rotterdam architects' association *Opbouw*, of which Oud had been the chairman for a few years

**in the twenties. The 'politicalization' of the profession and, by implication, of *Opbouw*, was cause for him to resign his membership – and thus become even more isolated. *The principles concerning aesthetics which the Board wishes to champion, are too general in purport to be included in specific political constellations – whatever they may be. A synthesis of this type, which the Board has been trying to implement of late, results in a limitation of the intended opinions which I do not wish to condone with my membership.*[94]**

**Although Oud's isolated position had various, often highly personal causes, he invariably gave his theoretical position as the underlying reason. That position was perfectly clear: architecture is art which arises spontaneously from life and would only freeze up in propagandist manifestos and too strictly organized associations; life presents itself concretely in the assignment, not in abstract politico-social scenarios; design does not follow function, but is a valuable and autonomous aspect in the design process (a slight change in emphasis compared with what he stated in 1933, when he did not consider art to be the beginning but the end);[95] the design is produced by the interaction of form and function. These relatively general opinions, the significance of which would, Oud was convinced, only be clear in real-life buildings, were countered by increasingly severe criticism of the architecture he saw springing up around him, and of the movements which seemed to validate it. For instance, CIAM and the central committee embodied, for Oud, the materialist, functionalist view he so abhorred. Such views were diametrically opposed to his conviction that form should stem from life. It was precisely this view that Oud quoted to explain and legitimize his isolation. *This has put me in a rather odd and isolated position among the modern architects and for that reason I have never been able to decide to take part in CIRPAC, as this has a disposition that is too purely materialistic in my opinion.*[96]**

**Oud, inspired by Wölfflin amongst others, tried to see the new architecture in a wider perspective. He hoped that the new style would measure up to that of past times, but it failed badly. The premises were probably more pure, but the *'ability' is undoubtedly far, far less.*[97] Oud banged this drum**

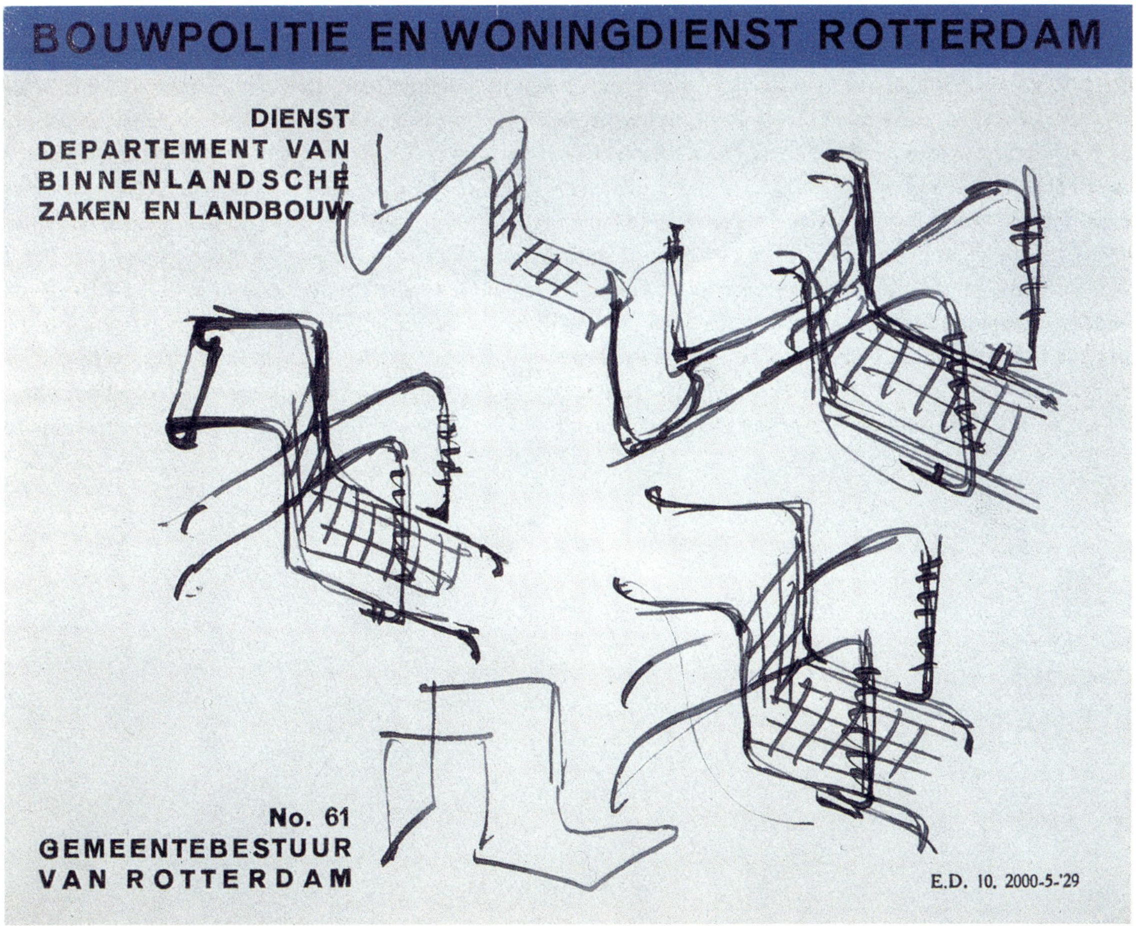

**Sketches by Oud for a tubular steel chair/
OUDJ-sn 41, NAI, Rotterdam**

constantly in the 1930s. Why applaud unsuccessful modern architecture just because it was modern? *Can no-one explain to me why in the world 'Nieuw Zakelijk' work cannot be properly conceived, have the right proportions or colour, why none of the musicality can be heard of what we can so splendidly achieve with the means at our disposal? ... The days of Hanna Höch's work may be behind us, but equally, the days of humdrum manoeuvring with steel girders, cranes, cupboards for shoes, brush and wash leather are behind us. Anyone still not knowing how to organize a house properly, will never learn!*[98] Anyone who wanted more, wanted to make architecture, was advised to consult architectural history, and the 'traditional' architects, for example H. Tessenow (1876-1950) whom Oud greatly admired. *Therefore I try to demonstrate that, from a spiritual point of view, the new architecture is no match for the earlier architecture and that it is just another aspect of evolution when we try to catch up... But I would consider it an enrichment if we succeeded in shaping the new architecture in such a refined manner that it had the refinements of Schmitthenner, but also our spirit of new architecture for one hundred per cent!*[99] The benefits of the new architecture had been reaped, and Oud no longer had any desire to continue elaborating on them endlessly. He felt it was time to stop *harping on about existing fundamentals and start working on achieved results.*[100]

Oud was not the only one to believe that modern architecture was threatening to end up as the opposite of architecture. The roots of that conviction can be found in his well-known lecture 'Ja und Nein' of 1925, but the thrust had changed. In the 1930s, resistance to 'undiluted' functionalism was growing. It was one thing to solve a problem optimally in a technical and economic sense, but architecture needed an artistic dimension which rose above that. This view produced a rift within 'the 8' and led to 'Group 32', which wanted to recapture the cultural dimension and was not averse to drawing on architectural history.[101] S. van Ravesteyn (1889-1983) did the same thing, in his highly personal way: he 'embellished' his modern idiom with references to the Baroque. Despite Oud's liking for 'embellished' architecture, he did not care for that. Van Ravesteyn's interiors recalled the 'spirit of my old aunt' rather than being 'joyfully designed by contemporary life'.[102] In 1938 this development was the reason for the architect's association 'Architectura et Amicitia' (A. et A.) to organize a workshop in Avegoor, addressing the dilemma from various sides. H. Buys sent Oud several contentions, some of which were decidedly critical. He warned that the conversion of third-rate designers to the new architecture was bound to take its toll eventually. He did not find the time ripe to accept Modernism at the level it had then achieved. *Elements of new style are still only sporadically present, yet are being reproduced, not very felicitously, in non-creative elements. It would attest to intolerable arrogance if the new architecture were to award itself a certificate of perfection,* as he put it in his contention no. 8, which was immediately followed by a hopeful statement of principles in which he rounded on any form of dogmatism, as well as on a return to traditionalism. *Many expressions of the new architecture contain such elements of a new beauty that it is merely a matter of time before the unarchitectonic shackles still binding it are shed, and catharsis and maturation can occur. However, this evolution is not advanced by a return to what may be considered to have been overcome, but by purification and enrichment of what has been accomplished.*[103] These attempts to reanimate modern architecture were not confined to the Netherlands. Le Corbusier – whom the 'renegade', younger modern Dutch architects lauded as the founder of a new decorative style – complained of the nostalgic desire in Paris to return to the style of 1900. In England, Modernism had completely fizzled out. *Lubetkin's studio is surrealist industrial art. But the English admire it like children,* Giedion lamented, as he regretfully regarded the decline of the Modern Movement in Europe.[104] *They are, as far as I can see, fatigue symptoms, in addition, the bill for those people who believed that one could manage with the functional, without painting, without feeling,* he wrote to L. Moholy-Nagy – thus implicitly bidding purely pragmatic functionalism farewell himself.[105] The biggest disappointment for Giedion was the new direction taken by Oud. Giedion visited Oud in Rotterdam in July 1938 and he saw Oud's entry for the Amsterdam city hall competition, amongst other things. Oud fell from his pedestal at that moment. He was *on a dangerous reactionary road,* but still claimed to be pursuing the same course as ten years earlier, when his well-known housing projects were born.[106] Giedion was convinced the opposite was true. To his mind, Oud had forced a radical breach. *It was a difficult evening*, he admitted in a letter to Van Eesteren. *Quite different from that with the '8'. They should concern themselves about him!*[107]

## Historicization

Giedion's gloomy outpourings on the loss of 'true' Modernism – i.e. Modernism according to the principles of CIAM (which was also in bad shape in the 1930s) – illustrate the change in position of the movement. Everywhere attempts were being made in the 1930s to embellish 'Nieuwe Bouwen', and in Giedion's opinion that signalled the end of modern architecture. Its ban in the Soviet Union and Nazi Germany marked the movement as a historical phenomenon in the second half of the 1930s, one of the many defunct 'isms' in the history of art and architecture. At the same time, however, the movement, marginalized as it was in Europe, was getting a foothold in the United States. There it changed from a rather oppositional, predominantly socialist-inspired avant-garde into an establishment house-style, embraced by elitist institutes like Harvard University and the MOMA. This shift in position was apparent, amongst other things, in growing numbers of historical, retrospective works, most of which were published in the United States. They typified European Modernism as a phenomenon which had functioned as a lever for new views on building – views which had then found their way to America and had gradually been accepted there. Mumford's *The Culture of Cities* (1938) echoes this point of view. Admittedly it is far wider in scope, but it does pay particular attention to Modernism. The book was a best-seller, which was a reason for Gropius to bring it to Giedion's notice. *I am really very much impressed by it, and I am very pleased that the book got so much publicity. Not only the 'New York Times', but also two of the largest magazines, 'Life' and 'Time', published articles with illustrations and last week the book ranked third on the best-sellers' list, amazing.*[108] That was the kind of publicity the Modern Movement needed, even though Gropius would have preferred a more profound discussion. Giedion, who travelled to Cambridge at Gropius's intercession to take up the Charles Eliot Norton lectureship at Harvard, could perhaps have supplied it. Giedion had planned to write a long standard work, to expose the historical roots of Modernism, and implicitly its historical necessity, an ambition he had cherished since the 1920s. He was not deterred by Mumford's monumental book and his magnum opus, *Time, Space and Architecture*, was published in 1941. The book did not appear in Europe until after the Second World War.
W.C. Behrendt (1885-1945) had already published his *Modern Building: Its Nature, Problems and Forms* in 1937, with a picture of Oud's housing at Hoek van Holland on the cover. Behrendt's positioning of Oud is typical. He identified him with his housing estates, but did not mention the most recent development in Oud's work. In these first historical retrospectives, Oud's work is featured as an important contribution to the growing flood of modern architecture which was now centring on America.

## Fine Architecture versus the International Style

Oud's design for the Amsterdam city hall – the plan with the monumental column which had so shocked Giedion – was not implemented, and the international press paid it no attention. The same initially applied to the design for the Bataafsche Importmaatschappij or BIM (later Shell) office building, which was completed in 1938. The first photos only reached the outside world in 1945, after the Second World War where it received a similar shocked reaction as the city hall design had produced in Giedion. Johnson was convinced that new stimuli were needed to protect Modernism from turning into a purely technocratic discipline. He was taking a stand against Gropius's influence and the consequences of the wartime economy for the construction industry, but was Oud's chosen course with the Shell Building the solution? *I suppose being in America now where we have had so little Berlage and where Wright has been such an individualist, we have taken too hard to the International Style. But there seems little attraction for me in a more traditional approach.*[109] And that is hardly surprising: what Oud had done with the Shell Building was diametrically opposed to the three basic principles of the International Style which Hitchcock and Johnson had postulated in 1932: the building appeared rather massive, especially in black-and-white photographs (the medium on which most foreign critics based their opinions), Oud had used traditional devices like symmetry and a generous amount of ornament. The building was the ideal manifesto of Oud's views in the 1930s, when he was fulminating against any form of formalism and was seeking to refine architecture. Of course, it was an experiment – *Better a failed attempt than successful rigidity!* he wrote to A. Roth. But Oud continued to support wholeheartedly the principal theme, to break through modern orthodoxy to achieve new architecture.[110] He did indeed seem to have passed beyond Modernism. But what had happened to Modernism in the meantime?

Social housing experiments, inspired by the New Deal, the MOMA's constant propaganda and the far from negligible influence of the 'Harvard Bauhaus' paved the way in the 1930s for an unexpectedly fast breakthrough of Modernism during the Second World War. But what kind of Modernism was it? Johnson complained about its anti-cultural character, for which he blamed Gropius. *Everyone here is working on the Existenz-Minimum which you remember was a great favorite of the Bauhaus. Gropius is the great leader here and no one that designs anything except a Harvard type building can win prizes. It is very discouraging.*[111] Initially the character of this Modernism was determined by the wartime economy, which had resulted in the rationing of building materials and necessitated austere building. Under its influence, the design and building process acquired a scientific character and had to comply with management principles, which had long been applicable in American business. First the objectives were determined in a businesslike way, and anything that was not efficient was omitted. Then the means were assessed with which the objectives were to be met. That entailed combining all existing, relevant know-how (the 'teamwork' principle) and dropping anything superfluous. The final step was execution – and as austere as possible. This management-style approach tied in with several basic principles of Functionalism, which was based on an analysis of the building assignment and also advocated restrained execution, inspired by modern industrialized production methods; much was expected from technological innovations. But did it lead to architecture? Or did it get stuck in a kind of production aesthetics?

Oud's criticism of post-war Modernism passed through different stages. It was more important than ever for the post-war reconstruction of the bombed parts of the Netherlands to clarify the position. The more so, as the Giedion-Gropius line in the United States seemed to have made a definite breakthrough. Oud's ideas had not evolved substantially since the 1930s, but his crusade against 'undiluted' Functionalism now fully coincided with his defence of the Shell Building. It caused him to take a step which was, for him, entirely unique. He had always tried to stay far away from codified dogmas and declarations of intent, but he now let himself be enticed into writing a manifesto. It comprised two points which tied in with the position he had taken in the 1920s: *Up to now the problem of modern architecture was: 1. To fix clearly and unconditionally the requirements of an edifice as to its practical use and construction. 2. To realize these requirements without compromise with the past in forms that are the direct expression of the demands to be met. As engineers do; as the science of structure does!* Oud then declared this stage to be closed. The result was admirable, but not as architecture. *In this way we have now reached, in the best utilitarian and domestic buildings, forms at the level of a good locomotive, a good car, a good dentist-tool. Sound technical forms which in their honesty become of cultural value!* But was that the kind of work with which modern architecture kept its promises? Oud followed the manifesto with a categorical denial. *It is a beginning: not, as some architects seem to think, already an end. It is the basis for a new architecture: a notable part of its grammar, but still not very much in the way of literature! It is good building, but not yet emotional building. Not yet: architecture!* And the latter was precisely what it was all about. *We must now strive to make good building into fine architecture!*[112]

In the following years Oud felt forced to fight on several fronts. What he had feared immediately after the Liberation came true: the American form of Modernism was threatening to become universal. A targeted propaganda offensive was developed in which the MOMA played a leading part. Exhibitions like *The lesson of wartime housing* and *Built in U.S.A. 1932-1944* proclaimed a new, if not universal American architecture and urbanism which seemed to tie in seamlessly with prewar European Modernism and proved capable of meeting

**'Frank Lloyd Wright' exhibition, Ahoy Rotterdam 1952/ OUDJ-67, NAI, Rotterdam**

'Frank Lloyd Wright' exhibition, Ahoy Rotterdam 1952/ OUDJ-67, NAI, Rotterdam

**the technocratic demands of the wartime economy. After a short break, the MOMA resumed its offensive, at the end of the 1940s, when the Cold War was demanding new imagery to convey American political and social ideals. What could be better suited to the purpose than Modernism? After Europe's cultural suicide during the war, a revival of the traditional and historical style elements of European culture was not exactly the obvious solution, and was, moreover, incompatible with America's freshly won status as a superpower. Socialist realism was the arch enemy's formal syntax and so was out of the question. There did not appear to be an alternative to Modernism in its new American form. Meanwhile, the MOMA was organizing retrospectives of the leading pioneers of the Modern Movement, including Mies van der Rohe, Gropius, Frank Lloyd Wright and Le Corbusier. Oud felt excluded and cared nothing for the American version of Modernism. *Modern architecture, which has largely lost sight of the emotional element, really gets my back up ... and I consider the Americans to be typical representatives of that. And they are still doing well too, because – with their freshness – they evidently have right on their side ... The architecture (is) fresh, but empty.*[113] Two buildings, which Oud considered to be among the most representative work of the post-war years and so belonging pre-eminently in the domain of architecture, were particular bones of contention: the headquarters of the United Nations in New York, and that of the UNESCO in Paris. Both pursued teamwork, so abhorrent to Oud, to the extreme: they had been designed by an alliance of architects and artists. They inspired Oud to a veritable crusade against teamwork and in favour of architecture as an individual spiritual achievement. It was quite a different point of view from his anti-individualism of the 1920s, when he championed the suprapersonal, general characteristics of the new style. From the early 1930s, when architects like Van Loghem suggested that pragmatic social relationships were determining design, with no intervention from the designer's personality, Oud set out a new course. In a letter to *Architektur der UdSSR*, of all things. *In architecture I reject collective labour (that is, in one single project). I see architecture – irrespective of my conviction that the principles can never be general enough – as a matter of personal synthesis. The work done by assistants is very vivid and valuable, but of secondary importance all the same.*[114] However, his arguments against teamwork and for individual artistic skill mark a new stage in Oud's post-war quest for a new platform on which to present himself as the representative of a pure kind of Modernism. His aversion to teamwork found support: from Frank Lloyd Wright, whom Oud had greatly admired since he saw Berlage's slides in 1912, and for whose work he mounted an exhibition at the Rotterdam 'Ahoy' in 1952. If anyone embodied the ideal of the architect as an individualist, it was Frank Lloyd Wright. He, too, had objected to the United Nations building. Oud immediately sought support from his American example. *I myself protested against the manner the building bureaucratically was conceived and I was happy to be informed that there is an article of protest of you too. [sic]*[115] When it seemed that the UNESCO building was going to be designed along similar lines, Oud again turned to Frank Lloyd Wright. *Did you read in the papers that there is again a 'team' for the preparation of the plan for the Unesco building in Paris (Gropius, Le Corbusier, Markelius a.s.o.). To supply us – I think – with a second U.N.-glass pearl. I should like very much to plead a bit in the press (or in the UN) for more idealism in the new building – for more architecture. Could not you and I (and Mumford) send a few words to the press as a kind of counteract? Why should the Giedion-gang again have the lead?*[116]**

**The final act in Oud's efforts to regain his pre-war position related directly to his place in history. It seemed far from secure. Again America was at the forefront. For example, in 1952, when the MOMA devoted an exhibition to *De Stijl*. It was not Oud, but Van Doesburg who was praised as the greatest architect of *De Stijl – a man as versatile as any figure of the renaissance.*[117] Of the 106 works on show, there were only four of Oud's projects: the site hut, the factory, the church at Kiefhoek and Café De Unie. What annoyed Oud most was the phrase in the accompanying brochure denying him the authorship of Cubism in architecture. Oud saw it as a deliberate attempt to remove him from architectural history. A MOMA publication of 1955, *Masters of Modern Art,* appeared to confirm this, naming Gropius, Le Corbusier and Mies van der Rohe as the founders of modern architecture, but making absolutely no mention of Oud. He hastened to demand an**

MEIN WEG IN 'DE STIJL'

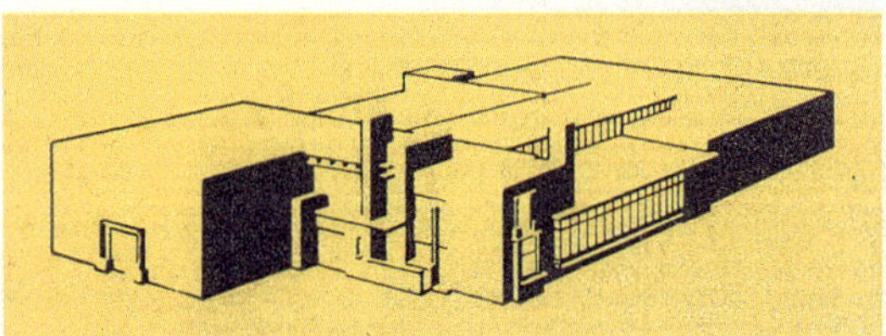

J.J.P. OUD

Cover of J.J.P. Oud, *Mein Weg in 'De Stijl'* (1960)/
Oud Archive, library, NAI, Rotterdam

**explanation from Johnson. *I initiated cubism in architecture in 1917 and 1919 and you are well aware of the influence going out from the 1932 'International Style' architecture in 'The Museum of Modern Art'. You also know that cubist architecture and later 'De Stijl' were of great profit to Le Corbusier, Mies and Gropius. Whereas Gropius had and has not a style of his own being more an educator than a creator. ... If America does not like my future, it could have at all events respect for my past that helped its architects too.*[118] Yet again it is clear that Oud considered himself – correctly – to be one of the founders of modern architecture. The manner in which Oud identified with the hero in Ayn Rand's novel *The Fountainhead* who was modelled on Frank Lloyd Wright, speaks volumes. He had not been accorded a place on the international stage and even his role in *De Stijl* had been misrendered, consequently he had to come up with a way of redressing misrepresentation. He immediately took up arms when he failed to receive due credit for his part in *De Stijl*: Oud, no-one else, had introduced Cubism into architecture. He was also the first to reject that 'visual artillery', for the very reason that it was too destructive of the architecture. The authors of books or articles who claimed otherwise (B. Zevi, H. Jaffé) could count on receiving an outspoken letter, in which Oud pointed out their errors. Whilst making historical corrections, Oud also maintained that *De Stijl* was alive and kicking, that it was a spiritual movement which had not dried up with the last issue of the magazine, but was searching for new substrates on which to develop further. His own work attested to that. Oud thus underlined his conviction that his personal oeuvre exhibited consistency and continuity. It was characterized by evolution, not interruptions; the Shell Building did not constitute a rift either. In other words, Oud refused to accept the blame for something of which he had accused Berlage twenty-five years earlier: a deviation from the course he had set for himself. Oud continued to hammer away on the ongoing line in his work, and that, too, is the essence of his *Mein Weg in 'De Stijl'* (My Progress in '*De Stijl*'), which gave it the character of an apology. His involvement in the series of *De Stijl* exhibitions resulted in later work being included as well – a form of presentation in which the MOMA did not, incidentally, wish to partici-**

**Notes**

**1.** Mrs Berlage to J.J.P. OUD, 26 September 1910, OUDJ-B, NAI, Rotterdam.
**2.** E. Thorn Prikker 'Willem C. Brouwer', in: *Nederlandsche Kunstnijverheid*, Rotterdam 1905, pp. 144-154.
**3.** T. van Doesburg, 'De nieuwe beweging in de schilderkunst', in: *De Beweging*, 12(1916)5, pp. 124-131; 12(1916)6, pp. 219-226; 12(1916)7, pp. 59-66; 12(1916)8, pp. 148-156; 12(1916)9, pp. 226-235. The article was also published independently in 1917.
**4.** T. van Doesburg to J.J.P. Oud, 24 February 1920, Fondation Custodia, Paris.
**5.** J. Huizinga, *Mensch en Menigte*, Haarlem 1918, p. 110.
**6.** H.P. Berlage to J.J.P. Oud, 7 March 1912, OUDJ-B, NAI, Rotterdam.
**7.** K. Lönberg-Holm to J.J.P. Oud, 15 February 1924, OUDJ-B, NAI, Rotterdam.
**8.** E. Mendelsohn, *Rußland – Europa – Amerika*, Basle, Berlin, Boston 1929, p. 6.
**9.** Quoted in a letter from P. Mondrian to J.J.P. Oud, 18 September 1921, Fondation Custodia, Paris.
**10.** P. Mondrian to J.J.P. Oud, 18 September 1921, Fondation Custodia, Paris.
**11.** P. Mondrian to J.J.P. Oud, 6 December 1921, Fondation Custodia, Paris.
**12.** J.J.P. Oud to P. Mondrian, Fondation Custodia, Paris.
**13.** P. Mondrian to J.J.P. Oud, 1 August 1922, Fondation Custodia, Paris.
**14.** P. Mondrian to J.J.P. Oud, 13 July 1922, Fondation Custodia, Paris.
**15.** J.J.P. Oud to P. Mondrian, Fondation Custodia, Paris.
**16.** P. Mondrian to J.J.P. Oud, 4 April 1922, Fondation Custodia, Paris.
**17.** Draft article for P. Johnson, 8 February 1933, OUDJ-vj 1001, NAI, Rotterdam.
**18.** J.J.P. Oud to G. Platz, 25 November 1925, OUDJ-B, NAI, Rotterdam.
**19.** J.J.P. Oud, 'Saenredam en Le Corbusier', draft text 5 October 1938, OUDJ-4-16, NAI, Rotterdam.
**20.** J.J.P. Oud to S. Giedion, 11 December 1928, GTA, Zurich.
**21.** K. James, *Erich Mendelsohn & the Architecture of German Modernism*, Cambridge (Mass.) 1997, pp. 48-78.
**22.** J.J.P. Oud's answer to a questionnaire on the future of the 'Kunstgewerbe', 1925, OUDJ-B, NAI, Rotterdam.
**23.** G. Rietveld to J.J.P. Oud, 24 April 1922, OUDJ-B, NAI, Rotterdam.
**24.** P. Behrens to J.J.P. Oud, 26 November 1922, OUDJ-B, NAI, Rotterdam.
**25.** J.J.P. Oud to T. van Doesburg, 16 December 1921, Fondation Custodia, Paris.
**26.** J.J.P. Oud to W. Hegemann, 21 July 1925, OUDJ-B, NAI, Rotterdam.
**27.** J.J.P. Oud to E. Mendelsohn, 11 October 1923, Kunstbibliothek, Berlin.
**28.** J.J.P. Oud to I. Falkenberg-Liefrinck, 28 May 1941, OUDJ-B, NAI, Rotterdam.
**29.** J.J.P. Oud, 'Piet Mondriaan' (draft for an opening address), November 1945, OUDJ-4-16, NAI, Rotterdam.
**30.** P. Mondrian to J.J.P. Oud, 4 October 1930, Fondation Custodia, Paris.
**31.** J.J.P. Oud to S. Giedion, 24 October 1927, GTA, Zurich.
**32.** J.J.P. Oud to F. Forbat, 7 December 1935, OUDJ-B, NAI, Rotterdam.
**33.** J.J.P. Oud to S. Giedion, 1927, GTA, Zurich.
**34.** J.J.P Oud to H. Buys, 22 May 1936, OUDJ-B, NAI, Rotterdam.
**35.** J.J.P. Oud to E. Mendelsohn, 31 August 1923, Kunstbibliothek, Berlin.
**36.** S. Jacobs, *Henry van de Velde. Wonen also kunstwerk, een woonplaats voor Kunst*, Louvain 1996.
**37.** L. Moholy-Nagy to J.J.P. Oud, 9 May 1922, OUDJ-B, NAI, Rotterdam.
**38.** H. van de Velde to J.J.P. Oud, 22 May 1922, OUDJ-B, NAI, Rotterdam.
**39.** J.J.P. Oud to W. Hegemann, 1925, OUDJ-B, NAI, Rotterdam.
**40.** J.J.P. Oud to H. Meyer, 1925, OUDJ-B, NAI, Rotterdam.
**41.** J.J.P. Oud to E. Mendelsohn, 31 August 1923, Kunstbibliothek, Berlin.
**42.** P. Behrens to J.J.P Oud, 26 November 1922, OUDJ-B, NAI, Rotterdam.
**43.** E. Stockmeyer to J.J.P. Oud, 17 October 1922, OUDJ-B, NAI, Rotterdam.
**44.** P. Behrens to J.J.P. Oud, 26 November 1922, OUDJ-B, NAI, Rotterdam.
**45.** J.J.P. Oud to W. Hegemann, 1925, OUDJ-B, NAI, Rotterdam.
**46.** J.J.P. Oud to A. Behne, 14 November 1920, Nederlands Letterkundig Museum, The Hague.
**47.** A. Behne to J.J.P. Oud, 12 October 1921, Nederlands Letterkundig Museum, The Hague.
**48.** A. Behne to J.J.P. Oud, 29 June 1923, Nederlands Letterkundig Museum, The Hague.
**49.** A. Behne to J.J.P. Oud, 3 October 1920, Nederlands Letterkundig Museum, The Hague.
**50.** A. Behne to J.J.P. Oud, 3 October 1920, Nederlands Letterkundig Museum, The Hague.
**51.** T. van Doesburg to J.J.P. Oud, 21 June 1921, Fondation Custodia, Paris.
**52.** J.J.P. Oud to E. Mendelsohn, 19 June 1926, OUDJ-B, NAI, Rotterdam.
**53.** J.J.P. Oud to W. Hegemann, 19 September 1926, OUDJ-B, NAI, Rotterdam.
**54.** J.J.P. Oud to E. Mendelsohn, 3 July 1926, OUDJ-B, NAI, Rotterdam.
**55.** S. Giedion to J.J.P. Oud, 22 June 1928, GTA, Zurich.
**56.** J.J.P. Oud to S. Giedion, 22

**pate in 1952, and which not appeal either to Bruno Zevi, who saw the exhibition in Rome in 1962.[119]**

**The manner in which Oud, towards the end of his life, was grappling with history, did not interrupt his isolation; on the contrary. Admittedly, he had become a national celebrity thanks to his pre-war pioneer's role, which was confirmed in the *De Stijl* exhibitions (which the Dutch government had helped to initiate). He received assignments of considerable distinction, such as the National Monument on Dam Square in Amsterdam, but by then he was long played out in international architecture. He had been a trailblazer for the evolution of the new architecture, but even in 1927, when he produced his best-known designs, he withdrew from the mainstream, and then finally cut himself off from it when it headed for America. That may have been his personal choice, but the reception of his post-war work and attitude certainly was not. The fact that he was seen as an outsider was all the more painful when the Giedion-Gropius line reached a dead end in the 1950s, CIAM was abolished and Oud's plea for 'fine architecture' appeared to be echoed in Giedion's call for a 'new monumentality', which also made a new form of Classicism acceptable. Things could hardly have been more hurtful for Oud. *Have you ever seen anything more banal than that 'Ambassy' in Athens, with which according to Mister Gropius, 'modern' tries to keep up with Greek tradition!* Oud wrote to Wiekart in 1962. Oud deemed the design for the Boston city hall even worse. *And how beautiful the Gropiuses consider it. ... If I recall how I'classicized' the 'Shell' back in 1938, and far more painstakingly, whilst people were ranting and raving at me (if I can put it that way), I sometimes fail to understand it all.*[120] Post-war modern architecture seemed to be playing an odd game with Oud. What was he to do to be acknowledged as the master of the Modern Movement once more? He was almost obsessed by that question in the fifties and sixties. He never succeeded in finding the answer.**

November 1927, GTA, Zurich.
**57.** J.J.P. Oud to S. Giedion, 22 November 1927, GTA, Zurich.
**58.** J.J.P. Oud to S. Giedion, 24 June 1928, CCA, Montreal.
**59.** J.J.P. Oud to S. Giedion, 24 June 1928, CCA, Montreal.
**60.** J.J.P. Oud to S. Giedion, 24 June 1928, CCA, Montreal.
**61.** J.J.P. Oud to S. Giedion, 11 December 1928, GTA, Zurich.
**62.** P. Johnson to J.J.P. Oud, 1931?, MOMA, New York.
**63.** H.-R. Hitchcock, P. Johnson, *The International Style*, 1995, New York, pp. 35, 36. (Original publication H.-R. Hitchcock, P. Johnson, *The International Style: Architecture since 1922*, New York 1932).
**64.** T. van Doesburg to J.J.P. Oud, 21 June 1921, Fondation Custodia, Paris.
**65.** T. van Doesburg to J.J.P. Oud, 21 June 1921, Fondation Custodia, Paris.
**66.** P. Mondrian to J.J.P. Oud, 22 May 1926, Fondation Custodia, Paris.
**67.** There, he also met Klee, Schlemmer and L. Moholy-Nagy, who were willing to commit themselves to the new magazine. Originally, the name *Één* (One) had been considered for which several typographic tests were run. The initial list of authors comprised Peter Alma, Walther Ayles, Adolf Behne, Walther Benjamin, D.A.M. Binnendijk, Ernst Bock, Menno ter Braak, Roger N. Baldwin, A. Fenner Brockway, Paul Biroukoff, Paul Collaer, C. Domela Nieuwenhuis, C. Van Eesteren, Von Ebneth, W. Gropius, E.J. Gumbel, V. Huszár, W. Kandinsky, Dan de Lange, El Lissitzky, Henri Laserre, B. de Ligt, P. Mondrian, H. Meyer, P. Meller, Pinaud, G. Rietveld, J. Romein. R. Rocker, H. Roland Holst, K. Schwitters, Slutzki, M. Stam, H. Stöcker, B. Vantongerloo, H. van de Velde, S. van Ravesteyn, A. Döblin.
A. Müller Lehning to J.J.P. Oud, 8 October 1926, OUDJ-B, NAI, Rotterdam.
**68.** J.J.P. Oud to A. Müller Lehning, 7 October 1927, OUDJ-B, NAI, Rotterdam.
**69.** A. Müller Lehning to J.J.P. Oud, 8 October 1926, OUDJ-B, NAI, Rotterdam.
**70.** Oud wrote in *i10* for example: 'Huisvrouwen en architecten' *i10* 1(1927)2; 'Internationale architectuur. Werkbund exhibition "die Wohnung" July-September 1927, Stuttgart', *i10*, 1(1927)6; and 'Aangepast bij de omgeving' *i10* 1(1927)10.
**71.** S. Giedion to C. van Eestern 21 November 1927, GTA, Zurich.
**72.** J.J.P. Oud to K. Moser, 22 July 1931, GTA, Zurich.
**73.** J.J.P. Oud to S. Giedion, 18 August 1928, OUDJ-B, NAI, Rotterdam.
**74.** J.J.P. Oud to W. Hegemann, 25 August 1927, OUDJ-B, NAI, Rotterdam. J.J.P. Oud to K. Moser, 4 January 1931, GTA, Zurich.
**75.** J.J.P. Oud to S.Giedion, 1928, OUDJ-B, NAI, Rotterdam.
**76.** J.J.P. Oud to S. Giedion, 24 October 1927, GTA, Zurich.
**77.** J.J.P. Oud to S. Giedion, 24 October 1927, GTA, Zurich.
**78.** J.J.P. Oud to S. Giedion, 1927, GTA, Zurich.
**79.** J.J.P. Oud, 'Saenredam en Le Corbusier', draft text 5 October 1938, OUDJ-B, NAI, Rotterdam.
**80.** J.J.P. Oud to S. Giedion, 24 June 1928, CCA, Montreal.
**81.** J.J.P. Oud to S. Giedion, 24 June 1928, CCA, Montreal.
**82.** J.J.P. Oud, 'Saenredam en Le Corbusier', draft text 5 October 1938, Oud Archive, NAI, Rotterdam.
**83.** J.J.P. Oud to H.P. Berlage, 11 October 1927, OUDJ-B, NAI, Rotterdam.
**84.** J.J.P. Oud to F. Schuster, 14 October 1933, OUDJ-B, NAI, Rotterdam.
**85.** Friedrich Gubler to J.J.P. Oud, 27 March 1927, OUDJ-B, NAI, Rotterdam.
**86.** *Rotterdamsche Courant*, November 1927.
**87.** A.H. Barr to P. Goodwin, 6 July 1936, MOMA, New York.
**88.** J.J.P. Oud to R. McGrath, 12 December 1934, OUDJ-B, NAI, Rotterdam.
**89.** J.J.P. Oud to E. Wedepohl, 12 October 1927, OUDJ-B, NAI, Rotterdam.
**90.** J.J.P. Oud to S. Giedion, GTA, Zurich.
**91.** H. Moscoviter, *Kwetsbare schoonheid. Monumenten in Rotterdam*, Delft 1994.
**92.** J.J.P. Oud to A. Roth, 5 August 1946, OUDJ-B, NAI, Rotterdam.
**93.** J.J.P. Oud to G. Rietveld, 11 March 1934, OUDJ-B, NAI, Rotterdam.
**94.** J.J.P. Oud to 'De Opbouw', 25 May 1933, OUDJ-B, NAI, Rotterdam.
**95.** Draft article for P. Johnson, 8 February 1933, OUD-vj 1001, NAI, Rotterdam.
**96.** J.J.P. Oud to F. Forbat, 7 December 1935, OUDJ-B, NAI, Rotterdam.
**97.** J.J.P. Oud, 'Kritiek?', 3 December 1935, typescript, OUDJ-4-16, NAI, Rotterdam.
**98.** J.J.P. Oud, 'Kritiek?', 3 December 1935, OUDJ-4-16, NAI, Rotterdam.
**99.** J.J.P. Oud to F. Forbat, 7 December 1935, OUDJ-B, NAI, Rotterdam.
**100.** J.J.P. Oud, 'Kritiek?', 3 December 1935, NAI, Rotterdam.
**101.** M. Bock et al., *Van het Nieuwe Bouwen naar een Nieuw Architectuur. Groep '32: Ontwerpen, gebouwen, stedebouwkundige plannen 1925-1945*, The Hague 1983.
**102.** J.J.P. Oud to Architectengroep 'De 8', 8 May 1937, OUDJ-B, NAI, Rotterdam.
**103.** H. Buys, 'Stellingen voor bespreking Avegoor', May 1937, typescript, OUDJ- 4-16, NAI, Rotterdam.

**104.** S. Giedion to C. van Eesteren, 31 August 1938, GTA, Zurich.
**105.** S. Giedion to L. Moholy-Nagy, 29 July 1938, GTA, Zurich.
**106.** S. Giedion to L. Moholy-Nagy, 29 July 1938, GTA, Zurich.
**107.** S. Giedion to C. Van Eesteren, 31 August 1938, GTA, Zurich.
**108.** W. Gropius to S. Giedion, 1 June 1938, GTA, Zurich.
**109.** P. Johnson to J.J.P. Oud, 1 January 1946, MOMA, New York.
**110.** J.J.P. Oud to A. Roth, 16 June 1946, OUDJ-B, NAI, Rotterdam.
**111.** P. Johnson to J.J.P. Oud, 27 April 1946, MOMA, New York.
**112.** J.J.P. Oud, 'Architecture to-day', Rotterdam, 11 May 1946, Getty Research Institute, Los Angeles, (correspondence Frank Lloyd Wright), Houghton library (Gropius archive), Cambridge (Mass.).
**113.** J.J.P, Oud to J.J. Vriend, 14 April 1956, Getty Research Institute, Los Angeles.
**114.** J.J.P. Oud to *Architektur der UdSSR*, 29 September 1933, OUDJ-B, NAI, Rotterdam.
**115.** J.J.P. Oud to Frank Lloyd Wright, 1 June 1948, Getty Research Institute, Los Angeles.
**116.** J.J.P. Oud to Frank Lloyd Wright, 25 May 1952, Getty Research Institute, Los Angeles.
**117.** A. Barr, 'de Stijl', in *de Stijl 1917-1928*, New York 1952, p. 7.
**118.** J.J.P Oud to P. Johnson, 28 August 1955, MOMA, New York.
**119.** B Zevi to J.J.P. Oud, 16 November 1960, OUDJ-B, NAI, Rotterdam.
**120.** J.J.P. Oud to K. Wiekart, 13 June 1913, OUDJ-B, NAI, Rotterdam.

# 1 Formative Years

**Drawing exercise, graphic design/
890126-box 7, 1*, Getty, Los Angeles**

# Education: Amsterdam, Delft and Munich

Jacobus Johannes Pieter ('Ko')[1] Oud was born on 9 February 1890 in Purmerend, the second of three children, all boys. The oldest brother, Pieter Johannes (1886-1968), went on to represent the Liberal Democratic Party in the Dutch Upper House and is best known as Mayor of Rotterdam (1938-1941; 1945-1952). His terms of office coincided with the period when his younger, architect brother was working on some major commissions in that city. According to the latter's son Hans, there was between the two brothers a *strong sense of rivalry that undoubtedly affected both their lives. It is no coincidence that P.J. Oud was later called the conscience of the parliament and his brother that of architecture.*[2]

Oud took his first steps on the road to a career in architecture in 1903 when, at the age of thirteen, he enrolled for the architecture course at the Quellinus School in Amsterdam. This school had evolved out of the applied arts and drawing course that P.J.H. Cuypers (1827-1921) had established in 1876 when confronted by a dearth of decorative sculptors during the building of the Rijksmuseum. For the first three years of its existence, the course was attached to the Rijksmuseum, but in 1879 Cuypers's closest colleague, E.C.E. Colinet (1844-1890) managed to persuade the Departement Amsterdam van de Maatschappij ter Bevordering van Nijverheid (Amsterdam Chapter of the Society for the Promotion of Industry) to set up an independent institute. The result was the Quellinus School which, after countless reorganizations, continues to live on in the Rietveld Academy, which was created in 1967. Some of the Netherlands' most illustrious architects taught at the Quellinus at one time or another, among them K.P.C. de Bazel, H.P. Berlage, J.F. Klinkhamer (1854-1928) and J.M. Lauweriks. One of the most influential teachers was J.H. de Groot (1865-1932), who was attached to the school from 1888 to 1917. De Groot specialized in the use of proportional systems and had written seven books on the subject. Another Quellinus teacher, H. Ellens (1871-?), developed a variation of this method in the form of grids and patterns that he arrived at by abstracting certain motifs. Both of these design methods existed side by side with experiments being carried out in the same period by De Bazel, Berlage and Lauweriks. Part of the Quellinus training took place in the workshop where furniture and architectural ornaments were made to order. Contrary to previous suggestions, this workshop probably had little in common with the medieval lodge.[3] Around 1890 the workshop was closed and the course reduced from five to three years with a corresponding increase in the number of lessons. From 1903 to 1906, Oud

Class photo, Purmerend primary school. Oud is kneeling in the second row from the front, third from right, *circa* 1900/ OUDJ-51, NAI, Rotterdam

attended practical classes in draughtsmanship and modelling, and theory classes in geometry, architectural and ornamental stylistics, anatomy and proportion. In 1906 he sat and passed the final examination.

This aesthetically oriented course did not, however, train students to be architects or architectural draughtsmen. In order to gain some practical experience of the architectural profession, Oud presented himself in 1907 at the offices of J.T.J. (Jos) Cuypers (1861-1949) and J. Stuyt (1868-1934). The latter came from Purmerend and was an acquaintance of Oud's father. Here Oud worked in an 'atelier'. Such ateliers were an important source of practical experience. The best known was the 'architecture atelier' run by Eduard Cuypers in his home on Jan Luykenstraat in Amsterdam and where at that moment M. de Klerk, P.L. Kramer and J.M. van der Mey were employed.[4] Jos Cuypers, who had been engaged since 1895 on the construction of the (Catholic) St. Bavo cathedral in Haarlem, joined forces with Stuyt in 1899 and when Oud entered their employ in 1907 they were busy with town halls in Heemstede (which Oud helped to draught) and Bloemendaal. It was a modern and specialized architectural firm with a considerable national reputation for both modern church architecture and middle-class residences. Oud undoubtedly gained a lot of practical experience while working for Cuypers & Stuyt, especially in the field of domestic architecture, both private and public. There were also the big ecclesiastical projects like the Haarlem cathedral and the church on Obrechtstraat, Amsterdam. Both were fine examples of an integrated, monumental architecture complete with detailed decorative programmes in the form of frescos, stained-glass windows and ornamental sculptures. They are in every respect the religious antithesis of such profane, and as often as not socialist-inspired, ensembles as Berlage's Stock Exchange.[5]

In 1908 Oud sat the entrance exam for the second class of the Rijksnormaalschool voor Teekenonderwijs (State School for Art Education) in Amsterdam. This institute was the result of an initiative of Victor de Stuers (1843-1916) who wanted to combine arts and crafts tuition with a teacher-training course in art in a government-funded school affiliated with the Rijksmuseum. The school commenced operation in 1881 in a few rooms in the still unfinished Rijksmuseum. The aim was to train teachers in modelling, and in freehand, architectural and technical drawing. The teaching staff included P.J.H. Cuypers, J.T.J. Cuypers and W. Kromhout, the last specializing in oriental architecture. To give the students practical teaching experience, a training school was set up in 1885 where, during the winter evenings, students from the highest classes gave lessons in freehand and mechanical drawing to children between the ages of eleven and fourteen.

Oud, too, taught at the training school as well as at the municipal art school in his home town, Purmerend. At the Rijksnormaalschool he met Corrie Berlage, the daughter of the leading Dutch architect at the turn of the century. They became friendly and from that moment Oud was a frequent

Students of the Rijksnormaalschool voor Teekenonderwijs in the garden of the Rijksmuseum, *circa* 1909/ OUDJ-59, NAI, Rotterdam (Photo E.F.H. Muller)

**visitor to the Berlage family home. It was there in 1912 that Oud first saw the 'slides' of Berlage's trip to America the previous year, which included photographs of work by Louis Sullivan and Frank Lloyd Wright.[6] During the 1908-1909 school year, Oud and Corrie Berlage served together on the executive committee of the Vereniging van Leerlingen (Student Association). The Vereniging mounted an annual exhibition, organized excursions and lectures and held competitions. Oud won second prize for architectural design in 1909 and first prize in the architectural drawing category in 1910. On 8 July 1910 Oud sat and passed the final exam of the Rijksnormaalschool.**

**To supplement a training that had so far been weighted in favour of the aesthetic aspects of design, Oud now proposed to enrol at Delft Technical College. The decision was evidently not an easy one, witness a letter from Mrs Berlage in which she invites the young man to come and talk it over with her husband.[7] It is strange that Oud, who was fairly well acquainted with the contemporary Amsterdam architectural scene, did not apply to the Rijksacademie voor Beeldende Kunsten (State Academy of Fine Arts) where a department of architecture had been established in 1908 on the initiative of the architectural society 'Architectura et Amicitiae'.[8] Instead, in September 1910, Oud enrolled for a two-year stint as a non-examination student at Delft. It was during this period that Oud made his first forays into the field of architectural journalism. They reveal an unqualified faith in the artistic and modernizing influence, not only of Berlage, but also of 'youngsters' like Kromhout and De Bazel. Writing also provided Oud with an outlet for his sense of frustration and disappointment at the fact that the invigorating wind of Amsterdam had yet to reach Delft. Oud felt that the training given at Delft was too narrowly focused on engineering and construction, with too little attention being paid to the aesthetic and artistic aspects of architectural design. In that respect architects lagged behind visual artists who, in the institution of the Rijksacademie voor Beeldende Kunsten, had an 'atelier' dedicated to discussion and the exchange of ideas: *Now the painters have stolen a march on us! If Amsterdam can pride itself on having an atelier where not only the technique but also the philosophy of art is studied, surely Delft too should hold gatherings for its architects – as the most aesthetically engaged element of the student corps – in order that the philosophy of architecture may be studied in addition to construction. It is a well-known fact that one of the greatest architects argues that an architect should also be a philosopher.*[9]**

**Not surprisingly, Oud did not last long at Delft. Armed with a solid letter of recommendation from Berlage, he departed for the office of Theodor Fischer in Munich, where he remained from 7 May to 31 July 1912. Theodor Fischer ran a celebrated architectural firm that attracted many young, international designers, among them Le Corbusier. Fischer also taught architecture at the Technische Hochschule and wrote regularly about what Winfried Nerdinger has called the relation between *Architektur und kulturelles Gedächtnis*.[10]**

**Student period in Delft, Oud is seated second from right, *circa* 1911/ OUDJ-59, NAI, Rotterdam (Photo J.C.C. Witte)**

Oud, of course, was already familiar with the 'style war' but in Fischer's office he learned how associations with historical examples could be integrated in highly original, distinguished formal concepts. And how ornament and typology enabled buildings to engage in a complex relationship with the location, the townscape and the collective memory of the surroundings. Fischer was not only an inspired teacher but also an influential architect–town planner. Along with Camillo Sitte (1843-1903) and Karl Henrici (1852-1927), he represented the architectural tendency in modern urbanism, which is to say, a movement that promoted an aesthetic monumental approach to town planning rather than the purely technical and utilitarian approaches favoured by planning professionals.[11] In the Netherlands it was above all Berlage who, from 1890 onwards, applied himself to the practical implementation of Sitte's rules and who, in the very years when he was advising and assisting the youthful Oud, was endeavouring to combine Sitte's monumental urban aesthetic with the economic realities of private and public housing which depended on land, construction and rental prices. Berlage's struggles with the planning of Amsterdam South (1900-1917) were not much different from Fischer's efforts in Munich which he described, in *Vorträgen über Baukunst* (Lectures on Architecture, 1918), as a battle with bureaucratic rules, regulations and codes: *The entire complicated chapter of land politics with the pitfalls of the Civil Code and the trap of the mortgage system; added to the rigorous ramparts of the building inspectors and the trenches of the hierarchic channels.*[12] In the short time that Oud spent in Munich he undoubtedly learned a lot from Fischer, especially in the field of urban design. Even after his departure, Oud kept in touch with Fischer and sent him his articles on the subject of town planning and in particular 'modular design'. Fischer's experiences and designs had a profound effect on Oud's ideas about the connection between architecture and urban culture. They laid the foundation for his own views on the role of the architect in *stedenbouwkunst* (the art of urban design); views that he adhered to throughout his life and which he shared with virtually no one else in the Netherlands, apart from his friend W.M. Dudok.[13]

After a stay of only three months Oud, who was no more successful than Le Corbusier had been a year earlier in securing a permanent place with the Munich firm, returned to the Netherlands and set up in practice for himself in Purmerend (1912). Looking back on these crucial years in the introduction to what was intended to be a richly illustrated monograph of his work published in England, Oud wrote: *There I built a movie theatre, a block of labourer-dwellings, with an assembly-room and some small houses. In the mean time my views on architecture, having been under the influence of "Cuypers en Stuyt" ecclesiastical, had changed.*[14] In the same manuscript, probably written in 1951 or thereabouts, Oud also referred to the influence of Berlage's 'rationalist tendency', a remark that has led many historians to place all of Oud's early work in Berlage's shadow, thereby unjustly neglecting the many and varied influences deriving from the English and German Arts and Crafts movements as well as from the work of De Bazel, Kromhout and Van der Mey.[15]

J.T.J. Stuyt/ Stuyt Archive, NAI, Rotterdam

**Notes**

**1.** After his marriage to Annie Dinaux his nickname changed to Bob.

**2.** H.E. Oud, *J.J.P. Oud. Architekt 1890-1963. Feiten en herinneringen gerangschikt*, The Hague 1984, p. 15; H.J.L. Vonhoff, *Bewegend Verleden, een biografische visie op mr. P.J. Oud*, Alphen 1969.

**3.** A. Martis, 'Het ontstaan van het kunstnijverheidsonderwijs in Nederland en de geschiedenis van de Quellinusschool te Amsterdam 1879-1924', in: *Nederlands Kunsthistorisch Jaarboek 1979*, vol. 30, Haarlem 1980, pp. 121-122; C.P. Krabbe, *Ambacht, Kunst, Wetenschap. Bevordering van de bouwkunst in Nederland (1771-1880)*, Zwolle, Zeist 1998.

**4.** H. Searing, 'Berlage or Cuypers? The Father of them all', in: H. Searing (ed.), *In Search of Modern Architecture. A Tribute to Henry-Russell Hitchcock*, Cambridge (Mass.), London 1982, pp. 226-244; B. Gerlagh, 'Eduard Cuypers (1859-1927)', in: *Het huis van de architect* (*De Sluitsteen. Jaarboek 1999*), pp. 40-41.

**5.** T. Eliëns, *H.P. Berlage (1856-1934). Ontwerpen voor het interieur*, Zwolle 1998, pp. 64-77.

**6.** H.P. Berlage to J.J.P. Oud, 7 March 1912, OUDJ-B, NAI, Rotterdam.

**7.** Mrs Berlage to J.J.P. Oud, 26 September 1910, OUDJ-B, NAI, Rotterdam.

**8.** M. Bock, *Architectura. Nederlandse Architectuur 1893-1918.* Amsterdam 1975, p. 35.

**9.** 'Opwekking', in: *Studenten Weekblad*, 10 March 1911; 'Over bouwkunst', in: *Schuitemakers Purmerender Courant*, 18 January 1911.

**10.** W. Nerdinger, *Theodor Fischer. Architekt und Städtebauer*, Berlin, Munich 1988, p. 90.

**11.** H. Engel, E. van Velzen, 'De vorm van de stad: Nederland na 1945', in: E. Taverne, *I. Visser, Stedebouw. De geschiedenis van de stad in de Nederlanden van 1500 tot heden*, Nijmegen 1993, pp. 276-283.

**12.** W. Nerdinger, *Theodor Fischer. Architekt und Städtebauer*, Berlin, Munich 1988, pp. 86-95; G. Schickel, 'Theodor Fischer als Lehrer der Avantgarde', in: V. Magnago Lampugnani, R. Scheinder (eds), *Moderne Architektur in Deutschland 1900 bis 1950. Reform und Tradition*, Stuttgart 1992, pp. 55-68.

**13.** H. van Bergeijk, *Willem Marinus Dudok. Architect-stedebouwkundige 1884-1974*, Naarden 1995, p. 68ff.

**14.** J.J.P. Oud, untitled English manuscript, OUDJ-5, NAI, Rotterdam. Covers childhood, education and work up to 1925. Erroneously dated at around 1926 by Hans Oud. Handwriting and language both suggest a much later date. In 1925 Oud's intellectual horizon was chiefly limited to the German-speaking countries. Oud Archive, NAI, Rotterdam.

**15.** G. Stamm, 'Het jeugdwerk van architect J.J.P. Oud 1906-1907', in: *Museumjournaal*, (1977)22, pp. 260-265; G. Stamm, *J.J.P. Oud. Bauten und Projekte 1906 bis 1963*, Mainz, Berlin 1984, pp. 15-19; H. Esser, 'J.J.P. Oud', in: C. Blotkamp (et al.), *De beginjaren van De Stijl 1917-1922*, Utrecht 1982, pp. 125-154.

# Aspiring Architect: Purmerend, Beemster, Aalsmeer and Heemstede

Oud designed some seven buildings in his home town of Purmerend, most of which were built. Outside Rotterdam there is no city in the Netherlands that can boast such a wide variety of building types – houses, a cinema, a clubhouse, shops – designed by Oud. This does not necessarily make Purmerend *the cradle of architectural world history*, however.[1] Most of the buildings are plain brick structures without too much in the way of ornamentation or dramatic spatial solutions. They are in tune with the prevailing tradition of anonymous urban architecture and are at best distinguished by an occasional quotation from an English or German architecture book. Some of them, moreover, are strongly influenced by Cuypers & Stuyt, the architectural practice where Oud had worked as draughtsman in the years 1907-1908. Oud was well-disposed towards his home town and in an article in the local paper (1913) he argued for effective aesthetic controls and for a return to simple, rational domestic architecture with attention to detail and architectural character: *Whereas Purmerend is lucky enough to have a development plan drawn up by Berlage, it is worth emphasizing that a sound arrangement of streets and squares is not alone in determining the aesthetic effects of a district (even though this is a basic requirement!), but that it is the buildings lining the streets that will ultimately do justice to the development plan or completely destroy it. ... To ensure that our urban expansion does not become an eye-sore for many years to come, the District Council needs to be invested with greater authority than is presently the case. ... Inferior buildings will slip through now and then of course and the new areas will not possess the beautiful simplicity of our remaining old towns (there are other reasons for this), but we will avoid the irritating blemishes that result when people who are not competent in such matters take to decorating and abandon the simple, rational building method that befits them. ... If it were at all possible, unqualified persons should be talked out of their unfortunate passion for decoration. If only they would rediscover the beauty of brick with its colourful scintillations and the effect of simple brickwork patterns in a large area of wall; if only they would try to recapture the ambience of an old room with the right lighting – not with brightly coloured cathedral glass and suchlike devices, but with simple, well-proportioned windows – and so much more that should be a matter of course; in other words, if only they would keep it completely simple for once and not resort to 'town hall language' in construction, any more than they do in their everyday speech, and replace a few false gables or Portland cement pinnacles with a sandstone sill or a nice keystone! That would be real progress.*[2]

Buffet Oud designed for J. Jongert, 1911. Collection Purmerends Museum/ OUDJ-ph 1913, NAI, Rotterdam (Photo F. Lievense)



**Notes**

**1.** G. Stamm, 'Bakermat 20ste eeuwse architectuur ligt in Purmerend', in: *Noordhollandsche Courant*, 31 July 1978. The phrase obviously does not come from Stamm himself who produced one of the earliest critical analyses of Oud's 'early' work. Cf. G. Stamm, *The Architecture of J.J.P. Oud*, Tallahassee 1978; G. Stamm, *J.J.P. Oud. Bauten und Projekte 1906 bis 1963*, Mainz, Berlin 1984.

**2.** J.J.P. Oud, 'Stadsschoon', in *Schuitemakers Purmerender Courant*, 8 June 1913, and continuation on 3 September 1913.

Presentation drawing, Heemstede Town Hall/ 890126-7, 1, Getty, Los Angeles

Bookcase for Annie Dinaux, 1915, Museum Boymans van Beuningen/ OUDJ-ph 1912, NAI, Rotterdam

## 1/ Oud-Hartog House

**Purmerend, 7 Venediën** **1906-1907**

Oud was sixteen when he designed this house for his aunt Alida Oud-Hartog. It was built on the foundations of an earlier house, with the staircase of the new house (behind the main building) being located on the site of the former kitchen. The flat facade is divided by sturdy windows, the most striking of which is the central, T-shaped window on the first floor. In the previously mentioned autobiographical sketch of 1951, Oud wrote of this house: *My first house I built at the age of 16. It was a house with a ground floor and two storeys, the highest of these being under the roof. It stands on a narrow plot between other houses: the architecture was a bit like that of english country-houses, which I admired greatly at that time as I did some years later studying the interesting book of Muthesius: das englische Haus. Some years later I built another small house of the same kind: a bit more refined and a bit under influence of the early works of Stuyt.*[1]

He wrote in the same vein about this house to his friend, the art critic W. Jos de Gruyter (1951): ... *those ribbon windows derive from the English country house. I read a lot about it when I started out as architect and used them in my very first house (partially) and wholly in a small house in Blaricum (1914). I well remember that in my first modern work – as independent architect – I had the greatest difficulty in omitting the glazing bars because the English country house in general was (and is) a great favourite of mine and I thought that idea of carrying the wall through as a lattice over the window as it were so very fine. Employing the window 'as opening' did not come easily to me. But as you will recall, English country houses ('the domestic architecture') stand or fall by the 'ribbon windows', which are the order of the day there.*[2]

Oud's retrospective association of the traditions of the English country house with this particular house are not entirely convincing. Windows with glazing bars were not confined to England at that time but were also a regular feature of the Dutch urban dwelling, as Leliman's well-known handbook on the subject makes clear.[3] Oud's first publication about the work of Muthesius dates from 1913 and until the celebrated country house in Blaricum (1915), there is nothing in his work to indicate a particular interest in the architecture of the English town and country house.

**Front view/ OUDJ-ph 1, NAI, Rotterdam**



**Notes**

**1.** J.J.P. Oud, English manuscript, OUDJ-5, NAI, Rotterdam.
**2.** J.J.P. Oud to W.J. de Gruyter, 23 January 1951, OUDJ-B, NAI, Rotterdam.
**3.** J.H.W. Leliman, *Het stadswoonhuis in Nederland gedurende de laatste 25 jaren*, The Hague 1920.

**Sources**

NAI: OUDJ-ph 1-3, OUDJ-B
Streekarchief Waterland, Purmerend: submission for building approval by Jacob van Voorst, drawing not signed (and probably not drawn) by Oud.

**Literature**

U. Barbieri, *J.J.P. Oud*, Rotterdam 1987, p. 12
H.E. Oud, *J.J.P. Oud. Architekt 1890-1963. Feiten en herinneringen gerangschikt*, The Hague 1984, pp. 18-20
S. Polano, *J.J.P. Oud Architettura Olandese*, Milan 1981, p. 12
G. Stamm, *J.J.P. Oud. Bauten und Projekte 1906 bis 1963*, Mainz, Berlin 1984, pp. 19-20

# 2/ Beets House

**Purmerend, 23 Herengracht** **1910**

In 1910, during Oud's spell as a 'trainee' draughtsman with the Amsterdam architectural partnership of Cuypers & Stuyt, the firm was engaged in building four town houses on the Herengracht in Purmerend, at numbers 14, 17, 18 and 23 respectively. The first house (no. 14) was designed by Jan Stuyt for Oud's father who was evidently not yet sufficiently confident of his son's architectural skills. Oud designed no. 23, an office-cum-dwelling that differed from the otherwise very similar house by Stuyt at no. 14 to the extent that Oud toned down the corbelling of oriel and piano nobile and brought them back into line with the facade plane. Oud was pleased with the result and published a photograph of it in the Delft student magazine, *Technisch Studenten Tijdschrift*.[1]

**Front elevation/ OUDJ-he 1, NAI, Rotterdam**

**Notes**
**1.** J.J.P. Oud, 'Woonhuis te Purmerend', in *Technisch Studenten Tijdschrift*, 2(1912)8, p. 228.

**Sources**
NAI: OUDJ-be 3001

**Articles**
J.J.P. Oud, 'Woonhuis te Purmerend', in *Technisch Studenten Tijdschrift*, 2(1912)8, p. 228

**Literature**
H.E. Oud, *J.J.P. Oud. Architekt 1890-1963. Feiten en herinneringen gerangschikt*, The Hague 1984, pp. 20-21

# 3/ Beerens House

**Purmerend, 54 Julianastraat** **1912**

This is exactly the type of house Oud had in mind when he argued for a simple, undecorated local domestic architecture in a local newspaper in 1913. The facade plane terminates in a parapet that conceals the flat roof. The row of openwork, geometric patterns in the parapet, and the sober stone ornamentation in the corbelling beneath the living room bay window and around the front door can be traced to the detailing of the housing blocks that Berlage had been building in various parts of Amsterdam since 1905. Oud would also have seen the details in the crown of another Berlage design, the newly completed office for De Nederlanden van 1845 in Amsterdam.[1]

**Front view/ OUDJ-ph 24, NAI, Rotterdam (Photo J.H.P. Coppens)**



**Notes**

**1.** H. Searing, 'Berlage and Housing, "the most significant modern building type"', in: *Nederlands Kunsthistorisch Jaarboek*, 25(1974), pp. 133-180; J. de Heer, 'Style and Dwelling Type: Berlage's Housing Projects' in: S. Polano (ed.), *Hendrik Petrus Berlage, Complete Works*, New York 1988, pp. 66-90.

**Sources**

NAI: OUDJ-ph 21-24, OUDJ-ju 3001
Streekarchief Waterland, Purmerend: 1911 folder 4, no. 153, building application and drawings

**Literature**


J. de Heer, 'Style and Dwelling Type: Berlage's Housing Projects' in: S. Polano (ed.), *Hendrik Petrus Berlage, Complete Works*, New York 1988, pp. 66-90

H.E. Oud, *J.J.P. Oud. Architekt 1890-1963. Feiten en herinneringen gerangschikt*, The Hague 1984, pp. 20-21

S. Polano, *J.J.P. Oud Architettura Olandese*, Milan 1981, p. 12

Searing, 'Berlage and Housing, "the most significant modern building type"', in: *Nederlands Kunsthistorisch Jaarboek*, 25(1974), pp. 133-180

G. Stamm, *J.J.P. Oud. Bauten und Projekte 1906 bis 1963*, Mainz, Berlin 1984, p. 20

# 4/ Moerbeek House

**Purmerend, Achterdijk** **1913-1914**

Even after he moved to Leiden in 1913, Oud continued to receive commissions for building projects in his home town of Purmerend. On 27 July 1914 he applied for a building permit on behalf of F. Moerbeek for a house that bears a strong resemblance in layout to the Houtman house on Zuiderweg in Beemster (cat. no. 8). Both dwellings have a main entrance and a living room at the front and a back room with kitchen at the rear separated by an alcove-bedroom. Upstairs are two bedrooms and a box room. The chief difference is that the Moerbeek house is smaller and more simply detailed.

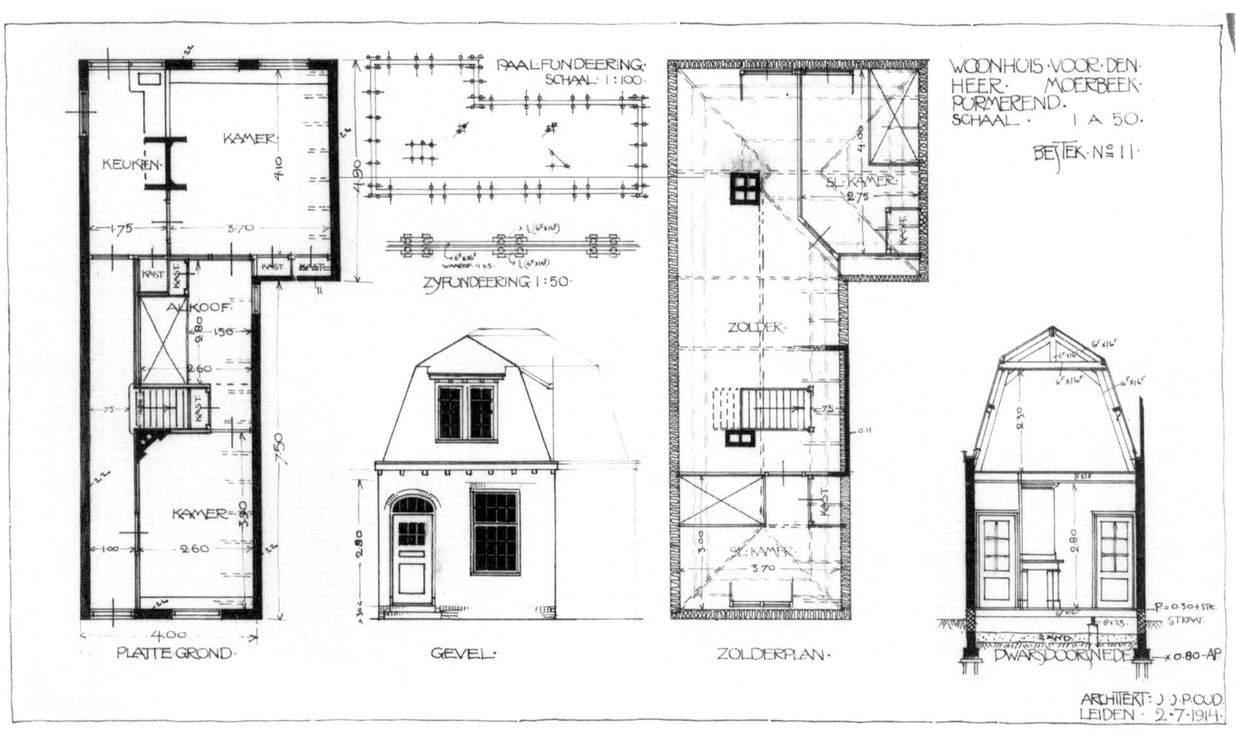


Various design views/ OUDJ-mo 1, NAI, Rotterdam

**Sources**
NAI: OUDJ-mo 1-2
Streekarchief Waterland, Purmerend: 1913-1914 folder 2, no. 338

**Literature**
H.E. Oud, *J.J.P. Oud. Architekt 1890-1963. Feiten en herinneringen gerangschikt*, The Hague 1984, p. 22

## 5/ Project for a Country House with Architect's Office

**Location unknown** **1915**

The design for a detached architect's home with office can be seen in the context of Oud's departure from Purmerend and his introduction to artistic circles in Laren, Bergen and Katwijk, where, since the end of the nineteenth century, architects like Berlage and De Bazel had built numerous country residences. It is the first of several design studies he was to produce in the coming years. It is unlikely that he made this design for himself; it is far too big for a fledgling architect. The ground floor contains both dwelling and office, with a separate entrance for the latter. The office consists of a room with library for the architect and a draughtsman's office with space for three drawing boards. Bedrooms and servant quarters are upstairs.

Perspective/ OUDJ-Ia 1, NAI, Rotterdam

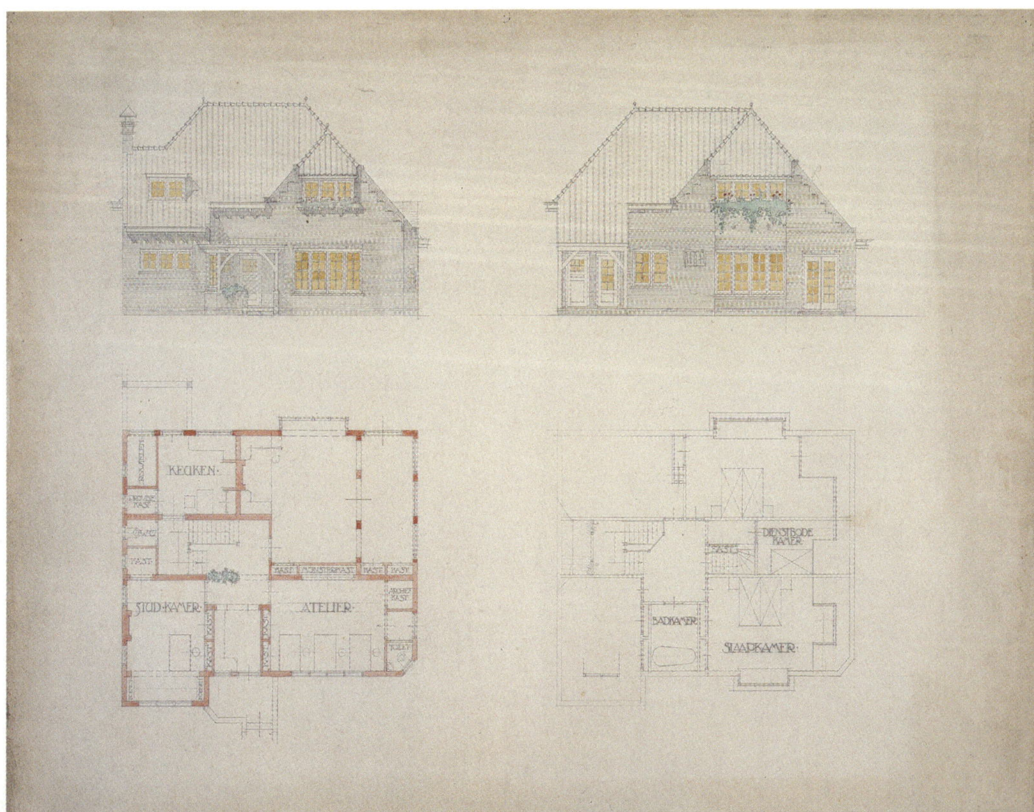


Elevations, ground and first floor plans/ OUDJ-Ia 2, NAI, Rotterdam



**Sources**
NAI: OUDJ-Ia 1-2

# 6/ Alterations to Two Shops with Upstairs Flats

**Purmerend, Hoogstraat**

**1914**

In 1913-1914, Oud was busy in both Purmerend and Heemstede with seemingly simple commissions such as connecting a shop and dwelling. The Purmerend commission entailed the alteration of two adjoining shops, each of which had an upstairs flat. In the absence of any record of the original state of the property, it is difficult to determine Oud's contribution to the present complex. The deep lot made it difficult to provide all the rooms with adequate natural light and to resolve the circulation without too much loss of space. The shop fronts were treated in much the same fashion as that of the Van Bakel shop-dwelling combination in Heemstede (cat. no. 11): the shop window is topped by a beam with room for the firm's name and is separated from the door by a sturdy-looking timber post.

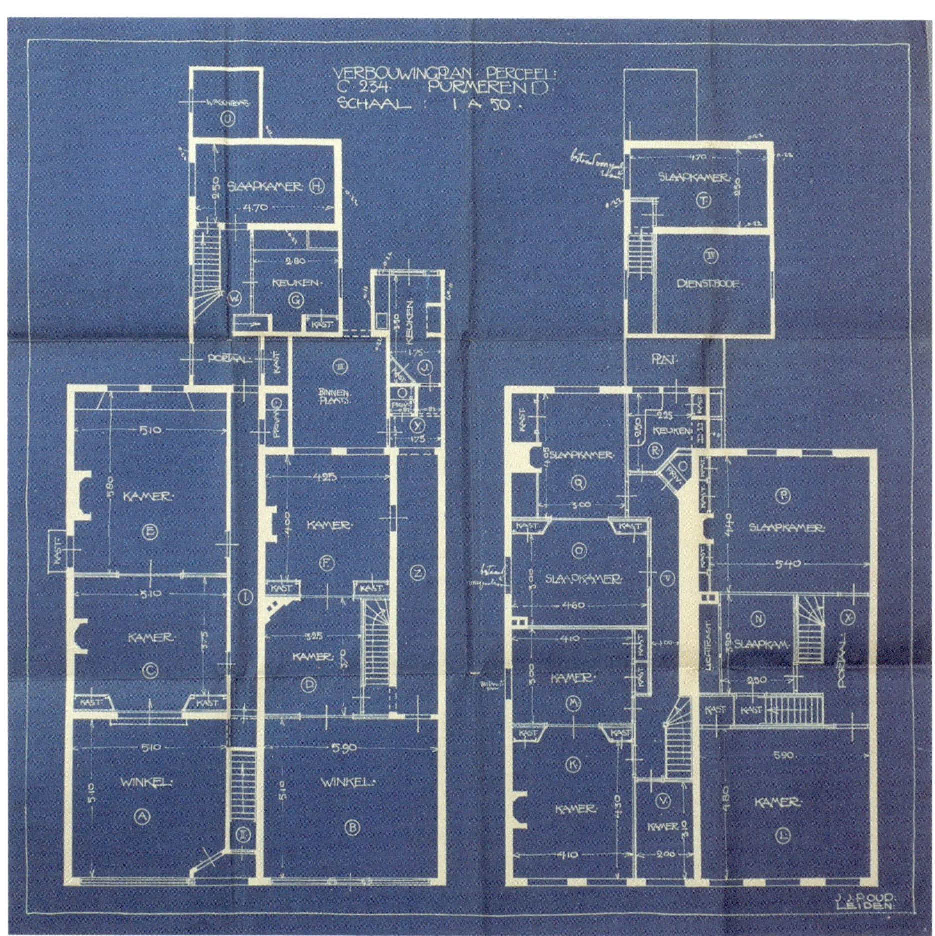


Plans of ground floor (left) and first floor/ Streekarchief Waterland, Purmerend

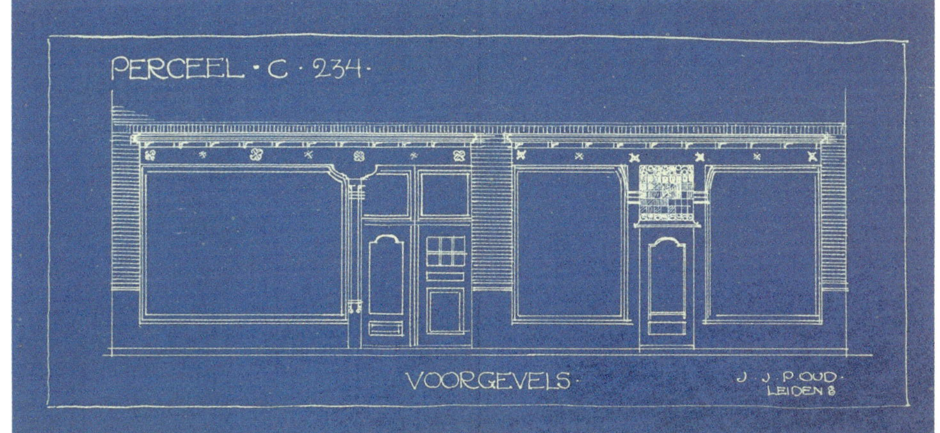


Elevations/ Streekarchief Waterland, Purmerend



**Sources**
Streekarchief Waterland, Purmerend: 1913-1914 folder 2

# 7/ Brand House

**Beemster, 159 Zuiderweg** **1912**

The Brand house is the first detached house designed by Oud and the first house for which he also designed the interior. The client was a Purmerend contractor and carpenter, H.J. Brand, who had built similar houses elsewhere in Beemster. Brand was also the man who made the buffet Oud had designed for J. Jongert in 1911. It is a typical Dutch rural dwelling with the entrance at the side. The ground floor is made up of a spacious kitchen at the rear and two 'mirror-image' living rooms (with respect to the incidence of light). The front facade is distinguished by the corbelling below the upstairs window, a feature Oud also used in a number of town houses in Purmerend. Set into the facing brickwork of the chimney piece in the sitting room was a panel bearing an allegorical painting of 'Repose' in the form of a farm worker leaning on a shovel. It was by the same J. Jongert who was to paint the frescos in the 'Vooruit' Working Men's Club in Purmerend and who, as graphic designer, also carried out commissions for Wed. G. Oud & Co. in Purmerend. Two years later, Oud built another dwelling on Zuiderweg (cat. no. 8).

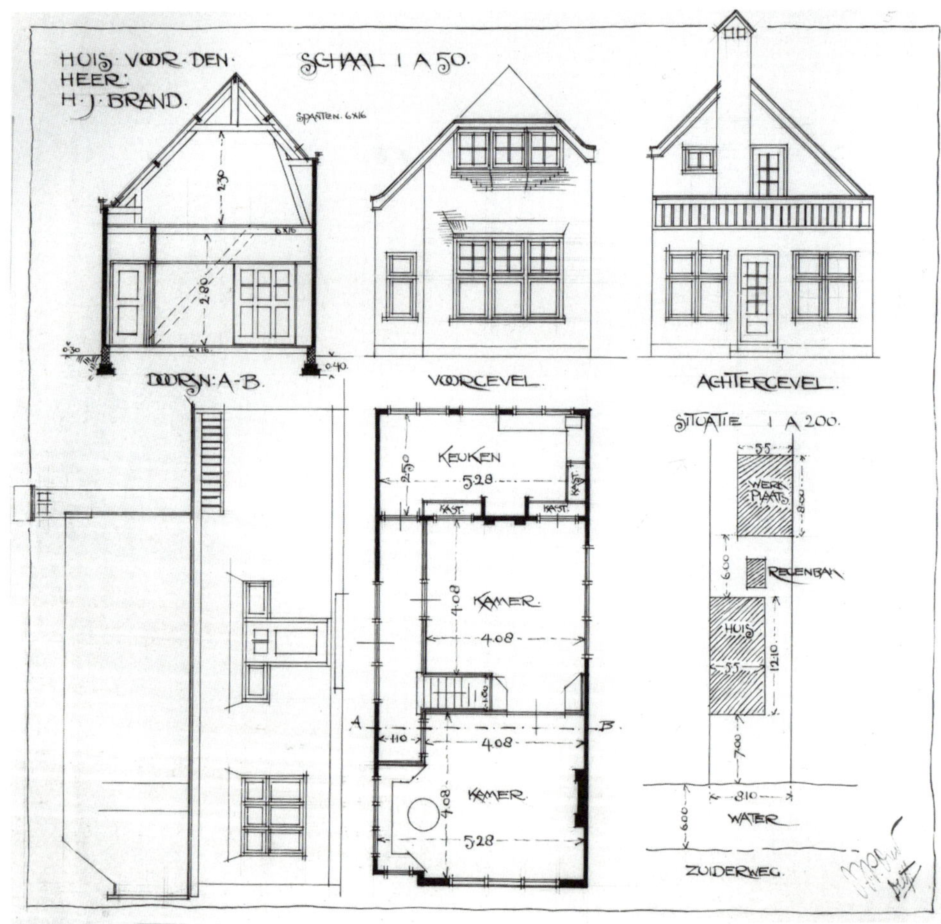


Various design views/ OUDJ-br 1, NAI, Rotterdam



**Sources**
Getty: 890126-box 4, F2
NAI: OUDJ-br 1-2, OUDJ-br 3001, OUDJ-ph 4-9
Purmerends Museum: photograph
Streekarchief Waterland, Purmerend: building application with drawing

**Literature**
U. Barbieri, *J.J.P. Oud*, Rotterdam 1987, p. 16
S. Polano, *J.J.P. Oud Architettura Olandese*, Milan 1981, p. 12
G. Stamm, *J.J.P. Oud. Bauten und Projekte 1906 bis 1963*, Mainz, Berlin 1984, p. 21

Interior back room/ OUDJ-ph 9, NAI, Rotterdam (Photo J.H.P. Coppens)

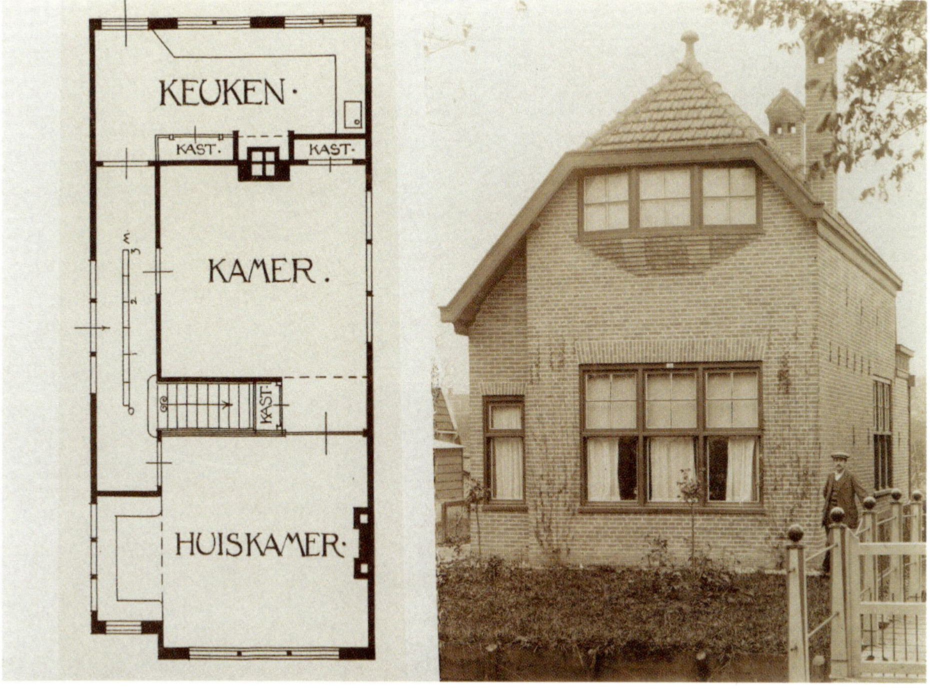


Plans of ground floor and front elevation/ OUDJ-ph 6, NAI, Rotterdam (Photo J.H.P. Coppens)

Interior front room/ OUDJ-ph 8, NAI, Rotterdam (Photo J.H.P. Coppens)

# 8/ Houtman House

**Beemster,**
**110 Zuiderweg**

**1914**

In 1914 Oud designed a detached house at 110 Zuiderweg in Beemster. It is quite different in layout from the other Zuiderweg house Oud had designed two years earlier for the contractor H.J. Brand (cat. no. 7). Unlike the Brand dwelling, the middle room on the ground floor was not intended as living space but as a bedroom. In addition, the main entrance here is not at the side but at the front. And, finally, the Houtman dwelling lacks a rear balcony.

**Front view/ OUDJ-ph 38, NAI, Rotterdam**



**Source**
NAI: OUDJ-hm 1, OUDJ-ph 38-39

**Literature**
S. Polano, *J.J.P. Oud Architettura Olandese*, Milan 1981, p. 12

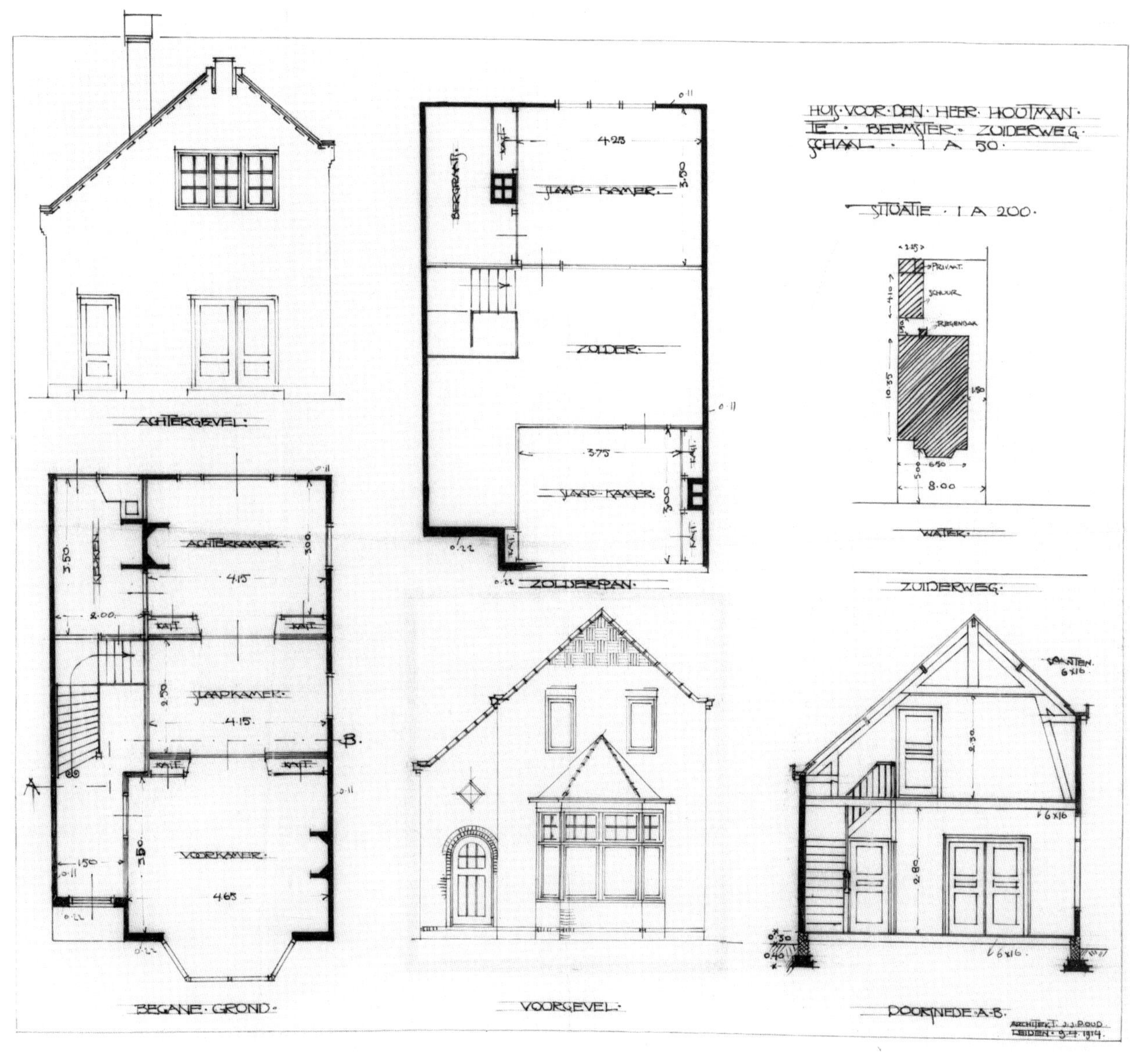


Various design views/ OUDJ-hm 1, NAI, Rotterdam

# 9/ G.J. Oud House

**Aalsmeer, 45 Uiterweg** **1912**

This detached house was built at the request of Oud's younger brother, Gerrit Oud. It is a fairly spacious country house with a compact, symmetrical plan. On the side facing the street is a terrace with an open loggia. But it was on the garden side that the suburban character of the house found an interesting architectural expression in the semi-circular balcony of the first-floor bedroom. Below it on the ground floor the facade was set back to make room, not for a door, but for a brick wall with wooden bench. Such 'inventions' but above all the 'clear and well-organized' overall ground plan of the house point to Oud's growing interest in the work of Hermann Muthesius, to whose country houses he devoted a first, short article in 1913.[1] In 1951, when Oud was trying to reconstruct the main influences in his architectural development, Muthesius was supplanted by Frank Lloyd Wright: *In this period Berlge lectured on the works of Frank Lloyd Wright which impressed me very much: a house in Aalsmeer was the reslut of it.*[2] This 'misremembrance' no doubt had something to do with the fact that after the Second World War Muthesius was virtually forgotten while Frank Lloyd Wright was a major success in post-war Europe. It was also tied up with the myth, carefully nurtured by Oud, that although the American had carried out some important groundwork, the road to modern architecture ran via the aesthetic of Cubism and that it was Oud himself who had set the ball rolling in that direction.[3]

**OUDJ-ph 27, NAI, Rotterdam**

**Notes**
**1.** J.J P. Oud, 'Landhäuser von Hermann Muthesius', in: *Bouwkundig Weekblad*, 33(1913), p. 589.
**2.** Oud to B. Schindler Esq., 1 February 1951, OUDJ-B, NAI, Rotterdam.
**3.** J.J.P. Oud, 'Der Einfluss von Frank Lloyd Wright auf die Architektur Europas', in: J.J.P. Oud, *Ter wille van een levende bouwkunst*, The Hague, Rotterdam 1962, pp. 34-39; M. van Stralen, 'Kindred Spirits: Holland, Wright, and Wijdeveld', in: A. Alofsin (ed.), *Frank Lloyd Wright. Europe and Beyond*, Berkeley 1999, pp. 45-65.

**Sources**
CCA: dr1984: 0006-0007
NAI: OUDJ-go 1-4, OUDJ-go 3001, OUDJ-ph 25-29, OUDJ-ph 1667, OUDJ-ph 1906-1907, OUDJ-B

**Articles**
J.J P. Oud, 'Landhäuser von Hermann Muthesius', in: *Bouwkundig Weekblad*, 33(1913)48, p. 589
J.J.P. Oud, 'Woonhuis te Aalsmeer', in: *Klei*, 5(1913)21, pp. 322-324
J.J.P. Oud, 'Woonhuis te Aalsmeer', in: *Nordische Baukunst*, 1914, November, p. 36
J.J.P. Oud, 'Woonhuis te Aalsmeer', in: *Bouwfragmenten*, vol. 14(1915)8

**Literature**
U. Barbieri, *J.J.P. Oud*, Rotterdam 1987, pp. 18-19
H.E. Oud, *J.J.P. Oud. Architekt 1890-1963. Feiten en herinneringen gerangschikt*, The Hague 1984, p. 19
S. Polano, *J.J.P. Oud Architettura Olandese*, Milan 1981, p. 12
G. Stamm, *J.J.P. Oud. Bauten und Projekte 1906 bis 1963*, Mainz, Berlin 1984, p. 27
M. van Stralen, 'Kindred Spirits: Holland, Wright, and Wijdeveld'., in: A. Alofsin (ed.), *Frank Lloyd Wright. Europe and Beyond*, Berkeley 1999, pp. 45-65

Front view/ OUDJ-ph 29, NAI, Rotterdam

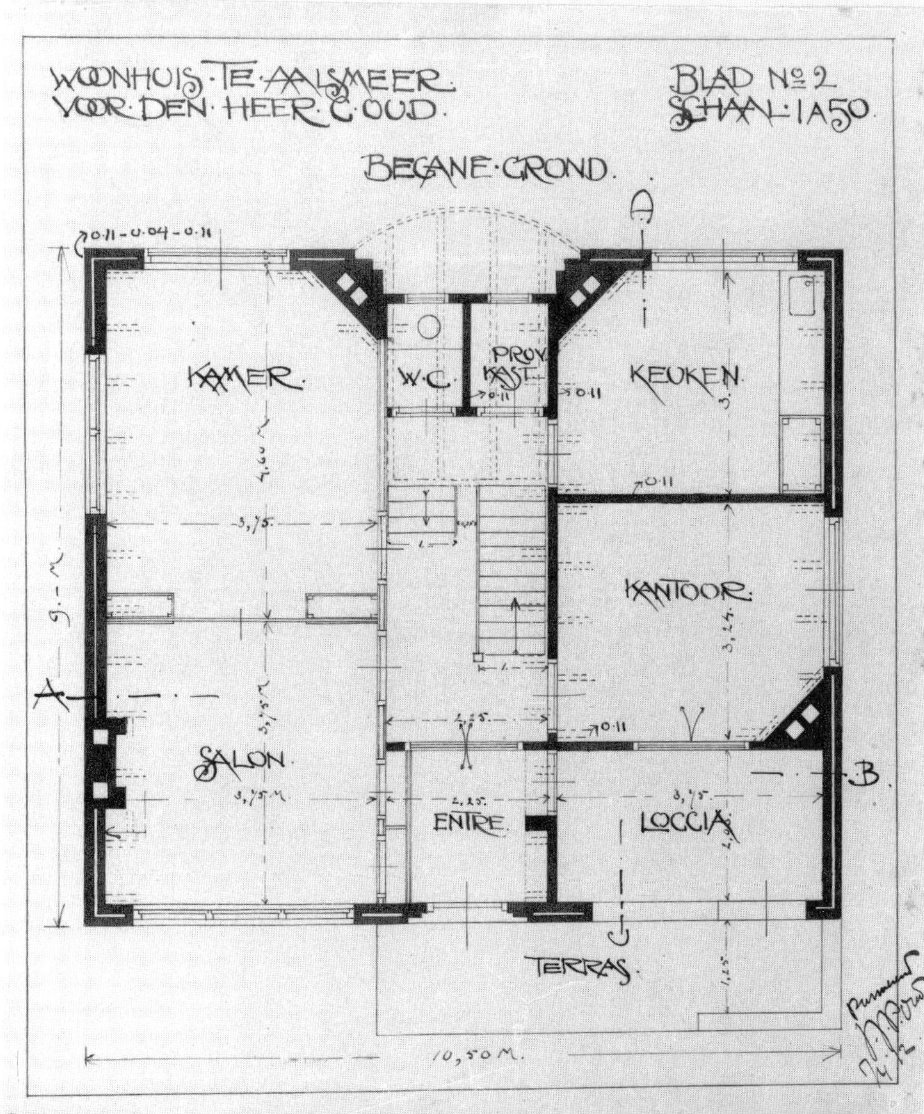


Plan of ground floor/ dr1984: 0006, CCA, Montreal

## 10/ Shop with Upstairs Flat (Van Lent)

**Heemstede, Kerklaan** **1913**

In 1913-1914 Oud built two shops in Heemstede, each of which prompted a modest but different compositional exercise. The Van Lent bicycle shop was given a taut street elevation with eye-catching details on the corner. The asymmetry resulting from the combination of shopfront and upstairs flat was corrected visually by the exaggerated timber frame of the doorway and, on the upper floor, a tile relief of a cyclist, made by W.C. Brouwer.

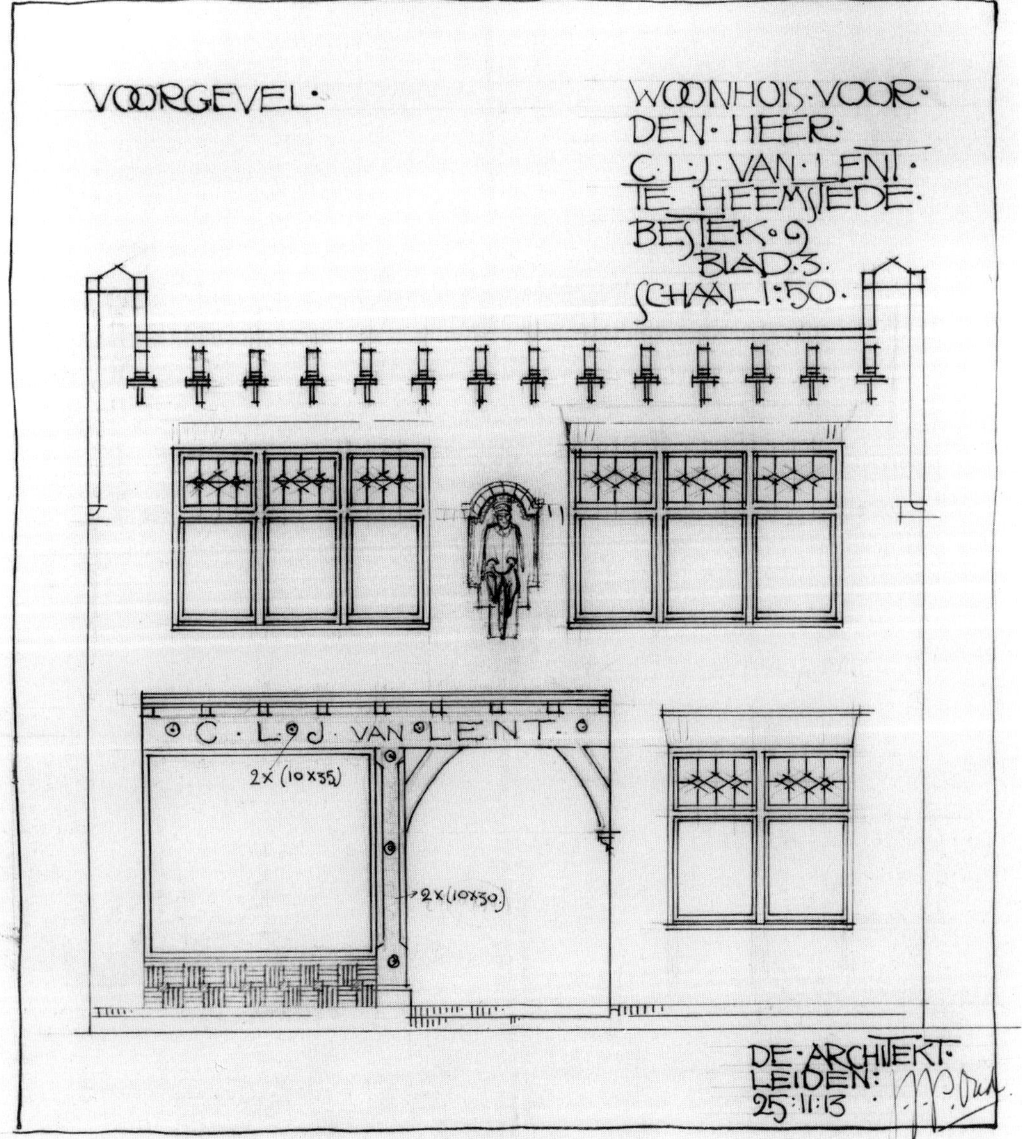


Front elevation/ OUDJ-wl 2, NAI, Rotterdam

**Sources**
CCA: dr1984: 0008, dr1984: 0476-0478, ph1984: 1002
NAI: OUDJ-wl 1-3

**Literature**
S. Polano, *J.J.P. Oud Architettura Olandese*, Milan 1981, p. 13

## 11/ Shop with Dwelling (Van Bakel)

**Heemstede, 41 Binnenweg** **1914**

Unlike the Van Lent bicycle shop on Kerklaan, the house and shop in the building on the Binnenweg formed a single typological whole, with the dwelling being accessed via the shop. This resulted in a remarkable facade composition at the rear. In contrast to the expressive, two-part street elevation, the rear elevation was conceived as a flat surface in which the windows and doors of the ground and upper floors formed the expressive elements of a single composition. This was probably the first time that Oud succeeded in uniting facade and plan to produce a coherent and intriguing architectural whole. Interestingly, at the end of his life, in *Architecturalia* (1963), Oud's only reference to the composition of the facades was of an anecdotal nature: *For instance in my youth I once had to build a shop with dwelling for an upholsterer (also undertaker!). It was one of my very first works. Filled with the highest regard for my profession, but still ignorant of the pitfalls ordinary life can pose for he who builds, and not yet sufficiently versed in avoiding them, I was fulsome in my praise of the living room window. It was one big window. My client had wanted two windows but I pointed out how even the light is with a single window and how splendid the shadow effect. Far better than with two windows, which give a diffuse light. To give him his due, he heard*

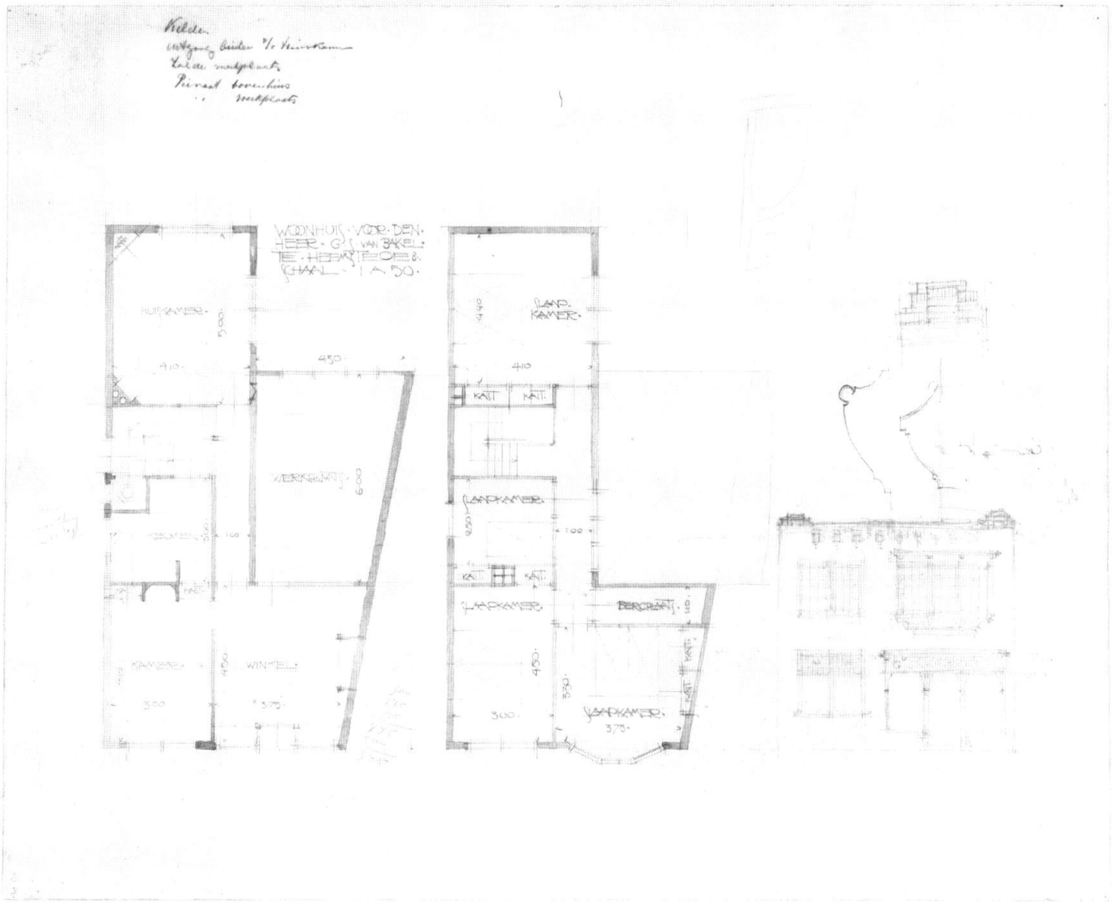

**Preliminary design, plans of ground floor (left), first floor (centre) and front elevation/ dr1984: 0009, CCA, Montreal**

**Rear view. From: G. Stamm, *J.J.P. Oud Bauten und Projekte*, Mainz, Berlin 1984**

**Notes**

1. J.J.P. Oud, *Architecturalia voor bouwheren en architecten*, The Hague 1963, pp. 15-16.

**Sources**

Bouw- en woningtoezicht Heemstede: four working drawings (specification no. 10)
CCA: dr1984: 0009, dr1984: 0479-0482
NAI: OUDJ-ww 1-4, OUDJ-ph 36-37, OUDJ-B

**Articles**

J.J.P. Oud, *Architecturalia voor bouwheren en architecten*, The Hague 1963, pp. 15-16

**Literature**

U. Barbieri, *J.J.P. Oud*, Rotterdam 1987, p. 17
H.E. Oud, *J.J.P. Oud. Architekt 1890-1963. Feiten en herinneringen gerangschikt*, The Hague 1984, pp. 22-23
S. Polano, *J.J.P. Oud Architettura Olandese*, Milan 1981, p. 13
G. Stamm, *J.J.P. Oud. Bauten und Projekte 1906 bis 1963*, Mainz, Berlin 1984, p. 23, p. 32

*me out patiently before finally saying: 'I dare say you're right, but with two windows I get a mortgage and with one window I don't. And I don't give a sh.t about beautiful light.' Ever since I have been extremely cautious with aesthetic arguments.*[1]

**Front view/ OUDJ-ph 37, NAI, Rotterdam**

# 12/ Essen-Vinckers Villa

**Blaricum, 37 Houtweg** **1915-1916**

The design for this country home passed through two stages, developing from the initial concept based on the traditional west-Netherlands farmhouse into a cottagey, scaled-down version of the country house. In both designs Oud struggled to accommodate the client's request for four bedrooms, including one on the ground floor. If, as is often claimed but seldom substantiated, this house displays an affinity with the country house architecture of Hermann Muthesius (about which Oud had written an article in 1913), it could at most be sought in the strong contrast effect of chimney and ridge line which together make for a forceful silhouette.[1] A more telling feature is the chimney.

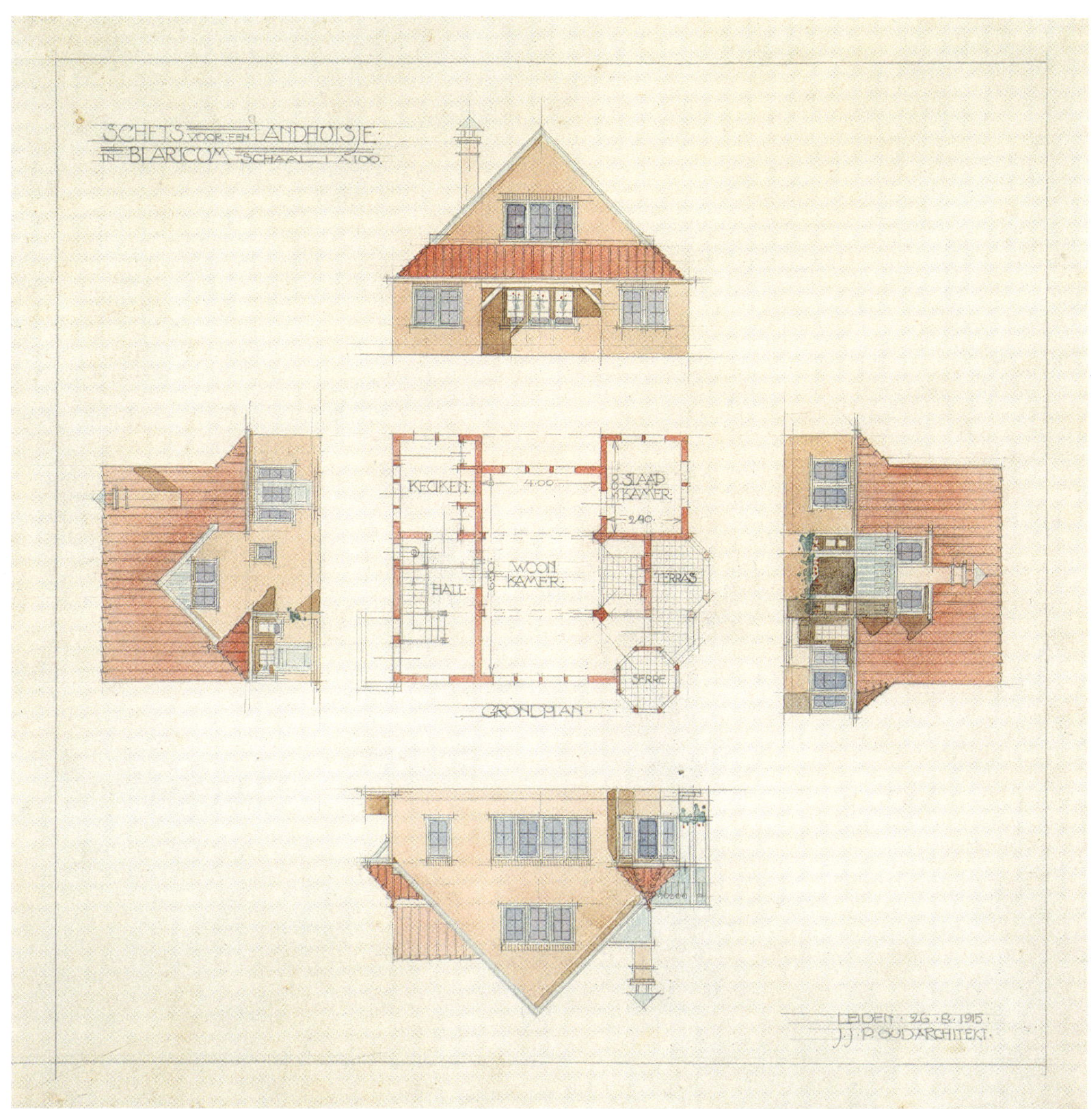


Plans of ground floor and elevations/ OUDJ-le 6, NAI, Rotterdam

**Notes**
**1.** J.J P. Oud, 'Landhäuser von Hermann Muthesius', in: *Bouwkundig Weekblad*, 33(1913), p. 589.

**Sources**
CCA: dr1984: 0012, ph1984: 0808-0809, ph1984: 1005-1008, ph1984: 0155
Getty: 890126-3**
NAI: OUDJ-le 1-8, OUDJ-le 3001, OUDJ-ph 44-51, OUDJ-ph 1903-1904, OUDJ-B

**Articles**
J.J P. Oud, 'Landhäuser von Hermann Muthesius', in: *Bouwkundig Weekblad*, 33(1913)48, p. 589
J.J.P. Oud, 'Landhuisje in Blaricum', in: *Bouwkundig Weekblad*, 37(1916)2, pp. 23-24
J.J.P. Oud, H. Kloot-Meyburg, *Landhuisbouw in Nederland*, Amsterdam 1921

**Literature**
U. Barbieri, *J.J.P. Oud*, Rotterdam 1987, pp. 20-21
S. Polano, *J.J.P. Oud Architettura Olandese*, Milan 1981, p. 12
G. Stamm, *J.J.P. Oud. Bauten und Projekte 1906 bis 1963*, Mainz, Berlin 1984, p. 27

Starting from a rather fortuitous and problematical alcove in the living room, it rises up out of the structure through the projecting dormer (and balcony) of the upper bedroom. This is a strategy more reminiscent of Frank Lloyd Wright than of Muthesius and his English-style country houses.

Side view/ OUDJ-ph 46, NAI, Rotterdam

Front view/ OUDJ-ph 45, NAI, Rotterdam

# 13/ House for Mr & Mrs Blaauw

**Alkmaar, Nieuwlandersingel** **1916**

In January 1916, Oud put the finishing touches to a design for a detached dwelling for the Blaauw family. The plan of this (unrealized) project is an elaboration of the houses Oud had designed a few years earlier for Moerbeek (cat. no. 4) and Houtman (cat. no. 8): with a hallway, staircase and kitchen along one side elevation, and the living room and back room on the other. The main difference is that the Alkmaar house is much more spacious with a full-fledged first floor. A conservatory on the living room side serves to temper the four-square orientation on the street. Another difference is that all the bedrooms are located on the upper floor.

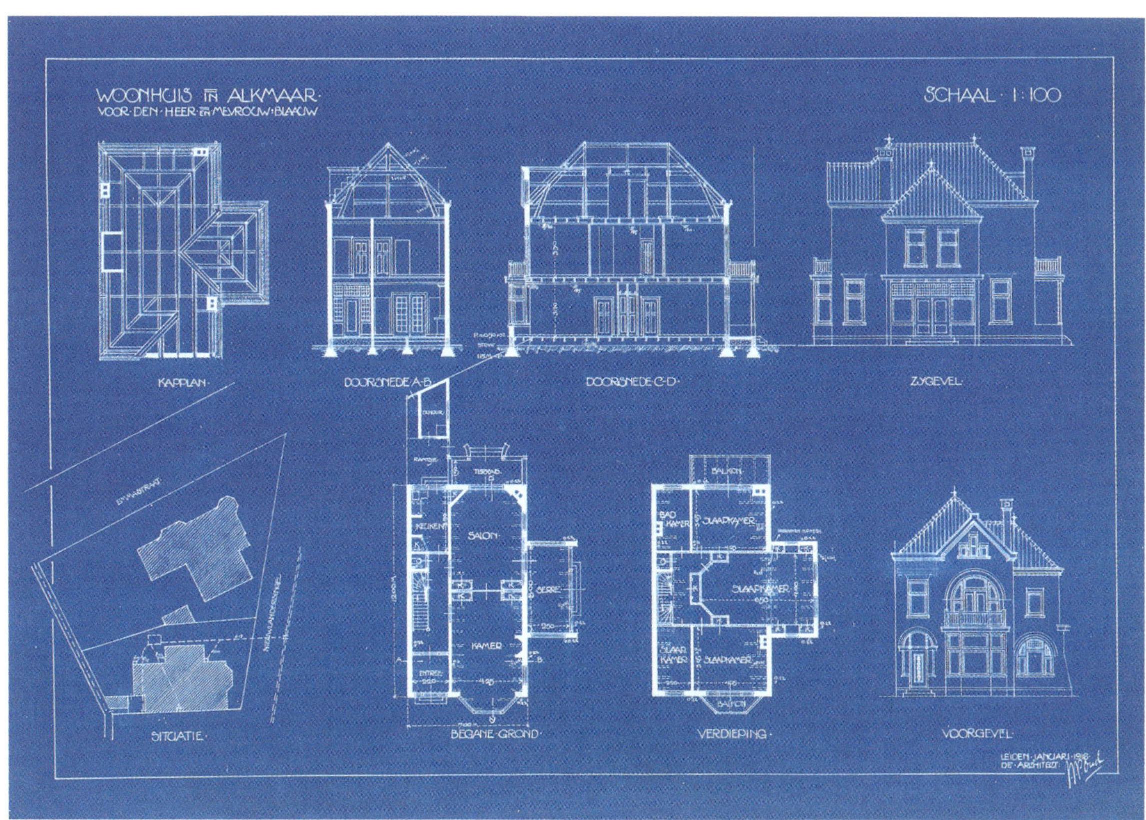


Various design views/ dr1984: 0486, CCA, Montreal



**Sources**
CCA: dr1984: 0486
Getty: 890126-12**

**Literature**
H.E. Oud, *J.J.P. Oud. Architekt 1890-1963. Feiten en herinneringen gerangschikt*, The Hague 1984, p. 233

# 14/ Design for Three Villas

**Velp** **1916**

All that remains of the design for three villas in Velp is a perspective drawing. It shows a deeply staggered front elevation, the result of the incorporation of terraces and balconies. This composition is similar to the beach elevation of Oud's design for a row of houses in Scheveningen (1917). For the villas in Velp, however, Oud also used arched brickwork for a loggia and entrance.
In the literature on Oud, this unrealized design has up to now been linked to three villas at numbers 11, 13 and 15 Zutphensestraat, Velp. Mistakenly, as it now appears, since that trio of houses, for which the client, a certain Mr Geerlings, applied for a building permit on 26 April 1912, were in fact designed by an architect by the name of Jacobse.

**Perspective of front elevation/ OUDJ-vv 1, NAI, Rotterdam**



**Sources**
Gemeentearchief Rheden: building permit and blueprint
NAI: OUDJ-vv 1, OUDJ-ph 61, OUDJ-ph 1780

**Literature**
H. Esser, 'J.J.P. Oud', in: C. Blotkamp (eds), *De beginjaren van De Stijl*, Utrecht 1982, p. 130
H.E. Oud, *J.J.P. Oud. Architekt 1890-1963. Feiten en herinneringen gerangschikt*, The Hague 1984, p. 23
S. Polano, *J.J.P. Oud Architettura Olandese*, Milan 1981, p. 13
G. Stamm, *J.J.P. Oud. Bauten und Projekte 1906 bis 1963*, Mainz, Berlin 1984, p. 32

# 15/ Stable

**Purmerend, Westersteeg** **1911**

One of the first commissions Oud undertook in Purmerend was a stable for a certain J. Eyck on whose behalf he applied for a building permit in July 1911. The permit was granted by the town council in September. The brick building consisted of a carriage room with street access at the front and several stalls at the back. The loft, which had a street-side loading hatch, was intended for storing hay.

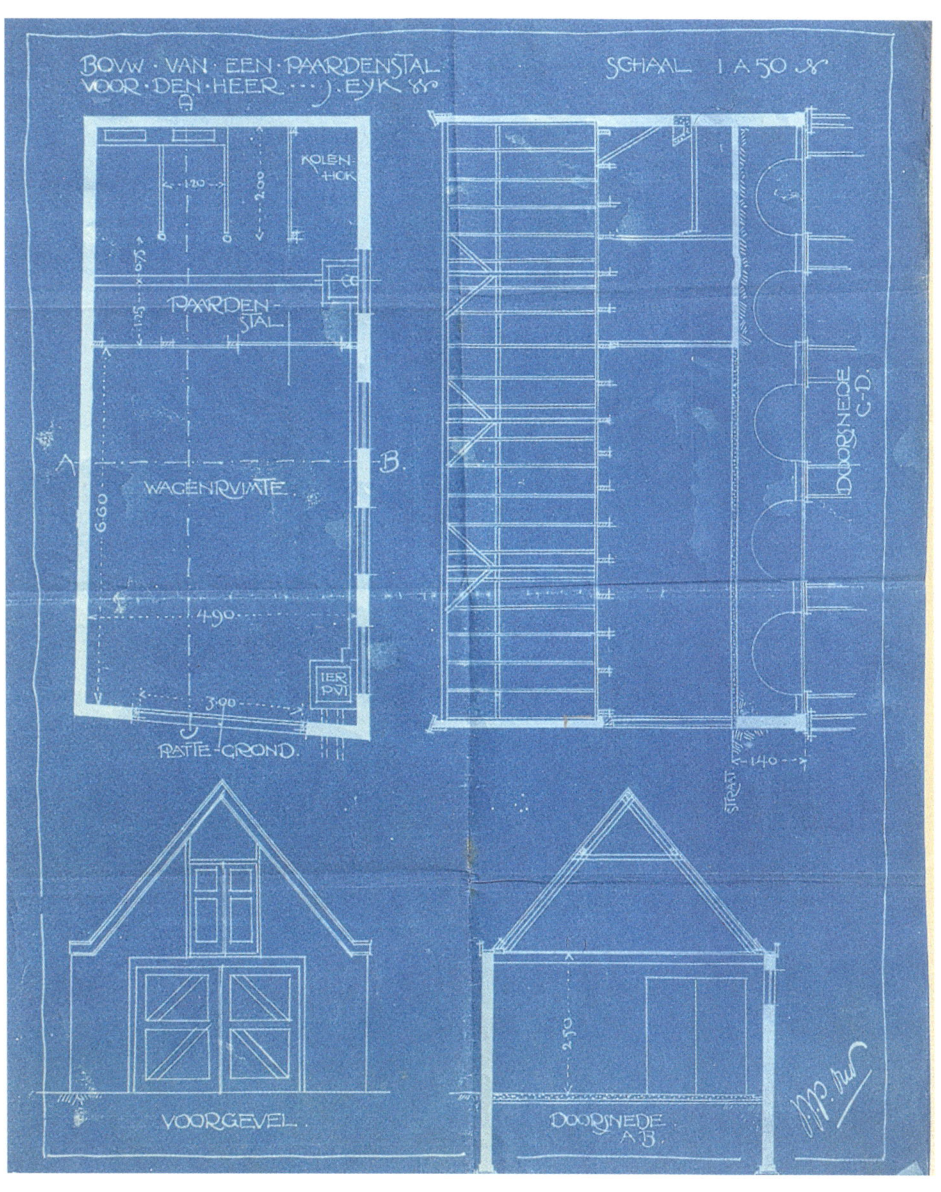


Ground floor plan, front elevation, long and cross sections/ Streekarchief Waterland, Purmerend

**Sources**
Streekarchief Waterland, Purmerend: submission for building approval 1911, folder 3, no. 134

# 16/ Building Complex for the 'Vooruit' Working Men's Club

**Purmerend, 23-26 Vooruitstraat / 10 Wilhelminalaan**

**1911 – 1912**

In the early decades of the twentieth century, working men's clubs were established in towns and cities all over the Netherlands, some, though not all, on a cooperative basis. In 1901-1907, for example, Berlage designed a 'Vereenigingsgebouw voor de arbeiderscoöperatie "Voorwaarts"' on Gedempte Slaak and Schoutenstraat in Rotterdam, which included a coffee house, bakery, grocer's shop, a garden and offices.[1] The construction of four dwellings and a club building for the 'Vooruit' Working Men's Club in Purmerend was a less politically motivated initiative of Oud's father. The main building contained a high-ceilinged meeting hall and had space for a handicrafts school on the first floor. Appended to the garden side was a block of four workers' houses. In elaborating his design, Oud made no attempt to amalgamate the two different building types – club hall and housing block – into a single concept. The main building is a striking, cubic structure, terminated by an attic under a pitched roof. The club hall is distinguished by two murals executed in fresco and representing 'Evening' and 'Morning'. In an article in *Klei* Oud wrote, not without pride: *The walls above the panelling have already been partially painted in fresco style and the white areas will be filled in later with figurative representations. These paintings are being carried out by and to designs by Mr J. Jongert of Purmerend. As far as I know, this is the first example of fresco painting – on any scale, at least – to have been carried out in modern times.*[2] Jongert's memoirs reveal that he had great difficulty mastering the fresco technique at first; the frescos were in fact not completed until 1917. When Jongert first made Oud's acquaintance, he was assisting R.N. Roland Holst with his monumental artwork in Berlage's Diamond Workers' Union building in Amsterdam. From 1909 Jongert and Oud were both teaching at the municipal art school in Purmerend.[3] A different form of collaboration between Oud and Jongert was the wooden sideboard that Oud designed around 1911 at Jongert's request and which was constructed by the carpenter H.J. Brand. The sideboard has a low backboard and a cutlery drawer behind the left-hand door. It is a plain piece of furniture, the occasional piece of wood carving providing the only decoration. It was originally unvar-

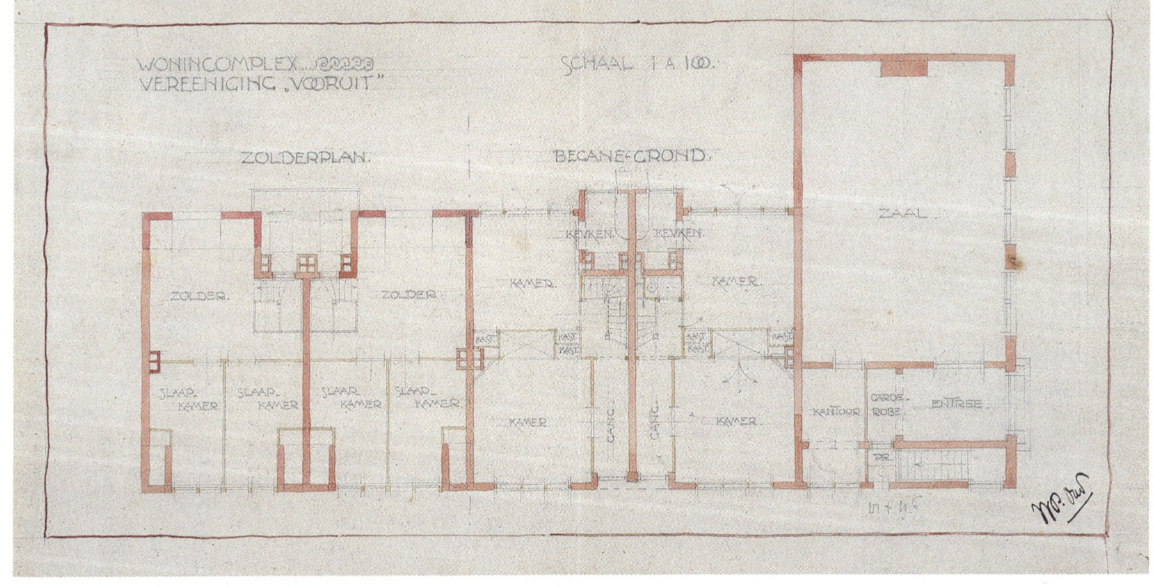


Ground floor plan/ OUDJ-vt 2, NAI, Rotterdam



**Notes**

**1.** S. Polano (ed.), *Hendrik Petrus Berlage. Complete Works*, New York 1988, p. 184.
**2.** J.J.P. Oud, 'Schoorsteen in het gebouw Werkmansver. "Vooruit" te Purmerend', in *Klei*, 4(1912)22, pp. 338-339.
**3.** J. Otsen, *De Purmerendse jaren van Jac. Jongert*, unpublished manuscript, Purmerend 1997.
**4.** E. Reinhartz-Tergau, *J.J.P. Oud: Architect. Meubelontwerpen en interieurs*, Rotterdam 1990, pp. 24-25.
**5.** G. Oud to J.J.P. Oud, 6 January 1951, OUDJ-B, NAI, Rotterdam.

**Sources**

CCA: dr1984: 0001-0003, ph1984: 0802-0804, ph1984: 0996-0998
Getty: 890126-box 4, F1
NAI: OUDJ-vt 1-2, OUDJ-vt 3001, OUDJ-ph 10-20, OUDJ-ph 1908, OUDJ-B
Streekarchief Waterland, Purmerend: 1911 folder 3, no. 120

**Articles**

J.J.P. Oud, 'Schoorsteen in het gebouw Werkmansver. 'Vooruit' te Purmerend', in: *Klei*, 4 (1912) 22, pp. 338-339

**Literature**


U. Barbieri, *J.J.P. Oud*, Rotterdam 1987, p. 15
H.E. Oud, *J.J.P. Oud. Architekt 1890-1963. Feiten en herinneringen gerangschikt*, The Hague 1984, p. 22
S. Polano, *J.J.P. Oud Architettura Olandese*, Milan 1981, p. 13
S. Polano (ed.), *Hendrik Petrus Berlage. Complete Works*, New York 1988, p. 184
E. Reinhartz-Tergau, *J.J.P. Oud: Architect. Meubelontwerpen en interieurs*, Rotterdam 1990, pp. 24-25
G. Stamm, *J.J.P. Oud. Bauten und Projekte 1906 bis 1963*, Mainz, Berlin 1984, p. 22

nished. It is presently housed in the Purmerends Museum.[4] The spatial detailing of the housing block stands in marked contrast to the uncomplicated connection of the mansard roof on the main building. There is an interesting interruption of the roof line at the rear of the building where the staircases were set back and the two kitchens pushed forward. Decidedly unusual for its time was the almost total glazing of the kitchen and living room on the garden side. In his doctoral thesis on his father's work, Hans Oud also drew attention to the unusual framework of latticed windows around the doors between the living rooms and the garden, suggesting that Oud returned to this device in the elaboration of the shops at Oud-Mathenesse in Rotterdam (1922). In 1951, probably with an eye to the English monograph he was then working on (see introduction, note 7), Oud asked his younger brother, Gerrit Kassen (1891-1985) for more details about this early design. The latter wrote with reference to the foundation stone: *Dear Ko, I got your postcard. The 'Vooruit' building and adjacent dwellings were built in 1911. The first stone was laid in August 1911 and the building and houses were occupied in April or May 1912. I remember because our housemaid Mina, who married Bernard Hartman in 1912, was the building's first caretaker. It is no longer possible to consult the stone because the building was sold some years back to the Apostolische Gemeente who had the name 'Vooruit' cemented over.*[5]

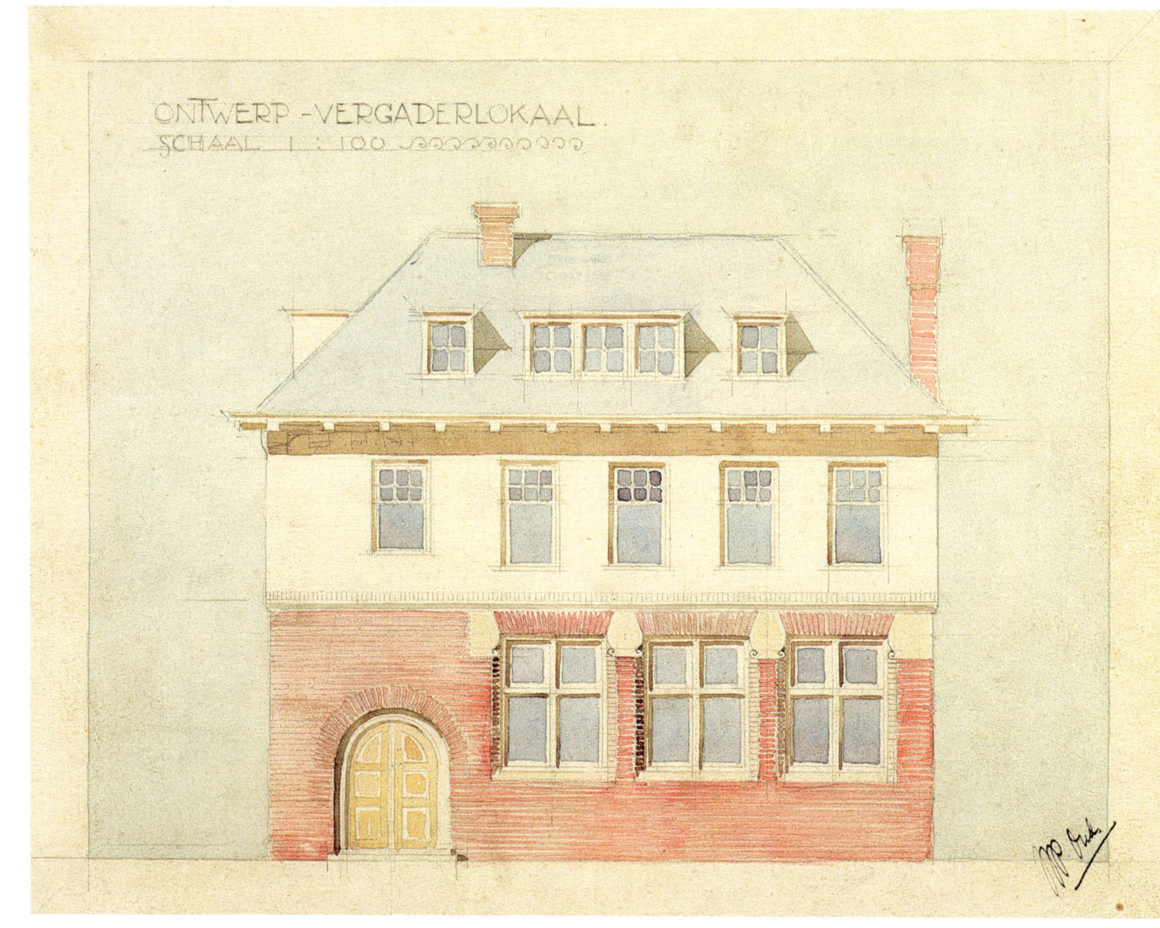


Wilhelminalaan elevation/ Getty, 890126-box 4, F1, Getty, Los Angeles

Vooruitstraat elevation/ 890126-box 4, F1, Getty Los Angeles

View from Vooruitstraat/ OUDJ-ph 15, NAI, Rotterdam

View from Wilhelminalaan/ OUDJ-ph 18, NAI, Rotterdam

Workers' houses, Vooruitstraat/ OUDJ-ph 19, NAI, Rotterdam

# 17/ Schinkel Cinema

**Purmerend, 16 Dubbele Buurt** **1912**

This movie theatre, designed for N.H. Schinkel, was Oud's first public building. It was a relatively modest auditorium (approximately 7.5 x 14 metres) with a narrow mezzanine at the front of the building for the film projector and above that, extending half the length of the auditorium, a small upstairs apartment consisting of one floor plus attic.[1] Both size and architectural detailing indicate a limited budget. On the front elevation the narrow vertical strips of leaded-light fenestration catch the eye, along with the tiled pilasters either side of the entrance that were produced in the atelier of W.C. Brouwer in Leiderdorp. Oud signed his design in December 1912, just before moving to Leiden. If he had not already met Brouwer in Amsterdam, he would undoubtedly have run into him at 'Kunst om de Kunst', a Leiden-based art society. Since about 1900, Brouwer had been an acknowledged authority on uncontrived ornament and hand-crafted architectural sculpture among architects like De Bazel, Lauweriks and Berlage. It is not clear whether the presence of Brouwer's art reflected the recent demise of the ceramics industry in Purmerend or, what is more likely, an attempt on the architect's part to enliven an unavoidably austere building with restrained but authentic architectural ceramics and in so doing raise it to the status of architecture.

**W.C. Brouwer, sculpture beside entrance/ OUDJ-ph 31, NAI, Rotterdam**

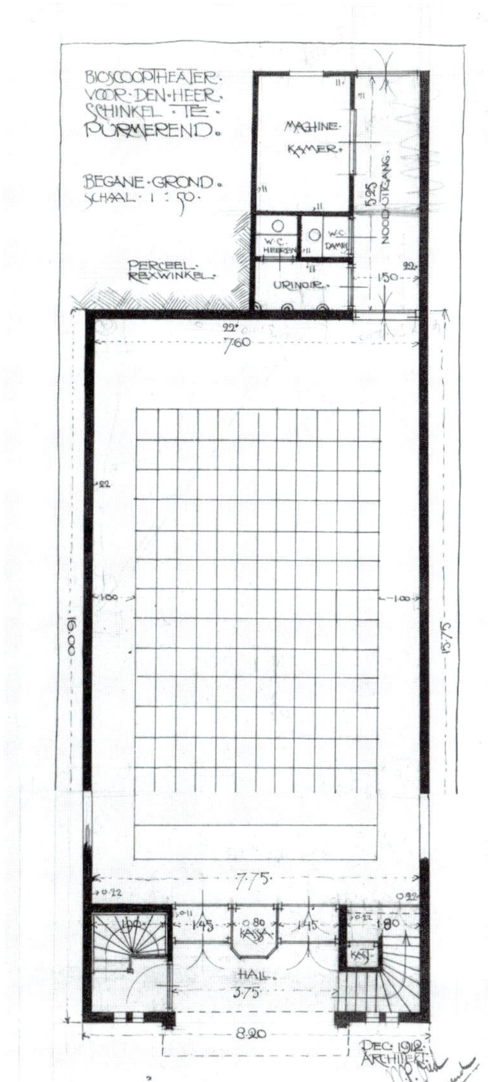


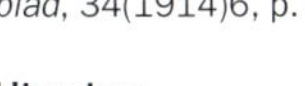

**Ground floor plan/ dr1984: 0004, CCA, Montreal**

**Notes**

**1.** J.J.P. Oud, 'Bioscooptheater te Purmerend', in: *Bouwkundig Weekblad*, 34(1914)6, p. 66.

**2.** M. Groot, K. Gaillard, 'Veelzijdige bedrijvigheid tussen ambacht en industrie', in: D. Wintgens Hötte, A. de Jongh-Vermeulen, *Dageraad van de Moderne Kunst. Leiden en omgeving 1890-1940*, Zwolle, Leiden 1999, pp. 125-127.

**Sources**

CCA: dr1984: 0004-0005, ph1984: 0805-0806, ph1984: 0999-1000
Getty: 890126-10**, 890126-box 2, F1, 890126-box 7, 4*
NAI: OUDJ-bc 1-4, OUDJ-bc 3001, OUDJ-ph 30-35, OUDJ-ph 1905, OUDJ-B
Streekarchief Waterland, Purmerend: four drawings (1912-1913)

**Articles**

J.J.P. Oud, 'Bioscooptheater te Purmerend', in: *Bouwkundig Weekblad*, 34(1914)6, p. 66

**Literature**

U. Barbieri, *J.J.P. Oud*, Rotterdam 1987, pp. 26-27
M. Groot, K. Gaillard, 'Veelzijdige bedrijvigheid tussen ambacht en industrie', in: D. Wintgens Hötte, A. de Jongh-Vermeulen, *Dageraad van de Moderne Kunst. Leiden en omgeving 1890-1940*, Zwolle, Leiden 1999, pp. 125-127
H.E. Oud, *J.J.P. Oud. Architekt 1890-1963. Feiten en herinneringen gerangschikt*, The Hague 1984, p. 19, p. 21
S. Polano, *J.J.P. Oud Architettura Olandese*, Milan 1981, p. 13

Perspective of front elevation/ 890126-10**, Getty, Los Angeles

Front view/ OUDJ-ph 32, NAI, Rotterdam

# 18/ Competition Design for a Village School

**Notional location** **1913**

In May 1913, Oud entered a design for a school complex in a competition organized by the Association of Dutch Brickmakers. Entrants were required to design a six-class primary school plus gym room, playground and a house for the head teacher, for a notional location in 'a big village and on the corner of two roads'. A special feature of the competition brief was the request to use 'brick products wherever possible', not just in the walls of the school and house, but also in the foundations and wall of the school yard. Oud designed an L-shaped school building and detached house. In the long wing of the school building, the classrooms are arranged on either side of a central corridor. The sports hall which, like the classrooms, was required to meet *stringent hygiene and efficiency standards*, was accommodated in the short wing. Oud's design, submitted under the codename H, was not among the prizewinners selected by a jury that included H.P. Berlage and J. Gratema (1877-1947).

**Perspective of village school with caretaker's dwelling/ 890126-5**, Getty, Los Angeles**

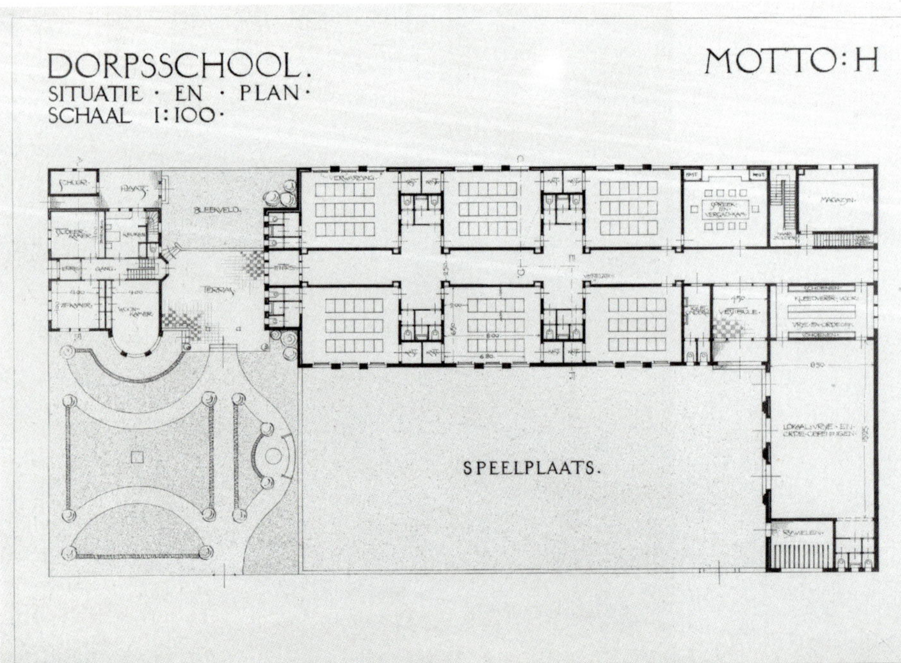


**Ground floor plan/ 890126-5**, Getty, Los Angeles**

**Sources**
Getty: 890126-5**

**Articles**
'Programma van de Nationale Bouwkundige Studieprijsvraag', in: *Klei*, 5(1913)4, pp. 63-64
'Nationale bouwkundige studieprijsvraag', in: *Klei*, 5(1913)12, pp. 177-178
'Nationale bouwkundige studieprijsvraag', in: *Klei*, 5(1913)14, pp. 209-211

# 19/ Extension to Wed. G. Oud Liqueur Distillery

**Purmerend, Peperstraat**

**1916**

Many of the commissions Oud received for shops and industrial buildings in Purmerend came to him via his family. The most interesting without a doubt was for the extension of the Wed. G. Oud & Co. liqueur distillery where Oud's father had been director until 1910. Management had then passed to two nephews, Kassen and Pieter Oud, who turned it into a flourishing business. Plans for an extension on the existing site were developed in 1915-1916 and Oud made the first design. On a typical industrial lot, he drew a rectangular shed measuring 33 by 8.5 metres and comprising a warehouse and a bottle-washing room, both over two floors, capped by a simple timber truss construction. The street facade reproduces the symmetrical composition of the existing building and invokes associations with the traditional (pre-industrial) warehouse. In the end, the plot of land turned out to be too small and it was decided to build a new factory on an industrial site on the outskirts of town. In 1919 the Alkmaar architect D. Saal and Oud, who was now living in Leiden, were jointly commissioned to produce a design for factory, warehouse and offices, a commission that culminated in one of Oud's best known and most frequently illustrated projects: the factory and warehouse at Purmerend (cat. no. 32).

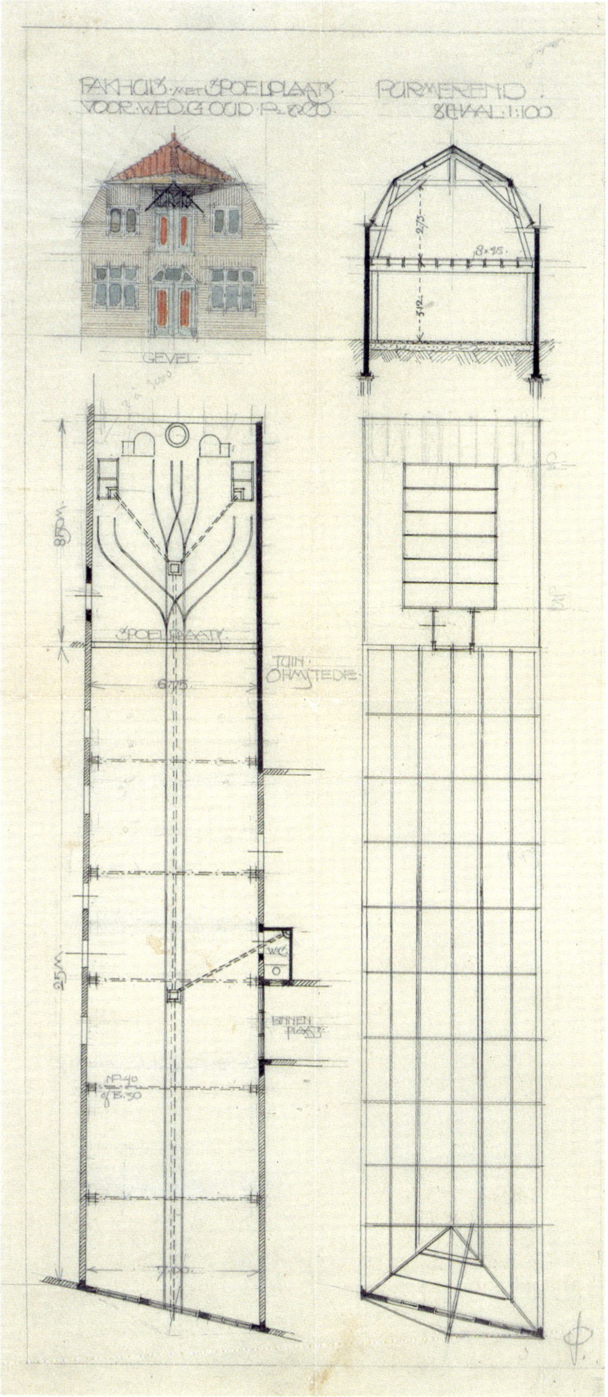

**Plans of ground floor and front elevation (left) and roof (right)/ OUDJ-pg 1, NAI, Rotterdam**



**Sources**
NAI: OUDJ-pg 1-2

**Literature**

U. Barbieri, *J.J.P. Oud*, Rotterdam 1987, p. 46
J. Otsen, 'De Purmerendse jaren van Jac. Jongert', unpublished manuscript, Purmerend 1997
G. Stamm, *J.J.P. Oud. Bauten und Projekte 1906 bis 1963*, Mainz, Berlin 1984, p. 47

**J.J.P. Oud in Leiden, on the wall the De Sphinx poster, designed by H. Kamerlingh Onnes, 1917. From: D. Wintgens Hötte (ed.),** ***Dageraad van de Moderne Kunst*****, Zwolle, Leiden 1999**

# Established Architect at Leiden

In 1913 Oud moved permanently from Purmerend to Leiden, where he set up as an independent architect. Nothing definite is known about his motives for moving. Perhaps he was following the example of Willem M. Dudok, whom he had got to know in Purmerend and who on 1 April 1913 had joined the Leiden public works department as engineer and deputy director (a post he exchanged on 1 July 1915 for that of director of public works with the city of Hilversum).[1] It is also conceivable that Oud had outgrown his home town – from a professional point of view, that is – and was attracted by the artistic ambience of places like Bergen, Laren, Voorburg and, of course, Leiden. The Leiden artistic scene (recently somewhat exaggeratedly described as having given birth to 'the dawn of modern art') was not confined to Leiden itself, but extended to the fashionable villages of Katwijk aan Zee, Noordwijk and Aerdenhout,[2] where architects like Kromhout, De Bazel and Berlage had been designing modern summer and holiday homes since the beginning of the century, a trend Oud was quick to join.

In Leiden Oud joined the Leids Tekengenootschap 'Kunst om de Kunst' (Leiden Art Society 'Art for Art's Sake') where he built up a new circle of friends that included Harm Kamerlingh Onnes, the ceramist W.C. Brouwer and Theo van Doesburg. Oud sought personal contact with the last when he heard that Van Doesburg was thinking of setting up a new society for artists. The letter in which he introduced himself to Van Doesburg reveals a self-assured young architect who is evidently looking for a new joint initiative in the field of architecture and visual art.[3] For his part, Van Doesburg, who was then living with his mother in Haarlem, was sceptical about Leiden's suitability as the location for an art society because, as he wrote in reply to Oud: *the Leidenaars of the new schools are still as good as ignorant. This is why I relinquished the chairmanship. Your letter, however, has served to keep alive the idea I once cherished and at the meeting last Wednesday I was struck by the fact that so many, of whom I would not have expected it, were actually in agreement with my ideas for a new society in a more modern spirit. I hope therefore that more people, imbued by the new sense of their time will support the society and in so doing also work towards achieving a general collaboration. I doubt whether the Leiden society we have established will satisfy you since it does not satisfy me either. ... For my part I believe that individual collaboration between the two of us will prove more fruitful. This is something I would like to discuss with you in person.* [4] This discussion duly took place and eventually led to five years of close friendship between Van Doesburg and Oud that were not confined to numerous interesting theoretical speculations on art and architecture, but also extended to exhibitions and joint building projects.

The new society did indeed get off the ground: the Leidsche Kunstclub de Sphinx began life on 31 May 1916, its main aim being *... to enhance the importance of art in all its forms (music, visual art, literature, etc.) but that of modern art in particular.*[5] Oud was the first chairman, Van Doesburg secretary. The committee had ambitious plans and immediately drew up a winter programme with *... various reading, lecture, musical and literary evenings, if possible three exhibitions of visual art and guided tours of our museums conducted by artists.* In the event, the committee did not survive its first exhibition, which opened in January 1917. Notwithstanding the committee's considerable aplomb – attested to by the official group photos taken at the opening – Sphinx's 'International Exhibition' was anything but representative of 'the new movement in painting' that Van Doesburg had written about in 1916 and that had prompted the setting up of the new society. The influence of what Van Doesburg somewhat disparagingly referred to as the 'Impressionists' was too strong. Besides, as far as Van Doesburg was concerned, Sphinx was not a club *that works together in colour and form to give shape to the spirit of the times.* When the committee was taken over by the Impressionists in mid-1917, Oud and Van Doesburg attempted to have their opponents thrown out of Sphinx altogether. Without success: it was they who were expelled.[6]

**Van Doesburg was by then busy with a completely new initiative, the foundation of a magazine (*De Stijl*), which suddenly became a real possibility in the course of 1917 as a result of several unexpected pieces of luck.**

**There is no evidence that Oud was as doctrinaire and internationally oriented with regard to the development of contemporary architecture and art at this time as Van Doesburg. Almost the contrary, in fact. Oud maintained and intensified his contacts with the ceramist W.C. Brouwer, for example, for whom Van Doesburg had little time. The same is true of the painter Kamerlingh Onnes and later of Chris Beekman. He also continued to visit the much older Berlage whose aesthetic austerity and social-philosophical leanings he defended against the impulsive attacks of the Amsterdam School architect Michel de Klerk.[7] Which is not to say that Oud developed an aversion to the architecture of the Amsterdam School in general in those years. Throughout his life he had enormous admiration for someone like Van der Mey and for the way the idea of the *Gesamtkunstwerk* had been given a contemporary interpretation in the Scheepvaarthuis. In short, the Leiden years, more so than those in Purmerend, were years of reflection and orientation regarding the future development of architecture. What direction it should take was anybody's guess. The only certainty was that contemporary art had a considerable head start.**

**Owing to the First World War there was also relatively little building in these years. The main projects were competition designs which remained on paper. To avoid national service, Oud accepted a modest commission from the Nederlandsche Bank as assistant to the Hague-based architect J.A.G. van der Steur who was busy building a Leiden branch on the corner of Kort Rapenburg and Galgewater. Although the position of assistant architect was somewhat beneath him at this point in his career, a declaration from the bank's directors served to keep him out of military service.[8]**



**Notes**

**1.** H. van Bergeijk, *Willem Marinus Dudok. Architect-stedebouwkundige 1884-1974*, Naarden 1994, pp. 16-18.

**2.** D. Wintgens Hötte, A. de Jongh-Vermeulen (eds), *Dageraad van de Moderne Kunst. Leiden en Omgeving 1890-1940*, Zwolle, Leiden 1999.

**3.** J.J.P. Oud to T. van Doesburg, 30 May 1916, Fondation Custodia, Paris; A. de Jongh-Vermeulen, P. van de Velde, 'De Leidsche Kunstclub De Sphinx. "Een Vereeniging die mee kan tellen"', in: D. Wintgens Hötte, A. de Jongh-Vermeulen (eds), *Dageraad van de Moderne Kunst. Leiden en Omgeving 1890-1940*, Zwolle, Leiden 1999, p. 174.

**4.** T. van Doesburg to J.J.P. Oud, 1 June 1916, Fondation Custodia, Paris.

**5.** *Catalogus der eerste tentoonstelling van werken van leden en genoodigden in de bovenzalen van de "Harmonie", Breestraat Leiden, 18 januari-31 januari 1917*, Leiden 1917.

**6.** J.F. Heijbroek, 'Het kortstondig bestaan van de Leidsche Kunstclub de Sphinx', in: *Leids Jaarboekje*, Leiden, 1980, note 15.

**7.** S. Frank, *Michel de Klerk 1884-1923. An architect of the Amsterdam School*, Ann Arbor 1980, pp. 84-86.

**8.** Leiden, Nederlandse Bank Archive, correspondence between J.A.G. van der Steur and the board of the Nederlandse Bank, October 1916, archive no. 1.412.21/99/60/1.

# 20/ Renovation of Rappard House

**Leiden, 45 Rapenburg** **1917**

The seventeenth-century property at 45 Rapenburg in Leiden came into the possession of A. Rappard Esq. at the beginning of the twentieth century. In 1917, Rappard, an engineer by profession, commissioned Oud to modernize the house, a task that included converting the rear section to a workshop/laboratory. Oud's plan also encompassed the reorganization of the transition between front and rear sections, in particular the stairs. However, a survey carried out in 1939 found the stairs still in their original position. The precise details of Oud's renovation are consequently unknown. Rappard sold 45 Rapenburg a year later, after which the property underwent several more major renovations.[1]

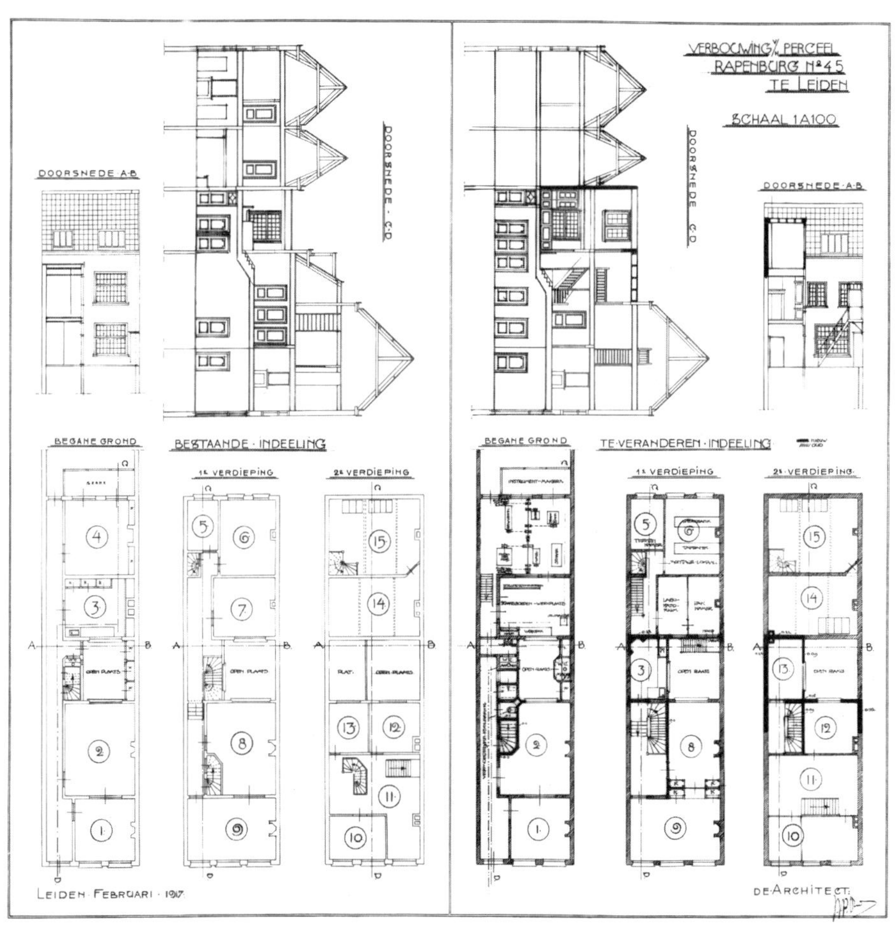


Various design views showing existing situation (left), renovation design (right)/ OUDJ-ra 1, NAI, Rotterdam



**Notes**

**1.** In Lunsing Scheurleer (1988) it is incorrectly stated that Oud's renovation involved the demolition of the rear section and its replacement by a smaller volume; in fact this occurred after the house was sold in 1919.

**Sources**

NAI: OUDJ-ra 1

**Literature**

U. Barbieri, *J.J.P. Oud*, Rotterdam 1987, p. 191

T.H. Lunsing Scheurleer et al. , *Het Rapenburg; Geschiedenis van een Leidse gracht*, Vol. IIIb Leiden, 1988

S. Polano, *J.J.P. Oud Architettura Olandese*, Milan 1981, p. 217

# 21/ Housing, Leiderdorp

**Leiderdorp, Munnikerweg /** **Lage Rijndijk**

**1914-1915**

In the second half of 1914, Dudok and Oud produced two designs for a working class neighbourhood for the 'Dorpsbelang' housing association in Leiderdorp. Both are recognizably based on a close study of Raymond Unwin's *Town Planning in Practice* (1908), a German translation of which had appeared in 1910. Unwin's book was at that moment the most complete guide to the solution of practical problems concerning urban layout, land division, and urban design as well as the linking and orientation of houses and housing blocks. In the second plan for Leiderdorp, presented in December 1914, the spatial context had been trimmed back in favour of the orientation and layout of the dwellings. But even in this more spartan, built version, the plan remains one of the most authentic examples of English (Parker & Unwin) garden city-inspired housing in the Netherlands. The entire scheme comprised 23 dwellings in two variants (Types A and B), plus a house with adjoining hairdresser and shop. Type A (18 dwellings) was a small house with a built-in kitchen in which the stove was located in an alcove under the stairs of all places. The ground floor also had space for a laundry and a small room that could be used as a bedroom. Upstairs were two more bedrooms and an attic. Type B, five of which were built, was more spacious, with a separate kitchen and an extra upstairs bedroom. The scheme was well received by the Leiden art world, at least that is the impression given by a laudatory article in the *Leidsch Dagblad* by W.C. Brouwer, the ceramist who was by now a friend of Oud and who lived and worked at 'Vrederust' along the banks of the Rhine not far from Leiderdorp. Brouwer's critique is illustrative of the popularity enjoyed by the aesthetic and ideological concept of the vernacular in the circles of cabinetmakers and potters, to which Oud too belonged at that time.

**Perspective/ OUDJ-ar 4, NAI, Rotterdam**

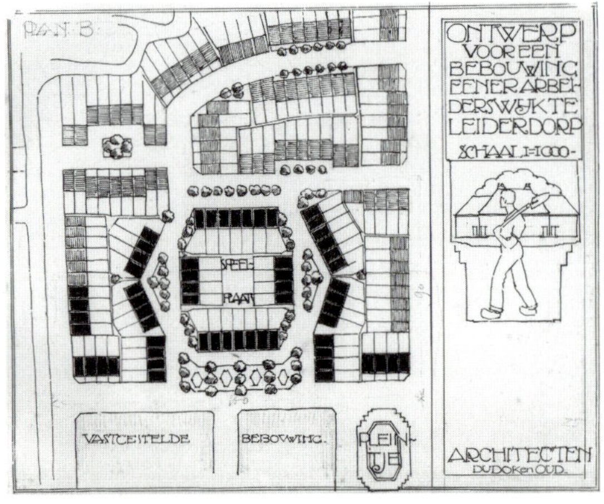


**Site plan/ OUDJ-ar 3, NAI, Rotterdam**

Type B dwelling (left) and Type A dwelling (right): plans of ground floor (bottom) and upper floor (top). From: F. Smit, *De droom van Howard. Verleden en toekomst van de tuindorpen*, Rijswijk 1991

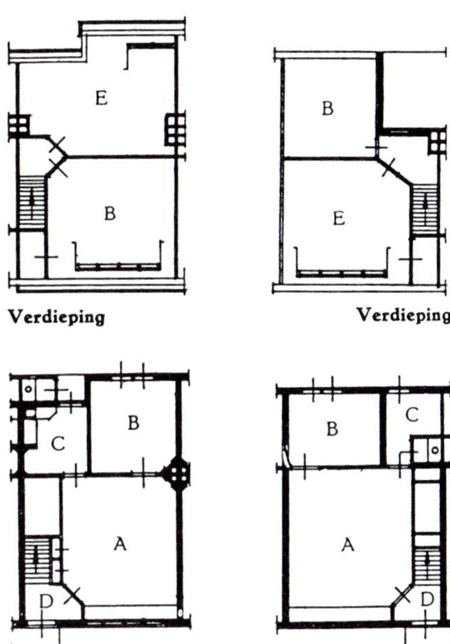


Design for a hairdressers' with dwelling, front elevation (top), plans of ground floor (centre) and first floor (bottom)/ 890126-box 7, 5*, Getty, Los Angeles

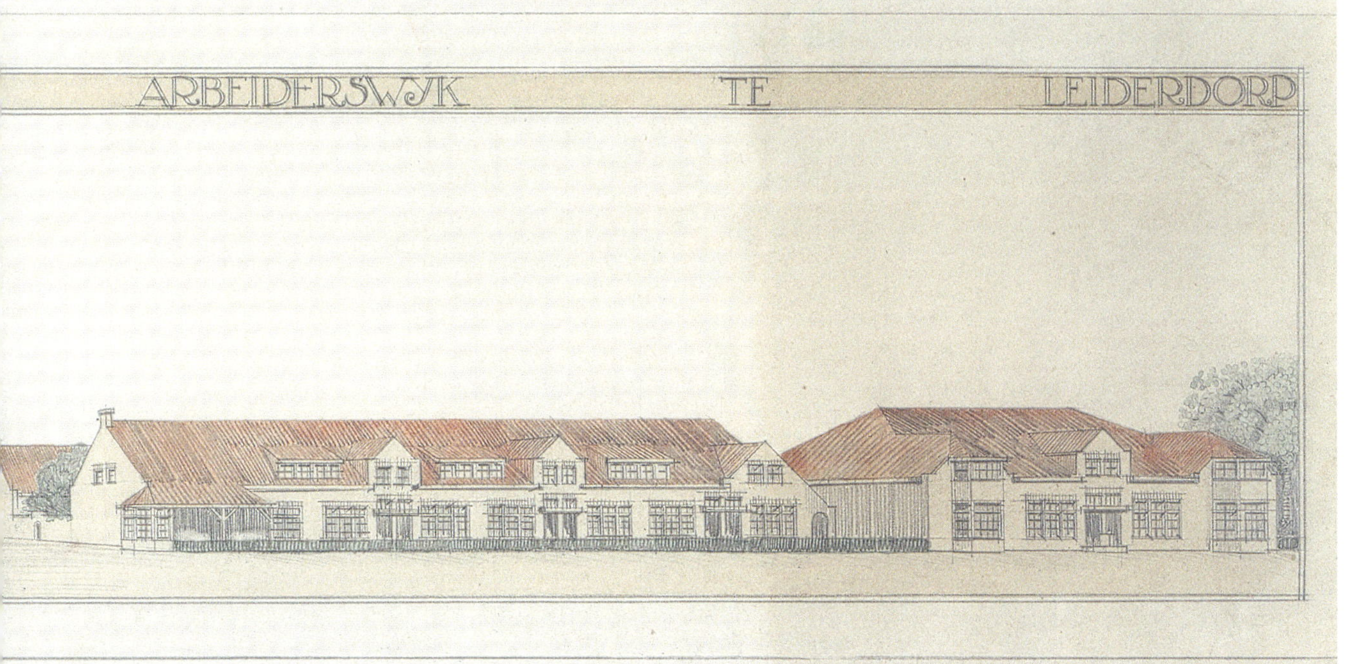




**Sources**
Bouw- en woningtoezicht Leiderdorp: two sheets (identical to those in the Oud Archive, NAI, Rotterdam)
CCA: dr1984: 0010-0011, ph1984: 1003
Getty: 890126-box 7, 5*, 890126-2**
NAI: OUDJ-ar 1-5, OUDJ-ar 3001, OUDJ-ph 40-43

**Articles**
W.C. Brouwer, 'Arbeiderswoningen', in: *Leidsch Dagblad*, 19 January 1916
J.J.P. Oud, 'Arbeiderswoningen te Leiderdorp', in: *Bouwkundig Weekblad*, 36(1915)11, p. 86
H.P. Berlage (et al.), *Arbeiderswoningen in Nederland*, Rotterdam 1921

**Literature**
U. Barbieri, *J.J.P. Oud*, Rotterdam 1987, pp. 24-25
H. van Bergeijk, *Willem Marinus Dudok. Architect-stedebouwkundige 1884-1974*, Naarden 1995, p. 133
H.E. Oud, *J.J.P. Oud. Architekt 1890-1963. Feiten en herinneringen gerangschikt*, The Hague 1984, pp. 22-23, p. 118
S. Polano, *J.J.P. Oud Architettura Olandese*, Milan 1981, p. 13
G. Stamm, *J.J.P. Oud. Bauten und Projekte 1906 bis 1963*, Mainz, Berlin 1984, pp. 24, 27

View of the district/ OUDJ-ph 40, NAI, Rotterdam

OUDJ-ph 41, NAI, Rotterdam

OUDJ-ph 43, NAI, Rotterdam

OUDJ-ph 42, NAI, Rotterdam

A while ago I was accorded some space in your magazine for a "talk" about the new H.B.S. at Leiden. This time it is for a group of working-class cottages that I request your indulgence.

In Leiderdorp the "Dorpsbelang" Association has built 24 cottages. In various price categories, they are now gradually becoming available for rent. Not all are complete but those which are now "livable", are so in the true sense of the word. They are charmingly grouped together in several blocks. Space has been left for a communal garden, while the simplicity of their construction accords perfectly with the rural surroundings. The sense of community is nicely demonstrated by connecting walls with here and there an arched gateway. The sociability of the "civic" Renaissance has been ... achieved here in spite of extremely limited resources. A wonderfully coloured (off-coloured) damp course, above this a very attractive brick in a warm colour which stands out all the better because of the grey jointing, shows once again what can be achieved with Dutch brick.

That the cottages are eminently livable is evidenced by fact that they all have one very large room that looks out over the road or over the countryside. Then there is another smaller sitting room or bedroom and a kitchen/kitchenette, while generous provision has been made for cupboards and a WC. Upstairs are several bedrooms (2 or 3) and usually an attic into the bargain. Small and comfortable, and everything ready to hand. Not a single cm. of ground has been wasted, and yet this is not apparent.

In townhouses built according to a formula of a sequence of rooms etc. one so often feels shut up in the long narrow house which has the same purpose, even the same form, as bond coupons. Here in Leiderdorp that is most certainly not the case. The paintwork is colourful. The beams warm orange-brown and the ceiling itself white. A refreshing approach! The gateway is perhaps a little on the small side, especially if young couples with a pram come to live here. But on the other hand, by restricting this space, the living room – which is the most important thing after all – is enviably spacious. For bicycles each cottage will have its own 3 x 1/2 M shed. Whereas the construction of working-class homes en bloc is a phenomenon of the modern times, and they are shooting up out of the ground by the dozens all over the place, this, I think is a task for the architect that entails many problems and which can contribute so much to whether such a neighbourhood fails or succeeds aesthetically speaking. In the case of Leiderdorp I think I can safely say that this work by the architects Dudok and Oud is an asset. An asset that merits imitation.

With polite thanks,
Respectfully,
Your obdt Servant
Willem Brouwer,
"Vredelust" Leiderdorp.

# 22/ Leidsch Dagblad Building

**Leiden, 1 Witte Singel** **1916-1917**

In 1916 Dudok and Oud signed the specifications and conditions *governing the bulk tender to be issued on behalf of Leidsch Dagblad plc for the construction of an office building and associated work.* The only signature on the working drawings, however, is that of Dudok. After the latter's departure for Hilversum, Oud took over day-to-day management of the construction work and supervision of the finishing. The ground floor contained the news room, the public lobby and the administrative department. Most of the first floor was taken up by a gallery. As the correspondence with Van Doesburg shows, Oud was also involved in the design of this space. In the first months of their acquaintance, Oud and Van Doesburg spoke and wrote at length about the ideal 'environment' for the exhibition of modern art. In his very first letter to Oud, Van Doesburg wrote: *It so happens that I recently received a letter from an art correspondent asking me in what kind of surroundings modern paintings, including mine, are seen to best effect. I subsequently spoke to him in person about this subject and indicated that the way to enjoy modern works is not of course the way people usually go about exhibitions: that is by hanging works that are sometimes of a very different nature in rows next to one another and moreover in surroundings that are worse than tasteless. Instead of galleries, in places where the products of the soul are displayed – at least sometimes – we need a new interior. And who is to produce the new interior? The Architect.*[1] Oud answered by return of post, sending Van Doesburg his article 'Over cubisme, futurisme, moderne bouwkunst, enz.' together with drawings for the *Leidsch Dagblad.* On 14 June, Van Doesburg replied that although he had not yet had time to read the article he had studied the drawings: *I like the plans for the Leidsch Dagblad.... It should above all be an intimate room. I have several plans in my head but cannot write it all down so quickly. I hope you will keep me informed about it. The light is everything in such a small room. It should fall in such a way as to intensify the materiality of the surroundings. The walls should be broken up by panelling, wainscotting. The benches fixed in the wall. ...I simply mention one or two things, without knowing of course whether you agree. Since you are building it yourself you will be in the best position to feel how it should be in relation to the exhibition of modern art.*[2]

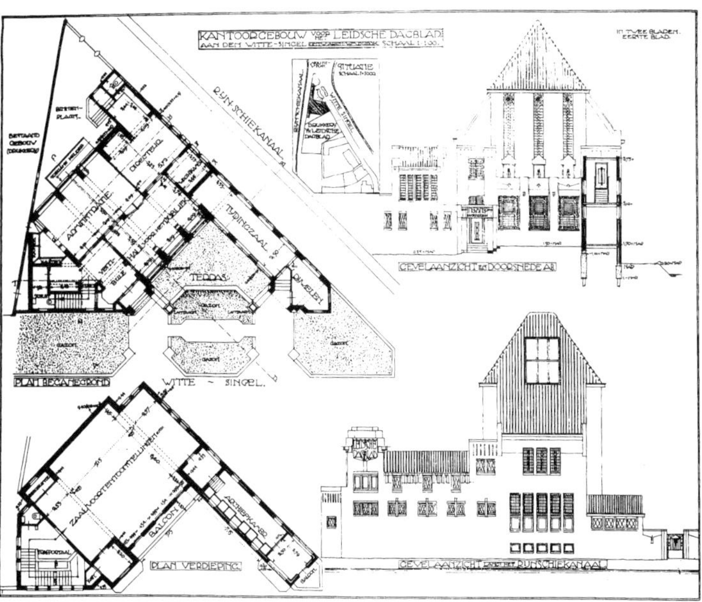


**Various design views/ Gemeentearchief, Leidsch Dagblad Company Archive, Leiden**

**Notes**

**1.** Van Doesburg to J.J.P. Oud, 1 June 1916, Fondation Custodia, Paris. Van Doesburg had spoken to Croiset, art critic with the *Dagblad voor Zuid-Holland en 's-Gravenhage*. As a result of this conversation, Van Doesburg penned an unpublished text about the same subject. E. van Straaten, *Theo van Doesburg. Schilder en architect*, The Hague 1988, pp. 12-13; A. de Jongh-Vermeulen, P. van de Velde, 'De Leidsche Kunstclub De Sphinx. "Een Vereeniging die mee kan tellen"', in: D. Wintgens Hötte, A. de Jongh-Vermeulen (eds), *Dageraad van de Moderne Kunst. Leiden en Omgeving 1890-1940*, Zwolle, Leiden 1999, pp. 176-181

**2.** Van Doesburg to J.J.P. Oud, 14 June 1916, Fondation Custodia, Paris.

**Sources**

Gemeentearchief Leiden: Leidsch Dagblad, Company Archive

**Literature**


H. van Bergeijk, *Willem Marinus Dudok. Architect-stedebouwkundige 1884-1974*, Naarden 1995, p. 147

J. Brink, 'Dudok's idee van een krantegebouw', in: *Leids Dagblad*, 9 July 1988

H. Fuchs, M. Maandag, H van de Schoor, *Vouwblad Dudok in Leiden*, Leiden 1990

E. van Straaten, *Theo van Doesburg. Schilder en architect*, The Hague 1988, pp. 12-13

# 23/ Competition Design for a Museum of Indonesian Art

**Notional location** **1914**

At the end of 1913, the Amsterdam architectural society Architectura et Amicitia (A. et A.) organized a competition for a Museum of Indonesian Art. Entrants were asked to submit a design for a museum building, cafeteria and caretaker's dwelling, plus landscaping for a notional location. The jury of A. et A. members included H.P. Berlage and W.J. Kromhout. In his entry Oud grouped the buildings around a central axis: the two auxiliary buildings he placed at either corner of the site beside the road while the museum building was set back at the centre of the site. This hierarchical layout was enhanced by the central section of the front elevation of the museum which was raised and decorated with sculpture. The museum itself had a symmetrical, axial plan with the sculpture rooms grouped around three adjacent courts. Given the incidence of light, the small galleries for painting were located at the front of the building and the rooms for applied art at the rear. Oud chose light-coloured materials for the facade cladding.

The jury rated Oud's design (coded O) fourth out of a total of eight entries. In the jury report, which was published in full in the society's journal in 1914, this assessment was justified as follows:

*Site: The building is well situated in relation to the garden design, although the arrangement of the garden is rather dull.*

*Plan: Overall there is a lack of large spaces. For a monumental building, it also lacks a grand vista in the central section. Some rooms, such as the bicycle accommodation and the storeroom are oddly situated with respect to the main entrance. Nor is there any organic connection between the courts and the garden.*

*Facade: An attempt has been made to give the front elevation a monumental character but the whole cannot be termed a success, although the proportions testify to diligent study.*

*Important detail: Too insignificant and an odd colour.*

*Drawing: Not bad, but in general rather superficially done, not yet conscientious enough for a competition.*[1]

**Front elevation/ 890126-4**, Getty, Los Angeles**



**Notes**

**1.** 'Juryrapport, Eereprijsvraag: "A. et A." 1914', in: *Architectura*, 22(1914)18, pp. 141-144.

**Sources**

Getty: 890126-4**

**Articles**

'Juryrapport, Eereprijsvraag: "A. et A." 1914', in: *Architectura*, 22(1914)18, pp. 141-144

'Ereprijsvraag 1914 van het genootschap "A. et A." te Amsterdam', in: *Architectura*, 21(1913)31, pp. 256-257

## 24/ Competition Design for an Old People's Home

**Hilversum** **1915**

Although the Netherlands was not a party to the First World War, construction stagnated during the war years for lack of building supplies. Architectural production was chiefly sustained by means of major design competitions. In his English autobiographical essay (1951) Oud had this to say about that period: *War came and brought wholly stand-still of building-works also for the neutrals. I could only be busy by prize subjects and so I made in this time projects for an old men's and old wives home, for a bathing house, a home for soldiers a.s.o. Still being persuaded of the necessity of a 'new style' to get beauty again in life and finding at that time, that this 'style' was brought already by Berlage, I thought everyone building like Berlage we will have the 'new style'.*[1] Such statements, more than thirty-five years after the event, may serve to confirm a myth that Oud himself had initiated in the 1920s, but they also obscure the complex background of Oud's early architecture. Even in the years when Oud was most closely involved with Van Doesburg and his search for a 'new style' was gaining momentum, he remained open to countless outside influences. His admiration for Berlage, for example, did not preclude interest in other domestic and international tendencies and architects. This, at any rate, is the message conveyed by his competition entries for an old people's home in Hilversum and for a military hostel in Den Helder, designs in which Oud drew not only on Berlage but also on the aesthetic devices of Dudok and Architectura et Amicitia (Kromhout and De Bazel). Even the inspiration for the famous Volksbadhuis, which is nearly always depicted in the literature as a copy of Berlage's Stock Exchange, is open to qualification. What the competition designs demonstrate is the relativity of the Berlagian legacy, an admiration for the artistic talent of Kromhout and Van der Mey and a more pragmatic confidence in traditional, rational compositional schemes. In that sense they are illustrative of Oud's efforts to link ideals of simplicity and efficiency to an artistic form expressive of his own time, a quest that was entirely in keeping with the tradition of nineteenth-century eclecticism.[2]

In 1914, the 'Verzorgingshuis te Hilversum' foundation organized a competition for a new home for able-bodied and

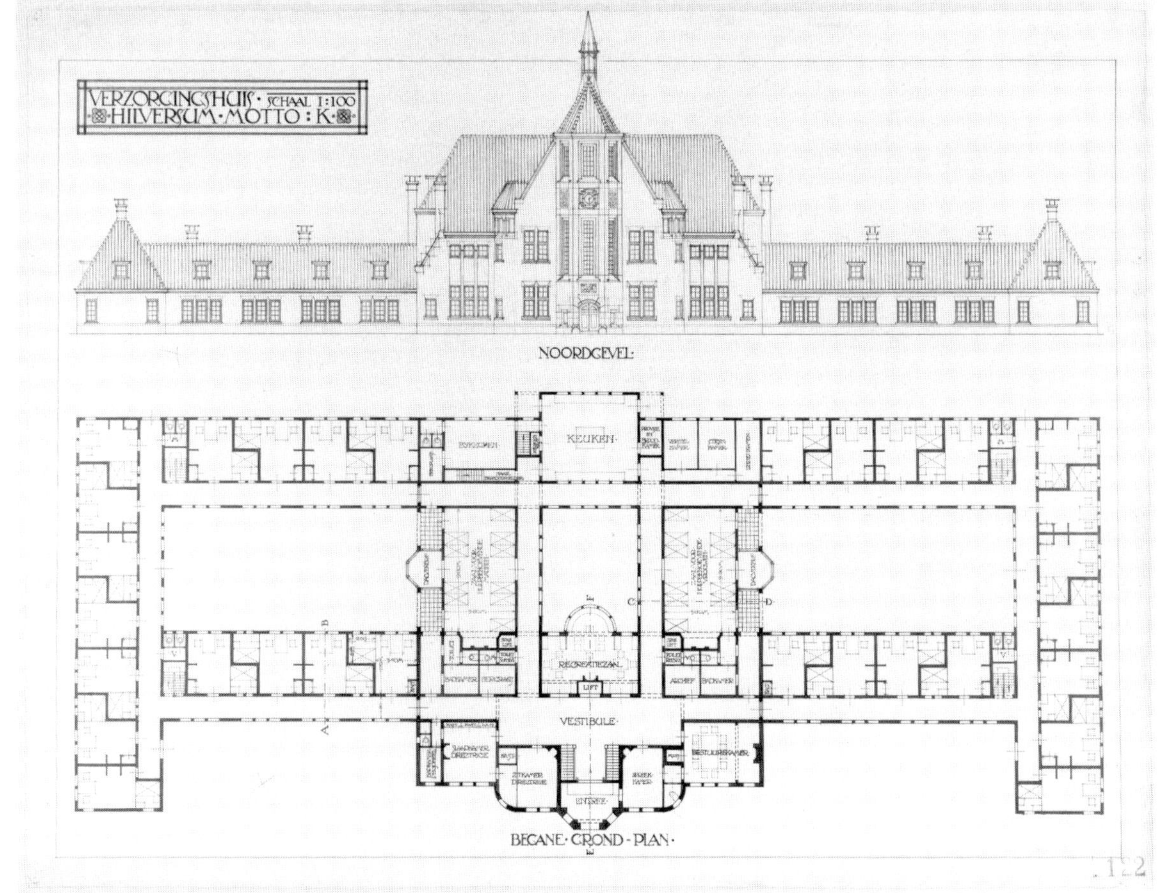


Front elevation and ground floor plan/ dr1984: 0483, CCA, Montreal

semi-invalid elderly people to be located on the outskirts of Hilversum. The competition brief called specifically for a sober and simple architecture. The jury was made up of H. Nieuwenhuizen, C. de Groot, J. Hingst, J.W. Hanrath and Jan Stuyt. Oud's ambitious designs was his first attempt at a public building. For the floor plan he resorted to the familiar Beaux-Arts layout of a central main building containing entrance and collective facilities, flanked by low-rise wings in which the rooms for the elderly residents are organized around open courts. Stylistically, as Herman van Bergeijk has already noted, the main building is closely related to the Leidsch Dagblad building on which Oud was currently working with Dudok.[3] But the Hilversum building was no office and Oud did his best to give the main building the character of an ample country house, beside which the residential wings stand somewhat awkwardly.
Although Oud's entry was not awarded a prize, several of the drawings were published in *Bouwfragmenten*.

**Perspective/ OUDJ-vh 1, NAI, Rotterdam**



**Notes**
**1.** U. Barbieri, H. Engel, B. Colenbrander, *Architectuur van J.J.P.Oud,* exhibition catalogue, Rotterdam 1982, p. 8.
**2.** A. van der Woud, *Waarheid en karakter. Het debat over de bouwkunst 1840-1900,* Rotterdam 1997, p. 355.
**3.** H. van Bergeijk, *Willem Marinus Dudok. Architect-stedebouwkundige 1884-1974,* Naarden 1995, p. 17.

**Sources**
CCA: dr1984: 0013, dr1984: 0483-0485, ph1984: 1004
NAI: OUDJ-vh 1, OUDJ-ph 56-57

**Articles**
'Prijsvragen. Stichting "Het Verzorgingstehuis" te Hilversum.', in: *Bouwkundig Weekblad,* 34(1914)28, pp. 342-345
'Prijsvraagontwerp', in: *Bouwfragmenten,* September 1915 no. 8

**Literature**
U. Barbieri, *J.J.P. Oud,* Rotterdam 1987, pp. 30-33
U. Barbieri, H. Engel, B. Colenbrander, *Architectuur van J.J.P.Oud,* exhibition catalogue, Rotterdam 1982, p. 8
H. van Bergeijk, *Willem Marinus Dudok. Architect-stedebouwkundige 1884-1974,* Naarden 1995, p. 17
H.E. Oud, *J.J.P. Oud. Architekt 1890-1963. Feiten en herinneringen gerangschikt,* The Hague 1984, pp. 18-20
S. Polano, *J.J.P. Oud Architettura Olandese,* Milan 1981, pp. 13-14
G. Stamm, *J.J.P. Oud. Bauten und Projekte 1906 bis 1963,* Mainz, Berlin , 1984, p. 29
A. van der Woud, *Waarheid en karakter. Het debat over de bouwkunst 1840-1900,* Rotterdam 1997, p. 355

# 25/ Competition Design for a Military Hostel

**Den Helder** **1915**

The background to this design is somewhat hazy. In 1909 Dudok built a distinctly Berlagian 'Tehuis voor Militairen' on Kanaalweg in Den Helder.[1] In 1911-1913, the young Piet Kramer realized his first big design commission, a hostel for Minder Marinepersoneel (Lower Naval Personnel) in Den Helder.[2] There is no documentary evidence to support Oud's claim (1951) that his design for a military hostel was a competition entry. The surviving materials (all the drawings were done on 27 and 29 December 1915) are more suggestive of an exercise in which Oud drew variations on the plans and facade compositions of existing buildings. In his sketch design he made use of Dudok's plan in which the entrance and staircase were placed off-centre in relation to the lounge and reading room which occupy the remainder of the ground floor. For the decorative finishing of the windows and especially the top of the tower, he borrowed freely from the rich arsenal of somewhat 'sentimental' architecture to be found in the work of Kromhout and the early products of the Amsterdam School, in particular Michel de Klerk's housing block on Johan Vermeerstraat and, of course, the Scheepvaarthuis by J.M. van der Mey, two buildings that he later also approvingly included in his *Holländische Architektur* (1926). The composition of the main elevation – from the relation of tower to building mass to the disposition of the windows – was based on a system of triangles, in accordance with the method Oud had learned as a student at the Quellinus School from J. de Groot.

Oud considered the design presentable enough to be displayed at Sphinx's 'International Exhibition' in January 1917, along with the 'cubist' paintings of Emil Filla and a couple of 'modern compositions' by Van Doesburg. In the light of the discussions then taking place between Van Doesburg and Oud, one could imagine that both men regarded the geometrical diagram stretched tautly over the facade plane as a step on the road to abstraction, to the reduction of architecture to a composition of geometrical shapes. Not that this was in itself so very new: equilateral triangles had been regarded by Cuypers as a representation of the divine Trinity and by theosophists like De Bazel and Lauweriks as symbols of a higher mystic reality.[3]

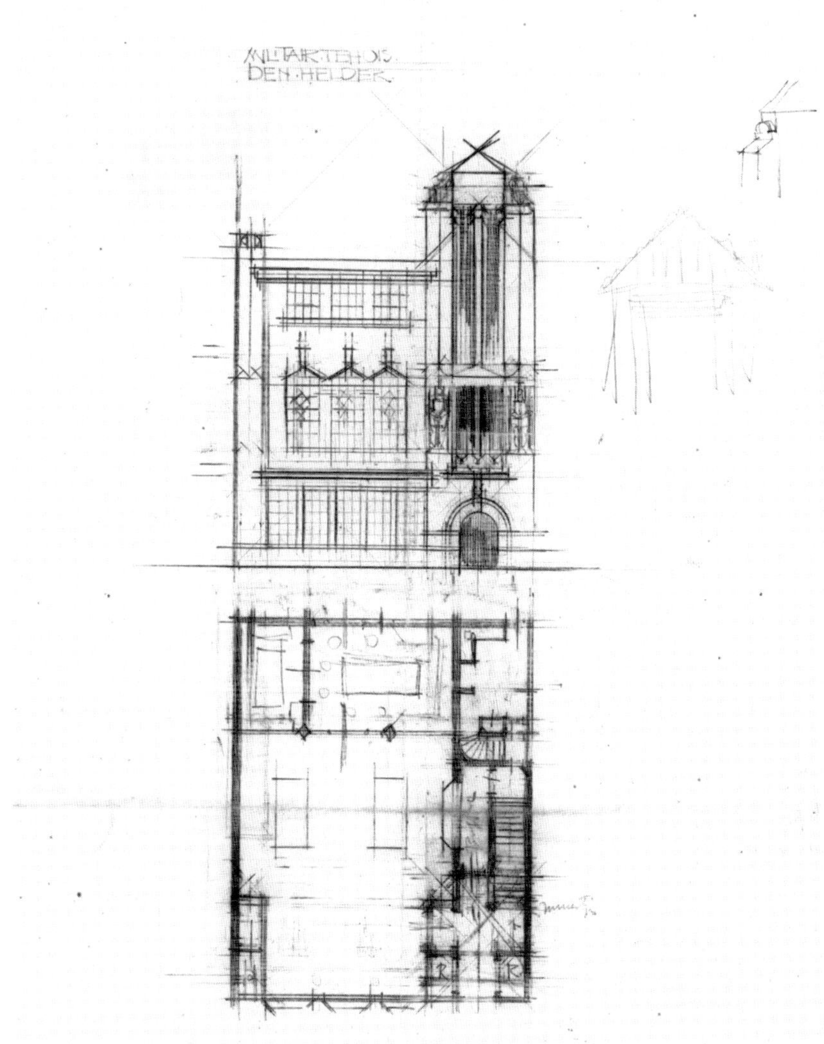


**Front elevation and ground floor plan/**
**NAI, OUDJ-mt 1, NAI, Rotterdam**

Front elevation/ 890126-box 7, 2*, Getty, Los Angeles



**Notes**

**1.** H. van Bergeijk, *Willem Marinus Dudok. Architect-stedebouwkundige 1884-1974*, Naarden 1995, pp. 128-129.

**2.** M. Casciato (ed.), *Architectuur en Volkshuisvesting. Nederland 1870-1940*, Nijmegen 1980.

**3.** A. van der Woud, *Waarheid en karakter. Het debat over de bouwkunst 1840-1900*, Rotterdam 1997, p. 352.

**Sources**

CCA: ph1984: 0810-0811, ph1984: 1009-1010
Getty: 890126-box 7, 2*, 890126-11**
NAI: OUDJ-mt 1-5, OUDJ-ph 58-59

**Articles**

W.M. Dudok, 'Nieuw tehuis voor militairen in Den Helder', in: *Bouwkundig Weeblad*, 33 (1913), pp. 464-468

**Literature**

U. Barbieri, *J.J.P. Oud*, Rotterdam 1987, p. 29
H. van Bergeijk, *Willem Marinus Dudok. Architect-stedebouwkundige 1884-1974*, Naarden 1995, pp. 128-129
H.E. Oud, *J.J.P. Oud. Architekt 1890-1963. Feiten en herinneringen gerangschikt*, The Hague 1984, p. 22
S. Polano, *J.J.P. Oud Architettura Olandese*, Milan 1981, pp. 13-14
G. Stamm, *J.J.P. Oud. Bauten und Projekte 1906 bis 1963*, Mainz, Berlin, 1984, p. 29
A. van der Woud, *Waarheid en karakter. Het debat over de bouwkunst 1840-1900*, Rotterdam 1997, p. 352

# 26/ Competition Design for Public Baths

**The Hague, notional location** **1914-1915**

Apart from Oud's own declarations on the subject, little is known about the origins of this design. In 1914 the Hague chapter of the Maatschappij tot Bevordering der Bouwkunst (Society for the Advancement of Architecture, precursor of the Royal Institute of Dutch Architects) organized a competition that was limited to local architects. H.P. Berlage was a member of the jury. Oud did not submit his design (there is no trace of a code) and evidently regarded the time spent on it as an exercise in style and design for which Berlage's Stock Exchange served as point of departure and teaching aid. In retrospect, however, (that is, in the 1950s) Oud accorded it much greater significance. In the previously quoted attempt at an autobiography in 1951, for example, he claimed that the bathhouse had been based wholly on Berlagian forms, in particular those of the Amsterdam Exchange. He expressed himself in similar terms in a letter to the putative publisher of this monograph.[1] Nonetheless, such pronouncements say more about Oud and his self-appointed place in Dutch architectural history than about the merits of the actual design. Three linked, round-arch portals are not enough to establish kinship with the Amsterdam Exchange. Compared with Berlage's Exchange, Oud's bathhouse is, as its function demands, a relatively simple and unpretentious building. The plan may be a typological echo of Berlage's building but it differs from it just as strongly in the almost obsessive symmetry and the lack of any form of architectonic drama. A good example of this is the 'dead' spot in the facade resulting from the sloping roofing of the entrance hall which internally, too, sorely lacks the *chiaroscuro* of the Stock Exchange vestibule.

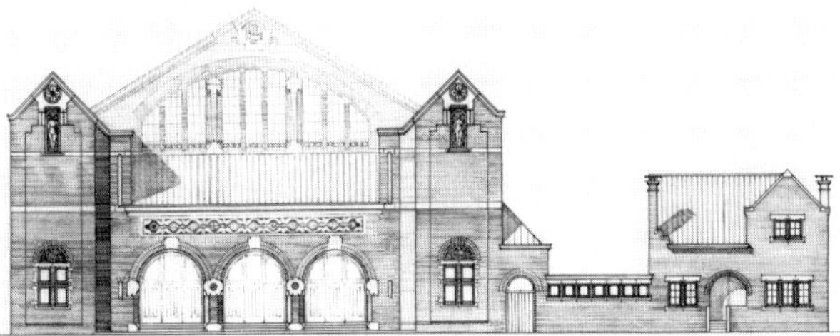

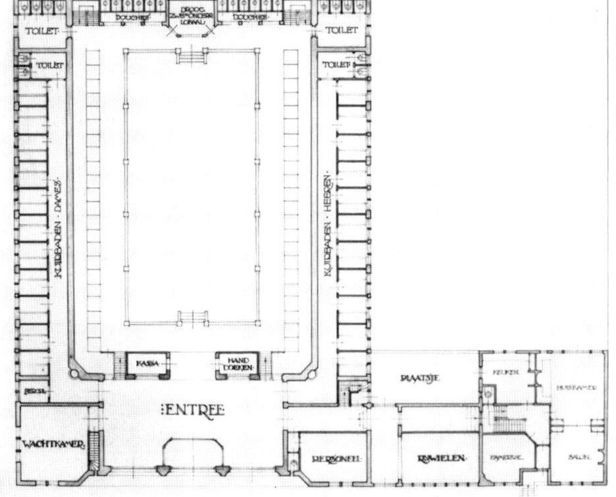


**Front elevation and ground floor plan/ OUDJ-vb 1, NAI, Rotterdam**

**Notes**

**1.** Oud to Dr. B. Schindler, 1 February 1951, OUDJ-B, NAI, Rotterdam.

**Sources**

CCA: ph1984: 0812, ph1984: 1011
NAI: OUDJ-vb 1, OUDJ-ph 52-55, OUDJ-5, OUDJ-B

**Articles**

A. Broese van Groenon, J.G. Robbers, 'Programma voor een studie-prijsvraag uit te schrijven door de Afdeeling 's Gravenhage van de Maatschappij ter Bevordering der Bouwkunst', in: *Bouwkundig Weekblad*, 34(1914)51, pp. 537-538
Anonymous, 'Rapport der jury', in: *Bouwkundig Weekblad*, 36(1915/1916)1, pp. 6-8

**Literature**

U. Barbieri, *J.J.P. Oud*, Rotterdam 1987, p. 28
H.E. Oud, *J.J.P. Oud. Architekt 1890-1963. Feiten en herinneringen gerangschikt*, The Hague 1984, p. 21
S. Polano, *J.J.P. Oud Architettura Olandese*, Milan 1981, pp. 13-14
G. Stamm, *J.J.P. Oud. Bauten und Projekte 1906 bis 1963*, Mainz, Berlin 1984, p. 29

# 27/ Project for the 'Helder' Junior Technical School

**Den Helder** **1917**

Ever since Günther Stamm's 1984 book on Oud, the drawing of the front elevation of the junior technical school has been regarded as a design for a new building in Den Helder.[1] However, this is unlikely given that a new junior technical school had been built in Den Helder as recently as 1907 and nothing is known about a commission or competition for a second school. It looks as if here, as in the last two projects, Oud was simply using an existing building to practise his art. The (abstract) site sketch supports the suspicion that this is an imaginary design. The drawings show that what Oud had in mind was not so much a building as an entire building complex consisting of an internal courtyard (playground) reached through a gateway building (with caretaker's lodge) and two buildings: a rectangular main building over three floors containing the classrooms and administration, and a much smaller, square building with workshops for electricians, machine operators and smiths. Judging by the articulation and detailing of the main building, the entire project looks like an architectural study based on the work of De Bazel whom Oud regarded, along with Kromhout and Berlage, as one of the founders of modern architecture in the Netherlands. The exterior, with its narrow windows framed by piers, its tall, imperforate roof area and its decorated, high plinth, is reminiscent of the headquarters of the Koninklijke Nederlandsche Heidemaatschappij in Arnhem (1912), the symmetrical composition and restrained monumentality of which would certainly have appealed to Oud.[2] From a distance, the cubic composition of De Bazel's office building bears a passing resemblance to the Kröller house in Wassenaar, designed by the Berlin architect Peter Behrens. So it could perhaps be said that Günther Stamm was indirectly correct when he claimed that Oud's junior technical school was influenced by Peter Behrens, an architect with whose work Oud was probably barely, if at all, acquainted at that time.

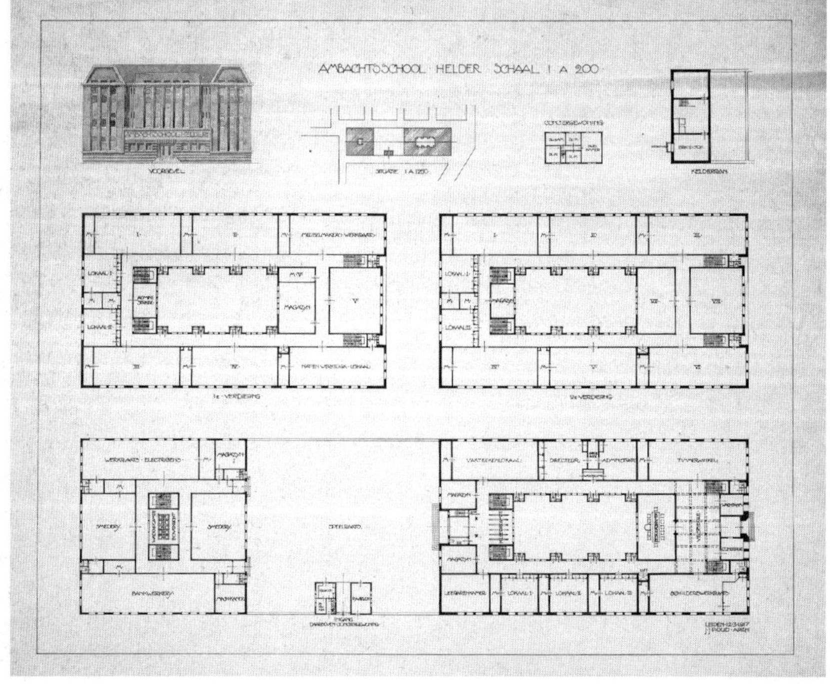


Various design views/ dr1984: 0014, CCA, Montreal



**Notes**

**1.** G. Stamm, *J.J.P. Oud. Bauten und Projekte 1906 bis 1963*, Mainz, Berlin 1984.

**2.** A.W. Reinink, *K.P.C. de Bazel – Architect*, Leiden 1965, pp. 136-138.

**Sources**

CCA: dr1984: 0014

**Literature**

U. Barbieri, *J.J.P. Oud*, Rotterdam 1987, p. 191

H.E. Oud, *J.J.P. Oud. Architekt 1890-1963. Feiten en herinneringen gerangschikt*, The Hague 1984, p. 22

S. Polano, *J.J.P. Oud Architettura Olandese*, Milan 1981, pp. 13-14

G. Stamm, *J.J.P. Oud. Bauten und Projekte 1906 bis 1963*, Mainz, Berlin , 1984, p. 29, p. 32

Haarlem, 13 nov. 1916

Dear Chap! Cordial thanks for your cordial telegram. Just arrived while we were eating, Lena will have told you everything. In all honesty I can no longer call any painting mine since I'm willingly parting with all my best work for the promised amount. You can imagine how wonderfully free I feel now. No need to do anything that in the slightest way conflicts with my spiritual nature. To be able to buy everything I need for my beloved calling. The best thing is [that] my uncommonly noble patron handed me an advance of 625 guilders. What trust, eh, uncommon. My faith in humanity has been strengthened by all this. You know yourself probably as well as I, the attitude people adopt when it comes to money and how slow people are to value someone's energy. I wanted to fly to Zurich that instant to embrace the man (and woman) to whom I owe this great piece of financial good luck. I hadn't counted on it at all. It had simply been mentioned in passing, until on 13 Nov. I suddenly received a letter to present myself at the Ned. H. Bank. The money for the magazine has been promised as well so that all ways lie open before me. Christ, old chap, when I realized what had actually happened, I felt I wanted to strike a statue from the first available paving stone. Things had been going badly, too, recently, but from 10 to 11 Nov. things suddenly took a turn for the better. ...articles arrived; proofs and other articles suddenly appeared. I made a lot of progress ... with my work. I developed my Dancer with sure confidence into a stylish whole. In short, everything went my way; summarum sum: the letter of 13th Nov. Strange – have I told you before – that all these sort of things happen on the 13th? The decisive missive arrived on the 13th. From my debut in 1908 I counted 66 x 13. The number of bank notes was 13 that was the 67th time. And 67 = 6.$_3$7. The sum of the figures. I don't know whether you are interested in astrological numbers, but from what I have learned my astrological position is 5 en$_{13}$8. Oh well, it's of no importance, the main thing is that I can now work, that I can finish everything. I am busy working on that glass window for you. Of course the swan should be coloured, pretty much as in the enclosed sketch. The background can not be cut from one piece of glass since this would be too weak. I shall work the connections into the motif as much as possible so that it doesn't show. Before I make the final drawing I'll visit [Borstman] and find out how much freedom I have. Huszár informed me in a note that [Borstman] didn't "appeal" to him. The glass Huszár used he deliberately allows to [harden] because the available glass is transparent. I shall get involved in everything so that it does justice to [both] of us. You can count on it. – I thank you for the addresses of the architects and will write to them about the magazine. I'm up to my ears in correspondence as I'm sure you understand. Inquire whether Berlage will collaborate on the magazine. I'll write him too about his collaboration. My book has still not been published and Waltman hasn't been in touch. If I get fed up I can take everything back. Let anyone who wants it write to Delft (Waltman) for a copy, perhaps that will get things moving. Wednesday a meeting of the Sphinx? I hope we can celebrate together afterwards. You still have to give a party too Oudje. I was really pleased that you ... are spared that rubbish for 5 mths. and then we shall see. If necessary I'll write to the minister that's bound to work!! But now to work. What price Michelangelo! What price Roggeveen! Doesburg! That Roggeveen indeed! I had harsh words with him. I had written a letter to the Editor of Theosofia. In it I claim that Monsieur de Winter "hoodwinks" people and I read this epistle to Roggeveen. He was apoplectic with rage and shouted: How dare you! Who do you think you are, to meddle in someone['s] life! That you're the only one who knows what art is?? I replied that I only knew what [scoundrels] were and if he took the side of such a charlatan, if he wasn't such a scoundrel, "what did he imagine he was then" no doubt that he was something of a painter etc.". You can imagine that I'd rather give him a wide berth than get involved with him again. His wife tried to patch things up and I pity her. She still imagines that Roggeveen is a genuine searcher. I heard a nice anecdote about a friend of Roggeveen, another painter of the dirty power politics. Job Hermes once asked him ([Boot]): hey [Boot] how did you get here, by bike" [Boot]: No, I don't cycle. H. how then? Someone else: Boot came by [hansom] cab". Now then old chap, all the best. Till Wednesday

Regards
From your friend Does
In Haarlem

Even if you don't join you can still come to my lecture but I advise you to become a member.

# *De Stijl*: Van Doesburg and Mondrian

*De Stijl* – the magazine, collaborators, contacts and events – played a dominant role in Oud's life as architect and architectural critic. As the correspondence with Van Doesburg reveals, Oud was closely involved in the founding of the magazine and the publication of the first issue. Van Doesburg had intended that Oud should act as its architectural editor but this he refused. He also refused – on principle – to sign any of the various manifestos issued by *De Stijl*, but this did not stop him from publishing seven major articles in *De Stijl* between 1917 and 1921. And despite having officially 'resigned' by that time, he also took part in the group exhibition in Paris in 1923. It was above all the *De Stijl*-inspired contacts and polemics – especially with Van Doesburg and Mondrian – that gave Oud the material for his essay 'Over de toekomstige bouwkunst en hare architectonische mogelijkheden' (On Future Architecture and its Architectonic Possibilities, 1921), one of the first theoretical reflections on the essence of modern architecture, either in the Netherlands or elsewhere. The ideas animating *De Stijl*, especially those concerning the amalgamation of architecture and art, led not only to a lot of discord and discussion, but also to projects that can be seen as architectural experiments embodying the aesthetic ideas of *De Stijl*: the sea-front housing at Scheveningen (1917), the factory and warehouse at Purmerend (1919), Villa 'Allegonda' at Katwijk aan Zee (1917), the De Vonk holiday house at Noordwijkerhout (1917-1918) and, finally, the first blocks of social housing at Spangen (1918-1921). Designed in a short period of time from 1917 to 1921, each of these projects is in its own way an example of 'plastic architecture' in which ideas about form, colour and space derived chiefly from painting were tested against architectural rules and practices. Fundamental disagreements with both Van Doesburg (December 1921) and Mondrian (August 1922) regarding the content of the magazine and the practical and theoretical consequences of painting's contribution to architecture did not result in a permanent break with either man. Oud remained on friendly terms with Mondrian. He followed Mondrian's development as a painter at first hand and assisted in every possible way with the raffling and sale of the artist's paintings in the Netherlands. With Van Doesburg things were a little more complicated: relations between the two men were distinctly chilly in the wake of their contretemps over Van Doesburg's colour design for Spangen (1921) and it was not until 1929 that Oud and Van Doesburg were once again on visiting terms. Despite this, Oud collaborated on the anniversary issue of *De Stijl* in 1927 and, after Van Doesburg's death in 1931, he co-ordinated the magazine's memorial issue.

After the Second World War, as art and architectural historians started to reconstruct the early *De Stijl* years, Oud became rather obsessed with the twists and turns of that period of his life. In common with many architects of his generation (Le Corbusier, Gropius, Frank Lloyd Wright), Oud was apprehensive about the historical account of his contribution to the Modern Movement in architecture. This was compounded in Oud's case by worries about how historians would depict his contribution to the theoretical ideas and vocabulary of *De Stijl*. In such attempts to anticipate the historians, the boundaries between fact and fiction occasionally became blurred. Oud's autobiographical jottings, begun in 1951 with a view to a full-length English monograph, eventually culminated in the slight, German-language publication, *Mein Weg in 'De Stijl'* (1960).[1]

### From Colour Composition to Architecture: Oud and Van Doesburg

On 2 August 1920, H.P. Berlage wrote to *The publisher Van Doesburg: Dear Sir, I write to remind you that I have cancelled my subscription to your publication, De Stijl, for the coming year.*[2] Berlage's decision, coming after the defection of the architects Robert van 't Hoff and Jan Wils, was one more step in a dramatic development which saw modern architecture steadily detach itself from the aesthetic ideals propagated by *De Stijl*. *De Stijl*, and Van Doesburg in particular, had come increasingly within the sphere of influence of the international Dada movement and Berlage was not the only erstwhile supporter to see this as a reason to withdraw. Berlage's decision, which provoked a Dadaist outburst from Van Doesburg, would certainly have affected Oud for it was a result of his personal appeal that Berlage had become a subscriber and tacit sympathizer in the first place. At the moment when this news reached the editors, Mondrian, Van Doesburg and Oud saw themselves – despite their relatively short acquaintance – as a tight-knit triumvirate firmly committed to promoting *De Stijl* by means of publications, exhibitions and joint projects in what were then the main centres of the Modern Movement: Weimar (Bauhaus) and Paris (*L'Esprit Nouveau*). From the correspondence between Oud, Van Doesburg and Mondrian it is abundantly clear that the two painters saw a major role in that endeavour reserved for Oud and some of his recent buildings, in particular the factory at Purmerend (1919). Nevertheless, it was Oud himself who, if not at the instigation then at least in the footsteps of Berlage (as well as many others, including Adolf Behne, Chris Beekman and W.C. Brouwer), gradually began to distance himself from everything associated with *De Stijl*, finally withdrawing altogether in the winter of 1921, at the end of what had been a tumultuous year for *De Stijl*. This decision was regarded, with some justification, by both Mondrian and Van Doesburg as a form of betrayal and as the chief cause of the ultimate failure of *De Stijl* as an international avant-garde undertaking.[3]

Information about Oud's contribution to the birth of *De Stijl* is scanty. In *Mein Weg in 'De Stijl'* Oud himself had this to say on the subject: *During nightly walks near Leiden Van Doesburg and I discussed ad infinitum the problems of the new impulse and the new movements in the arts. Marinetti's futuristic manifest was still foremost in our minds and we conducted a frequent correspondence with kindred spirits at home and abroad. Gradually the desire to have our own magazine emerged, a magazine that would be dedicated to the development of the new art and we thought up serious plans in that direction.*[4] This account, penned almost fifty years after the event, is broadly confirmed by a few lines from a letter Van Doesburg wrote to Oud in June 1921 in response to the latter's scepticism regarding the promises of the Parisian art dealer Léonce Rosenberg. Van Doesburg wrote Oud that it was unthinkable he should pull out for purely practical reasons: *I can't imagine this when I think of our unforgettable, idealistic conversations in Leiden when we saw one another every day and constantly followed one another's work.*[5] He was referring to the years 1916-1917 during which Van Doesburg designed numerous leaded lights for buildings designed by Oud and Wils and both men started writing down their ideas about the relation between architecture and painting. It is beyond dispute that Van Doesburg was the 'originator' of *De Stijl*, both movement and magazine. The enterprise was completely in line with the many plans and projects he had been mulling over since 1913. It is equally indisputable that Van Doesburg's introduction to the persons and work of Mondrian (1915) and Oud (1916) played a crucial role in the realization and development of that enterprise.[6] Oud was also the first person Van Doesburg contacted on 13 November 1916 about the promise of money for the magazine: *Christ, old man, when I realized what had actually happened, I felt I wanted to strike a statue from the first available paving stone.*[7]

However amicable and animated relations were in those early years, by 1920 the two friends were quarrelling about the significance of their respective contributions. In November 1920, coinciding with an alarming drop in the number of subscribers, they had their first skirmishes about the intellectual copyright of *De Stijl*, both as magazine and as aesthetic movement. In response to a query from Oud as to whom Van Doesburg wanted named (in a article by A. Behne) as founders or co-founders, Van Doesburg wrote: *If there had been joint consultations between the (first) editors and the founder (Van Doesburg) on the setting up of De Stijl, this would in my opinion justify the term* founders. *In reality the setting up, the* organization *and so on was my work, while the idea that preceded this was also mine and* mine *alone. What I mean to say is: if I hadn't done it, no one else would have done it. To that extent Lena, who did the most work has more right to be called co-founder and this needs showing for once. So it would be more accurate if you were to say that* you were an editor *as from the founding (1917) and the chief (and at that point the only) editor for architecture. Wils can certainly not say that.*[8] To which Oud replied the same day that he was not talking about *De Stijl* the magazine but the *idea, in which I certainly, to the extent that it concerns the architectural aspect, played my part (you knew nothing about architecture when we first met, as you well know) while the ideas about painting were not yours alone but also for example to a great extent from Piet Mondriaan. The whole point was the collective, not the personal, wasn't it, and Huszár's claim that you alone were 'De Stijl' was something you yourself always rejected.*[9] But Van Doesburg was not about to give in so easily. By return post he wrote: *Dear Oud-Dada: Of course the significance of De Stijl as a movement is the outcome of collective understanding. As a result of a letter from you to me about the connection between architecture and modern painting back in Haarlem, I started to form a clear vision of the future of visual art. I saw the possibility of a collaborative art-expression, that was reinforced by my discussions with Mondriaan, v/d Leck, Huszár etc. De Stijl as possibility is not therefore an individual conception, you are quite right on that point and I think it detracts from our fine, open relationship for us to start wrangling about that now. ...De Stijl as possibility can therefore be called collective, individual it certainly* is not *but the founding of the magazine De Stijl is the articulation of a general desire, a deed that to my mind would not have come about without my perseverance. This is what I wanted to say and I hope that we no longer misunderstand one another on this point. I have certainly learnt a great deal from you about architecture, but even when I first met you I believe I already had some intuitive understanding, because you will recall that apart from your work (the significance of which I may have been the first to recognize) I immediately admired Wright and specifically the house you reviewed in* De Stijl. *It was a revelation for me, as was the work of Mondriaan before I knew him personally. Influence is always reciprocal, that is something no one, fortunately, can avoid. I shall never in any way diminish your great service and significance in the De Stijl movement and in the organ too. Anyway, you know that is so when you consider that I begin by talking about you to everyone who visits me.*[10] A year later there was little trace of these sentiments. Van Doesburg was preparing for a full-scale, international campaign in which Oud – once again following in Berlage's footsteps – was depicted, with no hint of Dadaist levity, as a conservative, cowardly and anything but modern architect. What had gone wrong?

From the correspondence between Oud and Van Doesburg in 1920 and 1921, it is patently clear that Van Doesburg had ambitious plans, not just for *De Stijl* but also for Oud whom he saw – alongside Mondrian and himself – as the standard bearer of the movement. To that end he encouraged Oud to write theoretical articles about a wide range of subjects: about Frank Lloyd Wright, about standardization in housing construction, about the contemporary townscape, about technological developments and so on, and also to present his own designs in the form of perspective drawings made especially for the magazine. On that score Van Doesburg was successful: the articles Oud published in *De Stijl* in those years are among the most original of his entire written oeuvre and together form the prelude to his most important pronouncement on architectural theory, 'On Future Architecture and its Architectonic Possibilities' (1921), which was not, however, published in *De Stijl*, but in *Bouwkundig Weekblad*, the professional journal for architects. But all this was not enough for Van Doesburg. In Paris, Berlin and Weimar he was indefatigable in propagating *De Stijl* as a broad-based movement encompassing architecture, visual art and literature; he established contacts with all kinds of people who were in any way involved in the modern avant-garde in art; he looked for means of having Oud's *De Stijl* articles translated into French; he constantly asked for photographs and especially slides for magazines, exhibitions and lectures, and he even solicited design commissions for Oud, both in Paris and in the United States. Without exaggeration one could say that Van Doesburg did everything in his power in 1920 and 1921 to launch Oud internationally as a practising *De Stijl* architect. But Oud held back, possibly in response to pressure from Berlage and certainly from Van 't Hoff and Jan Wils. A typical instance of such hesitancy was his refusal to take part in the group exhibition of the international artists' association, La Section d'Or, in The Hague in the summer of 1920. He did not even turn up at the opening, on which occasion Van Doesburg gave an informal talk with slides and even spoke about Oud's work. Oud had been annoyed by the public humiliation of Jan Wils by

Van Doesburg, who missed no opportunity to depict the successful Hague architect as a conservative and above all lazy imitator of Frank Lloyd Wright. Oud stood by Wils, a stance Van Doesburg in turn was quite unable to understand. The day after the opening (where Jan Wils *was* in attendance), Van Doesburg wrote to Oud: *Let me just say that in the association building I said quite openly that* Wils and his ilk *are the real danger for the emergence of a universal plasticity. I indicated that the new style has to be experienced first hand and not imitated the way Wils does by copying Wright. I particularly stressed the fact that your work is infinitely more sympathetic because it has grown out of and through you, because it originated with you and was not copied. ...I don't understand how you can fail to be convinced that I see you as the* only *and most steadfast architect of the Nieuwe Beelding and as such will succeed in placing you in the international art scene. That's why it would be so wonderful Oudje, if out of our shared love of the new we could for once realize a* work *that I could present as a complete model.*[11] By 'work' Van Doesburg was of course thinking of something along the lines of Oud's design for the factory and warehouse at Purmerend (1919) and in the same letter he suggested that Oud should reconsider his refusal to exhibit the plans and especially the perspective drawings.

The next opportunity for collaboration presented itself in Paris where in 1920 Van Doesburg had come into contact with the gallery owner Léonce Rosenberg who was full of plans: for a magazine about the international avant-garde, for a country house and for a group exhibition of the work of *De Stijl*.[12] As far as the house was concerned, Van Doesburg had immediately thought of Oud and himself as designers but Oud was wary from the outset, probably on account of Mondrian's recent negative experience with Rosenburg as art dealer. Van Doesburg took a more relaxed view of the matter and was keen to deploy Oud, as *De Stijl* architect, against the growing strength of the 'rival' movement of *L'Esprit Nouveau* and in particular its protagonist, the Swiss architect Le Corbusier.

The 'Rosenberg affair' began with the publication of an article by Van Doesburg in *L'Art Monumental*. On 4 May 1920, Van Doesburg dashed off a euphoric letter to Oud, who was on the point of leaving for Germany and England: *The article in L'Art Monumental has already borne fruit. I received an effusive and enthusiastic note from Rosenberg, the man who is behind the new spirit in Paris and who is very sympathetic towards our cause. I replied at length: that it was not Utopian but that, on however limited a scale as yet, we had put it into* practice *etc. ...The Paris trip can now become a mission for the Nieuwe Beelding. The great World Discipline of NB is about to take off.*[13] Rosenberg resumed his plan for a new magazine and approached Van Doesburg for his cooperation. For *De Stijl* this was a wonderful opportunity *to proclaim the new intelligence we want to carry through in art from the Centre. ...In Rosenberg's magazine, if all goes well, we can have a leading say. And exhibit our work, too, of course.* As to architecture, Van Doesburg wanted to show other countries that in the Netherlands *De Stijl* was already being practised, notably through architecture and Oud's appointment to the Rotterdam Housing Authority: *We must prepare, with De Stijl and with the work, for the great historic moment when De Stijl becomes a reality. I shall not rest until I experience that moment.*[14] The plans for the magazine eventually came to nothing.

The next step was Rosenberg's request that *De Stijl* design a new country house for him. On 1 October 1920 Van Doesburg reported, once again in euphoric tones, that Rosenberg, who had already intimated that he regarded Oud as *one of the pioneers of the new civilization* was intending *in a few years' time, to build a model house in the Campagne with the assistance of De Stijl artists. He also wants a completely modern garden. A splendid plan, isn't it? It's not going to happen immediately but that's all for the best since it means we can discuss it at our leisure. In any case, since the plan appears to be firm, we can start on the design before then. This can turn into a demonstration that will knock them all dead.!!!*[15] At Van Doesburg's request, Oud sent photographs of his work from which Rosenberg selected the now classic suite of entrance hall, street composition, factory, warehouse and Rotterdam housing blocks. This was the start of the next plan: an exhibition in Rosenberg's gallery centred around a model of the future house, which would subsequently travel to England and the United States at the gallery owner's expense. The plans for both house and exhibition gained momentum in April 1921. Rosenberg produced a detailed building programme and even a few sketches and a concept for the exhibition. In a long letter to Oud, Van Doesburg stressed that the three of them, that is to say Van Doesburg, Mondrian and Oud, should *keep things in their own hands and discuss and supervise everything.* Mondrian felt that Oud should consult with Van 't Hoff about the design and that for *such a historic and aesthetic event, all minor disputes should be put aside.* Mondrian appears to have had definite ideas about the model which he imagined *in wood, tin and various materials, coloured and uncoloured.* Rietveld, rather than Van Tongerloo as Van Doesburg wished, should supervise the technical execution by *ordinary carpenters and house painters.*[16] But Oud remained suspicious of the whole enterprise, feeling that it would probably cost a lot of time and money and ultimately not lead to a building. Oud even approached Rosenberg directly and when no further information was forthcoming about the exact location and numerous other practical details concerning the construction, he pulled out.[17] Van Doesburg was furious and disappointed: *Quite frankly it's a mystery to me how you could want to give up this wonderful plan on such purely practical grounds as in your last letter (I mean the risk question).*[18] In September, writing from Weimar, Van Doesburg returned one last time to the plans and Oud's complaint that Rosenberg was out to acquire a good design on the cheap: *If he's only prepared to display a project at present, that is a precaution, because he* first *wants to* see *something. If we* don't *make it, we will be passing up a wonderful opportunity and since you would like to get away from Rotterdam (standardization) and I from Weimar, it would be* very important *for us to hazard the* given *opportunity. We shall simply regard Rosenberg as an Impresario. Naturally he will want to do well out of it, nicht wahr? And talk the rich folk into it. Once we have such a model (we can get it for next to nothing) I'll be able to exhibit it in New York with Man Ray. In fact nowhere is any good in Europe. I'd just as soon pack up tomorrow and move to America. With the whole gang: you, Lena, Nelly.*[19] Oud, however, stuck to his guns and Van Doesburg took up with the young architect Cornelis van Eesteren whom he had met earlier that year in Weimar. Oud did, however, take part in the *De Stijl* group exhibition in Galerie L'Effort Moderne (1923). On 1 October 1923 Van Doesburg cordially inquired whether he could still count *on principled work* from Oud: *Your factory would be ideal, don't you agree?*[20] Oud had already sent five large and two small photographs of his work to Rosenberg but let Van Doesburg know that he was not sure whether they were sufficiently 'principled': *probably not! Dada? No again. I can only justify them for myself. For that matter there are plenty of principled people around nowadays.*[21]

The squabbles concerning Jan Wils and Léonce Rosenberg were clear portents of a truth that the two erstwhile friends were forced to acknowledge at the end of 1921: that the long-cherished ideal of *together transforming the architectural scene*, would never be realized. The immediate cause of this realization was Oud's personal interference with the colour scheme Van Doesburg had designed for a housing block in Spangen.[22]

In 1918, Oud had taken up the post of architect with the Rotterdam Housing Authority. In a relatively short period of time, he designed several (public) housing schemes that in terms both of architecture and of town planning can be seen as a continuation of Berlage's housing schemes in Amsterdam. At the same time, Oud seized on the building activities in Spangen to lift the ongoing discussion with Van Doesburg about the relation between painting and its environment out of the realm of exhibition and museum architecture and to transfer it to that of the home in the modern metropolis. In 1918, Oud invited Van Doesburg to collaborate on two housing blocks in Spangen (I and V) by designing stained-glass transom lights for the front doors and a colour scheme for both inside and outside. He also asked Rietveld to develop prototypes of standard furniture for a model home display in one of the dwellings. From Oud's point of view, the commissions to Van Doesburg and Rietveld were part of an aesthetic experiment with standardization and as such subordinate to the architecture.

The theme of standardization – a favourite topic of discussion among public housing officials and architects in 1918 – had as yet no particular aesthetic significance for Van Doesburg and was seen mainly in terms of economy. For example, in a letter to Oud concerning the colour design for the dwellings he wrote: *I gave it a good deal of thought and made a lot of studies before finally hitting upon this solution which, apart from the expressive (destructive) effect, has the advantage of being cheap. This struck me as an advantage for standardization and I'm very curious what you will think of it. I think the design is well balanced in every respect and I am convinced that it will bring about a big change in monumental painting.*[23] The end result was two separate and relatively static designs, one a colour scheme for the street elevations in which Van Doesburg was eventually obliged by Oud to make various compromises, and the other a colour design for the interior where the traditional wallpaper (chosen by the tenants) was to be replaced by plastered and painted walls (determined by the architect) which in turn took no account of the furniture designed by Rietveld.

In June 1920, Van Doesburg received the first drawings for blocks VIII and IX from Rotterdam which he promptly put to one side for nearly a year. In the meantime, rather than abandoning the theme of 'monumental painting', he expanded it by linking it to his ideas about the townscape and standardization and above all to his notion of time and movement. It was not until May of the following year that Van Doesburg – still in Weimar – embarked on the first designs for the new blocks. In July, after a visit from Oud and his wife, Van Doesburg rethought the whole thing and a breakthrough occurred both in his artistic approach to the task and in the technical rendering of the solutions found. In September it emerged that because of the late start and his hectic way of working, Van Doesburg was seriously behind schedule, leaving Oud and the painters in Rotterdam cooling their heels, as it were, while they waited for detailed instructions. But Van Doesburg had still not achieved the *great revolution in monumental painting*, which consisted in picturing the interior and exterior, in other words the entire block, as a spatial and dynamic unit. In contrast to the first two Spangen blocks, interior and exterior spaces were no longer conceived as separate entities: Van Doesburg had devised a new method of working *namely, by first working from the inside and then letting the frames and so on continue on the outside so that inside and outside can be painted in a single colour.*[24] Van Doesburg was determined to go further than Mondrian whose studio walls, covered with colourful plasterboard rectangles, he characterized as two-dimensional paintings rather than an example of mastery of space through colour. The whole concept hung in the balance, however, so long as Van Doesburg had not received Oud's permission to do anything to 'the interior situation'.

By 1921, Van Doesburg had also changed his views on the architectural issue of standardization. Instead of trying to adjust technically and economically to standardization, he tried to neutralize its monotonous and structural aspects by means of the dissonant triad yellow-green-blue, which moved dynamically and quite independently of the architectural and typological logic, over and through the building in accordance with a detailed plan. To this end he designed unique colour plans in the form of *schematic impression(s) of the abstract movement (and countermovement) of each colour.* On 13 and 17 October 1921, Van Doesburg sent Oud the various designs for the facade surfaces along Pieter Langedijkstraat, Hagenstraat and Potgieterstraat. On 20 October, Oud wrote to say that he though the colour designs were 'superb' and that they were not at odds with the architecture of the blocks. On 25 October, Van Doesburg announced that he was studying 'the interior situation' and would send his initial suggestions as soon as possible. Then the problems started. First of all Oud sent a message via Van Doesburg's wife, Lena Milius, that yellow was not permitted. Van Doesburg was naturally disappointed. In defending the use of yellow, he changed tack and toned down the destructive effect in favour of the iconographical function of yellow in the modern townscape: *What an awful pity it is that I am not allowed to use yellow; because yellow is the very colour for introducing the vertical. I notice here (and it struck me in Berlin, Munich, etc.) that bright yellow is also the preferred colour for cars, mail vans, Underground and so on. In Paris the Nord–Sud carriages are* red-blue-yellow. *They are the proper colours for these times.*[25] But the problems were not confined to the colour yellow. Around 1 November, after one-third of the Langendijkstraat facade had been given an undercoat and the woodwork of the dormers on one of the end-faces of the same block had been given a final coat of lacquer, Oud suggested yet more changes. Oud's reaction had been negative from the outset. The reasons for his disapproval have been often, though rather superficially, discussed in the literature. Most art historians have simply stated that Oud was dismayed by the destructive effect of Van Doesburg's colour scheme on 'his' architecture and left it at that. The reality, as the lengthy and lively exchange of letters in November and December reveals, was more complicated and had more to do with Van Doesburg's radical pretensions regarding control of the total environment by art. Van Doesburg had three objectives in mind with his dynamic colour scheme for the facades of the corner blocks. First of all he wanted to relieve 'the somewhat monotonous quality of standardization'. In the second place, the dynamic colour scheme was intended to relieve the unavoidably static quality and horizontal effect of the very long and monotonous Langedijkstraat. The third function of Van Doesburg's colour scheme, which fanned out diagonally across the facade, was to point up the contrast between Oud's modern, flat-roofed municipal housing and the old-fashioned, pitched roofs of the spec-built block on the other side of the street. Oud was evidently unpersuaded by Van Doesburg's aesthetic arguments, witness the letter Van Doesburg wrote to him on 3 November categorically rejecting any changes to the colour scheme: *given the fact that full realization was agreed, given the fact that I am not a house painter but turn these things into art, given the fact that I am Van Doesburg,* I have, I assume, *the right to shout: NO-NO-NO. Either this way – or nothing.*[26] In response, Oud decided to call a halt to the paintwork and to wait for Van Doesburg's planned return to the Netherlands (in early December). In the meantime, Lena Milius, obviously at Van Doesburg's request, went to have a look at what was happening in Rotterdam. She reported to Van Doesburg in detail in a letter that paints a disconcerting picture of the mutual distrust between artist and architect. The extent to which relations were already troubled is apparent from the no-nonsense opening: *I shall be as brief as possible in my account, you already know that Oud no longer goes along with your ideas so there's no need for me to beat about the bush.* Oud had told Lena that Van Doesburg's passion for diagonals was at odds with his architecture but that the problem could easily be solved by executing the colour design for the rest of the facade in the same colour combination as that used for the dormers but in straight rather than oblique lines. But Lena, who was accompanied by Oud's wife during her visit, did not agree. She felt that Van Doesburg's plan, to the extent that it had been carried out, was even better than in the original drawings and she did not think that any changes should be made: *Then the truth came out and he said that he had come to the conclusion that colour simply did not work on brick and that he would be painting all the remaining blocks grey. I told him he'd do better to choose brown.* In the end it transpired that Oud wanted to 'be shot of the whole thing' and Lena advised Van Doesburg to withdraw altogether because even in a modified version the plan would not be carried out: *just think about the much more gratifying collaboration with De Boer. He at least is prepared to take risks.* Whereupon she continued: *I'm glad I went to see the block in question because now I don't mind so very much if the colour isn't used on it. They are very tall houses and on the other side of a very narrow little street are houses of the same height by someone else. When you enter it you feel hemmed in as if you're walking in a narrow gully and the walls are coming at you. ...Oud said colour made it look small, but I thought quite the opposite.*[27] Lena recommended that Van Doesburg should stop replying to Oud's letters, no doubt to the latter's annoyance. He wrote at least two more letters, one of which he did not send out of anger about Van Doesburg's public insult of yet another friend, Jaap Gidding. In it he dismissed Van Doesburg's accusation that he was afraid of 'small-minded gossip' and tried to interpret the conflict more in terms of principles and especially art theory. The key concept here was the 'motto of unintentionality' In the first letter, written immediately after Lena's visit, Oud had responded pragmatically, coolly and analytically. He could understand Van Doesburg's incomprehension of the sudden reversal in his appreciation for the colour design: *It's like this: as I wrote you at the time, I didn't like the colours at first, later on I did. In retrospect I now realize that I* greatly *admire the colours as design (painting), but that as soon as they are employed architecturally I accept them with reluctance or forced enthusiasm.* He went on to trace the disagreement to an artistic change of course within *De Stijl*: *You will have noticed that I show little interest in collaborating on 'De Stijl' in its present form. The problem is that what I* theoretically *appreciate (greatly appreciate) in 'De Stijl', I am putting less and less into* practice. *Contrary to the motto of unintentionality that we postulated, 'De Stijl' is intentionality from a – z. What I need is a crystal-clear, pure art of exceptional simplicity and the first issues of 'De Stijl' allowed that. Every means thereto – so long as it is serious – is good for that. But mixing something so* positive *as this with Dadaist nonsense ... is a daily source of irritation. I am no Dadaist and feel no inclination to become one.*[28] At the time of writing, Oud was still convinced that the conflict could be resolved, or at the very least discussed amicably. Van Doesburg, however, was livid and responded as if a work of art had been meddled with. On 14 December 1921, in a repetition of his break with Wils and Van 't Hoff, he took leave of Oud as architect of the Nieuwe Beelding in a letter full of hatred and recrimination: *I wasn't planning to write to you again. It would have attested to greater openness, if you had told me at once* honestly *that you – for whatever reason (but* I *maintain out of cowardice and fear of public opinion) – that you wanted to paint the houses brown or grey. You would have saved me a lot of work and disappointment. It would also have been more honest if you had said to me more than a year ago: Does, I can no longer go along with you and De Stijl, instead of behaving as if it was only lack of time that prevented you from writing. I told you openly back then in Rotterdam that I was afraid the municipal appointment would bureaucratize you in the worst sense: make you more pragmatic. Your wife defended you then, remember? Well then, when you were in Weimar recently I saw it with my own eyes, that the once cherished ideals (perhaps you still recall them at Leiden – when you were still independent) were no longer shared. So the treatment meted out to me was not so very unexpected! After all, with the earlier block everything had to be altered repeatedly, and I saw then with my own eyes that it was only out of fear of public opinion.*[29]

Oud's reply was intended to be read by Van Doesburg on his return to Leiden from Weimar, as the prelude to a lively discussion. This document, together with a final letter dated 16 December, gives a very clear picture of Oud's view of the conflict, a view fuelled by personal frustrations, concern for architectural integrity and rather amateurish notions of art theory. The fact was that Oud had turned his back on *De Stijl* because the aesthetic ideal of unintentionality had proved to be unworkable in practice, a development for which Oud held Van Doesburg as artist especially responsible. For example, in the letter that was never sent (probably written at the beginning of December 1921) he stated: *I wrote [to] you and Piet Mondrian all sorts of things about town planning that make me uneasy deep down; this colour problem is another thing of the same sort: should we be intentional or not? I continue to look for the most* natural *[solution] (as you did with the new cover of 'De Stijl'). Must something as relatively low down on the scale of unintentionality as these rows of workers' houses* really *be painted as you indicate? Deep down I believe that even this much simpler solution than your earlier one, still contains much too much aesthetic intentionality.*[30] Oud blamed the decline of the ideal of unintentionality on Van Doesburg's success with *De Stijl* in Weimar where he had put the idea of Nieuwe Beelding into practice with such theatricality (Oud was referring to the way Bauhaus students had decorated the theatre in Weimar under Van Doesburg's direction) that *the functional connection between architecture and art – the only justification (see also 'De Stijl') degenerated into decorative hoo-ha.*[31] The project in Rotterdam – and thus also that of De Stijl as aesthetic movement – ultimately miscarried because, in Oud's view at least, instead of adopting the modest role of 'house painter', Van Doesburg had ended up by behaving as an artist: *Once again in 'theory' workman, in practice you are the artist* – a reproach that led smoothly into a fundamental rejection of any artistic contribution to architecture: *That is indeed the crux of the matter: you know too little about architecture to be able to improve architecture through your art; you speak of a monumental style, but in 'Spangen' you murder the monumentality of my work by your lack of understanding. Which would not be so bad if you artists were as prepared to learn from us as we are from you. But here too everything remains theory.*[32] But Van Doesburg was not interested in this argumentation: he returned the letter unread with the comment that further correspondence would inevitably led to yet more misunderstandings.[33]

### Mondrian's 'Building'

Contrary to what he tried to suggest later on in life, it is highly unlikely that Oud met Mondrian in person more than three times (August 1920, June-July 1921 and August

1925).[34] The first written contacts date from January 1920. Although Oud never collaborated on a building or design with Mondrian, as he had with Van Doesburg, for a short span of time Mondrian meant a great deal to Oud. It was above all Mondrian's idiosyncratic notions about the *art* of building that inspired Oud to pull together various stray ideas about contemporary architecture into a more or less coherent theory. In August 1921, Oud sent Mondrian the text of the lecture he had given to the Rotterdam architectural society *Opbouw*: 'Over de toekomstige bouwkunst en hare architectonische mogelijkheden'. The same article was greeted enthusiastically by Van Doesburg in Weimar but Mondrian was irritated from the outset by the contents and import because Oud, in a repetition of his unattributed use of Van Doesburg's ideas in 1916, had made use of Mondrian's pamphlet *Le Neo-Plasticisme* (1920) without acknowledging the fact.[35] Oud's refusal to come out openly in favour of Neo-Plasticism (Nieuwe Beelding) was understandably construed by Mondrian as a betrayal of *De Stijl* as aesthetic theory and movement. This view was further strengthened by the conflict between Oud and Van Doesburg, a conflict in which Mondrian unhesitatingly took Van Doesburg's side. On the other hand, Oud's perverse and blinkered views about architecture challenged Mondrian to elaborate and spell out his own ideas about the translation of the principles of Neo-Plastic painting to architecture. With this, the initial irritation escalated into a fundamental disagreement about architecture as art and practice. In 1922, Mondrian published an article in *De Stijl* of which both the title – 'De realiseering van het Neo-plasticisme in verre toekomst en in de huidige architectuur' (The realization of Neo-Plasticism in the distant future and in contemporary architecture) – and the gist were a direct reference to Oud's lecture. In the article Mondrian excluded contemporary architecture from Neo-Plasticism and held out the prospect of a new architecture that would be entirely constructed of elements drawn from painting: colour, line and plane. The intellectual exchange of ideas between Mondrian and Oud thereupon came to an abrupt end, although the almost unbroken correspondence between the two men up to 1935 shows that this in no way affected their personal relationship.

The years when he felt closely involved with *De Stijl* cannot have been easy for Oud as architect. While Van Doesburg tried to present Oud internationally as an architect who was successfully implementing the ideas about the Nieuwe Beelding while in government employment, Mondrian saw the realization of Neo-Plasticism in architecture as something that would only happen in the very distant future, if at all. *Active participation in a movement*, according to Van Doesburg, *means for the architect: build and in such a way that the consequences of the ideology of a new 'expressive consciousness' become a fact.*[36] This was all going much too fast for Mondrian who believed that Neo-Plasticist ideas could not be realized in architecture until architects had solved the problems of material, form and function. But the more obsessed architects became with the practice of building, the less able they were to solve those problems theoretically and so they were doomed to a life 'outside art'. When Mondrian first came into contact with Oud in January 1920, he knew very little about the architect. He had not seen the 'famous' perspective drawing of the Purmerend factory when it first appeared in *De Stijl* (for which it had been specially made) and it is most unlikely that he had read the articles on townscape, technology and ornament that Oud had also published in *De Stijl*. Because most of Oud's side of the correspondence is missing, the dispute between Oud and Mondrian about the relationship between Neo-Plasticism and architecture has hitherto been analysed chiefly from Mondrian's point of view. Yet it is clear that Oud's stance, both in *De Stijl* and in his letters to Mondrian, had its roots in the day-to-day (Dutch) practice of building which had been in a state of economic and aesthetic ferment for the past twenty years and which was still in want of satisfactory formal concepts and design theories.[37] Oud was the first architect, at least in the Netherlands, to try to understand recent movements in art – Futurism and especially Cubism – and to present them as a model for an architectural practice geared to contemporary problems. Van Doesburg and Mondrian started out from quite the opposite angle. Different though their theories of art were, both men aspired to an (abstract) control of space, determined by colour and plane, that would eventually lead to a complete transformation if not abandonment of prevailing architectural conventions and models.

**The misunderstanding between Oud and Mondrian began, in fact, with the interpretation of the celebrated factory at Purmerend. In *Bouwkundig Weekblad* (1921) Oud explained this design as *an attempt at architectural expression by purely architectural means, in which the decorative element had not yet been completely conquered.*[38] In effect Oud was presenting his design as the culmination of the movement towards simplification, purification and the renunciation of ornament that reform-minded Dutch architects had been working at since the end of the nineteenth century. The term 'expression' (*uitbeelding*) may invoke echoes of Van Doesburg and Mondrian, but in this context it does not mean much more than the abstractional design of elements determined by function, material and construction. Abstraction achieved by means of stylization, Mondrian called it. On 16 December, Mondrian wrote to Oud in reference to the drawing (*a factory, I think*) which he thought very good, *the best I have ever seen in that field.*[39] What Oud undoubtedly regarded as an important step on the road to a new definition of architectural form, Mondrian evidently saw as a farewell to an architecture geared to formal plasticity and a cautious, partially successful step on the road to an architecture that was the *plastic expression of the aesthetic, harmonious relationship in space.* In the months following the publication of Oud's article in *Bouwkundig Weekblad* (1921) and that of Mondrian's article in *De Stijl* (1922), Oud's enthusiasm for Nieuwe Beelding and for the Neo-Plasticist theory of art gradually waned. In August 1921 he argued (quite in line with what was then being published in Dutch architectural magazines) that the new architectural aesthetic – in the sense of a theory of forms – would only appear via practice and that Neo-Plasticism could at best serve as a catalyst, as a means to purification.[40] This to the astonishment of Mondrian, of course, who saw Neo-Plasticism as a good deal more than a purgative. Such a conception of art might serve to elevate the practice of architecture but it could not turn architecture into *art*. According to Mondrian *'practice' could never call forth an architecture like Neo-Plasticism. Only a very different practice would be capable of doing that. And that practice is made quite impossible for us by the ties ... So I say once again: N.P. is possible in current architecture* up to a certain point. *But not as complete art.*[41] Oud for his part had no interest in this kind of (theoretical) distinction between architecture and art and firmly rejected any Neo-Plasticist claims on architecture that went beyond mere purification. The whole discussion between Mondrian and Oud acquired a somewhat bitter undertone as a result of Mondrian's by no means idle threat to throw in the towel as free and independent artist. On 6 December 1921 he wrote to Oud: *not a single artist is selling any more. All the good artists are in retreat: making compromises. I'd rather stop altogether. My friend Van Eck has offered me the chance of a job in market gardening, on his farm down south. I'm thinking of going there in January.*[42] Only to announce four days later: *I couldn't after all reconcile myself to my decision to accept the offer from my friend Van Eck. I had already decided as you saw but I've changed my mind. I will always prefer an uncertain existence here to a socially secure life down south.*[43] It is clear from numerous remarks that Mondrian, like Van Doesburg, blamed Oud's aloofness to a large degree on his Rotterdam appointment: I *know*, he wrote on 6 December 1921, *that you had to contend with 'society' (which now obliges me to stop!) but that you are a confirmed believer in N.P.*[44]**

**At the beginning of the summer the discussion took a new turn. In the meantime, the first of two instalments of Mondrian's article about Neo-Plasticism in architecture had appeared in *De Stijl*. It was evident from Mondrian's argumentation that Oud had attacked Neo-Plasticism on three fronts: to begin with he did not think that the 'new spirit' (*L'Esprit Nouveau*) coincided with Neo-Plasticism, and that it also manifested itself elsewhere, for example in technology. For this reason Oud also considered *De Stijl* too limited a movement for the future development of architecture. Secondly, he accused Neo-Plasticism, once again from the viewpoint of architecture, of ambivalence in that it professed a desire to merge with daily life while at the same continually shifting the moment at which this was to take place towards some mystical vanishing point. But the essence of Oud's objection derived from a growing perception of Neo-Plasticism (and *De Stijl*) as a pre-determined formal principle, divorced from technology, practice and concrete task, which would entail an irrevocable return to the (nineteenth-century) 'building in**

styles'. Mondrian's response to this misrepresentation of Neo-Plasticism was categorical: *It is pretty clear to me from what you write that you do* not *agree with me. The* thing itself, *the principles, the laws, what you will, I regard as* fixed. *You call this formgiving, this fixedness. ... What you call form is the logical and intuitive fixing of what practice has discovered. And all those technical difficulties cannot alter the plastic understanding, rather they confirm it: that's why you, who work in technology, are so much in agreement with me. But if you put off accepting the truth I think you will get lost in technology alone. Thus the essential difference between us is, I think, that you are against form fixing. And so against Neo-Plasticism and me, and that's an end of it.*[45] Whereas Oud saw Neo-Plasticism as a way of working, as a means of purifying, Mondrian believed that merely *looking* for purity was dangerous.

Form, practice and purification: these were the three points on which the discussion with Mondrian broke down. And just as Mondrian's standpoint hardened in the wake of Oud's conflict with Van Doesburg, so too did Oud's. After his break with *De Stijl*, Oud publicly branded Van Doesburg *a cubist of provincial consequence* and although he drew a distinction between Van Doesburg's work and that of Mondrian, the latter contained the same threat to architecture as Neo-Plasticism in general and *De Stijl* in particular.[46] This was why Mondrian was so concerned: *I don't doubt that you value my work but you'll appreciate that my work does not consist only of making* things*: there's a lot more to it.* In June 1922, when Mondrian had gradually started to realize that the break with Oud was fundamental, he wrote: *As long as you admire my paintings (that are a fairly good approximation of Neo-Plasticism in Painting) I may continue to hope that you would also admire a* building *by me – if I were able to build it. You should be able to imagine more or less how I would do it after my earlier Stijl articles and especially after the pamphlet and especially after the piece about to appear in De Stijl.*[47] Alas, Oud could not imagine it. In September 1922 he wrote that he expected absolutely nothing of Neo-Plasticism applied to space. *Your life is painting, mine is building. For my aims in architecture, for which I have been working now for 10 years, Van Doesburg's activities are more detrimental, especially since these activities have started to venture into architectural prophecy and propaganda. I can not and will not take this lying down and will oppose it wherever I can. I am glad to be able to tell you that this counter move is not directed at your work, for which I have the greatest respect and – as long as it does not address itself to space – the greatest expectations, and I do not see it as comparable with that of Van Doesburg, nonetheless I also touch upon your view. I hope that you will take this generally and not personally: if you artists did not encroach on my territory, I would certainly remain silent. Now I am driven to it.*[48]

Shortly after this, Mondrian informed his friend Kok: *I've had to break with Oud, because he opposes Does and*

**Notes**

**1.** Principle sources for Oud's role in the early years of *De Stijl* are: C. Blotkamp (et al.), *De beginjaren van De Stijl, 1917-1922*, Utrecht 1982; N.J. Troy, *The De Stijl Environment*, Cambridge (Mass.) 1983, pp. 75-77, 80-83; C. Blotkamp, *Mondriaan in detail*, Utrecht, Antwerp 1987, pp. 44-52; 66-75; 82-84; C. Blotkamp, (ed.), *De Vervolgjaren van De Stijl, 1922-1932*, Amsterdam, Antwerp 1996, pp. 364-396; Y.A. Bois (et al.), *De Stijl et l'Architecture en France*, Liège, Brussels 1985, pp. 11-24; E. Hoek (ed.), *Theo van Doesburg. Oeuvrecatalogus*, Bussum 2000.

**2.** Postcard (torn in half) from H.P. Berlage to T. van Doesburg, 2 August 1920, Fondation Custodia, Paris. Referring to this note, Van Doesburg wrote to Oud: *Berlage had already cancelled long ago and we'll cross him off ... What a mean little man addressing me as Messrs (publisher). You see the old coot means nothing to NP. Nothing.* T. van Doesburg to Oud, undated, Fondation Custodia, Paris.

**3.** Mondrian wrote to Oud: *Anyway, you withdrew from De Stijl and if there are weaknesses in De Stijl (which is quite understandable since there is almost nothing 'new') you are yourself to blame for not collaborating.* P. Mondrian to J.J.P. Oud, 1 August 1922, Fondation Custodia, Paris.

**4.** J.J.P.Oud, *Mein Weg in 'De Stijl'*, The Hague, Rotterdam 1960.

**5.** T. van Doesburg to J.J.P. Oud, 21 June 1921, Fondation Custodia, Paris; C. Blotkamp, *Mondriaan in detail*, Utrecht, Antwerp 1987, pp. 44-52; 66-75; 82-84; C. Blotkamp, (ed.), *De Vervolgjaren van De Stijl, 1922-1932*, Amsterdam, Antwerp 1996, p. 45.

**6.** C. Blotkamp (et al.), *De beginjaren van De Stijl, 1917-1922*, Utrecht 1982, pp. 28-29.

**7.** T. van Doesburg to J.J.P. Oud, 13 November 1916, Fondation Custodia, Paris.

**8.** T. van Doesburg to J.J.P. Oud, 11 November 1920, Fondation Custodia, Paris.

**9.** J.J.P. Oud to T. van Doesburg, 11 November 1920, Fondation Custodia, Paris.

**10.** T. van Doesburg to J.J.P. Oud, undated (November/December 1920), Fondation Custodia, Paris.

**11.** T. van Doesburg to J.J.P. Oud, 12 June 1920, Fondation Custodia, Paris.

**12.** Y.A. Bois (et al.), *De Stijl et l'Architecture en France*, Liège, Brussels 1985, pp. 25-90; N.J. Troy, *The De Stijl Environment*, Cambridge (Mass.) 1983, pp. 77-81. Regarding contacts between *De Stijl* and the Parisian art world see A. Martens, 'The introduction of modern art in Holland. Picasso as pars pro toto, 1910-1930', in: *Simiolus* 21(1992)3, pp. 205-211.

**13.** T. van Doesburg to J.J.P. Oud, 4 May 1920, Fondation Custodia, Paris.

**14.** T. van Doesburg to J.J.P. Oud, 4 May 1920, Fondation Custodia, Paris.

**15.** T. van Doesburg to J.J.P. Oud, 1 October 1920, Fondation Custodia, Paris.

**16.** T. van Doesburg to J.J.P. Oud, xx April 1921, Fondation Custodia, Paris.

**17.** L. Rosenberg to J.J.P. Oud, 6 September 1921, Fondation Custodia, Paris: *Comme la maison ... corresponde ni à une commande ni à un emplacement déterminé, il m'est impossible de répondre à vos questions! Je laisse donc libre d'établir une maquette pouvant aller sur terrain X, Y ou Z.*

**18.** T. van Doesburg to J.J.P. Oud, 21 June 1921, Fondation Custodia, Paris.

**19.** T. van Doesburg to J.J.P. Oud, 12 September 1921, Fondation Custodia, Paris.

**20.** T. van Doesburg to J.J.P. Oud, 1 October 1923, Fondation Custodia, Paris.

**21.** Oud to T. van Doesburg, undated (October/December 1923), Fondation Custodia, Paris.

**22.** The most important literature on the Spangen 'issue': E. van Straaten, *Klare en lichte, gesloten vormen, geaccentueerd door diepe en pure kleuren. Het werk van Theo van Doesburg in de architectuur*, Amsterdam 1992, pp. 50-54; 65-68; N.J. Troy, *The De Stijl Environment*, Cambridge (Mass.) 1983, pp. 73; 81-83; C. Blotkamp, (ed.), *De Vervolgjaren van De Stijl, 1922-1932*, Amsterdam, Antwerp 1996, pp. 366-369.

**23.** T. van Doesburg to J.J.P. Oud, 4 August 1919, Rijksdienst Beeldende Kunst, The Hague.

**24.** T. van Doesburg to J.J.P. Oud, 12 September 1921, Fondation Custodia, Paris.

**25.** T. van Doesburg to J.J.P. Oud, October 1921, Fondation Custodia, Paris.

**26.** T. van Doesburg to J.J.P. Oud, 3 November 1921, Fondation Custodia, Paris.

**27.** L. Milius to T. van Doesburg, undated, some time between 3 November and 4 December, Van Doesburg Archive, Rijksdienst Beeldende Kunst, The Hague; E. Taverne, D. Broekhuizen, 'De dissidente architecten: J.J.P. Oud, Jan Wils en Robert van 't Hoff', in: C. Blotkamp (ed.), *De Vervolgjaren van De Stijl 1922-1932*, Amsterdam, Antwerp 1996, p. 367.

**28.** J.J.P. Oud to T. van Doesburg, undated, second half November 1921, Fondation Custodia, Paris.

**29.** T. van Doesburg to J.J.P. Oud, 14 December 1921, Fondation Custodia, Paris.

**30.** J.J.P. Oud to T. van Doesburg, undated, second half November 1921, Fondation Custodia, Paris.

**31.** J.J.P. Oud to T. van Doesburg, 16 December 1921, Fondation Custodia, Paris.

**32.** J.J.P. Oud to T. van Doesburg, 16 December 1921, Fondation Custodia, Paris.

***because he only recognizes Neo-Plasticism in 'my' painting.***[49] **The fundamental disagreement between Mondrian and Oud did not result in a permanent rift, though their subsequent correspondence did acquire a lighter tone. Art-historical subjects were studiously avoided, to be replaced by practical notations relating to Oud's (repeatedly postponed) plans to visit Mondrian and the purchase and sale of paintings.**[50]

**33.** T. van Doesburg to J.J.P. Oud, 18 December 1921, Fondation Custodia, Paris.
**34.** See for example Oud's moving portrait 'Mondriaan, de mens', in: J.J.P. Oud, L.J.F. Wijsenbeek, *Mondriaan*, Zeist, Antwerp 1962, pp. 61-81.
**35.** Y.A. Bois, 'Mondrian and the Theory of Architecture', in: *Assemblage. A Critical Journal of Architecture and Design Culture*, 4(1987), pp. 103-130; P. Mondrian, *Le Néo-Plasticisme. Principe Général de l'Equivalence Plastique*, Paris 1920 (published in 1921); C. Blotkamp, *Mondriaan in detail*, Utrecht, Antwerp 1987, pp. 68-69.
**36.** T. van Doesburg, 'Terechtwijzigingen', in: *De Stijl*, 5(1922)9, pp. 141.

**37.** A. van der Woud, *Waarheid en karakter. Het debat over de bouwkunst 1840-1900*, Rotterdam 1997, p. 293ff.
**38.** J.J.P. Oud, 'Over de toekomstige bouwkunst en hare architectonische mogelijkheden', in: *Bouwkundig Weekblad*, 42(1921), pp. 147-160; C. Blotkamp, *Mondriaan in detail*, Utrecht, Antwerp 1987, pp. 68-69.
**39.** P. Mondrian to J.J.P. Oud, 16 December 1921, Fondation Custodia, Paris; Y.A. Bois, 'Mondrian and the Theory of Architecture', in: *Assemblage. A Critical Journal of Architecture and Design Culture*, 4(1987), p. 106.
**40.** This position can be reconstructed from a couple of sentences in a letter from Mondrian: *I don't agree that an architectural aesthetic has to come from experience: it is there but it can only be applied directly.* P. Mondrian to J.J.P. Oud, 30 August 1921, Fondation Custodia, Paris.
**41.** P. Mondrian to J.J.P. Oud, 18 September 1921, Fondation Custodia, Paris.
**42.** P. Mondrian to J.J.P. Oud, 6 December 1921, Fondation Custodia, Paris. The friend was Marinus Ritsema van Eck, who lived in the south of France and often visited Mondrian in Paris. It is thought that he also helped with the French translation of the pamphlet. See C. Blok (ed.), *Het Neo-Plasticisme. Algemeen Manifest van de Beeldende Gelijkwaardigheid*, Amersfoort 1994, p. 18.
**43.** P. Mondrian to J.J.P. Oud, 10 December 1921, Fondation Custodia, Paris.
**44.** The remark was prompted by the conflict with Van Doesburg. Mondrian wrote: *As far as Van Doesburg is concerned, he hasn't written to me about you but I could well imagine that he thinks badly of you, given what you have just written to me. Because I, too, almost get the impression that you don't consider N.P. suitable to be used or applied in this way. I know that you had to contend with 'society' (which now obliges me to stop!) but that you are a confirmed believer in N.P.. That's why I've started on an article that will clarify everything.* P. Mondrian to J.J.P. Oud, 6 December 1921, Fondation Custodia, Paris.
**45.** P. Mondrian to J.J.P. Oud, 13 July 1922, Fondation Custodia, Paris.
**46.** P. Mondrian to J.J.P. Oud, 1922 (probably August-September), Fondation Custodia, Paris.
**47.** P. Mondrian to J.J.P. Oud, 1922 (between March and July), Fondation Custodia, Paris; C. Blotkamp, *Mondriaan in detail*, Utrecht, Antwerp 1987, pp. 72-73.
**48.** J.J.P. Oud to P. Mondrian, undated (autumn 1922), Fondation Custodia, Paris.
**49.** C. Blotkamp, *Mondriaan in detail*, Utrecht, Antwerp 1987, p. 73.
**50.** Y.A. Bois, J. Joosten (et al.), *Piet Mondriaan 1872-1944*, Washington, The Hague, New York 1994.

# 28/ De Geus House

**Broek in Waterland, 3 De Erven** **1916**

In mid-1916, the mayor of Broek in Waterland, Mr de Geus, commissioned Oud to design an official mayoral residence. Oud produced two designs. Plan A is quite stylized, thanks to a plethora of Dudokian details such as the rather overstated entrance (with steps), the fenestration and in particular the dominant shape of the roof. The floor plan was less flamboyant and was based on the traditional rural notary's house. In plan B the floor plan was much the same but the facades were more restrained and thus more in keeping with the informal character of a rural residence. The client preferred version B and that is what was built. Oud himself was evidently proud of version B for he included it in Sphinx's first group exhibition in January 1917.[1] It was also praised by Van Doesburg in a review published in the same year: *It is pleasing to note that by this means the younger generation is moving forward with confidence. I say 'with confidence' but this does not apply to all, only to those who, like the architect Oud, strive after purity without losing the mystic element, the fervour. As an example of this I would like to take his pyramid-shaped 'country house in Broek-in-Waterland'.*[2] Van Doesburg had every reason to be enthusiastic about this house because thanks to Oud he received the commission for a stained-glass window in the back door, which was installed in January 1917. The commission to Van Doesburg was part of the intensive exchange of ideas that followed their first meeting in May 1916. Evert van Straaten has characterized the blossoming friendship between Oud and Van Doesburg thus: *They talked about the amalgamation of the arts 'in a single shared spiritual idea' but also about the fact that there should be no competition among artists, doubtless based on the intuitive awareness that everyone in fact thinks their own discipline is the most important. But Oud showed understanding for Van Doesburg's aspirations and before long the latter was describing Oud as 'a fine, sensitive young man with a lot of energy'.*[3] The commission to Van Doesburg predates August 1916. On 11 September, Van Doesburg wrote on a postcard from the Heilige Landstichting near Nijmegen: *I have made a sketch for the glass window. Lena will show it to you. I'm rather pleased with it myself. I've managed it without resorting to painting.*[4] It was his first 'monumental' commission which is all the more remarkable since Van Doesburg had absolutely no technical experience in the field. From certain correspondence it appears that Vilmos Huszár provided the necessary information about stained-glass technique. The composition in the back door is dominated by the Broek in Waterland coat of arms, a swan with a sheaf of arrows. The background is a busy composition of planes made up of fragments of circles, squares and triangles. The client was evidently satisfied with the result, for in 1917 Van Doesburg was commissioned to supplement the large window with four small transom lights.

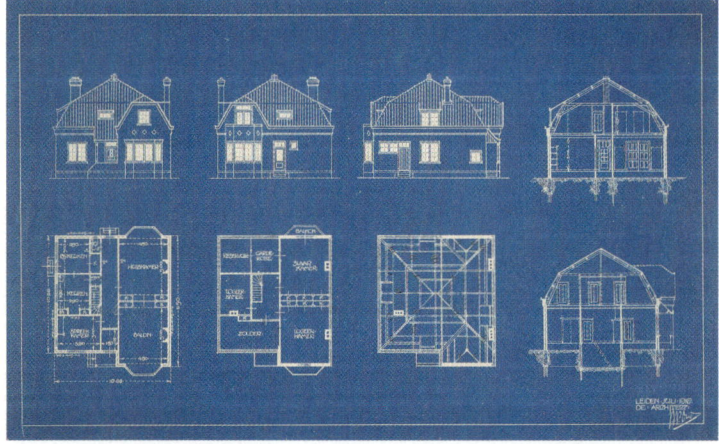

**Definitive design/ dr1984: 0488, CCA, Montreal**



**Notes**

**1.** A. de Jongh-Vermeulen, P. van de Velde, 'De Leidsche Kunstclub De Sphinx. "Een Vereeniging die mee kan tellen"', in: D. Wintgens Hötte, A. de Jongh-Vermeulen (eds), *Dageraad van de Moderne Kunst. Leiden en Omgeving 1890-1940*, Zwolle, Leiden 1999, pp. 181, 202.
**2.** T. van Doesburg, 'Schilderkunst', in: *Eenheid*, 3 February 1917.
**3.** E. van Straaten, *Theo van Doesburg. Schilder en architect*, The Hague 1988, pp. 24-25; E. van Straaten, *Klare en lichte, gesloten vormen, geaccentueerd door diepe en pure kleuren. Het werk van Theo van Doesburg in de architectuur*, Amsterdam 1992, pp. 31-35.
**4.** Postcard from Van Doesburg to Oud, 11 September 1916, Fondation Custodia, Paris.

**Sources**

CCA: dr1984: 0487-0488, ph1984: 1013
Getty: 890126-12**
NAI: OUDJ-ge 1-4, OUDJ-ph 60, OUDJ-ph 1779

**Articles**

T. van Doesburg, 'Schilderkunst', in: *Eenheid*, 3 February 1917
J.J.P. Oud, *Architecturalia voor bouwheren en architekten*, The Hague 1963, pp. 15-16

**Literature**

U. Barbieri, *J.J.P. Oud*, Rotterdam 1987, pp. 22-23
E. Hoek (ed.), *Theo van Doesburg. Oeuvrecatalogus*, Bussum 2000, nos. 500, 523
H.E. Oud, *J.J.P. Oud. Architekt 1890-1963. Feiten en herinneringen gerangschikt*, The Hague 1984, pp. 22-23
G. Stamm, *J.J.P. Oud. Bauten und Projekte 1906 bis 1963*, Mainz, Berlin 1984, p. 27, pp. 31-32
E. van Straaten, *Theo van Doesburg. Schilder en architect*, The Hague 1988, pp. 24-25
E. van Straaten, 'Glas-in-lood compositie I (1916) en vier bovenlichten in glas in lood (1917)', in: *Klare en lichte, gesloten ruimten, geaccentueerd door diepe en pure kleuren; Het werk van Theo van Doesburg in de architectuur*, Amsterdam 1990, pp. 31-35

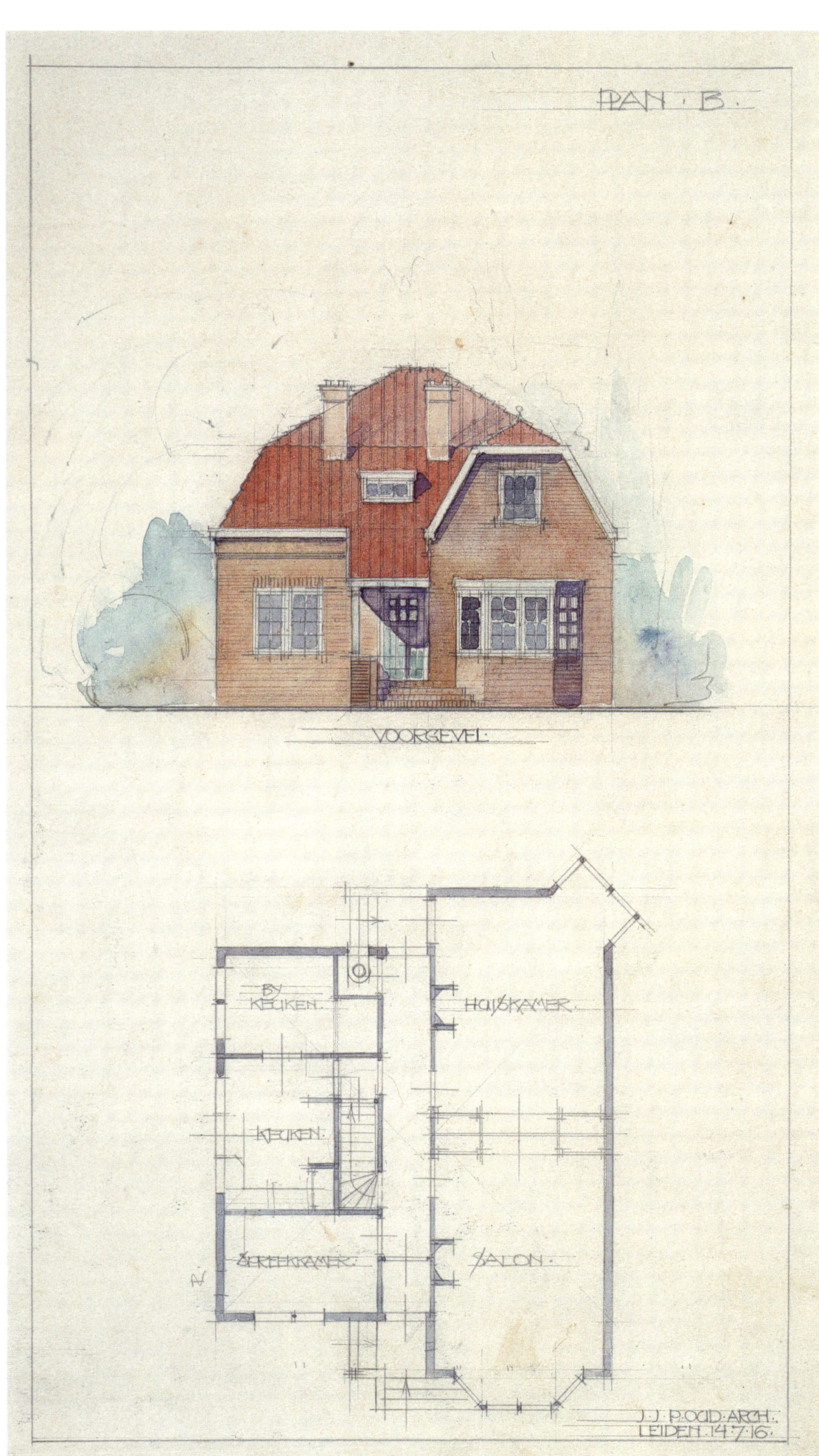


**Plan B: front elevation and ground floor plan/ OUDJ-ge 3, NAI, Rotterdam**

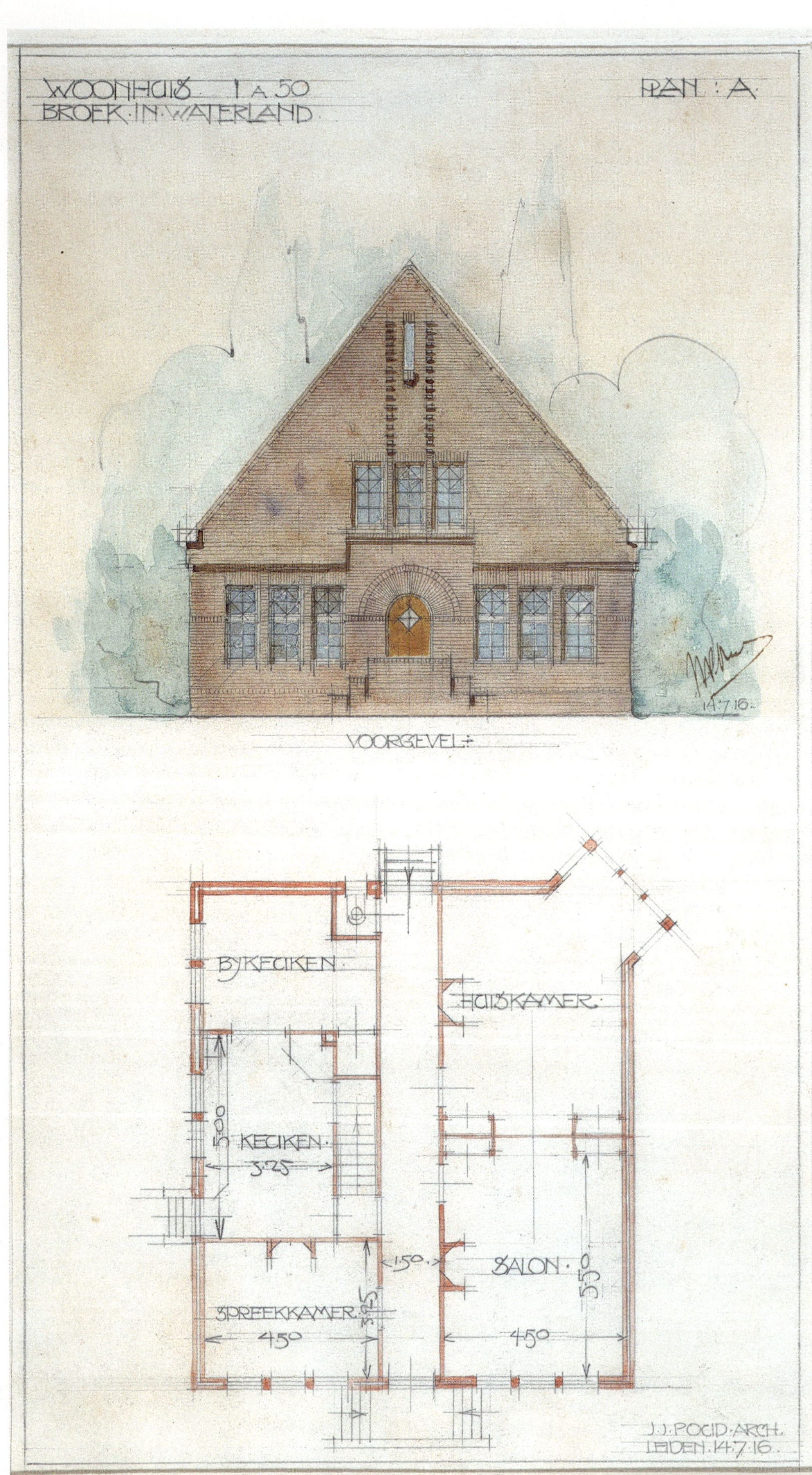


Plan A: front elevation and ground floor plan/
OUDJ-ge 4, NAI, Rotterdam

# 29/ Villa Allegonda

**Katwijk aan Zee, North Boulevard**

**1916/1917 – 1928**

During the period when he was directly involved in *De Stijl* (1917-1921), Oud designed a number of projects which very quickly came to be regarded as icons not only of *De Stijl*, but also of the Modern Movement in architecture. Oud himself played a not inconsiderable role in their promotion. From the correspondence between Van Doesburg and Oud it is evident that within *De Stijl* a lot of attention was paid to the presentation of these designs both in magazines and at exhibitions. For example, as early as 1920 Van Doesburg chose the factory and warehouse at Purmerend, the hall and staircase of De Vonk, the Strandboulevard and the street composition as typical *De Stijl* designs for one of the issues.[1] Shortly thereafter, he sent the same set of photographs to Paris to the gallery owner Léonce Rosenberg in order to convince the latter of Oud's special status as 'the' *De Stijl* architect.[2] In some instances – such as the factory at Purmerend – Oud produced, at Van Doesburg's instigation, handsome perspective drawings especially for presentation in magazines and at exhibitions. One of the most striking features of this form of 'marketing' of architecture through drawings and models – which eventually came to dominate the presentation of architectural history – is the exclusive focus on the pure form of the architectural object through the removal of all intrusive elements from the immediate surroundings, such as trees, passers-by and even neighbouring buildings.[3]
Among this suite of iconic buildings is one project that Oud himself consistently excluded because he had played such a minor role in the architectural design: Villa Allegonda. Nonetheless, during the 1930s critics increasingly 'identified' the villa as an important 'prototype' of the Modern Movement in architecture, the missing link between Adolf Loos's Villa Stein in Vienna (1910) and Le Corbusier's first white villas in the vicinity of Paris. Oud steadfastly rejected this honour, probably because he regarded the Villa Allegonda as an example of painter-designed architecture.
Villa Allegonda evolved in three stages.[4] Shortly after the turn of the century, the architect H.J. Jesse built three substantial summer houses in the dunes at Katwijk aan Zee. Two of the villas – 't Waerle and De Hoogcaete – belonged to the Leiden-based painter Menso Kamerlingh Onnes. The third villa, which was then called Sigrid, was occupied by the Norwegian painter Morgenstjerne Munthe, who subsequently sold it to the Rotterdam coffee and tea merchant, J.E.R. Trousselot. In 1916-1917 the villa was remodelled in accordance with the ideas of Menso Kamerlingh Onnes, who called in a friend of his son Harm – the architect J.J.P. Oud – to assist with the technical aspect. Kamerlingh Onnes designed an unusual, and in these surroundings somewhat exotic-looking, villa that in both plan and spatial composition was totally integrated into the coastal and dune landscape. What later (American) critics came to regard as an early example of European, 'cubist' architecture, was in fact nothing more than a trite echo of a North African vernacular

**First renovation/ OUDJ-ph 62, NAI, Rotterdam**

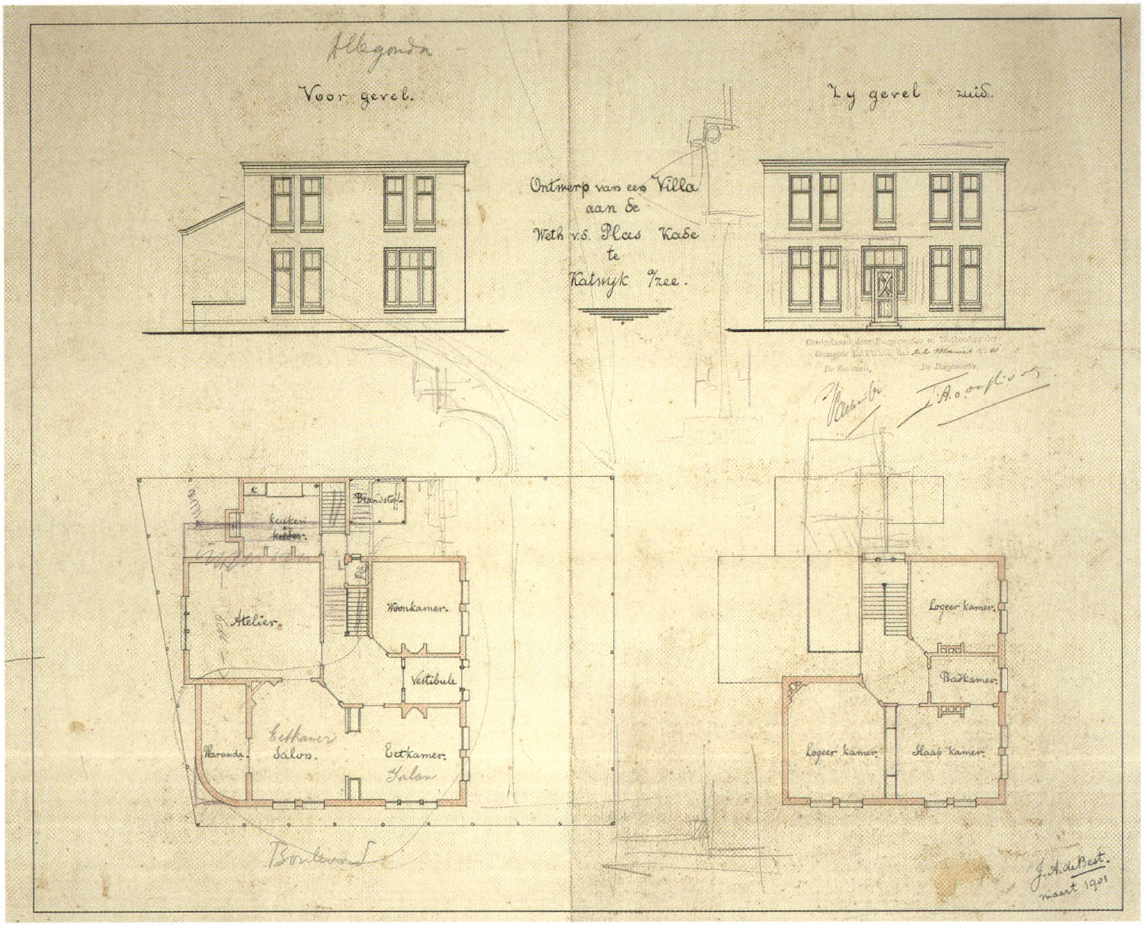

H.J. Jesse, Villa Sigrid/ dr1984: 0015, CCA, Montreal

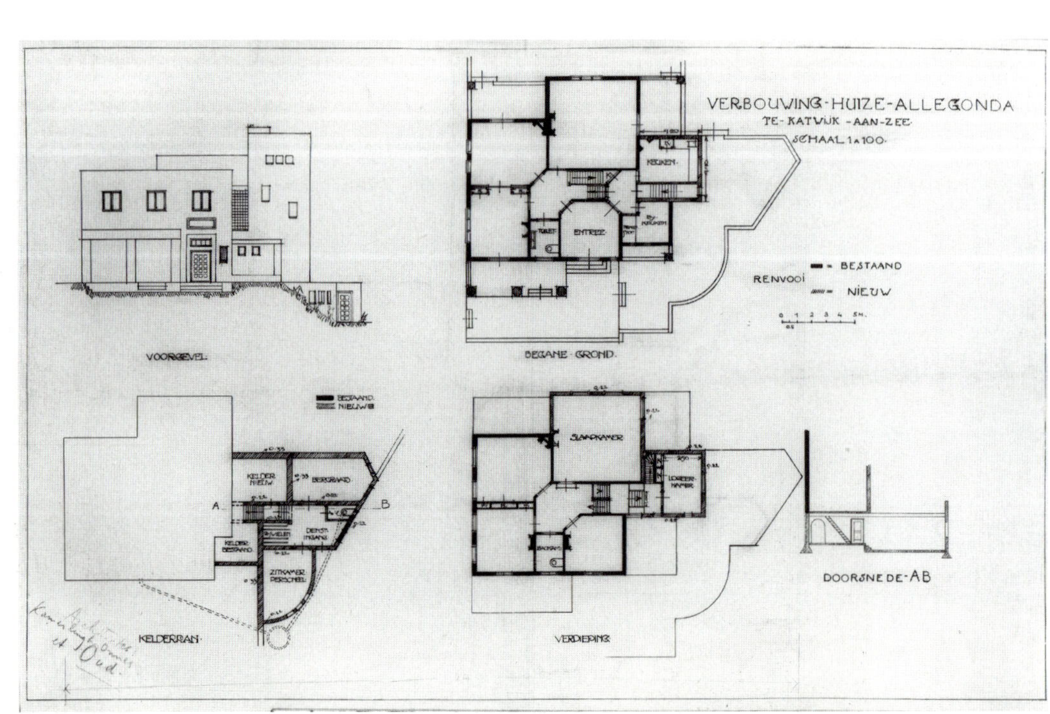


Plans of second renovation/ OUDJ-al 22, NAI, Rotterdam

architecture that Kamerlingh Onnes had fallen in love with on one of his many trips abroad. In this phase of the remodelling Oud's main responsibility, apart from draughting and technical advice, was to coordinate the contribution of artist friends from the Leiden artistic world (read *De Sphinx*: Theo van Doesburg, Harm Kamerlingh Onnes and W.C. Brouwer), without, however, attempting an 'aesthetic unity'. Oud probably also had some part in the colour scheme of the interior.[5] He had the woodwork painted in a greyish purple that displeased Van Doesburg who felt that primary colours would have been more in keeping with his own stained-glass windows (Composition II and V). Harm Kamerlingh Onnes, together with his father, designed the ornamentation in the dining room. He also designed a ceramic tile picture above the front door, which was produced in the Leiderdorp workshop of W.C. Brouwer. The correspondence with Oud reveals that Harm Kamerlingh Onnes also designed a stained-glass window for the building and that payment for this work was a long time in coming. On 25 April 1919 he wrote to Oud: *How are relations with Mr Trousselot? Haven't you even sent the bailiff round yet? I received the 1000 guilders for the window a month ago. I'm enclosing a small piece of a photo of it to let you see that such photos are pretty useless and I don't think it's worth sending the whole thing.*[6] In 1922 Oud mediated in the sale to Trousselot of one of Mondrian's paintings.[7]

In 1927, by which time Kamerlingh Onnes senior had died, the villa underwent another renovation. The living room was enlarged on the south side with a conservatory and a roof terrace while the 'Moorish' room decorated by father and son Kamerlingh Onnes was opened up with a (low) verandah on the sea side. In addition, Oud 'modernized' the architecture of the windows and of the pillars of the front verandah, and designed furniture for the conservatory such as dining room chairs, a table, armchairs and a cupboard. Nervous exhaustion and illness forced Oud to delegate the supervision of the work to Paul Meller. The renovation was carried out in consultation with Harm Kamerlingh Onnes whose correspondence with Oud reveals a quite independent and idiosyncratic view of architecture. In November 1927, in

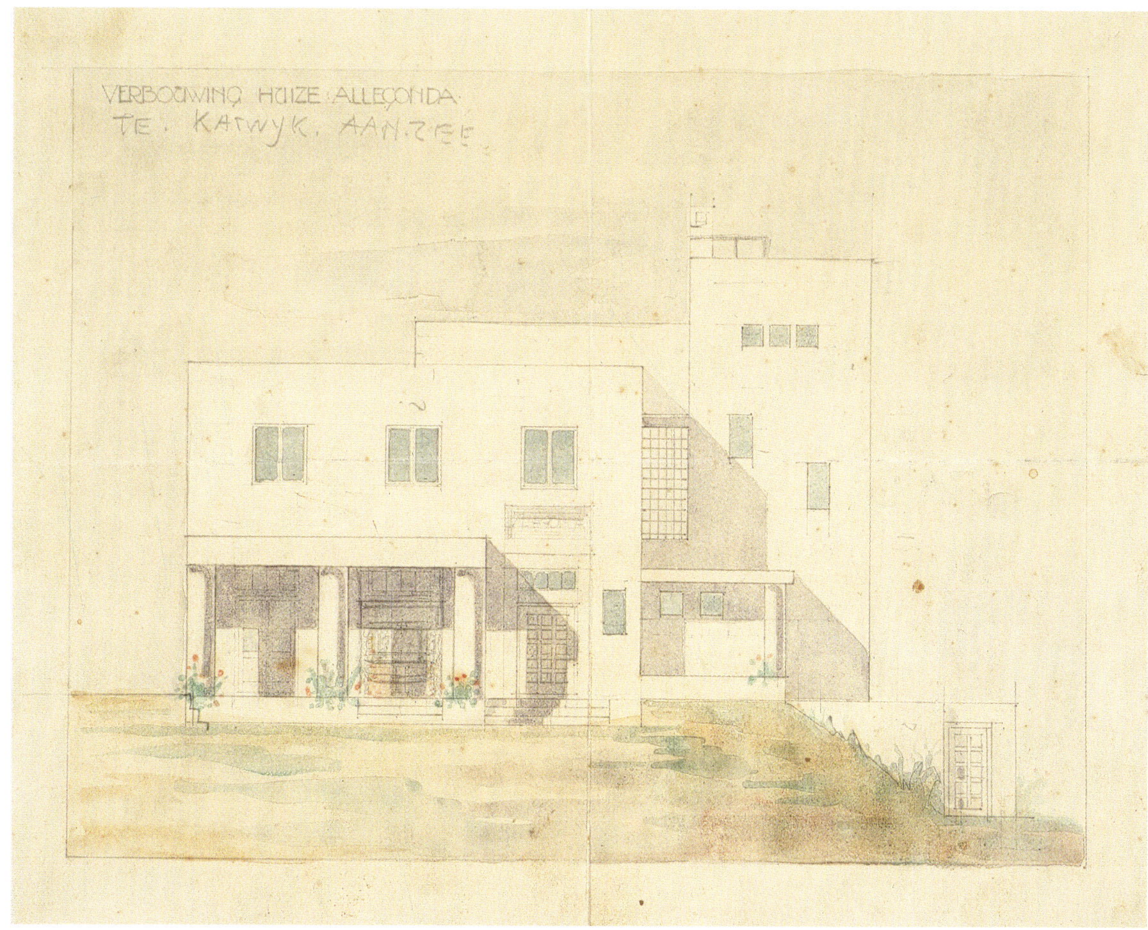


Boulevard elevation, first renovation/ dr1985: 0391, CCA, Montreal

Second renovation (right the conservatory)/
OUDJ-ph 66, NAI, Rotterdam (Photo E. van Ojen)

response to Oud's suggestions for the renovation he wrote: *In the sketch, the supporting pillars look a little narrow to me. It makes the building look a bit like concrete construction, something that I don't think my father intended. I think we'd do well to take a look at Moorish buildings, even though they're a bit heavy by modern standards.*[8]

The myth of the Villa Allegonda as an early example of 'cubist' architecture began with the Swiss architect Alfred Roth, who visited the villa in 1928.[9] By then the villa had already been linked to Oud in articles by Van Doesburg, Behne, Gropius and H. de Fries. But the main promoter of the Villa Allegonda as a precursor of a modern, functionalist style was Philip Johnson, who wanted to present it as such at the 1932 MOMA exhibition, *The International Style*. It seems reasonable to assume that he had visited the building together with Hitchcock and possibly in the company of Oud himself. In November 1930 he wrote Oud that he was planning to present the villa as the cradle of the modern aesthetic and that it would be the only building in the exhibition dating from before 1925. In the event, this plan came to nothing.[10] Even in the 1950s, when Oud was actively involved with the image-forming and myth-making surrounding his own contribution to *De Stijl*, he persistently omitted the Villa Allegonda from the suite of projects – the De Vonk holiday hostel, the factory at Purmerend and the Scheveningen esplanade – that he presented as examples of *De Stijl* architecture and as such as the true beginning of his career as modern architect.

**Second renovation, living room/ OUDJ-ph 1669, NAI, Rotterdam**



**Notes**

**1.** Van Doesburg to Oud, 1 October 1920, Fondation Custodia, Paris.
**2.** Van Doesburg to Oud, 8 December 1920, Fondation Custodia, Paris; Van Doesburg to Oud, 1 October 1920, Fondation Custodia, Paris.
**3.** B. Colomina, *Privacy and Publicity. Modern Architecture as Mass Media*, Cambridge (Mass.) 1996, p. 107ff.
**4.** G. Stamm, *J.J.P. Oud. Bauten und Projekte 1906 bis 1963*, Berlin 1984, pp. 38-41; C. Blotkamp, *Mondriaan in detail*, Utrecht, Antwerp 1987, pp. 49-52 (figure 24 is an unsigned front view drawn by Oud (1917), originally owned by H.H. Kamerlingh Onnes, now in the collection of the Getty Research Institute, Los Angeles; H. Esser, 'J.J.P. Oud', in: Blotkamp (et al.), *De Beginjaren van De Stijl*, Utrecht 1993, pp. 131-132.
**5.** A. de Jongh-Vermeulen, *Dageraad van de Moderne Kunst. Leiden en omgeving 1890-1940*, Zwolle, Leiden 1999, pp. 238-241; E. van Straaten, *Theo van Doesburg, schilder en architect*, The Hague 1988, pp. 28-31; H. Esser, 'J.J.P. Oud', in: Blotkamp (et al.), *De Beginjaren van De Stijl*, Utrecht 1993, pp. 131-132.
**6.** Harm Kamerlingh Onnes to Oud, 5 April 1919, OUDJ-B, NAI, Rotterdam.
**7.** P. Mondrian to Oud, 3 August 1922, Fondation Custodia, Paris.
**8.** Harm Kamerlingh Onnes, 10 November 1927, OUDJ-B, NAI, Rotterdam. Quoted by A. de Jongh-Vermeulen, *Dageraad van de Moderne Kunst. Leiden en omgeving 1890-1940*, Zwolle, Leiden 1999, p. 241.
**9.** A. Roth, *Begegnungen mit Pionieren*, Basle, Stuttgart 1973, p. 128
**10.** G. Stamm, *J.J.P. Oud. Bauten und Projekte 1906 bis 1963*, Mainz, Berlin 1984, p. 52.

**Sources**

CCA: dr1984: 0015, dr1985: 0391, ph1984: 1019, ph1984: 1020
Getty: 890126-box 7, 6*
NAI: OUDJ-al 1-24, OUDJ-al 1001, OUDJ-al 3001, OUDJ-ph 62-81, OUDJ-ph 1668-1669, OUDJ-ph 1781-1783, OUDJ-B

**Articles**

J.J.P. Oud, 'Verbouwing Huize "Allegonda", Katwijk aan Zee', in: *Bouwkundig Weekblad*, 39(1918)5, pp. 29-30
J.J.P. Oud, 'Glas-in-lood', in: *Bouwkundig Weekblad*, 39(1918)35, pp. 199-202
'Huize Allegonda', in: *L'Architecture vivante*, Winter 1924 (n.p.)
H. Hoste, 'Twee villa's aan zee', in: *De Telegraaf*, 27 April 1918

**Literature**

U. Barbieri, *J.J.P. Oud*, Rotterdam 1987, pp. 41-43

C. Blotkamp, *Mondriaan in detail*, Utrecht, Antwerp 1987

D.A. Buiskool, *De reis van Harm Kamerlingh Onnes, Brieven uit de Oost 1922-1923*, Hilversum 1999

B. Colomina, *Privacy and Publicity. Modern Architecture as Mass Media*, Cambridge (Mass.) 1996, p. 107ff

H. Esser, 'J.J.P. Oud', in: Blotkamp (et al.), *De Beginjaren van De Stijl*, Utrecht 1993, pp. 131-132

E. Hoek (ed.), *Theo van Doesburg. Oeuvrecatalogus*, Bussum 2000, nos. 530, 557

A. de Jongh-Vermeulen, *Dageraad van de Moderne Kunst. Leiden en omgeving 1890-1940*, Zwolle, Leiden 1999

H.E. Oud, *J.J.P. Oud. Architekt 1890-1963. Feiten en herinneringen gerangschikt*, The Hague 1984, pp. 38-39, pp. 106-108, p. 199, p. 201

E. van Straaten, *H.H. Kamerlingh Onnes schilder en keramist*, exhibition catalogue Leeuwarden, Arnhem, Kröller-Möller, 1981-1982

E. van Straaten, *Theo van Doesburg, schilder en architect*, The Hague 1988

S. Polano, *J.J.P. Oud Architettura Olandese*, Milan 1981, p. 18

A. Roth, *Begegnungen mit Pionieren*, Basle, Stuttgart 1973, p. 128

G. Stamm, *J.J.P. Oud. Bauten und Projekte 1906 bis 1963*, Mainz, Berlin 1984, pp. 40-41, p. 89

Second renovation, conservatory interior/ NAI, OUDJ-ph 69, NAI, Rotterdam (Photo E. van Ojen)

Second renovation, dining area in conservatory/
OUDJ-ph 70, NAI, Rotterdam

Second renovation, lounge area in conservatory/
OUDJ-ph 71, NAI, Rotterdam

**Renovation 1931, curved banquette in hall/ OUDJ-ph 72, NAI, Rotterdam**

J.J.P. Oud, 'Verbouwing Huize Allegonda Katwijk aan Zee', in: *Bouwkundig Weekblad,* 39(1918)5

# Remodelling Villa Allegonda Katwijk aan zee

The remodelling of the here illustrated villa Allegonda at Katwijk aan zee, owned by Mr J.E.R. Trousselot of Rotterdam, was worked out technically by me to a design by the artist M. Kamerlingh Onnes.
Basically, the extension comprised the provision of better service quarters, terraces, loggias and the construction of the tower and of a large bedroom. In connection with these additions the existing section was also modified so that little remained of the original aspect, as the photos show.
The consulting room of the existing house was turned into an entrance hall. The presence of a door set at an angle gave rise to a solution in which the service areas form an entity of their own.
A small hall is the centre of this service area and opens into the large hall, the entrance, the kitchen, the pantry and to the stair which provides access from the service entry in the basement and comes out on the highway running down along the dunes. The basement also contains: two large cellars, a servants' lounge, large storage area for suitcases, etc., bicycle accommodation, WC for the servants.
The living rooms remained unchanged except for the addition of loggias. The entrance and the hall have marble floors; the entrance also has a white marble wainscotting finished with a strip of light grey marble. On the spot where the entrance used to be, is the toilet.
On the ground floor of the tower is the kitchen. Above the kitchen is a guest room, reached from a landing that is in turn reached from a landing of the main staircase. From the landing in front of the guest room, another stair leads to the servants' room and then to the roof of the tower which affords a superb view over land and sea.
On the outside the building is entirely plastered with a mortar of Doorn lime and sand, not applied below the smoothing board but spread as evenly as possible without smoothing board to do justice to the material.
The roofing above the loggias is reinforced concrete; the colour of the paint is purple-grey (in the colour of shadow to cause the minimum of disruption to the large planes) everywhere.
The terraces are laid with 'quenast' [porphyry] tiles.
Set into the front facade is a ceramic name plate designed by H.H. Kamerlingh Onnes and fired by Willem C. Brouwer, while at the junction between the tower and the old section is a stained-glass window by Theo van Doesburg. The whole building fits wonderfully well into the surroundings and the choice of flat roofs is particularly felicitous beside the sea. All the more since the distribution of masses is very fine here and makes a successful termination of the North Boulevard. The building's very sober colour harmonizes beautifully with the pale dune landscape. Anyone who is familiar with our seaside resorts knows how often this (self-evident) requirement is flouted.

# 30/ De Vonk Holiday Hostel

**Noordwijkerhout, 34 Westeinde** **1917-1919**

Opinions about the relation between painting and architecture were far from unanimous in the early years of *De Stijl*. In 1917-1918, when the first issues of *De Stijl* appeared, the painters in particular engaged in lively speculation about 'the place of modern painting in architecture', with Van der Leck, Van Doesburg and Mondrian all presenting very different ideas on the subject.[1] Whereas Mondrian was convinced from the outset that the two forms of art were fundamentally incongruent, Van der Leck and Van Doesburg chose to emphasize the differences between their practitioners, the architect and the painter. Van Doesburg was much more consistent in this than Van der Leck, who saw architecture and painting as separate but, especially in their treatment of the plane, mutually enhancing and elucidating arts, whereby painting 'deconstructs' architecture's corporality into flatness.[2] For his part, Van Doesburg always emphasized the difference in *technique*: architecture combines, joins and, by means of meticulous proportions, produces solid, closed and plastic forms, whereas painting decomposes and opens up, in which it is the exact opposite of architecture. Although Van Doesburg saw the modelling of space as the main task confronting both architect and painter, 'space' for the modern visual artist was not a measurable, bounded area such as architects were wont to imagine, but *the notion of* extension *expressed by the one (for example, a line, a colour) to the other (for example the picture plane)*.[3] And he added that this notion of extension or space was the fundamental condition for all visual art. A notable feature of Van Doesburg's painterly notion of space in relation to architecture is his interest in what the observer *sees* and experiences while moving around the environment.[4] Unlike Mondrian, who saw space in static terms, Van Doesburg had always been interested in a dynamic imaging of space.

The robust De Vonk holiday hostel at Noordwijkerhout was designed and built in the very same years in which the columns of *De Stijl* were filled with speculations about architecture and painting and their mutual relationship. In that context, the project (in which the artists Van Doesburg and Harm Kamerlingh Onnes were also involved) can be seen as

**Rear elevation/ OUDJ-ph 1789, NAI, Rotterdam**

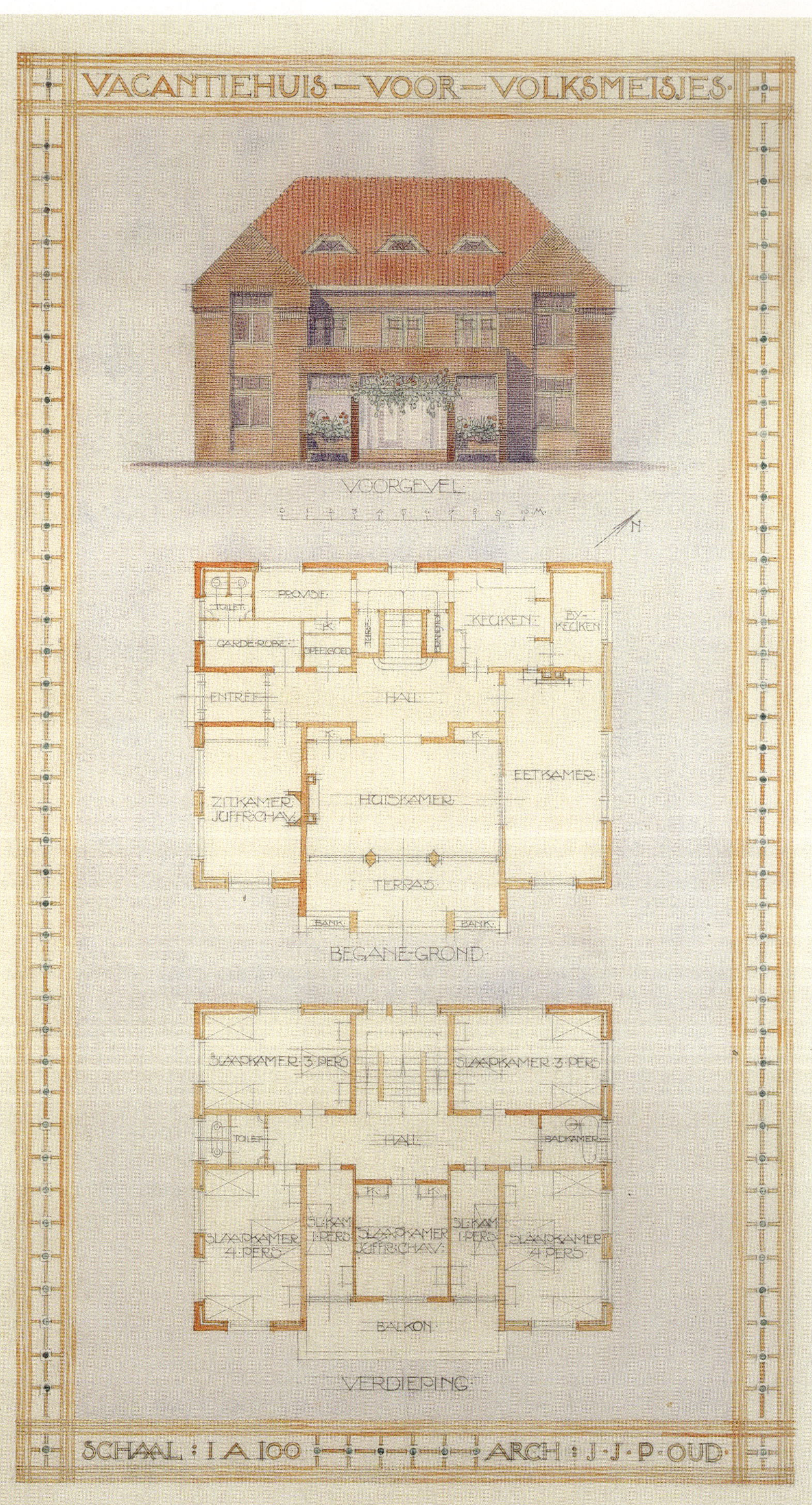


Front elevation (top), plans of ground floor (centre) and first floor (bottom)/ OUDJ-vo 1, NAI, Rotterdam

the most important contribution to that debate by an *architect*. A contribution that differed little from that of Van Doesburg in terms of stance and intensity and that cannot be explained otherwise than as a confirmation of the principle of strict division of labour, a principle at that moment shared, at least in theory, by both Rietveld and Van Doesburg. As far as Van Doesburg was concerned, this meant that painting and architecture should confine themselves to their own particular means of expression. The logical consequence of this for architecture was to free it from all means of expression that were not strictly architectural, such as colour. And that is exactly what Oud tried to do in the holiday hostel at Noordwijkerhout. De Vonk ('the spark') is not, as so often claimed in art-historical literature, an essentially 'retrograde' or conservative building that owes its place in the *De Stijl* pantheon to Van Doesburg's artistic devices. Nor is De Vonk, as G. Stamm thought, an early, slightly veiled experiment in 'cubist' architecture consisting of nothing but horizontal and vertical relationships and thus 'precursive' of the design for the Purmerend factory (1919).[5] De Vonk is exactly what it is: a massive, closed, exceptionally 'corporeal' brick building, designed on a rigidly symmetrical ground plan. It stands for everything that passed for a 'modern' building at that moment in Dutch architecture, by virtue of the emphasis on massing, (symmetrical) organization and measurable space as new, strictly architectural means of expression. It is an example of what Van Doesburg would later call 'a frontal architecture' which nonetheless conceals the unsuspected riches of two 'building sections' – staircase and corridor – where painter and architect, each using their own specialist resources, have encapsulated the 'four dimensions of space' in a new (time space) concept, in a new, collective monumental style.

The building owed its existence to the efforts of Emilie Knappert, a social reformer who in 1899 had founded the Leidsch Volkshuis, a social centre for the working classes modelled on Toynbee Hall in London.[6] De Vonk was intended as a centre where young girls from working class families in Leiden could be taught various skills and at the same time brought into contact with the delights and wholesome

**Hall at ground floor level with staircase. From: D. Wintgens Hötte (ed.), *Dageraad van de Moderne Kunst*, Zwolle, Leiden 1999**



**Notes**

**1.** Y.A. Bois, 'Mondrian and the Theory of Architecture', in: *Assemblage. A Critical Journal of Architecture and Design Culture*, 4(1987), pp. 104-106; J. Beckett, '"De Vonk", Noordwijk. An Example of early De Stijl co-operation', in: *Art History* 3(180), pp. 202-217.

**2.** R.W. Oxenaar, *Bart van der Leck tot 1920. Een primitief van de nieuwe tijd*, Utrecht 1976.

**3.** T. van Doesburg, *Grondbegrippen der nieuwe beeldende kunst* (1919), quoted here from the edition presented by S.U. Barbieri, C. Boekraad and J. Leering as: *Grondbegrippen van de nieuwe kunst*, Nijmegen 1983, p. 13.

**4.** First noted by C. Blotkamp, 'Theo van Doesburg', in: C. Blotkamp (et al.), *De Beginjaren van De Stijl*, Utrecht 1982, pp. 31-32.

**5.** G. Stamm, *J.J.P. Oud. Bauten und Projekte 1906 bis 1963*, Mainz, Berlin 1984, p. 43.

**6.** H. Esser, 'J.J.P. Oud', in: Blotkamp (et al.), *De Beginjaren van De Stijl*, Utrecht 1993, p. 135; H. van der Heide, 'De Vonk en de Vereeniging "Buitenbedrijf"', in: *Maatschappelijk Werk: Opstellen aangeboden aan Emilie Knappert op haar zeventigsten verjaardag*, Amsterdam 1930, pp. 253-260.

**7.** T. van Doesburg, 'Aanteekeningen over monumentale kunst. Naar aanleiding van twee bouwfragmenten (Hall in vacantiehuis te Noordwijkerhout. Bijlage 1)', in: *De Stijl*, 2(1918), no. 1, pp. 10-12.

**8.** E. van Straaten, *Klare en lichte, gesloten vormen, geaccentueerd door diepe en pure kleuren. Het werk van Theo van Doesburg in de architectuur*, Amsterdam 1992, pp. 45-48; A. Doig, *Theo van Does-*

effects of nature. In order to achieve this ideal, the 'Vereeniging Buitenbedrijf' foundation was established in 1911. In 1917, having amassed the necessary funds, the foundation approached the architect H.P. Berlage, who was a friend of Knappert's and a familiar figure in left-wing, social-democratic circles. Berlage had no time, however, and recommended his young friend and protégé J.J.P. Oud. If, as seems likely, the client had a clear notion of what she wanted, based on an existing holiday hostel such as the one at Bergen aan Zee, Oud's architectural contribution would have consisted less in devising a ground plan and facade layout than in the strict systematization and streamlining of available plans and models. Oud designed a compact building that in terms of monumentality – symmetrical facade composition, ground plan arranged along two axes – compares with the 'Helder' technical school designed in the same period (see nr. 27). There are also many similarities of detail, such as the vertical organization of the windows, the dark bands of the plinth and especially the crisp contours of the volume. De Vonk is an example of an international tendency towards monumentality in architecture which had resulted, since the 1890s, in buildings with classical compositions and details. This trend was intensified in Oud's case because of his interest in the residential architecture of Hermann Muthesius, an interest manifested in De Vonk not only in the detailing of the stairs – in particular the built-in benches – but above all in the way the cubism of the floor plan carried over into the structure as a whole. While the central location of the staircase and its 'furnishing' with benches may have been inspired (via Muthesius) by English country house architecture, the same can certainly not be said of the architectural detailing. The spatial effect of the staircase is the successful result of Van Doesburg's insistence that the architect confine himself to strictly architectural means. Oud detached the inside bend of the flight of stairs from the walls of the narrow passage around the staircase allowing light to fall on the built-in benches. This intervention was not only functional but also provided an opportunity to articulate the balustrade to match the strict measure of the treads and risers of the stairs. Van

**Hall at first floor level/ OUDJ-ph 96, NAI, Rotterdam**

*burg. Painting into architecture, theory into practice*, Cambridge, London etc. 1986, pp. 58-71; N.J. Troy, *The De Stijl Environment*, Cambridge (Mass.) 1983, pp. 17, 19, 23.

**9.** J.J.P. Oud, 'Over de toekomstige bouwkunst en hare architectonische mogelijkheden', in: *Bouwkundig Weekblad*, 42 (1921), pp. 147-160.

**10.** T. van Doesburg, 'Aanteekeningen over monumentale kunst. Naar aanleiding van twee bouwfragmenten (hall in vacantiehuis te Noordwijkerhout. Bijlage 1)', in: *De Stijl*, 2 (1918), no. 1, p. 12.

**11.** C. Blotkamp, 'In de periferie van De Stijl: H.H. Kamerlingh Onnes', in: *Jong Holland* 1 (1999), pp. 23-31.

**12.** Fondation Custodia, Paris. Two letters from T. van Doesburg to Oud ( 2 June and 12 July 1920) refer respectively to Van Doesburg's colour scheme for 'the entire holiday hostel' (the shutters and external fencing, for which drawings are requested) and to a technical solution for the perimeter fence. E. van Straaten, *Klare en lichte, gesloten vormen, geaccentueerd door diepe en pure kleuren. Het werk van Theo van Doesburg in de architectuur*, Amsterdam 1992, p. 46.

**Sources**

CCA: ph1984: 0793, ph 1984: 1016
Getty: 890126-8**, 890126-9**
NAI: OUDJ-vo 1-6, OUDJ-vo 3001, OUDJ-ph 96, OUDJ-ph 1787-1790, MAQV-538
RKD: Van Doesburg Archive

**Articles**

T. van Doesburg, 'Aanteekeningen over monumentale kunst. Naar aanleiding van twee bouwfragmenten (hall in vacantiehuis te Noordwijkerhout. Bijlage I)', in: *De Stijl*, 2(1918)1, pp. 10-12
H. Hoste, 'Het vacantiehuis te Noordwijk', in: *De Telegraaf*, 1 March 1919
J.J.P. Oud, 'Vacantiehuis Noordwijkerhout', Illustrations to T. van Doesburg, in *De Stijl*, 2(1918), pp. 10-12
Gratema, 'Vacantiehuis te Noordwijkerhout', in: *Klei*, 12(1920)2, pp. 13-19

**Literature**

Y.A. Bois, 'Mondrian and the Theory of Architecture', in: *Assemblage. A Critical Journal of Architecture and Design Culture*, 4(1987), pp. 104-106
U. Barbieri, *J.J.P. Oud*, Rotterdam 1987, pp. 36-39
S.U. Barbieri, C. Boekraad and J. Leerling (eds), *Grondbegrippen van de nieuwe kunst*, Nijmegen 1983
J. Beckett, 'De Vonk, Noordwijk; an example of early De Stijl cooperation', in: *Art History*, 3(1980)2, pp. 202-217
C. Blotkamp, 'Theo van Doesburg', in: C. Blot-

Doesburg described the plasticity of the staircase as follows: *By abandoning every external, non-architectural decoration and sculptural detail (figures, mouldings, etc.) the plastic rhythm of the architecture achieves its full* autonomous *expression. ...The ascending stair, the pierced walls, the side benches and the bench on the upper corridor, they all have a logical, functional meaning that expresses itself three-dimensionally in a single organic form. This form, from whatever side it is viewed, has a remarkably rhythmic effect.*[7] The effect of Oud's architectural spatial composition is complemented and enhanced by Van Doesburg's strictly *artistic* contribution in the form of tiled floor designs for the hall below and the landing above. Van Doesburg saw his tile compositions and the colour scheme he devised for the doors and wall surfaces as an example of spatial effect in 'the manner of painting-in-architecture' in which the architectural elements are stripped of their mass and corporality and thus turned into a means of 'painting' space.[8] Whereas Van der Leck conceived the relation between architecture and painting as pragmatic and functional, a matter of mutual influence, in De Vonk this relation is conceived as complementary; as a totality of independent, active and interacting forces in which the movement of the plastic art (the effect of the colour composition) is brought to rest by the contrary movement of the architecture. In De Vonk, two concepts of spatial art are *simultaneously* at work, and that gives the hall and its surroundings that rare tension and energy that Van Doesburg and Oud tried to achieve together in a new collective monumental *style*. Tried, for both Oud and Van Doesburg were critical of the final result. In a caption to a photograph of the hall, Oud wrote in 1921: *Hall. Painterly interior solution. Attempt at three-dimensional realization of the two-dimensional demonstrated in illustration 3 (Mondrian's* Composition, *1918), but the elements still appear too detached.*[9] Van Doesburg viewed De Vonk, like most of the collective projects realized in the early years of De Stijl, as merely the first step on the road to the ultimate goal of *monumental art: to place human beings in (rather than in front of) visual art and so enable them to take part in it, on a thoroughly modern footing.*[10] An assertion that makes C. Blotkamp's interpretation of the floor as a composition geared to human movement perfectly acceptable.[11]

That these aspects of De Vonk's genesis made it a superb experimental subject for the theoretical casuistry of a few *De Stijl* collaborators was not immediately grasped by everyone: not by contemporary architectural critics, nor for that matter by the socially-inspired client who may have thought that the abstraction had been carried too far, for in 1918 she commissioned Harm Kamerlingh Onnes to design five stained-glass windows halfway up the stairs. Much, of course, to the fury of Van Doesburg, who felt that the new, dark-coloured windows all but destroyed the effect of the light, one of the 'foremost aspects of spatial art'. He nonetheless retained his interest in De Vonk, wrote about it enthusiastically in *De Stijl* and in 1920 produced another (executed) colour design for the exterior woodwork (shutters and fencing).[12]



kamp (et al.), *De Beginjaren van De Stijl*, Utrecht 1982, pp. 31-32
C. Blotkamp, 'In de periferie van De Stijl: H.H. Kamerlingh Onnes', in: *Jong Holland* 1 (1999), pp. 23-31
A. Doig, *Theo van Doesburg. Painting into architecture, theory into practice*, Cambridge, London etc. 1986, pp. 58-71
H. Esser, 'J.J.P. Oud', in: Blotkamp (et al.), *De Beginjaren van De Stijl*, Utrecht 1993, p. 135
H. van der Heide, 'De Vonk en de Vereeniging "Buitenbedrijf"', in: *Maatschappelijk Werk: Opstellen aangeboden aan Emilie Knappert op haar zeventigsten verjaardag*, Amsterdam 1930, pp. 253-260
H.E. Oud, *J.J.P. Oud. Architekt 1890-1963. Feiten en herinneringen gerangschikt*, The Hague 1984, p. 22, pp. 39-41
R.W. Oxenaar, *Bart van der Leck tot 1920. Een primitief van de nieuwe tijd*, Utrecht 1976
S. Polano, *J.J.P. Oud Architettura Olandese*, Milan 1981, pp. 17-18
G. Stamm, *J.J.P. Oud. Bauten und Projekte 1906 bis 1963*, Mainz, Berlin 1984, pp. 41-44
E. van Straaten, *Klare en lichte, gesloten vormen, geaccentueerd door diepe en pure kleuren. Het werk van Theo van Doesburg in de architectuur*, Amsterdam 1992, pp. 45-48

by J. J. P. Oud

The monumental is by nature intrinsic rather than extrinsic. It can manifest itself in both the small and the large. Material factors play no role in this.

As such, one could superficially claim that a small country cannot have a monumental style. In the Netherlands there is room and need for a monumental style! Architecture, like Painting, is evolving in the direction of the universal and the monumental. It follows the line set by the Berlage School and is fundamentally opposed to the so-called Amsterdam School, where the monumental has been corrupted into something that is basically decadent.

Only the universal is important in attaining a style. A monumental style will emerge through a collaboration of artistic expressions operating within a purity of means, because collaboration is only possible when each art form operates within its own domain and eschews all impure elements. The defining feature of each art form comes to the fore in such a situation and the need for collaboration naturally makes itself felt.

The defining feature of Architecture is Plasticity. Architecture is plastic art: the art of spatial determination and as such expressing what is most universal in the townscape: in the single building and in the joining together and juxtaposition of buildings. Town planning is generally dominated by two factors: street and square. The street as a string of houses; the square as the focus of the streets.

The townscape is determined chiefly by the streetscape.

In determining the character of the modern street, it is necessary to proceed on idealistic and practical grounds from the streetscape as a whole. On idealistic grounds, as indicated above; on practical grounds, because in modern town planning private initiative will increasingly disappear and the construction of individual houses will be replaced by mass housing and perimeter blocks.

The modern streetscape, in sharp contrast to the old streetscape in which the houses are grouped arbitrarily, will be dominated by housing blocks in which the houses are so arranged as to create a rhythmic play of plane and mass.

The main task for the modern architect is therefore the perimeter block. This task, which requires government involvement, calls for a distinctive solution which it has not yet found in the blocks realized to date, in which traditional influences have continued to hold sway.

The characteristic beauty of the modern urban block will manifest itself in a very pronounced rhythm and acceptance of modern materials.

The radical renunciation of the sham roof occupies a prominent position, resulting in the acceptance of the flat roof and its consequences: the solution of horizontal spans by way of iron or concrete structures, the treatment of wall planes and wall openings in modern materials.

In this way the architecture of the perimeter block will to a large degree determine the character of the modern aesthetic in Architecture.

Leiden, 9-7-'17

# 31/ Seafront Terrace Housing (Strandboulevard)

Scheveningen 1917

Oud's design for the 'Strandboulevard' is an example of a project that since the moment of publication has always been seen in isolation from any concrete commission or actual site. Although the design exists in several forms – as model, as perspective sketch and as preliminary study – it has never been treated as a serious building project, but rather as an exhibition 'item' and an obligatory illustration in books and articles about *De Stijl*. From the moment when Theo van Doesburg, writing in the first issue of *De Stijl*, called it a springboard for a 'monumental mass housing based on purely plastic principles', which is to say a first-rate example of style-conscious building in the Netherlands, the Strandboulevard became a typical demonstration model. Oud never bothered to contradict this view of things and it was not until a year before his death that he admitted to the architectural historian J. Joedicke: *Those houses were designed for a cousin who subsequently went bankrupt so that nothing further came of the design.*[1] This statement is confirmed by source materials. The client was a property developer, the Maatschappij 'Oostduinen Scheveningen', involved in a building project on a site in Scheveningen between the 'esplanade and Gevers Deynotweg'. There is a 'land division plan' in which the site in question is subdivided into two strips of development, the first of which, along the esplanade, contains nine lots and the second, along Gevers Deynotweg, eleven. The two strips are separated by a (dead-end) internal street. It is quite possible that Oud received a (preliminary design) commission for the seafront block only. The nine lots in the subdivision plan are each nine metres wide, except for the middle one which is one metre wider and seems to have been intended to be a gateway building providing access to the internal street. If so, Oud ignored this in his design. He took a similarly cavalier approach in projecting the dwellings over the lots, treating the lot structure as little more than an opportunity for a rhythmic play of taut lines and blocks that slide in front, along and into one another according to an ingenious system of symmetries. The surviving drawings suggest that Oud designed a terrace of nine luxury units capable of being repeated ad infinitum. All rooms on all floors are reached via a single front door and a narrow staircase. Staggered composition aside, the floor plans for all three floors are identical: evidently at this stage of the design Oud was not yet interested in detailed domestic arrangements. All his attention was focused on the spatial–expressive effects of the residential function on the architecture of the terrace. The architectural design of the block as a whole is characterized by a stark contrast between the decidedly expressive, not to say cubic, articulation of the sea elevation and the decidedly flat wall of the rear elevation along the internal street. But in the last instance the design revolved around the front elevation – at least, this is the conclusion suggested by the many scrawls and sketches of this facade which appear to be an exercise in mastery of architectural

Model of Strandboulevard (NAI, MAQV-238), built *circa* 1951/ OUDJ-ph 90, NAI, Rotterdam

movement. One of these preliminary studies also shows that the Strandboulevard design did not start out as the unornamented, refined and white (rendered?) manifestation depicted later on, in particular by the model. At a certain stage of the design Oud had thought in terms of the same kind of ornamentation as used for De Vonk: masonry ornaments above the windows, wood panelling above the bay windows and (painted) railings for the terrace walls.[2] What ties Oud's Strandboulevard to *De Stijl* is not sundry stylistic or formal characteristics (what Oud was to dismiss as '*De Stijl* architecture' after 1921) but a 'different' architectural method, one which has less to do with Berlage and everything to do with Theo van Doesburg.

Unlike Villa Allegonda, where architecture and painting were more or less independent of one another and the dwelling was certainly not conceived 'as the true environment for the true painting' and also unlike De Vonk, where architect and painter were simultaneously engaged in 'shaping space' using different means, the Strandboulevard was a strictly architectural affair, an experiment in which the abstract method evolved in modern visual art was tested for its usefulness in architecture. As such, the project can be seen as a direct outgrowth of the many night-time conversations between Oud and Van Doesburg in Leiden in those years. Van Doesburg was also the first to acknowledge and formulate the significance of the Strandboulevard as an experiment in expressive architecture.[3] He saw Oud's Strandboulevard as a step towards architecture as 'monumental art', that is to say an architecture that serves the community by expressing universal values. It does this by not only using its true subject, space, in a functional sense, but also by expressing it visually, by means of abstract proportions. Thus are the conditions created for a new *style* that is characterized ethically by simplicity and self-restraint and aesthetically by the square. The square – as opposed to the 'scheefrond', a catch-all term of abuse for everything that is not square – is not just a functional form but first and foremost a concept that epitomizes the spirit of an age. In light of this somewhat cryptic position, Van Doesburg welcomed Oud's Strandboulevard as an example of style-conscious building. The true theme was 'space', not physical, material space, but space as *extension* in which *plane and mass are harmoniously resolved in relation to all spatial directions*, as Oud put it a year later in *De Stijl* in reference to a house by the American architect Frank Lloyd Wright.[4] This crystallization of space in height, breadth and depth resulted in a certain rhythm, a 'space–movement', that was in turn reinforced by horizontal and vertical profiles and frames of doors, windows and balconies and also, of course, by the alternation of light and dark resulting from the staggered facade. The architectural modelling of mass into space was not purely aesthetic; it also answered to the practical and/or functional purpose. If Oud's Strandboulevard was a springboard for a monumental art it was because in design-

**Site plan: the 'land division plan'/ 890126-13**, Getty, Los Angeles**

**Preliminary studies: plans of ground floor (left), first floor (centre) and second floor/ OUDJ-sc 15, NAI, Rotterdam**



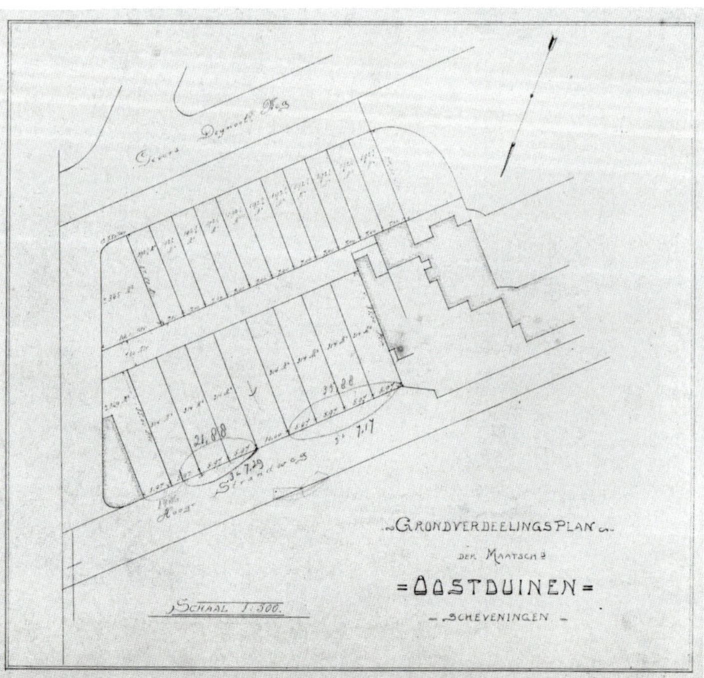


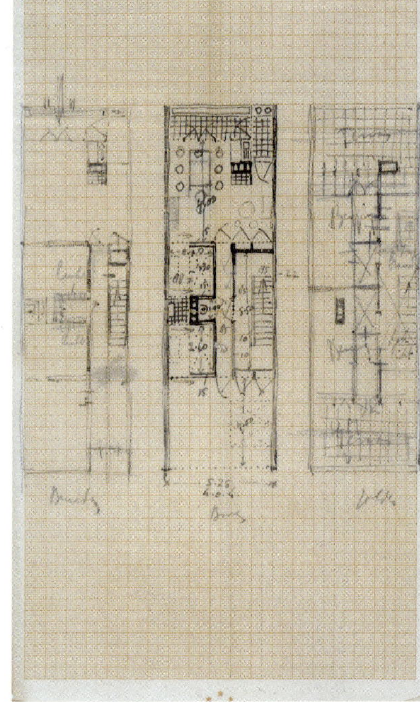

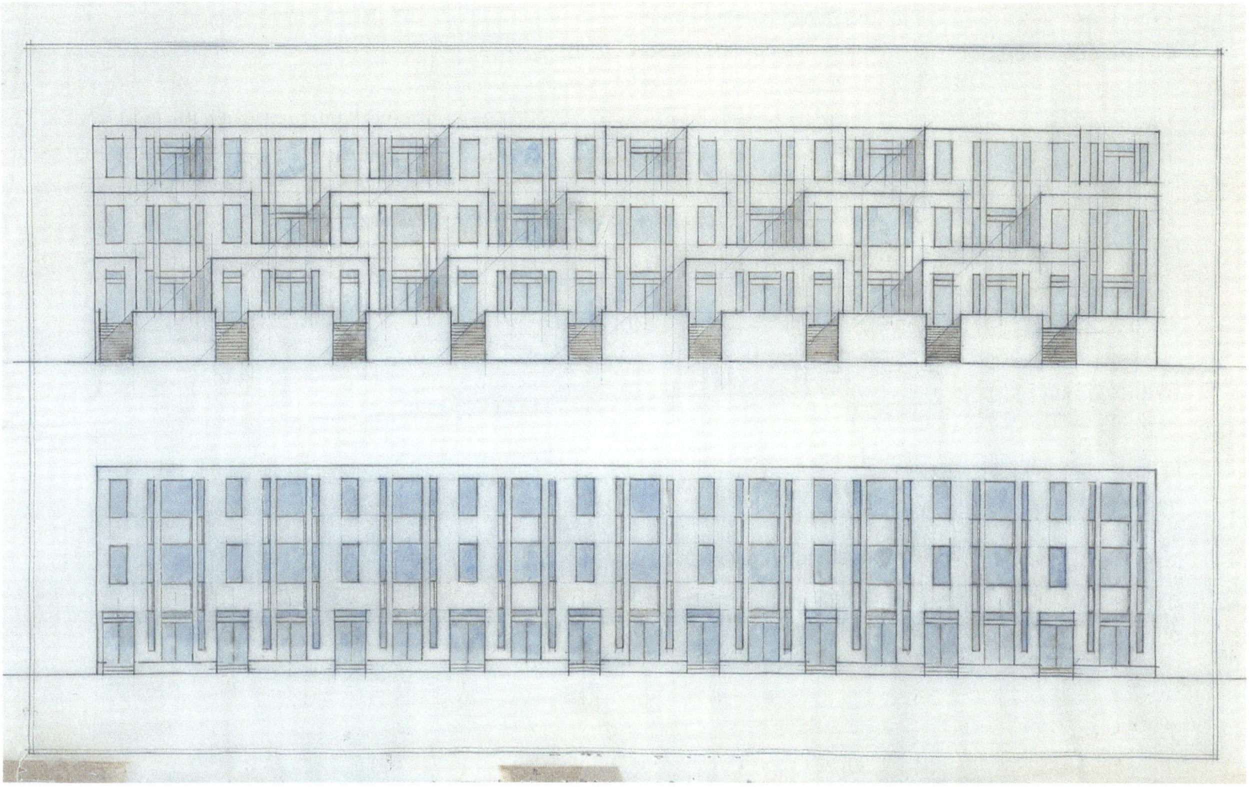

Final design (model-version): beach elevation (top) and inner street/ OUDJ-sb 7, NAI, Rotterdam

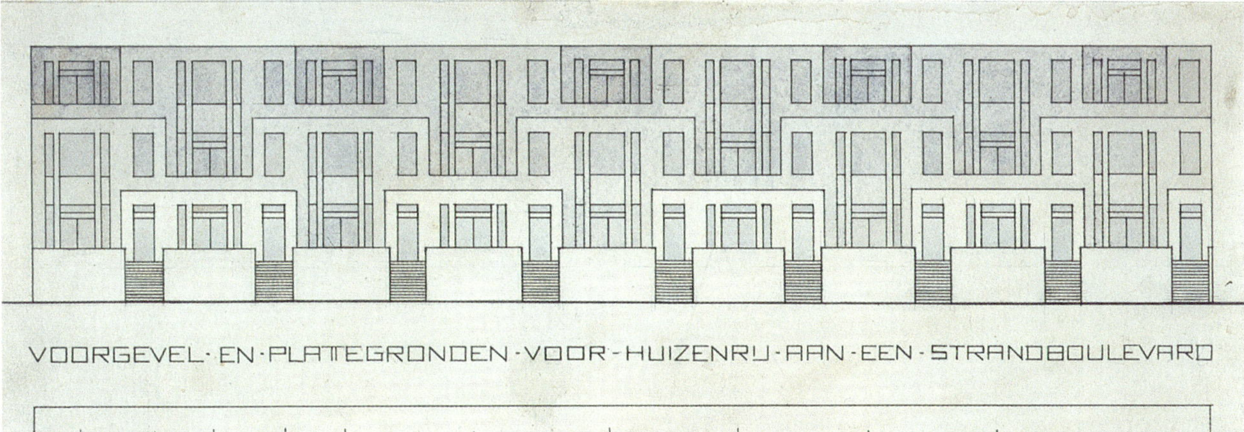


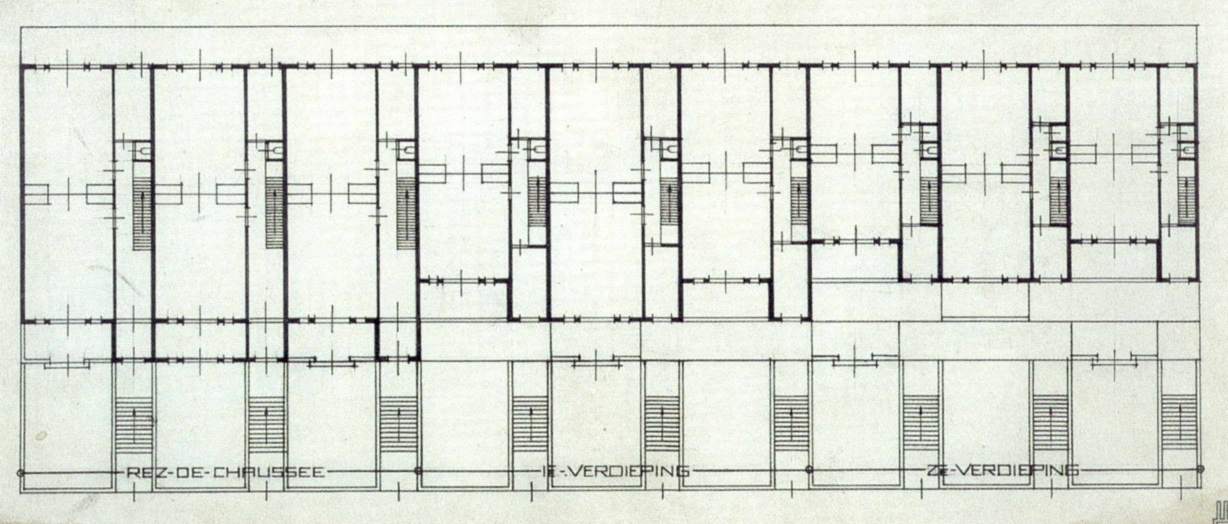


Final design (model-version): beach elevation (top) and plans of upper floors (bottom)/ OUDJ-sb 4, NAI, Rotterdam

ing his plan, the artist had concentrated on what happens inside and understood the unity of function in all the houses. It was this understanding that gave the motif of the horizontal and vertical relationships their eventual tension and expression and this was also the source of the striking 'similarity with good modern painting'.
Van Doesburg's interpretation was never contradicted by Oud, nor is it at odds with Oud's own contribution to the first issue of *De Stijl* entitled 'The Monumental Townscape'.[5] This short text has often been regarded as not much more than a summary of Berlage's urbanist ideas. Yet such a reading completely ignores the many turns of phrase and expressions borrowed from Van Doesburg which give the text a tone and content quite unlike anything by Berlage. In 1917 Oud was not yet working for the Rotterdam Housing Authority and his interest in the townscape was more in the nature of aesthetic speculation than based on any practical experience with mass housing construction.
The fact is that in 1917 Oud, too, was a strong proponent of monumental art, which he saw as emerging from a collaboration of all the different arts, but not before each art form had been individually purged of all (historical) ballast. Oud, like Van Doesburg, believed that the true subject of architecture is space. But not space as extension and dynamic datum as defined by the painter Van Doesburg, but space as *plasticity*. Literally: *Architecture as plasticity: the art of defining space and as such to express the most universal in the townscape: in the single building and in the combination and contraposition of buildings*. If this is Berlagian, it is Berlage engaged in a polemic with *De Stijl*. It followed that the most important task for the modern architect was the housing block, not as Berlage saw it, but the 'purified' housing block for which no aesthetic solution had yet been found. Before this could happen, architects first needed to acquaint themselves with recent developments in modern painting – in Cubism and Futurism – as previously referred to by Oud. There they would see how the new aesthetic was determined by 'rhythmic relationships of stone to space'. For the building block this meant the end of the 'sham roof' and the acceptance of *the flat roof with its consequences: the solution of horizontal spans by means of iron or concrete structures, the treatment of wall planes and wall openings in modern materials*.
Compared with Van Doesburg's critique, Oud's 'manifesto' is remarkably down-to-earth. Of course, it too is to some extent imbued with the idealistic notions of a new art that typified the early years of their friendship, but the main thrust of Oud's article is the plea for a division of labour, for setting the Berlagian legacy to rights, and in that sense 'The Monumental Townscape' is an indirect commentary on the design, made in that same year, for the Strandboulevard in Scheveningen.



**Notes**
**1.** Oud to J. Joedicke, 19 February 1962, OUDJ-B, NAI, Rotterdam.
**2.** Canadian Centre for Architecture, Montreal.
**3.** T. van Doesburg, 'J.J.P. Oud. Ontwerp voor een complex huizen voor een Strandboulevard', in: *De Stijl* 1(1917)1, pp. 13-14.
**4.** J.J.P. Oud, 'Architectonische beschouwing bij bijlage VIII', in: *De Stijl*, 4(1918)1, pp. 39-41.
**5.** J.J.P. Oud, 'Het monumentale stadsbeeld', in: *De Stijl*, 1(1917)1, pp. 10-11.

**Sources**
CCA: dr1984: 0019-0020, dr1984: 0489, dr1985: 0401, ph1984: 1014-1017
Getty: 890126-13**
NAI: OUDJ-sb 1-7, OUDJ-ph 82- 95, OUDJ-ph 1784-1786, OUDJ-B, OUDJ-sc 6-7, OUDJ-sc 15-16, MAQV-238 , OUDJ-sc 6-7, OUDJ-sc 15-16

**Articles**
T. van Doesburg, 'J.J.P. Oud. Ontwerp voor een complex huizen voor een Strandboulevard', in: *De Stijl* 1(1917)1, pp. 13-14
J.J.P. Oud, 'Architectonische beschouwing bij bijlage VIII', in: *De Stijl*, 4(1918)1, pp. 39-41
J.J.P. Oud, 'Het monumentale stadsbeeld', in: *De Stijl*, 1(1917)1, pp. 10-11

**Literature**
U. Barbieri, *J.J.P. Oud*, Rotterdam 1987, p. 35
H.E. Oud, *J.J.P. Oud. Architekt 1890-1963. Feiten en herinneringen gerangschikt*, The Hague 1984, p. 29, p. 44, p. 118
S. Polano, *J.J.P. Oud Architettura Olandese*, Milan 1981, p. 19
G. Stamm, *J.J.P. Oud. Bauten und Projekte 1906 bis 1963*, Mainz, Berlin 1984, pp. 32-40

T. van Doesburg, 'J.J.P. Oud. Ontwerp voor een complex huizen voor een strandboulevard', in: *De Stijl*, 1(1917)1

# J.J.P. Oud. Design for a housing complex for a seaside boulevard.

In this century of universal art reform it goes without saying that in architecture, too, the plastic consciousness is awakening. The artists among the architects have begun an offensive against the archaistic patchwork of their predecessors. The notion of an absolute architecture is reestablishing itself. The serious architect-artist is starting to reflect once more on the essential prerequisites of monumental art. Because the architect-artist remains tied to practice, his task consists in this: using space and expressing aesthetic relationships from the inside out. The exterior expresses the interior and both form a perfect unity: the building. Self-restraint and simplicity are primary conditions for style, in the best sense. To convey something of the essence of the new style in words we would have to say that the plastic consciousness of the modern workman sets the "square" against the "contortions" of the baroque. The square is not just a definition of the form, but the expression of a concept that characterizes the spirit of the times. An excellent example of style-conscious building of recent years in the Netherlands is the housing complex designed by the young Leiden architect, J.J.P. Oud. Plane and mass are harmoniously resolved in relation to all spatial directions. Space is as it were crystallized. There is a movement of planes and masses in depth, height, width, which lends the whole a certain rhythm. This architectural rhythm is strictly speaking: space-movement. This space-movement is further accentuated by the horizontal and vertical bands of the verandah doors, windows and frames. The effects of advancing light and receding shadow will amplify this movement still more. Because the artist, in designing his plan, concentrated on what happens inside and understood the unity of function in all the houses, he has been able to repeat a certain motif, both internally and externally. Not monotonously, but full of animated expression in a tension of horizontal and vertical relationships we see this motif dominate the whole. Because of this it bears a striking similarity to good modern painting.

With this design for a "Housing Complex for a Seaside Boulevard" a young Dutch architect-artist of the twentieth century has expressed the possibility of a monumental mass construction based on purely plastic principles.

v.D.

# 32/ Design for Factory and Warehouse

**Purmerend, Jaagweg** **1919-1920**

The designs for both the factory and the warehouse at Purmerend were, from their very inception, part of a publicity campaign, firstly that of Van Doesburg, who used them to support his presentation of *De Stijl* as a credible international avant-garde movement, and later that of Oud himself who produced them as evidence of his historic role as pioneer of international, modern architecture. As a result, their significance as designs for functional buildings on a real site has tended to be pushed into the background.
After plans for the expansion of the existing factory in the centre of Purmerend had been drawn up in 1916 and subsequently shelved, the company decided in 1918 to build a new factory on the outskirts of the town. In the meantime the distillery business had passed to two of Oud's cousins. As in 1916, the commission was awarded to the Alkmaar architect D. Saal, a childhood friend of one of the directors. Saal in turn brought Oud into the project with the result that Oud took on the design of both the factory and the warehouse. It appears from a letter from Van Doesburg to Oud that the first designs related to a store-cum-office – the warehouse – which was already put out to tender in January 1919. The surviving drawings (if, that is, they relate to this stage of the design) show a rectangular, window-less hall with a distillery projecting from the front elevation. The symmetrical layout gives the building an unmistakable classic look very similar to that of the celebrated factory by Gropius and Meyer at the 1914 Werkbund exhibition in Cologne. In the ensuing months Oud worked on a much larger expansion plan encompassing the entire works. From correspondence it emerges that Oud had not only informed Van Doesburg about the project at an early stage but that he had also invited him – in his capacity as artist, of course – to participate in the project. What the correspondence does not make clear is whether the commission was for stained-glass windows, a floor painting or a mural. On 24 June, Van Doesburg wrote: *If it goes ahead I would like to know beforehand whether your cousin insists on figurative work or whether I can be purely abstract. Even in the first case the possibilities are considerable. The art–architecture relationship can lead to a composition that expresses the new spirit.*[1] In addition Rietveld, who was 'mulling over' a bedstead for Oud's newborn son Hans, was engaged to produce a model. The first designs for the factory were made in the summer and autumn of 1919 and subsequently modified in consultation with the client. On 8 November 1919, Van Doesburg wrote to Oud: *Rietveld was here on Wednesday. He is waiting for the drawings of the factory so that he can cut it in wood, but in accordance with the latest, modified design. Can you send them to him yet?* But this was not all. In the same letter Van Doesburg asked Oud to make a black-and-white drawing of the factory for a poster to be sent around the world *by way of demonstration! I'm really enthusiastic about this idea. We still have the best architecture. All the modern-thinking people will like your architec-*

Perspective/ OUDJ-fa 20, NAI, Rotterdam

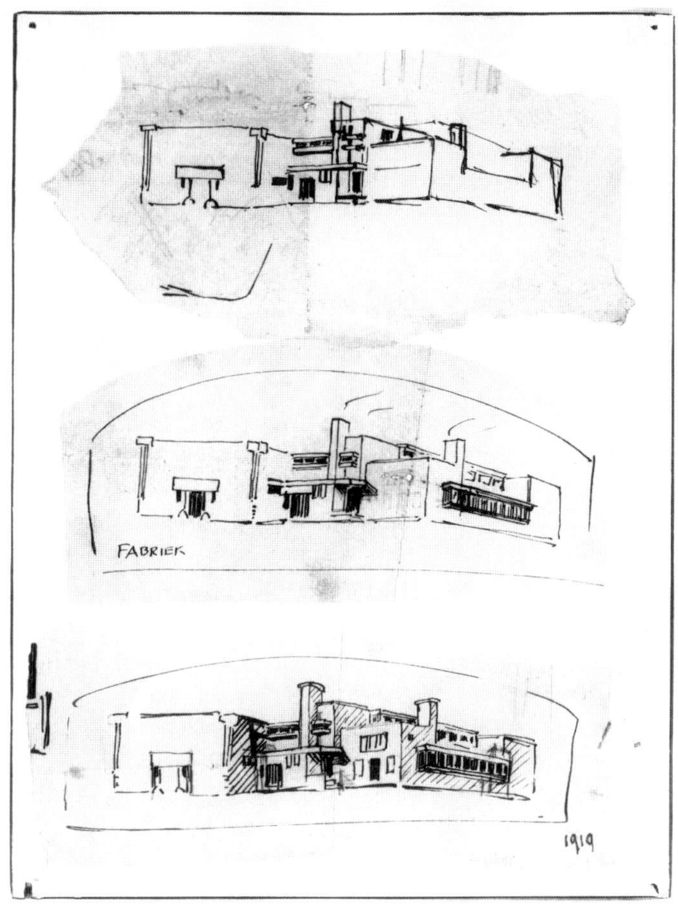


Sketches/ OUDJ-fa 19, NAI, Rotterdam

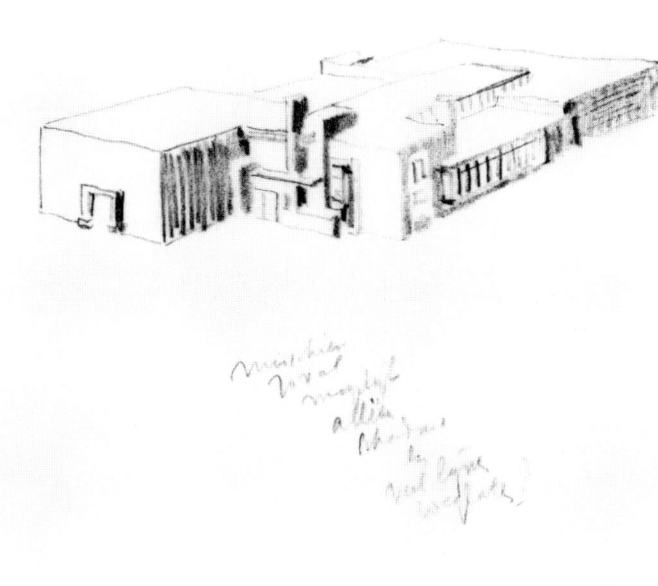

Sketch/ OUDJ-fa 1, NAI, Rotterdam

*ture.*[2] However, not long afterwards the plan was cancelled and it was decided instead to renovate the existing buildings in the town centre. In May 1922, there was renewed hope that the warehouse might go ahead after all, witness a postcard from Saal to Oud, but after a few months these plans went the way of the earlier ones.[3] This was all very frustrating for Van Doesburg who, with an eye to promoting *De Stijl* – as group, magazine and idea – in the artistic world of the French capital, had set his heart on being able to point to a building realized according to *De Stijl* principles. On 24 February 1920, Van Doesburg wrote to Oud from Paris, where he was staying with Mondrian, to say how extremely pleased he was that Oud had made a perspective drawing of the factory specially for *De Stijl*: *We were both very pleased about this since it shows the new spirit, which is still so rare in architecture, isn't it?*[4] A month later, in the famous letter demolishing Jan Wils, Van Doesburg wrote: *You don't know how happy I was to find your factory waiting for me on my return. Wonderful that something like this is possible, even if it hasn't been built (I'll never forgive your cousin. He is the one who stood in the way of realization and patronizes rubbish like Jongert).* A little further on he is close to issuing an order: *Make big propaganda drawings of the factory for events abroad. Don't forget that Wils will try to put a spoke in your wheels.*[5] Ten days later he returns to the subject: *Frans Netscher has asked for the factory with my article for the Holl. Revue. I've sent him the whole lot. Sure to be all right. It's a neutral magazine that publishes everything up to date. Oh! If only it had been built. That would have been something. It would have been an international success.*[6] All the indications are that at that moment Van Doesburg saw the factory and warehouse as the only pure, architectural prototypes of *De Stijl* ideas. Hence his incomprehension in the face of Oud's defence of Jan Wils's integrity: *I don't understand how you can fail to be convinced that I see* you *as the* only *and most steadfast architect of the Nieuwe Beelding and as such will succeed in placing you in the* international *art scene. That's why it would be so wonderful Oudje, if out of our shared love of the new we could for once realize a* work *that I could present as a complete model. That's why I would so much have liked the factory to go ahead and why the cancellation was a deep disappointment for me!*[7] In the ensuing years the factory was a regular feature of every exhibition and every publication devoted to *De Stijl*, beginning with the major exhibition in Rosenberg's gallery in Paris (1923), where the plan and photographs of a model were on show together with the famous perspective drawings. Oud's own views about his design are known only through remarks made in the 1950s when the factory was offered as proof of Oud's historical status as a pioneer of the Modern Movement in international architecture. There is only one indication of what he thought about the design in the years when he was actually working on it. In the published version of his celebrated

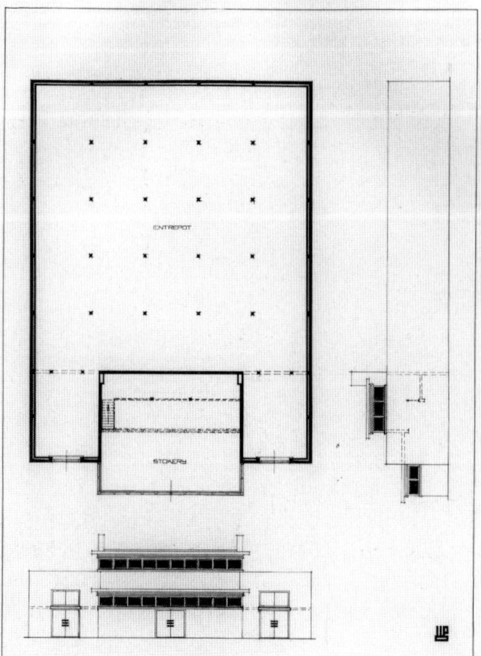

**Warehouse, plan and elevations/ OUDJ-fa 8, NAI, Rotterdam**

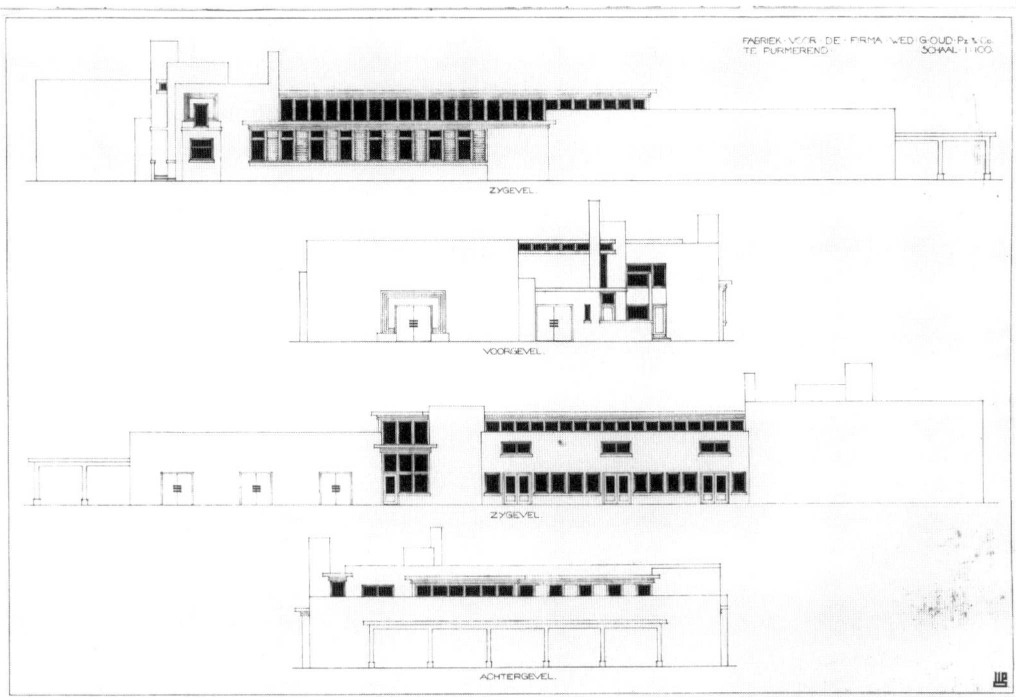


Elevations/ OUDJ-fa 10, NAI, Rotterdam

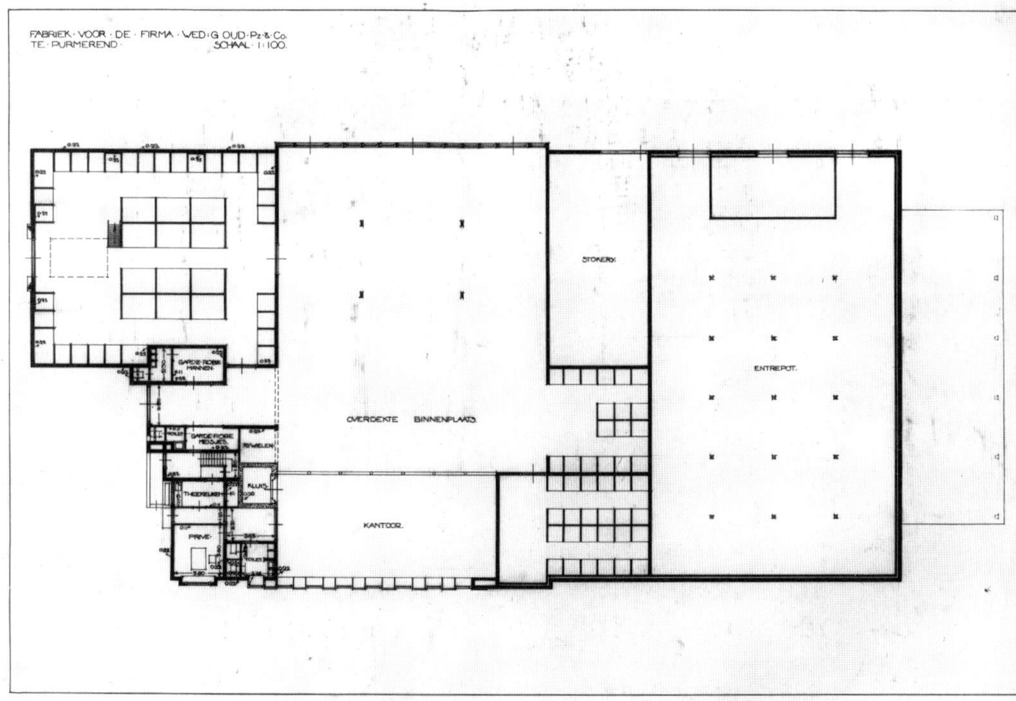


Plan of ground floor/ OUDJ-fa 11, NAI, Rotterdam

Opbouw lecture on the future of architecture he included the well-known perspective of the factory with the following caption: *attempt at architectural rendering by purely architectural means, in which the decorative element has not yet been entirely conquered (see e.g. the left-hand entrance door).*[8] Considering what was being achieved in Europe (and in the United States) at that moment in the field of modern architecture in general and factory building in particular, Van Doesburg's (if perhaps not Mondrian's) 'shock of recognition' must surely be a cause for mild astonishment.

The reason why the factory was such a successful model during *De Stijl*'s early years, was because it convincingly demonstrated that Cubism was a useful system not only for making abstract art, but also for making modern architecture. Plan and perspective – Van Doesburg insisted on this combination – showed that although the stage of decomposition and purification (of ornament and stylistic imitation) was not entirely finished, any more than it was in Neo-Plastic painting, it had already been followed by that of *integration.* In the first design phase, Oud elaborated on the earlier project of 1916, drawing a linear structure consisting of two volumes separated by a raised connecting-piece. In the second phase, which was to be rounded off with a model by Rietveld, the complex became a lot more compact and, in terms of plasticity, acquired a more pronounced character. Perspective sketches reveal how Oud had tried to organize and resolve the logic of the programme ('the ordering of the building's function') in a pure and monumental architecture,[9] characterized by self-restraint, absence of ornament and determination of proportions. In all known sketches and drawings, the factory is never presented front-on but always from an angle, with a full view of the entrance zone where 'the essence of architecture is evoked' in the taut balance of horizontal and vertical relationships of lines and masses.

There is no doubt that Oud, in his design of factory and warehouse, as in the graphic representation of that design, was strongly influenced by the American architect Frank Lloyd Wright. Notwithstanding all Oud's later misrepresentations on this point, Wright's buildings (and in particular, published drawings) offered a dramatic example of how a cubist approach could result in a 'plastic architecture'. Oud was already familiar with Wright's work via Berlage, of course, and also from books and magazines. But it was Theo van Doesburg who drew Oud's attention to Frank Lloyd Wright's importance as a 'cubist architect'. In an undated letter, probably from October 1920, Van Doesburg is quite definite on this point: *I have certainly learnt a great deal from you about architecture, but even when I first met you I believe I already had some intuitive understanding, because you will recall that apart from your work (the significance of which I may have been the first to recognize) I immediately admired Wright and specifically the house you reviewed in* De Stijl. *It was a revelation for me, as was the work of Mondriaan before I knew him personally.*[10] Van Doesburg taught Oud to look at Wright's work with different eyes, a process that was accelerated by his acquaintance with Wright's ideas about the new plasticity and space and, in particular, about technology and the machine. A case in point is the penetrating analysis in *De Stijl* of the famous Robie House in Chicago (1909), in which Oud calls attention to two architectural innovations that also appear in his own designs of this period: in the stairs in De Vonk, in the Strandboulevard and, of course, in the factory at Purmerend.[11] To start with, Oud was fascinated by Wright's solution of modern building issues – programme, building industry, technology, materials – in such a way as to produce pure architecture; that is to say, a method of building that expresses the functional organization from the inside out, in a 'conscious massing'. The second aspect was perhaps even more important and related to a 'new plasticity', the architectural variant of the pictorial conception of space as *extension.* By this Oud was referring to the dynamics of the building, achieved not through superficial details and ornaments, but by *a separation of the masses from the whole ... His masses slide backwards and forwards and left and right. There are plastic effects in all directions and this interpenetration opens up new aesthetic possibilities for architecture on a purely structural basis.* This description was suspiciously close to Van Doesburg's earlier description of the cubist approach in contemporary art. Under the influence of Wright's formal concepts and his designs (for buildings, furniture, etc.)

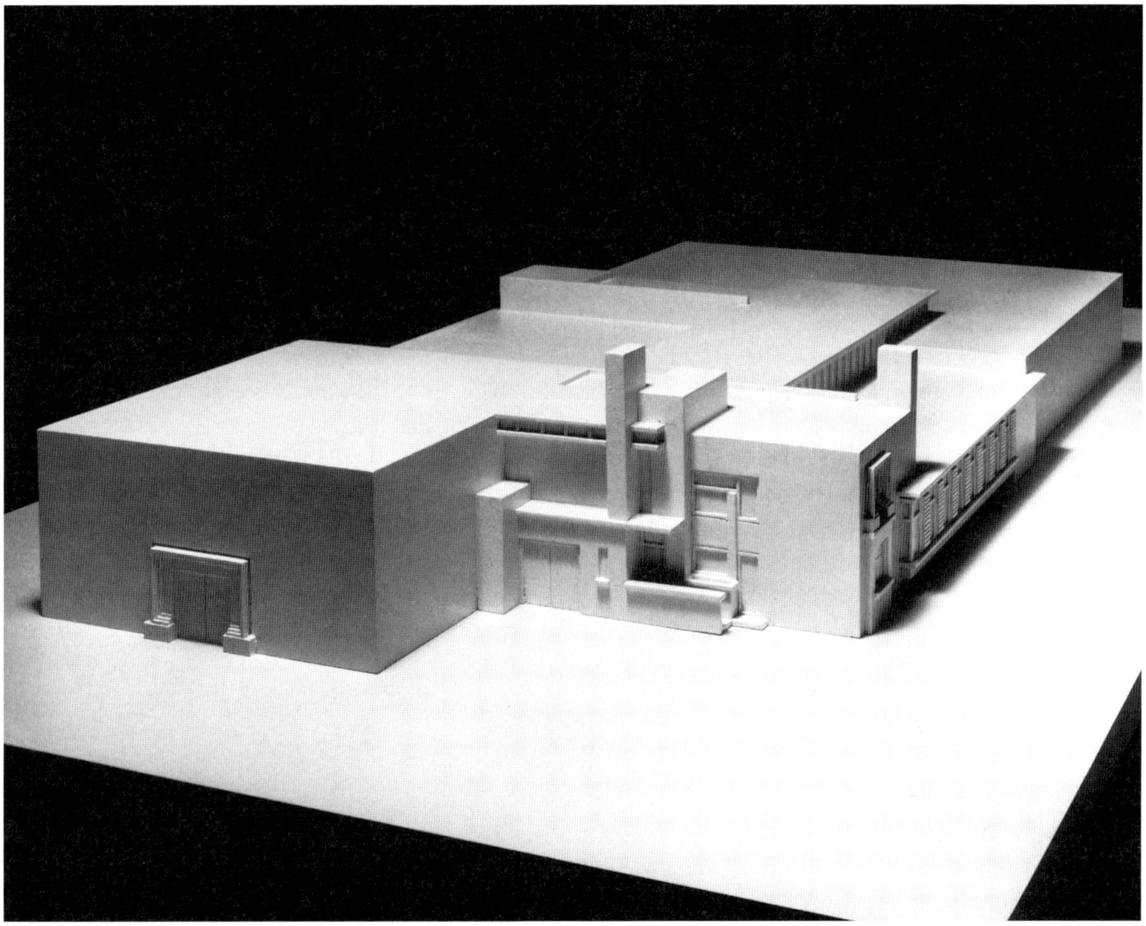

Model of factory (NAI, MAQV-224), built *circa* 1951/ OUDJ-ph 181, NAI, Rotterdam (Photo E. van Ojen)

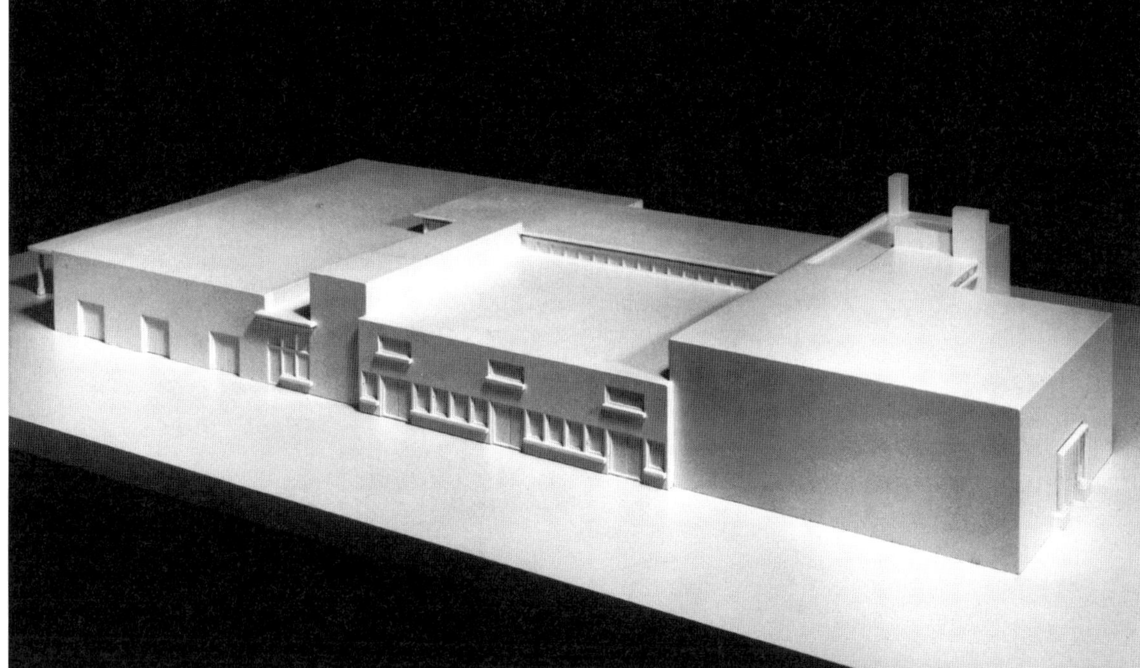

Model of factory (NAI, MAQV-224), built *circa* 1951/ OUDJ-ph 187, NAI, Rotterdam (Photo E. van Ojen)

based on mechanized production, Oud's original interest, not so much in Hermann Muthesius – whom he continued to admire all his life – but in the ideas of the Arts and Crafts Movement, on which his friendship with W.C. Brouwer among others was founded, was pushed into the background.

Oud's attitude to Wright reached a crisis, however, when it appeared that other architects associated with *De Stijl*, such as Van 't Hoff and Jan Wils, were also interested in Wright's work, even if this interest was, as Oud and Van Doesburg maintained, less theoretical and more superficial. From that moment the danger of imitation and formalism loomed large once more. Once again it was Theo van Doesburg who set the record straight and with such authority that Van 't Hoff – after his break – was virtually a non-person as far as *De Stijl* was concerned; Jan Wils was repeatedly denounced in public as a Wrightian imitator and copier, and Wright's name was deleted from the *De Stijl* annals in favour of terminology borrowed from Cubism. The high point of this drama was a commotion during a lecture by Mendelsohn in Gropius's house in Weimar in June 1921. Van Doesburg was present, as was H.T. Wijdeveld: *It was about Wright and on this occasion Wijdeveld mentioned Oud, Van 't Hoff and Wils as a group of Dutch followers of Wright. Whereupon I said that this might apply to Wils but not to you, nor to Van 't Hoff. That you had nothing at all to do with Wright.*[12] Van Doesburg had set out the line of action to be pursued vis à vis Frank Lloyd Wright and Oud, witness various letters to Gustav Platz (1926) and much later on to Philip Johnson (1951), Colin Rowe (1957) and Sigfried Giedion (1957)[13] among others, appears to have adhered to it until the day he died. The end result of this code of behaviour was that the Purmerend factory, instead of going down in history as an interesting, but by no means unique, example of European adoption of Wright's prairie house architecture, has been seen as a unique and highly original prototype of cubist architecture. In the mid-1920s, long after he had broken with *De Stijl* and Van Doesburg and was reaping international success with his white housing blocks at Rotterdam, Hoek van Holland and Stuttgart, Oud distanced himself from this terminology, too, preferring to describe the Strandboulevard and the factory as examples of an architecture of transition. The first signs of this change can be detected in an article in *De Stijl* in 1927: *Collaborating with colleagues from the free arts was attractive to me, and it was with great pleasure that I participated in the journal* De Stijl, *a pleasure which – in artistic terms – I never regretted! Through this collaboration I was able to transform the principles of plastic art into architecture. The result: cubist houses, interesting solely in their effort to achieve a pure architecture, well-balanced proportions, straight lines, tight forms, in short: a well-constructed architectural complex from the aesthetic viewpoint, with an inner vitality that architecture was lacking. But it wasn't properly understood: it was just a stage in the development towards a clear, simple, severe and pure architecture, but in general, all people saw were the romantic possibilities contained in the procedure. The amusement of accumulating cubes, prisms and so forth was born: an architecture without tension, accidental in composition, formless, a new decorative architecture, stamped 'cubist architecture' by a critic as blind as the artists were avid; a 'cubist architecture' which had less to do with cubism than the architecture that had come before it. Fortunately true cubism in architecture is almost never built! It was a spiritual movement, in preparation for the new architecture! The new architecture is the architecture that needed cubism's constructive force. Though it borrowed from cubism, it surmounted cubism's effects. The architecture of tomorrow has other tendencies...*[14]



**Notes**

**1.** H. Esser, 'J.J.P. Oud', in: C. Blotkamp (et al.), *De Beginjaren van De Stijl, 1917-1922*, Utrecht 1983, pp. 127-154.

**2.** T. van Doesburg to Oud, 8 December 1919, Van Doesburg Archive, Rijksdienst Beeldende Kunst, The Hague.

**3.** H.E. Oud, *J.J.P. Oud, Architekt 1890-1963. Feiten en herinneringen gerangschikt*, The Hague 1984, pp. 48-49.

**4.** T. van Doesburg to Oud, 24 February 1920, Fondation Custodia, Paris.

**5.** T. van Doesburg, 28 March 1920, Fondation Custodia, Paris.

**6.** T. van Doesburg, 7 April 1920, Fondation Custodia, Paris.

**7.** T. van Doesburg to Oud, 12 July 1920, Fondation Custodia, Paris.

**8.** J.J.P.Oud, 'Over de toekomstige bouwkunst en hare architectonische mogelijkheden', in: *Bouwkundig*

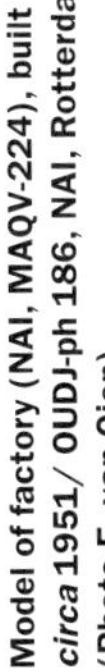

**Model of factory (NAI, MAQV-224), built *circa* 1951/ OUDJ-ph 186, NAI, Rotterdam (Photo E. van Ojen)**



*Weekblad*, 42(1921), pp. 147-160.
**9.** G. Stamm, *J.J.P. Oud. Bauten und Projekte 1906-1963*, Mainz, Berlin 1984, pp. 47-52.
**10.** T. van Doesburg to Oud, 1920, otherwise undated, Fondation Custodia, Paris.
**11.** J.J.P. Oud, 'Architectonische beschouwing bij bijlage VIII: woonhuis van Fred. C. Robie door Frank Lloyd Wright', in: *De Stijl* 1(1918)4, pp. 38-41.
**12.** Van Doesburg to Oud, 21 June 1921, Fondation Custodia, Paris.
**13.** M. van Stralen, 'Kindred Spirits: Holland, Wright, and Wijdeveld', in: A. Alofsin, *Frank Lloyd Wright and Beyond*, Berkeley 1999, pp. 45-65.
**14.** J.J.P. Oud, untitled, in: *De Stijl*, 7 (1927), pp. 38-41.

**Sources**
CCA: dr1984: 0024-0026, dr1984: 0499, ph1984: 0819-0821, ph1984: 0866, ph1984: 1027-1033, ph1984: 1042
Getty: 890126-box 3, F19, 890126-6**
NAI: OUDJ-fa 1-23, OUDJ-fa 3001, OUDJ-ph 1828-1829, OUDJ-ph 1670-1671, OUDJ-ph 179-187, OUDJ-B

**Articles**
J.J.P. Oud, 'Architectonische beschouwing bij bijlage VIII: woonhuis van Fred. C. Robie door Frank Lloyd Wright', in: *De Stijl* 1(1918)4, pp. 38-41
J.J.P. Oud, 'Over de toekomstige bouwkunst en hare architectonische mogelijkheden', in: *Bouwkundig Weekblad*, 42(1921)24, pp. 147-160
J.J.P. Oud, untitled, in: *De Stijl*, 1(1927)6, pp. 38-41

**Literature**
U. Barbieri, *J.J.P. Oud*, Rotterdam 1987, pp. 46-49
H. Esser, 'J.J.P. Oud', in: C. Blotkamp (et al.), *De Beginjaren van De Stijl, 1917-1922*, Utrecht 1983, pp. 127-154
H.E. Oud, *J.J.P. Oud, Architekt 1890-1963. Feiten en herinneringen gerangschikt*, The Hague 1984, pp. 48-49
S. Polano, *J.J.P. Oud Architettura Olandese*, Milan 1981, p. 14, pp. 20-22
G. Stamm, *J.J.P. Oud. Bauten und Projekte 1906-1963*, Mainz, Berlin 1984, pp. 44-53, p. 94
M. van Stralen, 'Kindred Spirits: Holland, Wright, and Wijdeveld', in: A. Alofsin, *Frank Lloyd Wright and Beyond*, Berkeley 1999, pp. 45-65

The year 1919 was the high point in the short collaboration between Van Doesburg and Oud. In addition to several building projects – De Vonk, the factory at Purmerend and two housing blocks at Spangen in Rotterdam – they were also working closely together on the magazine *De Stijl*. In the autumn, Van Doesburg consulted Oud about a wooden studio and cottage in the dunes. Probably Van Doesburg had put something down on paper himself and then asked Oud for technical and architectural advice. On 5 November 1919, he wrote to Oud: *Many thanks for your drawing of the cottage. It's wonderfully lucid and gives a good idea of the totality with those elevation drawings.* A few weeks later, when more information was available about a possible location in the dunes and the financial aspects of the project, the plans were modified and the possibility explored of a modest 'cottage with *upper floor on the same site*' for Van Doesburg and his mother. Despite Van Doesburg's enthusiasm – *I can't stop thinking about it, how it gives me a wonderful opportunity ... to exhibit in my own studio and to create the interior* – the project turned out to be well beyond Van Doesburg's means. The only relic of the whole project is a sketch of a 'Studio in the Dunes' unmistakably signed by Oud. The building is as flat as a box, stands on the top of a dune and is far from lucid, so it cannot be the drawing Oud sent in November. It does give some idea of the initial phase of the project before there was any talk of a 'double cottage'. The architecture of the studio in the sketch is indirectly related to that of the factory on which Oud was working at this time. The studio is a smooth, undecorated volume in which the vertical elements such as pillars, dormers and chimney are completely subordinate to the dominant, context-inspired horizontality. As in the factory, there is an attempt around the entrance at what Oud himself would at that time have called 'cubistic form tightening'.[1]

Sketch of studio/ OUDJ-hw 5, NAI, Rotterdam



**Notes**
**1.** Most of the information relating to the studio came from: E. van Straaten, *Theo van Doesburg. Schilder en architect*, The Hague 1988, pp. 71-72.

**Sources**
NAI: OUDJ-ds 1

**Literature**
G. Stamm, *J.J.P. Oud. Bauten und Projekte 1906-1963*, Mainz, Berlin 1984, p. 53
E. van Straaten, *Theo van Doesburg. Schilder en architect*, The Hague 1988, pp. 71-72

# J.J.P. Oud and H.P. Berlage

## Dutch Architecture

Oud was not only a skilled draughtsman, but a competent and effective writer. If there was one thing he learned from H.P. Berlage, whose acquaintance he made in 1910-1911, it was the value of newspapers and professional journals for propagating new architectural ideals and programmes. It was Berlage – to whom he listened long and intently during his student years – who introduced Oud to the leading German architectural theorists of his day: Sitte, Scheffler, Behrens, Wagner and especially Muthesius, and it was largely from Berlage's point of view that he read their writings. Berlage was also the major source of Oud's initially idealistic views about the relationship between art and society, a subject he also discussed at length during his Leiden period with the socially engaged ceramist W.C. Brouwer but which acquired a whole new meaning after his meeting with Theo van Doesburg. In the early years of *De Stijl*, therefore – and at the very moment when he was writing his most important theoretical contributions to the Modern Movement in architecture – Oud was caught in a curious conflict of views. Persuaded of the truth of Berlage's idealistic conceptions of beauty in society, he was simultaneously beguiled by the principles of a new art developed by Van Doesburg and Mondrian and of their relevance to a future architecture.

This dichotomy is evident in many of Oud's theoretical reflections on architecture. Oud was and remained a staunch Berlagian at a time when the master's authority was being severely tested by contemporary developments in architecture. While Van Doesburg had already drawn the obvious conclusion in 1920 and categorically declared that the Berlage of *Schoonheid in Samenleving* and *Pantheon der Menschheid* was 'blind to the great intellectual processes of his own day', Oud was never able to do this of his own accord.[1] Oud did not part company with Berlage until the end of the decade, when he was more or less driven to it by the latter's provocations.

Oud wrote quite extensively about the recent history of architecture in the Netherlands, the most comprehensive account being 'De ontwikkeling der moderne bouwkunst in Holland: verleden, heden, toekomst' (The Development of Modern Architecture in the Netherlands: Past, Present, Future, 1922-1923), which was the distillation of a lecture given countless airings both at home and abroad. Furnished with a wealth of illustrations, it eventually formed the core of the tenth in a series of Bauhaus booklets on contemporary architecture, *Holländische Architektur* (1926).[2] Gathered together in this anthology are all the themes and historical constructions that Oud was to continue to reiterate, virtually unchanged, throughout his life. This lends the book a decidedly dogmatic quality, something it has in common with the writings of Giedion, Gropius and even Le Corbusier. The most striking characteristic of Oud's reflections on Dutch architecture is the adherence to what A. van der Woud has called a strongly personalized view of history in which the historical process is reduced to 'a sort of father-son relationship'.[3] This is true, for example, of his long essay about Berlage (1919) but also of his rather neglected 1924 essay on the architecture of one of his teachers, Willem Kromhout.[4] A second characteristic is their explicitly 'operative' nature, in the sense that they were written from the perspective of Oud's own time and, in particular, his own architectural views. There is not a single text by Oud in which his own struggles with problems of form and style are not in evidence. In the 1919 essay on Berlage, for example, Oud analysed the Stock Exchange building in Amsterdam in the light of the aesthetic principles he was concurrently attempting to apply in his design for the factory at Purmerend. Likewise, in his brilliant essay on Willem Kromhout, he discussed the latter's Rotterdam offices and shops in relation to the principle of 'dynamic functionalism' developed by his German friend Erich Mendelsohn.

## Amsterdam School

For the rest, there was nothing very original about Oud's account of the development of Dutch architecture; in

H.P. Berlage/ Berlage Archive, NAI, Rotterdam

fact, it was quite banal. In broad outline it followed the '*cyclical*' theory posited around 1900, which saw architecture as passing through successive periods of decline, catharsis and resurgence. This process was linked at every stage to the individual efforts of particular 'heroes': Cuypers, Berlage, De Bazel, Kromhout and, by implication, J.J.P. Oud. Auke van der Woud, in his study of the nineteenth-century architectural debate in the Netherlands, characterizes this historical account as follows: *According to the prevailing view of history, Berlage, together with those members of the younger generation (Lauweriks, Van der Pek, De Bazel and Walenkamp), had produced the 'new direction', of which the Amsterdam Exchange (1898-1903) was the foremost built outcome. Berlage in turn, wrote Jan Veth in 1900, had a 'great master who preceded him in Dutch architecture'. This predecessor, Cuypers, was similarly recognized by the young guard of the 1890s as their master. So around 1900 it was decided, with the approval of all concerned, how the Netherlands had come to acquire a modern architecture: Cuypers's sound rational principles had inspired the younger generation and Berlage to make the breakthrough that had put an end to nineteenth-century architecture of historical styles. A century later, this version of events is still broadly accepted, although the picture has acquired more details and nuances in the meantime.*[5] Oud stuck to this historical picture throughout his life, gradually adding the missing links to his own day. The First World War figured as a major watershed in this account – even for the neutral Netherlands. Thus Oud argued that, from the perspective of 1918, when architecture was all about providing the most essential structures with a purely aesthetic form using limited means, it was difficult to comprehend that this principle should have been so fiercely fought for at the beginning of the century and that superficial ornament should for so long have overshadowed proportion and rhythm. While it had originally looked as if newly released forces in other countries (Wagner, Behrens, Van de Velde) might lead to a new international (architectural) style, that road had been quickly blocked by the chain reaction of Classicism and Romanticism in which the soberness and rationalism of Classicism unleashed such a general excess of fantasy that much of what had been achieved had since been lost. In his essay on Kromhout, Oud expressed it thus: *At the time there was a programme for an architecture, rationally based on the demands of life, which purely stated and functionally implemented would lead to an architecture that, having its origins in this life, would become a cultural monument of this life. This programme has been abandoned: it still awaits realization.*[6] In the Netherlands, the chief impediments to progress, at least as far as Oud was concerned, were the excesses of the Amsterdam School. As early as 1916 he had defended Berlage against the attacks of Michel de Klerk who accused Berlage of expending too much time and effort on social and philosophical problems and too little on the free play of forms. Oud took the opportunity to launch a fierce counter-attack on the barely formed ideology of the Amsterdam School: *And I would also like to present this case in more general terms than the personal issue. I see here a clash between two tendencies that are increasingly manifesting themselves in contemporary architecture, namely the universal and the particular tendency. And I cannot refrain from stating here how dangerous I think this particular tendency is for our architecture. For the beauty of this tendency, though it be 'sparkling new' and 'sensationally shocking', has the seeds of destruction within it. 'What shines is for the present moment born, the genuine remains for those to come.' And I regard the basis of this art as false and artificial. The subtlety, the decadent refinement of this art has nothing in common with* gemeenschapskunst *and it is a disease that will gnaw at our healthy architectural ideal. We have learnt – thanks to Berlage – that architecture is based on construction and not the other way around. But here we are taught to make habitability and construction subordinate, and to base* building *on* architecture, *in order to satisfy the vision of beauty entertained by these pioneers. But is this not the reinstatement of facade architecture; is this not the same old song sung in a new way? And in a way that is in danger of becoming popular and that is therefore temporary and limited!*[7] Oud's deep-seated objections to the aesthetic and social stance of the leaders of the Amsterdam School did not, however, prevent him from admiring their excellent draughtsmanship and professional skills. De Klerk's housing blocks and J.M. van der Mey's Scheepvaarthuis occupied a prominent place in his *Hollandse Architectuur* and not merely as a target of abuse. After all, the aesthetic exuberance and 'extreme lawlessness' of the Amsterdam School could even be said to have had a positive effect on the history of Dutch architecture, insofar as they liberated Berlage's disciples from the rigid formalism they were in danger of falling into. In the last instance, the Amsterdam School was not much more than a brief episode in that endless cycle of prescription and freedom in which architecture had been imprisoned since the middle of the nineteenth century: *In rejecting Berlage's design, the Amsterdam School had in this respect – albeit unintentionally – a liberating effect in the sense that it kept open the path to continuing development for Dutch architecture. Furthermore, however, its violation of all architectural logic provoked such a reaction that this – automatically – strengthened the efforts of a newly emerging movement which is increasingly contemplating applying itself once more to the style problem.*[8] It comes as no surprise that Oud regarded himself as the chief pacesetter of the new 'architectural movement'.

### Mendelsohn's 'Dynamic Functionalism'

Oud's assessment of the significance of the Amsterdam School took a different turn as a result of his correspondence and conversations with the German architect Erich Mendelsohn. Mendelsohn had first come to international attention through an exhibition in Berlin of some highly virtuoso sketches of Expressionist buildings (1919).[9] The Dutch architect T. Wijdeveld was so excited by this work that the following year he devoted almost an entire issue of *Wendingen*, the magazine of which he was editor, to Mendelsohn's architecture. In 1921 he invited the German architect to visit the Netherlands where Mendelsohn gave lectures in Amsterdam and Rotterdam and made his first acquaintance with the public housing architecture of J.J.P. Oud. Mendelsohn was impressed by the liveliness of the Dutch debate about architecture and town planning, in particular by the different responses in Amsterdam and Rotterdam to the challenges of the new, urban housing construction programme. As an outsider he had a keen eye for the unproductive, polarizing effects of an exaggerated contrast between the practical, objective approach of Rotterdam architects – in this instance Oud – and the more individualistic, visionary schemes of the architects of the Amsterdam School. While Dutch architects like Berlage, De Klerk and Oud were intent on pointing up their ideological differences, Mendelsohn saw those same differences as the springboard for a new, modern architecture: that of dynamic functionalism. Dynamic functionalism was in effect a plea for a modern method of building that was open both to contemporary programmes, materials and techniques and to the dynamics of urban culture. Mendelsohn's ideas about dynamic functionalism crystallized out in response to the radicalization of modern architecture in Germany where, under the influence of the Bauhaus and Walter Gropius, it was reduced to a manner of building geared entirely to function and production processes. In this situation, as Mendelsohn saw things, the Dutch architectural conflict between Amsterdam and Rotterdam took on the character of a universal debate about the principles of the future modern architecture. It is interesting to note that, at the moment when Bauhaus circles, led by Gropius and Meyer, were hailing the austere, geometrical architecture of *De Stijl* and of Oud in particular, for pointing the way towards a functional and constructional architecture, Mendelsohn was busy opening the Rotterdam architect's eyes to the many possibilities of the dynamic, rounded form as the expression of energy and tension not only of concrete and steel, but also of the context in which people built and consumed: the city. Oud and Mendelsohn met for the first time in August 1923, when Oud gave his lecture on 'The Development of Modern Architecture in Holland: Past, Present, Future' during Bauhauswoche in Weimar. In a letter to his wife, Mendelsohn gave a very detailed account of Oud's successful performance in the presence of Taut, Kandinsky, Feininger, Behne, Mies van der Rohe, Gropius and many others. Although Mendelsohn was impressed by Oud's lecture, he did not agree with him on every point. For example, he felt that Oud made too much of the contrast between Rotterdam and Amsterdam: *Amsterdam is unfaithful, deserts the newly found truth for graphic, emotional, romantic trivialities, loses itself in modern, varied trifles. Only simple things can be understood by the masses, in the end the individual accomplishments fail to gain significance*, was his concise summary of Oud's historical survey. But Mendelsohn did not agree with

**him: *This seems to me to be an understandable error in Oud's struggle. To quote Gropius, Oud is functional. Amsterdam is dynamic. Reconciliation of both notions is feasible, but not clearly visible in Holland. The former presupposes reason – a formed opinion on the basis of analysis, the latter the irrational – a formed opinion based on vision. The analyst – Rotterdam – rejects vision. The visionary, Amsterdam, fails to understand the cold realism. True, the primary element is the function, but function without sensual stimulus will just be construction. More than ever I persist in my reconciliation programme. Both are necessary, both have to find each other. If Amsterdam moves a step towards reason, if Rotterdam refrains from killing the fervour, the two will meet. Otherwise Rotterdam will freeze to death in construction, and Amsterdam will perish on the pyre of dynamism.*[10] Oud's lecture, and the correspondence that followed, led Mendelsohn to refine his theory of dynamic functionalism which in turn had a deep impact on Oud's architecture. Eloquent evidence of this can found in the Hoek van Holland housing scheme (1924), not only in the rounded shop windows, but more especially in the complex's predominantly horizontal character.**

**Although Mendelsohn did not manage to change Oud's views with respect to the Amsterdam School, he did succeed in softening Oud's appreciation of Expressionism, not as a style but as an aesthetic manifestation of urban dynamism, thereby opening the way for a less abstract (i.e. less *De Stijl*) and more cinematic view of the impact of urban life on architecture. This is evident, for example, in his analysis of the change in Kromhout's work after he moved to Rotterdam. In the port city, after having been passed over in the competition for the new town hall, Kromhout received a series of interesting commissions from the business world. In Oud's view this was not only a hopeful sign for the cultural future of Rotterdam, but also a stimulus for a Rotterdam version of what Mendelsohn referred to as *Grossbauform*: office and industrial buildings whose voluminous presence gave expression and coherence to the surrounding, urban environment.[11] Writing in the *Nieuwe Rotterdamsche Courant* in 1924, Oud had this to say: *The nature of the commissions, involving the city where he lived, were not without influence on Kromhout's work: its character changed. It acquired something of the nature of the environment in which he worked, something of the nervous energy and driving force. 'Action' entered his work, one could say – but one should above all not think of the formal symbol associated with that word – it became more or less expressionistic. The German architect Erich Mendelsohn, designer among other things of the Einstein tower, has formulated his view of architecture in a twofoldness: 'Dynamik-Funktion'. 'Funktion': the practical requirements which determine the aesthetic form from inside to outside; 'Dynamik': the impact of the urban (street) character – in the widest sense, including visually, etc. – on the design from outside to inside. An interaction, such as this, can also be felt in Kromhout's work, both the Amsterdam and the Rotterdam.*[12] But the Kromhout of Amsterdam was a very different architect from the Rotterdam Kromhout! While the first was predominantly horizontal, the latter was vertical. In demonstration of which Oud indulged in a lyrical impression of Kromhout's Rotterdam work that far surpassed all his earlier architectural studies, including the one on Berlage. Whereas Oud regarded the formal extravagances of the Amsterdam School as subjective and unmotivated because they occurred in outer residential districts in the shadow of urban activity, Kromhout's 'verticals' sprang from the economic vitality of the city centre. Oud wrote: *There is a vertical tendency in all cities where it is very busy – it can probably be explained purely in terms of economics – in Rotterdam just as well as in New York and London. The streets in cities like these are narrow – too narrow – traffic dominates all life on the ground and the latter is constantly, literally and figuratively, under threat. Just as material necessity prompts taller and ever taller buildings, it is conceivable that psychological necessity – in spontaneous symbolism – drives the architect to tower above the hurly-burly: a towering that in architecture may find a symbolic as well as a material realization.*[13] This necessity was what made the exuberant formal language of Kromhout's Rotterdam high-rise genuine and contemporary and that of the Amsterdam housing blocks unmotivated and thus romantic.**

## The 'Impressionistic' Architecture of H.P. Berlage

**In the received history of modern architecture, retold by Oud in *Holländische Architektur*, Berlage occupies a promi-**

nent place. The essence of Oud's view of Berlage can be found in an essay he wrote at Berlage's request for the Austrian art magazine *Kunst und Kunsthandwerk* (1919). In it, Berlage is presented as the architect who, from the 1880s onwards, had *liberated* Dutch architecture from the arbitrariness of historical styles and romantic imagination by redirecting its focus to contemporary social programmes and technological achievements. In Berlage's architecture, the fundamental laws of building – rhythm and proportion – gradually ousted the masquerade of ornamentation. Berlage did not so much give architecture a face-lift as overhaul its essence, from the inside out. Oud reconstructed this operation on the basis of a loose collection of criteria and dogmas drawn from Berlage's writings, in particular 'Bouwkunst en Impressionisme' (Architecture and Impressionism, 1893). They included pronouncements by Berlage pertaining first of all to the revaluation of space, surface, mass and detail and the consequences of this for architectural composition, secondly to the insertion and intelligibility of the individual building in both the spatial and the social environment, and thirdly to the relationship between architecture and technology.

Although Oud surveyed almost the whole of Berlage's oeuvre, in his stylistic analyses he concentrated on two buildings in particular: the Exchange (1896-1903) and the offices for 'De Algemeene' insurance company (1891-1894), both on Damrak in the heart of Amsterdam.[14] Oud focused on these two structures not because he regarded them as completely successful, but because they so clearly demonstrated Berlage's *struggle* with the straightjacket of architecture of historical styles. In his analysis of the Exchange a single detail – the asymmetry of the two towers on the Damrak elevation in the very first competition design (1883) – was all he needed to demonstrate what Berlage had in mind. Needless to say, in his first design for the Exchange, Berlage was still so completely caught in the bogus world of historical styles that the resulting building took very little account of the local situation and the programme of a modern stock exchange. Nonetheless, the grouping of volumes along two axes projected at right angles to one another, indicated a desire for simplicity, regularity and monumentality, qualities capable of bringing the building closer to reality. The interesting thing was that Berlage tried to achieve these qualities without adhering steadfastly to the potentially rigidifying central axes of symmetry. On the Damrak in 1883, Berlage introduced a new compositional principle by setting non-symmetrical but similar elements like towers alongside and opposite one another without this leading to contrived picturesque effects. In the later designs for the Exchange, but also in numerous office buildings of the 1890s, such as 'De Algemeene', Berlage applied this compositional method on a wider scale and with greater consistency so that the asymmetrical facade organization was horizontally and vertically corrected – straightened – by the harmony of unlike elements. This at least was the intention Oud discerned in these designs, an intention that Berlage was not, of course, able to realize fully. Berlage recognized the solution all right, but sought it chiefly in the rhythmic reiteration of details (ornaments, doors, windows, towers). *Our younger colleagues are particularly interested in solving this problem of asymmetrical and balanced design, not by changing details, but by changing the mass.*[15] By 'younger colleagues' Oud must have been thinking primarily of himself, for what else was his design for the factory at Purmerend (1919) than the determination of the harmonious relationship – 'beelding' Mondrian and Van Doesburg would have said – of unlike elements of mass and space without resorting to the standard device of symmetry. The Purmerend factory design marked the (only) brief encounter in Dutch architecture between Berlage and *De Stijl*.

In 'Bouwkunst en Impressionisme' Berlage had written: *architecture must be impressionistic precisely because it is a practical art. The times are not only favourable to this, they dictate it.*[16] Buildings should be so designed as to satisfy, by their orientation, form and organization, the conditions of location, programme and the current state of building technology. Fulfilment of these requirements would automatically result in simple basic forms, 'characteristic, large surfaces', 'defining lines' and 'impressionistic angular blocks'. Qualities that Oud detected in the executed design of the Amsterdam Exchange, which he regarded as the most complete manifestation of Berlage's artistic personality. This applied above all to the way the building was anchored in the cityscape. Taking his cue from Berlage, Oud analysed the Exchange as an example of 'impressionistic architecture', that is to say as a building whose expressive outer walls not only enclose the internal space or define the functional and ideological 'content' of the whole, but also lend form and structure to the surrounding urban space. In short, the Exchange was an instructive example of architecture according to the aesthetic principles of Sitte.[17] This being so, Oud placed Berlage's stock exchange building at the head of the rich tradition of architectural, monumental and symbolic urbanism to which Oud himself remained faithful throughout his life: *A result of a strong artistic will and a firm conviction, the building commands the area, not only because of the strong and closed effect of its mass and faces, but also due to its spiritual value, which lends it authority. Because of the limited distance to the neighbouring buildings the whole of the building is impressive only when seen from one point. Seen from this point it offers a view of the front and the shortened side facades, that roughly could be believed to be a triangular shape. The result is stability in the townscape, as the tower, a dominant vertical, enhances the way it is fitted into the street scene. The whole is enlivened with a lively silhouetting and a piquant positioning of the doors, windows and sides.*[18]

Impressionism in architecture is concerned not only with the positioning of the building in its (immediate) surroundings, but above all with intelligibility and principles of social equality. Building is a social affair. This is particularly true of public housing, as Berlage had impressed upon his colleagues in 1918 during the Amsterdam Housing Conference. In public housing necessity gives rise to large, aesthetically ordered blocks and the inescapable demands of the economy automatically result in an impressionistic architecture of large surfaces, solid lines and crisp silhouettes. And it was by means of this simplification, according to Oud, that Berlage succeeded in making architecture intelligible once more for the general public. After all, the importance of a great artist lies precisely in his ability to express the *unconscious* concerns of the masses in a highly personal way. Berlage was important not only because he proclaimed sound and rational views concerning an organic architecture – so had Cuypers – but more especially because he managed to embody those ideas in buildings by which he gave voice to his own time and established the formal language of an entire era. For this was where he differed from Cuypers: *Cuypers used his principles in connection with historic forms (ingeniously composed and elaborated), but this failed to move the majority of the people and so his influence on architecture was limited.* [19] The desire for intelligibility was also the source of Berlage's interest in advertising and in how advertising and graphics could be made part of the architectural composition. In this respect the 'De Algemeene' office building on Damrak was a forerunner of a 'werbewirksame Architektur' (publicity-conscious architecture) which evidently made little impression on Oud in 1919 but which he had plenty to say about in 1924 in connection with his design for the facade of Café De Unie.[20]

Despite Oud's many expressions of indebtedness to Berlage, as spokesman for the 'young guard' he was not uncritical of the master. In keeping with the tradition of the personalized and operative historiography he espoused, Oud used that criticism *to intensify his own sense of newness, of originality and to display it to others.*[21] As such, his 1919 historical analysis of Berlage's oeuvre was the immediate prelude to his celebrated 1921 lecture, 'Over de toekomstige bouwkunst en hare architectonisch mogelijkheden' (Architecture and the Future) which received almost instantaneous, international recognition as the first manifesto of what was shortly to become known as the architecture of the Modern Movement (or International Style). Criticism of Berlage was by no means new, of course. Van der Woud argues that his right to be considered the leader of the new tendency in architecture was not entirely uncontested in 1895: *After all the fine words and fine drawings of the young guard, the 'De Algemeene' building was seen as the first concrete indication of the tendency. But was it mere idle scandalmongering when* De Opmerker *wrote in 1895 that adepts of the new architecture were whispering among themselves that Berlage was 'still too caught up in the old', or was this really being said? The building was indeed full of references to historical style elements and the interior seemed to have been strongly influenced by the interiors of the 'official style'.*[22] Oud took up this criticism in 1919 when he noted that, rather than radiating originality of design, Berlage's buildings of the 1890s bore the signs of struggle and destruction. Many of Berlage's buildings were 'scarred' by his search for a rough, unworked, natural state of architecture and the accompanying objective spatial forms and methods of construction. Because of this consuming struggle, Berlage found it difficult to give his buildings an aesthetic form as well, which is why the buildings from that period seem rather primitive and almost medieval. This was particularly true of Berlage's handling of technology. In his later work, according to Oud, his pursuit of simplification remained stuck in the process of monumentalization begun earlier, and he was oblivious to the revolutionary nature of contemporary technology. Because of this, Berlage's work was in danger of becoming bogged down in aesthetic formalism. In our day and age, claimed Oud, cultural and economic necessity demanded the fullest possible use of the machine. The new methods of production arising from mechanization and standardization would, in combination with new materials, transform the outward appearance of the new architecture. Berlage had explained this often enough in his writings and had recently, in response to the prevailing housing shortage, even defended standardization of housing on aesthetic grounds. When it came to housing construction, Oud knew exactly what he was talking about for in 1918 (once again, thanks to Berlage) he had been appointed architect with the Rotterdam Woningdienst where he had begun – in Spangen and later in Tusschendijken, Mathenesse, etcetera – to carry out on an unprecedentedly large scale an aesthetic programme based on a scenario sketched (on paper, at least) by Berlage.[23]

### An Undecorated Architecture

In February 1921, Oud addressed the members of the Rotterdam-based architectural society *Opbouw* with 'Over de toekomstige bouwkunst en hare architectonische mogelijkheden'. The text of this lecture was better received in foreign than in Dutch architectural circles. In 1922 it was translated into German and Czech and the following year the French version appeared in *La Cité*. In 1928, an English summary appeared in the magazine *The Studio*.[24] In this internationally oriented essay, Oud summarized in lucid fashion all the themes and clichés currently circulating about the new architecture. And because he was the first to do so, he soon became a focus of interest. Seen from the perspective of his earlier texts on contemporary architecture and on Berlage and the monumental cityscape, Oud's lecture did not actually contain very much in the way of new insights; it was more of a logical continuation of the 1919 article on Berlage. This applies in particular to two axioms that were vigorously defended in the *Opbouw* lecture: the significance of modern painting and sculpture as exponents of the modern 'rhythm of life' and, secondly, the exemplary role of the industrial mass-produced article. While the first related to the necessary destruction of formal traditions, the second referred to the future manifestation of architecture.

That painters had shown the way out of the impasse of academic eclecticism was a fact of which many architects had already been convinced as early as 1890. It was around this time that terms borrowed from the world of painting, such as 'realism' and 'naturalism', started to crop up in architectural literature, especially in Germany, where they were linked to the new aesthetic of simplicity and austerity. Berlage preferred to speak of 'impressionism' but his meaning was identical. Realism, Naturalism and Impressionism were new tendencies in European painting that might serve as a model for architecture. Otto Wagner wrote: *In the sister art, painting, this realism has already made a breakthrough and therefore these modern 'plein air' genre paintings have a greater appeal for us than all historic paintings.* [25] This notion was revived in the years 1914-1916 by architects like Taut and Oud, with Impressionism and Naturalism being replaced by Futurism, Cubism and Constructivism. In 1914, in an article in *Der Sturm*, Bruno Taut showed how painters and sculptors like Fernand Léger, Wassily Kandinsky, Alexander Archipenko, Franz Marc and Robert Delaunay had stolen a march on contemporary architecture. This was not a matter of superficialities either, but a reversal of compositional principles that brought the visual arts into the domain of architecture: *The architect should also recognise that from the outset architecture has embodied the prerequisite established by the new art of painting: the freedom of the perspective and the restriction of individual points of view.* [26] Oud arrived at the same conclusions two years later after reading Van Doesburg's article about the new movement in painting ('De nieuwe beweging in de schilderkunst') in which he gave a detailed account of the working methods and aesthetic principles of Cubism, Futur-

**ism and abstract painting and sculpture. The same year found Oud explaining to his fellow architects in *Bouwkundig Weekblad* 'why this new painting so richly merits the attention of architects'.[27] In 1916 the reasons related chiefly to the ability of the new painting style to conjure 'sensations of reality' using purely painterly means of form and colour and without resorting to figurative representation. In this way modern painting literally and figuratively entered the realm of architecture, although at the level of the exhibition the proposed collaboration never got beyond the arrangement and 'stylistic presentation' of paintings that was also championed jointly by Oud and Van Doesburg in Leiden: *And then it will become apparent that when painting abandoned the imitation of nature in order to arrive at a stylistic painting, it entered a phase that is highly relevant to architecture because modern painters and modern architects are pursuing the same aim, namely the reproduction of emotion by pure means, free of distracting elements.*[28]**

**Oud reiterated and enlarged upon this argument in the *Opbouw* lecture, which reflected the many discussions Oud had had with Van Doesburg concerning the relationship between architecture and painting. By 1921 Oud had a clearer understanding of the importance of the 'fermentation process' of modern painting and sculpture for the future architecture, not in terms of external or stylistic characteristics but the process of transformation itself, which was a reflection of contemporary culture to which architecture had so far remained 'spiritually immune': *Architecture itself, culturally speaking the most important of all the arts, remains for the time being internally unaffected by this fermentation process. Spiritually unripe for the revolutionary sentiment that gave birth to Cubism ... outwardly it falls into one excess after another, unable to conquer its natural tendency towards the incidental, the decorative, in favour of a more spiritual conception in which the essence of architecture, the tense balance of forces expresses itself directly.*[29]**

**Architecture might not (yet) posses the intellectual resilience of modern painting and sculpture, but Oud expected that the material conditions of building – production methods, construction and materials – would automatically bring renewal. In keeping with the Berlagian division of architecture into utility object and art form, he pointed to industrially produced objects like 'cars, steamships, men's clothing, sports clothing, electrical and sanitary appliances, tableware' which were *more* receptive to a new aesthetic design, the freer they were of aesthetic conventions. By pointing out the 'natural beauty' of modern appliances, Oud was tapping into a theme that was already circulating in the Deutsche Werkbund (Van de Velde, Gropius, Muthesius) and elsewhere (Vienna: Adolf Loos; Paris: Le Corbusier) and in which the technical method of the engineer was favourably compared with that of the architect. In acknowledging the importance of technology and industrial products, Oud was simultaneously distancing himself from Berlage who missed no opportunity to point to the materialistic and banal aspects of technology and the danger they posed for the spiritual quality of architecture. Berlage's cultural reservations vis à vis the machine and technology put him at odds not only with contemporaries and peers like Otto Wagner, but with members of the 'younger generation' like Oud; however, it was not until the late 1920s that Berlage made this theme the core of his attack on the Modern Movement.**

**While the first part of Oud's lecture was devoted to architecture's failure to keep up with recent developments in visual arts and technology, in the second part he sought the answers to two questions: what would the architecture of the future look like, and which 'possibilities' (factors and developments) would enable architecture to attain that state? Oud was convinced that contemporary architecture was working towards the ideal of an 'undecorated architecture', an ideal he could for the time being only formulate negatively: *Architecture to-day knows nothing of terseness such as it is realised in the rhythm and the balanced composition of mutually related and interdependent parts, in which the changing of even the smallest detail is followed by a destruction of balance.*[30] This was the ideal of an a-historical classicism based on the fifteenth-century ideal of beauty developed by Alberti among others but without reference to the corresponding classical vocabulary of forms. How then to imagine what such an a-historical, classical architecture might look like? In order to avoid all association with any existing arsenal of forms, especially that belonging to one of the historical styles, Oud**

**defined the new architecture exclusively with reference to the forces that were 'helping to prepare the revolution in its design': modern production methods and new materials. Both were points on which Oud had previously had occasion to criticize Berlage's architecture, in particular his Exchange. For example, he regarded Berlage's architectural detailing, with its endless variations on a principal motif, as clear evidence of Berlage's preoccupation with traditional methods of production to the exclusion of machine-made detailing which – relatively fixed in form and colour – was characterized by perfect uniformity of similar details. Mass production and standardization automatically forced the architect to focus on the objective – the type – and to ignore the incidental and the subjective. They also led directly to the true elements of architectural composition: mass, plane and space. New materials like iron, glass and reinforced concrete played a complementary role vis à vis these production methods. Oud felt that in contemporary architecture, in Berlage's Exchange for example, steel and iron were being used in an inappropriate (primitive–medieval) manner. Because iron construction made it possible to withstand a maximum of forces with a minimum of materials, the typical manifestation of iron was not one of mass and plane, but of void and openness, in contrast to the closed quality of the wall plane. The use of glass, in the form of a plate-glass window for instance, made it possible to exchange the traditional effect of the window as a continuation of the wall for the evocation of opening, so that glass too contributed to the gradual defeat of architecture's appearance of heaviness. Whereas brick was poor at absorbing tensile stress, inconvenient for constructing large spans and rather coarse-looking unless finished with a smooth coat of plaster, concrete construction offered the advantage of a homogeneous frame, of unprecedentedly large horizontal spans and of precisely defined planes and masses. The technical properties of concrete opened the way to a new 'architectural plasticity' which, together with the expressive qualities of iron and glass, would result in a structural and aesthetic revolution and thence to the emergence of 'an architecture of optically immaterial, almost weightless appearance': to an undecorated architecture.[31]**

**Notes**

**1.** T. Van Doesburg, 'De taak der nieuwe architectuur', in: *Bouwkundig Weekblad*, 41(1920)50-51, p. 283.
**2.** D. Langmead, *J.J.P. Oud and the International Style. A Bio-Bibliography*, Westport (Conn.), London 1999, no. 117.
**3.** A. van der Woud, *Waarheid en karakter. Het debat over de bouwkunst 1840-1900*, Rotterdam 1997, p. 295.
**4.** J.J.P. Oud, 'Kromhout en zijn tentoonstelling', in: *Nieuwe Rotterdamsche Courant*, 2 October 1924; D. Langmead, *J.J.P. Oud and the International Style. A Bio-Bibliography*, Westport (Conn.), London 1999, no. 117, no. 82.
**5.** A. van der Woud, *Waarheid en karakter. Het debat over de bouwkunst 1840-1900*, Rotterdam 1997, p. 293.
**6.** J.J.P. Oud, 'Kromhout en zijn tentoonstelling', in: *Nieuwe Rotterdamsche Courant*, 2 October 1924.
**7.** Quoted in: S.S. Frank, *Michiel de Klerk 1884-1923. An Architect of the Amsterdam School*, Ann Arbor (Mich.), 1984, pp. 84-86; 279-280.
**8.** J.J.P. Oud, *Hollandse Architectuur*, Nijmegen 1983, p. 43.
**9.** K. James, *Erich Mendelsohn & the Architecture of German Modernism*, Cambridge (Mass.) 1997.
**10.** E. Mendelsohn, *Briefe eines Architekten* (ed. O. Beyer), Munich 1961, pp. 56-58.
**11.** K. Frampton, 'Einige Anmerkungen zu Mendelsohn', in: R. Schneider, W. Wang (eds), *Moderne Architektur in Deutschland 1900 bis 2000. Macht und Monument*, Ostfildern-Ruit 1998, pp. 61-70.
**12.** J.J.P. Oud, 'Kromhout en zijn tentoonstelling', in: *Nieuwe Rotterdamsche Courant*, 2 October 1924.
**13.** J.J.P. Oud, 'Kromhout en zijn tentoonstelling', in: *Nieuwe Rotterdamsche Courant*, 2 October 1924.
**14.** For an acute architectural-historical analysis of these buildings, see: M. Bock, *Anfänge einer neuen Architektur. Berlages Beitrag zur architektonischen Kultur der Niederlande im ausgehenden 19. Jahrhundert*, The Hague, Wiesbaden 1983.
**15.** J.J.P. Oud, 'Dr. H.P. Berlage und sein Werk', in: *Kunst und Kunsthandwerk*, 22(1919)6-8, pp. 189-228.
**16.** See I.B. Whyte, 'Modernist Dioscuri? Wagner and Hendrik Petrus Berlage' in: H.F. Malgrave (ed.), *Otto Wagner. Reflections on the Raiment of Modernity*, Santa Monica 1993, pp. 157-198, 193.
**17.** M. Bock, *Anfänge einer neuen Architektur. Berlages Beitrag zur architektonischen Kultur der Niederlande im ausgehenden 19. Jahrhundert*, The Hague, Wiesbaden 1983, p. 117.
**18.** J.J.P. Oud, 'Dr. H.P. Berlage und sein Werk', in: *Kunst und Kunsthandwerk*, 22(1919)6-8, p. 216.
**19.** J.J.P. Oud, 'Dr. H.P. Berlage und sein Werk', in: *Kunst und Kunsthandwerk*, 22(1919)6-8, pp. 203-204.
**20.** M. Bock, *Anfänge einer neuen Architektur. Berlages Beitrag zur architektonischen Kultur der Niederlande im ausgehenden 19. Jahrhundert*, The Hague, Wiesbaden 1983, pp. 171-228.
**21.** A. van der Woud, *Waarheid en karakter. Het debat over de bouwkunst 1840-1900*, Rotterdam 1997, p. 312.
**22.** A. van der Woud, *Waarheid en karakter. Het debat over de bouwkunst 1840-1900*, Rotterdam 1997, pp. 315-316.
**23.** J. De Heer, 'Stijl en woningtype: Berlages woningbouw', in: S. Polano (ed.), *Hendrik Petrus Berlage. Het complete Werk*, Alphen 1988, pp. 67-91.
**24.** J.J.P. Oud, 'Over de toekomstige bouwkunst en hare architectonische mogelijkheden', in: *Bouwkundig Weekblad*, 42(1921)24, pp. 147-160.
**25.** I.B. Whyte, 'Modernist Dioscuri? Wagner and Hendrik Petrus Berlage'in: H.F. Malgrave (ed.), *Otto Wagner. Reflections on the Raiment of Modernity*, Santa Monica 1993, p. 193.
**26.** I.B. Whyte, *Bruno Taut, Baumeister einer neuen Welt. Architektur und Aktivismus 1914-1920*, Stuttgart 1981, pp. 25-28.
**27.** J.J.P. Oud, 'Over cubisme, futurisme, moderne bouwkunst enz.', in: *Bouwkundig Weekblad*, 37(1916)20, p. 156.
**28.** J.J.P. Oud, 'Over cubisme, futurisme, moderne bouwkunst enz.', in: *Bouwkundig Weekblad*, 37(1916)20, p. 156.
**29.** J.J.P. Oud, 'Over de toekomstige bouwkunst en hare architectonische mogelijkheden', in: *Bouwkundig Weekblad*, 42(1921)24, p. 151.
**30.** J.J.P. Oud, 'Architecture and the Future', in: *The Studio*, 98(1928)429, p. 405.
**31.** E. Taverne, 'Bouwen zonder make-up. Acties van Oud tot behoud van de architectuur', in: *Wonen/TABK*, 11(1983)3, pp. 8-22.

J.J.P. Oud, 'Over Cubisme, futurisme, moderne bouwkunst, enz.', in: *Bouwkundig Weekblad*, 37(1916)20, pp. 156-157

# Cubism, Futurism, Modern Architecture, Etc.

It is becoming increasingly apparent that the new movement in painting is developing into a lofty and monumental style of painting which – now that the modern endeavour, which seemed to have come to a standstill, is once again manifesting itself on all sides – deserves to be drawn to the attention of architects because this painting, more so than in the past, is going to be relevant to them.

The evolution currently taking place in modern painting has now reached a stage in which it exhibits great intellectual affinity with architecture and in which closer contacts between the two arts appears to be imminent.

J. Havelaar, in a review of the work of Tielens in the 'Nieuwe Groene', has already drawn attention to this in passing, and I would now like to show in more detail why this new painting so richly merits the attention of architects.

Readers will be familiar with the fact that in reaction to Naturalism, Realism, Impressionism, etc., in other words to the kind of painting that manifested itself by emulating nature, (and after several painters had independently attempted to turn nature into a means rather than an end), a movement arose known as Cubism whose proponents attempted to arrive at a more stylistic representation of reality.

Soon other artists went even further down this road which resulted in an increasing separation of art and reality. Futurism was no longer satisfied with a constructed reality but attempted to capture different visual impressions in a single picture – 'the conflated representation of a rapid movement (by the combination in a single picture of different aspects and conditions with their interrelationships)'.

Not all developments are as clear-cut as the ones described here and there are many intermediate and transitional stages whose boundaries are difficult to define and which are only relevant as the indispensable links in the evolutionary chain.[1)]

Nonetheless, the intention of presenting *sensations of realities* without depicting the external reality itself, is manifesting itself with increasing clarity and the logical and ultimate consequence of this endeavour is accordingly a style of painting in which these feelings are rendered *directly* i.e. by purely painterly means: through form and colour.

This consequence has been embraced by the so-called 'abstract' artists and I would like to illustrate this outlook with a simple example taken from an interesting article by one of their members, Theo van Doesburg, in 'De Beweging'.

In it he states: 'Art comes into being as soon as *transformation* begins. When a painter paints an apple and this apple begins to change in the artist's mind, the outcome is Art. The apple assumes the qualities of the artistic mentality and this transformation causes the concept of "apple" in the natural sense to be ousted by the concept of "apple" in the symbolic sense. In other words, that part of the symbolic apple which differs from the natural apple is the sole artistic value of the painting. It is the artistic value because it is the emotional value, the content. The apple serves only as form, not as content. If a viewer sees only the apple – in the natural sense – he is perceiving the form only of the painting, not the content. It goes without saying therefore that the artistic value will increase as the natural value, the concept "apple", decreases.' He calls this direct, unmediated reproduction of emotion 'expressive' and he contrasts it with 'optical' reproduction where history, allegory or nature are part of the artistic product. Thus painting operates independently and abstractly and changes from *programme art* into *absolute art*. It becomes *symbolic* because it does not present any particular realities but only sensations of realities, and what Bolland [G.J.P.J. Bolland, Dutch philosopher 1854-1922] wrote about Architecture is equally applicable to Painting, namely:

'that through it, rather than directly, mind speaks to mind'.
Its proper field of action is the *plane*, because the plane is incompatible with the perspectival image. The plane is the canvas on which the painting is constructed and the painter can express himself on it in endless variations of form and colour, just as the musician reproduces his emotion on his instrument in sound and beat. This art will appear less frequently in the form of 'staffelei-malerei' (easel painting); architecturally speaking it is the ultimate 'applied art'.
The practitioners of this art will be able to 'animate' the planes with which we, as spatial artists, express our emotions, turning them into an essential element of space, capable of making it more intimate and moving. In the hallowed space, the gold and blue images will harmonize with the sublime chorales; in the banquet hall the brightly coloured visions will intensify the revellers' excitement.
As such, this style of painting will open up greater and more intense emotive possibilities for architecture, but architecture for its part will create an atmosphere in which the mind is receptive to this painting and there will be more or less reciprocity depending on the similarity in mental outlook between architect and painter.

A new development is impossible to predict and to what extent this logical consequence of painting will turn out to be the be-all and the end-all, I am not in a position to say. Theoretically it would seem to have a lot in its favour, but in practice it still remains to be seen whether its opponents are wrong when they claim that painting in general will become too irrelevant and too worldly as a result of the total disregard of the imitative element.
It should be realized, however, that it is impossible to evaluate this abstract painting at exhibitions of the kind mounted for Impressionist paintings. Only a stylistic manner of exhibiting can do justice to this art!
And then it will become apparent that when painting abandoned the imitation of nature in order to arrive at a stylistic painting, it entered a phase that – though less reactionary in a subsequent stage – is of highly relevant to architecture because modern painters and modern architects are pursuing the same aim, namely the reproduction of emotion by pure means, free of distracting elements.
In this endeavour they meet and complement one another! And now – now that the need for a closer connection among the arts is being felt everywhere – architects are able to view this sign in the proper context and through active interest lead us further along the road to an amalgamation of the arts in which emotion will be simultaneously reproduced in the rhythmic relationship of brick to space, in form and colour and in sound and beat.

Leiden 4. 6. 16. J.J.P. OUD



**1.** For more information on this development, see the articles by E. Wichman, Theo van Doesburg et al. on which I have drawn for this essay.

ing factor, and, in modern architecture, the purely structural should take precedence over the decorative aspect. This would hardly be a loss to architecture. In the Renaissance the organic design was lost, in other words, the aesthetic design no longer originated in organic coherence and continuous interaction with the practical and constructive form, but the aesthetic design only appeared to be linked to the organic, the constructive form.
With this basically erroneous idea the Renaissance completely spoiled architecture for us, in as much as from that time on there was no longer an organic architecture with an inner life, but only a semblance (nonetheless often generous and ingenious) of architecture, in which the essence had been lost, for the sake of the decor. Since then, the decor of architecture has been con- However, the outward appearance of an architectural work should not be seen as detached from the whole, but only in coherence with the design of the entire work and as its final result. This design is not only depending on the coincidental mood of the artist, but should, in first instance, also serve practical needs. In accordance with these needs an aesthetic spatial design should be created and, because in our days these needs are totally different from those in the days of the Gothic age or the Renaissance, the essence of our traditional architecture should be revived and not just its outward appearance. Materials, too, impose certain demands and, since our materials show characteristics that are basically different from the earlier ones, designs in the new architecture will have to undergo essential changes.
Especially in the years 1890 to 1919 much was contested that, today, in this period of economic straits, seems

be: to create the greatest comfort in the smallest space in an aesthetic design of the purest kind. In the architecture of our future days the proportions and the rhythm should prevail over decoration.
There is nothing new about this and only because of the war the solution of this problem must be speeded up; in this period we also have the advantage that resistance against this view has diminished due to the need for an economic use of materials. We, younger ones, hardly know this resistance and all this seems a matter of course to us. But it is not and I would like to remind you of the resistance the Modern Movement and the leading architects, who recognized and fostered this development, had to conquer.
Especially in the years 1890 to 1919 much was contested that, today, in this period of economic straits, seems



DR. H. P. BERLAGE UND SEIN WERK VON J. J. P. OUD-ROTTERDAM

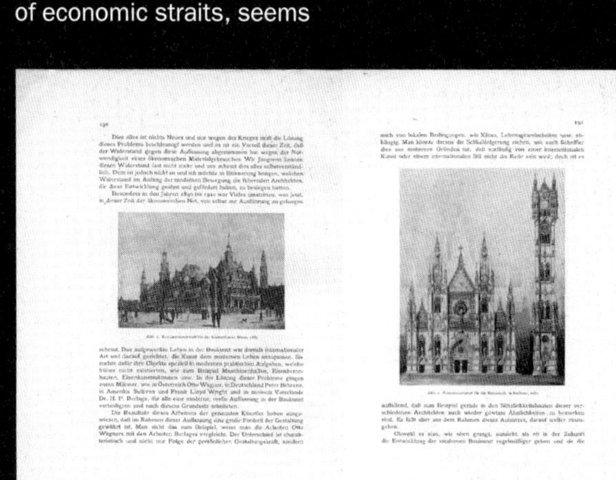

cal tasks, that did not exist before, as, for instance, machine engineering plants, reinforced concrete constructions, steel buildings etc. In solving these problems men like Otto Wagner in Austria, Peter Behrens in Germany, Sullivan and Frank Lloyd Wright in the USA and, in my country, Dr H.P. Berlage led the way: they all spoke out for a modern, realistic concept in architecture and followed this principle.

The results of the efforts by the above artists have shown that within the framework of this concept a great freedom of design is allowed. This is evident when, for instance, the works of Otto Wagner are compared to those of Berlage. The difference is characteristic and not just the consequence of personal designing power, but it also depends on local conditions, such as the climate, the way of life etc. This might lead to the conclusion industrial buildings by these various architects, certain similarities are noticeable. It falls outside the scope of this paper, however, to go into further detail.

Even if it looks, as I said earlier, as if the development of modern architecture will proceed more regularly and will move in the direction pointed out by the above-mentioned architects, it should not be forgotten that right now (and not only because of the war) we have reached a state of stagnation and reaction, which means a reversion. At the Cologne exhibition a return to classicism could already be observed. In Holland this Modern Movement, which in certain cases led to sober-mindedness, provoked a reaction; it unleashed an excess of fantasy and threatened to spoil what so far had been gained, in particular because the main representatives of this fantastic trend are extremely gifted and therefore carry design, but into a renewal of a form of outward decoration. Essentially, it has not brought any changes that add a cultural value to architecture.

With these movements in architecture, it is twice as necessary, because of the above principles, to realize their significance to modern life and for that reason I have accepted the request of the editors of this magazine with much pleasure, to say something about the work of the forerunner of the Dutch rational[1] trend in architecture, Dr H.P. Berlage.

Dr H.P. Berlage was born in Amsterdam on 21 February 1856. Initially he was more interested in painting, but as early as 1875 he enrolled as a student at the Technical College in Zurich and studied architecture under Larius and Stadler; the latter was a student and a supporter of Semper. Until the end of 1878 he stayed in Zurich. He then made a



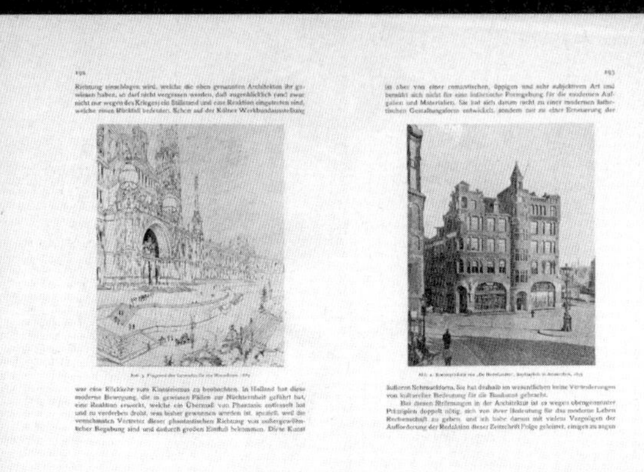

study tour of one year in Italy and, later, shorter trips to Germany, Austria and France. He started his professional activities as a draughtsman in the Bureau Sanders in Amsterdam, where he became a partner after a while. During this time he took part in the international competition for a Stock Exchange Building in Amsterdam; he won the fourth prize for a design that was not implemented. At the same time he was also a lecturer at the School for Applied Art, "Quellinus", in Amsterdam that was founded by Dr Cuypers.

For five years he worked together with Sanders and then he set up as an independent architect in Amsterdam. From then on he occupied an increasingly leading position and, with the realisation of the Amsterdam Stock Exchange (a new design he later carried out himself independently) he reached his prominent position in modern Dutch architecture which he championed and founded.

In 1914 he was appointed architect for business and residential buildings by the firm Wm. Müller & Co. in The Hague and this still keeps him occupied.

When Dr Berlage started his activities as an independent architect, there was some confusion in Dutch architecture, much like the situation in neighbouring countries. The historic development of Dutch architecture since the beginning of the nineteenth century can be summarized as follows: until the middle of the nineteenth century architecture was dominated by French classicism. More or less as a reaction to this, a tendency toward the Gothic and the Renaissance became manifest early in the second half of the century and gradually two schools developed: Romanticism and Eclecticism. The great building activity that had found expression in the area of Roman Catholic church building after 1850 began to influence the 'profane' architecture as well.

Although initially rigidly conventional, a more relaxed outlook developed in the building of churches with Dr Cuypers (the builder of the Amsterdam Rijksmuseum and of many churches). As a student and admirer of Viollet-le-Duc he thoroughly studied medieval architecture; its logical and constructive principles gradually led to his liberation from classicism and so he assisted in clarifying concepts concerning a rational architecture.

After 1870 a period came in which first Gothic motifs and little by little also motifs of the national Renaissance appeared, since foreign examples (disseminated through art magazines) were followed and refashioned, which resulted in the confusion referred to above. Berlage's great merit lies in the fact that in this period he gave guidelines to arrive at an architecture that would no longer be a combination of old or new styleforms, but an aesthetic design of social exigencies of its time.

Berlage did not come to the organic conception of architecture, as it manifests itself in his later works, overnight. In general, his development is similar to that of Otto Wagner and may be characterized by the words of Lux in his biography of Wagner, where he speaks about a development 'from architecture to the art of building'.

Berlage's first designs show a style of architecture in the spirit of the Renaissance. The motifs in the competition design for the Amster-

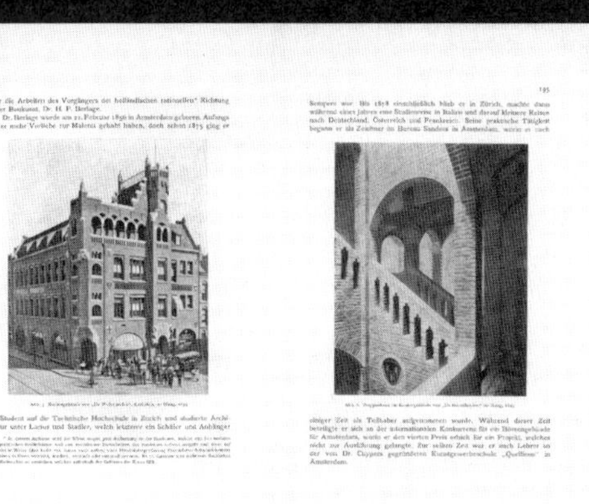

dam Stock Exchange (1885) (Fig. 1) – one of the earliest designs by Berlage I know – have mainly been derived from the national Renaissance. The arrangement of building sections round two axes that are at right angles to each other points to regularity and monumental art, although this design, in the effect of its mass and its silhouette, could be typified picturesque rather than monumental. A typical feature of a Stock Exchange Building was not found here (in those days of architecture of historical styles one was not so much concerned about expressing this); the above-mentioned use of two axes led to a sort of ambiguity in the composition, which resulted in an equivalence of the front and the side; this had disappeared in the design that was realised later, in 1898. The whole design, however, breathes a great knowledge of old style-forms and a skill to arrange these. It is remarkable that, with the symmetric construction of the side wall, the spires of both big towers are different. This could be explained from the designer's conviction that an exact symmetry of a work of art would lead to rigidity and therefore the artist would have tried to place equivalent rather than symmetric views next to and opposite each other. But especially in architecture of historical styles this problem is difficult to solve, since one is bound by existing forms; with these the parts cannot be composed in an inner coherence, but at best an outward harmony of forms is created. Since Berlage also failed to pursue this conception consequently in both parts of the façade, the desired result was not achieved and one gets the impression of something individual en forced.

In his later works Berlage has been able to find a beautiful and characteristic solution for this in details (also in the rhythmic repetition of a decoration); nevertheless, I do not know of any façade of his, in which he set himself this task in the greater masses as well. The solution of this problem of non-symmetric and equivalent design, not by reshaping details, but by reshaping the large faces in particular attracts the attention of our young ones.

How Berlage managed to immerse himself in the essence of old styles, is proved by his design for the façade of the Milan cathedral (Fig. 2). Although this façade reminds one in general of that of the Orvieto cathedral, nowhere have the details been copied as a matter of course, but has a uniform remodelling been created in coherence with the existing conditions; especially the tower is a great success, as it corresponds exactly with the shape and the essence of the whole and yet has become something very original in its appearance.

A grand finale of the architecture of historical styles he presented in his design for a mausoleum (entered for an international exhibition in Paris in 1889) (Fig. 3). In this design we see, more than in any other, how far his command of historic forms extended; here, practically all known styles, whose motifs are used to compose an edifice, are in evidence; the design may not be a uniform architectural design, but it already shows the urge for the monumental that is so apparent in Berlage's later work.

Even if this is chronologically not correct according to the designs and the works completed, I consider this



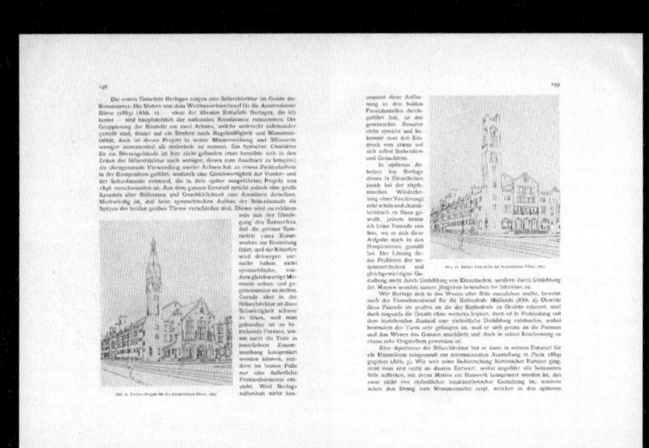

style, only reproducing or assembling work; this view first led to an interim period with the use of motifs from various different styles. However, this exhausts the possibilities of composing within the framework of the architecture of historical styles, and another step forward had to result in departing from this road in order to achieve designs that are really architectural. But this did not happen immediately and between this magnificent architectural parade and the first hesitant steps on the new road, which become more clearly visible in the building for the 'Algemeene Maatschappij van Levensverzekering en Lijfrente' in Amsterdam, there are smaller designs and completed buildings and living rooms on the top floor with its larger wall spaces and smaller windows, has in this instance, too, led to an ambiguity which is only partly disguised by the balcony on the right side wall. Apart from that, it is extremely amazing to make a comparison between this building and the 'Algemeene Maatschappij van Levensverzekering en Lijfrente' building. The structure of the façade of the latter really deviates very little from the structure of the façade of the former. All the elements appearing in the Focke & Meltzer building can actually be found again: the large shop windows, separated by columns, on the ground floor; the connecting piece: the balcony; both equally tall floors with ture, is quite significant in the detailed finishing of both façades. In the details of the later façade the new concept is revealed which, unlike the earlier one (which was more or less classic) could be said to be a very personal concept. This seems to contradict Berlage's principles, mentioned earlier, that do not aim at the special (the subjective) aspects, but at the general aspects in the art, but one should not forget that those general aspects are not in first instance related to the form, but are of a spiritual nature and, in the case of great artists, bear a more or less personal stamp in their outward appearance. The importance of great artists lies exactly in the fact that they

the outward language of forms of an entire era. Precisely the latter shows the difference between Cuypers and Berlage. Cuypers had used his principles in connection with historic forms (ingeniously composed and elaborated), but this failed to move the majority of the people and so his influence on architecture was limited. The details in the above-mentioned façade of the 'Algemeene Maatschappij van Levensverzekering en Lijfrente' building show the first step to the new form in Berlage's work. Here, as in many works from this period, one can still see the struggle to be freed from the traditional presence of the outward, historic details, whereas later, in Berlage's latest works this conquer the conventional and the material. Traces of this struggle are visible in many works, since they occasionally betray human tragedy as much as aesthetic emotion. After this period Berlage reminds us of the deeply serious artists in that group to which, for instance, Vincent van Gogh belongs as well (this group seems to be characteristic of that period). They are creators rather than virtuosos, in other words, they work with spiritual rather than with sensual means and never end up with a dead artistic pattern, because their creations rely on the awareness that art never exists, but always is born. So, every time he achieved a result, he detached himself from that achievement its meaning in his definition that "in a work of art the strength of the human spirit, visibly expressed in the material, is normative".
The building in question is also significant because of the strength of the artistic will, as is evident from every part of the façade. With this strength Berlage has roused Dutch architecture with its handed down academicism and with the temptation of widely available materials from its passivity and excited them to be active again in creating elementary art.
In the beginning this is most apparent from his concentration on detail.
The elaboration of detail in an architectural work generally performs a dual function; by comparison one could say: a passive one



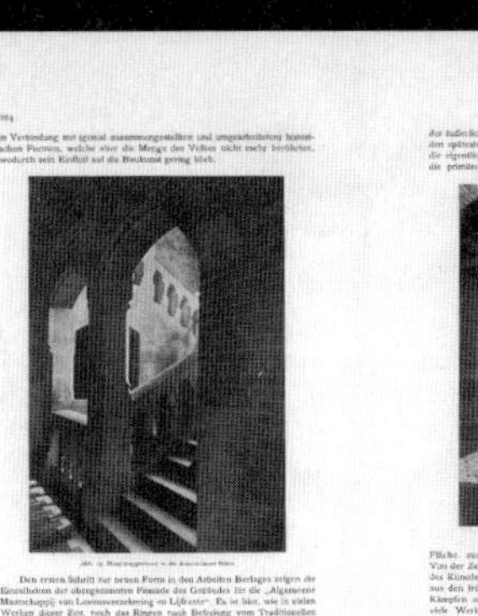

light, shade, colour, mass etc., in short as a general architectural means to shape the total architectural picture. The active function is performed in that the details are depicted independently to become artistic elements. Of course, in architecture of historical styles (the architecture of copying and assembly) this latter application is virtually out of the question. In classic art, too, the details were less active, less personal, but medieval art (and the Gothic art in particular) also managed to develop a individual charm, thanks to a very active attention to detail in its monumental buildings. The mastery of the architects in that era is revealed especially in the way in which these details are introduced; the passive effect in the total picture was not impaired by it, that is, the artistic value of the details was not brought into prominence, but only caught the eye when the details were examined more closely. As he did in his principles, which apply to all ages anyway, Berlage associated himself with medieval art in this respect as well. The and from the corresponding designs is never disadvantaged by smallish or pretentious detail, but, when we have a closer look, a great lyrical charm is revealed and we are constantly surprised by delicate features which were easily overlooked at first because of their excellent arrangement in the whole.

His details grow organically from the essence of the building, like branches from a tree trunk: they have not been copied or assembled, but are living organs of the work of art. So one can understand that for him the details must meet the highest standards and that he did not design or elaborate them himself, if he felt they fall outside his scope of architecture. In such events he invited the best artists of his day to co-operate with him and carry out sculpting or painting work etc. In the 'Algemeene Maatschappij van Levensverzekering en Lijfrente' building you will find sculpting work by Van Zijl and interior wall paintings by Derkinderen.

If suitable assistants were not available, for instance for making furniture or for objects himself. For the execution of these designs he founded, together with the master cabinetmaker Jac. van den Bosch, the workshops "'t Binnenhuis", which initially occupied a leading position in the new movement. Earlier, Berlage had already designed furniture in Renaissance style, but a revolution, similar to that in his architecture, took place in his furniture during this period. Nevertheless his principles were soon more clearly realised here than in his buildings designed in the transitional period. They are even presented with a certain bias and a propagandistic obtrusiveness, but in this particular case this seems to have been the better approach. We are too much tainted with historic traditions to be able to straightaway face new challenges with an open mind. As I mentioned earlier, this also affected Berlage's first buildings, and, consequently, they are, in the transitional period, spiritual adaptations and abstractions rather than aesthetic, new creations on the basis of elementary principles; it seems as if he

had grafted his new principles onto the old examples. In his furniture designed in this period this is not so much the case, as they show an archetype which corresponds with the practical needs and constructional requirements of the time. The fact that a new aesthetic design was not yet achieved, results from the one-sided structural view: material and construction are painstakingly respected, and so the results strike us as somewhat rough and not very decorative, but very convincing. There is a chair from this period, in which all round forms have been avoided and replaced by straight parts, as if rebelling against the structure of wood; as many as 36 wood joints were realised that were left visible with meticulous care.

This initial clinging to principles proves Berlage's artistic conscience; it does not allow any compromise, but eventually it had to submit to the dualism of idea and practice, the essence of architecture.

And so, in those days he faced the enormous task to solve in his works three different, often contradictory problems, that nonetheless cannot be considered separately, and to incorporate them harmoniously in an aesthetic design. First, he had to distance himself from the traditional form; secondly he had to determine approximately the contemporary archetype, as a compromise between practical and constructive requirements; thirdly, and at the same time, he had to express the latter aesthetically. In solving this problem he performed a gigantic task and with awe we regard the buildings in which the development matures and the individual quality of the artist gradually begins to reveal itself. This struggle can be sensed most clearly in the already mentioned 'Algemeene Maatschappij van Levensverzekering en Lijfrente' building, in the residence of professor Heymans in Groningen (1894) and in the office buildings for "De Nederlanden" in Amsterdam (Fig. 4) and in The Hague (1895) (Fig. 5). But in this respect the designs for the Amsterdam Stock Exchange are the most remarkable, because the entire development is comprised in the range of plans Berlage made for this building over the years. The 1885 design has already been discussed above. Twelve years later (1897) Berlage was commissioned to build the Stock Exchange building and after that he made the above range of designs.

The first of these plans (Fig. 8) bears only little resemblance to the old design, but it already contains the elements of the building as it was realised. Here, too, there still are traditional forms, and parts reveal the influence of Dr Cuypers, but compared to the earlier plan the dominance of the whole has become more generous, the conflict between side and front façades has been partly eliminated and the former shows a fairly closed front, which is extended in the longitudinal direction. The large wall faces with groups of relatively small windows, so characteristic for Berlage's later works, is evident here in its beginning. The dominant effect of the whole is, however, still uncertain. But then every following step shows improvements, by leaps: the front façade becomes increasingly more closed and the separate parts of the building take a definite shape, every time



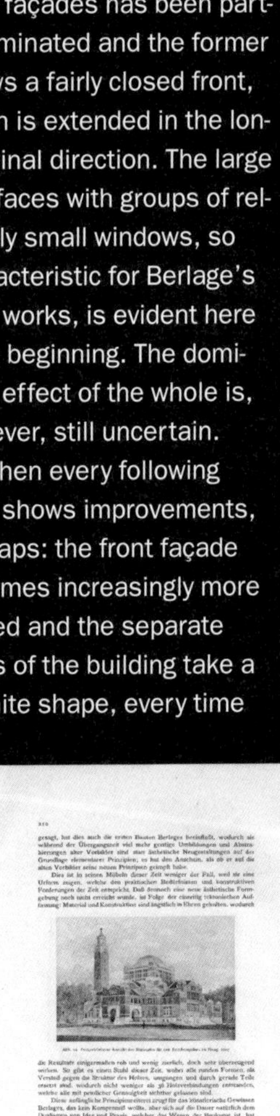

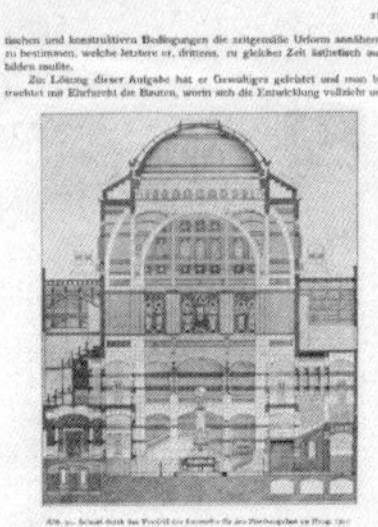

the tower commands the overall impression with increasing force, the component parts are merged, abstracted and led to the right places (Fig. 9, 10).

The highest level in his development is embodied in the completed building (Fig. 11), in which Berlage's personality expresses itself as an entity for the first time. A result of a strong artistic will and firm conviction, the building commands the area, not only because of the strong and closed effect of its mass and faces, but also due to its spiritual value, which lends it authority. Because of the limited distance to the neighbouring buildings the whole of the building is impressive only when seen from one point. Seen from this point it offers a view of the front and the shortened side façades, that roughly could be believed to be a triangular shape. The result is stability in the townscape, as the tower, a dominant vertical, advances its addition to the street scene.

The whole is enlivened with a lively silhouetting and a piquant positioning of the doors, windows and details. The central entrances (Fig. 12) and the top end of the tower are main points of the composition and, viewed separately, they belong to the most successful elements of the building. Doors and windows have, where possible, been united in groups, so that through the interruptions the walls do not suffer any disadvantage to the effect of their faces. The artist made the walls of Dutch bricks and so restored them to their old glory. He made the conscious choice to adapt the bright colour of this material to the atmosphere of the Amsterdam townscape; where, moreover, the enormous effort and pious devotion express a serious artistic spirit in every detail of this creation, it is difficult to understand the blunt remark by Lux, when he, in his ardour to honour the master Wagner, condemns this building as a "coarse tile shed which ultimately is offensive through its doctrinal puritanism".

Although this judgement fails to show any understanding of the nature of the work, public opinion initially shared the same view. But there were other factors that also played a role.

At the time the Amsterdam Stock Exchange was not just a first class artistic achievement, but its general significance overshadowed its artistic significance due to the principles underlying its development. The excitement it aroused during its construction and afterwards in circles of both artists and laymen must be attributed, at least partly, to Berlage's principles, as he was considered a danger to the arts due to their realistic basics. Therefore not only the building was ridiculed, but the architect, too, was maligned and scorned. Later there was a technical mishap that became the reason for fresh spiteful remarks and so the old story of derision and hostility, that so often is the lot of significant works of art at first, was repeated. To be sure, the witch hunt conducted at the time did not affect the artist's creative powers, but it robbed him of much happiness.

The Stock Exchange building marked the beginning of the artist's palmy days and the characteristic qualities of the design of this building can be found again in the major structures of this period.

They include, for instance: the residence of Mr Carel Henny in The Hague (1898)

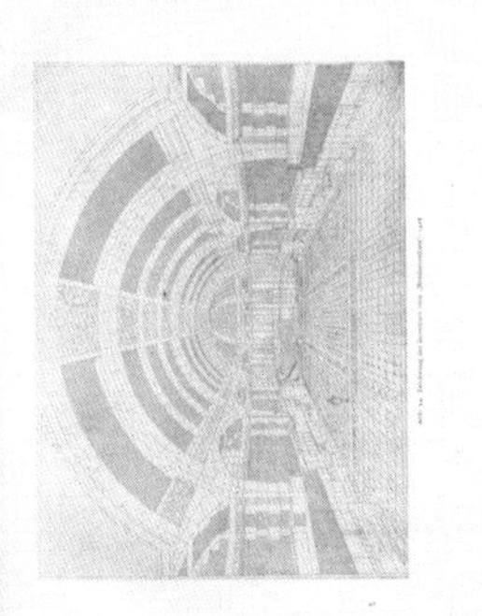

design for the urban expansion in The Hague (1908); the School for Industrial Art for Girls in Amsterdam (1908); the design for a

words, those parts of the building that are of the greatest practical importance, have been turned into the aesthetic main

This type of decoration is very characteristic of Berlage's work and can be found in many details, extending in a longitudinal

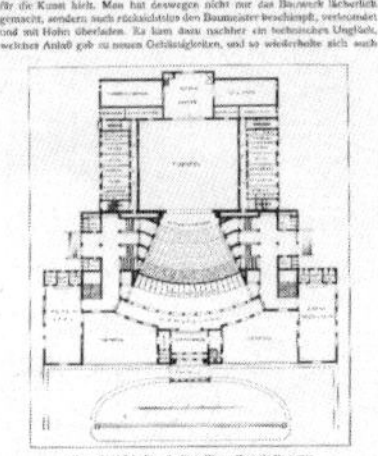

work they are again evident as wood carving.
In designing ends and separate parts that needed to be emphasised, too, he developed a wealth of fantasy in a similar fashion.
The motifs in the latter decorations and those mentioned before are mostly simple figures of abstract or abstracted depictions, cut out firmly and with sharp edges, achieving a fascinating effect.
In addition, his works include a type of decoration that is of a freer, more true-to-nature outlook and not so much constructively linked to architecture. These usually represent natural objects, occasionally with a symbolic meaning and enliven and stress certain components. In the first works produced after the transitional period we see columns with capitals and pedestals, which represent free adaptations of the traditional type. But the division in three parts gradually vanishes until in the end only the functional parts of the columns are highlighted, as was also common practice in medieval art.

notion, but they become increasingly constructive and angular.
For roof covering usually red tiles were used, for turrets sometimes cut stone slabs. Flat roof covering was also used.
Next to the unobtrusive colours of the natural stone material (occasionally enlivened by colourful glazed stones) he used rather bright, often primary colours for the painting of wood, iron etc.
When we consider the whole of Berlage's works from this period and imagine the general view on architecture in the days they came into existence, then we understand the agitation of the opponents and the admiration of the younger ones even better. Since he refrained from striving for success by means of the outward ornamental forms of a handed down world of forms, but abstracts, interiorises or reshapes the latter and puts them together in a simple style, his structures must have had an almost ascetic effect on their contemporary environment.
Both in the building of small

ence is now so evident in all areas that we are hardly able to still sense it to the same degree. But I remember how I sensed its artistic value when I first set eyes on the Stock Exchange building, but nevertheless was left with a sober impression. Later, it became clear to me that in the so-called puritanism of this building a passionate artistic spirit is inherent, that does not express itself in this manner for lack of imagination or creative power, but was restricted through the deliberate restraint of a sincere artistic conviction.
For, at heart, Berlage is not a harmonious, well-balanced artistic talent, as is demanded by the realisation of his principles, but a sensitive, temperamental personality who forces a strict discipline upon himself. His art develops under continuous restraint: with simplification and generalisation he strives for the monumental and the elevated.
In the above-mentioned works this was achieved in part only. In spite of the generous effect of mass and volumes and the integration

of details we still see a preference for lyrical emotional expression in the characteristic decorations mentioned earlier and a fondness of pictorial arrangements in the structural groups and the layout of plans. This is partly also the consequence of a natural-organic view on rationalism, which subordinates the aesthetic form to the coincidental practical conditions.[2] The deficiency of this view from an aesthetic point of view was recognised by the artist and gradually he adapted it in the sense that he recognised the natural requirements, but tried to find a rational solution in an aesthetic-constructive fashion. Some works from this first period already show this conception, but it mainly becomes apparent in Berlage's later works; because of the revolution in his views on other aspects as well, these can be counted as belonging to a new period in his creative work.

It must be admitted that the mixture of the monumental and the lyrical lends his first modern works a special charm; but in general it fails to be conducive to the uniformity of a work of art. Moreover, it really is that of medieval art and in the great variety of details it is consistent with the essence of the craft.

In our modern times cultural and economic needs demand the maximum use of machines. The changed production methods resulting from the use of machines and the subsequent standardisation will, together with the use of new materials have a far-reaching effect on the outward appearance of new architecture. In his articles Berlage has often pointed this out and, recently, bearing the prevailing housing shortage in mind, he defended the standardisation of houses for architectural reasons. The above factors will not be considered in mass production only, but will also have to have a strong influence on the construction when building better class residences and public buildings, lest the advantages of technical progress be withheld from the building trade for reasons of sentimental and romantic memories, and architecture would lag behind the times.

On the contrary, modern architecture has the duty to embrace technical improvements and to use them in an aesthetic manner. As I already explained in the beginning of this paper, this touches upon the heart of the matter, because new constructive and technical problems dominate building to such an extent that it can no longer be a matter of redesigning, but of fresh designs. The possibilities of producing bigger, jointless wall faces in every area of building techniques, as well as the need to mass-produce uniform building components, results in the promotion of architectural designs that concentrate on the total composition rather than on elaborate details; this means that the artist's individuality will emerge in the organism rather than in the organs. Plastic effect of mass and faces, proportion and rhythm will be the instruments of the new architecture.

This is therefore a continuation of Berlage's principles, which have not been fully realised in the works he created so far. The simplification in his later creations is the result of his pursuit of the monumental and the elevated ideals, not of a reversal due to the factors mentioned earlier. In the course of his development

his art, even in it simplest design, has an erudition which lends it valuable quality and great spirituality; on the other hand it precluded him from facing new tasks with an open mind. Intellectually Berlage accepted this and in his later works this is clearly visible; his training as an artist has steadily become more spiritualised and more complete but has not changed anything essential. Nevertheless, his buildings still show that they clearly have been influenced by the above, as is clearly proved by his works from the new period. The factors referred to before also play a part, since foreign influences also present themselves (German, American: the latter after he made a trip to America when Wright's work made a big impression on the architect). At this juncture, when the artist is still in his creative prime, it is hard to make any predictions regarding the final outcome of this development. We will have to leave this to the passage of time; all the same I wish to draw attention to two structures from this new period: they belong farmstead "De Schipborg" (1914) (Fig. 32 and 33), in which the needs of a farmer's life are architecturally represented in a sober and monumental manner. The second is an office building built for the firm Wm. Müller & Co. in London. (1914) (Fig. 31). It cannot be a coincidence that precisely the solution of this problem resulted in a work of great monumental quality. For Berlage has often compared the significance of office buildings for today's architecture with the significance of churches and palaces for the architecture in earlier centuries. The steel construction (which was fitted with a protective coating to resist the influence of the weather) and the business requirements led to a solution whose simple design consists mainly of a rhythmic series of white pillars; actually, in this narrow street a magnificent architectural effect is the result.

In the same period he also built shop-premises for the firm Meddens in The Hague (1914) (Fig. 30) and finished a design (inspired during a period of illness) for a monument "Pantheon of Humanity" (Fig. 35, 36, 37). Of the big plans now being carried out or in the process of preparation too little has been published to warrant a review.

I do not wish to conclude this paper without having pointed out that later too, the artist made designs for furniture and industrial art that experienced a development similar to that of his buildings. He also designed book jackets etc. and made a series of designs after motifs from the "Kunstformen der Natur" (Art forms in Nature) published by Häckel. In later years he was involved in the problems of urban development and planned urban expansion projects for The Hague and Amsterdam. Repeatedly he elucidated his principles and his views in papers and in lectures. In this respect it should be mentioned that his principles do not just refer to the rational view of architecture – as was discussed earlier –, but that he deems a combination with a spiritual ideal imperative. In his opinion this will be in keeping with socialism and a higher conception of business life. Finally, I want to

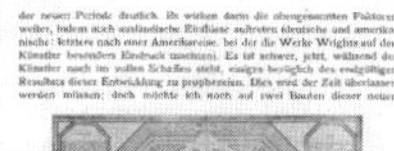

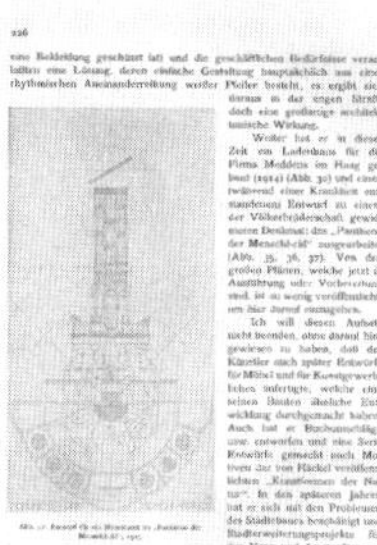

observe that in this paper I have only presented a few personal impressions of Berlage's creative work. In the steady development of art different notions come to the fore and time factors are to be considered; this means that an objective review of his works should be left to future generations.

All the same, Berlage's personality and his significance for modern Dutch architecture can be better judged by his contemporaries who partly witnessed his struggle, than by later generations who did not see the difficulties that had to be overcome and, in general, are more indifferent to the efforts than to the results. For that reason I emphasise again, with great respect, Berlage's enormous energy, effort and stamina which turned Dutch architecture from a lifeless tradition into an artistic reflection of contemporary social life again, and I add the wish that his creative power will benefit architecture for a long time to come.



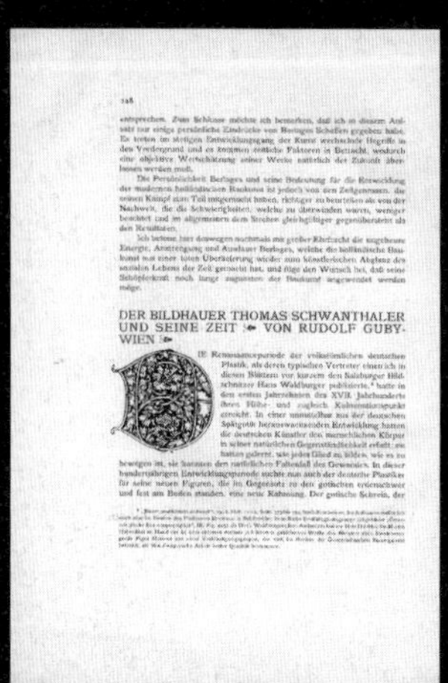
228

DER BILDHAUER THOMAS SCHWANTHALER UND SEINE ZEIT VON RUDOLF GUBY-WIEN

**1.** For the sake of brevity the particular trend in architecture that takes its departure from the social and practical needs and the technical progress in modern life and tries to solve these aesthetically in an organic way (that is, from the inside to the outside, without implying traditional decorative forms) has been referred to as modern, businesslike or rational. This should not be understood to include anything businesslike or rational which falls outside the realm of art.

**2.** This idea was propagated by Ruskin and it delayed the development of modern architecture considerably due to the priority given to sentimental and romantic values. This is eminently clear from the fact that over the years Berlage made additions to some of his buildings, when these suited the requirements of the occupants. But this does not conform to a purely aesthetic conception, for, in an aesthetic design each part is closely linked to the other parts and the smallest addition or removal would upset the balance of the entire composition.

J.J.P. Oud, 'Architecture and the future', in: *The Studio*, 96(1928)429, p.402-406, 453

# Architecture and the Future

By J.J.P. Oud.

Architecture is at a specially important period in its history. With the overthrow of formalism, it took a new lease of life, the consequences of which can at present be only faintly imagined.

Architecture has been slow to realise the benefits of our spiritual, social and technical progress. Not only is it not ahead of its time, it does not even keep pace with it. It has, in fact, a hindering effect on the necessary development of life. For it no longer places before itself as its aim the embodiment in a beautiful form of the most desirable type of dwelling-place; but, on the contrary, it sacrifices all to a traditional view of beauty, which, as it had its origin in other circumstances, is a hindrance to the development of life to-day. In other words, cause and effect have changed places. Thus it is that in building, the products of technical progress are not received with gratitude but are tested from the standpoint of a prevailing artistic outlook and, as a rule, because they are in contrast to this outlook they hold their place with difficulty against a pietistic architecturalism.

Art should be an expression of one's inner self, of a life-feeling. It is the life-feeling of a particular period and not formal tradition, which should determine the direction of its development. This life-feeling has never been more deeply stirred than at present. The stability of the old life-feeling is being undermined; new spiritual complexes are being formed. Yet architecture which has the task of holding up the mirror to the culture of its time is spiritually immune from all this movement, though it has been realised both in painting and in sculpture. However, though architecture is, in itself, unmoved by this change, change is coming about through force of circumstances.

Building-art is not, like the pure arts, exclusively the result of a spiritual process; it is also influenced by material factors. Its aim is the double one of being both useful and beautiful, and as the material circumstances change so architecture itself is changed and adopts new styles.

Architecture to-day knows nothing of terseness such as it is realised in the rhythm and the balanced composition of mutually related and interdependent parts, in which the changing of even the smallest detail is followed by a destruction of balance. What architecture to-day lacks in balance of that kind it makes up by the introduction of ornament. Ornament is the universal panacea for architectural impotence! While, on the other hand, unornamented buildings offers the greatest possible opportunities for pure architectural composition.

It is good to be able to record the presence of a tendency towards an unornamental architecture and yet this tendency is being continually hindered by the prevalence of the idea that, in the first instance, beauty and decoration are mutually inclusive terms.

Under the stress of circumstances and through the broadening of the æsthetic outlook, a self-formative type of architecture is at last becoming possible, an architecture which makes no use of other arts, but which in its constructive functionalism attains to beauty. And an architecture of this type requires no ornament for it is a complete organism in itself, in which all ornamentation is an individualisation of the part as distinct from the whole.

The substitution of machine-made articles – a social and an economic necessity – is also beginning to enjoy a wider scope. Originally opposed on æsthetic grounds, the use of machine-made productions is becoming more and more common. Though the use is restricted at present to subordinate tasks – mainly to the production of ready-made "detail" – it will extend to other more important tasks and so contribute its share to the evolution of the new styles. For the machines themselves possess endless possibilities for the development of an austerity and strictness of design, such as have not been heard of before.

New methods in the chemical, iron, glass and concrete industries are also playing their part in the revolutionary process which architecture is undergoing. For, for none of these materials can traditional forms be employed; indeed, tradional forms and ideas are frequently a hindrance to their adoption in building. This was the case, for example, with iron, which in spite of its obvious advantages as a building material was quickly shelved for "aesthecic" reasons.

The prospects, however, which are being opened out by the use of plate-glass and concrete are enormous. The latter holds aesthetic possibilities, which, when compared with the limitations to which brickbuilding is subject, cannot fail in the end to make for greater freedom in design.

As the last powerful factor in this new, revolutionary process, colour must be taken into account. In present-day architecture the colour element must, as a matter of course, be largely a matter of indifference. With the new processes, however, for the smoothing and colouring of roughcast and concrete, new possibilities occur for the greater and more deliberate use of colour in building. Thus, with these new processes, it is possible for the whole aspect of architecture to be changed.

In short, it follows that the new architecture, founded as it is on the actual conditions of life, will form a strong contrast to the architecture of the past. Without falling into any arid rationalism, it will be above all practical, and determined by the goal at which it aims.

J.J.P. Oud



Note. – The architect's views above given are from his book on Dutch Architecture, published by Albert Langen of

OVER DE TOEKOMSTIGE BOUWKUNST EN HARE ARCHITECTONISCHE MOGELIJKHEDEN

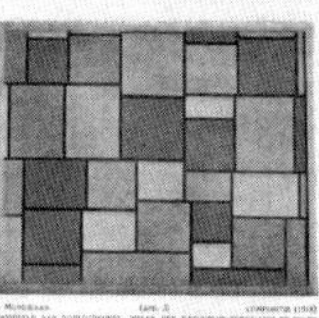

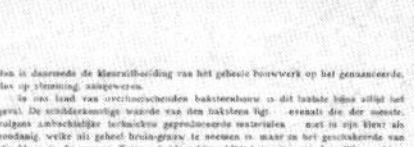

# 2 Pioneer of the ‘New Architecture’

**The Gemeentelijke Woningdienst of Rotterdam in 1918. Oud is seated in the first row, fifth from the right/ OUDJ-53, NAI, Rotterdam (Photo C. Kramer)**

# The Gemeentelijke Woningdienst in Rotterdam

During the years of his involvement with *De Stijl* (1917-1921), Oud was professionally immersed in his duties as architect with the Rotterdam Gemeentelijke Woningdienst (Municipal Housing Authority, 1918-1933). It was on the strength of this post that Van Doesburg sought to present Oud internationally as a practising *De Stijl* architect, a plan that was to founder dramatically on their second collaborative enterprise at Spangen in Rotterdam (1921). It was the bureaucratic, technical and economic aspects of this same job that served gradually to distance him from the intellectual and artistic sphere of Piet Mondrian. Nonetheless, it was also thanks to the Woningdienst that Oud was able to test his ideas about urban development, block organization, construction technology and the domestic floor plan against the practice of public housing construction. It enabled him to realize a small but impressive body of work that attracted a lot of attention, not only from architects and critics but also from housing reformers and public housing officials both at home and abroad. The Woningdienst also sent him on several study tours to find out what other countries were doing in the field of social housing, international trips that Oud also used to visit interesting architectural projects (such as Berlage's Holland House in London) and to give lectures, usually the *Opbouw* lecture 'Over de toekomstige bouwkunst en hare architectonische mogelijkheden' ('Architecture and the Future', 1921) which, given the number of translations it went through, may justifiably be regarded as the first international best-seller in the field of modern architectural theory.[1] The position with the Rotterdam Woningdienst also enabled Oud to undertake for himself what Van Doesburg had previously intended: the promotion abroad of J.J.P. Oud as a leading Dutch architect of modern housing. In common with other internationally active architects like Le Corbusier, Oud made clever use of the media. In newspapers, magazines, books (such as his *Bauhausbuch*) and exhibitions (the major shows in Paris and New York) he presented the same select suite of buildings from the same carefully chosen photographic viewpoints, thereby reducing complex buildings into highly legible and powerful images. Oud's texts were constructed in like manner: there, too, themes such as the evolutionary nature of Dutch architecture, the precursory role of Berlage, the tragedy of Frank Lloyd Wright and, finally, the idealization of contemporary art (Cubism), were so formulated, reiterated and paraphrased that they quickly acquired the character of incontrovertible myths.

Oud's friendship with Van Doesburg in the years 1916-1921 in no way precluded intensive contacts with H.P. Berlage. On the contrary, Oud regularly visited Berlage in Amsterdam; accompanied him to exhibition openings such as that of K.P.C. de Bazel in February 1916; attended lectures 'On Art' Berlage gave in his own home (March 1917); borrowed photographs, slides (of Holland House, for example) and above all books, including Karl Scheffler's monograph of Otto Wagner. Oud reciprocated with appropriate, homely presents – on one occasion a thermos flask for vacations – which were enthusiastically received by the Berlage family. In late 1916, Berlage asked Oud to come to Amsterdam 'to discuss a couple of matters',[2] one of which was a request that Oud should write a detailed article about Berlage in *Kunst und Kunsthandwerk*, a monthly magazine published by the Austrian Museum for Art and Industry. Oud agreed and the article eventually appeared, although only after a considerable delay and after Berlage had given his approval, in the April 1919 issue.[3] It is not impossible that another matter discussed on this occasion was Oud's appointment as architect with the recently established (1916) Rotterdam Gemeentelijke Woningdienst. Its first director was A. Plate, a civil engineer with a distinguished record of service in urban development and housing in the Dutch East Indies. Plate was a great admirer of Berlage and it was at the latter's urging that Oud received the public post in Rotterdam.

Van Doesburg and Mondrian were the first to point to the formative influence of the Rotterdam Woningdienst on Oud's development as architect,[4] which makes it all the more curious that there should be so little record of this in the literature about Oud. But then Oud himself was particularly keen to downplay the importance of this influence, lest it detract from his significance as an independent creative artist. Be that as it may, the constant changes in municipal housing policies, funding models and working coalitions kept Oud on his toes and forced him to keep coming up with new and different design solutions. When Oud joined the Woningdienst – in the last year before the First World War – he was immediately confronted with an enormous housing shortage and a political debate about the desirability of and need for municipal housing. Initially, Oud must have imagined that his slightly exalted, aesthetic ideas concerning standardization, the monumental townscape and construction technology were perfectly in keeping with the day-to-day practice of municipal housing policy. Partly as a result of Van Doesburg's encouragement, he saw himself functioning within the Woningdienst 'as a director who arranges mass products into an architectural whole'.[5] In that sense, Oud's early theoretical projects (which were also published in *De Stijl*), as well as the designs for the first Spangen blocks and the ambitious Tusschendijken plan, were tied up with a political ambition to 'widen the range of cheap housing'.[6] The fragile position of designers of municipal social housing became apparent in 1921 and again in 1923, when not only there was a realignment of political power at the local level, but, at the national level, the existing funding models were abandoned. Partly as a result of these developments, Oud found his activities at the Woningdienst severely curtailed. All of his subsequent housing projects for the city council were subject to special conditions and encountered considerable political and bureaucratic resistence. The 'Witte Dorp' (White Village), for example, was a temporary provision and as such located on a site earmarked for a park. The dwellings themselves were built as semi-permanent accommodation in accordance with the 1918 Housing Shortage Act. Oud's most successful Rotterdam housing scheme, at Hoek van Holland, had to be financed entirely by the city council and for that reason it was subject to extremely stringent conditions. After 1926, state funding for local housing was forthcoming only in the context of slum clearance and emergency accommodation. Oud's much-praised Kiefhoek estate was built under these terms although not without lengthy delays occasioned by the (municipal) approval procedures. Nor was Oud the only architect involved in social housing in Rotterdam in those years: Oud himself built on behalf of the city council, but in his capacity as a public official he was also concerned with the architectural and typological solutions of other architects (such as Michiel Brinkman in Spangen), who worked not for the city council but for private housing associations. This aspect of Oud's activities for the city council – bureaucratic supervision and adjustment of submitted building plans – has so far received little attention. It is also important that the evolution of the domestic floor plan and Oud's various typological choices and decisions should not be seen purely as steps in an autonomous and logically structured design process, but should also be analysed in the light of the prevailing political and bureaucratic views and differences of opinion concerning population policy in general and public housing in particular.

It is hard to imagine that Plate would have brought Oud into the Rotterdam Woningdienst on the strength of his articles in *De Stijl* in 1917 and 1918 on the monumental townscape and standardization in housing. At a time when the shortage of housing in Rotterdam was especially acute and both politicians and officials were struggling to formulate a municipal housing policy, Oud's pleas for an 'aesthetic approach to standard types' and for a 'stylistic street plasticity', to say nothing of his proposals for a 'monumental style' à la Berlage, would have struck many within the Woningdienst as distinctly odd. It is to Oud's credit, however, that during his collaboration with the social-democratic politician A.W. Heijkoop and the pragmatic Plate, he never renounced these architectural ideas but instead tried to render them acceptable, and that he remained open to foreign (German) experiences in the field of mass housing. On that score he no doubt profited from the contacts that Berlage – by virtue of his involvement with public housing in Amsterdam – had previously established with Walter Curt Behrendt, Karl Scheffler and Peter Behrens. This much is evident from one of his first articles about 'mass construction and street architecture' published in *De Stijl* in 1919, in which the problems of the architectural method, modern materials and aesthetic design were dealt with less abstractly and more from the perspective of everyday practice.[7] It is worthwhile reading this text in connection with the first large-scale housing schemes Oud built in Rotterdam, blocks I and V on Spaansche Bocht in Spangen (1918-1920). The main thrust of Oud's argument in *De Stijl* is the demand for a thorough reorganization of the construction industry coupled with the need to capitalize on new developments in construction technology and management. While the precise details of that reorganization are not spelled out, it is clear that Oud did not go nearly as far in this respect as certain groups within the Deutsche Werkbund (Muthesius, Behrens, Gropius) and that he was not acquainted with the radical proposals of Le Corbusier. In fact Oud does not touch on the economic aspects of the construction industry at all, merely the need to adjust architectural designs to meet the industry's changed conditions. In this process, cost-cutting measures like the placement of load-bearing walls perpendicular to the facade, narrower facades, the location of stairs in the centre of the buildings and standardization of a few components like frames and doors, went hand in hand with the search for a new street aesthetic. Actually, in theory and in practice, Oud stayed pretty close to Muthesius's careful prescriptions in *Kleinhaus und Kleinsiedlung* (1918). The first Spangen blocks show how much of this was feasible within the day-to-day reality of municipal house-building. In Spangen Oud was confronted with a street plan that precluded far-reaching economies in the design: *The site plan was more or less dictated by the building lines. The course of these lines, which meet at acute or obtuse angles and as far as Spaansche Bocht is concerned exhibit an irregular curved line, occasioned much time-consuming drawing and juggling in the making of the working drawings and in the construction. In general, a simple orthogonal, at any rate regular, street plan is essential for speedy and economic construction, which in these times is imperative. All good intentions in this direction come to naught if this is not taken into account when drawing up the street plans.*[8] In these first Spangen blocks, Oud worked with standard floor plans, altering various details (location of chimney, cupboards and windows) chiefly in order to achieve the required rhythm along the street frontage. However, the main theme of blocks I and V was a limited degree of standardization. 'Uniformity of parts' was achieved in the street elevation, where a single window and door model was used, albeit in various combinations, and in the profiles of internal window and door frames. In both cases the advantages had less to do with saving money in the construction than with saving time in the making of design and working drawings. Yet all these advantages were outweighed by the opportunities afforded by even this limited standardization for 'the aesthetic expression of the mass product', first and foremost in the architecture of the street elevation but also in that of the interior. Oud's ideas on this subject at that time were strongly influenced by theoretical debates within *De Stijl* and especially by his discussions with Van Doesburg, who as painter also had an active part in the colour scheme for the interior and exterior of the blocks. As far as the street elevation was concerned, Oud stated that the desired unity did not flow directly from the standardization of the ground plan and components but was arrived at in stages. At Spangen the sustained standardization resulted in a unity with a visually speaking ornamental effect. But it did not end here. Elaboration of this theme would, in the context of a less rigid standardization (with more scope for architectural input) result in a 'melodic-expressive street elevation' – which immediately brings to mind the celebrated design for the Strandboulevard at Scheveningen. Nor was this the end, either: *Absolute, harmonious, expression is only possible in the townscape* as a whole *(which must be made the aim), if the continuation of the street, which arises from the predominantly horizontal development, is interrupted by the explicitly vertical element, in the form of major corner treatments or free-standing buildings.*[9] Although these lines are from his article in *De Stijl*, Oud quoted them almost word-for-word in his commentary on the finished Spangen blocks, from which it must be concluded that in the rhythmic articulation of the street elevation (dictated by the bay width), Oud was *consciously* looking for 'a certain unobtrusiveness', the expressive significance of which only becomes visible at the point where the street becomes the city: at the corners of the block and in the vicinity of public buildings. It was precisely this architectural intention that Van Doesburg sought to oppose with his paintwork: in the first two blocks cautiously though unmistakably, in block IX some years later unacceptably (for Oud), with a dynamic, diagonal colour design that worked against the horizontal character of the street elevation. Whereas the artist Van Doesburg saw the street elevation as an autonomous plane, complete in itself, the architect and town planner Oud saw it as no more than one *element* in the much bigger composition of the city.

The notion of standardization as the starting point for aesthetic expression applied not only to the architecture of the street elevation but also, to the extent that Oud had any say in the matter, to the interior. This led at a later stage to the involvement of Rietveld as well as Van Doesburg. Unable to tinker much with the floor plan, Oud expended a lot of energy on interior design. For instance, the customary wallpapering was dispensed with and *the walls, by way of experiment, were provided at door-height with a picture rail below which the wall was rendered with coloured mortar, while the area above it, like the ceiling, was finished in white plaster.*[10] Van Doesburg's colour designs were restricted to the doors, the section of wall below the picture rail and the chimney piece. Oud's modifications to floor plan and interior were in keeping with contemporary ideas about housing reform and public education in public housing circles. The kitchen, for example, was kept deliberately small in order to prevent the working-class residents from using it as a living room as was their custom. The request to Rietveld for 'standard furniture' was another instance of this ideology. Initially asked to advise on the purchase of sound but inexpensive furniture for the model dwelling, Rietveld referred Oud to the Vroom & Dreesmann department store where he could buy chairs and a sideboard made by P.J.C. Klaarhamer for a factory in Zaandam. They were poorly made, of course, but Oud should not make too much of this: *After all, let's not pretend that we are working to please the populace, for there is no demand for this among the populace. Most of them have got no further than the desire to have something a little bit different. I know the people through and through on this point.*[11] In the end, Rietveld himself made a sideboard, a couple of chairs and a table for Spangen. Nonetheless, one wonders how Oud managed, in those years of acute housing and financial shortages, to secure additional funds for such expensive extras. One possible answer is related to the fact that several housing associations and speculative builders were also busy building in Spangen alongside the Woningdienst. Perhaps Plate and Heijkoop regarded the colourful finishing of the exterior and the sensible layout of the individual dwellings as desirable distinguishing features of public construction. This was suggested by Oud himself in his article on 'Architecture and Standardization in Mass Construction' in *De Stijl* (1918) in which he pointed to the 'anarchy' in the building industry resulting from the fact that private developers had already embraced 'an inferior version' of modern production methods (standardization). In essence this amounted to the non-aesthetic, and even worse, the hyper-aesthetic use of 'standard commercial types' for chimney pieces and upholstery fabrics, parquet floors and wall tiles and, at the architectural level, a whole range of 'luxury products such as newel posts and leaded lights'.[12] On the strength of these lines it is possible to imagine that the enlistment of Van Doesburg and Rietveld for the first Spangen housing blocks was no mere 'aesthetic game' at the expense of a tight public housing budget, but a politically sanctioned measure aimed at investing a new municipal initiative with added socio-cultural meaning.

That same desire to invest housing with social significance seems to lie behind the prominence given to the residential court, first in Spangen and later in Tusschendijken where it was furnished with numerous collective amenities in the form of sheds, pergolas and sand pits. Looking back, Plate's successor as director of the Rotterdam Woningdienst, M.J.I. de Jonge van Ellemeet compared Oud's orientation on a collective inner court with Michiel Brinkman's gallery-access flats which sought to compensate the disadvantages of multistorey living by other means: *Compared with the dynamic Amsterdam architecture there is a certain ruggedness – typical of the city – that even becomes a little dour when Oud in his municipal housing schemes deliberately moves daytime family life to the garden side and also expresses this shift in the street elevation. The dwelling itself in the meantime advanced by leaps and bounds both as self-contained accommodation for the closed family unit and in the rationalization of the floor plan in which the functional grouping of the various rooms was given increasing prominence. At the same time,*

*Brinkman, in his gallery flats, created a remarkable complex in which the aesthetic aspect was secondary, but in which a solution was found for certain inconveniences inherent to multi-storey buildings and moreover using purely functional means, in other words, entirely in line with the foregoing.*[13]

On 12 September 1921, Van Doesburg wrote to Oud: *I am very pleased by the rebelliousness in your letters. I sometimes (honestly and amicably) feared that standardization was making you too pragmatic.*[14] This was no doubt in reaction to an undated letter from Oud in which he had complained: *The municipal job bores me too. Now that my 1000 dwellings are under construction and I have mastered that standardization, the interesting part is over and I don't see the point of it any more.*[15] One can only guess at the reasons for Oud's despondency. He operated successfully within the Woningdienst and achieved rapid promotion which, judging from the reactions of Mondrian and Van Doesburg, was a source of pride. One possible explanation is the lack of sufficient (financial) scope for further research and experiment. After 1921, the political and financial conditions for municipal housing deteriorated swiftly. In Rotterdam the two social-democratic aldermen were ousted from the council and there came an end to the Woningdienst's experiments in subdivision, building materials, standardization and dwelling types. On top of this, the national government had started to withdraw from public housing in 1920; after 1921 it ceased to grant loans. In Rotterdam this meant that Oud's plans for 2,000 dwellings in Tusschendijken and Kromhout's for some 2,500 dwellings in Blijdorp were halved or shelved. Everything Oud designed in the field of social housing in Rotterdam after 1921 was overshadowed by two frustrating experiences: the end of a stimulating triumvirate of politics, management and architecture due to political and financial decisions in Rotterdam and beyond, and the conflict with Van Doesburg (and Mondrian) which put an end to the illusion of together – as architect and painter – achieving 'a mechanical, unintentional aesthetic'. In districts like Oud-Mathenesse, Hoek van Holland and Kiefhoek, Oud worked alone – without any outside input whatsoever – and he put all his energy into the careful, architectonic shaping of the daily reality of domestic life. Compared with the early Rotterdam projects, Oud's 'white residential architecture' is typical of the 'narrow margins outside mainstream housing construction' within which municipal housing construction was constrained to operate after 1921: *As a result, Oud's work fell outside the tumult of metropolitan operations. This was also literally the case, since the Witte Dorp, the Hoek van Holland terrace and Kiefhoek were fairly isolated locations and all entailed low-rise construction.*[16] The Witte Dorp is illustrative in this respect. Conceived as replacement accommodation for low-income, working-class families from inner-city slum clearance areas, in Oud's hands it became an instruction model of urban living. A small section of the Witte Dorp also fulfilled a special function as the final stage in a re-education programme for moderately asocial families. Oud-Mathenesse was a village-sized version of the residential square in which the complexity of urban life was reduced to a simple matter of living, shopping and playing. And the architecture contributed to this: it was sober, exemplary and completely dictated by standardization, both of the floor plan and of as many internal and external architectural elements as possible. The meticulous detailing was not altogether free of a certain paternalism. In reference to the finishing of the interior Oud wrote: *The living rooms are papered up to the picture rail, above that white. The wall and floor where the stove or cooker will stand is finished with a layer of red, hard-baked tiles. In the middle of the rear wall, a shelf has been built out above which there is room for a mirror and on which portraits, etc. can be placed: an interior so designed because experience has taught that residents are otherwise wont to arrange it in their own way.*[17]

The Witte Dorp makes explicit what Hoek van Holland and Kiefhoek were actually all about: a limited scheme aimed at bringing some prospects into the hopeless situation of a certain category of home-seekers. It was more about setting an example than attempting to solve the housing shortage. As such, these districts are early, and architecturally speaking, self-willed exercises in what would shortly come to be known in CIAM circles as *Die Wohnung für das Existenzminimum*, a topic on which there was still considerable disagreement in local government circles in Rotterdam. As such, they are also wholly in line with the research Oud had been conducting since 1917 into the architectural control of the industrially produced, urban housing block. Research that reached a provisional conclusion in 1931 with the studies for a residential neighbourhood of row housing in Blijdorp. Oud's architectural design work in those years was completely bound up with the search for a plan form that would allow 'maximum requirements to be contained in minimum spaces'. In the 'white housing' of the Witte Dorp, Hoek van Holland and Kiefhoek, Oud's researches focused on two aspects. From a town planning perspective, Oud concentrated on the urban district as a closed, monumental composition, as an autonomous architectural object whose symmetrical, some would say classical form, appeared to be a blatant contradiction of the ideals of unintentionality, openness and dynamism that characterized ideas about building and city in the early years of *De Stijl*. Secondly, Oud seized on the limiting (financial and programmatic) conditions of these three housing schemes to shift the focus of research from working methods, materials and design to 'the demands made by daily life'. By this he meant first of all the architectural control of new domestic techniques and appliances and, more broadly, knowledge of and the resulting architectural orchestration of 'the small conveniences called for by daily life'. In 1927, in one of the first issues of *i 10* – of which Oud was architectural editor – he wrote: *Yet there is only one way of arriving at a lively and a universal architecture, i.e. second by second, minute by minute, hour by hour repeatedly fathoming what is genuinely expected of the architect. In the resulting data lies the essential contact between life and architecture: the basis for a new unity, for 'style'.*[18] By way of illustration, he appended floor plans and a perspective drawing of the workers' dwellings, shops and warehouses at Hoek van Holland (1924-1928), a scheme that he was later to present as the true starting point of a 'new, plastic architecture' that had left all the uncertainties in form and style that still characterized the factory at Purmerend, for example, far behind it.

The final years of Oud's service with the Rotterdam Woningdienst, were marked by bouts of depression and a dearth of work. At the very moment when Oud's reputation as an architect of modern domestic living was internationally established and he was receiving numerous offers of guest lectureships and invitations to take part in major architectural exhibitions (like the one in New York in 1932), he resigned his post at the Gemeentelijke Woningdienst. The irony of that decision did not escape *Het Bouwbedrijf*, the leading magazine in the field of integrated construction at that time: *J.J.P. Oud, an architect who is very well known beyond our national borders and is certainly more valued outside our country than within it, is to leave the Rotterdam municipal service on 1 April 1933 and set up in private practice. For the sake of Dutch architecture it is to be hoped that this pioneer, this dedicated champion of new ideas in architecture, will enjoy a larger and more important sphere of action in private practice than as an official with a municipal service whose management was not entirely imbued with the spirit that animated Oud's works and aspirations.*[19] Although the accuracy of these observations is open to dispute, they were never actually contradicted by Oud himself. However, in view of developments in the field of public housing and the lack of resources and political will that effectively prevented local authorities from playing a major role in the housing market, it seems probable that Oud had little to gain by remaining with the Woningdienst. His research into a new working method, new materials and new design in public housing was finished. An international career beckoned but Oud withdrew to his home-cum-studio in Hillegersberg and from there, in defiance of CIAM, 'De 8' and 'Opbouw', commenced his battle against every attempt to re-evaluate modern architecture that was not rooted in actual building practice.

**Notes**

**1.** J.J.P. Oud, 'Over de toekomstige bouwkunst en hare architectonische mogelijkheden', in: *Bouwkundig Weekblad*, 42(1921)24, pp. 147-160. Oud's lecture was also published in: *Fruhlicht*, 1(1921/1922)4, pp. 113-118; *Baukunst* (1925), pp. 98-101; *La Cite*, (1923)5, pp. 73-85; *Stavba* (1922)109, pp. 177-192; and *Studio* (1928), pp. 401-406.

**2.** Postcard from H.P. Berlage to J.J.P. Oud, 14 April 1916, OUDJ-B, NAI, Rotterdam.

**3.** J.J.P. Oud, 'Dr. Berlage und sein Werk', in: *Kunst und Kunsthandwerk*, 22(1919)6/8, pp. 189-228.

**4.** Cf. letter from P. Mondrian to J.J.P. Oud, 18 September 1921, Fondation Custodia, Paris, and letter from T. van Doesburg to J.J.P. Oud, 14 December 1921, Fondation Custodia, Paris.

**5.** Quoted by H. Engel, 'De Kiefhoek. Een monument voor gemiste kansen', in: S. Cusveller (ed.), *De Kiefhoek, een woonwijk in Rotterdam*, Laren, Naarden 1990, p. 17.

**6.** Quoted by H. Engel, 'De Kiefhoek. Een monument voor gemiste kansen', in: S. Cusveller (ed.), *De Kiefhoek, een woonwijk in Rotterdam*, Laren, Naarden 1990, p. 19.

**7.** J.J.P. Oud, 'Architectonische beschouwingen: A. Massabouw en straatarchitectuur, B. Gewapend beton en bouwkunst', in: *De Stijl*, 2(1919)7, pp. 79-84.

**8.** J.J.P. Oud, 'Gemeentelijke volkswoningen, Polder " Spangen", Rotterdam', in: *Bouwkundig Weekblad*, 41(1920)37, p. 221.

**9.** J.J.P. Oud, 'Architectonische beschouwingen: A. Massabouw en straatarchitectuur, B. Gewapend beton en bouwkunst', in: *De Stijl*, 2(1919)7, p. 82.

**10.** J.J.P. Oud, 'Gemeentelijke volkswoningen, Polder "Spangen", Rotterdam', in: *Bouwkundig Weekblad*, 41(1920)37, p. 221.

**11.** G.T. Rietveld to J.J.P. Oud, 23 January 1920, OUDJ-B, NAI, Rotterdam.

**12.** J.J.P. Oud, 'Bouwkunst en normalisatie bij den massabouw', in: *De Stijl*, 1(1918)7, pp. 77-79.

**13.** M.J.I. de Jonge van Ellemeet, 'De Woningbouwvereenigingen en de architectuur', in: *Beter Wonen. Gedenkboek gewijd aan het werk van den Woningbouwvereenigingen in Nederland*, Amsterdam 1938, p. 67-91.

**14.** J.J.P. Oud to T. van Doesburg, 12 September 1921, Fondation Custodia, Paris.

**15.** H. Engel, 'De Kiefhoek. Een monument voor gemiste kansen', in: S. Cusveller (ed.), *De Kiefhoek, een woonwijk in Rotterdam*, Laren, Naarden 1990, p. 32.

**16.** J.J.P. Oud, 'Semi-permanente woningbouw "Oud-Mathenesse" te Rotterdam', in: *Bouwkundig Weekblad*, 45(1924)43, p. 418.

**17.** J.J.P. Oud, 'Semi-permanente woningbouw "Oud-Mathenesse" te Rotterdam', in: *Bouwkundig Weekblad*, 45(1924)43, p. 418.

**18.** J.J.P. Oud, 'Huisvrouwen en architectuur', in: *i 10*, 1(1927)2, p. 46.

**19.** Quoted by H. Engel, 'De Kiefhoek. Een monument voor gemiste kansen', in: S. Cusveller (ed.), *De Kiefhoek, een woonwijk in Rotterdam*, Laren, Naarden 1990.

Among the Woningdienst's tasks was the making and evaluation of 'subdivision plans' for those areas of the city earmarked for housing. While not of the same order as the urban design schemes for the city as a whole, they nonetheless included all the amenities necessary for daily life in a new district and as such they were full-fledged urban planning designs. In the early decades of the twentieth century, the town planning method developed at the beginning of the century by Berlage in his expansion plans for Amsterdam was regarded as exemplary and his 'handwriting' is also clearly discernible in the Rotterdam expansion plans. Berlage's plans were a collage of different urban planning layers. He used 'mass housing' as the raw material for the new city but articulated it meticulously in architectonic elements that formed the building blocks of a spatial composition. Typically, such a composition combined a hierarchical road system, hierarchical residential development (with the taller blocks lining the main roads), and public buildings as architectural markers of special places. The varied townscape produced by this method was further enriched in Rotterdam by an irregular base. On the one hand an obstacle to development, on the other hand the differences in height between polders, dikes and drainage canals gave direction to the spatial composition. P. Verhagen's plan for Spangen, drawn up in 1913 for his municipal employer, the Stadstimmerwerf, is one of the first examples in which topographical dictates were used as the basis for what in this case was still a fundamentally Berlagian plan. Spangen was a polder to the west of the city where the city council still owned a reasonably large tract of land, a fairly remarkable state of affairs, since Rotterdam had in the preceding decades squandered the lion's share of its own land. The availability of municipal land was one of the reasons why Spangen, despite its isolated location, was especially suitable for the construction of working-class housing; another reason was that the land could be built on without first having to be raised. Thus the topographical conditions did indeed help to determine the eventual plan.[1] Verhagen's plan set the tone for the spatial plans produced by the Woningdienst after 1918, some of them by Oud.

Oud, too, sought to employ the Berlagian urbanist idiom, and he, too, took account of topographical motifs. This is evident, for example, in his design for Varkenoordsche Polder, south of the river Maas. It is one of the few urban design plans by Oud to have survived, but he is known to have been involved in all the public housing schemes of the period, even those, like Varkenoordsche Polder, where the city council was not the client. The client in this instance was a private developer, N.V. Maatschappij Volkswoningen Vreewijk (N.V. Vreewijk for short), and the project was part of a green belt of garden suburbs, parks and lakes inspired by American examples. First mooted by influential private parties on the eve of the First World War, the green belt gradually started to take shape in the 1920s and 1930s. Varkenoordsche Polder was part of this chain; from there the green belt was to bear north across the river and so via the waterworks and Kralingen to Hilligersberg. Although the green belt was nominally one of a series of local and regional development plans, its implementation was virtually autonomous.[2] The first outcome was Vreewijk, a garden suburb laid out to a plan by Verhagen who had in the meantime left municipal service and set up in private practice with M.J. Granpré Molière and A.J.T.H. Kok. Much praised both at home and abroad, Vreewijk marked Verhagen's departure from Berlagian urban planning, with its strong architectural bias. Although architecture and planning are in perfect accord in Vreewijk, that was not the essence of the plan. The spatial plan is a simple, regular and fairly large-

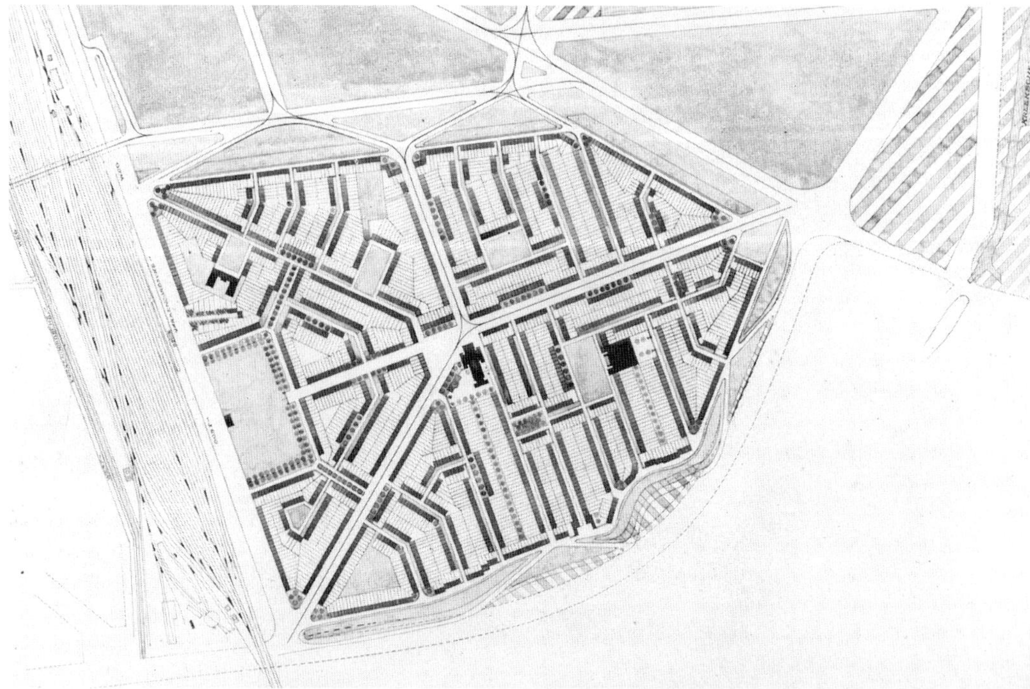

Lot plan/ 890126-33**, Getty, Los Angeles

scale axial cross with exceptionally precise contours and a very detailed green plan, strong enough to hold its own in any type of development. In other words, the spatial composition was disengaged from the architectural composition, and the plan from the faster and less predictable dynamics of the architecture. The Vreewijk development lacks the Berlagian hierarchical structure of the road network and the progression of squares with public buildings. The centre of the district is barely emphasized and it does not form the hub of the access roads, which lies on the edge of the district. N.V. Vreewijk wanted to develop Varkenoordsche Polder in similar fashion and it commissioned A. Siebers (1893-1978), who was then working for Granpré Molière, Verhagen & Kok, to draw up a masterplan. This plan met with objections from the Woningdienst, in particular from its director A. Plate, who was opposed to the whole idea of a green belt and would have preferred to turn Varkenoordsche Polder into an industrial zone. When this turned out to be impossible he opted for a garden suburb with a more urban aspect than Vreewijk. Oud's design for Varkenoordsche Polder was consequently in the nature of a counter-plan.

Oud retained the leafy, intimate character of a garden suburb of 1,300 to 1,400 dwellings. He connected the centre to the tram network and set aside land for collective amenities such as schools and churches that would not be built by N.V. Vreewijk. Oud's subdivision plan is pure Berlage. It is stratified and it relates a hierarchically organized road structure, centralized amenities and housing to one another and to the surrounding area. The backbone of the design is a diagonal road through the centre of the district. A second main axis runs from the centre to the north and forms the link with Rotterdam North. This road structure divides the district into three neighbourhoods where further access is provided by cross streets and side roads. As in Spangen, one of the axes is terminated by a playing field, which in turn abuts the railway yard separating Varkenoordsche Polder from Vreewijk. Depending on the nature of the terrain, the street pattern generates square or triangular parcels of land that are not filled with closed blocks but with 'open' development: rows of housing along the street, terminating in an end facade and private gardens at the rear. There is further differentiation in the form of footpaths, a few set-back rows (suitable for retail development), a traditional court development, axial layout and tree-planting. Along the south-west perimeter, the subdivision follows the windings of the dike. As could be expected, Oud's counter-proposal led to a difference of opinion with N.V. Vreewijk and Siebers. The main disagreement concerned Oud's centralized access system but there was also dissension about the placement of the housing rows: while Oud had opted for an orientation on the sun and a favourable position with respect to through traffic, Siebers and his client preferred rows and streets with a north-south alignment as in Vreewijk.[3] This allowed the road system to follow the natural course of the polder ditches, thereby minimizing the risk of subsidence.[4] When, after several months of negotiations, it became clear that the Woningdienst was not about to give in, Granpré Molière, Verhagen & Kok came up with a plan that addressed the Woningdienst's objections.

Oud's plan for Varkenoordsche Polder was never executed. Exactly one year after the plan was submitted, the city council announced that it first wanted to finish developing the land to the west of the railway yard. Otherwise the residential district currently being built in Rotterdam South would get too big and urbanization would proceed too slowly. In this, the council was following a recommendation (February 1922) of the Commissie voor Volkshuisvesting (Municipal Housing Commission) which, like Plate, was not keen to see a garden suburb on this site.



**Notes**

**1.** M. Steenhuis, *P. Verhagen*, monograph in the town planning series issued by the Nederlands Instituut voor Ruimtelijke Ordening en Volkshuisvesting (NIROV), manuscript October 2000.
**2.** For the IJsselmonde regional plan, see: K. Bosma, *Ruimte voor een nieuwe tijd*, Rotterdam 1993, p. 196 ff.
**3.** A. Siebers, 'Aantekeningen ten aanzien van de onderhandelingen over de Varkenoordsche polder, 1920-1921', handwritten manuscript in uninventoried section of the Siebers Archive, NAI, Rotterdam. With thanks to Marinke Steenhuis.
**4.** For the Vreewijk plans for Rotterdam South, see: L. de Klerk, *Particuliere Plannen*, Rotterdam 1998, p. 185, and for the plan by A. Siebers, p. 165.

**Sources**

Gemeentearchief Rotterdam: Secretarie Afdeling Volkshuisvesting Archive, dossier 245, 1921
Getty: 890126-33**
NAI: Siebers Archive, uninventoried section

**Literature**

K. Bosma, *Ruimte voor een Nieuwe tijd*, Rotterdam 1993
L. de Klerk, *Particuliere Plannen*, Rotterdam 1998
A. van der Valk, *Th.K. van Lohuizen*, Delft 1990

## 35/ Subdivision Plan for Mathenesser Polder

**Rotterdam/Schiedam, Nieuwe Havenspoorweg, Schiedamse Hoogen Zeedijk 1920**

Oud's subdivision plan for Mathenesser Polder came about in partnership with the urban planning analyst, T.K. van Lohuizen.[1] Oud regarded the collaboration with the newly appointed Van Lohuizen as a test case for the statistical survey, a key topic in the contemporary international town planning debate. He wanted to find out how the survey might contribute to the rationalization, standardization and efficiency of the urban development plan, and whether a more scientific approach to town planning could be reconciled with the pursuit of a monumental urbanism.

If the plan for Mathenesser Polder had been implemented, it might have turned out to be one of the most complete examples in Oud's oeuvre of the 'melodically expressive street wall' heralded in his 1919 article, 'Massabouw en straatarchitectuur'. The rhythmic composition of housing, businesses and collective amenities was based entirely on the results of Van Lohuizen's planning survey, which afforded a wealth of variations for the composition of the city. The survey made precise statements about the combination of various dwelling types, commercial spaces and public buildings. But Oud's design was not simply a neutral rendering of the building programme, nor a straightforward reproduction of the differentiated and functionalist-inspired composition of the city. It was also a differentiation of the hierarchy in the cityscape expressed in three-dimensional form. Even more than the plan for the garden suburb in Varkenoordsche Polder, the design for Mathenesser Polder is a small town in which schools, churches, a public library and other essential collective services are assigned a precisely determined, monumental place. The communal facilities function as visual highlights against the relatively neutral background of the housing; the axes, vistas and the detailing of the public space are once again a direct allusion to Berlage.

The Oud-Mathenesse district was intended to form the link between the suburban developments in Rotterdam West (Spangen, Tusschendijken) and the eastern extension of Schiedam. It was hemmed in by industry and docks to the south and railway lines to the north. The new district was supposed to accommodate a total of 35,000 inhabitants, almost as many as were then living in Schiedam. In the plan

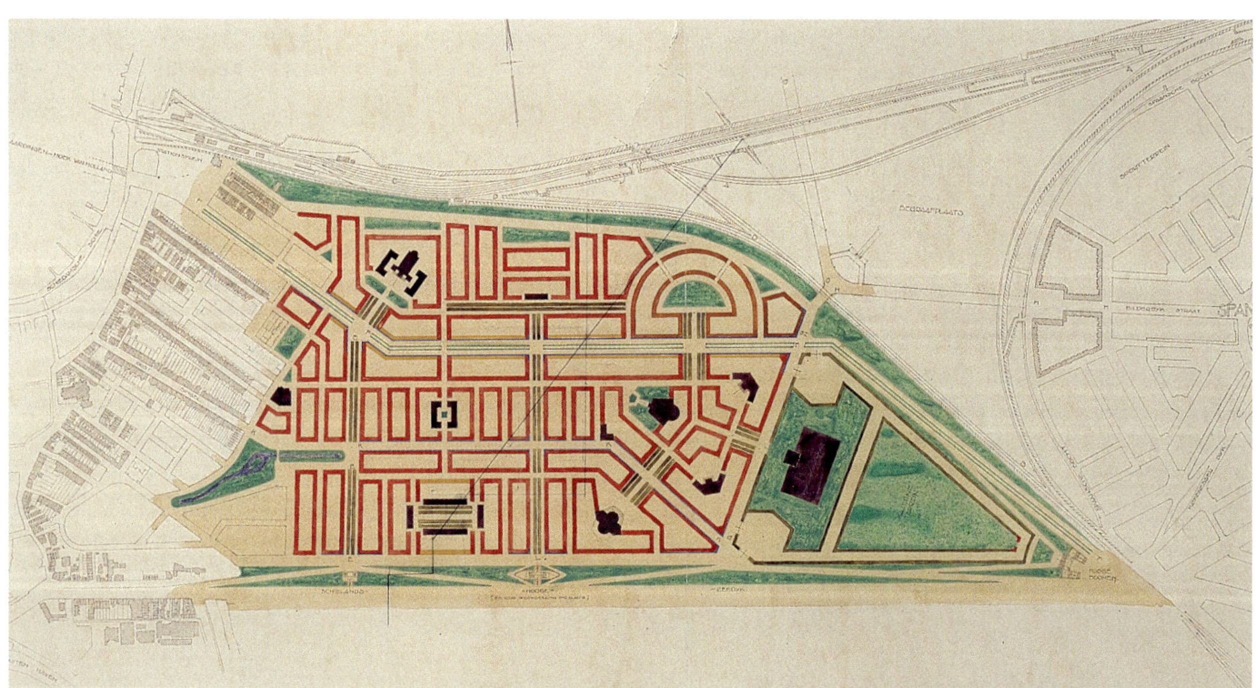

Lot plan/ OUDJ-wd 17, NAI, Rotterdam

commentary, probably written by Van Lohuizen, the location of the expansion area was justified on the grounds of Rotterdam's tendency to develop in a westerly direction. In that sense it was a counter-proposal to the more or less concurrent expansion plan (1921) for the southern shore of the Maas by Granpré Molière, Verhagen & Kok, who wanted to use the cheap land in Rotterdam South to alleviate the housing shortage. A large part of Oud-Mathenesse lay inside the municipality of Schiedam which in Oud's plan was incorporated in its entirety into the greater metropolitan area of Rotterdam. Because Oud-Mathenesse was quite a distance from the centre of Rotterdam, the plan commentary dwelt on the possibility of an electric express tramway.[2] The traffic systems – road network, tram tracks and railway lines – gave direction to the plan. The main access route for vehicular traffic ran through the middle of the district and was a continuation of Schiedamsche Weg and Mathenesser Weg. Van Lohuizen claimed that the road structure had not only been designed as efficiently as possible and with an eye to the existing and future situation, but that it had also served as the point of departure for the subdivision. The subdivision and land uses, which were precisely indicated on the map, were based on meticulous calculations. Van Lohuizen had used diagrams, graphs and comparisons of data such as land price, soil conditions, cost of street-laying and sewerage and operational costs to arrive at the 'ideal' subdivision types and building densities for the district, in which details such as block dimensions (block length, building depth, court width), building height, housing differentiation and street width and length were all laid down.[3] The plan provided for mainly north-south streets in combination with perimeter blocks. Along the main access roads the block development followed the cross street direction, which was east-west, in order to shield the houses in the neighbourhoods as much as possible from the high-speed (regional) traffic – a classic Berlagian theme. Housing with ground-floor shops was projected along the through roads. Most of the special buildings were designed as free-standing objects located far away from heavy traffic on squares in the neighbourhoods. These buildings were also linked to one another by a series of tree-lined avenues. Unlike Tusschendijken and Spangen, which were designed as purely working-class districts, this development was conceived as demographically mixed.[4]

Van Lohuizen and Oud presented their design at the very moment when the national government was withdrawing from the housing market. With large-scale municipal housing schemes like Spangen and Tusschendijken no longer a realistic proposition, the plan was modified to meet the demands of private developers. They showed little interest in the plan, however. Poor soil conditions made for expensive site preparation and foundations, and increased the possibility of engineering problems. The Rotterdam Woningdienst's initial development plans were confined to the site of the old army barracks in Oud-Mathenesse, which they planned to fill with emergency housing for people made homeless by slum clearance activities in the city centre. From 1922, Oud worked on his design for semi-permanent housing for this location, the so-called Witte Dorp, or 'white village' (see no. 42). Like the unrealized design for concrete housing in Spangen, the Mathenesser Polder expansion plan was a great disappointment for Oud, as witnessed by his life-long silence on the subject. The ill-fated collaboration with Van Lohuizen fuelled his fundamental criticism of another project in which Van Lohuizen played a major role, the 1935 Algemeen Uitbreidingsplan (General Extension Plan) for Amsterdam.[5]



**Notes**

**1.** The only writer to mention Oud's expansion plan for Mathenesser Polder is Arnold van der Valk. A. van der Valk, *Het levenswerk van Th.K. van Lohuizen 1890-1956. De eenheid van het stedebouwkundig werk*, Delft 1990, pp. 26, 32.

**2.** T.K. van Lohuizen, Toelichting ontwerp uitbreidingsplan Oud-Mathenesse, undated [1921], typescript, p. 24. Van Lohuizen Archive, dossier 7, item 8, NAI, Rotterdam.

**3.** A. van der Valk, *Het levenswerk van Th.K. van Lohuizen 1890-1956. De eenheid van het stedebouwkundig werk*, Delft 1990, p. 82.

**4.** T.K. van Lohuizen, Toelichting ontwerp uitbreidingsplan Oud-Mathenesse, undated [1921], typescript, p. 21. Van Lohuizen Archive, dossier 7, item 8, NAI, Rotterdam.

**5.** For Oud's criticism of the AUP, see: E. Taverne, D. Broekhuizen, J.J.P. Oud's Shell Building. Design and Reception, Rotterdam 1995, p. 99.

**Sources**

NAI: OUDJ-wd 17, T.K. van Lohuizen Archive, dossier 7

**Articles**

T.K. van Lohuizen, *Zwei Jahre Wohnungsstatistik in Rotterdam. Eine neue Methode der Statistiküber Wohnungsbedarf und Wohnungsvorrat*, Berlin 1922

**Literature**

H. van der Sloot, *Betrekkelijk tot tevredenheid. De woningbouwverenigingen in Schiedam*, Schiedam 1992

A. van der Valk, *Het levenswerk van T.K. van Lohuizen 1890-1956. De eenheid van het stedebouwkundig werk*, Delft 1990

*I have good expectations for the refinements which are possible in architecture thanks to mechanical production, but I fear that uncritical admiration of all that is mechanical will lead to a regrettable relapse.*

*I expect a crystallization of form leading to style by standardization of individual building components, but, in my view, it will be hard to fit the mass-produced standard house into the overall composition of the big city.*

These comments by Oud himself, both dating from 1925, could not be more ambivalent. In the years immediately before and after 1920, he was able to get closely involved in the cultural dilemmas occasioned by the modernization of the building production process. There were new products, new techniques and, in particular, a new definition of the craft, generated by advancing prefabrication and standardization. Standardization stands for limited variation in building components and typological choices, for reasons of efficiency and cost. Standardization means arranging work at the building site into a rigid pattern.

Standardization implies subservient or deferred artistry. The growing importance of this phenomenon was directly proportional to the growing prominence of large-scale housing projects in the list of architectural commissions. An exercise of this magnitude which had been spreading drastically from the start of the twentieth century, had to be dealt with systematically, and could not be solved with a succession of individual artistic decisions prompted by personal taste. Money was an important motive, but that also went with the nature of the assignment. A large housing project was not specifically designed for one user, but required an all-round organism with general stylistic connotations. Oud was aware of that, as his first written contribution (devoted to the monumental image of the city) in *De Stijl* demonstrated. The definition of the monumental cityscape was nicely in tune with his first Rotterdam housing-design work at the time. Oud presented in both a succinct view of what the new building exercise meant for the architect's work, on the face of it at the expense of the traditional substance of the profession. The profession was being redefined, in explicitly contextual rather than self-orientated terms. The central reference point in the theory which Oud proposed was the larger context of the cityscape as a whole. In that, the housing block featured as a basic unit of architectonic conception. He intended the sea of houses to be streamlined into a 'rhythmic play of plane and mass' in the street scene and housing block - that was architecture's main job. Architecture became to an increasing extent the art of relationships, rather than an art focusing on making single beautiful objects.

Oud's fascination with design meant that he did not hesitate to take the lead and capture territory virtually untrodden by civil servants and builders. The first two blocks in Spangen, numbers I and V, could not possibly have been designed as one complex, because they had been allocated in sections. Nevertheless, Oud tried to make the best of it, proposing to his colleagues that they 'weld' the segments together, by applying the black plinth bands and cornice lines throughout. Subsequent blocks in Spangen, in particular the unsurpassed block IX, and almost identical blocks in Tusschendijken - all designed and built just before and after 1920 - were a great leap forward and revealed far more than a few cosmetic tricks for joining up the separate parts. Here, the block was not a collection of tastefully designed interludes. It had advanced to become a repeatable prototype. Moreover, in its artistic essentials, it provided answers to questions on the true purpose of the architect's ideas: what is the relationship between the block's exterior and interior, how can the architectural standardization problem be surmounted, what will be the position of ornament and detail? Block IX is the condensed, smallest unit of the city as envisaged by Oud around 1920. Living focused consistently on the highly detailed inner courtyard, the standardized windows and doors were distributed rhythmically in a brick background, the corners of the blocks were developed to form an expressive ornament.

By 1920, Oud appeared to have examined the artistic purport of housing in considerable detail, repeatedly deriving inspiration from his favourite dialectic discourse on the regulating classicist impulse and its 'dematerialized' romantic counterpart. Were Berlage's 'impressionist' cityscapes still an operative example for him when he embarked on the Spangen and Tusschendijken projects? They certainly were. Oud was never to shake off the Berlage-like penchant for monumental order. He too aimed at large groups of buildings orchestrated into a cityscape which was cohesive even in the formal details. The direct outcome was a critical awareness of the less inflexible characteristics of modern urban planning, for instance the work of Cornelis van Eesteren in Amsterdam-West which developed from the mid-1930s onwards.

Standardization was less simple in theme in Oud's later work than it had been at Spangen and Tusschendijken. That fact was definitely affected by frustrations about the political, administrative and technical contexts of building, out of which the elan of around 1920 had rapidly evaporated. But when he was able to work in a congenial setting, especially at the Weissenhofsiedling in Stuttgart (1927), Oud was once more the brilliant conceptual builder of Spangen and Tusschendijken - this time on the scale of a small row of houses, two-and-a-half storeys in height. In the Weissenhofsiedlung Oud demonstrated his ingenuity in organizing the floor plan and fitting out the dwellings. The 'fundamental situation' suggested that he was still thinking in terms of a comprehensive concept for the city: the row of houses could, in his view, be repeated endlessly and was once more conceived as a prototype.

Yet Oud's ideas on the meaning of standardization began to alter subtly in the years following the definition of the monumental cityscape, and not only due to changing political reality in Rotterdam. The shift was occasioned by Oud's growing awareness that the matter of standardization was less important than architecture as an exalted undertaking. Projects such as the Hoek van Holland housing estate (designed in 1924) illustrated particularly well what Oud was to clarify in publications much later on: neutral architecture, mass designed and built, can be respected as 'background', the chief purpose of which is to allow space and provide a setting for individualist work of great architecture. Hoek van Holland was clearly not a matter of setting, but was a work of art in itself, unique and unrepeatable. Oud shifted his attention, slowly but surely, from the background of the cityscape to the polished work in the foreground. Accordingly, in his later work, starting with the much-debated Shell Building at the end of the 1930s, standardization was no longer a fundamental issue. From then on, Oud assumed the presence of a certain impressionist 'clutter' in the cityscape and went on to devote himself to the independent effect of art.

# 36/ Design for Standard Housing Types / Street Composition

1919

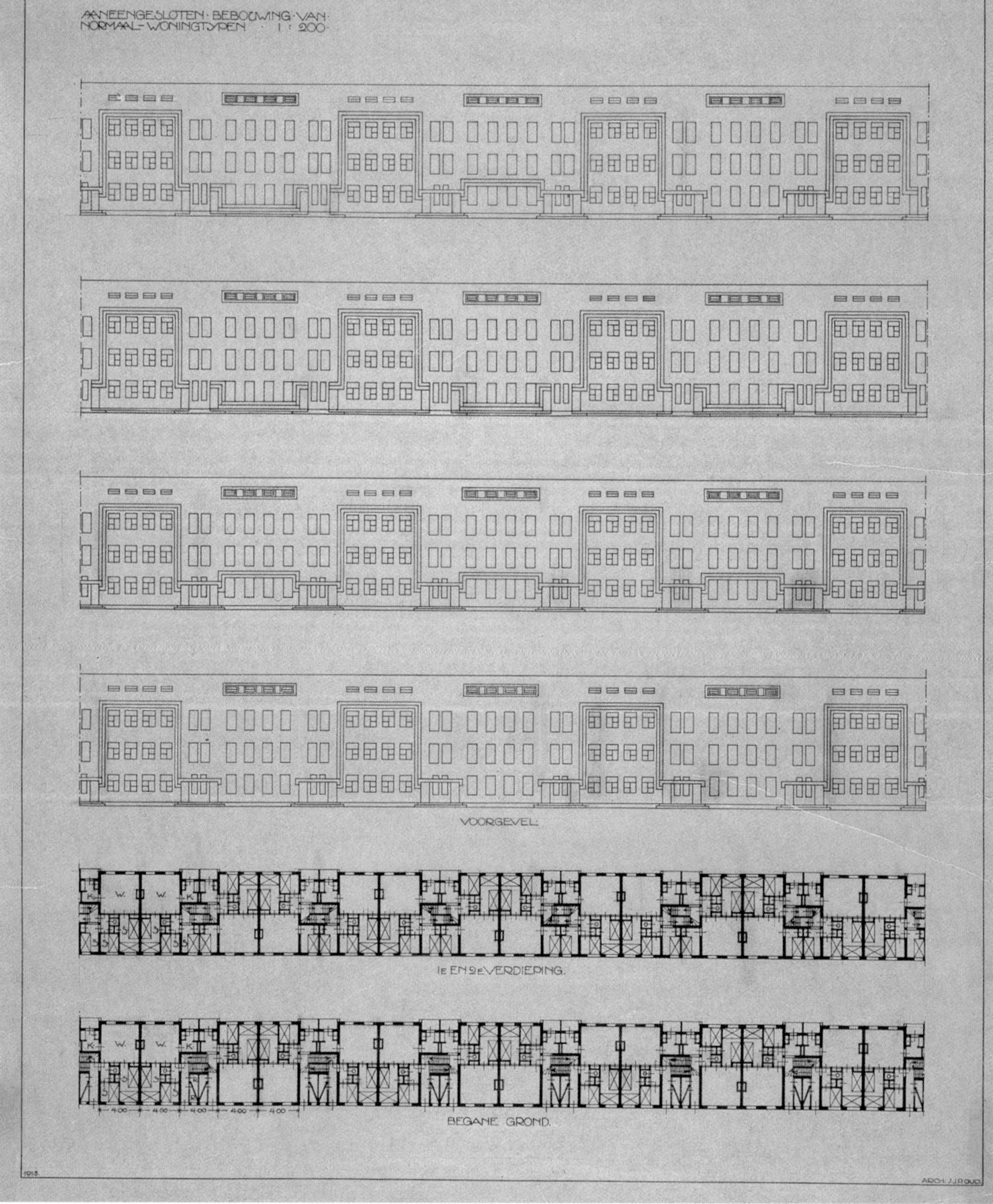


Elevation, plans of first and second floors, ground floor plan (bottom)/ OUDJ-nw 2, NAI, Rotterdam

When Oud joined the Rotterdam Woningdienst in the spring of 1918 he had two ambitions: as architect in government service to help solve the housing shortage, and as artist (in continual discussion with Theo van Doesburg) to explore the potential of mass housing for 'architectural expression', that is to say, its potential as the basis for a modern (contemporary) style. In both cases, the writings and buildings of H.P. Berlage were his starting point.

In 1918-1919, Oud published three articles in *De Stijl* on the architectural and town planning aspects of standardization in social housing. They were an architect's reaction to the conclusions of the conference on *Standardization in Housing* held in Amsterdam in February 1918 at which he was undoubtedly present and where he probably met the influential German art historian A.E. Brinckmann. In response to widespread resistence to the idea of standardization from architects and the labour movement, Berlage gave a lecture for *Architectura et Natura* 'Over normalisatie in de uitvoering van de woningbouw' (On Standardization in Housing Construction). This lecture had a mixed reception from most architects. Not so Oud, who, though he did not mention Berlage by name, was unequivocally positive in his first *De Stijl* article on 'Bouwkunst en normalisatie' (Architecture and Standardization). In his second article, 'Massabouw en straatarchitectuur' (Mass Construction and Street Architecture) Oud returned to the theme of the Amsterdam housing conference by way of a theoretical discourse on 'the representation of a terrace of working-class dwellings', based partly on a block he had designed for the Rotterdam Woningdienst for Spangen in Rotterdam. To begin with, the text and illustrations were a fairly brazen restatement of Berlage's views on the architectural townscape in the aesthetic terminology of *De Stijl*. Oud was deploying Berlage's ideas here as an argument in the ongoing debate with Van Doesburg about the limits and possibilities of a 'determined representation of the street'. At the same time, the design for the 'street composition' was part of a real, large-scale building experiment in which Oud explored the relation between housing block and mass housing at the level of ground plan and facade composition. Like the design for a double worker's dwelling (cat. no. 37), which was also published in *De Stijl*, the 'street architecture' drawing appears to have been part of a project Oud designed for the Rotterdam Woningdienst in 1918 and which he subsequently 'aestheticized' with a view to publication in *De Stijl*.

Oud writings on the technical and social aspects of mass housing in 1918-1919 attest more to his optimism about the future of *De Stijl* (and of its architectural component in particular) as aesthetic movement, than to familiarity with the technical aspects of standardization in housing construction. Like Berlage, Oud tended to skirt the practical and technical consequences of a systematic implementation of standardization in house building such as advocated during the Amsterdam housing conference, in particular by

**Perspective of elevation/ OUDJ-nw 1, NAI, Rotterdam**

representatives of the National Housing Board. J. van der Waerden, director of the Amsterdam Building Inspectorate had not only advocated standardization of building components and dwelling types, but had also argued for systematic implementation by means of government control of the production and distribution of building materials.[1] Although Oud firmly maintained that the outward appearance of future architecture should be dictated by modern building technology, he did not – any more than Van der Waerden or Berlage – go so far as to consider the unprecedented possibilities offered by reinforced concrete (including in the form of modular units) for standardized, large-scale housing construction. If the building used to illustrate his article was conceived as being built in concrete, it was for purely aesthetic reasons, in that concrete was perceived as providing the ideal basis for primary colour designs. Oud did however react, as had Van der Waerden and Berlage, to the fear expressed by architects and (potential) occupants that a centrally planned standardization would result in a stultifyingly monotonous environment. Like Berlage, he accused the workers not only of short-sightedness but of a lack of community spirit. The architects did not fare much better. According to Oud, the heart of the problem lay not in the degree or extent to which standardization should be implemented in housing construction, but in the ability of the artist–architect to recognize and to express the underlying principles of ordering, grouping and linking. Systematic implementation of standardization, according to Oud, was a precondition not only for the urgently needed reform of the building industry, but also for the status and especially the working method of the principal producer, the architect. When the essence of the architectural task was 'the aesthetic expression of the mass product', the architect would cease to be concerned with designing 'his own door or window' and become instead 'one who stage-manages mass products into an architectural whole: the art of relationships'. This firm pronouncement – which would surely have appealed to Mondrian and Van Doesburg – reveals that Oud, in the wake of Muthesius, Berlage and De Bazel, was in favour of only a limited form of standardization in house construction and that he saw this primarily in terms of the repetition of a fairly small number of dwellings, preferably designed by one architect. This was not quite what Van der Waerden meant by rigorous standardization. He envisaged national implementation of one standard type – a uniform dwelling – that could only be designed *by the most competent architects in collaboration with a few authorities in the field of construction and housing.*[2]

In 1919 *De Stijl* published Oud's 'Architectonische Beschouwing' (Architectonic Critique) an elaboration of his earlier article on mass housing containing designs made for the Rotterdam Woningdienst for a closed street elevation and for an ideal type of working-class dwelling in reinforced concrete (cat. no. 37). In these articles the technical and organizational modernization of the building industry was viewed purely in terms of its significance for the architectural design. According to Oud this was twofold: it concerned the aesthetic treatment of standard types and following on from this, the representation of 'a continuous development' in the form of a stylistic street expression of great monumentality. To judge how realistic these proposals were, it is necessary to realize that at the moment they were published, far more radical notions concerning standardization were circulating in social housing and town planning circles, notions in which architects were assigned a very different but every bit as ambitious a role. For example, in 1918, Van der Waerden argued that: *Coming up with a different dwelling layout, with rather pleasing strategies for components and so arriving at a new external order and a different stylistic concept, a kind of preparation that can take many years, must make way for the far greater task that circumstances now demand: grouping, realizing an urban development with prescribed types of dwellings, with standard dwellings. For those most deeply affected, there is one possible consolation: these standard dwellings need only be built until the housing shortage has been vanquished. After that there can be a return to the decentralized provision of housing, individual ideas, the so-called full contribution of individual architects, the solution of each case on its own.*[3]
Oud's proposal can be seen as the response of a serious designer to these sneering remarks addressed to architects by a leading housing reformer. Keeping as much as possi-

ble within the programme laid down by Van der Waerden (a single dwelling type of 36 to 40 squares, in nine different configurations), Oud produced an alternative ground plan that accommodated *maximum requirements in minimum spaces.* The individual floor plan was based on a system of squares with a bay-width of four metres. For the sake of economy, the facade detailing was limited as far as possible to the window openings of the living and bedrooms. The stairs were located at the centre of the individual premises and indirectly lit. The principal innovation of this design, compared with Oud's own Strandboulevard design and with housing blocks by Berlage and De Bazel in Amsterdam, is in the organization of the staircase. Every structural unit has two porch entrances, each serving six apartments. In actual fact, the stairwells contain *two* interlocking staircases: *Every left-hand front door gives access to the left-hand ground-floor flat, but on the first floor it serves the right-hand flat and on the second floor the left-hand one again. And vice versa.*[4] The splitting in two of the stairwell by a balustrade of discrete staircases that spiral around one another in a double helix, automatically resulted in a spatial organization in which the living and sleeping quarters in alternate pairs of dwellings were reversed in plan, a motif that Oud may have come across in German architectural literature, such as Peter Behrens and H. de Fries's informative book, *Vom sparsamen Bauen* (1918). This typologically dictated alternation offered new starting points for an aesthetic composition not only of the street elevation but also of the enclosed space of street and square. This was sorely needed since the elevation published in *De Stijl* turned out to be no more than a small portion of a super perimeter block with a total facade length of two hundred metres! The surviving drawings and the published perspective sketch show how Oud, in trying to get to grips with the relation between a lot-based block composition and the rhythmic articulation of the facade, looked for solutions now in the 'sky silhouette' (roof forms), now in the 'facade relief', wholly in the spirit of Van der Waerden. In the published design and the commentary, Oud stressed the ornamental (read: expressive) effect of the systematic standardization of all the units. In this, too, he appeared to fall in with Van der Waerden's diktat to the architectural community: *They should not spend much time in deliberation and must above all realize that the type, the variations, the composition of parts are fixed, but that their task consists solely ... in handling the type in its multiplicity in such a way that the dreaded uniformity does not give rise to something monotonous but that a harmonious whole is achieved.*[5] This pious hope was not shared by Oud, however. A high degree of standardization did not automatically lead to an acceptable 'street architecture': *elaboration of the idea (i.e. of standardization) could, in the case of a less stringent standardization, lead to a melodic-expressive street elevation. Complete, harmonious expression will only be possible in the townscape as a whole (which must be the ultimate aim), if the continuation of the street, which is a product of the predominantly horizontal development, is interrupted by conspicuously vertical elements in the form of substantial corner elements or freestanding buildings.*[6] And this is precisely what the published facade drawings of Oud's designs show: a 'melodic-expressive street elevation'. As in the Strandboulevard design, the strong relief of the street elevation, which in this case is supposedly dictated by the alternation of the dwelling layout, is not reflected in the ground plans. In this aesthetic interpretation of the effects of standardization on the townscape, Oud knew himself to be supported by the preparatory work of H.P. Berlage, in particular by the perspective drawings of *Plan Zuid.* He was also aware of what Berlage had said to his fellow architects in his lecture on *Standardization in Housing Construction* (1918): *All periods have produced fine examples of continuous and joined housing complexes. Well then, that will be your task as well, but on a scale such as never before. If the most talented young people among you address themselves to this problem, something exceptional can be achieved. For it is by the grouping, linking and stacking of the same units, to be compared with the design of a three-dimensional, cubic ornament [sic]. Street, square and buildings are mutually implicit in every urban design plan. Town planning is the creation of space with housing material.* [7]

A careful reading of Oud's *De Stijl* articles on architecture, standardization and 'streetscaping' throws up numerous



**Notes**

**1.** *Normalisatie in woningbouw. Voordracht gehouden door H.P. Berlage: preadvies uitgebracht door J. van der Waerden voor het woningcongres 1918 Amsterdam*, Rotterdam 1918.

**2.** J. van der Waerden, 'Maatregelen waardoor de bouw in massa bevorderd wordt. Normalisatie in de uitvoering, in het bijzonder wat betreft de te verwerken onderdeelen', in: *Normalisatie in woningbouw. Voordracht gehouden door H.P. Berlage: preadvies uitgebracht door J. van der Waerden voor het woningcongres 1918 Amsterdam*, Rotterdam 1918, p. 7.

**3.** J. van der Waerden, 'Maatregelen waardoor de bouw in massa bevorderd wordt. Normalisatie in de uitvoering, in het bijzonder wat betreft de te verwerken onderdeelen', in: *Normalisatie in woningbouw. Voordracht gehouden door H.P. Berlage: preadvies uitgebracht door J. van der Waerden voor het woningcongres 1918 Amsterdam*, Rotterdam 1918, p. 10.

**4.** H. Engel, 'Van huis tot woning. Een typologische analyse van enkele woningbouwontwerpen van J.J.P. Oud', in: *Plan*, 9(1981), p. 37.

**5.** J. van der Waerden, 'Maatregelen waardoor de bouw in massa bevorderd wordt. Normalisatie in de uitvoering, in het bijzonder wat

inconsistencies which are no doubt a reflection of the various circles in which Oud was moving at that time, in particular those of Berlage, Van Doesburg and the Rotterdam Woningdienst (A. Plate). The reason for Oud's involvement with 'mass construction and street architecture' was a large-scale housing block developed by the Rotterdam Woningdienst in the Spangen district (cat. no. 40). The principles Oud evolved in the course of this project he then deployed in the contemporary debate about standardization in housing construction and the aesthetic objections raised to this by architects. In his *De Stijl* article, Oud adopted Van Doesburg's method and, using a stylized reworking of the original design, presented architecture as a pure, abstract 'art of relationships' which in practice, however, was to be realized by means of Berlagian volumes and masses. Unlike Van Doesburg, whose views on architecture 'had gained momentum' in the wake of his categorical rejection of Berlage's architectural ideas as expressed in *Schoonheid in Samenleving* (Beauty and Society, 1919), Oud strove in his early work with the Rotterdam Woningdienst to achieve a workable compromise, which soon proved to be untenable in practice.



betreft de te verwerken onderdeelen', in: *Normalisatie in woningbouw. Voordracht gehouden door H.P. Berlage: preadvies uitgebracht door J. van der Waerden voor het woningcongres 1918 Amsterdam*, Rotterdam 1918, p. 10.

**6.** J.J.P. Oud, 'Architectonische beschouwingen. A. Massabouw en Straatarchitectuur', in: *De Stijl*, 2(1919)7, pp. 79-84.

**7.** H.P. Berlage, 'Over normalisatie in de uitvoering van den woningbouw', in: *Normalisatie in woningbouw. Voordracht gehouden door H.P. Berlage: preadvies uitgebracht door J. van der Waerden voor het woningcongres 1918 Amsterdam*, Rotterdam 1918, pp. 44-45.

**Sources**

CCA: dr1984: 0432, dr1984: 0434-0436, dr1984: 0443
MOMA: NC Drawings-blueprints
NAI: OUDJ-nw 1-6

**Articles**

J.J.P. Oud, 'Architectonische beschouwingen: A. Massabouw en straatarchitectuur; B. Gewapend beton en bouwkunst', in *De Stijl*, 2(1919)7, pp. 79-82

**Literature**

U. Barbieri, *J.J.P. Oud*, Rotterdam 1987, p. 45
J. de Heer, 'Stijl en woningtype: Berlages woningbouw', in: S. Polano, *Hendrik Petrus Berlage. Het complete werk*, Alphen 1985, pp. 67-91
H. Engel, 'Van woning tot woning', in: *Plan* 9(1981), pp. 34-39
H.E. Oud, *J.J.P. Oud. Architekt 1890-1963. Feiten en herinneringen gerangschikt*, The Hague 1984, pp. 45, 64
S. Polano, *J.J.P. Oud Architettura Olandese*, Milan 1981, pp. 19-20
H. Searing, 'Berlage and Housing, "the most significant modern building"', in: *Nederlands Kunsthistorisch Jaarboek*, 25 (1975), pp. 133-180
G. Stamm, *J.J.P. Oud. Bauten und Projekte 1906 bis 1963*, Mainz, Berlin 1984, pp. 58-59

# A. Mass Construction and Street Architecture

The spirit of the times is directed at broadening: broadening that is the product of deepening.

As a result it is once again thrown back on the crowd and consciously bases its developmental efforts on the existing cultural core that determines modern social and spiritual life.

Thus, the modern spirit, including in architecture, sets its goal further and does not confine itself to the individual (inside: the house), but to the crowd (outside: the street – the city).

In street development the individual, even the aesthetically designed*, house is contraband, and continuous street development as conscious street expression, a must.

Practically all the ingredients for this are available. Continuous street development, both of public housing and of better housing, will become the rule, piecemeal development more and more the exception.

Thoroughgoing reorganization of the building industry in the widest sense, by taking advantage of all the possibilities of modern technical and corporate development, is urgently needed. Economical and rapid, but not inferior, construction is the order of the day.

From this, the following a priori preconditions for the organization of such construction may be deduced:

Carefully worked out plan form, in the sense that maximum requirements are contained in minimum spaces; systematized construction as the result of economically efficient placement of structural walls (which affects the plan form in the first instance); economic production of standard materials; hard-headed management.

Means and objective determine one another in architecture: acceptance of the key concept should lead to new methods and materials and accordingly, in pure representation, to new aesthetic design.

Of energetic efforts in the direction of such a key concept and concomitant design, through mutual fertilization and continual exchange of ideas and practice there has been little sign up till now.** Sentimental-romantic traditions inhibit the evolution of the construction industry and withhold, as a result, important monumental–aesthetic tools from architecture.

The accompanying project illustrates another attempt to interpret a continuous development of public housing based on the above-mentioned considerations.

Regarding the composition of the ground plan, the following: A system of squares has been employed as aid. – The main walls are projected at right angles to the facades, at economically efficient intervals of 4 m.: the other walls, except for the facades, do not contribute to the construction and are light partition walls. Considering that this might lead to a more economic site subdivision, savings on sewerage and street construction and, structurally, to a smaller outer wall surface (with its drawbacks of costly treatment, cold, damp, condensation) an attempt was made to reduce the facade width. This led to the utilization of the facade surface as a whole for room illumination and to the acceptance of indirect and top light for the staircases. This naturally resulted in the placement of the staircases in the centres of the individual modules which also reduces the required hall space to a minimum.

Two staircases rotate, without any waste of space, in opposite directions, around the dividing wall, in a double helix, so that the stairwell actually contains two individual staircases that are completely separate from one another and which make it possible for no more than 3 families to share the one stair. The flights which make up each stair complex are separated at storey height by landings which are the mandatory minimum length of 1.2 m. (and no more!) and on which the entrance doors to the upper dwellings are located. Owing to the rotation of the stairs, these entrance doors are more to the front or to the rear, with the result that the living room and bedroom groups are alternately on the front or rear elevation. – Next to the entrances are bicycle storage spaces for the upstairs dwellings.

*Arbitrary stringing together of artistic fragments can never form a sculptural whole,

**The one heartening exception is Peter Behrens's book "Vom sparsamen Bauen" which consequently also displays new architectural solutions.

# 37/ Double Worker's Dwelling in Reinforced Concrete

**Rotterdam** **1919**

In the second part of his 'Architectonische beschouwing' (cat. no. 36), Oud speculated on the aesthetic potential of concrete, then a relatively new building material for large-scale housing construction. As in the first part on mass construction and street architecture, he illustrated his argument with one of his own designs. Here, too, text and design do not stand alone but are more in the nature of a two-way demonstration directed at Oud's *De Stijl* associates (in particular Van Doesburg and Van 't Hoff), and also at experts in social and municipal housing construction such as Berlage and Oud's superior at the Rotterdam Woningdienst, A. Plate. This dual 'focus' is reflected in the design of a 'double worker's dwelling' which could be seen as a *De Stijl* interpretation of Van der Waerden's standard plan for a freestanding, basic one-family dwelling.

In 'Kunst en machine' (Art and Machine), an indirect tribute to the work of the American architect Frank Lloyd Wright published in the December 1917 issue of *De Stijl*, Oud clearly distanced himself from what Auke van der Woud has called 'handcrafted mass housing': the *Arts and Crafts Movement*-inspired artisanal production of buildings and utensils in reaction to industrial and commercial production in the factory and on the building site. He also distanced himself from the associated communal ideal. From a professional point of view, therefore, the fourth issue of the first volume of *De Stijl* also marked the break with old friends like the ceramist W.C. Brouwer: *Where architectural expression is already arrived at through mechanical means (Wright), painting is in consequence obliged to adopt this mode of expression, there appears of itself a unified, pure expression of the spirit of the times. And that was Ruskin and Morris's cardinal mistake, to bring the machine into discredit by branding an imperfect use as the hallmark of its essence.*[1] In retrospect it is not entirely clear whether the debate about industrialization and standardization, as pursued in Dutch housing circles in the years 1917-1919, pushed architects like Oud, Van 't Hoff and Klaarhamer into the arms of Frank Lloyd Wright or whether it was the American master-builder who opened the eyes of his Dutch colleagues, starting with Van 't Hoff, to the architectural and ideological dimensions of reinforced concrete. If the latter, then according to Reyner Banham it was Van 't Hoff who apprised Oud (who had earlier learned to appreciate Wright through the eyes of Berlage and Van Doesburg) of the decisive role of reinforced concrete in the creation of a new, contemporary architecture.[2] From his texts and surviving drawings it would appear that Oud had two reasons for being interested in Wright's work in those years. Firstly, because reinforced concrete appeared to promise an 'architectural expression through purely architectural means' that was entirely complementary to the solutions being sought in painting by Van Doesburg and Mondrian.[3] Not just Oud, but Van 't Hoff, Wils and P.J.C. Klaarhamer also 'practised' Wright's new plastic expression, witness numerous contemporary sketches for street elevations, apartment blocks and private homes.

Secondly, Oud felt that the 'mechanized' realization of Wright's buildings had important implications for the division of labour in the production of buildings, in particular for the status of the construction drawings. Such a reaction can scarcely have been prompted by Wright's own, overly detailed drawings, but Oud's view of the changing status of the architect may have been influenced by the anti-artistic mentality of Rob van 't Hoff. If the main components of the building were delivered in a standard fashion by the factory, so that the architect on the building site had nothing much to do, where did that leave the design drawing? In his essay on Wright's Robie House, Oud wrote: *The architect of today is no longer constantly present on the building site, he simply comes to inspect, and in fact supervises the construction from his office. It is there he determines the shapes and proportions that will be executed by others. The degree of delicacy the design possesses as* drawing, *does not affect the aesthetic expression of the building. I do not mean to say that the architect's design is realized only as a* reproduction, *so that it would be possible, for example, to build 10 houses in accordance with the same design drawing that with mathematical certainty would lead to the same aesthetic effect, to the extent that this could still be said to concern the architect's work. Modern architecture will increasingly be reduced to determining relationships, in which it corresponds to modern painting.*[4]

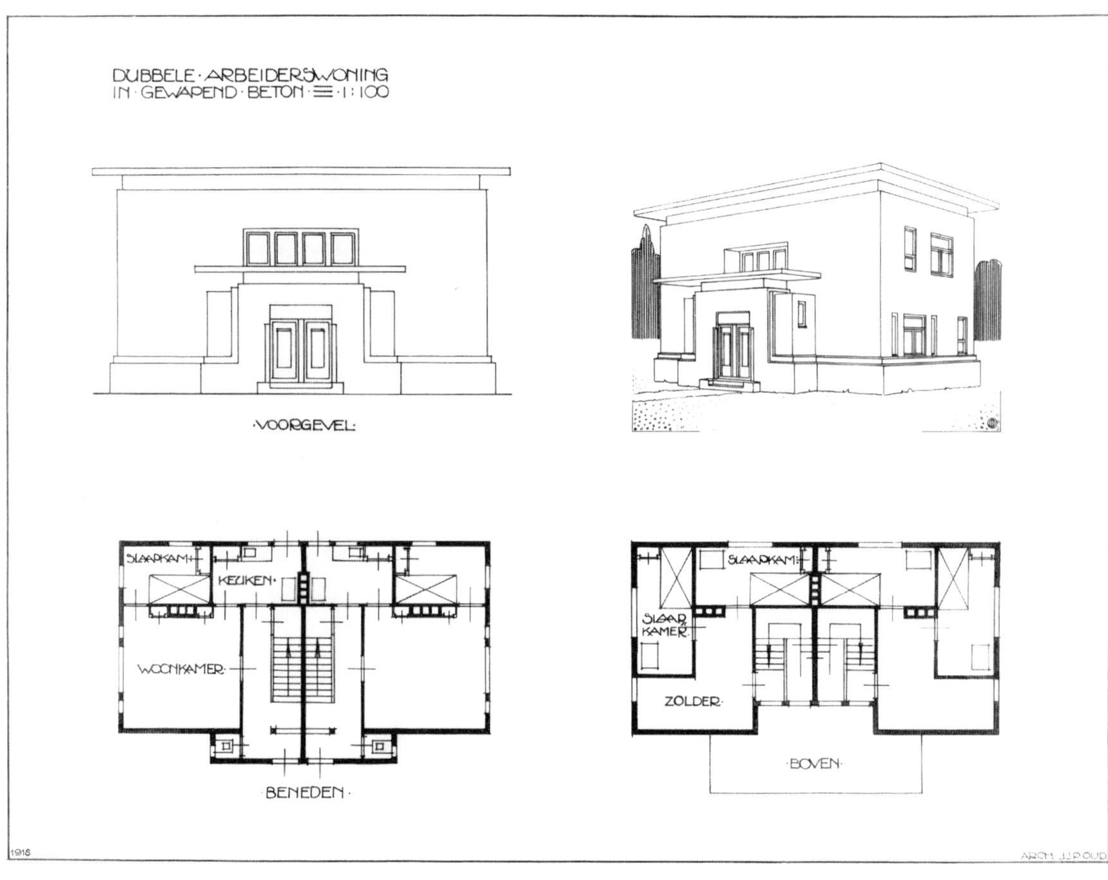


Front elevation and ground floor plan (left); perspective and first floor plan/ OUDJ-da 2, NAI, Rotterdam

The text of Oud's article 'Gewapend beton en bouwkunst' (Reinforced Concrete and Architecture) is symptomatic of the somewhat exalted tone of the debate among Dutch architects on the significance of reinforced concrete for a 'modern monumental architecture', in which the architectural control of both the structural and physical properties of concrete in the work of Frank Lloyd Wright was virtually proclaimed the model. The verbal euphoria is in strange contrast to the accompanying illustration of a design for a 'double worker's dwelling in reinforced concrete' which displays a far from spectacular use of concrete's much-vaunted structural possibilities. In the text, Oud argues that the new material is architecturally interesting because it does not share brick's disadvantages, such as the inability to absorb tensile stress, and renders superfluous such makeshift measures as 'suspending bricks from wire' as employed by the adherents of the Amsterdam School. Reinforced concrete provided a structural solution for the demand for horizontal spans and cantilevers prompted by the modern quest for a three-dimensional, spatial architecture in a system of strictly horizontal and vertical lines and planes. Thanks to reinforced concrete – and this was the lesson of Frank Lloyd Wright – it was now possible to transfer the Neo-Plastic aesthetic to architecture, in the same way as Rietveld was doing in his furniture. But whereas Rietveld had opted for an open, dynamic notion of space – and in so doing was the first to arrive at a 'balanced plastic expression' in space – Oud held to the importance of the closed plane. His position in 1918-1919 was similar to that of the painter Van der Leck who, in contrast to Mondrian, eventually opted for spatial flatness. In line with the decades-old architectural ideal of simplicity, monumentality and the flattest possible ('profoundly flat') facades, Oud claimed that *purer boundaries and more monumental, because more synthetic, surface effects could be achieved in concrete than in brick.*[5] A potential that could be further strengthened by a well-considered application of colour. The illustration accompanying the text, a design for a 'double worker's dwelling in reinforced concrete', succeeds only partially in elucidating the text. Given what is known of the project's origins, the drawing published in *De Stijl* would appear to be a perfect illustration of what Oud meant by 'an aesthetically rendered standard type': an edited version made especially for *De Stijl* of a design Oud had made for the Rotterdam Woningdienst. This is also apparent from the preliminary sketches in which the original technical drawings were manipulated into a 'modern' design and furnished with a Wrightian idiom. Oud sent them straight to Van Doesburg who reacted with delight: *I'm extremely enthusiastic about it! Wonderfully crisp and clear. The floor plans are first-rate too. A nice touch that they are different and transposed. I'll gladly reproduce them in De Stijl.*[6] Which he duly did. The surviving original construction drawings by contrast are totally devoid of architectural pretension. They were based on a standardized dwelling type and standard facade elements (doors, windows, rebates) as specified by Van der Waerden in 1918 and as (later) also used in numerous experiments with concrete in other cities. Although Rotterdam, like Amsterdam and The Hague, did not officially begin to experiment with concrete housing until 1920, the 'design for a double worker's dwelling', like that for the super perimeter block (cat. no. 36) were part of the public housing policy developed by A. Plate and A.W. Heijkoop, to use every available means – whether it be temporary housing, industrialized construction, standardization or concrete construction – to alleviate the acute housing shortage as quickly as possible. The economic and political situation in 1918-1919, in Rotterdam at any rate, was not such as would allow the experiment with concrete construction to be carried out by a specialized construction company under the direction of the Rotterdam Woningdienst. On the other hand, the pursuit of far-reaching industrialization of housing construction did lead to a considerable increase in the scale of the public and private house-building industry and to a better spatial organization of large-scale housing complexes. A joint study trip by Plate, Heijkoop and Oud to several German cities, including Bremen and Hamburg (1920), provided inspiration. The Dutch visitors were able to compare notes with the Hamburg Baudirektor, Fritz Schumacher, whose design for a 'Kleinwohnungssiedlung' in Hamburg-Langenhorn had been built by Kossel, a private construction firm that would later build Oud's contribution to the Weissenhofsiedlung. Oud reported on the Langenhorn project in detail, not in *De Stijl* of course, but in *Bouwkundig Weekblad*, in the same year as Plate made his first public pronouncement on standardization and the scaling-up and industrialization of the building industry in *Tijdschrift voor Volkshuisvesting en Stedebouw*. Finally, at the beginning of 1921, the Rotterdam city council decided to experiment with the construction of some two hundred concrete dwellings. Ironically, the Woningdienst, and with it Oud, was not involved in the experiment. The commission was awarded to two private construction firms (one of which was Kossel) who were also responsible for the drawing up the plans.[7] For this they engaged the services of outside architects such as Hardeveld and Pauw who had been carrying out important work in the field of concrete construction while Oud was busy elsewhere in the city realizing brick housing complexes (some of them white-rendered) for the Woningdienst (blocks I, V, VIII and IX in Spangen and blocks I-IV and VI in Tusschendijken).



**Notes**

**1.** J.J.P. Oud, 'Kunst en Machine', in: *De Stijl*, 4(1917), pp. 25-27.

**2.** R. Banham, Theory and Design of the First Machine Age, London 1960, pp. 154-155.

**3.** J.J.P. Oud, Architectonische beschouwingen bij bijlage VIII', in: *De Stijl*, 4(1918)4, pp. 38-41.

**4.** J.J.P. Oud, Architectonische beschouwingen bij bijlage VIII', in: *De Stijl*, 4(1918)4, pp. 41.

**5.** J.J.P. Oud, Architectonische beschouwing. B. Gewapend beton', in: *De Stijl*, 2(1919)7, pp. 82-84.

**6.** H. Esser, J.J.P. Oud, in: C. Blotkamp (et al.), De beginjaren van De Stijl 1917-1922, Utrecht 1982, p. 143.

**7.** M. Kuipers, *Bouwen in beton, experimenten in de volkshuisvesting voor 1940*, The Hague 1987, p. 118.

**Sources**

CCA: dr1984: 0021-0022, dr1984: 0490
NAI: OUDJ-da 1-4, OUDJ-ph 1793

**Articles**

J.J.P. Oud, 'Architectonische beschouwingen: A. Massabouw en straatarchitectuur, B. gewapend beton en bouwkunst', in: *De Stijl*, 2(1919)7, pp. 82-84

**Literature**

R. Banham, *Theory and Design of the First Machine Age*, London 1960, pp. 153-162
U. Barbieri, *J.J.P. Oud*, Rotterdam 1987, p. 44
S. Harth, 'Stadt und Region. Fritz Schumachers Konzepte zu Wohnungsbau und Stadtgestalt in Hamburg', in: H. Frank (ed.), *Fritz Schumacher. Reformkultur und Moderne*, Stuttgart 1994, pp. 157-182
M. Kuipers, *Bouwen in Beton, Experimenten in de volkshuisvesting voor 1940*, Zeist 1987, pp. 89, 104-107
H.E. Oud, *J.J.P. Oud. Architekt 1890-1963. Feiten en herinneringen gerangschikt*, The Hague 1984, pp. 46-47
S. Polano, *J.J.P. Oud Architettura Olandese*, Milan 1981, p. 20
G. Stamm, *J.J.P. Oud. Bauten und Projekte 1906 bis 1963*, Mainz, Berlin 1984, p. 44
E. Vermeulen, 'Robert van 't Hoff', in: C. Blotkamp (et al.), *De beginjaren van De Stijl 1917-1922*, Utrecht 1982, pp. 225-228
A. van der Woud, *Waarheid en karakter. Het debat over de bouwkunst 1840-1900*, Rotterdam 1997, pp. 396-407

# B. Reinforced Concrete and Architecture

The application of reinforced concrete has created greater freedom of expression for architecture which may contribute to the purification of the aesthetic element in design.
The limitations that brick, by virtue of its size and structure, imposes on architectural design (dependent on proportions, necessity of applying certain (curved) forms etc.) are familiar to every architect. The material's unsuitability for absorbing tensile stress makes it impossible to use it to construct major horizontal spans or cantilevers and makes it necessary to resort to auxiliary materials such as wood, iron, and so on (the combination of which with brick in such cases is seldom felicitously resolved) or to employ makeshift measures such as suspending the brick from iron wire, etc. (something of which the modern brick virtuosos are guilty).
The need for structural solutions of horizontal extensions in a homogeneous arrangement with the structure (that is after all the message of the afore-mentioned use of "suspended brickwork") also makes itself felt and is specifically modern. On the one hand it is the result of the emergence of modern materials (such as plate glass), which give no occasion for introducing intermediate supports, on the other hand of the modern architectural ambition to give genuine expression to the three-dimensional character of architecture, i.e. in sculpturally harmonious proportions, by creating sculptural effects from left to right, from front to back, from top to bottom. In particular as concerns the latter, the use of reinforced concrete has for the first time created the possibility of harmonious plasticity, because – unlike the old column and beam system, with which [working] from bottom to top it was only possible to build inwards (i.e. backwards) from bottom to top – it is now possible to build outwards (i.e. forwards) from bottom to top. If one adds to this, that in concrete it is possible to achieve* a purer planar delineation and a more monumental, because more synthetic, planar effect (because of the reduced need for structural aids like joints, lintels etc.) than in brick, while there is good reason to expect that in the future it will be possible to apply strong colour accents (while in brick it is the subtle colour that adds pictorial elements), one will have shown the aesthetic advantages of reinforced concrete that will guarantee it an important and vital place in the pursuit of a modern monumental architecture.
By way of added clarification respecting the "Double worker's dwelling in reinforced concrete" depicted here: they were designed as the termination of a little dead-end residential street and there are gardens on either side of the house. The walls are conceived as double: a structural wall, on which the roof rests, and (separated from the first by an interspace) an insulating wall. There is also an insulation space between the ceiling of the upper floor and the roof, the height of which is indicated by the frieze,
R'dam, May '19

*The plastered wall surface already has advantages in this respect.

# 38/ Design for Emergency Housing Below a Railway Viaduct

**Rotterdam, Voorburgstraat** **1918**

In 1918, after much discussion in municipal housing circles, the construction of emergency housing was laid down in law. The Woningnoodwet (Housing Shortage Act) made it possible for municipalities to start building housing with a limited lifespan of five to seven years secure in the knowledge that a government grant would cover ninety per cent of the total building costs. The provisions of the act were a cautious reaction to the national housing shortage, which had begun to assume alarming proportions by the end of the war due to lack of materials and soaring building costs. In the latter half of 1918, the Rotterdam city council and its public health committee debated a plan submitted by the Woningdienst (and signed by Oud) for the construction of emergency dwellings under the 49 arches of the railway viaduct serving the Hofplein line. In a meeting of the public health committee on 13 November 1918, at which the architect and town planner Granpré Molière was present, A. Plate let it be known that although he was opposed in principle to the idea of emergency housing, the housing shortage left no alternative. Furthermore: *for an amount of 3,600 guilders per dwelling a well-accessed accommodation would be obtained; people would soon adjust to the noise of the trains, as he knew from experience; the risk of depreciation of the surrounding area should not be taken too seriously for this would of course be dispersed accommodation and moreover a measure lasting 5, at most 10 years, as laid down by the Act.*[1] The plan was rejected in 1918; in June 1922 it was resubmitted – as temporary housing for unskilled workers – but again failed to gain council approval.

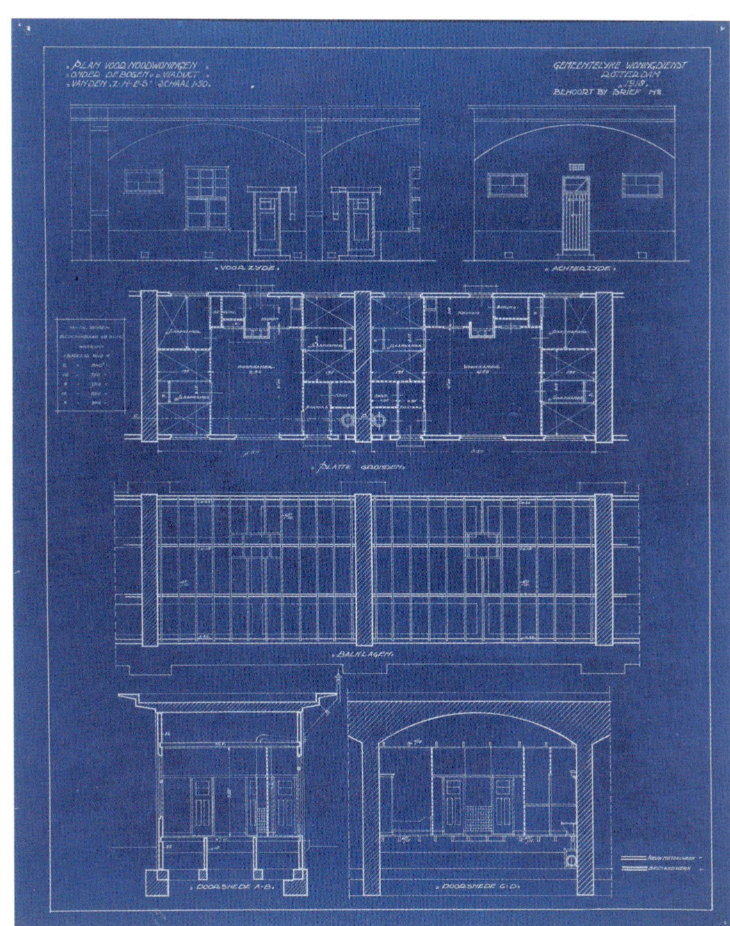

Plans/ OUDJ-nd 1, NAI, Rotterdam



**Notes**

**1.** Public Health Committee sub-committee A, meeting 13 November 1918, inv. no. 92, Gemeentearchief, Rotterdam.

**Sources**

GAR: *Handelingen 1922*, 15 June 1922, pp. 516-519; Published records 1922, no. 96, 28 March 1922, p. 429; Public Health Committee sub-committee A, inv. no. 57
NAI: OUDJ–nd 1, OUDJ-ph 1791-1792

**Literature**

H.G. van Beusekom, *Getijden der Volkshuisvesting. Notities ener geschiedenis van een halve eeuw*, Alphen 1955, pp. 79-103
H. Esser, 'J.J.P. Oud', in: C. Blotkamp (et al.), *De beginjaren van De Stijl 1917-1922*, Utrecht 1982, p. 142
H.E. Oud, *J.J.P. Oud. Architekt 1890-1963. Feiten en herinneringen gerangschikt*, The Hague 1984, p. 63, n. 21

# Material and Colour



The most radical change of course in Oud's oeuvre occurred around 1919. His work came under considerable production pressure. That was definitely the result of Oud's attempt to justify changes in production techniques as regards the nature of the assignment (housing) and the possibilities and impossibilities of mechanical production of components. Similarly, he subjected colour and material choice to critical analysis. As a result of his intellectual and artistic acknowledgement of these issues, the relatively carefree character of his earliest work made way for more stratified and complicated qualities, often expressed in visual friction in construction, composition and image. As a front-line modernist, he could have made things easy for himself if he had been satisfied just to indicate the aesthetic possibilities of new materials. In the early 1920s he did indeed sing the praises of the approaching revolutionary changes heralded by plate glass, reinforced concrete and steel. The three were paving the way for the demise of weighty architecture. In Oud's opinion, the new materials made it possible to achieve an 'architecture of optically immaterial, almost floating appearance', and that characteristic was precisely what he was originally looking for. In the collaboration with his friend Van Doesburg (which got dramatically out of hand) on the housing in Spangen, he sought to combat architectural weight with the striking, contrapuntal addition of 'destructive' colour to the standardized architectonics of the massive brick block. In his later work, the ambition for optical lightness was incorporated in the architecture itself. He achieved it by making the mass as transparent as possible and keeping the texture of the facades smooth and light, with a palette of bright blues, reds and yellows as support. In his investigation of the meaning of new production techniques, Oud had been somewhat ahead of his time as regards feasibility. And that was once more the case. He worked with the regular planes which determine the look of reinforced concrete before that material was readily available. The Oud-Mathenesse, Hoek van Holland and Kiefhoek projects were made in conventional brickwork and then finished with white plasterwork. Oud made his famous Café De Unie facade, as well as the Oud-Mathenesse site office, specifically to demonstrate a composition formed entirely of colour, and nothing else: both are examples of ethereal architecture, literally and figuratively.

It was not until the Weissenhofsiedlung that the whole gamut of ambitions concerning material, colour and process coincided with concrete, new building technology. Oud was able to use a prefabricated Kossel building system. The extremely fast construction of his Stuttgart houses, constructed at top speed from ready-made building slabs, was described by spectators as 'magical', even though the system was dogged by damp. Oud took a philosophical view of complications like that. When he encountered complaints about wet walls, he laconically remarked that the Dutch had a saying that you should have an enemy live in your new house for the first year, a friend for the second, and only move in yourself in the third year. *After all, a house needs time to overcome the limitations of its newness.*

Yet his interest in the effects of new methods and materials, combined with new colours, gradually changed direction as his ambitions became more profound. Those ambitions related both physically and metaphorically to the permanence of his work. Oud's archive contains numerous letters revealing that he joined battle *ad nauseam* with those supervising his housing projects who allowed sloppy work. He might criticize messy details, such as a washing-line which occupants had hung up of their own accord, but he was also enraged at the condition of the climate-sensitive plasterwork and incomplete

**or incorrect retouching of colour. His reaction was to develop the ideal of the 'tough' building: *What it amounts to ... is that one should deliver a building that is as complete and indestructible as possible.* Which meant a tectonically tangible building. Unprotected reinforced concrete had to be avoided; it had to be clad with weatherproof cut stone or glazed brick. But the paintwork was by no means straightforward either, for the man who at one time promoted Mondrian's colour scheme: *One should not, come what may, base on it anything essential in one's architecture.* That is why he preferred ceramics, tiles and glazes to paint. Oud liked to have massive doors and door frames, with no added colour and, from the late 1930s onwards, frequently opted for high-quality materials like aluminium and bronze.**

**From the Shell Building design onwards, Oud's trend toward the indestructible building combined with the equally far-reaching ambition at the end of the 1930s to make buildings intended to stand out from the surrounding clutter of mediocre buildings and secure a position for themselves somewhere at the top of the city's spatial pecking-order. Oud began devoting himself to the tectonically fully-fledged architectural object, of which the more successful ones also claimed, in a traditionally Semperian sense, to be the expression of a cultural idea. The Shell Building certainly had this dual pretension of being an autonomous building as well as a symbol. The symbolic intent proceeded from a hierarchical representation of the functioning of democracy. In the building, matter was elevated to idea.**

# 39/ Spangen Municipal Housing Scheme, Blocks I & V

**Rotterdam, Van Lennepstraat, Roemer Visscherstraat, Spaansebocht**
**1918-1920**

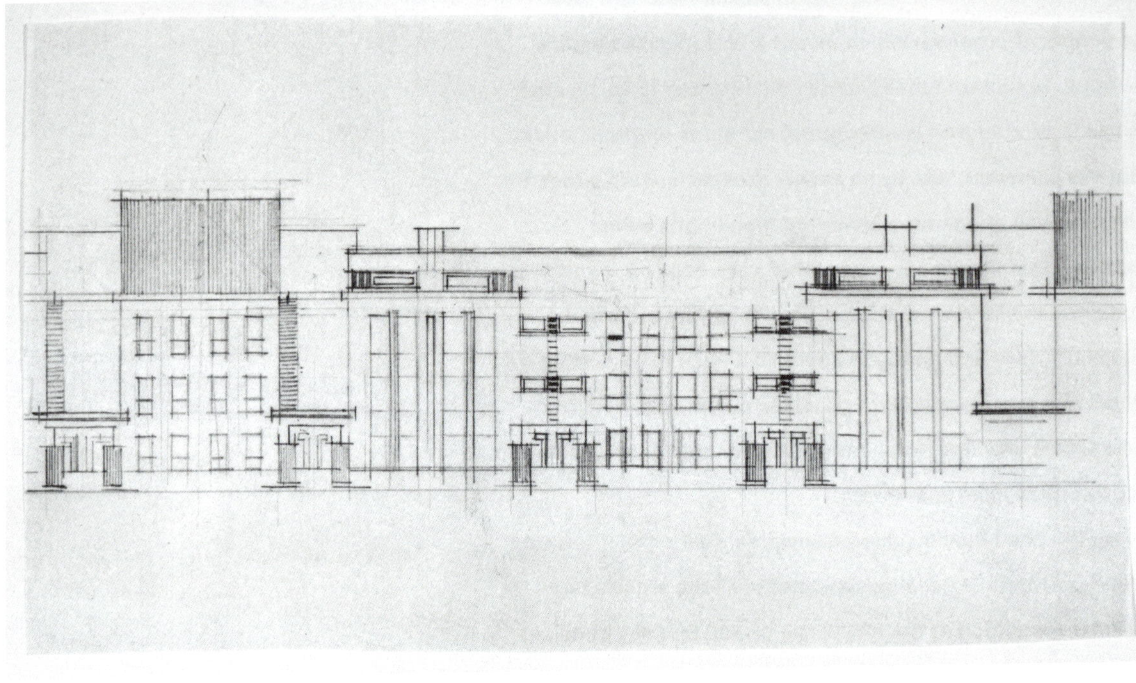

Variant of street elevation design/ dr1984: 0446, CCA, Montreal

Theo van Doesburg, colour scheme for living room/ OUDJ-sp 2, NAI, Rotterdam

In the course of 1918, work began on the huge municipal housing scheme in the Spangen polder. The spatial masterplan was drawn up by P. Verhagen under Berlage's supervision. The houses were designed by several different architects working for the Rotterdam Woningdienst and various housing associations. In August 1918, 242 dwellings were put out to tender. Designed by Oud, they formed part of two blocks either side of Bilderdijkstraat. The buildings fronting Bilderdijkstraat were built at almost the same time and contained spacious, middle-class dwellings designed (in consultation with Oud) by the office of Meischke & Schmidt. Gateway buildings gave access to the school buildings located in the inner courtyard, a solution Oud was not entirely happy with since *well-designed buildings of this importance are too valuable urban material to be withheld from the external aspect of the city.*[1] That this was no idle remark is evident from Oud's subdivision plan for Varkenoordsche Polder (1920) in which public buildings like schools and churches occupied a prominent place. Thanks to the housing shortage, the architecture of Oud's early projects for the Woningdienst was necessarily dominated by the debate about the economic and aesthetic aspects of standardization being conducted, not just in municipal housing authorities, but also in architectural and artistic circles, including *De Stijl*.

For the floor plan Oud availed himself of a 'standard type' previously used by, among others, J.E. van der Pek in The Hague and C.N. Goor in Rotterdam: a relatively small dwelling comprising one 'big' living room, two to four small bedrooms, a kitchen and toilet. In Spangen, the three pairs of flats per three-storey unit were reversed in plan, thus making it possible to provide access to the flats via a block of four doors instead of a single communal staircase. The two outermost doors opened directly into the ground-floor flats while each pair of flats on the upper floors shared a single street door. Although apparently identical from the outside, the dwellings differed from floor to floor. The ground-floor flats were the smallest with only two bedrooms and a small backyard. The (three bedroom) first-floor flat had access to its own laundry and storage area in the attic. The top flat was the largest: in addition to two bedrooms and a nursery in the attic, it had an extra bedroom for two in the attic (reached via an internal stair) as well as a laundry and storage area. Oud's interventions in the standard type were confined to 'aesthetic modifications' which came down to coordination of the block organization, adjustments to the floor plans and composition of the street elevation. For example, he changed the position of the chimney, windows and cupboards. Such typological 'emendations' not only added to the (collective) convenience, but also formed the basis of the rhythmical horizontal and vertical development of the building. The unity achieved by the alternation of windows and doors was accentuated by the three horizontal black bands of the base which linked all the doors together and, visually speaking, acted as a plinth for the unusual vertical strips of fenestration. Oud also managed, in his capacity as municipal official, to persuade the architects of the dwellings on the fourth side of the two blocks (on Bilderdijkstraat) to 'incorporate' elements of his street elevations (storey height, black bands, roof with cornice) into their facade architecture *so that there is no irksome interruption of the townscape as far as the complexes in question are concerned.*[2]

This town planning aspect also played a large role in Van Doesburg's colour design for the exterior. The commission to Van Doesburg was not entirely unexpected: in the street elevation Oud published in *De Stijl* in 1919 *the wall was conceived in white with primary colours for component parts.*[3] In Spangen, of course, there was no question of white rendered facades, let alone of concrete construction, only of painted woodwork. Van Doesburg's task as artist was precisely the same as the one that Oud, as architect, had set himself in designing the building: to devise a facade composition that reflected both the solidarity (typology, standardization) of the dwellings behind it, and the unity of the surrounding street- and townscape. Oud for his part resorted to the classical rules of architecture: symmetrical articulation of the main mass by dint of pronounced corner and centre projections, and, as a second layer over this, a division based on the classical order of entablature, pilaster and plinth that together define the wall as a repeatable, architectonic unit. Rather than challenging this order, Van

Doesburg's colour design added a sense of freedom and movement. Whereas in De Vonk Van Doesburg and Oud had worked separately and given the impression of cautiously testing the boundaries of each other's domain, at Spangen there was a sense of harmonious collaboration on a new, monumental beauty. The facade paintwork was realized in several phases. The point of departure was the streetscape as perceived by Van Doesburg from his studio in Leiden. Van Doesburg transformed this motif into an abstract composition of horizontal and vertical planes in what he called 'static colours': yellow, green and grey. Motif and colour scheme were first applied in the leaded lights above the front doors (in an unknown number of combinations) and subsequently to the wood of the doors themselves. Oud had imagined these doors *as large, bright patches of colour ... against a fairly neutral (colour) whole.*[4] From their correspondence it appears that Van Doesburg worked on two versions, one with a 'heavy' and one with a 'lighter' colour harmony, the second of which was evidently preferred by Oud. By the spring of 1919, all the doors were painted and the windows installed. In mid-August Van Doesburg finally came up with suggestions for the window frames, the dormer windows and the cornice. Here, too, he used the same motif and the same colour scheme but in a composition not of planes but of lines (for the standardized window components). In his facade composition Van Doesburg most certainly took account of the architectural 'conception' of the building and he respected Oud's black bands to the extent of repeating them in the dormer windows. But at the same time he succeeded, using purely aesthetic (painterly) devices of line, plane and colour, in achieving a rhythmic movement and a planar spatiality which, though it was the antithesis of Oud's sturdy formal expression, also served to strengthen the latter's expressive pretensions. Van Doesburg felt (quite rightly) that this design represented an important advance in 'monumental painting', one in which he *had finally got beyond the architecture-dependent corner treatment.*[5] This was so significant that Van Doesburg was convinced that his colour schemes were capable of achieving the unity in the townscape that Oud, too, was seeking

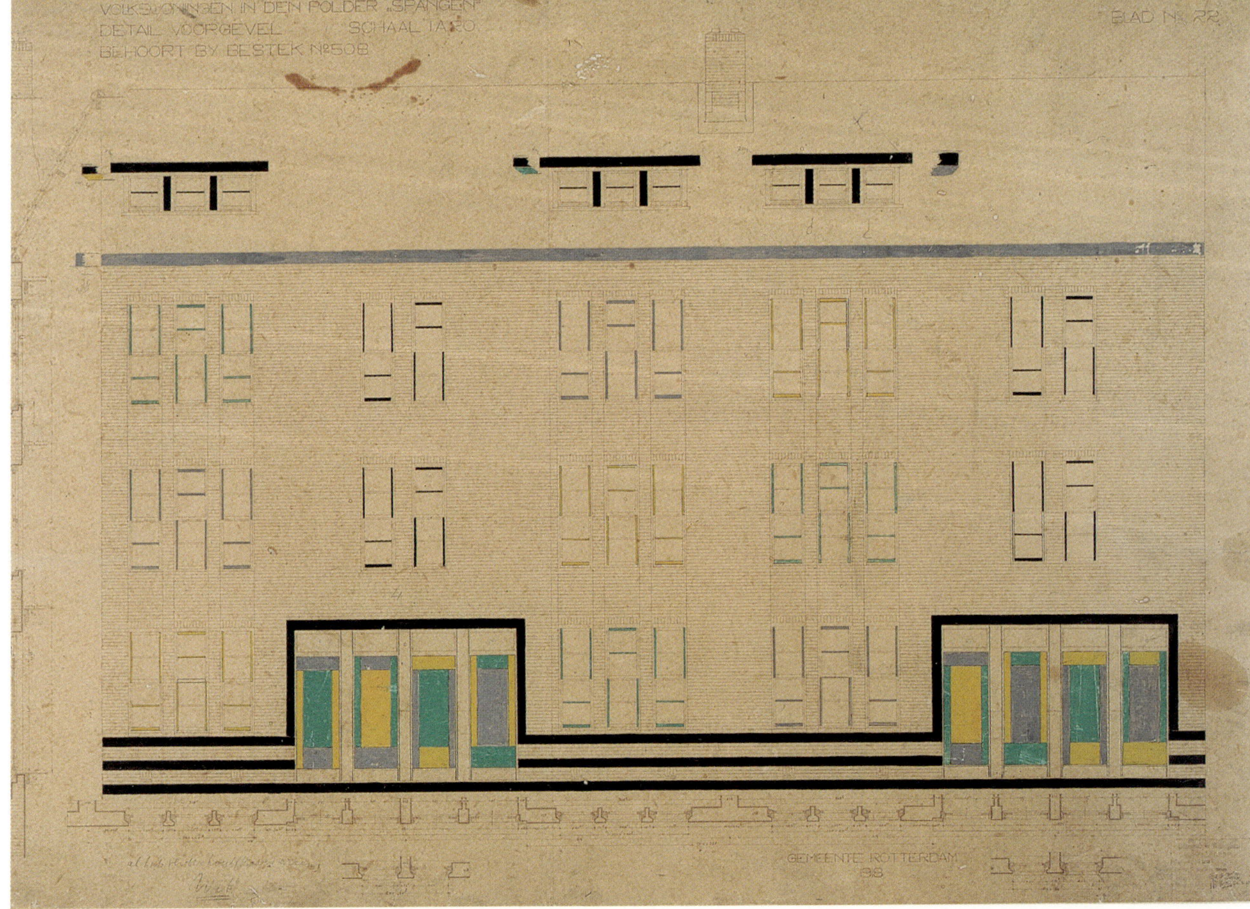


**Theo van Doesburg, colour scheme for street elevation/ OUDJ-sp 22, NAI, Rotterdam**

View of courtyard on building site/ OUDJ-ph 101, NAI, Rotterdam

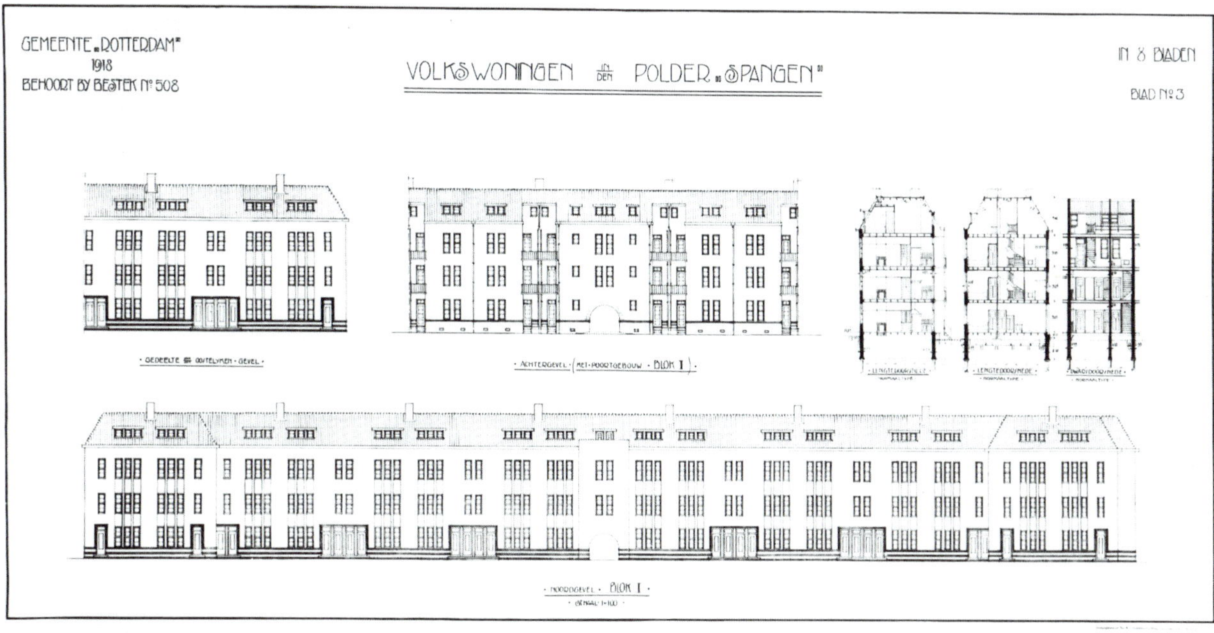



Elevations/ OUDJ-sp 15, NAI, Rotterdam

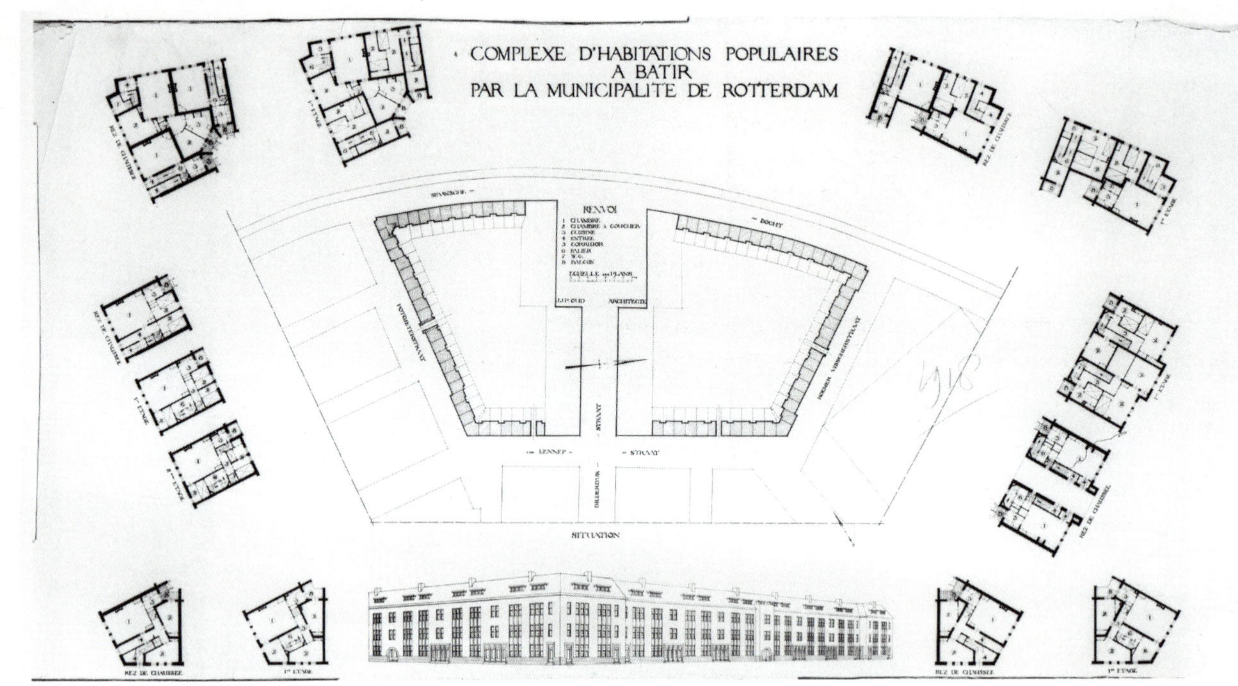


Various design views Spangen Block I (right) and Block V (left)/ OUDJ-sp 21, NAI, Rotterdam

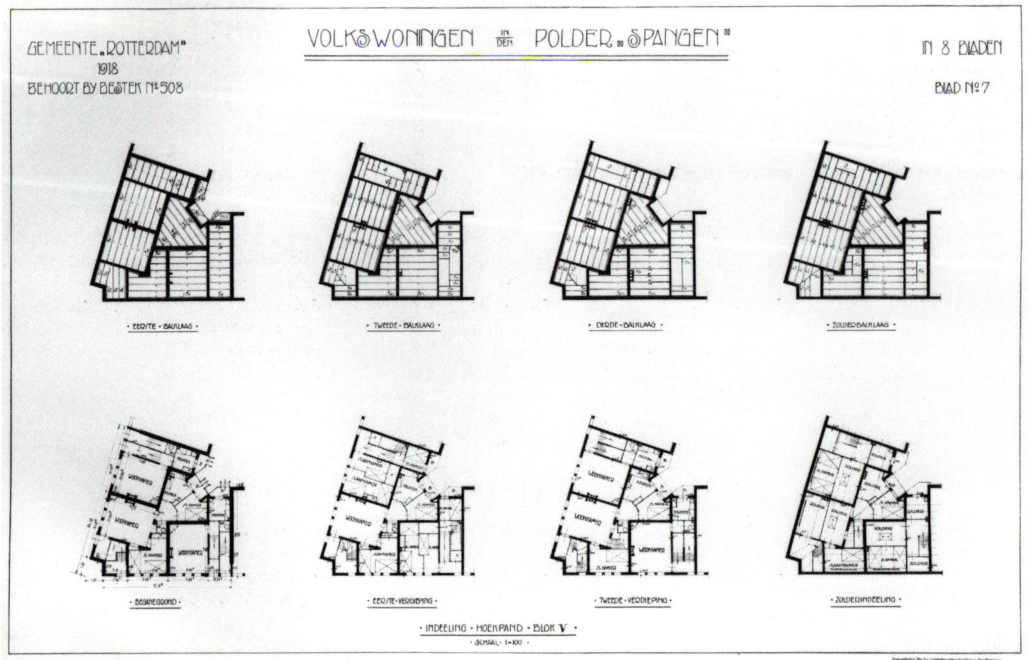


Plan for corner dwelling in Block V/ OUDJ-sp 19, NAI, Rotterdam

but which could not be fully realized because of the material limitations of the architecture (of the building block). Van Doesburg also produced the colour design for the interior. Here, too, his schemes were the expressive elaboration of objective facts (dictated by standardization of type and proportions), rather than the product of a colour fantasy. These objective facts formed the strict framework for the reworking of a motif – in this case a harmony of colours – noted during a holiday in Tilburg and which was built around the yellow colour stipulated by Oud. By way of clarification he wrote to Oud: *Without further explanation it sounds a bit crazy if I call these interiors 'late summer pastoral'. Don't be alarmed, it is all very simple and entirely suitable for standardization.*[6] The correspondence reveals that Van Doesburg was most anxious that Oud and his painters should keep to the exact shade of yellow so that the tension between the other three colours remained intact and thus also the link with the interior and the furnishings.

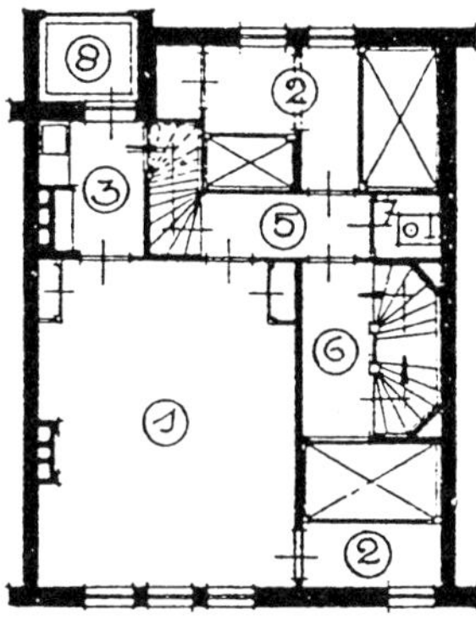


**Plan of standard type dwelling. From: J.J.P. Oud, 'Gemeentelijke Volkswoningen polder "Spangen", Rotterdam', in: *Bouwkundig Weekblad*, 41(1920)37**



**Notes**

**1.** J.J.P. Oud, 'Gemeentelijke woningbouw in "Spangen" en "Tusschendijken"', in: *Rotterdamsch Jaarboekje*, Rotterdam 1924, p. L.
**2.** J.J.P. Oud, 'Gemeentelijke woningbouw in "Spangen" en "Tusschendijken"', in: *Rotterdamsch Jaarboekje*, Rotterdam 1924, p. L.
**3.** J.J.P. Oud, 'Architectonische beschouwingen. A. Massabouw en straatarchitectuur', in: *De Stijl*, 2(1919)7, p. 82.
**4.** E. van Straaten, *Klare en lichte, gesloten ruimten geaccentueerd door diepe en pure kleuren. Het werk van Theo van Doesburg in de architectuur*, Amsterdam 1992; E. Hoek (ed.), *Theo van Doesburg. Oeuvrecatalogus*, Bussum 2000, pp. 242-243, 254-256.
**5.** E. Hoek (ed.), *Theo van Doesburg. Oeuvrecatalogus*, Bussum 2000, p. 255.
**6.** E. Hoek (ed.), *Theo van Doesburg. Oeuvrecatalogus*, Bussum 2000, p. 256.

**Sources**
CCA: dr1984: 0491-0497, ph1984: 0807, ph1984: 1043-1047
Getty: 890126-box 7, 8*
NAI: OUDJ-sp 1-22, OUDJ-sp 1001, OUDJ-ph 97-163, OUDJ-ph 1644, OUDJ-ph 1796-1817, OUDJ-ph 1820, OUDJ 1918-1919, OUDJ-B

**Articles**
J.J.P. Oud, 'Gemeentelijke volkswoningen, polder "Spangen", Rotterdam', in: *Bouwkundig Weekblad*, 41(1920)37, pp. 219-222
J.J.P. Oud, 'Gemeentelijke woningbouw in "Spangen" en "Tusschendijken"', in: E. van Wiersum (ed.), *Rotterdamsch Jaarboekje*, Rotterdam 1924, pp. XLIX – LV

**Literature**
U. Barbieri, *J.J.P. Oud*, Rotterdam 1987, pp. 66-71
H. Engel, 'De Kiefhoek, een monument voor gemiste kansen', S. Cusveller (ed.) , *De Kiefhoek, een woonwijk in Rotterdam*, Laren, Naarden 1990, pp. 20-21
E. Hoek (ed.), *Theo van Doesburg. Oeuvrecatalogus*, Bussum 2000, nos. 612, 631.i, 631.ii
H.E. Oud, *J.J.P. Oud. Architekt 1890-1963. Feiten en herinneringen gerangschikt*, The Hague 1984, pp. 58, 63-68, 112
S. Polano, *J.J.P. Oud Architettura Olandese*, Milan 1981, pp. 84-86
G. Stamm, *J.J.P. Oud. Bauten und Projekte 1906 bis 1963*, Mainz, Berlin 1984, pp. 58-59

Potgieterstraat elevation (left) Spaansche Bocht
Block V/ OUDJ-ph 157, NAI, Rotterdam

Spaansche Bocht elevation/ OUDJ-ph 155, NAI, Rotterdam

# Municipal Social Housing, "Spangen" Polder, Rotterdam.

The two housing blocks pictured here (municipal housing blocks I and V, "Spangen", Rotterdam) were designed in early 1918, put out to tender in August 1918 and completed in April of this year. Building costs averaged 4,825 guilders per dwelling. The contractor was Mr. Korevaar of Alblasserdam.

The layout of the general dwelling type in these blocks has been applied several times in Rotterdam; first of all by the architect C.N. van Goor. The layout of the standard type A reproduced here differs from the original type insofar as several cupboards, the chimney and the windows have been relocated in a quest for more regularity, which finds expression in the exterior and interior.

As is well-known, the kitchens of such dwellings are deliberately kept small, being treated more as a cooking and dishwashing area, in order to prevent the big room from being used for other than its real purpose and the kitchen being promoted to the status of living room. However, it appears that this, notwithstanding the limited dimensions, still occurs here.

As a result of previous difficulties in obtaining good paperer's cloth and wallpaper, and also because it was regularly found that the moisture generated by washing and cooking in the living rooms or the condensation on the walls, attacked the wallpaper, rendered it unsightly or loosened it, the walls, by way of experiment, were provided at door-height with a picture rail below which the wall was rendered with coloured mortar, while the area above it, like the ceiling, was finished in white plaster.

This has a much more satisfactory appearance; the painterly colour scheme of strongly contrasting colours (yellow, grey, blue, black) devised for the interior by Theo van Doesburg in relation to this wall treatment makes wallpaper superfluous. To what extent the aforementioned finishing of the walls of such dwellings will give satisfaction in the long term is impossible to say. There has been conflicting experience with this in various cities: it is claimed that it is more difficult to maintain than wallpaper because, in general, it is easier to hang new paper than to repair plasterwork. It is also said that the flat colour of the walls shows the dirt more than vari-coloured wallpaper where the decorative patterns absorb and conceal a multitude of imperfections. The ideal solution would be a hard, smooth, coloured surface that is washable. Although this is also greatly needed for hall panelling, it cannot be realized at reasonable cost. Metallizing is no solution, either, not only because it is expensive but also because as far as colour is concerned it is unpredictable while for the time being it does not seem possible to apply even, flat colours.

Regarding the interior finishing of the dwellings there is not much more to be said. The dividing walls are made of wood fibre and cement mortar (1 cement, 1 lime, 4 sand) 5 cm. thick. Efforts to arrive at a standard profile for the frames to be placed in such walls, such as to allow all kinds of combinations while the casing still produces a satisfactory whole, led to a type that afforded considerable time-saving during detailing and that could be improved on for new plans. As is well-known, the solution of the end plates used in the type of internal door frames normally (for such construction) employed in corners, at wall joins, etc. is far from handsome.

Above the front doors are stained-glass windows designed by Theo van Doesburg.

The site plan was more or less dictated by the building lines. The course of these lines, which meet at acute or oblique angles and as far as the Spaansche Bocht is concerned, exhibit an irregular curved line, occasioned much time-consuming drawing and juggling in the making of the working drawings and in construction. In general, a simple orthogonal, or at any rate regular, street plan, is essential for a speedy and economic construction, which in these times is imperative. All good intentions to this end come to naught, if this is not taken into account when drawing up the street plan.

As already said, the difficulties associated with this were also experienced in the plan described here. Even only slightly different corners necessitated individual solutions or, at the very least, for accurate execution, completely new work drawings.

Apart from these corners, several gateway buildings (3 with 4; 1 with 2 dwellings) were designed to provide access to the schools that will be built in the courtyards. The size of these gateway buildings was derived from the breadth of the standard types so as to maintain the rhythm of the fenestration.

Uniformity of parts was pursued for practical and aesthetic reasons (the latter on the grounds that a street elevation should not command attention for itself but, by means of a certain unobtrusiveness and uniform rhythmicality, set up a contrast with, and support the architectonic effect of, any major corner treatments or freestanding buildings). For that matter, the specification itself offered every motive for doing so in this case.

The economic advantages of this may, as far as the costs of preparation and work are concerned, have turned out be less than imagined in the initial enthusiasm, but they also have an impact on preparation and implementation costs. Economic comparisons on this score should not be limited to the building costs alone.

As far as windows and doors are concerned, the uniformity was carried through to such an extent that on the front elevations of both blocks only one window and one door model was used, while the necessary variation was sought by combining these elements into groups, a combination called for on practical grounds because of the dimensions of the various rooms which meant that some required a light surface area the size of 3, others of 1 or 2 standard window frames.

The grouping of the whole was achieved by shifting some units forwards or backwards.

The fourth side of each block is formed by the housing complexes – currently under construction – of the "Onze Woning" housing association. After consultation, their architects, Messrs Meischke and Schmidt, declared themselves prepared to incorporate storey heights, the 3 black bands of the plinth, the roof and cornice, etc. in their design so as to complete the blocks in such a fashion that there is no interruption of the outer walls.

# 40/ Spangen Municipal Housing Scheme, Blocks VIII and IX

**Rotterdam, Van Harenstraat, Jan Luijkenstraat, Pieter Langendijkstraat, 1919-1920**

Oud's early years with the Rotterdam Woningdienst were completely bound up with the housing shortage and the city council's efforts to tackle it in the short term by building a lot of new homes, quickly and above all cheaply. Thus social and economic conditions were no mere background to housing construction in Rotterdam in these years but the very basis of Oud's architectural endeavours. Nearly all of his plan commentaries contain a sentence along the lines of: *the design is based on the specific conditions and methods of our time, in correlation with which the architecture evolved.*[1] Henk Engel and Jan de Heer have pointed out that the main consideration in each of Oud's housing schemes is the relation between the layout of the dwelling, the organization of the housing block, the space created by the block and its expression in the elevations and corners. In successive housing projects, such as the one published in *De Stijl* (Straatcompositie/Street Composition, 1919), and more particularly those realized shortly afterwards at Spangen and Tusschendijken (and later at Hoek van Holland and Kiefhoek), Oud was constantly looking for ways of creating different, that is to say better, links between dwelling, block and public space. His study was rigorous inasmuch as he refused to work from 'aesthetic premisses' and proceeded instead by logically 'thinking through' the architectural implications of the obligatory structural and domestic demands. In that sense, the housing block designs for Spangen and Tusschendijken form a coherent whole.

Blocks VIII and IX at Spangen represented an important step forward for Oud because in addition to the link between the individual floor plan and the organization of the block, Oud (and the Woningdienst) tackled a new aspect of urban living: the space created by the block, in particular that of the inner courtyard. Because of the new domestic layout developed here and the exploration of the collective character of the courtyard, Oud regarded these two Spangen blocks as prototypes of the much bigger housing scheme he was to realize soon after that in the Tusschendijken district. The 'conquest' of the courtyard occurred in stages. The first subdivision plans for block VIII presupposed an urban block wholly designed and built by the Woningdienst. Two variants were developed: the first was a perimeter block in which the position of the living room alternated between the front and rear elevations. Oud published a segment of the ground plans and the accompanying elevation in *De Stijl* (Straatcompositie, 1919). The second variant was for a block with gallery access from the courtyard, a solution not unsimilar to the plan – strongly criticized by the city council – by Michiel Brinkman (and A. Plate) in which the galleries became virtual 'streets'. The decision to use or not to use galleries in block VIII was based the Woningdienst's studies of seasonal fluctuations in the incidence of light. As to floor plans, it was decided to use the 'standard dwellings' developed previously at Spangen, with the result that the idea of alternate front and rear living rooms was not systematically

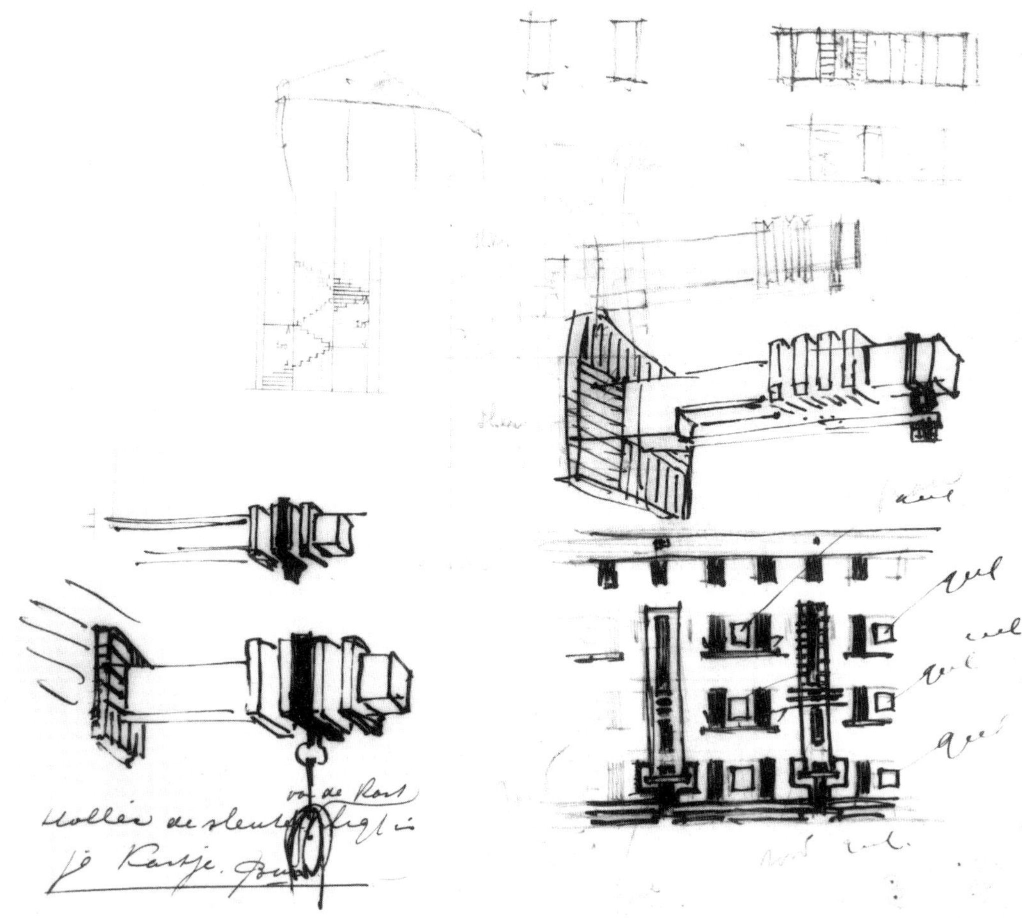

Sketches/ OUDJ-sg 2, NAI, Rotterdam

applied throughout the block. The opportunities for further experimentation were considerably restricted when it became clear that the greater part of the scheme would be built by private contractors.

In the execution of the plans for blocks VIII and IX, Oud faced three main problems: first of all the technical difficulties associated with fitting standard dwellings into an irregular street pattern; secondly, the collaboration with private developers, not just in the immediate vicinity but even within the individual blocks; and, finally, the external colour scheme of the facades, where he clashed with Van Doesburg concerning the compatibility of colour and brick and the aesthetic effect of a painterly composition on street- and townscape.

In block VIII Oud was faced with the difficulty of creating a lucid, architectonic unity when only a small part of the block (nineteen lots on Pieter Langendijkstraat) was to be built by the Woningdienst. In his negotiations with various private developers concerning the development of the other lots in the block, Oud reached a curious compromise whereby the short elevations, including the four corners, would be partly built by private contractors according to a Woningdienst design, and partly by the Woningdienst using floor plans developed by private contractors. From handwritten annotations on some of the working drawings, it appears that Oud's interest in the architectural treatment of the corner units (especially the Langendijkstraat–Van Harenstraat corner) was prompted mainly by his desire for a satisfactory juncture with block IX which was to be wholly built by the Woningdienst. Probably in an effort to win over the private developers, Oud produced two fine perspective drawings showing the short facades and corners on Pieter Langendijkstraat worked out in detail. From a town planning point of view, Oud was less than happy with this architectural 'cutting and pasting'. In his commentary he wrote: *Such a method – difficult enough to defend on architectural grounds – is unsatisfactory from a practical point of view as well. If one wishes to focus attention on the townscape as a whole yet without adversely affecting the architecture through mutual give and take, then a more recently applied*

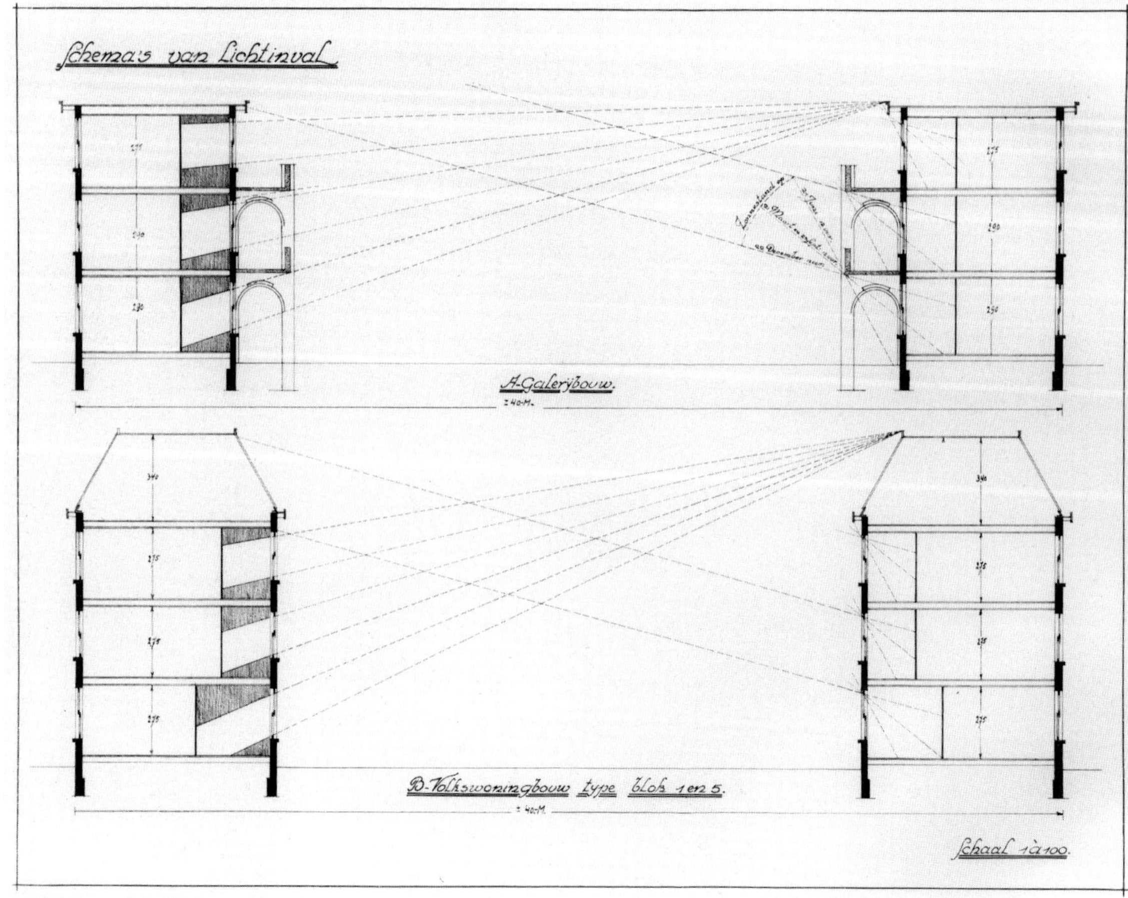


Diagram for calculating daylight levels for perimeter block development in Spangen/ OUDJ-sp 6, NAI, Rotterdam

*method is to be preferred in which the various building complexes are grouped and are linked to one another by means of small, slightly lower and more set back transitional objects. This preserves the individual expression of each complex, allowing them to manifest themselves as much as possible as separate entities, without however resulting in the disjointed appearance characteristic of contemporary streets. Not that this solution is entirely satisfactory either.*[2]
The importance Oud – and the Woningdienst – attached to the exemplary function of municipal construction vis à vis private builders soon became apparent in the conflict with Van Doesburg, where once again it was the relationship with the surrounding development that was at issue.
Coherence within the block (and with the immediate surroundings) was achieved by the already successfully used device of three black bands which in this case stopped either side of the doors instead of framing them as in blocks I and V. The horizontal and binding effect of the plinth was reinforced at floor height by the gentle rhythm of the small concrete canopies above the porches. At the corners these culminated in two long cantilevers above the shop windows which, as Oud informed Van Doesburg, emphasized the *vertical* character of the corners and simultaneously opened block VIII (at least on the corner with Van Harenstraat) to the 'characteristic' architecture of block IX.[3]
The adaptation of the standard floor plans to the specific conditions of a neighbourhood with long, narrow streets, represented an important step in the direction of a new 'living arrangement'. From the many versions Oud and the Woningdienst made for the accommodation of various standard-type dwellings above and alongside one another in a single structural unit, it appears that the main focus was on the problem of access – via staircases, corridors and porches. All manner of solutions were devised: four narrow corridors (and doors) side by side; a separate staircase flanked by two corridors; a communal porch, and so on. In each instance, however, the living rooms were located on the street side and the kitchens at the back. The two perspective drawings also date from this stage in which the internal layout of the dwellings was being tested for its

**Perspective of Block VIII/ OUDJ-sg 15, NAI, Rotterdam**

effect on the facade composition. The final version had a communal entrance for all four dwellings in a unit, which differed from floor to floor. The ground and first floors each contained a single dwelling while the two dwellings on the floors above were designed as maisonettes with kitchen and living room on the second floor and the bedrooms on the third (attic) floor. But the main difference compared with all the earlier housing complexes (by Oud and by the Woningdienst) was that half-way through the design process it was decided to locate *all* the living rooms on the back (i.e. courtyard) side. It is not clear exactly how and when they arrived at this decision but it appears to have been prompted by the need for more light in the living rooms. This at any rate was Oud's explanation: *Since the courtyard is usually considerably wider than the streets, the living rooms are located not on the streets but on the courtyard.*[4] According to this line of reasoning, it was a necessary (and for the Woningdienst understandable) corrective to the shortcomings of the street layout. The same dissatisfaction with the masterplan prompted Michiel Brinkman, in his almost simultaneously designed gallery-access block (located next to block VIII), to turn his back even more decisively on the street plan; in his case not even the perimeter block was spared. Oud did not go this far but the consequences of his modifications for the ambience and use of the individual dwelling and for the development of the urban block as collective housing block were no less decisive. His main innovation concerned the organization and architectural treatment of the courtyard. The presence of an open central area available for collective use was not in itself new – Amsterdam already boasted several impressive examples of the type. What was new was the way Oud tried to link the inner court to the layout of the dwellings and the composition of the housing block, thereby making the court the heart of a new 'living arrangement'. In block VIII, where the council controlled only half the area, he was only partially successful. In block IX a few simple architectural interventions turned a public area, reached through two entrances on the short sides of the block, into a modest residential court. In the centre of the court was a communal garden

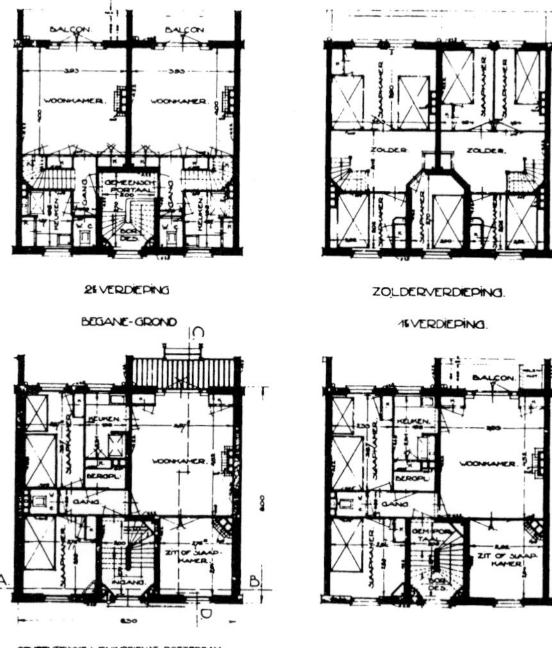


Plan of standard type dwelling. From: J.J.P. Oud, 'Gemeentelijke woningbouw "Spangen" te Rotterdam', in: *Bouwkundig Weekblad*, 44(1923)2

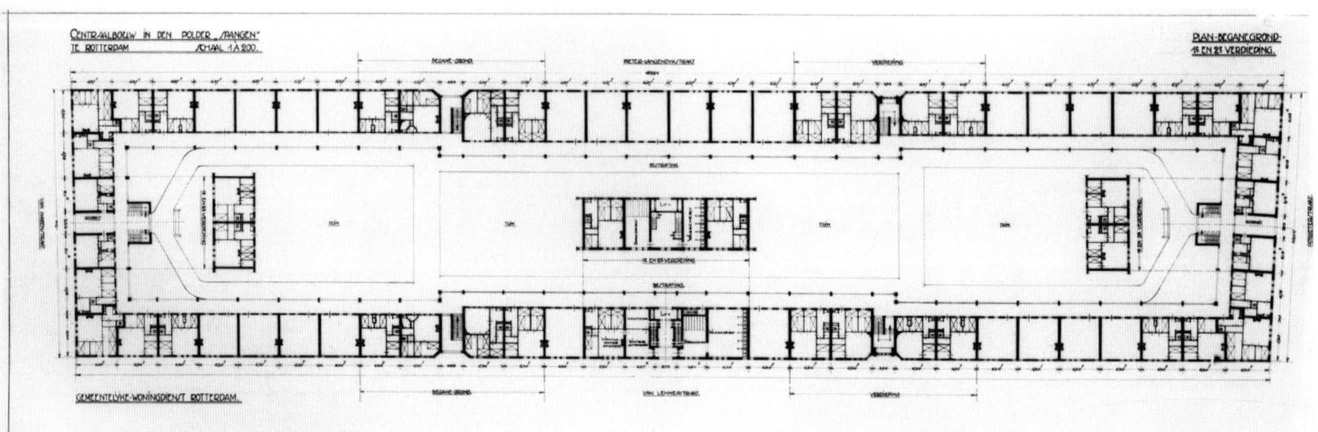


Variant of floor plan design, Block VIII ('Centraalbouw')/ OUDJ-sg 4, NAI, Rotterdam

encircled by a gravel path giving access to the (private) gardens belonging to the ground-floor dwellings. The internal organization of the block (into flats and maisonettes) and the design of the inner court came together – literally – in the structure of the court-side elevations. These were visually characterized by a composition of horizontal and vertical lines formed by the continuous balconies and their individual partition walls. It was while he was working on the detailing of block IX that Oud became aware of the architectural potentialities of the interior of the courtyard, potentialities he was soon able to exploit more fully in the Tusschendijken blocks. With most of the secondary spaces, kitchens and toilets moved from the back to the front, the street elevations acquired a different aspect. Gone was the rhythmic and plastic alternation of window bands, staircases and (painted) reliefs of the two perspective drawings. Instead Oud – now *freer in the determination of the architectural accent of the facades* – designed taut, flat walls with a minimum of variation.[5] This, in combination with the immediate surroundings, gave rise to a very stern and introverted streetscape. For Oud, this was the logical outcome of the social and economic conditions of public housing in the big cities. This, at least, is the import of one of the rare commentaries in which Oud defended himself against the alleged 'inhuman' character of his architecture and elaborated on the significance of the two aspects of urban life. The open space of the street stood for the vitality of urban traffic and commercial activity; that of the inner courtyard for the peace and quiet of domestic life. Acceptance of this contrast was the objective rationale behind the 'purification' of the building block as an element of a monumental, contemporary townscape: *I should like to point out that the most open-minded acceptance and most lucid rendering of the building programme (the basis of modern architecture in general) has led here to a contrast effect which strikes me – as such – as the architectural hallmark of the truly vibrant, big city. I am referring to the contrast between the practical, organizational requirements of the city as a hive of activity, and the need for peace and seclusion in domestic life which this automatically generates. Having accepted this antithesis (and only an architecture that is based on reality can be a true reflection of the culture of its age) the only way to achieve a city with character is to express this duality architecturally. If people insist on labelling one side of the image that the city presents as hard, inhuman and so on – which is quite usual for the kind of architecture depicted here – so be it. However, the reproach that is implicit in this – and which I reject on other grounds too – does not reflect on the designer, but on the basis which gave rise to the building in question: in this case the city as city. The nature of the city (once again as city: I am not talking about appropriately isolated and equipped residential areas, suburbs, etc. but only of that part of the city that gives it its character as such, in other words where business is at its most intensive) is, if you will, hard: to disguise this would result in something that, generally speaking, would not be better, simply more bland. Living in the city is a victory over the industry of the city: it calls for protection against that industry. To express this practically and aesthetically was the intention behind the design of the housing blocks reproduced here. The street equals industry, the inner courtyard equals domestic life. Both strictly separate and totally different in character. As far as the reality is concerned, from what I hear, the residents are generally satisfied.*[6]

This conception of the housing block as an anonymous urban element, subject to the laws of urban life, also proved to be the stumbling point in the conflict with Theo van Doesburg. In October 1921 Van Doesburg furnished a series of colour designs for the street facades of block VIII (Potgieterstraat and Pieter Langendijkstraat) and the street and courtyard facades of block IX (Van Harenstraat). From the correspondence with Oud it appears that he also made 'sketches' of facade compositions for an earlier version of block VIII. No drawings of this version are known, apart from the two perspective drawings mentioned earlier and a fairly rough sketch by Oud in which the colour (yellow) is specified for both the windows and the (wooden?) panels. Archival sources indicate that Van Doesburg's aim here, from the very outset, was a contrast effect: *colour* was used in contrast to the dominant mass of brick and *composition* against the dominant horizontality of the architecture. To this end he devised a *dissonant triad* (yellow, blue and green) and applied it in vertical bands on the long elevations, and in mainly diagonal bands on the short end-faces and the courtyard facades. According to Oud, the effect was the opposite of what Van Doesburg intended for it actually reinforced the horizontal character of the architecture. Oud's stated preference was to paint all the windows above one another in the same colour and *to vary the colour (of the doors as well!) along the length of the street. In this way the appearance of street changes constantly as one walks along it and never becomes monotonous. ... Such a street should in my view preserve the element of surprise in the* succession *and not, as in a more harmonious object, in the equilibrium as a whole ... this also has the potential to be* more interesting *in terms of painting.*[7] The deciding argument for Oud to end the collaboration with Van Doesburg on Spangen was an (unexpected) effect of the first colour scheme on block VIII. Van Doesburg and Oud were agreed that the colour scheme of the long and short elevations should be identical. But what no one at the Woningdienst had foreseen was that the effect of the concentration of colour on the much shorter and more dynamic – owing to the contrast between flat (Woningdienst) and pitched (private) roofs – Potgieterstraat facade, was to emphasize the contribution of private developers to the townscape. Van Doesburg had no objections to this effect: *I anticipated it. Indeed, I intended it, as a contrast with the static effect of*

**Elevations, Block IX/ OUDJ-ph 137, NAI, Rotterdam**

*the Langendijkstraat facade. This sparkling effect of colours in rhythmical order (the dormer windows) and oblique-angled perspective is what I expected and I do not have any difficulty with it. Be assured that you will think the same once it is* fully *realized.*[8] But it never got that far. Oud – and, one may assume, the Woningdienst too – felt that the colour scheme of the council-built housing block should have served to put the privately built housing in the shade. When it did not, Oud suggested to Van Doesburg that the two corner blocks be painted entirely in grey. Van Doesburg – understandably from his point of view – refused.
For Oud, the dramatic end of the collaboration with Van Doesburg at Spangen signified the end of the belief in a new, collective monumental style to be realized jointly by painter and architect. Around the same time when the two Spangen blocks were being painted grey on his orders, Oud wrote a review for *Bouwkundig Weekblad* of the colour schemes Karl Crayl had produced for several buildings designed by the Magdeburg city architect, Bruno Taut. The text can be read as a balanced comment on the recent developments at Spangen. Interestingly, Oud puts less emphasis on the destructive effect of colour (on the architecture) than on colour's ability to differentiate forms: *yellow is more radiant than red, red more than blue, and so on. Colour also magnifies or diminishes, makes things advance or retreat, i.e.* creates measure and plasticity. *Colour there-*

Pieter Langendijkstraat elevation, Block VIII/ OUDJ-ph 133, NAI, Rotterdam

Pieter Langendijkstraat elevation, Block VIII/
OUDJ-ph 111, NAI, Rotterdam



**Notes**

**1.** J.J.P. Oud, 'Gemeentelijke woningbouw in "Spangen" en "Tusschendijken"', in: *Rotterdamsch Jaarboekje*, Rotterdam 1924.
**2.** J.J.P. Oud, 'Gemeentelijke woningbouw "Spangen" in Rotterdam', in: *Bouwkundig Weekblad*, 44(1923)42, p. 17.
**3.** E. Hoek (ed.), *Theo van Doesburg. Oeuvrecatalogus*, Bussum 2000, p. 291.
**4.** J.J.P. Oud, 'Gemeentelijke woningbouw "Spangen" in Rotterdam', in: *Bouwkundig Weekblad*, 44(1923)42, p. 16.
**5.** J.J.P. Oud, 'Gemeentelijke woningbouw "Spangen" in Rotterdam', in: *Bouwkundig Weekblad*, 44(1923)42, p. 17.
**6.** J.J.P. Oud, 'Gemeentelijke woningbouw in "Spangen" en "Tusschendijken"', in: *Rotterdamsch Jaarboekje*, Rotterdam 1924.
**7.** E. Hoek (ed.), *Theo van Doesburg. Oeuvrecatalogus*, Bussum 2000, p. 291.
**8.** E. Hoek (ed.), *Theo van Doesburg. Oeuvrecatalogus*, Bussum 2000, p. 292.
**9.** J.J.P. Oud, 'Uitweiding bij eenige afbeeldingen', in: *Bouwkundig Weekblad*, 43(1922)43, pp. 421-422.
**10.** J.J.P. Oud, 'Uitweiding bij eenige afbeeldingen', in: *Bouwkundig Weekblad*, 43(1922)43, p. 423.

**Sources**

CCA: dr1984: 0023, dr1984: 0250-0252, dr1984: 0489, ph1983: 0320, ph1983: 0322
Getty: 890126-box 7, 8*
NAI: OUDJ-sg 1-18, OUDJ-sp 1001, OUDJ-ph 97-163, OUDJ-ph 1644, OUDJ-ph 1796-1817, OUDJ-ph 1820, OUDJ 1918-1919, OUDJ-B

**Articles**

J.J.P. Oud, 'Gemeentelijke woningbouw "Spangen" te Rotterdam' in: *Bouwkundig Weekblad*, 44(1923)2, pp. 15-20
J.J.P. Oud, 'Gemeentelijke woningbouw in "Spangen" en "Tusschendijken"', in: E. van Wiersum (ed.), *Rotterdamsch Jaarboekje*, Rotterdam 1924, pp. XLIX-LV
J.J.P. Oud, 'Uitweiding bij eenige afbeeldingen', in: *Bouwkundig Weekblad*, 43(1922)43, pp. 418-424

**Literature**

U. Barbieri, *J.J.P. Oud*, Rotterdam 1987, pp. 72-79
R. Dettingmeijer, 'De strijd om een goed gebouwde stad', in *Het Nieuwe Bouwen in Rotterdam 1920-1960*, Delft 1982, pp. 19-76
E. Hoek (ed.), *Theo van Doesburg. Oeuvrecatalogus*, Bussum 2000, no. 612, 671
H.E. Oud, *J.J.P. Oud. Architekt 1890-1963. Feiten en herinneringen gerangschikt*, The Hague 1984, pp. 58,

*fore has an enormous impact on the plastic effect of architecture. Every measure of colour, where painting and architecture work in harmony, is closely matched by a measure of architecture.* Differentiation of colour *simultaneously implies:* differentiation of form.[9] It is clear that at the time he wrote this, Oud had no sympathy at all for Van Doesburg's (and Crayl's) aesthetic ideas about a colour scheme based on *contrasts* and dissonant colour tones. An architecture based on the repetition of standardized elements was, according to Oud, incompatible with the principle of colour variation. That was the lesson of Spangen: *...the failure of similar attempts of my own, has convinced me of the correctness of this theoretical argument: such an interlocking of painting and architecture does not allow for an 'orderly' architecture: an alliance of this kind is only possible when both branches of art are permitted a great multiformity of relationships, that is to say in a very subjective, non-monumental architecture.*[10] It was a point of view that Oud was to stick to throughout his career and it was not until the mid-1950s that visual artists were once again welcome in his buildings.

**Mantelpiece of dwellings in Blocks VIII and IX/ OUDJ-ph 104, NAI, Rotterdam**

63-68, 112
S. Polano, *J.J.P. Oud Architettura Olandese*, Milan 1981, pp. 84-86
G. Stamm, *J.J.P. Oud. Bauten und Projekte 1906 bis 1963*, Mainz, Berlin 1984, pp. 59-60
E. Taverne, D. Broekhuizen, *J.J.P. Oud's Shell Building. Design and Reception*, Rotterdam 1995, pp. 336-368

# "Spangen" Municipal Housing in Rotterdam

The housing complexes depicted here (municipal housing, blocks VIII and IX, "Spangen", Rotterdam) were designed in 1919-1920. Essentially, they are based on one standard type and on one corner type (different for each block). Block IX also includes some warehouses and two gateways from the street to the inner court.
The standard type contains 4 dwellings; one dwelling on the ground floor and the same on the $1^{st}$ floor, while on the $2^{nd}$ floor a split occurs whereby the rooms of each of the two top dwellings are distributed over the $2^{nd}$ and $3^{rd}$ floors.
The above-mentioned spatial layout owes its existence to the wish to keep stair-climbing to the minimum: in this way, stair traffic, which during the day is mainly confined to the living areas, need usually extend over only 2 levels; the internal stairs, which only give access to the bedrooms, are by the nature of things less frequently used.
Most of the dwellings contain a living room and 3 bedrooms; in the dwellings on the ground and $1^{st}$ floors, the living room is placed "en suite" with the lounge or bedroom.
The stairs and contiguous floors and landings in the communal staircases are constructed of reinforced concrete; the floors, landings and steps are topped with magnesite flooring, protected at the front by iron nosings.
The structural and facade walls and the walls of the staircases are of brick; the secondary partition walls of wood fibre and cement mortar, reinforced at intervals of 0.90 m with 3/8 rods.
The block IX corner type contains a shop-dwelling unit below and for the rest conforms as far as possible to the standard type. The block VIII corner type also contains a shop-dwelling at street level, but the dwellings above are a little more spacious.
Since the width of the inner courts is usually much greater than the width of the streets, the living rooms are located not on the street side but overlooking the court. The latter is consequently surrounded by a continuous band of balconies onto which the living rooms open, while in its centre is a communal garden encircled by a path that provides access to the gardens belonging to the ground-floor dwellings. In later plans – presently under construction – based largely on the same dwelling type, a more sustained effort has been made to shift the residential aspect from the streets to the inner courts: the paths there are better designed, pergolas with benches provide residents with somewhere to sit, while for the children a handsome sandpit has been installed in the middle of the garden.
With respect to the architecture on the street sides, such an arrangement around an inner court has the added advantage of allowing more freedom in determining the architectural accent of the facades.
As far as block VIII is concerned, an attempt was made for town planning reasons (in this case: so that an overall picture emerges rather than the fragmented impression of a series of housing clusters) to create an architectonic transition from a private developer (which complex occupies the entire long elevation at the rear of the building block) to the municipal complex. The private builder cooperated willingly in this.
This transition, which occurs on the short sides of the block, links up with the "tower" of the municipal complex and is only partially visible in the photo. Such a method – difficult enough to defend on architectural grounds – is unsatisfactory from a practical point of view as well. If one wishes to focus attention on the townscape as a whole, yet without adversely affecting the architecture through mutual give and take, then a more recently applied method is to be preferred in which the various building complexes are grouped and are linked to one another by means of small, slightly lower and more set back transitional objects.
This preserves the individual expression of each of the complexes, allowing them to manifest themselves as much as possible as separate entities, without however resulting in the disjointed appearance characteristic of contemporary streets. Not that this solution is entirely satisfactory either.
The theory of town planning is sufficiently well set out in various handbooks nowadays to form a solid basis. But the practice is so complex that it is now time to focus all attention on it so that what has already been gained in the first instance should not be lost in construction.

R. Dec. 1922.
J.J.P. Oud

# Théo van Doesburg. The architect J.J.P. Oud "leader" of the "Cubists" in architecture?

"Do you believe that Cubism is truly dead?
"If so, from what disease did it die?"
(Survey by the "Revue de l'Epoque" March 1922)
Reply by Mr. I. K. BONSET: "Yes, from what disease? The short skirt"...

Issue 28 of "Bouwwereld" contains several excerpts from a speech by Mr JAN GRATAMA. The final passage might lead the reader to think that the architect OUD is "leader of the Cubists in architecture" and that he makes propaganda for this school of thought in "De Stijl". Furthermore, that a block of housing (namely "Spangen" in Rotterdam) should serve as an example of this so-called "Cubist" architecture.
This is for the most part untrue:
The architect J.J.P. OUD, since his appointment as city architect at Rotterdam, no longer plays any active part in "De Stijl".
Mr. OUD, who – theoretically at least – was for some time a faithful adherent and disciple of De Stijl ideas, has (with the exception of the hall in the Holiday Hostel at Noordwijkerhout) not realized any so-called "Cubist architecture". The housing complexes referred to, however much consultation and feeling for proper proportions went into their composition, cannot be counted an example of "Cubist architecture", unlike the design for a factory and warehouse, which, unfortunately, was never built.
Practical consequences, i.e. implementation of the ideas concerning a new form of expression in architecture, adhered to from around 1916 and afterwards occasionally "politely" and "cautiously" propagated, have – as far as I know – never been realized by OUD.
If by "villa" the villa "Allegonda" at Katwijk aan Zee is meant – which villa, although not flawless, could in outward appearance serve as an example of sound, if you will "Cubist" architecture (which it does, especially for the young German architects, who take their cue from Dutch architecture)[1)] – it should be mentioned here that we owe this "Cubist" effort to a design by the academic painter M. KAMERLINGH ONNES. It was not a "Cubist" but a "Romantic" effect that they were after here. The architect OUD, who made the plan technically feasible, played an intermediary role in this.
Now that experience has shown that it is necessary to struggle for the realization of the new spirit and Mr OUD has proven unequal to this struggle, it should be pointed out here that the architects ROBERT VAN 'T HOFF, JAN WILS, G. RIETVELD, PAUW and HARDEVELD (judging by the Concrete Houses in Rotterdam) have far more right to be called the pioneers of a "Cubist architecture".

Weimar 1922.

1) De Stijl ideas in particular have, since I have been living and working in Germany, been imitated by the architects MEYER-GROPIUS (theatre at Jena), FORBAT (Bauhaus housing estate), HILBERSEIMER, MENDELSOHN (houses at Charlottenburg) and many others.

## 41/ Tusschendijken Municipal Housing Scheme, Blocks I, III & V

**Rotterdam, Rösener Manzstraat, Gijsingstraat** **1920-1924**

On 8 October 1920, the Rotterdam city council approved a plan for eight blocks containing a total of 1,005 dwellings in the new Tusschendijken housing development (adjoining Spangen). In 1923, with blocks I-IV and block VI completed, construction was halted, no doubt because of the withdrawal of the special State funding provided for under the Housing Shortage Act. Design, bureaucratic groundwork and construction at Tusschendijken took place against a background of political bickering over the municipal housing programme. In September 1921, the socialist alderman, A.W. Heijkoop, resigned rather than carry out the council's instructions to negotiate with private contractors who had submitted plans for 'alcove dwellings' (in which curtained-off alcoves did duty as bedrooms), which had long since been phased out for hygienic reasons. In political (and official) circles in Rotterdam there had always been a strong preference for private enterprise in building. There were also financial and ideological objections to the proliferation of collective amenities in recent municipal housing schemes, such as galleries, raised 'streets', bath- and washhouses, interior decoration and communal gardens. Objections were also raised to the atmosphere of 'enforced collectivity' radiated by some of the housing blocks, which had the effect of making them seem even more insupportable than the average spec-built housing block. These circumstances were duly reflected in the Tusschendijken

**Perspective of elevations/ OUDJ-td 18, NAI, Rotterdam**

ARCHITECT J.J.P. OUD
GET. DOOR L.F. DUQUET

**Perspective of courtyard/ OUDJ-td 17 , NAI, Rotterdam**

## 41/ Tusschendijken Municipal Housing Scheme, Blocks I, III & V

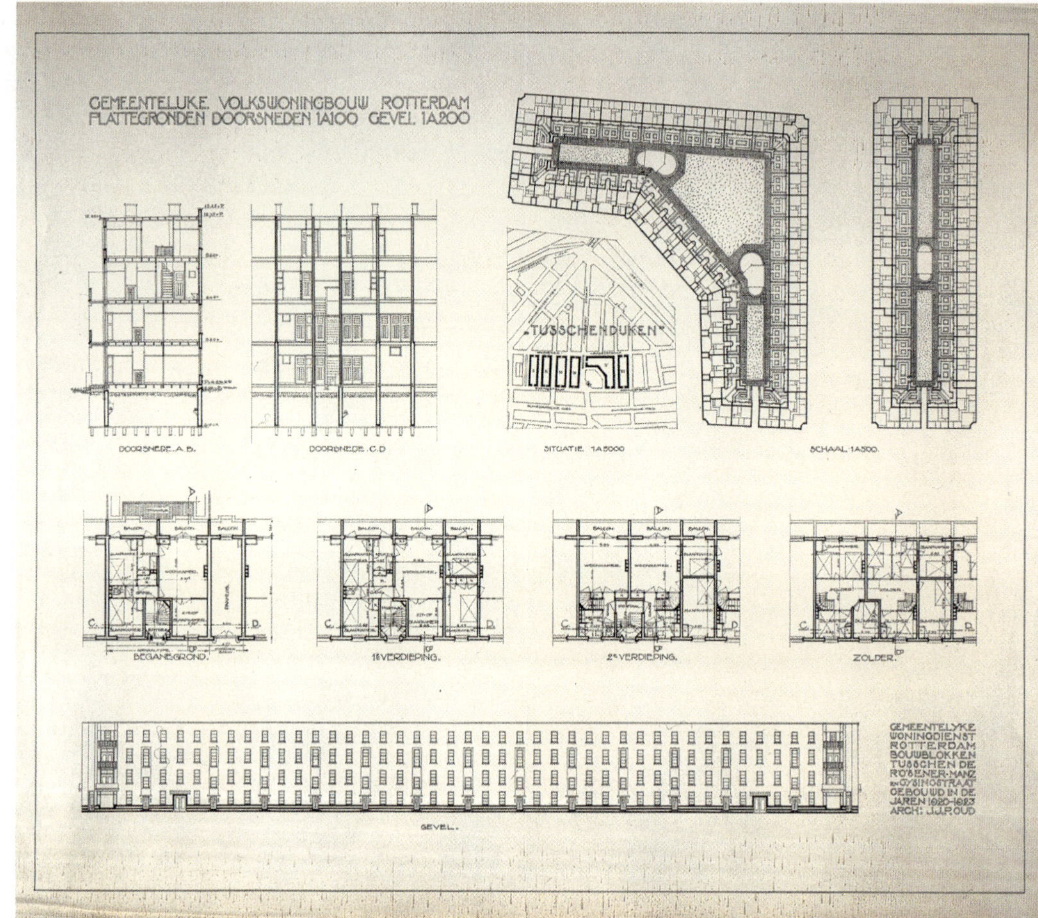


Various design views/ OUDJ-td 15, NAI, Rotterdam

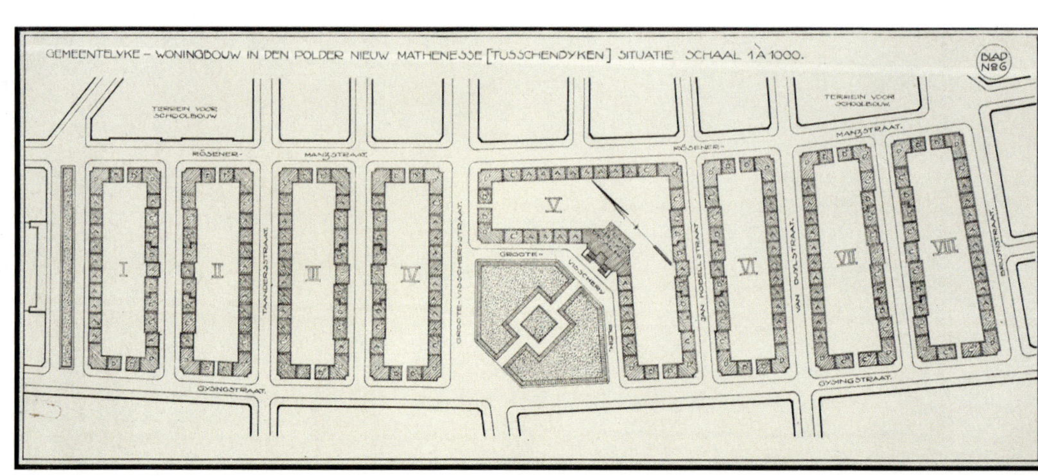


Site plan/ OUDJ-td 6, NAI, Rotterdam

blocks which, although they would not have won any prizes for structural or typological innovation, did succeed in elaborating and perfecting earlier innovations, in particular the inner courtyard.[1]

In Tusschendijken, the standard unit previously developed at Spangen (two flats plus two maisonettes with all living rooms on the courtyard side) was systematically employed in all eight blocks. With an eye to larger families, however, a number of bigger dwellings (four and five bedrooms) were included. This was achieved by inserting a bedroom-width module between the standard units. Depending on the situation, the front and rear rooms so created could be added to one or both of the adjoining standard dwellings. This had the virtue of not upsetting the systematic layout of floor plan and facade composition and of avoiding additional costs at the plan preparation stage and during construction. The larger dwellings were projected on the quietest streets and evenly distributed among the blocks so as to avoid overburdening the individual courtyards. At Tusschendijken the link between the individual dwellings and the green inner court was strengthened. The kitchens of the flats on the first two floors acquired outdoor access via a veranda and the storage sheds that had blocked residents' view of the central garden in Spangen were replaced by underground storage spaces. The content and design of the inner court received most of Oud's attention. It was as if he was determined, in the face of all the criticism, to increase his control over the shaping of this communal area and to leave nothing to chance. The private gardens for the ground-floor flats were rigidly enclosed by hedges, giving them a predetermined appearance. The same applied to the lawns, which were separated by 'light iron fences' from the encircling footpath (two-metre-wide concrete slabs); to the sandpit in the centre and especially to the benches for older people in the shadow of the pergolas at either end of the court. This was the culmination of the new living arrangement that Oud (and the Woningdienst) had been talking about in these years and which was soon to enter international architectural history as one of the icons of modern Dutch architecture (and town planning), thanks in part to the evocative pen and ink drawings made at Oud's behest by H.J. Jansen and L.F. Duquet, drawings that have graced every subsequent exhibition or publication devoted to the work of Oud (and *De Stijl*). The detailed drawings and carefully staged photographs of the Spangen and Tusschendijken housing schemes rapidly earned Oud an international reputation as an architect of contemporary living. As a result, the schemes became somewhat divorced from the political and economic conditions in which they were created. Not that these favourable opinions were shared by everyone in Oud's own circle, witness a letter from his friend W.C. Brouwers in 1923 in which he accused Oud of having betrayed his original, social ideals in his housing designs: *Your work amounts to a rabbit hutch, with a food rack. Is THAT love for the less well-off. Doesn't THAT rather DEGRADE him, and permanently erase any chance of joy. You're dangerous, because you take what is most sacred in human beings ... and toss it aside, and ignore it. IN FACT, destroy it.*[2] Wording aside, such negative sentiments were by no means unique, to judge from Oud's general rebuttal in an article about his housing schemes published in 1924. But there were also positive voices, like that of the Amsterdam architectural critic J.P. Mieras, who assessed the Spangen and Tusschendijken schemes on their metropolitan qualities, and who, ignoring the *De Stijl* trimmings, linked the pragmatic quality of Oud's architecture to the equally pragmatic character of the city of Rotterdam. Mieras's comments were in so far remarkable because they were based on his own observations rather



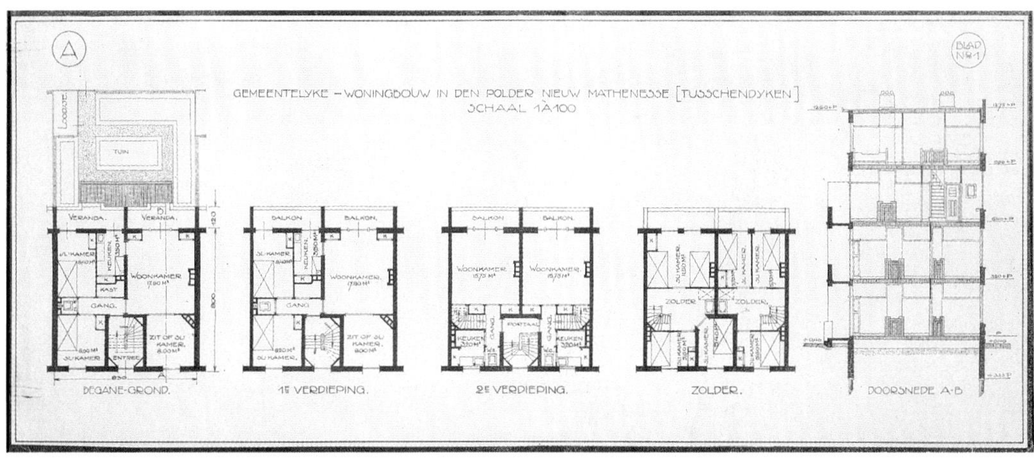

Plan of dwellings/ OUDJ-td 1, NAI, Rotterdam

than a photograph. This was why Mieras was the only critic to bestow any attention on the colour scheme that Oud – independently of Van Doesburg – had devised especially for the architecture of the rear elevations and the courtyards in Tusschendijken and which is not mentioned in any other source. After his visit to Tusschendijken Mieras wrote: *Oud is pragmatic. This is sometimes held against him as a not very artistic habit. The artist, it is said, is not pragmatic, distinguishes himself from his fellow men in fact by his lack of pragmatism. And art itself cannot be pragmatic. But Oud aspires to be pragmatic in his art.*[3] A claim Mieras went on to substantiate with an analysis of Tusschendijken: *Inside the complex ... which looks so very Oud-ish from the outside, are courtyards with a communal garden. These inner courts were a revelation for me. Unfortunately the photographs are quite unable to convey the charms of this architecture, and this may be precisely what sets it apart. It is perhaps a bit of an exaggeration to say that good architecture does not photograph well, only poor architecture photographs well. But it is often the case that good architecture contains few of the elements required by the objective lens. This courtyard too is entirely lacking in such elements, indeed, in the photo it could almost be mistaken for a speculative builder's courtyard. Now this is also partly because Oud is somewhat ascetic in his work. ...But in this court his architectural sentiments have prevented intellectual considerations from dominating. This court is a flawless space of splendid calm, not a dead but a vibrant, intimate calm and the very cleverly chosen colours impart a cheerful atmosphere. ...Oud has understood wonderfully well here that the cheerful tone of such a courtyard must be neutral and softly caressing and with his light colours and in particular with his brick colour, he has succeeded very well in this. This is not an architect's courtyard. When you are there you do not think of an architect. This courtyard is for the people. And they are in the photograph, because they belong there. Part of life takes place here and the setting is so designed as to render this significant, not to take some part of it away and claim it for itself because it is a work of art.*[4]

OUDJ-ph 1819, NAI, Rotterdam

OUDJ-ph 1820, NAI, Rotterdam



**Notes**

**1.** R. Dettingmeyer, 'De strijd om een goed gebouwde stad', in: *Het Nieuwe Bouwen in Rotterdam 1920-1960*, Delft 1982, pp. 32-33.

**2.** W.C. Brouwer to J.J.P. Oud, 13 Februari 1923, OUDJ-B, NAI, Rotterdam.

**3.** J.P. Mieras, 'Een boekje van een wereldstad', in: *Bouwkundig Weekblad*, 44(1923), pp. 361-364, 368-372, 375-378, 381-386. Quoted from: H. Engel, 'De Kiefhoek, monument voor gemiste kansen', in: S. Cusveller (ed.), *De Kiefhoek, een woonwijk in Rotterdam*, Leiden, Naarden 1990, pp. 28-30.

**4.** H. Engel, 'De Kiefhoek, monument voor gemiste kansen', in: S. Cusveller (ed.), *De Kiefhoek, een woonwijk in Rotterdam*, Leiden 1990, p. 30.

**Sources**

CCA: dr1984: 0027, [dr1984: 0253], dr1984: 0500-0506, ph1983: 0315-0319
GAR: Central Technical and semi-active records, Dienst Gemeentewerken Rotterdam
Getty: 840055**, 890126-15**
NAI: OUDJ-td 1-19, OUDJ-sp 1001, OUDJ-ph 164-178, OUDJ-ph 1672-1675, OUDJ-ph 1818-1819, OUDJ-ph 1821-1827, OUDJ-B

**Literature**

U. Barbieri, *J.J.P. Oud*, Rotterdam 1987, pp. 80-85
H.E. Oud, *J.J.P. Oud. Architekt 1890-1963. Feiten en herinneringen gerangschikt*, The Hague 1984, pp. 67-69, 112
S. Polano, *J.J.P. Oud Architettura Olandese*, Milan 1981, p. 86
G. Stamm, *J.J.P. Oud. Bauten und Projekte 1906 bis 1963*, Mainz, Berlin 1984, p. 69

**41/ Tusschendijken Municipal Housing Scheme, Blocks I, III & V**

OUDJ-ph 170, NAI, Rotterdam

Courtyard/ OUDJ-ph 177, NAI, Rotterdam

## 41/ Tusschendijken Municipal Housing Scheme, Blocks I, III & V

Gijsingstraat elevations/ OUDJ-ph 1827, NAI, Rotterdam

## 41/ Tusschendijken Municipal Housing Scheme, Blocks I, III & V

J.J.P. Oud, 'Toelichting woningbouw Tusschendijken', typescript, NAI, Rotterdam, OUDJ-td 1001

# Commentary, "Tusschendijken" housing

The type used in "Spangen" Blocks VIII and IX was also adopted, with one small modification, consisting in the fact that a balcony was added behind the kitchen and back bedroom of the ground-floor and first-floor dwellings (onto which these rooms open), as the standard type for a systematically conceived standardized plan for 1005 dwellings.
The dwellings here are divided among 8 blocks. The need to include larger dwellings, without this requiring too much extra work, resulted in the insertion of "intermediate units" the dimensions of which were derived from the rhythm of the window organization in the standard type; each intermediate unit contains 2 bedrooms. In the largest dwellings (type C) both these bedrooms were added to the standard type; for the medium-sized dwellings (type B) one bedroom was added to the standard type on the right and one to the standard type on the left of the intermediate unit.
These dwellings have been distributed evenly among the various blocks so that the number of children on the inner court of one block is no greater than on another. In addition, these dwellings face onto residential streets where traffic is less of a danger for children at play.
Since the streets are generally narrow compared with the courts, the courts around which the living rooms with balconies are situated must be made as pleasant as possible. Residential life is concentrated there, in other words, not on the street sides.
To this end the ground-floor dwellings have been given gardens surrounded by hedges, while the central section between these gardens is intended for communal use, for which there is an encircling path of concrete tiles, 2 m. wide, benches and pergolas, in addition to a sheltered sandpit for children.
On the corners of each block a shop has been projected, some with warehouse, while a public building, probably a bathhouse is envisaged for the urban square at the centre of the scheme.

# 42/ Oud-Mathenesse Municipal Housing Scheme (Witte Dorp)

**Rotterdam, Barendsestraat, Barkastraat, Aakstraat** **1922-1924**

In May 1922 the Rotterdam city council approved a plan to build 343 semi-permanent single-family dwellings, eight shop/dwelling units and a fire-engine shed in the former polder of Oud-Mathenesse. Owing to the various frictions surrounding municipal housing, construction did not get under way until March 1923. In August 1924 the first houses were completed and one of Rotterdam's most popular *and* most maligned residential districts was born. The complex was wholly designed by Oud who was responsible for both the site planning and the design of the dwellings and other buildings.

The Witte Dorp (White Village), as the housing estate was soon known, incorporated a number of strategies in the fields of urban planning, public housing and social work which Oud made the basis for an undecorated, introverted residential environment. Comparing the Witte Dorp with the huge Spangen and Tusschendijken housing blocks, critics both at home and abroad agreed that here, on the edge of the city, Oud had succeeded in creating an urban neighbourhood of remarkable intimacy; a neighbourhood with a village-like atmosphere that had not been achieved by pseudo-villagey means. In Oud's oeuvre, the Witte Dorp is the first of what Henk Engel has called 'the white-house architecture', a series of housing projects which, from the viewpoint of urban planning and public housing, stood somewhat on the sidelines of urban life, since their planning did not

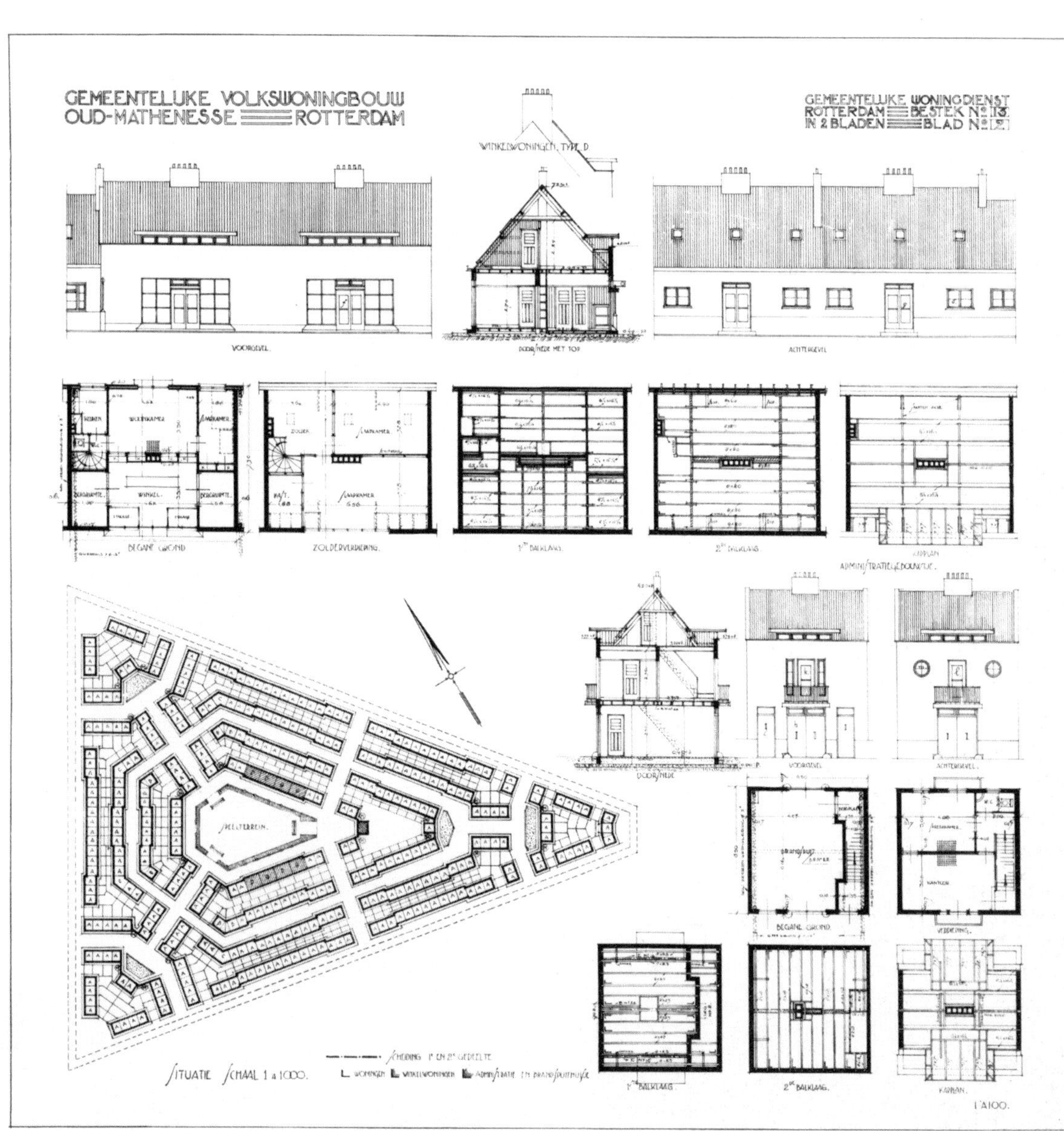


Design overview/ OUDJ-wd 11, NAI, Rotterdam

## 42/ Oud-Mathenesse Municipal Housing Scheme (Witte Dorp)

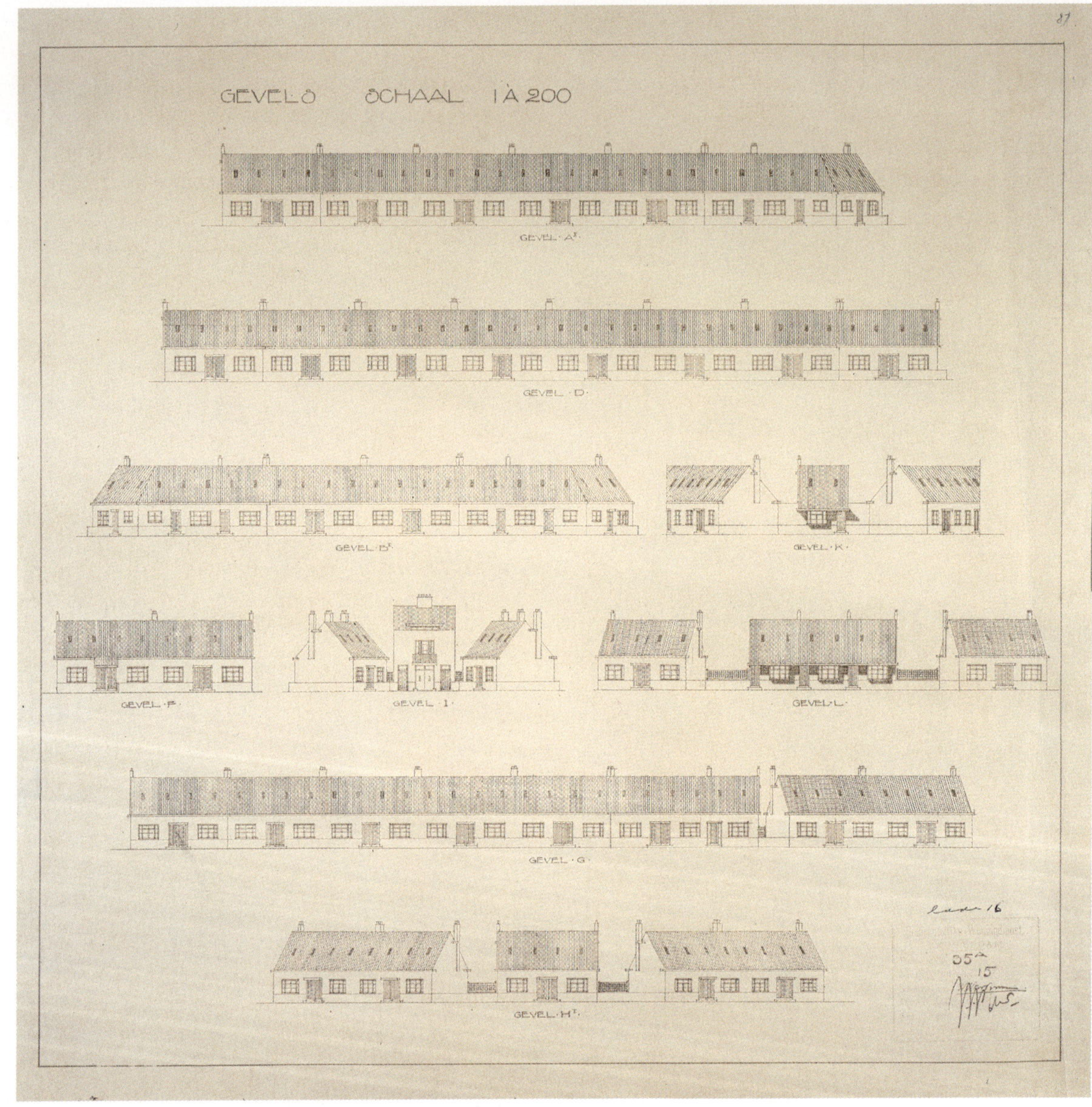


Elevations/ OUDJ-wd 14, NAI, Rotterdam

require or permit any form of structural and typological innovation. As a result, Oud was able to experiment more freely with the aesthetic of the street in the Witte Dorp. In the housing schemes designed for Hoek van Holland, Kiefhoek and Stuttgart, Oud reaped the benefits of this experience and proceeded to perfect the architectural detailing of daily life in and around the home.

Originally Oud and the Woningdienst had had much more ambitious plans for this tract of reclaimed land. Between 1919 and 1921, Oud and T.K. van Lohuizen (research engineer with the Woningdienst until 1928) had worked on a detailed development plan for Oud-Mathenesse (cat. no. 35). It envisaged a complete district of over 30,000 inhabitants, with housing, shops, fifteen schools, three churches, a public library, a public bathhouse and numerous businesses. Van Lohuizen was *responsible for drawing up the building programme, for the solution of traffic issues and for the method of funding.*[1] He also calculated the rental prices for seven different categories of dwelling based on the size and location of the lots in the masterplan. Oud must have been very disappointed to learn that this plan, like the equally large-scale Blijdorp development plan by Kromhout and Van Lohuizen (1919-1920), was to be shelved, partly because of the withdrawal of state funding. Instead, on the very triangle of land he had earmarked for a park, he found himself more or less forced to erect a humble little neighbourhood of semi-permanent dwellings. His disappointment – which was in sharp contrast to the euphoria in the national and international architectural press – is evident from the terse plan commentary, where he confined himself to supplying the technical details, and also from his letters where he made frequent reference to his desire to leave the Woningdienst at the earliest opportunity.

The indirect reason for the construction of 343 semi-permanent dwellings on this site was the shortage of cheap rental housing in Rotterdam. The first such working-class dwellings had been built in Rotterdam in 1914 by the Maatschappij voor Volkswoningen N.V., an 'approved organization' that played a major role in Rotterdam in the development of semi-permanent housing for the poorest members of the population.[2] Following the success of this housing type, which 'could be quickly and cheaply built and was nonetheless of good quality', the Woningdienst decided in 1917 to build a thousand such dwellings on the south bank of the river Maas. The immediate reason for choosing the Oud-Mathenesse site was the desire for affordable replacement housing for all those made homeless by large-scale slum clearance operations on the other side of the river. The council records stated that: *Since most of the occupants so displaced, given their social situation, are not eligible for the more expensive permanent dwellings, it will be necessary to devise a type of accommodation whereby it is possible, more so than in the provision of permanent dwellings, to take account of the financial capacity of those*

View of district/ OUDJ-ph 223, NAI, Rotterdam

*occupants.*[3] Arnold Reijndorp has shown that although the first residents were 'semi-invalid workers' (which meant that they were unable to afford the average rentals) this did not put them in the category of 'asocial families'. In any case, it was Oud's design rather than the nature of the residents that gave the Witte Dorp its introverted character. During the course of the planning and construction process, the council did however allocate 74 dwellings to the aforementioned Maatschappij voor Volkswoningen in order to enable 'reeducated' families to move on from the overcrowded transit centres to normal, sound and affordable housing. Owing to their cheap construction method, low rentals and functional layout, the dwellings in the Witte Dorp were ideally suited to the Maatschappij's educational strategy.
Whereas at Spangen Oud and the Woningdienst used every means available – the layout of the inner court, the aesthetically designed colour schemes and interior amenities – to differentiate their housing from that of private developers, in the Witte Dorp architecture and spatial planning were employed to prevent any association with the much-despised 'emergency dwellings'. There are few residential districts anywhere in the Netherlands where A.E. Brinckmann's famous pronouncement: *Städtebau heisst mit dem Hausmaterial Raum gestalten* ('City building is the creation of space with housing') has been put into practice so literally as in the Witte Dorp. In this Rotterdam neighbourhood houses, blocks, streets and square were stripped of their autonomy and merged into a townscape conceived as a single, sculptural whole. Here plan and architecture were in complete accord. The theoretical principles underlying this architectural approach to town planning had its origins in German architectural literature from the beginning of the century. They had first been put into practice in the Netherlands by Berlage, including in the expansion plan for Amsterdam South (1914-1917). While Oud's abortive development plan for Oud-Mathenesse (1921) had leaned heavily on the urban planning strategies of the second plan for Amsterdam South, the street and development plans for the Witte Dorp might almost have been excerpted from it.[4] The chief points of similarity are the severely geometrical street plan, the various short axes that come together at the (social) hub of the neighbourhood, the playground, and the introverted townscape. In the Witte Dorp the streetscape was not determined by repetition and contrast as in Spangen or Tusschendijken, but by the identical facades of the rows of houses on either side of the street. Every 'hiccup' in the street plan – a narrowing or widening of the access roads, a bend – had immediate repercussions in the architecture of the walls and was translated into a steeply pitched roof or a change in the facade. In the Witte Dorp the focus was firmly on the streetscape as a whole and it was onto the streets that the living rooms faced. The inner courts here played hardly any role as a communal area. This has led Roy Bijhouwer to hypothesize that in the Witte Dorp Oud's idea about 'the contrast between the industrious city and peaceful living' was worked out at a higher planning level.[5] As such, he sees the 'village' of Oud-Mathenesse – with the collective space of the square concealed at its centre – as an enlarged version of an urban block rather than as a garden village, the usual designation of the semi-permanent housing schemes.
The homogeneous and hermetic quality of the Witte Dorp was reinforced by the meticulous use of colour. Firstly in the vivid contrast between the white-rendered street elevations and roofs of bright red Dutch roof tiles. That colour scheme dominated the village as a whole and formed the background for the spatial composition created by the blue of the front doors, the yellow of the gutters, front-door frames



**Notes**
**1.** A. van der Valk, *Het levenswerk van Th. K. van Lohuizen. De eenheid van het stedebouwkundig werk*, Delft 1990, p. 26; Van Lohuizen Archive, dossier 7, no. 8: *Toelichting uitbreidingsplan voor het terrein tussen den Havenpoortweg Rotterdam 1921*, NAI, Rotterdam.
**2.** L. de Klerk, *Mooi werk. Geschiedenis van de Maatschappij voor volkswoningen, Rotterdam 1909-1991*, Rotterdam 1999
**3.** A. Reijndorp, 'Het Witte Dorp en de Rotterdamse Volkshuisvesting', in: B. Colenbrander (ed.), *Oud-Mathenesse: het Witte Dorp*, Rotterdam 1987, p. 62.
**4.** V. van Rossem, 'Een keerpunt in de Nederlandse stedebouw: Plan Zuid', in: K. Gaillard, B. Dokter (ed.), *Berlage en Amsterdam Zuid*, Rotterdam 1992, pp. 9-25; B. Colenbrander (ed.), *Oud-Mathenesse: het Witte Dorp*, Rotterdam 1987, p. 21.
**5.** R. Bijhouwer, 'Het Witte Dorp: aan de vooravond van een keerpunt', in: B. Colenbrander (ed.), *Oud-Mathenesse: het Witte Dorp*, Rotterdam 1987, pp. 74-75.
**6.** J.J.P. Oud, 'Over de toekomstige bouwkunst en hare architectonische mogelijkheden', in: *Bouwkundig Weekblad*, 42(1921)24, p. 160.

and canopies, and the white of the window casings. In the Witte Dorp Oud seized the opportunity to put into practice *for himself* what he had earlier advocated in *De Stijl* and in his 1921 *Opbouw* lecture: the combination of white-rendered masonry with primary colour schemes for the component parts. In the *Opbouw* lecture, which Oud had published before the break with Van Doesburg, the combination of brick and colour was firmly rejected on technical grounds in favour of glazed stone and rendered masonry. According to this line of reasoning, the colour scheme of the Witte Dorp was a technical and aesthetic experiment that anticipated future developments, especially in concrete construction. That indeed was the tenor of the *Opbouw* lecture: *the increasingly rapid succession of inventions for smooth and brightly coloured finishes for rendered and concrete surfaces opens up important prospects for the development of colour in architecture.*[6]

**Central square with transformer kiosk (foreground)/ OUDJ-ph 195, NAI, Rotterdam**



**Sources**
CCA: dr1984: 0437, dr1984: 0508-0510, ph1984: 0816, ph1984: 0818, ph1984: 1060-1067
Getty: 840055**, 890126-17**, 890126-18**
MOMA: NC Drawings-blueprints
NAI: OUDJ- wd 1-19, OUDJ- ph 188-223, OUDJ-ph 1677-1680, MAQV 0593, MAQV 111, VOOV 121-122, OUDJ-B


**Articles**
J. Badovici, 'Habitations à bon marché à Rotterdam, Oud-Mathenesse, maisons semi-permantentes', in: *L'Architecture Vivante*, 2(1925)I, pp. 10-13
M.J.I. de Jonge van Ellemeet, 'Woningbouw in Oud Mathenesse', in: *Tijdschrift voor Volkshuisvesting en Stedebouw*, 6(1925)3, pp. 62-64
J.J.P. Oud, 'Semi-permanente woningbouw "Oud Mathenesse" Rotterdam', in: *Bouwkundig Weekblad*, 45(1924)43, pp. 418-421
'Het witte dorp', in: *Klei*, 23(1931)12, pp. 137-142
L.C. van der Vlugt, 'De semi-permanente woningen in "Oud Mathenesse" te Rotterdam', in: *Bouwen*, 2(1925)11, pp. 161-164

**Literature**
U. Barbieri, *J.J.P. Oud*, Rotterdam 1987, pp. 86-93
R. Bijhouwer, 'Oud Mathenesse, tussen straatbeeld en woning' in: *Oase*, 4(1986)14, pp. 15-18
B. Colenbrander, (ed.), *Oud-Mathenesse, het Witte Dorp 1923-1987*, Rotterdam 1987
R. Dettingmeijer, 'De strijd om een goed gebouwde stad', in: *Het Nieuwe Bouwen in Rotterdam 1920-1960*, Delft 1982, pp. 33-35
H. Engel, 'De Kiefhoek, een monument voor gemiste kansen?' in: S. Cusveller (ed.), *De Kiefhoek, een woonwijk in Rotterdam*, Laren, Naarden 1990, pp. 30-38
H.E. Oud, *J.J.P. Oud. Architekt 1890-1963. Feiten en herinneringen gerangschikt*, The Hague 1984, pp. 58, 67, 74-77, 112, 117, 121
S. Polano, *J.J.P. Oud Architettura Olandese*, Milan 1981, pp. 86-87
G. Stamm, *J.J.P. Oud. Bauten und Projekte 1906 bis 1963*, Mainz, Berlin 1984, pp. 69-74
A. van der Valk, *Het levenswerk van Th.K. van Lohuizen 1890-1956. De eenheid van het stedebouwkundige werk*, Delft 1990, pp. 26-32

## 42/ Oud-Mathenesse Municipal Housing Scheme (Witte Dorp)

OUDJ-ph 194, NAI, Rotterdam

## 42/ Oud-Mathenesse Municipal Housing Scheme (Witte Dorp)

## 42/ Oud-Mathenesse Municipal Housing Scheme (Witte Dorp)

OUDJ-ph 198, NAI, Rotterdam

Shopping street on central square/ OUDJ-ph 206, NAI, Rotterdam

# "Oud-Mathenesse" Semi-permanent Housing, Rotterdam

The housing complex depicted here was begun on 19 March 1923 and completed on 20 August 1924. It comprises 343 dwellings, 8 shop-dwelling units, in addition to a small structure containing an administration office on the upper floor and storage space for a fire hose below.
Of the 343 dwellings, 331 are identical save for some changes in the aspect of the front door and in the front windows. These changes occur where the houses could not be strung together in pairs, resulting in a loss of balance. This has sometimes been restored by widening the aspect of the doors by means of a wooden frame for creepers, sometimes by means of projecting window frames so that the focus is shifted from the door to the window. In the latter case the less steeply pitched roof establishes the canopy. The roof also projects above some doors at the end: this too in connection with the restoration of the balance of the composition. All of which, it goes without saying, in combination with the grouping.
8 cottages (B) are corner dwellings of a standard type; 4 cottages (C) are corner dwellings of different, likewise standard type. The 8 shop-dwelling units (D) are all the same. The standard dwellings (A) contain downstairs: living room 3.80 x 4 m., bedroom 2 x 2.30 m., kitchenette 1.50 x 2 and WC. Upstairs 2 separate small bedrooms under the roof boarding, together with some attic space.
The living rooms are wall-papered up to the picture rail, above that white. An area of wall and floor has been clad with red, hard burnt tiles for a stove or cooker. In the centre of the rear wall a shelf has been built out, above which there is room for a mirror and on which portraits, etc. can stand: an interior so designed because experience has taught that otherwise residents will organize it in their own way.
The houses are built on slabs of reinforced concrete, 0.15 m. thick, laid directly on the ground (a layer of clay less than 1 m. thick, resting on a very unstable layer of peat, made any excavation dangerous). The reinforcement is double (top and bottom netting: 0.25 m. mesh, 6mm. wire). The main walls are of IJssel brick (0.16 m.), the facade walls are cavity walls: outer leaf of IJssel brick (0.08 m.) inner of sand-lime brick-on-edge (0.06 m.) The plinth is 1.00 m. high, facing brickwork, white joints: above the plinth the walls are plastered and finished with white rendering. The concrete slab, which projects 1 m. all round is laid with red tiles on the street side, terminating in a brick-on-edge coping of IJssel brick and iron fencing: the main aim of which is to protect the concrete from wear and to avoid the battered appearance resulting from its being walked on. The plinth of the shop-dwelling unit is of grey facing bricks; tiles in front of that also grey; area of wall below shop window in the same colour terrazzo tiles.
The roofing material is red Dutch roof tiles; the paint colour of the shops yellow, window casings white, windows frames and gutters yellow. Thanks to the cooperation of the service concerned, it was possible to include the transformer kiosk in the design.
Acacia Armata will be planted around the playground in the openings left for this purpose, the streets will be planted with espalier lindens, behind the wooden fences on the dividing walls, low shrubs.
The housing complex is intended to last 25 years. The contract sum for construction was 736,640 guilders, which came to approx. 2,050 guilders per standard dwelling. Contractor was P. van Loon in Dordrecht.
A park is planned on the site of the building in the future.

## 43/ Oud-Mathenesse Site Manager's Hut

**Rotterdam, Kanostraat**

**1923**

The construction of semi-permanent dwellings in Oud-Mathenesse commenced on 19 March 1923 and was completed 17 months later on 20 August 1924. One of the first structures to be erected was the site manager's hut which appeared in solitary splendour on the otherwise bare expanse in June 1923. On 6 June 1923 Rietveld sent Oud a postcard asking how the hut had turned out and whether the colours looked good outdoors.[1] The hut was intended, as indicated above the door, for the construction management and had facilities for construction meetings (including a 'drawing board') and meal breaks. The wooden building stood precisely in the middle of the small, triangular village square, directly opposite the 'administration office'. It remained in place even after the Witte Dorp had been completed, so it is fair to assume that the stark contrast between hut and dwellings was intentional on Oud's part. Though carefully slotted into the spatial layout of the Witte Dorp, it stood out because of the experimental nature of the architectural design. If the architecture of the surrounding residential streets can be characterized as an aesthetic reworking of the 'vernacular' (an extreme simplification of the typical 'Dutch house') the site manager's hut, with its ingeniously interlocking cubes, seems more like a demonstration model of a new, as yet unrealized architecture. Whereas its function refers to architecture as the practice of building, its form is intent on demonstrating that the new architecture is also art, with rules and qualities that Oud had been articulating since 1921 and defending, in vain, vis à vis Van Doesburg and Mondrian. In that sense, Oud's hut is a prototype of (*De Stijl*) architecture, yet another, in this case modern, variation on Laugier's famous 'hut'.
Although the hut appears to be made up of cubes, it is not an example of cubist architecture. Nor is it a three-dimensional rendering of a Neo-Plastic painting. The site hut is the outcome of the architectural treatment of three themes that Oud had not previously combined in such a fashion: geometry, cladding and, finally, colour. The rigid symmetry of the spatial layout of the Witte Dorp is reflected in the site hut. The dominant long axis continues in the narrow volume of the tall, top-lit corridor that runs from the door to the stove. Like almost all Oud's buildings from that period, the site hut design was based on a module. Yet Oud did not regard the laws of harmony and particular geometrical figures primarily as *a handy strategy for the development of the new art.*[2] Whereas in the work of De Groot, De Bazel or Lauweriks – which Oud had come to know during his training – they stood for a higher, mystical reality, for Oud symmetry, proportion and harmony symbolized the dominant role of technology in modern culture. In an interesting exchange of letters with the German architect Peter Behrens in the years 1920-1923, prompted by a lecture and publication in *Wendingen* of Behrens's 'Uber die Beziehungen der künstlerischen und technischen Probleme' ('About the Relation between Artistic and Technical Problems), Oud disputed the

**Elevations and ground floor plan/ dr1984: 0511, CCA, Montreal**

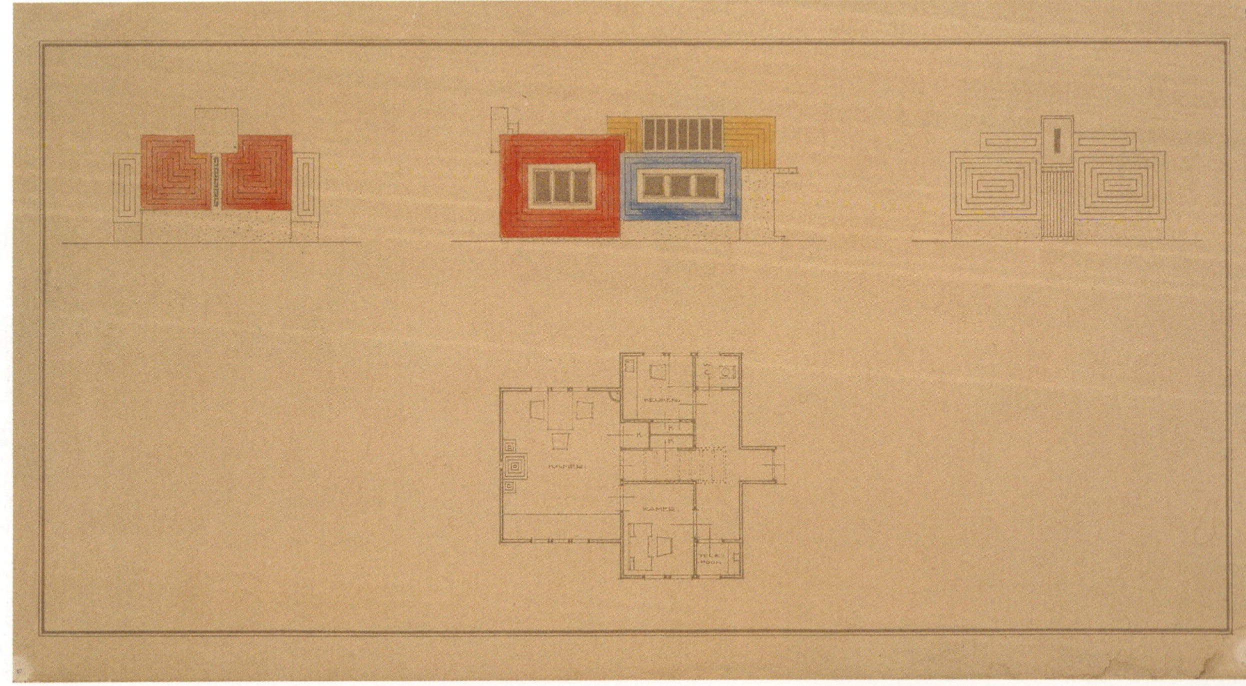

OUDJ-ph 230, NAI, Rotterdam

OUDJ-ph 233, NAI, Rotterdam

latter's contention that the modern age would benefit from the marriage and contrast of the classical and modern conceptions of art, and argued that only the classical position was able determine the aspect of contemporary culture: *When I say that, to me, the spirit of our times has classical tendencies in every respect (organization, typification, is generally regulated) this certainly does not imply that I reject romanticism. Perhaps it will play its part again – is Spengler right! – when our urge to mechanize is converted into mysticism again. It seems not at all impossible to me; but then we still need, in my opinion, the style, the artistic epitomization of our* technical *development.*[3] The discussion with Behrens makes clear that Oud's view of Classicism – by which he was not thinking of the formal idiom of Antiquity but *the spirit of Archimedes based on a mathematical thinking process* (Behrens) – was rooted in ideas and design concepts current in the circle around Peter Behrens, first in Düsseldorf (1903-1907) and thereafter in Berlin, in particular in the Behrens-dominated faction of the Deutsche Werkbund.[4]

His preliminary sketches show that Oud attached great weight to the pattern of the timber siding and to the decorative finishing of the wall and floor around the stove, which had the effect of turning the area into a quasi-ritualistic focus of the hut. The compelling pattern of concentrically laid planks was taken from Gottfried Semper's famous book *Der Stil in den technischen und tektonischen Künsten, oder praktische Aesthetik. Ein Handbuch für Techniker, Künstler und Kunstfreunde (1860-1863)* (Style in the Technical and Structural Arts, or Practical Aesthetics. A Textbook for Engineers, Artists and Friends of the Arts), a book that Oud had bought in November 1921 at Wasmuth's antiquarian bookshop in Berlin. Semper was also the source, probably via publications by and about Adolf Loos, of the ideas about enclosure and cladding as essential qualities of architecture on which the hut was based. It looks very much as if Oud's decision to finish the external walls with textile patterns drawn from the famous textbook also reflected a theoretical purpose. This was, after all, a clear allusion to Semper's idea of style as an intrinsic quality of architecture that

**Interior, with mantelpiece/ OUDJ-ph 249, NAI, Rotterdam**

uses technique and materials to give shape to an idea of beauty, in much the same way as natural organisms. In Semper's idealistic theory of style, the emphasis was not on the construction of space but, for historical, ethnographic and biological reasons, on the spatial enclosure and the cladding of objects which imparted the actual coherence to the form, function and construction of a building. As Auke van der Woud has demonstrated at length,[5] from the 1870s onwards, Semper's ideas had an enormous influence on architecture and applied arts education in the Netherlands, including those institutions where Oud received his architectural training in the early years of the twentieth century. Be that as it may, the hut was not designed until 1923, in the same year when Van Doesburg and Van Eesteren were working on the so-called Paris models in which Van Doesburg 'attempted to realize *De Stijl* in coloured architecture' (M. Bock) and in which the relation between function, form and structure was based on principles that were diametrically opposed to those of Semper (and by extension Oud).[6] Fascinating designs in which colour and space, in disregard of all the (classical) rules of architecture, achieved a new unity and a new manifestation.[7] Whereas in Van Doesburg and Van Eesteren's models the various functional spaces were 'thrown out' as it were from the centre, those in Oud's hut were magnetically held together by the central corridor which organizes the spaces into a dynamic composition of closed, interlocking cubes.

That Oud, too, was intent on 'realizing *De Stijl* in coloured architecture', is evident from the colour scheme for the hut, which employs the active colours of red, yellow and blue. Seen from the entrance, the two juxtaposed volumes are red and blue respectively, while the third, taller volume is painted yellow. The plinths are rendered in white and are also staggered on the various elevations, thereby enhancing the sense of the walls as ornamental cladding. This strategy also makes the hut seem lighter, so that it seems almost to float. The overall effect of the colour scheme is to reinforce the 'destructive' tendency of the architecture that is inherent to the hut as a provisional and temporary structure. This being so, what Oud had written a year earlier in reference to the colour scheme of a building by Taut also applies to the site hut: *thus arose an organic whole out of a jumble of planes, lines, masses, colours, the special thing about it being that it is free of all incidental ornamentation. There is indeed ornamentation in the form of colour, if you will, but it stands in an organic relation to the whole; there is tension between the two. The ornamentation is not as in the past an appendage: it permeates the architecture and the architecture permeates it in turn. This is an* architectural and artistic organism.[8]



**Notes**

**1.** G. Rietveld to J.J.P. Oud, 6 June 1923, OUDJ-B, NAI, Rotterdam.
**2.** A. Van der Woud, *Waarheid en karakter. Het debat over de bouwkunst 1840-1900*, Rotterdam 1997, p. 350.
**3.** J.J.P. Oud to P. Behrens, 6 November 1922, OUDJ-B, NAI, Rotterdam.
**4.** S. Anderson, *Behrens and a New Architecture for the Twentieth Century*, Cambridge (Mass.), London 2000, pp. 69-94.
**5.** A. Van der Woud, *Waarheid en karakter. Het debat over de bouwkunst 1840-1900*, Rotterdam 1997, p. 274.
**6.** M. Bock, 'Cornelis van Eesteren', in: C. Blotkamp (ed.), *De vervolgjaren van De Stijl 1922-1932*, Amsterdam, Antwerp 1996, pp. 241-294.
**7.** M. Bock, 'Cornelis van Eesteren', in: C. Blotkamp (ed.), *De vervolgjaren van De Stijl 1922-1932*, Amsterdam, Antwerp 1996, pp. 241-294.
**8.** J.J.P. Oud, 'Uitweiding bij eenige afbeeldingen', in: *Bouwkundig Weekblad* 43 (1922), pp. 418-424.

**Sources**

AKZO/Nobel archive, Sassenheim: E.P. van der Hoeven, reconstructie "Directiekeet" J.J.P. Oud, n.d.
CCA: dr1984: 0511, ph1984: 0822, ph1984: 1068-1074
Getty: 840055**, 890126-box 7, 10*
NAI: OUDJ-dk 1-10, OUDJ-ph 224-249, OUDJ-ph 1831, OUDJ-26, MAQV 373, OUDJ-B

**Articles**

*Dagblad van Rotterdam*, 28 June 1924
H.R. Hitchcock Jr., *J.J.P. Oud*, Paris 1931
J. Badovici, 'Petite maison semi-permanente à Rotterdam', in: *L'Architecture Vivante*, 2(1924)I, pp 29-37

**Literature**

U. Barbieri, *J.J.P. Oud*, Rotterdam 1987, pp. 94-97
B. Colenbrander, ( ed.), *Oud-Mathenesse, het Witte Dorp 1923-1987*, Rotterdam 1987
G. Fanelli, *Stijl-architectuur*, Stuttgart 1985, pp 134-140
H.E. Oud, *J.J.P. Oud. Architekt 1890-1963. Feiten en herinneringen gerangschikt*, The Hague 1984, pp. 78-79, 86
S. Polano, *J.J.P. Oud Architettura Olandese*, Milan 1981, p. 87
G. Stamm, *J.J.P. Oud. Bauten und Projekte 1906 bis 1963*, Mainz, Berlin 1984, pp. 74-76, 95

# 44/ Hoek van Holland Housing Scheme

**Hoek van Holland, 2e Scheepvaartstraat** **1924-1927**

In 1914, Hoek van Holland, a village located on estuary of the Nieuwe Waterweg, was annexed by the city of Rotterdam. The idea at the time of annexation was to develop Hoek van Holland as an up-market residential area and seaside resort along the lines of Bergen.[1] However, while potential villa residents were in short supply, the expansion of Rotterdam's dock industry ensured that the working-class population grew apace – and with it the housing shortage. From 1918 the residents of Hoek van Holland produced countless plans aimed at inducing the Rotterdam city council to provide social housing in the area. The times were far from favourable. In 1922 the national government discontinued its emergency housing construction subsidies and a year later the same fate befell the rental subsidy scheme. The result was to put public housing once more largely in the hands of private developers. Furthermore, there were plenty of local politicians and officials (including A. Plate at the Woningdienst) who felt that public housing should be put on a commercial footing (development and operation) rather than depending on endless government subsidies. In the circumstances, Rotterdam was not likely to be of much help to Hoek van Holland for the time being. To the extent that the council built any houses at all, they were either emergency dwellings or, as in the case of the Witte Dorp, semi-permanent accommodation for those left homeless by slum-clearance operations.

In the spring of 1921, the Rotterdam city council applied for a subsidy under the Woningwet on behalf of a plan put forward by the 'Hoek van Holland' housing corporation. The application was rejected and although the council appealed the decision, the result was a serious delay to the plans for Hoek van Holland. The council's decision to build its own working-class housing in Hoek van Holland, without state subsidy, was taken in late 1923. After satisfactory arrangements had been made regarding the funding, management and administration of the project, the Woningdienst/Oud received the commission to make a sketch plan for some forty dwellings. The scheme's political sensitivity and the narrowness of the margins for the design are evident from a statement by the then director of the Woningdienst: *It seems to me that for the time being no more than approx. 40 dwellings should be built, after which we can see what effect this has on the housing market and if necessary take further measures in this respect. The development should consist of workers' houses of no more than normal size. I have previously advised against subsidizing the construction of houses in the expectation of being able to rent rooms to seaside visitors; in the case of municipal housing this is certainly not to be recommended.*[2] The official archives reveal that several different plans were made, the deciding factors being the guarantee of sufficient tenants and adequate funding. The construction dossier shows that the planners started out with a building volume consisting of three rows of housing separated from one another by two

**Design variant showing buildings in side street (left)/ OUDJ-hh 34, NAI, Rotterdam**

**Design variant with two gateways (and six shops)/ OUDJ-hh 33, NAI, Rotterdam**

gateway buildings, thus allowing for a total of six shops at the ends. The building plan made public by the Woningdienst in June 1924, however, had only two, two-storey rows of housing separated by a centrally situated passageway. At this stage the plan envisaged 42 dwellings, including four with a shop, plus four warehouses. The dwellings – flats – were on both levels and came in four variations: one, two, three and four bedrooms. In August 1924 this plan came before the Rotterdamse Commissie voor Volkshuisvesting (Rotterdam Public Housing Committee) which was full of praise for the financial aspect of the plan but had little sympathy for its architectural form. Judging by the report of the director of the Woningdienst, De Jonge van Ellemeet, the objections centred on the austere design of the forty dwellings in a single building block, a type of development that was clearly at odds with what they were used to in Hoek van Holland and which was consequently perceived as 'metropolitan'. The plans were sent back with the request to look into the possibility of a different facade solution. According to the Woningdienst report, Oud had great difficulty with this. De Jonge van Ellemeet commended on this phase of the design process: *Complying with the Committee's request, I urged my staff to look for another solution; numerous sketches were made without a satisfactory solution being reached. It was not simply a matter of drawing a completely new facade. This is sometimes assumed in such cases, but the fact is that a good design poses the inescapable demand that floor plans, facades, etc. should form a single whole. ...Hence, a radical alteration of the appearance of the facade inevitably entailed a detailed reconsideration of the dwelling type.*[3] Oud's surviving sketches show that he did indeed explore a different, more traditional form for the block, in which the rounded shopfronts were replaced by orthogonal shop/flat units (with external stair). The revised design, which had been reduced to forty dwellings (in three rather than four types), four shops and two warehouses, in an effort to maintain the low rentals, was presented to the Committee on 20 June 1925. It rejected the new proposals and pronounced its preference for the earlier plan. On 17 September 1925 the original design (with adjustments) was approved by the Rotterdam city council at a meeting where alderman Heijkoop played on Oud's international reputation to win over the council. This despite the fact that Heijkoop, too, had recoiled from the very austere and ultramodern facade of the earlier design and initially called for something a bit less provocative: *We asked the Director to inquire of our chief Woningdienst architect whether he might not be able to attempt something in that direction. The chief Woningdienst architect, who is a highly gifted young man and held in esteem by nearly all Europe, did his best to comply and we all felt that the second project that resulted from these efforts was less successful than the first. Whereupon, with my layman's geniality, I abandoned my objections. I repeat:*

**Sketch for shop and gateway/ OUDJ-hh 14, NAI, Rotterdam**

*when all's said and done, I cannot coerce an artist; it does not befit a painter's apprentice to criticize Rembrandt and it certainly does not befit me to impose my standpoint on such a great architect, whom we have appointed chief architect at the Woningdienst. That is a question of taste.*[4] The project was put out to tender on 18 June 1926 and construction commenced in September; on 4 May 1927 the housing complex was completed.

In the realized version, the complex on 2e Scheepvaartstraat in Hoek van Holland comprised 41 dwellings, four shops, four warehouses and one centrally located passageway. In terms of domestic amenity, the floor plans were an improved version of those in the Witte Dorp. Two and three-room flats alternated on the ground floor while all the first-floor flats had three rooms (living room plus two bedrooms). The warehouses were 'concealed' in the kink either side of the gateway. Above this last was a public library and a flat for the librarian. From a structural point of view there is little of interest in the housing complex in Hoek van Holland. While elsewhere in Rotterdam private developers were freely experimenting with new industrial construction systems, Oud had to confine himself to a combination of concrete and brickwork. Inner and outer walls were built in brick (and plastered); the eye-catching, continuous balconies along the facades and the deep cantilevers above the shop windows were in concrete. All window frames were made of slender steel sections.

It is hardly surprising that the inhabitants of Hoek van Holland – and the aldermen they had lobbied – should have perceived the housing block as hard and anonymous. In many ways it was a link in the chain of austere housing blocks that Oud had worked on since producing the sketch for the seafront terrace at Scheveningen in 1917. At Hoek van Holland, a process that had seen the individual dwelling gradually absorbed into a new entity, that of the block, reached its logical conclusion. Whereas the terraced row of the Scheveningen esplanade and that of the street composition published in *De Stijl* had been presented as a fairly arbitrary excerpt, a mere fragment of a larger whole, the Hoek van Holland terrace was designed as a self-contained composition in which the individual dwellings were transformed into a single, classical building by dint of the simple reiteration of architectonic elements such as balconies, frames and plinths. It was a plastic and poetic elaboration, this time on the street elevation, of what Oud had previously attempted, in a much more primitive manner, on the courtyard elevations at Tusschendijken. Hoek van Holland, like the Witte Dorp, is an example of a form of town planning dictated entirely by architectural rules and motives. In this respect, the curved, glazed shopfronts command attention. They convert the horizontal lines of the continuous balconies into vertical, sculptural volumes that terminate the building in an elegant fashion and at the same time 'turn the corner'. The archives show that at every stage of the lengthy plan-

**Plan of dwelling, ground floor (left) and first floor/ OUDJ-hh 39, NAI, Rotterdam**



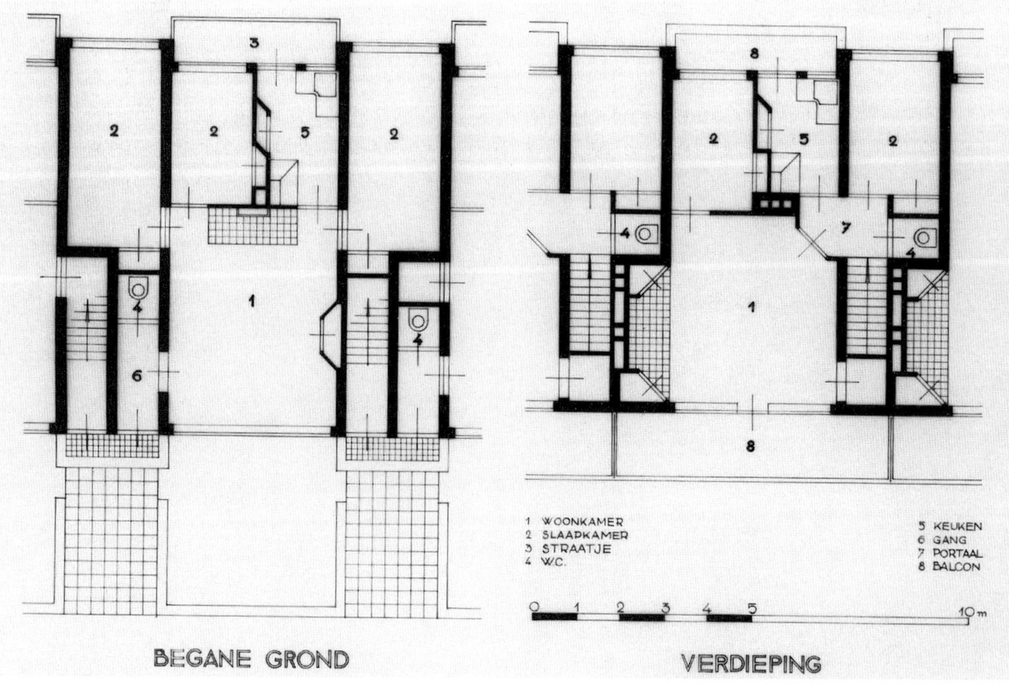

ning process, Oud did his utmost to keep the rounded shape of the shops in the design. Not simply because he believed that shops needed a big display area and a lot of 'exposure', but also on broader theoretical grounds. This can be inferred from several letters he wrote to El Lissitzky focusing on the issue of curved versus orthogonal forms and lines in relation to the design for Hoek van Holland. On 30 June 1924 El Lissitzky replied to a letter in which Oud had announced the rounded, mathematical forms of Hoek van Holland as an architectural 'innovation' vis à vis the *De Stijl* aesthetic: *It is symptomatic*, El Lissitzky wrote, *that we move on, that we reach a turning point again. You refer to Mondrian's point of view; which I do not know, for I do not understand Dutch. Doesburg never told me about it, except for the confrontation of art and nature. Here, I do not agree. The universal = horizontal + vertical, does not represent the universe, which only knows curves, not* straight *lines. For instance, the ball (not the cube) is the crystal of the universe. But we are unable to do anything with it (the ball), for it is the accomplished situation (death), therefore we concentrate on the properties of the cube, that allow us to arrange and rearrange it – and disturb it (life). The modern machine needs the 'round' element, for it has the* advantage *of circular movements as opposed to the* straight *forward and backward movements of man's hands and feet. When a dwelling, a house is a commodity to accommodate our bodies (as is our clothing), why should it not be round? But all this runs the risk of becoming academic scholasticism, when our living creation, our work, fails to prove it. I hope that your new design moves in that direction. And so I look forward with much interest, not only to the general drawing, but also a collotype of the plan and the pictures.*[5]
Seen in this light, the rounded corners of the housing complex at Hoek van Holland were no mere incident but the next step towards realization of the perspective Oud had sketched in his famous *Opbouw* lecture (1921). The gleam of the curved, plate glass windows, the smooth profiles of the inward-leaning concrete slabs and the seamless perfection of the white-rendered brickwork, brought within reach the modern style of which the industrially produced household appliance was a mere foretaste.

Although it is true that the Hoek van Holland terrace is a Rotterdam housing block turned around to face the street, and also, owing to the introduction of curved and rounded volumes, a polemical contribution to an international architectural debate, this is not to say that it was conceived without any thought for local conditions. Thanks to Oud's retrospectively written commentary, and more especially to the recent discovery of detailed specifications (including the colour scheme), we know that, just as seven years earlier the rhythm of the waves was the true motif for the architectural composition of the Strandboulevard, so the Hoek van Holland setting of dunes, beach and sea played an important role in the development of what Oud referred to at the time as the 'initial composition'. In 1927 he described it thust: *Hoek van Holland is neither city nor village (I mean in appearance). It has the flatness that characterizes the village because of its landscape; it has the high-rise that typifies the city because of the construction of downstairs and upstairs units. The beach and the fishing reinforce the tendency towards the open, rural and airy; the industry, the heavy traffic, the fort, contribute an atmosphere of more sophisticated life that invokes memories of urban activities and society. An attempt to represent this complex character as clearly as possible can be seen in the housing scheme (Hoek van Holland) depicted here: the horizontality of the building, with its long, unbroken lines, with its open-work fencing and its broad windows, alludes to the need for vastness and boundlessness (the advantages of the countryside): the tautness and smoothness of the exterior, the perfectionism of the details – simplicity in particular demands the greatest care – bespeak the refinement that distinguishes the city from the village. The light, bleached colour takes its cue from the dune landscape, while the front gardens, in their somewhat rigid demarcation, represent the less welcoming aspect of the city.*[6]
The colour scheme Oud chose for Hoek van Holland supported the compositional equilibrium of the block. That is to say, the use of colour added nothing to the expressive effect of windows, doors, balconies, chimneys and lower fronts, but at best enhanced it. For example, the use of colour reinforced the tripartite, horizontal structure of the

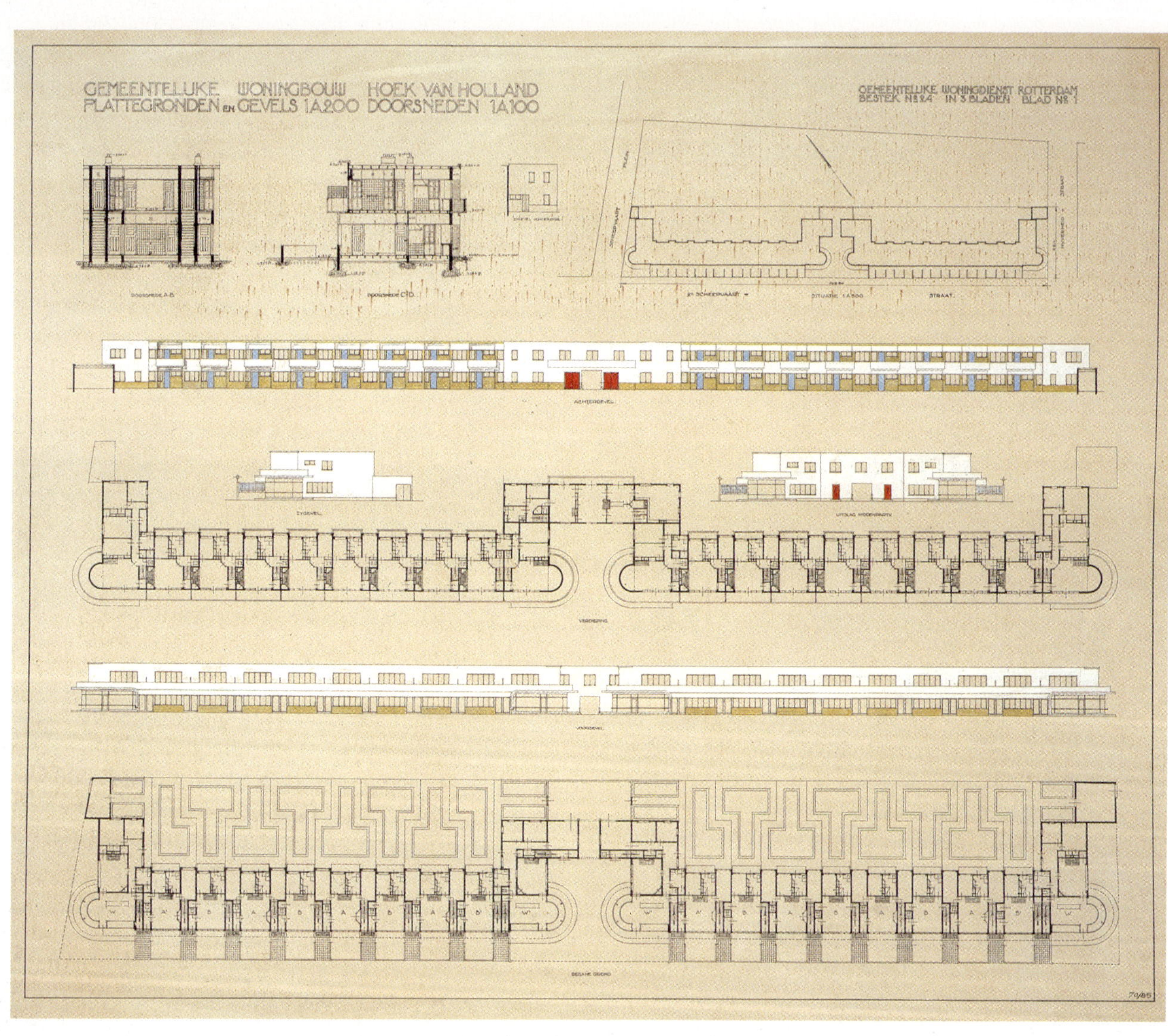


Various design views/ OUDJ-hh 47, NAI, Rotterdam

complex: first a forty-centimetre-high plinth, originally specified as grey facing stone but for reasons of economy executed in grey painted plasterwork. Next a band of yellow Frisian bricks up to windowsill height, demarcating the front gardens, and finally, the 'dune beige' rendering from windowsill height to roof edge. The dimensions and plasticity of the building were further intensified by the use of blue for front doors and balcony partitions and red for the street furniture.

When the Swiss art historian Sigfried Giedion asked the Woningdienst for suitable examples of what had come to be known internationally as 'die Wohnung für das Existenzminimum' for his booklet *Befreites Wohnen* (1929), Oud sent him several carefully composed photographs of the complex plus a section of the floor plan, on which he had noted, not without pride, the rentals of the two main dwelling types (type A, 5.75 guilders a week, type B 4.75 guilders a week).[7] Having already attracted the attention of groups in and around the Bauhaus with his articles and lectures, it is evident that Oud, with the construction and publication of Hoek van Holland, had finally joined the ranks both of the international movement of 'modern' architects and of the (German) housing reform movement. Oud had certainly done his bit to achieve this. In 1926 he included the project as a (new) illustration to the German version of his *Opbouw* lecture in *Holländische Architektur* (Bauhausbücher, no. 10), juxtaposing the perspective drawing and floor plans with a picture of one of Le Corbusier's villas. The piquancy of this did not escape Rietveld. On 17 January 1927 he wrote to Oud: *I've seen that Bauhaus booklet 10 of yours – haven't read it yet but I like the look of it. Best of all are those Hoek van Holland workers' dwellings. I can't examine the floor plans properly at that tiny scale, but it appeals to me enormously. The perspective too – especially that (detail of the cantilevered concrete slab above the shopfront) – that curve looks good in a floor plan too. I think it's the best I've seen yet. Le Corbusier always strikes me as very sober but I applaud the spirit.*[8]

**Project under construction with Oud and probably son Hans/ OUDJ-ph 260, NAI, Rotterdam**

Elevation, 2e Scheepvaartstraat/ OUDJ-ph 280, NAI, Rotterdam (Photo E. van Ojen)



**Notes**

**1.** The information in this text regarding the structural aspects of Hoek van Holland and its planning history came from M. Steenhuis, D'Laine Camp, M. Kamphuis, *Arbeiderswoningen in Hoek van Holland, J.J.P. Oud. Ontwerp, bouw, beheer en renovaties 1923-1999*, Rotterdam 1999.

**2.** M.J.I. de Jonge van Ellemeet to A. Heijkoop, 28 November 1923. Quoted in: M. Steenhuis, D'Laine Camp, M. Kamphuis, *Arbeiderswoningen in Hoek van Holland, J.J.P. Oud. Ontwerp, bouw, beheer en renovaties 1923-1999*, Rotterdam 1999, p. 13.

**3.** M.J.I. de Jonge van Ellemeet to A. Heijkoop, 13 November 1924. Quoted in: M. Steenhuis, D'Laine Camp, M. Kamphuis, *Arbeiderswoningen in Hoek van Holland, J.J.P. Oud. Ontwerp, bouw, beheer en renovaties 1923-1999*, Rotterdam 1999, p. 16.

**4.** *Handelingen der Gemeenteraad*, 17 September 1925. Quoted in: M. Steenhuis, D'Laine Camp, M. Kamphuis, *Arbeiderswoningen in Hoek van Holland, J.J.P. Oud. Ontwerp, bouw, beheer en renovaties 1923-1999*, Rotterdam 1999, p. 18.

**5.** El Lissitzky, *Proun und Wolkenbügel. Schriften, Briefe, Dokumente,* Dresden 1977, p. 125; Ed Taverne, 'Bouwen zonder make-up. Acties van Oud voor het behoud van de architectuur', in: *Wonen/TABK*, 3 (1983), pp. 8-22.

**6.** J.J.P. Oud, 'Woningbouw te Hoek van Holland', in: I.M. Dugteren, H. Dekking (eds.), *Het Groen-Wit-Groene Boek,* published on the occasion of the 10th anniversary of the Volksuniversiteit in Rotterdam, Rotterdam 1927, pp. 38-41.

**7.** S. Giedion, *Befreites Wohnen*, Zürich, Leipzig 1929, pp. 34-36.

**8.** G. Rietveld to J.J.P. Oud, 17 January 1927, OUDJ-B, NAI, Rotterdam.

**Sources**

CCA: dr1984: 0029, dr1984: 0438-0440, dr1984: 0454, dr1984: 0456, dr1984: 0512-0516, dr1985: 0277, ph1983: 0309-0313, ph1983: 0321, ph1983: 0464, ph1984: 0817, ph1984: 0824-0843, ph1984: 1075-1082
Getty: 890126-box3, F31, 890126-10**, 890126-14**, 840055**
NAI: OUDJ-hh 1-64, OUDJ-ph 258-295, OUDJ-ph 1832-1835, OUDJ-ph 1685-1690, OUDJ-ph 1695-1696, OUDJ-hh 1001, OUDJ-hh 3001, OUDJ-B

**Articles**

Adler, L. 'Neue Arbeiten von J.J.P. Oud, Rotterdam', in: *Wasmuth's Monatshefte für Baukunst*, 11(1927)1, pp. 32-38
'Complexe d'habita-

tions Hoek van Holland: architecte J.J.P. Oud', in: *Journal hebdomadaire d'information et de Critique*, 6(1927)5
G.F., 'Nieuwe Bouwwerken. J.J.P. Oud: Holländische Architektur', in: *Bouwkundig Weekblad*, (1927), pp. 95-96
'Gemeentelijke woningbouw te Hoek van Holland, architect J.J.P. Oud', in: *Bouwkundig Weekblad Architectura*, (1927)43, pp. 384-388
Klein, A., 'Neue Arbeiten von J.J.P. Oud', in: *Wasmuths Monatshefte für Baukunst*, 11(1927)7
Oud, J.J.P., 'Woningbouw te Hoek van Holland', in: *Het Groen-Wit-Groene Boek*, published on the occasion of the 10th anniversary of the Volksuniversiteit Rotterdam, 1927, pp. 38-42
Oud, J.J.P., 'Wohin führt das Neue Bauen: Kunst und Standard', in: *Die Form*, 3(1928)2, p. 61
Oud, J.J.P., 'Wohnhausgruppe in Hoek van Holland', in: *Die Form*, 3(1928)2, pp. 38-41
'Einer neuer Wohnungsbau von J.P. Oud, Stadtbaumeister von Rotterdam', in: *Der Baumeister*, 25(1927)11, pp. 297-301
Rogkerus, 'J.J.P. Oud: Arbeiterwohnungen mit Läden in Hoek van Holland', in: *Die Bauschau*, 3(1927)5, pp. 5-9

**Literature**

U. Barbieri, *J.J.P. Oud*, Rotterdam 1987, pp. 98-103
I. Grinberg, *Housing in the Netherlands, 1900-1940*, Delft 1977, pp. 93-94
H.E. Oud, *J.J.P. Oud. Architekt 1890-1963. Feiten en herinneringen gerangschikt*, The Hague 1984, pp. 79-82, 112, 122
S. Polano, *J.J.P. Oud Architettura Olandese*, Milan 1981, pp. 87-88
G. Stamm, *J.J.P. Oud. Bauten und Projekte 1906 bis 1963*, Mainz, Berlin 1984, pp. 76-77, 98

Shop beside gateway/ OUDJ-ph 1834, NAI, Rotterdam (Photo E. van Ojen)

Shop beside gateway/ OUDJ-ph 292, NAI, Rotterdam (Photo E. van Ojen)

Shop (left) and dwellings at end of row/ OUDJ-ph 287, NAI, Rotterdam

Project under construction/ OUDJ-ph 269, NAI, Rotterdam

Project, immediately after completion/ ph1983: 0321, CCA, Montreal

Central gateway with two shops/ OUDJ-ph 1835, NAI, Rotterdam (Photo E. van Ojen)

# 45/ Kiefhoek Workers' Housing

**Rotterdam, Groene Hilledijk**

**1925-1930**

In the latter half of the 1920s, the cost-effectiveness of workers' housing was a key concern in municipal housing circles, both inside and outside the Woningdienst. The Kiefhoek housing scheme, which occupied Oud intensively from 1926 to 1930, is illustrative of the difficulty of building sound and affordable housing, in particular for large families with a low income, while remaining within the prevailing margins of subsidized housing.[1] The solutions Oud and the Woningdienst came up with in Kiefhoek with respect to lot division, floor plans and operation were by no means exceptional and can to some extent be compared with the plans being developed around the same time in Schiedam and Rotterdam South by W. van Tijen on behalf of the N.V. Volkswoningbouw Rotterdam (a private construction firm he had set up together with A. Plate). Nonetheless, the two parties operated from very different viewpoints. While ambitions within the Woningdienst did not go beyond trying (often in the teeth of considerable political resistance) to come up with a cost-effective solution to the development of subsidized, brick-built 'single-family homes for subsistence-level occupants', Van Tijen's designs were pilot projects aimed at demonstrating the viability of a commercially based development of industrially produced social housing. During the years when Oud's social housing activities were restricted to the rationalization of block organization and floor plans, Van Tijen and Plate were staking everything on the industrialization of the construction process and trying to force through a transition from small-scale business to large-scale industrialized enterprise. In so doing they were indirectly implementing what Oud had referred to in *De Stijl* ('Bouwkunst en normalisatie bij den massabouw', 1918) as an imperative requirement of the modern age: 'the radical reorganization of the construction industry in the widest sense'.[2]

The immediate reason for the construction of Kiefhoek was the severe shortage of dwellings for large, low-income families following the resumption of slum-clearance operations in 1925. Although its own alarming report on the situation had resulted in the Rotterdam Woningdienst being requested in 1925 to draw up a plan for three hundred dwellings on the south bank of the Maas, the first designs did not reach the council's Finance Committee until October 1926. At that stage the plan envisaged approximately three hundred dwellings and a few shops. Nearly all the dwellings were of the same type: apartments on two levels below a flat roof, the living room facing the street and three bedrooms on the upper floor. All were equipped with special built-in conveniences such as a shower, an extra fitted wash basin, a fold-up ironing board, cupboards and a serving-hatch. This design was rejected by the committee because a majority of its members felt that the per dwelling building costs were too high. They also felt that the Woningdienst should first adapt existing (municipal) housing stock to the needs of this category of tenant. In March 1927, alderman Heijkoop

Plan of dwelling: ground floor (left) and first floor/ OUDJ-kh 32, NAI, Rotterdam



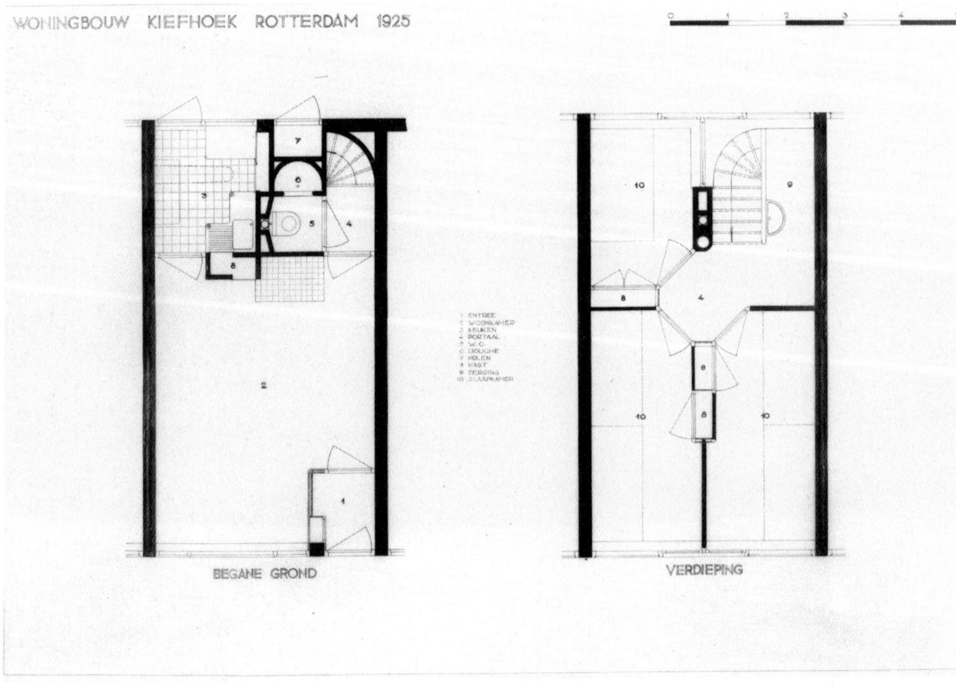

Aerial photo/ OUDJ-ph 300, NAI, Rotterdam

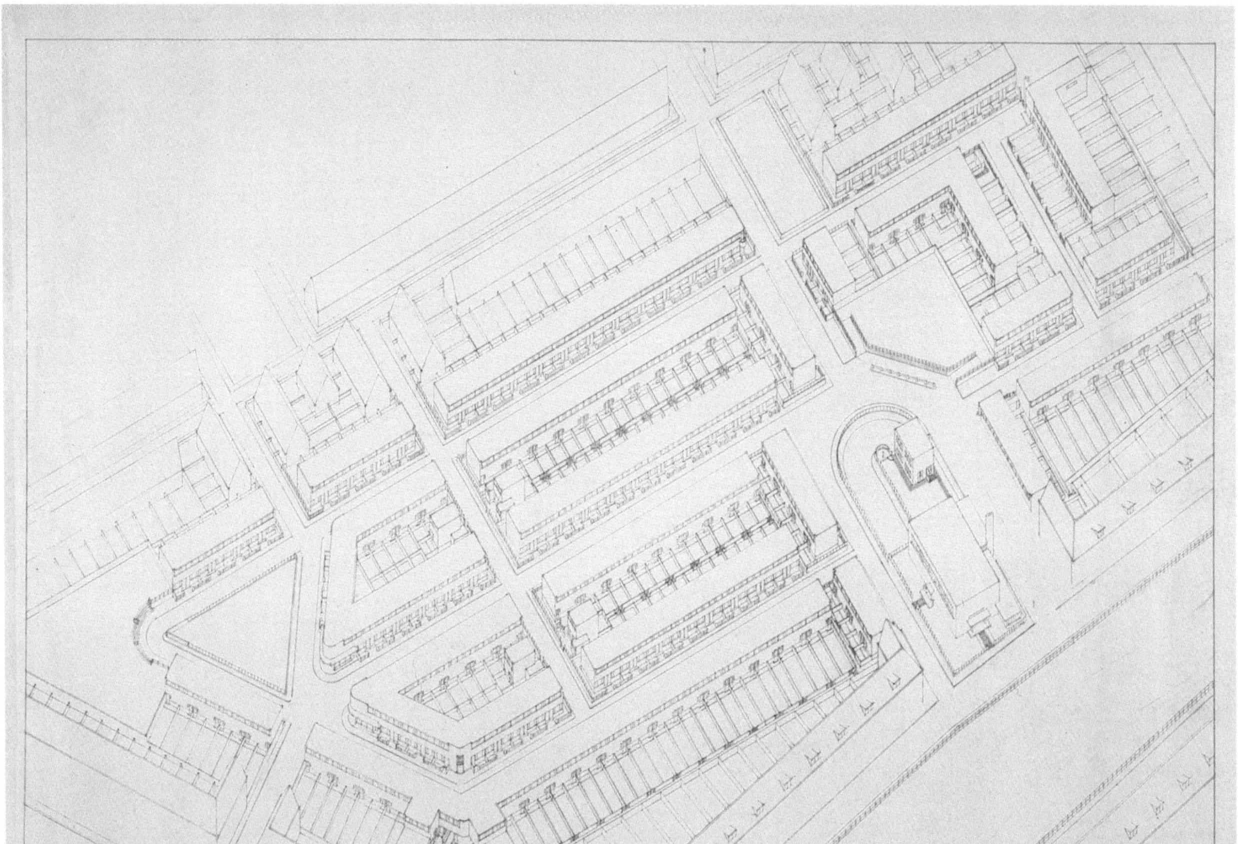

Isometric projection/ OUDJ-kh 34, NAI, Rotterdam

managed to persuade the council that only it – in combination with state subsidies – was capable of building sound and cheap dwellings for large, impoverished families. Under the pressure of the stringent economies imposed by the council and the national government, Oud set about simplifying his design, which was ready for tender in the course of 1928. At that point, the complex consisted of 291 dwellings, two shop/dwelling units, one dwelling with a hot-water boiler (to supply estate residents) and two warehouses. The quality of construction of the dwellings was greatly reduced and the aforementioned extra conveniences were either pared down or scrapped. Execution of the plan also suffered considerable delays: the last dwelling was not completed until 1930.

While the first (industrialized) housing scheme attempted by N.V. Volkswoningbouw Rotterdam foundered on the Woningdienst's determination, for town planning reasons, to locate the concrete dwellings on a site that was too expensive for 'true' working-class houses, Oud was saddled with a cheap site that presented him with well-nigh insoluble problems of spatial organization. The municipal housing estate was fitted into Hillepolder, a scene of Woningdienst activities since 1918. Originally intended, like the surrounding area, to be filled with concrete housing, the land between Hillevliet and Meerdervoort had been subdivided in 1923 according to a plan drawn up by the architect R.J. Hoogeveen. When Oud set to work here in 1926 he had to take account not only of the existing housing on all sides (Kiefhoek was to all intents and purposes 'built-in'), but also of a masterplan geared to multi-storey housing. Reviewing the project after the event, Oud's superior, De Jonge van Ellemeet, confirmed that Oud 'had not had much freedom with respect to the lot division, but had nonetheless produced an economical and yet interesting solution.'[3] Oud managed, thanks to clever use of dimensions, chamfers and constrictions, to transform a neutral and irregular street plan into the ground plan of an intimate village with space for three hundred units, without having recourse to the upstairs and downstairs dwellings used elsewhere in the district. Oud also succeeded in incorporating several collective facilities, such as a church,

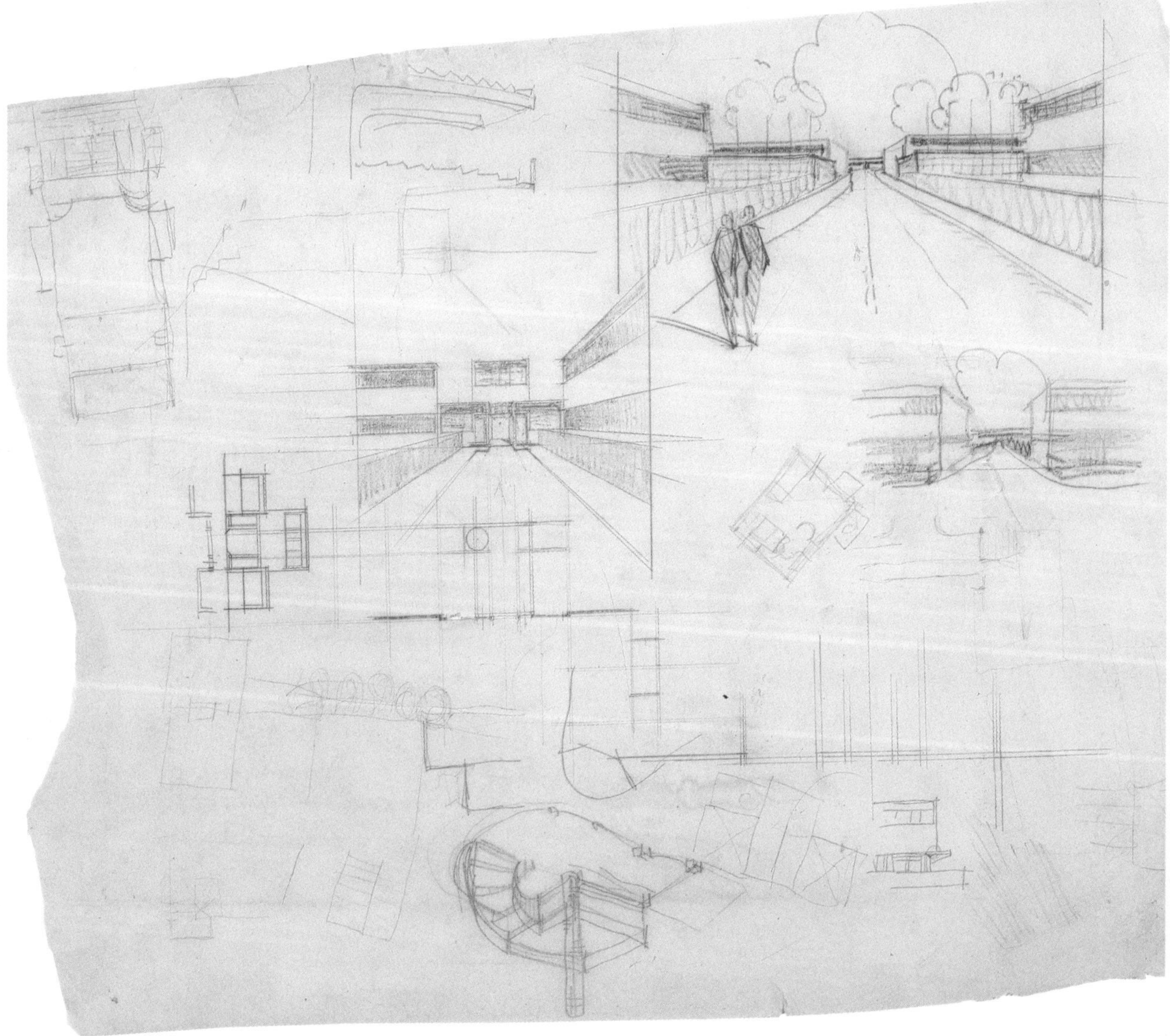

Sketches/ OUDJ-kh 29, NAI, Rotterdam

two play areas and a public garden, into a rational development plan geared to cost-efficiency. The introverted, villagey character was then imaginatively reinforced by the architectural detailing. The shops, for example, by their location and spacious, open architecture, enliven the entire plan. The best-known image of Kiefhoek is the symmetrical composition of the two curved shopfronts either side of the central and smartest street where they signal the estate's presence with a powerful entrance. In his affectionate analysis of Kiefhoek in 1963, Bakema remarked in reference to this solution: *the seemingly arbitrary oblique angles of the site plan are organized here into a lucid spatial form by means of architectural decisions (rounded corners, coherence of house walls, warehouses and play areas, bench).*[4] Elsewhere in the plan, too, Oud tried to correct irregularities of the plan by dint of symmetrical arrangements, such as the free-standing dwellings terminating the elongated blocks lining the main street. Sketches show that in Kiefhoek, too, Oud was preoccupied by the contrast between the intimacy of the tree- and house-lined inner courts, and the receding perspective of the residential street. Surviving sketches and preliminary studies constitute a regular training course for architecturally-oriented urban design. Sketches for corner structures, perspectives of courts and streets, show how universal elements like parapets, window strips, plinths and cornices were orchestrated to form a self-assured urban village.

It is interesting to compare the site and dwelling layout of Oud's Kiefhoek with that of Tuindorp, the housing scheme near Vreewijk designed almost concurrently by Van Tijen et al.[5] This plan for over five hundred dwellings owed much more than the Kiefhoek estate to German experiments with industrial housing production and rational house design, in particular those in Frankfurt.[6] Using industrial production methods similar to those developed in Germany, not just for the constructional system but also for numerous components and technical services, Van Tijen succeeded in creating a dwelling with a greater sense of space – a living room running the full length of the ground floor, for example – and greater amenity, thanks to technical services like central heating and good ventilation. For Van Tijen and Plate, these were the true *ingredients that were to change domestic life from a burden into a joy.* The same applied to the site layout which should be such that *every trace of drabness has been banished and made way for green, light and variation.*[7] The actual implementation of a programme that would undoubtedly have been endorsed by Oud and De Jonge van Ellemeet, was vastly different from that of Kiefhoek. Although the Tuindorp plan of N.V. Volkswoningbouw Rotterdam provided for more than just housing, the shops, schools, community buildings and pubs were anonymous (rather than architectural) details in the sustained lot division of north-south oriented housing rows. The lot plans and intriguing perspective drawings made by Van der Vlugt at Van Tijen's behest, suggest an urban space intent on nothing more than being a fresh and green environment for individual living. The street- and townscape Van Tijen had in mind was inextricably bound up with the system of lot division and the resulting repetitions. He felt no need at all to follow the Kiefhoek example by treating the rows architecturally and making them subordinate to a coherent street- and townscape.

The importance Oud attached to the closed street- and townscape meant that here and there obvious advantages of sun, light and air were subordinated to aesthetic considerations. In the north-west corner of Kiefhoek, for example, the housing blocks were substantially set back from the building line, a strategy that did not result in any extra sunlight for the dwelling or its front garden but which did result in a more spacious and symmetrical streetscape. Nonetheless, the Kiefhoek estate marked a high point in the history of Dutch housing architecture because it struck the right balance between meticulous research and aesthetic design. Oud himself, in a commentary directed at German professionals, called the dwelling type developed in the Kiefhoek estate a 'Wohn-Ford', whereby he was thinking not so much about the industrial production methods that preoccupied Le Corbusier, as the sophisticated floor plan that incorporated such standard extras as woodwork, tiling, cupboards, colour.[8] Oddly enough, it was Van Loghem, a frequent opponent of Oud in *de 8 en Opbouw* circles, who recognized Kiefhoek as a successful model of a modern living environment: *The modern individual feels at home in the functional, simple, well-lit dwelling which makes optimum use of technology. Anyone who has followed me closely [i.e. is familiar with Van Loghem's criticism of the villagey character of Vreewijk] will understand on a visit to "de Kiefhoek" what an important step has been taken, and with what proper understanding a housing estate has been created here for the modern worker. Everything is smooth, the long, big windows cast an abundance of light into all the rooms. Even the staircases are brightly lit. ...I hereby salute the designer of "de Kiefhoek" for the brilliant way in which he has managed, with a facade width of no more than four metres for each dwelling, to achieve a maximum spatial effect. For this is what true architecture is all about. It is not just a question of dividing space up – it is impossible to turn 4 metres into 5 metres – but the big architectural problem is that we must, by the judicious juxtaposition and interpenetration of spaces* enhance the sense of space.[9] Nor was Van Loghem the only architect to be interested in Kiefhoek. During the design process Oud was in regular contact with Gerrit Rietveld who was himself then engaged, together with T. Schröder-Schräder, in a study of various aspects of the small dwelling. In 1928 he wrote to Oud: *I'm curious to see how you solve the small dwelling. It seems to me that small dwellings, provided they are well appointed, represent an enormous* simplification *of life. I'm working on an interesting plan in the direction of simplified living, in other words industrialization of the work, and if it comes off I think something could be made of it.*[10] The theme of simplicity had already been touched on in an exceptionally candid letter written a year before: *I trust you are well? I'm very curious to see your little houses – I'm becoming more and more interested in small houses. I was working for a lady in Bergen. She was very taken with the design – but suddenly I was so fed up with the whole thing – all that meticulously planned living and sitting – this is how you eat, this is exactly how the food is brought in, that's where you sit to look outside – that's where you sit when there are visitors, this one sits here and that one sits there and you turn that chair around and then you sit there. Her final demand was that when she looked at the house standing there on the chosen*

**Project under construction/ OUDJ-ph 303, NAI, Rotterdam**

Street with shops (left)/ OUDJ-ph 316, NAI, Rotterdam

OUDJ-ph 319, NAI, Rotterdam



**Notes**
**1.** S. Cusveller, 'Niet zonder slag of stoot; wat er aan de bouw van de Kiefhoek vooraf ging', in: S. Cusveller (ed.), *De Kiefhoek, een woonwijk in Rotterdam*, Laren, Naarden 1990, pp. 41-54.
**2.** T. Idsinga, J. Schilt, *Architect W. Van Tijen 1894-1974*, The Hague 1990, pp. 226-236; L. de Klerk, 'Volkshuisvesting als onderneming, Ir. Auguste Plate 1881-1953', in: *En dat al voor de arbeidende klasse*, Rotterdam 1992, p. 179.
**3.** M.J.I. de Jonge van Ellemeet, 'De gemeentelijke woningbouw "Kiefhoek" te Rotterdam', in: *Tijdschrift voor Volkshuisvesting en Stedebouw*, 12 (1931), 5, pp. 101-106.
**4.** J.B. Bakema, 'Architect Oud 5 april 1963', in: *Forum*, 2 (1963), pp. 92-95.
**5.** T. Idsinga, J. Schilt, *Architect W. Van Tijen 1894-1974*, The Hague 1990, pp. 231-235.
**6.** G. Kähler, *Wohnung und Stadt. Hamburg, Frankfurt, Wien. Modelle sozialen Wohnens in den zwanziger Jahren*, Braunschweiz, Wiesbaden 1985, pp. 183-280.
**7.** E. van der Hoeven, 'De Kiefhoek in 1930', in: S. Cusveller (ed.), *De Kiefhoek, een woonwijk in Rotterdam,* Laren, Naarden 1990, pp. 55-84.
**8.** J.J.P. Oud, 'Eine Städtische Siedlung "De Kiefhoek, Rotterdam"', in: *Der Baumeister*, 28(1930)11, pp. 425-432; J.J.P. Oud, 'Ein Stadtviertel von "Wohn-Fords" in Rotterdam', NAI, Rotterdam.
**9.** J.B. van Loghem, 'Nederlandsche bouwmeesters: "De Kiefhoek" te Rotterdam – Architect J.J.P. Oud', in: *De Groene Amsterdammer,* 5 April 1930.
**10.** J.J.P. Oud to G. Rietveld (1928), NAI, Rotterdam.
**11.** G. Rietveld to J.J.P. Oud (1927). NAI, Rotterdam.
**12.** U. Barbieri, 'Oud als internationaal bouwmeester', in: S. Cusveller (ed.), *De Kiefhoek, een woonwijk in Rotterdam*, Laren, Naarden 1990, pp. 85-92.

**Sources**
CCA: dr1984: 0030-0035, dr1984: 0442, dr1984: 0445, dr1984: 0448, dr1984: 0453, dr1984: 0519-0536, dr1985: 0278, ph1984: 0845-0855, ph1984: 1086-1096,

*spot it should appear friendly and inviting or perhaps even smile upon her. It wasn't ill-meant, but I simply couldn't bear it at that moment and I spoilt it.*[11]

Even before the first Kiefhoek dwellings were finished, the site plan and floor plans were exhibited and discussed at the third CIAM congress in Brussels (1930), alongside a plan by Duiker and a design for a housing estate (with row housing) in Utrecht by Gerrit Rietveld. Together with the more or less concurrently designed Weissenhofsiedlung housing – which can be read as the de luxe version of Kiefhoek – the Kiefhoek municipal housing estate laid the foundation for Oud's international reputation as an architect of modern living.[12]

**OUDJ-ph 320, NAI, Rotterdam (Photo E. van Ojen)**



ph1985: 0151
Getty: 840055**, 890126-box 3, F14, 890126-18**
NAI: OUDJ-kh 1-104, OUDJ-ph 296-370, OUDJ-ph 1643, OUDJ-ph 1694, OUDJ-ph 1697-1698, OUDJ-ph 1700, MAQV 504, VOOV 123-127, VOOV 167, OUDJ-B

**Articles**

W.C. Brouwer, 'Ingezonden', in: *Bouwkundig Weekblad Architectura*, 51(1930)46, pp. 381-383
M.J.I. de Jonge van Ellemeet, 'De gemeentelijke woningbouw "Kiefhoek" te Rotterdam', in: *Tijdschrift voor Volkshuisvesting en Stedebouw*, 12(1931)5, pp. 101-106
'Kiefhoek', in: *Klei*, 23(1931)11, pp. 125-135
J.B. van Loghem, 'Nederlandsche Bouwmeesters', in: *De Groene Amsterdammer*, 5 April 1930
A. Otten, '"De Kiefhoek" te Rotterdam', in: *Bouwkundig Weekblad*, 51(1930)45, pp. 369-371
J.J.P. Oud, 'Eine Städtische Siedlung in Rotterdam', in: *Der Baumeister*, 28(1930)11, pp. 425-432
J.J.P. Oud, 'Die Städtische Siedlung "Kiefhoek" in Rotterdam', in: *Die Form*, 5(1930)14, pp. 357-369
J.J.P. Oud, 'Siedlung "Kiefhoek" in Rotterdam', in: *Zentralblatt der Bauverwaltung*, 51(1930)10
J.J.P. Oud, 'The £ 213 house', in: *The Studio*, 103(1931)456, pp. 175-179
A.J. van der Steur, 'Architect en het experiment, een overdenking naar aanleiding van de Kiefhoek', in: *Bouwkundig Weekblad*, 51(1930)46, pp. 379-381

**Literature**

J.B. Bakema, 'architect Oud 5 april 1963 †', in: *Forum*, 17(1963)2, pp. 92-95
U. Barbieri, *J.J.P. Oud*, Rotterdam 1987, pp. 104-109
S. Cusveller (ed.), *De Kiefhoek, een woonwijk in Rotterdam*, Laren, Naarden 1990
I. Grinberg, *Housing in the Netherlands, 1900-1940*, Delft 1977, pp. 96-100
E. van der Hoeven, *J.J.P. Oud en Bruno Taut; ontwerpen voor een nieuwe stad Rotterdam-Berlijn*, Rotterdam 1993, p. 42
H.E. Oud, *J.J.P. Oud. Architekt 1890-1963. Feiten en herinneringen gerangschikt*, The Hague 1984, pp. 67, 81, 88-93, 112, 122-123, 164-165
S. Polano, *J.J.P. Oud Architettura Olandese*, Milan 1981, pp. 88-89
G. Stamm, *J.J.P. Oud. Bauten und Projekte 1906 bis 1963*, Mainz, Berlin 1984, pp. 80-84

OUDJ-ph 324, NAI, Rotterdam (Photo E. van Ojen)

OUDJ-ph 336, NAI, Rotterdam

Living room interior/ OUDJ-ph 369, NAI, Rotterdam (Photo Kamman)

J.J.P. Oud, 'The £ 213 house. A solution to the re-housing problem for rock-bottom incomes in Rotterdam', in: *The Studio*, 101(1931)456

# The £ 213 House

A solution to the re-housing problem for rock-bottom incomes in Rotterdam by architect J.J.P. Oud

The houses here reproduced were erected by the Municipality of Rotterdam on the south bank of the river Maas. They are expressly designed to house the poorest elements of the working-class (employing this now-invidious distinction in its old sense) and, though the accommodation had to be large enough for "large" families (two parents, three girls and three boys, each) it was imperative to keep the actual building costs within 2400 guilders (circa £ 213) per house. Three hundred such houses, in all, were needed.

The problem for the architect was, accordingly, an interesting one. Its solution was found along the lines indicated by Henry Ford in his production of cars that were to be both good and cheap – namely, the practical construction and production methods, standardisation permitting of all components being factory-made, and economical organisation of space and material – "Dwelling Fords," in fact.

Space does not permit of going into the technical details, but in general it may be said that the plan of the houses is as compact as possible with no room wasted on corridors. Also the design allowed for the use of either concrete or brick, according to prices ruling this materials, a factor which, in Holland, is largely affected by the demand. Equally, the maintenance of a good standard in joiners' work (apt otherwise to be degraded in mass-production) was ensured by designing the joinery items in relation to each other so that exactness of fit had unavoidably to be maintained.

There is but one eduction pipe to each house, combining drainage of the flat roof, kitchen sink and lavatory, and this is combined with the one, central, chimney-stack, which has the advantage that the former is ensured against freezing since, as the kitchen range combines cooking with heating the living room, there is a certainty of a fire being maintained in cold weather.

The accommodation consists of living room, kitchen and lavatory, at street level; a bedroom for the parents and one for the boys and another for the girls, on the first floor beneath the flat roof; in the entrance are pegs for clothes and space for the gas, water and electricity meters, so that the intrusion of Municipal officials into living rooms is avoided. A little barn, a kind of drying loft, and some cupboards complete the tale.

Originally, a shower-bath, coal storage and a water draw-off on the upper storey were projected, but had to be abandoned on account of cost. It is highly desirable that the margin of cost should be increased, to allow of these being included, on the score of the great importance of health and cleanliness.

Since there was no possibility of individual variation, the architecture of the houses was based consequently on uniformity, and the complex as a whole draws its character from proportion, colour and grouping. The fences, some shops, and two playing-grounds for the children support, by their interchange, the impression of simplicity of the whole, while a church belonging to the little village forms something of a culminating point in the general flatness. Finally the bright colours of the houses and the flowers in the gardens help to lend the element of gaiety that houses of this type need, and which they can by such means be given without extra expense. OUD.

# 46/ Kiefhoek Church

**Rotterdam, Groene Hilledijk** **1927**

The church of the Hersteld Apostolische Gemeente (New Apostolic Church) fulfilled the same function in Kiefhoek as the site manager's hut in Oud-Mathenesse: intended as architectural symbol and prototype, it also served as the centripetal focus of an environment defined by housing. This dual function may also explain the remarkable fact disclosed by the surviving sketches, that whereas Oud never hesitated for a moment over the ground plan and overall shape of the building itself, when it came to integrating it programmatically and aesthetically into the housing estate, he tried out several versions.

As the site plan drawn up by Hoogeveen in 1923 reveals, a generous space had been reserved for a church on the northern perimeter of the Kiefhoek estate, along Groene Hilledijk.[1] It is the only area where Kiefhoek breaks through the surrounding development. How much importance Oud attached to the design of this semi-public building can be gauged from the manner in which he obtained the commission to design it. He gave a detailed account of this episode in *Architecturalia voor bouwheren en architecten* (Architecturalia for clients and architects, 1963),[2] a book that was not entirely free of vanity. When it transpired that the Hersteld Apostolische Gemeente was interested in the Kiefhoek location, Oud offered to do the design free of charge 'for the sake of the unity of the complex'. Oud designed a symmetrically organized, orthogonal church hall with no decoration apart from the strips of fenestration on two of the four elevations. On the north-west side of the church hall were two lower blocks for the vestry and storage (bicycle shed). The symmetrical composition of the front elevation was another example of the way an architectural decision served to turn 'the seemingly arbitrary oblique angles of the site plan' – in this case, the junction of Eemstein and Hillevliet – into 'a lucid spatial form'. The axis of symmetry was carried through, via the church building and a flagpole in the green, right into the heart of the street plan of the estate. In fact Oud designed an ensemble consisting of three elements – a church, a verger's house and a green – which he rearranged repeatedly during the design phase until he had achieved a satisfactory architectural unity.

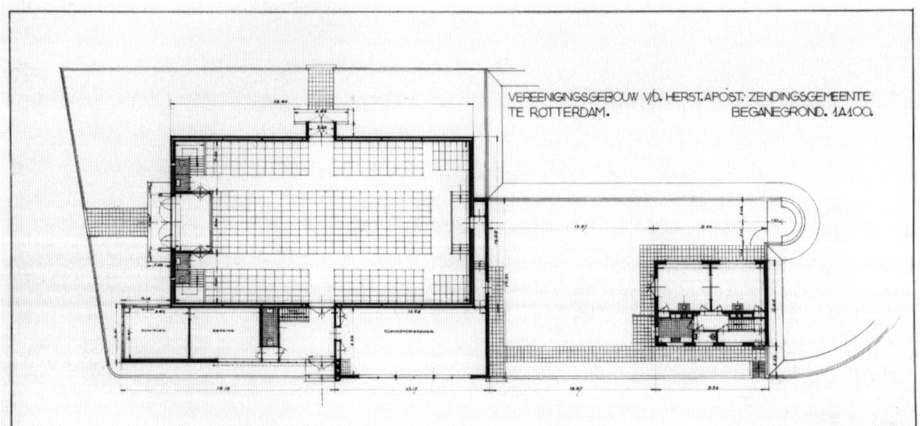


**Ground floor plan of church (left) and verger's house/ OUDJ-kk 18, NAI, Rotterdam**

**Perspective of church/ OUDJ-kk 23, NAI, Rotterdam**

The sketches show that Oud initially planned to accommodate the entire ensemble in the classical figure of a hippodrome (racecourse) divided lengthwise by a wall, with a flagpole as turning point, and terminated by a semicircular stone wall. Oud did not take the classical example as a literal model but as a 'Großbauform', as Erich Mendelsohn has done in Berlin. The main problem was to make the church and public space accessible on all sides via paths, steps and gates and also to orientate it visually in relation to the surrounding buildings. In the final version, the dwelling, church and green formed a compact compositional whole and all that remained of the figure of the hippodrome was a simple general shape.
There has been much speculation about the origin and significance of the orthogonal, undecorated church hall, probably because Oud himself was silent on the subject.[3] If one accepts Jan de Heer's analysis of Van Doesburg's views on a 'formless' architecture, the church building in Kiefhoek could be characterized as a copybook example of a Berlagian 'form–type architecture'.[4] In *Schoonheid en Samenleving* (Beauty and Society), which was published in 1919 and which Van Doesburg analysed at length – and astutely – in a series of articles published the following year, Berlage had resolutely rejected the relevance of abstract art to contemporary architectural design as claimed by Oud and Van Doesburg. Instead, he stuck to the material basis, to efficiency, as the true basis of architecture. According to De Heer: *Berlage visualized a prototype of architecture that is constructed using different means at different times throughout the course of history and that acquires a specific art form in accordance with the construction method and historic circumstances.*[6] What did such a prototype look like according to Berlage? In *Schoonheid en Samenleving* he wrote *To move on to the pure concept of building, because this must bring us to the clear explanation of the problem of architecture as a revelation of art, it could be said: 'building is space-making with the aim of providing human beings with accommodation'. ...Now, in its simplest arrangement, a space is formed by six planes: by the floor, four walls and a roof, the prototype of which is a rectangular*

**Isometric projection of church (left) and verger's house (right) dr1984: 0095, CCA, Montreal**

*parallelopiped. And then building is a matter of self-motivation, by means of building materials to put together, to 'construct' such a space.*[7] Berlage went on to describe in careful detail the elements of that rectangular box: floor, walls and roof, as well as doors and windows, which together comprised 'the whole concept of architecture', after which he concluded that no other elements were necessary for the composition of a building than those of the wall, roof and opening *and that is why the germ of the structure as artistic issue resides in these elements alone.*

It is tempting, in the light of Berlage's idea of the art form being anchored in a fixed basic form, to regard Oud's church building as a derived form, as an abstracted basilica. Yet is it not much more a built statement about the 'architectural effect' of the alternation of open and closed spaces (inner courts, atria), of the contrast between closed wall plane and window opening and of the significance of top and side lighting for the 'psychological' character of the space? The process cautiously and almost playfully begun in the Oud-Mathenesse site hut reached its apotheosis in the church building at Kiefhoek: the abandonment of Van Doesburg's 'dynamic spatial concept', which is not well served by a preconceived architectural concept of form and wants nothing to do with 'the monotonous repetition and rigid equality of two halves, the mirror-image, symmetry', which are precisely the features that define Oud's church. In his first design for a public building, Oud opted not for *De Stijl* but for a 'modern style' which, according to Berlage, should at any rate be an example of *gemeenschapskunst*, but for which there were at that moment no hard and fast aesthetic ground rules. Perhaps Oud's church at Kiefhoek could be seen as an honest attempt to formulate the problem of the modern building style without any assistance from modern artists and without having recourse to Berlagian formal concepts.

**View of estate with church/ OUDJ-ph 377, NAI, Rotterdam**

288

Church under construction/ OUDJ-ph 373, NAI, Rotterdam



**Notes**

**1.** S. Cusveller, 'Niet zonder slag of stoot; wat er aan de bouw van de Kiefhoek vooraf ging', in: S. Cusveller (ed.), *De Kiefhoek, een woonwijk in Rotterdam,* Laren, Naarden 1990, p. 51.
**2.** J.J.P. Oud, *Architecturalia voor bouwheren en architecten,* The Hague 1963, pp. 10-11.
**3.** E. van der Hoeven, 'De Kiefhoek in 1930', in: S. Cusveller (ed.), *De Kiefhoek, een woonwijk in Rotterdam,* Laren, Naarden 1990, pp. 80-83.
**4.** J. De Heer, 'Stijl en woningtype: Berlages woningbouw', in: S. Polano (ed.), *Hendrik Petrus Berlage: het complete werk*, Alphen 1988, pp. 67-90.
**5.** T. Van Doesburg, 'De taak der nieuwe architectuur', in: *Bouwkundig Weekblad*, (1920), 50, pp. 278-280; 51, pp. 281-283; (1921), 2, pp. 8-10.
**6.** De Heer, 'Stijl en woningtype: Berlages woningbouw', in: S. Polano (ed.), *Hendrik Petrus Berlage: het complete werk*, Alphen 1988, p. 70.
**7.** H. P. Berlage, *Schoonheid in samenleving*, Rotterdam 1919, p. 10.

**Sources**

Getty: 890126-box 7 14*
MOMA: NC Drawings-blueprints
NAI: OUDJ-kk 1-32, OUDJ-kk 1001, OUDJ-kk 3001, OUDJ-ph 371-401, OUDJ-ph 1701, OUDJ-B


**Articles**

H. P. Berlage, *Schoonheid in samenleving*, Rotterdam 1919, p. 10
T. van Doesburg, 'De taak der nieuwe architectuur', in: *Bouwkundig Weekblad*, (1920), 50, pp. 278-280; 51, pp. 281-283; (1921), 2, pp. 8-10
J.J.P. Oud, *Architecturalia voor bouwheren en architecten,* The Hague 1963, pp. 10-11

**Literature**

U. Barbieri, *J.J.P. Oud*, Rotterdam 1987, pp. 110-112
S. Cusveller (ed.), *De Kiefhoek, een woonwijk in Rotterdam,* Laren, Naarden 1990
J. de Heer, 'Stijl en woningtype: Berlages woningbouw', in: S. Polano (ed.), *Hendrik Petrus Berlage: het complete werk*, Alphen 1988, pp. 67-90
H.E. Oud, *J.J.P. Oud. Architekt 1890-1963. Feiten en herinneringen gerangschikt*, The Hague 1984, pp. 93-94
S. Polano, *J.J.P. Oud Architettura Olandese*, Milan 1981, pp. 88-89
G. Stamm, *J.J.P. Oud. Bauten und Projekte 1906 bis 1963*, Mainz, Berlin 1984, pp. 80-84

# 47/ Five Row Houses in the Weissenhofsiedlung Stuttgart 1926-1927

Rear elevation/ OUDJ-ph 406, NAI, Rotterdam

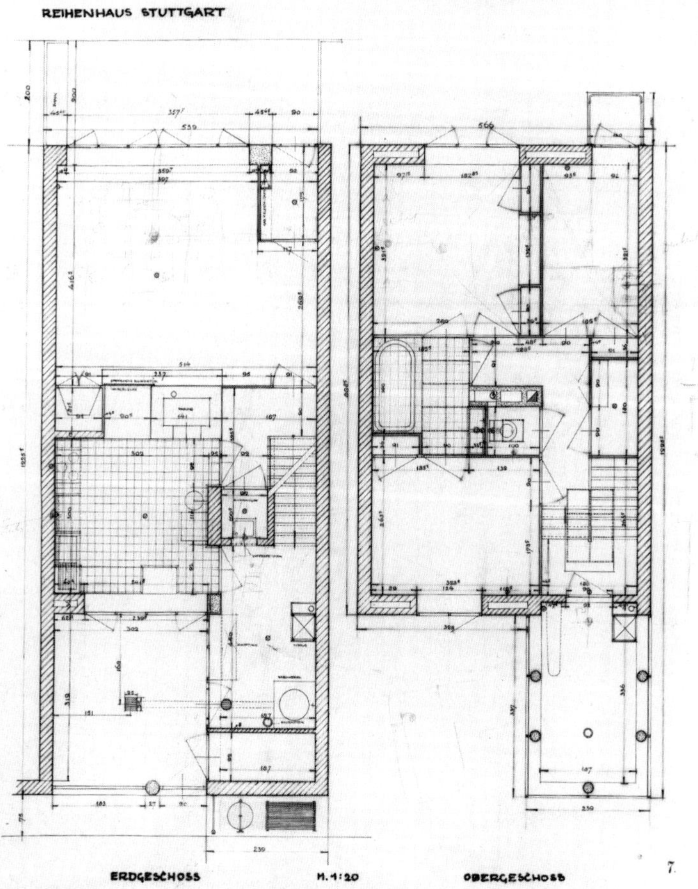


Plans/ OUDJ-st 19, NAI, Rotterdam

During the period 1925-1927, Oud was involved in the international exhibition of modern construction techniques and domestic culture in Stuttgart. The brainchild of the regional branch of the Deutsche Werkbund, the idea was adopted – despite strong political opposition – by the Stuttgart city council, which incorporated the construction of some forty model homes into its regular municipal housing programme. The leading players in the preparation, planning and execution of the housing estate were Gustaf Stotz, manager of the regional branch of the Werkbund and his chosen artistic director, Mies van der Rohe who, in close consultation with the municipal authorities, bore final responsibility for both the masterplan and the choice of architects.[1] The exhibition's motto and thus also its objective, underwent several changes in the course of the preparations. The original idea was that the model homes should be built and managed by local contractors and housing associations. For this reason Stotz wanted in the first instance to build for big families, and to use small, single-family dwellings and larger housing blocks as prototypes and demonstration models for innovations in the field of technology, construction and architecture. The first covenants (June 1925) were not about the exhibition of buildings but about the experiment with new principles and techniques for serial housing *production*. During the years when the Weissenhofsiedlung initiative was launched, the German business community was greatly exercised by standardization and rationalization and within the construction industry schemes were devised for the radical industrialization of the building trade.[2] Opinions as to what this would mean for architecture were divided, especially within the Deutsche Werkbund. Thus differences of opinion that dated from before the First World War and ran right through the so-called modern and the more traditionally-oriented architectural circles, left their mark on the Weissenhofsiedlung. Before long, the city council abandoned the programme for large families and reached an agreement with the Werkbund whereby the Weissenhofsiedlung would consist mainly of homes for the 'gebildete Mittelstand' (educated middle classes). This removed the economic basis for standardization and rationalization and for the experiment with new building materials and construction methods. Under the leadership of Mies van der Rohe, who had himself lost his belief in the architectural significance of rationalization and standardization midway through the planning, most of the architects appeared to have seen standardization and 'Typisierung' (development of types) chiefly as a pretext for formal and aesthetic experiments in their designs for spacious and comfortable villas and apartment buildings. This shift in interpretation altered the nature of the whole event and the Weissenhofsiedlung became an exhibition devoted to modern domestic culture in the widest sense. In the dwellings architects experimented variously with new materials, building systems, construction methods and with 'domestic efficiency' (layout and design). The end result was an exhibition of 'modern' architectural solutions to the diverse problems of the contemporary dwelling. Although the exhibition had been planned for 1926, the official opening did not take place until 23 July 1927, at which time many of the dwellings, including Oud's row of five, were still far from completion. The Weissenhof estate encompassed 21 separate projects, a total of 63 dwellings. They were designed by 17 architects and furnished by 55 interior designers. Dispersed across the site and through the city centre, were exhibitions about the new materials and construction methods used in the dwellings, about home economics and domestic technology and about what various countries had to offer with respect to the production, design and furnishing of the contemporary dwelling. Oud was responsible for the selection and presentation of the Dutch entry.

The considerable practical experience of Dutch architects – Oud in particular – in the field of social housing, did not go unremarked by the organizers. At a given moment, Mies's short list of prospective participants included the names of four Dutch architects: Oud, Stam, Van Doesburg and Van Loghem. In the end this was narrowed down to Oud and Stam whose projects were assigned a prominent position either side of Mies van der Rohe's own dominant, hill-top apartment block. The Stuttgart invitation came at an awkward moment for Oud: in addition to his work on major housing schemes like Kiefhoek, the final months of 1926 saw him working on his competition entry for the Rotterdam

Stock Exchange (cat. no. 57), the outcome of which was to cast him into a long and deep depression. Oud's contribution to the Weissenhofsiedlung was by contrast a great success, not least because in Stuttgart a more generous budget enabled him to implement more fully what he had experimented with in Rotterdam: the small dwelling as a synthesis of new materials, construction methods and form, guided by the principles of simplicity, efficiency and functionality.
Oud had received early notice of the plans for an exhibition of model homes in Stuttgart. In June 1925 he had shown Stotz around recent housing schemes in Amsterdam, The Hague and Rotterdam. His subsequent correspondence with Stotz and Mies van der Rohe reveals that Oud urged the inclusion of foreign architects, by which he was thinking principally of himself and Le Corbusier. He also intimated that such an exhibition ought really to have been held in the Netherlands (and in Rotterdam, of course)![3] The Germans for their part skilfully exploited Oud's excellent reputation among (German) housing reformers and architects, inviting him to submit articles for both local newspapers and the professional press and to give a lecture on his own work and on model projects elsewhere in the Netherlands to an audience composed of members of the Stuttgart city council and architectural organizations; this lecture duly took place on 23 October 1925. In January 1926 Oud was approached again, this time to write a letter to the city council in support of the plan. Oud reacted enthusiastically to the model and programme Mies van der Rohe produced in the autumn of 1925. In January 1926 he wrote to Stuttgart: *I was greatly interested in reading the programme of the exhibition 'Die Wohnung der Neuzeit' (The Dwelling in Modern Times). I was particularly delighted to read about the plan to set up a small-scale 'pilot settlement'. To do this in such a comprehensive and fascinating manner as pictured here is very modern indeed; in a striking fashion it would show the great progress made all over the world in the field of house-building. …For a long time it has been proved that today there are plans for the construction of houses that are the same for the whole world and that are recognized by prominent figures as similar. The modern architect feels*

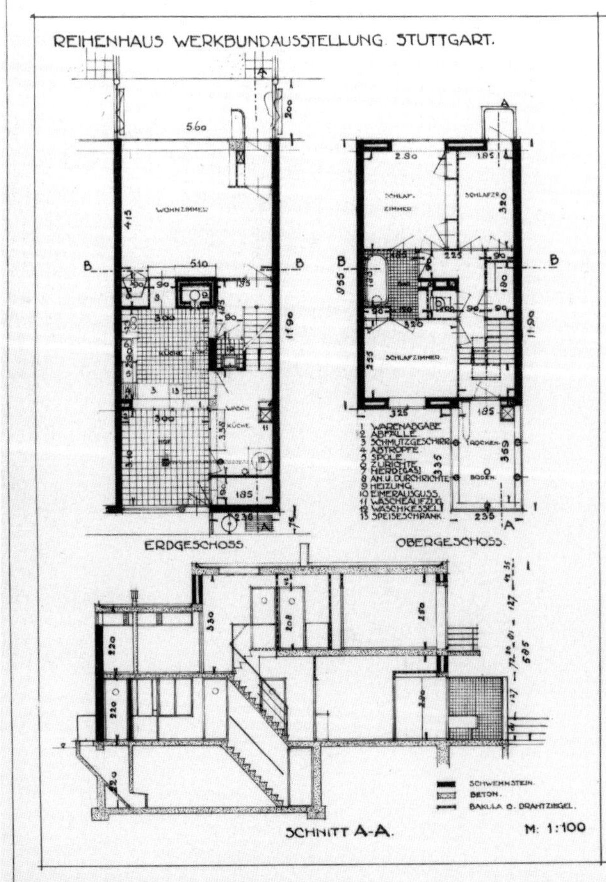


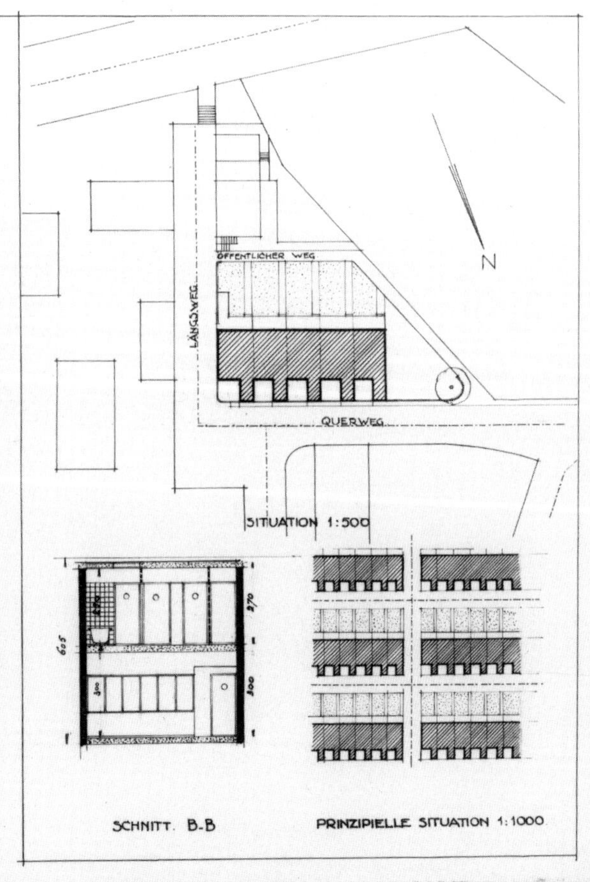


Various design views/ OUDJ-st 40, NAI, Rotterdam

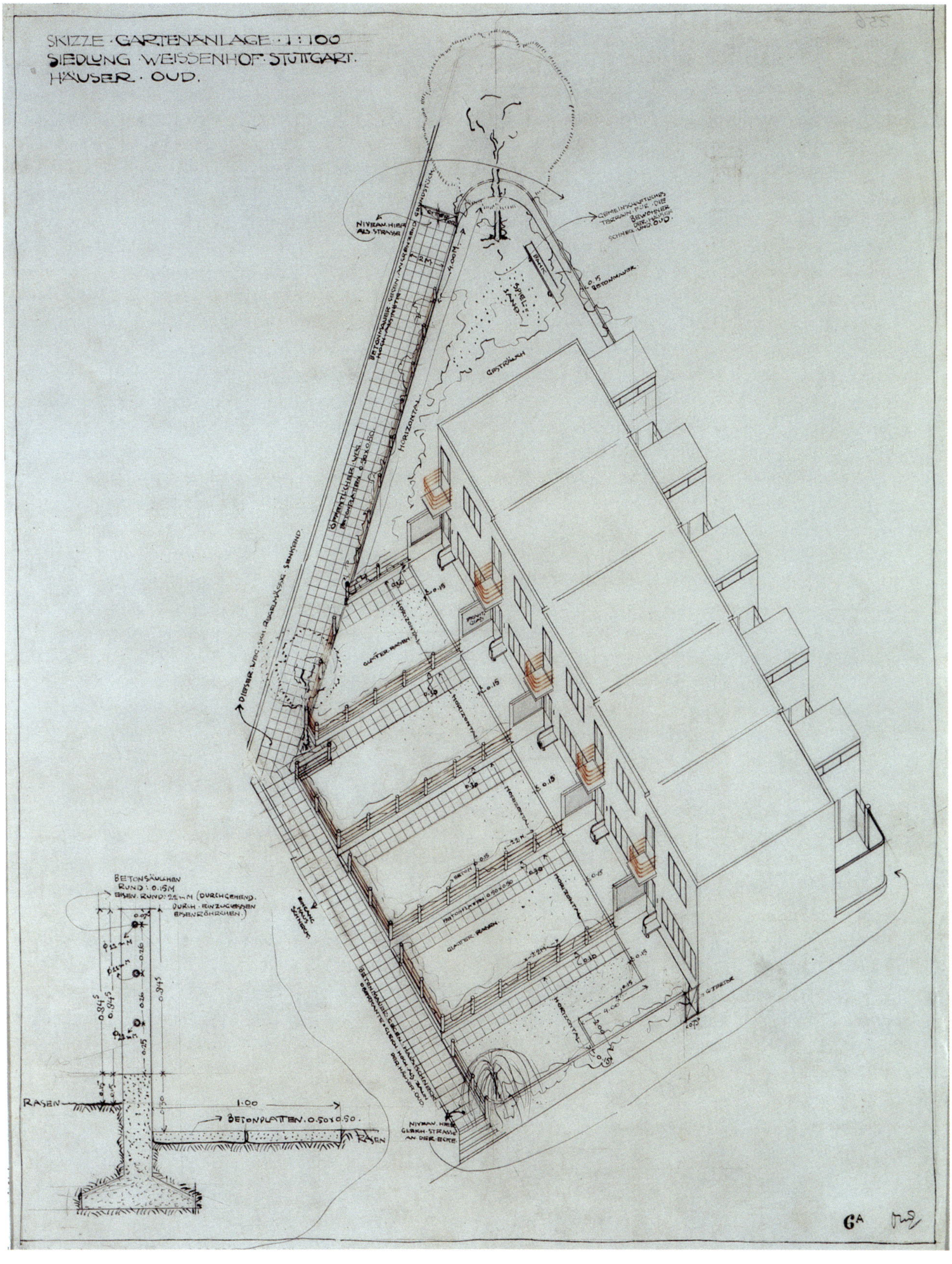

Isometric projection/ OUDJ-st 17, NAI, Rotterdam

*embarrassed to build a house that is not less expensive than any house of the same type and size built so far. At the same time, he also feels ashamed if that house is not also better than the older houses mentioned before. Study of the material, the construction and the actual building etc. made him accept this as a foregone conclusion. If you will allow me to speak for myself for an instant, I can add that I have been criticized for many things in my practice (which roughly includes the construction of 2000 houses by now), but never, not even today, now that I am building a large block with 8 contractors for their account, have I been reproached for my construction being more expensive or of poorer quality or less practical than other houses of the same type: the opposite is true. I state this because I would be happy to support an enterprise that at last translates so much experience into action and will again show so many new possibilities, albeit with a certain envy as this was planned in Stuttgart and not by us.*[4] But in the course of 1926 his initial euphoria cooled somewhat. When the official invitation arrived in mid-August 1926, and Oud learned that he would have to go to Stuttgart again to discuss the details of the planning, location and construction of his contribution and that the first designs had to be submitted in October of that year, he tried to withdraw on account of 'a big project' on which he was working (no doubt the Rotterdam Stock Exchange Competition). Stotz and Mies would not hear of it. On 9 September, Mies asked Oud to design two buildings on the corner of the two access roads to the Siedlung: a two-storey block containing four apartments and a single-family dwelling. Oud temporized, refusing to travel to Stuttgart and asking for written information about the dwelling types requested by Mies and about the required architectural expression: *I would like some elucidation. Do you impose specific requirements of an architectural nature, or, have certain details been determined by the colleagues in Stuttgart that I should take into account?*[5] On 15 November he received a reply from Mies van der Rohe who hoped that Oud had completed his 'important work' in the meantime and that he would now be able to give all his attention to the Stuttgart business. In reaction to Oud's technical queries about typology, construction and materials, Mies stressed that it was the question of domestic amenity – not of building – that should inform the design of the individual dwellings: *We want to tackle the living function and the problem of the economic management of a household.*[6] As an example of the kind of domestic aspirations entertained by housewives in Germany and in particular in Stuttgart, Mies sent the building brief for an efficient home drawn up by Stuttgart housewives, as well as guidelines for the kitchen and kitchen fittings by Erna Meyer, which were based on her *Der neue Haushalt* (The New Household, 1925), which appeared in a Dutch translation a couple of years later.[7] This was a direct hit where Oud was concerned. Both the 'conditions' laid down by the housewives and Meyer's guidelines confirmed him in his own (vague) notions about the significance of 'everyday life' as the basis for a new architecture. In 1927 he published the German housewives' building programme in the magazine *i10*. Ultimately, he made Erna Meyer's ideas about the location and layout of the kitchen and about rational household work the basis for his housing design, thereby ensuring himself a lasting reputation within the household efficiency movement in both Germany and the Netherlands.

Oud made the first designs in December, while on sick leave in Italy.[8] All the indications are that he began with the single-family home and then tried, using the experience gained in Rotterdam, to turn it into a row of houses. In any event, he suggested that his houses be situated on the north side of Pankokweg and that the back gardens originally planned be replaced by enclosed kitchen yards. In early January he received a letter from Mies announcing that the council was keen to economize and that the estate would therefore have to contain a higher proportion of cheaper single-family dwellings. Mies had chosen Oud and Stam as the architects to be asked to modify their designs accordingly. *As I assume,* Mies wrote to Oud, *that you have not yet finalized your plans, I would like to ask you to start work on these houses in addition to the small single-family dwelling. In the view of the town council, houses in this price range are possible in a closed row.*[9] This was precisely the letter the hard-pressed Oud had been waiting for. He replied by return post, not without a touch irony: *It seems that the gift*

Rear elevation/ OUDJ-ph 414, NAI, Rotterdam

Street elevation/ OUDJ-ph 408, NAI, Rotterdam

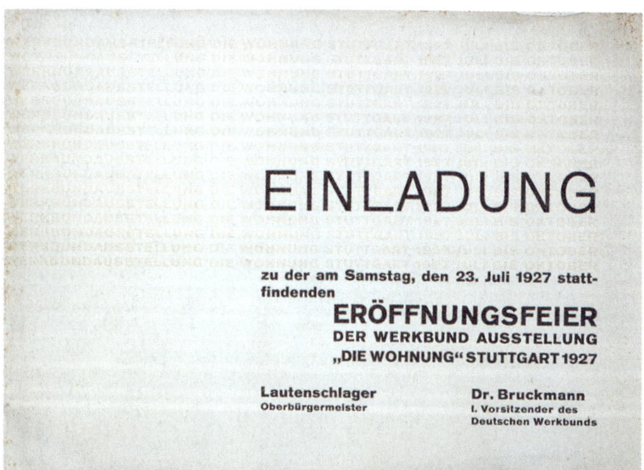

EINLADUNG

zu der am Samstag, den 23. Juli 1927 stattfindenden

**ERÖFFNUNGSFEIER**
**DER WERKBUND AUSSTELLUNG**
**„DIE WOHNUNG" STUTTGART 1927**

**Lautenschlager**
Oberbürgermeister

**Dr. Bruckmann**
I. Vorsitzender des Deutschen Werkbunds

Invitation to the opening of 'Die Wohnung' exhibition/ OUDJ-st 3001, NAI, Rotterdam

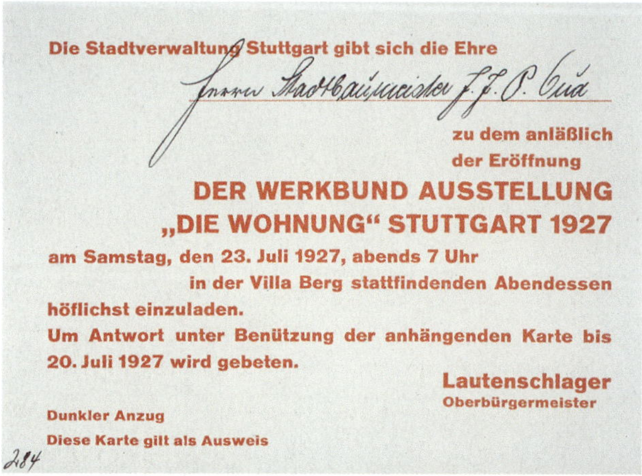

Die Stadtverwaltung Stuttgart gibt sich die Ehre

Herrn Stadtbaumeister J. J. P. Oud

zu dem anläßlich
der Eröffnung

**DER WERKBUND AUSSTELLUNG**
**„DIE WOHNUNG" STUTTGART 1927**

am Samstag, den 23. Juli 1927, abends 7 Uhr
in der Villa Berg stattfindenden Abendessen
höflichst einzuladen.
Um Antwort unter Benützung der anhängenden Karte bis 20. Juli 1927 wird gebeten.

**Lautenschlager**
Oberbürgermeister

Dunkler Anzug
Diese Karte gilt als Ausweis

284

*of prophecy has taken command of me, for my designs (the preliminary design will actually be finalized quite soon) have been executed exactly in accordance with your papers (that have only just arrived). I intended to suggest that we build rows of* single-family dwellings*! Hopefully, the proposed type will be agreed to, so that we can make rapid progress.*[10] In the end, Oud also abandoned the idea of one free-standing single-family dwelling and four row houses – he did not like the idea of putting a quasi-bungalow alongside the simple row houses – and in mid-January he sent a design for a terrace of five identical single-family dwellings to Stuttgart and Berlin. On 17 January 1927 he wrote to the project architect, R. Döcker: *Following a letter from Mr Mies van der Rohe, single-family dwellings have been designed instead of flats. Instead of 4 houses I have designed 5 houses of one type. First of all, this would make the construction cheaper because a special type would be relatively more expensive; secondly, the designing of a type demands a lot of time (more time than I can afford due to the delay caused by my illness) and it is better to produce* one *good type than two bad ones.*[11] Oud did not neglect to ask Erna Meyer in Munich for help and advice. Meyer had let Mies van der Rohe know that she was greatly disappointed by the quality of the designs so far, in particular that by Le Corbusier. Oud's plans, by contrast, were warmly received by Erna Meyer and they formed the basis of an intensive and extremely professional exchange of ideas between the architect and the home economist.[12] As a result, Oud was able to refine his dwelling in the months that followed until it was a veritable 'Ford home', a model of domestic efficiency. Oud's Weissenhof row houses are interesting not only from the standpoint of household efficiency but also from a town planning perspective. Unlike most architects, Oud did not design houses as an arbitrary object or row but as part of an urban fabric. In the model dwellings at Stuttgart – and subsequently at Blijdorp – Oud abandoned the principle of the perimeter block and developed a new kind of streetscape. In Stuttgart, Oud carried the contrast between living and utility spaces worked out with Erna Meyer over into the immediate surroundings and into the pattern of the spatial layout. In addition to a model dwelling, Oud designed an experimental proposal for a neighbourhood subdivision for the Weissenhofsiedlung (see page 292). In it the dwellings are grouped in terraces in accordance with the principles of open row housing, with the 'front' of the houses in one block facing the 'back' of the houses in the next block. The result is a lively streetscape with the north-facing, functional kitchen yards on one side and the south-facing gardens and living rooms on the other. In this arrangement the distinction between the front and back of the dwellings is removed or, as Henk Engel puts it: *the two sides are distinguished only by their character (consistent with their function) and according to Oud should be equally 'respectable': in other words, not a presentable street on*

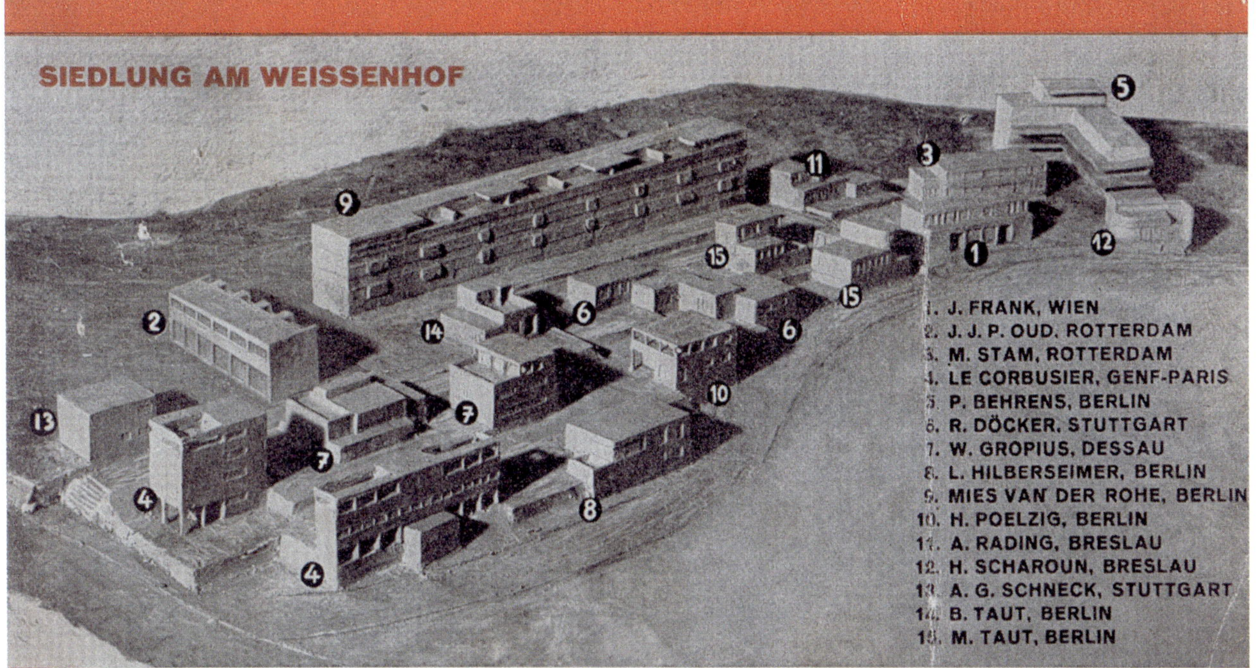


**Overview of dwellings at the Weissenhofsiedlung/ OUDJ-st 3001, NAI, Rotterdam**

Kitchen/ OUDJ-ph 1839, NAI, Rotterdam

Living room/ OUDJ-ph 1838, NAI, Rotterdam

Living room/ OUDJ-ph 415, NAI, Rotterdam

*one side and on the other a lane.*[13] In the commentary on the actual plan itself, that is to say, on the block of five dwellings, Oud went a step further by suggesting that on the other side of the street from the gardens, a communal garden with a sandpit for the children and, if desired, even an extra dwelling of the same type – but rotated through 90 degrees – might be built. Oud's attention to the spatial setting did not go unnoticed, and not just in Stuttgart. In the context of Dutch urban planning and housing, Oud's proposal was an early and important contribution to the architectural debate about the residential district that was to reach a provisional conclusion in the celebrated preliminary report of the two architectural societies 'de 8' and 'Opbouw': 'De organische woonwijk in open bebouwing' (Open planning and the Organic Housing Estate,1932).

The extent to which Oud saw the immediate surroundings as an enlargement of the individual house can be gauged from the floor plan which was designed as a link in the path followed by the occupants from street to garden. As Pommer and Otto have rightly remarked, the ground floor circulation system is quite unusual, describing a serpentine course that starts at the entrance at the side of the scullery and proceeds via the kitchen and around the stairs, to the living room and the street, without benefit of non-functional spaces like a corridor. The fluid passage through the quite constricted spaces is reinforced by a visual communication system of windows, glazed doors and service hatches.[14] In this sense, the kitchen was located and designed as the fulcrum of daily life in the dwelling. For all Oud may have heeded the strict and at times faintly risible instructions of Frau Meyer with regard to the precise layout and technical equipment of the kitchen, the kitchen and scullery were no arbitrary insertions but an integral part of a dwelling preoccupied with the details of daily life. It was these small details that sent housing reformers at home and abroad into raptures: the outer door of the kitchen yard that could be opened automatically from the kitchen; the coal deliveries to the cellar via an outside trapdoor; the mechanism (later sacrificed to cost-cutting) allowing the wet wash to be raised to a drying space above the scullery; the service hatch between kitchen and living room through which meals could be served and an eye kept on the children; central heating with individual radiators in the various rooms (later reduced, again because of the cost, to a hot air heating system with duct openings from the kitchen); and numerous other amenities that Oud had long had in mind but which he had been unable to implement in Rotterdam for lack of money. Although Oud had for technical reasons wanted to build the external walls in sandstone, to save money the dwellings were executed entirely in concrete, according to a monolithic (poured-concrete) system developed by Paul Kossel. Oud had inspected this construction method on a trip to Hamburg and Bremen with Plate in 1920 and it had also been used extensively in Rotterdam. Oud was kept meticulously informed as to the technical details and the subsequent finishing, the practices of local contractors and builders, the application of colour and the fitting out by different architects via an informative and entertaining correspondence with the young Hungarian architect Paul Meller who had been added to the Stuttgart building team to speed up the construction work.[15] Meller reported in detail on the official opening of the exhibition (in July) and the reactions of the first visitors to the as yet unfinished dwellings. It was not until 6 September that all five houses (numbered 5 to 9) were completely ready: number 5 was to have been fitted out by Mart Stam but remained empty; number 6 was furnished by a local interior designer, Rudolf Lutz; number 7 by Van Ravesteyn (to Meller's horror) and



**Notes**

**1.** There are numerous well-documented studies of the Weissenhofsiedlung: K. Kirsch, *Die Weissenhofsiedlung. Werkbundausstellung 'Die Wohnung'- Stuttgart 1927*, Stuttgart 1987; R. Pommer, C. F. Otto, *Weissenhof 1927 and the Modern Movement in Architecture*, Chicago, London 1991; W. Tegethoff, 'Weissenhof, 1927, Der Sieg des neuen Baustils', in: *Jahrbuch des Zentralinstituts für Kunstgeschichte, I (1987)*, pp. 195-228.

**2.** R. Pommer, C. F. Otto, *Weissenhof 1927 and the Modern Movement in Architecture*, Chicago, London 1991, pp. 61-71.

**3.** R. Pommer, C. F. Otto, *Weissenhof 1927 and the Modern Movement in Architecture*, Chicago, London 1991, pp. 45-46.

**4.** K. Kirsch (ed.), *Briefe zu Weissenhofsiedlung*, Stuttgart 1997, pp. 48-49

**5.** R. Pommer, C. F. Otto, *Weissenhof 1927 and the Modern Movement in Architecture*, Chicago, London 1991, pp. 242

**6.** K. Kirsch (ed.), *Briefe zu Weissenhofsiedlung*, Stuttgart 1997, pp. 124-125; R. Pommer, C. F. Otto, *Weissenhof 1927 and the Modern Movement in Architecture*, Chicago, London 1991, pp. 242-243

**7.** R. Pommer, C. F. Otto, *Weissenhof 1927 and the Modern Movement in Architecture*, Chicago, London 1991, p. 243; K. Kirsch, *Die Weissenhofsiedlung. Werkbundausstellung 'Die Wohnung'- Stuttgart 1927*, Stuttgart 1987, pp. 33-35; F.M. Hartveld, *Moderne Zakelijkheid. Efficiency in wonen en werken in Nederland, 1918-1940*, Amsterdam 1994, pp. 159-215.

**8.** Pommer quotes from a letter Oud wrote to Mies van der Rohe, dd. 23 December 1926: 'Heute zurück: erst heute Ihr Brief. Machte in Italien eine Skizze, welche jetzt eingetragen wird' ('Returned today: only got your letter today. Made a sketch while in Italy which I am now submitting'). R. Pommer, C. F. Otto, *Weissenhof 1927 and the Modern Movement in Architecture*, Chicago, London 1991, p. 243.

**9.** R. Pommer, C. F. Otto, *Weissenhof 1927 and the Modern Movement in Architecture*, Chicago, London 1991, p. 243; K. Kirsch (ed.), *Briefe zu Weissenhofsiedlung*, Stuttgart 1997, pp. 138-139.

**10.** R. Pommer, C. F. Otto, *Weissenhof 1927 and the Modern Movement in Architecture*, Chicago, London 1991, p. 243; K. Kirsch (ed.), *Briefe zu Weissenhofsiedlung*, Stuttgart 1997, p. 140.

**11.** R. Pommer, C. F. Otto, *Weissenhof 1927 and the Modern*

number 9 was furnished by the architect F. Kramer with furniture made by the Frankfurter Hausrat, a firm operated by the city of Frankfurt. 'Haus 8' was fitted out by Oud himself. The living room was furnished with a steel table and chairs designed especially for Stuttgart and lamps made by Gispen, a well-known Rotterdam interior design firm. A contemporary photograph shows a Mondrian-like painting hanging from a suspension system devised by Oud. Oud also designed the colour scheme for the walls (yellow), doors and cupboards; the rest of the dwelling was finished in white. And of course there was the fully fitted kitchen, designed largely in accordance with Erna Meyer's guidelines (see page 298).[16]

Oud's houses were favourably received by the professional press, both in Germany and elsewhere. In the highly critical report issued by the Reichsforschungsgesellschaft für Wirtschaftlichkeit in Bau und Wohnungswesen (1929), Oud's floor plan and kitchen layout were among the few designs singled out for commendation.[17] A particularly enthusiastic review by Edgar Wedepohl appeared in *Wasmuth's Monatshefte für Baukunst*, after the editor-in-chief, Werner Hegemann had earlier called Oud's houses one of the low points of the whole exhibition. This was especially surprising given the fact during these years Oud had maintained an exceptionally cordial and practical correspondence with Hegemann about numerous matters, including

**Pali Meller (left) and Oud *circa* 1928/ OUDJ-52, NAI, Rotterdam**

*Movement in Architecture*, Chicago, London 1991, p. 244.
**12.** K. Kirsch (ed.), *Briefe zu Weissenhofsiedlung*, Stuttgart 1997, pp. 91-92, 145-150
**13.** H. Engel, 'De Kiefhoek, een monument voor gemiste kansen?', in: S. Cusveller, *De Kiefhoek, een woonwijk in Rotterdam,* Laren 1990, pp. 32-36
**14.** R. Pommer, C. F. Otto, *Weissenhof 1927 and the Modern Movement in Architecture*, Chicago, London 1991, pp. 116-122.
**15.** K. Kirsch (ed.), *Briefe zu Weissenhofsiedlung*, Stuttgart 1997, pp. 94, 192-194; 196; 201-203; 211ff.
**16.** K. Kirsch (ed.), *Briefe zu Weissenhofsiedlung*, Stuttgart 1997, p. 97.
**17.** R. Pommer, C. F. Otto, *Weissenhof 1927 and the Modern Movement in Architecture*, Chicago, London 1991, pp. 66-67
**18.** K. Kirsch (ed.), *Briefe zu Weissenhofsiedlung*, Stuttgart 1997, pp. 212-215.
**19.** J.J.P. Oud to S. Giedion, 1927, GTA, Zurich.
**20.** R. Pommer, C. F. Otto, *Weissenhof 1927 and the Modern Movement in Architecture*, Chicago, London 1991, pp. 158-166; 272-274.

**Sources**
CCA: dr1984: 0070-0071, dr1984: 0546-0552, ph1983: 0457-0462, ph1983: 0066, ph1983: 0858-0863, ph1983: 0963, ph1983: 1100-1105, ph1985: 0319-0320
Getty: 840055**, 890126-box 7, 12*, 890126-box 7, 13*
MOMA: NC Drawings-blueprints
Museum Boymans van Beuningen: inv. no. V2.1-1745 a/b
NAI: OUDJ-st 1-OUDJ-st 76, OUDJ-st 1001-1002, OUDJ-st 3001-3002, OUDJ-ph 404-415, OUDJ-ph 1704-1705, OUDJ-ph 1709-1710, OUDJ-ph 1914-1917, MAQV 153, MAQV 156, OUDJ-B

**Articles**
J.J.P. Oud, 'Toelichting tot een woning-type van de Werkbundausstellung "Die Wohnung", Stuttgart 1927', in: *i10*, 1(1927)11, pp. 383-386
T. van Doesburg, 'Architectuurvernieuwingen in het buitenland. De architectuurtentoonstelling in "Die Wohnung" te Stuttgart', in: *Het Bouwbedrijf*, 4(1927), pp. 556-559

**Literature**
U. Barbieri, *J.J.P. Oud*, Rotterdam 1987, pp. 118-125
E. Holsappel, *Ida Falkenberg-Liefrinck (1901). De rotanstoel als opmaat voor een betere woninginrichting*, Rotterdam 2000
H.E. Oud, *J.J.P. Oud. Architekt 1890-1963. Feiten en herinneringen gerangschikt,*

the competition for the Rotterdam Stock Exchange. Not that the adverse opinion affected their friendship. Oud was more surprised by the many positive reactions elicited by his unassuming little houses. He wrote Wedepohl: *Of course, I was pleased with your review in 'Wasmuth's Monatshefte'; primarily, because I highly value you as a critic, secondly as I hardly expected my house to arouse any significant interest at the exhibition; however, it is only an attempt to build a proper private dwelling: a problem that hardly plays a part in the field of architecture. Since these days everything, even the smallest thing, should be architecture, I had not expected my un-architectural house to attract the attention it did.*[18] He wrote in similar terms to S. Giedion.[19] To what extent this was all a pose inspired by his distaste for Le Corbusier's 'performance' at Stuttgart, is unclear. It did not prevent Oud from answering Wedepohl's critique in detail and holding forth in letter form on just about every aspect of the dwelling, in particular the colour.
All in all, the five workers' dwellings and other designs by Oud (Mathenesse, Tusschendijken and Hoek van Holland) on show elsewhere in the city, attracted a lot of international attention on account of their unspectacular but well-considered solutions. They also secured Oud a permanent place in the Modern Movement at the very moment when it was starting to become institutionalized.[20]

**Oud (centre), his wife and Laslo Moholy-Nagy at Kijkduin, *circa* 1926/ OUDJ-51, NAI, Rotterdam**

The Hague 1984, pp. 93-94, 98-106, 112, 200
S. Polano, *J.J.P. Oud Architettura Olandese*, Milan 1981, p. 88
G. Stamm, *J.J.P. Oud. Bauten und Projekte 1906 bis 1963*, Mainz, Berlin 1984, pp. 86-89
E. Taverne, D. Broekhuizen, 'De dissidente architecten: J.J.P. Oud, Jan Wils en Robert van 't Hof' in: C. Blotkamp, *De vervolgjaren van de De Stijl 1922-1932,* Amsterdam, Antwerpen 1996, pp. 377-379

**Rotterdam, Blijdorp** **1931-1932**

In the second half of 1931, Oud worked on his last prewar municipal housing scheme: a design comprising a total of 306 workers' dwellings and eighteen single-storey buildings with apartments for the elderly. The scheme was part of Witteveen's 1929 Blijdorp expansion plan and was located to the north of Rotterdam's city centre. Oud, like Van Tijen & Van der Vlugt who were busy designing another (also unrealized) building block on Vroeselaan, ignored the perimeter blocks Witteveen had prescribed for this location and came up with an alternative block organization.[1] From the point of view of both urban and domestic spatial organization, this plan marked a decisive – final – stage in Oud's research into the typology and architectural expression of the urban block. At the same time, Oud's plan for Blijdorp could be seen as a personal comment on the large-scale housing schemes simultaneously being designed by Van Tijen, Van den Broek, Merkelbach, Stam and Van Loghem and in particular on the 'organic, open-row housing estate' designed jointly by *de 8 en Opbouw* (1932).

The first proposals to develop Blijdorp Polder as a residential area, date from 1920 when the architect W. Kromhout was commissioned to draw up a masterplan for an estate of 2,500 dwellings. The task included supervision of both the design and execution of the dwellings and 'architectural supervision of the rest'. During implementation Kromhout was to collaborate with the Woningdienst (A. Plate) and the Public Works department, in particular with its director, A.C. Burgdorffer, who had produced an earlier development plan for Blijdorp, approved in 1914. Burgdorffer's plan, which was itself a revised version of the plan drawn up by G.J. de Jong (1906), was abandoned in 1920 because of inadequate links with the existing city and more especially because of plans to locate the city's main railway station inside the planning area.[2] Kromhout drew a rigidly symmetrical plan (1921) in which the main station, wholly in the tradition of Berlage's Plan Zuid for Amsterdam, formed the starting point and terminus of a longitudinal axis along which the city park (with lake and bridge) was situated. The housing programme was conceived almost entirely in the form of perimeter blocks. In his entertaining, retrospective (1927) commentary on the plan, Kromhout sketched the idealistic atmosphere in which the alderman, Woningdienst (Plate, Oud) and architect worked on the plan: *It was a joy in those days to enter the Alderman's room, because there was action and ambition, the unity had not yet been beaten into a fragmented plurality that after one, two years would already evaporate into nothing. On one occasion Heykoop and I went to Vreewijk, i.e. on the southern shore of the Maas, where Granpré Molière and de Roos and Overeijnder had already filled whole districts with housing. There was a barely standardized ditch crossed at some point by a little bridge. I looked over the railing and saw a lot of empty sardine tins glinting on the bottom. Heykoop echoed my own thoughts with a "So what, let the lads eat sardines..." It*

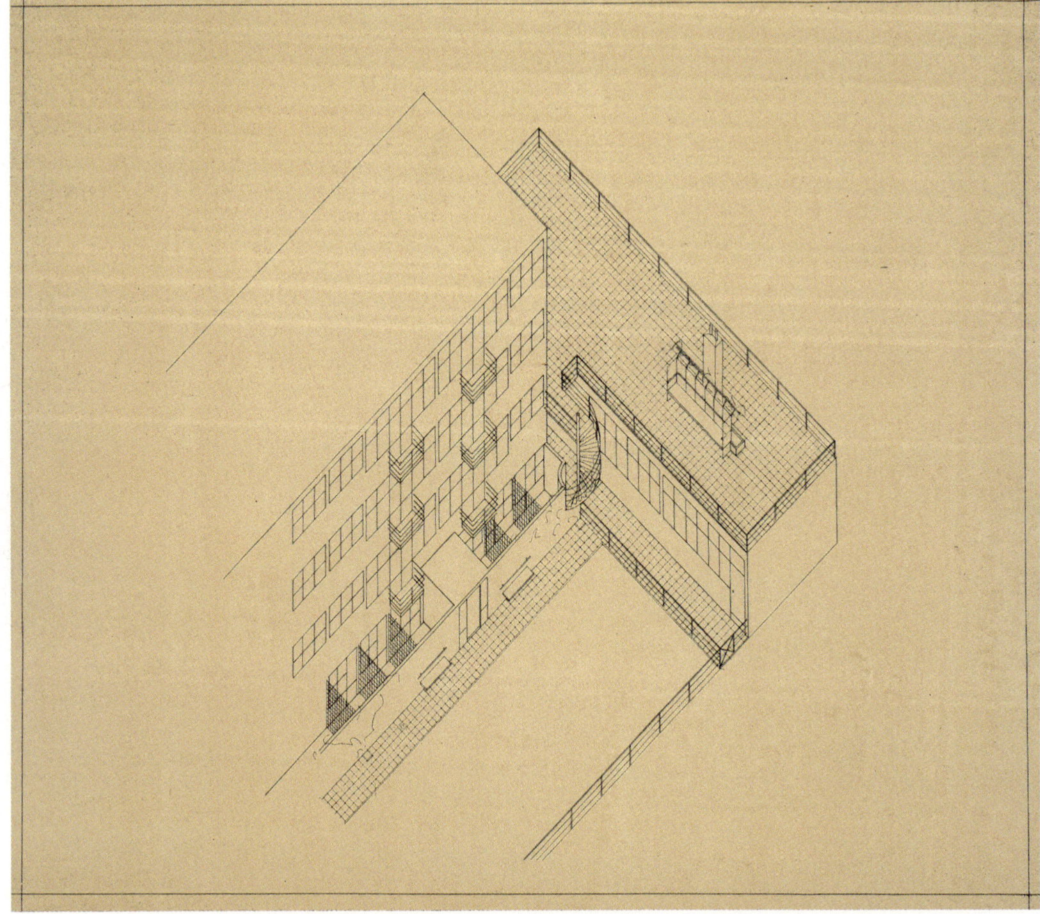

**Isometric projection of low-rise development and end of housing row/ dr1984: 0557, CCA, Montreal**

Perspective of courtyard/ OUDJ-bd 14, NAI, Rotterdam

*was with this attitude that the commission and the design came about. Now, six years later, looking over the parapet of my bridge there in the park, I cannot see a single one of the sardine containers I certainly still saw gleaming defiantly while I was designing. But that pollution by the residents did not last long for: 'We have to give them something beautiful, they have get used to it and then before very long you'll see how everyone cooperates to keep our park, the plantation and their own little garden in order.'*[3] But Heijkoop and Kromhout's visions never materialized, for the same reasons that Oud's almost contemporaneous design for Tusschendijken never realized its full potential. Although the outlines were laid down in a framework plan, the national government's withdrawal from the housing market put implementation out of the question. For the record, Oud, who had probably recommended Kromhout for the task, was very enthusiastic about the plan for Blijdorp. In 1924, in a review of a retrospective exhibition of Kromhout's work, he bracketed the plan for Blijdorp with the American Hotel in Amsterdam as successful examples of a harmonious combination of freewheeling fantasy and formal constraint:
*Another of his works is full of promise: it is the excellent plan for the development of part of Blijdorp, that is also on show in the exhibition and that, with its parks, lakes and terrace-style housing development might – had it been implemented – have become one of the finest areas of Rotterdam.*[4]

At the beginning of the 1930s, the planning of Blijdorp resumed. In the meantime the area's urban significance had altered as a result of W.G. Witteveen's General Expansion Plan for Rotterdam (1928), in which Blijdorp Polder was a vital link in the new system of major thoroughfares. In Witteveen's revised development plan of 1929, Blijdorp was transformed from a somewhat introverted garden village into an urban district tailored to the demands of infrastructure and amenities in which the public gardens envisaged by Burgdorffer and Kromhout had become the focal point of an urban parkway of regional proportions. More problematical was the way Witteveen had conceived the nature and distribution of the housing – working- and middle-class dwellings – in the district and the question of how these were to remain affordable in light of the cost of developing streets, squares and parks. On either side of the central parkway, Witteveen had projected middle-class housing along residential streets twelve to fifteen metres wide, arranged in 45-metre-deep blocks. The working-class housing was to be located in the 'more monumentally conceived section of the plan' to the west: around the harbour for the poorest families and in the blocks behind for the slightly better-off. It was clear that Witteveen's Blijdorp had little in common with Heijkoop's original ideal of a 'worker's town'. In the long run the high land price ruled out the development of workers' housing, thus putting paid to the experimental plans not only of Oud but also of N.V. Volkswoning-

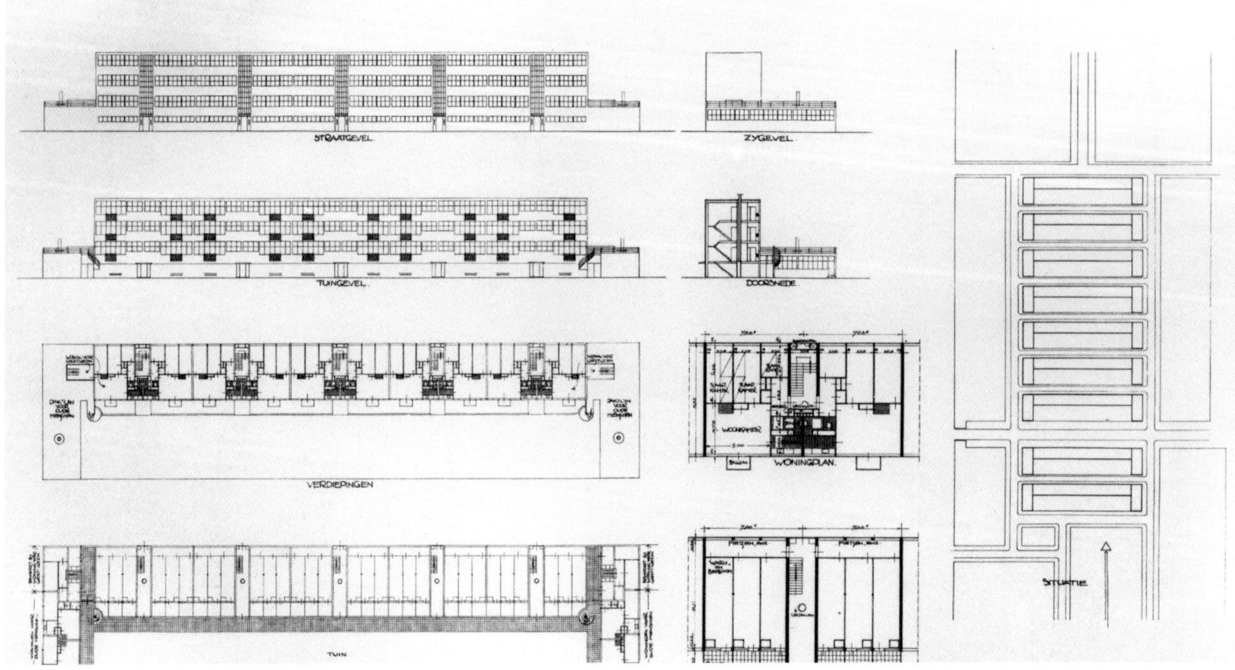


**Various design views/ OUDJ-bd 3, NAI, Rotterdam**

bouw Rotterdam (Plate, Van Tijen and Van der Vlugt).[5]
On a site where Witteveen had projected four perimeter blocks, Oud designed a subdivision consisting of nine, east-west oriented housing slabs. He explained the background to this spatial layout in a manifesto-like plan commentary.[6]
In the design for municipal housing in Blijdorp, Oud was looking for an acceptable compromise between the perimeter block and the principle of open row housing. It is clear that, architecturally speaking, he preferred the perimeter block, but that new ideas about what constituted good housing forced him to consider the option of the well-oriented, freestanding row. The disadvantage of such blocks, certainly when applied en masse, was that they did not make for a very architectonic street- or townscape. Following on from the subdivision principle he had devised for the housing block at Stuttgart (cat. no. 47), Oud designed a new urban unity for Blijdorp, one in which street and communal garden are combined and, together with the front and rear elevations of the apartment blocks, give rise to a varied streetscape. The key element in this composition is the communal garden. In contrast to the rigid subdivision chosen by Van Tijen for both the 'multi-storey plan' in Rotterdam South and for an 'organic housing estate', Oud elected to give his nine housing blocks an east-west orientation. Although this did not give the best incidence of sunlight in the dwellings, it did have the virtue of ensuring south-facing gardens. And these, as the various, beautifully detailed perspective drawings make clear, are the essence of Oud's Blijdorp scheme, in terms both of urban planning and domestic amenity. In order to achieve such a town- and streetscape in which street and garden, front and rear elevation are united in a single composition, it was necessary to subject household arrangements (especially at the rear) to stricter rules.
It is no accident that a large part of Oud's (unpublished) commentary was devoted precisely to this aspect: *The complex comprises a total of 306 dwellings. The majority (270) of these dwellings contain: living room, kitchen, WC, 3 bedrooms, (one for the parents, 2 with space for 2 beds for the children), cupboards. The lowest living level is situated +2m above street level; the +2m-high space below is used to accommodate separate laundry and storage space for each family, in addition, as access to these areas, a wide hallway on either side of the stair where bicycles or prams can be parked temporarily. Behind each of these laundry and storage areas is a small fenced-off yard where the residents can hang their wash to dry in the open air. I arrived at the layout for this type because in practice a lack of laundry and storage space is repeatedly redressed by the fact that everywhere one goes one encounters an untidy, messy and vexatious condition that could be remedied by general rules, caused by residents throwing fuel, rubbish etc. into the gardens and hanging washing all over the place. Not only does this situation detract from decent and agreeable occupancy, the disorderly picture it presents to the outside*

**Plan of two dwellings/ OUDJ-bd 3, NAI, Rotterdam**

307

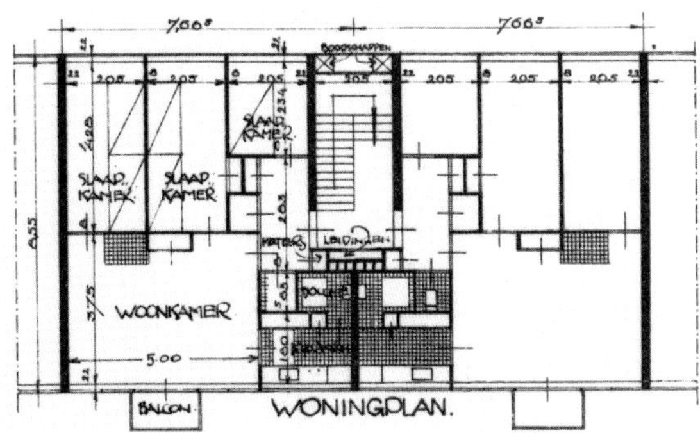


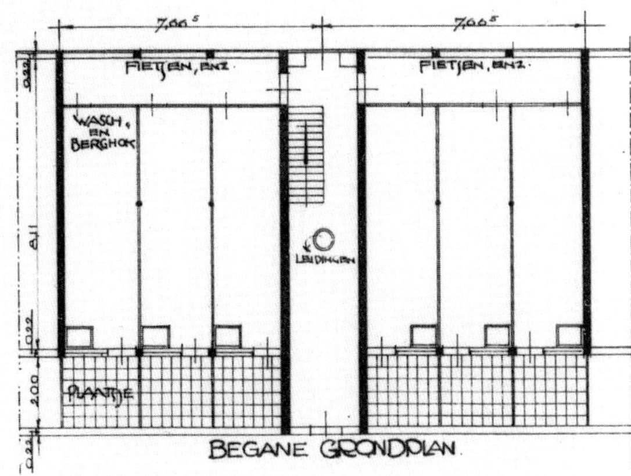

*world lowers the tone of the houses and thus also the whole appearance of the district, resulting in a lowering of the standard of occupants and dwelling. I believe that the solution I now propose will answer this completely, which in this case is all the more important because in the already indicated and still to be explained layout of these blocks I wished to take advantage of the possibilities offered by 'Zeilenbau' (row housing) to make the friendliness that usually characterizes the back side of dwellings – as a result of landscaping – subservient to the general aspect.*[7]
In Blijdorp the contrast between living and utility spaces achieved in the Weissenhof dwellings was largely surrendered, some would say sacrificed, to the architecture of the streetscape. All the dwellings are accessed by stairs leading to both the street and the garden. Living room and kitchen overlook the garden and also have a large balcony. In their totality, the balconies lend the southern facade a sculptural, horizontal rhythm that is in stark contrast with the flat north facade opposite where the only articulation is a vertical window provided by the central staircases. In Blijdorp the typological category of the dwelling has indeed vanished in favour of a new entity, that of the apartment block. The (provisional) main features of this new entity are the collective staircase and individual balconies which, against a background of uniform ribbon windows, reveal in opposite ways the articulation of the blocks into five structural units

**Perspective of courtyard with rows of housing, view from the low-rise development/ OUDJ-bd 15, NAI, Rotterdam**

Perspective of courtyard, view from low-rise development/ OUDJ-bd 13, NAI, Rotterdam

Bird's-eye view/ OUDJ-bd 17, NAI, Rotterdam

(each containing six dwellings). The collective character of the new, urban living arrangement is further confirmed by the arrangement and design of the space between the blocks. In Rotterdam, unlike in Stuttgart, there is no rigorous separation between residential and through traffic streets; on the contrary, the traffic is part of the total composition of garden and street. Actually, the Blijdorp design is not an example of pure row housing since the gardens on the short end-faces are closed off by 'single-storey wings' containing apartments for the elderly and additional bedrooms for the large families housed at either end of each main block. This 'low enclosure' also affords the garden, which connects along its length *with the adjoining street (separated from it by a fence) a measure of tranquillity while at the same time preventing through traffic.* The low-rise block has a tiled roof terrace that links up with the tiled path in front of the laundry areas via an ingenious system of stairs. Just as in Oud's earlier design for the inner courtyards of the Tusschendijken housing blocks, not a metre of the garden–street is left empty: *Rest assured that in the public streets that run between these rows, one-way traffic will be stipulated (and there is nothing against that), so that a single carriageway width of 4.5m will suffice, giving (according to Public Works data) footpaths 2m wide along the houses and 1m wide along the gardens. The advantage of this layout is that the communal gardens brighten up the street and make it seem wider (no dwelling is located on a narrow street as is customary elsewhere), but all look out front and back over wide expanses in which the gardens are located, while at the same time the street traffic is visible, which is something that this category of residents desires. So as not to spoil the appearance of the gardens from the street and of the gardens themselves, the previously mentioned laundries have been placed behind 2m-high walls. It is thus entirely justifiable to forbid the occupants of these blocks to hang washing to dry etc. on the balconies: they have plenty of opportunity for this below and the wall hides all activity of this nature from view. The garden itself is encircled by a tiled path with the occasional bench: children may play there and for this purpose there are one or two sandpits.*[8]

In the end, Oud's design for public housing at Blijdorp was never realized. This was not only because of high land prices and the imposition of tougher building conditions in the new estate, but more especially because of the repercussions of Oud's new subdivision. Although he designed another version of the plan with eight instead of nine blocks, in which numerous architectural details such as the balconies and roof terraces had been scrapped, when it came to tendering, this plan, too, turned out to be too expensive for social housing.[9]

Around 1930, Oud was certainly not the only Dutch architect occupied with the modification of the perimeter block, with new development and subdivision systems, with problems of orientation and of development along through roads. The most radical proposals in this direction were made in the aforementioned preliminary report about *De organische woonwijk in open bebouwing* (Open Planning and the Organic Housing Estate, 1932) in which house building practices in the Netherlands were tested against the 'modern concept of building'. In which context, the experiments in Blijdorp also earned a brief mention: *Its influence (i.e. the open manner of building) is clearly visible in the new development plans of our big cities. The 'Landlust' plan at Amsterdam, for example, is based largely on the new principles (of the 'modern concept of building'). The 'Blijdorp' plan at Rotterdam, having initially been laid out in the form of perimeter blocks with typical 'monumental' intentions, has been recast on several points in the spirit of greater openness, while there has also been no lack of proposals to go even further this direction. However, in this case the defects of the original subdivision present a strong obstacle to sound solutions.*[10] In writing this, Van Tijen (the main author of this report), was probably thinking not only of his own block on Vroeselaan, but also of Oud's blocks. Naturally Oud would, by virtue of his position at the Woningdienst, have been familiar with the main ingredients of what Van Tijen referred to as the 'modern concept of building'. It had been the subject of considerable research by the Woningdienst during the 1920s. The difference was that Oud attempted to realize the solutions arrived at by Van Tijen, Merkelbach, Van den Broek, Van Loghem and others within

**Notes**

**1.** T. Idsinga, J. Schilt, *Architect W. van Tijen 1894-1974,* The Hague, n.d., pp. 249-252.

**2.** E.J. Hoogenberk, *Het idee van de Hollandse stad. Stedebouw in Nederland 1900-1930 met de internationale voorgeschiedenis,* Delft 1980, pp. 141-144.

**3.** W. Kromhout, 'Het plan "Blijdorp" te Rotterdam', in: *Tijdschrift voor Volkshuisvesting en Stedebouw,* 8(1927)5, pp. 106-115.

**4.** J.J. P. Oud, 'Kromhout en zijn tentoonstelling', in: *Nieuwe Rotterdamsche Courant,* 2 October 1924.

**5.** W.G. Witteveen, 'Uitbreidingsplan voor het noordelijk en noordwestelijk stadsdeel (Blijdorp) te Rotterdam', in: *Tijdschrift voor Volkshuisvesting en Stedebouw,* 10(1929)8, pp. 169-179.

the ideals of the hierarchically composed, architectonic streetscape as formulated and executed by Berlage.[11] In Blijdorp Oud was not trying to create an 'organic housing estate' in the sense of an environment in which the various functions of living, working, circulation are integrated in a logical and lucid manner. These were technical questions which, while they impacted on the architecture were not part of its essence. In Blijdorp Oud was concerned with finding a solution to the key question that had occupied him throughout his years at the Woningdienst: that of the relationship between mass housing construction and urban design.



**6.** J.J.P. Oud, Blijdorp explanatory notes, OUDJ-bd 1001, NAI, Rotterdam.
**7.** J.J.P. Oud, Blijdorp explanatory notes, OUDJ-bd 1001, NAI, Rotterdam.
**8.** J.J.P. Oud, Blijdorp explanatory notes, OUDJ-bd 1001, NAI, Rotterdam.
**9.** H.E. Oud, *J.J.P. Oud. Architekt 1890-1963. Feiten en herinneringen gerangschikt,* The Hague 1984, pp. 108-110.
**10.** T. Idsinga, J. Schilt, *Architect W. van Tijen 1894-1974,* The Hague n.d., pp. 249-252.
**11.** E.J. Hoogenberk, *Het idee van de Hollandse stad. Stedebouw in Nederland 1900-1930 met de internationale voorgeschiedenis,* Delft 1980, pp. 254-257.

**Sources**

CCA: dr1984: 0124, dr1984: 0126 – 0143, ph1984: 0898 – 0901, ph1984: 1147 – 1151
Getty: 890126-box 2, F8b, 890126-22**
NAI: OUDJ-bd 1 – 18, OUDJ-bd 1001, OUDJ-ph 1841, OUDJ-B

**Articles**

W. Kromhout, 'Het plan "Blijdorp" te Rotterdam', in: *Tijdschrift voor Volkshuisvesting en Stedebouw,* 8(1927)5, pp. 106-115
W.G. Witteveen, 'Uitbreidingsplan voor het noordelijk en noordwestelijk stadsdeel (Blijdorp) te Rotterdam', in: *Tijdschrift voor Volkshuisvesting en Stedebouw,* 10(1929)8, pp. 169-179

**Literature**

U. Barbieri, *J.J.P. Oud,* Rotterdam 1987, pp. 113-116
M. Casciato (ed.), *Architectuur en Volkshuisvesting. Nederland 1870-1940,* Nijmegen 1980, pp. 149-152
H. Engel, 'De Kiefhoek, monument voor gemiste kansen?', in S. Cusveller (ed.), *De Kiefhoek, een woonwijk in Rotterdam,* Laren 1990, pp. 55-84
L. de Klerk, *Mooi Werk. Geschiedenis van de Maatschappij voor Volkswoningen, Rotterdam 1909-1999,* Rotterdam 1999, pp. 54-58
H.E. Oud, *J.J.P. Oud. Architekt 1890-1963. Feiten en herinneringen gerangschikt,* The Hague 1984, pp. 108-112
G. Stamm, *J.J.P. Oud. Bauten und Projekte 1906 bis 1963,* Mainz, Berlin 1984, pp. 109-110

# 49/ Project for the Kallenbach House

Berlijn, Grünewald

1921-1922

Perspective/ OUDJ-ka 7, NAI, Rotterdam

On 12 October 1921, Oud received a letter from the German architectural critic, Adolf Behne, with a request that he produce an 'Ideenskizze' for a modest, eight-room house in Berlin-Grünewald. The clients – initially Behne spoke only of a musically-inclined lady – had approached the Hungarian painter Moholy-Nagy who had suggested Oud on the strength of an article by Behne about recent architecture in the Netherlands.[1] Oud agreed almost immediately, which was surprising in itself considering the disappointing outcome of a similar commission from the French gallery owner Rosenberg only a few months earlier. It is not inconceivable that, in addition to the name and reputation of Adolf Behne, Oud's ambition to return to private practice tempted him to accept the invitation. The design for Haus Kallenbach marks the moment when Oud set about establishing his career as an international architect in word and deed. Though the design occupies a modest place in the totality of Oud's output, it was something of a succès d'estime in German professional circles and, effectively framed by numerous lectures and illustrated publications, it contributed to the consolidation of a cool, objective ('sachliche') tendency in German architecture of the early 1920s.

Adolf Behne played a crucial role in the introduction of modern Dutch architecture, especially that of Oud, to the German-speaking professional world.[2] Although the correspondence between Behne and Oud did not commence until September 1920, they must have met earlier that year, probably in the summer when Behne, together with his wife, undertook an exhausting tour of the Netherlands, calling on Berlage, Kromhout, Verhagen and Wijdeveld and visiting several Dutch cities including Amsterdam, Alkmaar, Gouda, Bergen and Rotterdam. He was one of the first of a long line of foreigners to visit the summer house at Katwijk and the holiday house at Noordwijkerhout: *I was very pleased with both, not because a certain principle was pursued in these works, but because the designer shows an artistic sensitivity. As it is, I do not know any dogma in the arts. I also visited Park Meerwijk. If I fail to like these buildings, it is not because I am principally opposed to such conceptions, but because I detect little artistic sensitivity in them.*[3] In the winter of 1920-1921 Behne published his impressions in *Feuer* and *Wasmuth's Monatshefte für Baukunst*, the first of a series of articles that was to culminate in 1929 in the celebrated *Holländische Baukunst der Gegenwart*. Although Oud frequently disagreed with Behne, his letters and articles nonetheless contributed to the latter's depiction of Dutch architecture in general and his own in particular. He was especially helpful in acquiring and supplying illustrative material for the book.

Partly thanks to Behne, Oud's name fairly soon became familiar in German architectural and artistic circles, especially those around the Bauhaus. Even though the Berlin-Grünewald project came to nothing, Oud's design certainly did his reputation no harm. Quite the contrary, in fact.

Owing to economic circumstances, very little building was carried out in Germany immediately after the First World War, except in the private sector where the construction of fashionable villas in the leafy suburbs, especially around Berlin, experienced a veritable boom. It is a striking fact, for example, that of 35 projects undertaken by the Gropius/Meyer architectural practice between 1919 and 1925, over half were for free-standing country houses. In her monograph of Adolf Meyer, Annemarie Jaeggi remarked: *In spite of enormous difficulties with regard to the supply of building materials, lower land prices have stimulated investment of capital saved from the war in safe real estate.*[4] So when Gropius and Meyer, who had been invited to submit a sketch design along with Oud and Hilberseimer, addressed themselves to the Kallenbach house, they had little or no practical experience with large-scale public housing construction, but all the more with villa construction. Villa Kallenbach was only one of an impressive series of suburban villas designed by Gropius and Meyer, such as Villa Sommerfeld, Haus Soeckle, Hause Otte, in which they had experimented with numerous stylistic models and patterns and drawn liberally on the Wasmuth 'bible' on the American architect Frank Lloyd Wright. Their clients were academics at the top of the university hierarchy and entrepreneurs who had grown rich during the war. Municipal and building association construction was in any case out of the question until 1925 because of the lack of an adequate financial-economic policy. This meant that in the Weimar Republic –

unlike in the Netherlands – the evolution towards a functionalist, modern architecture did not proceed via public housing construction but via the construction of free-standing, fashionable villas. Many German architects were fascinated by Oud – the correspondence with Behne, Taut and Meyer makes this quite clear – precisely because he had carried out pioneering work in both the collective and the private sector. This also explains the frequent requests for drawings and photographs of Villa Allegonda at Katwijk (just as frequently refused by Oud who did not count it among 'his' designs). Oud was, by force of circumstances, a specialist in what the Germans called 'Siedlungsbau', but had little or no experience with expensive villa construction. Oud was also at this moment, partly under the influence of Van Doesburg, in the process of distancing himself from the method and principles of Frank Lloyd Wright. The invitation to submit a design for a country house in Berlin gave him the opportunity to address himself to other, purely architectural, problems than those of large-scale housing construction. This is evident from the long letter in rather clumsy German that he wrote to Behne (15 October 1921) accepting the commission and requesting further details about the site and orientation: *I was very pleased with your letter and I would very much like to make a sketch of my ideas as requested. For a long time I wanted to produce something that is detached, something that, with my present working team, is not really possible. About four years ago I accepted an appointment by the town council with much enthusiasm and many idealistic expectations, but I feel I have to reconsider my initial opinion that this was the way to achieve the best results. It is not that I am unhappy with the results I have achieved so far; at the time, I desired to build blocks of houses and design street architecture and in that field I have had much more to do than I could possibly have managed as a private architect. However, the problem of town planning has not really been sufficiently solved in my opinion and is too much influenced by restraining circumstances, that more or less harmonious solutions cannot be realized.*[5] What it amounted to, Oud wrote to Behne, was that he had recently come to the conclusion that he knew little about the technical, financial and especially political problems surrounding urban development to be able to realize his architectural ideas and 'einheitliche Gestaltungen' in the townscape. In addition, the government was clearly in the process of withdrawing from the housing market so that there was a danger that before long municipal commissions would dry up. And even if the prospects were not exactly rosy, Oud was seriously thinking about leaving municipal service and setting up as in private practice. Which was why Behne's invitation to make a sketch design for a villa in Berlin was actually quite opportune.

The surviving designs for Haus Kallenbach produced by Gropius/Meyer and Oud illustrate their very different positions, the outcome of their different national and personal histories. The villa designed by the German duo is a good example of the ideal of an 'expressive architecture' pursued by many German architects in the immediate post-war years. It was an architecture completely under the spell of expressive form, which appealed less to reason than to the senses and emotions. In an architecture concerned with form and colour, diagonals played both an organizational and a symbolic role. In Haus Kallenbach as designed by Gropius and Meyer the orthogonal composition of the ground plan is traversed at an angle of 45 degrees by a diagonal system within which house and garden are brought to an abstract unity. Such a projection was a copybook example of Frank Lloyd Wright's version of 'system-based design'. The diagonals also appear to organize the three-dimensional composition of the house but in fact they do so only in a superficial manner. As Nerdinger and Jaeggi have remarked, the numerous triangular bay windows, balconies and alcoves are not the result of the architectural penetration of cubic volumes but are simply appendages and extensions aimed at visual effect: *A penetration of the body is hinted at, rather than actually taking place, for it develops from the framework, not from the volume.*[6] In fact, Gropius and Meyer's Haus Kallenbach appears to have been conceived with little if any thought for the functional requirements of the design brief and more with a view to creating an expressive overall impression, a visually spectacular ensemble. By contrast, Oud, who did not get around to making a detailed perspective drawing in the first round, pro-

duced a design that comes across as extremely cool, sober and functional.
Oud's design scrupulously attempted to satisfy the clients' demands, in particular with regard to location and orientation on the plot and the internal organization of the rooms. It is more than likely that not only Oud but the clients, too, were familiar with Hermann Muthesius's *Wie baue ich mein Haus* (1915) which contained detailed rules regarding 'die Stellung des Hauses auf dem Grundstück' (siting the house on the plot of land). Oud's decision to place the house right at the back of the site and to angle the front facade away from the street, was taken not only with a view to possible future extensions but also for reasons of privacy, sunlighting and use of the garden. These, after all, were the advantages of a detached country house over its city cousin which was compelled to conform to streets and building lines. As Muthesius had written: *As a rule, the prospective resident of a house comes from a town and then it is usually difficult for him to distance himself from his ideas of urban life. One of these ideas is that the front of the house should be facing a street and that the street side of the house is at the same time the side where he lives. This is the situation with a town house. It has houses on both sides and, as the light from the garden is usually less bright than that from the street, the main living rooms should necessarily be on the street side. However, for a country house different conditions apply. It is detached on all sides, no side is at a disadvantage compared with the other three. Consequently, we are offered the possibility of supplying as much air and light to all rooms as is desired. Another consequence is that the four sides can be made use of effectively, depending on the difference in exposure to the sun. This means that rooms where the sun is most required, are planned on the side with more sunshine, and those rooms that can do with less sunlight on the sides that are less exposed to the sun. Sunlight is required in all living rooms and bedrooms, it is less necessary in most other rooms. A second advantage of a country house, at least as important, is that direct access from the house to the surrounding garden can always be created. After all, the garden, this must be stressed, is an*

Various design views/ OUDJ-ka 4, NAI, Rotterdam



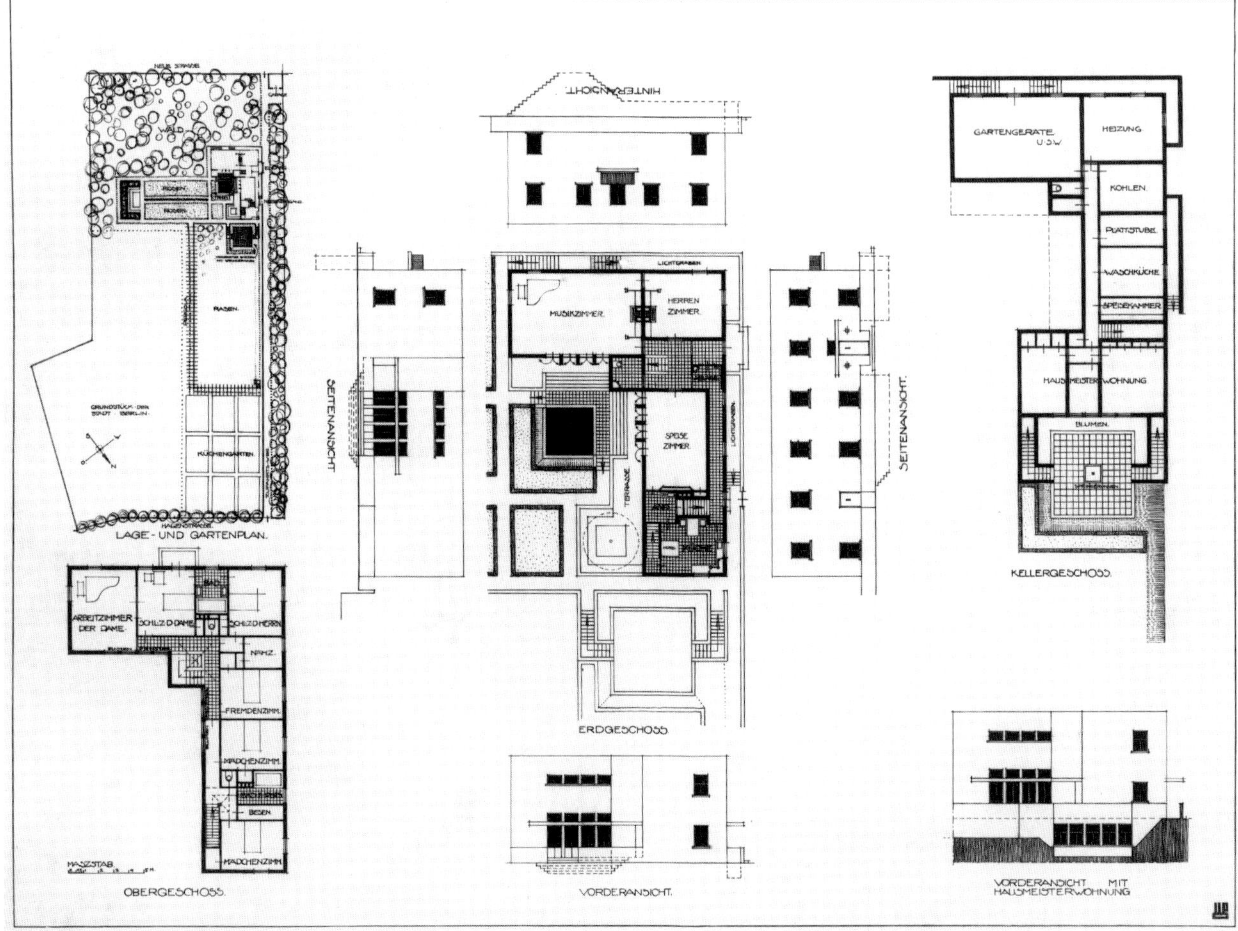

*inseparable part of the country house: a house without a garden will never be a country house.*[7]
The house itself, also in the spirit of the German version of the English country house propagated by Muthesius, is designed as a symmetrically organized, angular building. The two most important formal rooms – the music room and dining room – are symmetrically balanced around the axis which runs from the internal angle via the windowless staircase to link the house with terraces, pool and rose beds. The concentration of living in the angle is reinforced architecturally by the concrete cantilevers above the French windows, a horizontal accent that balances the vertical column of the staircase. House and gardens were originally designed on a module of 1.10 metres; later, at the request of Kallenbach, who probably found the house too compact vis à vis its surroundings, this was changed to 1.20 metres and even, to Oud's distress, to 1.30 metres. Because Kallenbach did not wish to adjust the height of the house and the individual rooms accordingly, the building was in danger of becoming seriously out of proportion, especially since the original module not only guaranteed the harmonious proportions of the individual rooms but also determined the layout of the facades and the dimensions of smaller parts, from windows to individual sanitary fittings.
One of the most unexpected components of the plan concerned the facilities for the servants. The main servants' rooms were located in the basement, including the flat for the 'Hausmeister'. Daylight entered via large 'light trenches' (Lichtgräben) running part-way round the house. In addition, the service flat opened into a sunken garden with flower-boxes and fountain *so that the servants, too, might have the opportunity of sitting outside in summer in the vicinity of the house without either group of occupants (family members and servants) experiencing any loss of freedom.*[8]
Although Oud emerged the winner from the invited competition, he derived little pleasure from the Berlin adventure. On 31 January 1922, Kallenbach informed Oud via Moholy-Nagy that he wished to consult with him; the meeting duly took place on 25 February in Berlin. Despite the fact that Kallenbach had already followed Oud's advice and engaged a local architect to supervise construction, it was still quite uncertain whether the project would go ahead. Kallenbach also felt that the rooms on the ground floor should be more spacious.[9] Back in the Netherlands, Oud made two new series of drawings in which the whole building, in response to the demand for larger rooms, was based on the desired modules of 1.20 and 1.30 metres. In the smaller version, which Oud preferred, the smoking room was 4.25 by 5.40 metres; the dining room 4.40 by 7 metres; the music room 9.20 by 5.40 metres. Oud wrote that he thought these proportions very fine, actually better than in the original plan.[10] He posted the new drawings and an accompanying letter on 12 March after which nothing more happened. On 9 May he received a long letter from Moholy-Nagy who had just spo-

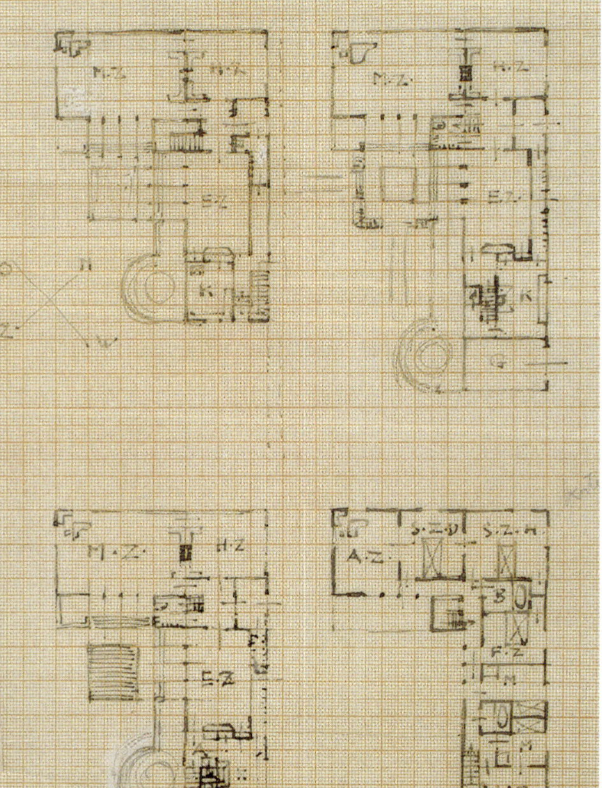

Ground floor and basement (bottom right)/ 0.415 B.2, Letterkundig Museum, The Hague

Design for corner dwelling/ OUDJ-hw 5, NAI, Rotterdam



**Notes**
**1.** A. Behne to J.J.P. Oud, 21 October 1921, Letterkundig Museum, The Hague.
**2.** A. Behne, *Architekturkritik in der Zeit und über die Zeit hinaus: 1913-1946*, Basle, Bern, Boston 1994; A. Behne, *The Modern Functional Building* (Texts & Documents. Introduction by Rosemarie Haag Bletter. Translation by Michael Robinson; The Getty Research Institute for the History of Art), Santa Monica 1996.
**3.** A. Behne to J.J.P. Oud, 3 October 1921, Letterkundig Museum, The Hague.
**4.** A. Jaeggi, *Adolf Meyer, der zweite Mann. Ein Architekt im Schatten von Walter Gropius*, Berlin 1994, p. 139.
**5.** J.J.P. Oud to A. Behne, 15 October 1921, OUDJ-B, NAI, Rotterdam.
**6.** A. Jaeggi, *Adolf Meyer, der zweite Mann. Ein Architekt im Schatten von Walter Gropius*, Berlin 1994, pp. 147-150; W. Nerdinger, *Walter Gropius*, Cambridge (Mass.), Berlin 1985/ 1986, pp. 48-51; W. Pehnt, *Die Architektur des Expressionismus*, Stuttgart 1998, pp. 113-115.
**7.** H. Muthesius, *Wie baue ich mein Haus. Berufserfahrungen und Radschläge eines Architekten*, Munich 1925 (4), p. 80.
**8.** J.J.P. Oud, 'Ontwerp voor een landhuis in Berlijn', in: *Bouwkundig Weekblad*, 43(1922)35, p. 344.

ken to Kallenbach and from the latter's attitude had formed the impression that it would be fruitless to invest any more energy in the project. Oud had already reached this conclusion himself and in April had informed Kallenbach in writing – with a copy to Moholy-Nagy – that he wished to withdraw from the project.[11]
The somewhat disappointing outcome of the Kallenbach project was by no means the end of Oud's activities in Germany. At the precise moment when Oud and Kallenbach were arguing about the dimensions of the latter's villa, Oud was negotiating with Adolf Meyer – his rival in the invited competition for the Kallenbach house, no less – about the German translation of his 'Opbouw' lecture. This was published in *Frühlicht* in the summer of 1922, despite the disapproval of the editor-in-chief, Bruno Taut.[12] The main illustration was Oud's design for Haus Kallenbach, for which occasion Oud probably also got around to making the fine perspective drawing. The German version of Oud's text, meticulously translated (and edited) by Meyer, together with the drawings for Haus Kallenbach, formed the core of the countless lectures Oud went on to hold in the ensuing years in numerous places and on all manner of occasions in Germany, beginning with the celebrated Bauhauswoche in Weimar in the summer of 1923. Even before the publication in Germany, Oud's 'design for a private house in Berlin' appeared in *Bouwkundig Weekblad* with the same illustrations. It prompted a spontaneous, if somewhat cryptic, response from Gerrit Rietveld: *I consider your house above all honest in the sense of straight. That long facade put me in mind of palazzo Strozzi in Florence, not because of any similarity in outward appearance, but as pure stylistic expression without trimmings – And so it goes throughout the house. – it's almost intentionally unintentional. Oh yes, that's what I wanted to say to you. Be especially careful not to see too much unintentionality in mechanical things. They are less that at the moment than you and I for example – More about this anon. Isn't the pool a bit small? This corner [line to a sketch of the concrete edge of the centrally situated pool] seems to me something of a central point on the garden side and that being so I'm bothered by that point created underneath by the steps. Perhaps I still need to get over that. For the rest all I wish is to see it finished.* [13]
Rietveld's remarks about 'unintentionality', a much-discussed theme within *De Stijl* circles, probably had less to do with the architecture of Haus Kallenbach than with one or two passages from Oud's lecture, 'Over de toekomstige bouwkunst en hare architectonische mogelijkheden', which also appeared in the same issue of *Bouwkundig Weekblad.*



**9.** H. Kallenbach to J.J.P. Oud, 13 February 1922, OUDJ-B, NAI, Rotterdam.
**10.** J.J.P. Oud to H. Kallenbach, 12 March 1922, OUDJ-B, NAI, Rotterdam. The series of drawings is in the Letterkundig Museum in The Hague.
**11.** L. Moholy-Nagy to J.J.P. Oud, 9 May 1922, OUDJ-B, NAI, Rotterdam.
**12.** The correspondence between Oud and Adolf Meyer (January-May 1922), together with several draft versions of the translation, are in the Oud Archive in the NAI in Rotterdam. The translation appeared under the title '"Uber die zukünftige Baukunst und ihre architektonische Möglichkeiten" Ein Programm von J.J.P. Oud. Leiter des städtischen Bauamts in Rotterdam', in: *Frühlicht* (1921/22)4, pp. 113-118; A. Jaeggi, *Adolf Meyer, der zweite Mann. Ein Architekt im Schatten von Walter Gropius,* Berlin 1994, pp. 152-154.
**13.** G. Rietveld to J.J.P. Oud, 24 April 1922, OUDJ-B, NAI, Rotterdam.

**Sources**
CCA: dr1984: 0028, dr1984: 0507
Getty: 890126-box 7-9*
NAI: OUDJ-ka 1-8, OUDJ-ph 1676, OUDJ-ph 1830, OUDJ-ph 1862, OUDJ-26, OUDJ-B

**Articles**
J.J.P. Oud, 'Ontwerp voor een landhuis in Berlijn', in: *Bouwkundig Weekblad,* 43(1922)35, p. 344

**Literature**
U. Barbieri, *J.J.P. Oud,* Rotterdam 1987, pp. 50-51
H.E. Oud, *J.J.P. Oud. Architekt 1890-1963. Feiten en herinneringen gerangschikt,* The Hague 1984, pp. 72-73
S. Polano, *J.J.P. Oud Architettura Olandese,* Milan 1981, p. 86
G. Stamm, *J.J.P. Oud. Bauten und Projekte 1906 bis 1963,* Mainz, Berlin 1984, pp. 54-57

# Design for a private house in Berlin

The accompanying design for a private house at Grünewald in Berlin came about as the result of an invitation to participate in a limited entry competition, together with Gropius and Hilbersheimer. After it had been selected for construction, several difficulties arose which caused me to decide against realization. The plans to build were later abandoned.

For the genesis of the design, the following is of importance.

The building site was enclosed front and back by roads, on either side by open development; the plot was L-shaped and house and garden had to be so placed that enlargement of the construction as a result of the later addition of a smaller plot that would turn the original plot into a near square, remained possible. At the rear of the site were pine trees; along this ran a forest road (Neue Strasse).

To allow the garden to profit from the sun, the house was placed as close as possible to the north-west boundary. Only a windbreak and driveway running from front to back are on this side which is 'closed' in terms of architecture and consequently also conceived as more or less "official"; the living quarters are more "open" to the garden which is separated from the driveway by low walls.

The siting of the house at the back of the plot was dictated by the wish to be as far as possible from the main road and to spare as many trees as possible. In order that the fairly close proximity of the forest road should not result in undue loss of freedom for the occupants, the house was designed as an L-shape so that day-to-day domestic activities can take place in the inner angle of the building free from the curiosity of passers-by.

In this corner, therefore, the domestic life of the family is concentrated: music room and dining room with terraces in front are there; steps lead down from this to the path around a pond sited approximately 80 cm below ground level; rose beds are located opposite the big doors topped by an awning and flower-box windows.

Underpinning the interior layout was the wish for spacious rooms that could be served by a small staff. Hall and corridors were consequently kept to a minimum; the service corridor between hall and kitchens, also including the service entrance (and the entrance to the caretaker's flat), was required to insulate the dining room against the north-west. Various service quarters, etc., are located in the basement and illuminated by big "light trenches" ("Lichtgräben"). The caretaker's flat, which was also located in the basement, imposed higher demands regarding lighting levels, and so prompted the design of a sunken garden with flower boxes and fountain and accessible by an outdoor flight of stairs, so that the servants, too, might have the opportunity of sitting outside in summer in the vicinity of the house without either group of occupants (family members and servants) experiencing any loss of freedom. In order that this sunken garden should not end up looking like a hole or a grotto, the lawn ("der Rasen") in front was excavated to half the depth of the sunken garden; the difference in height with the adjoining ground-level garden areas was solved by inserting a pergola (right on the boundary of the possible additional plot) from where one has a view over the lower-lying garden section.

On the upper floor, around the upper hall, are the living areas and bedrooms of the family members; on the other side, more to the front, are the servants' living quarters accessed by a separate service stair; the two sections of the upper floor are completely separated from one another by a door across the corridor. The upper hall has flower-box windows and light from above.

The house is conceived in white with iron window and door frames and the doors entirely flat and painted in a bright colour. Internally all the necessary services etc. were projected as much as possible as built-in and -on; the lower and upper halls were intended to be laid with marble; the furniture, as much as possible fixed, was designed in relation to the whole.

J.J.P. OUD

In the 1920s, modernism had all the appearances of an international movement. Avant-garde groups sprang up everywhere, as often as not around magazines dedicated to reporting on what was happening in other countries. One of the most active 'cells' was in the Czech city of Brno, the capital of Moldavia. Oud soon came into contact with his Czech counterparts and in 1924 and 1925, as part of a lecture series entitled 'For a New Architecture', he gave his celebrated lecture on 'The Development of Modern Architecture in the Netherlands' in Prague and Brno.[1] In 1928, his contacts with central European architects brought him a commission to design an apartment complex in Brno. Precise details about the commissioning situation in Brno are unknown, but the typology of the building Oud designed suggests the world of private clients where real estate was regarded as a sound investment. Oud's design can be viewed as an attempt to combine the principles of urban housing and villa construction recently worked out and applied respectively in Stuttgart and Berlin. Unlike the 1917 design for an apartment complex at Scheveningen, where the individual dwellings occupied several floors and were linked side by side, at Brno Oud opted for one dwelling per floor, stacked one on top of the other above a communal ground floor containing the porter's flat, garage, laundry area and storage space. The advantage of this set-up was that the individual dwellings were less fragmented. As in Villa Kallenbach, he made separate living arrangements for residents and their servants. The two groups were accommodated in separate wings which ran parallel to one another and were partially staggered. The area where the two wings met contained the central circulation system: the main residents' staircase, the service lift and the lobby. Around this zone were grouped the kitchens, dining rooms and living rooms of the various apartments. The bedrooms were located at the far ends of each wing. At the end of the servants' wing was a separate staircase for staff. 'Service' areas such as the servants' wing, the main entrance, the entrance to the garage and the corridor serving the bedrooms, were all located on the street side. The three bedrooms, living room and dining room faced the garden. The connection between apartment and garden was strengthened by balconies running the full length of the residents' wing and providing direct access to the garden. To safeguard the residents' privacy on the garden side, the windows in the garden elevation of the servants' wing were very small. For the same reason, the previously planned roof terrace on this wing was scrapped. Instead, Oud allocated the narrow garden on the street side as a recreation area for servants.[2]

Isometric projection/ OUDJ-hb 1, NAI, Rotterdam



**Notes**

**1.** The information about modern architecture in Czechoslovakia and Poland comes from: W. Lesnikowski (et al.), *East European Modernism. Architecture in Czechoslovakia, Hungary & Poland between the Wars 1919-1939*, London 1996 and V. Slapeta (et al.), *Die Brünner Funktionalisten. Moderne Architektur in Brünn (Brno)*, Innsbruck 1985. For the Czech magazines see also: D. Elliot (et al.), *Devetsil. Czech avant-garde art, architecture and design of the 1920s and 30s*, London 1990.

**2.** J.J.P. Oud, 'O budoucím stavitelství a jeho architektonickych moznostech', in: *Stavba*, 1(1922)10, pp. 177-192.

**Sources**

The Carnegie Museum of Art (Pittsburgh, PA), The Heinz Architectural Center: 94.37
CCA: dr1984: 0096-0097, dr1984: 0099-0103
Getty: 890126-19*
NAI: OUDJ-hb 1-6

**Articles**

J.J.P. Oud, 'O budoucím stavitelství a jeho architektonickych moznostech', in: *Stavba*, 1(1922)10, pp. 177-192

**Literature**

U. Barbieri, *J.J.P. Oud*, Rotterdam 1987, p. 192
D. Elliot (et al.), *Devetsil. Czech avant-garde art, architecture and design of the 1920s and 30s*, London 1990
W. Lesnikowski (et al.), *East European Modernism. Architecture in Czechoslovakia, Hungary & Poland between the Wars 1919-1939*, London 1996
H.E. Oud, *J.J.P. Oud, Feiten en herinneringen gerangschikt*, The Hague 1984, p. 108
V. Slapeta (et al.), *Die Brünner Funktionalisten. Moderne Architektur in Brünn (Brno)*, Innsbruck 1985
V. Slapeta (et al.), *Czech Functionalism 1918-1938*, London 1987
G. Stamm, *J.J.P. Oud. Bauten und Projekten*, Mainz, Berlin 1984, p. 109

## 51/ House for Mrs H.H. Johnson

Pinehurst,
North Carolina, USA

1931

Perspective of living room/ Royal Institute of British Architects, London

In the autumn of 1931, Oud worked feverishly on the design of a house for the mother of Philip Johnson. Oud had first come into contact with Johnson in 1930 via the art and architectural historian Henry-Russel Hitchcock. It was the start of a long friendship. Drawings and a model of the house were exhibited in the *Modern Architecture – International Exhibition* that opened at the Museum of Modern Art in New York on 9 February 1932.[1] The commission for the house and the invitation to take part in the exhibition illustrate the international impact of Oud's work after his success at the Weissenhofsiedlung in Stuttgart. More importantly, however, Oud, thanks partly to the Americans, acquired a different perspective on the contemporary architectural scene in Europe and on his own place within it. While Lewis Mumford and Catherine Bauer, the militant champions of the 'Modern Housing' movement in the United States, were primarily interested in Oud as a social housing reformer, Johnson and Hitchcock propagated a typically art-historical picture of Oud's architecture which, with its explicit qualities of form, colour, proportion and materials seemed certain to appeal to an affluent American public.[2] Oud's meticulously designed buildings – together with the architecture of Mies van der Rohe and Le Corbusier – featured largely in the promotion of modern architecture in the United States in that they provided an alternative to the more radical tendencies in European architecture geared to technology, function and construction (Gropius, Hannes Meyer, Stam and Giedion) for which there was scant interest in America.

The American appreciation and interpretation did not fail to have an effect on Oud. In the very years when he was trying to get away from the Woningdienst and was setting up in private practice in a leafy Rotterdam suburb, they prompted a radical reversal in his ideas about architecture. It is beyond dispute that in the years between 1927 and 1932, under the influence of the Americans, Oud finally turned his back on the period of purification, searching and experimentation and turned to the professional refinement and completion of modern building as style. It was a tendency that he also saw around him in the Netherlands (Groep '32) and in Europe and of which he regarded himself, along with Mies van der Rohe, as a key protagonist and 'leader'. This at least is the import of an essay on 'De Nieuwe Bouwkunst Beweging in Europa' (The New Architectural Movement in Europe) published in 1933 and again in 1935. The essay ('sermon' according to Donald Langmead) ends on a prophetic note: *When I cast an eye over the movement as a whole (whereby I take the liberty of including for the sake of completeness the important activity in America and Japan), I am delighted to be able to conclude that aesthetic experiments of all kinds are increasingly disappearing in favour of working according to universal guidelines: that art is slowly but surely turning into style.*[3]

Oud never set foot in America. Although the trip to the United States was as natural for architects in the twentieth century as a trip to Italy had been in earlier centuries, Oud declined every invitation to visit or settle there. His poor state of health and the lack of social security were the main reasons. However, this did nothing to diminish his fascination with the country – with the metropolitan culture of jazz, film, detective stories, advertising and clothing. Oud's knowledge of American architecture came from magazines (*Architectural Record*, *Bouwbedrijf* and others) and from his many foreign friends: in the first instance Erich Mendelsohn, Karl Lönberg-Holm, Werner Hegemann and Frederik Kiesler, and in the second Lewis Mumford, Henry-Russell Hitchcock and Philip Johnson. Between 1923 and 1925, he received lively reports from the young Danish architect Karl Lönberg-Holm who informed him about the state of American architecture, architectural education, the work practices of the big architectural firms, the personality of Wright, popular Wright imitations, and, of course, about the futuristic qualities of the American street- and cityscape where traffic, car parks, advertising, automobiles and movie houses seemed like an early fulfilment of all the promises of European modernism. *The hygienic, clean interiors are unforgettable. The toilets in the stations (built, or rather decorated, in the style of Roman baths), lunchrooms, subways, new tramcars, factories, offices. Most of Europe's attempts at modernization have already been solved here. In Europe it remains a formalism. Here it taken for granted, an everyday thing. And in accordance with the age-old law of action and reaction,*

*Americans look back longingly to the Romantic past. Hence the town hall basement in the Woolworth building (executed in extravagant neo-gothic style and labelled by Mendelsohn in his book as 'The tragic expression of present-day America'). Photos of the 'Ford factory' where I consume my daily portion of calories – a micro-world of nickel, glass and stone, a machine for eating (Corbusier-Saugnier) – would put the whole Bauhaus exhibition in the shade.*[4] Lönberg-Holm illustrated his letters with fascinating photographs which ended up, via Oud, in Erich Mendelsohn's *Amerika: Bilderbuch eines Architekten* (1926).[5]
Oud also received visits from many American architects and critics, especially after the first publications (1928 and 1929) of the young American art historian Henry-Russell Hitchcock who came into contact with Oud in 1927, once again via Berlage. The year 1929 saw the publication of Hitchcock's Ph.D. thesis *Modern Architecture: Romanticism and Reintegration*, that indirectly led to the major exhibition on modern architecture in New York in 1932. Hitchcock had previously asked Oud for photographic material, in particular of his own (early) work to which Hitchcock had devoted a separate chapter of his book. This had appeared in February 1928, as a prepublication, in the American art journal *The Arts*.[6] This article presented an interpretation of Oud's architectural development and the qualities of the individual buildings that was completely at variance with European opinion. In Hitchcock's view (which for once was never contradicted by Oud), the true watershed in Oud's development, as also for Le Corbusier and Gropius, was the year 1922. On this reading, the Witte Dorp marks the moment when Oud distances himself from the rejection of the romantic tendencies in contemporary architecture and for the first time exploits the 'vocabulary' developed in Spangen and Tusschendijken in a truly convincing manner. It ushers in a phase of purification that was to bring Oud, via the site manager's hut at the Witte Dorp and the facade of Café De Unie, to the total mastery of form, colour, proportion and materials exhibited at Hoek van Holland (1926) where Oud realized the architectural equivalent of abstract painting. It was Hitchcock who drew Oud's attention to the fact that in the housing block at Hoek van Holland – and to a lesser extent in the design for the Rotterdam Exchange – the architectural possibilities of the architecture of the future were established once and for all. As an art historian of American origin, with a sound schooling in the Anglo-Saxon tradition of scholarship and aesthetics, Hitchcock was interested in the aesthetic manipulation of the technical framework of architecture, by which he meant not so much matters like construction or standardization, as the subtle treatment of (glazed) shop fronts, steel window frames and the architectural handling of colour: *Here is the complete master of the new manner now devoid of even such inherited elements as tiled roofs and wooden window frames: and at last he is content to let color speak discreetly, as in all good architecture. The yellow brick basement, the dark grey band beside the blue door, the black iron work with merely a touch of red about the lighting fixtures, provide against the reduced white plaster quite enough color in these exquisite buildings. The ribbon windows and the long balconies made possible by the reënforced concrete construction are used to emphasize the subtlety of proportions now magnificently simple: while in the corner stores the necessary elements of construction are turned into positively lyric ornament. These buildings are surely of a quality equal to any which the new manner has achieved in France or Germany.*[7]
Oud was understandably flattered by this publication. When in 1928 André Lurçat, the editor of the 'Les Maîtres de l'Architecture Moderne' series published by the French *Cahiers d'Art*, approached him about the possibility of a book about his work, he nominated Hitchcock as author even though Lurçat had intended entrusting the introduction to Piet Mondrian.[8] The upshot was that Hitchcock expanded his existing text by a few pages and – at Oud's direction – revised it. He also asked Oud to furnish the illustrations. To underscore his thesis about Oud's heroic struggle with Berlagian romanticism, he suggested including some of the early designs that he had evidently seen at Oud's home, such as the competition designs for a bath house and for an elderly people's home at Hilversum (cat. nos. 24, 26). He also asked for new illustrations of the villa at Katwijk and especially of Haus Kallenbach in Berlin which Hitchcock considered illustrative of Oud's second period, that of intellectual

catharsis and experimentation with a new aesthetic vocabulary.[9] Such interventions were not without repercussions. Precisely in the years when the relationship with Berlage reached crisis point and the place Oud had accorded himself in the prevailing, strongly personalized history of contemporary architecture was consequently starting to look rather shaky, Hitchcock sketched a different historical picture of his development. One in which the view of contemporary architecture (shared by Oud) as a historical development dominated by a 'sort of father–son relationship' was exchanged for an objective, art-historical process of styles. Now Oud's entire architectural output could be easily slotted into the early historiography of the Modern Movement. Thanks to Hitchcock Oud, together with Gropius, Le Corbusier and Mies van der Rohe, was proclaimed a 'New Pioneer'.

In the young Philip Johnson, Hitchcock's interpretation and eloquent presentation of Oud's architectural 'performance' effected a 'Saul–Paul conversion', as he was to describe it in 1982, in a *festschrift* devoted to Hitchcock.[10] In the summer of 1930 Johnson and Hitchcock toured Europe looking at the work of 'the finest masters among the moderns': Le Corbusier, Gropius and Oud. It was during this study tour, which included a visit to Oud in Rotterdam, that the two men hit upon the idea of a new, more generally accessible edition of Hitchcock's thesis. The result was *The International Style* (1932), a book which, though separate from the exhibition and catalogue of the famous 1932 MOMA exhibition, certainly influenced the format of the exhibition.[11] Both Hitchcock and Johnson consulted closely with Oud on the content and layout of this publication. As the previously quoted letter of August 1930 from Hitchcock to Oud makes clear, the two authors considered a variety of titles such as *Architecture Still* and *Doch noch ein Baustil*, working titles that underscore the polemical nature of the project and show to what extent it was no longer, in 1930, the academism of the architecture of historical styles against which the 'Modern Movement' set itself, but rather the 'anti-aesthetic functionalist' movement within its own ranks, headed by S. Giedion. In the end it was Johnson who used Hitchcock's picture of Oud as an international, modern architect in his fight against the conservatism and romanticism of historical styles in American architecture: as *curator* through the organization of the MOMA exhibition (1932) and the accompanying publications; as *patron* through the commissioning of a house for his mother and through countless attempts to arrange guest lectureships as well as official university appointments.[12]

In the two hectic years leading up to the big exhibition, Johnson and Oud maintained a lively correspondence that sheds an unprecedented light on the American contribution to the Modern Movement's change of course and on the consequences this had for Oud's national, and more especially, international reputation. The letters leave no doubt that Johnson wanted to present Oud (together with Mies van der Rohe) to the American public as the chief protagonist of 'the modern style', in the realization of which he left no stone unturned. From one of the earliest letters Johnson wrote to Oud (July 1930) it would appear that Oud's *Bauhausbuch* (1926) served as a model for Johnson and Hitchcock's joint enterprise. Johnson had even started on an English translation but found Oud's text too complicated. The original plan was to produce a book featuring eighty photographs of 'the masterpieces in the style' accompanied by a short and accessible introduction by Hitchcock. The principal aim was to make 'propaganda for modern architecture in America'. But there was also a German market for the taking, not only for Oud – about whose qualities, according to Johnson, the

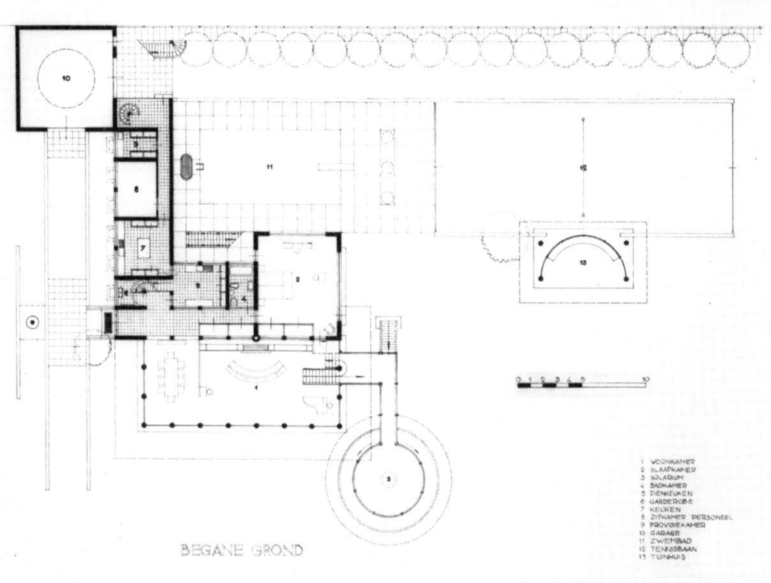


Plan of ground floor/ OUDJ-vj 5, NAI, Rotterdam

German public was completely ignorant – but also for Hitchcock who, with a German edition of the book could capture a place in German architectural criticism. But neither critics nor publishers in Germany were much interested in a project Johnson described in a letter to Oud as follows: *Of course the criticism will be purely aesthetic much to the distress of our German sachlich friends who think of nothing but sociology. We want to discuss new materials, brick again and tile etc.; then colors and street planning. But principally the aesthetic foundation of the style. The German critics are too apt to claim that the style has other than aesthetic foundations, whereas the point of the book will be to show just what this aesthetic foundations is and how it came about.*[13] Even specialist German publishers, used as they were to the books of Behrendt, Behne, Platz, Gropius, Muthesius, Giedion and Mendelsohn, were reticent: *A great criticism of the book here seems to be that we have no Rote Fade in the book: it is just to be a collection of photographs plus some abstruse criticism; the public will not buy such a book unless there is some catch word such as Eisen und Eisenbeton. In vain do we tell the publishers that it will be the first book to deal with the style as a whole in the world and with nothing but the style, nothing by Dudok, nothing by Mallet-Stevens, nothing like the Swedish Town Hall. But apparently the purity of the book has not any appeal to the publishers in Germany.*[14] Johnson also asked Oud if he had any suggestions for the book but Oud replied that he would prefer to write such a book himself. By which he was probably referring to the essay on European architecture that appeared in 1933 in the English magazine *Studio* and which, after Johnson's unsuccessful efforts to get it published in America, appeared in a longer Dutch version in 1935.[15] Oud also expressed surprise about the book's working title: *Why are people not more interested in books with titles containing words like 'Gestaltung', 'dynamic', 'Seele' or 'Raumgefühl'. 'Modern man, wrote Döblin, 'has solved all problems by setting them to one side and making toothpaste instead.'*[16]

As might be expected, there was close consultation about the way Oud's work should be presented both in the book

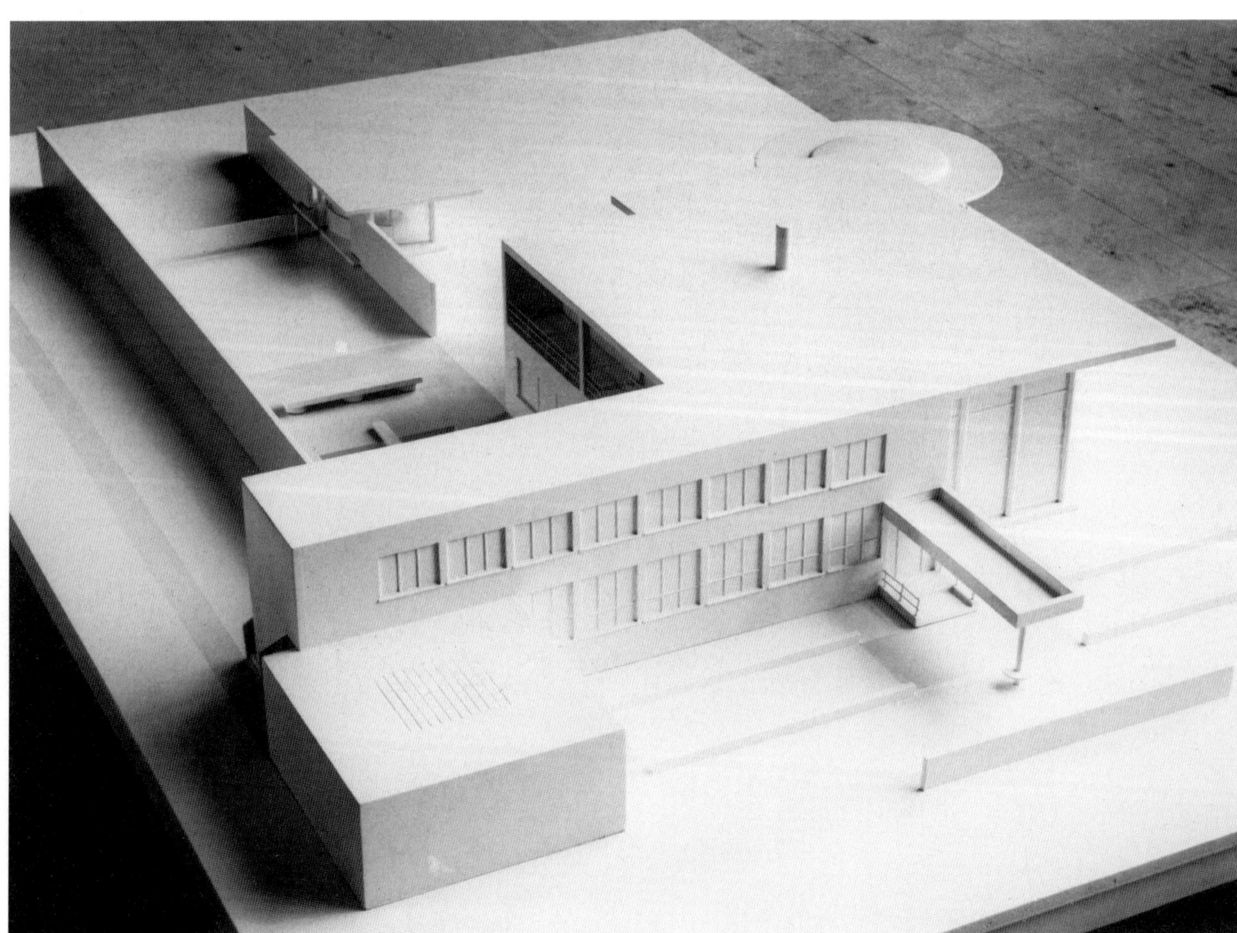

Model (NAI, MAQV-272), probably 1951/ OUDJ-ph 438, NAI, Rotterdam

and in the exhibition. The two-stage design of the Villa Allegonda at Katwijk played a crucial though controversial role in these negotiations (cat. no. 29). It must have been rather galling for Oud to find a building to which he had contributed relatively little as architect the object of so much attention in the international architectural world. The house attracted a succession of celebrated visitors such as Alfred Roth – who encountered his first Mondrian painting at the Villa – Bruno Taut, Adolf Behne, Hannes Meyer, Erich Mendelsohn, and of course Hitchcock and later Philip Johnson.[17] Oud also had great difficulty preventing the house from appearing under his name in foreign magazines and books. For Johnson and Hitchcock the Katwijk summer house was a compelling example for the American public of how easily the 'modern style' could be incorporated into one's own home. Johnson's reasoning failed to convince Oud: *I can understand your not wanting to publish the Katwijk house,* Johnson wrote on the boat going back to New York, *but we wanted it to show two things: the birth and development of the modern aesthetic, and the best* Umbau. *The difference for instance, between the east porch (1927-1931) and the west porch (1917), is the difference between the fully completed idea of no-weight as against the uncompleted attempt to reach this feeling ... The post on the west porch are thick and obviously support the roof. The post on the east give only definition to the surfaces, and the porch is a volume and not a weight. Then also Katwijk* is of such early date. *...Then again Katwijk is an* Umbau. *What can be done simply with an old house to make it absolutely modern?*[18] Oud remained adamant however and the Katwijk villa was withheld from the American public.

The discussion concerning the content and intention of the book and how best to present Oud's work in the exhibition, formed the real backdrop to the design of a house for Mrs H.H. Johnson at Pinehurst, North Carolina. From the moment that the idea for an exhibition was born, it was clear that the core would consist of a series of models of realized designs. In June 1930, during Johnson's first visit (in the company of Hitchcock) to Oud in Rotterdam, some months before he saw Mies van der Rohe's Villa Tugendhat

**Model (NAI, MAQV-272), probably 1951/ OUDJ-ph 437, NAI, Rotterdam**

Model (NAI, MAQV-272), probably 1951/
OUDJ-ph 439, NAI, Rotterdam

in Brno, he sounded Oud out about designing a house for his family. The model and drawings would be included in the MOMA exhibition. On 12 June Johnson wrote to his mother: *If we ever, ever build, I would have perfect confidence in him even on the other side of the ocean, something which I can not say of Le Corbusier.*[19] At that point he had not yet been to Brno and it is possible that, in retrospect, he regretted asking Oud rather than Mies van der Rohe to be his architect. What Oud thought about the commission can be gauged from a letter of 12 November of the same year. It was the period when he was toiling over the Blijdorp housing scheme (cat. no. 48) and looking forward to finally being able to make a major building: *I think I could do now a big thing after so many experiences with other things and it must be 'herrlich' to make important buildings in good material, to make 'Raum' has also to do something with architecture and until now the 'Raum' I could make were nearly only streets: interesting also of course but it has to be combined with 'Raum' inside also and the labour dwellings of very low prices are not the best objects for this.*[20] This enthusiasm was not immediately translated into concrete plans. As so often in Oud's career, he now tried to duck earlier agreements, much to the dismay of Johnson who wrote him on 8 July: *So you see how important it is for my head and position to get the model. And I am sure you underestimate the importance of it for yourself. After all consider that I am propagating* only you and Mies van der Rohe.[21] The first sketches date from just before the end of that month and may also have been discussed with Johnson. The actual design process did not get under way until the moment when Johnson had wanted to have the model in New York. It was not until 12 December 1931, after numerous agitated telegrams from New York, that the final design drawings were ready to be passed on to the model builder.
In this spacious villa designed for an American clientele, Oud abandoned the radical principle of *Elementare Gestaltung* that he had developed in the Exchange design. If anything, the design is a somewhat contrived application of the aesthetic principles of volume, rhythm and texture formulated by Hitchcock and Johnson in *The International Style*. It can also be seen as a frank 'conversation piece' in which Oud comments on the solutions of other 'leaders' of the modern style: Frank Lloyd Wright, Le Corbusier and above all Mies van der Rohe. Mies inspired the spacious, completely open living and dining room; Le Corbusier the expressive gesture of the internal and external stair; Wright the 'free-standing pavilion' of the sun room. The references are purely associative and are evidently intended to stamp Villa Johnson as a 'key monument' of the emergent International Style.
Despite Oud's repeated requests for photographs and maps of the site, he finally had to make do with a cursory land registry map and verbal information from Johnson. Oud placed the house on the north-west side of the plot so as to afford the living room maximum profit from garden and sunlight. The villa is wedged into a right angle between two driveways so that the garage – replete with a mechanical turntable – functions literally as a hinge. On the north side a low wall, swimming pool and tennis court block the view of the 'very ugly' neighbouring development.[22] Domestic activity is concentrated in the rectangular living room which offers unrestricted views of the surrounding landscape on three sides. Here the villa presents itself as an *open* house: that is to say as an ensemble that does all it can to facilitate diverse contacts between the house's occupants, guests and staff. The large living space extends over two storeys, is devoid of columns and dividing walls and has a slightly centrifugal effect because of the free-standing stair leading to the sun room and to the balcony and guest rooms. Spiral and straight-run stairs also dominate the facade architecture and afford *'free' access to the garden or the swimming pool* from the servants' wing, master bedroom and sun room. Not all solutions seem equally felicitous. Because the client wanted an all-round view from the living room, the sun room was detached from the house and set on a sizeable column, but whether this is to the advantage of the view from the living room is a moot point. The same applies to the siting, exposure and layout of the guest quarters. Virtually north-facing, with windows shaded by the roof overhang, and – to the client's dismay – served by only one bathroom, the three identical guest rooms are more suggestive of a Dutch apartment than a luxurious American

country house. One also gets the impression that Oud was trying to compensate for architectural shortcomings by means of all sorts of electrical and mechanical installations. In his design commentary he wrote: *all the lower windows in the large living area can be pushed up and the upper windows down. The large window in the downstairs bedroom can be pushed all the way down (door and all), the door can also be opened separately.*[23] The technical features of the sun room – a cylindrical, glazed pavilion with an openable roof – were quite spectacular. The villa's deep roof overhang created a covered sun terrace accessed through French windows. In this way Oud transformed an annex derived from Frank Lloyd Wright – for example, the free-standing library of his Studio in Oak Park, Chicago (1898) or the two pavilions either side of the Glasner House in Glencoe, Illinois (1908) – into a transparent pavilion that looks like an enlarged version of the rounded shop fronts at Hoek van Holland, the project responsible for Philip Johnson's 'conversion'.[24]

The construction and shipping of the model was no simple matter. Money was a major stumbling block. For example, Oud had wanted to use colour and to have a separate model of the living room (with furnishings); he did in fact make a perspective sketch of this. On 20 December, when the model was still being made, he wrote Johnson: *The house has given me a lot of work. I saw quite new possibilities in it but it will have to be worked out to develop these fully. I hope you will like it though it is very simple. But to make it simple asks most of your time.*[25] In the end, the model arrived in New York just in time to be reassembled, photographed and printed in the catalogue in which Oud was handsomely represented by a twenty-page article. According to Johnson, Mies van der Rohe and Oud were the architects who attracted the most attention at the show: Oud above all because of the photographs of Hoek van Holland, Mies, of course, because of the model and drawings of the Tugendhat House. Le Corbusier found little favour with the American public because, according to Johnson, Americans did not like houses on pilotis. Oud's *House for Mrs H.H. Johnson* was not very successful, chiefly because of the quality of the (cardboard) model: *If only your model had been as graphic as that of Mies van der Rohe's with furniture, original colour, and glass, I think your house would be as much admired as his, but as it is, the Tugendhat House attracts most of the rich people, as might be expected.*[26] Apart from a few casual remarks from the client and exhibition visitors, the Johnson House attracted little critical attention, except from Frank Lloyd Wright (a great admirer of Oud according to Johnson) who disapproved of the sun room *because it is not organically part of the house.*[27] This was a fairly mild – and legitimate – reaction from Wright who viewed European modernism's invasion of America in much the same way as Berlage had viewed CIAM's declaration of principles at La Sarraz in 1928: as a personal attack and challenge. He defended himself in numerous pamphlets, reviews and statements, even penetrating the columns of *De 8 en Opbouw.*[28] The contacts with Oud did not suffer as a result, however. In February 1934, Wright sent Oud a prospectus of the Taliesin Foundation in which the latter's name appeared in the list of 'Friends of the Fellowship' and to which Oud reacted enthusiastically.[29]

The house for Johnson's mother never did get built owing to the financial impact of the Depression years on the Johnson family. This did not, however, affect the contacts between Johnson and Oud. Johnson was particularly active on Oud's behalf, trying to capitalize on the Dutch architect's growing popularity and fame in the United States to arrange visiting lectureships and even permanent university appointments.



**Notes**

**1.** T. Riley, *The International Style: Exhibition 15 and the Museum of Modern Art,* New York 1992.
**2.** G. Radford, *Modern Housing for America. Political struggles in the new Deal Era,* Chicago, London 1996, pp. 59-84.
**3.** J.J.P. Oud, *Nieuw Bouwkunst in Holland en Europa (1935).* Introduction B. Colenbrander, Amsterdam 1981, p. 30.
**4.** P. Hefting, 'America beschreven door K. Lönberg-Holm aan J.J.P. Oud', in: *Museumjournaal,* 4(1975), pp. 155-160.
**5.** M. Bock, *Nederlandse architectuur 1880-1930: Americana*, Otterloo, Amsterdam 1975, pp. 98-106; P. Hefting, 'America beschreven door K. Lönberg-Holm to J.J.P. Oud', in: *Museumjournaal,* 4(1975), pp. 155-160.
**6.** D. Langmead, *J.J.P. Oud and the International Style. A Bio-Bibliography*, Westport, London 1999, p. 52; P. Scrivano, 'J.J.P. Oud e l'architettura olandese negli scritti di Henry-Russell Hitchcock', in: *Zodiac* 18(1997), pp. 90-103.
**7.** H.-R. Hitchcock, 'The architectural work of J.J.P. Oud', in: *The Arts* 2(1928), pp. 102-103.
**8.** J.L. Cohen, *André Lurçat 1894-1970. Autocritique d'un moderne*, Luik 1995, p. 93; H. Jannière, 'L'Architecture Vivante' en 'Cahiers d'Art' , in *Casabella,* 57(1993)603, pp. 46-53.
**9.** H.R. Hitchcock to J.J.P. Oud, 10 August 1930, OUDJ-B, NAI, Rotterdam.
**10.** P. Johnson, 'An Architect's Preface', in: H. Searing (ed.), *In Search of Modern Architecture. A Tribute to Henry-Russell Hitchcock*, New York, Cambridge (Mass.), London 1992, p. viii.
**11.** F. Schulze, *Philip Johnson. Life and Work,* New York 1994, p. 50ff; T. Riley, *The International Style: Exhibition 15 and the Museum of Modern Art,* New York 1992., pp. 12-15.
**12.** P. Scrivano, 'International Style Twenty Years After: la trasformazione di un'idea', in: P. Bonafazio, S. Pace, M. Rosso, P. Scrivano (a cura di), *Tra Guerra e Pace. Società, cultura e architettura nel secondo dopoguerra*, Milan 1998, pp. 118-127.
**13.** P. Johnson to J.J.P. Oud, July 1930, OUDJ-B, NAI, Rotterdam.
**14.** P. Johnson to J.J.P. Oud, July 1930, OUDJ-B, NAI, Rotterdam.
**15.** Oud to P. Johnson, 22 July 1930, Johnson/Oud correspondence, Museum of Modern Art, New York.
**16.** Oud to P. Johnson, 22 July 1930, Johnson/Oud correspondence, Museum of Modern Art, New York.
**17.** C. Zarrelli, *Alfred Roth. La Testimonanza di un protagonista. Il*

**Exhibition *Modern Architecture – International Exhibition*, room with work by Oud/ Installation Photographs, Museum of Modern Art, New York**



*Movimento Moderno tra le due guerre*, Milan 1993, pp. 35-36; A. Roth, *Begegnung mit Pionieren*, Basel, Stuttgart 1973, p. 49.
**18.** P. Johnson to J.J.P. Oud, 17 September 1930, OUDJ-B, NAI, Rotterdam.
**19.** T. Riley, *The International Style: Exhibition 15 and the Museum of Modern Art*, New York 1992, p. 35.
**20.** T. Riley, *The International Style: Exhibition 15 and the Museum of Modern Art*, New York 1992, p. 35.
**21.** P. Johnson to J.J.P. Oud, 8 July 1931, OUDJ-B, NAI, Rotterdam.
**22.** J.J.J. Oud, 'Ontwerp voor een huis in Pinehurst (U.S.A.)', in: *De 8 en Opbouw*, 3(1932)23, p. 229.
**23.** Commentary on the design, OUDJ-vj 1001, NAI, Rotterdam.
**24.** N. Levine, *The Architecture of Frank Lloyd Wright*, Princeton (N.J.) 1996, pp. 26; 50-51.
**25.** J.J.P. Oud to P. Johnson, 20 December 1931, MOMA, New York.
**26.** P. Johnson to J.J.P. Oud, 16 April 1932, OUDJ-B, NAI, Rotterdam.
**27.** P. Johnson to Oud, 14 July 1932, OUDJ-B, NAI, Rotterdam.
**28.** N. Levine, *The Architecture of Frank Lloyd Wright*, Princeton (N.J.) 1996, pp. 218-220; 'Het manifest van Frank Lloyd Wright', in: *De 8 en Opbouw* 3(1932)18, pp. 177-179.
**29.** M. Bock, *Nederlandse Architectuur 1890-1930: Americana*, Otterloo, Amsterdam 1975, p. 105.
**30.** P. Johnson to J.J.P. Oud, 23 November 1933, OUDJ-B, NAI, Rotterdam.
**31.** M. van Stralen, 'Kindred Spirits: Holland, Wright and Wijdeveld', in: A. Alofsin (ed.), *Frank Lloyd Wright. Europe and Beyond*, Berkeley 1999, pp. 45-65.

**Sources**
CCA: dr1984: 0104 - 0119, dr1984: 0279, dr1984: 0288, ph1983: 0302-0308, ph1983: 0314, ph1983: 0503
Getty: 840055*, 890126-21**, 890126-33**
NAI: OUDJ-vj 1-15, OUDJ-vj 1001, OUDJ-vj 3001, OUDJ-ph 416-439, OUDJ-ph 1712-1715, MAQV 272
RIBA: RAN 8/B/13

**Articles**
H.-R. Hitchcock, 'The architectural work of J.J.P. Oud', in: *The Arts* 2 (1928), pp. 102-103
P. Johnson, A. Barr, H.-R. Hitchcock, *Modern architecture: International Exhibition*, MOMA, New York 1932
P. Johnson, H.-R. Hitchcock, *The International Style: architecture since 1922*, New York 1932
J.J.P. Oud, 'Ontwerp voor een huis in Pinehurst (U.S.A.)', in: *De 8 en Opbouw*, 3(1932)23

In November 1933 he offered Oud a two-month visiting lectureship at the Museum of Modern Art and Columbia University. It would probably result in an American commission for Oud: *I cannot promise any theaters to build but since I am already building a house myself with my friend Jan Ruthe-berg, it would not surprise me at all to find something for you.* Adding by way of further inducement: *I am not sure whether it is a compliment to you but I discover that all my trys at designing my house come out looking much more like yours than like Mies'. It seems your style gives a better more wholesome discipline than that of any of the other great moderns.*[30]

Unlike H.T. Wijdeveld, who usually accepted similar invitations from Frank Lloyd Wright, Oud responded with his customary refusal. Instead, he sent a revised version of his *Studio* article about European architecture, although neither Johnson nor the editors of American magazines showed much interest in publishing it.[31]



**Literature**

U. Barbieri, *J.J.P. Oud*, Rotterdam 1987, pp. 126-127

J.L. Cohen, *André Lurçat 1894-1970. Autocritique d'un moderne*, Liège 1995, p. 93

H. Jannière, ' 'L'Architecture Vivante' e 'Cahiers d'Art' , in *Casabella*, 57(1993)603, pp. 46-53

*Nederlandse Architectuur 1890-1930: Americana*, Otterloo, Amsterdam 1975, p. 105

N. Levine, *The Architecture of Frank Lloyd Wright*, Princeton (N.J.) 1996, pp. 218-220

H.E. Oud, *J.J.P. Oud Architekt, Feiten en herinneringen gerangschikt*, The Hague 1984, pp. 110-111

G. Radford, *Modern Housing for America. Political struggles in the new Deal Era*, Chicago, London 1996, pp. 59-84

T. Riley, *The International Style: Exhibition 15 and the Museum of Modern Art*, New York 1992

F. Schulze, *Philip Johnson. Life and Work*, New York 1994, p. 50ff

P. Scrivano, 'International Style Twenty Years After': la trasformazione di un'idea', in: P. Bonafazio, S. Pace, M. Rosso, P. Scrivano (a cura di), *Tra Guerra e Pace. Società, cultura e architettura nel secondo dopoguerra*, Milan 1998, pp. 118-127

P. Scrivano, 'J.J.P. Oud e l'architettura olandese negli scritti di Henry-Russell Hitchcock', in: *Zodiac* 18(1997), pp. 90-103

G. Stamm, *J.J.P. Oud. Bauten und Projekten 1906 bis 1963*, Mainz, Berlin 1984, pp. 110-115

# Design for a House in Pinehurst (U.S.A.)

So far as the distribution of rooms is concerned, the drawings and model speak for themselves. Deep overhangs were requested against the sun; views out on 3 sides of the large living room were asked for (resulting in the raised position of the "sun room"); a major requirement was to hide the view of a neighbouring, very ugly, house on the swimming pool and tennis court side. All activity in the house is concentrated as much as possible in the large living room. Next to the entrance (a hall was not required) is the eating area; an open hearth for the evenings is located beneath the balcony used by the guests; a stair in the living room is not intended to divide, but merely to bridge the height difference with the "sun room" and the guest rooms; the guests are given a sense of freedom by a row of cupboards – 2m high – which affords a break without quite separating. This task – creating contact on all sides among the occupants – was further resolved by not isolating the service stairs (beside the entrance); the only separation is a 1m-high solid balustrade: people on either side can still see one another. The "sun room", the outside balcony of the guest rooms and the downstairs bedroom all have "free" access to the garden and the swimming pool. The lower windows in the large living room can be pushed up and the upper windows down. The big window in the downstairs bedroom can be pushed down completely (together with the door it contains); the (glazed) door can also be opened separately. In the garage is a turntable (shopping in the village is via the path beside the swimming pool and tennis court). The chauffeur's flat is above the service entrance. Parts of the side wall of the stairs to the chauffeur's flat have been omitted to admit light for washing the car in the open air. The "sun room" has a roof that can be opened.

# 52/ Gravestone, E.T.J. Dinaux

**Heemstede, 2 Herfstlaan** **1925**

Oud's oeuvre includes two designs for graves. In 1925 he designed a gravestone for E.T.J. Dinaux (1860-1925), a relative of his wife's, who was buried in the public cemetery at Heemstede. In 1932, when his mother died, he designed a family grave at Driehuis-Westerveld where his parents and his younger brother Gerrit Kassen and his wife are buried. Several features of the grave at Heemstede recall Oud's almost contemporaneous design for the front elevation of Café De Unie: the emphasis on the lettering, which is clearly legible and strongly outlined, the asymmetrical composition of materials, primary colours and orthogonal shapes with the odd rounded accent, and the frontal composition with a strong relief effect. The grave covering consists of four parts: a base of yellow brickwork is topped by an unpolished stone slab. At the head of the grave are two stone slabs with raised lettering against a red background.

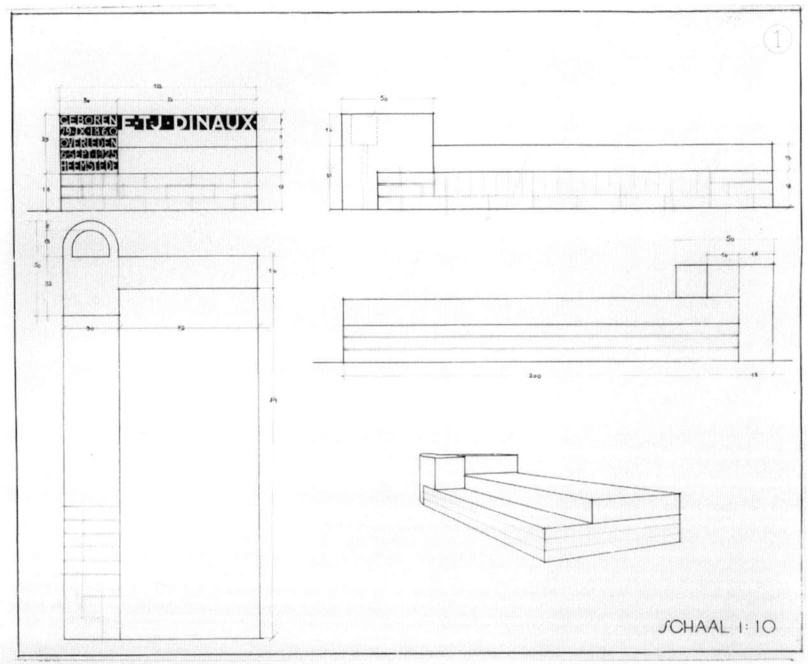


Various design views/ OUDJ-gd 2, NAI, Rotterdam

OUDJ-ph 2001, NAI, Rotterdam (Photo P.S. Goedhart)



**Sources**
Getty: 890126-1**
NAI: OUDJ-gd 1-4

# 53/ Gravestone

**Driehuis, 6 Duin en Kruidbergerweg** **1932**

Oud's parents are buried in a family grave at Westerfeld Cemetery in the province of North Holland. Oud designed the grave when his mother, N.T. Oud-Janszen, died in 1932. Other family members buried there are Oud's father, H.C. Oud (1939), his younger brother Gerrit Kassen (in the 1960s) and the latter's wife (in the 1980s). The names of the last two are on a separate headstone. When Oud himself died on 4 April 1963, he was cremated in the Westerfeld crematorium and his ashes scattered there in the special lake area set aside for this purpose. Compared with the grave Oud had designed for E.T.J. Dinaux in the 1920s, the grave for his parents is simpler and less contrived: there is no compositional play of forms and colours. Instead, forms and colours are the means of expression. The design consists of a rectangular border of white stone accentuated by metal tubing. At the head of the grave is a partially sunken block of stone with bronze lettering.

OUDJ-ph 1716, NAI, Rotterdam



**Sources**
Getty: 890126- box 7, 19*
NAI: OUDJ-gj 1-3, OUDJ-ph 1716

# Oud and the Public Building

In addition to his celebrated housing schemes, Oud designed several more representative buildings, such as a stock exchange, an adult education centre, a modernist café, and various items of furniture. Although he viewed public housing as an important, though extremely onerous, task, Oud never regarded it as the be-all and end-all of contemporary architecture but rather as an opportunity for developing and refining his own style. Nevertheless, architecture it certainly was and at the cutting edge of the new style. Public housing was housing for the 'masses' – a potent concept in the 1920s and 1930s and the subject of numerous dissertations and sundry strategies geared to their 'edification'. The masses were simultaneously acclaimed and feared as the 'shapers' of the society of the future. They were the product of a volatile modern industrial society. The United States, according to Lewis Mumford, was in a transitional phase between what he called the 'paleo-technological' and the 'neo-technological' stages of development, in which the contours of what would later come to be known as the consumer society were already discernible. Things took a different course in the Soviet Union, where the masses – the workers – had assumed power and were busy shaping society via the organs of the state. In the Netherlands, and especially in Rotterdam, the Dutch city most influenced by the masses, everything seemed to happen at once. While the socialists prepared the workers for their future role, the port barons and industrial elite applied themselves to the task of giving shape to the city of the future. Their efforts resulted in garden suburbs built by private developers and even in large-scale regional development plans complete with American-inspired green belts. What set Rotterdam apart in these inter-war years was that these private plans were nearly always taken on board by the municipal town planning department. In Rotterdam, the future of the city seemed to be tied up with the future of the masses and it goes without saying that public housing played a major role in both. It appeared to be the perfect instrument for creating a new city and even a new culture. Moreover, mass housing construction was at the forefront of fundamental developments in architecture; not for nothing did people talk about 'Ford housing'. In other words, social housing, appeared to be in the front line of fundamental cultural, architectural and urban planning developments and Oud was very much aware of this.

Nevertheless, the design of public housing was not without its drawbacks. In the first place, there were the practical problems of tight budgets and the constant pressure to economize. Innovative ideas recommended in the manifestos of avant-garde movements turned out to be extremely difficult to realize in practice and the results were seldom a cause for euphoria. Then again, because municipal housing construction was a highly sensitive issue in local politics, there was no certainty that a scheme, having been designed, would ever in fact be built. Finally, there were the unexpected structural problems that had a habit of manifesting themselves only after the occupants had moved in. Furthermore, housing turned out to be much less susceptible to standardization than cars, say, and almost impossible to mass produce. Even the material that seemed to be ideally suited to this task – concrete – was in practice the source of a good many problems. *But I must observe that a concrete contractor cannot build concrete houses just like that,* Oud wrote to Giedion when the latter proposed replicating Oud's Stuttgart housing experiment in Zurich. *We have had some very bad experiences in this area: on the one hand a house should be waterproof etc., on the other hand it should be nailable, porous, soundproof etc. Without such experience mistakes will always be made, mistakes the building trade engaged in concrete construction in general will be blamed for.*[1] But more important from Oud's point of view than all these practical and technical obstacles, was the conviction that although housing belonged to the domain of architecture, it was not central to it. For this, its representational role in the cityscape was too limited. This was related to practical constraints but also, in his view, to institutional considerations:

housing did not lend itself to representation, let alone to spectacle. This conviction coincided with Oud's ideas about the city. Habitation was a basic ingredient of the city, but not its essence. In Oud's view the city was a complex organism in which important public facilities, which merited a dominant role in the city plan, formed the structuring elements. *Habitation is of great importance [but] could never be a reason for subordinating the plan of the city entirely to housing: a contemporary tendency!*[2] Despite the undeniable impact that the masses and technology were having on the modern metropolis, it was not subordinate to them: it was an organism with a symbolic significance that manifested itself in the representational architecture of buildings occupying a higher place in the social hierarchy and in the position of these buildings in the fabric of the city. Seen in this light, the public building had a special architectural *and* urban significance.

During his employment with the Rotterdam Woningdienst, Oud designed a number public buildings, most of which were never built. Curiously enough, the only one that was built – Café De Unie – was intended as a temporary infill. Moreover, in Oud's view, it lay outside the main trajectory of modern architecture: for him it was a project *in which I purposely stress the 'temporary nature of the form' – the destructive too, to protect myself from becoming rigid in my search for unambiguous forms;* it was, like the site hut at Oud Mathenesse, a Dadaist-like provocation, a token of the need to demolish the old rather than a contribution to 'the new'.[3] Insofar as Oud designed this building as a provocation, he was completely successful, so successful in fact that the Café De Unie facade was reproduced so frequently both at home and abroad that it joined the select suite of images that defined Oud's reputation. In fact, the unrealized projects are a more accurate reflection of Oud's approach to the design of the public building. The essence of the Volksuniversiteit, for example, is determined by the almost Constructivist manner in which the functions are expressed in the building. Each of his public building designs appears as a collage of fragments within a fully controlled overall plan form. Hotel Stiassni was similar to the Volksuniversiteit, but it also stood out because of the way it was located within the existing urban context. The most controversial of the unrealized designs was that for the Rotterdam Exchange. Here, too, several sections, each with its own function, were combined in a perfectly controlled whole which, like the hotel, was emphatically inserted into the existing urban setting such that the latter assumed a completely different character. The Exchange, a monument of the new commercial culture, also functioned as a vehicle for an exuberance of illuminated advertising, one of the main ingredients of the metropolitan cityscape. The symbolic character of the Volksuniversiteit, the Hotel and the Exchange did not derive from non-programmatic additions: their symbolism was, to use Oud's own term, completely unintentional. After each element had been abstracted and reduced to its essence, they were assembled into a logical whole, the essence of which was a perfect symbiosis with the given location.[4] Oud's public buildings were an extension of – not a break with – the idiom he had developed in his public housing.



**Notes**

**1.** J.J.P. Oud to S. Giedion, 24 October 1924, GTA, Zurich.

**2.** J.J.P. Oud to J. Posener, 20 August 1935, OUDJ-B, NAI, Rotterdam.

**3.** J.J.P. Oud to B. Adler, 14 October 1927, OUDJ-B, NAI, Rotterdam.

**4.** The only other Dutch architect working along these lines at the time was J. Buys, 'Interieurs van architect J.J.P. Oud, Hillegersberg', in: *Het landhuis*, 1936; outside the Netherlands there was Le Corbusier's competition design for the League of Nations building in Geneva and E. Mendelsohn's investigation of 'Großbauformen'. K. James, *Erich Mendelsohn & the Architecture of German Modernism*, Cambrdige (Mass.), 1997.

# 54/ Design for the Volksuniversiteit

**Rotterdam, Land van Hoboken** **1924-1927**

At the beginning of the 1920s, the Rotterdam Volksuniversiteit (Institute of Adult Education) conceived a wish to have its own premises. In 1924 a building committee was established for this purpose and Oud was commissioned to make a design. The plans were ambitious: the brief called for a large, multi-purpose building containing a generous events hall (receptions, concerts, theatre), an auditorium, three or four smaller lecture theatres and other spaces for the institute. The first drawings date from late 1924 and early 1925 and are based on a building in two sections – an educational block and a large events hall – which could be built separately if need be. The front part of the building is two storeys high and contains an auditorium, several smaller rooms and various ancillary spaces. Behind this is a large theatre with foyers, dressing rooms and cloakrooms. The theatre is triangular in plan with a rounded apex flanked by wings containing various facilities. A fly tower makes up the rear of the complex. In one of the earliest sketches, the fly tower is crowned by a sculpture group and the theatre section is topped by a tent roof stretched between the two wings. The final version reveals an unadorned fly tower and a flat roof. The second design dates from 1927 and is much more detailed. The size suggests that the building was intended to house other organizations besides the Volksuniversiteit. In addition to a reception room for 1,000 people and accommodation for the Volksuniversiteit, the design contains several apartments. The first sketches reveal a dynamic structure with an overhead bridge that seems to float in the air, an apartment tower and a deeply cantilevered hall at the tip of the complex. The choice of location had fallen on Land van Hoboken, the undeveloped grounds of a former country estate, for which W.G. Witteveen, head of the Rotterdam town planning department, was currently drawing up a masterplan. Witteveen transformed the site into a green lung with development, consisting mainly of public buildings, schools and villas, restricted to the edges. A defining feature of Witteveen's design was the manipulation of the direction of vision: by reining in the greenery at a number of places, he created a succession of vistas that lead the visitor into the park. On the rim of the park this

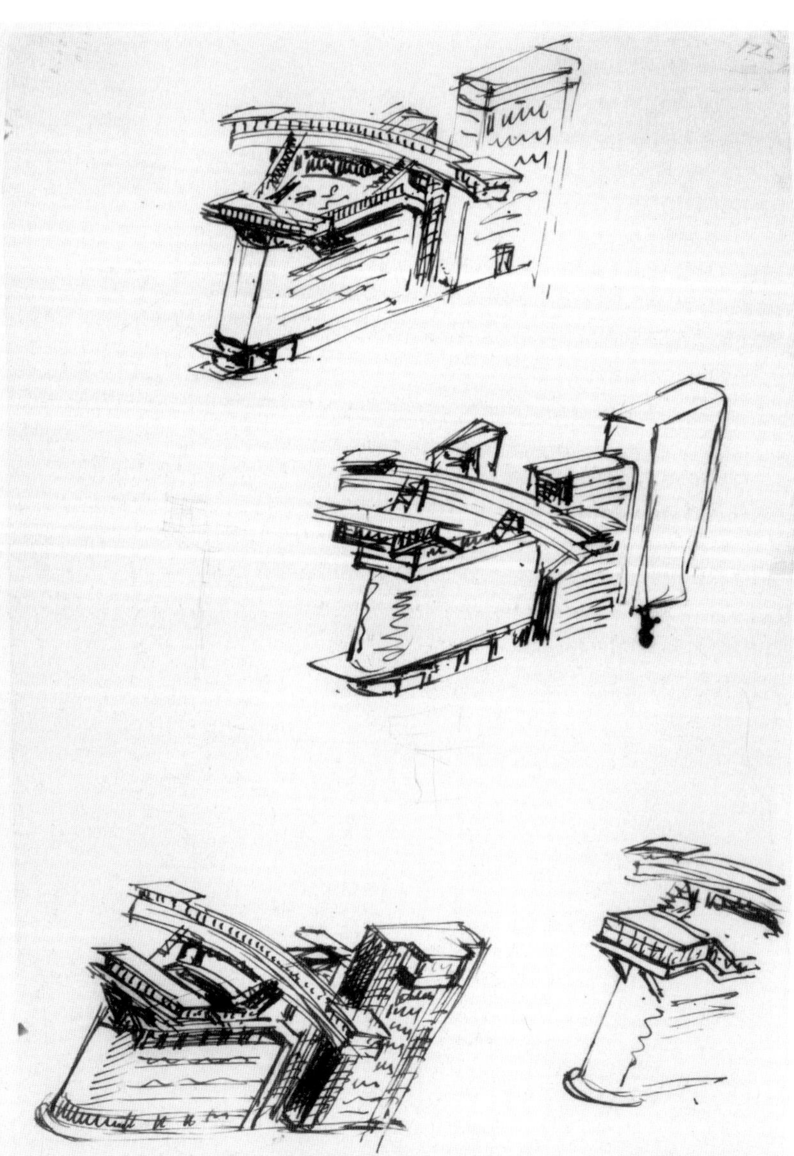

Sketches, second design/ OUDJ-vu 2, NAI, Rotterdam

gave rise to triangular and trapezium-shaped areas. Oud made use of this feature in his second design for the Volksuniversiteit. The triangular complex encloses an interior courtyard spanned midway by a raised walkway that serves as a communicating space. The scheme's initiators had originally intended using this design to attract potential financiers, but the exorbitant price tag (over two million guilders) made this rather unrealistic. Oud consequently drew a third, still smaller version that was no longer designated for a specific location. For this design he reverted to his initial proposal (1924-1925), halving the volume and combining all the functions in the lower, orthogonal volume. The design was reproduced in a circular, accompanied by an explanation by the architect. *The sketch for a Volksuniversiteit building reproduced below is not designed for a specific site. Its purpose is to indicate the space that would be required for the present work of this Association. The floor plan is of the ground floor. On either side of the entrance are offices and an interview room, behind this, around an internal courtyard – so arranged with a view to the desired quiet – to the left, a lecture room seating 400 (with facilities for showing films), to the right, two lecture rooms seating 250 and 150. The latter is intended for physics and chemistry classes and will be fitted out with tiered seating and provision made for film projection, the installation of an epidiascope and the carrying out of experiments. The large auditorium seating 1,000 has separate entrances at the rear of the building. The sketch shows only one solution. It is perfectly possible to bring the large auditorium into closer contact with the other lecture rooms. The second storey is not indicated on the drawing. It contains the small club rooms and the room for the teaching and administrative staff, together with a small gallery. The porter's flat is also located on this floor. The large auditorium is constructed over two storeys. In front of this hall is a lobby with cloakrooms; above this is a foyer. The courtyard could serve as an overspill area during intervals in fine weather; the roof, too, could be used for open-air activities, for example in summer. This sketch plan, which is intended as clarification of several requirements related to the Volksuniversiteit edu-*

**Isometric projection, second design/ NAI, OUDJ-vu 20, NAI, Rotterdam**

*cation programme, can be worked out in detail entirely in accordance with specific wishes and in relation to the future location of the building. The drawing is intended solely to show interested parties what a future Volksuniversiteit building should contain.*[1] This version, too, remained unexecuted.

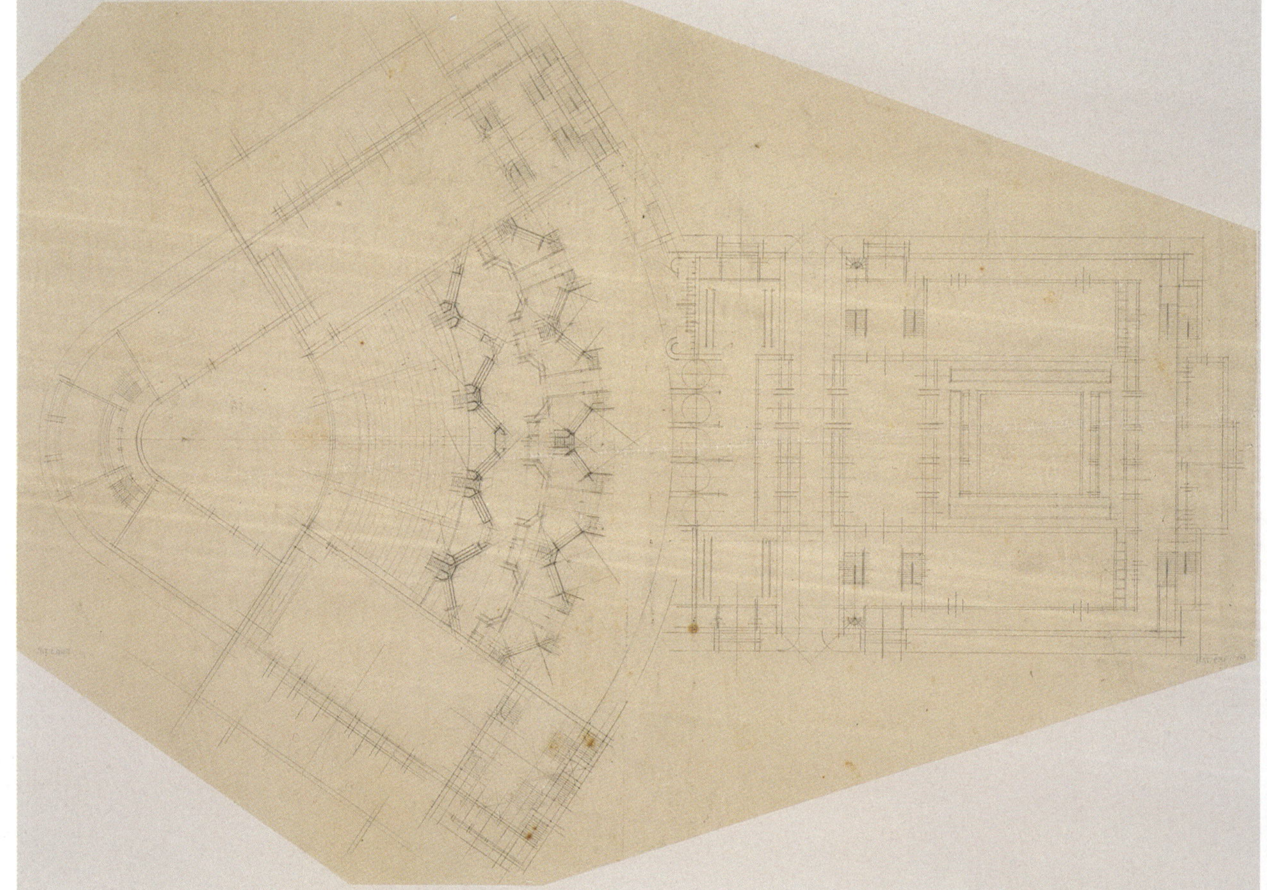

**Ground floor plan, first design/ dr1984: 0072, CCA, Montreal**

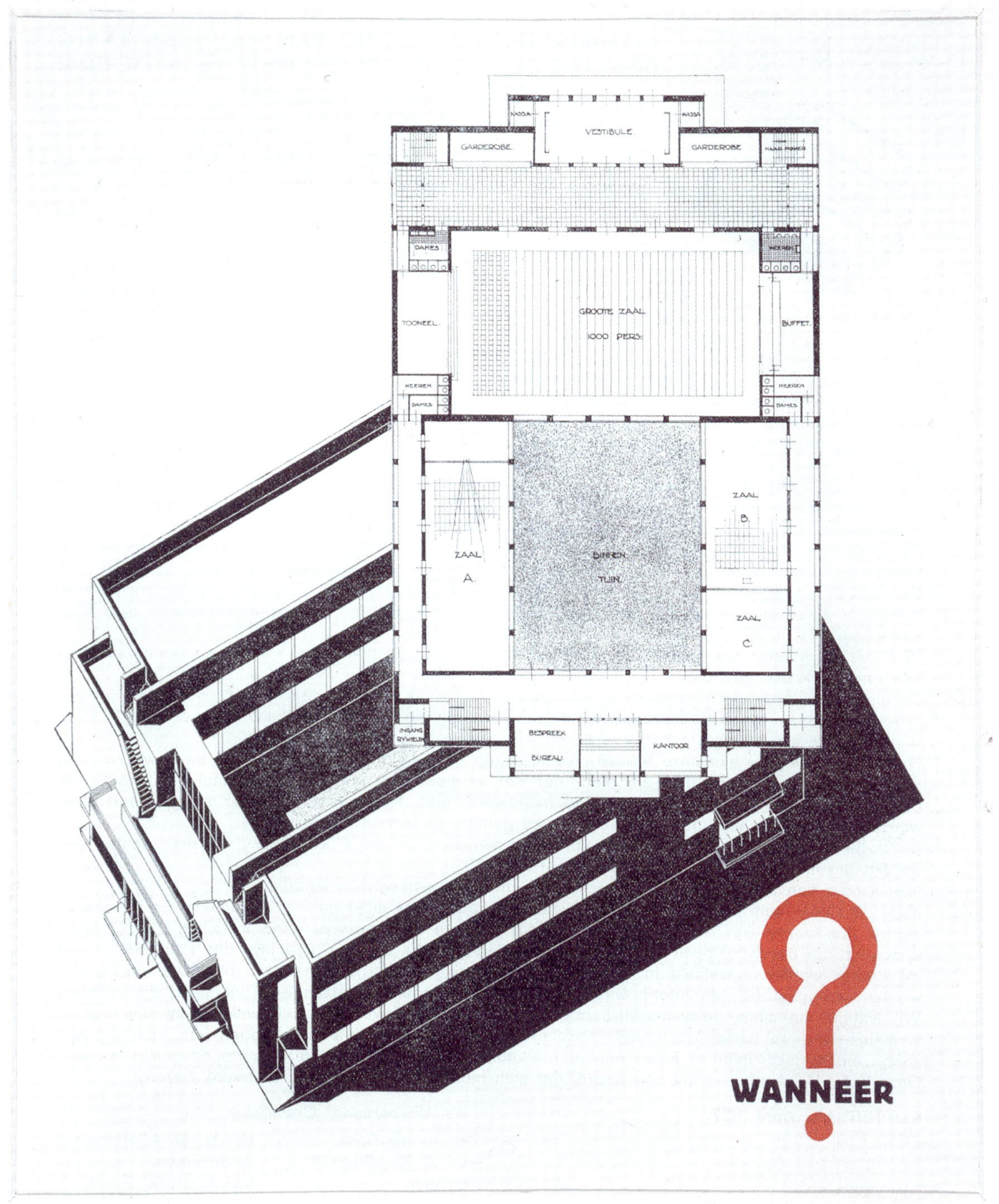


Isometric projection and ground floor plan, third design/ OUDJ-vu 21, NAI, Rotterdam



**Notes**

**1.** Committee for the celebration of the tenth anniversary of the Volksuniversiteit of Rotterdam, 'Feestuitgave bij het tien-jarig bestaan der Volksuniversiteit', Rotterdam 1927, printer's proof with manuscript changes, p. 3, 890126-box 3, F7, Getty Research Institute, Los Angeles.

**Sources**

CCA: dr1984: 0072-0078, dr1984: 0553, dr1984: 0075:002
GAR: Volksuniversiteit Archive
Getty: 890126-box 3, F7
NAI: OUDJ-vu 1-OUDJ-vu 20

**Literature**

U. Barbieri, *J.J.P. Oud*, Rotterdam 1987, pp. 58-59
W.C. Mees, 'De Rotterdamsche Volksuniversiteit', in: E.O.H.M. Ruempol (ed.), *Gedenkboek Rotterdam 1328-1928*, Rotterdam 1928, pp. 515-518
L. Ott, *Naar wijder horizon. Vijftig jaar Volks-Universiteit te Rotterdam*, Rotterdam, The Hague 1967
H.E. Oud, *J.J.P. Oud. Architect 1890-1963. Feiten en herinneringen gerangschikt*, The Hague 1984, pp. 82-83
S. Polano, *J.J.P. Oud, architettura Olandese*, Milan 1981, p. 14
G. Stamm, *J.J.P. Oud. Bauten und Projekten*, Mainz, Berlin 1984, pp. 99-103

Front elevation/ OUDJ-cu 3, NAI, Rotterdam

Oud designed the facade and floor plans of Café De Unie in his capacity as municipal architect after the client's own plans had been thrice rejected by the city's building inspectorate (the newly merged Bouwpolitie & Woningdienst). Oud's input is a typical example of *Bauberatung*, whereby a municipal authority assigns one of its own architects to a private developer, a not uncommon practice in large-scale housing schemes in Rotterdam. The development in this case concerned a narrow, ten-metre-wide plot on Calandplein, two blocks south of the projected site of the new stock exchange building. Wedged between two stately, Neo-Classical buildings (occupied by a secondary school and a charitable institution) it was considered by many in Rotterdam to be an inappropriate location for a café. *But if a café doesn't belong on a big and busy thoroughfare, where does it belong?*, Oud mused, and proceeded to design a facade that lived up to the critics' worst fears.[1] He was encouraged to experiment by the fact that the building had a proposed life span of only ten years. In essence, this commission offered him the opportunity to design something other than housing for once and to make a modern facade that related to contemporary urban life complete with illuminated signs, form and colour. Advertising was a major theme in *De Stijl* circles (as it was at the Bauhaus) and Oud had undoubtedly discussed it at length with Van Doesburg. There is a delightful letter from Van Doesburg to Oud (February 1920) in which the writer gives an exhilarating impression of Paris and of the 'unintentional' role played by advertising in the cityscape: *It was perfect spring weather, we [Mondrian and Van Doesburg] sat outside. Just like a film! It was the busiest time of day and it was impossible to cross Place de la Concorde or Place de l'Opéra without exercising great caution. Mondrian does this quite calmly, by the way, as if he were walking around his studio. Just as earlier painters drew one another's attention to particular features in a tranquil landscape, so we did the same with respect to certain taut movements or the great beauty of a modern shop front with its taut areas of plate glass and iron. The great thing is that it is so natural, so unintentional, while the intentional, mostly baroque, is overloaded and ugly. Paris is perfect, just as it is. Noise + movement dissolve into a certain atmosphere. This is full of an implicit charm. Those who have not seen Paris at work have a mistaken conception of the noise + movement + advertising. ... When I left Brussels and was riding in the tram in the dark to Gare du Midi, I was struck just as here by the tremendous role advertising plays in the cityscape. I have meditated on this at length and hope later to be able to have a more informed discussion about it with you. The question is, of course, whether present-day economic and industrial life will convert this reality of advertising, for the most part based on individualism, into a better culture. Which I doubt. If individualism as such were to disappear it would no longer be necessary for everyone to use their facade to advertise their wares. The facades of the department stores are at present nothing but outsize business cards, behind which the architectural picture is lost (which is just as well!).*[2] The facade design and primary sources suggest that Oud saw the Café De Unie assignment as an opportunity to parade himself as a *De Stijl* architect, even though he no longer had any formal ties with the movement.

The facade of Café De Unie – constructed of boards, cement rendering and glass – has a fragile appearance that is wholly in keeping with the establishment's limited life span. Oud himself remarked that *The critic who wrote in a local paper that 'the whole fell apart somewhat' was therefore in some sense not far wrong: form and colour were intended, in the destructive character of their manifestation, to emphasize the element of impermanence.*[3] But this is not the essence of the design. In the Café De Unie, architecture and advertising are combined in a completely logical way. The lettering and illuminated signs were not tacked onto the facade *afterwards* but 'composed as a whole beforehand'. This resulted, not in a flat composition or a built version of a Neo-Plastic painting, but in a facade *in relief* to which the advertisements had been applied with an eye to both visual expression and commercial (and architectural) function. The viewpoint from which Oud had the Café photographed on various occasions – diagonally rather than front on – indicates to what extent the composition was intended to capture the casual gaze of passers-by in the street, by day and by night. At the same time, Oud ensured that the facade was able to hold its own as an individual, architectural entity vis à vis the intimidating monumentality of its neighbours: *The extent to which the adjoining buildings have been taken into consideration and respected in achieving this [contrast effect], is evident from the shape and position of the illuminated signs, all of which are directed 'inwards', that is to say, mounted in such a way as to maximize their effectiveness for passers-by on all sides, but purely on and from their own territory: the areas of these illuminated signs that are turned towards the neighbouring properties are designed to be blank. This separation is also carried through in the recesses of the café walls at the facade interfaces, which serves to enhance the autonomy of all the objects concerned.*[4] The notion of working from 'outside to inside' was Oud's recalcitrant commentary on Rietveld's method of working. In 1921, Oud and Rietveld had corresponded about a building in the narrow Kalverstraat in Amsterdam where 'in a variegated row of colourful and inviting shops', Rietveld had been commissioned to design a 'striking but nonetheless "distinguished" and "spacious"-looking store'.[5] To make the building look wider, Rietveld abandoned the concept of a continuous facade surface and, working from inside to outside on the principle that 'if not in breadth then in depth', he dissolved the shop front into a spatial composition of volumes and planes. Oud felt that for all its would-be unintentionality, the facade nonetheless had something intentional about it, which did not, however, prevent him from including a picture of it in his *Holländische Architektur* (1926). This same 'objection' can in fact be levelled at Café De Unie where an asymmetrical facade was somewhat artificially placed in front of an otherwise symmetrically organized interior. Another factor contributing to the 'intentional' or artificial nature of the building, was of course the colour scheme which was quite a change from what Oud generally permitted in his housing schemes. Café De Unie is the most colourful building in Oud's entire oeuvre. The choice of colour was undoubtedly connected with the architectural interpretation of the advertising aspect. Oud wrote: *As far as the colour is concerned, the right top corner is vermillion red, the left-hand window frame canary yellow; the aforementioned recesses at the facade interfaces are grey as is the half cylinder above one of the illuminated signs; the topmost covering cylinder element is yellow. The lower front is ultramarine blue with black end piers, the front door, grey; the windows above the lower front yellow, grey and white with black corners. The letters of the illuminated signs are white on a blue background, yellow light box and yellow on the sides; the facework is white.*[6] Such an explosion of colour makes the facade flatter and more graphic to the extent that it serves to correct the apparent projection of the upper section vis à vis the lower, slide-out window. On the facade of Café De Unie colour integrates the lettering into an abstract, planar composition that answers to only one logic, that of 'from outside to inside: advertising!'[7] There are numerous indications that Oud regarded the design of Café De Unie as an experimental moment in his own development as architect-artist. There is an interesting exchange of letters with the Swiss architect Hannes Meyer, which reveals that Oud was definitely aware of the Dadaist implications of the notion of 'destruction'. In July 1925, Meyer (the future director of the Bauhaus (1927-1930) sent Oud a linocut, one of a series, with a request for his opinion.[8] Meyer's interest in Oud stemmed from his hope that the Dutch architect would be able to help him to develop an abstract vocabulary for the future architecture. Provoked by the radical, anti-formalist tendencies of the editors of *ABC. Beiträge zum Bauen* (M. Stam, El Lissitzky), Meyer was investigating the foundations of 'der neuen Gestaltung' in



**Notes**

**1.** J.J.P. Oud, 'Een café', in *Bouwkundig Weekblad,* 46, no. 31 (1925), pp. 397-400.
**2.** T. van Doesburg to J.J.P. Oud, 24 February 1930, Fondation Custodia, Paris.
**3.** J.J.P. Oud, 'Een café', in *Bouwkundig Weekblad,* 46, no. 31 (1925), p. 399.
**4.** J.J.P. Oud, 'Een café', in *Bouwkundig Weekblad,* 46, no. 31 (1925), p. 399.
**5.** E. Taverne, D. Broekhuizen, 'De dissidente architecten: J.J.P. Oud, Jan Wils en Robert van 't Hoff, in: C. Blotkamp (ed.), *De vervolgjaren van De Stijl 1922-1932*, Antwerp, Amsterdam 1996, p. 373.
**6.** J.J.P. Oud, 'Een café', in *Bouwkundig Weekblad,* 46, no. 31 (1925), p. 400.
**7.** J.J.P. Oud, 'Een café', in *Bouwkundig Weekblad,* 46, no. 31 (1925), p. 400.
**8.** H. Meyer to J.J.P. Oud, 31 July 1925, NAI, Rotterdam.
**9.** *Hannes Meyer 1889-1954. Architekt Urbanist Lehrer*, Berlin, Frankfurt, 1989, pp. 60, 74, 168.
**10.** J.J.P. Oud to H. Meyer, NAI, Rotterdam.
**11.** J.J.P. Oud, 'Café-Restaurant "De Unie", Rotterdam', in *Die Form*, 1, 4 (1926), pp. 79-81; W. Dexler, 'Reklame im Stadtbilde', in *Die Schaulade*, 3, 5 (1928), pp. 269-275.

**Sources**

CCA: dr1984: 0517, dr1984: 0518,

Coolsingel with Café De Unie facade/ OUDJ-ph 254, NAI, Rotterdam

*De Stijl* and *L'Esprit Nouveau* circles. It was probably this that had brought him to Oud in Rotterdam. He also hoped that Oud would introduce him to Mondrian because he needed to speak to a 'strong, absolute artist' about various problems relating to abstract art.[9] Meyer had previously visited Oud in Rotterdam, on which occasion he had invited the architect (who had once again intimated that he was keen to leave the Woningdienst) to visit Switzerland for a winter sports holiday and for a 'Verjüngungskur' (rejuvenating cure). In 1928, he offered Oud a contract as lecturer in architecture at the Bauhaus in Dessau. Oud invoked the aesthetic of Café De Unie in his detailed analysis of the artistic qualities of Meyer's linocut. He wrote that he found the linocut too contrived, too constrained and above all too decorative. He pointed to the innovations of the Constructivists who had *brought tension – freedom, too – and also restraint instead of disintegration: openness, air and light, instead of mood, distress and semidarkness*, qualities that Oud had experienced in the wonderful hall of the community centre and the Co-op Theater in Freidorf, but which he sorely missed in the advertising graphics: 'too much glue'. Oud wrote that he himself needed to let go artistically, not only in order to arrive at new forms, but more particularly so as not to get bogged down in what had already been achieved. This was why it was necessary constantly to destroy what has once been achieved: *The café therefore is a release and a diversion, a joke, Dada, however, also great seriousness!*[10]

And that Oud was serious about Café De Unie is evidenced by the competition design for the new Rotterdam Exchange (1926; cat. no. 57), in which the facades of the shops and cafés in the low structure fronting Coolsingel were organized in the same manner as Café De Unie and, architecturally speaking, were dominated by advertising, illuminated or otherwise. This was also how Café De Unie was received by the foreign architectural press. Design and commentary were published in their entirety in *Die Form*, the organ of the Deutsche Werkbund, as early as 1926. Two years later Walter Dexel presented 'De Unie' in a supplement of the German *Die Schaulade deutscher Wert- und Kunstarbeit* as *the first genuine example of a uniform attempt to perfect architecture and advertising.*[11]



dr1984: 0537, ph1984: 0823, ph1984: 1083, ph1985: 0149, ph1095: 0152
Getty: 890126-box 3, F21
NAI: OUDJ-cu 1-8, OUDJ-cu 3001, OUDJ-ph 250-257, OUDJ-ph 1683-1684, OUDJ-B

**Articles**

'Café De Unie', in: *Gross Deutsch Hotel Rundschau*, 16 October 1926
'Café De Unie', in: *Die Form*, 1(1926)4
K. Begeer, *Holland, Arts and Crafts 1900-1926*, Amsterdam 1927
H. Meyer, 'Die neue Welt', in: *Das Werk*, (1926)July, pp. 206-209
J.J.P. Oud, 'Een café', in: *Bouwkundig Weekblad*, 46(1925)31, pp. 397-400
A. Stoffels, 'Das Kaffeehaus De Unie von Architekt J.J.P. Oud', in: *Österreichische Bau- und Werkkunst*, 2(1926), p. 329
E.E. Strasser, *Neuere Holländische Baukunst*, München-Gladbach, 1926

**Literature**

U. Barbieri, *J.J.P. Oud*, Rotterdam 1987, pp. 54-57
R. van de Lugt, 'La ricostruzione del café De Unie a Rotterdam', in: *Domus*, (1987)April
H.E. Oud, *J.J.P. Oud, Feiten en herinneringen gerangschikt*, The Hague 1984, pp. 84-86
S. Polano, *J.J.P. Oud. Architettura Olandese*, Mainz 1976, p. 87
G. Stamm, *J.J.P. Oud. Bauten und Projekten 1906 bis 1963*, Mainz, Berlin 1984, pp. 77-80

# *A café*

*In Kunst und Wissenschaft, sowie in Tun und Handeln, kommt alles darauf an, dasz die Objekte rein aufgefaszt werden und ihrer Natur gemäsz behandelt werden.*
*Goethe*

It is actually no light undertaking, to comment in other than purely practical terms on a building: it is so tempting in retrospect to reconstruct the pre-history after one's own fashion (there are some choice stories of this kind in circulation!), but above all – the result must survive in everyday life without our intervention and so in general it is better forego this kind of mediation from the start.
The case in question is nevertheless somewhat unusual as regards remit: it also caused – less unusual in these times – a few pens [1)] and especially tongues to move and the many unsympathetic utterances that it provoked sometimes testify to so little knowledge of the underlying objective facts that some explanation would seem to be in order here.
For the construction of the premises concerned, three separate designs were submitted to "Bouwpolitie en Woningdienst" [Building Inspectorate and Housing Authority], all of which were rejected on aesthetic grounds. It concerned, as the illustrations show, the erection of a café on Calandplein, the continuation of the big and busy Coolsingel boulevard. It was to be built between two distinguished-looking buildings, the Erasmiaansch Gymnasium and Maria Catharina Van Doorn's Liefdegesticht van Weldadigheid, and to remain for a period of 10 years, no more and no less.
What should a café on this site look like? "There should never have been any café there at all" people said later. But if a café doesn't belong on a big and busy thoroughfare, where does it belong?
When "Bouwpolitie en Woningdienst" took it upon itself – to prevent further delay and an unsightly facade – to make a new design for the owner by way of "Bauberatung" [building advice], all parties were agreed that it [a café] was completely appropriate to the setting. In making the design, therefore, I left the café for what it was, which is to say a place for eating and drinking that by all the right and appropriate means, such as illuminated signs, graphics, form, colour, etc., does all it can to focus attention on itself. In this I departed from the normal procedure insofar as those means were not invoked at a later stage as is usually the case, with all the untidy and bland consequences that entails, but were composed beforehand into a whole which one may find beautiful or ugly but the purity of intention of which cannot be denied. If the aspect thus arrived at is judged to contain, in terms of conception, an offence against the townscape (which I categorically reject: I believe in a new beauty of more brilliant possibilities on the aforementioned basis) then critics should rather turn against conditions, which are the cause, than against the outcomes, which are effect.
If the exterior, as it is, is thus nothing but the outcome of a scrupulous acceptance of the stated requirements, the fact that the building would last for only 10 years was an added stimulus in the same direction. So the critic who wrote in a local paper that "the whole fell apart somewhat" was to some extent not far wrong: form and colour were intended, by virtue of the destructive character of their manifestation, to emphasize the element of impermanence, although by the same token – it goes without saying – the aim was to produce a balanced composition, be it that the balance sought was of a more "shallow" nature, unstable rather than stable.
As far as the neighbours are concerned, the main thing was to establish the right kind of mutual relationship between the facades. To make the café a linking element between the adjoining buildings was inadmissible; for example: the latter would have been brought down to the level of the first, which would rightly have provoked protests. What was needed here on the contrary was to keep the café completely autonomous and in this way to try by means of rational con-

trast to respect the value of the one and the other.
We have been taught – and it was by no means the most modern who decreed ad nauseum – that everything that arises organically from the essence of an age goes well with the authentic product of the essence of another age (the oft-quoted example of this is the Palace on the Dam and the Nieuwe Kerk). Without wishing to commend the harmony here – I adduce in my defence that with all respect, the architecture of the adjoining properties can hardly be regarded as "the authentic product of its age" – so without commending the harmony, I nevertheless feel that a contrast effect has been achieved that is far from objectionable. The extent to which the adjoining buildings were taken into consideration and respected in achieving this, is evident from the shape and position of the illuminated signs, all of which are directed "inwards", that is to say, mounted in such a way as to maximize their effectiveness for passers-by on all sides but purely on and from their own territory: the surfaces of these illuminated signs that are turned towards the neighbouring properties are entirely closed. This demarcation is moreover carried through in the recesses of the café walls at the facade interfaces which serves to enhance the autonomy of all the objects concerned.
There is not much more to be said, in fact. As far as the colour is concerned, the top right corner is vermillion red, the left-hand window frame canary yellow; the afore-mentioned recesses at the facade interfaces are grey as is the half cylinder above one of the illuminated signs; the upper covering cylinder element is yellow. The lower front is ultramarine blue with black end piers, the front door, grey; the windows above the lower front yellow, grey and white with black corners. The letters of the illuminated signs are white on a blue background, yellow light box and yellow on the sides; the facework is white. The paint process used on the walls, which is guaranteed colour-fast, is "Hermacolor".
We built from the inside out! That little things inside are no longer so perfectly reflected on the outside as was designed, should not be laid at our door: what was behind the facade, turned out to be difficult to control according to our design owing to lack of authority. This meant that the interior, too, was beyond our concern.
The material was cement rendering on herring-bone steel and planks. The planks – if more explanation is required – were separated by grooves (to localize the stretching where it would be least inconvenient); that the contractor made our planks in cement and applied our rendering to sandstone is one of the many experiences of "Bauberatung" that must be gone through in order to be able to avoid them on a following occasion. The top part of the facade projects – in two senses from inside to outside, because of the sliding of the lower windows. The "tower" contains a stair to the flat roof with an entrance door under the canopy.
The rest is logic from outside to inside: advertising! "From outside to inside", it is perhaps as well to emphasize it once again here, for the inside to outside of a functional architecture is sometimes also from outside to inside. But an explanation of this play on words is too ponderous for this simple affair.
July, '25. J.J.P. OUD.

1) The elegantly launched torpedo of your submarine hero "Periscopius" had not yet struck me when I wrote this.

# 56/ Hotel Stiassni

**Brno, Theatergasse/ Palackystrasse** **1926**

The invitation to participate in a design competition for a large hotel/leisure complex in the centre of Brno can be seen as a measure of Oud's growing international reputation. The other participants were the *éminence grise* of German modern architecture, Peter Behrens, and a Czech contemporary, Arnost Wiesner (1890-1971). Oud's (unbuilt) design was published in *Wasmuth's Monatshefte für Baukunst* and exhibited in Brno together with the other entries.[1]

One side of the site faced the freestanding municipal theatre, on the other side was a square with two separate railway stations for goods and people. The surrounding, dense development consisted for the most part of ground-level shops, restaurants and businesses topped by three levels of dwellings. These formed the backdrop for one or two monumental buildings and squares. The plan was to demolish the existing development on the site in two stages, starting with a triangular section on the corner of Theatergasse and Palackystrasse and then moving on to the more northerly, rectangular section of the site. At the same time, the station square would be upgraded by the removal of the goods station.[2]

Oud designed an eight-storey building (just within the maximum building height), dropping to six storeys at the rear. Because of this lower rear section and the low-key, functional architecture, the building made no attempt to compete for attention with nearby public buildings such as the monumental city theatre and the neighbouring 'Künstlerhaus'. As in his design for the Rotterdam Exchange, Oud respected the existing hierarchical make-up of the townscape – unlike Behrens who used facade cladding, a tower and a striking awning to set his building apart.[3] Oud also took account of the new traffic situation in his design. The canopy above the main entrance on the corner was echoed in the roof overhang which served to emphasize the corner and give both sides equal weight.

As required by the building programme, Oud situated a cinema, plant (heating, ventilation) and the kitchen in the two basement levels. Each of the top five floors contained 28 hotel rooms ranged along a central corridor. Oud's proposal for the ground floor layout was striking. He projected a swimming pool in one wing and a restaurant in the other and between the two a landscaped courtyard café. The three areas could be combined into one by opening big French doors. This arrangement served to enhance the attraction of the shops beside the swimming pool and restaurant as well as the cafés and rental offices on the first and second floors. Large windows along the street afforded passers-by a view of people relaxing in the swimming pool, restaurant and courtyard. Oud's design provided for an urban building whose shop fronts, balconies and exaggerated awning all served to emphasize its commercial role in the streetscape.[4]

None of the competition entries was realized. A short time

Preliminary studies for Hotel Stiassni/ OUDJ-hs 1, NAI, Rotterdam

Perspective/ OUD-J-hs5, NAI, Rotterdam

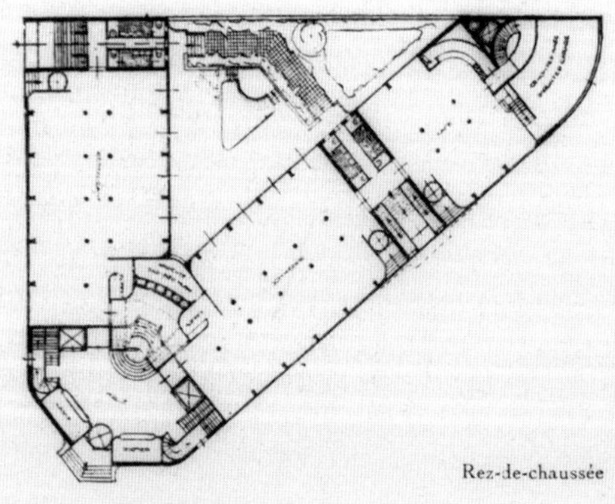


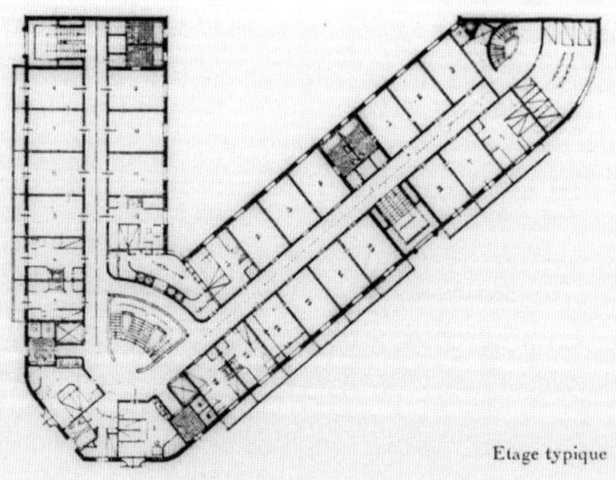


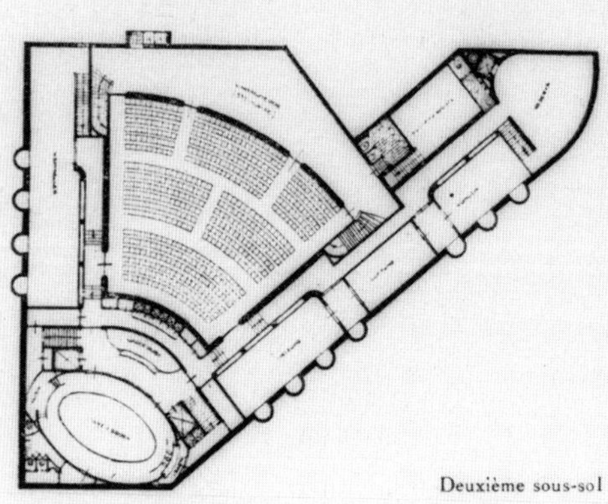


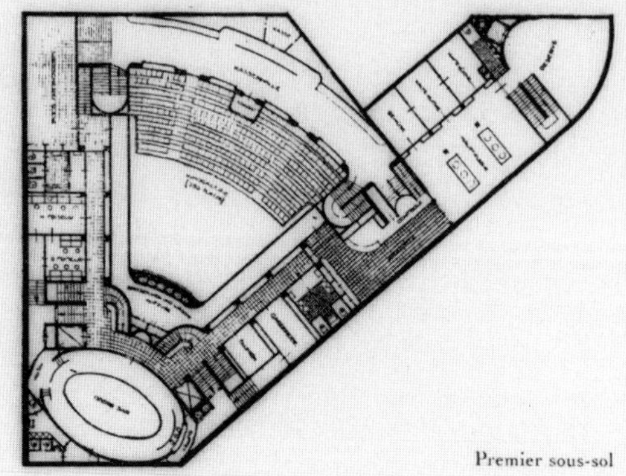


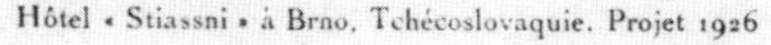
Hôtel « Stiassni » à Brno, Tchécoslovaquie. Projet 1926

Plan of ground floor (top left), second basement, (bottom left), hotel floors (top right) and first basement (bottom right)/ L 67469, RKD, The Hague

later, however, Wiesner made another plan for the same site and this one did get built. In the new design the shops, restaurant and cinema on the lowest levels were retained, but the hotel rooms were replaced by offices for a life insurance company.[5]

Perspective/ dr1984: 0545, CCA, Montreal

349 **Notes**

**1.** Oud was alerted to the exhibition of competition entries by the Brno-based architect Heinrich Blüm. H. Blüm to J.J.P. Oud, 10 April and 3 May 1926; J.J.P. Oud to H. Blüm, 18 April [1926], OUDJ-B, NAI, Rotterdam.

**2.** Details of the urban design plans for the area were included in the competition programme: Anonymous, 'Programm für das Projekt eines Stadthotels', typescript, undated [1925/1926], p. 2, Oud Archive, NAI, Rotterdam.

**3.** For Behrens's design for Hotel Stiassni see: H.J. Kadatz, *Peter Behrens. Architekt-Maler, Grafiker und Formgestalter 1868-1940*, Leipzig 1977, pp. 102-103.

**4.** For Oud's commentary on his entry see: [J.J.P. Oud], 'Erläuterungsbericht zum Entwurf für ein Stadthotel in Brünn', typescript, undated [February 1926], p. 5, OUDJ-hs 1001, NAI, Rotterdam.

**5.** The present address of the complex designed by Wiesner is Divadelni-Strasse 3. V. Slapeta (et al.), *Czech Functionalism 1918-1938*, London 1987, pp.30, 154.

**Sources**

CCA: dr1984: 0050-0062, dr1984: 0539-0545
Getty: 890126-box 7, 11**
MOMA: NC Drawings-blueprints
NAI: OUDJ-hs 1-9, OUDJ-hs 1001, OUDJ-ph 403, OUDJ-B

**Articles**

'Neue arbeiten von J.J.P. Oud, Rotterdam', in: *Wasmuth's Monatshefte für Baukunst*, 11(1927)1, pp. 32-34

**Literature**

U. Barbieri, *J.J.P. Oud*, Rotterdam 1987, pp. 62-63
Lesnikowski, W. (et al.), *East European Modernism. Architecture in Czechoslovakia, Hungary & Poland between the Wars 1919-1939*, London 1996
H.E. Oud, *J.J.P. Oud, Feiten en herinneringen gerangschikt*, The Hague 1984, pp. 97-98
V. Slapeta (et al.), *Die Brünner Funktionalisten. Moderne Architektur in Brünn (Brno)*, Innsbruck 1985
V. Slapeta (et al.), *Czech Functionalism 1918-1938*, London 1987
G. Stamm, *J.J.P. Oud. Bauten und Projekten 1906 bis 1963*, Mainz, Berlin 1984, p. 103

# 57/ Competition Design: Rotterdam Exchange

**Rotterdam, Coolsingel** **1926**

In the autumn of 1926, Oud worked under enormous pressure on a competition design for a new stock exchange building on the Coolsingel boulevard in Rotterdam. In fact, as A. Plate stated in 1947, the project entailed a complex of buildings and a variety of uses, the economic feasibility of which was by no means certain.[1] The brief of the invited competition asked not only for a new building but also for an urban planning concept for the surrounding area. Oud's entry for both the multi-purpose complex and the spatial context, was his first and most radical design for a mayor public building. At the same time it marked an unequivocal turning point in his architectural career, insofar as in this design he finally abandoned the Berlagian aesthetic of *Schoonheid en Samenleving* and embarked on a highly functional, non-figurative and non-symbolic architecture. This eventually brought him into open conflict with Berlage (the chairman of the jury) who was coincidentally engaged in harrying the modern movement in architecture on several domestic and international fronts. Oud's poor showing in the competition and the concomitant loss of face at home and abroad, as well as the debate about the future direction of modern architecture triggered off by the Exchange design competition, plunged Oud into a deep psychological crisis and led to a complete reversal in his view of architecture.

*It seems to the designer, that the impact of the Exchange Building on the future urban layout cannot be very great.*[2] This was the first, somewhat cryptic sentence of Oud's design commentary. The rest of the text reveals a decided lack of enthusiasm for the building's location on Coolsingel where it was obliged to fall into line with the Town Hall and the Post & Telegraph Office. Moreover, the Coolsingel location distanced the Exchange from the city's vital north-south axis and the link to the new main highway to The Hague. It also meant that there was no chance of making the Rotterdam Exchange – like Berlage's Amsterdam Exchange – a spatial focus of the city. This, in Oud's eyes fatal, decision dated from before the war. The first plans for a new Exchange had evolved in the context of radical public and private schemes for a new city core that had been around since the beginning of the twentieth century. Large-scale slum clearance operations in the Zandstraatkwartier were followed by the carving out of traffic corridors (Meent), the filling in of canals (Coolvest) and in particular by the construction of squares, thoroughfares, shopping streets and urban boulevards (Hofplein, Coolsingel). In fact, in the years immediately prior to the First World War the spatial groundwork had been laid for an entirely new city centre of which the Town Hall (1912-1920), the Post & Telegraph Office (1913) and the Exchange (1926-1940) formed the actual architectonic heart.[3] The first plans for a new Exchange located on Coolsingel, dated from 1913-1914 when city council debated (and sanctioned) the compulsory purchase of a city block between two streets earmarked for widening. The result was a huge building site of over 10,000 $m^2$,

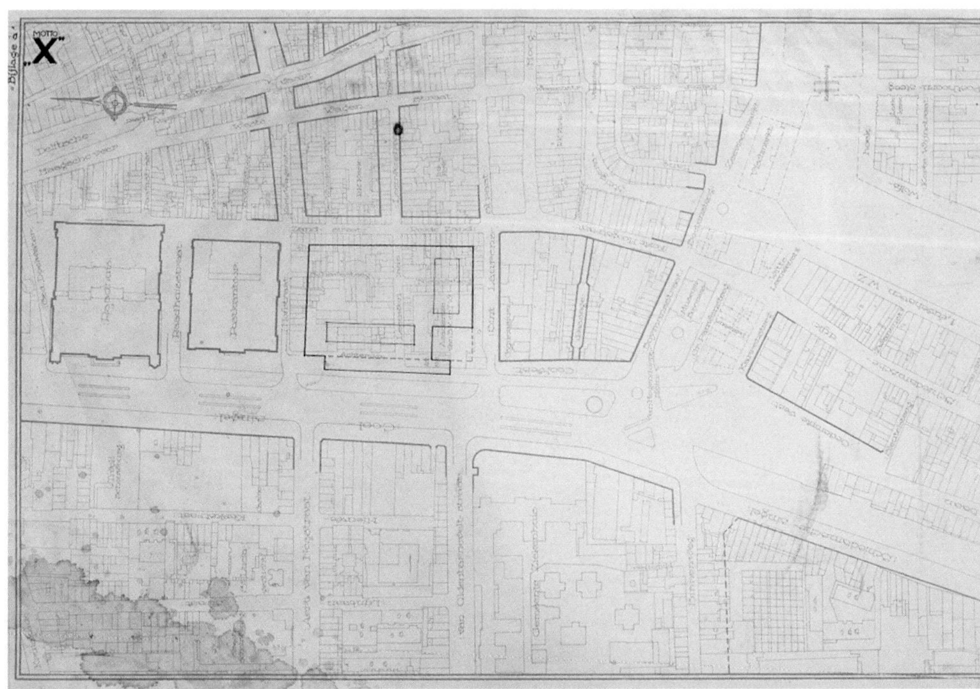


Site plan/ OUDJ-bs 25, NAI, Rotterdam

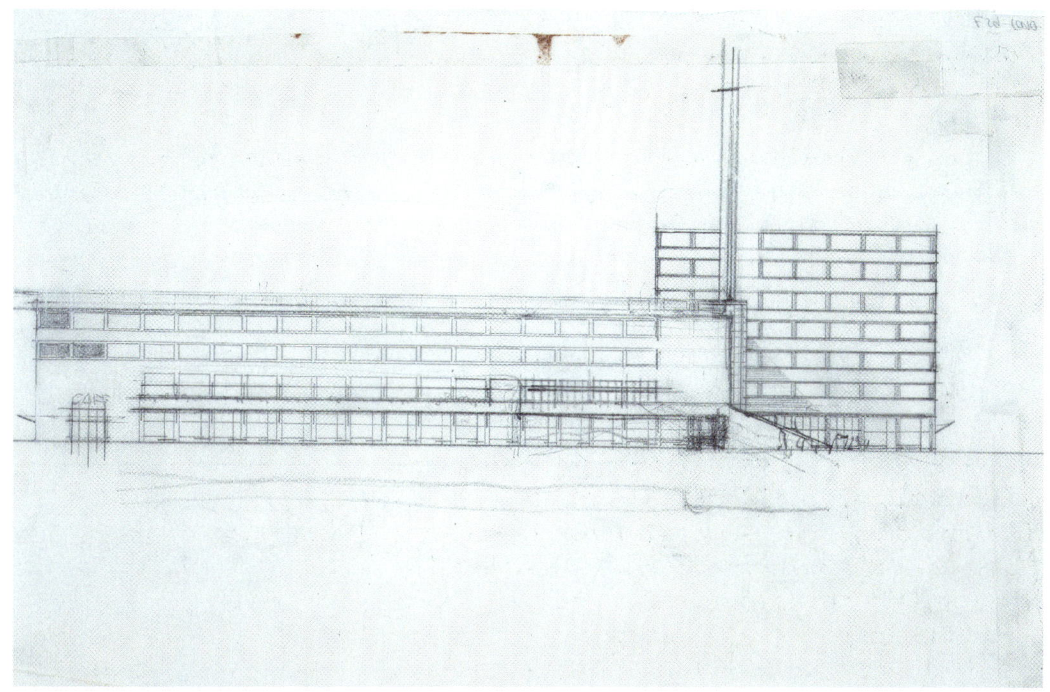

Coolsingel elevation/ OUDJ-bs 7, NAI, Rotterdam

Coolsingel elevation/ OUDJ-bs 5, NAI, Rotterdam

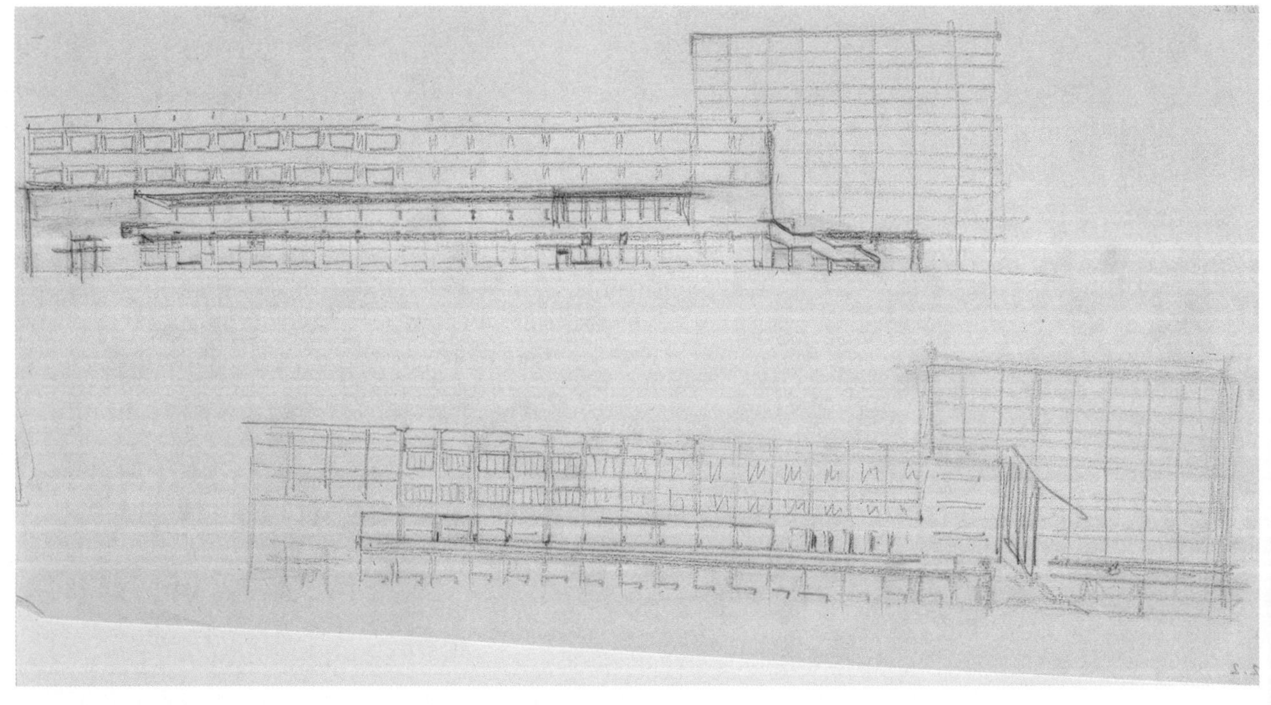

Coolsingel elevation/ OUDJ-bs 2, NAI, Rotterdam

Sint Laurensstraat elevation (south side)/ OUDJ-bs 3, NAI, Rotterdam

many times larger than was needed for the new Exchange (the existing Exchange covered only 3,780 m$^2$). At the time, it seemed an ideal spot. It would, the council argued, put the new Exchange right at the heart of the city *while it would also stand alongside the central Post and Telegraph Office and on the main roads from both stations – Delftsche Poort and Zuid Hollandsche Electrische Spoorweg Maatschappij – into the city, which will shortly gain in significance from the building of the Town Hall and the aforementioned Post Office and which also, should the Exchange also be built there in the future, be entirely taken up by large and monumental buildings on that side, something that is all the more appealing when one considers that the Doelenterrein also belongs to the City and will before long be at the City's disposal once more. As such, the Exchange building will itself contribute to the further formation of the character of the main road and the placement of this building on that particular spot, right next to Van Hogendorpplein and the existing development to the south of St. Laurensstraat, may from that point of view in our opinion be considered a felicitous idea.*[4]

The First World War considerably delayed everything to do with large-scale construction, from expropriation procedures to site preparation, but above all planning and execution. It was not until the spring of 1925 that the idea of a new Exchange building was picked up again, this time at the initiative of the private sector, in the person of the Rotterdam grain merchant, P. Penn. A special Beurs Comité (Exchange Committee) was set up to clear the way politically and financially for the construction of a new commodity exchange. Committee members were drawn from the worlds of trade, shipping and commerce and included several well-known local figures such as A. Plate, the former director of the Woningdienst, the banker W.C. Mees, and a future chairman of the Chamber of Commerce, K.P. van der Mandele. The aim of this private initiative was set out at the very first meeting of the committee: *to erect a building that would be as satisfactory as possible from an urbanistic viewpoint and that would also be an architectural asset.*[5] From the very first contacts between the committee and the city council, the latter's prewar decisions regarding the future location of the new Exchange were a bone of contention. At 10,652 m$^2$, the allocated site was much too large for the projected Exchange footprint of 7,500 m$^2$. The council objected to the committee's plan to develop only part of the plot because of the adverse effect this would have on the appearance of Coolsingel, while the committee feared operating deficits and architectural blandness if a quarter of the site were to be allocated to semi-permanent office space. W.C. Mees neatly summarized the difficulties and their consequences for the programme of the new Exchange building: *Usually one takes as much land as one needs for a house, yet in this case the house is supposed to become as big as the piece of land. In effect, that is turning things on their head.*[6] The consultations between the city council and the committee ended in victory for the council. The decision to use the entire plot meant that the building programme, which provided for a maximum building volume of 25,000 m$^3$, including a large hall (4,500 m$^2$) and various meeting rooms (2,000 m$^2$), would have to be 'embellished' with offices, shops, a restaurant and other facilities such as a theatre and a cinema. In early January 1926, the jury was selected and a building committee appointed. The jury was made up of three architects, H.P. Berlage (chairman), W.G. Witteveen (public works department) and A.G. van der Steur (independent), plus two members of the Exchange committee. The building committee, whose job was to draw up the building programme and select the participating architects, consisted of the jury and two other members of the Exchange committee, one of whom was A. Plate. Six architects were invited to take part in the competition, three from Rotterdam – Granpré Molière, J.J.P. Oud and W. Kromhout – and three from elsewhere – W.M. Dudok, H.F. Mertens and J. F. Staal. In drawing up the programme, the building committee was once again confronted with the problem of the building's spatial orientation on an overlarge plot on Coolsingel. Partly on the advice of Berlage, the building committee reached a remarkable compromise whereby the new Exchange building would remain a permanent element of the monumental street wall established by the Town Hall and Post & Telegraph Office, while at the same time being linked programmatically to the uncertain future of Van Hogendorpplein, the

353

**Town Hall facade (left) with Post Office (centre) and Exchange Building (right) on Coolsingel. From: J.J.P. Oud to B.J. Koldewey, 29 October 1935/ OUDJ-B, NAI, Rotterdam**

square on the south side of the site. In consultation with the council it was decided to combine the competition for a new Exchange building with an ideas competition for Van Hogendorpplein. Participants were to be permitted to design shops and offices independently of the Exchange programme and in so doing to make use of plots scheduled for clearance to the south or east of the new Exchange. In a discussion of the building programme between the building committee and the six architects, Berlage confirmed that the city council had left the planning of the area around the southern termination of Coolsingel (Van Hogendorpplein) to the competition jury, a decision that was not to everybody's liking. Furthermore, the proposals for Van Hogendorpplein would be evaluated in connection with Berlage's second design for Hofplein (1926). And, as if all this was not enough, Witteveen pointed out that the architects should also take account of a projected new east–west connection via Blaak in the direction of Van Hogendorpplein and Vischmarkt.[7]

If the municipal decision to appoint Berlage as architect of the new Amsterdam Exchange on Damrak had been a cause of consternation, the fact that the plans for and construction of the Rotterdam Exchange and its environs had been left entirely to private initiative provoked a storm of criticism, particularly in socialist circles.[8] Likewise the choice of architects, which many people (including members of the city council) felt had unfairly discriminated against local architects. There was also criticism of the building programme. Jan Tinbergen, at that point attached to the Economische Hogeschool (School of Economics) in Rotterdam, observed that a great many programme components had nothing to do with the Exchange as such, and he questioned the need for a large restaurant and 11,000 $m^2$ of office space on Coolsingel, to say nothing of the shops in the widened St. Laurensstraat. He was not the only person to view the overloaded programme as a misconceived imitation of America, where high land prices meant that public buildings were often part of a conglomeration of bars and restaurants, offices and commercial services. But such solutions were quite unnecessary in a city like Rotterdam! Tinbergen warned the Rotterdam authorities that if they accepted the committee's proposals for the new Exchange complex, they would be introducing an elephant into the city, an outsized building that would forever dominate the cityscape.[9] All these objections were trenchantly summarized by the architect H.A. Maaskant in 1947 in his critique of the finished building designed by J.F. Staal: *We readily acknowledge the Rotterdammers' energy, but this building has much too much.*[10]

Oud's entry is intriguing because, of the six competition designs, it was the only one that unconditionally took all the compromises and uncertainties of programme and site as its starting point. Oud took an active part in the various discussions between the building committee and the competition architects, which resulted in substantial adjustments to the building programme. He also consulted Werner Hegemann in Germany about recent literature on commodity exchange buildings in Europe and the United States, although with little result.[11] And of course he also tried to imagine to what uses the new complex on Coolsingel might be put. In one of the few (early) texts on his approach to designing (1933) he had this to say: *For small jobs I usually see the general composition straightaway. Bigger jobs I visualize first by entrusting all parts of the assignment (rooms etc.), their number and size, to a sheet of paper. I prepare the organic arrangement of these elements in the composition by making repeated visits to the places where the life my work has to provide a background for, actually occurs.*



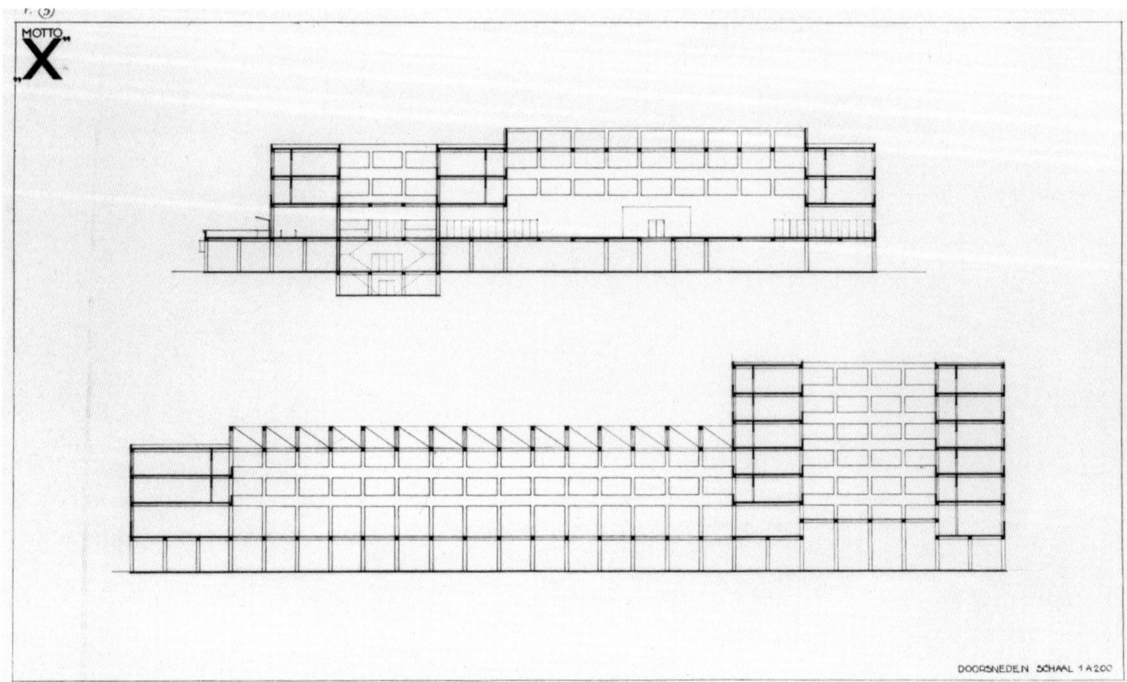


**Long and cross sections/ OUDJ-bs 35, NAI, Rotterdam**

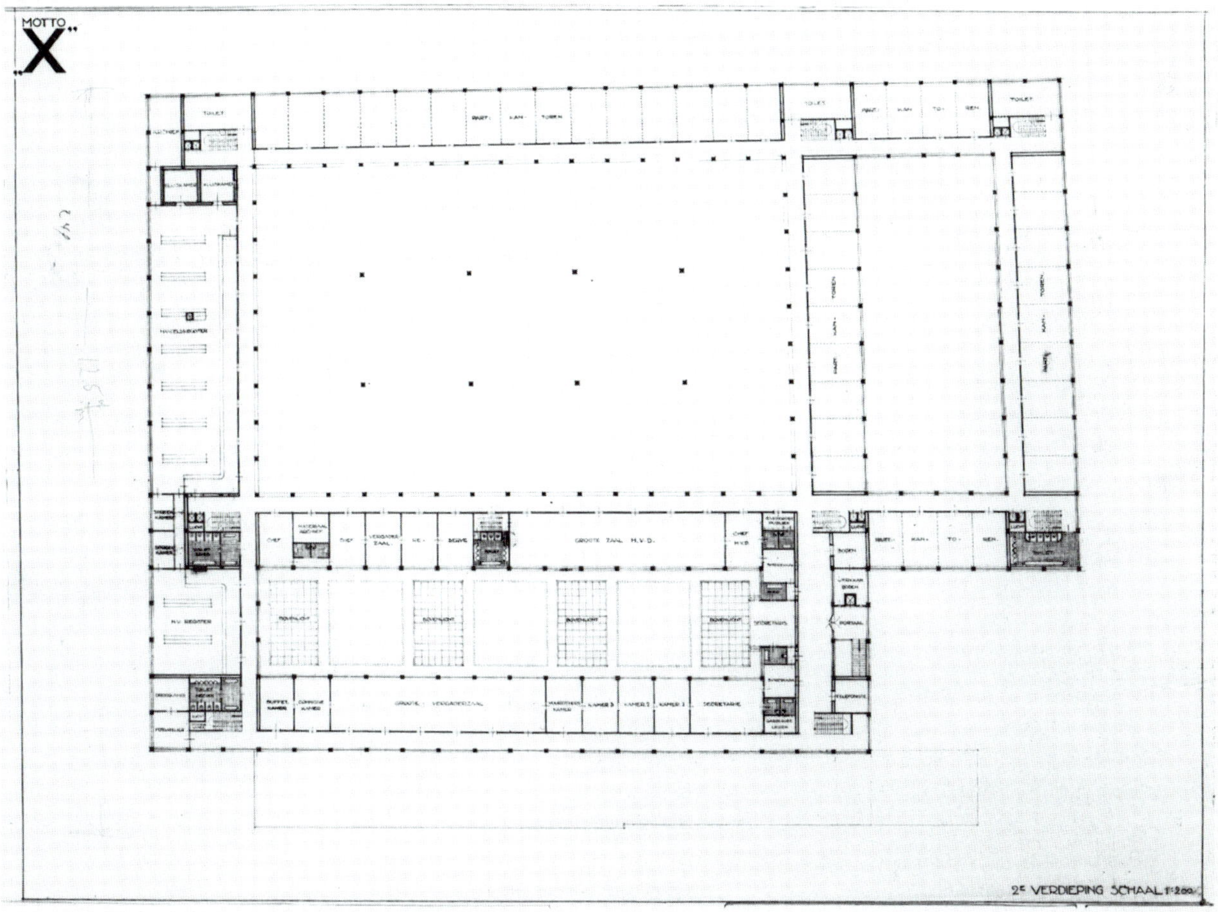

Plan of second floor/ OUDJ-bs 34, NAI, Rotterdam

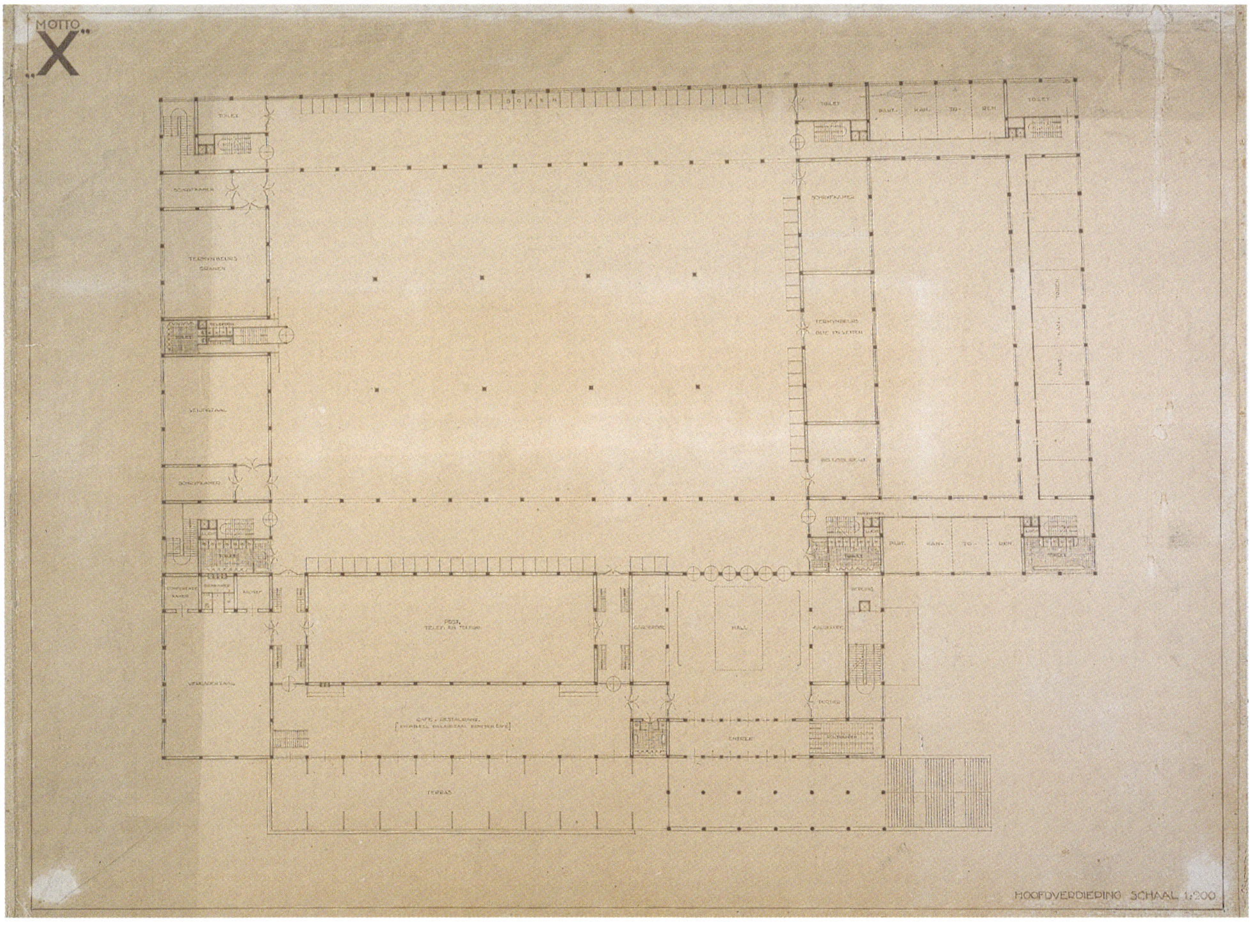

Plan of main floor/ OUDJ-bs 33, NAI, Rotterdam

*There I expose myself to the activities, each time adopting a different role (that of a visitor, a merchant, a doorman, a charwoman etc.). In this way I designed: stock exchange, hotel, cinema, districts, urban extension plans, etc.*[12] There is no reason to distrust this outpouring, which is wholly borne out by the spatial and architectural organization of his Exchange design. This was to a large degree determined by two themes: the vitality and vibrancy of Coolsingel as the beating heart of Rotterdam, and the need for spatial flexibility and multi-functionality imposed by the uncertain and bloated programme. The first theme Oud addressed by way of a subtle spatial insertion of the building into the existing context; the second by a highly radical, architectural exploitation of the chosen construction system.

Just as Dudok, for example, tried to reinforce the order and calm of the street wall by means of the powerful silhouette and massing of his Exchange building, so Oud too sought to establish a broad connection between the three buildings.[13] In Oud's view the Exchange was not some *representative darling, but [a] living part of the urban hustle and bustle.*[14] The connection he sought had less to do with monumentality and everything to do with the dynamism of Coolsingel as urban boulevard. This dynamism is made visible and tangible by a subtle juggling of two building lines. The long elevation on Coolsingel is aligned with (and the same height as) the Post Office, while the prescribed alignment with the Town Hall is applied to an apparently subordinate, front structure containing shops or a department store and a restaurant. This 'frontispiece' is the key to Oud's design in terms both of urban aesthetics and of programme. The front building, with its steps, provides a lead-up and climax towards the Town Hall. Seen from Hofplein, on the other hand, a climax is reached in the high-rise of the office building, which has the effect of neutralizing the outer wall of the Post Office.[15] In addition, the low front building functions, with its outdoor stair, as a prelude to the main entrance of the Exchange and the terraces in front of the Beurs Café. While the ten-metre-wide, open outdoor stairs (plus three escalators and the entrance to the Chamber of Commerce inside the building) are a gesture of vitality in the direction of Coolsingel, for the rest the building resolutely turns its back on the monumental Coolsingel street wall and focuses all its energy on the south side where, at the point where the pedestrian routes of city and building intersect, a plaza emerges, a genuinely 'busy' corner close to Calandplein. All the horizontal and vertical movements converge here and Oud wanted to reinforce this with a substantial technical installation (telecommunications?) on the roof; in the event this was reduced to a flagpole. In his design commentary, Oud wrote: *It seems to the designer that the total layout so created has the further advantage that visitors to the Exchange would be able to fill in the time until the Exchange opens on the little square that will arise – away from the traffic – at the foot of the stairs to the side of the office building, so that they remain outside the stream of pedestrian traffic while the Coolsingel aspect, as a result of this overall organization, is furnished with a vitality that is wholly in keeping with the character of our city.* [16]

Just as he had used the building lines to withdraw the building from the enforced monumental frontality of the Coolsingel wall, so Oud elevated the column arrangement he had chosen for the construction system into the vehicle for what was in many respects a vague and unstable programme. Oud was quite clear about this in his commentary: the constructional system *arose in correlation with the programmatic requirements of the building.*[17] Moreover, and this was greatly held against him by the jury (read: Berlage), Oud allowed the constructional system to steer both the plan and the facade composition, in short the architecture. The essence of the architectural statement in Oud's Exchange design is neither form nor function but the construction method itself. As such, it is a unique example in Oud's development as a designer of *Elementare Gestaltung* as espoused by Mies van der Rohe, Hans Richter, El Lissitzky and Werner Graeff, the editors of *G. Material zur elementaren Gestaltung*, with whom Oud corresponded regularly in these years.[18] The organization of the floor plan and the arrangement of the windows were not subordinate to a specific composition; on the contrary, they were independent, *atypical*, and neutral vis à vis the hybrid and unstable nature of the programme. In his design commentary Oud put it succinctly: *The chosen structural system is reinforced concrete construction: for a building of this consequence the most usual, economical and practical. The basis was an intercolumniation of 5 m. centre-to-centre: a spacing that is economical and in practice allows an internal division into rooms of 5 m. or multiples thereof, which makes it possible to place 2 double desks or multiples thereof in front of one window. This column system dominates both the plan form and the exterior. In the floor plan all the building components are so designed that they can always be changed around within the framework of this system without affecting the exterior. Staircases, toilets, halls, rooms, corridors, etc. have the same windows, thus allowing for continual change, a precondition for a building like the present one. For example, corridors can be shifted left or right, while the offices can, if required, be projected either side of a central corridor without adversely affecting the architecture.*[19]

The Exchange design and accompanying commentary together form one of the few instances – apart from earlier remarks on the subject in *De Stijl* and the *Opbouw* lecture (1921) – in which Oud expressed his opinion on the architectonic aspects of concrete construction. His ideas in the mid-1920s appear to have been sharply radicalized by the polemical articles of Mies van der Rohe, such as the one about office buildings (*Bürohaus*) in the first issue of the magazine *G* (1923). Here every form of aesthetic speculation, of architectural doctrine and formalism was rejected and the office building objectively defined as a building of work, organization, clarity and economy. In terms of building materials, hard concrete (skeleton) is contrasted with pliable dough (skin). As in Oud's Exchange, the module is based on the most efficient organization of the work place and the column distance is set at five metres, resulting in a (three-dimensional) grid that is applied throughout the building.[20] The association with Mies's proposed identification of architecture with concrete, steel and glass, is even discernible in a letter Oud wrote to S. Giedion describing 'his' Exchange: *The whole thing is a large construction of glass, mounted in concrete, with shops, neon lights etc. In its function very lively, as is required to serve its purpose and, for the rest, so it seems to me, very clear in its architecture.*[21]

Oud grasped the opportunity offered by the associated ideas competition for the area around Van Hogendorpplein to place his Exchange at the centre of a new road and traffic system. If Rotterdam went ahead with plans to improve the existing north–south and east–west connections by widening several streets in the city centre, these would necessarily intersect at Van Hogendorpplein. The Boymans Museum would have to disappear. The block to the north of this (adjacent to the new Exchange) would suddenly become a unique location for an 'important building'. At any rate it gave Oud the opportunity to project a substantial building that in height, building line and mode of construction was a continuation of the Exchange office tower in the direction of Van Hogendorpplein, thereby allowing the Exchange to *slot naturally into the development along Blaak.*[22]

In the jury's view, Oud's competition design offered too few starting points to warrant second-round refinement. Although they commended the spatial orientation in general and the opening up of the building at the plaza in particular, they felt that *the architecture was inappropriate to the purpose and the location.*[23] The kind of architecture they had in mind can be inferred from their review of the winning design in the second round, that of J.F. Staal: *He [Staal] also succeeded in developing an expressive but very controlled and distinguished architecture that offers every guarantee that should the commission be awarded to him, a monumental building worthy of the Rotterdam merchant will be achieved.*[24] This outcome was a bitter disappointment for Oud and it appears that he was quick to apprise his friends in Germany of the dramatic dénouement. A letter from Oud to Giedion suggests that Walter Gropius had been aware of the results of the jury's deliberations at an early stage but, because of the confidential nature of the information, was unable at first to undertake any action on Oud's behalf.[25]

On 3 May 1927, the day before the Exchange committee decided to hold a second round (in which Mertens, Dudok and Staal were invited to take part), Gropius wrote to Oud: *Your stock exchange story keeps going through my head and I would like to do anything that may prevent things from going wrong. I wrote a long letter to Berlage and I actually started by setting forth my ideas about the two architectural*

Perspective/ dr1984: 0046, CCA, Montreal

Isometric projection/ OUDJ-bs 12, NAI, Rotterdam

*trends in Holland. And I then linked up with your case. Of course, I have no idea how he will react. Anyway, I believe it is really necessary that you, with the many essential contributions you make, should succeed with a large building that cannot be ignored.*[26] Gropius did, however, try via jury member Van der Leeuw to get Oud into the second round instead of Dudok, but the jury was immovable. Two weeks later, Bruno Taut wrote a long letter to Berlage relating his impressions of Dutch architecture during a brief vacation in the Netherlands. He also touched in passing on the matter of the Exchange: *During my brief stay in Rotterdam I was very pleased to come upon Oud's clear architectural conception, further developed and matured in his new work. His group of houses at Hoek van Holland already overcomes the theoretical rigidity that is always fated to be the mark of an initial tendency. What I found to be confirmed in his design for the Rotterdam Exchange were especially the accuracy and clarity of his conception, which largely and so in the end completely and adequately corresponds with the excellent arrangement of the plan. I also feel that the arrangement of the walls will lend this rather unattractive place something substantial, at least as far as this is still possible, when we take into consideration the buildings that have been put up haphazardly in that neighbourhood without any sense of composition. Looking at the flowing, light and, in its kind, wonderful housing project at Hoek van Holland I am under the impression that Oud will be able to add a similar touch to the construction of the Exchange, that will surpass the skeleton-type structure.*[27] Taut had intended calling on Berlage himself during his vacation but the latter was in Switzerland to discuss with Karl Moser the adjudication of the international competition for the League of Nations building at Geneva.

Towards the end of his life Berlage, probably unintentionally at first, played an important role in the international reputation of modern architecture both as movement and as a method of building. This was a consequence of his active involvement in major architectural design competitions at Rotterdam and Geneva and also of his (disappointing) inaugural speech at the founding of CIAM in La Sarraz (1928). On all these occasions Berlage adopted a critical if not dismissive attitude towards the aspirations and direction of modern architecture; an attitude he subsequently tried to substantiate theoretically in lectures and articles, which in turn brought him into conflict, in the Netherlands at any rate, with the 'young guard', including Oud. In effect, Berlage's stance – and the reactions it provoked – marked 'the end of unrestrained, or at least carefree, experimentation with innovations in architecture', at least in Oud's case. When Berlage wrote to him in September to compliment him on his Stuttgart houses, Oud wrote back: *Your letter pleased me more than I can say. I have mentioned to you once before that I have the painful feeling that you are less and less enamoured of my work, whereas I am firmly convinced that I am following your teaching and that I, more than anyone else, am working in the direction indicated by you.*[28]

Berlage was the only member of the older generation present at the first CIAM gathering in La Sarraz and during the congress the differences separating Berlage and the younger generation manifested themselves on several fronts. In the months following his return home, Berlage toured the country with a lecture entitled *Het congres van La Sarraz. Over de internationale architectuur* (The La Sarraz congress. On international architecture), in which he – one of the founders of modern architecture – was highly critical of the principal 'mottos' of international architecture.[29] In so doing he deliberately forced a rift in the early, person-

359 **Notes**

**1.** A. Plate, 'Rotterdams Beurs', in: *Forum* 2(1947)9/10, pp. 262-263.
**2.** J.J.P. Oud, 'Motto "X". Toelichting tot het voorlopig schetsontwerp voor een beursgebouw te Rotterdam'. Typescript, undated [15 November 1926], Oud Archive, NAI, Rotterdam.
**3.** For the (pre) history of the Exchange, see: P. Penn, *Beursgebouw*, Rotterdam 1940, pp. 15-18; J.A. Feith, *De Koopmansbeurs te Rotterdam. De ontstaansgeschiedenis van een in de architectuurgeschiedenis miskend gebouw* (Architectural History paper – University of Groningen), Groningen 1995.
**4.** J.A. Feith, *De Koopmansbeurs te Rotterdam. De ontstaansgeschiedenis van een in de architectuurgeschiedenis miskend gebouw* (Architectural History paper – University of Groningen), Groningen 1995, pp. 18-10.
**5.** J.A. Feith, *De Koopmansbeurs te Rotterdam. De ontstaansgeschiedenis van een in de architectuurgeschiedenis miskend gebouw* (Architectural History paper – University of Groningen) Groningen 1995, p. 26.
**6.** J.A. Feith, *De Koopmansbeurs te Rotterdam. De ontstaansgeschiedenis van een in de architectuurgeschiedenis miskend gebouw* (Architectural History paper – University of Groningen) Groningen 1995, p. 27.
**7.** Minutes of the Bouwcommissie meeting of 8 April 1926, p. 7. Idem, copy of letter from W.G. Witteveen to H.W. Dudok, 26 July 1926, Berlage Archive 128, NAI, Rotterdam.
**8.** M. Bock, 'De beurs van Berlage. Het ontstaan van een conceptie', in: M. Bock (et al.), *De inrichting van de Beurs van Berlage. Geschiedenis en Behoud*, Zwolle 1995, pp. 6-24.
**9.** H. Engel, 'Architecture without characteristics. On sustainability in architecture', in: *The Architecture Annual 1995-1996. Delft University of Technology*, Rotterdam 1997, pp. 66-72.
**10.** H.A. Maaskant, 'Rotterdams Beursgebouw', in: *Forum* 2(1947)9/10, pp. 275-276.
**11.** The editors of *Wasmuth's Monatshefte für Baukunst* to J.J.P. Oud, 19 June 1926; J.J.P. Oud to W. Hegemann, 19 September 1926. Hegemann sent a special issue devoted to the 'Ulmer Münsterplatzfrage'of *Städtebau. Monatshefte für Stadtbaukunst, Städtischer Verkehrs-, Park- und Siedlungswesen*, 3/4 (1925), NAI, Rotterdam.
**12.** J.J.P. Oud, 'Wie ich arbeite'. Typescript, 29 September 1933. Published in French in *L'Architecture d'Aujourd'hui*, 5(1933)2, pp. 58-59. See also

alized historiography of the Modern Movement as presented by Oud, Gropius, Le Corbusier and especially Giedion. He was particularly scathing about the way certain principles that had guided the renewal of architecture since the beginning of the century in both Europe and the United States had been raised to the status of dogma, such as pure construction as the basis of the 'new world of forms' or the ban on ornament. Berlage ended his lecture by musing on what he saw as the contradictory character of the 'international movement' in architecture which, in reacting in a somewhat 'forced' manner to academic stylistic architecture and to every form of false monumentality, had itself fallen into the trap of 'formalism'. He wondered whether *in the place of the disputed formalism a new formalism is not involuntarily manifesting itself, as a result of the unconditional combination of three building materials, concrete, iron and glass and this last even to a maximum according to the dogma of 100 per cent.* It was as if all the certainties about the future of contemporary building as propagated in circles around magazines like *G*, *ABC* and to some extent *de 8 en Opbouw* had been banned by decree. And as if that were not enough, he also wondered *whether, in the light of such propaganda for the new style it does not appear as if the building material has become an end in itself and as if the architect who continues to use wood rather than concrete should be regarded as totally backward?*[30] Berlage was convinced that the architecture now presenting itself as international was of a temporary and provisional nature only, that it was the exponent of a civilization in transition and as such still lacking the human dimension. According to this line of reasoning Oud's Exchange was an interesting building but it manifestly lacked the artist's touch needed to turn the mechanical character into a social idea, into style. In Dutch architectural circles the debate only really got going when Berlage, in an interview in the social-democratic newspaper *Vooruit* (13 February 1932), made a frontal attack on the 'insensitivity' of the new objectivity and repeated his contention that the preoccupation of modern architects with the objective and technical aspects of society could not of itself lead to 'art'. Not long afterwards the first reactions appeared in *de 8 en Opbouw*, including a temperate and above all defensive one from Oud and a radical and aggressive one from Duiker. In his defence, Oud fell back to the positions he had erected in 1921 in his *Opbouw* lecture.[31] Modern architecture might be based on technology – contemporary building materials and construction methods – but the motivation for the new form had been and still was developments in visual art, film and science. If this connection had initially led to a measure of formalism – *horizontal and vertical lines, floating slabs, corner windows, etc. were very popular for a while* – architects were now indeed in danger of going too far in the other direction. Oud did, however, dispute the existence of purely objective modern buildings devoid of aesthetic value. But that was not really the point. The major gain of the past decade, according to Oud, was that thanks to modern architects *building had once more been put at the service of people, in order to produce for them the healthiest, most practical and pleasant objects for everyday use.* The search for this had led to numerous improved insights with regard to orientation, technical services and the design of dwellings, offices and factories, insights that together formed the true ethos of modern architecture, the 'moral value' Berlage set so much store by.

Berlage's position on the Exchange issue and in the verbal skirmishing that followed, caused Oud's artistic vocation to take a different (in the sense of defensive) turn, away from a tradition he himself had previously so carefully constructed and propagated on numerous occasions. In his strongly



J.J.P. Oud, *Architecturalia voor bouwheren en architecten,* The Hague 1963, p. 25.

**13.** H.W. van Bergeijk, *Willem Marinus Dudok. Architect-stedebouwkundige 1884-1974,* Naarden 1995, pp. 190-191; 'Geen sensaties, niet ultramodern, maar één organisch geheel. De Rotterdamse nieuwe Beurs', in: *Forum* 36(1993)3/4, pp. 99-122.

**14.** J.J.P. Oud, 'Beursproject Rotterdam 1926', in: *i 10. Internationale Revue,* 2(1928)14, p. 25. This article saw the first publication of the famous isometric drawing.

**15.** J.J.P. Oud to B.J. Koldewey, 29 October 1935 (with explanation of the X motto), OUDJ-B, NAI, Rotterdam.

**16.** J.J.P. Oud, 'Motto "X". Toelichting tot het voorloopig schetsontwerp voor een Beursgebouw te Rotterdam'. Typescript, undated [15 November 1926], p. 2, Oud Archive, NAI, Rotterdam.

**17.** J.J.P. Oud, 'Motto "X". Toelichting tot het voorloopig schetsontwerp voor een Beursgebouw te Rotterdam'. Typescript, undated [15 November 1926], p. 2, Oud Archive, NAI, Rotterdam.

**18.** F. Neumeyer, *Mies van der Rohe. Das kunstlose Wort. Gedanken zur Baukunst,* Munich 1986, p. 130 ff.

**19.** J.J.P. Oud, 'Motto "X". Toelichting tot het voorloopig schetsontwerp voor een Beursgebouw te Rotterdam'. Typescript, undated [15 November 1926], p. 2, Oud Archive, NAI, Rotterdam.

**20.** F. Neumeyer, *Mies van der Rohe. Das kunstlose Wort. Gedanken zur Baukunst,* Munich 1986, pp. 299-300.

**21.** J.J.P. Oud to S. Giedion, 5 May 1927, GTA, Zurich.

**22.** J.J.P. Oud, 'Beursproject Rotterdam 1926', in: *i 10. Internationale Revue,* 2(1928)14, p. 25.

**23.** J.J.P. Oud to B.J. Koldewey, 29 October 1935, OUDJ-B, NAI, Rotterdam.

**24.** Letter accompanying the Report on the second round, addressed to A.J.H. Goudriaan, September 1928, Beurs van Koophandel Archive, Rotterdam.

**25.** J.J.P. Oud to S. Giedion, 5 May 1927, GTA, Zurich.

**26.** W. Gropius to Oud, 3 May 1927, OUDJ-B, NAI, Rotterdam.

**27.** B. Taut to J.J.P. Oud, 17 May 1927 (with copy of letter from Taut to H.P. Berlage of the same date), OUDJ-B, NAI, Rotterdam.

**28.** J.J.P. Oud to H.P. Berlage, 11 October 1927, OUDJ-B, NAI, Rotterdam.

**29.** M. Bax, '"Het congres van La Sarraz". Een lezing van berlage uit 1929', in: *Jong Holland* 7(1991)14, pp. 44-51; M. Bock, *Anfänge einer neuen Architektur Berlages.*

personalized view of the history of the new Dutch architecture (adopted from Berlage, as it happened), Berlage's rejection effectively deprived the younger generation of the opportunity to locate its searching and experimenting within the 'great' tradition of the modern style which, at the beginning of the century, had heralded a new era in Dutch architecture. In the final analysis, Oud laid the responsibility for this entirely at Berlage's door: *His principles, abstract and prophetic enough in writing, became in the reality of his feeling, thinking and doing always Berlage-ideas in Berlage-forms. The disadvantage of this was that we, his young disciples, were initially able to believe that we were observing his principles, whereas he had the impression that we were going against him. It was his tragedy, as well as ours.*[32]



*Beitrag zur architektonischen Kultur der Niederlände im ausgehenden 19. Jahhundert,* The Hague, Wiesbaden 1983, pp. 45-50.
**30.** M. Bax, '"Het congres van La Sarraz". Een lezing van Berlage uit 1929', in: *Jong Holland* 7(1991)14, pp. 46-51.
**31.** M. Bock (et al.), *Groep '32. Ontwerpen, gebouwen, stedebouwkundige plannen 1925-1945,* The Hague 1983, pp. 22-25.
**32.** J.J. P. Oud, 'Dr. H.P. Berlage 1856-1934', in: *de 8 en Opbouw,* 18(1934)5, p. 151.

**Sources**
CCA: dr1984: 0036-0049, dr9184: 0537, dr1984: 0538, ph1984: 1098, ph1984: 1099
Getty: 890126-20**
MOMA: NC Drawings-blueprints
NAI: OUDJ-bs -36, OUDJ-ph 402, OUDJ-ph 1702-1703, OUDJ-bs 1001-1003, OUDJ-bs 3001, MAQV 639, PBRO
The Art Institute of Chicago: 1 drawing

**Articles**
P., 'De projecten voor Rotterdams Beurs', in: *Het Vaderland,* 9 February 1929
B.J. Koldewey,'De nieuwe Beurs te Rotterdam', in: *Het R.K. Bouwblad,* 7 (1935)6
A. Otten, 'Rotterdamsche problemen', in: *Bouwkundig Weekblad,* (1929)21
J.J.P. Oud, 'Beursproject Rotterdam 1926', in: *i10,* 2(1928)14

**Literature**
U. Barbieri, *J.J.P. Oud,* Rotterdam 1987, pp. 60-61
H. Engel, 'Architecture without characteristics', in: *Jaarboek TU Delft,* 1995-1996
H.E. Oud, *J.J.P. Oud. Architekt 1890-1963. Feiten en herinneringen gerangschikt,* The Hague 1984, pp. 94-97
G. Stamm, *J.J.P. Oud. Bauten und Projekte 1906 bis 1963,* Mainz, Berlin 1984, pp. 84-86

# 3 New Architecture in Crisis

**Oud on the beach at Kijkduin/ OUDJ-53, NAI, Rotterdam**

# Oud's Designs after Leaving the Woningdienst

By the middle of the 1930s, European modernism was looking distinctly shaky, assailed as it was by external threats and irreconcilable internal differences. In the Soviet Union, long extolled as the country where the creation of a new society was accompanied by the most daring experiments, including in architecture and town planning, modernism was ousted by socialist-realism, a visual vocabulary with greater popular appeal. Popular appeal – *volkstümlich* – was the preference of the National Socialist regime in Germany as well, and there, too, it spelled the end of the modernist avant-garde. The consequences of Germany's defection from the modernist camp were far graver than the Soviet Union's volte-face, for Germany was the heartland of modernism and German its medium of communication. The other European countries where modernism appeared to have taken root were Czechoslovakia, Hungary, Austria, Switzerland and the Netherlands, but with the exception of the last two, these countries, too, fell prey to nationalist dictatorships that paved the way for an end to modernism. In England the movement led a marginal existence and in Italy ornamentation and decoration appeared to have transformed modern building into a representational style that had nothing to do with the original principles of the movement. Even in France, which could boast a modernist master in the person of Le Corbusier and where such prominent designers as A. Lurçat (1894-1970) and Mallet Stevens (1886-1945) were counted as belonging the Modern Movement, the modernists failed to become the architectural mainstream.[1]

But it was not just the context of modernism that deteriorated. Inside the movement, too, there were visible signs of a reaction. During the 1930s there was a polarization of views between orthodox functionalists and a group of mainly younger architects who promoted the autonomous cultural dimension of the design. They regarded the pursuit of architectural beauty as one of the fundamentals of the profession and were no longer prepared to subordinate this to a puritanical functionalism; in this respect Le Corbusier was regarded as an exemplar by many Dutch members of the young guard. Giedion, the secretary of CIAM, spoke of a 'romantische Reaktion',[2] as well he might, since such views were diametrically opposed to those prevailing within CIAM – yet even that organization rarely met any more, buffeted as it was by political opposition and economic recession. All these trends lent weight to the perception that modernism had had its day in Europe.

The result was a veritable exodus to the United States where architects of the calibre of Gropius, Mendelsohn and Mies van der Rohe were received with open arms, along with many avant-garde artists, including Piet Mondrian. Between 1933 and 1935, English supplanted German as the 'official' language of the Modern Movement, a development that can be clearly traced in Oud's voluminous correspondence. The shift of focus from Europe to the United States was not without consequences for the character of the Modern Movement. Modernism shed the stigma of a socialist-inspired countermovement and was embraced as a cultural phenomenon by some of the most elitist cultural institutions in America, including Harvard University and the Museum of Modern Art (MOMA). As a result of this metamorphosis, modern architecture suddenly found itself required to design representational buildings for a new type of client: the wealthy business world. In the depressed 1930s this task was not so urgent, but in the decades that followed demand boomed.

The 1930s were also a period of drastically altered circumstances for Oud. The termination of his employment at the Woningdienst in 1933 brought with it great uncertainty, notwithstanding the transitional period on reduced pay to which he was entitled. Although Oud set himself up in private practice, he decided against establishing a full-fledged office; he worked from home and never had more than two draughtsmen in his employ. Major commissions failed to materialize and until the late 1930s he was dependent on the design of furniture, interiors and villas (many of which were never realized). A modest highpoint was his collaboration on the fitting

**out of the SS *Nieuw Amsterdam*, the Rotterdam-built flagship of the Holland America Line. His fortunes finally turned in 1938 when the Bataafsche Importmaatschappij (BIM, later Shell) chose him to design its new head office in The Hague. Only then was Oud able to put into practice his ideas about the design of the representational public building, ideas he had earlier experimented with in his competition design for the new town hall at Amsterdam.**



**Notes**

**1.** J.L. Cohen, *André Lurçat 1894-1970; autocritique d'un moderne*, Liège 1995.

**2.** S. Giedion to L. Moholy-Nagy, 29 July 1938, GTA, Zurich.

Founded in Antwerp in 1921 by M. Seuphor, *Het Overzicht* was one of several interwar magazines that aspired to become a platform for the international avant-garde. In the beginning, as its subtitle – 'Arts, Letters and Humanity' – suggested, it cast its net wide, but over the years its focus narrowed to the visual arts. Unlike Theo Van Doesburg with *De Stijl*, M. Seuphor and J. Peeters, the chief editors of *Het Overzicht* did not wish to form a movement, but rather a network of avant-garde artists. An important step in this direction were the contacts already made by one of the editors, the artist J. Peeters, as secretary of the Kring Moderne Kunst Antwerpen (Antwerp Modern Art Circle). There were intensive contacts with Van Doesburg, for example, with the Italian Futurist Marinetti, with H.N. Werkman of the Groningen painters' society 'De Ploeg', with Paul Dermée of *L'Esprit Nouveau* and H. Walden of *Der Sturm*. The collaboration was not limited to the articles and projects that these and other artists published in the magazine. From 1923 onwards, the cover of each issue was designed by a different artist. As well as Oud, cover designs were made by L. Moholy-Nagy and R. Delaunay among others.[1]

The contact between Oud and *Het Overzicht* was also through Peeters, who approached Oud in 1922 to write an article for the magazine. After some initial reluctance, Oud eventually produced 'Aforismen' (Aphorisms, 1923).[2] At the end of 1923 Peeters asked Oud to design the cover of the twenty-first issue. Once again Oud was reticent at first, on this occasion because the design had to be delivered in the form of a linocut which was outside his experience.[3] The design was finished at the beginning of 1924. It was composed as a contrast between a coloured area and letters, with the letters at the top and bottom of the page and the coloured area in between.

Cover design/ OUDJ-ty 3, NAI, Rotterdam

Cover design/ OUDJ-ty 2, NAI, Rotterdam



**Notes**

**1.** H. Henkels (ed.), *Seuphor* Haags Gemeente Museum, The Hague 1976, pp. 8-15.
**2.** J. Peeters to J.J.P. Oud, 2 February 1922, Oud Archive, Nederlands Letterkundig Museum, The Hague.
**3.** Postcard from J.J.P. Oud to J. Peeters, undated [1923], Oud Archive, Nederlands Letterkundig Museum, The Hague.

**Sources**

NAI: OUDJ-ty 2-3

**Literature**

H. Henkels, (ed.), *Seuphor*, Haags Gemeente Museum, The Hague 1976, pp. 8-15

# 59/ Cover for *Rotterdam. Outlines of Extension and Housing*



*Rotterdam. Outlines of Extension and Housing 1924* was an English-language booklet about urban planning in Rotterdam, produced by the Gemeentelijke Woningdienst. After a brief introduction about the city's identification with port activities, an outline of the city's development, plans for expansion, inner-city slum clearance and road building programmes, it presented several recently completed housing schemes, giving details of the location, access roads and type of construction and so on. With the exception of the development along the Kralingse Plas in the northeast corner of the city, most of the projects featured were on the south bank of the Maas where land prices were lowest. In addition to two concrete-built complexes, Hillepolder by J.M. van Hardeveld and Bloemhof by J. Hulsebosch, there was a 'flat-building' on Beukelsdijk by L.C. van der Vlugt, an urban square development in Spangen by Meischke & Schmidt, Oud's Tusschendijken blocks and the Vreewijk 'garden city' by Granpré Molière, Verhagen and Kok.
Oud was responsible for the publication's design. Although he is not mentioned specifically, it is known that Oud designed the cover and perhaps also the page layout and the maps.[1] The inner pages, like the cover are divided into two columns. At first glance, the design does not seem very adventurous for a supposedly avant-garde architect employed by the Woningdienst. Its originality only becomes apparent upon use, when the reader discovers that the booklet has been folded twice. The pages are folded and bound along the spine in the normal way but the resulting square has been folded in two between the columns to produce a rectangular booklet. On the right-hand section of the cover (the front, when folded double) is the title of the publication: *Rotterdam*. The sub-title, *Outlines of Extension and Housing 1924*, is on the left-hand section. There is a visual allusion to the booklet's contents in the form of a map of Rotterdam and a schematic representation of housing.
In 1925 Oud designed a cover for a special issue of *Der Neubau* devoted to 'Die Volkswohnung' (public housing).

Cover design/ OUDJ-ty 4, NAI, Rotterdam



**Notes**
**1.** These can be found in OUDJ-ty 1-13, NAI, Rotterdam.

**Sources**
NAI: OUDJ-ty 1-13, Oud Library

**59/ Cover for *Rotterdam. Outlines of Extension and Housing***

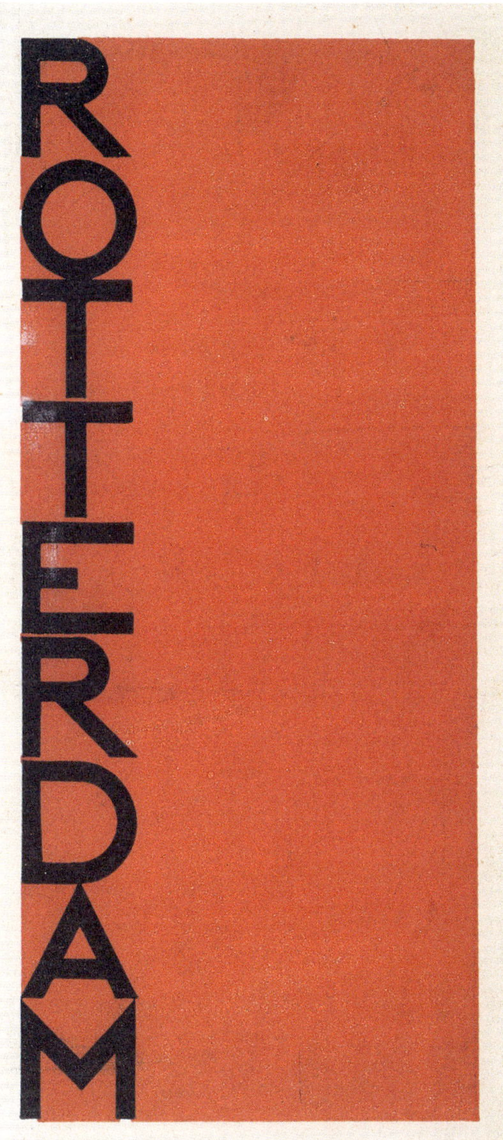


Cover design/ OUDJ-ty 1, NAI, Rotterdam

# 60/ Writing Paper, Envelope and Cover for *De Opbouw, democratisch tijdschrift voor Nederland en Indië* 1935-1936

In July 1935, at the request of the magazine's secretary, B.W. Kranenburg, Oud designed new stationery for *De Opbouw*. Oud also 'promised' *to take another look at the Monthly's cover with a view to discussing possible changes to it.*[1] In August 1935, Oud sent Kranenberg a sketch design with the request to agree in principle after which he would himself conduct the subsequent correspondence with the printers (Van Gorcum & Co.). He explained his design on this occasion as follows: *Mindful of the scholarly nature of the magazine I did not make the design too exuberant. ...My idea is: cover on (not too thin) white paper, pre-printed (a year at a time for example) with the blue colour. This means that for each issue the black text can be easily arranged and printed on the prepared cover. Except for the one-off blue printing, which is not expensive, this entails no extra costs. If a change of colour were wanted after one year, a different colour could be chosen, which would also make it easier to locate an issue from a particular year. It may be that even the colour is considered a bit much for a scholarly magazine, but nowadays it is necessary to call attention to a magazine and so I think it would be a good idea to do it like this. The blue should be: cobalt blue (not too dark).*[2] The (final?) proof was dispatched in May 1936; the design was probably used for the first time in June of that year.

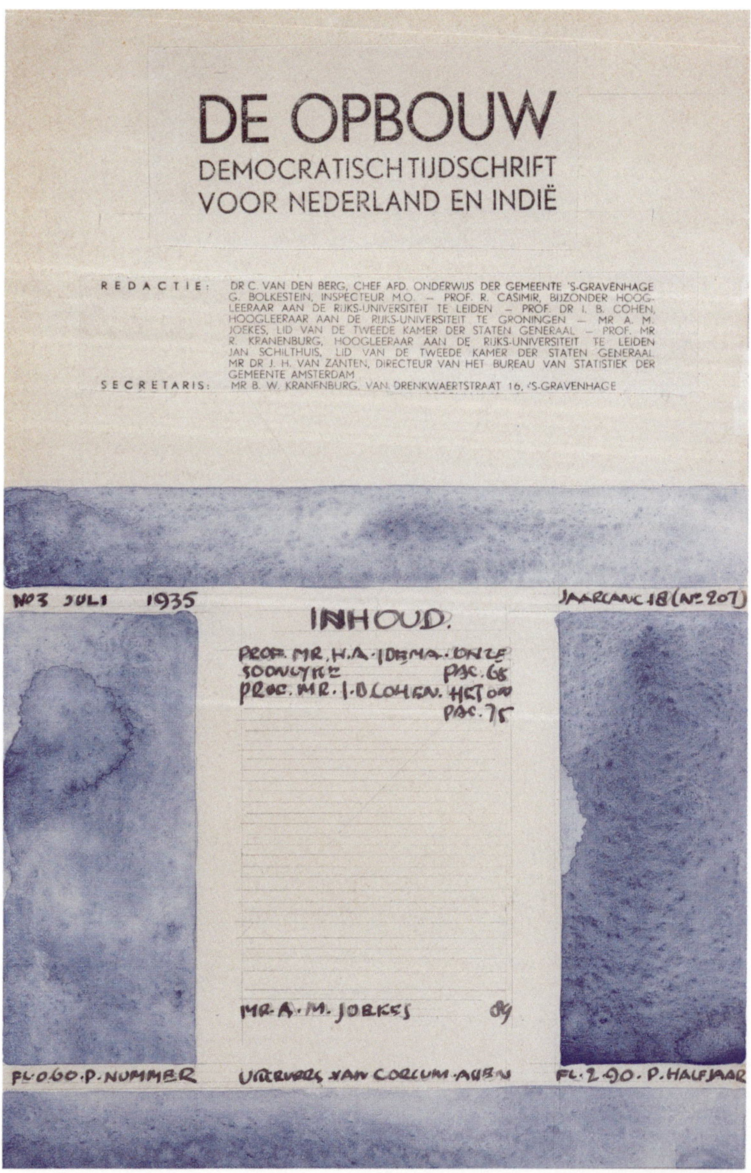


Cover design/ OUDJ-ty 6, NAI, Rotterdam

**Notes**
**1.** J.J.P. Oud to Van Gorcum & Co., 2 August 1935, OUDJ-B, NAI, Rotterdam.
**2.** J.J.P. Oud to B.W. Kranenburg, 27 August 1935, OUDJ-B, NAI, Rotterdam.

**Sources**
NAI: OUDJ-ty 6, OUDJ-ty 3001, OUDJ-B

**Articles**
*De Opbouw, democratisch tijdschrift voor Nederland en Indië*, 19(1936)2 (no. 218), June 1936

# 61/ Piano Lamp / Giso 404

**1927**

In July 1927, Oud's friend Harm Kamerlingh Onnes married Titia Easton. For their wedding gift, Oud designed a piano lamp which he had made by W.H. Gispen. Gispen took the design into production and it subsequently became known as Giso 404. The lamp has a round base and an asymmetrically attached cylinder that is held in balance by a massive sphere. This balancing act of stereometrical forms evokes associations with Bauhaus experiments. The only surviving sketch for the lamp shows a version in which the arm is attached to the centre of the cylinder, but this symmetrical variant was never made. Later on, probably in the 1950s, the asymmetry was reversed but the precise reason for this change is unknown.

**Piano lamp. From: W.H. Gispen, 'Techniek en Kunst', in: *Wendingen*, 9(1928)2**



**Sources**

ICN: R12315
Museum Boymans van Beuningen: inv. no. V2.2-1621
NAI: OUDJ-kh (sketch on drawing of Kiefhoek)

**Literature**


A. Koch, *W.H. Gispen; een modern eclecticus (1890-1981)*, Rotterdam 1988, pp. 33, 56-58

B.A. Laan, A. Koch (eds), *Collectie Gispen; meubels, lampen en archivalia in het NAI, 1916-1980*, Rotterdam 1996, pp. 95-96

H.E. Oud, *J.J.P. Oud. Architekt 1890-1963. Feiten en herinneringen gerangschikt*, The Hague 1984, p. 199

E. Reinhartz-Tergau, 'Een Gispenlamp van 1987 J.J.P. Oud', in: *Jong Holland* 3(1987)1, pp. 34-37

# 62/ Cabinet for the Domela Nieuwenhuis Collection

**Rotterdam, Museum Boymans van Beuningen** **1925**

In 1924, the committee responsible for the Dutch entry in the Exposition Internationale des Arts Décoratifs et Industriels to be held in Paris in 1925, asked Oud to submit material. He was not overly enthusiastic, especially since the French organizers had ruled out German participation. On the other hand, Oud was disinclined to heed his German friends' call to boycott the exhibition. He decided that he would only take part if he were allowed to exhibit five photographs instead of the three requested by the committee. These photographs of the Witte Dorp, Tusschendijken and De Vonk were among the 255 architectural photographs exhibited in rooms designed by H.T. Wijdeveld. In addition, the city of Rotterdam entered a wooden cabinet Oud had designed for a collection of some three thousand prints amassed by A.J. Domela Nieuwenhuis. The commission came from D. Hannema, the director of Museum Boymans, where this collection was housed. *Some time ago you mentioned that you rather like designing furniture. Now the following situation has arisen, for which I am calling on your help. The city council has agreed to grant a sum of money for the construction of a cabinet, which will be its entry in the coming Decorative Arts exhibition in Paris, for the graphic collection of Domela Nieuwenhuis. I would greatly appreciate it if you would be willing to make the design for it. I have already approached the committee's chairman, Mr de Bie, who will be happy to accept a piece furniture designed by you.*[1] The cabinet, which was made by the Rotterdam cabinetmaker M. van Dort, consists of two sections, each conceived as a separate module. The top part of both modules has two doors over the full width, each door emblazoned with the monogram of Museum Boymans – MBR. The bottom section is narrower and has only one door. Sketches reveal the extent to which Oud experimented, especially with the lower section. Although he devised various decorative corners, it was the plainest version that was executed. Oud's cabinet received a 'Diplôme de Médaille d'Or' in the architecture section and a 'Diplôme de Médaille D'Argent' in the interior and furniture design section. Back home, the Dutch entry came in for a lot of criticism. The committee was accused of having made an unbalanced selection

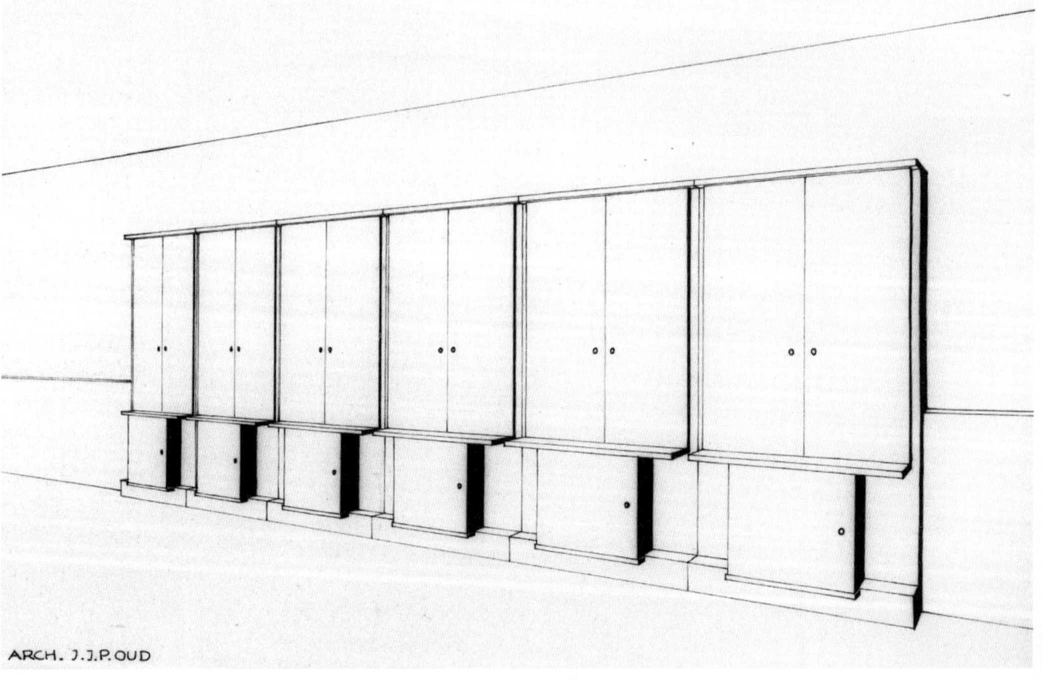


**Perspective of wall units/ OUDJ-kb 6, NAI, Rotterdam**



**Notes**
**1.** D. Hannema to J.J.P. Oud, 26 January 1925, OUDJ-B, NAI, Rotterdam.
**2.** T. van Doesburg, 'Het fiasco van Holland op de expositie te Parijs in 1925', in: *De Stijl*, 6(1925)10/11, pp. 157-158.

**Sources**
CCA: ph1983: 0323, ph1984: 1097
Getty: 890126-20**
NAI: OUDJ-kb 1-6, OUDJ-ph 1694, OUDJ-16, OUDJ-B

**Articles**
*L'art Hollandais a l'exposition internationale des arts decoratifs et industriels modernes; Paris 1925*, Amsterdam 1925, pp. 69, 149
T. van Doesburg, 'Het fiasco van Holland op de expositie te Parijs in 1925', in: *De Stijl*, 6(1925)10/11, pp. 157-158
G. Friedhoff, 'Holland en Denemarken te Parijs', in: *Bouwen*, 3(1925), pp. 97-104

**Literature**
M. Mosler, *D. Hannema. De geboren verzamelaar*, Rotterdam 1995
H.E. Oud, *J.J.P. Oud. Architekt 1890-1963. Feiten en herinneringen gerangschikt*, The Hague 1984, p. 199
E. Reinhartz-Tergau, *J.J.P. Oud, architect: meubelontwerpen en interieurs*, Rotterdam 1990, pp. 44-45

weighted in favour of Amsterdam artists from the Arti et Amicitiae circle. Van Doesburg complained in *De Stijl* about the absence of a collective entry by the magazine's contributors, a protest echoed by several (foreign) artists and architects. He refused to submit work as an individual and lambasted Oud's contribution: *Nor was there any reason to fear the collaboration of the vacillating architect Oud. He had already long since converted to the Liberty-Wendingen style (see the cottagey "Oud Mathenesse" at Rotterdam and the decorative facade architecture of the café "De Unie"). His confession (to the effect that: I like straight lines – but I don't see why curved ones shouldn't be acceptable as well), as published in Gustav Kiepenheuer's Almanak is the entertaining catechism of a muddle-head. Composition: 30% doubt; 30% fear; 33% small-mindedness; 2% understanding and 5% modernity. When one recalls the honest beginnings of this architect, one can only marvel at how, as a result of wholesale practice, the respected objectivity has degenerated into a commercial traveller's mentality. While the Dutch art press, which beats that of all other countries in terms of backwardness, may appeal to the fact that the architect Oud has joined the Wendingen group in spirit and in fact and in so doing supported the suppression and exclusion of the New Style, the Style artists themselves have long since ceased to number Mr Oud among their colleagues.* [2]

**OUDJ-ph 1694, NAI, Rotterdam**

# 63/ Design for Royal Begeer Silver Factory

1934-1935

In 1934, Oud's contacts with the family of the director (A. Plate) of the Woningdienst, put him in touch with Mr G.J.A. Begeer of the eponymous silver factory in Voorschoten, whom he managed to interest in several designs. Oud's dealings with Begeer are a good illustration of his active pursuit of design commissions in the years following his departure from the Woningdienst. *Since I am currently able to cope very well with the pressure of work, I came up with the idea that it might perhaps be worth trying to make something along the lines that we talked about. I have designed lamps, furniture, book covers, etc. in the past... Leerdam once suggested that I should design glass, so why not try to realize something in silver or the like. Of course, I have no idea whether you are interested in anything of the kind and I certainly have no wish to foist it upon you. But should it contain something that appeals to you too, I would be very happy to come and discuss it with you at a time and place to be determined later.*[1] From the correspondence it appears that Oud did indeed work on designs for the factory in the spring of 1935: two models for a doorknob and one for a letterbox.[2] The models were not taken into production.



**Notes**

**1.** J.J.P. Oud to G.J.A. Begeer, 6 December 1934, OUDJ-B, NAI, Rotterdam.

**2.** J.J.P. Oud to Waldherr, 2 April 1935, OUDJ-B, NAI, Rotterdam.

**Sources**

NAI: OUDJ-B

**Literature**

H.E. Oud, *J.J.P. Oud. Architekt 1890-1963. Feiten en herinneringen gerangschikt*, The Hague 1984, p. 114, n.168

# 64/ Furniture Designs for Metz & Co

**1933-1934**

In the early 1930s, Joseph de Leeuw, director of the interior design firm Metz & Co, invited a number of artists and architects to design furniture for the firm. Oud was one of them and the fourth ex-*De Stijl* associate, alongside Van der Leck, Huszár and Rietveld, with whom Metz worked. The presentation of Oud's first four chairs took place at the exhibition 'Het stalen meubel in 1934' (Steel Furniture in 1934), which opened in December 1933 in the 'cupola' Rietveld had designed on the roof of Metz's Amsterdam store. It was Oud's first commercial furniture commission. His four chairs (numbered o1 to o4) all had chromium-plated tubular steel frames and well-cushioned backs, seats and armrests. The most striking feature of the designs are the ingenious frames. The o1 is the simplest of the series, with four straight legs and a well-padded seat; the o2 is a variation of the o1 with armrests. In the o3 the extremely short arms turn into the rear supports which angle sharply backwards and then, where they meet the ground, angle forwards to join up with the front supports in a kind of central 'leg' below the seat. In the o4 the front and rear supports cross one another just below the seat. A short while later, two armchairs were produced, the o5 and o6, which elaborated on the Z-frame of the o3 and were part of the original commission. In 1934, the series was augmented with the o7.[1] This model was made in six versions (o7a to o7f), varying from table chairs without arms to thickly upholstered easy chairs. The only common feature was the graceful, swept-back rear support. There are also designs for a small table that, according to jottings on the drawings, was designed to go with the o7 chair and which is identified on some of the drawings as o8. There are no indications that this table was ever taken into production.

Unlike designers such as Mies van der Rohe and Stam who exploited the lightness and elasticity of steel, the frames of Oud's chairs were not at all elastic and, with their sometimes very thick cushions, were anything but light. They elicited a lot of criticism. The best-known objection is that of J.B. van Loghem, who dubbed Oud's chairs 'a cross between an elephant and a deer.[2] About the o7 series, however, the press was enthusiastic. In 1955, O. van Tussenbroek called

**Display of furniture by Oud in the cupola of Metz & Co's shop in Amsterdam (design G.T. Rietveld, 1933)/ OUDJ-ph 443, NAI, Rotterdam (Photo Spies / d'Oliviera)**



**Notes**

**1.** O. van Tussenbroek included several models of the o7 in his 1955 book, dating them to 1934. However, this series was not mentioned in the original contract with Metz. O. van Tussenbroek, 'Bij werken van J.J.P. Oud', in: *Interieur*, 68(1955)525.

**2.** J.B. van Loghem, 'De stoel gedurende de laatste veertig jaar' in: *De 8 en Opbouw*, 6(1935)1.

**3.** O. van Tussenbroek, 'Bij werken van J.J.P. Oud', in: *Interieur*, 68(1955)525; G. Rietveld, 'Verschillende interieurs door architect J.J.P. Oud', in: *De 8 en Opbouw* 10(1939)3.

**4.** W.J. de Gruyter, 'Het nieuwe gebouw van Metz & Co. te Den Haag', in: *Elsevier's Geïllustreerd Maandschrift*, November 1934, pp. 63-65.

**Sources**

CCA: dr1984: 0124, dr1984: 0126-0143, ph1984: 0898-0901, ph1984: 1147-1151

Gemeentearchief Amsterdam: Metz Archive: METZ.01-METZ.39

Getty: 890126-box 7-16*, 890126-box 7-17*

NAI: OUDJ-mz 1-131, OUDJ-mz 3001, OUDJ-ph 443-460, OUDJ-ph 1842-1843, OUDJ-ph 1717-1718, OUDJ-B

**Articles**

W.J. de Gruyter, 'Het nieuwe gebouw van Metz en Co. te Den Haag', in: *Elsevier's Geïllustreerd Maandschrift*, November 1934, pp. 63-65

J.B. van Loghem, 'De stoel gedurende de laatste veertig jaar' in: *De 8 en Opbouw*, 6(1935)1, p.1

J.J.P. Oud, 'Tentoonstelling Liberty' in: *De 8 en opbouw*, 5(1934)2, p. 2

J.J.P. Oud, 'Van hout tot staal', in: *De Groene Amsterdammer*, 19 January 1935

H. Hoste, 'metaalmeubelen', in: *Opbouwen. Halfmaandelijks tijdschrift voor architektuur, tevens orgaan der Vlaamse architektenvereniging*, 4(1934)1, p. 14

H. Hoste, 'Ouds Nieuwe Metaalmeubelen', in *Opbouwen*, 4(1934)15, pp. 129-131

O. van Tussenbroek, 'Bij werken van J.J.P. Oud' in: *Interieur*, 68(1955)525, pp. 361-365

**Literature**

U. Barbieri, *J.J.P. Oud*, Rotterdam 1987, p. 189

P. Dupuits-Timmer, *Metz de creatieve jaren*, Rotterdam 1995

P. Dupuits-Timmer, 'De tijden veranderen. Bij de heropening van het eerste Haagse filiaal van Metz & Co.', in: *Jong Holland*, 4(1988)2, pp. 563-574

H.E. Oud, *J.J.P. Oud. Architekt 1890-1963. Feiten en herinneringen gerangschikt*, The Hague 1984, pp. 114, 200, 201

T. Overtoom, *J.J.P. Oud*

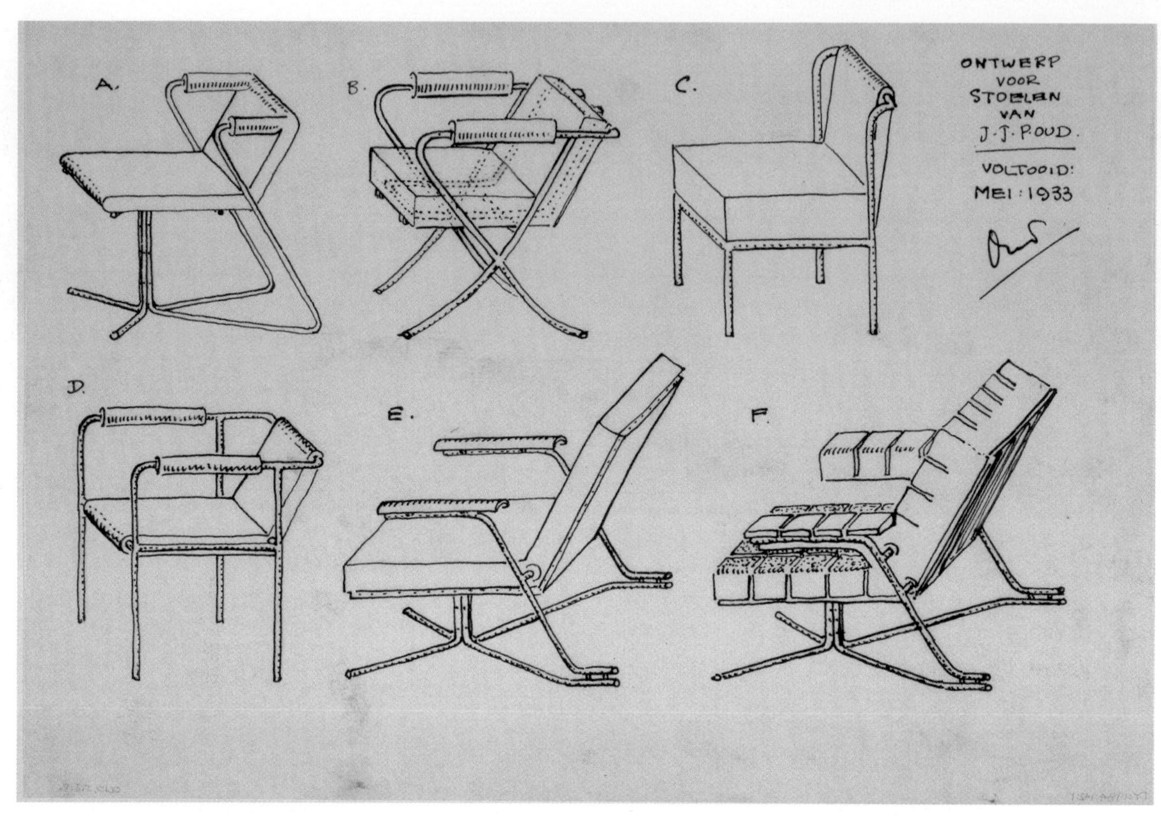


Various design views accompanying the contract, 1933/ dr1984: 0142, CCA, Montreal

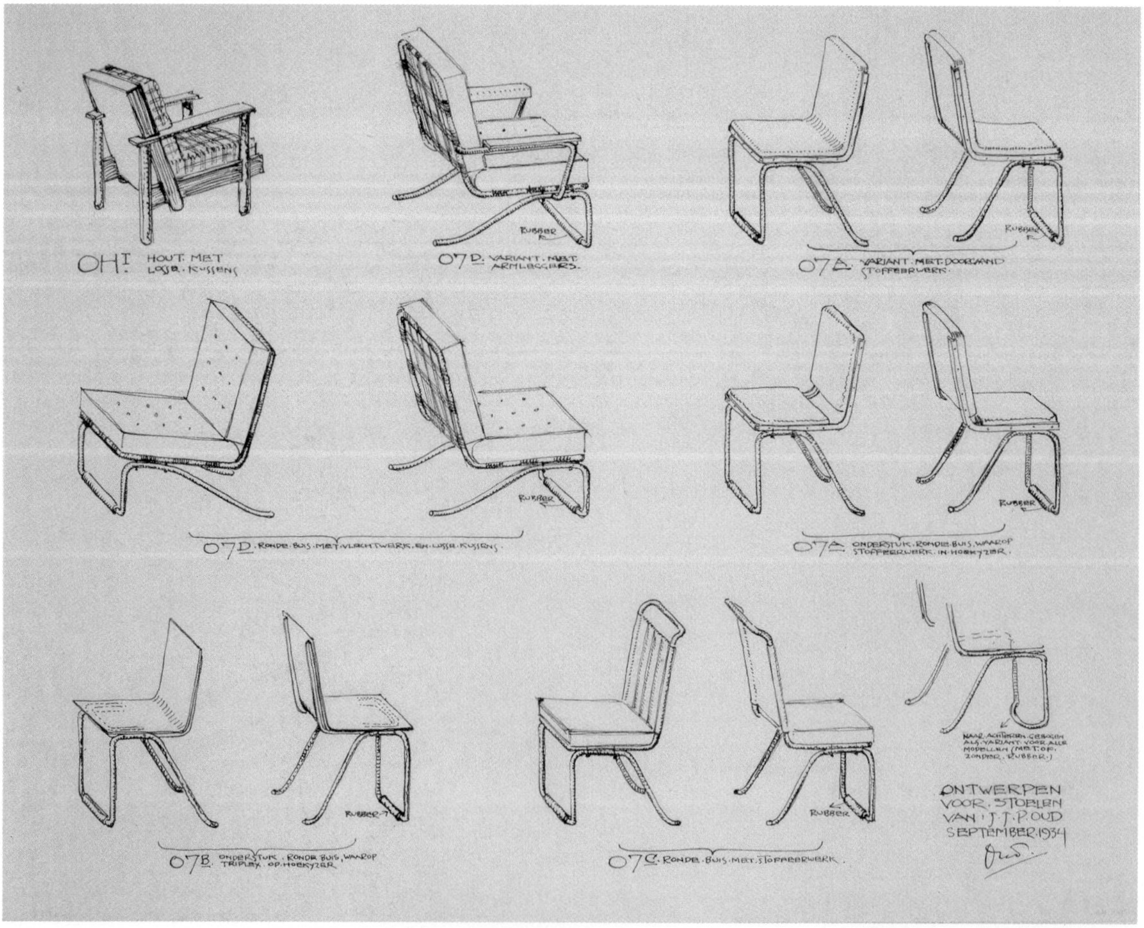

Various design views accompanying the contract, 1933/ dr1984: 0143, CCA, Montreal

the o7 with triplex back the best thing Oud had ever made, and Rietveld expressed his appreciation for the easy chair version of the o7 (with or without armrests), calling it a total success in spatial terms.[3] W.J. de Gruyter was full of praise in *Elsevier's Geïllustreerd Maandblad.*[4] Nonetheless, the idea of marketing the chairs in America came to nothing, as did an attempt by the Museum of Modern Art in New York to acquire one of the chairs for its collection in 1948. Metz did not have a single specimen left.

Model o7d/ OUDJ-ph 450, NAI, Rotterdam

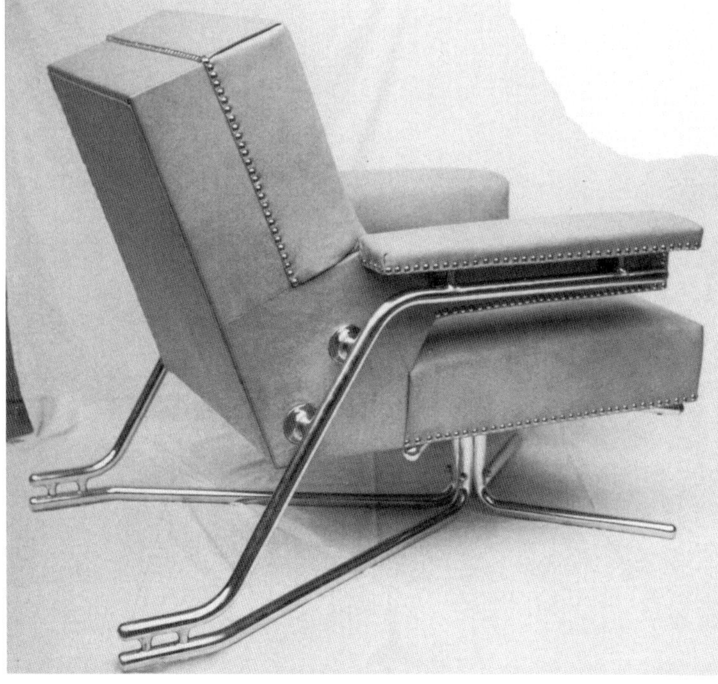

Model f/ OUDJ-ph 459, NAI, Rotterdam (Photo Kamman)

Model o7a/ OUDJ-ph 446, NAI, Rotterdam (Photo Co-op 2)

377 *als ontwerper van meubelen: een onderzoek naar 327, niet eerder geïnventariseerde, schetsbladen,* paper, Groningen University 1996
T. Overtoom, 'De geëigende vorm. J.J.P. Oud als ontwerper van stalen meubelen', in: *Jong Holland. Tijdschrift voor kunst en vormgeving na 1850,* 15(1999)3, pp. 28-44
E. Reinhartz-Tergau, *J.J.P. Oud architect: Meubelontwerpen en interieurs,* Rotterdam 1990, pp. 90-109
O. van Tussenbroek, *Achter blinkende vensters,* Leiden, 1950

People viewing my contributions to the "Steel Furniture in 1934" exhibition will notice that I have not striven above all else for lightness in the sense of limited weight, as is customary for steel chairs. Although I acknowledge that there are on the one hand advantages in this lightness, on the other hand I feel that there are disadvantages associated with it which I wanted to avoid in this group of furniture.
Of seating in general I demand that it should provide 'rest' (I leave aside here the instances in which sitting is more of a pause – a very brief pause – from other work). The sense of 'rest' demands first and foremost: stability.
I regard it as a major disadvantage of a lot of steel chairs that, in their easy portability and their elasticity (spring), they do not provide this rest (either in reality or in appearance).
In addition, I cannot see the sometimes deliberate tendency to make a point of the fact that this is "steel" furniture, as anything but a "hobby". That steel must be used as steel is self-evident for the kind of opinions we are dealing with here. With a lot of steel furniture, chairs in particular, the steel is emphasized to such an extent as to give rise to something "hairpin-like" which, precisely because of the exaggeration, has ended up losing the dynamism inherent to steel.
In addition to this, tubular steel is not "physical" enough to work convincingly as mass: a lot of steel chairs are ambivalent objects in a room because they are too insubstantial to help to determine the space, yet on the other hand they are too substantial to seem to disappear as it were, leaving the original space intact. Steel should be no more used for itself than other materials: it must serve us just like the other materials.
In my models I have done my best to avoid the disadvantages I have indicated.
I simply do not believe that people would in the long run be satisfied with the primitive way of sitting that is still intrinsic to many steel chairs. People today are no less disposed to sitting "comfortably" than those of the past (rather the opposite in fact).
So first of all I have concentrated on the function of sitting. Truly comfortable sitting: easy, softly enclosed if possible, supple. In making these qualities my priority, I feel the need for "materiality", of "mass". The object on which or in which a person sits should be softly voluminous. Neutralizing this mass for the eye of the beholder, is steel's special quality. The very contrast generated here causes the steel to disappear from view and frees the floor to resume its role as spatial determinant. Sitting, one seems to be suspended in space. The space as such, notwithstanding the greater mass it contains, remains more intact.
To the extent that there is a principle to these chairs of mine, I would express it thus: softness and stability for the act of "sitting", appearance of massiveness neutralized by steel.

# 65/ Knitting Chair

1950

The 'knitting chair' Oud designed in 1950 occupies a special place in his catalogue of furniture designs. Unlike his other items of furniture, Oud did not design this chair for a particular client or interior, but developed the model on his own and then offered it for sale. The easy chair, which has a tubular-steel frame and an upholstered seat and back, is reminiscent of the series Oud had designed in the 1930s for Metz. The frame of the backrest crosses the frame of the legs at the level of the seat so that there are no real armrests. Oud's construction, in which the components were simply screwed together, did away with the expensive and time-consuming welding of the frame. He had a prototype made and asked Metz & Co whether they would be interested in marketing the model. *The chair is – in my opinion – elegant to look at, does not take up too much space and has an unusual shape. I would be grateful for a prompt reply, since I have already had an offer for it from a factory. I would prefer to maintain the association with you however: in view of the past and because I set more store by the cachet my chair has in your surroundings, than as a factory-made mass product.*[1] Metz was interested but in the end did not take up the proposal. Despite Oud's suggestion that he could sell the design elsewhere, it was never taken into production.

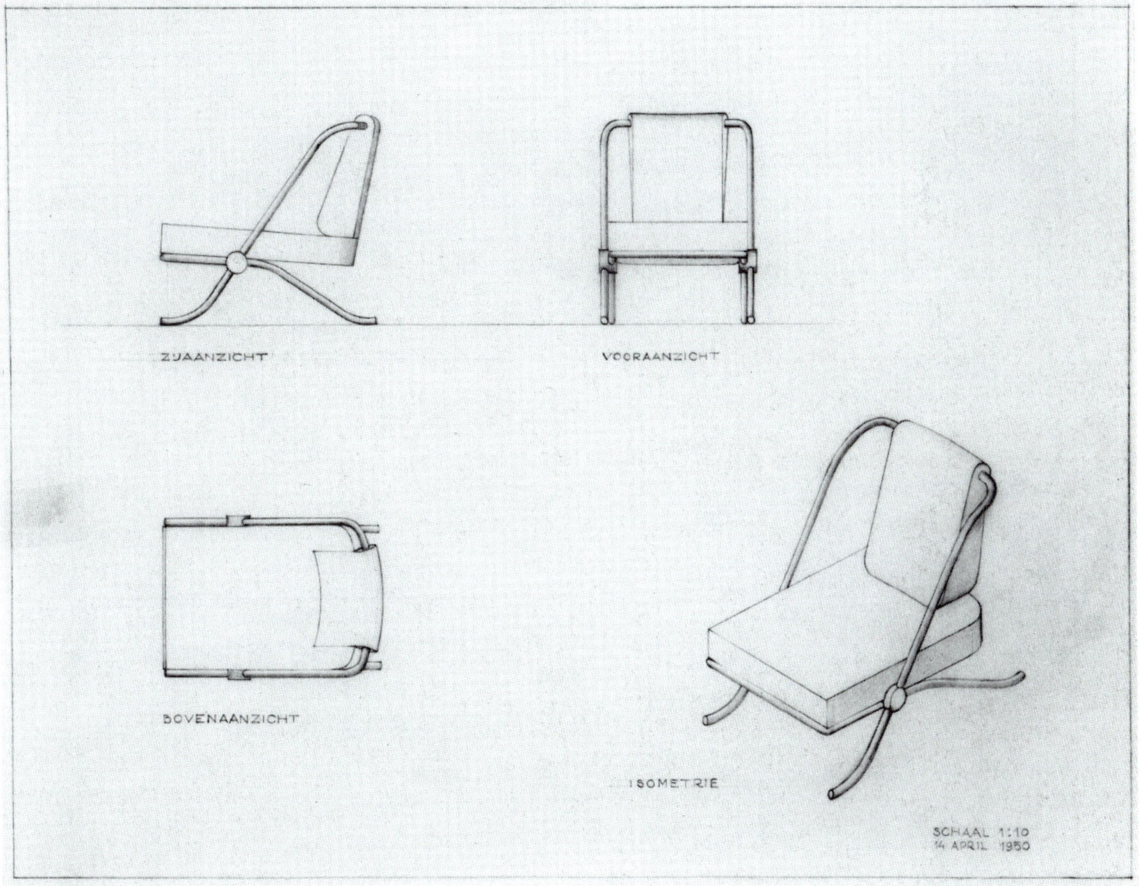

Various design views/ OUDJ-so 20, NAI, Rotterdam

Prototype of Knitting Chair, Museum Boymans van Beuningen/ OUDJ-ph 995, NAI, Rotterdam (Photo F. Lievense)

**Notes**

**1.** J.J.P. Oud to Metz & Co, 6 November 1950, OUDJ-B, NAI, Rotterdam.

**Sources**

Museum Boymans van Beuningen: knitting chair, inv. no. V2.1-1673

NAI: OUDJ-so 2, OUDJ-so 4-20, OUDJ so-22-24, OUDJ-ph 1025, OUDJ-ph 1844

**Literature**


T. Overtoom, *J.J.P. Oud als ontwerper van meubelen: een onderzoek naar 327, niet eerder geïnventariseerde, schetsbladen*, paper, Groningen University 1996, pp. 62-63

T. Overtoom, 'De geëigende vorm. J.J.P. Oud als ontwerper van stalen meubelen', in: *Jong Holland. Tijdschrift voor kunst en vormgeving na 1850*, Vol. 15 (1999)3, pp. 42-43

E. Reinhartz-Tergau, *J.J.P. Oud, architect: meubelontwerpen en interieurs*, Rotterdam 1990, pp. 183-187

# 66/ Interior of M.J.I. de Jonge van Ellemeet's Study

**Rotterdam, Coolsingel** **1930-1931**

In the mid-1920s, the Rotterdam Woningdienst and the Bouwpolitie (Building Inspectorate) were merged.[1] The new director was M.J.I. de Jonge van Ellemeet who had succeeded A. Plate as head of the Woningdienst in 1923. In 1930 he asked Oud, who was departmental head at the time, to redecorate his study at the Rotterdam town hall. The director's suite had been created in 1926 by dividing up the existing large room. It appears that this division was altered again during the refurbishment in 1930.[2] Oud's involvement was restricted to the study where, in addition to two built-in cupboards between the windows and a wardrobe against the opposite wall, Oud designed several pieces of furniture: a desk with telephone table and office chair, and a conference table and chairs. The desk, which bears a strong resemblance to the tables Oud had made for Villa Allegonda and the Weissenhofsiedlung, has a metal underframe surmounted by a heavy wooden desktop. Interestingly, the legs were not painted as with the earlier tables, but chromium plated, as also the legs of the office chair. The commodious seat is straight at the front and rounded at the back. The back and armrests, which consist of a single piece of tubing that follows the rounded shape of the seat, are encased in a thick red leather-clad roll. As E. Reinhartz-Tergau has remarked, the chair bears a striking resemblance to the *siège tournant* designed by Le Corbusier and Charlotte Perriand (1929); sketches confirm that this was indeed a source of inspiration.[3] The square-shaped telephone table has a wooden top (painted black) and chromium legs. The conference table is of a completely different type from the desk; its underframe, also of chromium-plated tubular steel, is quite complex. To go with the table, Oud designed six conference chairs that are not visible in the archival photographs; presumably they were never made.[4] Several versions were made, all based on the same principle: four straight legs, a square seat and back. Some versions had armrests. As well as the chairs, the drawing shows a waste-paper bin beside the desk and a low, round metal table with armchair. Presumably these, too, were never made. The interior of the director's room has not been preserved.

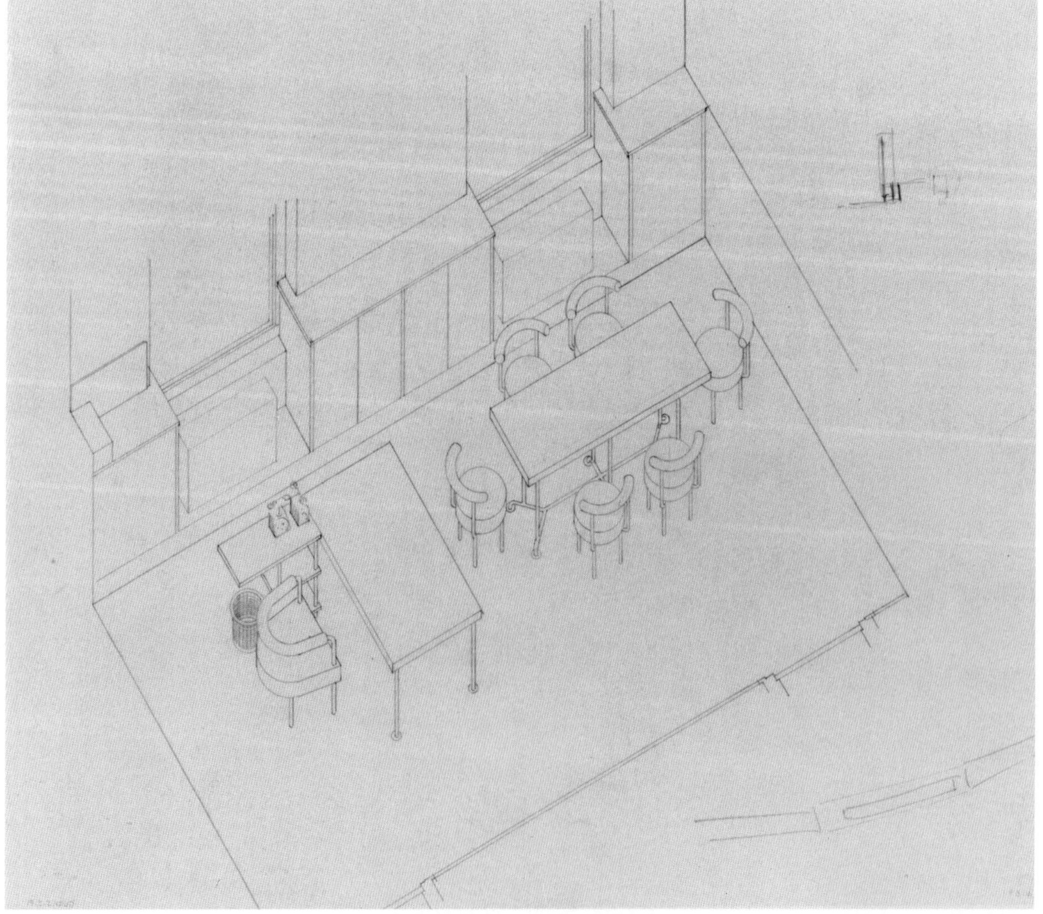

Isometric projection/ dr1984: 0069, CCA, Montreal

OUDJ-ph 441, NAI, Rotterdam

OUDJ-ph 442, NAI, Rotterdam



**Notes**

**1.** It is not entirely clear in which year the departments merged; 1930, the year suggested by Reinhartz-Tergau (1990), is demonstrably incorrect. According to H. Engel in *De Kiefhoek* (p.19) the two departments merged in 1924, while the council's own record, *Handelingen*, mentions the year 1926.

**2.** *Handelingen 1932*, 24 February 1932, p. 397, Gemeente-archief, Rotterdam.

**3.** E. Reinhartz-Tergau, *J.J.P. Oud, architect: meubelontwerpen en interieurs*, Rotterdam 1990, p. 85. See also the sketches of 'Le Corbusier-Perriand-bureaustoel' on the following sheets in the Oud Archive: OUDJ-m157, OUDJ-m143, OUDJ-m188. There is also a remarkably similar chair by W.H. Gispen.

**4.** Contemporary photographs of the interior show wooden chairs.

**Sources**

CCA: dr1984: 0063-0069, ph1984: 0902
Getty: 890126-box 7, 15*
NAI: OUDJ-je 1-15, OUDJ-ph 440-442, OUDJ-ph 1711, OUDJ-ph 1840

**Literature**

H.E. Oud, *J.J.P. Oud. Architekt 1890-1963. Feiten en herinneringen gerangschikt*, The Hague 1984, p. 200
T. Overtoom, *J.J.P. Oud als ontwerper van meubelen: een onderzoek naar 327, niet eerder geïnventariseerde, schetsbladen*, paper, University of Groningen 1996, pp. 22-23
T. Overtoom, 'De geëigende vorm. J.J.P. Oud als ontwerper van stalen meubelen', in: *Jong Holland*, 15(1999)3, pp. 28-44
E. Reinhartz-Tergau, *J.J.P. Oud, architect: meubelontwerpen en interieurs*, Rotterdam 1990, pp. 84-87

# Design Process and Office Organization



Work at Oud's architectural office proceeded along the lines of the nineteenth-century 'atelier'. The architect was the undisputed leader of the design and building process, but made use of draughtsmen, technical experts and – sometimes – artists to work out his inspired ideas. For draughtsmen, a period in an atelier was often an essential part of their architects' training. That was how Oud had learnt the ropes himself. Everything in the atelier was geared to effectuating the architect's 'vision', which Oud considered to be of a highly personal nature. Not that this point of view conflicted for him with working on a new, general style – the important mission which he took as the aim of modern architecture.

Oud believed that every assignment required the personal involvement of the designer. Architecture was, in his opinion, *a social and manly matter ... and not an occasion for fireworks or platitudes.*[1] It was a lonely exploration, precluding fads, a serious, difficult profession. He described his working method on several occasions, sometimes with reference to Mondrian. That was not unusual: the way he kept on starting afresh, plodding on step by step, was very similar to Mondrian's approach to his paintings. Oud was convinced that the emotion during painting and the emotion conveyed with the end result were closely connected. *For many it is inconceivable – yet it is true – that the effect radiated by these paintings stems from a powerful, inner emotion during their creation.*[2] It was exactly the same in architecture; there, too, it was essential to convey emotion. At the beginning of every design there was a flash of inspiration, usually a hastily sketched idea on a handy scrap of paper: a restaurant bill, an envelope, a tram ticket. Oud tended to read detective stories to escape from his despair when a plan got stuck; then a solution invariably presented itself automatically. It was, as he explained at the end of his career, the beginning of a new struggle: *Then my day is further on spoilt by the flow of my mind (or soul or whatever you like to name it) which will steadily take its course in connection with the newly found progress of the plan.*[3]

Then everything had to be redrawn, with sometimes dozens of variants placed side by side. In this way, Oud hoped to retain the integrity of the original idea; moreover, he compared the more elaborate plans with his initial rough sketches.

Oud's view of the essence of architecture and, by extension, of the architect's position, explains why he always kept his practice as small as possible. Many of his colleagues founded big offices, which grew rapidly, especially in the 1950s, but Oud was satisfied with one or two draughtsmen, who worked with him in his home. When large projects like the Shell headquarters had to be built, there would be an on-site office to support the small atelier, but the staff of the former were on the client's payroll. Then, too, Oud continued to exercise control over the design. For instance, he would demand to be part of the building management team (which, apart from the architect, usually included the client, the contractor and the site foreman). Most of the contractual drawings and the working drawings were made at the site office. Some work was contracted out to specialized firms (services engineering, concrete construction, lift, metalwork) which had often been involved in the earlier design stage.

In the more than fifty years in which Oud worked as an architect – from 1906 until his death in 1963 – his method seemed to become more and more of an anachronism. The building process underwent great changes. Oud noted how all the sectors relating to construction were obliged to economize, and put their operations on a more scientific and commercial footing. Architectural practices were not immune either: there, too, specialization and division of labour were unavoidable. Oud felt this was dangerous, since it threatened to undermine

**the architect's fundamental task as the coordinator of the design and its implementation. The articles he wrote after the Second World War particularly express concern about what he considered to be 'fatal' teamwork, in which the essence of the atelier – entailing an all-out effort to realize the architect's vision – was lost. But even more important was the fact that, in practice, he went looking for the most suitable alliances, in which, on the one hand, specialisms could be turned to best advantage and, on the other hand, the architect could maintain his leading position. He seized the post-war reconstruction of the Netherlands as a test case for new coalitions with the client, contractor, technical adviser, supplier, project manager and artists, as well as with new institutions in the field of architecture, such as the 'Bouwcentrum' (Information and Development Centre for Building and Housing).**

**Notes**
**1.** J.J.P. Oud to S. Giedion, 2 August 1938, GTA, Zurich.
**2.** Draft contribution for an exhibition catalogue on Mondrian's work, 1954, OUDJ-4-16, NAI, Rotterdam.
**3.** J.J.P. Oud to Vangetti, 16 August 1960, OUDJ-B, NAI, Rotterdam. The following aphorism could well be typical: "The less I work/The more I do." Notebook. Getty Research Institute, Los Angeles.

# 67/ Architect's study

**Rotterdam, Burgemeester de Villeneuvesingel 29** **1933-1935**

In 1933, Oud redesigned his own study in the house at Hillegersberg, the Rotterdam suburb where he had lived since 1929. The new interior comprised two 'comfortable' armchairs, a hearth, a couple of fitted cupboards and a plan chest. The two armchairs, a low and a high model, had a straight seat, round timber legs, wide, straight armrests and a slightly reclined back. Both chairs had cushions upholstered in blue and white checked material. The wooden frames were painted in white gloss. Oud produced at least five designs for the tiled hearth, finally settling on the plainest. To the left of the hearth, attached to the wall, was a fold-down table, to the right a simple, open-fronted plan chest. Of the remaining furnishings, nothing is known. The choice of materials is interesting: although he was simultaneously engaged in designing tubular steel furniture for Metz. & Co., Oud chose wood for his own study. Numerous sketches show a mixture of wooden and steel furniture.[1]

**J.J.P. Oud in his study, circa 1951/ OUDJ-56, NAI, Rotterdam**



**Sources**
CCA: dr1984: 0144, ph1984: 0857
Museum Boymans van Beuningen: inv. nos. V2.1-1732, V2.1-1733, V2.1-1734, V2.1-1743, V2.1-1744 a/b, V2.1-1749
NAI: OUDJ-io 1 – 41, OUDJ-ph 1721-1722, OUDJ-ph 1845

**Literature**
H.E. Oud, *J.J.P. Oud. Architekt 1890-1963. Feiten en herinneringen gerangschikt*, The Hague 1984, p. 201

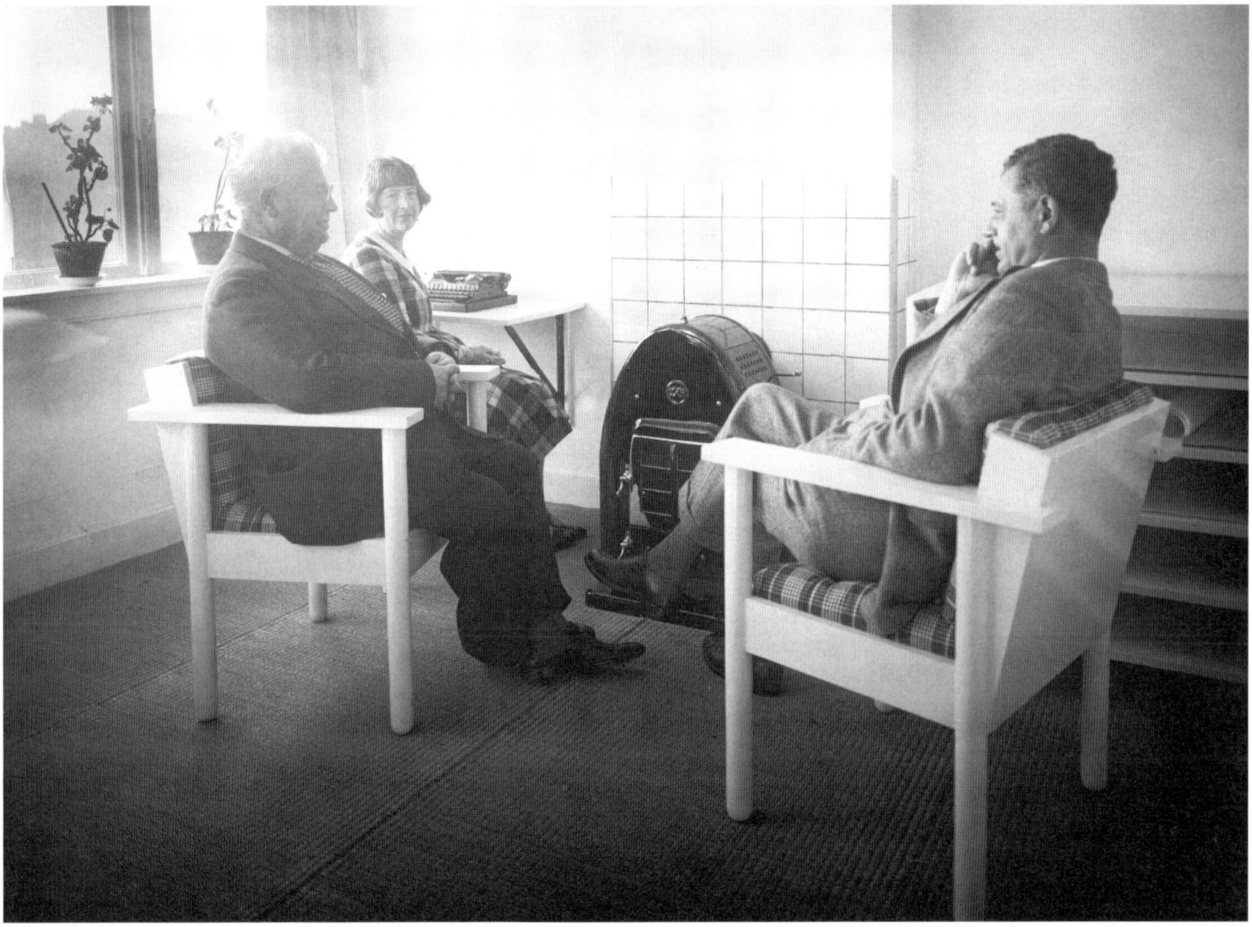

P.J. Oud (left), Annie Oud-Dinaux (centre) and J.J.P. Oud (right)/ OUDJ-56, NAI, Rotterdam

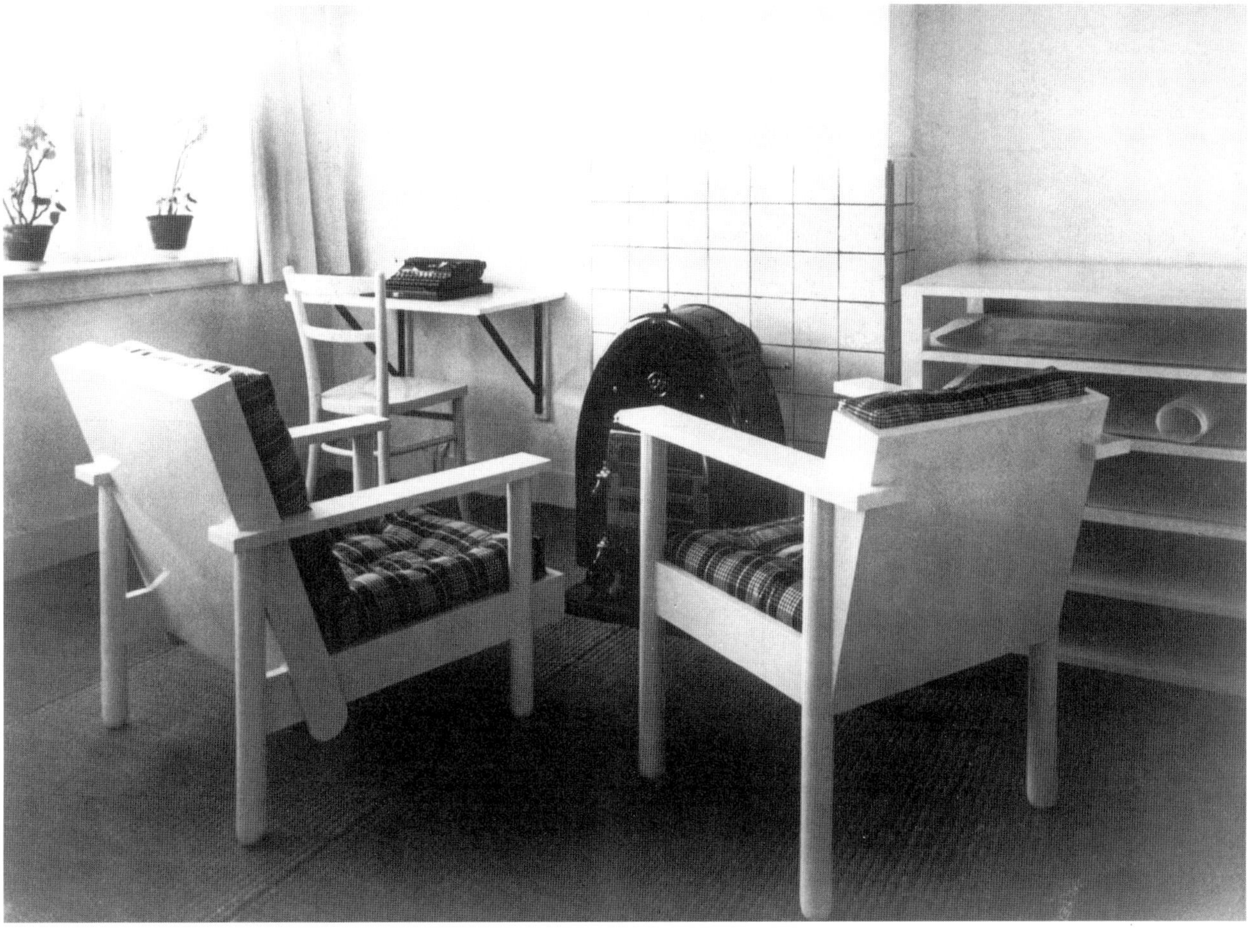

OUDJ-ph 1845, NAI, Rotterdam

# 68/ Interiors for Dr. D. Hannema

**Rotterdam, 25 Westerkade and 6 Javastraat** **1934, 1937**

Library, 25 Westerkade/ OUDJ-ph 461, NAI, Rotterdam (Photo Kamman)

Oud designed two interiors for D. Hannema (1895-1984), the director of Museum Boymans from 1921 to 1945. In 1934 he had designed the interior of Hannema's upstairs apartment at 25 Westerkade, and two years later, when Hannema moved to a townhouse on Javastraat, he was called in again. In the Westerkade apartment Oud designed the study and a library. The walls of the study were painted white and the floor was laid with sisal. On either side of the fireplace, which he had remodelled, he placed two wooden bookcases that could be closed off with light-blue curtains. Below the window Oud designed a built-in cupboard and in front the fireplace he placed a plain wooden table with drop-leaves at either end and a white rubberized top.[1] Behind the table was one of Oud's o3 chairs, upholstered in pale yellow cowhide. For the rest, the room contained a writing table with a wooden top and steel legs painted in a light blue, very similar to the table Oud used in Villa Allegonda. The chair he designed to go with the writing table bears a striking resemblance to Le Corbusier's *fauteuil au dossier basculant* of 1928 and had a frame of light-blue-painted tubular steel, a natural leather seat and back, and leather armrests. The library design was very austere. Three walls were lined with tall, wooden bookcases. The cases for the walls left and right of the door had curtains while the case against the rear wall was fitted with twelve plywood sliding doors. A notable feature is the illumination: the light source was located above a transparent ceiling which produced a very restful, diffuse light in the room. Oud called it a *kleines abstraktes Bibliothekzimmer* (a small, abstract library).[2] According to the drawings, Oud designed two more items for this interior: a draught excluder of wood and glass and a small, half-round, wooden table; the table is in the Hannema collection. Interestingly, the chair visible in the photo of the library is a variant of the Metz o3, with a different frame: where the rear supports touch the ground, they make a right angle to form a bar, instead of running forward to connect with the front supports.

In Hannema's next house, Oud furnished the entrance and the staircase with several curtains and stair carpet, and advised on the hanging of a number of art works from Han-

Study, 25 Westerkade/ OUDJ-ph 462, NAI, Rotterdam

nema's collection.[3] He furnished the back room with existing (antique) furniture and for either side of the fireplace, which he faced with Euville stone, he designed two low wooden bookcases. The front room was fitted out exclusively with furniture of his own design. The Westerkade desk and chair were reused and placed immediately in front of the big window. For the stove Oud designed a plain surround of pale-veined white marble. On either side he placed built-in beechwood bookcases. The seating arrangement in front of the hearth consisted of a rug by Het Paapje and two wooden armchairs and a round coffee table. The armchairs had straight arms and a slightly reclined back. The sides of the chair were closed, although as the many sketches attest, Oud had long experimented with open sides. The chairs were executed in pale maple- and candlewood and upholstered in natural leather. To go with the chairs there was a stool in a darker wood with a cloth-covered seat. The coffee table had a wooden top set on a metal ring and painted tubular steel legs. The table had been designed for the Westerkade interior at the same time as the desk and chair. In the centre of the room hung a cone-shaped ceiling lamp that does not appear in the drawings but which was probably designed by Oud; the model is similar to the lamp he later made for his own house in Wassenaar.

**Interior front room, 6 Javastraat/ OUDJ-ph 465, NAI, Rotterdam**



**Notes**

**1.** O. van Tussenbroek, 'Architect J.J.P. Oud. Verbouwing van een woning te Rotterdam', in *Interieur. Tijdschrift voor woninginrichting*, 58(1941)408, pp. 293-295.
**2.** J.J.P. Oud to M. Seegers, 28 November 1951, OUDJ-B, NAI, Rotterdam.
**3.** A.C.A.W. baron van der Feltz, *Beschrijvende catalogus kunstnijverheid Hannema-De Stuers Fundatie*, Zwolle 1980.

**Sources**

CCA: ph1984: 0869, ph1984: 0870, ph1984: 1120-1123, ph1984: 0897, ph1984: 1119
Gemeentearchief Amsterdam: Metz Archive: METZ.10, METZ.35 -39
Hannema-De Stuers Fundatie: inv. no. 842, 843, 937, 938, 1028, 1029, 3127
NAI: OUDJ-ih 1-35, OUDJ-ph 461-466, OUDJ-ph 1846-1848, OUDJ-B

**Articles**

G. Rietveld, W. van Gelderen, 'Verschillende interieurs door architect J.J.P. Oud', in: *De 8 en Opbouw*, 10(1934)3, pp. 21-30
O. van Tussenbroek, 'Architect J.J.P. Oud. Verbouwing van een woning te Rotterdam', in *Interieur. Tijdschrift voor woninginrichting*, 58(1941)408, pp. 293-295
O. van Tussenbroek, 'Bij werk van J.J.P. Oud als meubelontwerper en binnenhuisarchitect', in*: Interieur. Tijdschrift voor woninginrichting*, 68(1955)525, pp. 361-365

**Literature**

W. Boerhave Beekman, *Hout: van oerwoud tot interieur*, Deventer 1939
H. Buys, 'Interieurs van architect J.J.P. Oud, Hillegersberg', in: *Het Landhuis*, 1936, p. 156
A.C.A.W. baron van der Feltz, *Beschrijvende catalogus kunstnijverheid Hannema-De Stuers Fundatie*, Zwolle 1980
M. Mosler, *Dirk Hannema, de geboren verzamelaar*, Rotterdam 1995
H.E. Oud, *J.J.P. Oud. Architekt 1890-1963. Feiten en herinneringen gerangschikt*, The Hague 1984, pp. 93-94, 201
T. Overtoom, *J.J.P. Oud als ontwerper van meubelen: een onderzoek naar 327, niet eerder geïnventariseerde, schetsbladen*, paper Groningen University 1996
T. Overtoom, 'De geëigende vorm. J.J.P. Oud als ontwerper van stal- en meubelen', in: *Jong Holland. Tijdschrift voor kunst en vormgeving na 1850*, 15(1999)3, pp. 28-44
E. Reinhartz-Tergau, *J.J.P. Oud, architect: meubelontwerpen en interieurs*, Rotterdam 1990, pp.110-121

On 3 January 1936, the Rotterdam Droogdok Maatschappij laid the keel of the largest ship ever built in the Netherlands: the *Nieuw Amsterdam*. The client was the Rotterdam-based Holland-America Line (HAL) which planned to use the ship for a regular service between Rotterdam, Southampton and New York. As the company's flagship it was to be fitted out with a luxury to rival that of the even larger American and French ocean liners. The ship boasted two swimming pools, numerous sporting facilities, a theatre and cinemas, and both the 288 first-class and 86 second-class cabins had their own shower or bath and toilet – an unprecedented luxury for those days. The fit-out was completed on 23 April 1938. The *Nieuw Amsterdam* was seen as a visiting card for Rotterdam and the Netherlands and the national press accordingly devoted many pages to the ship and its furnishings. It embarked on its maiden voyage to New York on 10 May 1938.

The commission to furnish the entire ship had been awarded to the architectural firm of Brinkman & Van der Vlugt in early 1936. After Van der Vlugt's death in April that year and at the suggestion of HAL's director W.H. de Monchy, the commission was cancelled and a large number of architects and artists were invited to assume responsibility for part of the interior design. Subject to the company's approval, each architect could invite artists of their choice to work with them. *Elsevier* magazine dubbed it 'trail-blazing experimentation'.[1]

The liner had three classes, each with its own separate social areas. The prestigious Grand Hall and the Ritz Carlton Lounge for passengers in Saloon (First) Class were fitted out by Wijdeveld, the Lounge and Smoking Room for passengers in Tourist (Second) Class by Oud, who also designed the first-class swimming pool. For the lounge on the lower promenade deck Oud used mainly wooden furniture. In the centre of the room was a circular parquet dance floor laid in a geometric pattern; behind this at one end of the room was a stage with a grand piano. At the back of the stage was a curved wall and behind this a 'completely soundproof' projection booth. The long, satinwood clad walls were punctuated by fitted cabinets containing the life

Tourist Class Smoking Room/ OUDJ-ph 477, NAI, Rotterdam (Photo E. van Ojen)

jackets (accessible from the deck). Between these cabinets were large, circular windows with a diameter of one and a half metres. In front of the windows hung yellow-green net curtains and heavy drapes of green peau-de-suède. The furniture comprised banquettes mounted in front of the cabinets and a lot of wooden chairs with rounded, shell-shaped backs. These chairs were upholstered in finely corded velvet in the same grey-green colour as the legs of the square and round occasional tables. Beside the door was a clock designed by Elisabeth Spaniër-Dammers, executed in millefiore glass. The one dramatic element of the Tourist Lounge was the bright red, hand-knotted carpet which Oud had designed together with Hans Polak of Het Paapje carpet weavers in Voorschoten. The red ground was strewn with patches in a different colour and interspersed with images representing, on the one side typically American images (skyscrapers, a jazz band) and on the other side typical Dutch ones (windmills, milk carts).

The Smoking Room, located directly behind the Lounge and accessible from it, was more simply furnished. The natural cork floors were laid with dark brown, hand-knotted rugs. The walls were panelled with limed oak. Between the two entrance doors was a long reading/writing table ('continental style' according to the company) and in the alcoves along the walls to the left and right were tables and chairs.[2] On the other short wall was a hearth with an electric fire and above it a bronze swimmer by John Raedecker. The ceiling and wall above the hearth were covered with leather and bronze strips. Near the electric fire were several club chairs upholstered in brown leather and reminiscent of the armchairs Oud designed in the same period for Hannema. The rest of the lounge was furnished with wooden chairs of a slightly different design from the chairs in the Lounge. The reading table was flanked by two small bronzes (Negro and Negress) by Han Wezelaar.

The most striking and the most functionalist interior Oud designed for the *Nieuw Amsterdam* was that of the first class swimming pool, hidden deep in the prow of the ship (E deck). Oud used white, semi-matt Delft tiles for the walls and floor, and sea-green tiles for the pool itself. Instead of the wooden furniture he had favoured for the lounges, here he opted for tubular steel as being more in keeping with the room's function. The otherwise purely functional space was enlivened by several metal figures by Spaniër-Dammers.

Press reactions were divided. Many papers and magazines (including foreign ones) applauded the grandeur and conspicuous luxury and saw the ship as a model of Dutch applied and visual arts. The unique collaboration between the numerous architects and artists was warmly welcomed as serving to bring architecture and art closer together. *The Studio* saw the ship and its interior as a *truly national effort* and opined that the interior represented *a further stage in the progress of modern thought*, with more feeling, more expressiveness and more fantasy. *The result is not merely*

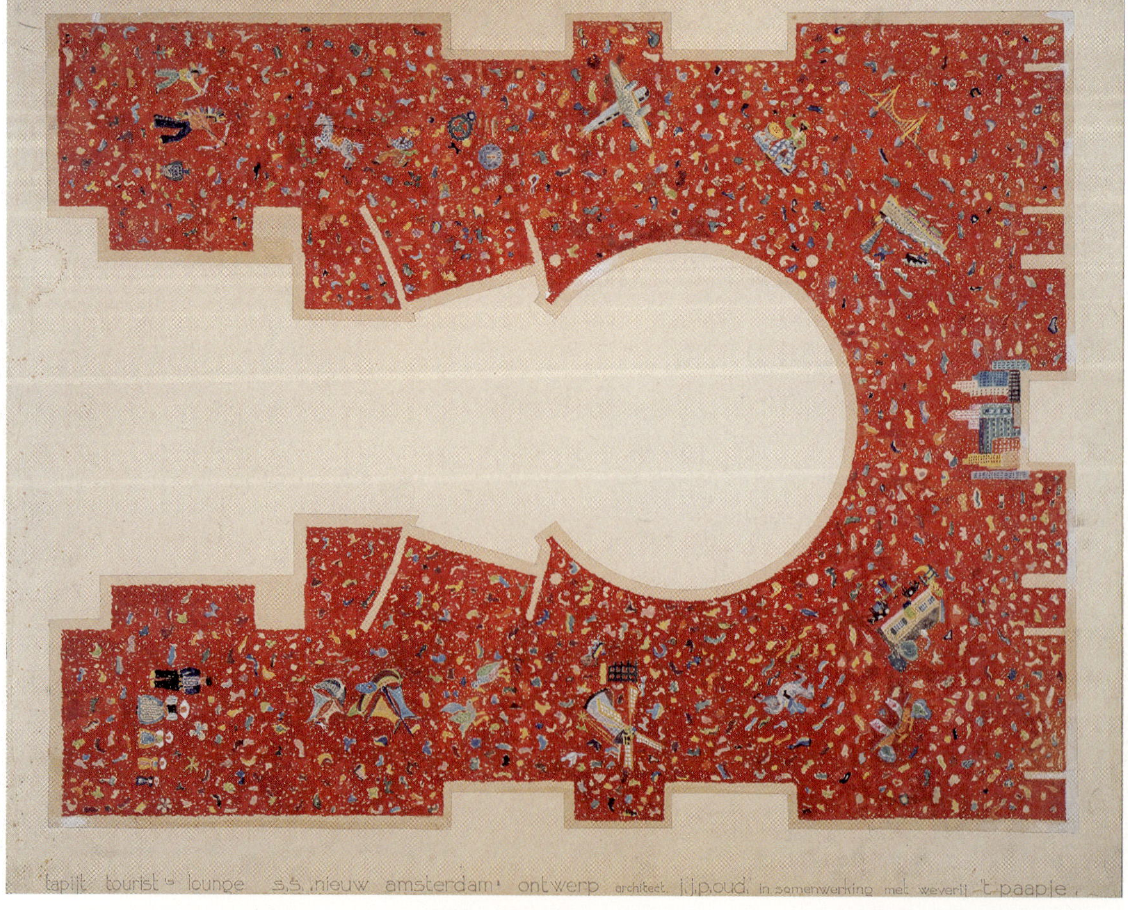


Design for carpet in Tourist Class Lounge/ OUDJ-na 586, NAI, Rotterdam

Tourist Class Lounge/ OUDJ-ph 1732, NAI, Rotterdam

Reading Table in Tourist Class Lounge/
OUDJ-ph 1731, NAI, Rotterdam

*decoration applied – it is decoration that springs from the very nature of the architectural treatment.*[3] Nonetheless, the restlessness occasioned by the welter of styles and the alleged 'gold-leaf romanticism' of the interior was severely criticized. In *Elsevier* the ship was likened to a steam carousel, while Stam dismissed it as an experiment of *very limited success.*[4] Yet even in these critical articles, Oud's contribution was seen as an agreeable exception. The way he had combined function and aesthetics in the swimming pool came in for particular praise. In *De 8 en Opbouw* Van Gelder called Oud's contribution a breath of fresh air: *The wooden chairs in the lounges are well-considered attempts to keep working according to the tried and tested methods and testify to more character than all that carry-on with tubular steel or attempts to show how many possible and impossible ways there are of bending plywood. The orthogonality of the frame and the legs does however constitute a disturbing dualism with the rounded form of the backs. ... As such there are numerous solutions and details that testify to deliberate simplicity that make one feel that in this interior work Oud has moved from the realms of abstraction to the ordinary but always completer and sounder human arena.*[5]

After the Second World War, when the *Nieuw Amsterdam* had been used to transport troops, the ship was partially refurbished. It was deployed on the transatlantic route until 1971 and for three years after that it was used as a cruise liner.

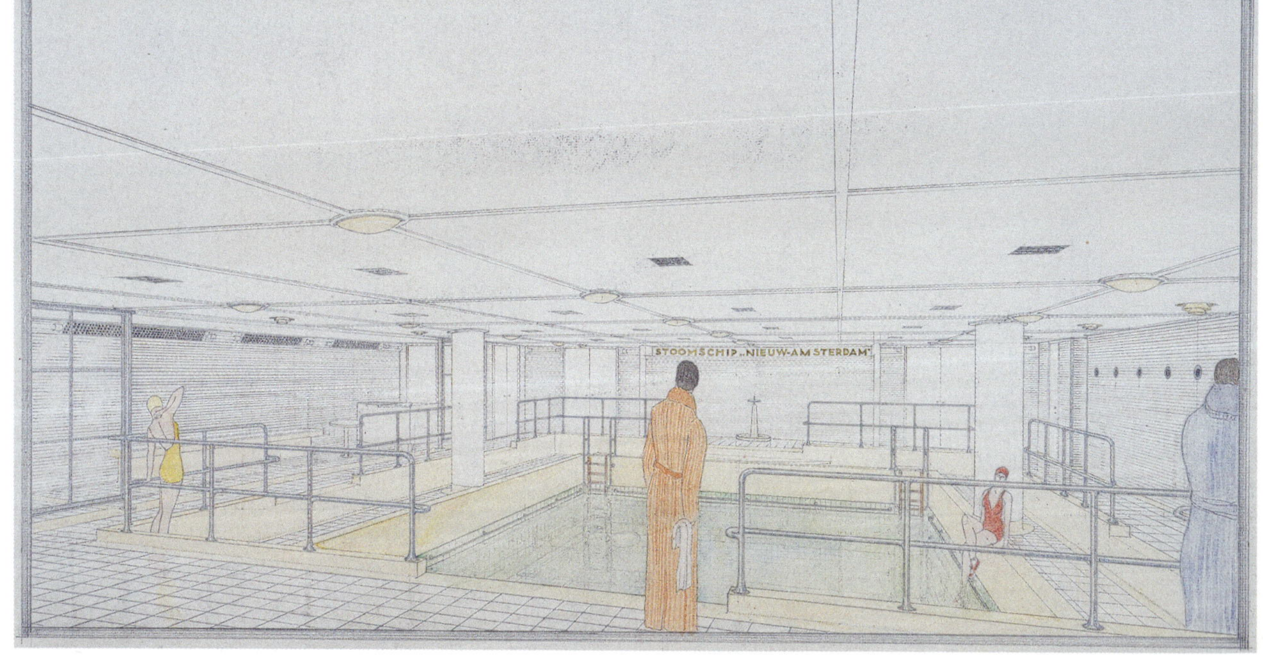


**Perspective of First Class swimming pool/ OUDJ-na 589, NAI, Rotterdam**



**Notes**

**1.** J.G. van Gelder, 's.s. Nieuw Amsterdam 1938', in *Elsevier's Geïllustreerd Maandschift*, 48(1938), p. 308.

**2.** *Nieuw Amsterdam: Facts and Figures*, Rotterdam, 1938.

**3.** 'The Nieuw Amsterdam: a Floating Palace of Art', in: *The Studio*, 116(1938)544, pp. 3-18.

**4.** W. Retera Wzn, 'Opmerkingen over de "Nieuw Amsterdam" in het algemeen en over de hutten (het slapen) in het bijzonder', in: *Elsevier's Geïllustreerd Maandschift*, 48(1938)5, pp. 318-323; M. Stam, 'Het passagiersschip de "Nieuw Amsterdam"', in: *De 8 en Opbouw*, 9(1938)12/13, p. 128.

**5.** W. van Gelderen, 'Verschillende interieurs door architect J.J.P. Oud', in: *De 8 en Opbouw*, 10(1939)3 , pp. 26-27.

**Sources**

CCA: dr1984: 0562-0566, ph1984: 0871, ph 1984: 1124

Gemeentearchief Rotterdam: HAL Archive

Getty: 890126 – box 3, F33

Hannema-De Stuers Fundatie: 1030, 1031

Museum Boymans van Beuningen: inv. no. V2.1-1735, V2.1-1736, V2.1-1738, V2.1-1747

NAI: OUDJ-na 1-589, OUDJ-na 3001, OUDJ-ph 471- 481, OUDJ-B

**Articles**

'De samenwerking tusschen directie en architecten. Een gesprek met den heer J.J.P. Oud', in: *NRC*, 23 April 1938, p.7

'D.S.S. "Nieuw Amsterdam"', special issue of *Schip en Werf*, n.d. [1938]

*Elsevier's Geïllustreerd Maandschrift*, Nieuw Amsterdam nummer, 48(1938)5 (May 1938, containing articles by: Gelder, J.G. van, 'S.S. "Nieuw Amsterdam", 1938, een inleiding' [pp. 301-310], Traa, C. van, 'De ruimten voor eten en drinken aan boord van de "Nieuw Amsterdam"' [pp. 310-318], Retera Wzn, W., 'Opmerkingen over de "Nieuw Amsterdam" in het algemeen en over de hutten (het slapen) in het bijzonder' [pp. 318-323], Hammacher, A.M., 'Het schip en zijn versierde ruimten' [pp. 323-331])

W. van Gelderen, 'Verschillende interieurs door architect J.J.P. Oud', in: *De 8 en Opbouw*, 10(1939)3, pp. 26-30

J.W. de Gruyter, 'De aesthetische inrichting van de Nieuw Amsterdam II', in: *Het Vaderland*, 3 May 1938

T.B.F. Hoyer, *Nieuw Amsterdam 1626-1936*, Haarlem, Rotterdam, 1938

J. Niegeman, 'De "Nieuw Amsterdam"', in: *De 8 en Opbouw*, 9(1938)12/13, pp. 128-129

*Nieuw Amsterdam, Facts and Figures*, Rot-

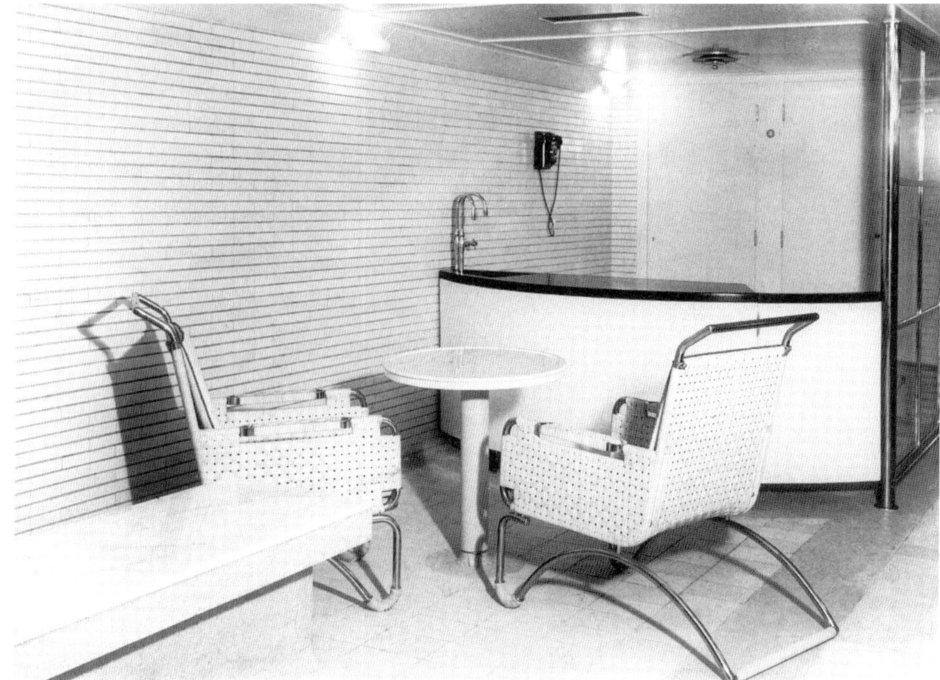

**Tubular steel furniture in the First Class swimming pool/ OUDJ-ph 1730, NAI, Rotterdam**

**First Class swimming pool/ OUDJ-ph 1729, NAI, Rotterdam**



terdam, 1938
M. Stam, 'Het passagiersschip de "Nieuw Amsterdam"', in: *De 8 en Opbouw*, 9(1938)12/13, pp. 119-128
'The Nieuw Amsterdam: a Floating Palace of Art', in: *The Studio*, 116(1938)544, pp. 3-18
O. van Tussenbroek, 'Werk van J.J.P. Oud voor de "Nieuw-Amsterdam" en de "Noordam"', in: *Intérieur* 58(1941)402 , pp. 115-118
O. van Tussenbroek, 'Bij werk van J.J.P. Oud als meubelontwerper en binnenhuisarchitect', in: *Interieur. Tijdschrift voor woninginrichting*, 68(1955)525, pp. 361-365

**Literature**

U. Barbieri, *J.J.P. Oud*, Rotterdam 1987, pp. 136-136
A.C.A.W. Baron van der Feltz, *Beschrijvende catalogus kunstnijverheid Hannema-De Stuers Fundatie*, Zwolle 1980
G. Hoogewoud, 'De nieuw-amsterdam. Overal een andere (luxe) vormgeving', in: *Wonen/TABK*, 5-74, pp. 25-28
H.E. Oud, *J.J.P. Oud. Architekt 1890-1963. Feiten en herinneringen gerangschikt*, The Hague 1984, pp. 135, 136, 202
T. Overtoom, 'De geëigende vorm. J.J.P. Oud als ontwerper van stalen meubelen', in: *Jong Holland. Tijdschrift voor kunst en vormgeving na 1850*, 15(1999)3, pp. 28-44
E. Reinhartz-Tergau, *J.J.P. Oud, architect: meubelontwerpen en interieurs*, Rotterdam 1990, pp. 122-141
'S.s. Nieuw Amsterdam', in: *Schip en Werf*, 41(1974)5, pp. 104-106

For a ship is more: it is intended to be "lived" in. And certainly not lived in as a machine for living. ...
For shipboard life can be monotonous. Have you ever talked to people who make a lot of long sea voyages? However beautiful the sea, wind and clouds, it gradually palls. The mind needs to keep active. There must be something to experience and to see on board! People want to smoke, drink, play, dance, and eat! The room where people dance has a different aspect from the room where people eat. The nursery should look different from the library. "Arid" architecture no longer suffices here. It is not just "space" that must be created, but "atmosphere" too. On top of the construction we must introduce an emotion through mood into building.
As such, ship architecture introduces a topic that land/house architecture still studiously avoids: the music in building. ...
Not that this means that we must hark back to the riches of the past, quite the reverse. But nor must we cling rigidly to the Spartan little shed that is currently presented to us as architecture. We must try to go a step further and to allow the richness/fullness of life to resound in architecture in our own language. This is bound to go awry at first, but more awry than now, when everything is so straight, it certainly cannot go.
We must not allow ourselves be materialistically pushed in the direction of an architecture of fatalistic tedium, rather we must [achieve] spiritual rapport with an architecture that is once again full and rich; that is once again composed with music; that once again knows order and hierarchy.

# 70/ Dining Room interiors for MS *Zaandam* and MS *Noordam*

**1937-1938**

On the strength of the results of the commissions for SS *Nieuw Amsterdam*, the HAL's board of directors invited some of the same architects and artists to design various parts of the interior of two other, smaller HAL ships, the 'combi-liners' MS *Noordam* and MS *Zaandam*, which were designed to carry both passengers and freight on the fortnightly Rotterdam–New York–Philadelphia run. The *Noordam* entered service in September 1938, her sister ship four months later. Both ships, which had 125 cabins in one class only, were fitted out in almost identical fashion. Oud designed the interiors of both the dining rooms. The dining room walls were panelled in teak, the columns with Coromandel wood. The teak furniture was upholstered in green leather and the floor was laid with a reddish-brown carpet. The entrance to the T-shaped dining rooms was located in the relatively short leg of the T. To one side of the entrance was the buffet, while the wall opposite was lined with mirror glass. The bar of the T was a long, fan-shaped space. The wall opposite the entrance was punctuated by nineteen portholes with flattened sides. Along the walls were square tables with four or five chairs and in the middle of the room round tables with six to eight chairs. Cabinets were placed beside the two columns. John Raedecker and Han Wezelaar were each asked to make two statuettes for one of the two ships. Raedecker's Medusa and Fortuna ended up gracing the dining room of the *Zaandam*, Wezelaar's dancer and harlequin that of the *Noordam*. Above the buffet in both ships was a clock with a carved surround made by Han Richters.

The *Zaandam* was sunk during the Second World War; the *Noordam* survived and was refubished in 1946.Oud was not consulted.

**Dining Room/ OUDJ-ph 1778, NAI, Rotterdam**



**Sources**

Gemeentearchief Rotterdam: HAL Archive

Museum Boymans van Beuningen: inv. no. V2.1-1741

NAI: OUDJ-za 1-za 4, OUDJ-za 3001, OUDJ-ph 482 -486

**Articles**

'De jongste aanwinst van de H.A.L. vaart proef. De Noordam beteekent een experiment', in: *Rotterdamsch Nieuwsblad*, 15 September 1938, p.1

*D.S. Motorschip "Noordam"*, HAL brochure, [1938]

'Het interieur van het D.S.M.S. Noordam', in: *NRC*, 15 September 1938

*Noordam, Zaandam*, Rotterdam 1939

O. van Tussenbroek, 'Werk van J.J.P. Oud voor de "Nieuw-Amsterdam" en de "Noordam"', in: *Intérieur* 58(1941)402, pp. 115-118

**Literature**

H.E. Oud, *J.J.P. Oud. Architekt 1890-1963. Feiten en herinneringen gerangschikt*, The Hague 1984, p. 136

T. Overtoom, 'De geëigende vorm. J.J.P. Oud als ontwerper van stalen meubelen', in: *Jong Holland. Tijdschrift voor kunst en vormgeving na 1850*, 15(1999)3, pp. 28-44

E. Reinhartz-Tergau, *J.J.P. Oud, architect: meubelontwerpen en interieurs*, Rotterdam 1990, pp. 142-147

Renesse is a small village on the North Sea coast of the island of Schouwen-Duiveland in Zeeland, where Oud frequently took his holidays in the 1930s. Tourism was a growing business and many of the inhabitants of Renesse hoped to profit from it, among other things by renting and building holiday accommodation. During Christmas 1933, Oud was approached by J. Oudkerk, a building contractor and owner of Den Ruigenhoek, the house where Oud and his family spent their holidays, to design a 'standard' holiday cottage. Oudkerk was to build a prototype in May 1934. This first show model, costed at 3,000 guilders excluding land, was supposed to persuade other interested parties to build one of their own. Nothing came of the idea, however. In the middle of the depression there was little interest and less money for such enterprises.

The two-storey cottage Oud designed could accommodate six people. There was a living room, kitchen and one bedroom on the ground floor and two more bedrooms upstairs. The latter opened onto a landing which overlooked the living room below and connected with a stair leading to a small storage loft. In the definitive design a shower, which had been absent from the sketch design, was added beside the kitchen. The inner and outer walls and the chimney were brick, the rest of the construction was timber.

In 1935, when the Amsterdam furniture maker Willem Penaat (1875-1957) showed some interest in the plan, Oud explained the choice of construction method in terms of practical and economic considerations. *I designed such a house – for the sake of economy in 'indigenous' materials (which I enjoyed doing, too) – and in such a way that it could be assembled by the village carpenter. It was to cost (including my fee) 2,900 to 3,000 guilders (only the land would be extra).*

*...Shall I come and discuss it some time? And take a good look at this little house. I really enjoyed designing it: but of course it is more or less a country cottage, i.e. in truth 'countryfied', as we all are on holiday. Actually for cheap construction it's better to keep it primitive: I'd rather make a good primitive building, than a clumsy structure that looks 'modern'. That smooth look, etc., always costs a lot of money if it is done properly (and otherwise there's no point). You probably have the same experience with your furniture.* On this occasion, too, the plan came to nothing.

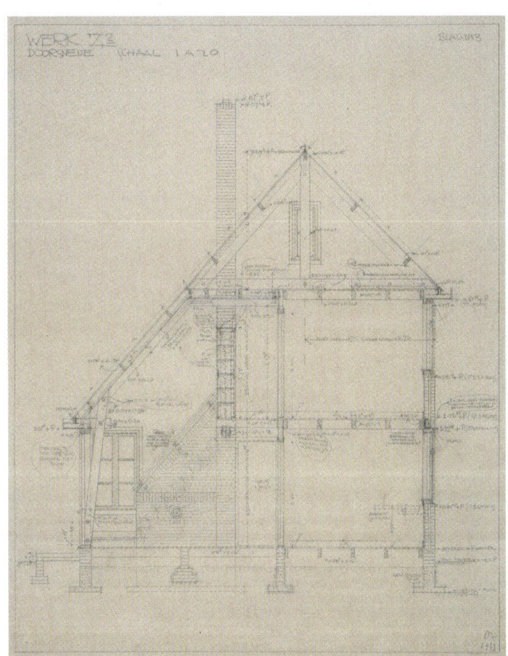

Contract design, section/ OUDJ-wz 3, NAI, Rotterdam

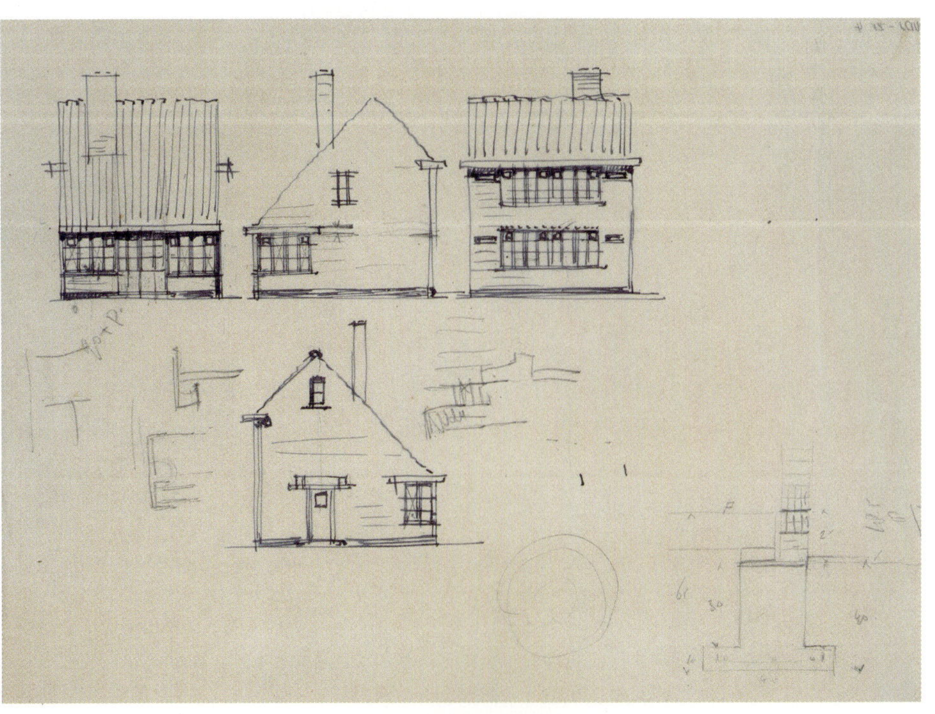

Elevations / OUDJ-zr 4, NAI, Rotterdam

**Sources**
Getty: 890126-box 7, 16*
NAI: OUDJ-zr 1-22, OUDJ-zr 1001, OUDJ-wz 1-12

**Literature**
U. Barbieri, *J.J.P. Oud*, Rotterdam 1987, pp. 130-131
H.E. Oud, *J.J.P. Oud. Architekt 1890-1963. Feiten en herinneringen gerangschikt*, The Hague 1984, p. 114

# 72/ Design for a House on a Deep Site

1933

One of Oud's first attempts to establish himself as an independent architect after leaving the Woningdienst in 1933, was this – unbuilt – design for a house for an unknown client and location. Oud resolved the challenge presented by an extremely narrow, deep site by placing a long, narrow house lengthwise on the plot in such a way that both end elevations sat on the property line. The only free space was along the two side elevations: on the east side this took the form of a narrow entranceway, on the west side a garden with patio and a fixed garden bench. The ground-floor plan was geared to this layout and to the occupants' privacy: the facade bordering the entranceway was closed and behind it were the hall, kitchen and the wall units of the living room. On the other side a study area and the living room enjoyed an expansive view of the garden. This principle was continued on the upper floor where a central hallway was flanked on the one side by wall units and on the other, overlooking the garden, the bedrooms. Unlike the Kallenbach house, there was no provision for a live-in servant. The servant had access to the kitchen and from there, via a servant's room, to the living room, bedrooms and bathroom, without unduly disturbing the occupants.
In 1934, a year after it was made, Oud tried to sell the design again, on which occasion he emphasized the separation between private and servant quarters. *The intention in this house was to keep the paths of the occupants and the servant as separate as possible. There is no need for the servant to enter the space overlooking the garden, behind the servant's room and kitchen, so that this could become a sort of parlour, 'Herrenzimmer' or what you will (one would not be disturbed by people going upstairs, either, since this space can be closed off with curtains). For the rest the idea was that visitors would not be 'subjected' to kitchen activities (often unavoidable in modest-sized houses): food smells, views into the kitchen, etc. are to all intents and purposed impossible here.*
*A cellar can be reached from the servant's room and from the yard, with a view to coal deliveries, hanging out the wash, etc. The yard is entirely enclosed. A lot of cupboard space upstairs is a universal requirement.*
*The bedrooms face the east, the living room the west (the south can sometimes be too hot).*
*This house was planned for a particular site but is of course capable of other possibilities.*[1]

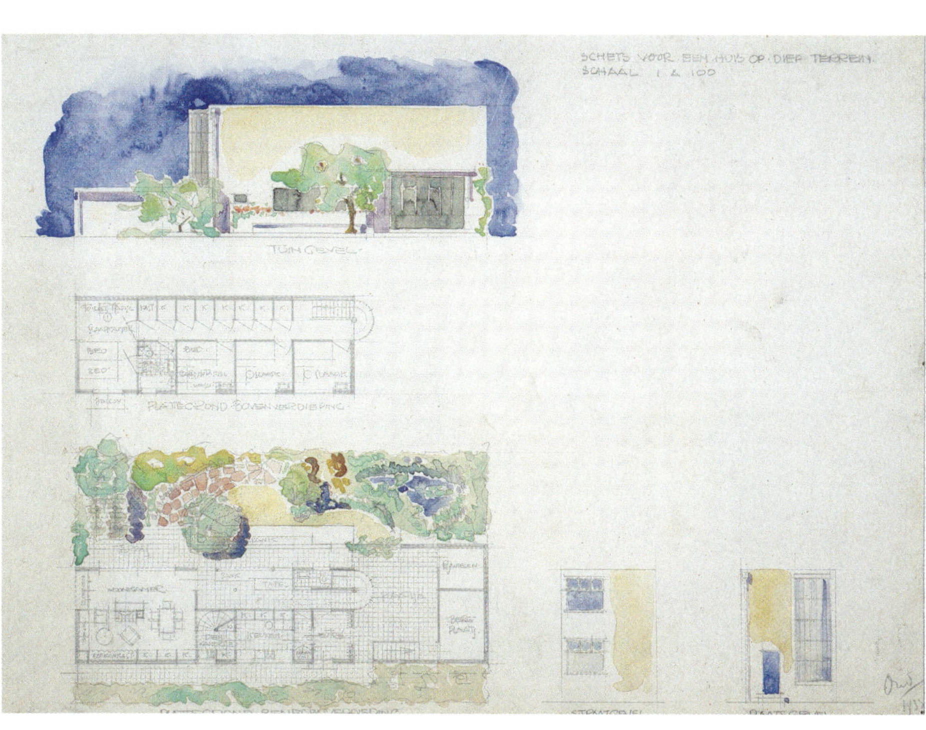


**Various design views/ OUDJ-dt 9, NAI, Rotterdam**



**Notes**
**1.** J.J.P. Oud to J. Leopold, 26 May 1934, OUDJ-B, NAI, Rotterdam.

**Sources**
NAI: OUDJ-dt 1-9

**Literature**
U. Barbieri, *J.J.P. Oud*, Rotterdam 1987, p. 129
G. Stamm, *J.J.P. Oud. Bauten und Projekten 1906 bis 1963*, Mainz, Berlin 1984, pp. 115-116

# 73/ Project for a Row of Six Houses



In 1934 Oud made a sketch design for a row of six dwellings. The context of the design is unclear. In the only known sketch for this project, one of the dwellings is rendered in reasonable detail but the remaining five are sketchily drawn. What is clear is that the dwellings were intended to be reversed in plan in pairs. The design displays many similarities with the design for a terrace of studio dwellings that Oud made a year later. One important difference is that the studio dwellings were topped by a mono-pitch roof.

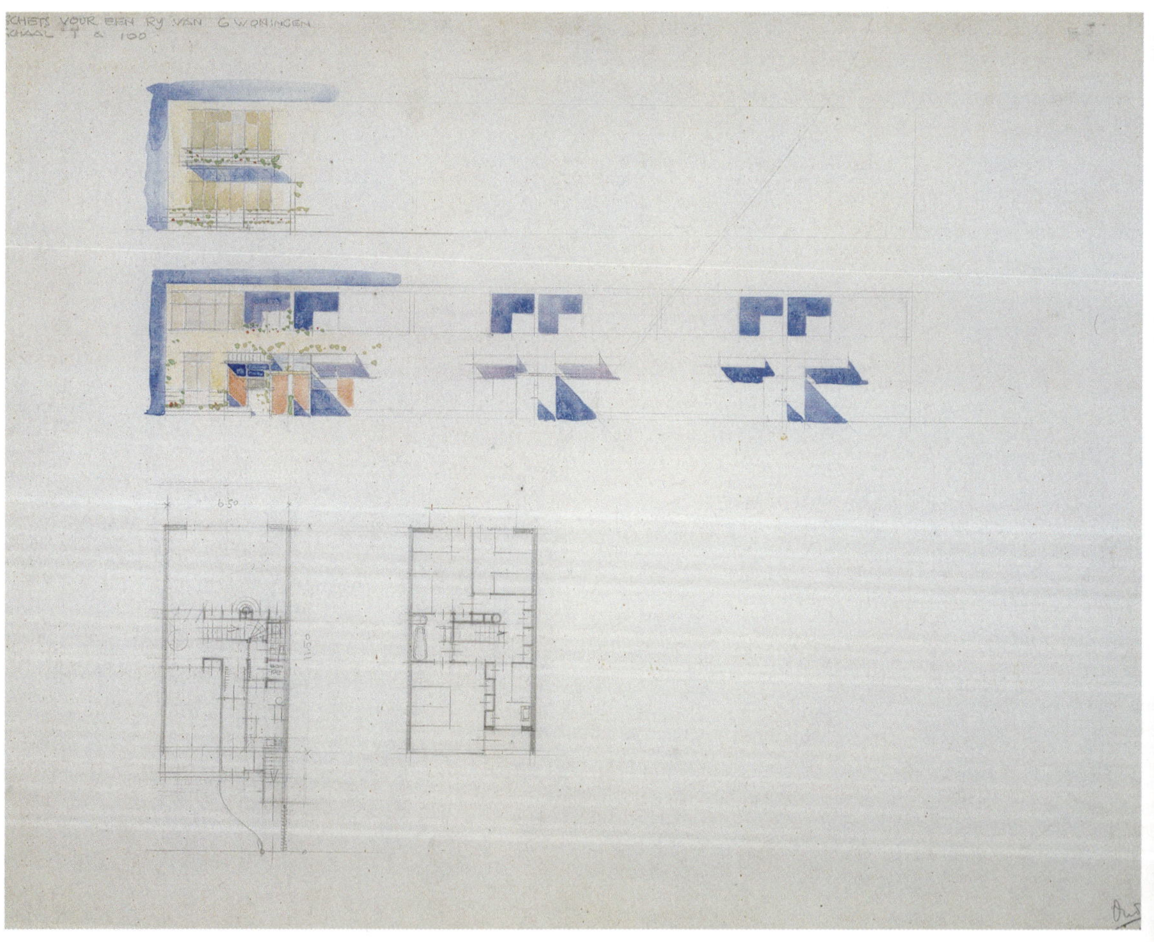


Various design views/ OUDJ-rw 1, NAI, Rotterdam



**Sources**
NAI: OUDJ-rw 1

**Literature**
G. Stamm, *J.J.P. Oud. Bauten und Projekte 1906 bis 1963*, Mainz, Berlin 1984, pp.115-116

# 74/ Project for a Private House for the Dinaux Family

**Haarlem** **1934**

In 1934 Oud's in-laws asked him to design a house for them in Haarlem. There is a strong resemblance between this design and Oud's 1933 design for a House on a Deep Site (cat. no. 72). In both designs there is a clear distinction between the garden and street elevations. The closed front elevation indicates that this is where the servants' quarters are located. The garden elevation, by contrast, is very open, with a lot of glass. As with the House on a Deep Site, Oud included a closed yard between the dwelling and the garage. The living room opens onto a covered terrace. This generously conceived home with spacious rooms was never realized.

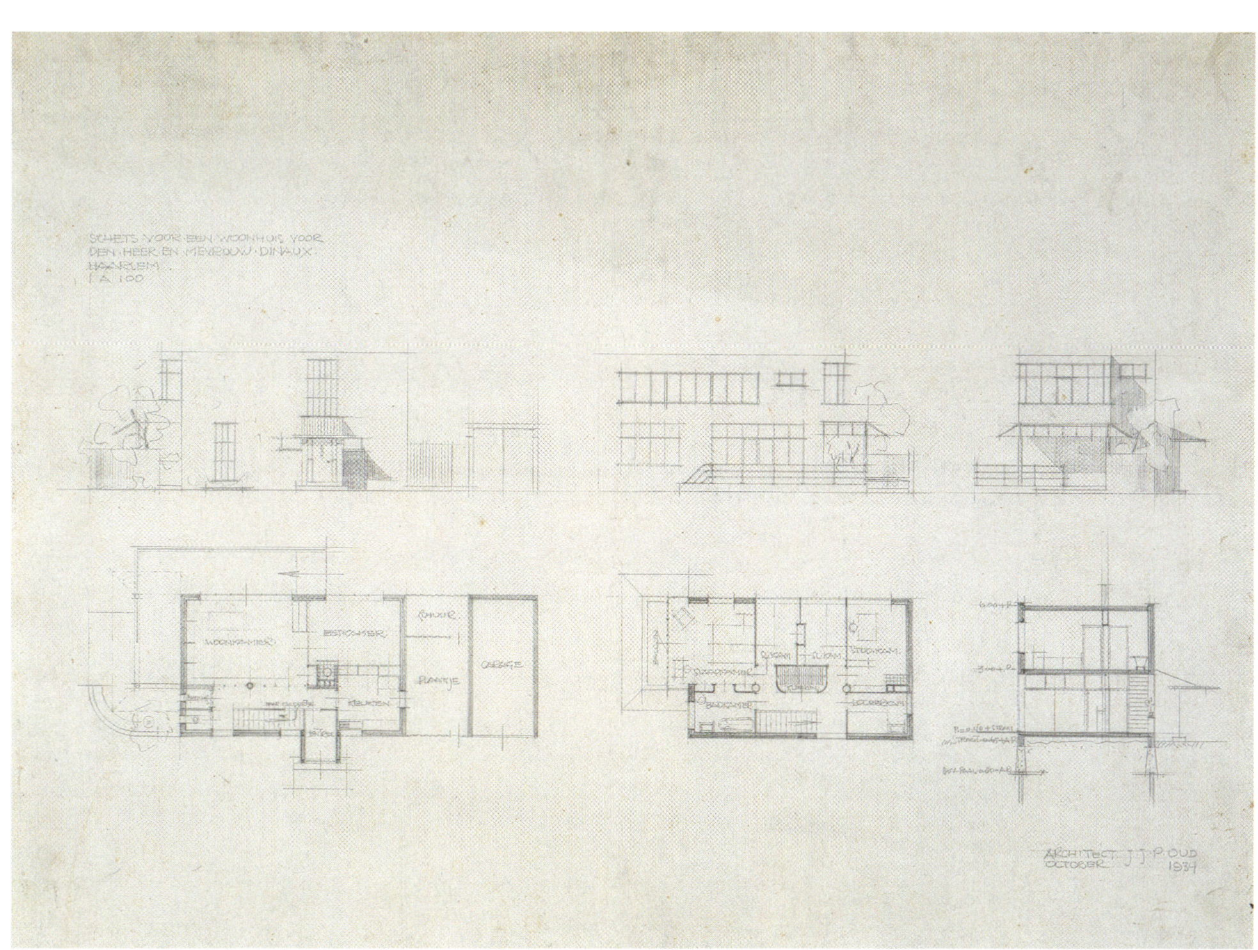


Various design views/ OUDJ-wx 2, NAI, Rotterdam



**Sources**
Getty: 890126-1**
NAI: OUDJ-wx 1-2,
OUDJ-wx 1001

**Literature**
U. Barbieri, *J.J.P. Oud*, Rotterdam 1987, p. 132
G. Stamm, *J.J.P. Oud. Bauten und Projekte 1906 bis 1963*, Mainz, Berlin 1984, p. 115

In 1935, Oud designed several studio dwellings under a single, monopitch roof, in connection with which he consulted Zanstra, Giesen & Sijmons, who had built similar dwellings in Amsterdam.[1] Oud's design shows a ground floor with dining room, kitchen and toilet at the front and a studio at the rear. The upper half-floor contains two bedrooms with balcony, and a wardrobe and a picture chest on the landing overlooking the studio. The spiral staircase connecting the two floors begins in the studio. It is not clear whether this layout was similar to that of the detached studio dwelling about which Oud corresponded in February of that year with Mrs Ooms-Vickers.[2]

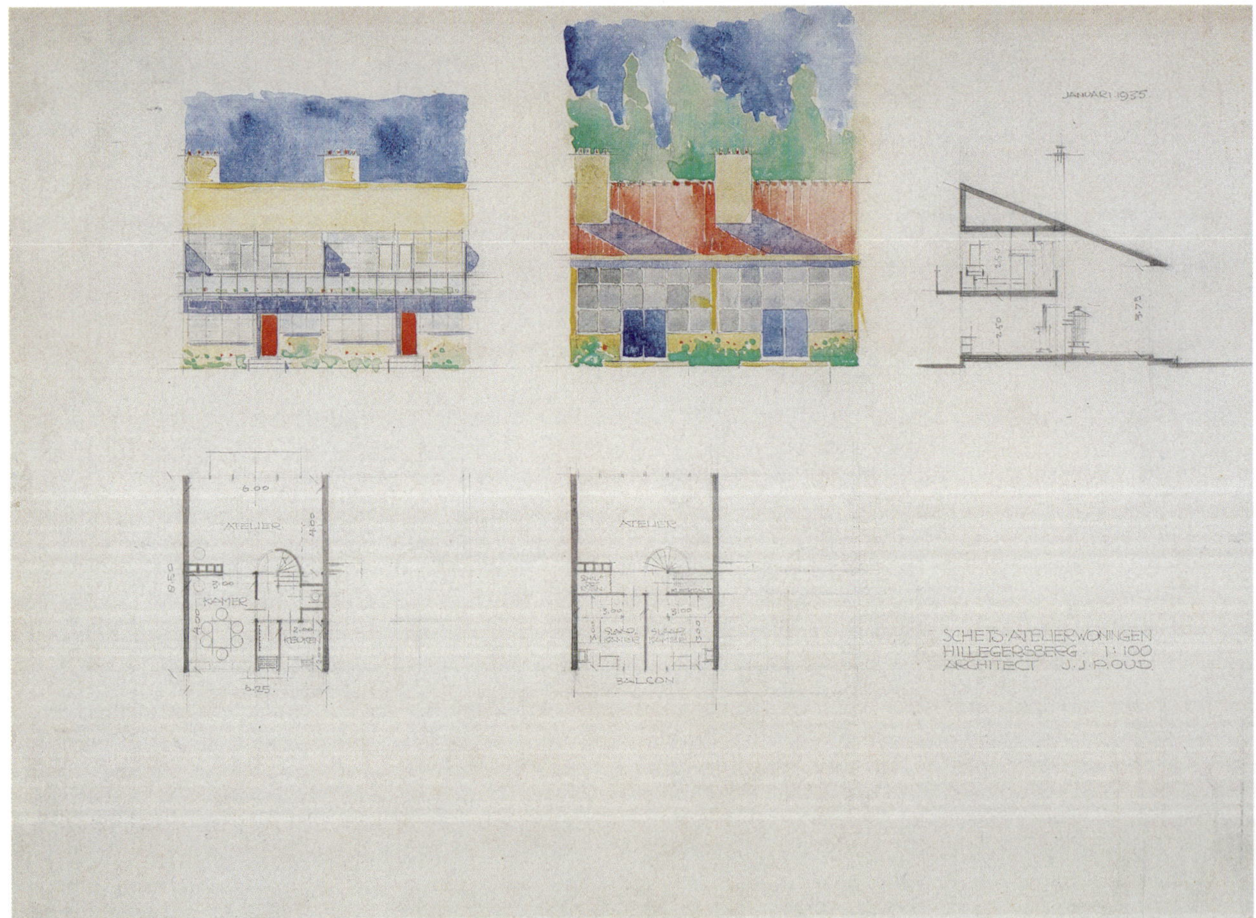


**Various design views/ OUDJ-at 2, NAI, Rotterdam**



**Notes**
**1.** Zanstra, Giesen & Sijmons to J.J.P. Oud, 25 January 1935, OUDJ-B, NAI, Rotterdam.
**2.** C.J. Ooms-Vinckers to J.J.P. Oud, 22 February 1935, OUDJ-B, NAI, Rotterdam.

**Sources**
CCA: dr1984: 0153 – dr1984: 0156
NAI: OUDJ-at 1 – 2, OUDJ-at 1001

**Literature**
U. Barbieri, *J.J.P. Oud*, Rotterdam 1987, p.133
G. Stamm, *J.J.P. Oud. Bauten und Projekte 1906 bis 1963*, Mainz, Berlin 1984, p. 116

# 76/ Project for a Private House in Blaricum

**Blaricum, Bussumerweg** **1935**

In 1935 Oud designed a house with monopitch roof on Bussumerweg in Blaricum. The identity of the client is unknown. The contrast between the closed street facade and the open garden elevation is even stronger than in his previous designs. The house opens up to the garden as it were, an effect further reinforced by the fact that the roof is highest on the garden side. Oud devoted special attention to the staircases. The internal stair is visible on the outside through a semi-circular glazed stairtower. On the garden side an external stair links the terrace with the balcony and the bedrooms.

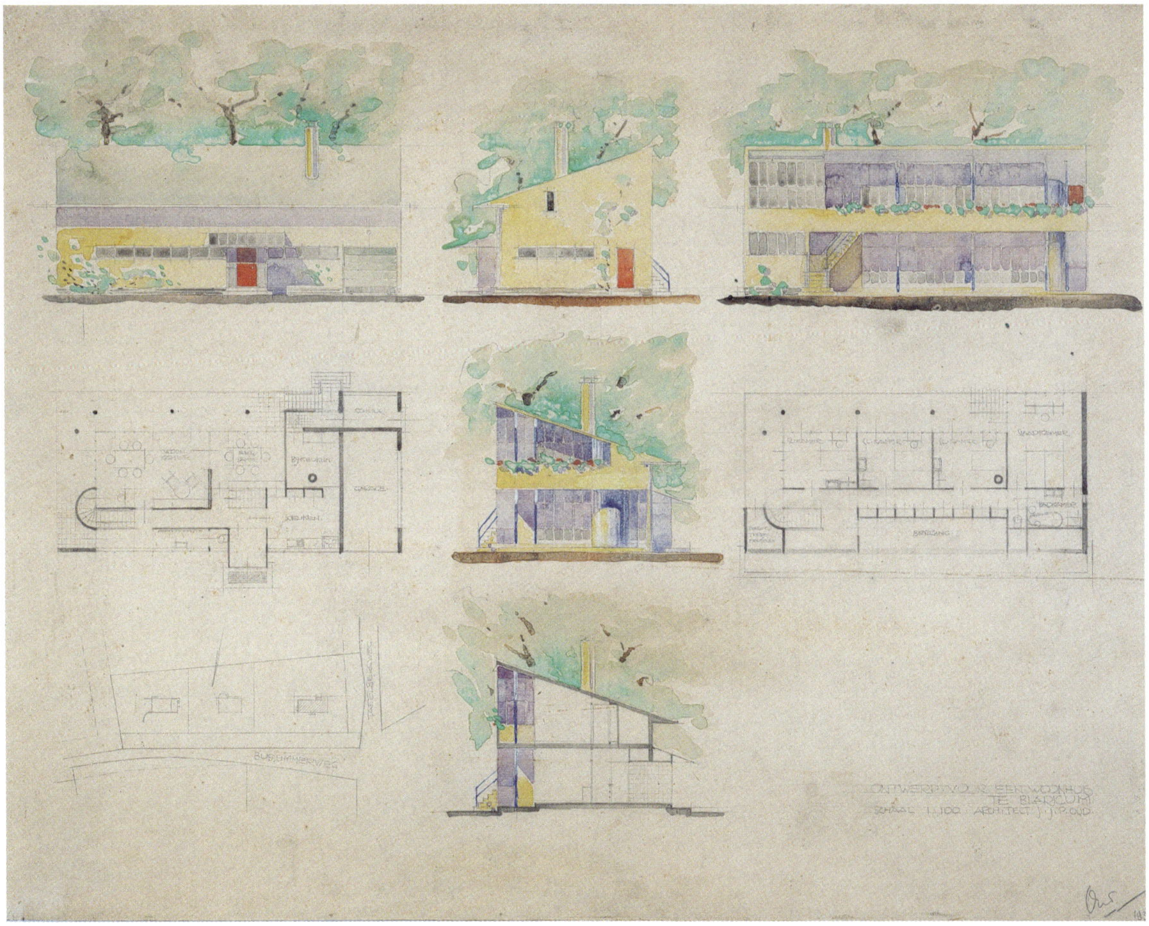

Various design views/ OUDJ-bl 10, NAI, Rotterdam



**Sources**
NAI: OUDJ-bl 1-32,
OUDJ-ph 467-470,
OUDJ-ph 1723-1724,
MAQV 375

Model/ MAQV-375, NAI, Rotterdam

# 77/ Design for a Private House for Mr & Mrs Pfeffer de Leeuw

**Blaricum, Bussumerweg 35** | **1935-1936**

Oud made two designs for a house for Pfeffer de Leeuw. The first of these has a flat roof and rather austere elevations, except for one of the short sides which is animated by a semi-circular external staircase and a roofed terrace. The local (Gooi) council rejected the flat roof as inappropriate to the district, whereupon Oud produced a second plan. He was evidently dissatisfied with the results of his attempts to provide the existing design with a pitched roof. He blamed his difficulties with this plan on the 'shock of the modern' which he subsequently denounced in a review of a colleague's design which had met a similar fate at the hands of the same 'aesthetic police'.[1] On the advice of his client, Oud reverted to an earlier design for a house with a monopitch roof, also in Blaricum (cat. no. 76). Although this design had never actually been built, it had received council approval. In the end, this house, like the one on which it was based, remained unbuilt.

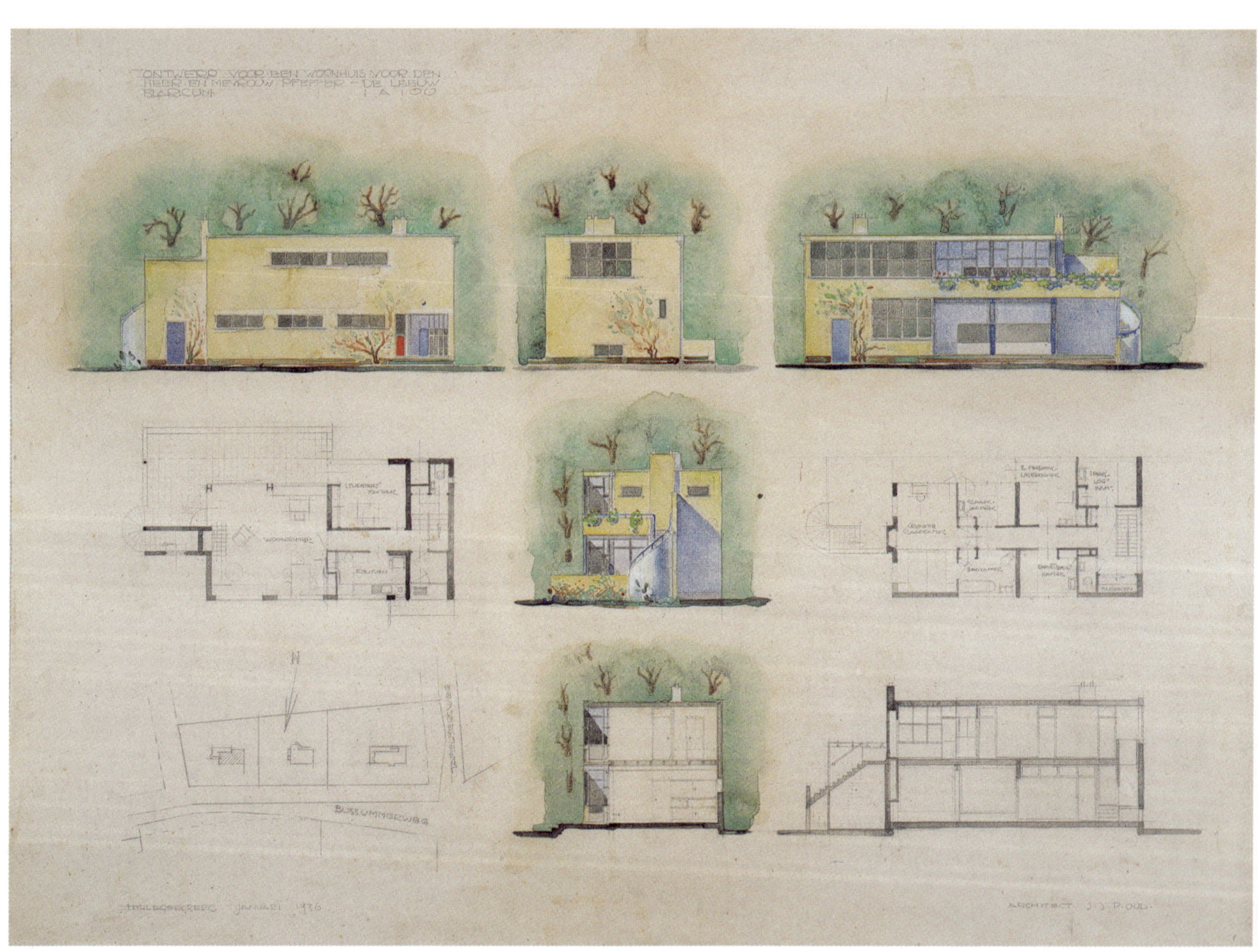

Various design views/ OUDJ-bl 2, NAI, Rotterdam



**Notes**
**1.** J.J.P. Oud, 'Atelierwoning te Blaricum. Arch. Hausbrand', in *Bouwkundig Weekblad*, 57(1936)34, p. 357.

**Sources**
CCA: dr1984: 0158-0160, dr1985: 0279
Getty: 890126-box 7-18*
NAI: OUDJ-bl 1-32, OUDJ-ph 467-470, OUDJ-ph 1723-1724, MAQV 375

**Articles**
J.J.P. Oud, 'Atelierwoning te Blaricum. Arch. Hausbrand', in: *Bouwkundig Weekblad*, 57(1936)34, p. 357

**Literature**
U. Barbieri, *J.J.P. Oud*, Rotterdam 1987, p. 134
G. Stamm, *J.J.P. Oud. Bauten und Projekte 1906 bis 1963*, Mainz, Berlin 1984, p. 117

# 78/ Design for a Holiday Cottage for Mr & Mrs Pfeffer de Leeuw

**Laren, Hertenweg**

**1935**

As well as asking Oud to design a home for them in Blaricum, the Pfeffer de Leeuws also commissioned him to design a country cottage in nearby Laren. The sketch design dates from September 1935 and is similar to other designs for houses from this period. The holiday cottage was conceived as surrounded by woods and Oud sought to derive maximum profit from this setting by employing a lot of glass, especially on the west facade which is also the most detailed. The side facades are more closed and slightly set back. The dimensions are generous for a holiday cottage, with a living room, kitchen and study on the ground floor and five bedrooms – two large and three small – upstairs.

Various design views/ OUDJ-zp 1, NAI, Rotterdam

**Sources**
CCA: dr1984: 0158-0160, dr1985: 0279
NAI: OUDJ-zp 1

# 79/ Director's House, Maatschap De Wilhelminapolder

**Wilhelminapolder, Westhavendijk 6**

**1936-1937**

The house Oud designed for the director of Koninklijke Maatschap De Wilhelminapolder marks the moment when, having resigned from the Rotterdam Woningdienst, he actually started to build again, as opposed to designing. It is curious therefore that he himself made so little mention of this commission, which he probably owed to contacts with the client made during one of his frequent summer holidays in Zeeland. In this design Oud distanced himself from his other 1930s villa designs which, with their splendid (modern) exteriors of white facades, taut shapes and large expanses of glass were in danger of fuelling a new formalism, something Oud regarded as undesirable. De Wilhelminapolder company was responsible for developing and renting out the farmland around the village of Wilhelminapolder. Appropriately, the rear of the house looked out over the polder managed by the Maatschap. It was the appointment in 1936 of a new director, A. Minderhoud, that prompted the company to demolish the existing dwelling (except for a small office section) and to erect a new house on the same site. Oud drew the design for this in late 1936. Construction was supervised by a local architect, C. van Maris of Goes. The house had a decidedly formal front aspect with a ground floor raised slightly above street level and above the front door a relief by Han Richters depicting the company's coat of arms and farmers reaping the harvest. The garden elevation by contrast was very open with ample windows, French doors, a bay window and a terrace. The ground floor contained the main entrance, kitchen, living room and office. On the upper floor, which included a bathroom, and bedrooms for at least ten people, the link between house, garden and polder was reinforced by the large balcony of the main bedroom.

**Front and rear views (Photos D. Broekhuizen)**



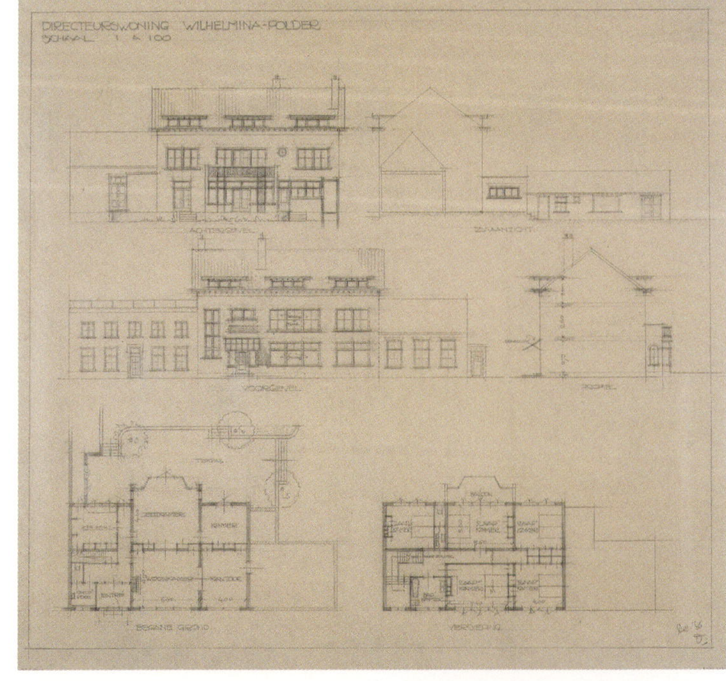


**Various design views/ dr1984: 0157, CCA, Montreal**

**Sources**
CCA: dr1984: 0157
Rijksarchief Zeeland, Middelburg: Maatschap De Wilhelminapolder Archive, inv. 963, 1035, 1042, 1045

**Literature**
A.M. de Jongh (ed.), *De Wilhelminapolder. Een beeld van een grootlandbouwbedrijf*, Goes 1996
Y. Koopmans, *Muurvast en gebeiteld. Beeldhouwkunst in de bouw 1840-1940*, Rotterdam 1994, pp. 180-181
Y. Koopmans, *Muurvast en gebeiteld. Beeldhouwkunst in de bouw 1840-1940*, Rotterdam 1997, p. 320
G.J. Lepoeter, 'Bij het 175-jarig bestaan van de Wilhelminapolder (1984)', in: *Zeeuws Tijdschrift*, 34 (1984) 161-178

# Oud and the Public Building

The public buildings Oud designed in the 1930s are very different from his projects of the 1920s. They illustrate a change of outlook related to his need to distance himself from the views espoused by Giedion and Gropius in particular, views that had to some extent become institutionalized in CIAM. Oud regarded the expression of a building's function and the search for the most efficient and economic resolution of the task as yesterday's challenge, something that architects should by now have left behind them and this is precisely what Oud, mindful of Wölfflin's lessons, now tried to do. If this critical attitude had already led him to query the established axioms of modernism (in his famous 'Ja und Nein' lecture of 1925), in the 1930s he appeared to be deliberately distancing himself from them. Nor did he see functionalism as the architectural touchstone. It was an ideological rather than a formal criterion. At issue was the development of architecture towards a new style; most modern designs failed this test, which put them outside the domain of architecture in Oud's view. In the designs he made for public buildings in the 1930s, Oud explored the possibilities and limits of a contemporary, representational architecture without having recourse to historical styles. This quest resulted in a fundamental change of course.

Unlike in the previous decade, Oud no longer distilled the representational character from the programme and he tried to get away from the composition of objectively and functionally designed components and of their interaction with the surrounding city. The differentiation of function seems less explicit in his designs for the Amsterdam Town Hall and the Shell Building than in the plans for the Volksuniversiteit and the Exchange. While the composition of volumes is more clear-cut in the Town Hall and the Shell Building, in the facade finishing, the choice of brick and the application of a rich ornamentation they introduce new elements into Oud's work. Reduction had made way for addition, abstraction for embellishment.

How to explain this change? Oud himself insisted that he never abandoned the principles of his work of the 1920s. After all, they were the years of *catharsis* when, by dint of research and experiment, architecture was purged of all historical ballast and tested for new formal possibilities. Moreover, the 1930s designs were in line with Oud's notion that the public building belonged to a higher order that was far more suited to the creation of architecture than public housing. That the designs for the Town Hall and Shell Building ushered in a new phase in his work, was never denied by Oud. However, he vehemently opposed critics who claimed that this new path was incompatible with what had gone before and even accused him of betraying his original principles. After the international publication of the Shell Building this controversy became the red thread running through the rest of his architectural and critical work.

Oud is the originator of the all-too-frequently quoted aphorism 'Ornament is the universal panacea for architectural impotence', but that does not mean he was an existential enemy of ornament like Adolf Loos, with his publication *Ornament und Verbrechen* (Ornament and Crime). However, they both were acutely aware of the fact that, at the dawn of the twentieth century, the functioning of ornament was in utter confusion; that it was invariably used to disguise a complete failure to address a new building programme. And that justifies an aggressively rhetorical tone concerning the subject of ornament. The very fact that they highlighted the issue of decorative detail in architecture served to clarify its purpose. It was perfectly clear to Oud, as it was to Loos, that twentieth-century architecture could not automatically thrive on the foundations of existing codes. It set its own standards. And that applied to ornament as well. The discovery of new compositional and tectonic harmonies, facilitated by reinforced concrete, steel and polished plate glass, itself constituted a sufficiently ambitious and grand exercise. The necessity of decorative extras was never even acknowledged as a problem. Nevertheless, from the start of his experiments, Oud did not go overboard with ornament; it did not always form a specifically demonstrable entity in the composition. Even with his disciplined examination of the housing block, culminating directly in the typologically perfected order of block IX in Spangen, ornament has a mature presence, created from nothing, as an authentic example of the discovery of form. The surface composition may be based on the rhythm of the doors and windows against the masonry background, but the corner treatment is explicitly ornamental, with ridges, cornices and striking window-piers. They are the anchors in Oud's urban model, which was based on the repetition of similar basic components (housing blocks), but also required precisely positioned interruptions in the background. That was the purpose of ornament.

It was remarkable that, from the start, Oud was obsessively inclined in his ornamental ambitions to do something that had never been done before, if only to flout tardy academic conventions. The Witte Dorp, a semi-permanent housing scheme devoid of sound foundations and costing next to nothing, came straight after the prototypes of Spangen and Tusschendijken. It is less disciplined, 'liberal' even in decorative treatment. Impermanence - which with the Witte Dorp actually amounted to a useful life of over a half a century – also meant freedom in Oud's view. The project became a veritable gem, thanks to its formal virtuosity, beginning with the master plan and going on to conquer and overrun the entire three-dimensional composition. With the housing terrace at Hoek van Holland, the ornamental impulse (comparable with block IX) lies chiefly in the components which are intended to complete the regularity of the composition. This time it was primarily the detailing of the rounded ends. Oud went to great lengths to discover how to refine this symmetrical block down to the smallest detail - and that is what made him the classicist among modernists, even in the mid-1920s. Ornament, or at least the ornamental intention, was part and parcel of architecture for him, either in order to make a complete, self-contained jewel, or as part of a wider architectural concept, after the example of the Spangen estate.

The 'jeweller' retained his vitality after the Witte Dorp. In the early 1930s – a period of decided halfheartedness in his oeuvre – he came up with a strange line in furniture, made mainly for Metz & Co. With its somewhat frenetic lineation, it was destined to be a commercial fiasco. Yet the chairs in particular do have a curious, eccentric appeal. They were actually studies of conceivable specifications of form and material, rather than studies of function, although some of Oud's chairs, especially the 'knitting-chair', are quite comfortable. The mannerism of Oud's lineation was occasionally also reflected in a larger object than a chair, namely a real building. The post-war Bio-Convalescent Home for Children is an assembly of detached pavilions, some of which served purely as 'follies'. The boiler house with flat and the observation tower are entirely ornamental, with, of necessity, an additional functional specification. Later he also applied that sequence – the initial purpose being pure form, followed by a function because it was required – in the three-sided tower of the Congress Centre. As a result, users of the complex have always looked in vain for a lasting use for this magnificent transparent stack of triangular floors.

Oud circumnavigated the compositional objective, with his exploration of form without specific function, more than any other Dutch modernist. He was asked to design the national monument on Dam Square. He also went further than his contemporaries in the way in which he made room for ornament alongside strictly functional elements in the spatial programme. The 'culture shock' of the Shell Building was to a large extent due to the generous application of adornments (designed by the architect himself) in stone, bronze, reinforced concrete, tiling, majolica and so on. Yet anyone who takes a good look at the earlier work, particularly in Spangen and Hoek van Holland, must recognize that the Shell Building was on the same track, as regards method. However, Oud gave this building more prominent urban significance. The Shell Building was not one in a series, so not part of the 'clutter' of the city. It was explicitly intended as a self-referring composition, the motive of which was further explained by ornamental additions. Firstly, the building literally said something about the principal and occupant – Shell – with the obvious rendering of a shell, arduously depicted here and there by the architect himself. Secondly, the building represented, figuratively, a crucial but eloquent component of an ideal hierarchy, which Oud reduced to what he tended to describe as 'a good democracy'. Thanks to the ornament, in step with the composition of volumes, the substance of the building was elevated to another level - one in which substance acquired significance. After the war, Oud pursued the same process, though he was somewhat deterred by the ideological objections against the Shell Building. He did not exactly shy away from drastic compositions and strategies, as is borne out by the eccentricities of the Bio-Convalescent Home for Children and the Congress Centre, for instance, yet he did avoid exploring the ostentatious hierarchy further, and its realistic support in a visual programme. The decoration of a building like De Utrecht is certainly striking, but far more diffuse in meaning than was customary for the pre-war Oud.

# 80/ Competition Design for the Amsterdam Town Hall

**Amsterdam, Frederiksplein, Oosteinde, Westeinde** **1936-1937**

Perspective of courtyard/ OUDJ-rh 47, NAI, Rotterdam

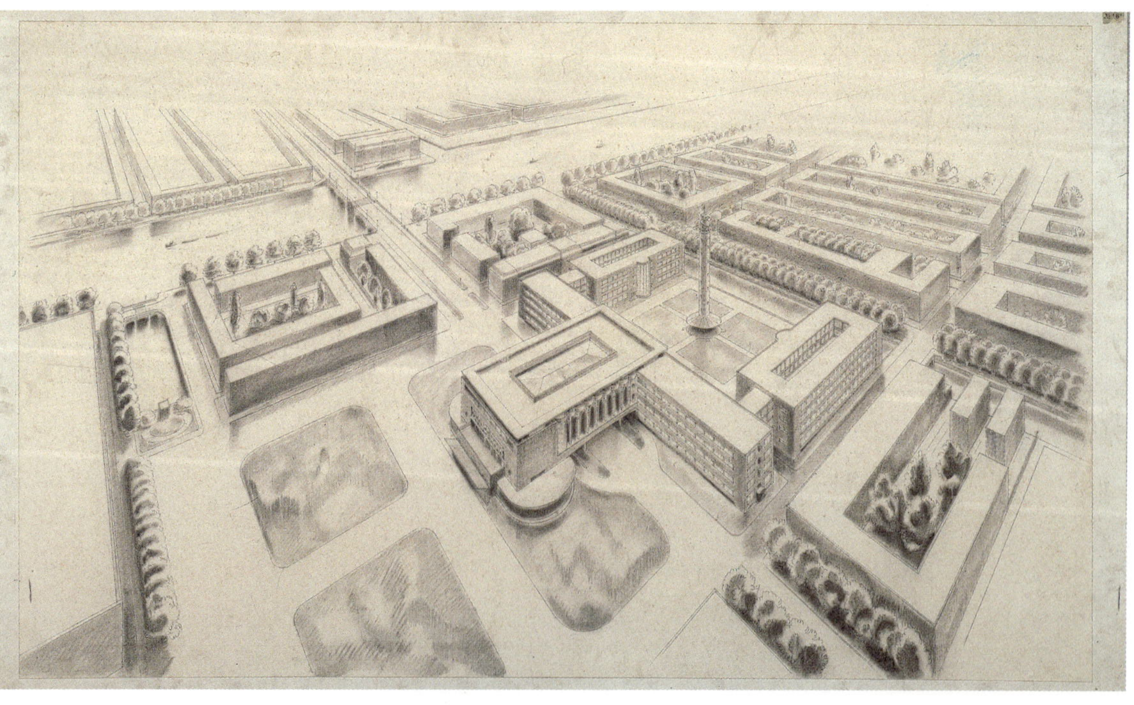

Bird's-eye view/ OUDJ-rh 48, NAI, Rotterdam

No design task in the 1930s was more contentious than that of the town hall. It led to heated debates within *De 8 en Opbouw* and even to the break-up of *Groep '32*.[1] This is really not so surprising for the town hall is a highly symbolic building and it was precisely on this point that opinions were so sharply divided. Could the demand for symbolism be combined with a functional and objective approach to architecture? Could it be reconciled with the egalitarian tendencies of modern mass society? Could the inevitably high costs be justified against the background of a still unresolved housing shortage? Nor did the problems end with the acceptance of the representational function of architecture, for the question then arose as to how this was to be expressed. Was it permissible to draw on the arsenal of architectonic resources of the past? Were symmetry and ornamentation still acceptable? Did costly materials or vast proportions offer a way out? Oud threw himself wholeheartedly into the debate surrounding the competitions for town halls in The Hague (1930) and Huizen (1938) but when it came to his own entry for the Amsterdam town hall competition (1936), he retreated into silence.
The town hall design Oud sent to the jury in August 1937 was first and foremost an investigation of the spatial orchestration of the cityscape by means of the precise placement of open and closed spaces, views over water features, vistas, axial perspectives and building above roads. On the south side of the site Oud placed a court that was open on one side to the canal (Stadhouderskade) and for the rest surrounded by three office wings. On the north side, the more open Frederiksplein bordered a busy thoroughfare (Weteringschans-Sarphatistraat). Straddling this road – with an entrance on the square and a link to the other three wings – was a fourth office wing containing the most important formal functions such as the council chamber, various function rooms and the civic hall. The enclosed court was restricted to local traffic (public servants, visitors and bridal parties), while Frederiksplein, which sat atop an underground car park, was intended for through traffic. On this square, exactly in line with the Utrechtsestraat axis, was the formal main entrance, intended chiefly for ceremonial occasions like state visits and inaugurations. Access to the courtyard was via two portals in the side wings. While the horizontal volumes were attuned by virtue of their placement, facade composition and height to the surrounding development and street pattern, Oud used the vertical accent of the tower in the courtyard to stress the building's importance for the city as a whole.
The internal organization differed from wing to wing. At the centre of the main wing, extending through several floors, was a spacious lobby. Ranged around this were the council chamber, function rooms, the main wedding room and, on the top floor, a cafeteria with roof terrace for the staff. The wing along Frederiksplein contained offices organized along a central corridor, the two transverse wings were situated

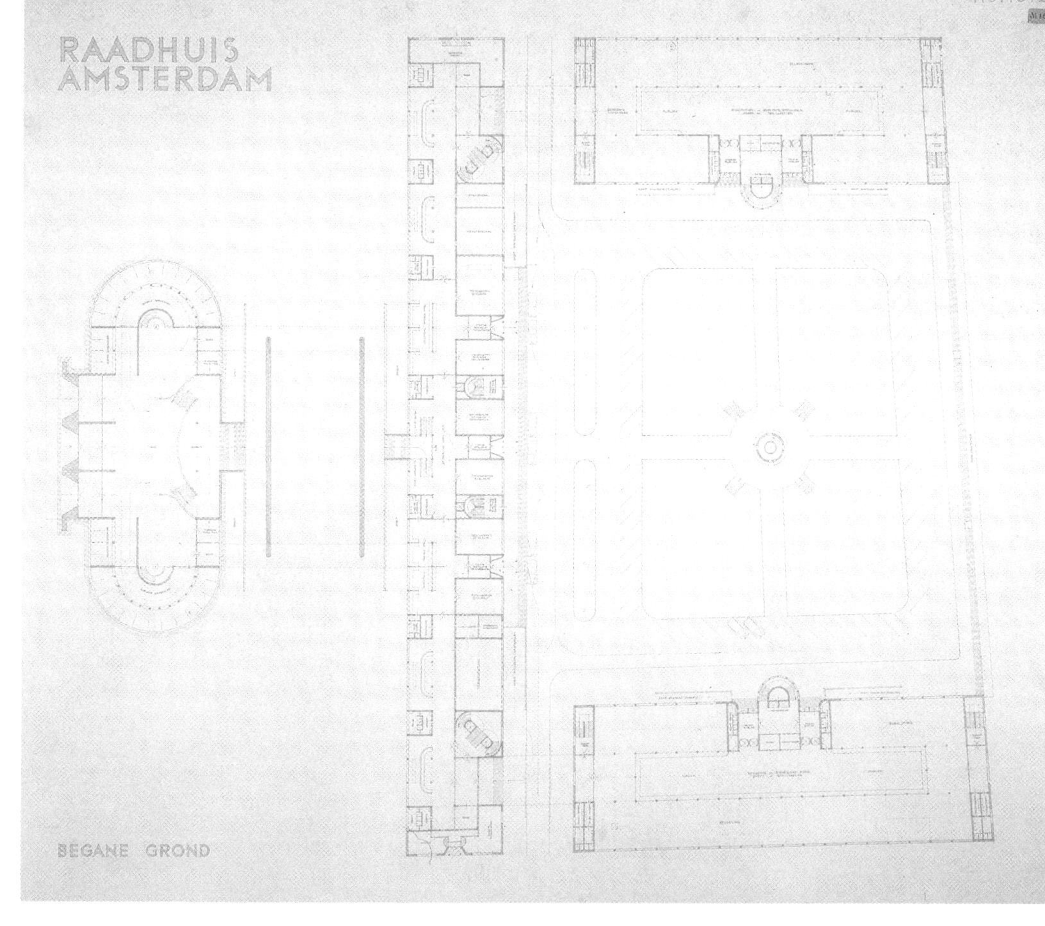


Ground floor plan/ OUDJ-rh 39, NAI, Rotterdam

409

around a small open court with promenade and offices. In stark contrast to the uniformly anonymous facades of his Rotterdam Exchange design ten years previously, Oud envisaged rich decoration for the town hall facade. There was also a marked difference between the anonymous treatment of the office areas and the abstractly ornamented window units and loggias of the representative areas. On top of this, the entrance and the highest point of the building were decorated with figurative carvings. The main entrance was accentuated by lions holding the Amsterdam coat of arms and the tower was crowned by a globe and 'Koggeschip' (a medieval merchant ship), a symbolic representation of Amsterdam as a centre of international trade. While these last two ornaments were conceived in colourful majolica, the remaining facade decorations were to be executed in light-coloured brick and stone.

The outcome of the competition was a huge disappointment for Oud. To begin with, he was not even among the four architects invited to refine their design by a jury that included the architects S. van Ravesteyn, M.J. Granpré Molière and A. van der Steur. But equally wounding no doubt was Le Corbusier's negative remarks upon inspecting the anonymous entries on display in the Stedelijk Museum in Amsterdam. In this analysis, which was published in *De 8 en Opbouw* in 1940, Le Corbusier was particularly scathing of the infrastructure in Oud's design: *The road system is confused, it is a tree without trunk. Here we see the characteristic tendency of an architecture that proceeds from empty interiors and not from the natural birth of an organism.*[2] S. Giedion, whom Oud had visited in 1938, was shocked. *He is on a dangerous path of reaction*, he wrote to L. Moholy-Nagy.[3]

**Sketch of reception room balcony/ OUDJ-rh 6, NAI, Rotterdam**

**Notes**

**1.** For the debate about the competitions see Bock (ed.), *Van het Nieuwe Bouwen naar een Nieuwe Architectuur. Groep '32. Ontwerpen, gebouwen, stedebouwkundige plannen 1925-1945*, The Hague 1983, pp. 96-100.

**2.** Le Corbusier, 'Le Corbusier over de raadhuisprijsvraag', in *De 8 en Opbouw*, 4(1940), pp. 30-40.

**3.** S. Giedion to L. Moholy-Nagy, 29 July 1938, GTA, Zurich.

**Sources**

CCA: ph1984: 0872-0877
Getty: 890126-box 3, F32
NAI: OUDJ-rh 1-48, OUDJ-rh 1001

**Articles**

Le Corbusier, 'Le Corbusier over de raadhuisprijsvraag', in: *De 8 en Opbouw*, 4(1940), pp. 30-40

**Literature**

J.H. Albarda, 'Herinneringen aan Oud', in: *Jong Holland*, 4(1987)11, pp. 21-23
U. Barbieri, *J.J.P. Oud*, Rotterdam 1987, p. 135
H.E. Oud, *J.J.P. Oud. Architekt 1890-1963. Feiten en herinneringen gerangschikt*, The Hague 1984, pp. 137
G. Stamm, *J.J.P. Oud. Bauten und Projekte 1906 bis 1963*, Mainz, Berlin 1984, p. 131

# 81/ Head Office of the Bataafsche Import Maatschappij (Shell)

**The Hague, Wassenaarseweg**

**1937-1942, 1946-1948 (restoration)**

In 1937 the board of the Bataafsche Import Maatschappij (BIM, the Batavian Import Company, better known as Shell) decided to build a new head office.[1] Its existing offices were on Carel van Bylandtlaan in The Hague, alongside those of the parent company, the Bataafsche Petroleum Maatschappij. The new BIM building, it was revealed in December 1937, would be built on the estate of Countess M.A.O.C. van Bylandt, on the corner of Wassenaarseweg and Floris Grijpstraat. An exhaustive in-house study of the company preceded the drawing up of the building programme. The entire organization was analysed and a model devised for its future operation. The BIM's technical department drew up a provisional building programme on the basis of this report.[2] From the outset it was laid down that the building was to cost no more than one million guilders, including services, architect's fee and the site office, but excluding the furnishings. As well as spelling out the conditions governing a possible future extension, the building programme also focused on the building's representational function. The designer was to *bear in mind that the building was to be perfectly visible from Wassenaarscheweg and that, as a conspicuously large office building, it should be a dignified yet unambiguous advertisement for "Shell". ...The architecture should from the outset incorporate an eye-catching illuminated sign for "Shell" without in any way allowing this to diminish, in a more or less banal fashion, the architecture of the whole. Accommodate the installation of floodlight illumination of the front and side elevations.*[3] The initial building was to house six hundred employees with the possibility of future extension to provide office accommodation for 1,800 people. The building programme contained precise indications as to the orientation of the building volume on the site. The front facade with main entrance conformed to the building line of the houses on Wassenaarseweg; the service entrance was around the corner on Floris Grijpstraat. In essence the task was to design the tallest possible building on the smallest possible base. Reinforced concrete was stipulated for the support structure and steel for the window frames. Even the heights of the individual storeys were laid down in advance. Windows had to be designed to a precise module so that partition walls could be moved if necessary. The BIM board also had definite ideas about the character of the office building and proffered, by way of example, the BPM building and the KLM office in The Hague (designed by Roosenburgh and Verhave & Luijt). The new head office was required to be unpretentious and functional yet distinguished.

As soon as the location and building programme had been settled, the BIM set about organizing an invitational competition involving four architects: Oud, A.J. Kropholler, D. Roosenburg and G. Friedhoff. The first meeting between the invited architects and the building committee, at which the need to allow for possible future expansion was emphasized, took place on 10 January 1938. The architects then

Sketch of front elevation (centre) and rear elevation (bottom left) of office building, and service station (bottom right)/ OUDJ-bm 1, NAI, Rotterdam

## 81/ Head Office of the Bataafsche Import Maatschappij (Shell)

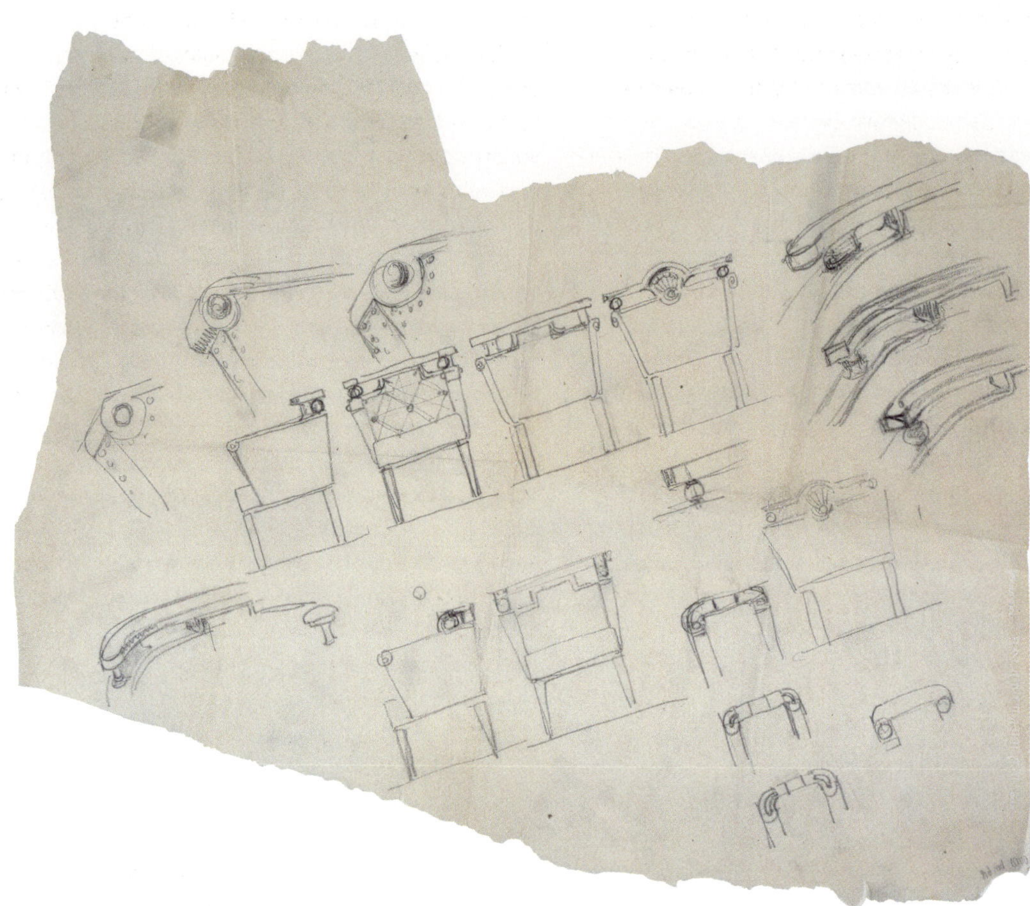

Sketches for an office chair/ OUDJ-bm 618, NAI, Rotterdam

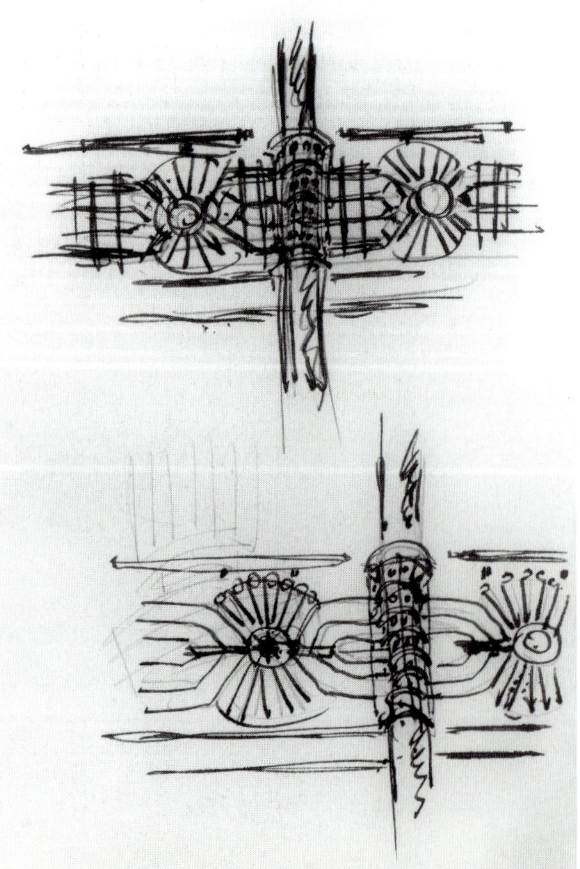

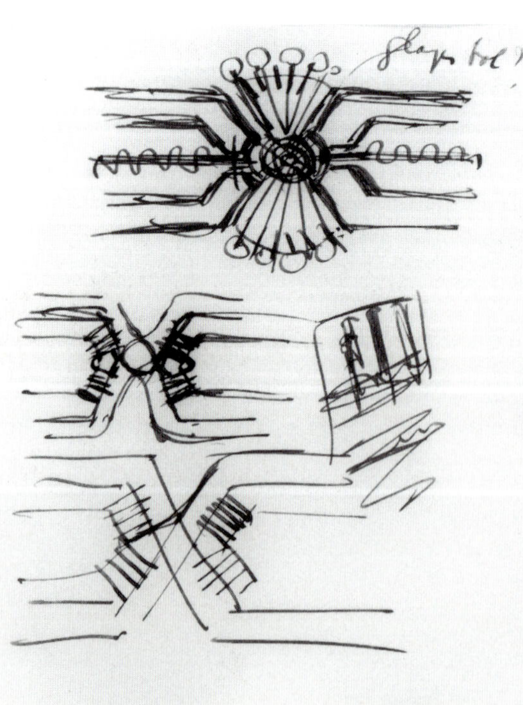

Sketches for the facade of the stairwell at rear/ OUDJ-bm 71 and 70, NAI, Rotterdam

had three months in which to work on the design. Oud's explanatory notes reveal that he kept as close as possible to the terms of reference. The basic plan-form was a familiar type: a rectangular block with rooms ranged either side of a central corridor. The offices were separated by movable partitions. In the middle of the rear facade was the main staircase and behind it a low structure containing the multifunctional recreation hall: company cafeteria during the day and theatre or cinema in the evening. The low structure, which was surrounded by a landscaped garden, consisted of a passageway perpendicular to the main building with, at right angles to it (on the west side) the recreation hall. Oud proposed a two-stage extension programme. During the first stage the low-rise structure would be raised to the same height as the main building and in the second stage a third office block would be built on the north side, parallel to and similar in plan to the first, thus giving rise to an H-shaped ground plan. The location of the service station was dictated by practical and traffic engineering considerations but because it looked out over the garden, Oud felt that it should at all events be *somewhat romantic*.

The BIM board was immediately enthusiastic about Oud's design.[4] Admitted to the building committee on 25 April 1938, he spent the entire summer and autumn incorporating modifications and refining the detailing in order to have the design ready for tendering in January 1939. The main contractor was NV Timmerfabriek De Concurrent of Bergambacht. Oud chose a yellow IJssel brick and a beige Euville stone from Belgium for the central section of the front and rear elevations and the window surrounds. The basement facade was partly in beige stone and partly in concrete with a grey surface layer: Oud wanted a massive plinth to complement the light brick. In addition to the fixed furnishings, Oud designed office furniture specifically for the BIM: a conference table and chairs executed in 1947, a seating area and a workspace for the director which was probably not designed until 1946. Earthworks got under way in September 1939. No sooner had the first pile been driven into the ground than mobilization was proclaimed on 29 September. Since stopping work would have resulted in cancelled contracts, the BIM board

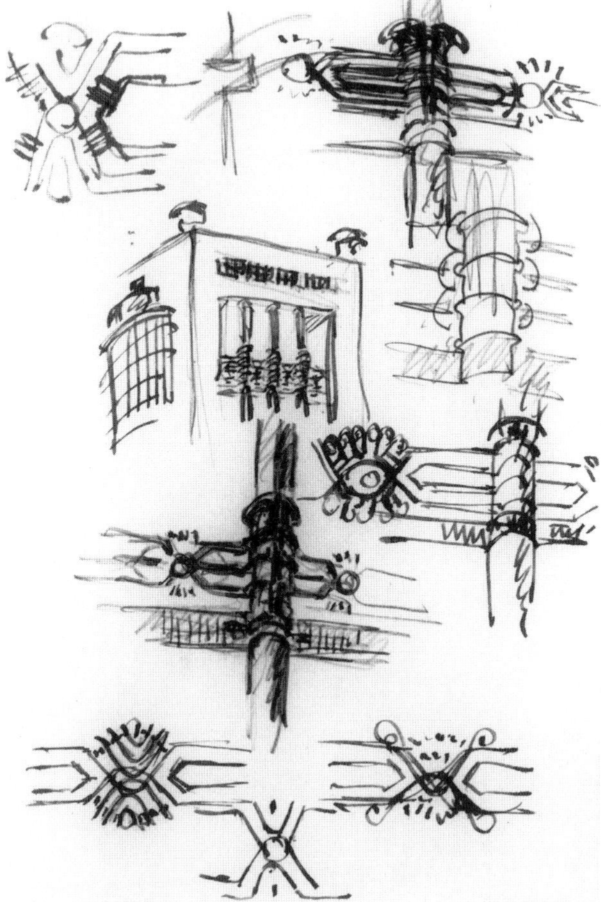

Sketches for the facade of the stairwell at the rear/
OUDJ-bm 73 and 72, NAI, Rotterdam

decided to proceed with the construction but to realize only the absolute minimum required to produce a serviceable office building. As a consequence, landscaping was curtailed and the main building and service station were built without the internal and external bronze ornamentation. Most of the contracts were carried out according to plan and the building was occupied in the course of 1941. Towards the end of the war, on 18 and 30 March 1945, the building was damaged by Allied bombing. Immediately after the war, Oud set about restoring it.

In the Netherlands, the Shell Building met with a positive reception in the 1940s, but the foreign architectural press was highly critical. Many of Oud's foreign friends were frankly dismayed by what appeared to be a wrong turning in his architectural career. Oud attempted to forestall criticism by pointing to the innovative nature of his design. Philip Johnson was one of the prewar friends he tried to convince in this way: *We have to explore always new terrains. I myself I am sure that I did a bit of this in the Shell-building again and I hope that you too will find after studying it that I am right. If it is "conventional" to use anew the rules that as long as the world rolls has reigned good architecture than I am glad that I am "conventionally".*[5] Johnson reacted very sceptically: *I do not know what to say. Maybe I ought to wait until I can see you and we can talk over the whole thing together. Frankly, to me the building looks like a return to Dutch tradition rather than the next step in international architecture. It is International only if Berlage was an International architect. No one but a Dutchman could have built it just that way. That is fine, but why call it International? I am afraid I am as old fashioned as poor Giedion. Do you not agree, after seeing the pictures in the book?*[6]

The review in *The Architectural Record* was equally harsh: *Here, now, is Oud himself resorting to embroidery. The plan of the Shell Building is hard to distinguish from straight academic. Its major forms seem to be not enascent from the problem but are recognizable as repertory out of the architect's notebook. The very insistent, heavy, separate, imposed pattern of 'decoration' seems visually related not to a keen process of expanding apperception but rather to the pleasant reminiscences of peasant art.*[7] Oud responded immediately and thus the Shell Building became the subject of a polemic that was to determine his position in international architecture of the late 1940s. *The Shell building is an effort to strive again after architecture as a matter of the soul. As a consequence you will find in it resources that through the ages have proved to be good bearers of psychological feeling: of forms that have some underlying substance for universal apprehension. They concern geometry, symmetry, harmony, proportion. Also now and then: hierarchy. Further: questions like those of modules, ornament, and so on are faced. Different styles are based on such objective aesthetic frameworks, and time has shown that with the m just as much variety in outward appearance is*

Ornamentation above main entrance/ OUDJ-ph 811, NAI, Rotterdam

## 81/ Head Office of the Bataafsche Import Maatschappij (Shell)

OUDJ-ph 807, NAI, Rotterdam
Ornamentation rear elevation/ OUDJ-ph 790, NAI, Rotterdam



**Notes**

**1.** For a detailed description of the events surrounding the construction of the Shell Building, see: E. Taverne, D. Broekhuizen, *J.J.P. Oud's Shell Building. Design and Reception*, Rotterdam 1995.
**2.** Report by Management's Control of the General Course of Affairs (the body set up to study the corporation), 19370930, Shell Archive, The Hague, and Programma van Eisen, 19371207, Shell Archive, The Hague.
**3.** Programma van Eisen, 7 December 1937, Shell Archive, The Hague.
**4.** Apart from Oud's design, only that of Friedhoff has been preserved. All that is known about the other two designs comes from a critical comparison by art historian J.G. van Gelder, who saw all four designs at an exhibition and published reviews in the *NRC* and *Elsevier*. He detected similarities between the designs of Friedhoff and Kropholler and between those of Roosenburg and Oud.
**5.** J.J.P. Oud to P. Johnson, 18 December 1945, OUDJ-B, NAI, Rotterdam.
**6.** P. Johnson to J.J.P. Oud, OUDJ-B, NAI, Rotterdam.
**7.** 'Mr. Oud embroiders a theme. Shell "I.B.M." Building, the Hague. J.J.P. Oud, Architect', in: *Architectural Record*, 6(1946), pp. 80-84. The translation was Oud's own work, OUDJ-bm 1001-1008, NAI, Rotterdam.
**8.** J.J.P. Oud, 'Speech delivered by Mr J.J.P. Oud to members of the International Association of art Critics during their visit to the Shell Netherland Building at the Hague on the 9th July 1951' typescript, 4 July 1951, NAI, Rotterdam.

**Sources**

CCA: dr1984: 0199-0207, dr1984: 0260, dr1984: 0450-0451, dr1984: 0466, dr1984: 0561, dr1985: 0376, ph1984: 0878-0880, ph1984: 0895-0896
Getty: 890126-box 3, F14, 890126-1**
MOMA: NC Drawings-blueprints
Museum Boymans van Beuningen: inv. no. V2.1-1737, V2.1-1740
NAI: OUDJ-bm 1-975, OUDJ-bm 1001-1008, OUDJ-bm 2001-2004, OUDJ-bm 3001-3002, OUDJ-ph 487-859, OUDJ-ph 1849-1850,

## 81/ Head Office of the Bataafsche Import Maatschappij (Shell)

Perspective, detailed competition design, 1938/ OUDJ-bm 109, NAI, Rotterdam

Perspective, detailed competition design, 1938/ OUDJ-bm 108, NAI, Rotterdam

Extension variant with two office wings and low connecting corridor/ OUDJ-ph 500, NAI, Rotterdam

## 81/ Head Office of the Bataafsche Import Maatschappij (Shell)

*possible as with the human skeleton which has been the basis for millions of shapes of men and women. I may explain that with the Shell building I tried to avoid a lot of mistakes such as I made in former works which were praised now and then by my colleagues from over the Ocean. ...The ornament is not used to conceal mistakes in architecture: the building itself could do without it, but it stimulates its meaning. It is – to quote Frank Lloyd Wright – "of the building, not on it' ... In the same manner the groundplan of the Shell building became its shape: it is not a dead academic figure, as suggested by American friends, but it grew out of the need for the pleasant rather than only the useful form in which functionalism expresses itself delightfully.*[8]

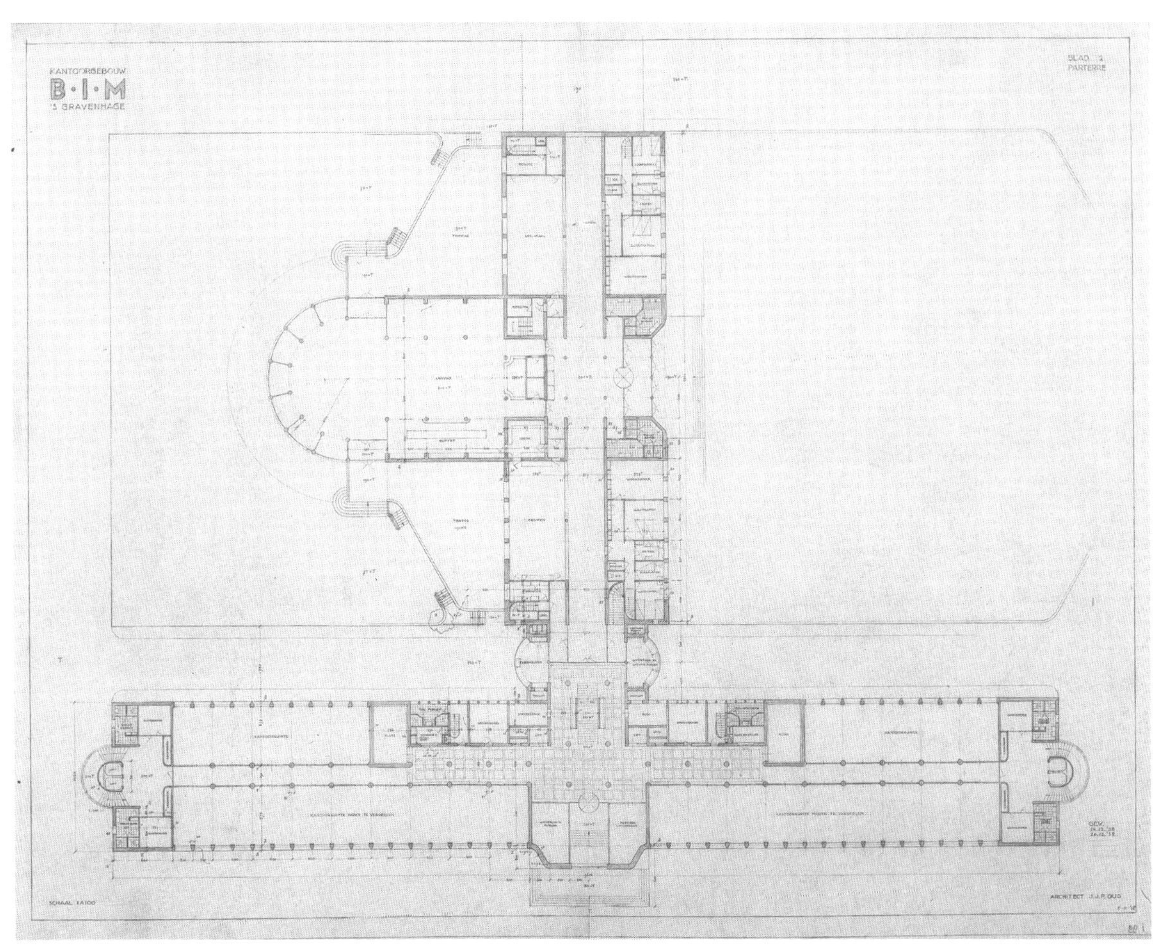


**Ground floor plan detailed competition design, 1938/ OUDJ-bm 99, NAI, Rotterdam**

OUDJ-ph 1646-1666, OUDJ-ph 1733-1740, OUDJ-ph 1920, VOOV-168

**Articles**

J.G. van Gelder, 'Ontwerpen voor het nieuwe gebouw der Bataafsche Import Maatschappij in Den Haag', in: *Elsevier's Geïllustreerd Maandschift*, 49(1939), pp. 353-354

J.H. de Haas, 'Kantoorgebouw voor de Shell Nederland N.V. te 's Gravenhage', in: *Bouwbedrijf en Openbare Werken*, 2(1947), pp. 11-16, 21-24, 31-34

'Mr. Oud embroiders a theme. Shell "I.B.M." Building, the Hague. J.J.P. Oud, Architect', in: *Architectural Record*, 6(1946), pp. 80-84

E. Mulhern, 'Netherlands Architects set the pace. Oud followed Neoplasticists in Functional Design, in: *Knickerbocker Weekly*, 27(1943), pp. 34-37

'Ontwerpen voor het nieuwe gebouw der Bataafsche Import Maatschappij', in: *Nieuwe Rotterdamsche Courant*, 4 April 1939

'Oud in de Amerikaanse Pers', in: *Forum*, 2(1947)2/3, pp. 71-72

'The Shell Building The Hague. Architect J.J.P. Oud', in: *Journal of the Royal Institute of British Architects*, 53(1946)5, pp. 162-166

'Shell Head Office of The Hague: views and plans', in: *Journal of the Royal Architectural Institute of Canada*, July(1950), pp. 220-221

A. Staal, 'Het gebouw der B.I.M. Architect Oud's jongste werk. Vruchtbare vooruitgang', in: *De Telegraaf*, 13 June 1941

J.J. Vriend, 'Het nieuwe kantoorgebouw voor de B.I.M. door architect J.J.P. Oud', in: *De Groene Amsterdammer*, 12 January 1946

**Literature**

U. Barbieri, *J.J.P. Oud*, Rotterdam 1987, pp. 138-143

H.E. Oud, *J.J.P. Oud. Architekt 1890-1963. Feiten en herinneringen gerangschikt*, The Hague 1984, pp. 138-143, 154, 202

S. Polano, *J.J.P. Oud Architettura Olandese*, Milan 1981, pp. 14-15

G. Stamm, *J.J.P. Oud. Bauten und Projekte 1906 bis 1963*, Mainz, Berlin 1984, pp. 124-128

E. Taverne, 'Neo-De Stijl of Neo-Monumentalisme. Het Shell-gebouw van J.J.P. Oud te 's Gravenhage', in: W. Denslagen, (et al.), *Bouwkunst. Studies in vriendschap voor Kees Peeters*, Amsterdam 1993, pp. 515-527

E. Taverne, D. Broekhuizen, *J.J.P. Oud's Shell Building. Design and Reception*, Rotterdam 1995

# 81/ Head Office of the Bataafsche Import Maatschappij (Shell)

Rear elevation with canteen (right)/ OUDJ-ph 744, NAI, Rotterdam (Photo D. Renes)

Office wing and service station/ OUDJ-ph 767, NAI, Rotterdam (Photo D. Renes)

## 81/ Head Office of the Bataafsche Import Maatschappij (Shell)

Facade of main stairwell at rear and entrance to canteen/ OUDJ-ph 1920, NAI, Rotterdam

Bomb damage 1945/ OUDJ-ph 587, NAI, Rotterdam

# 81/ Head Office of the Bataafsche Import Maatschappij (Shell)

Decorative ending of main staircase handrail/ OUDJ-ph 691, NAI, Rotterdam

## 81/ Head Office of the Bataafsche Import Maatschappij (Shell)

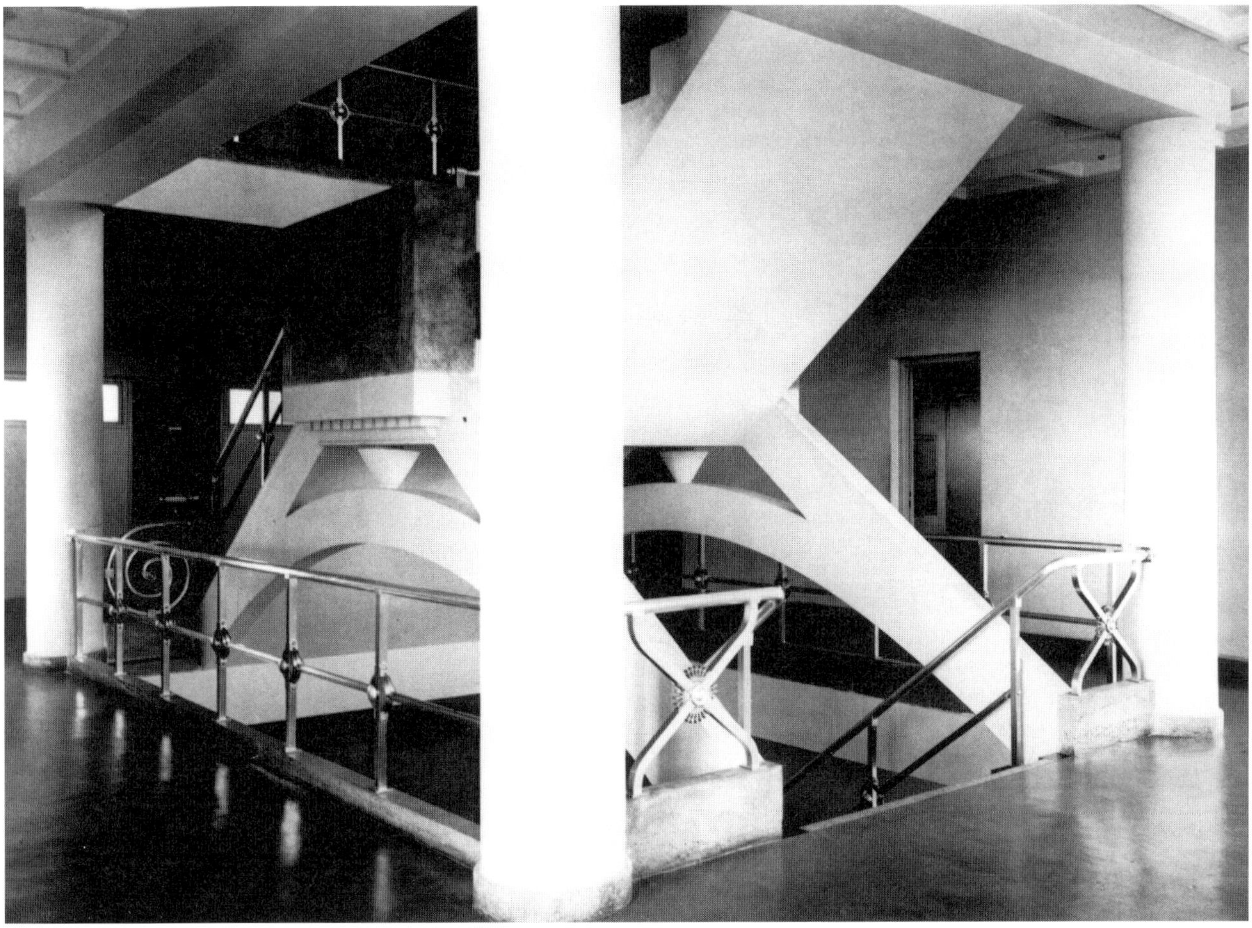

Main staircase/ OUDJ-ph 690, NAI, Rotterdam

Board Room/ OUDJ-ph 835, NAI, Rotterdam

# 4 War and Recovery

VERBODEN
TE VISSEN

**Canteen with terrace in garden of Shell Building/ OUDJ-ph 727, NAI, Rotterdam**

# Wartime Reconstruction

The architectural views Oud developed in the 1930s had their culmination in his work during the Second World War. This five-year period, during which the Netherlands was occupied by Nazi Germany, marked a crucial phase in the development of Dutch architecture in which lasting changes were made to the context in which that architecture came about. What the occupiers and their Dutch collaborators had in mind was clear: a local version of the prevailing (officially sanctioned) German architecture which had gradually deserted its original 'volkstümliche' (popular) ideals in the course of the 1930s. Vernacular architecture had receded into the background to be replaced on the one hand by a megalomaniac architecture that found its apotheosis in Albert Speer's reconstruction plans for Berlin, and on the other hand by a bureaucratic, standardized design method tailored to the demands of the war economy. These obsessions fuelled German criticism of the first reconstruction plans for Rotterdam, which were considered to be lacking in grandeur and monumentality. In this situation, the ideological map of the Dutch architectural world underwent a dramatic change. As in Dutch society as a whole, individual differences were set aside for the duration and an effort was made to present a united front to the occupiers and their Dutch representatives. This led to numerous joint study groups, of which the *Kerngroep*, whose members included J.F. Berghoef, S.J. van Embden, B. Merkelbach, W. van Tijen and P. Verhagen, was one of the best known. The *Kerngroep* and the many-branched network of study groups that grew up around it, tried to arrive at a common basis for post-war architecture, which would undoubtedly pose different demands from the ones Dutch architects had been accustomed to before the war. While their researches focused on the organizational and functional aspects of construction, views about architectonic expression also changed in response to the occupation. German domination resulted in a revaluation of traditional Dutch architecture. Whereas its historicizing associations had made it unacceptable in the 1930s, especially to modern architects, these same associations now gave it an explicitly anti-German aura which even the modernists found attractive. Thus was the basis laid for that typical Dutch 'shake-hands' style, a fusion of traditional and modern often referred to as a marriage between brick and concrete. In the meanwhile, commissions gradually dried up. Dutch investors put their building plans on hold and, unlike in Germany, where state-financed construction was booming, the Germans did not authorize any large-scale construction works – apart from military installations, that is. A shortage of materials and labourers was already making it increasingly difficult to carry out construction work when a total building freeze was proclaimed in 1942 and all construction work ceased. This may explain why relatively few architects joined the Kultuurkamer, membership of which was a precondition for practising as an architect during the occupation. The exception to this general picture was 'Reconstruction'. It was subject to different rules and quite a lot of construction work was carried out under its auspices, especially in the early years of the war.

No sooner were the occupation forces in place, than work started on integrating the Dutch economy with that of the Third Reich. This long-term objective soon made way for the urgent task of assimilating Dutch industry with the Ger-

National Historic Monuments Commission, Oud is eighth from right (seated)/ OUDJ-59, NAI, Rotterdam

man war economy. Although it obviously functioned differently in the occupied Netherlands than in Germany or the Allied countries, the system was to some extent the same: the production of goods and services was subject to priority schedules, raw materials, semi-finished products and building and other materials were rationed, the available manpower was deployed systematically and in part under duress, and there was an overall effort to step up production by working as efficiently as possible, which in turn promoted rationalization and standardization. The war effort required an extensive government machinery which in the occupied Netherlands was staffed largely by Dutch planning professionals who justified their seeming collaboration by a desire to avoid the disastrous consequences of a German-imposed planning system. Their involvement does, however, help to explain why the various mechanisms introduced during the occupation were later accepted without too much political debate and integrated into the post-war Dutch planning system – they were not after all the result of German decree.

Dutch architecture in the immediate post-war years can be characterized as the cumulation of a number of trends: the necessary assimilation of a spate of rules and regulations, the inevitable scarcity of some materials, the need for standardization and experiments with prefab mass produced systems and mechanized construction, and the willingness of different groupings within architecture to work together. What is striking is how rapidly Dutch historicism, which had enjoyed a brief resurgence during the occupation, disappeared around 1945. Shake-hands architecture proved of similarly short duration and by the early 1950s, the American-oriented International Style was starting to make its appearance in the Netherlands, too.

During the occupation Oud kept aloof from the increasingly intense architectural debate. He was still busy with the completion of the Shell Building and he also managed to carry off one of the most prestigious reconstruction commissions in Rotterdam: Hofplein. Unlike most of his colleagues, he had his hands full and he evidently did not share their enthusiasm for endless meetings and study. He devoted all his time to a more urgent problem: the spatial and architectural reconstruction on Rotterdam. The same body that had been responsible since 1940 for overseeing the reconstruction of the Netherlands, also embarked upon a thorough-going economic and scientific rationalization of architecture and in so doing created an environment in which Oud's architectural and town planning ideals were severely tested.

German forces invaded the Netherlands on 10 May 1940; four days later the Dutch army capitulated. The immediate cause was the devastating bombing of Rotterdam followed by German threats to reduce other Dutch cities to ashes in similar fashion. Shortly before the capitulation, the Dutch high command set up the Regeringscommissariaat voor de Wederopbouw (Government Agency for Reconstruction) to look after Dutch interests in the repair of war damage. J.A. Ringers was appointed head of this new government agency which subsequently became part of the civil administration of the occupier. After the queen and government had fled to England, the most senior civil servants, including Ringers, formed a College van Secretarissen-Generaal (College of Permanent Secretaries). This College remained in office throughout the occupation and Ringers remained a member of it until his arrest in April 1943. Even then, he continued to direct the Regeringscommissariaat right up until his transportation to German concentration camps in 1944: the agency had succeeded in becoming an autonomous island within the government apparatus, where other rules applied. So long as its operation fitted in with the occupiers' policy, they left it alone and even



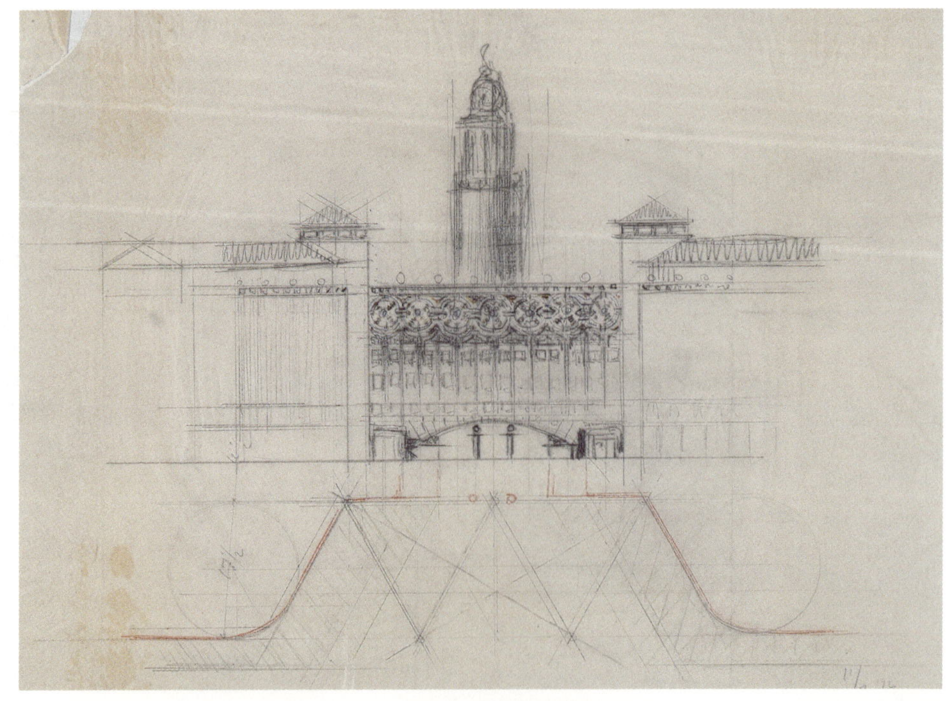

Facade of gateway building opposite Town Hall on Coolsingel / OUDJ-hp 25, NAI, Rotterdam

prevented interference from Dutch Nazis who could not boast experts of the calibre of those with whom Ringers surrounded himself.

Ringers saw himself as a pragmatic technocrat and he staffed his Regeringscommissariaat with like-minded engineers and economists. He made no secret of his anti-German feelings and continued to base himself on the mandate he had received from the Dutch high command. For a long time the German occupiers turned a blind eye to this and it was not until they caught him in an act of political resistance – making preparations for a transitional government to take over after the 'inevitable' German defeat – that he was forced to step down. By then he had largely accomplished his mission, which went a lot further than forestalling direct German interference in the reconstruction: Ringers had built his agency into an instrument of spatial and socio-economic planning in which the construction industry, which had also been placed in his care in 1941 as a logical consequence of his reconstruction responsibilities, was assigned a key role. The service he set up formed the basis for the post-war Dutch planning bureaucracy which was to make a major contribution to the creation of the welfare state. This differed on essential points from the prewar government set-up and there can be no doubt that Ringers deliberately promoted the switch to a planned and more benevolent society.

The Regeringscommissariaat formed a direct link between economic planning, spatial planning and architecture. At Ringers' behest, various bodies were established, such as Stichting Ratiobouw (Institute for Technical, Economic and Organizational Studies for the Building Industry), aimed at improving architecture's ability to initiate and execute large construction programmes, in particular in public housing. To this end, the financial and logistical consequences and the costs in terms of material and labour needed to be much more precisely calculated than in the past and this in turn was a powerful argument for standardization. This transformation was a logical result of the war economy. The manner in which priorities were determined and building flows directed was virtually identical, as were the consequences for architecture. In this respect developments in the occupied Netherlands displayed great similarities to those in, for example, England and the United States: architecture was subsumed in planning and itself appeared to be increasingly subject to new management strategies. The form taken by this 'scientifically based' architecture was fairly new but the principles accorded wonderfully with both the introduction of scientific principles in business and government and modern architecture's prewar penchant for rationalism and technology. Its influence was decisive and was one of the factors that served to marginalize the stylistic debates between the various architectural schools.

Although Ringers did not involve himself in the aesthetic aspect of architecture and town planning, he did subject the architects permitted to work on the reconstruction programme to a stringent selection procedure, for which purpose he set up regional committees of architects charged with vetting the quality of the chosen designers. Their advice was not formally binding – clients were free to choose their own architect – but in practice it was seldom disregarded. Initially Ringers' preference was for a regionally inspired architecture but, as in other countries with a rigid war economy, this fairly vague vision tended to fade into the background as the consequences of planning and standardization started to make themselves felt. His involvement with town planning went a good deal further: he withdrew municipal councils' power to accept or reject reconstruction plans and set up a College van Algemene Commissarissen voor de Wederopbouw (College of General Commissioners for Reconstruction) under

**Perspective of gateway building opposite Town Hall on Coolsingel/ OUDJ-hp 35, NAI, Rotterdam**

P. Verhagen to advise him on this matter. Ideals that had been circulating among town planners since the 1920s, in particular the desire for a National Plan made up of regional plans, could count on a favourable reception from Ringers.

For a long time, the focus of the Regeringscommissariaat's work lay in Rotterdam, the most heavily damaged city. Special arrangements were made for Rotterdam. Instead of setting up a full-fledged design office within the Regeringscommissariaat, Ringers decided to co-opt the existing Rotterdam town planning department. The result was the Adviesbureau Stadsplan Rotterdam (Rotterdam Town Plan Advisory Section, ASRO), made up of Rotterdam public servants and headed by W.G. Witteveen who had occupied this position since 1924, be it in municipal service. The ASRO's remit was to draw up a reconstruction plan for the city and to start implementing it as soon as possible. ASRO was also left to determine the architectural aspect of the plan and Rotterdam duly acquired its own architects' committee which operated in much the same way as in other parts of the country. One unique feature of the Rotterdam situation was that the city was divided up into different districts, each with its own supervisor. The supervisor's task was to coordinate the architectural designs in his district, a labour-intensive job that usually culminated in a large number of perspective drawings. The final result was first vetted by Witteveen, which often resulted in further adjustments. The post of supervisor was an official appointment and its holder was barred from accepting architectural commissions in their own district.

Most of the regulations drawn up within the framework of reconstruction remained in force after liberation. The architects' committees disappeared, however, and in 1951 the final political verdict on reconstruction plans was handed back to the municipalities. The dearth of aesthetic motives within the Regeringscommissariaat had no lasting effect on post-war architecture, unlike the rationalization, standardization and scientific principles it introduced.

Oud was involved with reconstruction until long after the war. As a member of the Rijkscommissie voor de Monumentenzorg (National Historic Monuments Commission) he was in an excellent position to assess the results throughout the country. As supervisor, he was responsible for the Vredenburg district in Utrecht until shortly before his death. But his involvement with reconstruction dated back to the war years in Rotterdam, where he was active both as architect and as supervisor. In the lists drawn up by the Rotterdam architects' committee, Oud enjoyed the highest status and this entitled him to jobs in key areas of the city. Evidence of his prominence was his appointment as supervisor of Coolsingel, the main boulevard in both old and new Rotterdam. This job was soon passed to his friend J. Klijnen when Ringers, on Witteveen's recommendation, asked Oud to supervise the new Hofplein development. This commission went much further the usual supervisor's job in that Oud was permitted to determine the architectural character of the square independently of the plans of the architects who would eventually build there. It appeared that Oud would be free to develop his own architectural-spatial vision of Hofplein. It was an ideal commission and it helped him to get through the war years in relative financial comfort. Apart from Hofplein, he also worked on one or two shops and a bank, also in Rotterdam. His designs from this period elaborate on the idiom for which he had laid the basis in his plan for the Amsterdam Town Hall and the Shell Building. He did this with perfect conviction, apparently untroubled by any premonition of the scathing criticism this new course was to encounter after 1945.

At the beginning of the twentieth century, Hofplein developed into Rotterdam's principal spatial planning bottleneck. This was a direct result of the westward shift of the city centre and the transformation of Coolsingel, which joined the square at an angle, into a central boulevard. The Coolsingel's metamorphosis from urban canal to major boulevard was crowned by the filling in of the canal and the construction of a new town hall (H. Evers), the Post & Telegraph Office (G.C. Bremer) and, eventually, a new Exchange, to a design by J.F. Staal. Hofplein, which formed the northern point of the triangular historical street plan, changed from a relatively peripheral link between the city centre, the Delftse Poort railway station and the new districts to the west, into a busy, centrally located traffic intersection surrounded by cafés, cinemas and the terminus of the Hofplein railway line. In the midst of this bustle, the historic Delftse Poort gateway was becoming more and more of an obstacle. In consequence, the number of plans made for this square, which more than any other spot in the city epitomized metropolitan life in Rotterdam, was well nigh endless. The best known are the two proposals by H.P. Berlage, the first of which Oud analysed at length in *Het Hofplein-plan van dr. Berlage* (1922).[1]
The bombing of May 1940, tragic though it was, also opened up the possibility of a permanent solution to the Hofplein problem by sweeping away all the buildings in the area, including the gateway building. The first reconstruction plan by W.G. Witteveen began by eradicating the awkward kink in the transition from Coolsingel to Hofplein: Witteveen shifted the square westwards so that Coolsingel now fed into it directly. At this spot Witteveen projected a hexagonal traffic square fed by four thoroughfares. On the east side, the square devolved into an oblong 'entertainment plaza' with space for cinemas and theatres. This oblong space continued under the railway viaduct to the new Hofplein station. Witteveen wanted to make the viaduct bridging as slender and subtle as possible so that it would not form a visual barrier and the underpass would transmute smoothly into a generously conceived 'parkway' leading to Kralingse Bos. In 1942, J.A. Ringers overruled Witteveen and held a competition for Rotterdam's two main squares – Hofplein and Blaak

Final site plan / OUDJ-hp 287, NAI, Rotterdam

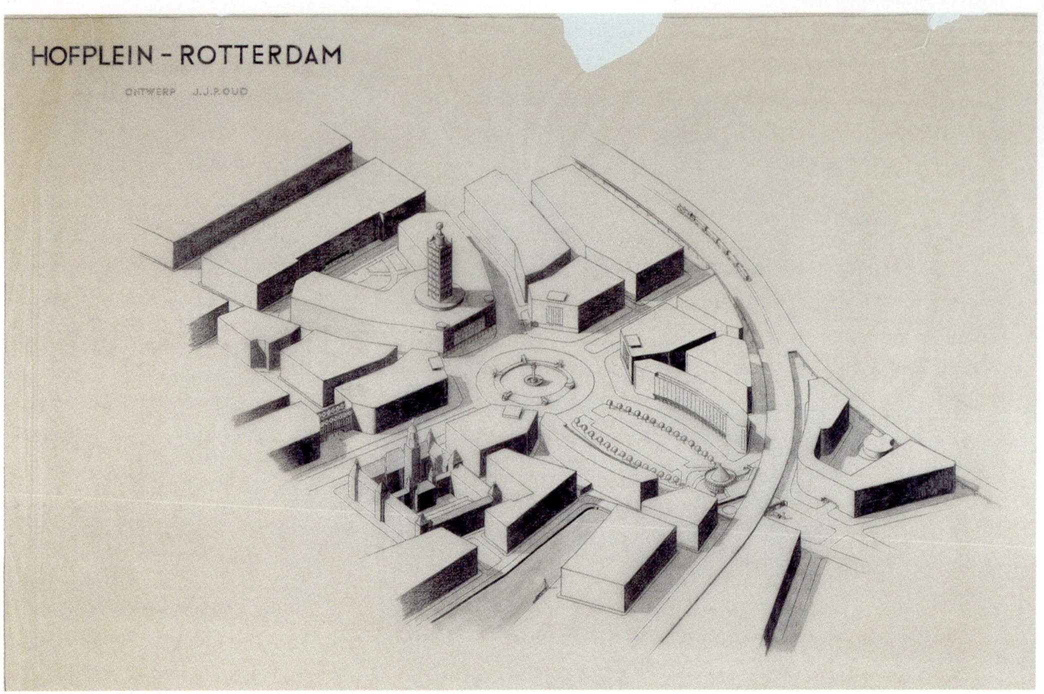


Bird's-eye view of final design/ OUDJ-hp 290, NAI, Rotterdam

Bird's-eye view of final design/ OUDJ-hp 298, NAI, Rotterdam

– but the results were disappointing. Shortly afterwards, Oud was appointed supervisor of the Hofplein redevelopment, whereupon he handed supervision of the Coolsingel development to his friend Jos Klijnen, although he continued at first to supervise the section adjoining Hofplein, including the street wall opposite the Town Hall, where he envisioned the viaduct as a built-over link with Raadhuisplein.[2]

Oud's involvement with Hofplein went far beyond what was customary for supervisors, who were not even supposed to design the street facades in the areas for which they were responsible. Yet this is precisely what Oud was expected to do at Hofplein. Oud's concept for Hofplein, which was all but finished by February 1943, divided the square into three parts: a traffic loop linked to an entertainment plaza on the east side of the railway viaduct and a circular café that served to mask the view of the viaduct. Oud proposed replacing the tower building on the west side, that was intended as a showroom for Dutch industry, by a new town hall, an idea shared by Witteveen. The spatial composition consisted of a sequence of different shapes: a circular traffic roundabout, an oval entertainment plaza with deeply curved walls, and a rectangular extension that flowed into a broad axis. *By creating contrasts an attempt has been made to generate a varied spatial picture that avoids monotony specifically through mutual contrasts. ...In my plan I have tried to introduce a rhythm in the sequence of pictures. First you have the decidedly 'hard' traffic square, then the more congenial 'leisure square' with trees and perhaps stalls, finally arriving, after the intermezzo of a somewhat darker viaduct underpass (which will need to be well laid out) at the spacious and leafy 'outdoor square'. Each square with a development appropriate to its nature and consequently varying in appearance.*[3] This concept did however introduce two elements that served to check the sense of visual flow that was Witteveen's planning trademark: the oval entertainment plaza, which intercepted the gaze instead of leading it further, and the built-over viaduct. At the very first discussion of Oud's plan, Witteveen objected to the tripartite organization and rejected the oval entertainment plaza out of hand. Instead of ordering Oud to revise his supervision design, Witteveen came up with a completely new plan in the expectation that Oud would once again attend to the architectural elaboration. Now it was Oud's turn to demur.

In Witteveen's new design, Hofplein was considerably smaller and the traffic and entertainment squares were combined. Witteveen justified this solution by referring to the wish of Dutch Railways to rebuild Hofplein Station on the west side of the viaduct, thereby removing the need to have the square continue beneath the viaduct. Oud was not impressed: *If an elongated square of such dimensions is to appear to some extent as a closed form, the walls should be interrupted as little as possible. But that is practically impossible here since several and fairly large openings are*

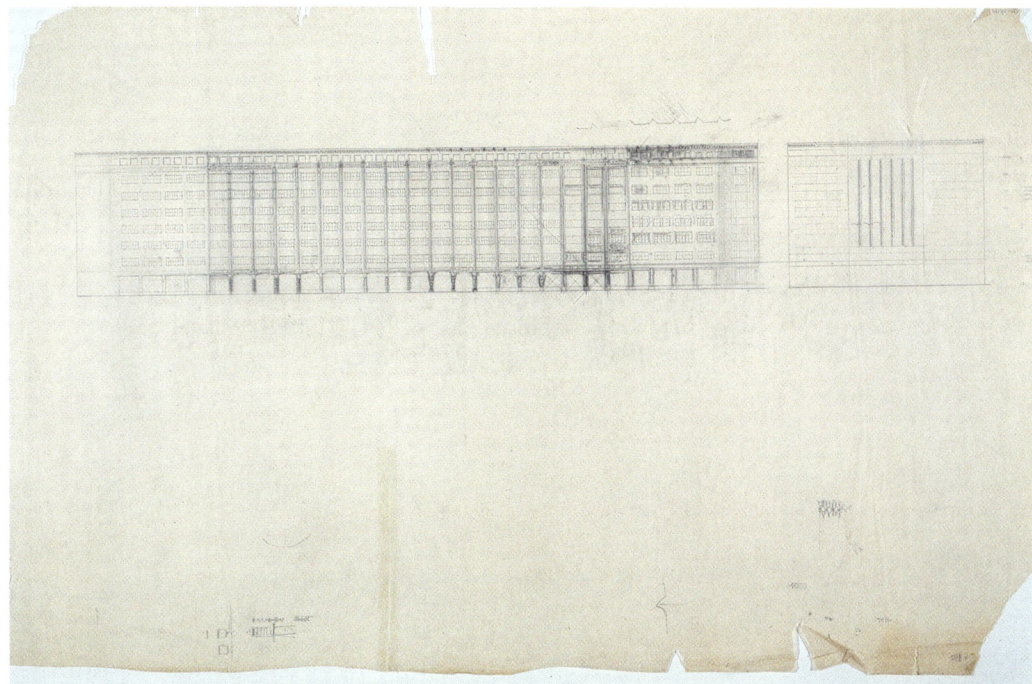

**Design for facade of buildings on traffic square (left) and entertainment square (right)/ OUDJ-hp 160, NAI, Rotterdam**

*needed.* Witteveen tried to close the gaps visually with small, architectural elements, but these 'diminutive closure motifs' were not enough to save the plan.[4]

The conflict between Oud and Witteveen was irreconcilable: Oud refused to do the architectural elaboration for the new plan and Witteveen declined to integrate the new location of Hofplein Station into the earlier plan. Oud accused Witteveen of unfairness: *That you now swing around so radically at a moment when we were practically agreed ... I can only ascribe to the fact that you regard my design as an 'alien' element in the city, that is to say not as an unqualified piece of Witteveen.*[5] At the heart of the quarrel were conflicting ideas about the three-dimensional composition of the city. Witteveen wanted to impose this compulsorily on supervisors and architects and this was the Achilles heel of his urban masterplan. It was this, rather than the type of architecture he proposed, which was by no means explicitly modern, that led to the demise of his plan. Once again, Rotterdam dignitaries and business tycoons played an interesting role. Used to exerting considerable influence over urban development, they now took the lead in getting Witteveen's proposal replaced by a new design. To this end they enlisted the services of a group of architects calling themselves Opbouw Rotterdam (OPRO). One of OPRO's leading lights was P. Verhagen. He had been arguing since the 1920s for a looser alliance between architecture and urbanism (see cat. no. 34 for his role in the plan for Varkenoordsche Polder), and in his position as 'elder statesman' within OPRO he was in at the birth of a completely new reconstruction plan, the 'Basisplan' drawn up by Van Traa, Witteveen's assistant and secretary, in which the third dimension was omitted from the urban design plan. All of a sudden, the disagreement between Oud and Witteveen turned into a rearguard action. Oud resisted a change of tack that went against his concept of the city as a three-dimensional composition – a belief he paradoxically shared with Witteveen, his opponent in the plan for Hofplein. The Basisplan reduced Hofplein to a traffic square fed by four roads and unrelated to the surrounding buildings.



**Notes**

**1.** An overview of all the plans can be found in H.E.M. Berens, *Planontwikkeling Hofplein 1915-1945. Grootsch zonder grootsch te heten*, paper, University of Groningen 1989.

**2.** K. Schipper, J. van Geest, *Jos. Klijnen*, Rotterdam 1999, pp. 48-49.

**3.** J.J.P. Oud to H.W. Mouton, 16 October 1943, semi-active records, Ministry of Housing, Physical Planning and Environment, The Hague.

**4.** J.J.P. Oud to H.W. Mouton, 16 October 1943, semi-active records, Ministry of Housing, Physical Planning and Environment, The Hague.

**5.** J.J.P. Oud to W.G. Witteveen, 10 January 1944, semi-active records, Ministry of Housing, Physical Planning and Environment, The Hague.

**Sources**

CCA: dr1984: 0165, dr1984: 0208-0249, dr1984: 0254-0258, dr1984: 0261-0264, dr1984: 0266-0278, dr1984: 0280-0282, dr1984: 0285-0308, dr1984: 0312-0324, dr1984: 0328-0347, dr1984: 0458, dr1984: 0457, ph1984: 1125-1131
Getty: 890126-23**, 890126-33**
NAI: OUDJ-hp 1-314, OUDJ-hp 1001-1040, OUDJ-hp 1001-1012, OUDJ-hp 3001, OUDJ-ph 860-879

**Articles**

A.Gs. [A. Glavimans], 'Architect J.J.P. Oud: Geef Rotterdam zijn kern terug. Niet gezellig, maar keihard van energie', in: *Elseviers Weekblad*, 4 November 1950
Anonymous: 'Mr Oud embroiders on a theme' in: *Architectural Record* 100(1946)6, pp. 80-84
Anonymous, 'Oud in de Amerikaanse Pers', in: *Forum*, 2(1947)2/3, pp. 71-72
De Gruyter, *Architect J.J.P. Oud. 1890-1950*, exh. cat. Museum Boymans, Rotterdam 1951, pp. 11-12
J.J.P. Oud, *Het Hofplein-plan van dr. Berlage*, Haarlem 1922 (Inst. voor Volkshuisvesting, Serie voor Stedebouw no. 1)
S. van Ravesteyn, 'Kunstenaars dienen Rotterdam op te bouwen', in: *Het Parool*, Opbouwnummer, 10 May 1947, p. 5

**Literature**

U. Barbieri, *J.J.P. Oud*, Rotterdam 1987, pp.144-145
D. Broekhuizen, *De Stijl toen / J.J.P. Oud nu*, Rotterdam 2000, p. 56-85
H.E. Oud, *J.J.P. Oud, Feiten en herinneringen gerangschikt*, 1984, pp. 143-148
S. Polano, *J.J.P. Oud. Architettura Olandese*, Mainz 1976, p. 14
G. Stamm, *J.J.P. Oud. Bauten und Projekten 1906 bis 1963*, Mainz, Berlin 1984, pp. 128-130
E.R.M. Taverne, 'Ouds

**Sketches for Town Hall facade/ OUDJ-hp 223, NAI, Rotterdam**

**Sketch for the facade of the café near viaduct/ OUDJ-hp 111, NAI, Rotterdam**

433 ontwerp voor het Hofplein. Een veronachtzaamde periode uit de stedebouwkundige geschiedenis van Rotterdam', in: *Plan*, (1981)9, pp. 30-34

# Oud and the Visual Arts



The visual arts do not necessarily feature logically in architecture for every architect. For Oud, architecture and the visual arts were, however, complementary. Moreover, both showed the way forward, to the new style which went with the modern culture emerging at the beginning of the twentieth century. Oud was convinced that painting was far in advance of architecture. After he had met Theo van Doesburg, he was tempted into several remarkable experiments in which architecture and the visual arts were fused. It involved breaking with traditional architecture, which was replaced, as it were, by a kind of three-dimensional art. And it had its consequences for the relationship between the architect and the painter. Van Doesburg's colour schemes for Oud's housing estates in Spangen caused a furious row centring on Van Doesburg's work, but above all on the relationship between art and architecture. In addition, there was an underlying pragmatic argument. Oud's job with the Rotterdam Woningdienst restricted his freedom to carry out artistic experiments in social housing. He could no longer allow himself the same freedom as an architect with his own practice, as he had had when designing the De Geus house and De Vonk.

Consequently, Oud was obliged to review the relationship between the visual arts and architecture. Although he continued to believe firmly that modern, abstract art and the new architecture were imbued with the same spirit and pointed in the same direction, he now believed that the two disciplines should follow their own courses. This seemed to be an attempt to tie in with relationships which had prevailed in former stylistic periods, especially in the Middle Ages, and which pioneers of architectural innovation like G. Semper had already tried to revive in the nineteenth century. Oud came to the conclusion that the visual arts, when used in architectural surroundings, could never equal it. And, accordingly, the artist could never have the same position as the architect. He never revised that point of view. After the conflict with Van Doesburg in the 1920s, Oud did not work with other artists during his time as architect of the Woningdienst; the stained glass windows which Vilmos Huszár designed for the New Apostolic Church in the Kiefhoek estate were an exception, but it was the the church that had commissioned Huszár. After Oud set up his own practice in 1933, he again made overtures to various artists. He worked with Han Wezelaar, John Raedecker and E. Spaniër-Dammers on interior designs for the Holland-America Line. Oud encountered John Raedecker

Vilmos Huszár/ OUDJ-ak 5 , NAI, Rotterdam

Han Wezelaar/ OUDJ-ak 4, NAI, Rotterdam

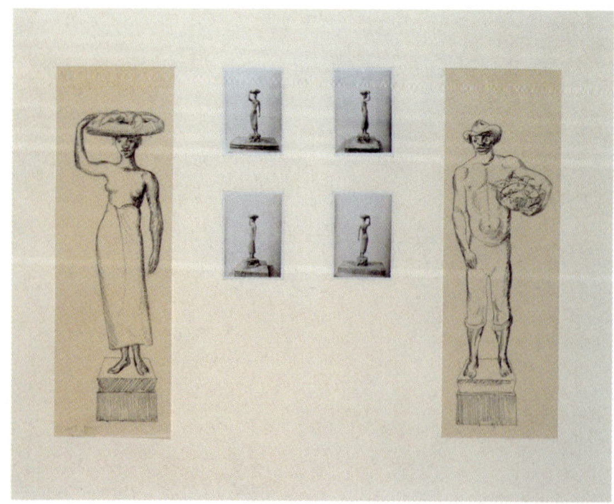

again, for the design of the National Monument on Dam Square. His relationship with Raedecker was probably the most intense post-war contact he had with an artist, and also involved work for the Spaarbank – Savings Bank – and De Utrecht in Rotterdam. Raedecker was commissioned for the National Monument and although Oud had had considerable influence in the overall design, he had learnt his lesson and stuck to the clearest possible division of tasks. That division reflects his ideas on teamwork, which he had vigorously opposed in the 1940s and '50s. The artistic connotation of an architectural design was the territory of the architect, and no-one else. Cooperation with others could only harm the designer's personal vision. That was not only the case when fellow-architects got involved in a design, but also when artists were involved. True, they did add something to the edifice, but the way in which they did so and the extent of their freedom was determined entirely by the architect. There are examples which illustrate this: the sculpted figures Aart van den IJssel 'added' to the design on the 'Spaarbank' headquarters. Although this sculptural work is literally built into the architecture, it is a distinct addition and not part of the building.

Oud avoided experiments allowing the visual arts greater scope. *After my efforts in those days I have become rather wary of the utmost consequence of that striving. I am, however, still convinced of the necessity to take the greatest care with the colourful element in architecture; I want to involve the painter (artist) - allow him considerable freedom - but I want to be in charge.*[1] In other words: the architect as a 'total' artist, so responsible for the totality.

John Raedecker/ OUDJ-ak 1 and 3, NAI, Rotterdam

**Note**
**1.** J.J.P. Oud, quoted in 'Schilder en Architect' (Painter and Architect), in: *De Groene Amsterdammer*, 13 January 1951.

Side elevation on Librijesteeg (left)/ OUDJ-ph 942, NAI, Rotterdam (Photo F.E. de Wilde)

The Spaarbank building occupies a curious place in Oud's oeuvre by virtue of its long and arduous genesis. Although he secured the commission in 1942, the bank was not completed until 1957. The project was part of the design research that Oud embarked upon during the Second World War. Oud obtained the Spaarbank commission through the intervention of the Adviesbureau Stadsplan Rotterdam (Advisory Bureau Rotterdam Town Plan, ASRO) which was dissatisfied with the plan produced by the bank's regular architect, A.A. van Nieuwenhuyzen of Van der Heyden & Van Nieuwenhuyzen. ASRO's architecture committee considered Van Nieuwenhuyzen too light-weight for this commission and on 9 February 1942 demanded that Oud be appointed chief architect. Van Nieuwenhuyzen stayed on as technical adviser. He was responsible, in collaboration with the board of the Spaarbank, for drawing up the building programme, a chief requirement of which was direct contact between counter staff and clients. In tackling the design, Oud made use of organization diagrams to help him plot the position of the various functions within the building and relational diagrams to help him determine the most efficient floor plan and the appropiate typology. He made the combination of these diagrams with existing typologies the starting point for his own design.

The initial design was presented to the Spaarbank's board on 15 April 1942; a detailed version was sent to ASRO in October of that year. The plan envisaged five floors on top of two basement levels and a ground floor; the top floor was probably intended for rental offices. It took a further two years to reach agreement with ASRO. One reason for this long delay was the difficulty in fitting Oud's proposed module into the spatial framework of the block maps. The symmetry desired by Oud was also difficult to reconcile with the oblique corners stipulated by ASRO. The elaboration of the final design also took a long time: what with the position taken by ASRO and modifications called for by the Spaarbank, the design was not ready for tendering until 1952.

The Spaarbank building was very lavishly executed. For the external facades, Oud chose a glazed brick. Natural stone was in frequent evidence both inside and out: the window

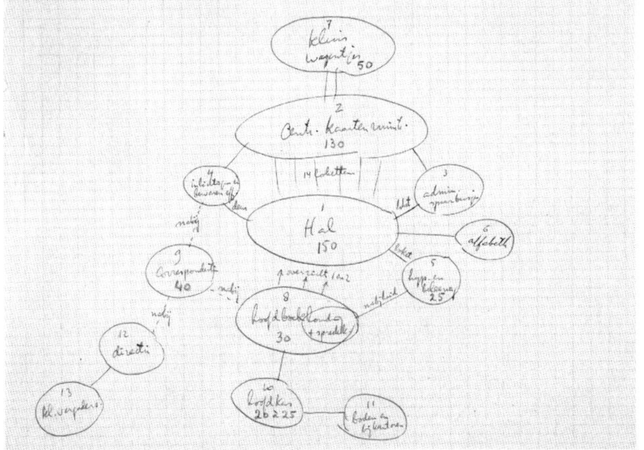


**Diagram of space allocation, main hall/ OUDJ-sk 16, NAI, Rotterdam**



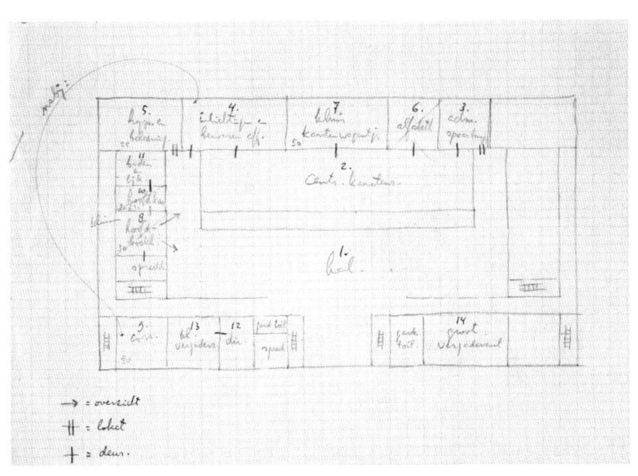


**Sketch plans of main floor/ OUDJ-sk 17, NAI, Rotterdam**

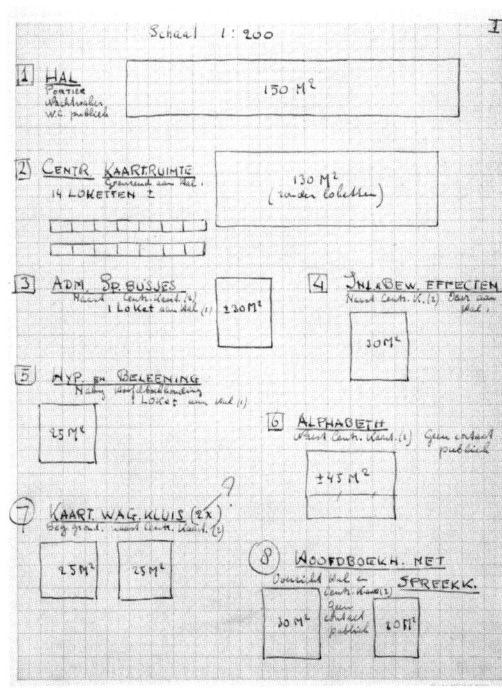


**Rooms drawn to scale/ OUDJ-sk 18, NAI, Rotterdam**

and door casings were in yellow-grey Euville (a French limestone), while the floors and walls of the main public areas were faced with white-grey Roman travertine. The main hall was dominated by the white frosted glass of the ceiling and the counter screens, and the light stone of the floor and counter. Chromium-plated and silver-coloured metal was used for the window frames and grilles and for the banisters. Colour was used to give quiet emphasis to some elements: pale yellow ash for wall panelling in the boardroom, gold-coloured anodized aluminium for the wall of the main lobby, and a pale pink plinth of Swedish granite.

Oud's opinions on the use of ornamentation altered during the course of the design process. Whereas the initial designs contained a lot of abstract decorations designed by Oud himself, in the final plan, Oud subordinated these to the sculptures by Aart van den IJssel (b. 1922), who had replaced W.L. Reijers (1910-1958), with whom Oud had quarrelled. The iconographic programme was carried by animal figures embodying the virtues of thrift and caution. In consultations between the architect and the board it was decided to restrict the representations to creatures found in the natural environment of the building. The Museum voor Onderwijs (Museum for Education) was consulted and duly recommended the hamster, hedgehog, badger, squirrel, bee and ant. They were all creatures that gather and husband, an appropriate theme for a bank. The first sculptures were finished in May 1957.

The first sketches for the furniture appeared at the end of 1946. At that moment Oud was also working on the furniture for the Shell Building and the initial ideas for the Spaarbank chairs are almost identical to the early designs for the boardroom chairs and table for the Shell Building. In 1954 the designs acquired a more definite character, one that departed from the first sketches. Oud had come to the conclusion that the building should be animated by colour accents and he wanted to use the furniture for this purpose. His starting point was the chair he had designed for Hannema's library (cat. no. 68). Instead of wood alone, he opted for a combination of wood and metal. Oud designed two models: a low, wide Morris chair and a somewhat higher,

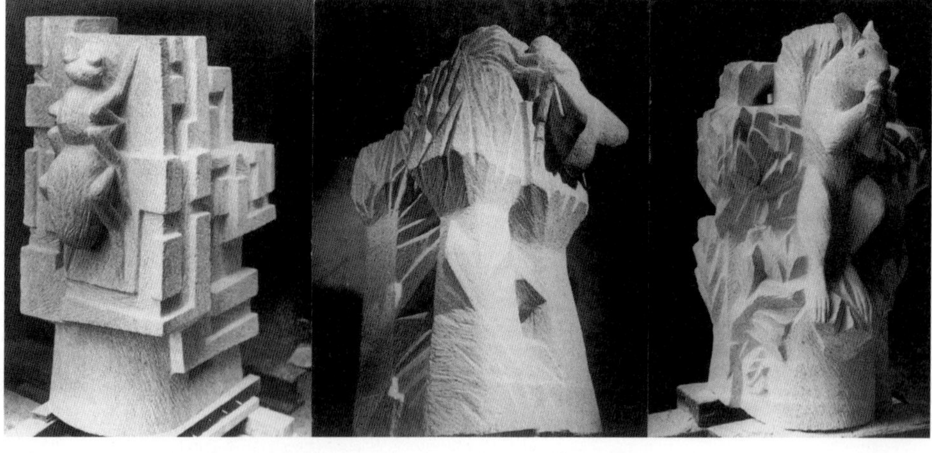

**'Thrifty Animals' by Aart van den IJssel, studio display: ant, bee and squirrel/ OUDJ-ph 959, NAI, Rotterdam**




**Sources**
CCA: dr1984: 0125, dr1984: 0284, dr1984: 0447, ph1984: 0903-0905, ph1985: 0157
Getty: 890126 – box 2-F3
Museum Boymans van Beuningen: inv. no. V2.1-1742, V2.1-1748
NAI: OUDJ-sk 1-634, OUDJ-sk 1001-1006, OUDJ-sk 2001, OUDJ-sk 3001, OUDJ-ph 880-961, OUDJ-ph 1741-1742, OUDJ-ph 1851-1853, CGOU-vsb 1-141, OUDJ-B

**Articles**
'Architect J.J.P. Oud ontwierp nieuwe Spaarbank voor R'dam', in: *Maasbode*, 13 October 1953
G.H.M. Delprat, *Hoofdkantoor der Spaarbank te Rotterdam*, 1904
'Dieren als voorbeeld voor spaarzaamheid', in: *De Rotterdammer*, 18 May 1957
'Een nieuwe Spaarbank voor Rotterdam, in: *Maasbode*, 10 October 1953
H.E. Oud, 'Nieuw hoofdkantoor voor de Spaarbank te Rotterdam', in: *Bouw*, 6(1951)19
'De Spaarbank te Rotterdam in een nieuwe behuizing', (1959)
K. Wiekart, 'De moderne architectuur en wij', in: *Compositie*, 7(1962)1

**Literature**
U. Barbieri, *J.J.P. Oud*, Rotterdam 1987, pp. 146-151
D. Broekhuizen, *De Stijl toen / J.J.P. Oud nu*, Rotterdam 2000, pp. 56-85
H.E. Oud, *J.J.P. Oud. Architekt 1890-1963. Feiten en herinneringen gerangschikt*, The Hague 1984, pp. 148-150, 202-203
G. Stamm, *J.J.P. Oud. Bauten und Projekte 1906 bis 1963*, Mainz, Berlin 1984, p. 133

narrow office chair. Both chairs had a base of chrome-plated tubular steel topped by a wooden frame onto which the cushions were mounted. Two different colours of imitation leather were used: powder blue for seat and sides, pale yellow for the back. To go with the Morris chair, which had an extra headrest, Oud designed a low occasional table with a round top, and to accompany the office chairs, a six-leaf conference table. The conference table and the seating arrangement were intended for the main conference room and the boardroom of the Spaarbank, located on the first floor.

Four loose rugs, two red, one blue and one yellow, provided the finishing touch to the interior. The weaver Betty Hubers produced a blue wall hanging with red and yellow accents that was hung in the corridor near the board's quarters.

**Front elevation/ OUDJ-sk 556, NAI, Rotterdam**

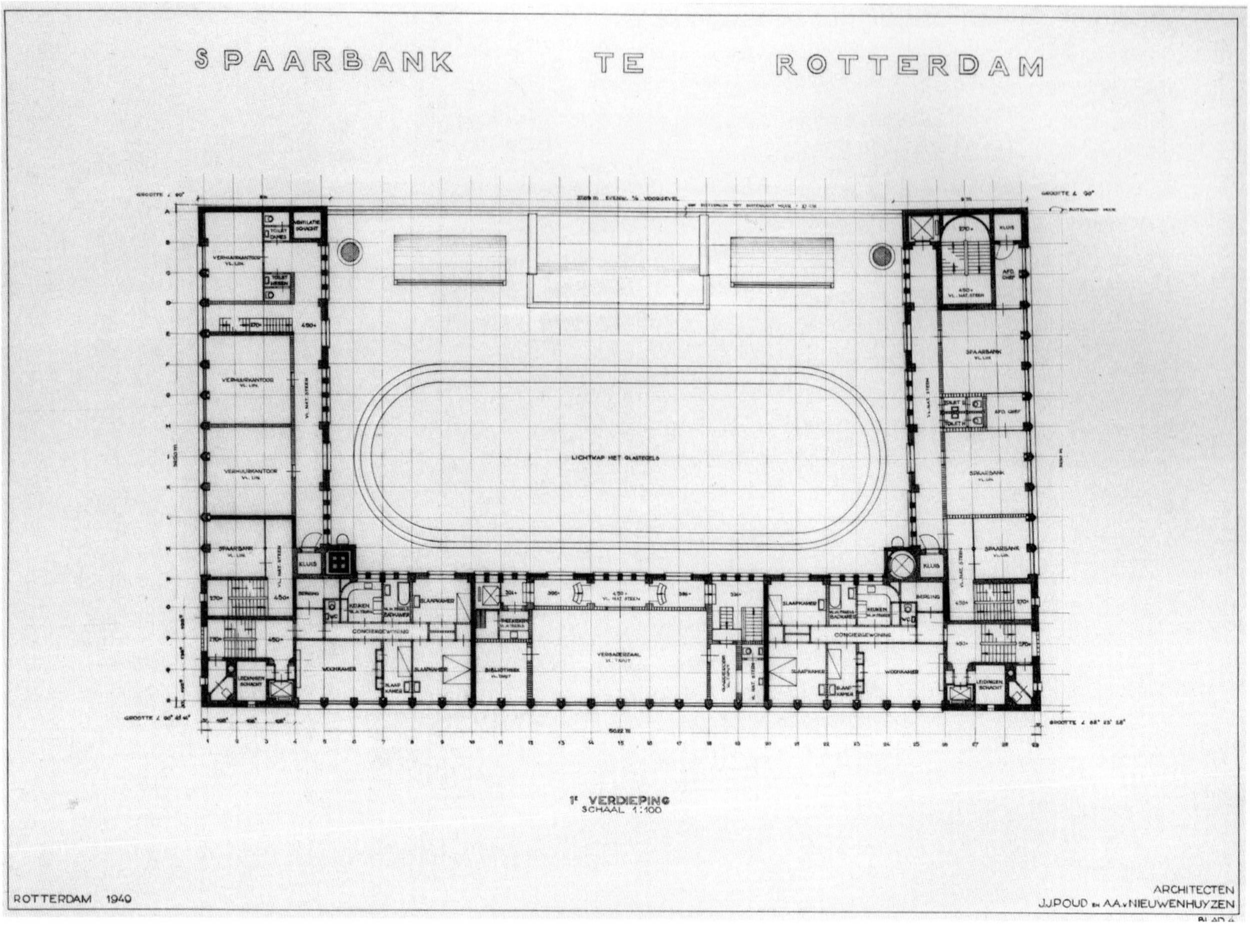

SPAARBANK TE ROTTERDAM

1e VERDIEPING
SCHAAL 1:100

ROTTERDAM 1949

ARCHITECTEN
J.J.P.OUD EN A.A. v NIEUWENHUYZEN

First floor plan/ OUDJ-sk 552, NAI, Rotterdam

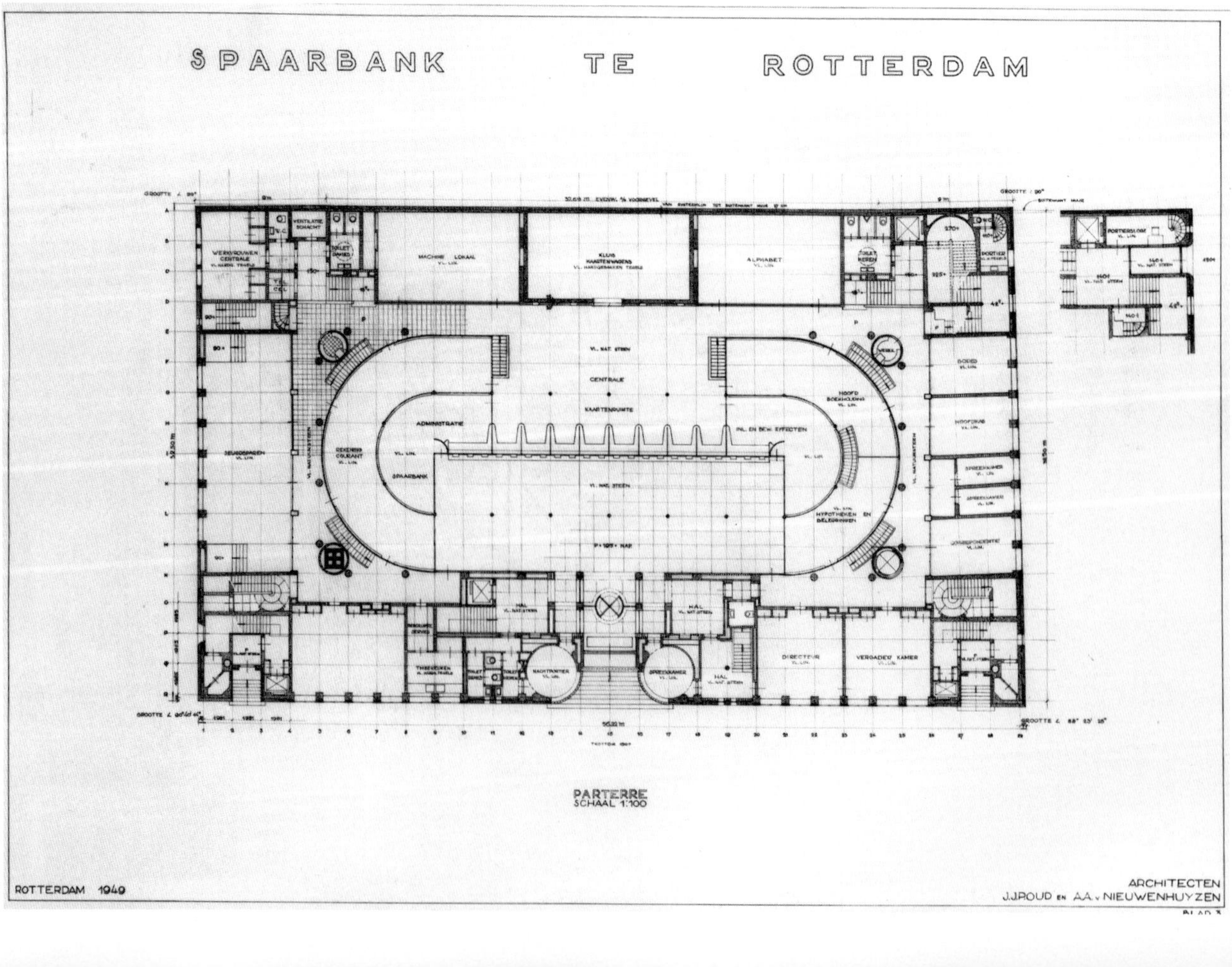

SPAARBANK TE ROTTERDAM

PARTERRE
SCHAAL 1:100

ROTTERDAM 1949

ARCHITECTEN
J.J.P.OUD EN A.A. v NIEUWENHUYZEN

Ground floor plan/ OUDJ-sk 551, NAI, Rotterdam

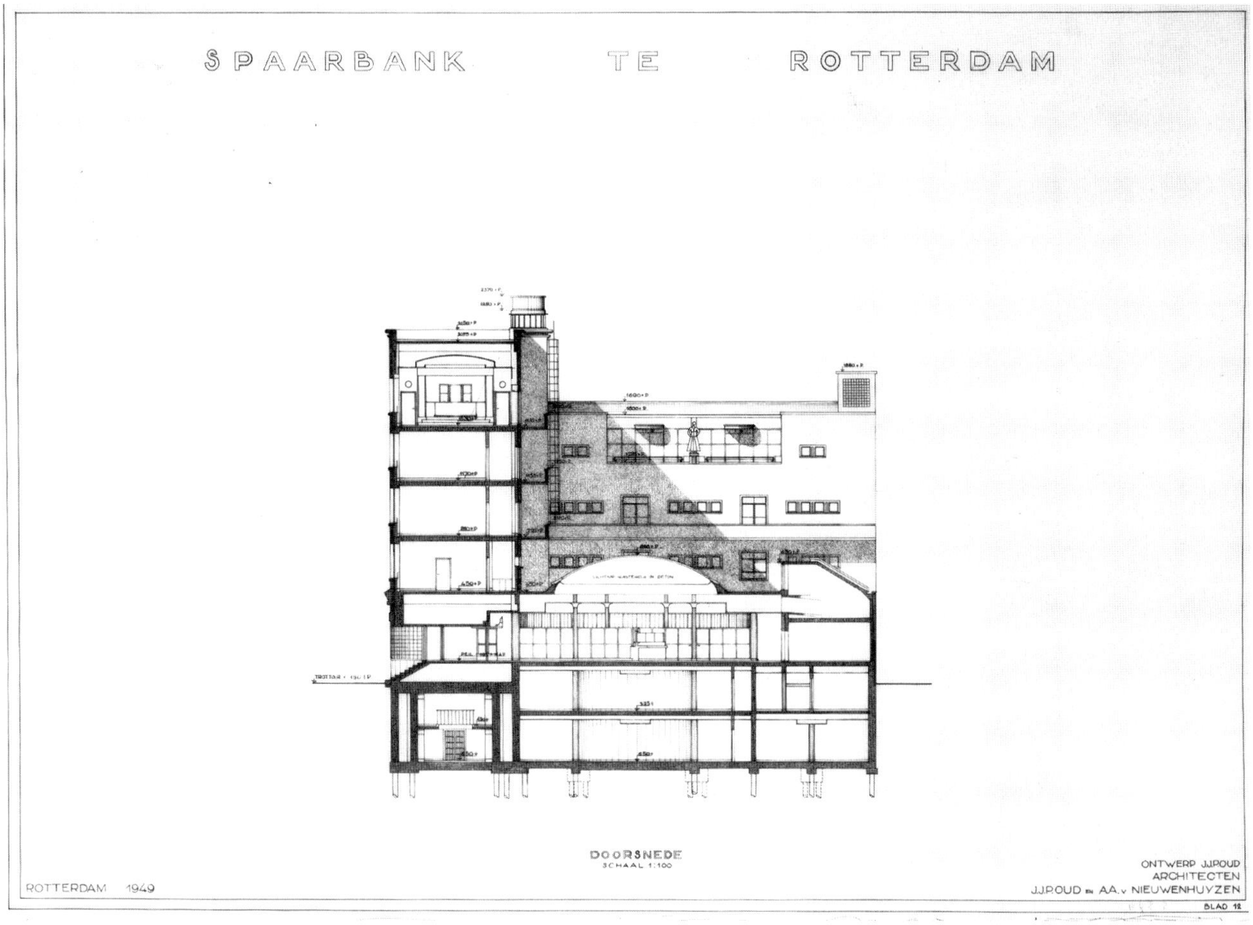

SPAARBANK TE ROTTERDAM

DOORSNEDE
SCHAAL 1:100

ROTTERDAM 1949

ONTWERP J.J.P.OUD
ARCHITECTEN
J.J.P.OUD EN A.A.v NIEUWENHUYZEN
BLAD 12

Section/ OUDJ-sk 574, NAI, Rotterdam

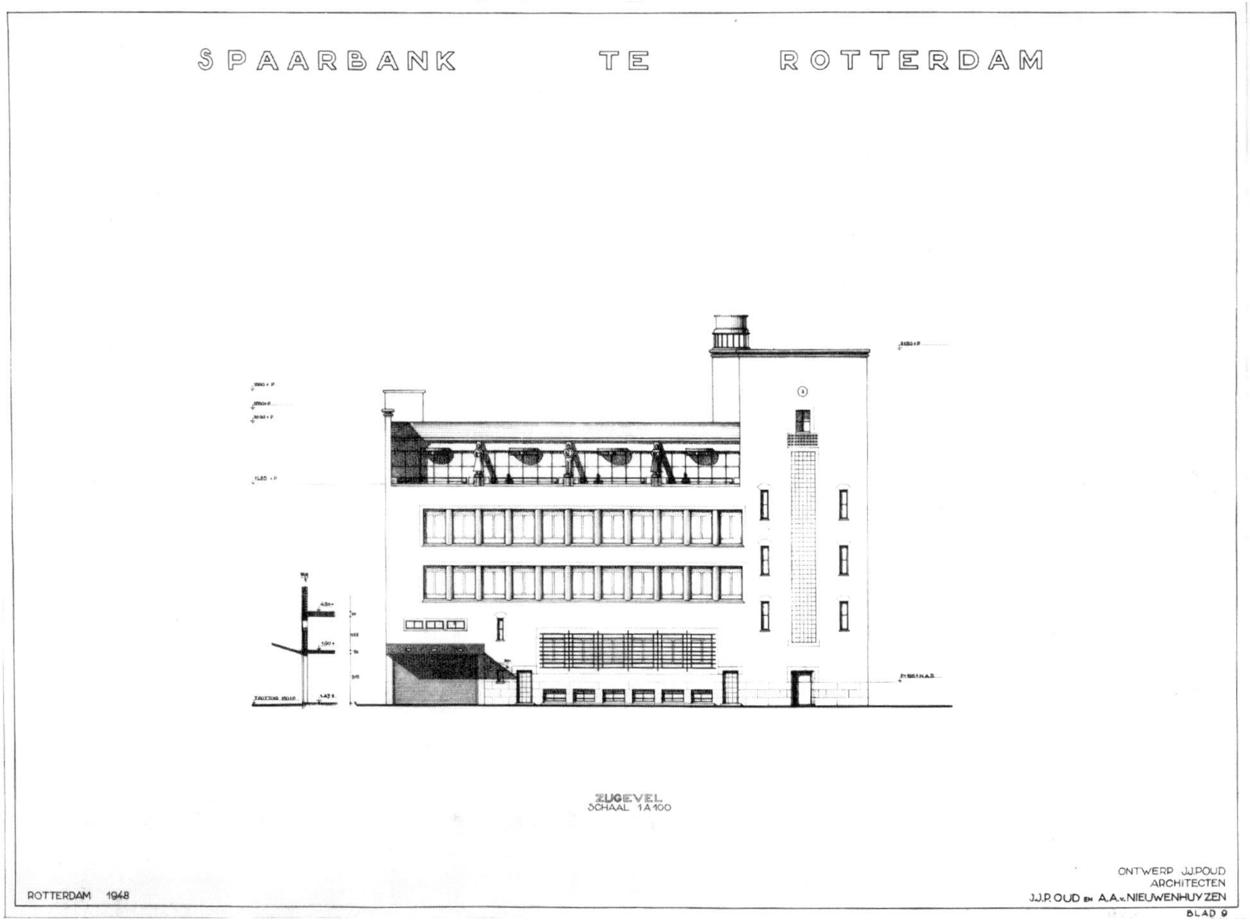

SPAARBANK TE ROTTERDAM

ZIJGEVEL
SCHAAL 1 A 100

ROTTERDAM 1948

ONTWERP J.J.P.OUD
ARCHITECTEN
J.J.P. OUD EN A.A.v. NIEUWENHUYZEN
BLAD 9

Librijesteeg elevation/ OUDJ-sk 561, NAI, Rotterdam

Front facade/ OUDJ-ph 905, NAI, Rotterdam (Photo Jan Versnel)

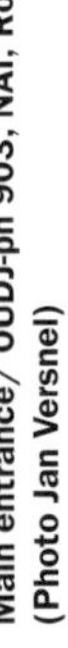

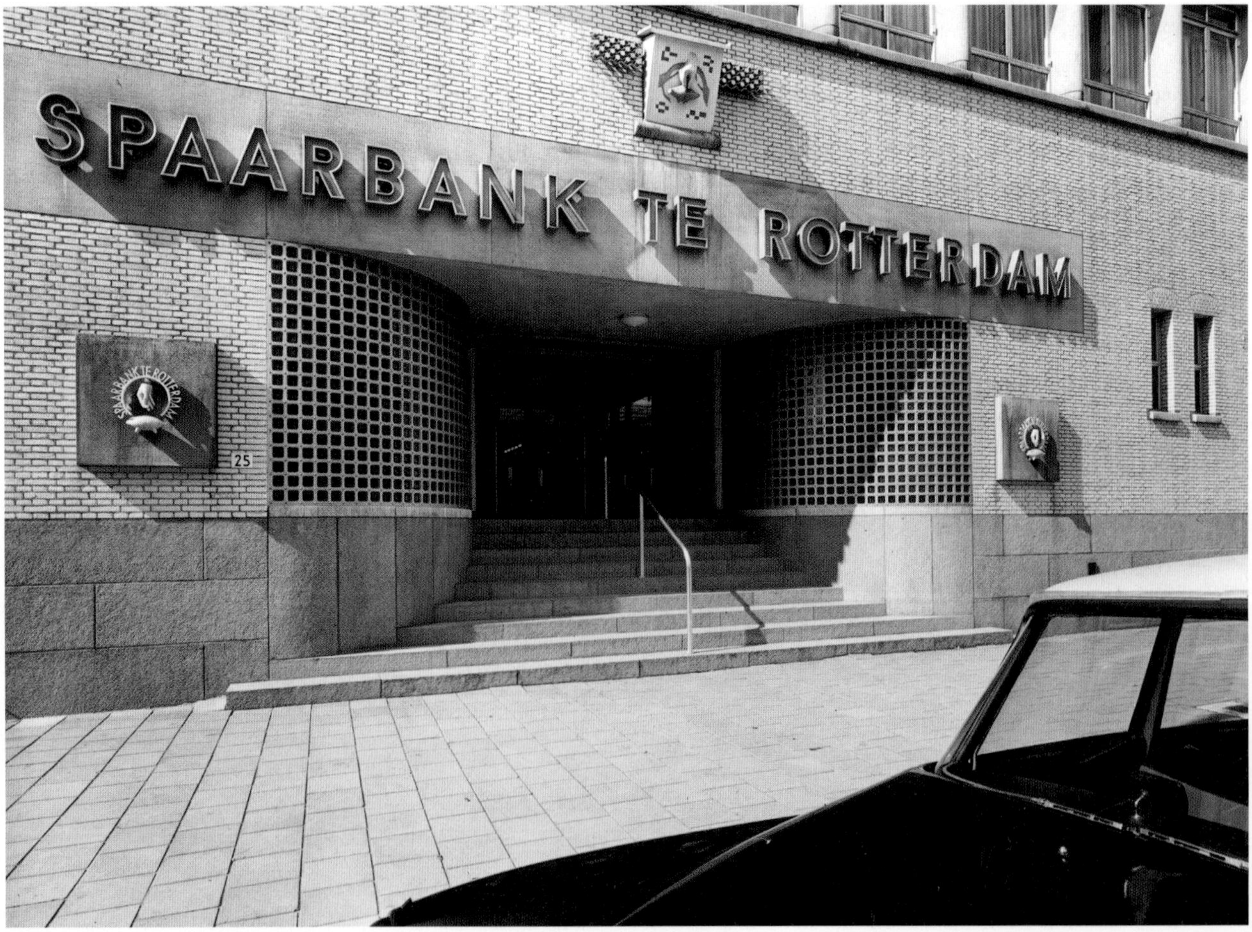

Main entrance/ OUDJ-ph 903, NAI, Rotterdam (Photo Jan Versnel)

Courtyard elevation/ OUDJ-ph 910, NAI, Rotterdam
(Photo Jan Versnel)

Main entrance/ Oud Archive, library, NAI, Rotterdam
(Photo F.E. De Wilde)

Central hall/ OUDJ-ph 930, NAI, Rotterdam
(Photo Steef Zoetmulder)

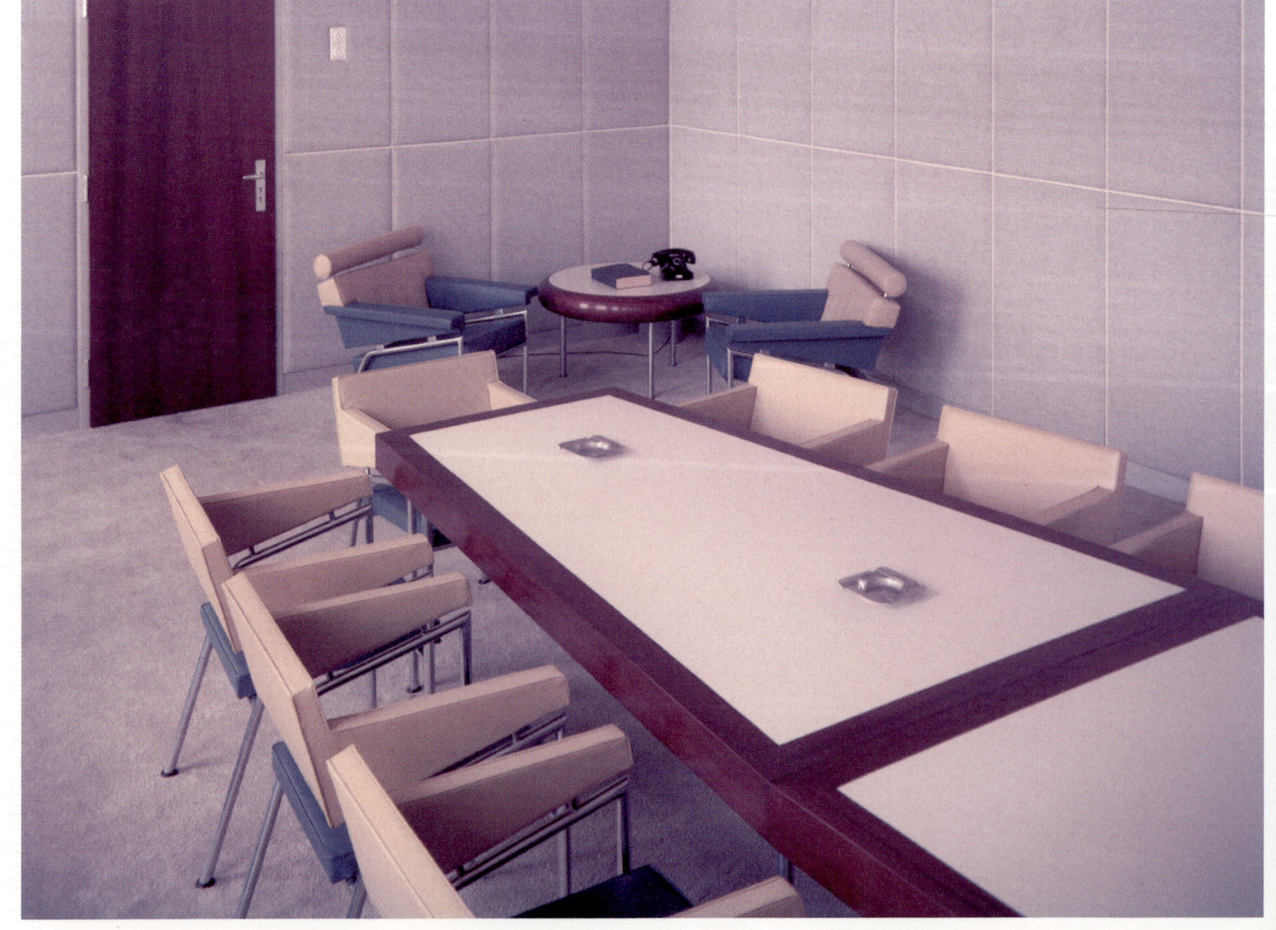

Board Room/ Oud Archive, Library, NAI, Rotterdam
(Photo F.E. de Wilde)

Canteen/ OUDJ-ph 925, NAI, Rotterdam (Photo Jan Versnel)

Board Room/ OUDJ-ph 921, NAI, Rotterdam (Photo Jan Versnel)

# 84/ Design for Shops and Dwellings for Olveh

**Rotterdam, Parkweg**

**1942**

In August 1942, Olveh, a life insurance company based in The Hague, commissioned Oud to design a branch office on the corner of Parkweg and Van Oldenbarneveldstraat in Rotterdam. To render the construction cost-effective, the building was to contain shops and flats in addition to the company's offices. Oud projected three shops on the Parkweg side and one on Van Oldebarneveldstraat. Five floors were intended for flats, the sixth and top floor for the Olveh office. The company's name was emblazoned in large letters on the roof: identification and advertisement. The design remained unrealized.

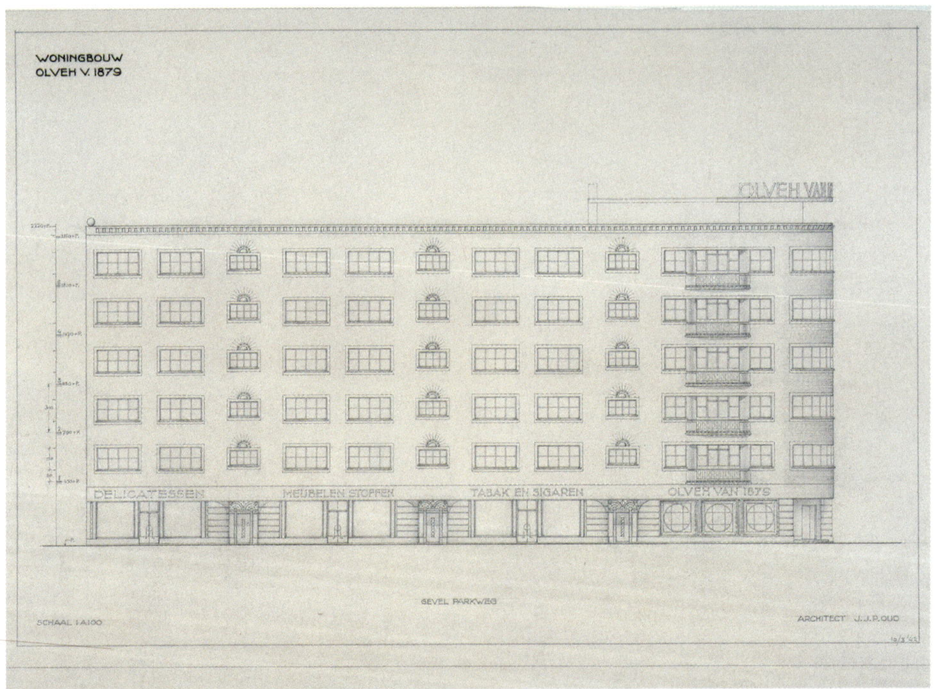


Front elevation/ OUDJ-ov 96, NAI, Rotterdam

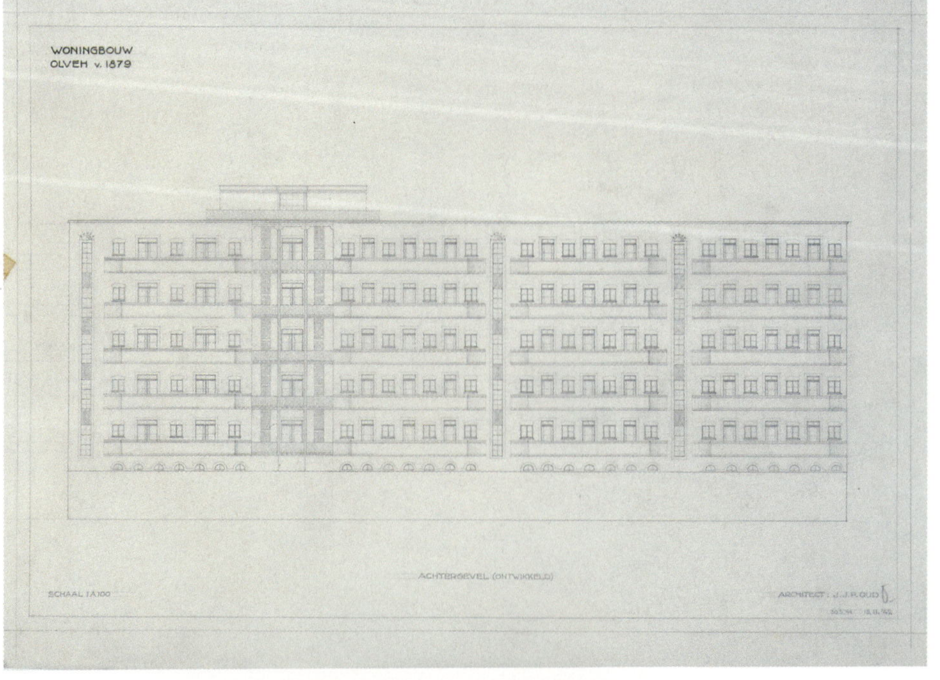


Rear elevation/ OUDJ-ov 97, NAI, Rotterdam



**Sources**

CCA: dr1984: 0161-0164, dr1984: 0166-0198, dr1984: 0287, dr1984: 0325, dr1984: 0326, dr1984: 0430
Getty: 890126-24**
NAI: OUDJ-ov 1-133, OUDJ-ov 1001

**Literature**

H.E. Oud, *J.J.P. Oud. Architekt 1890-1963. Feiten en herinneringen gerangschikt*, The Hague 1984, p. 239

# 85/ Meddens & Zoon Store

Rotterdam, Blaak

1944

The first contacts between Oud and the Meddens firm dated from May 1944. Oud was asked to prepare a plan so that construction could start as soon as the war was over. As well as an architect, the firm had already engaged a contractor and an engineering consultant. The plain exterior of Oud's design concealed a fairly complex internal layout. The Meddens store occupied the basement and ground floor. The basement floor contained a hairdressing salon as well as the hat and sportswear departments. The cash desk was on the ground floor where Oud had also projected a void with fitting rooms. The first floor was intended for rentable offices, the four remaining floors probably for apartments. In the event, this design, like the Olveh building, came to nothing.

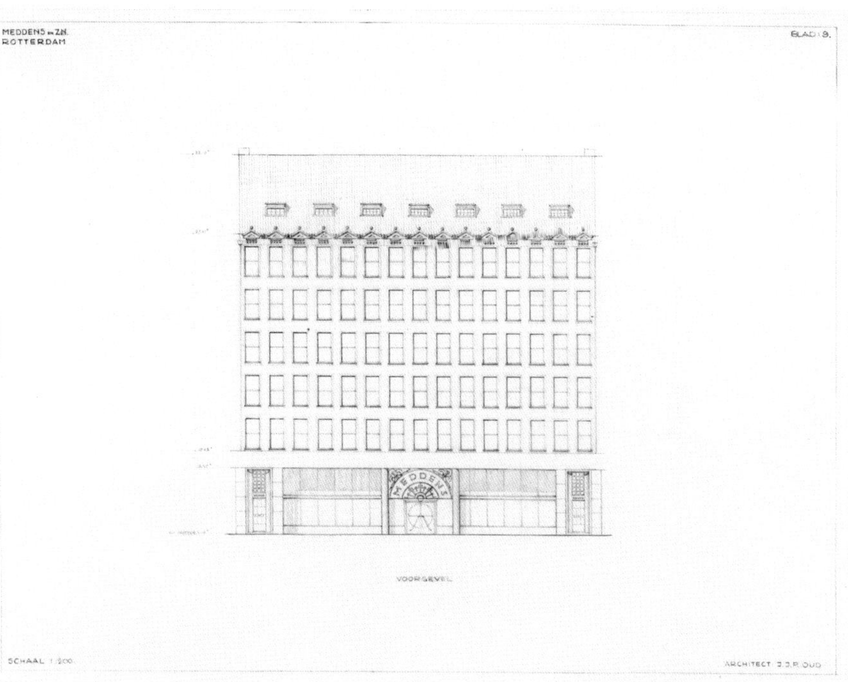


Front elevation/ OUDJ-md 58, NAI, Rotterdam

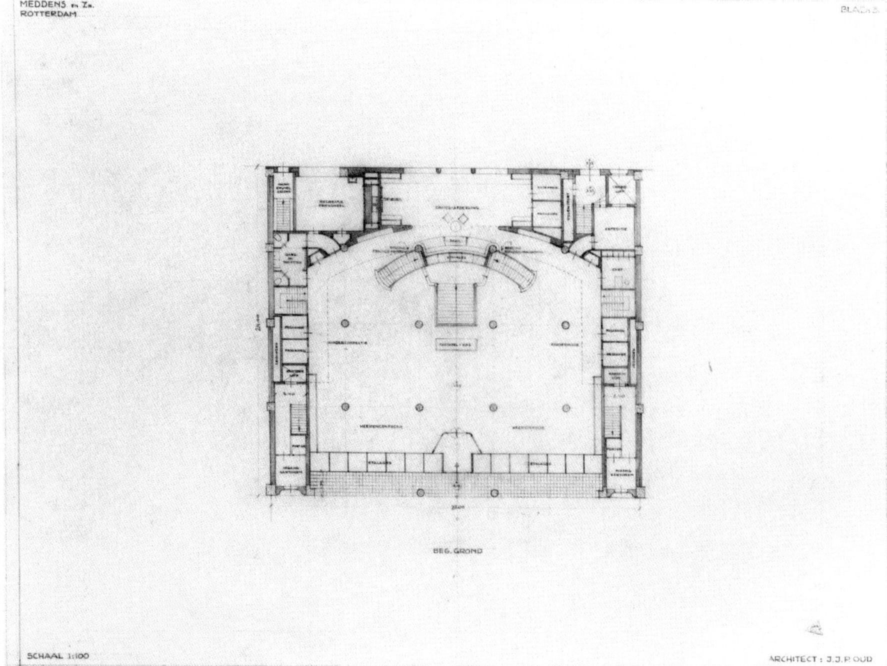


Ground floor plan/ OUDJ-md 52, NAI, Rotterdam



**Sources**
NAI: OUDJ-md 1-105, OUDJ-md 1001

**Literature**
H.E. Oud, *J.J.P. Oud. Architekt 1890-1963. Feiten en herinneringen gerangschikt*, The Hague 1984, p. 239

# Commemoration

Immediately after liberation, the Netherlands was awash with plans for the erection of war memorials. Memorials constituted a unique design task in that they involved finding an artistic expression for strong feelings of national identity. In several cases, moreover, the position of the memorial in the town-scape played a major role. This last aspect linked the topic of memorials to the theme of the *new monumentality* that had been much discussed at an international congress held in America in the early 1940s and at which Giedion, Léger and Sert had broached the same theme in their 'Nine Points on Monumentality', albeit in relation to architecture.[1] The idea that war memorials were particularly suited to the exploration of this theme was shared by Philip Johnson. He corresponded about it with Oud and Frank Lloyd Wright, among others, but his hopes of developing a specifically American approach foundered on the disappointing lack of interest shown by his compatriots.[2] The monuments Oud designed, which included the National Monument on Dam Square in Amsterdam and the military monument at Grebbeberg, were architectural-spatial exercises whose primary purpose was their message: commemoration of the war. Oud's involvement with war monuments necessarily brought him into contact with an extensive bureaucracy established to bring order to the multiplicity of commemorative plans. Yet it does not appear to have caused him many problems, any more than another potentially vexatious aspect of monument design, the division of work among the various designers. Like Rietveld, Oud was in favour of one person being in charge, whether it be the architect or the sculptor. On his own projects he himself was in command.

Oud interpreted the war monument as a living part of the city, as a place with which the populace should be able to identify. He was opposed to the notion that such sites should above all inspire awe, nor did he think that they should be a platform for displays of political or military might. His designs, in which he worked closely with sculptors like J.W. and J.A. Raedecker, reflect this conviction, which was not always shared by his clients.

Oud at the National Army Monument at Grebbeberg/ OUDJ-ph 1045, NAI, Rotterdam



**Notes**

**1.** See E. Taverne, D. Broekhuizen, *J.J.P. Oud's Shell Building. Design and Reception*, Rotterdam 1995.

**2.** P. Johnson to J.J.P. Oud, 5 September 1945, 25 September 1945, 5 October 1945, 31 July 1946, OUDJ-B, NAI, Rotterdam; P. Johnson to J.J.P. Oud, 27 April 1946, 20 May 1946, Johnson Papers, MoMA, New York; J.J.P. Oud to P. Johnson, 18 December 1945, OUDJ-B, NAI, Rotterdam.

# 86/ Design for a Monument for De Nederlanden van 1845

**The Hague, Meer en Bosch Park**

**1943-1945**

In late 1943, J.G.H. Sauveplanne, the managing director of De Nederlanden van 1845, an insurance company for which both Berlage and Dudok had previously designed buildings, approached Oud with the request that he design a monument for The Hague. Oud had been recommended by Jan Kalf, director of the Rijksbureau voor Monumentenzorg (National Historic Monuments Commission) and a good friend of Oud's.[1] The idea was to present the monument to the people as part of the celebrations of the firm's centenary in 1945. Sauveplanne asked Oud to keep the plan a secret because it was supposed to be a gift to the inhabitants of The Hague and also because there was no knowing at this stage of the war whether it was going to be possible celebrate the anniversary at all. Oud presented his first design in June 1944. When Dudok was subsequently invited to draw up a reconstruction plan for The Hague, Oud made a new design that was integrated into the expansion plan ('Uitbreidingsplan West') that had been drawn up in 1927 by the local Dienst Stedebouw en Volkshuisvesting (Town Planning and Housing Department) and which now fell within Dudok's remit. This second design for a *Herdenkingsplaats in parkaanleg. Idee voor een monument* (Memorial in Park Setting. Concept for a Monument) was set in Meer en Bosch Park and consisted of two parts: a dense wood traversed by footpaths and organized along a central longitudinal axis; and at the end of this axis a large expanse of water encircled by trees. Half-way along the central axis was a circular open area, the meeting point of six footpaths. It was here that Oud projected his design for the memorial.

The central element of the memorial is a pillar, its verticality a visual counterbalance to the otherwise horizontal layout. The pillar is at the centre of a concentric composition of pool, decorative paving, benches and paths. The architectural design is embellished with sculpture groups, inscriptions and reliefs depicting high points in the history of The Hague. Oud eschewed nostalgia and included a power station, railway bridges, harbours and aircraft. Commerce, traffic and industry were after all major constituents of the modern cityscape and by pointing up the constructive role played in society by large companies, the monument tied in

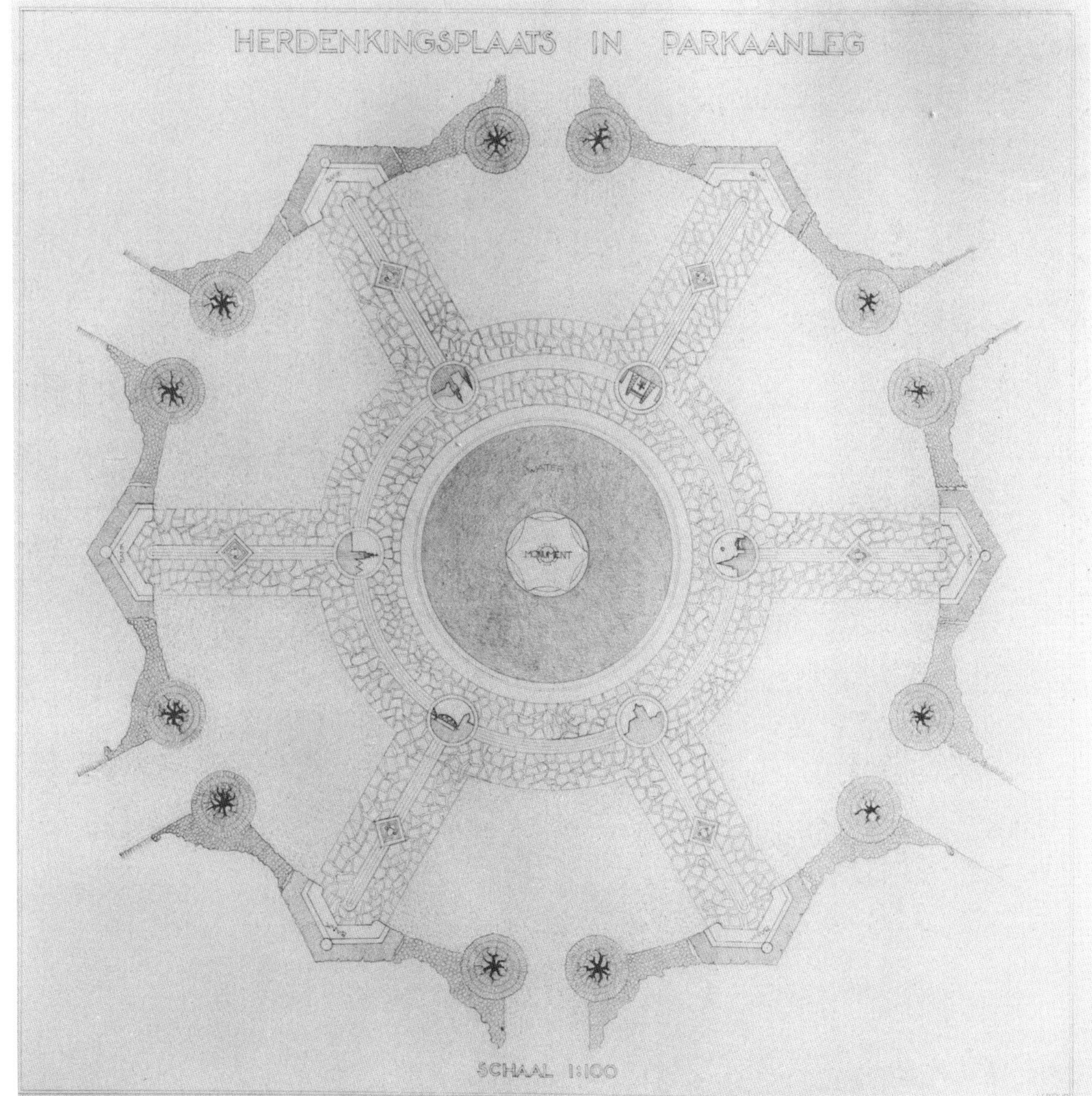


Site plan/ OUDJ-hd 1, NAI, Rotterdam

with the client's ambitions. In addition, the bands of geometric motifs around the upper half of the pillar and the crowning sculpture alluded to the De Nederlanden logo. The lions were a reminder that De Nederlanden was a Dutch company. In light of the parlous condition in which the country found itself in the spring of 1945, the board decided to abandon the planned celebrations, including the monument. At the client's request, the plans were not made public; the design was also absent from the retrospective exhibition of Oud's work in Museum Boymans van Beuningen in 1951.

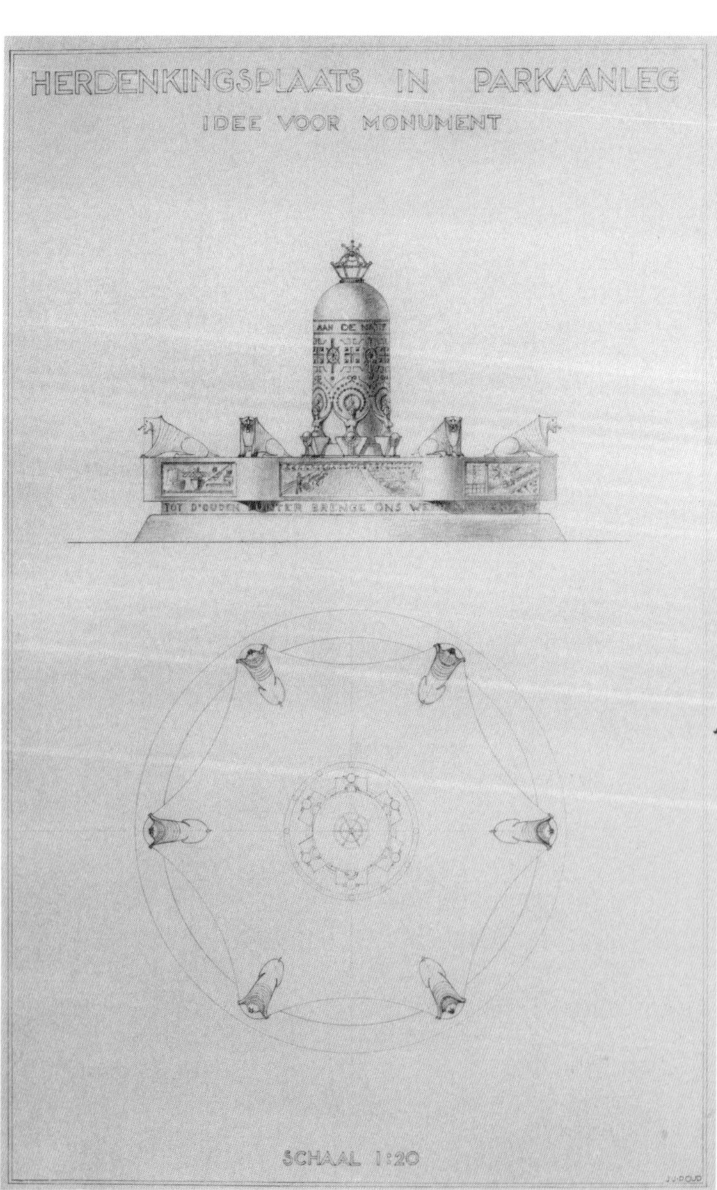


**Sculpture group seen from the side and above/ OUDJ-hd 2, NAI, Rotterdam**



**Notes**

**1.** J.G.H. Sauveplanne to J.J.P. Oud, 18 December 1943, OUDJ-hd 1001, NAI, Rotterdam.

**Sources**

CCA: dr1984: 0265, dr1984: 0279, dr1984: 0283, dr1984: 0288
Getty: 890126- box 7-20*
NAI: OUDJ-hd 1-OUDJ-hd 22, OUDJ-hd 1001, OUDJ-ph 1641-1642, OUDJ-B

**Literature**

D. Broekhuizen, *De Stijl toen / J.J.P. Oud nu*, Rotterdam 2000, pp. 138-149
G. Stamm, *J.J.P. Oud. Bauten und Projekte 1906 bis 1963*, Mainz, Berlin 1984, p. 128

## 87/ Grebbeberg National Army Memorial

**Rhenen, Rijksstraatweg**

**1948-1953**

In December 1947, the Stichting Nationaal Leger Monument Grebbeberg (Grebbeberg National Army Memorial Foundation, established 22 October 1946) invited Oud to design a national memorial to the fallen at Grebbeberg, the hilly, wooded site of a major battle in May 1940.[1] It was to be partially financed from the 'cent protest' organized during the war by Rhenen's mayor, Bosch van Rosenthal. Instead of being handed over to the occupying power, the bronze cents had been collected and hidden away for the benefit a national monument to be erected after the war. Part of the hoard was to be melted down for a bronze bell that would act as a direct reminder of this act of civil disobedience. The programme for the memorial consisted of two parts – a modification of the existing cemetery and a new memorial site – which were physically separated by the old Utrecht–Arnhem trunk road. In the preparation of the design and in discussions during construction, differences of opinion emerged between civilian representatives, in particular the mayor and Oud, and the army. The army seized every opportunity to press for a more military-looking memorial incorporating images of battle and heroism. Oud and Bosch van Rosenthal wanted to emphasize universal values, such as equality and tolerance. The upshot was that the reliefs planned for the inner surface of the curved walls were eventually abandoned. Oud accompanied his plan with a detailed commentary but this was never published.
Work began, on the cemetery section of the plan, in 1949. John Raedecker and his son Noeki were responsible for the two stone lions and cross at the entrance. The graphics were by Jan van Krimpen. The wall around the cemetery (replacing the existing hedge) was built by the army's Engineering Corps, which had a major say in the project on behalf of the Ministry of War. The large number of parties involved (national government, local council, military authorities and a host of commissions and committees) made for endless delays. The cemetery section was not finished until 1951; work on the memorial only got under way in 1952. The project was also dogged by lack of funds, which inevitably left its mark on the original design: the stone slabs Oud had intended using for the path linking the two parts of the scheme were dropped.

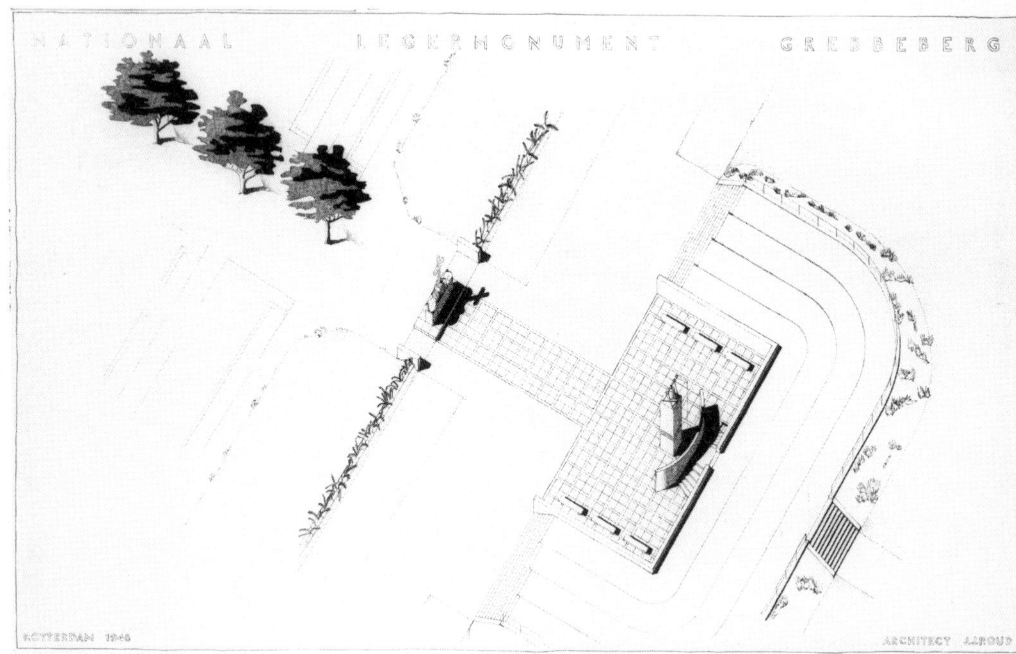


Isometric projection/ OUDJ-gr 65, NAI, Rotterdam

On 15 April 1953 the commemorative bell was cast at the Eijsbouts foundry in Asten; Eijsbouts and two other foundries were jointly responsible for the bell's realization. After the bell had been installed, the memorial was dedicated and presented to the state during an official ceremony on 4 May 1953. In 1956, at the request of the military authorities, Oud designed a receptacle for an urn containing the ashes of fallen soldiers. This small pillar was never executed.

**Casting the bell for the army monument, 1953. Oud is third from left/ OUDJ-ph 1049, NAI, Rotterdam (Photo Anefo)**



**Notes**

**1.** O.A.G. Kauffmann to J.J.P. Oud, 29 December 1947, OUDJ-gr 1001-1003, NAI, Rotterdam.

**Sources**

CCA: dr1984: 0385-0387, dr1984: 0350-0354
Getty: 890126-box 7, 21*
NAI: OUDJ-gr 1-111, OUDJ-ph 1026-1050, OUDJ-ph 1746, OUDJ-ph 1856-1857, OUDJ-gr 1001-1003, OUDJ-gr 2001, OUDJ-gr 3001

**Articles**

'Nationaal legermonument Grebbeberg', in: *Bouw*, 8(1953)37, pp. 713-714

**Literature**

U. Barbieri, *J.J.P. Oud*, Rotterdam 1987, p. 154
D. Broekhuizen, *De Stijl toen / J.J.P. Oud nu*, Rotterdam 2000, pp. 150-165
H.E. Oud, *J.J.P. Oud. Architekt 1890-1963. Feiten en herinneringen gerangschikt*, The Hague 1984, pp. 150-151
G. Stamm, *J.J.P. Oud. Bauten und Projekte 1906 bis 1963*, Mainz, Berlin 1984, p. 136

Entrance to cemetery with sculpture group/ OUDJ-ph 1036, NAI, Rotterdam (Photo D. Renes)

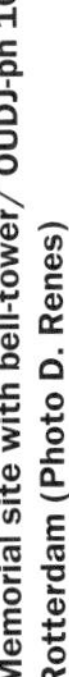

Memorial site with bell-tower/ OUDJ-ph 1035, NAI, Rotterdam (Photo D. Renes)

The main priority was to design a layout that would ensure that during ceremonies and the laying of wreaths at the monument, those present would be standing facing the graves. Since it also seemed unacceptable to place that part of the monument against which the wreaths are laid with its back to the cemetery, and because only the road side affords adequate space for troop line-ups, the visitor encounters this important, double-sided monument at the entrance to the cemetery.
It consists of two recumbent lions, symbolizing victory over death and faith in the resurrection and eternal life, between which – separated from them by a pedestal – the Cross. The base contains an inscription and the Dutch coat of arms. To achieve the double-sided effect, one of the lions looks forwards, the other backwards.
On the other side of the road is a "memorial site" where authorities and speakers can take up their positions on ceremonial occasions, after having entered the site via the woods from the rear and past the segment-shaped wall.
To accommodate the troops who will line up around the memorial site, this area has been raised in the manner of an amphitheatre. The "memorial site" is surrounded by a low wall.
In the middle of the "memorial site" is a small, square-shaped tower supporting a bronze bell which – conditional on the minister's consent – will be cast from the bronze cents concealed from the Germans during the occupation and collected for this purpose by the mayor of Rhenen. On remembrance day this bell will ring out and announce the solemnities to the surrounding area. The segment-shaped wall will have reliefs on the inner side or carving on top in the form of a continuous frieze of figures visible on all sides.
The floor of the "memorial site" is made of stone slabs, laid between lines of square basalt cobblestones set far enough apart to allow moss to grow between them. This floor continues locally in the form of a "runner" across the road to the entrance. It is over this path that people walk to lay a wreath.
For ordinary days, several benches for visitors have been installed at the "memorial site".
The cemetery is envisioned as separated from the hedge by low walls of hand-shaped bricks, covered with a rough, half-round, concrete rim and below – abutting the road – ending in boulders. The aim is to achieve a natural-looking transition from the road to the cemetery, as an indication that the dead are part of us and are not separated from us.
Still in the future: closure of the road to through traffic so as to lend the whole a dignified character.

# 88/ National Monument on Dam Square

**Amsterdam, Damplantsoen** **1946-1956**

Immediately after the war, schemes for sites of remembrance and war memorials abounded. In an effort to bring some kind of order to this chaos, the government of the day set up a number of memorial committees under the general coordination of the Centrale Commissie voor Oorlogs- en Vredesgedenktekens (Central Commission for War and Peace Memorials). In 1946, the commission decided to investigate the feasibility of a single National Monument commemorating the war. J. Henrick Muller, director of the Prins Bernhardfonds, was asked to undertake this investigation. One of the most important decisions – the location – was already laid down in his terms of reference: if he found in favour of a single national monument, it would stand in the middle of Dam Square in Amsterdam. A preliminary specification for a national monument, drawn up in 1947, called for a rich and expressive programme. It was to reflect *the fact itself of the five years of war and occupation and of the subsequent liberation. The suffering caused by oppression, the sense of powerlessness in the face of superior strength, the irreparable sorrow caused to so many of us, the lawlessness, the material distress and fear for life; the dogged resistence, the faith and the pride of the powerless, the solidarity of all, who knew themselves to be one against the oppressor; the inner certainty of victory, the expectation of liberation, the eventual triumph and deliverance from the leaden burden, all this we as a nation wish to pass on to our descendants, as the experience from a dark period that almost spelt the end of our national existence.*[1]

While preparations for a national monument were in full swing, plans were also afoot for a municipal memorial in Amsterdam. In the spring of 1946, the Comité Oorlogsmonumenten Amsterdam (Amsterdam War Memorials Committee, COMA) had approached the sculptor John Raedecker to produce a design for a monument to be erected on one of three locations: Weteringplantsoen, the main entrance to Vondelpark or Museumplein. Raedecker experimented with four variations, each of which featured a sculpture group supported by a purely architectonic element: an obelisk, a colonnade, an arch and a gateway. In his definitive design, for the Weteringplantsoen site, Raedecker settled on the obelisk version. On the initiative of the mayor, A.J. d'Ailly, the two schemes were combined. Raedecker's design for Weteringplantsoen was to be erected on the Dam Square location earmarked for a national monument. Since it was expected that it would be years before the national monument was ready for dedication, a temporary memorial to a design by A. Komter and A.J. van der Steur was erected on the Dam: eleven urns symbolizing the Dutch provinces were placed in a four-metre-high, semicircular brick wall.

The planning and decision-making surrounding the permanent monument were as slow as expected. D'Ailly was appointed chairman of a working committee charged with overseeing the realization of the national monument on Dam Square. It decided, in consultation with Raedecker, to

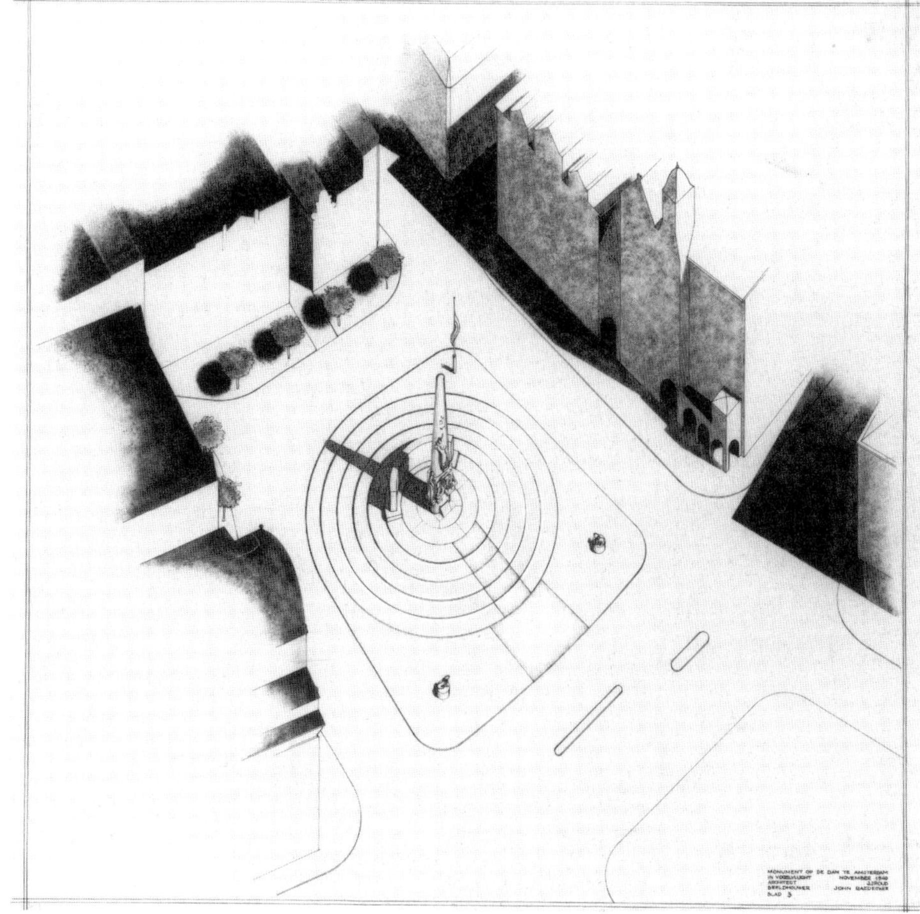

**Isometric projection of site/ OUDJ-dm 124, NAI, Rotterdam**

Model, whereabouts unknown/ OUDJ-ph 1058, NAI, Rotterdam

The first wreath-laying ceremony, 1956/OUDJ-ph 1063, NAI, Rotterdam (Photo Nationaal Photo Persbureau)

involve an architect in the design. With the mayor's approval, Raedecker chose Oud, who duly accepted the commission on 25 November 1948. Oud's remit was to produce a spatial design for a memorial consisting of sculptures on an architectural base, and a repository for urns. The collaboration between sculptor and architect was based on three principles: the integration of the independently conceived sculpture into the architecture of support and socle, incorporation of elements of Raedecker's plan for Weteringplantsoen (such as the terraced surround) and use of three-dimensional models of clay, plaster, cardboard, wax or wood and combinations of these as the principal means of communication between sculptor and architect. The budget was 300,000 guilders, half of which had been raised by a national fund-raising campaign involving the sale 'Dam certificates' costing cost fifty cents each and representing one square centimetre of Dam Square. The remaining half of the budget had still to be found.
Raedecker and Oud's design for the National Monument on Dam Square aquired definite shape in 1949. Oud's first proposal (April 1949), however, was judged too expensive. Although half the sculptures had to be dropped, Oud insisted on retaining the original concept: an obelisk flanked by sculpture groups and behind them an urn wall. At the end of 1949, Oud and Raedecker presented their final design. It faced the Royal Palace and was anchored in the existing urban structure by its position at the intersection of the three alleys that debouch into the square.
On 24 January 1950, Oud and Raedecker explained their proposal at a meeting of the Centrale Commissie, making it clear that they were not prepared to tolerate any interference from the commission. They dismissed criticism to the effect that the monument lacked grandeur and that its orientation on the palace undermined its autonomy. In a letter to the sculptor Han Wezelaar, Oud justified his response by referring to the role of the individual artist vis à vis the (collective) commission: *I take the view – even in these times – that the individual is better when it comes to art than the group. I am wholly in favour of democracy but in return for the liberty others take to interfere in everything, I demand for myself – as fellow-democrat! – the liberty to act without this interference. ...If the Commission is of the opinion that I have not succeeded, it must seek support for its viewpoint from the Minister and reject the design. I hope that it will do this quickly for I have other things to do besides this empty talk. I shan't scowl at any Commission member because he renounces us, but I shall resist their interference as long as I can. In my opinion it is none of their business and they are exceeding their authority. I have no need of art judges and besides, another's criticism can never be sharper than my own. So advise them to go ahead and reject the design. There are more highly placed people who are fed up with this Commission, and perhaps in this way we shall be rid of another Commission. And if not, I shall bow out and John will choose another architect who is more compliant.* [2]
On 27 September 1950, the Centrale Commissie officially submitted Oud and Raedecker's design to the minister. The latter gave it his approval after which nothing more stood in the way of its execution. Italian travertine was used for the socle, unpolished Vaurion for the sculptures and polished Vaurion for the cladding of the obelisk. It took four years to carve the sculptures in which task Raedecker was helped by four assistants. Oud remained in the background during this period. The carving was all but finished when on 12 January 1956, just a few months before the completion of the monument, John Raedecker died.
Oud wrote of the Monument on Dam Square: *For me the essence of the Dam monument is that it expresses*



**Notes**
**1.** Werkcommissie der Nationale Monumentencommissie voor Oorlogsgedenktekens, Nota betreffende het aantal, de plaats en de betekenis van nationale gedenktekens op te richten ter herdenking der gebeurtenissen 1940-1945. Undated typescript, Sandberg Collection, Nationale Monumentencomissie voor Oorlogsgedenktekens Dossier, Stedelijk Museum, Amsterdam.
**2.** J.J.P. Oud to H.M. Wezelaar, OUDJ-B, NAI, Rotterdam.
**3.** J.J.P. Oud, 'Het Dammonument', typescript (OUDJ-dm 1001), NAI, Rotterdam.


**Sources**
Amsterdams Historisch Museum: John Raedecker Archive, A.4041and A.40411
CCA: dr1984: 0355-0357
Gemeentearchief Amsterdam: Archive of the Comité van Oorlogsmonumenten te Amsterdam, Archive of the Werkcomité voor het tot stand brengen van een Nationaal Monument op de Dam te Amsterdam
Getty: 890126-25 **
NAI: OUDJ-dm 1-125, OUDJ-ph 1051-1093, OUDJ-ph 1747-1748, OUDJ-dm 1001-1003, OUDJ-dm 3001-3005, MAQV 378, OUDJ-B
Stedelijk Museum Amsterdam: Sandberg Collection, Nationale Monumentencomssie voor Oorlogsgedenktekens Dossier

**Articles**
'B. en W. van Amsterdam stellen voor: Kostloze grond voor nationaal monument op de Dam', in: *Algemeen Handelsblad*, 5 July 1952
D.A.M. Binnendijk, 'De tekst van A. Roland Holst op het Nationaal Monument. Een teken aan de muur', in: *Algemeen Handelsblad*, 19 May 1956
R. Blijstra, 'Nationaal Monument en Erebegraafplaats', in: *Forum*, 12(1957)3
'Dam zal tot een groot plein worden', in: *Algemeen Handelsblad*, 25 March 1950
'Dam-monument goedgekeurd', in: *Het Parool*, 1 March 1951
'Definitieve oplossing Midden-Damterrein. Totale verandering van aanzicht', in: *De Nieuwe Dag*, 2 March 1950
'Dorp op de Dam. Achter hoge schuttingen verrijst het Nationaal Monument', in: *Trouw*, 17 December 1955
'Gedachten in steen

*strength. In the representation of misery in the large relief, Raedecker depicted people who are suffering for the sake of the strength that is within them. These are no weaklings who undergo defeat like beaten curs, but grimly tense die-hards who are powerless as lions driven into a corner. The lament over the tragedy, which the relief expresses, comes to the viewer not through grieving supernumeraries, not as cries of despair from defeated people, but through the voice of nature. Through the lamentation and fury of the dogs. A fate is unfolding; not a drama. ... And it is no accident ... that the basic shape of the pillar displays no similarity to a truncated pylon for example, but that it is possible to see in it an upright sword. The monument is intended as an expression of a peace-loving and tranquil nation. But a nation that has suffered; that has weathered this suffering, and that in prosperity and adversity has maintained its strength.*[3]

On 4 May 1956, the National Monument on Dam Square was unveiled by Queen Juliana. The most important part of the elaborate ceremony was the installation of the urns that were carried from the Nieuwe Kerk to the monument by war orphans.

Urn wall with text by Adriaan Roland Holst/
OUDJ-ph 1073, NAI, Rotterdam

460 van dichters en classicus', in: *De Volkskrant*, 5 May 1956
'Het groote monument wordt geboren', in: *NRC Handelsblad*, 8 June 1946
'In het hart van de hoofdstad staat een witte zuil', in: *Het Vrije Volk*, 4 May 1956
'Koningin onthuld Nationaal Monument', in: *Alkmaarsche Courant*, 5 May 1956
'Midden-Damterrein voor Nationaal Monument', in: *Het Parool*, 5 July 1952
J.P. Mieras, 'Monument op het Damplantsoen', in: *Bouwkundig Weekblad* 66(1948)4
'Monument op de Dam. Ontwerp van Raedecker en Oud aanvaard', in: *De Tijd*, 1 March 1951
'Het Nationale Monument', in: *Cobouw*, 11 May 1956
'Het Nationaal Monument op de Dam', in: *Bouw*, 148(1950)5
'Het Nationaal Monument op de Dam', in: *Nieuwbouw Nederland*, 3(1956)3/4
'Nationaal monument op de Dam door koningin Juliana onthuld', in: *NRC*, 4 May 1956
'Nationaal Monument op Dam in Amsterdam', in: *De Nieuwe Dag*, 27 March 1950
'Nationaal Monument zal aanzien van Dam grondig veranderen', in: *Het Parool*, 25 March 1950
'Nationaal Monument zal er nu eindelijk komen', in: *Het Vrije Volk*, 29 March 1952
'Nationale oorlogsgedenkteekens', in: *Bouwkundig Weekblad*, 65(1947)9
'Ontwerp monument op de Dam goedgekeurd', in: *Algemeen Handelsblad*, 1 March 1951
'Ontwerp Nationaal Monument door minister aanvaard', in; *Het Parool*, 1 March 1951
'Ontwerp Oud-Raedecker aanvaard', in: *De Volkskrant*, 2 March 1951
'Oorlogsmonumenten', in: *Bouwcentrum*, 2(1947)41
J.J.P. Oud, 'Dam-monument', in: *Elsevier's Weekblad*, 13 October 1956
J.J.P. Oud, 'Het Dam-monument', in: *Maatstaf*, 4(1956)
J.J.P. Oud, 'Het Dam-monument in de verdrukking', in: *Algemeen Handelsblad*, 20 December 1960
J.J.P. Oud, 'John Raedecker', in: *De Groene Amsterdammer*, 21 January 1956
J.J.P. Oud, 'Mensen op de treden hinderen mij niet', in: *De Telegraaf*, 2 September 1959
J.J.P. Oud, 'Een monument ontstaat', in: *De Groene Amsterdammer*, 13 February 1954
J.J.P. Oud, 'Nationaal Monument', in: *NRC*, 10 March 1961
J.J.P. Oud, 'Het Nationaal Monument op de Dam. Repliek arch. Oud', in: *Bouw*, 5(1950-b)23
J.J.P. Oud, 'Nationaal Monument op de Dam', in: *Bouwkundig Weekblad*, 74(1956)22
J.J.P. Oud, 'Het Nationale Monument op de Dam en de politie', in: *De Groene Amsterdam-*

Sculpture group on obelisk/ OUDJ-ph 1075, NAI, Rotterdam



*mer*, 11 April 1959
J.J.P. Oud, 'Nationaal Monument op de Dam in Amsterdam', in: *Bouwt in beton*, (1956)
'J.J.P. Oud en John Raedecker zullen Dam-monument uitvoeren', in: *Het Parool*, 25 January 1949
J.M. Prange, 'Nationaal Monument geen eenheid', in: *Het Parool*, 7 May 1956
'Raadsleden bekeken een maquette', in: *De Waarheid*, 23 April 1952
'Raedeckers kunst en het monument op de Dam', in: *NRC*, 12 May 1956
'Raedeckers Nationaal Monument een indrukwekkende schepping', in: *Alkmaarsche Courant*, 5 May 1956
H. Redeker, 'John Readecker en het Nationaal Monument', in: *Forum*, 12(1957)3
W.J.H.B. Sandberg, 'Schuldig aan het monument op de Dam', in: *De Volkskrant*, 9 August 1969
K. Sarneel, 'John Raedecker en het nationale monument', *De Linie*, 12 May 1956
'Scheuren in monument op Amsterdamse Dam', in: *Cobouw*, 27 March 1959
M.G.W. Schiphouwer, 'Het monument op de Dam', in: *Werk in Uitvoering*, 5(1955)9
E. van Tetterode, 'Dam monument bijna voltooid', in: *Natuursteen*, (1956)108
'Tijdelijk monument midden-Dam-terrein Amsterdam', *Forum*, 2(1947)8
'Voorstel aan de Raad: Nationaal monument wordt waardig en groots', in: *De Nieuwe Dag*, 5 July 1952
J.J. Vriend, 'Het nieuwe nationale monument op de Dam', in: *De Groene Amsterdammer*, 3 June 1950

**Literature**

U. Barbieri, *J.J.P. Oud*, Rotterdam 1987, pp. 154-155
D. Broekhuizen, *De Stijl toen / J.J.P. Oud nu*, Rotterdam 2000, pp. 166-191
D. Carasso, 'Een monument voor de natie', in: *Jong Holland*, 3(1987)1
Y. Koopmans, *Muurvast en gebeiteld. Beeldhouwkunst in de bouw 1840-1940*, Rotterdam 1997
H.E. Oud, *J.J.P. Oud. Architekt 1890-1963. Feiten en herinneringen gerangschikt*, The Hague 1984, pp. 150-152
G. Stamm, *J.J.P. Oud. Bauten und Projekte 1906 bis 1963*, Mainz, Berlin 1984, pp. 136
E. Stevens, 'Het Nationale Monument op de Dam', in: *Toonbeeld*, 1(1990)2
B. Stigter, 'Beelden om nooit te vergeten', in: *Kunst + kunstbeleid in Nederland*, Amsterdam 1993

# 89/ Alternative Restoration Plan for Sint Laurenskerk

Rotterdam, Grotekerkplein

1950

Isometric projection/ OUDJ-It 9, NAI, Rotterdam

During the bombardment of Rotterdam in May 1940, the 15th-century Sint Laurenskerk was severely damaged. A special committee was invoked that same year to look into the feasibility of restoration. Oud sat on the committee on behalf of the bodies responsible for the preservation of historic buildings; the chairman was J.A.G. van der Steur. The committee concluded that the historical importance of the building justified restoration and in 1948 A. van der Steur and J.C. Meischke presented their first design. They proposed to rebuild the nave around a reinforced-concrete frame and to separate it from the tower. Since these solutions were historically indefensible, the Rijkscommissie was divided in its reaction. Oud and L.O. Wenkebach in particular were fiercely opposed. Oud was of the opinion that restoration meant complete reconstruction. This would easily cost eight to ten million guilders and in Oud's view the citizens had *troubles enough already without being burdened with such an expense.*[1] He felt it was a travesty to build a *dead copy* of a church – one which concealed a modern construction behind a gothic facade – in the twentieth century.[2] Moreover, the old nave was far too big for its religious function.

At the presentation of the detailed plan by Van der Steur and Meischke two years later, Oud produced an unsolicited alternative. He proposed restoring the tower but replacing the nave with a modern, much smaller building standing apart from the tower. Between tower and church he projected a contemplative space with greenery and water, a place *imbued with devotion. It will be an oasis in this part of the city. People will be able to retreat there from the bustle of the city and will be better able to reflect on how to prevent the misery of war than in a St. Laurens rebuilt in the old style. Which I am convinced, incidentally, will never get beyond the stage of the initial impetus.*[3] One of Oud's ideas was to place Zadkine's controversial bronze, *De Verwoeste Stad* (*The Destroyed City*) in this space.

Publication of the plan in *De Groene Amsterdammer* and elsewhere elicited many declarations of support from colleagues and ordinary citizens alike. Mieschke, however, lashed out at Oud, even comparing him to Goebbels.[4] Other

Isometric projection of church/ OUDJ-lt 6, NAI, Rotterdam

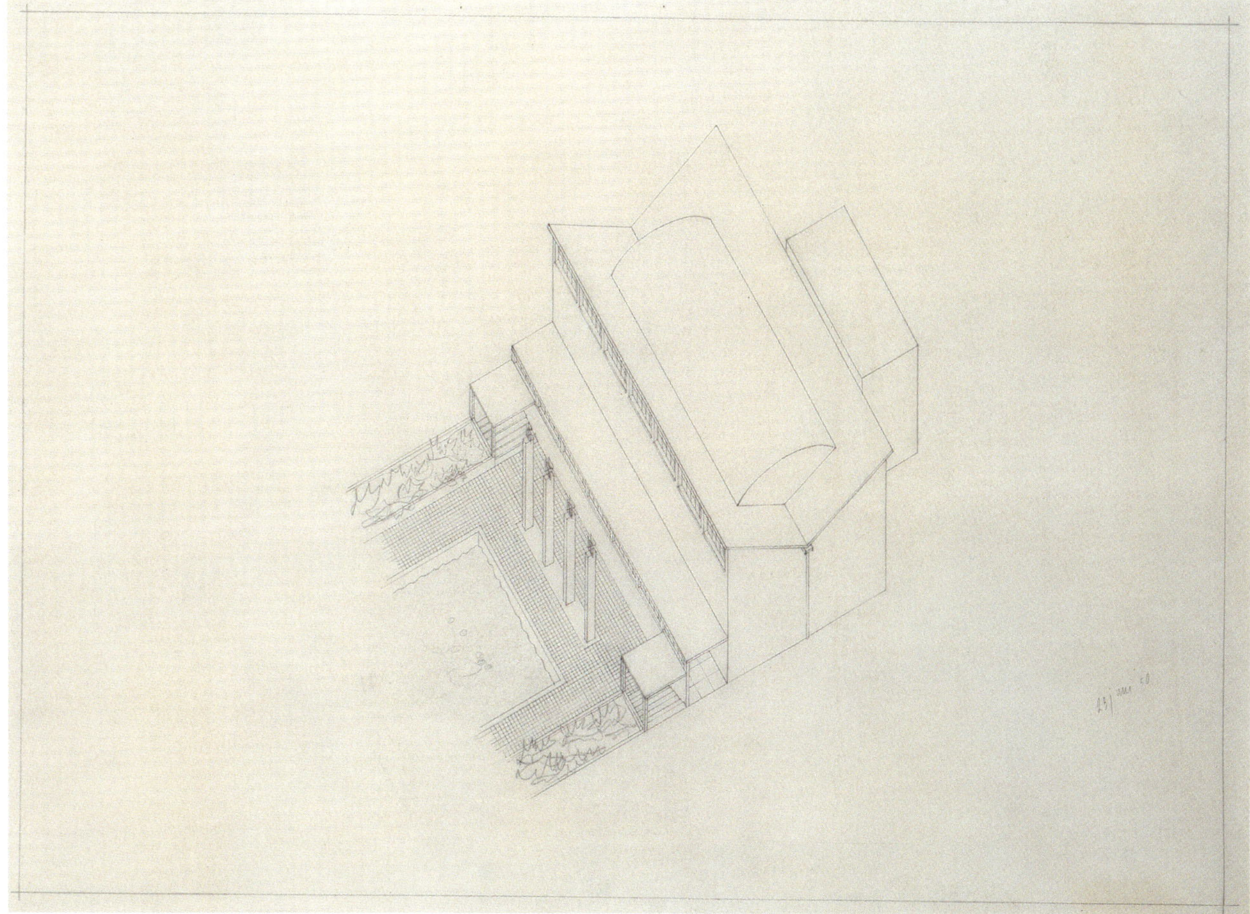

opponents spoke slightingly of *a mini-square* that could never attain to the grandeur of the old Sint Laurens, especially since Oud's church building was in their view too small for its symbolic function. Oud was unimpressed. *My plan has the potential to generate new cultural values. It is on a human scale and within human comprehension. It does not aspire to any extravagant effects but in its modest nature it is capable of a deeply religious effect. An effect more profound than would be possible if it were confined to a church building. The intention here is not at all a "little square", but a broad space imbued with higher sentiments.*[5] Oud's plan was disregarded and tower and nave were restored in accordance with a modified plan by Van der Steur and Meischke.

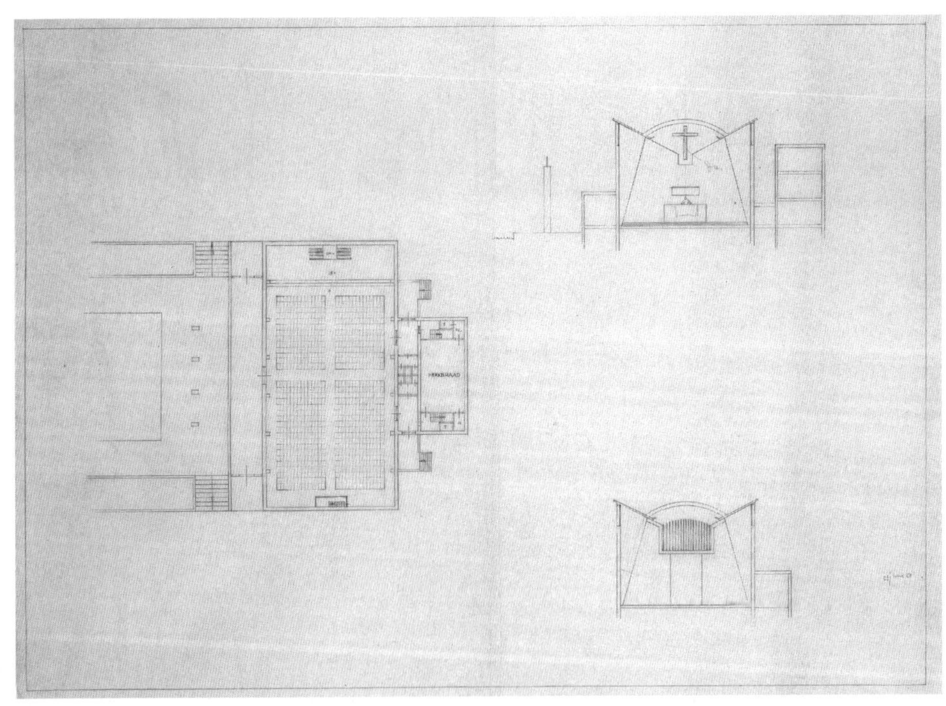

**Ground floor plan and cross sections of church/**
**OUDJ-lt 7, NAI, Rotterdam**



**Notes**

**1.** J.J.P. Oud to De Rijkscommissie voor de Monumentenzorg, 6 July 1948, OUDJ-B, NAI, Rotterdam.
**2.** J.J.P. Oud, 'Rotterdams St. Laurens', in *Bouw*, 5(1950)40, p. 659.
**3.** A.B[oeken], 'Het voorstel van J.J.P. Oud voor de Sint Laurens te Rotterdam', in: *Forum*, 5(1950)8, p. 309.
**4.** J.C. Meischke to J.J.P. Oud, August 1950, OUDJ-B, NAI, Rotterdam.
**5.** J.J.P. Oud, 'Architect Oud beantwoordt ds Den Hertog', in: *Het Rotterdams Parool*, 3 August 1950.

**Sources**

CCA: dr1984:0369
Getty: 890126-27**
NAI: OUDJ-lt 1 – 13, OUDJ-lt 1001, OUDJ-lt 3001, OUDJ-B

**Articles**

A.B[oeken], 'Het voorstel van J.J.P. Oud voor de Sint Laurens te Rotterdam', in: *Forum*, 5(1950)8, pp. 307-309
'Architect Oud heeft nieuw plan voor herbouw St. Laurens', in: *De Rotterdammer*, 28 July 1950, p. 2
F.J. Brevet, 'Rotterdams St Laurens: een grote kerk?', in: *De Groene Amsterdammer*, 19 August 1950, with reply from Oud
Den Hertog, 'Ds Den Hertog en architect Meischke tegen het plan-Oud', in: *De Rotterdammer*, 4 August 1950, p. 5
J.J.P. Oud, 'Architect Oud beantwoordt ds Den Hertog', in: *Het Rotterdams Parool*, 3 August 1950
J.J.P. Oud, 'Rotterdam en de St. Laurens', in: *Bouw*, 5(1950)36, p. 595
J.J.P. Oud, 'Rotterdam en de St. Laurens', in: *De Groene Amsterdammer*, 29 July 1950, p. 11
J.J.P. Oud, 'Rotterdams St Laurens', in: *Bouw*, 5(1950)40, pp. 658-659

**Literature**

U. Barbieri, *J.J.P. Oud*, Rotterdam 1987, pp. 152-153
D. Broekhuizen, *De Stijl toen / J.J.P. Oud nu*, Rotterdam 2000, pp. 120-137
H.E. Oud, *J.J.P. Oud. Architekt 1890-1963. Feiten en herinneringen gerangschikt*, The Hague 1984, pp. 152-153

At the end of 1950, the board of the Wieringermeer section of the Northeast Polder Works organized an ideas competition for a 'polder tower' at Emmeloord. It was to serve as a water tower but its main purpose was as a landmark in the new and largely empty polder landscape. Oud was expressly invited to take part in the competition and was the only participant to be offered an honorarium. He produced two proposals, one in accordance with the competition brief and one that deviated from it but which he regarded as his true design. *Designer made project E (project in accordance with the brief) with reluctance. It strikes him as mistaken to build a carillon between two water reservoirs if the intention is to give the tower a purpose geared to height. In addition, it creates ambivalent structural requirements, while the carillon is too low down to be able to function properly. So this project was made so as not to circumvent the terms of reference, but the designer would prefer project Motto E (variant) to be regarded as his real proposal. There is all the more reason for this since there is virtually no difference in price between the two.*[1]

Both designs show a concrete, cylindrical volume. In Motto E the carillon is located about halfway up the tower and there is a separate bell suspended at the top of the tower. In the alternative plan, Oud placed the carillon at the top of the tower and used the vacant space in the middle to house the polder records office. A salient feature is the staircase which, together with the lift shaft, was placed outside the plan of the actual tower. *The stairs are more generously conceived than is usual for such an object. The reason is that the designer has included in the tower various spaces he thinks will be useful for life in the Polder and which will therefore be able to pay for themselves. In addition, the idea of having the stairs on the outside is to help reinforce the representational function of the tower.*[2]

None of the 170 entries was awarded a prize and Oud's design did not make it past the 'second sorting'. The built design was by H. van Gent and was completed in 1959.

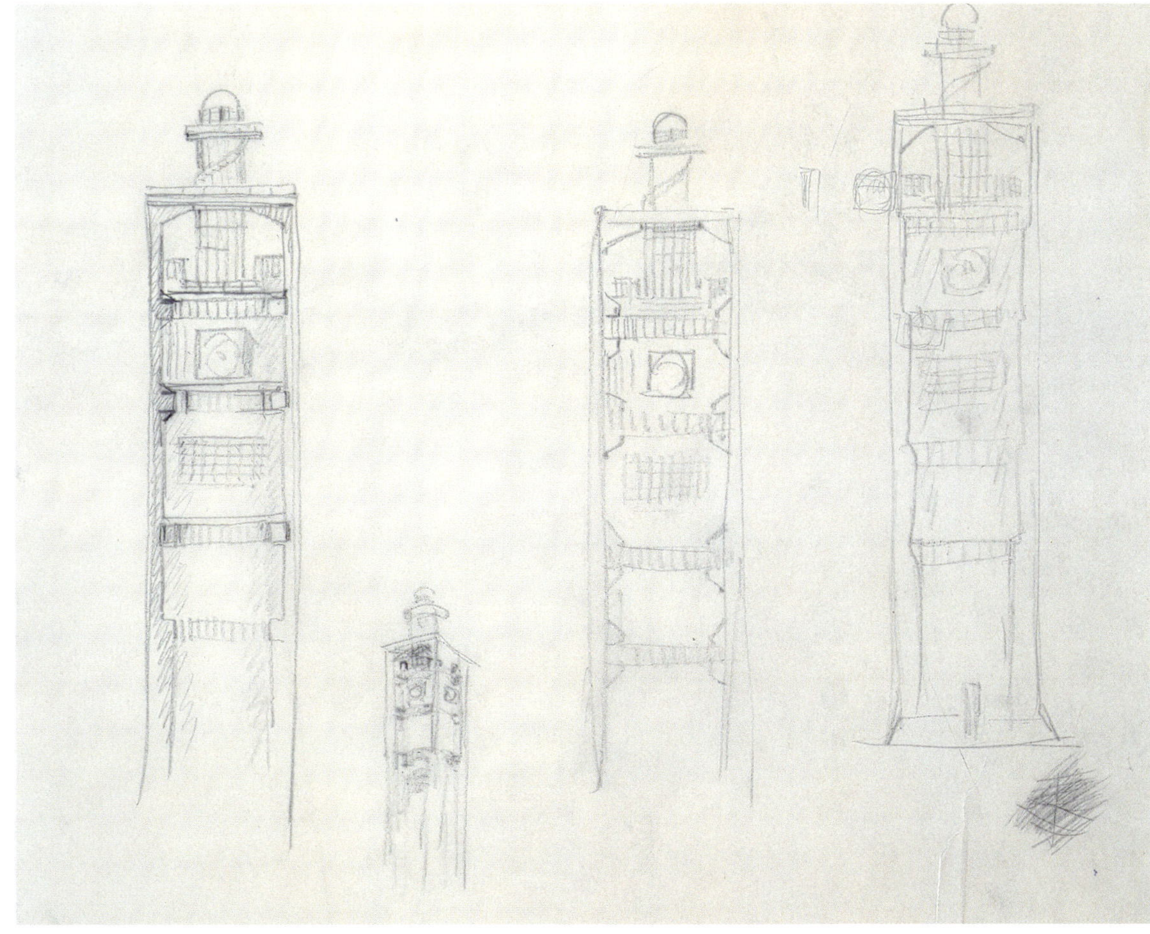

Cross sections/ OUDJ-pt 12, NAI, Rotterdam

Perspective/ OUDJ-pt 22, NAI, Rotterdam

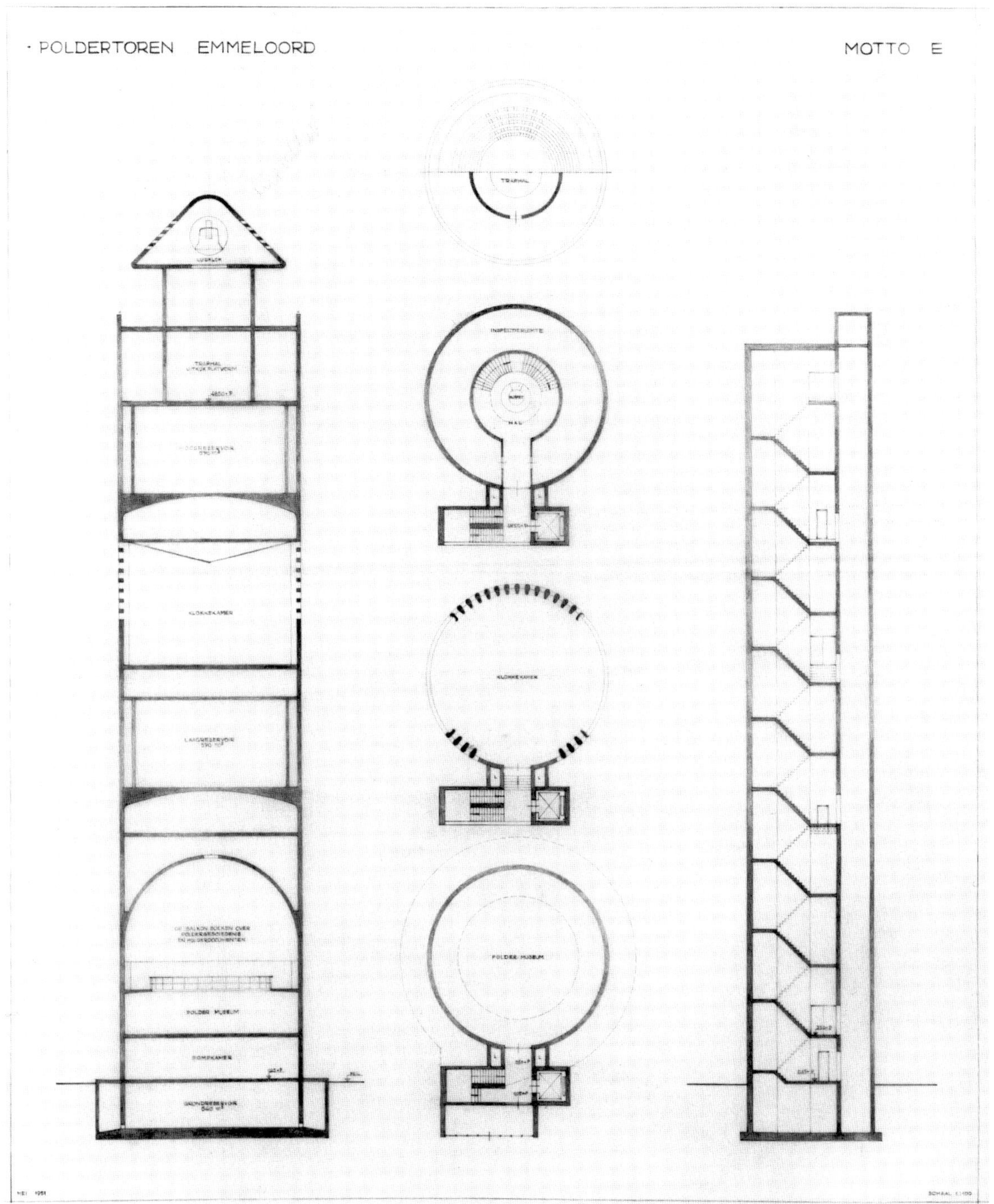


Various design views/ OUDJ-pt 17, NAI, Rotterdam



**Notes**

**1.** J.J.P. Oud, 'Toelichting' (OUDJ-pt 1001), NAI, Rotterdam.

**2.** J.J.P. Oud, 'Toelichting', (OUDJ-pt 1001), NAI, Rotterdam.

**Sources**

CCA: dr1984: 0391
NAI: OUDJ-pt 1-33, OUDJ-pt 1001, OUDJ-ph 990-993

**Articles**

*Bouwkundig Weekblad*, 9 January (1951)2, p. 23
*Bouwkundig Weekblad*, 24 April-1 May (1951)17-18, p. 187
*Bouwkundig Weekblad*, 8-15 May (1951)19-20, pp. 203-204

**Literature**

H.E. Oud, *J.J.P. Oud. Architekt 1890-1963. Feiten en herinneringen gerangschikt*, The Hague 1984, p. 239

# Struggle for a 'Fresh Architecture'

After the war, Oud embarked enthusiastically on what should have been, and to some extent was, a new chapter in his career. The disastrous reception of the Shell Building was a bitter pill to swallow, but it did not prevent him from presenting himself as an authority in the field of modern architecture. If anything, the opposite was true. Only now did Oud emerge as a national figure, a status given final confirmation by his design for the National Monument on the Dam in Amsterdam. Oud was the recipient of many special awards. On 25 September 1955 he received an honorary doctorate from Delft Technical College with F.J. Berghoef acting as his 'promoter'. In his address, Berghoef stressed that Oud was to be admired above all for his wilful singularity: *His works are unquestionably cool, verging on the cold. But just as Vermeer recorded the figures, the fabrics, the colours and the gleams of light in his Delft room with a cool passion, just as Saenredam noted the buildings before which he seated himself in unbroken avid attention, so Oud with penetrating acuity gives shape in his works to the social reality of the 20th century: in his public housing the actuality of the orderly, reasonably prosperous masses, in his office buildings the self-assurance of the economically powerful corporation. And behind the seeming lack of emotion one detects in both the tensions of the age. In his work, Oud is a realist who sees through reality with uncommon clarity and who makes no concessions whatsoever in order to embellish or to soften it. Oud's work is architecturally speaking of an extraordinary purity; its essence is completely embedded in dimensions and proportions. In this it resembles the abstract architecture of the Greeks and it possesses the clarity of Classical humanist architecture; in his best works, Oud attains an uncomplicated grace – I know this is the atmosphere he prefers.*[1] The much-valued honorary doctorate gave

Oud beside a drawing for the Congress Centre, late 1950s/ OUDJ-56, NAI, Rotterdam (Photo C. Ferguson)

Oud the official recognition appropriate to his prominent position within the Dutch architectural establishment. In this respect there is a parallel with the fortunes of former fellow-modernists like Gropius and Mies van der Rohe in that like them, Oud 'arrived', socially and financially, after the war. But there the comparisons end, for Oud's role in the further development of international modern architecture was played out. Though he did everything in his power to return to this stage, he did not succeed. Henceforth his sphere of influence was effectively restricted to the Netherlands; from now on it was mainly developments in Dutch architecture that determined his work.

Oud had begun his offensive on behalf of a 'fresh' architecture even before the negative reception of the Shell Building reached him, and as it became clear that his international role was finished, he intensified his battle. The first skirmish was prompted by the post-war reconstruction of The Hague, for which Dudok had drawn up a masterplan. Oud was indirectly involved as a result of his plan for a monument for De Nederlanden van 1845. When Dudok's plan came under fire from self-styled 'progressive' architects unwilling to go along with the underlying principles of Dudok's design, Oud was undoubtedly reminded of the fate of Witteveen's reconstruction plan for Rotterdam. Although Oud had fought bitterly with Witteveen, he shared the latter's opinion that it was the job of urban development plans to define the third dimension, in other words, that they should include an architectural component. After Witteveen had been forced to step down, architecture and urban planning in Rotterdam were divorced, a development that was no doubt sanctioned from the wings by P. Verhagen, town planning adviser to the Ministry of Public Works and Reconstruction. If criticism of Dudok's reconstruction plan were to gain ground, the same thing was in danger of happening in The Hague. Oud accordingly launched a campaign among his fellow reconstruction supervisors (the 'Commission of 5') aimed at gathering all who were 'fresh in spirit' around him.[2] He even toyed with the idea of launching a new magazine along the lines of *Das Werk* or *L'homme et l'architecture* and sounded out the journalist J.J. Vriend about the idea. While the criticism of Dudok's plan was the immediate pretext for this campaign, his real motives lay deeper. Oud saw in the criticism of Dudok's plan an expression of a new, *bureaucratic* spirit. *Civil engineers are now deciding on the reconstruction of our nation*, Oud complained. *Zwiers gone – Abspoel gone – the bureaucracy is growing at an alarming rate. Ringers kowtows to Z.Y. van der Meer (with whom the BNA even wanted to request an audience – I inquired whether one should say Sire or simply Your Majesty, but it turned out to be a mistake, Mieras wrote back) this man [who] is certainly a dictator, now has a finger in public housing too and thus indirectly in the National Plan.*[3] According to Oud, the bureaucratic machine Ringers had built up during the occupation and which had remained in place after liberation, was getting completely out of hand and stood in the way of a free development of modern architecture. That Oud should have fulminated simultaneously against the progressive young architects intent on preserving The Hague from what they saw as an outdated, traditional reconstruction, and against the Hague bureaucracy is not surprising, for in his view it was precisely this combination that had put paid to the architectural and artistic reconstruction plan for Rotterdam. It seemed to him that a crude form of architecture corresponding to the International Style (which he regarded as an Americanized form of European modernism as codified by Giedion and Gropius around 1930) was conspiring with an ever-expanding network of rules, regulations and above all prohibitions aimed at cutting costs.

Oud was fairly mild towards the younger generation of

Oud receiving an honorary doctorate from Delft Technical College, 1955/ OUDJ-57, NAI, Rotterdam

architects. When he fulminated against an anti-individualist, non-architectural interpretation of modernism (teamwork was his particular bugbear), he preferred to direct his shafts at Gropius or Giedion. At the other end of the architectural spectrum lurked an equally great danger in Oud's eyes, the traditionalism of the Delft School. The latter took its name from Delft Technical College where Oud himself had briefly studied in the 1910s and where the training in architecture and town planning had been dominated since 1924 by Granpré Molière. Leading alumni of the Delft School appeared to have secured key positions in Ringer's reconstruction bureaucracy from where they were getting involved in most of the reconstruction plans. Oud reproached the traditionalists with a lack of faith in the future. *Kindly-disposed and full of diffidence the Delft gentlemen seem. But their tyranny reaches much deeper than the tyranny of those who exhibit greater power. For they do not target the outer man, rather they attack man in his soul. So caught up are these architects in their exclusive interpretation of what constitutes architecture that they fail to notice that they are committing downright tyranny against others whose opinions differ from theirs.*[4] An attempt at reconciliation by Granpré Molière, who impressed on Oud the importance of achieving a common stance, was rejected out of hand: *No, just as building for you is a 'higher calling', so is it for me and I could at the very least reproach you for the fact that you could forget this for a single moment. Be that as it may, what is most important to me in architecture is being thwarted by your influence.*[5]

What Oud had always regarded as the best platform for his ideas, his own work, displayed a gradual departure from the methods for enhancing architecture he had developed in the 1930s. His work became more astringent and he returned to playing with volumes determined by their function. This is most evident in a series of public buildings which include his competition entry for a new head office for Hoogovens (a commission of comparable importance to the Shell Building), his design for the Zuid-Holland provincial offices and his town hall plans for Groningen, Rhenen and Almelo. Oud failed to break back into his prewar specialism, public housing. The network of rules and regulations was particularly dense here, constantly refuelling Oud's aversion to bureaucracy. An open letter to the Minister of Reconstruction and Public Housing, correspondence with this minister and an informal radio interview had no effect and after a (failed) experiment with social housing in Arnhem, he turned his back on this field of endeavour.

Oud's campaign against the International Style, which he attempted to conduct at an international level, his distaste for bureaucracy and his opposition to the Delft School, are typical of the solitary position he adopted after the war and which was reflected in the somewhat hybrid character of his later work. Neither the importance of the commissions he secured nor the honours that started to come his way could induce him to break out of his self-imposed isolation. In 1952, when he noticed that *Opbouw* had once again become a mouthpiece for ideas he did not share, he cancelled the membership he had renewed in 1945. He was also remarkably reticent vis à vis the most influential political-social philosophy around 1945: that of humanistic socialism. Thanks to his editorial work for *i10* and his wide reading, he was well versed in this philosophy, which had crystallized out during the occupation in a German hostage camp. Its core element, the proposed reconciliation of the individual and mass society, can only have appealed to him. That he nonetheless remained aloof is undoubtedly related to the policies of the first postwar government, which were based on this philosophy. In practice, humanistic socialism led in Oud's view to the bureaucracy he so ardently detested. In response to a personal invi-

Oud in Vierhouten/ OUDJ-57, NAI, Rotterdam

tation to join the Nederlandse Volksbeweging (NVB, Dutch Popular Movement), which was based entirely on this philosophy, Oud made no bones about his views: *since the liberation I have kept myself well informed about the N.V.B, because I initially thought I might have a certain sympathy for it. ...After the brief practical experience I am now thoroughly persuaded that* this *socialism will bring us nothing good. This type of government interference leads to rigidity, not to renewal. Even to actual deterioration in many respects. What is more, it kills all creative energy.*[6]

Perhaps the most eloquent evidence of Oud's idealistic concept of his heroic but lonely mission, is his immense admiration for a book by the American writer Ayn Rand: *The Fountainhead* (1943). It describes the vicissitudes of the architect Howard Roark who, despite endless setbacks and massive opposition, eventually succeeds in his mission to practise and propagate a modern, functional and ahistorical architecture. Roark's struggle was that of the individual against the collective, a theme that seemed to be highly topical in the context of the Cold War. In 1949, the book, an immediate best seller, was made into an equally successful film by King Vidor. Oud received a copy of the book from the author herself, with the inscription *To J.J.P. Oud, with my sincere appreciation for your contribution to modern architecture* – a token of esteem Oud must surely have treasured. The character of Howard Roark was based on Frank Lloyd Wright and the whole book can be read as a plea for individual creativity and against everything that stands in its way, especially teamwork. It was for this very reason, that Oud was a great admirer of Wright and in 1951 he got to supervise an exhibition of Wright's work in Rotterdam. The Dutch city was the exhibition's last port of call in a tour that had included Florence, Munich and Paris, but thanks to Oud's involvement, the Rotterdam version acquired a special slant, which Oud discussed with his American mentor in Paris. The exhibition – like *The Fountainhead* – can be read as propaganda for the individually creative architect. Oud displayed a similar wilfulness in his own work. Over all his later works, however, hung the shadow of the Shell Building and the manner of its reception. Oud did not find it easy to be simultaneously wilful and modern, and his wilfulness appears to have been more in the nature of a mental and defensive idée fixe than a spontaneous source of personal creativity.

Cover of collection of articles on the Delft School, circa 1947/ Los Angeles, Getty, 890126-22**



**Notes**

**1.** Address by J.F. Berghoef, Oud Archive, NAI, Rotterdam.
**2.** J.J.P. Oud to J.J. Vriend, 17 August 1946, Getty Research Institute, Los Angeles. For the reconstruction of The Hague see: M. Provoost, 'De wederopbouw van Den Haag', in K. Bosma, C. Wagenaar, *Een geruisloze doorbraak. De geschiedenis van architectuur en stedebouw tijdens de bezetting en wederopbouw van Nederland*, Rotterdam 1995, pp. 317-329.
**3.** J.J.P. Oud to J.J. Vriend, 17 August 1946, Getty Research Institute, Los Angeles.
**4.** J.J.P. Oud, 'Wij bouwen weer op?' in *De Groene Amsterdammer*, 21 December 1946.
**5.** J.J.P. Oud to M.J. Granpré Molière, 25 July 1946, OUDJ-B, NAI, Rotterdam.
**6.** J.J.P. Oud to the secretariaat of the Nederlandse Volksbeweging, 3 January 1946, OUDJ-B, NAI, Rotterdam.

# 91/ Urban Design and Supervision of Vredenburg / Jaarbeurs Site

**Utrecht, Vredenburg**

**1949-1961**

In January 1949, Oud was asked to design a plan for Utrecht's problematical Vredenburgplein. For years a traffic bottleneck, the square was also regarded as an eyesore by the city council. This was largely due to the Jaarbeurs exhibition complex, which occupied the entire west wall, and to the many wooden huts erected on the square as temporary exhibition space. The original square design by Berlage (1919) had been severely compromised, not least by the ever-expanding Jaarbeurs. Accordingly, the council asked Oud to produce a design for the 'future configuration of the square' in consultation with the architect of the Jaarbeurs, C. Wegener Sleeswijk. His plan was to address *the shape and layout [of the square], possible enclosure by development along the street frontages, the siting and general appearance of new development in the area (especially that of the Jaarbeurs) and guidelines for the treatment of the existing square frontages.*[1] Supervision of the plan's implementation was part of the commission.

Oud took the expansion plans for the Jaarbeurs as his starting point: a fourth building located in the south corner of the square between the third building and the Beatrixhal, and a semi-circular secretariat building on the corner opposite. In Wegener Sleeswijk's original plan of 1946, the 'fourth building' closed off the entire south-east side of the square. Oud suggested replacing this with a twelve-storey tower block that would give the horizontally oriented square a vertical caesura and a clear-cut termination. And since it occupied a much smaller area than the building proposed by Wegener, the square would benefit from greater openness on this side. *In my plan I consequently set out from the volumes of the Jaarbeurs, which I accepted in its neutrality. I did, however, wish to provide it with two important accents designed to give it a beginning and an end. The first accent is the so-called "Jaarbeurs tower" which contains the new extension. The other accent is an architectonic elaboration of the existing entrance which I want to give greater emphasis and also allow to contribute spatially to the new set-up. ...This made it possible to allocate the Jaarbeurs a significant space in a way that benefits the overall appearance of square and architecture because the existing buildings now find visual support. ...*

*The fact that I introduced such a decidedly vertical element as the "Jaarbeurs tower" is a result of my need for a volume on Vredenburg that could become a confrontational focus, a centre of the visual image of the square. Only in this way do I see a possibility of affording Vredenburg such solidity of appearance as will enable it to give rest to the eye.*[2]

The entrance to the tower was flanked by a terrace and a sizable sculpture group. A gently raked ramp connected the Jaarbeurs tower to the secretariat, which Oud placed at the north-east corner of the square. This was the same position as in Wegener Sleeswijk's plan but Oud gave it a form that fitted in with the new circulation routes. Modifications to these routes formed the core of Oud's plan: car traffic was

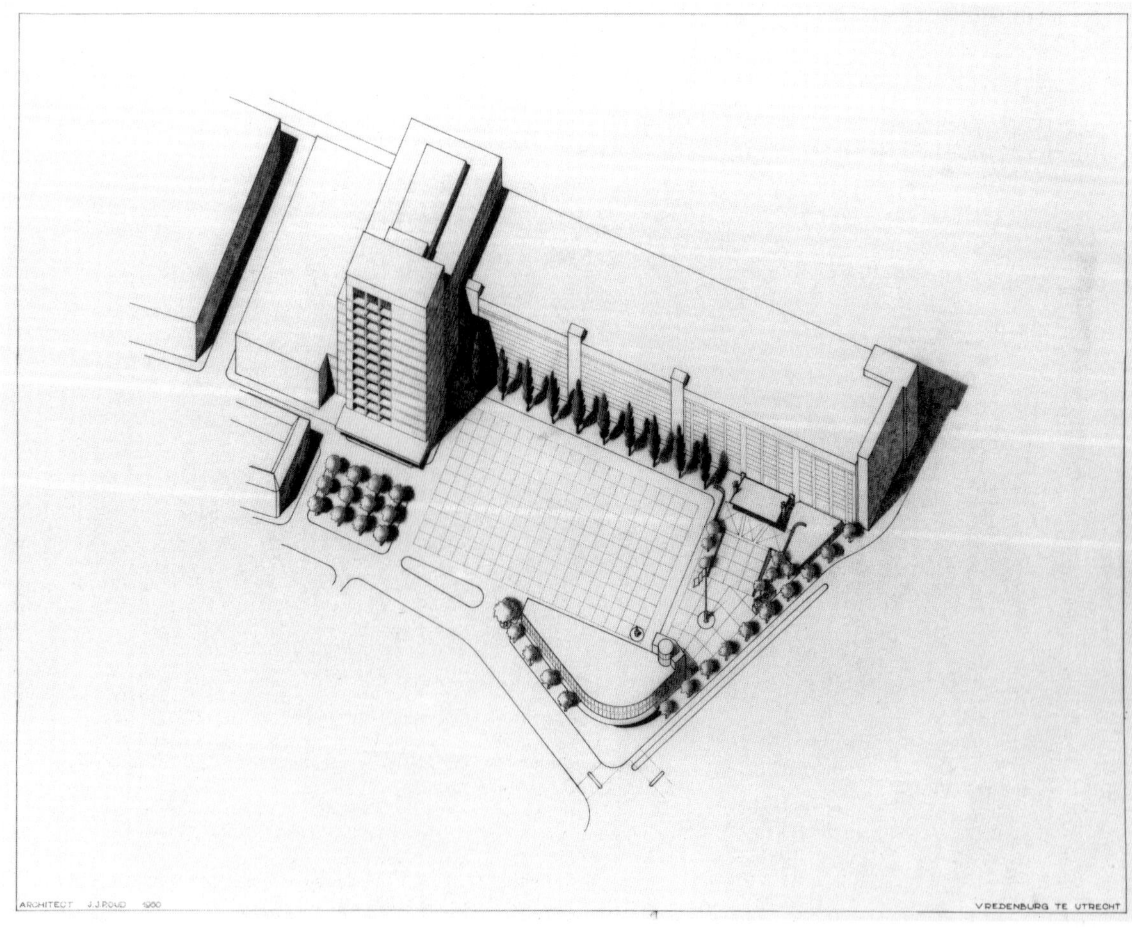


Isometric projection of site/ OUDJ-vr 14, NAI, Rotterdam

able to flow more smoothly and there was space reserved for buses on the north-west side. The central section of the square was closed to all vehicles but taxis. Oud wanted the street facades to be as 'rough' as possible; and vis à vis the taut lines of the Jaarbeurs complex he saw no need for a fixed cornice height. Oud's most striking intervention was the siting of a large, half-round facade opposite the secretariat. Press reactions to the unveiling of the plan in March 1951 were uniformly favourable. Frequent reference was made to the 'fifty-metre-high Jaarbeurs tower', usually with a reassuring subheading to the effect that it would not compete with the spire of the Dom.

However, square residents complained that the secretariat closed off the square too much. The city council, which had already approved the plan, started to have doubts and even considered banning the whole secretariat building. In order to gain more control over the Jaarbeurs building plans, the council decided to develop the new premises itself and rent them out to the Jaarbeurs. Wegener Sleeswijk's plan was set aside and because Oud could not act as supervisor *and* architect, the commission for the new development went to Merkelbach & Elling. In 1957 P. Elling (1897-1962) designed a six-storey administration building in the angle between the two exhibition halls – in effect a combination of the fourth building and the secretariat. It was completed in 1962.

No part of Oud's original proposal was implemented, although he continued to air his views about the outer walls. By the time the council presented its new Structure Plan, Oud's traffic solutions were out of date. He was convinced that it was his opposition to the plans of the German traffic engineer Feuchtinger, who in 1958 proposed filling in the canals to make way for access roads, that had led the council to terminate the supervisory contract in 1961.[3] Oud expressed his disappointment in a letter to Elling. *I consider it [the final plan] a very meagre result for all the effort invested in it by me and others, including yourself. I am consequently unable to accept it. The plan no longer even corresponds to the model I was shown during my last discussion at the town hall and to which I gave my approval, be it without much enthusiasm.*

*As supervisor I will shortly have little more to do with Vredenburg. The Secretariat, on which you are now working, occupies the most important place. I would be happy if they were now to determine the square as a whole in consultation with you. Perhaps, in conjunction with your building, you may be still be able to offer some fruitful impetus. Little by little, everything that gave the square some expressive possibilities has disappeared so that in my opinion it now promises to become a bleak square. What can be done to counteract this, I do not know. I have done everything in my power to furnish the square with a certain allure. But there are forces active in Utrecht (terrestrial rays or whatever) that make it impossible ever to arrive at a result of any consequence. My experience, unfortunately, is that because of this it is impossible to get the necessary foothold to achieve anything.*[4]



**Notes**

**1.** City of Utrecht to J.J.P. Oud, 31 January 1949, OUDJ-vr 1001-1006, NAI, Rotterdam.

**2.** G.A. Leeuwenberg, 'Het Vreeburg-van-nu verschrikking voor het oog', in: *Utrechts Katholiek Dagblad*, 13 March 1951.

**3.** J.J.P. Oud to J. Engelman, 5 June 1960, OUDJ-vr 1001-1006, NAI, Rotterdam.

**4.** J.J.P. Oud to J. Elling, 6 June 1960, OUDJ-vr 1001-1006, NAI, Rotterdam.

**Sources**

CCA: dr1984: 0358-0368
Getty: 890126-7**
NAI: OUDJ-vr 1-20, OUDJ-vr 1001-1006, OUDJ-vr 3001, OUDJ-ph 1755-1756, OUDJ-B

**Articles**

'Architect Oud zegt: Vreeburg heeft thans geen positieve kwaliteiten', in: *Nieuw Utrechts Dagblad*, 13 March 1951, p. 2
'Architecten zijn niet gebonden aan hoekbebouwing', in: *Nieuw Utrechts Dagblad*, 14 May 1954
K. Jakobs et al., *De ideale stad 1664-1988*, pp. 99-100,
Anon., 'Jaarbeurstoren van 50 m. hoogte', in: *Utrechts Katholiek Dagblad*, 3 March 1951, pp. 1-2
'Oud ziet Jaarbeurstoren als zwaartepunt van het nieuwe Vredenburg', *Utrechtsch Nieuwsblad*, 13 March 1951, p. 3
'Plan Oud: eindelijk de oplossing van het Jaarbeursvraagstuk', in: *Het Vrije Volk*, 14 March 1951
'De toekomstige vorm van Utrechts voornaamste plein', in: *Nieuwe Rotterdamsche Courant*, 14 May 1954

**Literature**

R. Dettingmeijer, 'Een gebouw als optelsom van grijpbare elementen en ruimten. Muziekcentrum voltooit Vredenburg', in: *Wonen/TABK*, (1979)24, pp. 21-45
R. Dettingmeijer, 'Van Fockema Andreae tot renovatie HC', in: *De ideale stad. Ideaalplannen voor Utrecht*, Utrecht 1988, p. 75-114
A.H. Okazaki, 'Architect Oud and Vredenburg Square', in *Kunst in Utrecht* 5(1967)5/6
H.E. Oud, *J.J.P. Oud. Architekt 1890-1963. Feiten en herinneringen gerangschikt*, The Hague 1984, p. 239

# 92/ Design for Standard Type Workers' Dwellings

1947

Before the war, Oud's international reputation was based largely on his celebrated social housing schemes and so it is remarkable that after his departure from the Rotterdam Woningdienst he should have remained aloof from commissions in this sector. Nonetheless, public housing was high on the political agenda in post-war Holland. Housing construction was an integral part of the national government's socio-economic policy of keeping wages and prices low in order to strengthen the international competitiveness of the Dutch economy. Low wages presupposed low rentals and this in turn resulted in attempts to reduce construction costs in the public housing sector. The friction between the desired – and implicitly promised – decent quality, and the continuous pressure to keep building costs low, dominated the debate about post-war housing. It was against this background that Oud designed a standard type for working-class housing in 1947. When the Minister for Post-War Reconstruction and Housing, Mr J. in 't Veld, personally joined in the debate in 1950, Oud sent him this design in order to show that the only solution to the dilemmas confronting public housing lay in highly sophisticated floor plan design. *It is once again a design for very small dwellings that I made for my own pleasure and in which, in my opinion, a fairly large family would be very well accommodated. This type too is not wide, 4.70 m. centre to centre, and can therefore be built without intermediate support. Downstairs it has one large living room, a bedroom for the parents (with wall bed) and kitchen. Upstairs is a shower and two bedrooms for the children. If necessary I would have no hesitation about putting two beds (with stepladder) one above the other in these bedrooms. Children like them and if the ventilation is good, there is nothing against them. Such sleeping cubicles represent a saving that should be readily used, as long as the living space is generous. In the living space of this type, one has a sense of space because there is a balcony in the living room onto which the bedrooms open and which serves to dispel the cramped feeling that otherwise attends small dwellings. Whether it will be possible to persuade workers into this kind of dwelling straight away, I would not dare to predict. I am, however, convinced that once they are in they will never want to leave again. Everything has been thought of in these dwellings and most of the components should be immediately available from the factory. Not much plastering and as far as the finishing and appearance inside and out is concerned, spic and span. If the "Kiefhoek homes" were Ford houses, then I venture to call these, which are a bit better, "Citroën houses".*[1]

The housing blocks, like those at the Weissenhofsiedlung in Stuttgart and Blijdorp in Rotterdam, were projected in accordance with the principle of row housing. The dwellings consisted of two sections of different height joined together. Thanks to the staggering, the living room appears very spacious and the dwelling provides more room than the front facade would appear to suggest.

Bird's-eye view of site/ OUDJ-sw 6, NAI, Rotterdam



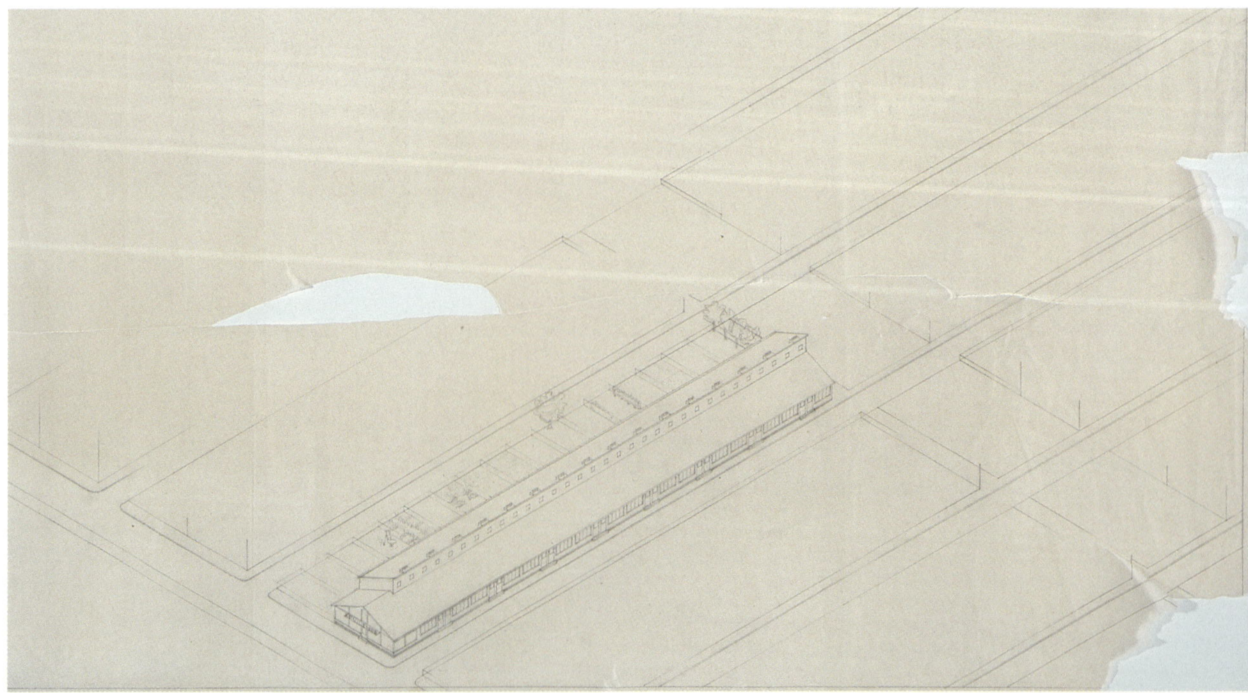

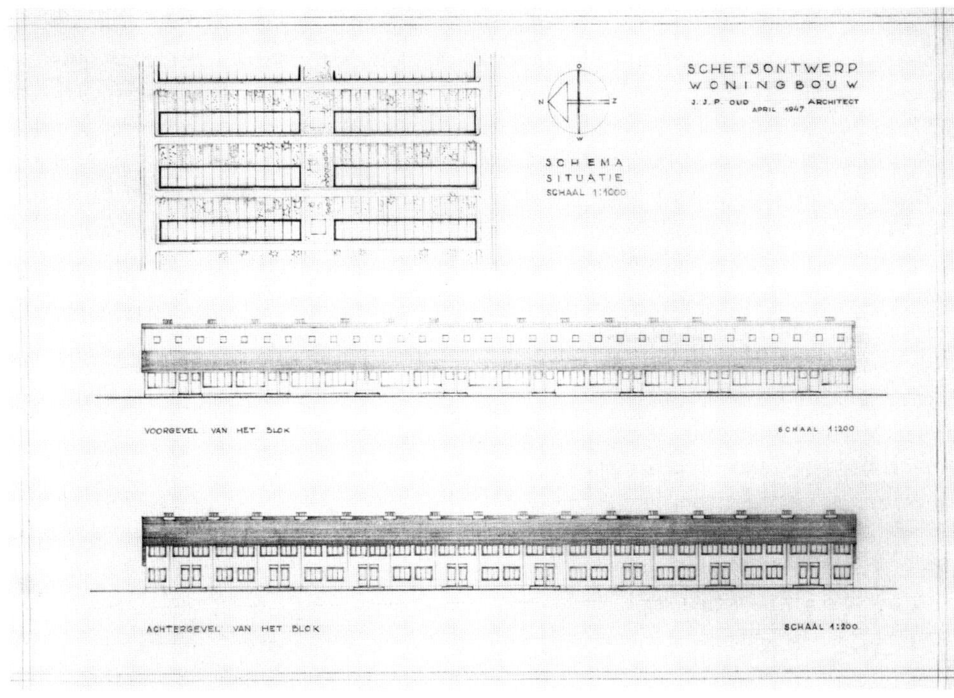


Site plan (top) and elevations/ OUDJ-sw 9, NAI, Rotterdam

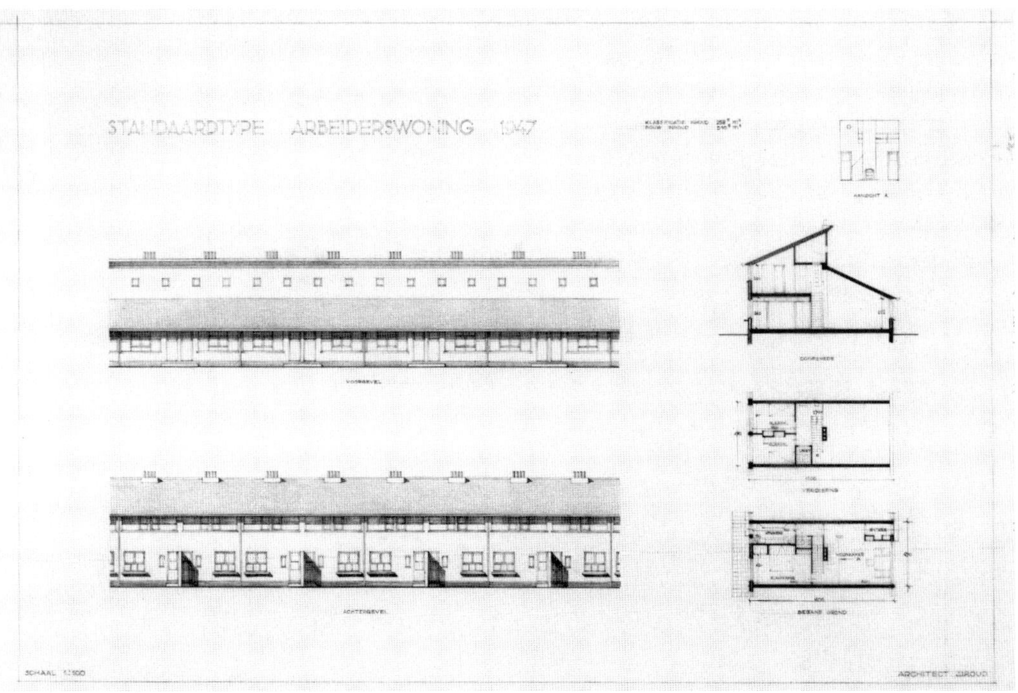


Elevations, section and plans/ OUDJ-sw 11, NAI, Rotterdam



**Notes**
**1.** J.J.P. Oud to J. in 't Veld, 14 December 1950, OUDJ-B, NAI, Rotterdam.

**Sources**
NAI: OUDJ-sw 1-25, OUDJ-B

**Articles**
J.J. Oud, 'Standaard-type arbeiderwoningen', in: *Bouw,* 8(1953)15, p. 270

**Literature**
H.E. Oud, *J.J.P. Oud. Architekt 1890-1963. Feiten en herinneringen gerangschikt,* The Hague 1984, p. 165

# 93/ 360 Dwellings at Arnhem

**Arnhem, Presikhaaf**

**1951-1953**

In 1951, Oud's contacts with the housing minister J. in 't Veld gained him a commission to design 360 dwellings in the Arnhem district of Presikhaaf. The project was carried out on behalf of the Catholic housing association, St. Eusebius, under the supervision of the Ministry of Post-War Reconstruction and Housing. The objective was to achieve lower than average building costs. Oud drew six identical housing units, each consisting of three rows. The location of the rows, along the edges of a plot, created the opportunity for a closed inner courtyard. The gallery-access flats Oud proposed ran up against objections from the client who was afraid that they would not be very popular. Moreover, this type was considerably more expensive than the average, which was contrary to the terms of reference. This first plan vanished and was replaced by a design based on standard floor plans produced by the Centrale Woningstichting Arnhem (Arnhem Central Housing Association). Oud's task now was to fit these floor plans into his original spatial plan. The changes this necessitated led once again to an unacceptable rise in building costs so that Oud was forced to drop most of the alterations.

Execution was no less laborious than the design process. Oud's suggestions for improvements to the finishing prompted serious disagreements with the contractor. *I do so wish*, Oud wrote to him, *that you would believe that I have not the slightest intention of making your work difficult or expensive. As I have frequently told you, it is in my interest to ensure that you make a good job of it. You chose me yourself and I so appreciate this that I wish to hamper you as little as possible. That goes without saying. But put yourself in my place for once. You would like me to restrict myself to the facades and take the rest on trust. But how can I do that? Just as you have a reputation to uphold in the contracting business, so have I as architect. I cannot take the risk of careless work inside that would be credited to me, now can I? No one would believe that I had had nothing to do with the inside.* [1]

The Arnhem project was a big disappointment to Oud so it is little wonder that he did not assist in its publication and hardly ever referred to it.

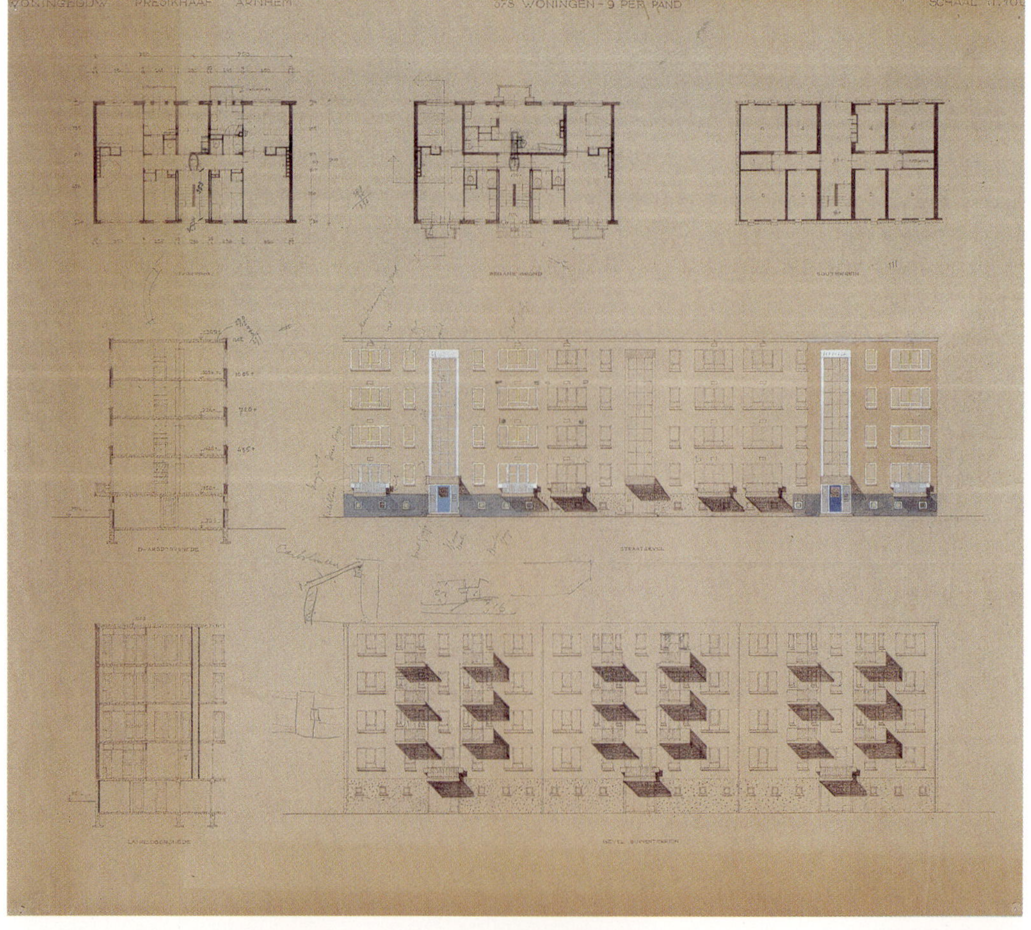


**Final design for walk-up flats/ OUDJ-pk 67, NAI, Rotterdam**

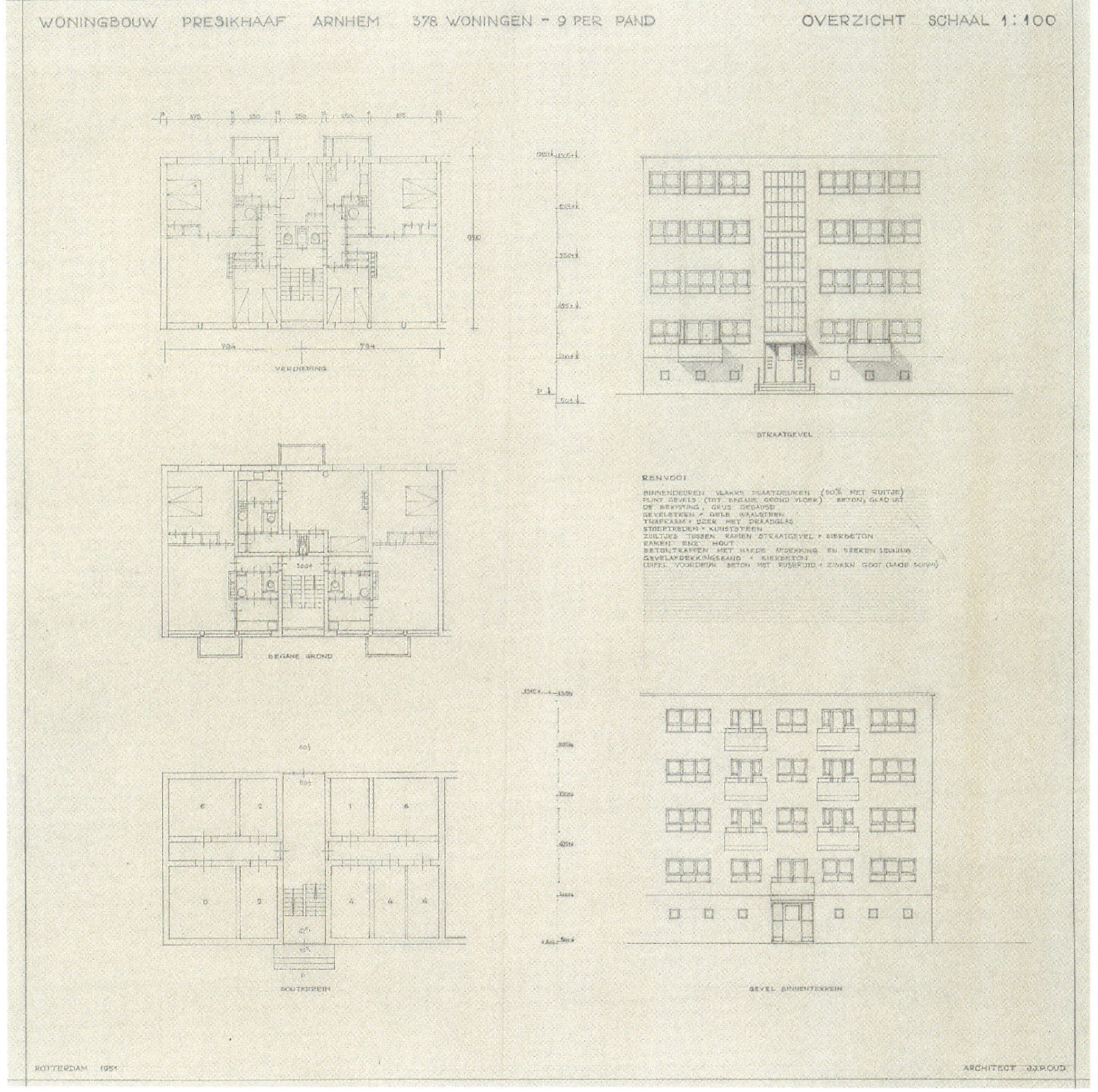


**Preliminary design for walk-up flats/ OUDJ-pk 39, NAI, Rotterdam**



**Notes**

**1.** J.J.P. Oud to J.M. Krijger, 6 February 1952, OUDJ-pk 1001-1004, NAI, Rotterdam.

**Sources**

NAI: OUDJ-pk 1-69, OUDJ-pk 1001-1004, OUDJ-pk 2001, OUDJ-ph 1361-1369, OUDJ-ph 17657-1760, OUDJ-B

**Literature**

U. Barbieri, *J.J.P. Oud*, Rotterdam 1987, p. 193
D. Broekhuizen, *De Stijl toen / J.J.P. Oud nu*, Rotterdam 2000, pp. 192-213
H.E. Oud, *J.J.P. Oud. Architekt 1890-1963. Feiten en herinneringen gerangschikt*, The Hague 1984, p. 165
G. Stamm, *J.J.P. Oud. Bauten und Projekte 1906 bis 1963*, Mainz, Berlin 1984, p. 137

Porch/ OUDJ-ph 1365, NAI, Rotterdam
(Photo D. Renes)

IJsselaan facades/ OUDJ-ph 1367, NAI, Rotterdam (Photo D. Renes)

# 94/ Design for a Double House for the De la Court Family

**Overveen, Lombar Petrilaan** **1950**

In 1950, the De la Court family commissioned Oud to design a double house: a single-storey home for their parents/ in-laws and next to it a two-storey house for themselves. The design comprised two separate, interlocking dwellings. Sketches show that from the outset Oud worked on the basis of two discrete dwellings, each with a quite distinct design, fused into a single house. The motif of interlocking dwellings, which refers to his design for standard-type workers' dwellings, is reinforced by the fact that the roof of the lower house continues through the taller house, as it were, to reappear on the side elevation in the form of a canopy over the two entrances.

The house for the older couple consists of a single storey under a low roof. It is distinguished by a tall chimney, which lends the little building an almost industrial appearance, and two flower boxes incorporated into the rear elevation. The second dwelling, which is cuboid, is unusual in that the living room and main bedroom are located on the upper floor. The ground floor contains the children's bedroom, the kitchen and the dining room. Philip Johnson, to whom Oud sent his plan, thought it exceedingly odd. *I have always seen wit in your madness. Your direction interests me, but baffles. Especially the house for two families at Bloemendaal – which I find mysterious beyond comprehension.*[1] In the event, the plan was never executed. Fear that growing international tension would erupt into a new crisis, persuaded the older members of the De la Court family to abandon the whole idea.

**Isometric projection of site/ OUDJ-dw 22, NAI, Rotterdam**

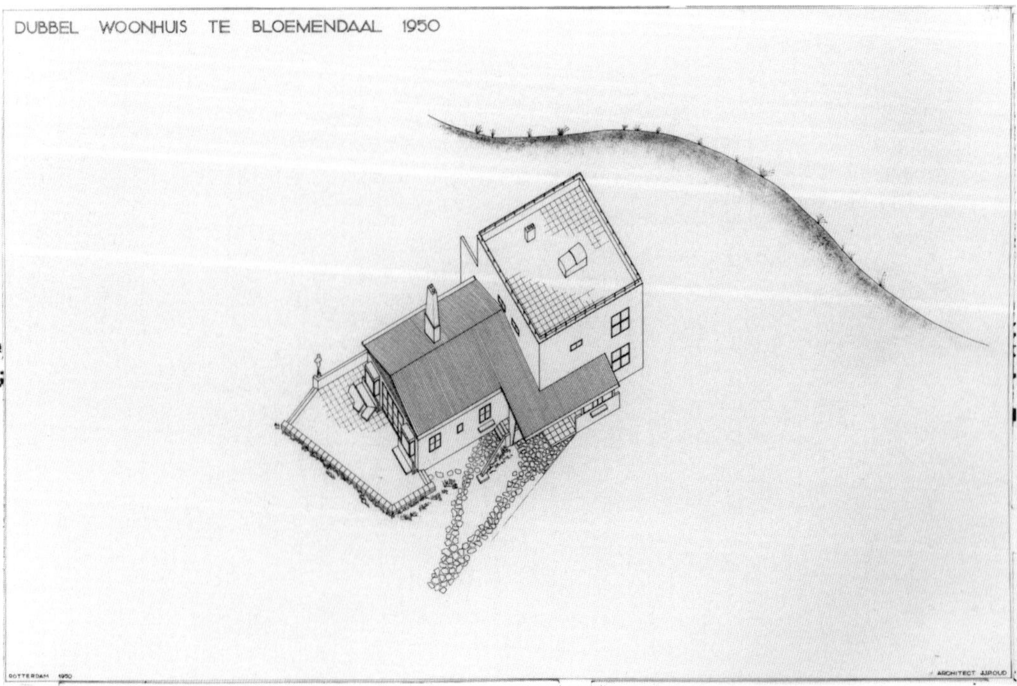




**Notes**

**1.** P. Johnson to J.J.P. Oud, 25 January 1954, OUDJ-B, NAI, Rotterdam.

**Sources**

NAI: OUDJ-dw 1-25, OUDJ-dw 1001, OUDJ-B

## 94/ Design for a Double House for the De la Court Family

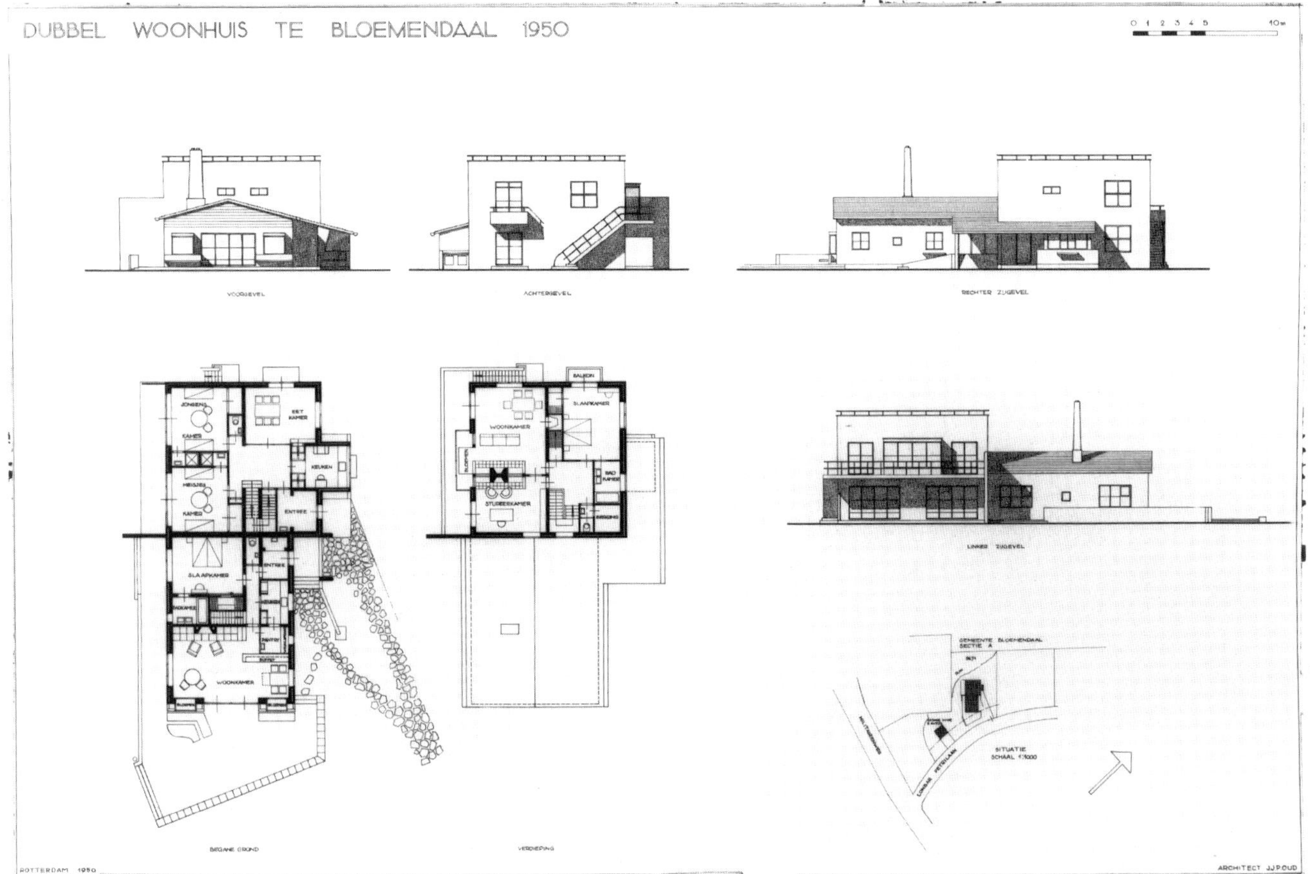


Various design views/ OUDJ-dw 23, NAI, Rotterdam

# 95/ Design for Gatekeeper's Lodge, Hoge Veluwe National Park

**Otterlo** **1957**

In late 1957, Oud designed a gatekeeper's lodge and ticket booth for the Stichting Nationaal Park De Hoge Veluwe. As it was intended to be the main entrance to the Park, the latter's administrators were keen to acquire a good-looking building that *could hold its own amongst the other architectural work on the Hoge Veluwe and in terms of architecture considerable care could be spent on it.*[1] Oud designed a forester's hut along the lines of his designs for the Bio Convalescent Centre (cat. no. 106) and the house for E. Plate (cat. no. 96). The two-storey building was orthogonal in plan, had a shed roof, steel-framed ribbon windows and several small balconies. On the left side was a small annexe for ticket sales. Brick walls beside the building defined a small square that linked up with the original entrance gate a little way behind. Oud made several colour schemes, all based on white walls with areas of primary colours. Oud completed the design in December 1957 and in order to reduce the costs, came to an agreement with the contractor of the nearby Bio Convalescent Centre that the two could be built at the same time. However, permission from the Ministries of Culture and Finance to actually start building was so long in coming that this proved impossible and prices had risen so much in the meanwhile that the original tenders were rendered obsolete. In July 1960 it was finally decided to cancel the whole plan.

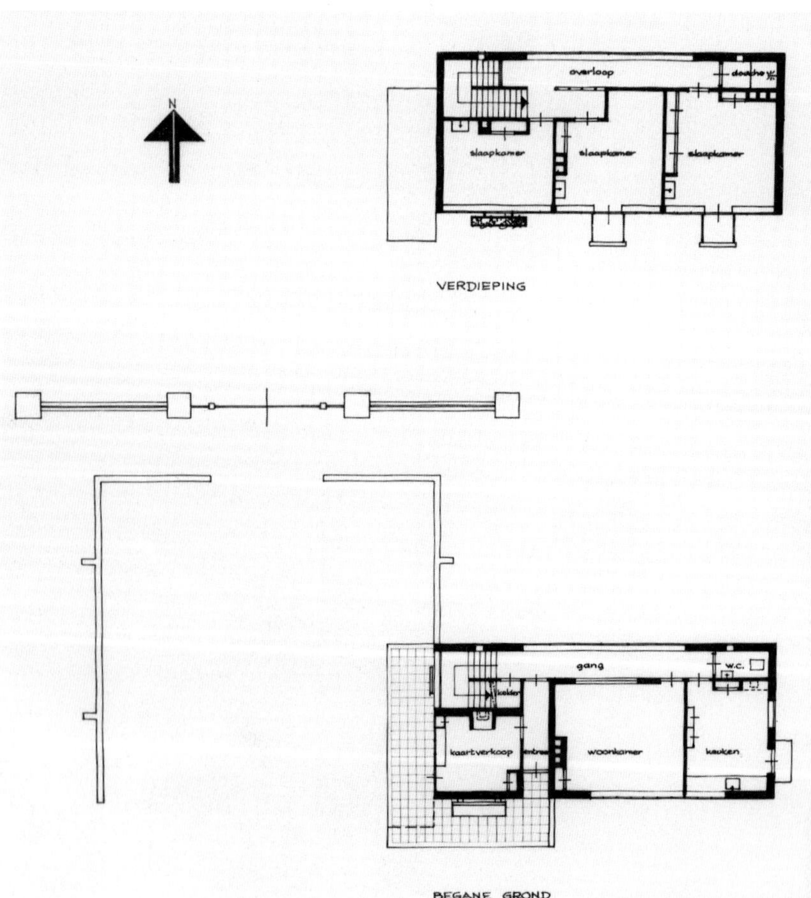


**Plans of ground floor (bottom) and upper floor (top)/ Oud Archive, library, NAI, Rotterdam (Photo E. van Ojen)**



**Notes**

**1.** J.J.P. Oud to J.H. van Tuil, 23 July 1960, OUDJ-B, NAI, Rotterdam.

**Sources**

CCA: dr1984: 0474-0475, dr1985: 0280-0282
Getty: 890126-31**
NAI: OUDJ-ow 1-25, OUDJ-ow 1001, OUDJ-ph 1636-1637, MAQV 376, OUDJ-B

**Literature**

*De Hoge Veluwe, 60 jaar natuur, cultuur en architectuur*, 1995

## 95/ Design for Gatekeeper's Lodge, Hoge Veluwe National Park

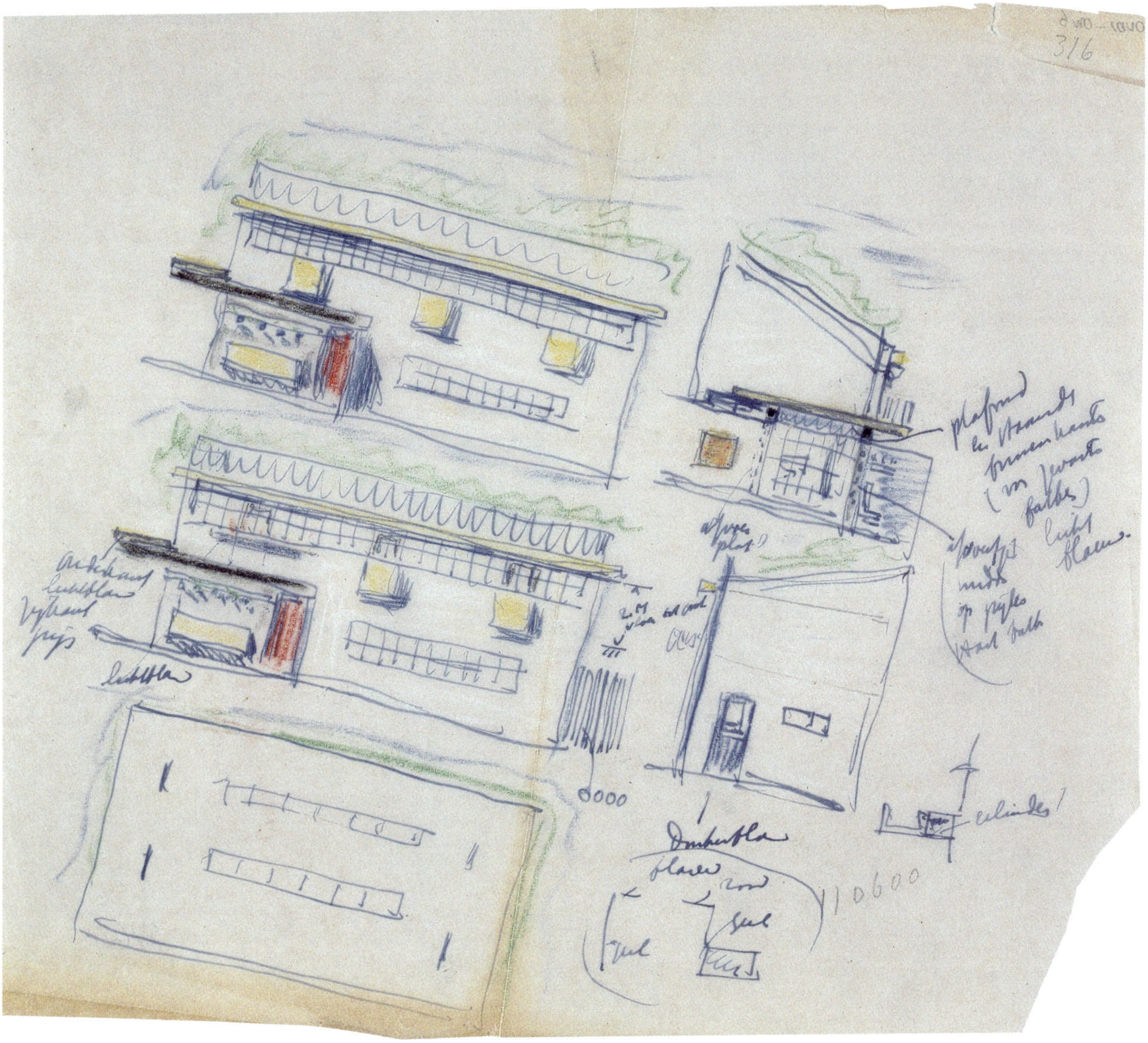

Facade sketches/ OUDJ-ow 6, NAI, Rotterdam

Perspective/ OUDJ-ow 25, NAI, Rotterdam

## 96/ Design for Plate House

**Voorburg, Park Leeuwenstein** **1960**

In 1960, as a friendly gesture, Oud designed a house for E. Plate, the son of his former director at the Rotterdam Woningdienst. The design, for a spacious lot in leafy surroundings, has several features in common with the various design studies for houses Oud made in the 1930s (cat. nos. 72, 77 and 78): the contrast between the closed street facade and open garden side, the colourful presentation, and the two interlocking volumes. Plate thought the proposal too expensive and since Oud felt that a cheaper solution could only be achieved by making a completely new plan, he decided to withdraw.

Perspective/ OUDJ-pl 66, NAI, Rotterdam

Perspective/ OUDJ-pl 65, NAI, Rotterdam

## 96/ Design for Plate House

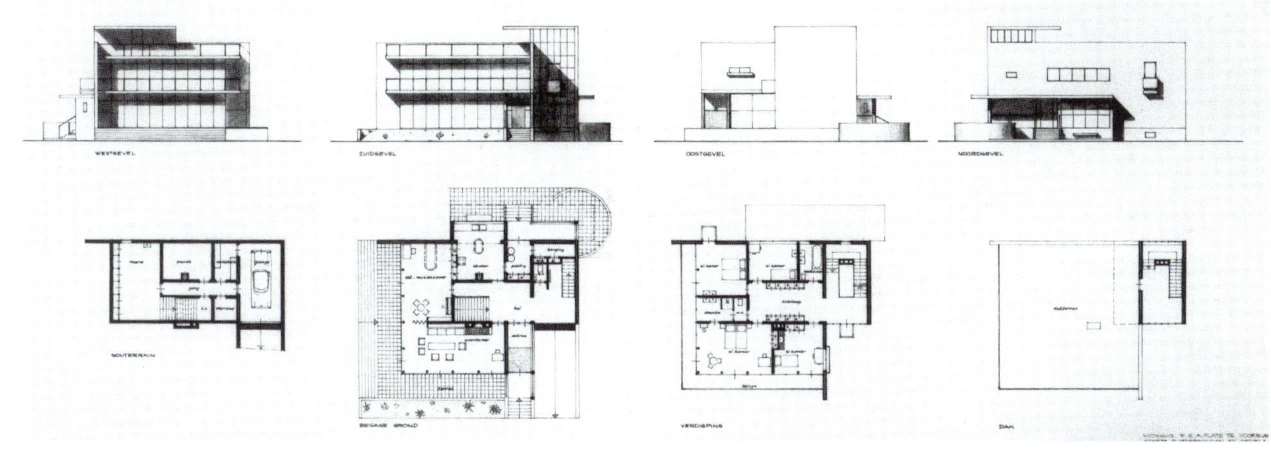


Compilation/ OUDJ-pl 58, NAI, Rotterdam

Model/ MAQV-377, NAI, Rotterdam



**Sources**
Getty: 890126-29**
NAI: OUDJ-pl 1-66, OUDJ-pl 1001, OUDJ ph 1638-1640, OUDJ-ph 3001, MAQV 377, OUDJ-B

**Articles**
J.J.P. Oud 'Tradition in einem Einfamilienhaus', in: *Traditionen, Jahrbuch Freie Akademie der Künste*, Hamburg 1961

**Literature**
U. Barbieri, *J.J.P. Oud*, Rotterdam 1987, p. 187
H.E. Oud, *J.J.P. Oud. Architekt 1890-1963. Feiten en herinneringen gerangschikt*, The Hague 1984, pp. 194-195
G. Stamm, *J.J.P. Oud. Bauten und Projekte 1906 bis 1963*, Mainz, Berlin 1984, p. 139

This house was designed in 1960 for a family of a husband, a wife and two sons.
In the basement there is a garage underneath the staircase and, next to it, a small workshop, a hobby room.
In addition, there is a spare room – accessible from the hall by a wide staircase – that can be used as a playroom for the children, as a spare room, or as a dressing room when there are many guests etc.
Finally there is a pantry in the basement with a dumbwaiter, a wine cellar and the central heating boiler.
On the ground floor one enters the hall; the rooms are arranged round it. The living room and the dining room (also the music room) are separated by a folding partition. The outside walls of these rooms are glass walls looking out on a terrace that lies about one metre above the surrounding garden.
The kitchen, with a serving hatch to the dining room, has a connection with a pantry and a store room.
Behind the kitchen there is a terrace for the kitchen staff and a low round wall, behind which buckets etc. can be shifted out of the way: at the same time they can work out in the open.
The first floor has four bedrooms, a shower closet, a toilet and a bathroom arranged round the hall. All the way around – above the ground floor terrace – there is a balcony.
The staircase leads all the way up to the roof, where sunbathing is an option.
The following materials were selected: for the exterior walls coloured glazed bricks, mainly blue and yellow, to the basement black. Casements, windows and doors: aluminium with double glazing. Floors in the hall and the spare room: coloured floor tiles.
The facades facing north and east have been made as 'open' as possible, for climatic reasons, and otherwise the house has been designed as a fairly closed building.
The size of the house is about 1200 $m^3$.
The cost of construction is about 150,000 guilders (165,000 DM)

# 97/ Competition Design for the Head Office of Nederlandse Hoogovens & Staalfabrieken

**IJmuiden/Velsen** **1947-1948**

In 1947, the Koninklijke Nederlandse Hoogovens en Staalfabrieken (Royal Dutch Blast Furnaces and Steel Factories, KNHS) at IJmuiden invited four architects to design a new head office building. Although the building was to be realized in several stages, the brief stipulated that it should have a distinct presence as from the completion of the first section. Oud's rivals on this occasion were W.M. Dudok, D. Roosenburg and H.T. Zwiers. The location was a site near the factory, which already contained several sheds and which was bisected by the main access road of the complex. Dudok and Zwiers decided to put all departments together in a single building placed athwart the main road. The monumental gateway buildings so produced were well received by the KNHS. Oud and Roosenburg broke the design up into a main building, located along the main road, and several smaller buildings (for the design and construction office, for example) and a car park located on another part of the site. Oud's main building stood with its side elevation facing the main road and the front facade at right angles to it. He employed a concrete frame which allowed for a freely subdivisible building that could be built in three phases. Although the board acknowledged that Oud had made optimum use of the available space, his plan was not considered sufficiently impressive-looking. The commission was awarded to Dudok, whose building had a monumental appearance even in a partially completed state.

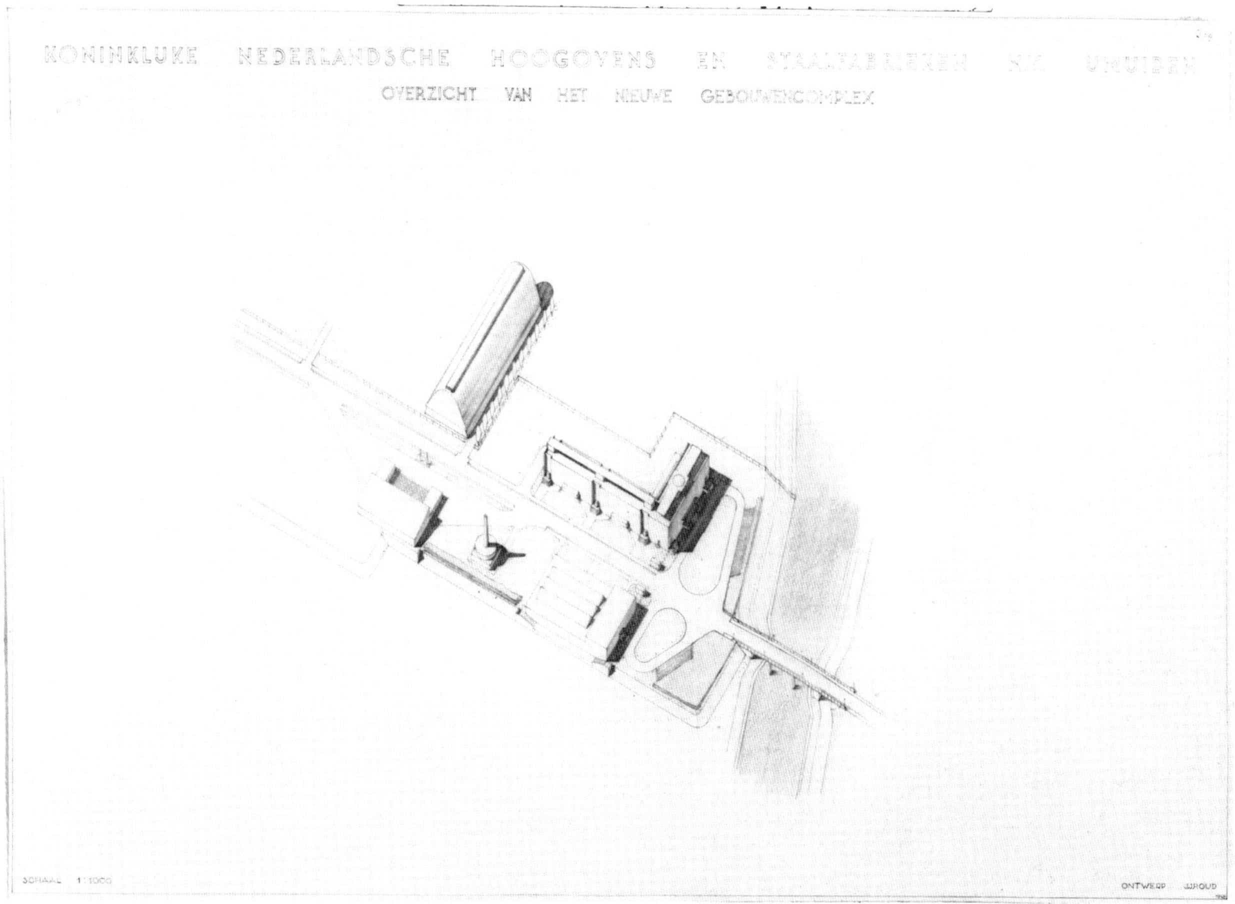

Isometric projection of site/ OUDJ-ho 1, NAI, Rotterdam

Perspective main facade office building/ OUDJ-ho 12, NAI, Rotterdam



**Sources**
CCA: dr1984: 0348-0349, ph1984: 0881, ph1984: 1132
Getty: 890126-24**
Hoogovens Archive
NAI: OUDJ-ho 1 – 40, OUDJ-ph 995 –1024

**Articles**
J. de Jager, W. van Someren, 'Hoofdkantoor Hoogovens', in: *Forum*, 5(1950)10, pp. 388-395
C. Wolterbeek, 'Het nieuwe Hoofdkantoor der Hoogovens', in *De Ingenieur*, 62(1950)52, pp. A581-A582

**Literature**
U. Barbieri, *J.J.P. Oud*, Rotterdam 1987, p. 152
H. van Bergeijk, *W.M. Dudok. Architect-stedebouwkundige 1884-1974*, Naarden 1995, p. 291-294
H.E. Oud, *J.J.P. Oud. Architekt 1890-1963. Feiten en herinneringen gerangschikt*, The Hague 1984, p. 239
G. Stamm, *J.J.P. Oud. Bauten und Projekte 1906 bis 1963*, Mainz, Berlin 1984, p. 133

## 98/ Main and Service Buildings for the Dutch Reformed Church

**The Hague, Oostduinlaan/ Wassenaarseweg** **1949-1959**

In 1946, the Stichting Oostduin, a foundation representing the General Synod of the Dutch Reformed Church, the Central Church Council and the Reformed Church of The Hague, purchased fourteen hectares of land on the edge of The Hague with a view to building a religious centre. Each of the four components of the complex was to be designed by a different architect: H.T. Zwiers was approached to design the nursing home, J.F. Berghoef the old people's home and F.A. Eschauzier the retreat house-cum-conference centre; to Oud fell the honour of designing the main building and associated administration buildings. The unbuilt portion of the site was designated as a publicly accessible urban park. Inside the main building, the suites of offices occupied by the three initiators of the scheme were to be clearly separated from one another, but the section with halls and meeting rooms was for joint use. Oud produced two sketches, one for the central section of the site and another for one of the corners. The centrally located building was a linear sequence of volumes, the highest rising to four storeys. The alternative was more compact and had six floors. The client preferred the first solution but thought it was too big and too expensive so that Oud was obliged to design a smaller version. However, his proposal did not find favour with the advisory committee whose task it was to vet development plans in the Province of South Holland. *We consider the location and massing of the synod building designed by architect Oud to be unacceptable. Not only does the long mass divide the handsome property into several small pieces, which in our view amounts to a total sacrifice of the natural beauty of the country estate, but the superb north-west park corner is also compromised in an unacceptable fashion. We therefore find that a more compact, perhaps slightly higher building volume, is to be preferred for the synod building.*[1]
Oud did not agree. *I regard the Committee's proposal, namely to build higher, as quite unacceptable. I am very happy with the position as it presently determined. ...I embarked on this task with great pleasure and believe that I can make something of consequence for you. Now that the original intention is gradually starting to be diluted, however, I miss something of the "strength" that could have made this centre so spiritually significant. I greatly regret this. It is also why also I vigorously oppose proposed changes to the big building.*[2] Despite the support of the client and his colleagues, Oud felt compelled to return the commission in 1959. By then, lack of money had obliged the client to sell off part of the site and it would have been virtually impossible to reach a satisfactory spatial solution on the remaining piece of land.

Perspective/ OUDJ-dg 91, NAI, Rotterdam

## 98/ Main and Service Buildings for the Dutch Reformed Church

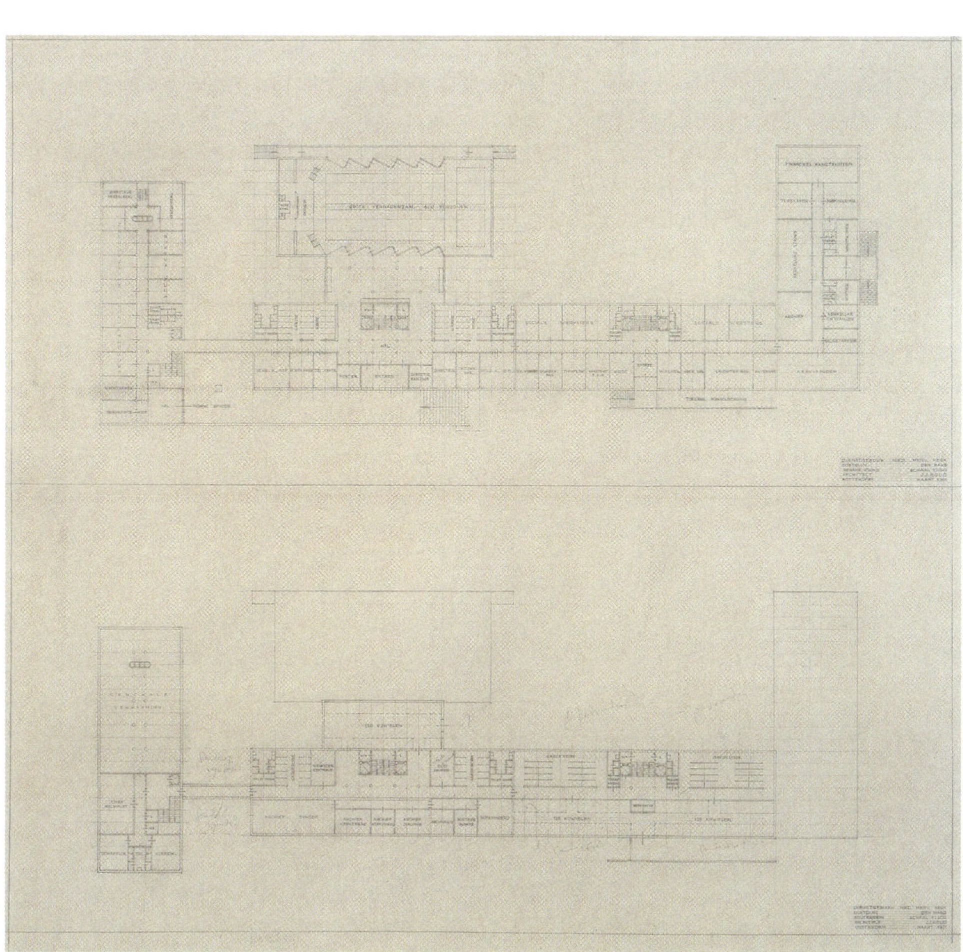

Plans/ OUDJ-dg 93, NAI, Rotterdam



**Notes**

**1.** Provinciale Commissie voor de Uitbreidingsplannen in Zuid-Holland to J.F. Berghoef, 4 August 1953, OUDJ-B, NAI, Rotterdam.

**2.** J.J.P. Oud to De Kock van Leeuwen, 8 August 1953, OUDJ-B, NAI, Rotterdam.

**Sources**

CCA: dr1984: 0472
NAI: OUDJ-dg 1-148, OUDJ-dg 1001, OUDJ-dg 3001, OUDJ-ph 1357-1360, OUDJ-B

**Articles**

'Op "Oostduin" zal iets groots worden verricht', *De Rotterdammer*, 1 May 1948, p. 4
*Kerkelijk centrum op landgoed Oostduin*, n.y., n.p. (D1.20)

**Literature**

U. Barbieri, *J.J.P. Oud*, Rotterdam 1987, pp. 152-153
H.E. Oud, *J.J.P. Oud. Architekt 1890-1963. Feiten en herinneringen gerangschikt*, The Hague 1984, p. 164
G. Stamm, *J.J.P. Oud. Bauten und Projekte 1906 bis 1963*, Mainz, Berlin 1984, p. 139

# 99/ Esveha Office/Warehouse

**Rotterdam, 25 Delftsestraat** **1947-1950**

When the Hague-based stationary wholesaler Esveha decided to build a new office/warehouse in Rotterdam, Oud was engaged as 'aesthetic consultant' working alongside the Rotterdam architect H. Breur C.M.Gzn. Oud was supposed to concentrate on the front and rear elevations and the 'broad outlines of the interior work'.[1] In reality, however, Oud designed the whole complex. The preliminary design was ready by December 1947 and the building was completed in 1950. Oud projected the showroom in the basement while the ground floor was occupied by the dispatch office, storerooms, offices and sales area. The first floor contained the flat for the caretaker couple and one storeroom; the rest of the storerooms were on the floor above. The composition of the front and rear facades displayed similarities with the BIM building: full-height pilasters divided the facade into eight bays.[2] Between the pilasters on every floor were eight identical aluminium window units, an innovation for those days; an alternative arrangement of clustered windows was dropped. The roof had a shallow overhang while the base took the form of a granite plinth.

When the reconstruction supervisor for this area demanded that the designer of the adjoining building, for the Warmond company, model his design on the Esveha facade, Oud rebelled. He sought support from the client, appealing to the latter's business interests. *A while ago I noticed that the appearance of the Esveha building has been seriously marred because the authorities – in an access of sensitivity – have ordered the neighbour to conform. ...As a result, the autonomy of the Esveha building (and in my view it is also in your commercial interest that it should continue to speak for itself) has been severely prejudiced. ...Warmond would be better served by this solution, too, for at the moment it is as if their volume is part of yours.* [3]

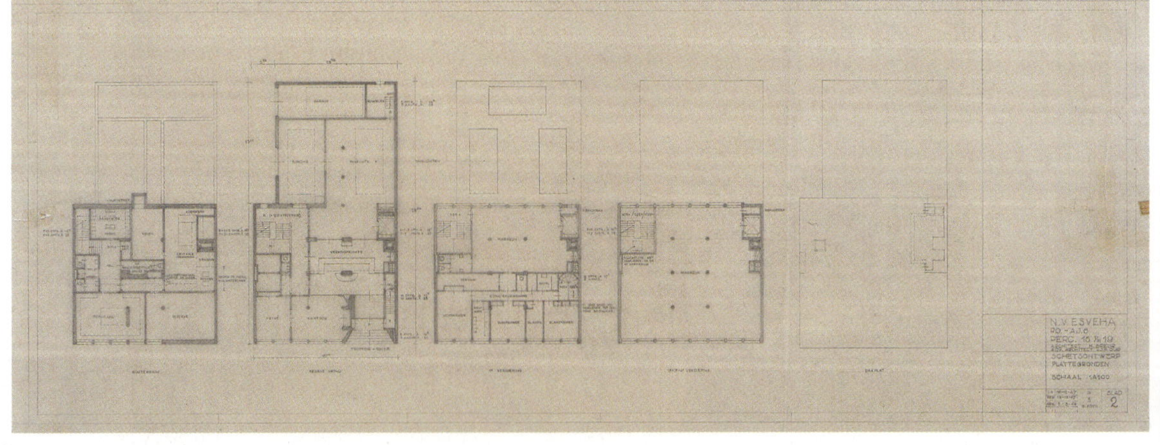


Plans/ OUDJ-es 32, NAI, Rotterdam



**Notes**

**1.** A.C.G. Hartog to J.J.P. Oud, 30 October 1947, OUDJ-B, NAI, Rotterdam.
**2.** Oud himself referred to these columns on one of the sketches as 'BIM columns', OUDJ-B, NAI, Rotterdam.
**3.** J.J.P. Oud to H. Zadoks, 14 October 1955, OUDJ-B, NAI, Rotterdam.

**Sources**

CCA: ph1984: 0882, ph1984: 1133-ph1984: 1139
Gemeentearchief Rotterdam: working drawings
NAI: OUDJ-es 1-38, OUDJ-es 1001, OUDJ-es 3001, OUDJ-ph 962-989, OUDJ-ph 1743-1745, OUDJ-ph 1854-1855, OUDJ-B

**Articles**

'Building in the Netherlands', in: *The Journal of the Royal Institute of British Architects*, 60(1953)5
J. Niegemann, 'Baubrief eines hollandischen Architekten' in: *Vom Bauen in Holland*, offprint (?) from *Der Bauhelfer*, 1949, pp. 495-502

**Literature**

U. Barbieri, *J.J.P. Oud*, Rotterdam 1987, p. 156
D. Broekhuizen, *De Stijl toen / J.J.P. Oud nu*, Rotterdam 2000, pp. 112-119
H.E. Oud, *J.J.P. Oud. Architekt 1890-1963. Feiten en herinneringen gerangschikt*, The Hague 1984, p. 153
G. Stamm, *J.J.P. Oud. Bauten und Projekte 1906 bis 1963*, Mainz, Berlin 1984, pp. 132-133

Rear elevation/ OUDJ-ph 975, NAI, Rotterdam (Photo J. Vrijhof)

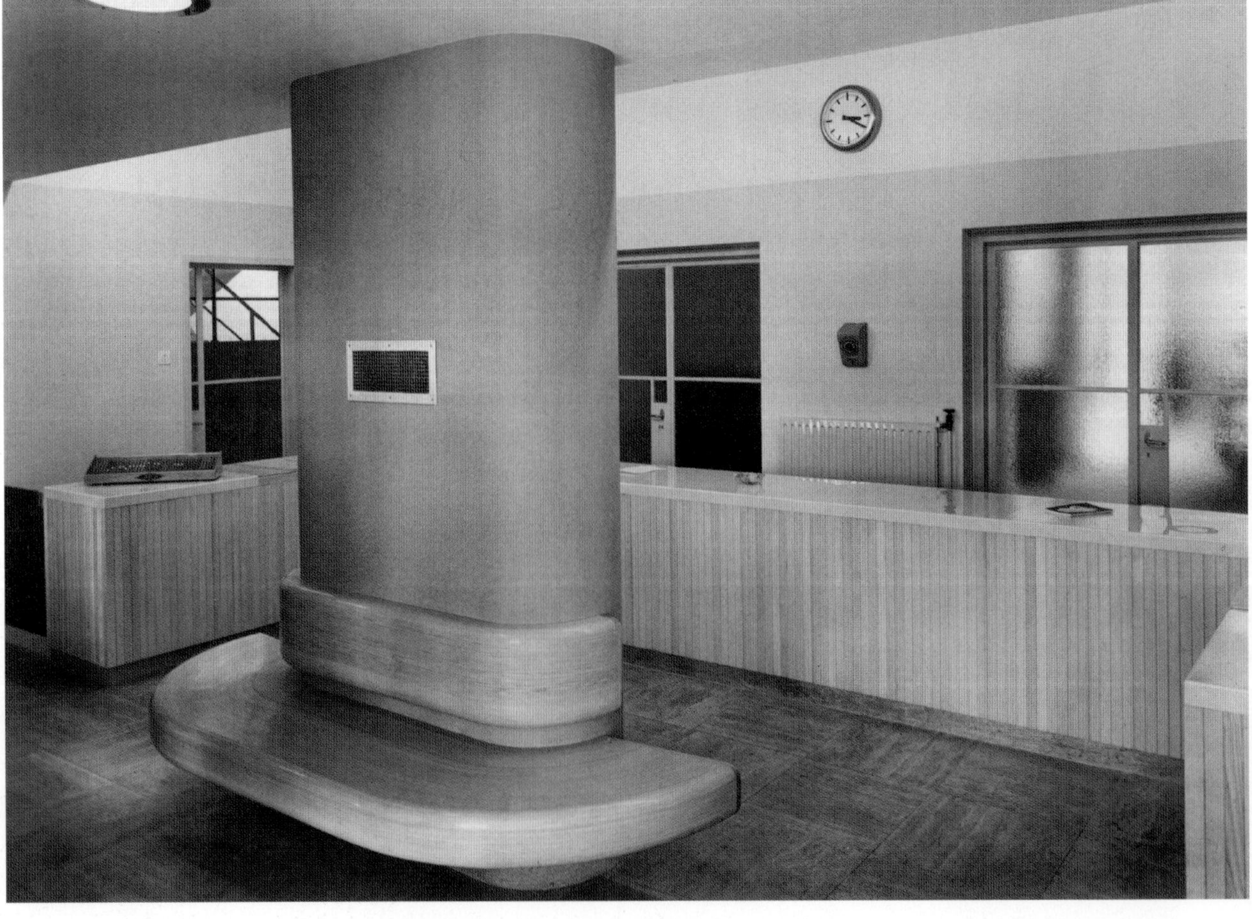

Main hall/ OUDJ-ph 985, NAI, Rotterdam (Photo J. Vrijhof)

Front elevation/ OUDJ-ph 988, NAI, Rotterdam (Photo J. Vrijhof)

# 100 Facade NV Chemische Industrie De Adelaar Office

**Apeldoorn, 16 Kanaal Zuid**

**1950-1952**

In 1950, Oud designed a new facade for the office of the De Adelaar chemical factory in Apeldoorn. On the assumption that the client would provide for 'a reliable builder' to take care of the technical aspects of the design on the spot, he declined to supervise the work himself. He did, however, declare his willingness to defend the design if necessary before the Schoonheidscommissie (local aesthetic review committee).[1] Oud had initially planned to execute the facade in grey Waal bricks and fair-faced concrete lintels. When this material turned out to be unavailable, he settled on a 'reddish facing brick'. It was two years after the design was finished before the facade was completed.

OUDJ-ph 1372, NAI, Rotterdam

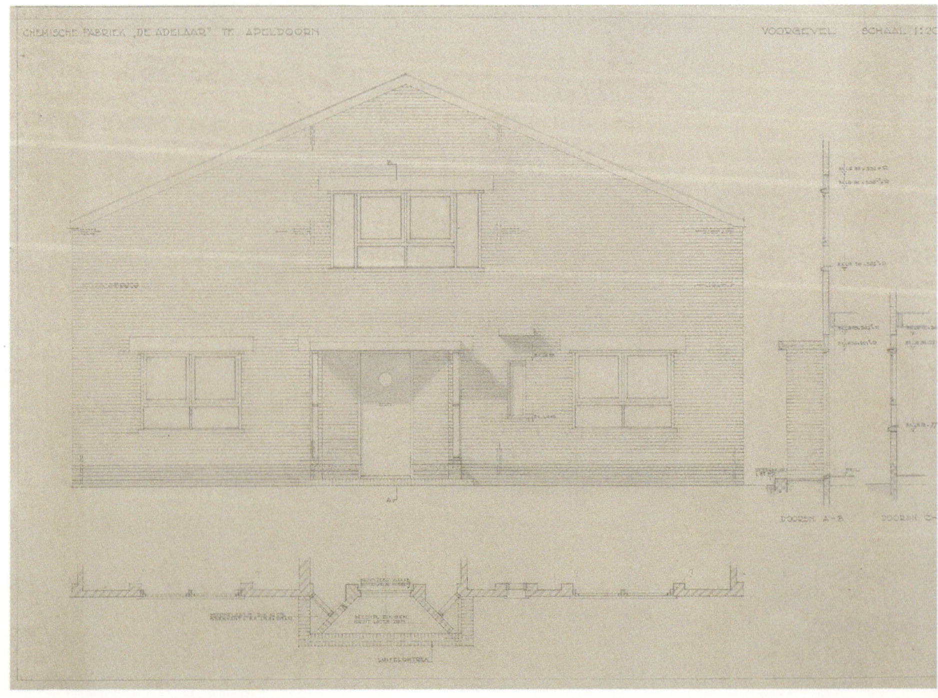


Design for facade/ OUDJ-ad 1, NAI, Rotterdam



**Notes**

**1.** J.J.P. Oud to A.B. Huber, 27 December 1950, OUDJ-B, NAI, Rotterdam.

**2.** J.J.P. Oud to A.B. Huber, 13 November 1951, OUDJ-B, NAI, Rotterdam.

**Sources**

NAI: OUDJ-ad 1-2, OUDJ-ad 1001, OUDJ-ph 1370-1379, OUDJ-B

# 101 Design for Development on Velperplein in Arnhem

**Arnhem, Velperplein**

**1951-1953**

At the end of 1951, Oud was approached by the Nationale Levensverzekingsbank to make a preliminary design for a plot of land the company had its eye on. The function of the new building had not yet been decided and depended on the conditions laid down by Arnhem city council. While waiting for the outcome, Oud made a few studies of the most appropriate development for the location. In the event, the negotiations over the purchase of the plot came to nothing and Oud refused a request to make a plan for a plot elsewhere in Arnhem.

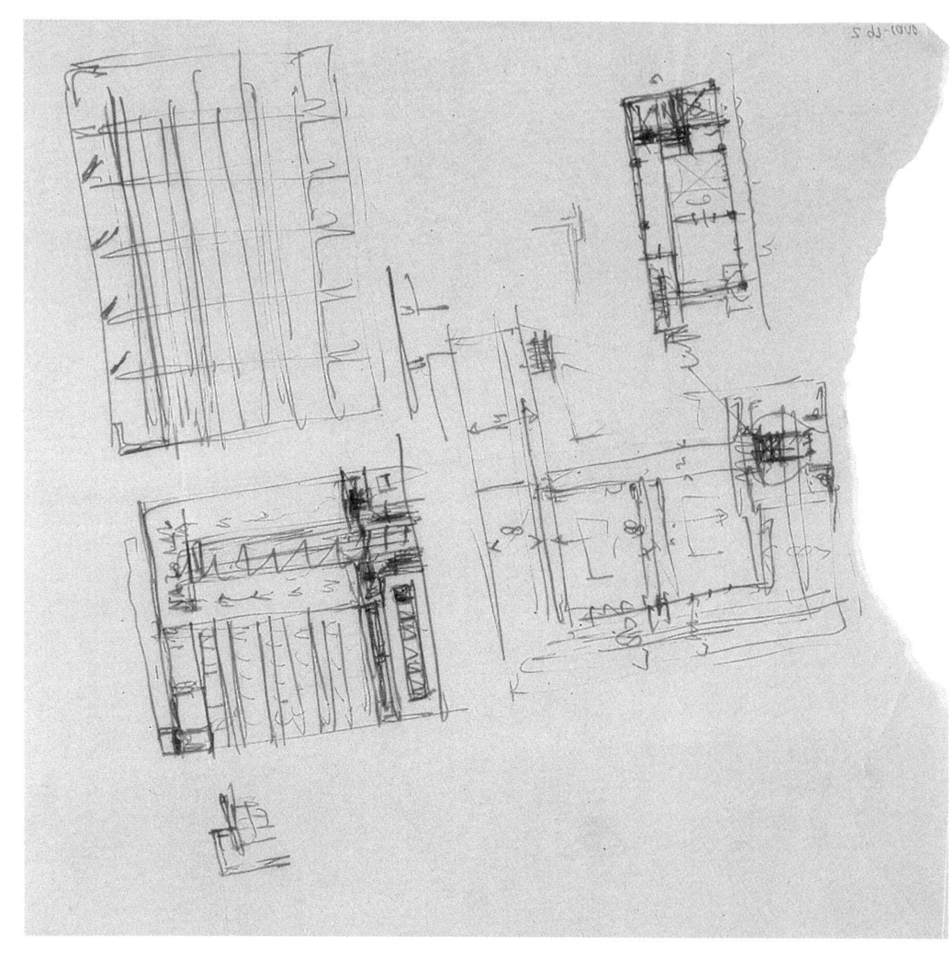

Sketches/ OUDJ-lb 2, NAI, Rotterdam



**Sources**
NAI: OUDJ-lb 1-2, OUDJ-lb 1001

# 102 Competition for Zuid-Holland Provinciehuis

**The Hague, Benoordenhoutseweg, Koningskade** **1951-1952**

In 1950, the Province of South Holland decided to build itself a new office complex. As well as replacing the bomb-damaged building on Korte Voorhout and accommodating two provincial services (the registry office and the department of transport and communications) currently occupying a number of houses, the new provincial headquarters was to include an official residence for the provincial governor. At the urging of the BNA (Royal Institute of Dutch Architects), an advisory committee was set up to supervise the building plans. It consisted of P.F.O.R. Sickinghe (Steward of the Royal Palaces), G. Friedhoff (government architect), J. Leupen (chief architect, Amsterdam) and the architect S. van Ravesteyn. The BNA also recommended holding a competition among a select group of architects drawn from different parts of the country. The invited architects were J.J.P. Oud, based in Rotterdam, W.S. van de Erve and M.P.J.H. Klijnen from The Hague, F.P.J. Peutz from Heerlen and J.W.H.C. Pot of Amsterdam.
The proposed location of the new building, the site of a former zoo on the corner of Koningskade and Benoordenhoutseweg, fitted in with the post-war reconstruction plan drawn up by the architect-town planner W.M. Dudok in 1946. Dudok had designed a grid of roads punctuated by a number of 'centres': concentrations of buildings for city, provincial and national government and for cultural facilities (but no obvious main centre). The provincial government cluster had been projected more or less where the provincial government now proposed to build its new quarters.
Oud's design, which more or less toed the building line on Koningskade and Benoordenhoutseweg, formed a fairly solid wall along these busy streets. Its height – four storeys – matched the other buildings on Koningskade and in its final form, the design was dominated by the horizontality of the facade composition which echoed the movement of the urban traffic.[1] The concentration of the building volume at the south-west corner of the site resulted from the request to retain the zoo building at the north-east corner until after the new provincial offices had been built. As Oud himself explained in his commentary on the design, the composition of the building derived in large part from the building programme.[2] The brief called for the governor's residence

Perspective/ OUDJ-pr 18, NAI, Rotterdam

to be placed on the south-east part of the site, close to the ceremonial section containing a State Room and a Salle des Pas Perdus (a reception room). The third main component was a largely autonomous office section for the provincial services which were in turn required to be directly connected to the ceremonial section. This resulted in a main volume along Benoordenhoutseweg (with the ceremonial section in the middle), two office wings (one for each service) at right angles to the main volume on the corner with Koningskade and the governor's residence on the other corner. Oud expressed the various functions in the street facade by means of a slight staggering of the building line and building height, and variation in detailing.

Both in the design commentary and in a brief description of the building written for *The Architectural Review* in England, Oud emphasized the building's 'lightness' which found expression in a number of ways.[3] For example, Oud envisaged a light-coloured brick combined with aluminium frames for the facade, while the building as a whole sat atop a black stone plinth. The State Room on the inner courtyard was raised on slim columns and the first flight of the main staircase leading to the State Room had a glazed support while the stairs themselves, instead of being in line with the main entrance proceeded upwards at a slight angle; above the staircase, the ceiling was punctured by a narrow, irregularly shaped void. At the top of the stairs on the first floor, a narrow corridor led to the State Room. In the Salle des Pas Perdus, which was conceived with large areas of glazing front and back, the floor area was augmented by a balcony suspended from the ceiling on thin, steel columns. Oud referred to this specifically in his article for *The Architectural Review*: *The festival room (between representative hall and dwelling of the governor) has open connection with a large garden (with trees, flowers, pool). The balconies in this room are all "free" from wall: they "sail" – so to see – through space and activate this (especially when there are not so many people). By this free arrangement of the balconies it will not be missed when there are not people on the balconies. They help to give a lively aspect to the room. It gives movement to the ceiling.*[4] The last two sentences

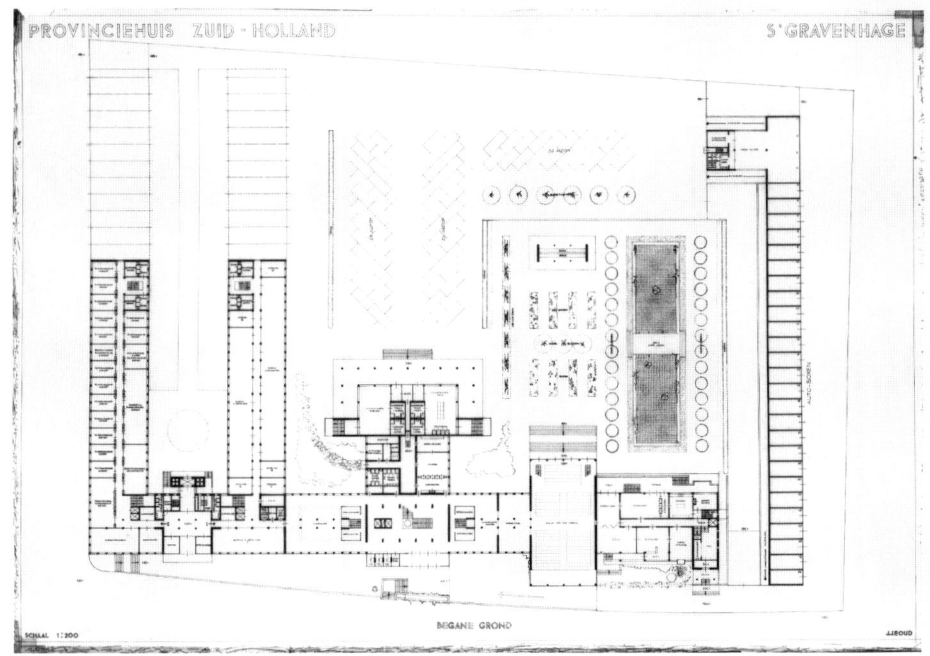


Ground floor plan/ OUDJ-pr 8, NAI, Rotterdam

497

**Notes**

**1.** OUD-pr 1-4, NAI, Rotterdam.

**2.** J.J.P. Oud, 'Toelichting J.J.P. Oud. Provinciehuis te 's-Gravenhage', undated typescript [1952], OUDJ-pr 1001, NAI, Rotterdam.

**3.** J.J.P. Oud, 'Toelichting J.J.P. Oud. Provinciehuis te 's-Gravenhage', undated typescript [1952], OUDj-pr 1001, NAI, Rotterdam; J.J.P. Oud to J.M. Richards, 18 June 1953, with enclosure: 'Description for design for a Governemental Building The Hague', OUDJ-pr 1001, NAI, Rotterdam.

**4.** J.J.P. Oud, 'Description for design for a Governemental Building The Hague', OUDJ-pr 1001, NAI, Rotterdam.

**5.** For the jury report see: H.G.J. Schelling, 'Plannen voor nieuw Provinciehuis van Zuid-Holland te 's-Gravenhage. Opmerkingen naar aanleiding van de meervoudige opdracht', in: *Bouwkundig Weekblad*, 71(1953)21-22, pp. 165-177.

**6.** H.G.J. Schelling, 'Plannen voor nieuw Provinciehuis van Zuid-Holland te 's-Gravenhage. Opmerkingen naar aanleiding van de meervoudige opdracht', in: *Bouwkundig Weekblad*, 71(1953)21-22, pp. 165-177, 168-169.

**7.** J.J.P. Oud to S. van Ravesteyn, 20 February 1953, OUDJ-B, NAI, Rotterdam.

refer to Oud's second aim with this design: to convey a sense of the building's vitality to the users.
None of the entries was entirely to the jury's liking and the detailed report on each design contained a mixture of praise and censure.[5] Klijnen's design was considered daring and spatially interesting but it was criticized for the absence of any functional logic. Oud's design was commended for its facade but not for its plan. Oud was also chided for 'somewhat cramped proportions'. *The architecture is very fine and of an unerring harmony and scale, the pleasing silhouette effect is achieved by natural means. The entrance for the ceremonial section with the built-out glazed volume of the phone booths, topped by massive sculpture, was less favourably rated, however. ...The composition of the prescribed main the spaces in the ceremonial section lacks clarity: the central entrance hall with the apparently floating staircase and lift box comes across as cramped; the stairs to the State Room and the narrow approach lacks distinction.*[6] The design by Peutz, whose building was the most voluminous of all the entries, was praised for its plan and for the spacious and stately (axial) entrance. Although the jury was less happy with the facades, this was the design it chose for implementation.
The rejection of his design was a deep disappointment for Oud. Where he had tried to achieve a new monumental expression with the help of powerful architectural means like construction, space and materials (rather than size or axes), he was accused of employing cramped dimensions. Oud felt misunderstood. He had seized the Provinciehuis commission as an opportunity to pursue his search for a new monumental architecture by way of a large public building. In a letter to Van Ravesteyn he drew a comparison with two other, equally strongly criticized, competition designs: the Rotterdam Exchange (1926) and the design for the Shell Building (1938-1948). He claimed that his competition entries were invariably subject to unjust criticism.[7]
The jury ignored Oud's request to reconsider its verdict. The winner, Peutz, produced a modified design in 1953 based on total building costs of approximately 12 million guilders. In the new design, the tower and the governor's residence were scrapped.

498

**Sources**
CCA: ph1984: 0883-0886
NAI: OUDJ-pr 1-47, OUDJ-pr 1001, OUDJ-pr 3001, OUDJ-ph 1380-1404, OUDJ-ph 1761-1764, OUDJ-ph 1861, OUDJ-B

**Articles**
J.G.E. Luyt, 'Provinciehuis voor Zuid-Holland', in: *Bouw*, 8(1953)10, pp. 179-183
H.G.J. Schelling, 'Plannen voor nieuw Provinciehuis van Zuid-Holland te 's-Gravenhage. Opmerkingen naar aanleiding van de meervoudige opdracht', in: *Bouwkundig Weekblad*, 71(1953)21-22, pp. 165-177
F.H. Warnaars, 'Het provinciehuis van Zuid-Holland', in: *Katholiek Bouwblad*, 20(1953)15, pp. 225-273
F.H. Warnaars, 'Het provinciehuis van Zuid-Holland', in: *De Ingenieur*, 65(1953)38, pp. 179-190

**Literature**
W.M.J. Arets, W.H.J. van den Bergh (et al.), *F.P.J. Peutz. Architect 1916-1966*, Eindhoven 1981, pp. 321-324
U. Barbieri, *J.J.P. Oud*, Rotterdam 1987, p. 157
H. van Bergeijk, *Willem Marinus Dudok*, Naarden 1995, pp. 269-281
I. van Huik, 'Ingebed in het karakteristieke groen. Dudok en Den Haag in de jaren 1930-1950', in: V. Freijser (ed.), *Het veranderend stadsbeeld van Den Haag*, Zwolle 1991, pp. 99-142
H. Oud, *J.J.P. Oud. Architect 1890-1963. Feiten en herinneringen gerangschikt*, The Hague 1984, pp. 167-169
K. Schipper, J. van Geest, *Jos Klijnen*, Rotterdam 1999, pp. 58-63, 124-125
G. Stamm, *J.J.P. Oud. Bauten und Projekte 1906 bis 1963*, Mainz, Berlin 1984, p. 137

# 103 Design for an Extension to Groningen Town Hall

**Groningen, Grote Markt**

**1948**

During the liberation of the northern provinces of the Netherlands in April 1945, the Grote Markt in Groningen was largely destroyed. Only the Martini Tower and Church, J.O. Husly's Classical town hall, the Renaissance Goudkantoor (1635) and the south face of the square survived the fighting, the rest was razed to the ground. The council had wanted to extend the Town Hall even before the war and the devastation seemed to afford an ideal opportunity to realize this ambition. The post-war reconstruction plan of M.J. Granpré Molière, who had risen to prominence in the 1930s as a philosophically inclined theorist of Dutch traditionalism, formed the framework for the first, historicizing design by his pupil J. Vegter. This immediately became an issue in the fierce controversy that flared up around post-war reconstruction in Groningen and that was dominated by the struggle between 'Delft' (traditionalism) and Nieuwe Bouwen (Dutch Functionalism). It was against this discordant background that a local committee, with the blessing of the Chamber of Commerce, invited the architects J.H. Emck and E. Reitsma to develop an alternative, modern plan. Emck consulted Oud about the town hall extension which because of its size, the historicizing style and the awkward integration of the Goudkantoor had become a major bone of contention. It is reasonable to assume that Oud's alternative proposal for the town hall extension dates from this period. In the siting of the volume vis à vis the adjacent street, and the inclusion of a number of shops on the ground floor, Oud's plan is similar to that of Emck and Reitsma. A striking difference is the facade ends which are built out to the front so that the building 'embraces' a little square and the extension acquires a distinctive character. Whether Oud's plan had any official status is unknown. It played no role in the eventual resolution of the town hall issue. Vegter replaced his earlier historicizing sectional design by a modern-looking, white marble block that was linked to both the Goudkantoor and the old town hall by a 'footbridge'.

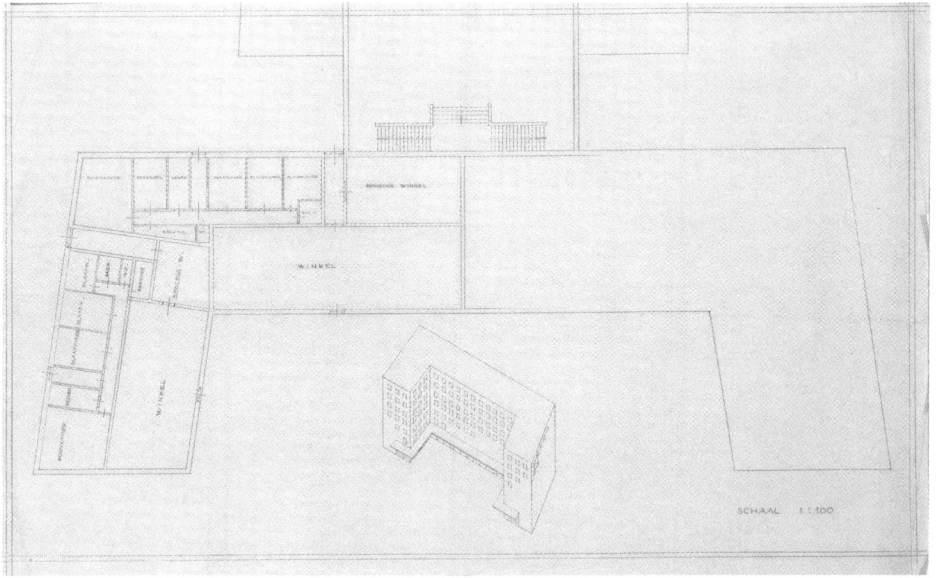


Plan and isometric projection/ OUDJ-rg 1, NAI, Rotterdam

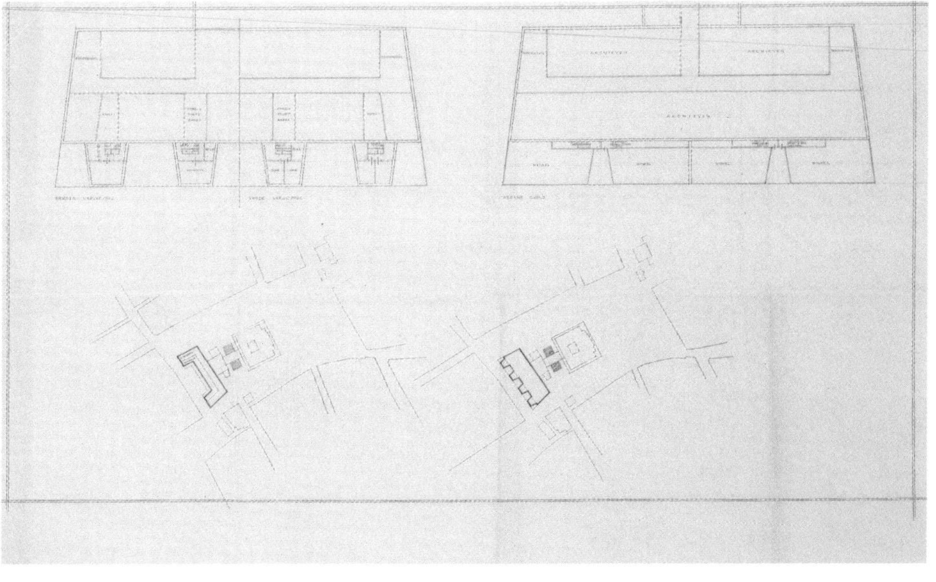

Various design views/ OUDJ-rg 2, NAI, Rotterdam



**Sources**
NAI: OUDJ-rg 1-5

**Literature**
H.E. Oud, *J.J.P. Oud. Architekt 1890-1963. Feiten en herinneringen gerangschikt*, The Hague 1984, p. 235
C. Wagenaar, *Tussen grandezza en schavot. De ontwerpen van Granpré Molière voor de wederopbouw van Groningen*, Groningen 1991, pp. 108-109

# 104 Rhenen Town Hall

**Rhenen, Herenstraat** **1958-1960**

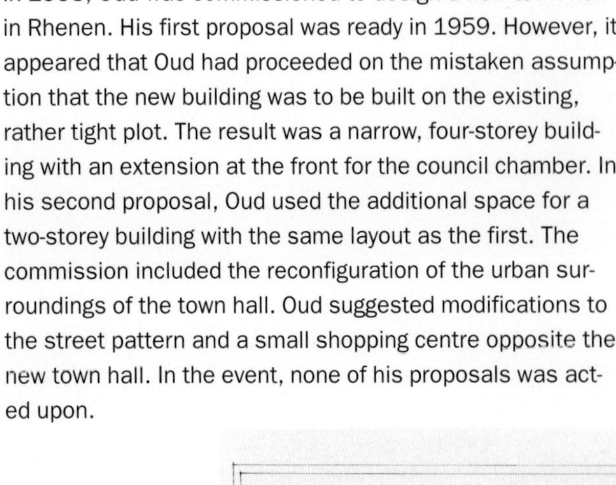

In 1958, Oud was commissioned to design a new town hall in Rhenen. His first proposal was ready in 1959. However, it appeared that Oud had proceeded on the mistaken assumption that the new building was to be built on the existing, rather tight plot. The result was a narrow, four-storey building with an extension at the front for the council chamber. In his second proposal, Oud used the additional space for a two-storey building with the same layout as the first. The commission included the reconfiguration of the urban surroundings of the town hall. Oud suggested modifications to the street pattern and a small shopping centre opposite the new town hall. In the event, none of his proposals was acted upon.

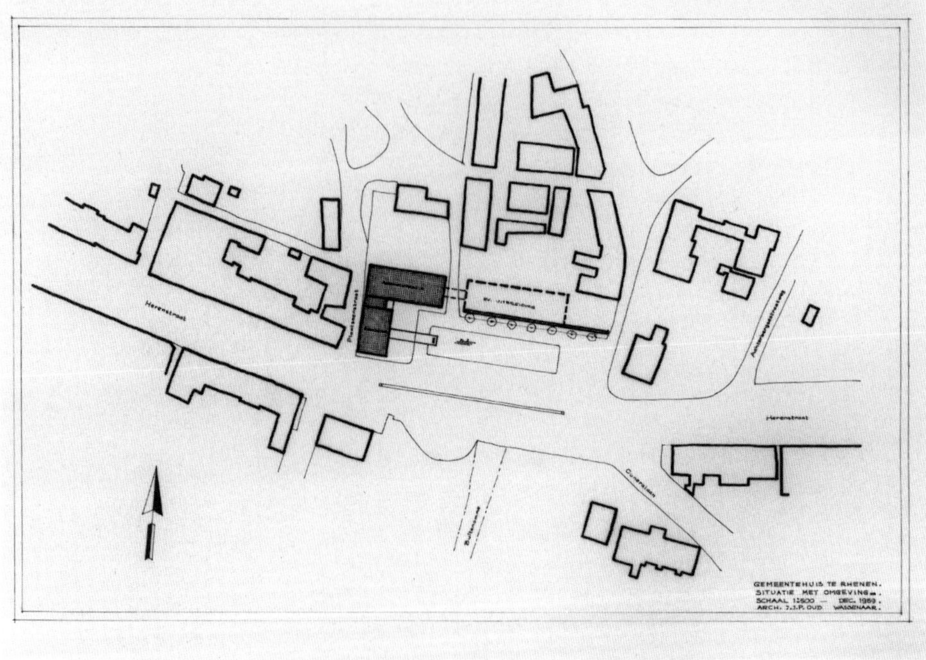


Site plan first design/ OUDJ-rr 26, NAI, Rotterdam

Perspective first design/ OUDJ-rr 23, NAI, Rotterdam

**Sources**
Getty: 890126-box 3, F3
NAI: OUDJ-rr 1-43, OUDJ-rr 1001

**Literature**
H.E. Oud, *J.J.P. Oud. Architekt 1890-1963. Feiten en herinneringen gerangschikt*, The Hague 1984, p. 235

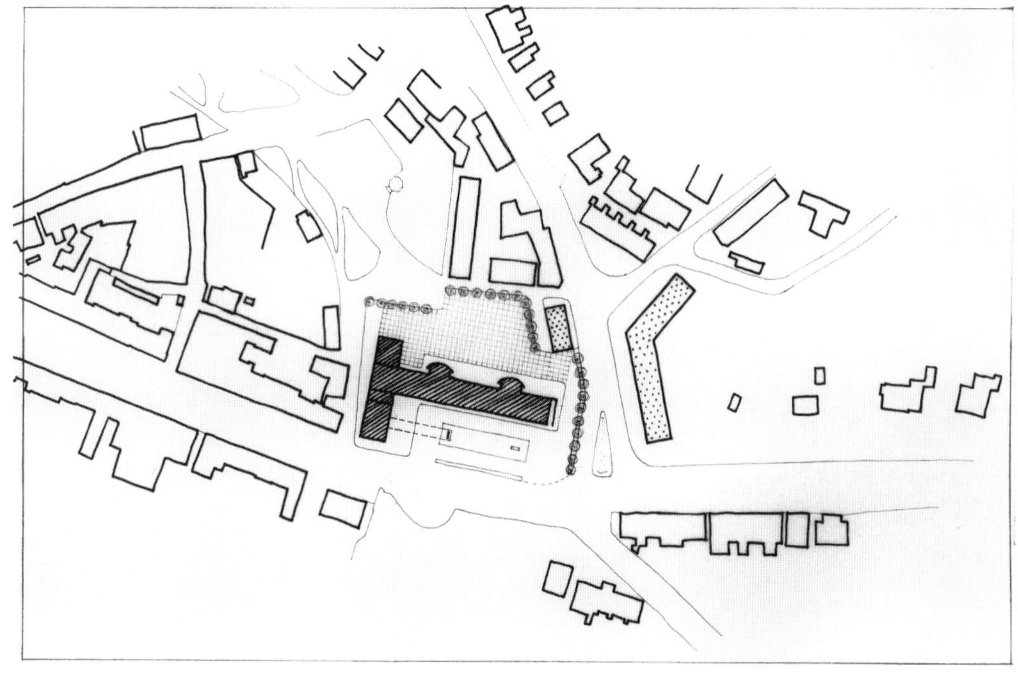

Site plan second design/ OUDJ-rr 22, NAI, Rotterdam

Perspective second design/ OUDJ-rr 18, NAI, Rotterdam

501

J.J.P. Oud to Rhenen town council, 25 February 1960, 890126-30**, Getty Research Institute, Los Angeles

The new Town Hall follows a linear development along the road. The administrative section is located in this longitudinal block (two floors plus a basement), while the Council Chamber (perhaps also wedding room) is located at the head of the forecourt.
The layout of the town hall is briefly as follows:
The recessed corner contains the normal Town Hall entrance with doorman, etc. After the vestibule is a substantial stairhall leading, on the first floor, to the Mayor's room and next to it the wedding room for everyday use (all of this with ancillary spaces etc.). This hall also contains the passage to the service flat behind, while the Council Chamber etc. can be accessed from the front.
The Council Chamber can be used for special wedding events and is accessed from the outside via a canopied entrance. This is also useful for receiving important visitors.
The offices ... are accommodated in the longitudinal volume. The idea is that people will park at the back of the building from where two "service entrances" (with entrance halls) lead to the wide corridors for the public (with waiting areas in these corridors). The busiest departments (located on the ground floor) can thus reached separately from outside.

# 105 Almelo Town Hall

**Almelo, 1 Stadhuisplein** **1962-1973**

When Almelo town council decided in the mid-1950s to build a new town hall, it was naturally keen to engage a competent architect for this prestigious commission. The committee of the council reached the unanimous conclusion that J.J.P. Oud was in every respect the most suitable designer and its proposal was officially endorsed by the full council on 28 June 1962. The sketch plans were already at a fairly advanced stage and there were drawings and a model when Oud died in April 1963. Oud's design envisaged three main sections: a central slab for the administrative departments, a triangular section containing the council chamber, and a low, orthogonal volume with two wedding rooms and a civic reception room. The three aspects of council responsibilities were thus reflected in the building. The council was so enthusiastic about this proposal that it decided to go ahead and build it. Hans Oud and Harm Dethmers were subsequently given the job of developing the design and supervising the construction. Altered circumstances made some modifications to the design inevitable. Financial constraints led to a number of changes, such as the scrapping of the double corridor system that Oud had used satisfactorily in his design for De Utrecht (no. 108). More crucial, however, were the modifications occasioned by the change of location to the site of a former textile factory Palthe. The orientation, effected by rotating the design, was changed. As such, the final building was different from the one conceived by Oud.

Perspective/ OUDJ-sa 31, NAI, Rotterdam



**Sources**
CCA: dr1984: 0441, ph1984: 0893-0894
Gemeentearchief Almelo: Stadhuis Dossier
Getty: 890126-30**
NAI: OUDJ-sa 1-48, OUDJ-sa 3001, MAQV 327

**Articles**
'Industriestad Almelo kreeg een aristocratisch stadhuis', in: *De Tijd*, 17 September 1973

**Literature**
U. Barbieri, *J.J.P. Oud*, Rotterdam 1987, p. 188
M. Kuper, *Het stadhuis van Almelo; Het laatste ontwerp van J.J.P. Oud*, Almelo 1995
H.E. Oud, *J.J.P. Oud. Architekt 1890-1963. Feiten en herinneringen gerangschikt*, The Hague 1984, pp. 195-196
'Raadhuis voor Almelo', in: *Bouw* 19 (1964) 4, p. 126

Perspective/ OUDJ-sa 32, NAI, Rotterdam

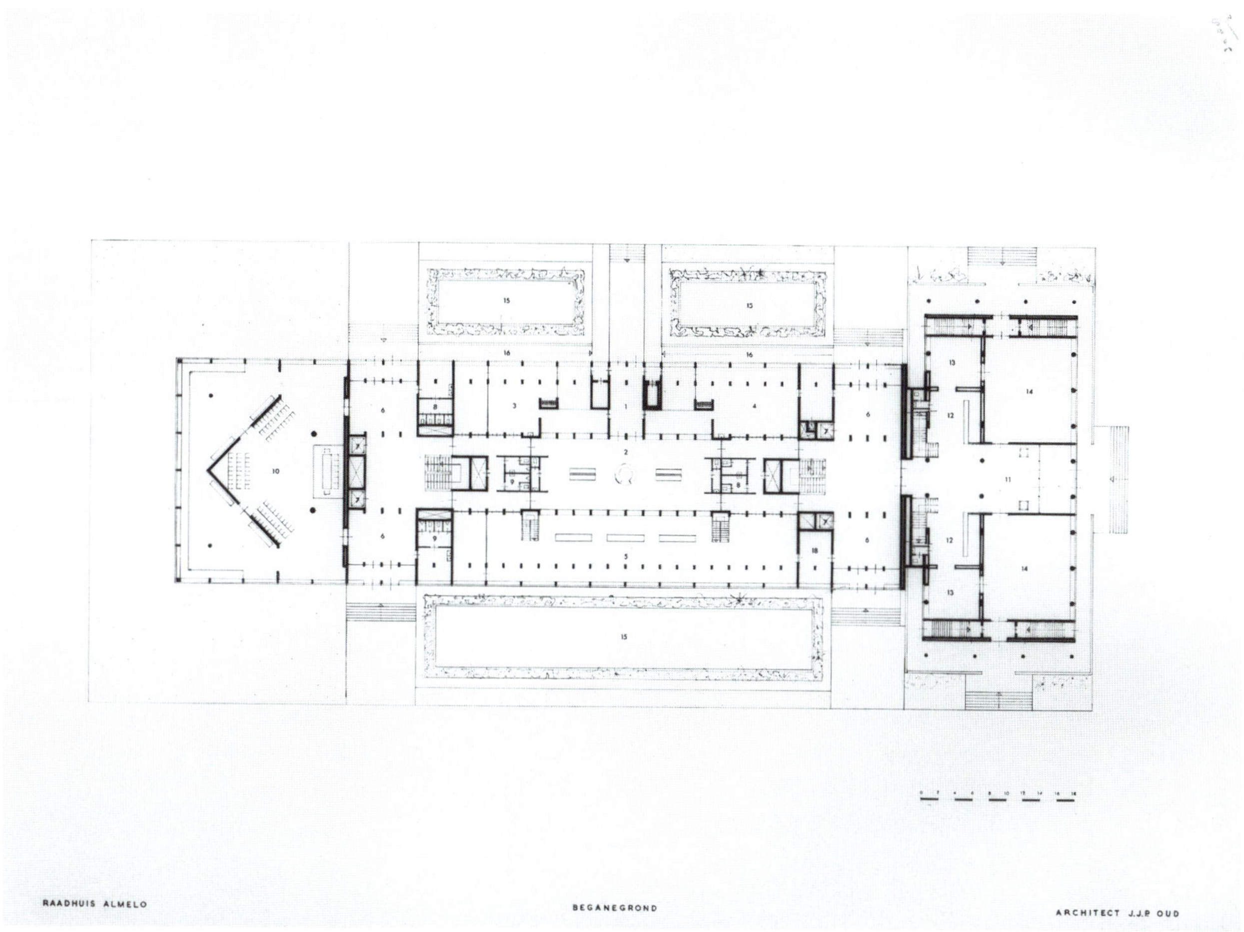

RAADHUIS ALMELO

BEGANEGROND

ARCHITECT J.J.P. OUD

Ground floor plan/ OUDJ-sa 27, NAI, Rotterdam

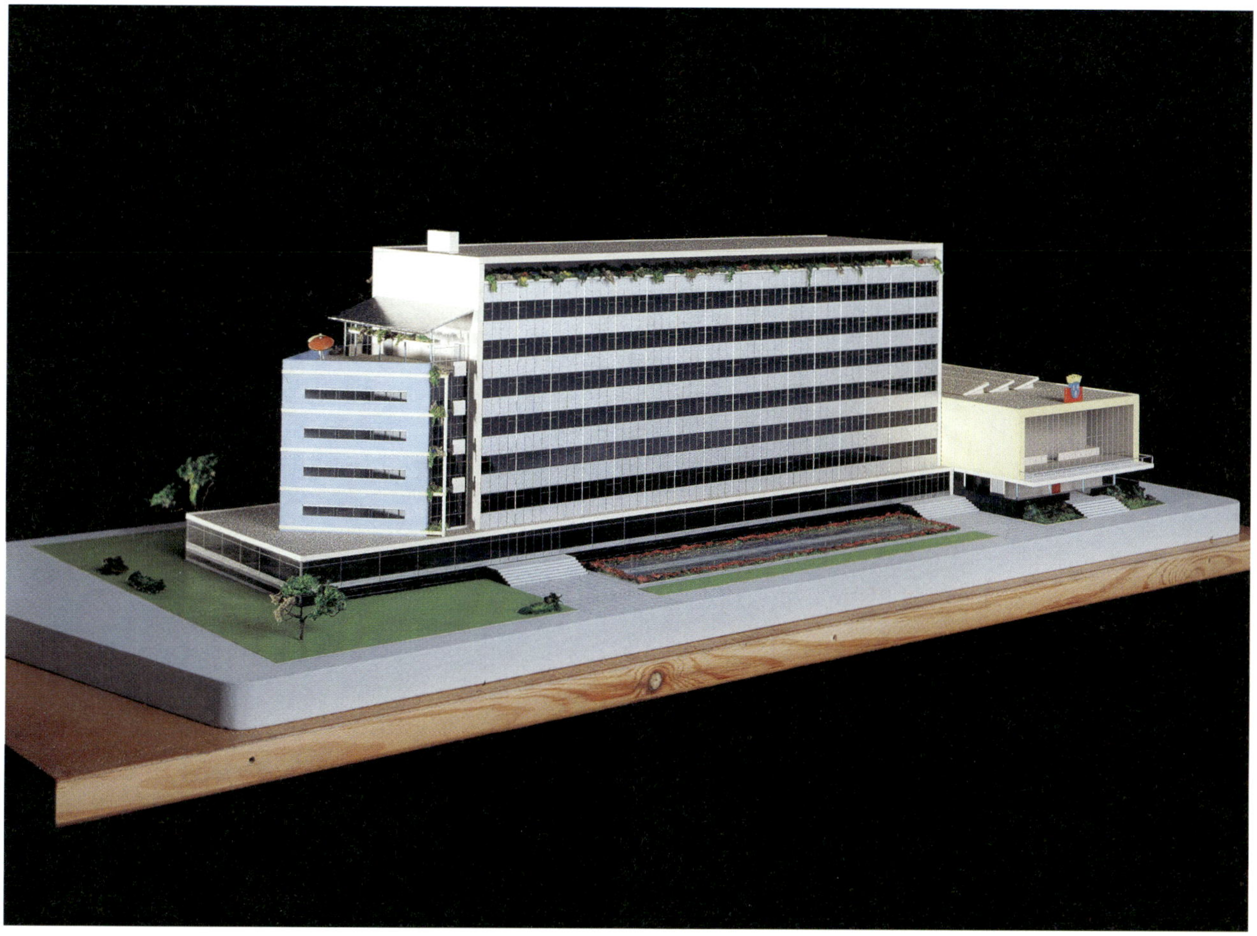

Model/ MAQV-327, NAI, Rotterdam

**Oud in his house in Wassenaar, circa 1961. From: J.J.P. Oud, 'De wereld wordt mooier door meer grote dingen', in: *Visie*, (1961)12**

# *De Stijl* – Then and Now

The criticism and incomprehension that followed the publication of the Shell Building came as a disagreeable surprise to Oud and he saw it as a deliberate attempt to oust him from the history of the Modern Movement. That this movement was now an accepted part of history was evidenced by the many retrospective articles, books and exhibitions devoted to it from the early 1950s, in which echoes of Wölfflin's artistic evolution theory could be heard: modernism was consistently presented as the only appropriate style for the modern world and the logical outcome of a historical process embodied by the work of the generation of pioneers active in the decades following the First World War. Anyone who opposed this process would wind up on the sidelines and place themselves outside modern society. This was the message of a view of history that looked like becoming generally accepted in the 1950s. Its basis had been laid by the movement's own protagonists, in particular Giedion (Oud even talked of a 'Giedion Gang'). In Oud's view the official interpretation reflected the principles of the post-war International Style which he regarded as synonymous with the surrender of the artistic dimension of architecture and the hated axiom of teamwork, two offshoots of the CIAM doctrine for which Giedion and Gropius had laid the basis in the 1920s and which Oud had opposed even then. Since his designs for public buildings in the 1930s, Oud's work had developed in a different direction, as Giedion had duly noted in relation to the competition entry for the new Amsterdam town hall. If this had seemed to be a mere incident at the time, the Shell Building showed that Oud was in earnest. His rich, representational architecture, with its unambiguous reference to Classicism, was patently at odds with post-war, Americanized modernism and consequently not part of its historical evolution. Not only was there no place in modernism's new self-image for Oud's work after the Shell Building, it also seemed as if his historical contribution to the movement in the 1920s was being denied. Oud was not honoured as a founder of modernism: MOMA devoted special exhibitions to Gropius, Le Corbusier and other pioneers, but not to Oud.

Oud fought on several fronts to correct this 'false' image of his person and his work. Whenever he came across what he regarded as an inaccurate account of his contribution to modernism in an article or a book, he would immediately write the author or publisher a stiff letter, often drawing their attention to the general literature of the 1920s and 1930s where he had most certainly been honoured as a pioneer. In his work meanwhile he returned to the roots of his artistic development. Rather than tracing his route backwards from the present, he went straight back to the beginning and from there attempted to reconstruct his artistic evolution. For him the beginning lay in *De Stijl*. After the designs made during the ten years between 1936 and 1946, he also started to refer to *De Stijl* again in his work. The use of colour in particular attested to this, but also the pursuit of reduction (compared with the exuberance of the Shell Building and his design for the Spaarbank) and his attempts to link up with the new avant-garde in the visual arts, in the person of Karel Appel. Finally, he sought a more theoretical, or at least verbal, basis for his present course. The red thread running through all this was the unwavering assertion that his work had never for one moment deviated from the straight line leading back to *De Stijl*. It was not so much a matter of form, he told Bakema, but of spirit. That it should have been Bakema with whom he discussed this matter, was no accident: Bakema was one of the leaders of a revolt within CIAM in which the young guard reminded the established order of the pioneering work from before the war, and accused them of having betrayed its spirit.[1] Oud clearly resented the fact that Bakema recognized this spirit in his earlier work, but not in his post-Shell Building work. *I only wish to point once again to the spirit of the building: you behave, in my opinion, a bit like the geese in the Capitol, who are always pointing to their forefathers in order to prove their own importance. In the process, you use the same few clichéd examples (a few of which you forget, as you would know if you were to go more deeply into the origins of the new building, such as would become clear to you for example from*

*American books of the 1930s). The details of that history are too little known here. Anyway, it's not the examples that matter but the spirit behind them. That is more important than the results. The results keep diverting attention from the spirit.*[2] Again and again Oud insisted on the continuity in his work which, according to him, was imbued from start to finish with the same spirit. And that was the spirit of *De Stijl*. This claim became the starting point for his numerous attempts to reclaim his historical pioneering role.

The most explicit of these was a German-language booklet, *Mein Weg in 'De Stijl'*, written around 1957-1958. Oud wrote the manuscript in German and had it corrected by Kees and Erica de Wit. The booklet was published in 1960 by Nijgh & Van Ditmar. The front cover depicted the 1919 design for the factory at Purmerend and a monogram Oud used in the 1920s. In keeping with Oud's ambition to see *De Stijl* ideas as an ongoing spiritual movement, the text was not confined to the period when Oud identified with the *De Stijl* group, but covered the whole of his oeuvre. Likewise the illustrations. In addition to celebrated projects like the Kiefhoek and Hoek van Holland housing schemes and typical *De Stijl* designs like the Purmerend factory and the Scheveningen Strandboulevard, the book also contained pictures of later projects like the Shell Building, Esveha, the Grebbeberg monument and De Utrecht. On the back cover there was even a drawing (in the same style as the drawing of the factory on the front cover) of the yet-to-be-built Congress Centre in The Hague.

What prompted the writing of this booklet is unknown. It began with an account of how Oud had got to know Theo van Doesburg and Mondrian. This was followed by an introduction sketching the general outlines of *De Stijl*, after which Oud proceeded to justify the manner in which he had applied its principles. This he did with reference to his projects, which were woven into the text in more or less chronological order. When he came to his design for the Shell Building in 1938, Oud emphasized the continuity in his work where others had seen a breaking point. He was in no doubt that the Shell Building was a logical consequence of what had gone before. *When, in 1938, I was given the commission to build the administrative office for Shell Nederland N.V. in The Hague, I accepted it with much pleasure. It gave me the opportunity to try and banish the restlessness I had developed due to those facts. 'Shell' is a company of considerable standing and I did my best to express this in my architectural design. In doing that I had, unwittingly, stirred up a hornets' nest! In the New York magazine, 'Architectural Record', a promoter normally favouring me and my work, a few critics called me a traitor of my own principles, principles they had just started to consider very attractive. Far be it from me to declare that my endeavour to shape architecture with more subtle, varied and expressive qualities was an immediate success. There is some truth in the reproach that I had reverted to my love for aesthetic order and precision, inclining towards the classical.*[3] Even the Shell Building contained traces of *De Stijl* principles, as did his later work. The problem, according to Oud, lay in the fact that *De Stijl* principles had a different meaning in architecture than in visual art. *The means available to architecture do not allow the same freedom in design as do painting and sculpture. These two only have to follow the laws of aesthetics, whereas on the other hand the means employed by an architect must, first and foremost, incorporate realities. If he fails to do that adequately, building becomes anti-social: turning its back on life. Individual, not universal. Failing to 'shape Style (Stijl)'! For that reason architecture cannot focus exclusively on mere proportions and abstract three-dimensional effects, the impasse in which 'De Stijl' initially got stuck. In construction the proportions and the three-dimensional designs should simultaneously serve a useful purpose. Life should be realized in a beautiful form, not just the abstract spirit.*[4] Oud ended his essay with his personal credo: *To find a form for architectural building, based on the new, free aesthetics, to make this form fuse with the social conditions of our times and to allow the external aspect of this form, too, to develop into a type of building that corresponds with today's social existence, consistent with its inherent subtle distinctions.*[5]

Reactions to the book were for the most part positive (leaving aside criticism of the faulty German). It helped that *De Stijl* was very much en vogue around this time. Several Dutch and foreign museums had held or were planning exhibitions about *De Stijl* in which Oud was prominently represented. In 1949, the Stedelijk Museum in Amsterdam had mounted a *De Stijl* exhibition that was subsequently shown in New

York and Rome before concluding at Museum Boymans van Beuningen in Rotterdam in 1951. For the *De Stijl* exhibition held in London in 1958, Oud made some new drawings of his earlier designs. *Mein Weg in 'De Stijl'* was distributed to visitors to an exhibition in Rome in 1960.

With *Mein Weg* the circle closed for Oud. He had returned, not only to the origins of his work, but to the very roots of architecture. There was a direct link from his oeuvre, via *De Stijl*, to the foundations of western culture, to which modern architecture was in his view the most recent contribution. In this respect, too, he was convinced of the continuity and of the slow, big movements in the evolution of art and culture which, despite the radical innovations that were sometimes necessary, continued uninterrupted. The consequence of the great purification at the beginning of the twentieth century was not, as adherents of some post-*De Stijl* movements (such as CIAM and the International Style) seemed to think, that architecture should abandon its artistic mission and merge into a modern form of building. Nor did it mean that the personality of the artist-architect should be banished to the background. On the contrary, its importance remained undiminished. Only the personal creativity of the architect was capable of elevating building into architecture. Of course the new architecture was functionalist, but it was more than that, just as literature was more than writing. Oud, too, was a functionalist, for this was the connection with general developments in society. But the essence of Oud's functionalism was neither technocratic nor organizational. Oud himself characterized his oeuvre as 'poetic functionalism'.[6] This was what linked his architecture, via *De Stijl*, to the great tradition of architecture in which experiments like the Shell Building were but minor ripples. The ultimate message of *Mein Weg* was Oud's unshakable faith in the evolution of this poetic functionalism.

Annie Oud-Dinaux in Munich at an exhibition about Oud (1965)/ OUDJ-58, NAI, Rotterdam

**Notes**

**1.** C. Wagenaar, 'Jaap Bakema and the fight for freedom', in Sarah Goldhagen, Réjean Legault, *Anxious Modernism*, Cambridge (Mass.), Montreal, 2000.
**2.** J.J.P. Oud to J. Bakema, 16 March 1959, Getty Research Institute, Los Angeles.
**3.** J.J.P. Oud *Mein Weg in 'De Stijl'*, 1960, pp. 31-32.
**4.** J.J.P. Oud *Mein Weg in 'De Stijl'*, 1960, pp. 34.
**5.** J.J.P. Oud *Mein Weg in 'De Stijl'*, 1960, pp. 34-35.
**6.** U. Barbieri, Henk Engel, B. Colenbrander, *Architect J.J.P. Oud*, Rotterdam 1981-1982.

# 106 Bio Convalescent Centre for Children

Arnhem, 6 Wekeromseweg

1952-1960

Sports building/ OUDJ-bo 404, NAI, Rotterdam

Main building/ OUDJ-bo 403, NAI, Rotterdam

Oud's design for the Bio Convalescent Centre in Arnhem was closely bound up with his views on the development of modern architecture,[1] which according to him depended largely on the achievements of a few individuals and manifested itself in a few crucial buildings. In 1952 he seized the commission for the convalescent centre as an opportunity to demonstrate that modern architecture had outgrown the radical and experimental stage of the 'pioneering' period of the 1920s. With this design Oud proved that modernism in architecture had not succumbed to the threat of idle formalism and expressionless architecture that had loomed large in the 1930s and later. On the contrary. The building complex in the Arnhem woods demonstrated quite clearly that modern architecture was alive and well. Oud had not only remained true to its functionalist principles but had developed them further. The motivation for this polemical, historiographical theme Oud found in large measure in the commission itself. By virtue of its function – a rehabilitation centre for inner-city (working-class) children who where undernourished and sickly – it begged comparison with one of the icons of the Modern Movement, the Zonnestraal Sanatorium in Hilversum (1926-1928) by Duiker, Bijvoet and Wiebenga. In the 1950s, moreover, the principles of the 'pure' beginnings of modernism, to which Zonnestraal in Oud's view so strongly attested, came under attack from, among others, Aldo van Eyck.[2] Van Eyck polemicized against the 'old' modernism in speech and writing, and, most compellingly, in the form of a concrete design: the Municipal Orphanage in Amsterdam (1955-1960). On the completion of the Convalescent Centre in Arnhem, which more or less coincided with that of the Orphanage, Oud urged the editors of *Forum* to review the two projects.[3] His plea fell on deaf ears and it was left to the architect Van Tijen to make the connection in the course of an article on the history and future of Dutch architecture published in the magazine in 1961. Oud's building played only a marginal role in his thesis, however.[4]

The commissioning situation Oud faced in Arnhem was quite different from the one encountered by the designers of Zonnestraal. At Hilversum one architect (Berlage) had acted as consultant to the client and the three architect-engineers had produced the design, whereas at Arnhem one architect was in charge of the whole design process: J.J.P. Oud. The client had approached Oud for this commission because it was looking for an architect-artist capable of offering sufficient counterweight to a functionally overloaded programme. He was assisted in this task by his son (an expert in hospital architecture) and by an advisory committee. The members of this committee, which had been set up especially for this project, fell into two categories: medical specialists in the field of child convalescence and paediatrics, and members of Bouwcentrum, a national advisory body in the field of construction. In setting up this committee, the client, the Stichting Bio-vacantieoord (Bio Holiday Centre Foundation), a private charitable institution, was honouring the dual objective that had informed its foundation in 1927. This was geared on the one hand to filling the gap in the government health care system by providing medical care for sick children (initially undernourished inner-city children, later polio patients and physically disabled children) and on the other to initiating research in the field of child rehabilitation.

In 1952, the advisory committee produced a blueprint for a convalescent centre which functioned as a guideline for Oud's design.[5] The most important aspect of the chosen building programme was the pavilion set-up. Although considerably more expensive than concentrated construction, pavilions were preferred on psychological and medical

511

Children's pavilion/ OUDJ-bo 412, NAI, Rotterdam

grounds. The design was to include day and night accommodation for the children and for the nursing and medical staff, a sports building (with swimming pool and gym) and an outpatients' clinic. The maximum number of patients was set at 120, which worked out at ten pavilions each for twelve children, six girls and six boys. Since the nursing of polio patients entailed a much lengthier stay than the average six weeks spent at the centre by inner-city children, the committee felt that a school was essential.

In 1955, three years after the advisory committee had drawn up its first functional diagram for a convalescence centre, Oud submitted a final design. In the intervening period he had been obliged to adjust his plans several times to take account of financial cutbacks, new medical insights and other centres in the Netherlands, or as a result of consultations with yet more experts. In the executed design, all the buildings were organized along a central axis. At the head of this axis, along the access road, the main building fronted and protected the complex as a whole with its wide facade. The centre of the axis was formed by the boiler house, not only because of its location, but also because of its form. Owing to its relative height (required for the flue), conical roof and ring-shaped dwelling, the boiler house dominated the constellation of buildings. Although Oud regarded its prominent location as a disadvantage, the client had insisted on the location and the combination of boiler house and caretaker's dwelling for reasons of economy. Oud tried to offset this defect by visually emphasizing the sports building which terminated the axis by adding an observation tower. This, in combination with the vertically oriented pitched roof of the main building and the tall boiler house produced a clear trio of buildings along the central axis. Arranged either side of this spine were a total of ten pavilions, although the budget initially allowed no more than six (three on either side) to be built. Here the rigid symmetry of the complex was broken by the oblique siting of the pavilions which was the most favourable alignment with respect to sunlight, wind and outlook. The school building, which was not part of Oud's design and was later built to a design by Hans Oud in the years 1962-1965, was located to the left of the axis right at the back of the site. A chapel at an angle to the front of the site, which was included in Oud's design (1955), remained unbuilt for financial reasons. The medical pavilion was for the same reason incorporated in a reduced form into the main building.

That Oud saw his design in terms of 'perfecting' the Zonnestraal Sanatorium is evident in the detailing. In contrast to the Zonnestraal finishing, which because of the use of painted sheet metal and plastering was unsuitable for the Dutch climate and the rough treatment of children, Oud opted for glazed brick. Though relatively expensive, it was extremely robust, durable and maintenance-free, advantages Oud emphasized in his design commentary. In keeping with his personalized view of history, he presented the use of brick in terms of a personal journey of discovery during his career. In 'Waarom ik van het toepassen van baksteen afstapte en op grond waarvan ik er weer toe terugkeerde' ('Why I stopped using brick and subsequently returned to it' 1960) he studiously avoided all mention of Zonnestraal and referred to his white housing schemes of the 1920s as his training ground. In the design for the row of shops and dwellings at Hoek van Holland, for example, the plastering had given rise to a lot of technical problems which he had managed overcome in later projects through the 'discovery' of a bright, light-coloured (white, cream or beige) brick. Although he had first experimented with this in the Shell Building, it was only at Arnhem that he had been able to use it to his satisfaction. Only there did he hit upon the right

512

**Boiler house with caretaker's dwelling/ OUDJ-bo 406, NAI, Rotterdam**

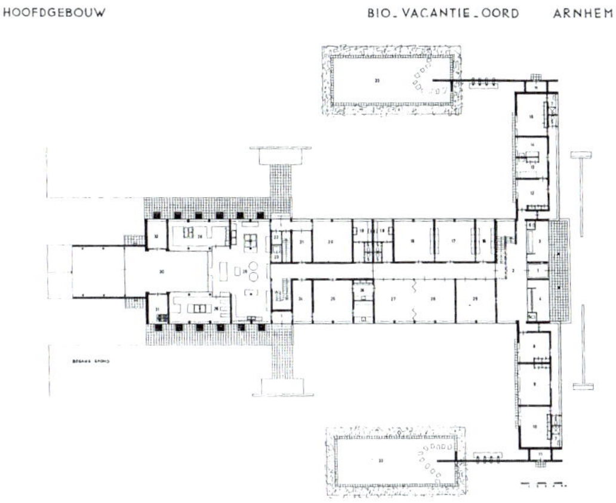

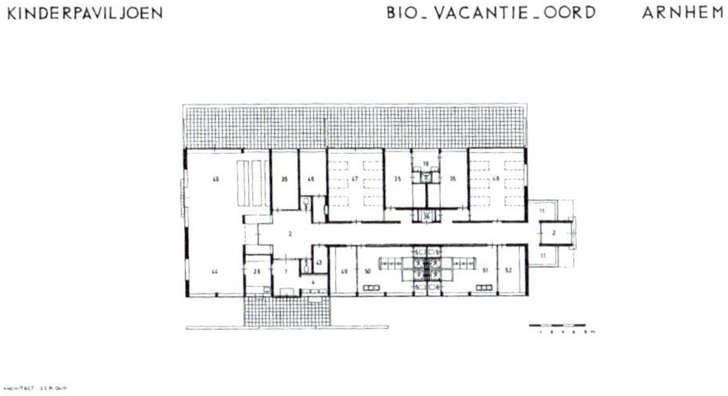

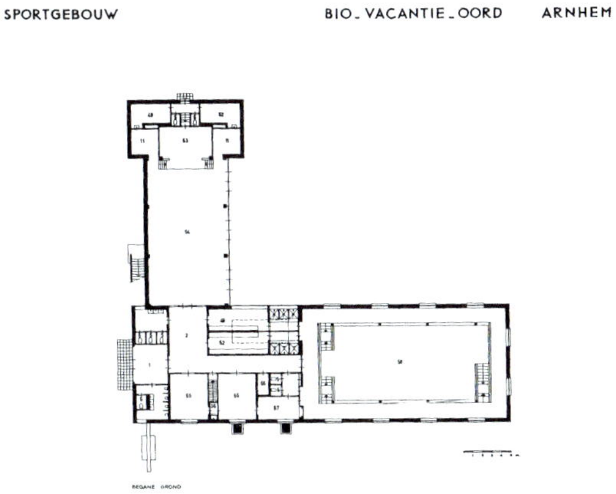

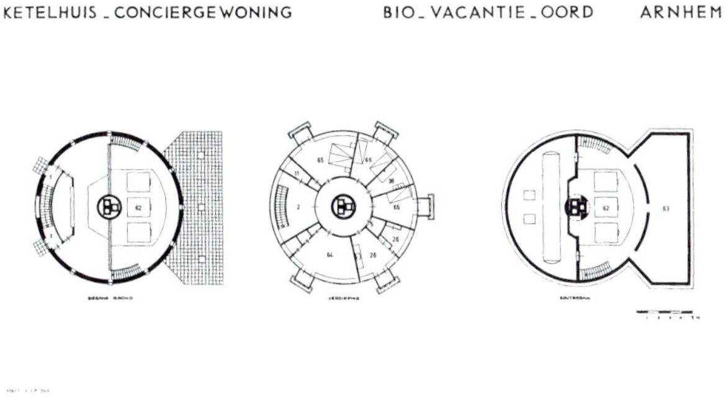

HOOFDGEBOUW
BIO_VACANTIE_OORD
ARNHEM

KINDERPAVILJOEN
BIO_VACANTIE_OORD
ARNHEM

SPORTGEBOUW
BIO_VACANTIE_OORD
ARNHEM

KETELHUIS_CONCIERGEWONING
BIO_VACANTIE_OORD
ARNHEM

Plans of ground floor main building, children's pavilion, sports building and boiler house with caretaker's dwelling/ Oud Archive, library, NAI, Rotterdam

513

SITUATIE BIO_VACANTIE_OORD ARNHEM
1952

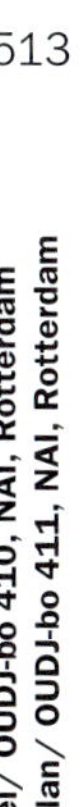

Chapel/ OUDJ-bo 410, NAI, Rotterdam
Site plan/ OUDJ-bo 411, NAI, Rotterdam

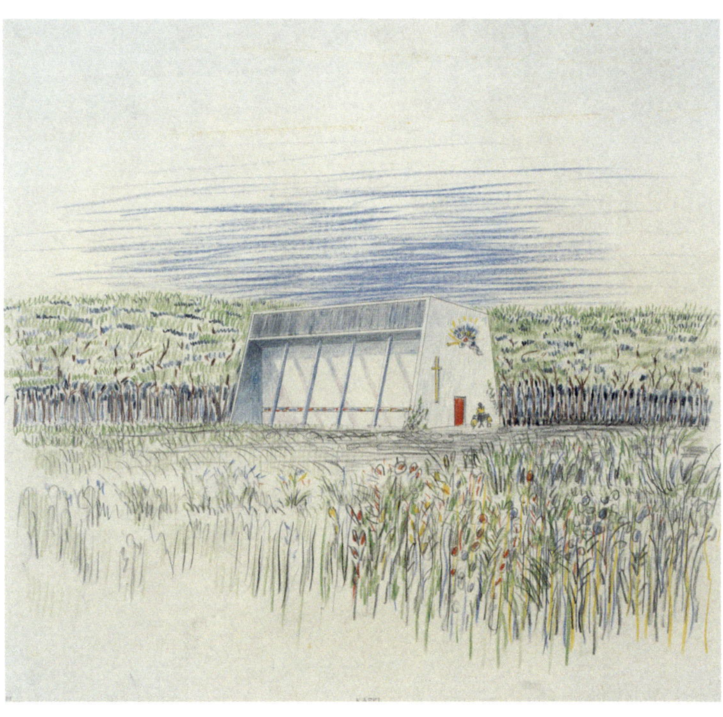

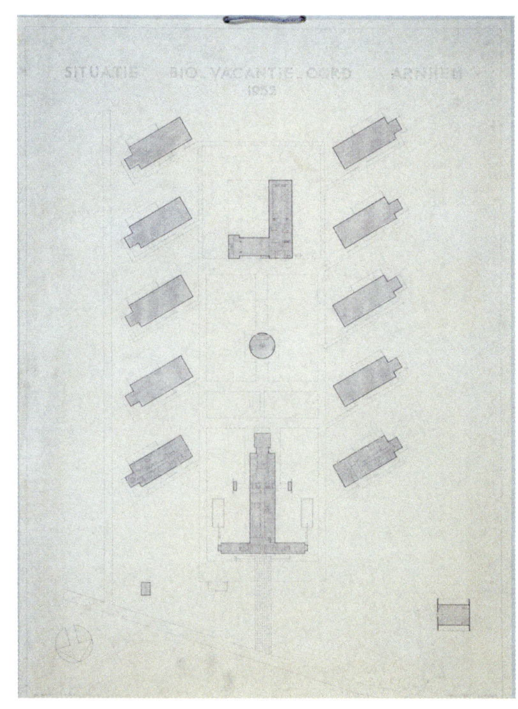

composition and treatment: *The special difficulties that I originally saw as being associated with building in brick were: typical brick constructions like upright courses, stretchers, arches, large corbels, etc., which interfere with the closed aspect of the flawless whole which I seek. Likewise my desire – for the same reason – to place the windows in the front of the facade seemed to be difficult to satisfy in brick. Wall copings without substantial frames was another difficulty that I had to solve (complicated, one-off solutions do not satisfy me: I look for logical solutions that can be constructed in the normal way because only on such a basis can building have a universal value). It would be going too far to recount in this article how I solved this to my own satisfaction. Anyone who is interested should look at the works themselves. At any rate, basically I succeeded and I have the feeling that I am now able to do more with brick than I felt I could expect from plastering. Large areas, with permanently bright colours!*[6]

Aside from the glazed brick, Oud opted for a predominantly grey-white colour scheme enlivened by splashes of primary colour on the eaves, doors and ventilation grilles. The wall beside the entrance to the sports building was faced with bright blue glazed tiles. Here and there the form was enlivened, too: fixed benches and garden walls executed in the same materials as the buildings served to soften the austerity of the basic architectural layout. A striking element of the detailing was the visual art, which had been completely absent in the Zonnestraal complex. The tile picture by Karel Appel above the entrance to the main building, the sculpture by Rudy Rooyackers on the playground beside the sports building, and the fish by Aart van den IJssel beside the pond on the forecourt were an integral part of the complex, not only because of their use of material (glazed ceramics) but also because their subject matter – a circus act, animals in the jungle, a fish – were designed to appeal to children. The tile picture in particular became a defining feature of the complex. The commission had gone to Appel only after the Spanish artist Joan Miró had withdrawn through lack of time. In presenting his design to Oud in 1960, Appel described the tableau as *a lively circus act primarily of colour ... Depicting from left to right: two dancing clowns, an animal balancing a couple of coloured cubes and a ball on its nose, and throwing another ball into the air with its back, and another creature with open mouth and big teeth throwing another big coloured ball in the air and finally a sad little coloured clown.*[7]

**One of the children's pavilions/ OUDJ-ph 1517, NAI, Rotterdam (Photo Spies / d'Oliviera)**

514

**Observation tower atop sports building/ OUDJ-ph 1519, NAI, Rotterdam (Photo Spies / d'Oliviera)**

515

**Notes**

**1.** C. Wagenaar, 'Honestly, from within', in: *Archis*, (1998)12.
**2.** For the 'generational conflict' of the *Forum* editors and in particular Van Tijen's position in it, see: T. Idsinga, J. Schilt, *Architect W. van Tijen 1894-1974,* The Hague 1990.
**3.** J. Huijts to J.J.P. Oud, 3 March 1960, OUDJ-B, NAI, Rotterdam.
**4.** W. van Tijen, 'Discussie-avond A. et A.', in: *Forum*, 15(1960/1961)9, pp. 318-320.
**5.** Bouwcentrum, 'Rapport inzake stichting Bio-vacantieoord van een Koloniehuis B' (text and drawings), typescript, 12 April 1952, Hans Oud Archive, acquisition no. 96.009, NAI, Rotterdam.
**6.** J.J.P. Oud, 'Waarom ik van het toepassen van baksteen afstapte en op grond waarvan ik er weer toe terugkeerde', in: *Baksteen*, May 1960.
**7.** C.K. Appel to J.J.P. Oud, 9 April 1960, OUDJ-B, NAI, Rotterdam.

**Sources**

CCA: ph1985: 0156
Getty: 890126-26**
NAI: OUDJ-bo 1-458, OUDJ-bo 1001, OUDJ-bo 2001, OUDJ-bo 3001, OUDJ-ph 1404-1520, MAQV 275, MAQV 374, OUDH-acquisition no. 96.009, OUDJ-B

**Articles**

*Het bio-boekje*, 1992
'Bio Vacantie-oord

Entrance to main building/ OUDJ-ph 1486, NAI, Rotterdam




nabij Arnhem', in: *Bouw*, 10(1955)44
'Bio-herstellingsoord te Arhem officieel geopend', in: *Cobouw*, 24 June 1960
J. van Goethem, 'Colonia Bio-Holiday ad Arnhem', in: *l'Architettura. Chronacle & storia*, VII(1961)1
W.A. Jacobsen, 'Voor lichamelijk gehandicapte kinderen bouwde Nederlandse bioscoopbond herstellingsoord te Arnhem', in: *Technische Gids*, 18 June 1960
G. Kühne, 'Oud und die Klassik. "Bio Herstellingsoord" in Arnhem/Niederlande', in: *Bauwelt*, 51(1960)40
P. Man 'Dit is van uw dubbeltjes gebouwd', in: *Libelle*, 27(1960)35
H. Oud, 'Bio-mytylschool te Arnhem', in: *Bouw*, 20(1965)45
J.J.P. Oud, 'Waarom ik van het toepassen van baksteen afstapte', in: *Baksteen*, (1960)3
J.J.P. Oud 'Bio-herstellingsoord te Arnhem', in: *Bouw*, 15(1960)44
J.J.P. Oud 'Bio-herstellingsoord te Arnhem', in: *Bouwkundig Weekblad*, (78(1960)23
J.J.P. Oud 'Bauen für Kinder', in: *Kontraste. Jahrbuch Freie Akademie der Künste*, Hamburg 1960
J.J.P. Oud 'Architect dr. J.J.P. Oud keerde terug tot toepassing van baksteen', in: *Cobouw*, 24 June 1960
J.J.P. Oud 'Het Bio-Herstellingsoord te Arnhem', in: *Ons Profiel*, (1961)3
'Recent works of a pioneer', in: *Progressive Architecture*, XLII(1961)6
'The Record reports', in: *Architectural Record*, (1956)
Verschoor, 'Bio-Herstellingsoord bij Arnhem', in: *Bouwwereld*, 56(1960)20
J.J. Vriend, 'Oud's Bio Herstellings-oord Arnhem', in: *De Groene Amsterdammer*, 2 July 1960
K. Wiekart, 'Het nieuwste werk van J.J.P. Oud', in: *Vrij Nederland*, 21(1960)9


**Literature**


U. Barbieri, *J.J.P. Oud*, Rotterdam 1987, pp. 171-179
D. Broekhuizen, *De Stijl toen / J.J.P. Oud nu*, Rotterdam 2000, pp. 234-255
J. C. Ludi, et al., *Analyse du Bio-herstellingsoord, Arnhem, J.J.P. Oud, 1952-1960 1ère année 1989-1990*, EAUG, Zurich 1989
N. Mens, A. Tijhuis, *De architectuur van het ziekenhuis*, Rotterdam 1999
H. Oud, *J.J.P. Oud. Architect 1890-1963. Feiten en herinneringen gerangschikt*, The Hague 1984, pp. 169-177
G. Stamm, *J.J.P. Oud. Bauten und Projekte 1906 bis 1963*, Mainz, Berlin 1984, p. 139
J.T. van Taalingen, *Nederlandse Bioscoopbond 60 jaar*, Amsterdam 1978
C. Wagenaar, 'Honestly, from within', in *Archis*, 12(1998), pp. 67-74

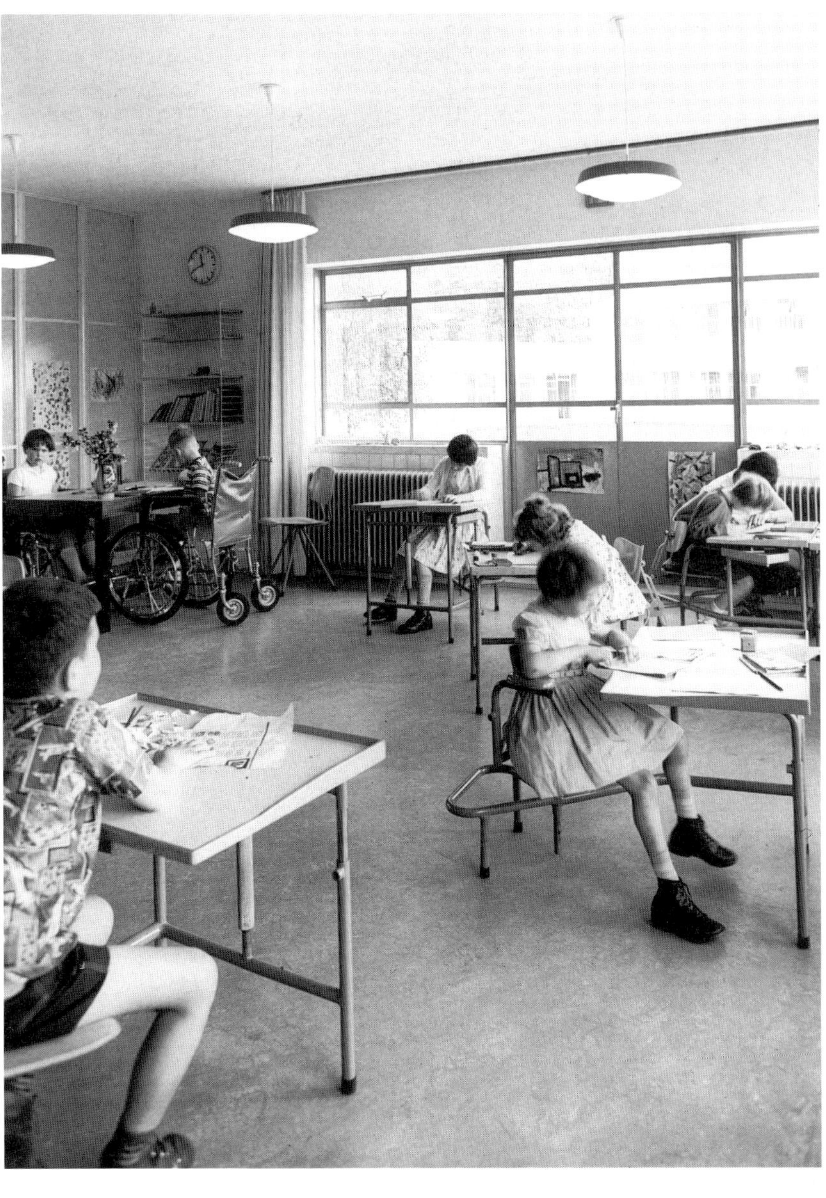

Pavilion interior/ OUDJ-ph 1490, NAI, Rotterdam
(Photo Publicam)

517

Children's pavilions and boiler house/ Oud Archive, Library, NAI, Rotterdam

Main building, boiler house and sports building/ Oud Archive, Library, NAI, Rotterdam

Sports building/ Oud Archive, Library, NAI, Rotterdam

In 1954, the Haags Gemeentemuseum commissioned Oud to design a gallery for glass objects from the Mulier Collection. The room was also to serve as a transitional space between the lobby and the museum proper. Oud proposed placing a half-height wall along the long axis of the room with five triangular display cases on either side. More display cases were to be inserted into the two side walls. The walls were finished with glazed white bricks and stone. The ceiling consisted of sheets of wire glass, and the floor was laid with white marble. For the triangular display cases Oud suggested a framework of chrome-plated copper with glass top and sides and a concrete slab for the base. A light fitting was placed above the case and a fluorescent light in the front angle; the display cases in the side walls were lit from below.
The museum's board was initially enthusiastic but later on objections were raised and it was decided not to implement Oud's plan. Not long afterwards, however, work commenced on a remodelling of the room according to a concept that to Oud's eyes looked like a watered-down version of his original proposal. He reacted with disappointment. *I am forced to point out to you ... that the room I designed for you was the creation of a space that I had spent great care and time in detailing in order to conjure up an atmosphere that would undoubtedly have brought about a metamorphosis in your museum along the lines that we talked about. That this is not the same as the tasteful placement of a few display cases, which I could also have attempted, goes without saying. You no doubt realized this, when you noticed how much more securely such cases sit in such a space when they are part of a total design: such as now arranged by yourselves.*[1]

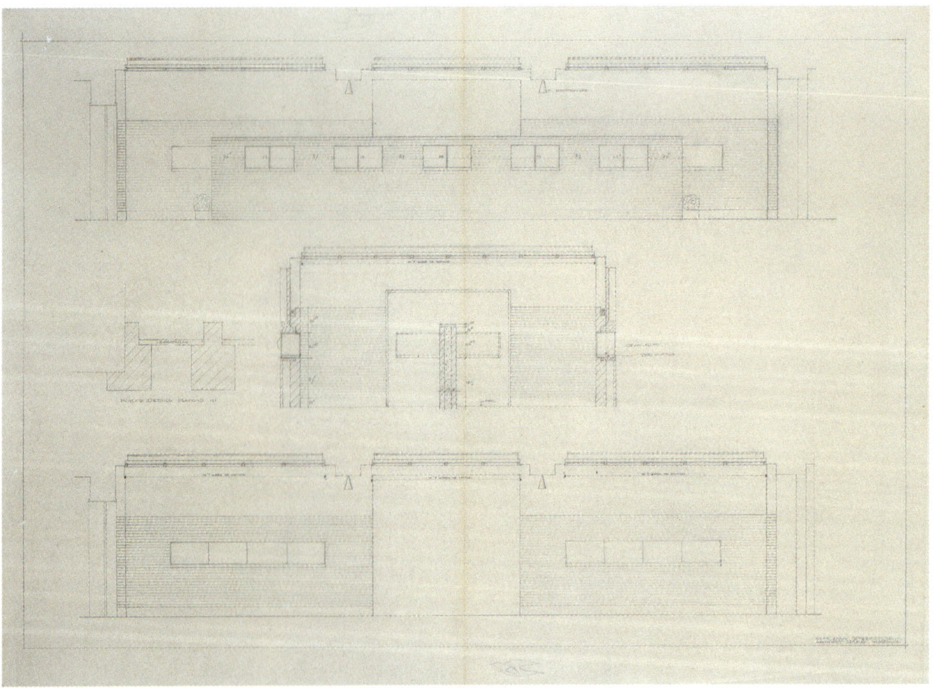

**Various design views/ OUDJ-gm 3, NAI, Rotterdam**



**Notes**
**1.** J.J.P. Oud to the board of the Gemeentemuseum, 10 April 1956, OUDJ-gm 1001, NAI, Rotterdam.

**Sources**
NAI : OUDJ-gm 1-4, OUDJ-gm 1001

**Literature**
H.E. Oud, *J.J.P. Oud. Architekt 1890-1963. Feiten en herinneringen gerangschikt*, The Hague 1984, pp. 182-183, 185-194
E. Reinhartz-Tergau, *J.J.P. Oud, architect: meubelontwerpen en interieurs*, Rotterdam 1990, pp. 188-189

## 108 De Utrecht

**Rotterdam, Coolsingel** **1954-1961**

One of the buildings that survived the 1940 bombardment of Rotterdam was the Handel & Nijverheid office building on Coolsingel, owned by the De Utrecht life insurance company. However, since the building did not fit in with Witteveen's reconstruction plan, it was destined to disappear anyway. The land was compulsorily purchased by the city council and De Utrecht was assigned a new plot, slightly behind the old one. The existing building continued to be used for many years after the war and it was not until 1954 that De Utrecht approached Oud to design its new premises. The choice fell on Oud because he *could be regarded as representative for this city.*[1]
Oud's design for the combined office and department store building shows the extent to which, in searching for a contemporary representational and urban architecture, he fell back on the formal arsenal of architecture and visual art of the 1920s and 1930s.[2] The architectural detailing and the use of materials and colour were largely inspired by work from this period by the Russian artist El Lissitzky. Key elements of De Utrecht, such as the texture of the aluminium panels used to clad the facade, the metal cage construction of the stairwells and lifts and the tension between visual art and architecture, were based on the *Kabinett der Abstrakten*, an exhibition space the artist had designed in 1927 for the Landesmuseum in Hanover. The walls of this gallery were finished with strips that presented a different aspect as the visitor moved around the room. This effect was the due to the way they were mounted and to the fact that the front and sides of the strips and the wall behind were painted in different shades of grey. In De Utrecht Oud used aluminium sheets with vertical grooves and a partially matt finish. They lent the building a transparency that was further enhanced by a colour scheme that was also based on Lissitzky's work. The two bands of glazed tiles either side of the curtain wall, and the black stone bands either side of the ground floor entrances are an allusion to Lissitzky's series of lithos depicting the comic strip story of two squares, that had been published in *De Stijl* in 1922. As such De Utrecht can be regarded as the most successful example in Oud's oeuvre of the perfection of the programme he had formulated in

Perspective Coolsingel elevation/ OUDJ-ut 32, NAI, Rotterdam

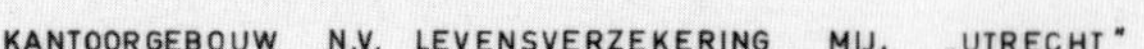


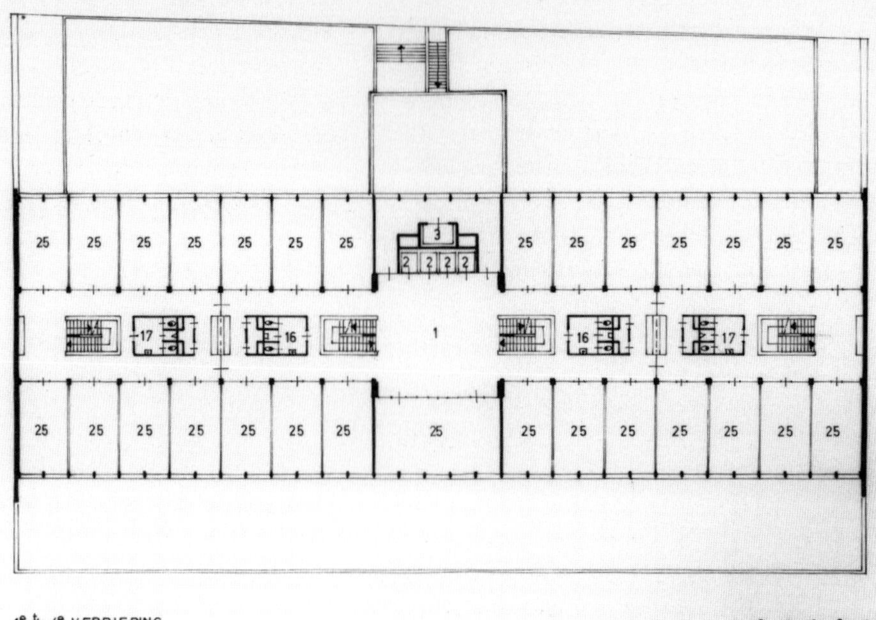


Plan of office floor/ OUDJ-ut 137, NAI, Rotterdam

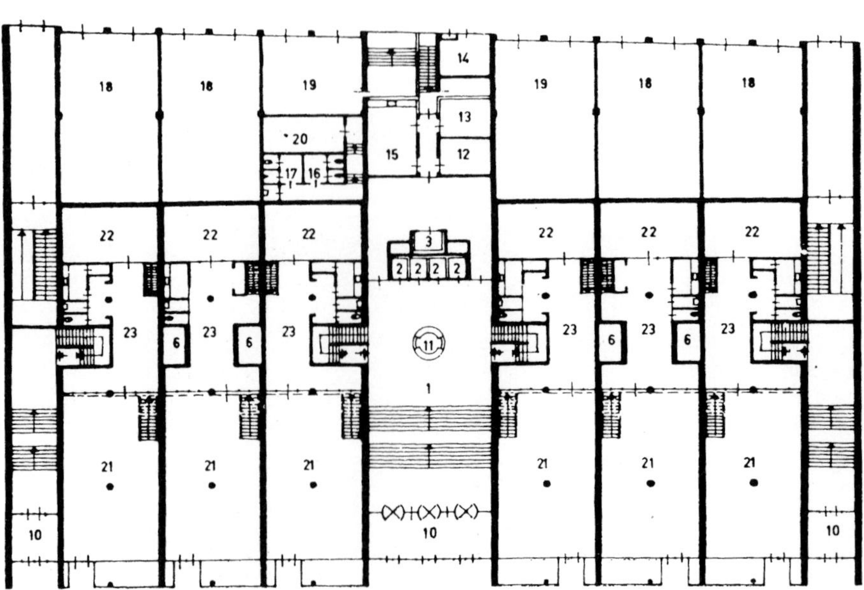

Ground floor plan/ OUDJ-ut 136, NAI, Rotterdam

1921 in 'Over de toekomstige bouwkunst en hare architectonische mogelijkheden' (Architecture and the Future).
As in Lissitzky's gallery in Hanover, Oud deployed 'real' art throughout the building. Sculptures depicting Foresight and The Rewards (an allusion to the client's insurance business) were placed high up on either side of the front facade. Wall hangings depicting fantastical creatures, designed by Karel Appel, contributed to the relaxed atmosphere of the canteen. The most striking art works were four reliefs by the artist Cesar Domela in the foyer of the office building. The abstract reliefs, consisting of metal arabesques and coloured stone mosaics, were mounted on the four black stone walls. Because Oud was afraid that they might otherwise detract from the architectonic spatial effect, they were not allowed to exceed 75 by 75 centimetres.
In its volumetric composition, De Utrecht refers to the Lijnbaan shopping street (Van den Broek & Bakema, 1948-1953). A broad, low substructure for shops formed a 'plinth' for a narrow, tall building volume containing offices.
The most striking – and audacious – aspect of Oud's proposal was his choice of the double-corridor system. *The system was also – after much study – employed in the big Dijkzicht Hospital in Rotterdam. In essence it means that you make double corridors between which are the service areas, such as cloakrooms, toilets, staircases, lifts, broom cupboards, etc., while on both sides [are] the offices which are a good 7 m. deep. One disadvantage is the lack of daylight (that is to say in the middle only) so that the corridors and so on have to be artificially illuminated. But this is unavoidable in such deep construction anyway: for the rest the advantages are considerable.*[3]
The building was constructed in stages. The first part to be completed was the office section at the rear, after which the old office building was demolished and work began on the Coolsingel facade. The front elevation was set back one and a half metres behind the official building line for Coolsingel and the area in front paved with eye-catching red tiles. Continuous bands of aluminium-framed windows gave this facade a strong horizontality. The ground-floor shop front was almost entirely of glass above a low plinth of Swedish granite. The awnings Oud placed above the shop windows were intended not only to protect people from the weather but also to induce them to enter the shops by easing the transition from outside to inside. The materials of the facade were continued on the inside. The profiled steel cladding used for the spandrel panels also lined the rear wall of the main lobby. The non-colours black, white and grey predominated in the interior, relieved here and there with cobalt blue and light yellow accents. The floor covering in the corridors was dark blue. The doors were painted a different colour on each floor, making it easier for people to find their way around the building.

525

**Notes**
1. 'Kantoorgebouw op de Coolsingel', in *Bouw*, 10(1955)28.
2. For a detailed discussion of the design, construction and reception of De Utrecht, see: D. Broekhuizen, *De Stijl toen / J.J.P. Oud nu*, Rotterdam 2000, pp. 256-276.
3. J.J.P. Oud to D. Schuitemaker, 27 February 1954, OUDJ-B, NAI, Rotterdam.

**Sources**
CCA: ph1984: 0891, ph1984: 0892
Getty: 890126-26**
NAI: OUDJ-ut 1-142, OUDJ-ut 1001-1002, OUDJ-ut 2001, OUDJ-ut 3001, OUDJ-ph 1521-1598, OUDJ-ph 1765-1769, OUDJ-ph 1860

**Articles**
'Bau-Strukturdetails', in: *Detail*, (1962)3
M. Cerruti, 'Pallazo per uffici a Utrecht', in: *L'Architettura*, 8(1962)
'Kantoorgebouw op de Coolsingel', in: *Bouw*, 10(1955)28
'Een nieuw aluminium gevel aan de Coolsingel', in: *Constructies*, 4(1962)1
'Ontwerp Kantoorgebouw', in: *Bouwbedrijven en Openbare Werken*, 32(1955)24
J.J.P. Oud 'Kantoorgebouw voor "De Utrecht" te Rotterdam', in: *Bouwkundig Weekblad*, 80(1962)2

**Literature**
U. Barbieri, *J.J.P. Oud*, Rotterdam 1987, pp. 166-169
D. Broekhuizen, *De Stijl toen / J.J.P. Oud nu*, Rotterdam 2000, pp. 256-277
J.L.J.M. Gerwen, N.H.W. Verbeek, *Voorzorg & de Vruchten*, 1995
H.E. Oud, *J.J.P. Oud. Architekt 1890-1963. Feiten en herinneringen gerangschikt*, The Hague 1984, pp. 178-181
G. Stamm, *J.J.P. Oud. Bauten und Projekte 1906 bis 1963*, Mainz, Berlin 1984, p. 139

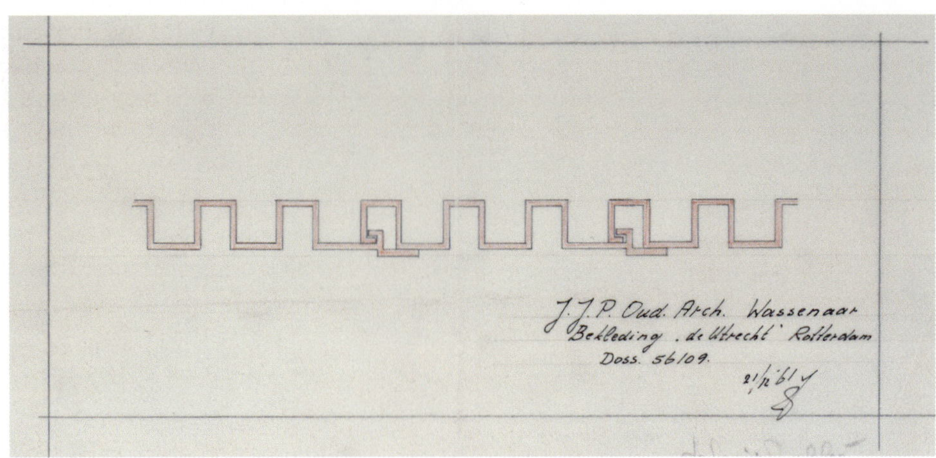


Section facade cladding/ OUDJ-ut 128, NAI, Rotterdam

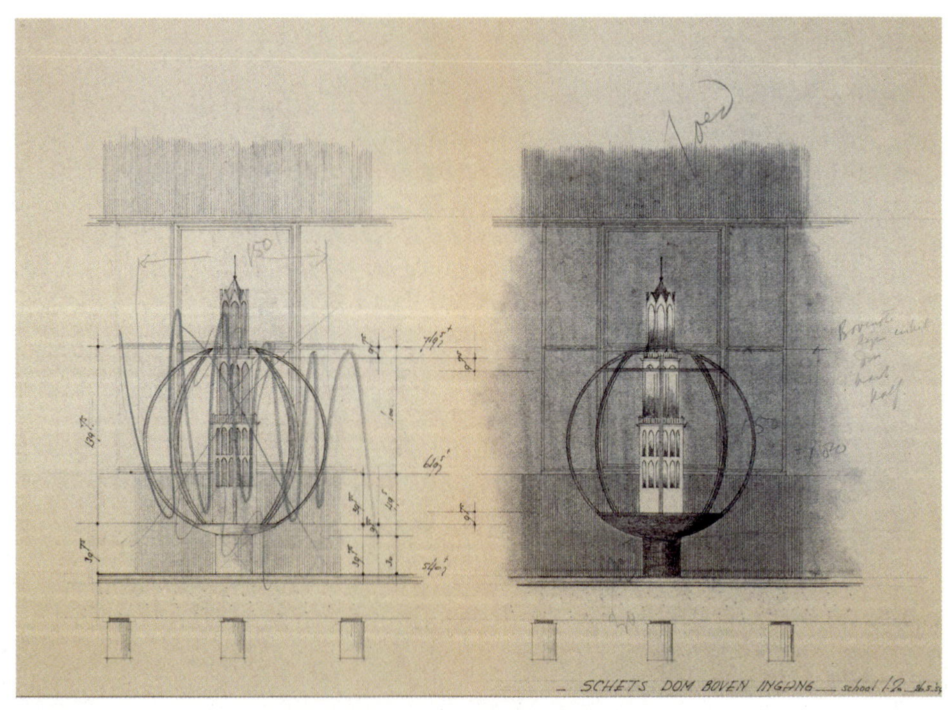


Design of Domtoren model above main entrance to office section/ OUDJ-ut 119, NAI, Rotterdam

Main entrance to office section/ OUDJ-ph 1550, NAI, Rotterdam

Coolsingel elevation/ OUDJ-ph 1542, NAI, Rotterdam (Photo Bart Hofmeester)

MAATSCHAPPIJ UTRECHT
GILDE INTERIEUR
DATA INTERNATIONAL
DD-33-06

Office section lobby with two reliefs by Cesar Domela/ OUDJ-ph 1566, NAI, Rotterdam (Photo Jan Versnel)

Hall of top floor office section with wall hanging by Karel Appel/ OUDJ-ph 1570, NAI, Rotterdam (Photo S. Zoetmulder)

# 109 Tweede Vrijzinnig Christelijk Lyceum

**The Hague,**
**131 Goudsbloemenlaan**

**1949-1956**

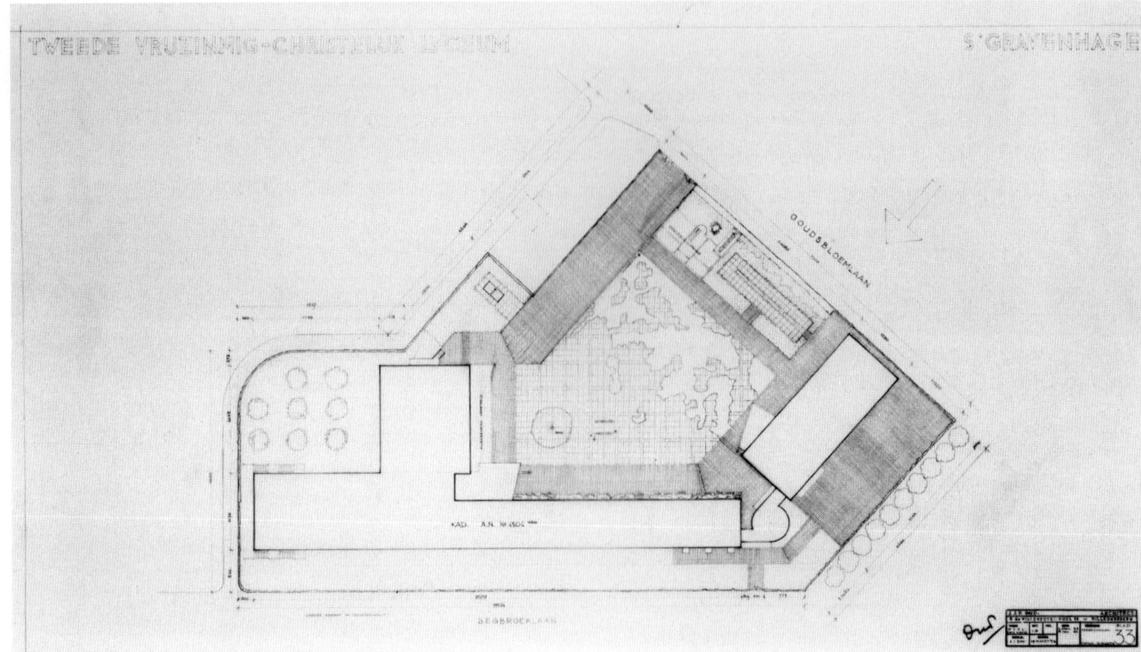


Site plan/ OUDJ-vc 527, NAI, Rotterdam

Isometric projection school building/ OUDJ-vc 108, NAI, Rotterdam

The design for the Tweede Vrijzinnig Christelijk Lyceum in The Hague is illustrative of Oud's standpoint in the discussion with both the political and the architectural world about industrialized building. It is a demonstration model of a modern, monumental architecture tailored to a particular situation. With it Oud distanced himself from the officially endorsed tendency to standardize school designs. His building illustrates how unique factors like location and particular requirements of the school board determine the typological and stylistic appearance of the building.
In Dudok's post-war reconstruction masterplan (1946), the school was slotted into the Herbouwplan Sportlaan (Reconstruction Plan for Sportlaan). The fact that the new building was intended to be a centre for Dalton teaching, secured it the status of experimental school and allowed the designer a little more room for manoeuvre with respect to the oppressive regulations governing school construction. The school board wanted a large auditorium and was opposed to long corridors. In most respects, the first design, which Oud presented to the board in January 1950, conformed to Dudok's planning guidelines. The main difference was that the building was one storey higher than originally stipulated (four levels instead of three) which served to distinguish it from the surrounding housing. Oud placed the long, tall block containing the auditorium and classrooms along Segbroeklaan. At right angles to this he placed a wing with practical classrooms and at an angle to one of the ends a separate gymnasium building connected to the main wing by a circular stairtower. The playground, enclosed on three sides by these three volumes was open towards the neighbourhood. While the facades on the street side were closed, those facing the playground and residential area were by contrast very open. At the official opening J.B. Bakema linked this to *De Stijl*. In *Forum* he argued that the Lyceum design represented a return to Oud's prewar level in that it was architecturally and urbanistically designed as 'a composition of independent planes, columns and facade sections' that engaged openly with the 'total space'. But at least as important, according to Bakema, was that in a period of increasing industrialization and bureaucratization, Oud had suc-

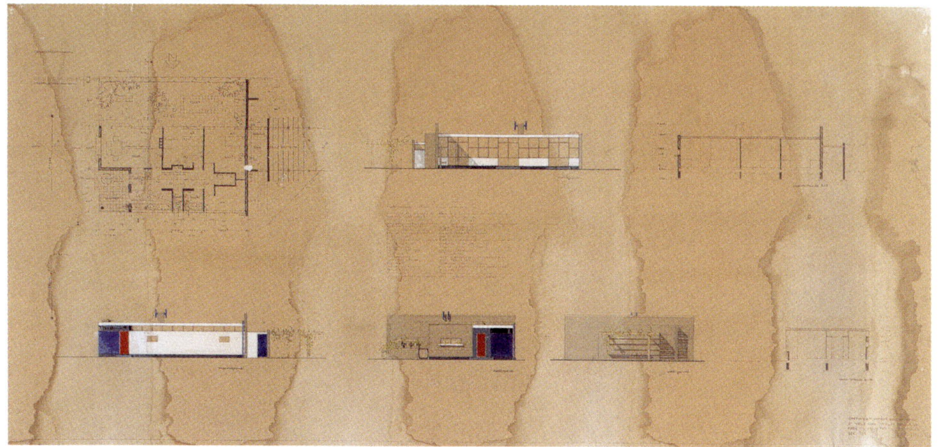
**Various design views caretaker's flat/ OUDJ-vc 495, NAI, Rotterdam**

533

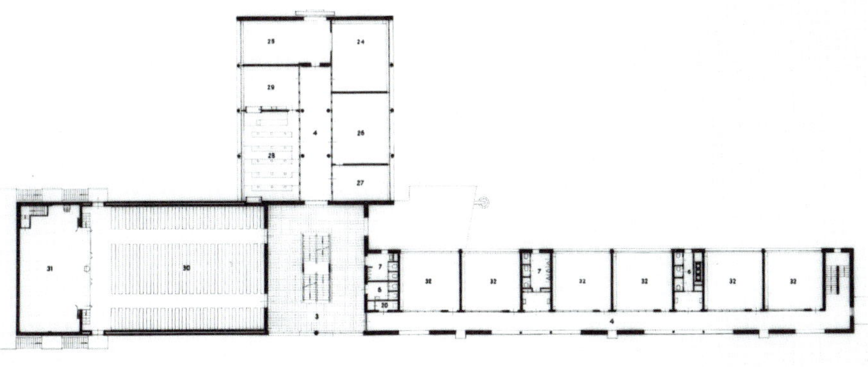

**Ground floor plan/ OUDJ-vc 496, NAI, Rotterdam**

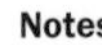

Segbroeklaan elevation, right the gymnasium wing/ OUDJ-ph 1858, NAI, Rotterdam (Photo Jan Versnel)

Playground facades/ OUDJ-ph 1194, NAI, Rotterdam

Sculpture by Rudy Rooyackers/ OUDJ-ph 1214, NAI, Rotterdam (Photo F.E. de Wilde)

**Notes**

1. J.B. Bakema, 'Het "Tweede Vrijz.-Christ. Lyceum" van Oud gezien in verband met de architectuurontwikkeling', in *Forum*, 11(1956)7, pp. 229-232. For a detailed discussion of the design, execution and reception of this building, see: D. Broekhuizen, *De Stijl toen / J.J.P. Oud nu*, Rotterdam 2000, pp. 214-233.
2. J.J.P. Oud, 'De Stijl – Toen en nu', in: *De Groene Amsterdammer*, 12 January 1957.

**Sources**

CCA: dr1984: 0370-0380, dr1984: 0473, ph1984: 0888-0890, ph1984: 1140-1146, ph1985: 0154
Gemeentearchief Den Haag: Dienst Stadsontwikkeling Archive, Tweede VCL Dossier
Getty: 890126-28**, 890126-box 3, F22
NAI: OUDJ-vc 1-535, OUDJ-vc 1001-1005, OUDJ-vc 2001, OUDJ-vc 3001, OUDJ-ph 1094-1356, OUDJ-ph 1749-1750, OUDJ-ph 1858-1859

**Articles**

J.B. Bakema, 'Het "Tweede Vrijz.-Christ. Lyceum" van Oud (1956) gezien in het verband met de architectuurontwikkeling', in: *Forum*, 11(1956) 7 (September 1956), pp. 228-254
J.E. Carriere, *Op de Drempel. Orgaan van het 2e VCL*, special edition, 4-8 September 1956

ceeded in realizing a powerful architectonic form. In this it resembled his prewar work when, despite parsimonious subsidy schemes for social housing, he had nonetheless managed to accomplish pioneering work.[1]

The building has also been linked to *De Stijl*, in the first place by Oud himself, because of the use made of visual art. Not so much because of the iconographical programme of sculpture and paintings (which related to the building's function), but because of the deliberate use of the autonomous effects of visual art in the building. The Hague school building is an interesting attempt – certainly in the context of the contemporary 'revival' of monumental art and of *De Stijl* (J. Baljeu, D. van Woerkom, Liga Nieuw Beelden) – to give an entirely contemporary form to the collaboration of architects and artists. The Lyceum in The Hague contained work by, among others, the sculptors Wessel Couzijn (relief of *The Men of Emmaus* in the auditorium) and Rudy Rooyackers (sculpture of relay runners in the gymnasium), who worked under the strict direction of the architect. Oud had two paintings by Karel Appel installed in the main hall where, because they were mounted on free-standing panels, they were able to retain their significance as individual works of art. Oud explained this solution as follows: *Because I consider painting and sculptures absolutely essential in a complete architectural work, I assigned two <u>free-standing</u> wall panels to Karel Appel and I believe that in so doing I was able to let the tensions of building and painting work together in the space itself without inhibiting the individual effect of either expression. I probably arrived at this arrangement via recollections from my "Stijl" days.*[2]

**Main entrance school building/ OUDJ-ph 1197, NAI, Rotterdam (Photo Jan Versnel)**




H. Dethmers, 'Tweede Vrijzinnig Christelijk Lyceum te 's Gravenhage', in: *Bouw*, 12(1957)35, pp. 850-859
'Hollande. College Catholique a La Haye', in: *l'Architecture d'Aujourd'hui*, 28(1957)72, pp. 20-21
G. Kazemier 'Het tweede Vrijzinnig Christelijk Lyceum te 's-Gravenhage', offprint from *Forum* 11(1956)7, p. 5
G. Kazemier 'Het Tweede Vrijzinnig Christelijk Lyceum te 's Gravenhage', in: *Bouwkundig Weekblad*, 75(1957)3, pp. 29-36
L. Mariani, 'Recenti opere di Jacobus Johannes Pieter Oud', in: *l'Architettura, cronache e storia*, 2(1956)11, pp. 342-351
L. Mariani, 'Architettura popolare de Jacobus Johannes Pieter Oud', in: *Edilizia Popolare* (1957)15, pp. 34-40
J.J.P. Oud 'Genormaliseerde scholenbouw. Een bouwterrein is iets anders dan een laboratorium', in: *De Groene Amsterdammer*, 11 April 1953, p. 3
J.J.P. Oud 'Nieuw Lyceum te Den Haag', in: *Bouw* 8(1953)49, pp. 18-23
J.J.P. Oud 'De Stijl – toen en nu', in: *De Groene Amsterdammer*, 12 January 1957, p. 9
W. van Tijen, 'De architect als ontwerper voor bouwbedrijven', in: Bouwkundig Weekblad, 71(1953)3/4, pp. 29-30
W. van Tijen, 'Industrialisatie van het bouwen en de Erecode van de BNA', in: Bouwkundig Weekblad, 71(1953)9/10, pp. 73-74
J.A.A. Verlinden, 'Pedagogische aspecten van de bouw en de inrichting van scholen', in: *Weekblad O.K.W-mededelingen*, 1956, no. 42, pp. 1-12
J.J. Vriend, 'Nieuwe school van architect Oud', in: *De Groene Amsterdammer*, 29 September 1956, pp. 9, 12

**Literature**
U. Barbieri, *J.J.P. Oud*, Rotterdam 1987, pp. 158-165
D. Broekhuizen, *De Stijl toen / J.J.P. Oud nu*, Rotterdam 2000, pp. 214-233
P. Groenendijk, 'Tweede Vrijzinnig Christelijk Lyceum Den Haag (1956)', in: T. Boersma, T. Verstegen (ed.), *Nederland naar School. Twee eeuwen bouwen voor een veranderend onderwijs*, Rotterdam 1997, pp. 236-239
H.E. Oud, *J.J.P. Oud. Architekt 1890-1963. Feiten en herinneringen gerangschikt*, The Hague 1984, pp. 161-164
G. Stamm, *J.J.P. Oud. Bauten und Projekte 1906 bis 1963*, Mainz, Berlin 1984, p. 139

Awning over main entrance to school building/
OUDJ-ph 1196, NAI, Rotterdam (Photo Jan Versnel)

Relay runners, sculpture by Rudy Rooyackers on gymnasium wing/ OUDJ-ph 1203, NAI, Rotterdam (Photo Jan Versnel)

Main stairwell with mural by Karel Appel/ OUDJ-ph 1213, NAI, Rotterdam

Preliminary study by Karel Appel for mural in main stairwell/
OUDJ-ph 1211, NAI, Rotterdam (Photo F.E. de Wilde)

# Library Order



After Oud had stopped working for the Rotterdam Woningdienst in 1933, he worked 'from home', without a large practice. He had the occasional assistant who was virtually a lodger. Oud liked working in that way and the set-up suited his ever-increasing individualism. In many respects he had an awkward relationship with the group, the social collective. As a result, participation in CIAM was an undertaking Oud opted to avoid; it also meant that he kept up incessant vituperation against 'round-table architecture', in which the building was the end result of a cooperative process. Nevertheless, the collective association was not forbidden territory in all respects. However much he tried to avoid the everyday, amorphous reality of intercourse with others, he was fascinated by the collective as an artistic and intellectual base, as a 'concept'. The central theme of the housing at Spangen and Tusschendijken is set in the force field between the collective 'medium' of the cityscape and the singly identifiable counterpoint. That also applies to much of Oud's later work, though the balance between the collective and the distinctive tipped increasingly towards the latter. After the Shell Building, careful observers could not fail to notice that Oud sought expressly to make his buildings stand out against the neutral background. In his later work the spatial context became less important, but the independent quality of the individual building all the more so, as if the oeuvre were becoming introspective. But within Oud's progressively autonomous compositions, the same dialectic persisted between general and particular: the expressive exception (in the form of ornament, colour and isolated motif) was materializing on top of the regular pattern of the composition based on the main features. In this way, the formless point of departure of the programme was elevated to an expressive order.

In his buildings Oud dealt with the idea of the group by means of composition, sublimation. That process applied equally to his intellectual 'habitus', to the way he charged himself up for his buildings by reading and studying, and to the independent theoretical universe he created in his articles and books. In terms of intellectual education, he was also concerned with fashioning a formless premise into a meaningful pattern. And that was not an easy process. The introvert (which Oud was, to a certain extent) had to open up to new influences from outside, to ideas and theories of varying substance. His oeuvre (as an architect, as well as an essayist) was far more profoundly influenced by this than one would expect from an individualist who did not take any signs, other than his own impulses, seriously. Oud's library reflects his intellectual avidity, faithfully. The preserved book collection illustrates the interest of an autodidact, who sought the idealistic collective and seriously tried to connect up with 'his own kind', in time and space.

What exactly does this library, which is still largely intact, consist of? It is quite considerable in size, although not excessive (some 3,000 titles) and very varied in make-up. Oud was not one of those architects who are only interested in like-minded, contemporary colleagues. There are in fact remarkably few monographs on contemporary architects, although Oud was happy to make an exception for the megalomaniacal prose of his role model Frank Lloyd Wright. He was also tempted to purchase occasionally one of the numerous publications by and about Le Corbusier, out of irritation at this contemporary, whom, as a writer, he criticized mercilessly at times. The art history and theory content of Oud's bookshelves is far more extensive. With his reading, he got through roughly the same programme as H.P. Berlage, immersing himself, like his predecessor, some thirty years his senior, in the almost complete works of Karl Scheffler, Fritz Schumacher and Walter

Curt Behrendt, and in the basic art-historical literature of Jacob Burckhardt, Heinrich Wölfflin and A.E. Brinckmann which he had acquired almost in their entirety.

The foundations of Oud's knowledge on the theory and history of his profession were laid around 1915. He prepared his own essays and historical sketches as he read. His 1919 study of Berlage is an outstanding determinist attempt to provide a historical introduction to his own assignment, with Berlage as the brilliant protagonist. Oud must have studied with passion. From the start, the intellectual context he created for himself contained a great deal of philosophy. The bombastic shadow of the Dutch Hegelian G.J.P.J. Bolland hangs over his early prose. Bolland has meanwhile been forgotten, but in those days he was widely read - including by young Oud. In addition, the library contains a wealth of original writings on philosophy, including work by Arthur Schopenhauer and Immanuel Kant. Not that their influence is immediately apparent in Oud's work.

Oud was extremely interested in psychoanalysis as a scientific discipline since his depressions forced him to withdraw from normal social intercourse for long periods. He devoured Sigmund Freud and Carl Jung, one book after another. There he undoubtedly encountered material for analogies which he was to use repeatedly in the second half of his life to explain the meaning of his buildings – the analogy between an architectural hierarchy and the 'ranking' of a good democracy, or with respect to father-son relations. Were Oud's buildings thus the conveyors of characteristics which penetrate the very core of human nature? That attractive thought is open to further speculation.

The intellectual giants in Oud's imaginary universe are offset by a flood of light, and not-so-light literature with which he amused himself: it did indeed have relatively amorphous foundations, full of bourgeois facetiousness, kitsch and fun. The two worlds sometimes mixed. When Oud first encountered the work of Ayn Rand, the writer of *The Fountainhead*, shortly after the war, he was completely sold on it. The authoress devoted hundreds of melodramatic pages to the absurd notion that the Messiah could have assumed the guise of an architect, misunderstood but valiant in the extreme. Oud revelled in it. He particularly enjoyed the book's dramatic portrayal of the relationship between the genius and the masses. He contacted Ayn Rand - something he often did if he recognized a kindred spirit or felt he must put something right in a work. It transpired that she knew his name, he proudly noted when the return mail from America arrived, and appreciated his contribution to modern architecture. Something of the prestige of Frank Lloyd Wright, on whose machismo *The Fountainhead* was based, reflected on him.

# 110 Design for Kiefhoek District Library

**Rotterdam, Hendrik Idoplein**

**1956-1957**

In the 1950s, the Kiefhoek district felt the need of its own library building and the Rotterdam public works department approached Oud to design it. Oud was delighted to be asked even though the location, the playground on Hendrik Idoplein, caused him a few headaches. *The playground itself ... was not overgenerous to begin with and so I think it wise to remind the council that in connection with the principles concerning play areas it would be a very good idea if space could be found elsewhere for the little building.*[1] Oud made a sketch design in which he took the unusual shape of the lot in one of the corners of the triangular district as his starting point. He projected one large and two smaller volumes in the three corners of the site. Although the library is on the same scale as the existing buildings, its design is clearly of a later date. Funding difficulties prevented the design from being built.

Perspective/ OUDJ-gb 12, NAI, Rotterdam

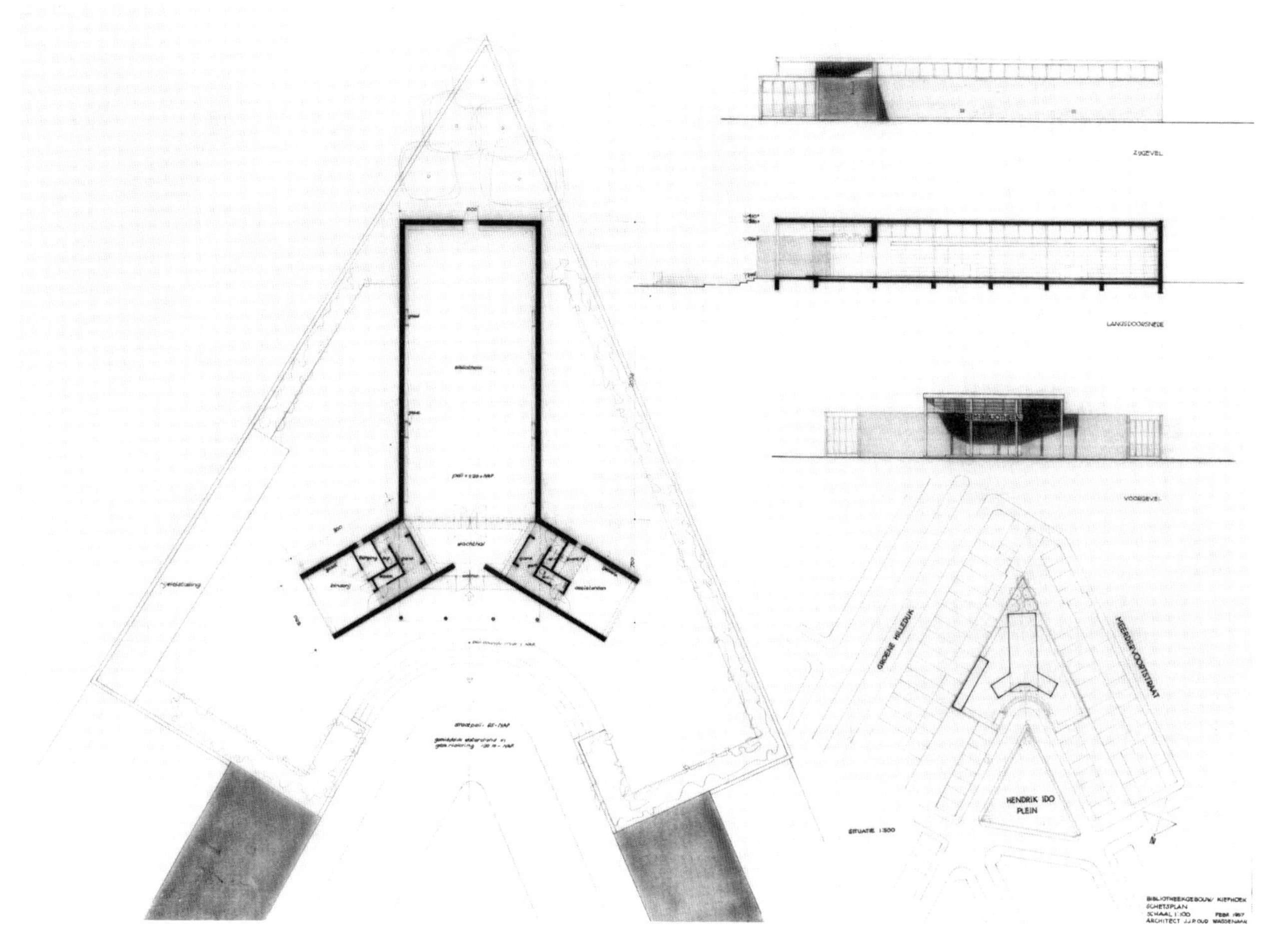


Various design views/ OUDJ-gb 13, NAI, Rotterdam



**Notes**

**1.** J.J.P. Oud to J. Poot, 18 December 1956, OUDJ-B, NAI, Rotterdam.

**Sources**

NAI: OUDJ-gb 1-15, OUDJ-ph 1633-1635

**Literature**

H.E. Oud, *J.J.P. Oud. Architekt 1890-1963. Feiten en herinneringen gerangschikt*, The Hague 1984, p. 140

# 111 Netherlands Congress Centre

**The Hague, Johan de Witlaan, Zorgvliet** **1956-1963**

In his post-war reconstruction plan for The Hague (1946), Dudok proposed building a large cultural centre suitable for international conferences, concerts and shows on a site in the Zorgvliet district adjacent to Berlage's Gemeentemuseum. After Dudok's departure in 1951, it was decided to combine the theatre, concert hall and congress centre in one multi-functional complex. It was hoped that by extending the Gemeentemuseum and establishing an education museum and conservatorium, Zorgvliet would develop into the cultural heart of The Hague. These ambitions were affirmed in a report presented in the spring of 1956 by an ad hoc committee set up to study the congress centre idea. The report also suggested putting the architect of the congress centre in charge of supervising the whole scheme. His task should not be limited to *drawing up a detailed plan for the congress centre, but should also extend to the spatial layout of the entire site set aside for the cultural centre.*[1] In 1956, in accordance with the committee's stated preference, the city council invited Oud to design the congress centre, thereby handing him one of the most prestigious commissions of the period.

The brief called for a conference hall seating three thousand people and below that a huge function room, reception rooms, a music room and a room for theatrical performances; the two wings were to contain various meeting rooms, kitchens, toilets and so on and a flat for the director. Oud's aim was to make a 'humane' building. *It was my intention that all levels of the population; that anyone who has anything to do with the building – be it for duty or pleasure – should be able to move around it pleasantly and easily. That there should be – to the extent possible – "space" on all sides. That everything that takes place here should feel "at home". Some might call this democratic, but "humane" strikes me as more to the point.*

*The building is not intended to be pompous, but truly "humane". With its feet firmly on the ground and thus able to cast its gaze far and high.*

*The material in which the building will be realized is of a simple nature. Sober, with here and there a touch of colour. Dignified, but not overawing.*[2]

Putting this into practice was no simple matter however. The first conceptual plans turned out to be unfeasible and were replaced by a sketch plan in which the quality of the acoustics was of prime importance. A detailed version of this design was ready in 1958. The most striking element was an imposing, seventeen-storey, triangular tower which concealed the complex's chimney stack and contained three hotel rooms per floor. Oud's plan was highly commended both at home and abroad. There were favourable reviews in German and Italian architectural magazines and one German newspaper spoke of *Jakobus J. Pieter Ouds genialer Entwurf.*[3] The Dutch press even floated the idea of transferring the general assembly of the United Nations to The Hague – a plan greeted with some astonishment in the United States.

Financial difficulties delayed construction, however. It was another four years before the first pile was driven and Oud used the delay to introduce a few changes – the conference hall became oval, the balconies were reshaped and a royal box added. In 1960, however, he suggested a drastically reduced main hall: *a hall seating 1500 people in which not only congresses but also plays, concerts, ballet etc. can be held. Such a hall will probably be used every day and thus be able to support a permanent core of personnel. By treating the original large vestibule and cloakroom space (partially) as a covered "street" (arcade with display cases, etc.) I have achieved excellent separate entrances to "all" the spaces (main hall, small halls, reception room, sport) which*



**Notes**

**1.** Report of Commissie Ad Hoc inzake het Congresgebouw. The Hague, Gemeentearchief, Gedrukte Verzamelingen, 1956 no. 343, pp. 1-19.

**2.** Congress Centre design notes, undated manuscript, (OUDJ-cg 1001-1005), NAI, Rotterdam.

**3.** *Frankfurter Rundschau*, 3 October 1958.

**4.** J.J.P. Oud to the mayor of The Hague, 9 January 1960, OUDJ-B, NAI, Rotterdam.


**Sources**

CCA: dr1984: 0259, dr1984: 0311, dr1984: 0327, dr1984: 0388-0427, dr1984: 0461-0465, dr1984: 0469-0471
Gemeentearchief Den Haag: Gedrukte Verzamelingen, 1953 ff.
Getty: 890126-box 3, F10, 890126-box 3, F12, 890126-box 3, F13, 890126-box 3, F16, 890126-box 3, F25, 890126-box 3, F26, 890126-box 3, F27, 890126-box 3, F28, 890126-box 4, F4, 890126-32**, 890126-33**
NAI: OUDJ-cg -887, OUDJ-cg 1001-1005, OUDJ-cg 2001, OUDJ-cg 3001-3003, OUDJ-ph 1599 -1632, OUDJ-ph 1770-1777, MAQV 379, MAQV 607, VOOV 117-120

**Articles**

'Architect Oud over het nieuwe Haagse Congresgebouw', in: 13(1958)43
'Congresgebouw officieel open over een jaar. Creatie J.J. Oud in laatste fase', in: *Haagsche Courant*, 11 March 1968, p. 27
'Congresgebouw voor 's Gravenhage', in: *Bouw*, 13(1958)38
'Het congresgebouw van 's Gravenhage', in: *Bouwen en Wonen*, 5(1958)8
'Cultural Centre The Hague Holland', in: *Architectural Design*, 29(1959)10
'Cultural centre for The Hague', in: *Architectural Record*, February 1959
'Den Haag hat Millionenpläne', in: *Holland Land und Leute*, (1959)1
'Ein Grossprojekt: das neue Kongressgebäude im Haag', in: *Schweizer Baublatt*, 70(1959)7
H.J. de Haas, 'Ontwerp voor een congresgebouw te 's Gravenhage', in: *Bouwbedrijf en Openbare Werken*, 35(1958)21
'Hollande Centre culturel de la Haye', in: *Techniques & Architecture*, 18(1958)6
'Een Nederlands Congresgebouw dringende noodzaak voor ons land', in: *Polytechnisch Tijdschrift*, 14(1959)11/12
'Nog eens het Haagse Congresgebouw', in: *Bouwbedrijf en Openbare Werken*, 35(1958)26
'Nouvelle salle de congres a la Haye', in: *L'Architecture d'Aujourd'hui*, 29(1958)80
'Ontwerp voor een congresgebouw te 's Gravenhage', in:

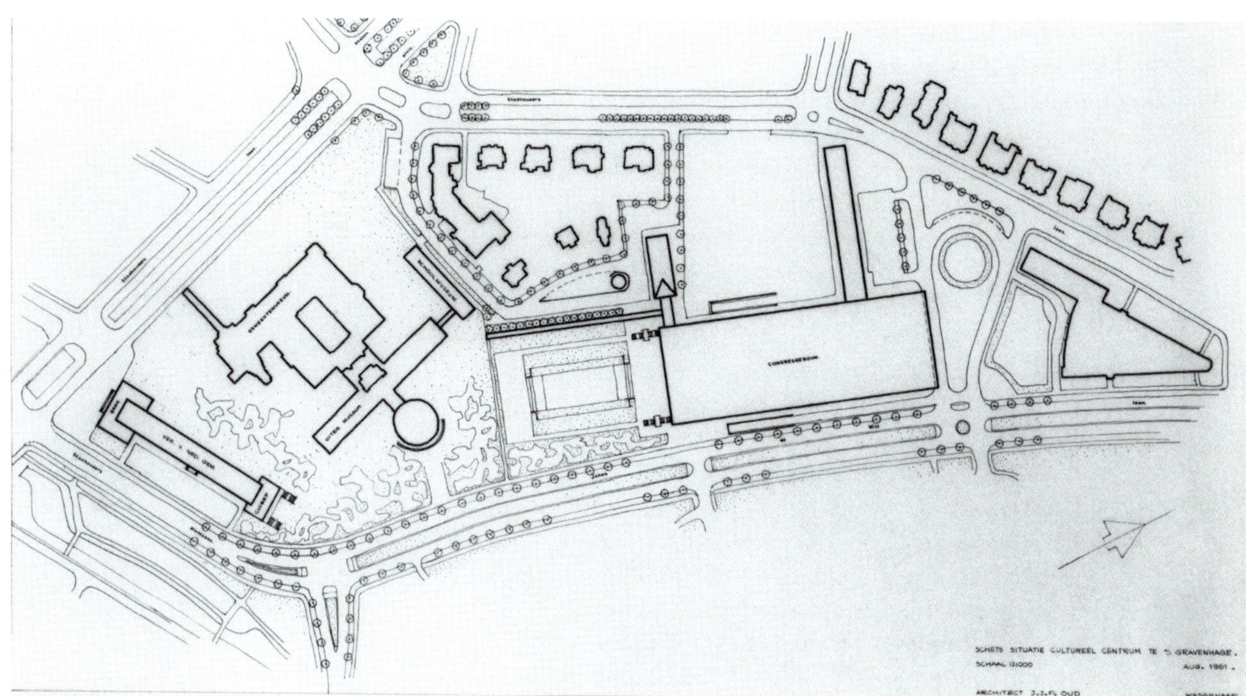


Site plan: Gemeentemuseum with design for extension (left), Congress Centre (centre)/ OUDJ-cg 531, NAI, Rotterdam

Isometric projection preliminary design: extension of Gemeentemuseum (left), Congress Centre/ dr1984: 0399, CCA, Montreal

*will greatly ease the operating costs through savings on heating, etc. I have made the main hall "parterre" so that there are fewer steps to climb, a reduced fire risk, and a much shorter walking distance to the seats. The introduction of the "arcade" has generated a congenial waiting area outside, while the route inside has been considerably shortened: something that is psychologically very important for a pleasant break. This change has also enabled me to use the roof for many branches of outdoor sport. The transformation from Conference Hall etc. to Theatre etc. can be effected very smoothly. The interrelationship of the spaces is the same if not better and the dimensions of the foyers, etc. are "more humane": i.e. more humane on those occasions when the building is not completely full (in my view one of the biggest objections to the plan with the big hall).*[4]

In January 1960 the Stichting Congresgebouw 's-Gravenhage, the foundation set up to run the complex, instructed Oud to produce a detailed design of this version. In autumn it seemed as if it might finally be possible to start building. The final modifications had been made – the hotel rooms in the tower were replaced by flats for the 'majordomos' of important productions – the site office was fitted out, and there seemed to be nothing more standing in the way of the plan's implementation. In the event, it was 1962 before the necessary government approval was issued, and by the time the first sod was turned Oud had died. His son, Hans Oud, took charge from that moment onwards. The building was officially opened on 14 March 1969.



*Bouwbedrijf en Openbare Werken*, 35(1958)22
'Het ontwerp voor een Cultureel Centrum te 's Gravenhage', in: *Bouwwereld*, 54(1958)42
'Het ontwerp voor het Haagse Congresgebouw', in: *Bouwbedrijf en Openbare Werken*, 35(1958)23
J.J.P. Oud 'Het congresgebouw van 's Gravenhage', in: *'s Gravenhage*, 13(1958)9
J.J.P. Oud 'Das Kongresgebäude im Den Haag', in: *STZ*, 57(1960)30/31
J.J.P. Oud 'Kulturzentrum Den Haag', in: *Bauen + Wohnen*, (1959)2
M. Reneman, 'Haags congresgebouw grandioze mislukking', in: *De Nieuwe Linie*, 22 March1969
L. Ronchi, 'Il Centro culturale a L'Aja', in: *L'Architettura*, 39(1959)9
'Schetsontwerp van dr JJP Oud. Congresgebouw en het cultureel centrum zullen f 35,- miljoen kosten', in: *Nieuwe Haagse Courant*, 10 September 1958
'Stoutmoedig plan in Den Haag', in: *Horeca*, 6(1958)38
'This is what The Hague Congress Building will look like', in: *International Associations*, 11(1959)1
'Watchful widow', in: *Holland Herald*, 1(1966)2
B. Zevi, 'Theo van Doesburg – Morgen', in: *Museumjournaal*, 14(1969)2

**Literature**
U. Barbieri, *J.J.P. Oud*, Rotterdam 1987, pp. 180-186
H.E. Oud, *J.J.P. Oud. Architekt 1890-1963. Feiten en herinneringen gerangschikt*, The Hague 1984, pp. 182-194
G. Stamm, *J.J.P. Oud. Bauten und Projekte 1906 bis 1963*, Mainz, Berlin 1984, pp. 139-144

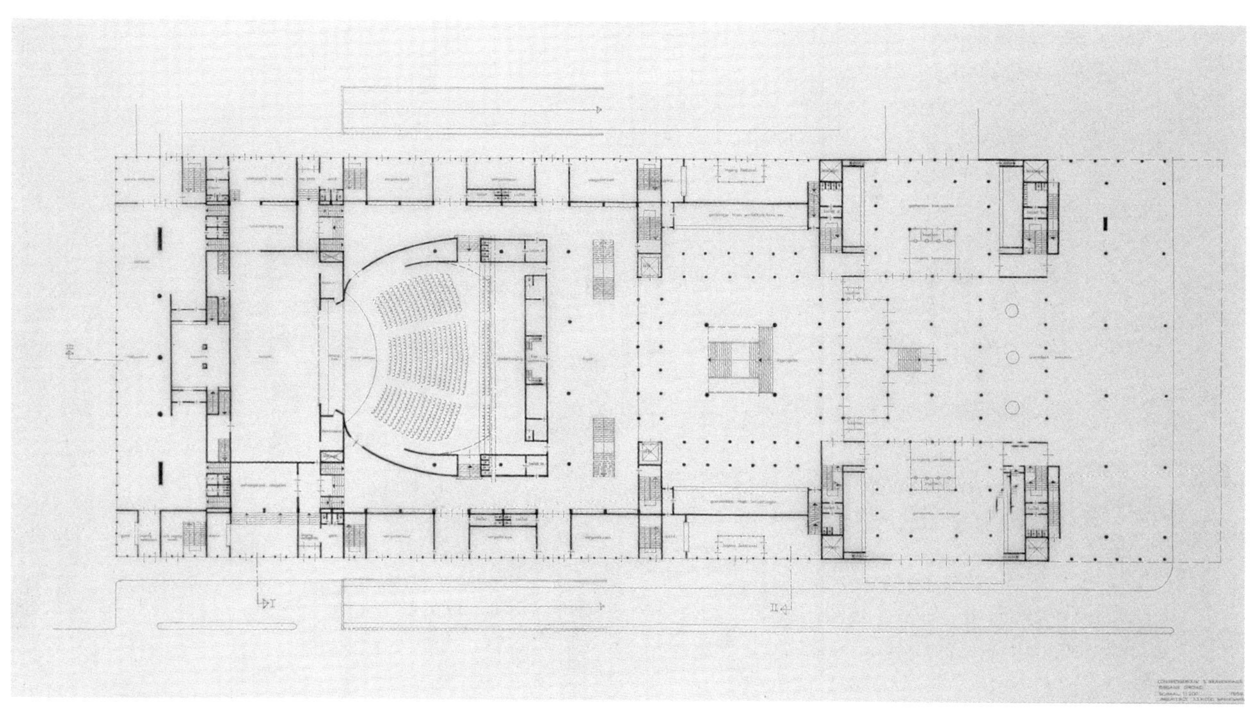

Ground floor plan Congress Centre/ OUDJ-cg 438, NAI, Rotterdam

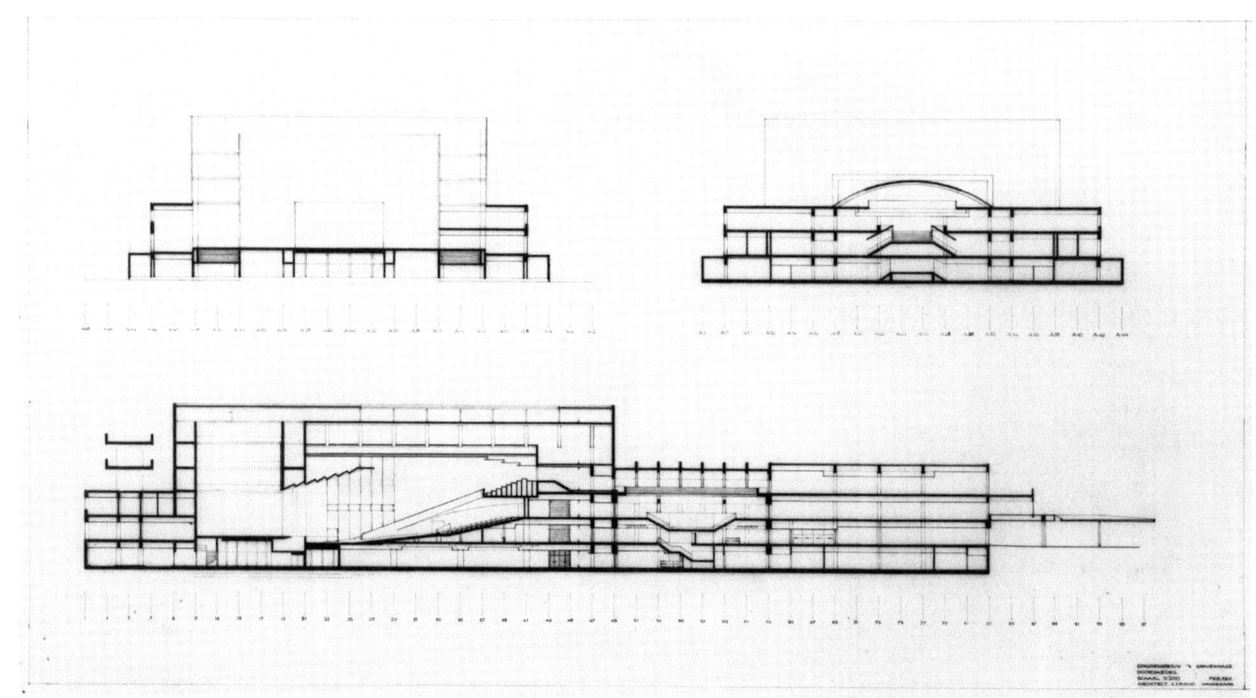

Sections, Congress Centre/ OUDJ-cg 550, NAI, Rotterdam

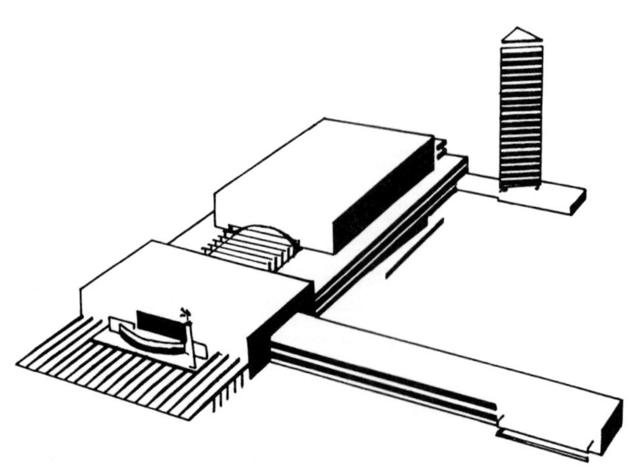

**Sketch for back cover of *Mein Weg in 'De Stijl'*, 1961/ Oud Archive, library, NAI, Rotterdam**

Perspective rear elevation/ dr1984: 0416, CCA, Montreal

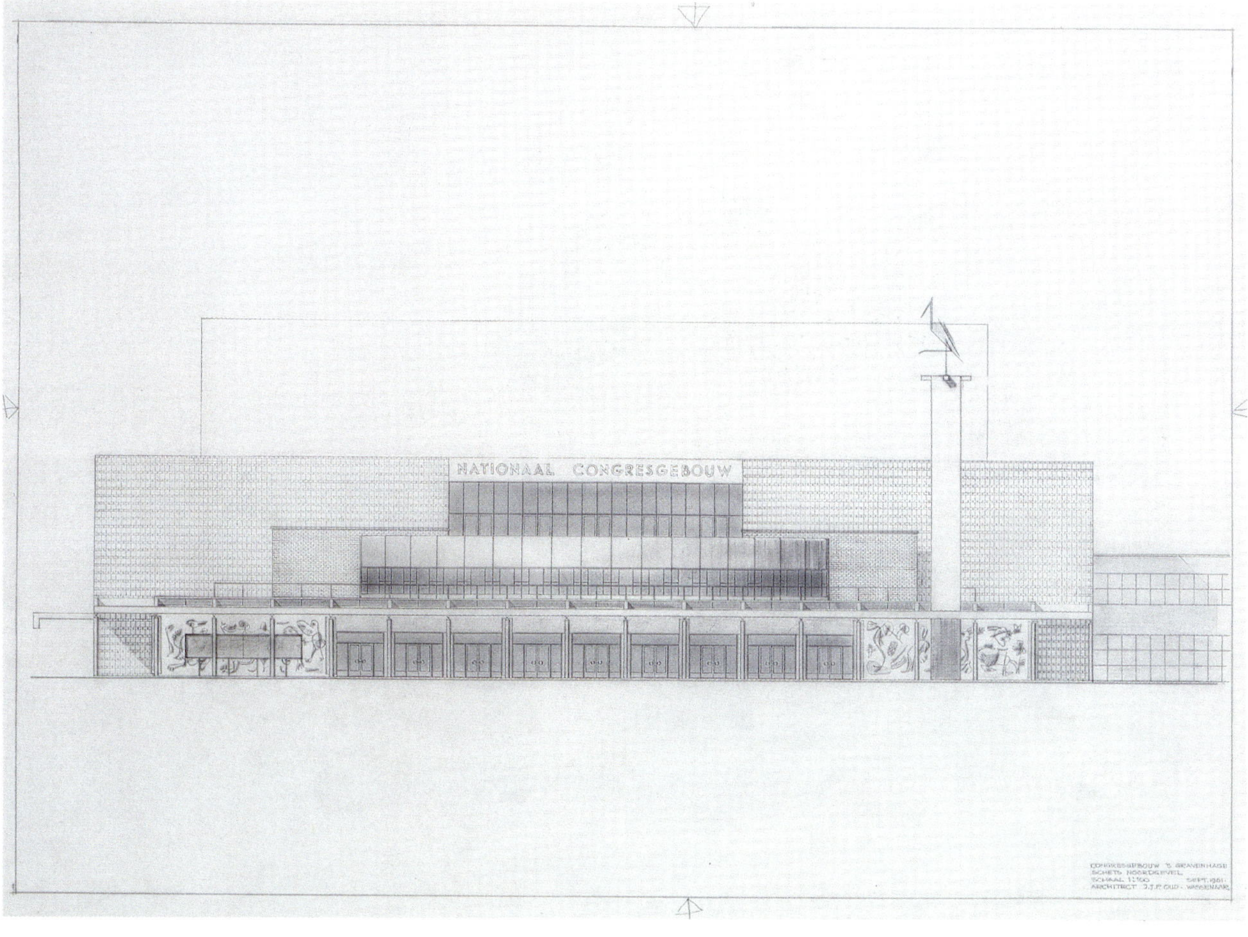

Front elevation with main entrance / Rotterdam, NAi, OUDJ-cg 773

Rear elevation (Photo Ger van der Vlugt)

## List of Original Documents

102 W.C. Brouwer, 'Arbeiderswoningen', in: *Leidsch Dagblad*, 19 January 1916

111 T. van Doesburg to J.J.P. Oud, 13 November 1916, Fondation Custodia, Paris

138 J.J.P. Oud, 'Verbouwing Huize Allegonda Katwijk aan Zee', in: *Bouwkundig Weekblad*, 39(1918)5

144 J.J.P. Oud, 'Het monumentale stadsbeeld', in: *De Stijl*, 1(1917)1

149 Th. van Doesburg, 'J.J.P. Oud. Ontwerp voor een complex huizen voor een strandboulevard', in: *De Stijl*, 1(1917)1

169 J.J.P. Oud, 'Over cubisme, futurisme, moderne bouwkunst, enz.',in: *Bouwkundig Weekblad*, 37(1916)20

171 J.J.P. Oud, 'Dr. H.P. Berlage und sein Werk', in: *Kunst und Kunsthandwerk*, 22(1919)6-8

182 J.J.P. Oud, 'Over de toekomstige bouwkunst en hare architectonische mogelijkheden', in: *Bouwkundig Weekblad*, 42(1921)24

209 J.J.P. Oud, 'Architectonische beschouwingen: A. Massabouw en straatarchitectuur', in: *De Stijl*, 2(1919)7

214 J.J.P. Oud, 'Architectonische Beschouwingen: B. Gewapend beton en bouwkunst', in: *De Stijl*, 2(1917)7

226 J.J.P. Oud, 'Gemeentelijke Volkswoningbouw polder "Spangen", Rotterdam', in: *Bouwkundig Weekblad*, 41(1920)37

237 J.J.P. Oud, 'Gemeentelijke woningbouw "Spangen" te Rotterdam', in: *Bouwkundig Weekblad*, 44(1923)2

238 Th. van Doesburg, 'De architect J.J.P. Oud "voorganger" der "kubisten" in de bouwkunst?', in: *De Bouwwereld*, 30(1922)21

246 J.J.P. Oud, 'Toelichting woningbouw Tusschendijken', typescript, NAI, Rotterdam, OUDJ-td 1001

255 J.J.P. Oud, 'Semi-permanente woningbouw "Oud Mathenesse" Rotterdam', in: *Bouwkundig Weekblad*, 45(1924)43

285 J.J.P. Oud, 'The £ 213 house. A solution to the re-housing problem for rock-bottom incomes in Rotterdam', in: *The Studio*, 101(1931)456

318 J.J.P. Oud, 'Ontwerp voor een woonhuis in Berlijn' , *Bouwkundig Weekblad*, 43(1922)35

331 J.J.P. Oud, 'Ontwerp voor een huis in Pinehurst (U.S.A.)', in: *De 8 en Opbouw, 3(1933)23*

345 J.J.P. Oud, 'Een Café', in: *Bouwkundig Weekblad*, 46(1925)31

378 J.J.P. Oud, 'Van hout tot staal. Ontwikkelingen van den stoel', in: *De Groene Amsterdammer*, 9 January 1935

394 J.J.P. Oud, 'The Building and the Ship', unpublished manuscript, NAI, Rotterdam, OUDJ-na 3001

456 J.J.P. Oud, 'Toelichting Nationaal Legermonument Grebbeberg', undated typescript, NAI, Rotterdam, OUDJ-gr 1001

486 J.J.P. Oud, 'Plate House Plan Commentary', German typescript, 1962, NAI, Rotterdam, OUDJ-pl 1001

502 J.J.P. Oud to Rhenen town council, 25 February 1960, 890126-30**, Getty Research Institute, Los Angeles

# Index of Personal Names

# Index of Place Names

# Bibliography


*Arranged alphabetically according to author's name (anonymous works also listed alphabetically)*

**Anonymous**

Anonymous, 'Architect J.P. Oud ontwierp een nieuwe Spaarbank voor R'dam', in: *Maasbode*, 13 October 1953

Anonymous, 'Architecten zijn niet gebonden aan hoekbebouwing', in: *Nieuw Utrechts Dagblad*, 14 May 1954

Anonymous, 'Architect Oud heeft nieuw plan voor herbouw St. Laurens', in: *De Rotterdammer*, 28 July 1950

Anonymous, 'Architect Oud over het nieuwe Haagse Congresgebouw', in: *Bouw* 13(1958)43, p. 1115

Anonymous, 'Architect Oud zegt: Vreeburg heeft thans geen positieve kwaliteiten', in: *Nieuw Utrechts Dagblad*, 13 March 1951

Anonymous, *L'Art Hollandais a l'exposition internationale des arts decoratifs et industriels modernes; Paris 1925*, Amsterdam 1925

Anonymous, 'Details zu Strukturformen der Architektur', in: *Detail*, (1962)3, pp. 230-250

Anonymous, *Het Bio-boekje. Over de Stichting Bio-kinderrevalidatie*, n.p. [Arnhem] 1992

Anonymous, 'Bio Vakantie-oord nabij Anhem', in: *Bouw*, 10(1955)44, pp. 906-909

Anonymous, 'Bio-herstellingsoord te Arnhem officieel geopend', in: *Cobouw*, 24 June 1960

Anonymous, 'Building in the Netherlands', in: *The Journal of the Royal Institute of British Architects*, 60(1953)5, pp. 171-174

Anonymous, 'B. en W. van Amsterdam stellen voor: Kostloze grond voor nationaal monument op de Dam', in: *Algemeen Handelsblad*, 5 July 1952

Anonymous, *De Sphinx. Catalogus der eerste tentoonstelling van werken van leden en genoodigden in de bovenzalen van de "Harmonie", Breestraat Leiden, 18 januari - 31 januari 1917*, Leiden 1917

Anonymous, 'Complexe d'habitations Hoek van Holland: architecte J.J.P. Oud', in: *Journal hebdomadaire d'information et de critique*, 6(1927)5

Anonymous, 'Congresgebouw officieel open over een jaar. Creatie J.J.P. Oud in laatste fase', in: *Haagsche Courant*, 1 March 1968

Anonymous, 'Congresgebouw voor 's Gravenhage', in: *Bouw*, 13(1958)38, pp. 980-985

Anonymous, 'Het congresgebouw van 's Gravenhage', in: *Bouwen en Wonen*, 5(1958)8, pp. 235-238

Anonymous, 'Cultural Centre, The Hague, Holland', in: *Architectural Design*, 29(1959)10, p. 429

Anonymous, 'Cultural centre for The Hague', in: *Architectural Record*, 125(1959)2, p. 14

Anonymous, 'Dam zal tot een groot plein worden', in: *Algemeen Handelsblad*, 25 March 1950

Anonymous, 'Dam-monument goedgekeurd', in: *Het Parool*, 1 March 1951

Anonymous, 'Definitieve oplossing Midden-Damterrein. Totale verandering van aanzicht', in: *De Nieuwe Dag*, 2 March 1950

Anonymous, 'Den Haag hat Millionenpläne', in: *Holland Land und Leute*, (1959)1

Anonymous, 'Dieren als voorbeeld voor spaarzaamheid', in: *De Rotterdammer*, 18 May 1957

Anonymous, 'Dorp op de Dam. Achter hoge schuttingen verrijst het Nationaal Monument', in: *Trouw*, 17 December 1955

Anonymous, 'Eereprijsvraag 1914 van het genootschap "A. et A." te Amsterdam', in: *Architectura*, 21(1913)31, pp. 256-257

Anonymous, 'Einer neuer Wohnungsbau von J.P. Oud, Stadtbaumeister von Rotterdam, in: *Der Baumeister*, 25(1927)11, pp. 297-301

Anonymous, 'Gedachten in steen van dichters en classicus', in: *De Volkskrant*, 5 May 1946

Anonymous, 'Gemeentelijke woningbouw te Hoek van Holland, architect J.J.P. Oud', in: *Bouwkundig Weekblad*, 47(1927)43, pp. 384-388

Anonymous, 'Het groote monument wordt geboren', in: *Nieuwe Rotterdamsche Courant*, 8 June 1946

Anonymous, 'Ein Grossprojekt: das neue Kongressgebäude im Den Haag', in: *Schweizer Baublatt*, 70(1959)7, pp. 19-22

Anonymous, 'In het hart van de hoofdstad staat een witte zuil' in: *Het Vrije Volk*, 4 May 1956

Anonymous, 'Hollande Centre culturel de la Haye', in: *Techniques & Architecture*, 18(1958)6, pp. 70-71

Anonymous, 'Hollande. College Catholique a La Haye', in: *L'Architecture d'aujourd'hui*, 28(1957)72, pp. 20-21

Anonymous, 'Huize Allegonda', in: *L'Architecture Vivante*, (1924)4, pp. 43-44

Anonymous, 'Industriestad Almelo kreeg een aristocratisch stadhuis', in: *De Tijd*, 17 September 1973

Anonymous, 'Het interieur van het D.S.M.S. Noordam', in: *Nieuwe Rotterdamsche Courant*, 15 September 1938

Anonymous, 'Jaarbeurstoren van 50m. hoogte', in: *Utrechts Katholiek Dagblad*, 13 March 1951

Anonymous, 'De jonge aanwinst van de H.A.L. vaart proef. De Noordam beteekent een experiment', in: *Rotterdamsch Nieuwsblad*, 15 September 1938

Anonymous, 'Juryrapport, Eereprijsvraag: "A. et A." 1914', in: *Architectura*, 22(1914)18, pp. 141-144

Anonymous, 'Kantoorgebouw op de Coolsingel', in: *Bouw*, 10(1955)28, pp. 574-576

Anonymous, 'Kiefhoek – Het witte dorp', in: *Klei*, 23(1931)11, pp. 125-142

Anonymous, 'Midden-Damterrein voor Nationaal Monument', in: *Het Parool*, 5 July 1952

Anonymous, 'Monument op de Dam. Ontwerp van Raedecker en Oud aanvaard', in: *De Tijd*, 1 March 1951

Anonymous, *D.S. Motorschip "Noordam"*, H.A.L. brochure, [1938]

Anonymous, 'Mr. Oud embroiders a theme. Shell "I.B.M." Building, the Hague, J.J.P. Oud, Architect', in: *Architectural Record*, 100(1946)6, pp. 80-84; translation published under: Anonymous, 'Oud in de Amerikaanse pers', in: *Forum*, 2(1947)2/3, pp. 71-72

Anonymous, 'Nationaal legermonument Grebbeberg', in: *Bouw*, 8(1953)37, pp. 713-714

Anonymous, 'Het Nationale Monument', in: *Cobouw*, 11 May 1956

Anonymous, 'Het Nationaal Monument', in: *Nieuwbouw Nederland*, 3(1956)3/4, p. 3

Anonymous, 'Nationaal monument op de Dam door Koningin Juliana onthuld', in: *Nieuwe Rotterdamsche Courant*, 4 May 1956

Anonymous, 'Nationaal Monument op de Dam in Amsterdam', in: *De Nieuwe Dag*, 27 March 1950

Anonymous, 'Nationaal Monument zal aanzien van Dam grondig veranderen', in: *Het Parool*, 1 March 1951

Anonymous, 'Nationaal Monument zal er nu eindelijk komen', in: *Het Vrije Volk*, 29 March 1952

Anonymous, 'Nationale oorlogsgedenkteekens', in: *Bouwkundig Weekblad*, 65(1947)9, pp. 69-70

Anonymous, 'Een Nederlands Congresgebouw dringende noodzaak voor ons land', in: *Polytechnisch Tijdschrift*, 14(1958)11/12, pp. 182b-189b

Anonymous, 'Neue arbeiten von J.J.P. Oud, Rotterdam', in: *Wasmuth's Monatshefte für Baukunst*, 11(1927)1, pp. 32-34

Anonymous, 'Een nieuwe aluminium gevel aan de Coolsingel', in: *Constructies*, 4(1962)1, pp. 9-13

Anonymous, 'D.S.S. "Nieuw Amsterdam"', *Schip en Werf*, [special issue] 1938

Anonymous, 'Nieuw Amsterdam-nummer', in: *Elseviers Geïllustreerd Maandschift*, 48(1938)5

Anonymous, *Nieuw Amsterdam: Facts and Figures*, Rotterdam 1938

Anonymous, 'The Nieuw Amsterdam: a floating Palace of Art', in: *The Studio*, 116(1938)544, pp. 3-18

Anonymous, 'Een nieuwe Spaarbank voor Rotterdam', in: *Maasbode*, 10 October 1953

Anonymous, 'Nog eens het Haagse Congresgebouw', in: *Bouwbedrijf en Openbare werken*, 35(1958)26, pp. 292-294

Anonymous, *Noordam, Zaandam*, Rotterdam 1939

Anonymous, 'Nouvelle salle de congres a la Haye', in: *L'Architecture d'Aujourd'hui*, 29(1958)80, p. IX

Anonymous, 'Ontwerp kantoorgebouw voor de N.V. levensverzekerings-Mij. "Utrecht" aan de Coolsingel te Rotterdam', in: *Bouwbedrijf en Openbare Werken*, 32(1955)24

Anonymous, 'Ontwerp monument op de Dam goedgekeurd', in: *Algemeen Handelsblad*, 1 March 1951

Anonymous, 'Ontwerp Nationaal Monument door minister aanvaard', in: *Het Parool*, 1 March 1951

Anonymous, 'Ontwerp Oud-Raedecker aanvaard', in: *De Volkskrant*, 2 March 1951

Anonymous, 'Het ontwerp voor een Cultureel Centrum te 's Gravenhage', in: *Bouwwereld*, 54(1958)42, pp. 1133-1139

Anonymous, 'Het ontwerp voor het Haagse Congresgebouw', in: *Bouwbedrijf en Openbare werken*, 35(1958)21, pp. 215-223, 35(1958)22, pp. 227-229

Anonymous, 'Oorlogsmonumenten', in: *Bouwcentrum*, 2 (1947)41, p. II

Anonymous, 'Op "Oostduin" zal iets groots worden verricht', in: *De Rotterdammer*, 1 May 1948

Anonymous, 'Oud ziet Jaarbeurstoren als zwaartepunt van het nieuwe Vredenburg', in: *Utrechtsch Nieuwsblad*, 13 March 1951

Anonymous, 'Plan Oud: eindelijk de oplossing van het Jaarbeursvraagstuk', in: *Het Vrije Volk*, 14 March 1951

Anonymous, 'Prijsvraagontwerp verzorgingstehuis Hilversum', in: *Bouwfragmenten*, (1915)8, n.p.

Anonymous, 'Prijsvragen. Stichting "Het verzorgingstehuis" te Hilversum', in: *Bouwkundig Weekblad*, 34(1914)28, pp. 342-345

Anonymous, 'Provinciehuis voor Zuid-Holland', in: *Bouw*, 8(1953)10, p. 179

Anonymous, 'Raadhuis voor Almelo', in: *Bouw*, 19(1964)4, p. 126

Anonymous, 'Raadsleden bekeken een maquette', in: *De Waarheid*, 23 April 1952

Anonymous, 'Raedeckers kunst en het monument op de Dam', in: *Nieuwe Rotterdamsche Courant*, 12 May 1956

Anonymous, 'Raedeckers Nationaal Monument een indrukwekkende schepping', in: *Alkmaarsche Courant*, 5 May 1956

Anonymous, 'Recent works of a pioneer', in: *Progressive Architecture*, XLII(1961)6, pp. 72-73

Anonymous, 'The Record Reports', in: *Architectural Record*, 119(1956)1, p. 300

Anonymous, 'Rapport der jury', in: *Bouwkundig Weekblad*, 36(1915/1916)1, pp. 6-8

Anonymous, 'De samenwerking tusschen directie en architecten. Een gesprek met den heer J.J.P. Oud', in: *Nieuwe Rotterdamsche Courant*, 23 April 1938

Anonymous, 'Schetsontwerp van dr. J.J.P. Oud. Congresgebouw en het cultureel centrum zullen f35,- miljoen kosten', in: *Nieuwe Haagse Courant*, 10 September 1958

Anonymous, 'Scheuren in monument op de Amsterdamse Dam', in: *Cobouw*, 27 March 1959

Anonymous, 'The Shell Building The Hague. Architect J.J.P. Oud', in: *Journal of the Royal Institute of British Architects*, 53(1946)5, pp. 162-166

Anonymous, 'Shell Head Office in The Hague: views and plans', in: *Journal of the Royal Architectural Institute of Canada*, (1950)July, pp. 220-221

Anonymous, 'Stoutmoedig plan in Den Haag', in: *Horeca*, 6(1958)38

Anonymous, 'De toekomstige vorm van Utrechts voornaamste plein', in: *Nieuwe Rotterdamsche Courant*, 14 May 1954

Anonymous, 'This is what The Hague Congres Building will look like', in: *International Associations*, 11(1959)1, p. 62

Anonymous, 'Tijdelijk monument midden-Dam-terrein Amsterdam', in: *Forum*, 2(1947)8, p. 211

Anonymous, 'Voorstel aan de Raad: Nationaal Monument wordt waardig en groots', in: *De Nieuwe Dag*, 5 July 1952

Anonymous, 'Watchful widow', in: *Holland Herald*, 1(1966)2, pp. 20-21

**A**

L. Adler, 'Neue Arbeiten von J.J.P. Oud, Rotterdam', in: *Wasmuth's Monatshefte für Baukunst*, 11(1927)1, pp. 32-38

J.H. Albarda, 'Herinneringen aan Oud', in: *Jong Holland*, 3(1987)4, pp. 21-23

S. Anderson, *Behrens and a New Architecture for the Twentieth Century*, Cambridge (Mass.), London 2000

W.M.J. Arets, W.H.J. van den Bergh (e.a.), *F.P.J. Peutz. Architect 1916-1966*, Eindhoven 1981

**B**

J. Badovici, 'Petite maison semi-permanente à Rotterdam', in: *L'Architecture Vivante*, 2(1924)I, pp. 29-37

J. Badovici, 'Habitations a bon marché à Rotterdam, Oud-Mathenesse, maisons semi-permanentes', in: *L'Architecture Vivante*, 2(1925)I, pp. 10-13

J.B. Bakema, 'Het "Tweede Vrijz.-Christ. Lyceum" van Oud (1956) gezien in het verband met de architectuurontwikkeling', in: *Forum*, 11(1956)7, pp. 229-254

J.B. Bakema, 'Architect Oud 5 April 1963 †', in: *Forum*, 17(1963)2, pp. 92-95

R. Banham, *Theory and Design in the First Machine Age*, London 1960

U. Barbieri, *J.J.P. Oud*, Rotterdam 1987

U. Barbieri, H. Engel, B. Colenbrander, *Architectuur van J.J.P. Oud*, exh.cat. Rotterdam (Lijnbaancentrum RKS) 1981-1982

U. Barbieri, C. Boekraad, J. Leering, *Theo van Doesburg. Grondbegrippen van de nieuwe beeldende kunst*, Nijmegen 1983

A.H. Barr, 'de Stijl', in: P. Johnson, A.H. Barr, *De Stijl 1917-1928. The Museum of Modern Art Bulletin*, XX( 1952/ 1953)2, pp. 7-12

M. Bax, '"Het congres van La Sarraz". Een lezing van H.P. Berlage uit 1929', in: *Jong Holland*, 7(1991)4, pp. 44-51

J. Beckett, '"De Vonk", Noordwijk. An Example of early De Stijl co-operation', in: *Art History* 3(1980)2, pp. 202-217

A. Behne, *The Modern Functional Building* [Introduction by Rosemarie Haag Bletter, translation by Michael Robinson], Santa Monica 1996

A. Behne, *Architekturkritik in der Zeit und über die Zeit hinaus: 1913-1946*, Basle, Berne, Boston 1994

H.E.M. Berens, *Plantonwikkeling Hofplein 1915-1945. Grootsch zonder grootsch te heten*, doctoral thesis, Groningen University1989

H. van Bergeijk, 'Geen sensaties, niet ultramodern, maar één organisch geheel. De Rotterdamse Beurs', in: *Forum*, 36(1993)3/4, pp. 99-122

H. van Bergeijk, *Willem Marinus Dudok. Architect-stedebouwkundige 1884-1974*, Naarden 1995

H.P. Berlage, *Schoonheid in samenleving*, Rotterdam 1919

H.P. Berlage (et al.), *Arbeiderswoningen in Nederland*, Rotterdam 1921

H.G. van Beusekom, *Getijden der Volkshuisvesting. Notities ener geschiedenis van een halve eeuw*, Alphen 1955

R. Bijhouwer, 'Oud-Mathenesse, tussen straatbeeld en woning', in: *Oase*, 4(1986)14, pp. 15-18

D.A.M. Binnendijk, 'De tekst van A. Roland Holst op het Nationaal Monument. Een teken aan de muur', in: *Algemeen Handelsblad*, 19 May 1956

J.-A., Birnie Danzker, C. Blotkamp, Sj. Ex, E. van Straaten, *Theo van Doesburg. Maler – Architekt*, Munich 2000

C. Blok, *Piet Mondrian, Le néo-plasticisme=Het Neo-Plasticisme. Algemeen Manifest van de Beeldende Gelijkwaardigheid*, Amersfoort 1994

C. Blotkamp (et al.), *De beginjaren van De Stijl 1917-1922*, Utrecht 1982

C. Blotkamp (et al.), *De vervolgjaren van De Stijl 1922-1932*, Amsterdam, Antwerp 1996

C. Blotkamp, *Mondriaan in detail*, Utrecht, Antwerp 1987

C. Blotkamp, 'In de periferie van De Stijl: H.H. Kamerlingh Onnes', in: *Jong Holland*, 15(1999)1, pp. 23-31

R. Blijstra, 'Nationaal Monument en Erebegraafplaats', in: *Forum*, 12(1957)3, pp. 62-88

M. Bock, *Architectura. Nederlandse Architectuur 1893-1918*, exh.cat Amsterdam (Architecture Museum) 1975

M. Bock, *Anfänge einer neuen Architektur. Berlages Beitrag zur architektonischen Kultur der Niederlände im ausgehenden 19. Jahrhundert*, The Hague, Wiesbaden 1983

M. Bock (et al.), *Van het Nieuwe Bouwen naar een Nieuwe Architectuur. Groep '32. Ontwerpen, gebouwen, stedebouwkundige plannen 1925-1945*, The Hague 1983

M. Bock (et al.), *De inrichting van de Beurs van Berlage. Geschiedenis en Behoud*, Zwolle 1995

A. B.[A. Boeken], 'Het voorstel van J.J.P. Oud voor de Sint Laurens te Rotterdam', in: *Forum*, 5(1950)8, pp. 307-309

W. Boerhave Beekman, *Hout: van oerwoud tot interieur*, Deventer 1939

T. Boersma, T. Verstegen (eds), *Nederland naar school. Twee eeuwen bouwen voor een veranderend onderwijs*, Rotterdam 1997

Y.-A. Bois (et al.), *De Stijl et l'Architecture en France*, Liège, Brussels 1985

Y.-A. Bois, 'Mondrian and the Theory of Architecture', in: *Assemblage. A Critical Journal of Architecture and Design Culture*, 2(1987)4, pp. 103-130

Y.-A. Bois, J. Joosten, A.Z. Rudenstine, *Mondriaan 1872-1944*, Washington, The Hague, New York, 1994

P. Bonifazio, S. Pace, M. Rosso, P. Scrivano (eds), *Tra Guerra e Pace. Societa, cultura e architettura nel secondo dopoguerra*, Milan 1998

K. Bosma, *Ruimte voor een nieuwe tijd. Vormgeving van de Nederlandse regio 1900-1945*, Rotterdam 1993

F.J. Brevet, 'Rotterdams St Laurens: een grote kerk?', in: *De Groene Amsterdammer*, 19 August 1950

J. Brink, 'Dudok's idee van een krantegebouw', in: *Leids Dagblad*, 9 July 1988

D. Broekhuizen, *De Stijl toen / J.J.P. Oud nu. De bijdrage van architect J.J.P. Oud aan herdenken, herstellen en bouwen in Nederland (1938-1963)*, Rotterdam 2000

A. Broese van Groenon, J.G. Robbers, 'Programma voor een studie-prijsvraag uit te schrijven door de Afdeeling 's Gravenhage van de Maatschappij ter Bevordering der Bouwkunst', in: *Bouwkundig Weekblad*, 34(1914)51, pp. 537-538

W.C. Brouwer, 'Arbeiderswoningen', in: *Leidsch Dagblad*, 19 January 1916

W.C. Brouwer, 'Ingezonden', in: *Bouwkundig Weekblad*, 51(1930)46, pp. 381-383

D.A. Buiskool, *De reis van Harm Kamerlingh Onnes. Brieven uit de Oost 1922-1923*, Hilversum 1999

H. Buys, 'Interieurs van architect J.J.P. Oud, Hillegersberg', in: *Het Landhuis*, 1936, pp. 154-156

**C**

D. Carasso, 'Een monument voor de natie', in: *Jong Holland*, 3(1987)1, pp. 2-23

J.E. Carriere (et al.), *Op de drempel. Orgaan van het 2e VCL*, 4-8 September 1956

M. Casciato (ed.), *Architectuur en Volkshuisvesting. Nederland 1870-1940*, Nijmegen 1980

M. Cerruti, 'Palazzo per uffici a Utrecht', in: *L'Architettura. Cronache e storia*, VIII(1962)79, pp. 38-42

J.-L. Cohen, *André Lurçat 1894-1970. Autocritique d'un moderne*, Liège 1995

B. Colomina, *Privacy and Publicity. Modern Architecture as Mass Media*, Cambridge (Mass.) 1996

B. Colenbrander (ed.), *Oud-Mathenesse, het Witte Dorp 1923-1987*, Rotterdam 1987

Le Corbusier, 'Le Corbusier over de raadhuisprijsvraag', in: *De 8 en Opbouw*, 11(1940)4, pp. 39-40

S. Cusveller (ed.), *De Kiefhoek, een woonwijk in Rotterdam*, Laren, Rotterdam 1990

**D**

G.H.M. Delprat, *Hoofdkantoor der Spaarbank te Rotterdam*, Rotterdam 1904

H. Dethmers, 'Tweede Vrijzinnig Christelijk Lyceum te 's Gravenhage', in: *Bouw*, 12(1957)35, pp. 850-859

R. Dettingmeijer, 'Een gebouw als optelsom van grijpbare elementen en ruimten. Muziekcentrum voltooit Vredenburg', in: *Wonen/TABK*, 7(1979)24, pp. 21-45

R. Dettingmeijer, 'De strijd om een goed gebouwde stad', in: W. Beeren (et al.), *Het Nieuwe Bouwen in Rotterdam 1920-1960*, Delft, Rotterdam 1982, pp. 19-76

R. Dettingmeijer, 'Van Fockema Andreae tot renovatie HC', in: *De ide-*

ale stad. Ideaalplannen voor Utrecht*, Utrecht 1988, pp. 75-114

W. Dexler, 'Reklame im Stadtbilde', in: *Die Schaulade*, 3(1928)5, pp. 269-275

T. van Doesburg, 'De nieuwe beweging in de schilderkunst', in: *De Beweging*, 12(1916)6/7/8/9

T. van Doesburg, 'Schilderkunst', in: *Eenheid*, 3 February 1917

T. van Doesburg, 'J.J.P. Oud. Ontwerp voor een complex huizen voor een Strandboulevard', in: *De Stijl*, 1(1917)1, pp. 13-14

T. van Doesburg, 'Aantekeningen over monumentale kunst. Naar aanleiding van twee bouwfragmenten', in: *De Stijl*, 2(1918)1, pp. 10-11

T. van Doesburg, 'De taak der nieuwe architectuur', in: *Bouwkundig Weekblad*, 41(1920)50, pp. 278-280; 41(1920)51, pp. 281-283 and 42(1921)2, pp. 8-10

T. van Doesburg, 'De consequentie van de pen en de teekenhaak. Terechtwijzingen', in: *De Stijl*, 5(1922)9, p. 141

T. van Doesburg, 'Het fiasco van Holland op de expositie te Parijs in 1925', in: *De Stijl* 6(1925)10/11, pp. 156-159

A. Doig, *Theo van Doesburg, Painting into architecture, theory into practice*, Cambridge (London) 1986

W.M. Dudok, 'Het nieuwe tehuis voor militairen in Den Helder', in: *Bouwkundig Weekblad*, 33(1913)38, pp. 464-468

P. Dupuits-Timmer, 'De tijden veranderen. Bij de heropening van het eerste Haagse filiaal van Metz & Co.', in: *Jong Holland*, 4(1988)2, pp. 15-21

P. Dupuits-Timmer, *Metz & Co. De creatieve jaren*, Rotterdam 1995

**E**

T. Eliëns, *H.P. Berlage (1856-1934). Ontwerpen voor het interieur*, Zwolle 1998

D. Elliot (et al.), *Devetsil. Czech avant-garde art, architecture and design of the 1920s and 30s*, London 1990

H. Engel, 'Architecture without characteristics. On sustainability in architecture', in: H. Bekkering (et al.), *The Architecture Annual 1995-1996. Delft University of Technology*, Rotterdam 1997, pp. 66-72

**F**

G. Fanelli, *Stijl-architektur*, Stuttgart 1985

J.A. Feith, *De Koopmansbeurs te Rotterdam. De ontstaansgeschiedenis van een in de architectuurgeschiedenis miskend gebouw*, doctoral thesis, Groningen University 1995

A.C.A.W. van der Feltz, *Beschrijvende catalogus kunstnijverheid Hannema-De Stuers Fundatie*, Zwolle 1980

H. Frank (ed.), *Fritz Schumacher. Reformkultur und Moderne*, Stuttgart 1994

S. Frank, *Michel de Klerk 1884-1923. An Architect of the Amsterdam School*, Ann Arbor 1980

V. Freijser (ed.), *Het veranderend stadsbeeld van Den Haag*, Zwolle 1991

G. Friedhoff, 'Holland en Denemarken te Parijs', in: *Bouwen*, 3(1925), pp. 97-104

G.F.[G. Friedhoff] 'Nieuwe boekwerken. J.J.P. Oud: Holländische Architektur', in: *Bouwkundig Weekblad*, 47(1927)10, pp. 95-96

H. Fuchs, M. Maandag, H. van de Schoor, *Vouwblad Dudok in Leiden*, Leiden 1990

**G**

J.G. van Gelder, 'S.S. Nieuw Amsterdam 1938', in: *Elseviers Geïllustreerd Maandschrift*, 48(1938)5, pp. 300-310

J.G. van Gelder, 'Ontwerpen voor het nieuwe gebouw der Bataafsche Import Maatschappij in Den Haag', in: *Elseviers Geïllustreerd Maandschrift*, 49(1939)5, pp. 353-354

Anoniem [J.G. van Gelder], 'Ontwerpen voor het nieuwe gebouw der Bataafsche Import Maatschappij in Den Haag', in: *Nieuwe Rotterdamsche Courant*, 4 April 1939

W. van Gelderen, 'W. van Gelderen over de Opbouw-tentoonstelling', in: *De 8 en Opbouw*, 5(1934)12, pp. 103-104

W. van Gelderen, 'Verschillende interieurs door architect J.J.P. Oud', in: *De 8 en Opbouw*, 10(1939)3, pp. 25-27

B. Gerlagh, ´Eduard Cuypers (1859-1927)´, in: *Het huis van de architect. De Sluitsteen. Jaarboek 1999*, Arnhem 1999, pp. 40-41

J.L.J.M. Gerwen, N.H.W. Verbeek, *Voorzorg & de Vruchten. Het verzekeringsconcern AMEV*, Amsterdam 1995

S. Giedion, *Befreites Wohnen*, Zurich, Leipzig 1929

J. van Goethem, 'Colonia Bio-Holiday ad Arnhem', in: *l' Architettura. Cronache e storia*, VII(1961)1, pp. 36-42

J. Gratema, 'Vacantiehuis te Noordwijkerhout', in: *Klei*, 12(1920)2, pp. 13-19

D.I. Grinberg, *Housing in the Netherlands, 1900-1940*, Delft 1977

W.J. de Gruyter, 'Het nieuwe gebouw van Metz & Co. te Den Haag', in: *Elseviers geïllustreerd maandschrift*, 44(1934)11, pp. 63-65

W.J. de Gruyter, 'De aesthetische inrichting van de Nieuw Amsterdam II', in: *Het Vaderland*, 3 May 1938

**H**

H.J. de Haas, 'Kantoorgebouw voor de Shell Nederland N.V. te 's-Gravenhage', in: *Bouwbedrijf en Openbare Werken*, 24(1947)2, pp. 11-16, 24(1947)3, pp. 21-24, 24(1947)4, pp. 31-34

H.J. de Haas, 'Ontwerp voor een congresgebouw te 's Gravenhage', in: *Bouwbedrijf en Openbare Werken*, 35(1958)21, pp. 215-223

Ds. Den Hartog, 'Ds Den Hartog en architect Meischke tegen het plan-Oud', in: *De Rotterdammer*, 4 August 1950

F.M. Hartveld, *Moderne Zakelijkheid. Efficiency in wonen en werken in Nederland, 1918-1940*, Amsterdam 1994

H. van der Heide, 'De Vonk en de Vereeniging "Buitenbedrijf"', in: Anonymous, *Maatschappelijk Werk. Opstellen aangeboden aan Emilie Knappert op haar zeventigsten verjaardag, 15 juni 1930*, Amsterdam 1930, pp. 253-260

J.F. Heijbroek, 'Het kortstondig bestaan van de Leidsche Kunstclub de Sphinx', in: *Leids Jaarboekje, nummer 72*, Leiden 1980, pp. 155-162

P. Hefting, 'America beschreven door K. Lönberg-Holm aan J.J.P. Oud', in: *Museumjournaal*, 21(1975)4, pp. 155-160

H. Henkels (ed.), *Seuphor*, exh.cat. The Hague (Haags Gemeentemuseum) 1976

H.-R. Hitchcock, 'The architectural work of J.J.P. Oud', in: *The Arts*, XIII(1928)2, pp. 97-103

H.-R. Hitchcock, *J.J.P. Oud (Cahier d'Art)*, Paris 1931

H.-R. Hitchcock, P. Johnson, *The International Style: Architecture since 1922*, New York 1932

E. Hoek (ed.), *Theo van Doesburg. Oeuvrecatalogus*, Utrecht, Otterlo, Bussum 2000

E. van der Hoeven, *J.J.P. Oud en Bruno Taut: ontwerpen voor een nieuwe stad Rotterdam-Berlijn*, Rotterdam 1993

E. Holsappel, *Ida Falkenberg-Liefrinck (1901). De rotan stoel als opmaat voor een betere woninginrichting*, Rotterdam 2000

E. J. Hoogenberk, *Het idee van de Hollandse stad. Stedebouw in Nederland 1900-1930 met de internationale voorgeschiedenis*, Delft 1980

G. Hoogewoud, 'De nieuw-amsterdam. Overal een andere (luxe) vormgeving', in: *Wonen/TABK*, 2(1974)5, pp. 25-28

H. Hoste, 'Twee villa's aan zee', in: *De Telegraaf*, 27 April 1918

H. Hoste, 'Het vacantiehuis te Noordwijk', in: *De Telegraaf*, 1 March 1919

H. Hoste, 'Metaalmeubelen', in: *Opbouwen. Halfmaandelijks tijdschrift voor architektuur, tevens orgaan der Vlaamse architektenvereniging*, 4(1934)1, p. 14

H. Hoste, 'Ouds nieuwe metaalmeubelen', in: *Opbouwen. Halfmaandelijks tijdschrift voor architektuur, tevens orgaan der Vlaamse architektenvereniging*, 4(1934)15, pp. 129-131

T.B.F. Hoyer, *Nieuw Amsterdam 1626-1936*, Haarlem, Rotterdam 1938

I. van Huik, 'Ingebed in het karakteristieke groen. Dudok en Den Haag in de jaren 1930-1950', in: V. Freijser (ed.), *Het veranderend stadsbeeld van Den Haag*, Zwolle 1991, pp. 99-142

J. Huizinga, *Mensch en Menigte*, Haarlem 1918

**I**

T. Idsinga, J. Schilt, *Architect W. van Tijen 1894-1974*, The Hague [1990]

**J**

S. Jacobs, *Henry van de Velde. Wonen als kunstwerk, een woonplaats voor Kunst*, Louvain 1996

W.A. Jacobsen, 'Voor lichamelijk gehandicapte kinderen bouwde Nederlandse bioscoopbond herstellingsoord te Arnhem', in: *Technische Gids*, 18 June 1960, pp. 511-517

A. Jaeggi, *Adolf Meyer, der zweite Mann. Ein Architekt im Schatten von Walter Gropius*, Berlin 1994

J. de Jager, W. van Someren, 'Hoofdkantoor Hoogovens', in: *Forum*, 5(1950)10, pp. 388-395

K. Jakobs (et al.), *De ideale stad 1664-1988, ideaalplannen voor de stad Utrecht*, exh.cat. Utrecht (Centraal Museum)1988

K. James, *Erich Mendelsohn & the Architecture of German Modernism*, Cambridge (Mass.) 1997

H. Jannière, ' 'L Architecture Vivante' en 'Cahiers d'Art', in: *Casabella*, 57(1993)603, pp. 46-53

P. Johnson, A.H. Barr, H.-R. Hitchcock, *Modern Architecture: International Exhibition*, New York 1992

P. Johnson, H.-R. Hitchcock, *The International Style: architecture since 1922*, New York 1932

A.M. de Jongh (ed.), *De Wilhelminapolder. Een beeld van een grootlandbouwbedrijf*, Goes 1996

M.J.I. de Jonge van Ellemeet, 'Woningbouw in Oud-Mathenesse', in: *Tijdschrift voor volkshuisvesting en stedebouw*, 6(1925)3, pp. 62-64

M.J.I. de Jonge van Ellemeet, 'De Gemeentelijke Woningbouw "Kiefhoek" te Rotterdam', in: *Tijdschrift voor volkshuisvesting en stedebouw*, 12(1931)5, pp. 101-106

M.J.I. de Jonge van Ellemeet, 'Meeningen van anderen', in: *Het Bouwbedrijf*, 12(1932)26, p. 333

M.J.I de Jonge van Ellemeet, 'De woningbouwvereenigingen en de architectuur', in: *Beter wonen. Gedenkboek gewijd aan het werk van den Woningbouwvereenigingen in Nederland*, Amsterdam 1938, pp. 67-91

**K**

G. Kazemier, 'Het tweede Vrijzinnig Christelijk Lyceum te 's Gravenhage', [offprint from] *Forum*, 11(1956)7

G. Kazemier, 'Het Tweede Vrijzinnig Christelijk Lyceum te 's Gravenhage', in: *Bouwkundig Weekblad*, 75(1957)3, pp. 29-36

K. Kirsch, *Die Weissenhofsiedlung. Werkbundausstellung 'Die Wohnung'- Stuttgart 1927*, Stuttgart 1987

A. Klein, 'Neue Arbeiten von J.J.P. Oud', in: *Wasmuth's Montatshefte für Baukunst*, 11(1927)7, pp. 294-298

W. Kleinerüschkamp, *Hannes Meyer 1889-1954. Architekt Urbanist Lehrer*, Berlin, Frankfurt am Main 1989

L. de Klerk, H. Moscoviter, *En dat al voor de arbeidende klasse. 75 Jaar Volkshuisvesting Rotterdam*, Rotterdam 1992

L. de Klerk, *Particuliere plannen*, Rotterdam 1998

L. de Klerk, *Mooi Werk. Geschiedenis van de Maatschappij voor Volkswoningen, Rotterdam 1909-1999*, Rotterdam 1999

H. van der Kloot-Meyburg, *Landhuisbouw in Nederland*, Amsterdam 1921

A. Koch, *W.H. Gispen; een modern eclecticus (1890-1981)*, Rotterdam 1988

B.J. Koldewey, 'De nieuwe Beurs te Rotterdam', in: *Het R.K. Bouwblad*, (1935)7, p. 6

Y. Koopmans, *Muurvast en gebeiteld. Beeldhouwkunst in de bouw 1840-1940*, Rotterdam 1994

Y. Koopmans, *Muurvast en gebeiteld. Beeldhouwkunst in de bouw 1840-1940*, Rotterdam 1997

C.P. Krabbe, *Ambacht, Kunst, Wetenschap. Bevordering van de bouwkunst in Nederland (1775-1880)*, Zwolle, Zeist 1998

W. Kromhout, 'Het plan "Blijdorp" te Rotterdam', in: *Tijdschrift voor Volkshuisvesting en Stedebouw*, 8(1927)5, pp. 106-115

M. Kuipers, *Bouwen in Beton*, Zeist 1987

G. Kühne, 'Oud und die Klassik. "Bio-Herstellingsoord" in Arnhem/Niederlande', in: *Bauwelt*, 51(1960)40, pp. 1163-1167

M. Küper, *Het stadhuis van Almelo; Het laatste ontwerp van J.J.P. Oud*, Almelo 1995

**L**

B.A. Laan, A. Koch (ed.), *Collectie Gispen; meubels, lampen en archivalia in het NAi, 1916-1980*, Rotterdam 1996

V. M. Lampugnani, R. Schneider (ed.), *Moderne Architektur in Deutschland 1900 bis 1950. Reform und Tradition*, Stuttgart 1992

D. Langmead, *J.J.P. Oud and the International Style. A Bio-Bibliography*, Westport, London 1999

G.A. Leeuwenberg, 'Het Vreeburg-vannu verschikking voor het oog', in: *Utrechts Katholiek Nieuwsblad*, 13 March 1951

J.H.W. Leliman, *Het stadswoonhuis in Nederland gedurende de laatste 25 jaren*, The Hague 1920

G.J. Lepoeter, 'Bij het 175-jarig bestaan van de Wilhelminapolder (1984)', in: *Zeeuws Tijdschrift*, 34(1984), pp. 161-178

W. Lesnikowski (et al.), *East European Modernism. Architecture in Czechoslovakia, Hungary & Poland between the Wars 1919-1939*, London 1996

N. Levine, *The Architecture of Frank Lloyd Wright*, Princeton (N.J.) 1996

J.B. van Loghem, 'De stoel gedurende de laatste veertig jaar', in: *De 8 en Opbouw*, 6(1935)1, p. 1

J.B. van Loghem, 'Nederlandsche bouwmeesters: "de Kiefhoek" te Rotterdam – Architect J.J.P. Oud', in: *De Groene Amsterdammer*, 5 April 1930

T.K. van Lohuizen, *Zwei Jahre Wohnungsstatistik in Rotterdam. Eine neue Methode der Statistik über Wohnungsbedarf und Wohnungsvorrat*, Berlin 1922

J.C. Ludi (et al.), *Analyse du Bio-herstellingsoord, Arnhem, J.J.P. Oud 1952-1960 1ère année 1989-1990 EAUG*, Zurich 1989

T. H. Lunsing Scheurleer (et al.), *Het Rapenburg; Geschiedenis van een Leidse gracht, Deel IIIb*, Leiden 1988

J.G.E.Luyt, 'Provinciehuis voor Zuid-Holland', in: *Bouw*, 8(1953)10, pp. 179-183

El Lissitzky, *Proun und Wolkenbügel. Schriften, Briefe, Dokumente*, Dresden 1977

**M**

H.A. Maaskant, 'Rotterdams Beursgebouw', in: *Forum*, 2(1947)9/10, pp. 275-276

H.F. Malgrave (ed.), *Otto Wagner. Reflections on the Raiment of Modernism*, Santa Monica 1993

P. Man, 'Dit is van uw dubbeltjes gebouwd', in: *Libelle*, 27(1960)35

L. Mariani, 'Recenti opere di Jacobus Johannes Pieter Oud', in: *L' Architettura, Cronache e storia*, II(1956)11, p. 342-351

L. Mariani, 'Achitettura popolare de Jacobus Johannes Pieter Oud', in: *Edilizia Popolare*, (1957)15, pp. 34-40

A. Martens, 'The introduction of modern art in Holland. Picasso as pars pro toto, 1910-1930', in: *Simiolus* 21(1992)3

A. Martis, 'Het ontstaan van het kunstnijverheidsonderwijs in Nederland en de geschiedenis van de Quellinusschool te Amsterdam 1879-1924', in: *Nederlands Kunsthistorisch Jaarboek 1979, deel 30*, Haarlem 1980

E. Mendelsohn, *Russland – Europa – Amerika*, Basle, Berlin, Boston 1929

E. Mendelsohn (ed.), *Brief eines Architekten*, Munich 1961

N. Mens, A. Tijhuis, *De architectuur van het ziekenhuis*, Rotterdam 1999

J.P. Mieras, 'Monument op het Damplantsoen', in: *Bouwkundig Weekblad*, 66(1948)4, pp. 26-27

P. Mondriaan, *Le Néo-Plasticisme. Principe Général de l'Equivalence Plastique*, Paris 1920

H. Moscoviter, *Kwetsbare schoonheid. Monumenten in Rotterdam*, Delft 1994

M. Mosler, *Dirk Hannema. De geboren verzamelaar*, Rotterdam 1995

E. Mulhern, 'Netherlands architect set the pace', in: *Knickerbocker Weekly*, 3(1943)27, pp. 34-37

H. Muthesius, *Wie baue ich mein Haus. Berufserfahrungen und Radschläge eines Architekten*, Munich 1925

**N**

W. Nerdinger, *Walter Gropius*, Cambridge (Mass.), Berlin 1985-1986

W. Nerdinger, *Theodor Fischer. Architekt und Städtebauer*, Berlin, Munich 1988

J. Niegeman, 'De "Nieuw Amsterdam"', in: *De 8 en Opbouw*, 9(1938)12/13, pp. 128-129

J. Niegemann, 'Baubrief eines Holländischen Architekten', in: *Vom Bauen in Holland*, offprint from *Der Bauhelfer*, (1949), pp. 495-502

F. Neumeyer, *Mies van der Rohe. Das kunstlose Wort. Gedanken zur Baukunst*, Munich 1986

**O**

A.H. Okazaki, 'Architect Oud and Vredenburg Square', in: *Kunst in Utrecht*, 5(1967)5/6

J. Otsen, 'De Purmerendse jaren van Jac. Jongert', unpublished manuscript, Purmerend 1997

A. Otten, 'Rotterdamsche problemen', in: *Bouwkundig Weekblad*, 50(1929)21, pp. 161-168

A. Otten, '"De Kiefhoek" te Rotterdam', in: *Bouwkundig Weekblad*, 51(1930)45, pp. 369-371

H.E. Oud, 'Nieuw hoofdkantoor voor de Spaarbank te Rotterdam', in: *Bouw*, 6(1951)19, pp. 319-321

H.E. Oud, 'Bio-mytylschool te Arnhem', in: *Bouw*, 20(1965)45, pp. 1676-1679

H.E. Oud, *J.J.P. Oud. Architekt 1890-1963. Feiten en herinneringen gerangschikt*, The Hague 1984

T. Overtoom, *J.J.P. Oud als ontwerper van meubelen: een onderzoek naar 327, niet eerder geïnventariseerde, schetsbladen*, doctoral thesis, Groningen University 1996

T. Overtoom, 'De geëigende vorm. J.J.P. Oud als ontwerper van stalen meubelen', in: *Jong Holland*, 15(1999)3, pp. 28-44

R.W. Oxenaar, *Bart van der Leck tot 1920. Een primitief van de nieuwe tijd*, Utrecht 1976

**P**

W. Pehnt, *Die Architektur des Expressionismus*, Stuttgart 1998

P. Penn, *Beursbouw Rotterdam*, Rotterdam 1940

A. Plate, 'Rotterdams Beurs', in: *Forum*, 2(1947)9/10, pp. 262-263

S. Polano, *J.J.P. Oud, Architettura Olandese*, Milan 1981

S. Polano (et al.), *Hendrik Petrus Berlage. Het complete werk*, Alphen 1985

S. Polano (ed.), *Hendrik Petrus Berlage, Complete Works*, New York 1988

R. Pommer, C.F. Otto, *Weissenhof 1927 and the Modern Movement in Architecture*, Chicago, London 1991

J.M. Prange, 'Nationaal Monument geen eenheid', in: *Het Parool*, 7 May 1956

**R**

G. Radford, *Modern Housing for America. Political struggles in the New Deal Era*, Chicago, London 1996

H. Redeker, 'John Raedecker en het Nationaal Monument', in: *Forum*, 12(1957)3, pp. 89-96

E. Reinhartz-Tergau, 'Een Gispenlamp van 1927 J.J.P. Oud', in: *Jong Holland*, 3(1987)1, pp. 34-37

E. Reinhartz-Tergau, *J.J.P. Oud: Architect. Meubelontwerpen en interieurs*, Rotterdam 1990

A.W. Reinink, *K.P.C. de Bazel – Architect*, Leiden 1965

M. Reneman, 'Haags congresgebouw grandioze mislukking', in: *De Nieuwe Linie*, 22 March 1969

W. Retera Wzn. 'Opmerkingen over de "Nieuw Amsterdam" in het algemeen en over de hutten (het slapen) in het bijzonder', in: *Elseviers Geïllustreerd Maandschrift*, 48(1938)5, pp. 318-323

G.T. Rietveld, 'Nieuwste werken van J.J.P. Oud', *de 8 en Opbouw*, 10(1939)3, pp. 21-23

T. Riley, *The International Style: Exhibition 15 and the Museum of Modern Art*, New York 1992

Rogkerus, 'J.J.P. Oud: Arbeiterwohnungen mit Läden in Hoek van Holland', in: *Die Bauschau*, 3(1927)5, pp. 5-9

L. Ronchi, 'Il Centro culturale a L'Aja', in: *L'Architettura. Cronache e storia*, IV(1959)39, pp. 626-629

A. Roth, *Begegnungen mit Pionieren*, Basle, Stuttgart 1973

**S**

W.J.H.B. Sandberg, 'Schuldig aan het monument op de Dam', in: *De Volkskrant*, 9 August 1969

K. Sarneel, 'John Raedecker en het nationale monument', in: *De Linie*, 12 May 1956

H.G.J. Schelling, 'Plannen voor nieuw Provinciehuis van Zuid-Holland te 's-Gravenhage. Opmerkingen naar aanleiding van de meervoudige opdracht', in: *Bouwkundig Weekblad*, 71(1953)21-22, pp. 165-177

M.G.W. Schiphouwer, 'Het monument op de Dam', in: *Werk in Uitvoering*, 5(1955)9, pp. 254-256

K. Schipper, J. van Geest, *Jos. Klijnen*, Rotterdam 1999

R. Schneider, W. Wang (eds), *Moderne Architektur in Deutschland 1900 bis 2000. Macht und Monument*, Ostfildern-Ruit 1998

F. Schulze, *Philip Johnson. Life and Work*, New York 1994

P. Scrivano, 'J.J.P. Oud e l'architettura olandese negli scritti di Henry-Russell Hitchcock', in: *Zodiac*, 18(1997), pp. 90-103

H. Searing, 'Berlage or Cuypers? The father of them all', in: H. Searing (ed.), *In search of Modern Architecture. A Tribute to Henry-Russell Hitchcock*, Cambridge (Mass.), London 1982, pp. 226-244

H. Searing, 'Berlage and Housing, "The most significant modern building type"', in: *Nederlands Kunsthistorisch Jaarboek 1974, deel 25*, Haarlem 1974, pp. 133-180

V. Slapeta (et al.), *Die Brünner Funktionalisten. Moderne Architektur in Brünn (Brno)*, Innsbruck 1985

V. Slapeta (et al.), *Czech Functionalism 1918-1938*, London 1987

H. van der Sloot, *Betrekkelijk tot tevredenheid. De woningbouwverenigingen in Schiedam,* Schiedam 1992

A. Staal, 'Het gebouw der B.I.M. Architect Oud's jongste werk. Vruchtbare vooruitgang', in: *De Telegraaf*, 13 June 1941

M. Stam, 'Het passagiersschip de "Nieuw Amsterdam"', in: *De 8 en Opbouw*, 9(1938)12/13, pp. 119-128

G. Stamm, 'Het jeugdwerk van architect J.J.P. Oud 1906-1917', in: *Museumjournaal*, 22(1977)6, pp. 260-265

G. Stamm, *J.J.P. Oud. Bauten und Projekte 1906 bis 1963*, Mainz, Berlin 1984

G. Stamm, *The Architecture of J.J.P. Oud*, Tallahassee 1978

G. Stamm, 'Bakermat 20ste eeuwse architectuur ligt in Purmerend', in: *Noordhollandsche Courant*, 31 July 1978

M. Steenhuis, D'Laine Camp, M. Kamphuis, *Arbeiderswoningen in Hoek van Holland, J.J.P. Oud. Ontwerp, bouw, beheer en renovaties 1923-1999*, Rotterdam 1999

M. Steenhuis, *P. Verhagen*, monografie in de stedenbouwkundige reeks van het Nederlands Instituut voor Ruimtelijke Ordening en Volkshuisvesting (NIROV), manuscript October 2000

A.J. van der Steur, 'Over den architect en het experiment, een overdenking naar aanleiding van de Kiefhoek', in: *Bouwkundig Weekblad*, 51(1930)46, pp. 379-381

E. Stevens, 'Het Nationale Monument op de Dam', in: *Toonbeeld*, 1(1990)2, pp. 5-10

B. Stigter, 'Beelden om nooit te vergeten', in: F. van den Burg (ed.), *Kunst en Beleid in Nederland, deel 6*, Amsterdam 1993, pp. 13-62

C.W. Stortenbeker, A. van der Woud (et al.), *De Hoge Veluwe, 60 jaar natuur, cultuur en architectuur*, Hoenderloo 1995

E. van Straaten, *Theo van Doesburg. Schilder en architect*, The Hague 1988

E. van Straaten, *Klare en lichte, gesloten ruimten, geaccentueerd door diepe en pure kleuren. Het werk van Theo van Doesburg in de architectuur*, Amsterdam 1992

E. van Straaten, *H.H. Kamerlingh Onnes. Schilder en keramist*, tent.cat. Leeuwarden, Arnhem 1981-1982

M. van Stralen, ´Kindred Spirits: Holland, Wright and Wijdeveld´, in: A. Alofsin (ed.), *Frank Lloyd Wright. Europe and Beyond*, Berkeley 1999, pp. 45-65

**T**

J.T. van Taalingen, *Nederlandse Bioscoopbond 60 jaar*, Amsterdam 1978

E.R.M. Taverne, 'Ouds ontwerp voor het Hofplein. Een veronachtzaamde periode uit de stedebouwkundige geschiedenis van Rotterdam', in: *Plan*, (1981)9, pp. 30-34

E.R.M. Taverne, 'Bouwen zonder makeup. Acties van Oud voor het behoud van de architectuur', in: *Wonen/TABK*, 11(1983)3, pp. 8-22

E.R.M. Taverne, 'Neo-De Stijl of Neo-Monumentalisme? Het Shell-gebouw van J.J.P. Oud te 's-Gravenhage', in: W. Denslagen (et al.), *Bouwkunst. Studies in vriendschap voor Kees Peeters*, Amsterdam 1993, pp. 515-527

E.R.M. Taverne, I. Visser (eds), *Stedebouw. De geschiedenis van de stad in de Nederlanden van 1500 tot heden*, Nijmegen 1993

E.R.M. Taverne, D. Broekhuizen, *Het Shell-gebouw van J.J.P. Oud: ontwerp en receptie / J.J.P. Oud's Shell-Building: design and reception*, Rotterdam 1995

E.R.M. Taverne, D. Broekhuizen, 'De dissidente architecten: J.J.P. Oud, Jan Wils en Robert van 't Hoff', in: C. Blotkamp (et al.), *De vervolgjaren van De Stijl 1922-1932*, Amsterdam, Antwerp 1996, pp. 365-396

W. Tegethoff, 'Weissenhof, 1927, Der Sieg des neuen Baustils', in: *Jahrbuch des Zentralinstituts für Kunstgeschichte*, I(1987)

E. van Tetterode, 'Dam monument bijna voltooid', in: *Natuursteen*, (1956)108, pp. 70-71, 83

E. Thorn Prikker, 'Willem C. Brouwer', in: *Nederlansche Kunstnijverheid*, Rotterdam 1905

N.J. Troy, *The De Stijl Environment*, Cambridge (Mass.) 1983

O. van Tussenbroek, 'Werk van J.J.P. Oud voor de "Nieuw Amsterdam" en de "Noordam"', in: *Interieur. Tijdschrift voor woninginrichting*, 58(1941)402, pp. 115-118

O. van Tussenbroek, 'Architect J.J.P. Oud. Verbouwing van een woning te Rotterdam', in: *Interieur. Tijdschrift voor woninginrichting*, 58(1941)408, pp. 293-295

O. van Tussenbroek, *Achter Blinkende Vensters*, Leiden 1950

O. van Tussenbroek, 'Bij werk van J.J.P. Oud als meubelontwerper en binnenhuisarchitect', in: *Interieur. Tijdschrift voor woninginrichting*, 68(1955)525, pp. 361-365

W. van Tijen, 'De architect als ontwerper voor bouwbedrijven', in: *Bouwkundig Weekblad*, 71(1953)3/4, pp. 29-30

W. van Tijen, 'Industrialisatie van het bouwen en de Erecode van de BNA', in: *Bouwkundig Weekblad*, 71(1953)9/10, pp. 73-74

**V**

A. van der Valk, *Het levenswerk van Th.K. van Lohuizen 1890-1956. De eenheid van het stedebouwkundige werk*, Delft 1990

J.A.A. Verlinden, 'Pedagogische aspecten van de bouw en de inrichting van scholen', in: *Weekblad O.K.W-medelingen*, (1956)42, pp. 1-12

E. Vermeulen, 'Robert van 't Hoff', in: C. Blotkamp (et al.), *De beginjaren van De Stijl 1917-1922*, Utrecht 1982, 207-232

Verschoor, 'Bio-Herstellingsoord bij Arnhem', in: *Bouwwereld*, 56(1960)20, pp. 521-526, 584

L.C. van der Vlugt, 'De semi-permanente woningen in "Oud-Mathenesse" te Rotterdam', in: *Bouwen*, 2(1925)11, pp. 161-164

H.J.L. Vonhoff, *Bewegend verleden, een biografische visie op mr. P.J. Oud*, Alphen a/d Rijn 1969

J.J. Vriend, 'Het nieuwe kantoorgebouw voor de B.I.M. door architect J.J.P. Oud', in: *De Groene Amsterdammer*, 12 January 1946

J.J. Vriend, 'Het nieuwe nationale monument op de Dam', in: *De Groene Amsterdammer*, 3 June 1950

J.J. Vriend, 'Nieuwe school van architect Oud', in: *De Groene Amsterdammer*, 29 September 1956

J.J. Vriend, 'Oud's Bio Herstellingsoord Arnhem', in: *De Groene Amsterdammer*, 2 July 1960

**W**

C. Wagenaar, *Tussen Grandezza en Schavot. De ontwerpen van Granpré Molière voor de wederopbouw van Groningen*, Groningen 1991

C. Wagenaar, *Welvaartsstad in wording. De wederopbouw van Rotterdam 1940-1952*, Rotterdam 1992

C. Wagenaar, '"Gewoon echt, van binnen uit" Het Bio-vakantieoord van J.J.P. Oud', in: *Archis*, (1998)12, pp. 67-74

F.H. Warnaars, 'Het provinciehuis van Zuid-Holland', in: *Katholiek Bouwblad*, 20(1953)15, pp. 225-273

F.H. Warnaars, 'Het provinciehuis van Zuid-Holland', in: *De Ingenieur*, 65(1953)38, pp. 179-190

I.B. Whyte, *Bruno Taut, Baumeister einer neuen Welt. Architektur und Aktivismus 1914-1920*, Stuttgart 1981

K. Wiekart, 'Het nieuwste werk van J.J.P. Oud', in: *Vrij Nederland*, 21(1960)9

K. Wiekart, 'De moderne architectuur en wij', in: *Compositie*, 7(1962)1, pp. 9-15

D. Wintgens Hötte, A. de Jongh-Vermeulen (eds), *Dageraad van de Moderne Kunst. Leiden en omgeving 1890-1940*, Zwolle, Leiden 1999

W.G. Witteveen, 'Uitbreidingsplan voor het noordelijk en noord-westelijk stadsdeel (Blijdorp) te Rotterdam', in: *Tijdschrift voor Volkshuisvesting en Stedebouw*, 10(1929)8, pp. 169-179

C. Wolterbeek, 'Het nieuwe Hoofdkantoor der Hoogovens', in: *De Ingenieur*, 62(1950)52, pp. A581-A582

A. van der Woud, *Waarheid en karakter. Het debat over de bouwkunst 1840-1900*, Rotterdam 1997

C. Zarelli, *Alfred Roth. La Testimonanza di un protagonista*, Milan 1993

B. Zevi, 'Theo van Doesburg – Morgen', in: *Museumjournaal*, 14(1969)2, pp. 58-63

P. Zwart, 'De projecten voor Rotterdamse Beurs, 1928. De victorie der pathetische architectuur', in: *Het Vaderland*, 3 February 1929

# Published Articles by J.J.P. Oud

*Articles are listed according to first publication, followed where applicable by details of any subsequent full or partial publication, whether the text appeared in instalments or entailed an afterword*

**1911**

Anonymous [J.J.P. Oud], 'Over Bouwkunst', in: *Schuitemakers Purmerender Courant*, 18 January 1911

J.J.P. Oud, 'Opwekking", in: *Studentenweekblad*, 10 March 1911

J.J.P. Oud, 'Arbeiderswoningen van J. Emmen', in: *Technisch Studententijdschrift*, 15 March 1911

**1912**

J.J.P. Oud, 'Schoorsteen in het gebouw der werkmansvereeniging "Vooruit" te Purmerend', in: *Klei*, 4(1912)22, pp. 338-339

**1913**

J.J.P. Oud, 'Ingezonden', in: *Bouwkundig Weekblad* 33(1913)13, pp. 155-156

J.J.P. Oud, 'Onze eigen bouwstijl', in: *Bouwkundig Weekblad*, 33(1913)19, pp. 223-224

J.J.P. Oud, 'Landhäuser von Hermann Muthesius', in: *Bouwkundig Weekblad*, 33(1913)48, p. 589

J.J.P. Oud, 'Stadsschoon', in: *Schuitemakers Purmerender Courant*, 8 June 1913 and 3 September 1913

J.J.P. Oud, 'Naar aanleiding van "Van de Scheepvaarttentoonstelling"', in: *De Wereld*, 18 July 1913

J.J.P. Oud Oud, 'Duitsche Kunst', in: *De Wereld*, 3 October 1913

**1914**

J.J.P. Oud, 'Bioscooptheater te Purmerend', in: *Bouwkundig Weekblad* 34(1914)6, pp. 64-66

J.J.P. Oud, [Aalsmeer house], in: *Nordische Baukunst*, November 1914, p. 36

**1915**

J.J.P. Oud, 'Architecten met de pen', in: *Bouwkundig Weekblad* 35(1915)6, pp. 44-45

J.J.P. Oud, W.M. Dudok, 'Arbeiderswoningen te Leiderdorp', in: *Bouwkundig Weekblad*, 36(1915)11, pp. 85-87

**1916**

J.J.P. Oud, 'De moderne en modernste bouwkunst', in: *Bouwkundig Weekblad*, 36(1916)46, pp. 341-343

J.J.P. Oud, 'Landhuisje in Blaricum', in: *Bouwkundig Weekblad*, 37(1916)2, pp. 23-24

J.J.P. Oud, 'Over cubisme, futurisme, moderne bouwkunst, enz.', in: *Bouwkundig Weekblad*, 37(1916)20, pp. 156-157
- J.J.P. Oud, 'Over cubisme, futurisme, moderne bouwkunst, enz.', in: *De Nieuwe Amsterdammer*, 23 September 1916

**1917**

J.J.P. Oud, 'Gedachten over bouwkunst', in: *Gedenkboek uitgegeven ter herinnering aan het 10-jarig bestaan der Vereeniging van Leerlingen der Rijksnormaalschool voor Teekenonderwijzers*, Amsterdam n.y. [1917], pp. 36-38

J.J.P. Oud, 'Het monumentale stadsbeeld', in: *De Stijl*, 1(1917)1, pp. 10-11
- J.J.P. Oud, 'Het monumentale stadsbeeld', in: J.H. van den Broek (et al., eds), *De Stijl*, exh.cat. Stedelijk Museum (Amsterdam) 1951, p. 74

J.J.P. Oud, 'Ingezonden', in: *Holland Express* 10(1917)40, p. 479

**1918**

J.J.P. Oud, 'Verbouwing huize "Allegonda" Katwijk aan zee', in: *Bouwkundig Weekblad*, 39(1918)5, pp. 29-30

J.J.P. Oud, 'Glas-in-lood van Theo van Doesburg', in: *Bouwkundig Weekblad*, 39(1918)35, pp. 199-202
- afterword: J.J.P. Oud, 'Ingezonden', in: *Bouwkundig Weekblad*, 39(1918)42, p. 242

J.J.P. Oud, 'Kunst en machine', in: *De Stijl*, 1(1918)3, p. 25-27
- J.J.P. Oud, 'Kunst en machine'in: J.H. van den Broek (e.a., red.), *De Stijl*, exh.cat. Stedelijk Museum (Amsterdam) 1951, pp. 75-76

J.J.P. Oud, 'Architectonische beschouwing bij bijlage VIII', in: *De Stijl*, 1(1918)4, pp. 39-41
- reprinted in part as: J.J.P. Oud, 'Architectonische beschouwing', in: J.H. van den Broek (et al., eds), *De Stijl*, exh. cat. Stedelijk Museum (Amsterdam) 1951, p. 76-77

J.J.P. Oud, 'Bouwkunst en normalisatie bij den massabouw', in: *De Stijl*, 1(1918)7, pp. 77-79
- reprinted in part as: J.J.P. Oud, 'Bouwkunst en normalisatie bij den massabouw', in: J.H. van den Broek (et al., eds), *De Stijl*, exh.cat. Stedelijk Museum (Amsterdam) 1951, pp. 77-78

**1919**

J.J.P. Oud, 'Dr. H.P. Berlage und sein Werk', in: *Kunst und Kunsthandwerk*, 22(1919)6-8, pp. 189-228

J.J.P. Oud, 'Architectonische beschouwing: A. Massabouw en straatarchitectuur, B. Gewapend beton en bouwkunst', in: *De Stijl*, 2(1919)7, pp. 79-84
- reproduced in part as: J.J.P. Oud, 'Massabouw en straatarchitectuur', in: J.H. van den Broek (et al., eds), *De Stijl*, exh.cat. Stedelijk Museum (Amsterdam) 1951, p. 78

J.J.P. Oud, 'Boekbespreking. "Dr. Otto Grauttoff, Formzertrümmerung und Formaufbau in der Bildenden Kunst"', in: *De Stijl*, 2(1919)10, p. 113-114
- reproduced in part as: J.J.P. Oud, 'Boekbespreking', in: J.H. van den Broek (et al., eds), *De Stijl*, exh.cat. Stedelijk Museum (Amsterdam) 1951, p. 78

J.J.P. Oud, 'Oriëntatie', in: *De Stijl*, 3(1919)2, pp. 13-15
- reproduced in part as: J.J.P. Oud, 'Oriëntatie', in: J.H. van den Broek (et al., eds), *De Stijl*, exh.cat. Stedelijk Museum (Amsterdam) 1951, p. 79

**1920**

J.J.P. Oud, 'Architectonische beschouwing bij bijlage III', in: *De Stijl*, 3(1920)3, pp. 25-27

J.J.P. Oud, 'Het bouwen van woningen in (gewapend)-beton' [part I], in: *Bouwkundig weekblad*, 41(1920)15, pp. 89-94
- J.J.P. Oud, 'Het bouwen van woningen in (gewapend)-beton' [part II], in: *Bouwkundig weekblad*, 41(1920)23, pp. 131-136
- reproduced in part in: Anonymous/ J.J.P. Oud, 'Betonbouw in Duitschland. Het oordeel van een Nederlands deskundige daarover', in: *Het Vaderland. Extra-Weekblad ter bestrijding der Woningcrisis*, 17 April 1920

J.J.P. Oud, 'Gemeentelijke volkswoningen, polder "Spangen", te Rotterdam', in: *Bouwkundig Weekblad*, 41(1920)37, pp. 219-222

J.J.P. Oud, 'De "Building Exhibition" te Londen', in: *Tijdschrift voor Volkshuisvesting*, 1(1920)4, pp. 97-98

**1921**

J.J.P. Oud, 'Over de toekomstige bouwkunst en hare architectonische mogelijkheden', in: *Bouwkundig Weekblad*, 42(1921)24, pp. 147-160

- J.J.P. Oud, 'Bouwkunst', in: *Nieuwe Rotterdamsche Courant*, 9 and 10 March 1921
- J.J.P. Oud, 'Über die zukünftige Baukunst und ihre Architektonischen Möglichkeiten', in: *Frühlicht*, 1(1921/1922)4, pp. 113-118
- J.J.P. Oud, 'O budoucím stavitelství a jeho architektonickych moznostech', in: *Stavba*, 1(1922)10, pp. 177-192
- J.J.P. Oud, 'Over de toekomstige bouwkunst en hare architectonische mogelijkheden', in: *Vlaamsche Arbeid*, 12(1922), pp.165-174
- J.J.P. Oud,' L'architecture de demain et ses possibilites architectoniques', in: *La Cité*, 4(1923)5, pp. 73-85
- J.J.P. Oud, 'L'Architecture de demain et ses possibilités architectoniques', in: *Bulletin de "L'Effort Moderne"*, (1924)4, 5, 6
- J.J.P. Oud, 'Über die zukünftige Baukunst und ihre Architektonischen Möglichkeiten', in: *Baukunst*, 1(1925)5, pp. 88-100
- reprinted in part as: J.J.P. Oud, 'Architecture and the future', in: *The Studio*, XCVI(1928)429, pp. 401-406, 453
- J.J.P. Oud, [Japanese translation of: 'Over de toekomstige bouwkunst en hare architectonische mogelijkheden'], in: *Shinkenchiku*, 4(1928)1, pp. 53-61
- reprinted in part as: J.J.P. Oud,'Over de toekomstige bouwkunst en hare architectonische mogelijkheden', in: *Forum*, 6(1951)5/6, pp. 148-150
- reprinted in part as: J.J.P. Oud,'Over de toekomstige bouwkunst en hare architectonische mogelijkheden', in: J.H. van den Broek (et al., eds), *De Stijl*, exh.cat. Stedelijk Museum (Amsterdam) 1951, pp. 79-80

J.J.P. Oud, 'Naar aanleiding van de Amsterdamse tentoonstelling voor woninginrichting', in: *Tijdschrift voor volkshuisvesting*, 2(1921)7/8, pp. 196-199

J.J.P. Oud, 'De ontwerpen van het tweede kamer-gebouw', in: *De Telegraaf*, 15 September 1921

**1922**

J.J.P. Oud, 'Het Hofplein-plan van Dr. Berlage', in: *Nederlands Instituut voor Volkshuisvesting. Serie voor stedebouw*, (1922)1, pp. 3-11

J.J.P. Oud, 'Boekaankondiging. Naar aanleiding van "Arbeiderswoningen in Nederland", in: *Tijdschrift voor volkshuisvesting*, 3(1922)1, pp. 18-19

J.J.P. Oud, 'Bouwkunst en kubisme', in: *De Bouwwereld*, 21(1922)32, p. 245

J.J.P. Oud, 'Ontwerp voor een woonhuis in Berlijn', in: *Bouwkundig Weekblad*, 43(1922)35, pp. 341-344

J.J.P. Oud, 'Uitweiding bij eenige afbeeldingen', in: *Bouwkundig Weekblad*, 43(1922)43, pp. 418-424

J.J.P. Oud, untitled, in: *De Stijl*, 5(1922)12, pp. 207-208

J.J.P. Oud, 'Het Haagsche raadhuis', in: *De Telegraaf*, 18 June 1922

O [J.J.P. Oud], 'Nieuwe uitgaven. Het woonhuis I: Zijn Bouw, door Jan Wils', in: *De Telegraaf*, 8 June 1922

**1923**

J.J.P. Oud, 'Gemeentelijke woningbouw "Spangen" te Rotterdam', in: *Bouwkundig Weekblad*, 44(1923)2, pp. 15-20

J.J.P. Oud, 'Bij een Deensch ontwerp voor de "Chicago Tribune"', in: *Bouwkundig Weekblad*, 44(1923)45, pp. 456-457

J.J.P. Oud, 'De architectuurweek te Weimar. Het "Ariadische ballet" – een mechanisch cabaret', in: *De Telegraaf*, 28 August 1923

J.J.P. Oud, 'Bruno Taut. Ter inleiding', in: *Utrechts Provinciaal en Stedelijk Dagblad*, 26 September 1923

J.J.P. Oud, 'K.P.C. de Bazel', in: *Bouwkundig Weekblad*, 44(1923)50, pp. 513-514
- J.J.P. Oud, [part of] 'In memoriam K.P.C. de Bazel', in: *Forum*, 6(1951)5/6, p. 150-151

J.J.P. Oud, 'Geschakelde aforismen over kunst en bouwkunst', in: *Het Overzicht*, (1923)15, p. 41

**1924**

J.J.P. Oud, 'Schoonheidscommissies II; Antwoord van J.J.P. Oud', in: *Bouwkundig Weekblad*, 45(1924)4, pp. 50-51

J.J.P. Oud, '"Vers une architecture" van Le Corbusier-Saugnier', in: *Bouwkundig Weekblad*, 45(1924)9, pp. 90-94

J.J.P. Oud, 'Kromhout en zijn tentoonstelling' in: *Nieuwe Rotterdamse Courant*, 2 October 1924

J.J.P. Oud, 'Semi-permanente woningbouw "Oud-Mathenesse", Rotterdam', in: *Bouwkundig Weekblad*, 45(1924)43, pp. 418-421

J.J.P. Oud, 'Gemeentelijke woningbouw in "Spangen", en "Tusschendijken"', in: *Rotterdamsch Jaarboekje*, Rotterdam 1924, pp. XLIX-LV

J.J.P. Oud, 'Kunst, Handwerk und Maschine', in: *Thüringer Allgemeine Zeitung*, 13 July 1924

J.J.P. Oud, 'Die Entwicklung der modernen Baukunst in Holland: Vergangenheit, Gegenwart, Zukunft', in: *Schweizerische Bauzeitung*, 83(1924)12, pp. 134-137
- J.J.P. Oud, 'Vyvoj nové myslenky v moderním stavebním umení holland-ském', in: *Stavba*, III(1924/1925)5, p. 96

**1925**

J.J.P. Oud, 'Ja und nein, Bekenntnisse eines Architekten', in: *Europa Almanach*, Potsdam 1925, pp. 18-20
- J.J.P. Oud, 'Von der Technik. Aus J.J.P. Oud: Ja und nein, Bekenntnisse eines Architekten', in: *Das Werk*, XI(1924)12, p. 336
- J.J.P. Oud, 'Ja und nein, Bekenntnisse eines Architekten', in: *Wasmuths Monats Hefte für Baukunst*, IX(1925)4, pp. 140-146 (correction 209-210)
- J.J.P. Oud, 'Ja und nein, Bekenntnisse eines Architekten', in: *Werkbund Gedanken*, 17 October 1925
- J.J.P. Oud, 'Ja und nein, Bekenntnisse eines Architekten', in: *Bouwkundig Weekblad*, 46(1925)35, pp. 431-432
- J.J.P. Oud, 'Von Technik und Baukunst', in: *Innen-Dekoration*, 36(1925)August, p. 292
- J.J.P. Oud, 'Ja und nein, Bekenntnisse eines Architekten', in: *Kvart*, (1930)2
- J.J.P. Oud, [part of] 'Ja und Nein: Bekenntnisse eines Architecten', in: *Forum*, 6(1951)5/6, pp. 151-152

J.J.P. Oud, 'Een café', in: *Bouwkundig Weekblad*, 46(1925)31, pp. 397-400
- J.J.P. Oud, 'Café-Restaurant "De Unie", Rotterdam', in: *Die Form*, (1926)4, pp. 79-81

J.J.P. Oud, 'The influence of Frank Lloyd Wright on the architecture of Europe', in: *Wendingen*, 7(1925)6, pp. 85-89
- J.J.P. Oud, 'De invloed van Frank Lloyd Wright op de architectuur in Europa', in: *Architectura*, 30(1926)7, pp. 78-82
- J.J.P. Oud, [Japanese translation of: 'De invloed van Frank Lloyd Wright op de architectuur in Europa'], in: *Shinkenchiku*, 4(1928)1, pp. 62-74
- J.J.P. Oud, 'Wplyw Franka Wright'a na architekture europejska', in: *Architektura i Budownictwo*, (1933), pp. 188-189

J.J.P. Oud, 'De Bauhaus-Bücher', in: *Bouwkundig Weekblad*, 46(1925)51, pp. 587-588

J.J.P. Oud, 'Erziehung zur Architektur', in: *Sociale Bauwirtschaft*, 5(1925)4, pp. 25-28
- J.J.P. Oud, 'Erziehung zur Architektur', in: *Odbudowa, Reconstruction Economique*, V(1925)3
- J.J.P. Oud, 'Wychowanie przez architekture', in: *Praesens. Kwartalnik Modernistów Czerwiec*, (1926)1, pp. 4-5

**1927**

J.J.P. Oud, untitled, in: *De Stijl*, VII(1927)79/84, pp. 39-40

J.J.P. Oud, 'Woningbouw te Hoek van Holland', in: I.M. van Dugteren, H. Dekking (eds), *Het Groen-Wit-Groene Boek. Uitgegeven ter gelegenheid van het 10-jarig bestaan der Volks-universiteit te Rotterdam*, Rotterdam 1927, pp. 38-42

J.J.P. Oud, 'Erläuterungsbericht', in: *Bau und Wohnung. Die Bauten de Weissenhofsiedlung in Stuttgart errichtet 1927 nach Vorschlägen des Deutschen Werkbundes im Auftrag der Stadt Stuttgart und im Rahmen der Werkbund Ausstellung 'Die Wohnung'*, Stuttgart 1927, pp. 87-94

J.J.P. Oud, 'De bouw van een raadhuis te Enschede en de prijsvraag voor het gebouw van den Volkenbond', in: *Nieuwe Rotterdamsche Courant*, 4 October 1927

J.J.P. Oud, 'Richtlijn', in: *i 10*, 1(1927)2, p. 2

J.J.P. Oud, 'Huisvrouwen en Architecten', in: *i 10*, 1(1927)2, pp. 44-46

J.J.P. Oud, 'Internationale architectuur', in: *i 10*, 1(1927)6, pp. 204-206

J.J.P. Oud, 'Aangepast bij de omgeving', in: *i 10*, 1(1927)10, pp. 349-350

J.J.P. Oud, 'Toelichting tot een woningtype van de Werkbundausstellung "die Wohnung", Stuttgart 1927', in: *i 10*, 1(1927)11, pp. 383-384

J.J.P. Oud, 'Wohin führt das neue Bauen: Kunst und Standard', in: *i 10*, 1(1927)11, pp. 385-386
- J.J.P. Oud, 'Wohin führt das neue Bauen: Kunst und Standard', in: *Neue Züricher Zeitung*, 9 September 1927
- J.J.P. Oud, 'Wohin führt das neue Bauen? Kunst und Standard', in: *Der Kreis*, 4(1927)12, pp. 705-707
- J.J.P. Oud, 'Wohin führt das neue Bauen: Kunst und Standard', in: *Die Form*, 3(1928)2, p. 61

J.J.P. Oud, 'Das Flache in Holland', in: *Das Neue Frankfurt*, 1(1926/1927)7, pp. 189-192

**1928**

J.J.P. Oud, 'Wohnhausgruppe in Hoek van Holland', in: *Die Form*, 3(1928)2, pp. 38-41
- J.J.P. Oud, 'huizen te hoek van Holland', in: *Red*, 28 October 1928, p. 56

Anonymous [J.J.P. Oud], 'Brieven over Bouwkunst. Tentoonstelling Olympische Kunst', in: *Nieuwe Rotterdamsche Courant*, 14 July 1928

J.J.P. Oud, 'Beursproject Rotterdam 1926', in: *i 10*, 2(1928)14, pp. 25-29
- J.J.P. Oud, 'Toelichting bij het ontwerp motto: X voor een beurs te Rotterdam', in: *Bouwkundig Weekblad*, 50(1929)6, pp. 41-43

J.J.P. Oud, Tentoonstelling Olympische kunst, in: *Nieuwe Rotterdamsche Courant*, 14 July 1928

O [J.J.P. Oud], 'A.G. Sneck, Der Stuhl', in: *i 10*, 2(1928)15, pp. 64-65

J.J.P. Oud, 'Ein tägliches Problem des Städtebaues', in: *Berliner Börsen-Courier*, 4 November 1928

J.J.P. Oud, 'Das fliessende Leben. Der natürliche Weg des Architekten', in: *Innen-dekoration*, XXXIX(1928) May, p. 209

J.J.P. Oud, 'Observaties van J.J.P. Oud' [on H.P. Berlage and M. de Klerk], in: *Shinkenchiku*, 4(1928)1, p. 52

**1929**

Anonymous [J.J.P. Oud], 'Brieven over bouwkunst. Moderne architectuur', in: *Nieuwe Rotterdamsche Courant*, 19 July 1929

J.J.P. Oud, 'In memory of Peter van der Meulen-Smith, 1902-1928', in: *i 10*, 2(1929)19, pp. 122-123

O. [J.J.P. Oud], 'Boekbespreking. Erich Mendelsohn: Russland, Europa, Amerika – Ein architektonischer Querschnitt', in: *i 10*, 2(1929)19, pp. 135-136

O. [J.J.P. Oud], 'Boekbespreking. Julyus Vischer, Ludwig Hilberseimer: Beton als Gestalter', in: *i 10*, 2(1929)19, pp. 135-136

**1930**

J.J.P. Oud, 'Die städtische Siedlung "De Kiefhoek" in Rotterdam', in: *Die Form*, 5(1930)14, pp. 357-369
- J.J.P. Oud, 'Eine Städtische Siedlung in Rotterdam', in: *Der Baumeister*, 28(1930)11, pp. 425-432
- J.J.P. Oud, 'Rotterdam város "Kiefhoek" lakótelepe', in: *Tér és Forma*, 4(1931)1, pp. 11-17
- J.J.P. Oud, 'Siedlung "Kiefhoek" in Rotterdam', in: *Zentralblatt der Bauverwaltung*, 51(1931)10, pp. 149-153
- J.J.P. Oud, [The Kiefhoek in Rotterdam], in: *L'Architecture d'Aujourd'hui*, (1931)4, pp. 2-8

J.J.P. Oud, [untitled], in: T. Tzara (ed.), *Adolf Loos. Festschrift zum 60. Geburtstag*, Vienna 1930, p. 41

J.J.P. Oud, 'Mysli', in: *Praesens*, (1930)2, pp. 87-90

**1931**

J.J.P. Oud, 'The £ 213 House. A solution to the re-housing problem for rock-bottom incomes in Rotterdam', in: *The Studio*, 101(1931)456, pp. 175-179
- J.J.P. Oud, '£ 213 a house; a Solution to the Re-housing Problem in Rotterdam', in: *Creative Art*, 8(1931)3, pp. 174-179

**1932**

J.J.P. Oud, untitled [In Memoriam Theo van Doesburg], in: *De Stijl*, (1932) final number, pp. 46-47

J.J.P. Oud, 'De "nieuwe zakelijkheid" in de bouwkunst', in: *De Jonge Gids*, 6(1932)11, pp. 174-179
- J.J.P. Oud, 'De "nieuwe zakelijkheid" in de bouwkunst', in: *De 8 en Opbouw*, 3(1932)23, pp. 223-228

J.J.P. Oud, 'Ontwerp voor een huis in Pinehurst (U.S.A.)', in: *De 8 en Opbouw*, 3(1932)23, pp. 228-229

**1933**

J.J.P. Oud, untitled [Waarom schoonheidscomissies?], in: *De 8 en Opbouw*, 4(1933)9, p. 73

J.J.P. Oud, 'Towards a new architecture. The European Movement', in: *The Studio*, 105(1933)481, pp. 249-256, correction: 105(1933)487, p. 233

J.J.P. Oud, 'Wie ich arbeite', in: *Architektur der U.d.S.S.R.*, (1933)6, p. 27
- J.J.P. Oud, 'Comment je conçois ma tache ...', in : *l'Architecture d'Aujourd'hui*, 5(1935)2, pp. 58-59

**1934**

J.J.P. Oud, 'Tentoonstelling Liberty', in: *De 8 en Opbouw*,5(1934)2, p. 9

J.J.P. Oud, 'Dr H.P. Berlage, 1856-1934', in: *Bouwkundig Weekblad*, 55(1934)51, pp. 26-27
- J.J.P. Oud, 'Dr H.P. Berlage, 1856-1934', in: *de 8 en Opbouw*, 5(1934)18, pp. 149-152

J.J.P. Oud, 'De stalen stoel voortbrengsel van kunstnijverheid?', in: *Nieuwe Rotterdamsche Courant*, 4 April 1934

J.J.P. Oud, 'Huis Allegonda te Katwijk aan Zee', in: *Linoleumnieuws*, (1934)7, pp. 12-14

Anonymous [J.J.P. Oud], '"Enerverend geluid moet worden geweerd." Bouwmeester Oud over de geluidsstichting', in: *De Telegraaf*, 29 August 1934

J.J.P. Oud, 'Ingezonden. Ik dacht zoo: over Jan Jans en zijn oordeel', in: *De 8 en Opbouw*, 5(1934)16, p. 140

J.J.P. Oud, 'Stadt ohne Denkmähler? Eine Umfrage', in: *Prager Tageblatt*, 31 March 1934

J.J.P. Oud, 'Stellung und Aufgabe des Architekten', in: *Deutsche Bauzeitung*, 68(1934)50, pp.975-976
- J.J.P. Oud, 'Plaats en taak van de architect', in: *Nieuwe Rotterdamsche Courant*, 2 February 1935
- J.J.P. Oud, 'Plaats en taak van de architect', in: *Cobouw*, 12 February 1935

**1935**

J.J.P. Oud, 'Uitbreidingsplan voor Groot-Amsterdam', in: *De Telegraaf*, 18 June 1935

J.J.P. Oud, 'Toekomstig Amsterdam onder de loupe', in: *De Telegraaf*, 20 June 1935

J.J.P. Oud, 'Uitbreidingsplan is een "programma-plan"', in: *De Telegraaf*, 21 June 1935

J.J.P. Oud, 'Men moet het nieuwe bouwen zijn kans geven', in: *De Telegraaf*, 31 March 1935

J.J.P. Oud, 'De lezing van architect Oud. Een rechtzetting en een nadere toelichting' in: [*De Telegraaf*], 15 November 1935

J.J.P. Oud, 'Het nieuwe bouwen. Landelijke architectuur. Geen grondslag voor komende bouwkunst', in: *De Groene Amsterdammer*, 7 December 1935
- Afterword: J.J.P. Oud, 'Oud antwoordt:', in: *De Groene Amsterdammer*, 4 January 1936

J.J.P. Oud , 'Van hout tot staal. Ontwikkelingsgang van den stoel', in: *De Groene Amsterdammer*, 19 January 1935

Oud, .J.J.P., 'Boekbespreking. Raymond McGrath. "Twentieth Century Houses"', in: *De 8 en Opbouw*, 6(1935)1, pp. 11-12

**1936**

J.J.P. Oud, 'Mies van der Rohe', in: *De 8 en Opbouw*, 7(1936)6, pp. 71-72

J.J.P. Oud, 'Leen van der Vlugt', in: *De 8 en Opbouw*, 7(1936)10, p. 112

J.J.P. Oud, 'Zullen de beste krachten wel aan een prijsvraag deelnemen?', in: *De Groene Amsterdammer*, 4 April 1936

J.J.P. Oud, 'Het nieuwe bouwen. Tegenstanders en meelopers', in: *De Groene Amsterdammer*, 5 September 1936

J.J.P. Oud, 'Atelierwoning te Blaricum. Arch. F. Hausbrand', in: *Bouwkundig Weekblad*, 57(1936)34, pp. 357-360

**1938**

J.J.P. Oud, 'Saenredam en Le Corbusier', in: *De 8 en Opbouw*, 9(1938)21, pp. 217-218

**1939**

Oud, J.J.P, 'Bij den dood van twee bouwmeesters. Theodor Fischer en Bruno Taut', in: *Nieuwe Rotterdamsche Courant*, 6 January 1939

J.J.P. Oud, 'Een oordeel van J.J.P. Oud, arch.', in: *Cobouw*, 24 January 1939

**1945**

J.J.P. Oud, 'Hoofdkantoor Bataafsche Import Maatschappij te 's-Gravenhage', in: *Bouwkundig Weekblad*, 63(1945)2, pp. 14-21

J.J.P. Oud, 'Piet Mondriaan', in: M. Seuphor (et al.), *P.M. Piet Mondriaan herdenkingstentoonstelling*, exh.cat. Amsterdam (Stedelijk Museum) 1946, pp. 29-34

**1946**

J.J.P. Oud, 'Durven en niet durven in de architectuur', in: *Bouw* 1(1946)29, pp. 613-614, 620

J.J.P. Oud, 'De dictatuur van de "Delftse School" en de volkshuisvesting', in: *De Vrije Katheder*, 24 July 1946

J.J.P. Oud, 'De Delftsche School en synthese in architectuur', in: *Bouwkundig Weekblad*, 64(1946)24, p. 222

J.J.P. Oud, 'Vorm en Vrijheid', in: *Bouw*, 1(1946)3, p. 5

J.J.P. Oud, 'Wij bouwen weer op?', in: *De Groene Amsterdammer*, 21 December 1946
- J.J.P. Oud, 'Wij bouwen weer op?', in: *De Opbouw. Orgaan van de aannemersbond en patroonsbond afdeling Amsterdam*, 1(1947)1, pp. 11-13

J.J.P. Oud, 'Architecture today', in: R. Mc.Grath (ed.), *Architecture in Ireland. Yearbook for 1946. The Royal Institute of Architects in Ireland*, London 1946, pp. 27-28

**1947**

J.J.P. Oud, 'Mr. Oud replies', in: *Architectural Record*, 101(1947)3, p. 18

J.J.P. Oud, 'Oud in de Amerikaanse pers. Bouwen of architectuur?', in: *Forum*, 2(1947)2/3, pp. 72-73

J.J.P. Oud, 'Meeningen over de Delftsche school', in: *De Groene Amsterdammer*, 22 February 1947

J.J.P. Oud, 'Het Delftsche Bouwen', in: *De Groene Amsterdammer*, 19 April 1947

J.J.P. Oud, 'Bouwen in het Zuiden', in: *De Groene Amsterdammer*, 14 June 1947

J.J.P. Oud, 'Het geloof van een architect', in: *De Groene Amsterdammer*, 23 August 1947

J.J.P. Oud, 'Vragen en antwoorden over de wederopbouw in ons land', in: *Bouw*, 2(1947)18, p. 147

J.J.P. Oud, 'Walcheren', in: *Bouw*, 2(1947)33, p. 275

J.J.P. Oud, 'Delftse School en namaakantiek', in: *De kampioen*, 62(1947)10, p. 308

J.J.P. Oud, untitled ['Stand van zaken'], in: *Forum*, 2(1947)8, pp. 190-191

**1948**

J.J.P. Oud, 'Drie nieuwe professoren in Delft', in: *De Groene Amsterdammer*, 17 January 1948

J.J.P. Oud, 'Ontmoedigende plaatjes', in: *De Groene Amsterdammer*, 7 August 1948

J.J.P. Oud, 'The UN-building', in: *Journal of the RIBA*, 55(1948)8, pp. 363-364

J.J.P. Oud, 'The UN-building', in: *Journal of the RIBA*, 55(1948)12, p. 560

J.J.P. Oud, 'Het gebouwencomplex voor de U.N.', in: *Forum* 3(1948)2, pp. 38-40
- J.J.P. Oud, 'United Nations headquarters', in: *AIA-Journal*, 1948, pp. 278-280

**1949**

J.J.P. Oud, 'Bouwen en pseudo-bouwen', in: *De Groene Amsterdammer*, 22 January 1949
- J.J.P. Oud, [part of] 'Bouwen en Pseudo-bouwen', in: *Forum*, 6(1951)5/6, p. 151

J.J.P. Oud, 'Restaureren tot er de dood op volgt', in: *De Groene Amsterdammer*, 26 February 1949, (afterword 2 April 1949)

J.J.P. Oud, 'Groot 's-Gravenhage', in: *De Groene Amsterdammer*, 19 March 1949

J.J.P. Oud, 'Restaureren', in: *De Groene Amsterdammer*, 2 April 1949

J.J.P. Oud, 'Bouwen zonder Make-up', in: *De Groene Amsterdammer*, 29 October 1949

J.J.P. Oud, 'Clarity in Town Planning', in: *Housing and Town and Country Planning*, 4(1949)2, pp. 19-21
- J.J.P. Oud, 'Duidelijkheid in de stedebouw', in: *Forum*, 4(1949)4, pp. 127-130
- J.J.P. Oud, 'Clarity in Town Planning', in: *Journal of the RIBA*, 58(1951)5, pp. 193-195
- J.J.P. Oud, 'Duidelijkheid in de stedebouw', in: *Ruimte*, 1(1953)1, pp. 20-24

J.J.P. Oud, 'Contemporary English Architecture', in: *The Architectural Times*, 1(1949)1, p. 24
- J.J.P. Oud, 'L'Architettura moderna in Inghilterra', in: *Metron Architettura*, 7(1952)45, pp. 10-12

J.J.P. Oud, untitled ['De enquete van de V.N. Pessimisten en optimisten'], in: *Vrij Nederland*, 30 April 1949

**1950**

J.J.P. Oud, 'Architect Oud beantwoordt ds den Hartog. "Beschouw mijn voorstel als de aanzet tot een meer doorwerkt plan"', *Het Rotterdamsch Parool*, 3 August 1950

[J.J.P. Oud] , 'Het Nationaal Monument op de Dam', *Bouw*, 5(1950)14, pp. 234-235

J.J.P. Oud, 'Het nationaal monument op de Dam. Repliek arch. Oud', in: *Bouw*, 5(1950)23, p. 363

J.J.P. Oud, 'Kunst, die leeft', in: *Het [Rotterdamsch] Parool*, 1 February 1950

J.J.P. Oud, 'Architectuur-critiek en architectuur', in: *De Groene Amsterdammer*, 14 January 1950
- J.J.P. Oud, 'Waarderingsvermogen en kritiek omtrent bouwkunst', in: *Bouw*, 11(1956)20, pp. 430-431
- J.J.P. Oud, 'Die architekten und die Kritiker', in: *Kontrapunkte. Jahrbuch Freie Akademie der Künste*, Hamburg 1956/1957, pp. 57-61
- J.J.P. Oud, 'Architectuur-critiek en architectuur', in: *Bouwkundig Weekblad*, 77(1959)33/34. pp. 405-406

J.J.P. Oud, 'Moeilijkheden van de dag', in: *De Groene Amsterdammer*, 11 February 1950

J.J.P. Oud, 'De Commissies en de Instanties', in: *De Groene Amsterdammer*, 15 April 1950
with afterword: J.J.P. Oud, 'Verder dit', in: *De Groene Amsterdammer*, 22 July 1950

J.J.P. Oud, 'Kunst, die leeft', in: *Het Rotterdamsch Parool*, 1 February 1950

J.J.P. Oud, 'Rotterdam en de St. Laurens', in: *De Groene Amsterdammer*,

29 July 1950
- J.J.P. Oud, 'Rotterdam en de St. Laurens', in: *Bouw*, 5(1950)36, p. 595
- J.J.P. Oud, 'Rotterdams St. Laurens', in: *Bouw*, 5(1950)40, pp. 658-659
- J.J.P. Oud [adapted by Albert Boeken], 'Het voorstel van J.J.P. Oud voor de Sint Laurens in Rotterdam', in: *Forum*, 5(1950)8, pp. 307-309

J.J.P. Oud, 'Architect Oud beantwoordt ds Den Hartog. Beschouw mijn voorstel als de aanzet tot een meer doorwerkt plan', in: *Het Rotterdamsch Parool*, 3 August 1950
- J.J.P. Oud, 'Wederwoord', in: *De Rotterdammer*, 4 August 1950
- J.J.P. Oud, 'Rotterdams St. Laurens', in: *Bouw*, 5(1950)40, p. 659

J.J.P. Oud, untitled [reply to: F.J. Brevet, 'Rotterdams St Laurens: een grote kerk?'], in: *De Groene Amsterdammer*, 19 August 1950

J.J.P. Oud, 'Geef Rotterdam zijn kern terug!', in: *Elseviers weekblad*, 4 November 1950

J.J.P. Oud, 'Zweden-Nederland 1-0', in: *De Groene Amsterdammer*, 16 December 1950

J.J.P. Oud, 'Otto van Tuss[ch]enbroek, Achter blinkende vensters', in: *Intérieur*, 63(1950)463, p. 323

**1951**

J.J.P. Oud, 'Schilder en architect', in: *De Groene Amsterdammer*, 13 January 1951

J.J.P. Oud, 'Ruimte-problemen', in: *De Groene Amsterdammer*, 28 April 1951

J.J.P. Oud, 'Bouwkunst, verkeer en Amsterdamse binnenstad', in: *De Groene Amsterdammer*, 8 December 1951
- J.J.P. Oud, 'Bouwkunst en verkeersactiviteit', in: *Bouw*, 7(1952)8, p. 139

**1952**

J.J.P. Oud, 'Bouwen en "Team-work"', in: *De Groene Amsterdammer*, 9 February 1952
- J.J.P. Oud, 'Building and Team work', January 1951
- J.J.P. Oud, 'Bauen und teamwork', in: *Der Architekt*, 1(1952)6, pp. 93-95
- J.J.P. Oud, 'Architettura e lavoro in collaborazione', in: *Metron Architettura*, 7(1952)45, pp. 7-10
- J.J.P. Oud, 'Building and Teamwork', in: *Architectural Association Journal*, LXXIII(1958)818, pp. 144-146

J.J.P. Oud, 'L'Edificio della Shell Olandese', in: *Metron Architettura*, 7(1952)45, pp. 12-15
- J.J.P. Oud, Speech delivered by Mr. J.J.P. Oud to members of the International Association of Art Critics during their visit to the Shell Netherland Building at the Hague on the 9th July 1951, Den Haag 1951
J.J.P. Oud, 'Die Weissenhof-Siedlung. Ein Brief J.J.P. Ouds an die Stuttgarter', in: *Stuttgarter Zeitung*, 4 April 1952

J.J.P. Oud, 'Frank Lloyd Wright', in: *De Groene Amsterdammer*, 17 May 1952

J.J.P. Oud, 'fllw', in: Anonymous, *Frank Lloyd Wright*, exh.cat Rotterdam (Ahoy building) 1952

J.J.P. Oud, 'Wright's betekenis voor het nieuwe bouwen', in: *De Groene Amsterdammer*, 1 July 1952

J.J.P. Oud, 'Architect en supervisor', in: *De Groene Amsterdammer*, 3 May 1952
- Afterword: J.J.P. Oud, 'Onderschrift', in: *De Groene Amsterdammer*, 14 June 1952

J.J.P. Oud, 'Bouwkunst of industrial design? Het gebouw voor de Unesco in Parijs', in: *De Groene Amsterdammer*, 1 November 1952

J.J.P. Oud, 'Stationspostgebouw Den Haag', in: *Forum*, 7(1952)11, pp. 320-331

J.J.P. Oud, 'Geef kunstenaars royaler kansen in Rotterdam', in: *Nieuwe Rotterdamsche Courant*, 30 January 1952

**1953**

J.J.P. Oud, 'Architectuur: lichtend symbool of grootste gemene deler?', in: *Bouw* 8(1953)4, pp. 60-61

J.J.P. Oud, 'Genormaliseerde scholenbouw. Een bouwterrein is iets anders dan een laboratorium', in: *De Groene Amsterdammer*, 11 April 1953
- J.J.P. Oud, untitled [caption to article by Van Tijen], *De Groene Amsterdammer*, 2 May 1953
- J.J.P. Oud, 'Genormaliseerde scholenbouw en industriële productie. Bouwterrein is iets anders dan een laboratorium', in: *Bouw*, 8(1953)24, pp. 461-462. (postscript p. 464)

J.J.P. Oud, 'Nieuw Lyceum te Den Haag', in: *Bouw*, 8(1953)49, pp. 18-23

J.J.P. Oud, 'Standaardtype arbeiderswoningen', in: *Bouw*, 8(1953)15, pp. 270-271

**1954**

J.J.P. Oud, 'Studieprijsvraag voor een Wijkcentrum Amsterdam-Noord', in: *Forum*, 9(1954)9/10, pp. 391-394

J.J.P. Oud, 'Architectuur en prijsvragen', in: *De Groene Amsterdammer*, 23 January 1954

J.J.P. Oud, 'Een monument ontstaat, het Dammonument en pantoufles', in: *De Groene Amsterdammer*, 13 February 1954

J.J.P. Oud, 'Nog eenmaal: de Gulden Snede. Architect Oud contra architect Slebos', in: *Bouw*, 9(1954)14, p. 274

J.J.P. Oud, 'Building in the Netherlands', in: *De Groene Amsterdammer*, 2 October 1954

J.J.P. Oud, 'Neue Form oder neue Architektur', in: *Die Spur des Menschen. Jahrbuch Freie Akademie der Künste*, Hamburg 1954, p. 94

**1955**

J.J.P. Oud, 'Deze sit-down regelingen verstoren de bouw-harmonie', in: *Algemeen Dagblad*, 5 August 1955

J.J.P. Oud, 'Mondriaan', in: *De Groene Amsterdammer*, 12 February 1955 (correction 19 February 1955)
- J.J.P. Oud, 'Mondriaan', in: P. Bucarelli (ed.), *Piet Mondrian*, Roma 1956/1957, pp. 7-18

J.J.P. Oud, 'Kantoorgebouw op de Coolsingel', in: *Bouw*, 10(1955)28, pp. 574-576

**1956**

J.J.P. Oud, 'John Raedecker', in: *De Groene Amsterdammer*, 21 January 1956

J.J.P. Oud, 'Het Dam-monument', in: *Maatstaf*, 4(1956)[6], pp. 405-410

J.J.P. Oud, 'Nationaal Monument op de Dam te Amsterdam', in: *Bouwkundig Weekblad*, 74(1956)22, pp. 266-268
- J.J.P. Oud, 'Nationaal Monument op de Dam in Amsterdam', in: *Bouwt in beton*, (1956)1, pp. 18-19
- J.J.P. Oud, 'Het Dam-monument (Amsterdam)', in: *Openbaar Kunstbezit*, 1(1957), pp. 18c-18d

J.J.P. Oud, 'Dam-monument'' in: *Elsevier's Weekblad*, 13 October 1956

J.J.P. Oud, 'Preface', in: H.L.C. Jaffé, *De Stijl 1917-1931. The Dutch Contribution to Modern Art*, Amsterdam 1956, pp. v-vi

J.J.P. Oud, '50 jaar moderne kunst in de U.S.A. en het ontwerp voor de U.S.A.-ambassade in Londen', in: *De Groene Amsterdammer*, 16 June 1956

J.J.P. Oud, 'Industrial design en bouwkunst', in: *Bouw*, 11(1956)34, p. 738

J.J.P. Oud, 'Boekbespreking', in: *Forum*, 11(1956)10, pp. 355-356

**1957**

J.J.P. Oud, 'De Stijl - Toen en nu', in: *De Groene Amsterdammer*, 12 January 1957

J.J.P. Oud, 'Is architectuur vogelvrij?', in: *De Groene Amsterdammer*, 20 July 1957

J.J.P. Oud, 'Ten geleide', in: J.J. Vriend, *Nieuwere Architectuur*, Bussum 1957, n.p. [5-6]
- J.J.P. Oud, 'Nieuwere architectuur', in: *De Groene Amsterdammer*, 8 February 1958.

**1958**

J.J.P. Oud, 'J.J.P. Oud, Von Ihm Selber', in: *Das Einhorn. Jahrbuch Freie Akademie der Künste*, Hamburg 1957/1958, pp. 188-192

- J.J.P. Oud, 'Selbstdarstellung', in: *Profile. Jahrbuch Freie Akademie der Künste*, Hamburg1967

J.J.P. Oud 'De architectuur van de Nederlandse afdeling op de wereldtentoonstelling Brussel 1958', in: *Forum*, 13(1958)6, pp. 158-124

J.J.P. Oud, 'Het congresgebouw van 's Gravenhage', in: *'s-Gravenhage*, 13(1958)9, pp. 32-36

J.J.P. Oud, 'Industriële vormgeving', in: *De Groene Amsterdammer*, 18 January 1958

J.J.P. Oud, 'Le Corbusier', in: *De Groene Amsterdammer*, 12 April 1958

J.J.P. Oud 'Over de samenwerking voor de tentoonstelling in Brussel', in: *De Groene Amsterdammer*, 26 April 1958

J.J.P. Oud, 'Henry Ford in Alkmaar', in: *De Groene Amsterdammer*, 8 November 1958

J.J.P. Oud, 'Nut van auto's in de stad wordt steeds meer twijfelachtig', in: *Nieuw Utrechts Dagblad*, 29 November 1958

J.J.P. Oud, 'Sette maniere di accettare una nomina ad accademico', in: *l'Architettura. Cronache & storia*, IV(1958)8, p. 570

J.J.P. Oud, untitled [Een kroonjaar van Rietveld], in: *Forum*, 13(1958)3, p. 80

J.J.P. Oud, 'Repliek van dr. Oud', in: *Bouwbedrijf en Openbare werken*, 35(1958)23, p. 250

**1959**

J.J.P. Oud, 'Das Kulturelle Zentrum in Den Haag', in: *Fundamente. Jahrbuch Freie Akademie der Künste*, Hamburg 1959, pp. 108-109

J.J.P. Oud, 'Open brief aan de Raad der gemeente Wassenaar', in: *De Wassenaarder*, 6 August 1959

J.J.P. Oud, 'Het nationale monument op de dam en de politie', in: *De Groene Amsterdammer*, 11 April 1959

J.J.P. Oud, "'Mensen op de treden hinderen mij niet." 't Is vooral een blij monument', in: *De Telegraaf*, 2 September 1959

J.J.P. Oud, 'Over het Dammonument', in: *Nieuwe Rotterdamsche Courant*, 2 November 1959

J.J.P. Oud, 'Frank Lloyd Wright', in: *De Groene Amsterdammer*, 18 April 1959

J.J.P. Oud, 'Professor L.O. Wenckebach, in: *De Groene Amsterdammer*, 13 June 1959

J.J.P. Oud, 'Kuststad Nederland. Waar de blanke top der duinen ...', in: *De Groene Amsterdammer*, 25 July 1959
- J.J.P. Oud, 'Randstad dreigt kuststad te worden', in: *Bouw*, 14(1959)33, pp. 943-944

J.J.P. Oud, 'Naschrift', in: *De Groene Amsterdammer*, 12 September 1959

J.J.P. Oud, 'Verkeer stedebouw en professor Feuchtinger', in: *De Groene Amsterdammer*, 12 December 1959

**1960**

J.J.P. Oud, 'De aannemer zij volledig team-lid', in: *Bouw*, 15(1960)7, p. 180

J.J.P. Oud, 'Gebruik het monument beschaafd', in: *Algemeen Dagblad Rotterdam*, 6 September 1960

J.J.P. Oud, 'Het Dammonument in de verdrukking', in: *Algemeen Handelsblad*, 20 December 1960

J.J.P. Oud, '6 March 1960', in: *Forum*, 15(1960/1961)4, p. 128

J.J.P. Oud, 'Waarom ik van het toepassen van baksteen afstapte en op grond waarvan ik er weer toe terugkeerde', in: *Baksteen*, (1960)3, pp. 1-5
- J.J.P. Oud, 'Architect dr. J.J.P. Oud keerde terug tot toepassing van baksteen', in: *Cobouw*, 24 June 1960

J.J.P. Oud, 'Bauen für Kinder', in: *Kontraste. Jahrbuch Freie Akademie der Künste*, Hamburg 1960, pp. 110-112

J.J.P. Oud, 'Bio-herstellingsoord te Arnhem', in: *Bouw*, 15(1960)44, pp. 1306-1311
- J.J.P. Oud, 'Bio Herstellingsoord te Arnhem', in: *Bouwkundig Weekblad*, 78 (1960) 23, pp. 507-515
- J.J.P. Oud, 'Het Bio-Herstellingsoord te Arnhem', in: *Ons Profiel*, (1961)3, pp. 4-5
- J.J.P. Oud, 'Bio-Zentrum, Arnhem, Holland', in: *Schweizerische Technische Zeitschrift*, 59(1962)27, pp. 529-537

J.J.P. Oud, 'J.J.P. Oud commenta l'editoriale del n. 50', in *: l'Architettura. Cronache & storia*, V (1960)11, pp. 795-796

J.J.P. Oud, 'In welk dor brein is de gedachte opgekomen ?', in : *De Tijd - Maasbode*, 4 June 1960

J.J.P. Oud, 'Voorkeuren', in: *Elseviers Weekblad*, 19 March 1960
- J.J.P. Oud, 'Preferenza', in: *Casabella*, (1961) 249, p. 53

**1961**

J.J.P. Oud, 'Architektur und Baudetail heute', in: *Detail*, (1961)1, pp. 4-5

J.J.P. Oud, 'Co-Operation between Painters, Sculptors and Architects', in: *International Association of Plastic Arts*, (1961)41, p. 11

J.J.P. Oud, 'J.J. Vriend 65 jaar', in: *De Groene Amsterdammer*, 15 July 1961

J.J.P. Oud, 'De melodie van de ruimte', in: *De Groene Amsterdammer*, 18 March 1961

J.J.P. Oud, 'De wereld wordt mooier door meer grote dingen', in: *Visie*, (1961)12, pp. 16-17

J.J.P. Oud, 'Nationaal monument', in: *Nieuwe Rotterdamsche Courant*, 10 March 1961

J.J.P. Oud, 'Tradition in einem Einfamilienhaus', in: *Traditionen. Jahrbuch Freie Akademie der Künste*, Hamburg 1961, pp. 94-96

**1962**

J.J.P. Oud, 'Mondriaan, de mens', in: L.J.F. Wijssenbeek, J.J.P. Oud, *Mondriaan*, Zeist 1962, pp. 61-81

J.J.P. Oud, 'Het carnaval der architecten', in: *De Groene Amsterdammer*, 10 February 1962
- J.J.P. Oud, 'The Architects' Carnival', in: *Delta*, 5(1962)3, pp. 15-21

J.J.P. Oud, 'Recreatie-kust-Holland of Manchester aan zee?', in: *De Groene Amsterdammer*, 13 October 1962

J.J.P. Oud, 'Hoge gebouwen, Bouwspreiding en "Architectuur-reservaten"', in: *De Groene Amsterdammer*, 22 December 1962 (correction 5 January 1963)

J.J.P. Oud 'Geen Hoogbouw', in: *Televisier*, 6 October 1962

J.J.P. Oud, 'Benauwd', in: *Algemeen Dagblad*, 11 October 1962

J.J.P. Oud 'Eemshaven', in: *De Nieuwe Stem*, March 1962

J.J.P. Oud, 'Oswald Wenckebach', in: *De Groene Amsterdammer*, 17 November 1962

J.J.P. Oud, 'Kantoorgebouw voor "De Utrecht" te Rotterdam', in: *Bouwkundig Weekblad*, 80(1962)2, pp. 40-45
- J.J.P. Oud, 'Kantoorgebouw voor de levensverzekeringsmaatschappij Utrecht aan de Coolsingel te Rotterdam', in: *Bouw*, 18(1963)16, pp. 470-475

J.J.P. Oud, 'Boston City Hall', in: *Architectural Forum*, (1962)October, p. 19

# Published Articles by J.J.P. Oud

**Separate Publications by J.J.P. Oud**

J.J.P. Oud, *Holländische Architektur, Bauhausbuch nr. 10*, Munich 1926
Geständnis [1926]
Die Entwicklung der Modernen Baukunst in Holland: Vergangenheit, Gegenwart, Zukunft (Ein Vortrag) [1922-1923]
über die Zukünftige Baukunst und ihre architektonischen Möglichkeiten (Ein Programm) [1921]
Der Einfluss von Frank Lloyd Wright auf die Architektur Europas (Ein Essay) [1925]

J.J.P. Oud, *Holländische Architektur, Bauhausbuch nr. 10*, Munich 1929 (second, enlarged edition of *Holländische Architektur* (1926))
Geständnis [1926]
Die Entwicklung der Modernen Baukunst in Holland: Vergangenheit, Gegenwart, Zukunft (Ein Vortrag) [1922-1923]
Über die Zukünftige Baukunst und ihre architektonischen Möglichkeiten (Ein Programm) [1921]
Der Einfluss von Frank Lloyd Wright auf die Architektur Europas (Ein Essay) [1925]
Ja und Nein, Bekenntnisse eines Architekten [1925]
Wohin führt das Neue Bauen: Kunst und Standard [1927]

J.J.P. Oud, *Holländische Architektur, Bauhausbuch nr. 10*, Munich 1926 (facsimile edition Mainz, Berlin 1976 with a postscript by H.L.C. Jaffé)
Geständnis [1926]
Die Entwicklung der Modernen Baukunst in Holland: Vergangenheit, Gegenwart, Zukunft (Ein Vortrag) [1922-1923]
über die Zukünftige Baukunst und ihre architektonischen Möglichkeiten (Ein Programm) [1921]
Der Einfluss von Frank Lloyd Wright auf die Architektur Europas (Ein Essay) [1925]

J.J.P. Oud, *Hollandse architectuur*, Nijmegen 1983 (translation of: J.J.P. Oud, *Holländische Architektur, Bauhausbuch nr. 10*, Munch 1926, with a foreword by S.U. Barbieri, J. Leering and C. Boekraad)

J.J.P. Oud, *Nieuwe Bouwkunst in Holland en Europa*, Amsterdam 1935
- J.J.P. Oud, 'De "nieuwe zakelijkheid" in de bouwkunst', in: *Maandblad 1935. Perspectieven van een wordende cultuur*, 2(1935)4, pp. 4-16
- J.J.P. Oud, 'De nieuwe bouwkunstbeweging in Europa', in: *Maandblad 1935. Perspectieven van een wordende cultuur*, 2(1935)4, pp. 17-30
- J.J.P. Oud, *Nieuwe Bouwkunst in Holland en Europa*, Amsterdam 1935 (reprint Amsterdam 1981 with a postscript by B. Colenbrander)

Trautrottl, Heinz [pseudonym for J.J.P. Oud], 'Ja. Eben. Künstler-erlebnisse. Gedankenvolles und Gedankenleeres von Heinz Trautrottl', [Wassenaar] September 1956

J.J.P. Oud, 'Zijn er nog architecten? Rede gehouden op de Hogeschooldag van de T.H. te Delft op 10 January 1959', The Hague 1959
- J.J.P. Oud, 'Zijn er nog architecten', in: *De Groene Amsterdammer*, 7 February 1959
- J.J.P. Oud, 'Tot slot', in: *De Groene Amsterdammer*, 4 April 1959
- J.J.P. Oud, 'Zijn er nog architecten', in: *Katholiek Bouwblad*, XXVI(1959)9, pp. 136-138
- J.J.P. Oud, 'Zijn er nog architecten', in: *Bouwkundig Weekblad*, 77(1959)9, pp. 110-111

J.J.P. Oud, *Mein Weg in 'De Stijl'*, Den Haag, Rotterdam 1960
- J.J.P. Oud, 'La mia strada in "De Stijl"', in: *Casabella*, (1961)256, pp. 24-31
- J.J.P. Oud, 'Mijn weg in de stijl', in: *Plan*, 12 (1981)6, pp. 16-25

J.J.P. Oud, *Architecturalia, voor bouwheren en architecten*, The Hague 1963

**Collections / Translations**

J.J.P. Oud, *Ter wille van een levende bouwkunst. Een keuze uit zijn schrifturen, verzameld en ingeleid door K. Wiekart*, The Hague, Rotterdam n.y.[1962]
Het monumentale stadsbeeld (1917)
Kunst en machine (1917)
Over de toekomstige bouwkunst en haar architectonische mogelijkheden (1921)
Ja und nein: Bekenntnisse eines Architekten (1925)
Der Einfluss von Frank Lloyd Wright auf die Architektur Europas (1925)
Wohin führt das neue Bauen: Kunst und Standard (1927)
Wij bouwen weer op? (1946)
Het U.N.O.-gebouw te New York (1948)
Bouwen en pseudo-bouwen (1949)
Clarity in town-planning (1949)
Bouwen zonder make up (1949)
Architectuurkritiek en architectuur (1950)
Architect en schilder (1951)
Ruimteproblemen (1951)
Het gebouw 'Shell Nederland N.V., 's-Gravenhage' (1951)
Bouwkunst, verkeer en Amsterdamse binnenstad (1951)
Bouwen en team-work (1952)
Bouwkunst of industrial design? Het gebouw voor de Unesco in Parijs (1952)
Architectuur en prijsvragen (1954)
Inleiding prijsvraag A. et A., Amsterdam (1954)
De Stijl – toen en nu (1957)
Is architectuur vogelvrij? (1957)
Le Corbusier (1958)
Henry Ford in Alkmaar (1958)
Zijn er nog architecten? (1959)
Prof. L.O. Wenckebach (1959)
De melodie van de ruimte (1961)

J.J.P. Oud, *Architettura Olandese. A cura di Sergio Polano*, Milan 1981
Architettura olandese
Introduzione [1926]
Lo sviluppo dell'architettura moderna in Olanda: passato, presente, futuro (una conferenza) [1922-1923]
Sull'edilizia del futuro e le sue possibilità architettoniche (un programma) [1921]
L'influenza di Frank Lloyd Wright sull'architettura europea (un saggio) [1925]
Appendice:
L'immagine della città monumentale [Het monumentale stadsbeeld, 1917]
Arte e macchina [Kunst en machine, 1918]
Architettura e normalizzazione nell'edilizia di massa [Bouwkunst en normalisatie bij den massabouw, 1918]
Orientamento [Oriëntatie, 1919]
De Stijl 1917-1927 [untitled, 1927]
La questione dell'Onu [The U.N. Building, 1948]
Chiarezze nella pianificazione urbana [Clarity in Town-planning, 1949]
L'edificio della Shell olandese [Het gebouw 'Shell Nederland N.V., 's-Gravenhage', 1951]
Architettura e lavoro in collaborazione [Building and Team-work, 1952]
Preferenze [Preferenties, 1960]
La mia strada in De Stijl [Mein Weg in 'De Stijl', 1960]

J.J.P. Oud, *Mi Trayectoria en "De Stijl". Selección, Traducción e Introducción Charo Crego*, Valencia 1986
Mi trayectoria en De Stijl [Mein Weg in 'De Stijl', 1960]
La evolución de la arquitectura moderna en Holanda: presente, pasado, futuro [Die Entwicklung der Modernen Baukunst in Holland: Vergangenheit, Gegenwart, Zukunft (Ein Vortrag), 1922-1923]
Sobre la arquitectura del futuro y sus posibilidades arquitectónicas [Over de toekomstige bouwkunst en haar architectonische mogelijkheden, 1921]
La influencia de Frank Lloyd Wright en la arquitectura europea [Der Einfluss von Frank Lloyd Wright auf die Architektur Europas (Ein Essay), 1925]
Sí y no: confesiones de un arquitecto [Ja und nein: Bekenntnisse eines Architekten, 1925]
¿A dónde va la nueva arcuitectura? Arte y normalización [Wohin führt das neue Bauen: Kunst und Standard, 1927]
El movimiento de la Nueva Arquitectura en Europa [Nieuwe Bouwkunst in Holland en Europa, 1935]
Arquitecto y pintor [Architect en schilder, 1951]
Le Corbusier [Le Corbusier, 1958]

# Colophon

This publication coincides with an exhibition of the same title held in the Netherlands Architecture Institute, Rotterdam, from 18 May to 9 September 2001.
Design Exhibition: Bureau Van der Wijst, Marijke van der Wijst, with Wim Poppinga

The publication of this book was made possible in part through the financial support of the Prins Bernhard Cultuurfonds, Amsterdam, the Oranje Nassagroep, Amsterdam, Sikkens Foundation, Sassenheim, Rotterdam 2001 and the Foundation Architectuurhistorisch Onderzoek Groningen.

Design: Joseph Plateau grafisch ontwerpers, Amsterdam
Concept: Bernard Colenbrander, Cor Wagenaar
Written and edited by: Ed Taverne, Cor Wagenaar, Martien de Vletter
With contributions by: Dolf Broekhuizen, Bernard Colenbrander, Maartje Taverne, Sander van Wees
Copy Editing: Marianne Lahr, Robyn de Jong-Dalziel
Translation Dutch-English: Robyn de Jong-Dalziel
Translation 'Lonely Explorations along the Horizon of our Times' and Short Essays: Wendy van Os
Translation 'Dr. H.P. Berlage und sein Werk', Preface, Introduction and Quotations from German: Pierre Zeevaarder
Translation French-English (p. 156): Brian Holmes
Reproduction Photography NAI: Martien Kerkhof, Studio Retina, Amsterdam
Lithography and Printing: Drukkerij die Keure, Bruges (B)
Binding: Delabie, Marken (B)
Production: Astrid Vorstermans
Publisher: Simon Franke



Available in North, South and Central America through D.A.P./Distributed Art Publishers Inc, 155 Sixth Avenue 2nd Floor, New York, NY 10013-1507, Tel. 212 6271999, Fax 212 6279484.

Available in the United Kingdom and Ireland through Art Data, 12 Bell Industrial Estate, 50 Cunnington Street, London W4 5HB, Tel. 181 7471061, Fax 181 7422319.

Printed and bound in Belgium
isbn 90-5662-199-8